The IEBM Handbook of Management Thinking

Titles from the International Encyclopedia of Business and Management Library

International Encyclopedia of Business and Management, 2nd edition
Edited by Malcolm Warner
8 Volume set, Hardback 1-86152-161-8, September 2001
IEBM Online 1-86152-656-3

Concise International Encyclopedia of Business and Management
Edited by Malcolm Warner
1 volume edition, hardback, 1-86152-114-6

Pocket International Encyclopedia of Business and Management
Edited by Malcolm Warner
Paperback, 1-86152-113-8

The IEBM Dictionary of Business and Management
Edited by Morgen Witzel
Paperback, 1-86152-218-5

The Encyclopedia of Marketing
Edited by Michael J. Baker
Hardback, 1-86152-304-1
Paperback, 1-86152-635-0

Regional Encyclopedia of Business and Management
Edited by Malcolm Warner
4 volume set, hardback, 1-86152-403-X

IEBM Handbook Series

The IEBM Handbook of Economics
Edited by William Lazonick
Hardback, 1-86152-545-1

The IEBM Handbook of Human Resource Management
Edited by Michael Poole and Malcolm Warner
Hardback, 1-86152-166-9
Paperback, 1-86152-633-4

The IEBM Handbook of Information Technology in Business
Edited by Milan Zeleny
Hardback, 1-86152-308-4
Paperback, 1-86152-636-9

The Handbook of International Business
Edited by Rosalie L. Tung
Hardback, 1-86152-216-9
Paperback, 1-86152-631-8

The Handbook of Management Thinking
Edited by Malcolm Warner
Hardback, 1-86152-162-6
Paperback, 1-86152-632-6

The IEBM Handbook of Organizational Behaviour
Edited by Arndt Sorge and Malcolm Warner
Hardback, 1-86152-157-X
Paperback, 1-86152-634-2

http://www.iebm.com

The IEBM Handbook of Management Thinking

Edited by
Malcolm Warner

THOMSON
™
LEARNING

Australia • Canada • Mexico • Singapore • Spain • United Kingdom • United States

The IEBM Handbook of Management Thinking

Copyright ©1998 Thomson Learning

First published by International Thomson Business Press
The Thomson Learning logo is a trademark used herein under license.

British Library Cataloguing-in-Publication Data
A cataloguing record for this book is available from the British Library

First edition (Hardback) 1998
Paperback edition 2001

Typeset by Hodgson Williams Associates, Cambridge
Printed in the UK by TJ International Ltd, Padstow, Cornwall

ISBN 1-86152-632-6

Thomson Learning
Berkshire House
168-173 High Holborn
London WC1V 7AA
UK

http://www.thomsonlearning.co.uk

Contents

List of Contributors

Professor Etsuo Abe
Professor of Business History
School of Business Administration
Meiji University
Tokyo
Japan

Professor Roy J. Adams
Emeritus Professor of Industrial Relations
DeGroote School of Business
McMaster University
Hamilton
Canada

Dr Peter H. Antoniou
Pomegranate International
California
USA

Dr Roger E. Backhouse
Professor of the history and philosophy of economics
Department of Economics
University of Birmingham
England

Professor Greg J. Bamber
Director, Graduate School of Management
Griffith University
Brisbane
Australia

Professor Philippe Baumard
Department of Management
University of Versailles
Paris
France

Dr Martin Beirne
Senior Lecturer and Director of
Undergraduate Management Programmes
Department of Management Studies
Universityof Glasgow Business School
Scotland

Professor Philippe Bernoux
Directeur de Recherches
Groupe Lyonnais de Sociologie Industrielle
Centre National de la Recherche
Scientifique
Université Lumiére Lyon II
France

Dr Pierre Berthon
Distinguished Senior Research Fellow
Cardiff Business School
University of Wales, Cardiff
Wales

Professor Jack Birner
Department of Economics
Faculty of Economics and Business
Administration
University of Maastricht
The Netherlands

Professor Christopher Boone
Professor of Organizational Behavior and
Organization Theory
Faculty of Economics and Business
Administration
University of Maastricht
The Netherlands

Dr Richard E. Boyatzis
Professor and Chair
Department of Organizational Behavior
Associate Dean for Executive Education
Programs
Weatherhead School of Management
Case Western Reserve University
Cleveland, OH
USA

Dr E.F.L. Brech
Visiting Research Fellow
The Open University Business School
The Open University
Milton Keynes
England

Professor William Brown
Montague Burton Professor of Industrial
Relations
Faculty of Economics and Politics
University of Cambridge
England

Professor Richard Butler
Professor of Organizational Analysis, The
Management Centre and Chair of Graduate
School of Social Sciences and Humanities
University of Bradford
England

Kees Camfferman
Faculteit der Economische Wetenschappen
Vrije Universiteit
Amsterdam
The Netherlands

Dr Adrian Campbell
School of Public Policy
University of Birmingham
England

Kellie Caught
Australian Centre in Strategic Management
Queensland University of Technology
Brisbane
Australia

Professor Joseph L. C. Cheng
Department of Business Administration
College of Commerce
University of Illinois at Urbana-Champaign
USA

Professor Victoria Chick
Department of Economics
University College London
England

Professor Peter Clark
Commerce Department
University of Birmingham
England

Professor Stewart R Clegg
School of Management
Faculty of Business
University of Technology, Sydney (UTS)
Australia

Dr Robert F. Conti
Associate Professor
Management Department
Bryant College
USA

Professor James Curran
Emeritus Professor of Small Business
Studies
Small Business Research Centre
Kingston University
Kingston upon Thames
England

Professor Barbara Czarniawska
Gothenburg Research Institute
School of Economics and Commercial Law
Gothenburg University
Sweden

Professor Sandra J. N. Dawson
KPMG Professor of Management Studies
and Director, Judge Institute of
Management Studies
University of Cambridge
England

Dr Mark Dibben
Department of Management Studies
University of Aberdeen
Scotland

Professor Paul Edwards
Industrial Relations Research Unit
Warwick Business School
University of Warwick
England

Professor J.E.T. Eldridge
Department of Sociology
University of Glasgow
Scotland

Professor Raul Espejo
Centre for Systems Research
School of Management
University of Lincolnshire and Humberside
Lincoln
England

Professor Robert L. Flood
Director, Centre for Systems Studies
University of Hull
England

Dr Frank Furedi
Reader in Sociology
Darwin College
University of Kent at Canterbury
England

Dr Richard Gillespie
Museum of Victoria
Melbourne
Australia

Dr Ian Glover
Lecturer of Management and Organization
Department of Management
University of Stirling
Scotland

Dr Pauline Graham
Research Fellow
Department of Engineering
University of Bradford
England

Professor Prabhu S. Guptara
Group Director and Chairman, Advance:
Management Training Ltd
Farnham
England
Organisational Learning and
Transformation
Union Bank of Switzerland
Wolfsberg Executive Development Centre
Ermatingen
Switzerland

Professor Jerald Hage
Director, Centre for Innovation
Department of Sociology
University of Maryland at College Park
USA

Dr Charles Hampden-Turner
Judge Institute of Management Studies
University of Cambridge
England

Dr Frank Heller
Director, Centre for Decision Making
Studies
The Tavistock Institute
London
England

Dr Geoffrey M. Hodgson
University Lecturer in Economics
Judge Institute of Management
University of Cambridge
England

Elaine C. Hollensbe
School of Business
University of Kansas
Lawrence
USA

Dr Dian-Marie Hosking
Aston Business School
Aston University
Birmingham
England

Dr Yao-Su Hu
Vice President (Academic)
Hong Kong Shue Yan College
Hong Kong
and Honorary Fellow
Science Policy Research Unit
University of Sussex
Brighton
England

Professor Mike C. Jackson
Lincoln School of Management
University of Lincolnshire and Humberside
England

Robin John
Head of Division of Strategy and Marketing
South Bank University Business School
London
England

Dr Matthew R. Jones
Judge Institute of Management Studies
University of Cambridge
England

Professor Pat Joynt
*PowerGen Professor of Management
Development
Henley Management College
Henley-on-Thames
England
and Norwegian School of Management
Sandvika
Norway*

Dr Ian Kessler
*Fellow
Templeton College
and School of Management Studies
University of Oxford
England*

Dr Maurice Kirby
*Department of Economics
The Management School
Lancaster University
England*

Professor Bruce Kogut
*The Wharton School
University of Pennsylvannia
USA*

Dr R.M. Lala
*Director, Sir Dorabji Tata Trust
Bombay
India*

Dr David C. Lane
*Operational Research Department
London School of Economics and Political
Science
England*

Professor Russell D. Lansbury
*Faculty of Economics
Sydney University
New South Wales
Australia*

Dr Frederic S. Lee
*Department of Economics
De Montfort University
Leicester
England*

Professor Anne Loft
*Copenhagen Business School
Denmark*

Professor Ray Loveridge
*Director of Research
Aston Business School
Aston University
Birmingham
England
and Editor of Human Relations
Tavistock Institute
London
England*

Professor Craig Lundberg
*School of Hotel Administration
Cornell University
Ithaca
New York
USA*

Dr Kevin McCormick
*School of Social Sciences
University of Sussex
Brighton
England*

Professor Kenneth D. Mackenzie
*Edmund P. Learned Distinguished
Professor
School of Business
The University of Kansas
Lawrence
USA*

Dr Geoff Mallory
*The Open University Business School
The Open University
Milton Keynes
England*

Professor Roger Mansfield
*Director
Cardiff Business School
University of Wales, Cardiff
Wales*

Professor Roderick Martin
*Department of Management Studies
University of Glasgow Business School
Scotland*

Professor Noah M. Meltz
*Professor of Economics and Industrial
Relations
and Principal, Woodsworth College
University of Toronto
Canada*

Professor Shunsaku Nishikawa
*Faculty of Business and Commerce
Keio University
Tokyo
Japan*

L.I Okazaki-Ward
*Senior Research Fellow
Cranfield School of Management
Cranfield University
Bedford
England*

Dr Nick Oliver
*Judge Institute of Management Studies
University of Cambridge
England*

Dr Robert Pitkethly
*School of Management
University of Oxford
England*

Professor Leyland Pitt
*Cardiff Business School
University of Wales, Cardiff
Wales*

Professor Michael Poole
*Professor of Human Resource Management
Cardiff Business School
University of Wales, Cardiff
Wales*

Professor Derek S. Pugh
*Visiting Research Professor of International
Management
The Open University Business School
The Open University
Milton Keynes
England*

Alfonso Reyes
*Departamento de Ingenieria Industrial
Universidad de Los Andes
Colombia*

Professor Jacques Richard
*Université-Dauphine
France*

Professor Martin Ricketts
*Professor of Economic Organization
University of Buckingham
England*

Professor George Ritzer
*Department of Sociology
University of Maryland at College Park
USA*

Sheila Rothwell
*Before her death, Director of Centre for
Employment Policy Studies
Henley Management College
Henley-on-Thames, England*

Dr Chris Rowley
*Senior Lecturer
Department of Human Resource
Management and Organizational Behaviour
City University Business School
England*

Thekla Rura-Polley
*Postdoctoral Research Fellow
School of Management
Faculty of Business
University of Technology, Sydney (UTS)
Australia*

Donald Rutherford
*Lecturer in Economics
Department of Economics
University of Edinburgh
Scotland*

Professor Chris Smith
*School of Management
Royal Holloway
University of London
Egham, Surrey
England*

Dr Gillian Stamp
*Director, Brunel Institute of Organisation &
Social Studies (BIOSS)
Brunel University
Uxbridge
England*

Dr Rosemary Stewart
Emeritus Fellow and Director
Oxford Health Care Management Institute
Templeton College
University of Oxford
England

Professor John Storey
The Open University Business School
The Open University
Milton Keynes
England

Carolyn Strong
Lecturer in Marketing
Cardiff Business School
University of Wales, Cardiff
Wales

Dr Monir Tayeb
Department of Business Organization
Heriot-Watt University
Edinburgh
Scotland

Professor Jean-Claude Thoenig
Department of Organizational Behavior
INSEAD
Fontainebleau
France

Dr Louise Thornthwaite
School of Industrial Relations
Griffith University
Brisbane
Australia

Dr Richard C.S. Trahair
Faculty of Social Sciences
La Trobe University
Bundoora
Victoria
Australia

Professor Peter Walton
HEC Management Studies
University of Geneva
Switzerland

Professor John P. Wanous
Department of Management and Human
Resources
Fisher College of Business
The Ohio State University
Columbus
USA

Professor Malcolm Warner
Fellow
Wolfson College and
Judge Institute of Management Studies
University of Cambridge
England

Professor John King Whitaker
Georgia Bankard Professor of Economics
University of Virginia
Charlottesville
USA

Dr Richard Whittington
Reader in Strategy
Said Business School
University of Oxford
England

Professor Barry Wilkinson
Business School
University of Bath
England

Professor Arjen van Witteloostuijn
Professor of Competitive Analysis and
Market Behavior
Faculty of Economics and Business
Administration
University of Maastricht
The Netherlands

Morgen Witzel
London Business School
and Durham University Business School
England

Professor John Cunningham Wood
Dean
College of Business
University of Notre Dame Australia
Fremantle
Western Australia

Professor Emeritus Basil S. Yamey
Department of Economics
London School of Economics and Political
Science
England

Professor Mohamed Zairi
SABIC Professor of Best Practice
Management
The European Centre for Total Quality
Management
University of Bradford
England

Professor Stephen A. Zeff
Jesse H. Jones Graduate School of
Administration
Rice University
Houston
Texas
USA

Professor Milan Zeleny
Graduate School of Business Administration
Fordham University at Lincoln Center
New York
USA

Acknowledgements

The publishers would like to thank the following for permission to use copyright material:

Ansoff, H. Igor (1918–)
Levels of turbulence; Hypothesized success triplets
Reproduced by permission of Ansoff Associates.

Handy, Charles (1932–)
Diagram to illustrate the four types of organization /Greek deities in *Gods Of Management*, p19, Arrow 1979.
Reprinted by permission of Charles Handy.

Miles, Raymond E. (1932–) and Snow, Charles, C. (1945–)
Diagram from *Organizational Strategy, Structure and Process* (1978) p24
Reproduced by permission of McGraw-Hill, New York.

Porter, Michael E. (1947–)
The five competitive forces that determine industry competition; Generic strategies; The value chain
Reproduced by permission of Macmillan Press Ltd.

Senge, Peter (1947–)
Figure 1: Deep Learning Cycle; Figure 2: Organizational architechture
From *The Fifth Discipline Fieldbook: Strategies and Tools for Building a Learning Organization* by Peter M. Senge, Art Kleiner, Charlotte Roberts, Richard B. Ross, Bryan J. Smith, published by Nicholas Brealey Publishing Ltd, Tel: (0171) 430 0224, Fax: (0171) 404 8311.
Also from *The Fifth Discipline Fieldbook: Strategies and Tools for Building a Learning Organization*: by Peter M. Senge, Art Kleiner, Charlotte Roberts, Richard B. Ross, Bryan J. Smith, published by Doubleday/Currency, 1540 Broadway, New York, NY 10036.

Thompson, James David (1920–73)
A typology of decision making
From *Comparative Studies in Administration*, James D. Thompson et al. (eds), copyright © 1959 by University of Pittsburgh Press. Reprinted by permission of the University of Pittsburgh Press.

Toyoda family
The Toyoda family: Members in Director Positions with Toyota. Permission granted by Elsevier Science.
Critical differences between Fordism , neo-Fordism and lean production in 'Towards lean management? international transferability of Japanese management studies to Australia', Shadur, M. A. and Bamber, G. J., from *The International Executive*, 36 (3) Copyright © 1994 John Wiley & Sons, Inc. Reprinted by permission of John Wiley & Sons, Inc.

Introduction

This volume brings together the major contributions to management thinking in the twentieth century with some of the earlier ones that fed into this mainstream. Together, they represent a body of both theory and practice that has influentially shaped modern business and management. The collection expands upon an initial foundation, namely the *International Encyclopedia of Business and Management* (1996) which attempted to create a worldwide reference work in its field both in terms of subjects and authorships. Published in six volumes (and followed by concise and pocket editions) the IEBM attempted to create a benchmark for not only topic and country entries but also biographical ones, and covered the following subject areas:

- Accounting and finance
- Business economics
- Comparative management
- Industrial relations/HRM
- International business
- Manufacturing management/operations
- Marketing
- OR and Systems/MIS
- Organization behaviour
- Strategy

Defining management

Asking the key question 'what is management?' is a legitimate concern at this point. We need to not only look at its essence but also its scope. Whether it is a cohesive field of study, what are its constituent parts and where its boundaries lie are also important queries. There are no easy answers. If we have learnt anything in recent times, it is that there is 'no one way'. Once upon a time, there was something called 'scientific management'. Writers like Taylor thought that they could concoct a 'science' of management; others like Fayol

and Barnard evoked 'principles' of management and so on. The audience for such notions arose for a sound set of reasons: the need for managers to 'make sense' of what they were doing and the environment in which it was taking place. If they could do so, they could have a better chance of shaping and controlling the process.

Putting it simply, management is what managers are seen to do. So, observation was prior to theorizing. Practice invoked theory; theory in turn illuminated practice. As a consequence, there are many management thinkers who were mainly or at some point in their lives practitioners, like Taylor, the Gilbreths, Bedaux or Fayol, but also wrote extensively, at least in the pre-1945 period. After this date, academics and especially business school academics begin to predominate, but not exclusively. Some of those we have included from the nineteenth and twentieth centuries have been industrialists like Bata, Ford, Ibuka, Sloan, Tata and so on, who have not only created their own ways of running companies whether in North America or elsewhere, but have also written about this in more or less schematic ways.

We have tried here to present management thinking as a cumulative set of both theories and practice, accumulating over time, and built up by key, individual thinkers on the subject. The presentation is thus biographical. Many of these individuals, singly or with colleagues, 'stand on the shoulders of giants', that is to say they have amplified the work of their precursors, some directly and others indirectly. In some cases, a specific contribution is almost unthinkable without the work of earlier ones. The work of the so-called 'management gurus' represents a social process by which management ideas are invented and often but not always applied by the originators. Whilst not all would endorse the 'guru' concept, it has some use in explaining how management ideas occur and spread. There was also an interaction between the individuals and the environments they find themselves in. Many were creatures of their times: others *made* history.

How such theories emerge as critical depends on how far they legitimize what managers think is 'managerially correct' and will fit their needs. New ideas must supercede what has gone before and replace the existing conventional wisdom. Managers of course seek a 'holy grail', normally to produce an end to the 'us' and 'them' divide in business, many of the supposed 'solutions' aiming to create industrial harmony. But as no one theory can solve all problems, the search is always on for the next path to salvation.

As Huczynski (1997: 234) points out:

From the turn of the century onwards management gurus have played a central role in the manufacture, transmission and application of management knowledge. To explain their influence, one has to understand both the nature of managerial work and the needs it creates among occupants of managerial positions. Those ideas which meet their needs are likely to be the most popular. Moreover, the nature of management itself also predisposes the profession to look to management gurus for guidance since, at one and the same time, these gurus develop, represent and also act as conduits for the application of their ideas into organizations.

Whether or not one accepts the so-called 'guru concept', there are clearly bodies of knowledge in the management field and many of these are distinctive. Hucyzinski (1997: 234) cites six of these:

- bureaucratic (Max Weber)
- scientific management (Frederick Taylor)
- classical management (Henri Fayol)
- human relations (Elton Mayo)
- neo-human relations (Douglas McGregor)
- guru theory (Tom Peters/Rosabeth Moss Kanter)

Popularity creates reputations; success breeds success in the field. The resultant synthesis is essentially a pragmatic one: their contribution rests on acquired reputations in either the primary domain of management or in those directly influencing it. How broadly management is defined is moot however; some see it as more widely defined than others. We take here a rather 'catholic' view of what it encompasses. This step may explain the rather diverse set of contributions we have included. We have for instance gone beyond the usual list of 'writers on organization' (see Pugh, Hickson and Hinings 1964 and subsequent editions). Our roster is much longer; we have cast our net much more widely but we have kept in mind that their writings have to be theoretical, at least in the sense that they are trying to derive generalizations applicable to a wide spectrum of managerial and organizational contexts, whether they were theorists, researchers or practitioners: 'theory and practice are inseparable' (1964: 8).

Establishing boundaries

Such thinking thus extends beyond the borders of management as more narrowly defined. We have of course included the 'classics' in the field, such as Taylor, Fayol, Barnard and so on. The reasons for including such thinkers is self-evident. Many of these are normally categorized as key 'management theorists' and we would not dispute their place.

Indeed, Huczynski (1997: 234) is right to emphasize that management ideas are associated with individuals or groups of individuals; further, that such names become identified with the concept. Taylor, for example, *was* 'scientific management'.

At any one point in time, one school of thought may rule the roost. Some speak of 'paradigms' (Kuhn 1970); others use the lesser term of 'metaphor' (Morgan 1997). The latter believes that 'all theories of management are based on explicit images or metaphors that lead us to see, understand, and manage organizations in distinctive yet partial ways' (1997: 4). If weaker, ideas may exist at the margins. Factions may form and vie to predominate.

Normally, the list of such management writers extends from the end of the nineteenth century up to the present day. Yet economic activity goes back much further than that and such activity was 'managed' for a very long time (see Warner 1984; Warner and Witzel 1997). There were early transnational banks like the Medicis or trading corporations like the East India Company. What they actually did was not however conceptualized as such in modern terms. There existed in effect *management before 'management' as a subject.* But there were no well-known 'names' or 'gurus' in management at that stage.

The term 'management' as we know it in the English language dates from Shakespeare's days. The term has Latin, Italian and French roots. It comes from the Latin 'manus' meaning 'hand' but also 'power' or 'jurisdiction'. The Italian term 'maneggiare' appeared in the late Middle Ages in connection with property management and business; the French 'manegerie' also came into use. The English word 'manage' first appeared in 1561, 'manager' in 1588, and 'management' in 1589, relating mostly to land usage. According to the Shorter Oxford English Dictionary (1993: 1197) it was first used in its modern context in 1670. It meant to 'handle' business affairs, as opposed to its earlier meaning of 'handling' a sword or a horse.

However, what we call 'modern management' is essentially a twentieth century phenomenon. 'Management studies' is even more novel as a subject but this depends on national definitions of the subject and what is included. The US developed 'business administration' as a university-level subject in the late nineteenth century but the Germans had taught 'business economics' overlapping with this curriculum not long after and the Japanese almost in parallel had initiated high-level 'commerce' courses (see Locke 1996). What in fact is seen as 'management' may vary cross-culturally and may be wider or narrower, depending on the academic, professional or country context. In many US business schools, for example, there is a concentration on 'hard' quantitative subjects; in others, 'soft' qualitative ones may prevail. Even MBA courses may have different emphases and in some countries they may not exist at all. Aspirant managers in these countries like Germany or Japan study engineering or technical subjects, often in a business and industrial context.

Criteria for inclusion

What then were the criteria for inclusion and exclusion of key figures in management thinking? Inevitably, many of the examples included are Anglo-American by origin; none the less, we have attempted to avoid the ethnocentric. However, it must be recognized that the majority of 'guru' figures were North American and most of these were actually born in the US. For example, Taylor, Barnard, Sloan, Follett and many others were native-born Americans. Most had conventional middle-class backgrounds and were university educated. Hardly any of them had gone to the newly emerging US business schools, like Wharton, Harvard and the like.

Although a few emigrated from Western or Eastern Europe in their earlier years, it is surprising that these were rather few in number. Some management thinkers who are in this category are Argyris, Drucker, Fiedler and Lewin. They also were university educated but not in business-related subjects. Some were social scientists proper.

British management writers (see Child 1969) are thinner on the ground vis a vis their North American counterparts. Some like Urwick, Vickers and so on achieved great success and high status as practitioners; later academic teacher figures like Burns, Pugh and the Aston Group as well as Woodward made their marks. More popular writers like Parkinson gained a wider readership. In economics, British contributions in both micro and macro domains were prominent, such as Marshall and Coase vis a vis the theory of the firm and many others in the macro environment of business activity. Boulding, who also contributed to systems thinking, was British born. Schumacher was born in Germany but made his name when living in Britain.

Continental Europeans are most prominently represented by Bedaux, Crozier, Fayol, Limpberg, Michels, Schmalenbach and Weber. Several, like Fayol or Weber, did not become widely known until after World War II when they acquired more widely diffused translations. Pacioli, who is credited with 'inventing' double-entry accounting in Renaissance Florence, was a recognized figure from way back, however.

Although many of the entries admittedly focus on British or North American thinkers, as they rightly deserve, enough have their roots elsewhere across the world, especially in Asia. We have for example included several Japanese contributions to management thinking, some of these never previously covered in such compilations, such as Ishikawa, Ohno, Morita and Ueno. Additionally, a number of women writers on management have been included, such as L. Gilbreth, Follett, Kanter and Woodward.

Management over time

The contributions to management thinking may be analyzed both across time as well as space (i.e. their country of origin or activity). They have both a historical dimension as well as a geographical one and within each set of parameters they can also be assessed by discipline and theme. The time line shown in Figure 1 seeks to show the development of management ideas over time. It is, however, extremely difficult to pinpoint exactly when someone made his or her contribution to this development. Some key figures from the last century are still influential today. Some people made their impact at an early age while their contemporaries may have spent a lifetime building on and developing their approaches. We have, therefore grouped our 'management thinkers' together roughly by date of birth.

Most of the contributions are 'modern' as opposed to 'post-modern' but it is difficult to draw the line. We have deliberately chosen 'established' thinkers as they had already made their impact. Indeed, most of these figures are recognized *post hoc*. At the time, they were mostly unknown to the academic world, let alone to practising managers.

Many, however, deal with 'post-modern' phenomena involving new technology as well as globalization and their consequent employment, managerial, organizational, marketing and associated consequences. Writers like Handy, Womack and Jones, McLuhan, Morgan, Ohmae, Nonaka and Toffler have been included here.

Management by disciplines

Disciplinary bases have also played a role in the way we think about management. They may also be clustered according to discipline or subject, although some may be classified as interdisciplinary.

Accounting and finance

Perhaps the earliest contribution to management thinking we have included is that of Pacioli, who lived in Renaissance Florence, although accounting was found in ancient Babylon and biblical times (Wyatt 1997). In the twentieth century, more complex methods were needed. In the US and Germany, for example, accounting developed as a university subject, distinct but related to economics. Some recent contributions include Benson, Limpberg, Paton and Schmalenbach, for instance. Hopwood's work on behavioural accounting has also been added.

Business economics

Business economics is concerned with firms, markets and industries but in the field, economists are commonly involved with 'descriptions and forecasts of behaviour in a macro-economic environment' (Kay 1997: 44). An early influence on how we think about such links was Adam Smith in the eighteenth century. Many economists subsequently added to our understanding of business but were not necessarily 'management thinkers' per se. Some added greatly to our knowledge of the business environment and are therefore included. While we have noted most of the

	General Management	Organizational Behaviour	Marketing	Strategy	OR/Systems and MIS	Manufacturing Management	Industrial Relations/HRM	Comparative Management	Business Economics	Accounting and Finance
4th Century BC										
Sun Tzu, 4th Century BC				■						
Fifteenth century										
Pacioli, Luca (c. 1445-1517)										■
1700 - 1800										
Smith, Adam (1723-90)				■		■			■	
1801 - 1900										
Mill, John Stuart (1806-73)								■	■	
Iwasaki Yataro (1834-85)										
Fukuzawa, Yukichi (1835-1901)	■									
Fayol, Henri (1841-1925)	■					■				
Marshall, Alfred (1842-1924)									■	
Taylor, Frederick Winslow (1856-1915)	■	■		■		■	■			
Veblen, Thorstein Bunde (1857-1929)			■							
Ford, Henry (1863-1947)	■					■	■			
Weber, Max (1864-1920)	■	■								
Toyoda family (1867+)	■			■		■				
Follett, Mary Parker (1868-1933)	■	■				■				
Gilbreth, Frank Bunker (1868-1924) and						■				
Gilbreth, Lillian Evelyn Moller (1878-1972)						■				
Lewin, Kurt (1870-1947)		■								
Schmalenbach, Eugen (1873-1955)				■						■
Watson, Thomas (1874-1956)	■			■		■				
Sloan, Alfred Pritchard, Jr (1875-1966)	■			■		■				
Bata, Tomas (1876-1932)	■									
Michels, Roberto (1876-1936)		■								
Limperg, Theodore (1879-1961)										■

Name	General Management	Organizational Behaviour	Marketing	Strategy	OR/Systems and MIS	Manufacturing Management	Industrial Relations/HRM	Comparative Management	Business Economics	Accounting and Finance
Mayo, George Elton (1880-1949)		■					■			
Keynes, John Maynard (1883-1946)									■	
Ueno, Yōichi (1883-1957)		■					■			
Schumpeter, Joseph (1883-1950)	■									
Matsushita, Konosuke (1884-1989)	■			■		■				
Bedaux, Charles E. (1886-1944)										
Barnard, Chester Irving (1886-1961)	■	■								
Perlman, Selig (1888-1959)							■			
Paton, William Andrew (1889-1991)										■
Urwick, Lyndall Fownes (1891-1983)	■			■						
Gulick, Luther Halsey (1892-1993)	■			■						
Vickers, Sir Geoffrey (1894-1982)					■					
Wiener, Norbert (1894-1964)					■					
Means, Gardiner Coit (1896-1988)									■	
Blackett, Patrick Maynard Stuart (1897-1974)					■					
Hayek, Friedrich August von (1898-1992)									■	
Deming, William Edwards (1900-93)				■		■				
1901-1920										
Von Bertalanffy, Ludwig (1901-72)					■					
Tata, Jehangir Ratanji Dadabhoy (1904-93)	■			■						
Juran, Joseph M. (1904-)						■				
McGregor, Douglas (1906-64)							■			
Maslow, Abraham H. (1908-70)	■						■			
Galbraith, John Kenneth (1908-)									■	
Ibuka, Masaru (1908-97)										
Benson, Harry (1909-95)										■
Shingo, Shigeo (1909-90)				■		■				

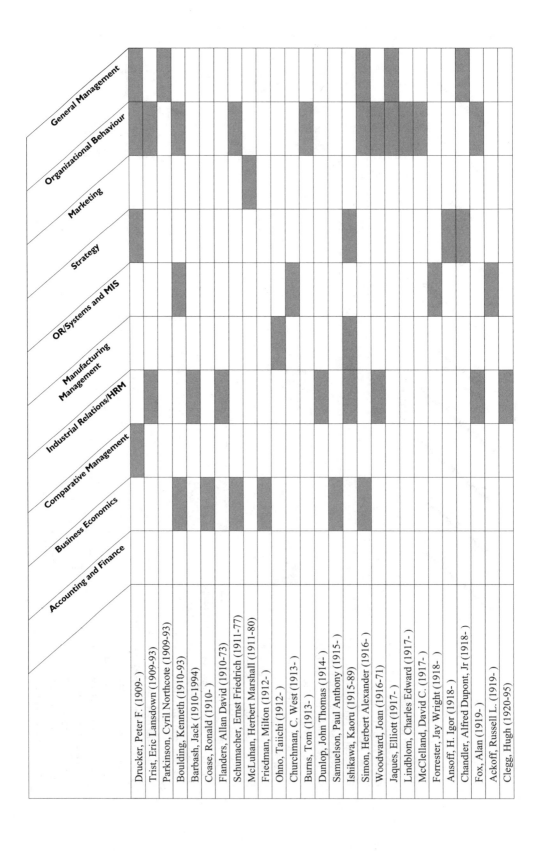

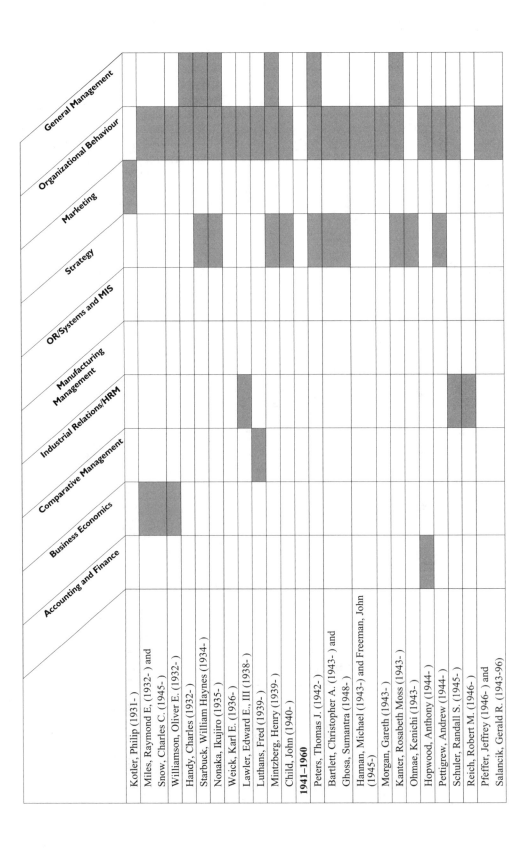

	General Management	Organizational Behaviour	Marketing	Strategy	OR/Systems and MIS	Manufacturing Management	Industrial Relations/HRM	Comparative Management	Business Economics	Accounting and Finance
Kochan, Thomas (1947-)							■			
Porter, Michael E. (1947-)				■					■	
Kotter, John (1947-)	■	■								
Adler, Nancy (1948-)		■						■		
Senge, Peter (1947-)	■	■		■						
Hammer, Michael (1948-)				■		■				
Tung, Rosalie L. (1948-)		■		■			■	■		
Womack James P. (1948-) and Jones, Daniel Theodore (1948-)				■		■				
Parasuraman, A (1948-), Zeithaml, Valarie (1948-) and Berry, Leonard L. (1942–)			■							
DiMaggio, Paul (1951-) and Powell, Walter W. (1951-)		■								
Hamel, Gary (1954-) and Prahalad, C.K. (1941-)	■			■						
Aston Group (1960s)		■						■		

major contributions to business economics, micro-economics and the theory of the firm, (Mill, Marshall, Coase, Means, March and Cyert, Simon for instance) we have thus also included several thinkers who have added to our understanding of the macro-economic or wider environment in which the firm operates (Keynes, Friedman, Galbraith, Schumpeter, Samuelson, Veblen and so on). We have particularly emphasized those economists whose work has overlapped with studies of the new institutionalism, managerial behaviour and organization behaviour.

Comparative management

We have included several comparative and cross-cultural writers on management here, including Hofstede, Luthans, Porter and Tung, who have written about the subject comparing different countries' systems. There is clearly an overlap with international management as a subject here.

Industrial relations/HRM

Industrial and labour relations involves 'the study of the employment relationship' and is an interdisciplinary subject (Poole 1997: 264). Industrial and labour relations, personnel administration and later HRM have all been for some years important parts of management thinking. Many have been accused of being pro-managerial and focusing on harmony of interests between management and labour, especially the forerunners of the subject such as Taylor, Follett and Mayo in the pre-World War II period. After 1945, the impact of the human relations school and the neo-human relations thinkers was also similarly criticized. Not all the writers on IR/HRM may be easily tarred with the same brush. We have included here writings on the subject as diverse as those of Perlman, Barbash, Dunlop, Strauss, Kochan, Reich, Schuler and Strauss from one side of the Atlantic; Flanders, Clegg and Fox from the other. Braverman, who was outside the consensus, and who wrote on 'labour process', has also been added. Several writers on organization behaviour, such as Gouldner, Mayo, Maslow, Herzberg, Ishi-

kawa, Ueno and Woodward contributed insights that impinged considerably on the IR/HRM area.

Manufacturing management

In this group, we find Taylor, the Gilbreths, Bedaux, Ford, Sloan, Watson from the US who made a substantial impact on manufacturing management and operations, whether in terms of theory and/or practice. In Japan, Ishikawa, Ohno, Matushita, Morita, Shingo and the Toyodas and so on shaped not only national but worldwide manufacturing practices. Total Quality Management (TQM) emerged there via Deming and Juran but had originally emanated from the US. Womack and Jones later analyzed this 'lean manufacturing' phenomenon.

Marketing

Although Smith wrote about markets long ago, marketing as a subject is more recent (see Baker and O'Brien 1997). In 1776, Smith wrote that 'Consumption is the sole end and purpose of production'. Marketing is important because it represents 'the interface between organization and the consumer' (1997: 428). Here we have added contributions by writers such as Berry, Levitt and Kotler as well as McLuhan, who enhanced our understanding of media and hence advertising. Veblen's notion of 'conspicuous consumption' also overlaps here.

OR/Systems and MIS

Operations research (OR) links 'the behaviour of operating systems made up of nature, people and machines' with each other (Miser 1997: 507). Blackett, Rivett and others made seminal contributions to this field. Thinking about systems in ways that could be described as modern vis a vis social science and business stem from the 1940s (Checkland 1997: 667). Systems which had been thought of in biological terms before this were extended to wholes of any kind, 'to systems in general' (1997: 667). From von Bertalanffy, Boulding, Vickers and Wiener to Ackoff, Beer, Checkland, Churchman, and Forrester, such thinking whether in its 'hard' or 'soft' varieties produced what became known as the 'systems movement'. It moved on from seeing the world in everyday language terms to specific modelling processes.

Organization behaviour

One of the strongest contingent comes from organization behaviour (OB), a discipline but also a 'cross-disciplinary endeavour' (Sorge 1997: 523) where we have a wide range of contributions. OB has a complex history and is interdisciplinary, stemming from economics, industrial relations, production, psychology, sociology and the like (see Warner 1996). We have here included early contributors like Taylor, Weber, and have proceeded via Follett and Mayo to most recent figures such as Child, Hannan and Freeman, Senge and Weick.

We can see within OB several strands of thought or sub-themes, such as in bureaucracy, where we have a line from Michels and Weber, to Burns and Stalker, Crozier, Downs and Pugh and the Aston Group, with an emphasis on organizational structure. Decision making is another parallel strand here, with March and Cyert, Lindblom, Simon and others who have contributed. Group behaviourists include Jaques, Mayo, and Lewin, who 'discovered' the role of the informal group on organizations. Knowledge-based systems is a another sub-theme where Nonaka, as well as Starbuck and colleagues, have made their mark. Leadership is a major heading where we must note the work of Weber, Fiedler and Kotter. Motivation, where Maslow, Herzberg, and so on, form a conceptual lineage, is also represented. In organizational economics, we find the work of Boulding and Williamson. In organizational learning, we have Argyris, Bennis, Schon and Senge. Power is a key concept; here we have included Crozier as well as Pfeffer and Salancik. On strategy and structure, Chandler is represented. Organization and technology. as well as socio-technical

systems, are long-standing contributions: Taylor, Emery and Trist, Thompson, and Woodward may be considered here.

Strategy

The application of strategy to business problems is 'of relatively recent origin' (Mansfield 1997: 656). A long list of contributions here runs from Sun Tzu in ancient China to Chandler, who was one of the first modern thinkers to link strategy to structure. We have also included later figures such as Hamel and Porter. 'Strategic choice', a key concept emphasized by Child and which overlaps with OB, may also be spoken of in this category.

Overlapping contributions

Some contributions are hard to pigeon-hole, as they could be placed in more than one slot. They are often interdisciplinary in nature, as they cross over from say economics to OB, as in the case of Williamson, or from OB to strategy, such as Pettigrew. Some contributions are in OB but may be seen as international business, like Adler, Hofstede, Luthans or Tung.

Many of the contributions relate to general management (see Warner and Witzel 1997), a fundamental anchor of the subject area and one which we believe can integrate many of the sub-themes into it. We include here Barnard, Drucker, Fayol, Fukuzawa, Handy, Gulick, Kanter, Kotter, Parkinson, Peters and Urwick, for example.

Conclusions

We may conclude that there are a number of over-arching strands that characterize the work of the authors included in this volume. Contributions have taken a number of forms, mainly conceptualization, terminology, methodology and practice.

Conceptualization

The most important contributions are often at the level of theory and conceptualization, that is, seeing the subject afresh and inventing a new concept. Many of the authors we have included here qualify on this criterion but not all. Some not readily associated with management, like Weber, would help us more clearly conceptualize notions like 'bureaucracy' or 'leadership' for instance. Major management thinkers like Taylor would conceptualize 'scientific management'; this would also be linked to introducing new terminology and new methods as well as contributing to practice. Von Bertalanffy on 'systems thinking' was a major conceptual breakthrough. Simon, a Nobel prize winner in economics, added to our insights into 'programmed and non-programmed' decision making. March and Cyert would conceptualize the 'behavioural theory of the firm' and so on. Such insights have proved fundamental contributions to management thinking.

Terminology

Adding to our vocabulary in the subject is an important addition to knowledge. This may also be linked to conceptual advances as well as innovations in practice. Morgan (1997) has seen some of these concepts as 'metaphors'; which translate into terms used by consultants and practitioners which may be later legitimized by academics (Alvesson and Wilmott 1996: 92). These would include 'cultures' and 'organisms' amongst many others. But not all of these entered the everyday language of managers. More technical terms may have wider usage. Terms like 'Just In Time' (Ohno) may be cited here as a term which has clearly entered the managerial language. Hammer on 're-engineering' is another noteworthy addition. Where terminology went into the common parlance of managers, the chances were higher that it would be internalized and lead to changes in practice.

Methodology

Devising new methods of investigation are also important; i.e. how to investigate a management problem. Some of these developments, like the Hawthorne research and Mayo's work for example, led to advances in studying group behaviour. Some manage-

ment thinkers developed new research instruments, such as the Aston Group in their studies of organizational structure. Lawler in his area of specialization devised new tools for studying payments systems. Fiedler did something similar in the field of leadership studies. These are research methodologies but new management methods of a technical nature may appear vis a vis day-to-day practice as in manufacturing, to which we now turn.

Practice

Adding new practices as well as theoretical approaches in management is clearly essential. A major addition to practice was in the case of Ford, for example. Some were basically practitioners but were able to reflect and write about how they went about improving practice, like Sloan. Bata in Czechoslovakia, Tata in India or, more recently, Morita in Japan, would fall into this category. But as we move forward in historical time from around the turn of the century, we see the role of the practitioner-theorist becoming less evident and professional academics and consultants (or those combining these two roles) becoming more predominant. The management 'guru', often an entrepreneurial academic in a university-based business school, becomes the organization's 'witchdoctor' (see Clark and Salaman 1996).

Summing-up

To sum up, very few management thinkers contributed to all of the above four categories. Most made their mark in one or possibly two of them. Nearly all of them have changed 'received wisdom' in their respective subfields or in the field as a whole. Critics may disapprove of their work in 'improving upon' established ways of managing and working (see Alvesson and Wilmott 1996: 9). Nevertheless, they have all made their mark historically and in contemporary practice in one way or another. Yet we must not go so far as to 'reify' such management thinking, to use Silverman's (1970) term in this context. In any event, managers prefer 'theoretical guidance which is, above all, easily understandable'

(1997: 241). Whether or not much (or indeed any of this) has a 'scientific' basis is moot, however. Even so, the historian of management ideas can note the distinctive contributions; evaluation is less easy.

Structure of the volume

We have arranged the entries alphabetically for easy reference and included cross-referencing to other key contributions where appropriate. There are two indexes, one by subject and the other a detailed, general index. Each chapter contains an initial list of biographical details and major writings, then a summary of their contribution. Their career and work is then described and evaluated, with conclusions to follow. Finally, annotated references and further reading are provided.

References

Alvesson, M. and Willmott, H. (1996) *Making Sense of Management: A Critical Introduction*, London, Thousand Oaks and New Delhi: Sage Publications.

Baker, M.J. and O'Brien, E.M. (1997) 'Marketing', in M. Warner (ed.) *Concise International Encyclopedia of Business and Management*, London: International Thomson Business Press, 449–455.

Checkland, P. (1997) 'Systems', in M. Warner (ed.) *Concise International Encyclopedia of Business and Management*, London: International Thomson Business Press, 667–673.

Child, J. (1969) *British Management Thought*, London: George Allen and Unwin.

Clark T.A.R. and Salaman G. (1996) 'The management guru as organizational witchdoctor', *Organization* 3, 1: 85–107

Huczynski, A. (1997) 'Guru concept', in M. Warner (ed.) *Concise International Encyclopedia of Business and Management*, London: International Thomson Business Press, 234–242.

Kay, J. (1997) 'Business economics', in M. Warner (ed.) *Concise International Encyclopedia of Business and Management*, London: International Thomson Business Press, 44–52.

Kuhn, T.S. (1970) *The Structure of Scientific Revolutions*, Chicago, Ill.: University of Chicago Press.

Locke, R.R. (1996) *The Collapse of the American Management Mystique*, Oxford: Oxford University Press.

Mansfield, R (1997) 'Concept of strategy', in M. Warner (ed.) *Concise International Encyclopedia of Business and Management*, London: International Thomson Business Press, 656–667.

Miser, H.J. (1997) 'Operations research', in M. Warner (ed.) *Concise International Encyclopedia of Business and Management*, London: International Thomson Business Press, 507–522.

Morgan, G. (1997) *Images of Organizations* (new edition), Thousand Oaks, London and New Delhi: Sage Publications.

Poole, M. (1997) 'Industrial and labour relations' in M. Warner (ed.) *Concise International Encyclopedia of Business and Management*, London: International Thomson Business Press, 264–282.

Pugh, D.S., Hickson, D.J. and Hinings, C.R. (1964 and subsequent editions) *Writers on Organizations*, Harmondsworth, Middlesex: Penguin Books.

OED (1993) *Shorter Oxford English Dictionary*, Oxford: Oxford University Press.

Silverman, D. (1970) *The Theory of Organizations*, London: Heinemann.

Sorge, A. (1997) 'Organizational behaviour' in M. Warner (ed.) *Concise International Encyclopedia of Business and Management*, London: International Thomson Business Press, 523–539.

Warner, M. (1984) *Organizations and Experiments: Designing New Ways of Managing Work*, Chichester and New York: John Wiley.

Warner, M. (ed.) (1996) *International Encyclopedia of Business and Management*, London: International Thomson Business Press, 6 volumes

Warner, M. (ed.) (1997) *Concise International Encyclopedia of Business and Management*, London: International Thomson Business Press.

Warner, M. and Witzel, M. (1997) 'General management: back to the future', *Human Systems Management*, (in press).

Wyatt, A. (1997) 'Accounting', in M. Warner (ed.) *Concise International Encyclopedia of Business and Management*, London: International Thomson Business Press, 1–10.

All articles referred to in the *Concise International Encyclopedia of Business and Management* can also be found in the full six-volume *International Encyclopedia of Business and Management*.

Ackoff, Russell L. (1919–)

Personal background

- born in 1919, Philadelphia, USA
- assistant instructor in philosophy, University of Pennsylvania 1941–2, 1946–7
- served in the US army, 1942–6
- assistant professor at Wayne University, Detroit, 1947–51
- associate professor and professor, Case Institute of Technology, 1951–64
- professor of systems sciences and Anheuser-Busch professor of management science; chairman of the Department of Statistics and Operations Research and the Department of Social Systems Sciences; director of the Management Science Centre and the Busch Centre: University of Pennsylvania, 1964–86
- Anheuser-Busch Professor Emeritus of management science, University of Pennsylvania, 1986–
- chairman of the board of INTERACT, the Institute for Interactive Management, Philadelphia, 1986–

Major works

Methods of Inquiry (with C. West Churchman)(1950)

Introduction to Operations Research (with C. West Churchman and E.L. Arnoff)(1957)

A Manager's Guide to Operations Research (with P. Rivett)(1963)

Fundamentals of Operations Research (with M. Sasieni)(1968)

On Purposeful Systems (with F.E. Emery) (1972)

The Art of Problem Solving (1978)

Creating the Corporate Future (1981)

A Guide to Controlling Your Corporation's Future (with E. Vergara and J. Gharajedaghi)(1984)

Revitalizing Western Economies (with P. Broholm and R. Snow)(1984)

Management in Small Doses (1986)

Ackoff's Fables (1991)

The Democratic Corporation (1994)

Summary

The work of Russell L. Ackoff has had a significant impact upon many fields in business and management. Wherever he has had his say, Ackoff is without compromise in promoting messages of participation, creativity, problem dissolving, improving the future, and plan or be planned for. In this, he has generated a whole too massive to cover here. Nevertheless, there are perhaps four main contributions that stand out and provide a representative account: operations research, interactive planning, circular organization, and fables and foibles. Along with Churchman, he largely co-defined operations research in its early years (1950s). By the 1970s, however, he concluded that operations researchers had failed to change with the times. An operational and tactical mode dominated, whilst corporate managers had moved into a strategic mode. In addition, by the 1980s, teachers of operations research taught and learnt from textbooks and had little practical experience. Ackoff, who admits he is market-led, responded in accordance with his observations. He moved out of operations research. He began a new phase of work that addressed purposeful systems of corporations and systems of interacting problems ('the mess') that characterizes them. By the 1980s, Ackoff had consolidated his ideas in a participatory approach labelled interactive planning. Interactive planning encourages people to conceive unconstrained idealized designs and to invent ways of realizing them. In the 1980s, and particularly in the 1990s, Ackoff's concern for participation surfaced in another guise; a structural notion for a circular organization. The circular organization is in fact a democratic hierarchy. In creating his own future, summarized above, Ackoff had many notable experiences, which he has consolidated, often with humour, in publications of fables and foibles. An account of Ackoff would not be complete without at least brief reference to this side of the man's intellectual character.

I   Biographical data

Russell L. Ackoff was born in 1919 in Philadelphia, USA. He graduated with a Bachelors degree in Architecture in 1941 and straight away joined the University of Pennsylvania as assistant instructor of Philosophy. This redirection of interest was sparked off in 1939 when he joined a course on his degree entitled 'modern philosophy', offered by C. West Churchman. Here began a remarkable professional relationship that continued until 1958, and a lifelong friendship. Details of Ackoff and Churchman's collaboration are given in the piece on Churchman (see CHURCHMAN, C.W.).

In the years of World War II (1942–1946) Ackoff was drafted into the USA army, but he kept in communication with Churchman and thus was able to complete his PhD in the philosophy of science under Churchman's guidance (1947). Ackoff then took up posts as assistant professor in philosophy and mathematics at Wayne University, Detroit (1947–1951), methodological consultant with the USA Bureau of Census (on six months leave from Wayne University, 1950), and associate professor and professor of operations research as well as director of the Operations Research Group, Case Institute of Technology (1951–1964). In this period he also accepted the Joseph Lucas visiting professorship of operations research at the University of Birmingham in the UK (1961–1962).

Ackoff continued his magnificent career on return to the University of Pennsylvania (1964–1986). He held professorships in systems sciences and management science. He became chairman of the Department of Statistics and Operations Research and the Department of Social Systems Sciences. He assumed the directorship of the Management Science Centre and the Busch Centre, and also accepted a visiting professorship at the National Autonomous University of Mexico (1975–1976).

In 1986, Ackoff left academia to establish INTERACT, the Institute for Interactive Management at Bala Cynwyd, Pennsylvania, of which he is chairman of the board. INTERACT is a self-funding institute that generates income through consultancy, advisory and training services, employing Ackoff's interactive planning and circular organization.

Ackoff's distinguished career is displayed in a cabinet's worth of awards. He received Doctor of Science (Honorary) from the University of Lancaster, UK (1967) and from Washington University, St Louis (1993), and Doctor of Law (Honorary) from the University of New Haven (1997). He received the silver medal from the UK Operational Research Society (1971) and the George E. Kimball medal from the USA Operations Research Society (1975). He received the annual award (1979) for outstanding contribution to the art and science of planning from the Southern California Corporation of Planners Association. He became foreign member of the Russian Academy of Natural Sciences (1995) and has been a fellow of the American Statistical Association since 1965. In 1993, he received the American Society for Training and Development award.

A practitioner at heart, Ackoff has applied his approaches in more than 300 corporations and government agencies. A few of the well known ones are ALCOA, American Airlines, Anheuser-Busch, AT&T, the Department of Justice, Eastman-Kodak, Ford, General Electric, General Foods, the Government of Mexico, IBM, the Internal Revenue Service, Monsanto, the National Science Foundation and the US army and air force.

Each of the four main contributions mentioned in the summary above that stand out and provide a representative account of Ackoff's work – operations research, interactive planning, circular organization, and fables and foibles – is elaborated on below.

2 Operations research

Operations research in the 1950s and 1960s promised to satisfy Ackoff's appetite for doing real, practical work that philosophy did not offer and,with Churchman, he largely co-defined it in its early years (1950s). *Introduction to Operations Research* (1957, with Churchman and Arnoff) was the first international textbook in the field and in the 1960s he co-produced *A Manager's Guide to Operations Research* (1963, with P. Rivett) and *Fundamentals of Operations Research* (1968, with M. Sasieni) (see RIVETT, B.H.P.). In this trilogy, he heads a comprehensive account of operations research, emphasizing the importance of a mixed team approach: an organization is diverse and requires at least equal diversity in operational research teams. The mixed team approach distinguished North American operations research from operational research in the UK, and points to a systemic interest in managing the whole.

In the 1960s, Ackoff states, operations researchers learnt that their techniques were best suited to certain types of problem: machines and machine-like behaviour. Operations research problems tended to be operational and tactical in nature, rather than strategic and normative, and such problems came to define this method of research. At the same time, Ackoff reckons, problems of corporations were changing. After World War II, demand rose rapidly and production responded, which posed problems well suited to the technology of operations research. By the early 1960s, Western industry had built more production capacity than required to meet demand. Corporate leaders with purposeful behaviour switched attention to handling competition for demand and creation of new demand. Most operations researchers stuck with their techniques and focused on operational and tactical problems. Thus a gap developed between corporate manager's needs and operations researcher's provision. Operations research thus became relegated to lower levels of management.

Further changes, in Ackoff's view, led to a widening gap. There were limits to growth obtainable by manipulating marketing variables. Corporations increasingly turned to internal development of new products and services. This required strategic planning, in Ackoff's thinking, not operational and tactical problem solving; it required dealing with complex systems of interacting problems that Ackoff labels 'messes'. It was the failure of operations research to change with the times that moved it down and even out of organizations. At the same time, Ackoff observes, instructors increasingly taught and learnt from textbooks, not from practice. Ackoff concludes that by the 1980s professional operations research journals were almost completely devoid of discussion about real, practical issues, and isolation of operations research from the real world was virtually complete. (Since the 1980s, however, a soft operational research movement based mainly in the UK has attempted to redirect the field of study.)

Ackoff, who admits he is market-led, responded in accordance with his observations. He moved out of operations research and began a new phase of work that addressed purposeful systems of corporations and the 'messes' that characterize them. Ackoff's work came together in an approach called interactive planning.

3 Interactive planning

At every stage of a diverse career, Ackoff has maintained a commitment 'to improve the future'. He does not claim to be a scholar in this regard (although his biographical data defies the denial), but instead, Ackoff says, he works out his own thoughts rather than thoughts of others. Interactive planning is one result of this. It asks what can be done *now* to create the future, not what the future will be independently of what we do now. The aim is to assist participants of an organization to design a desirable future for themselves and to invent ways of bringing it about. This reflects Ackoff's firm belief in the maxim, *plan or be planned for*.

Interactive planning builds on the premise that obstructions to change sit mainly in the minds of participants rather than separately in the problem context. Obstructions are often nothing more than assumptions made by participants. Ackoff dismisses approaches that attempt to surface and sweep away assumptions because the task is not practically feasible. There are probably thousands of assumptions, and in any case, how would we know when all assumptions had been surfaced and dealt with critically? Rather, Ackoff advocates formulating an idealized design and seeking creative ways of achieving it. Participants assume that existing fixtures of the problem context were destroyed last night, and so consider what ideal future they can choose today, now they are freed up in this way. In a process of closing the gap between their ideal future and the future they are already in if no changes are made, participants find that obstacles; dissolve' – that is, they disappear out of participants' minds.

Interactive planning is a methodology that leverages the preceding ideas into the world of practice, and is set out in *Creating the Corporate Future* (1981). An instrumental version is given in *A Guide to Controlling Your Corporation's Future* (1984). The methodology has five stages:

- formulate the mess
- ends planning
- means planning
- resource planning
- design of implementation and control.

The original contribution of interactive planning is located in the first three stages that are elaborated on below.

Formulate the mess

As noted, Ackoff's notion of mess is a complex system of interacting problems.

Formulating the mess aims to get to grips with an organization's mess and thus work out the future the organization is already in if it did nothing about things. This involves synthesizing the following three types of study yielding a reference scenario vital to means planning:

- *systems analysis* – formulate a detailed picture of the organization as it is today in terms of its processes, structure, culture, and its relationship with its environment
- *obstruction analysis* – surface existing obstructions to corporate development
- *preparation of reference projections* – animate the output of systems analysis and obstruction analysis to generate plausible projections about future performance.

Ends planning

This is where idealized design is located. Idealized design encourages participants to design the organization they would have today if they were free to choose any design they desired. This is qualified as follows:

- the design must be *technologically feasible*, not science fiction
- the design must be *sustainable* and this means it must demonstrate qualities of a learning organization.

Three strategic steps are followed:

- *select a mission* – formulate a general-purpose statement that generates commitment and direction
- *specify desired properties of the design* – based on the ideal mission, formulate a picture of the ideal properties of the design in terms of processes, structure, culture, and its relationship with its environment
- *idealized design* – move from idealized properties to a detailed idealized design.

Ackoff recommends passing through these steps twice – once constrained by the environment and once unconstrained by it.

Significant differences suggest an additional task of bringing about changes in the environment.

Means planning

The reference scenario and idealized design are compared and strategies for closing the gap are generated. This needs to be a highly creative process. Later stages can be likened to Juran's project-based approach to clearing up quality failure cost, except projects aim at some ideal future(see JURAN, J.M.). Strategies become clearly defined projects in terms of purposes, resource requirements, ownership, time scale and measures of performance. In this way, means planning moves into *resource planning* and *design of implementation and control*.

Interactive planning promises many benefits. Participation generates motivation and commitment, and thus unlocks much potential creativity. It aims to achieve consensus among participants and thus increases changes of smooth implementation. It reminds us that, in Vicker's terms, it is participants' own 'mind traps' that prevent participants from achieving their ideal future.

Criticisms have been levelled at interactive planning. A consensus world view assumes all participants are willing to engage in open and free debate. What if there are knowledge-power plays at work? People may wittingly or unwittingly act in this way. There is no indication in interactive planning of how to recognize and manage contexts of this sort.

Ackoff responds to this criticism as just another obstruction that dissolves if participants are creative in finding ways around resistances, for example, from powerful stakeholders. A counter-argument is that Ackoff can only claim that he has not in his experiences come across 'irresolvable conflict' simply because the scope of his projects do not challenge his client's fundamental interests. Ackoff then points to a picture on his office wall of a violent management–union clash and then a letter from the union some time later thanking him for dissolving the conflict. The debate continues.

An extended discussion of Ackoff's interactive planning is located in Flood and Jackson (1991: 144–165), where a case study is also presented.

3 Circular organization

Ackoff's concern for participation surfaces in another guise, in a structural notion for a circular organization. The circular organization is in fact a democratic hierarchy. It is a form of organization that is meant to cater for more active contribution of people in co-defining their involvement in the organization. It opens the way for organizational members to operate Ackoff's interactive planning amongst other things. *Creating the Corporate Future* (1981) provides a first account of the circular organization, whilst *The Democratic Organization* (1994) is the main reference text. Each account is written in Ackoff's typical precise fashion, captured in the summary below.

There are three principles put forward by Ackoff that exemplify his notion of participation through structure:

- the absence of an ultimate authority
- the ability of each member to participate directly or through representation in all decisions that affect him or her directly
- the ability of members, individually or collectively, to make and implement decisions that affect no-one other than the decision maker(s).

The main structural characteristic of a circular organization is the board. A board is a body of people from a local area in the organization. Every person in a position of authority is a compulsory member of their own board. Each board, except the ones at the top and the bottom of the hierarchy, has a minimal membership: the manager whose board it is, that manager's immediate subordinates, and that manager's immediate superior. Any board may, as seen fit, add members from within or beyond the organization as long as it improves representation of the principle stakeholders. The number of representatives should not exceed the number of subordinates, thus maintaining a majority with the latter.

Boards at the lowest level of the hierarchical organization should include all their subordinates. If the number is too large for all to serve on one board, they should be divided into semi-autonomous work groups. Each group selects a leader who reports to the lowest level manager. The leader has a board comprising themselves, the lowest level manager and all members of the group.

There are six responsibilities of each board:

- to plan for the unit whose board it is
- to make policy for the unit whose board it is
- to co-ordinate plans and policies of the immediately lower level
- to integrate plans and policies - its aim with those immediately below it and those at higher levels
- to improve the quality of work life of the subordinates of the board
- to enhance and evaluate performance of the manager whose board it is.

The circular arrangement overcomes some of the concerns levelled at traditional hierarchy, such as Weber's bureaucracy. It enhances people's chances of participating and making a rapid and meaningful contribution. It breaks with strict verticalness thus introducing more responsibility throughout the organization. It does this by spreading participation, whereas bureaucracy spreads responsibility only in terms of an individual's competency. The circular organization increases flexibility to respond to changing circumstances, although much still depends on the nature and extent of governing rules. Of the numerous options to organizational design, circular organization may have an advantage since it complements the traditional hierarchy that dominates today's organizations, rather than radically overhauling it with the danger of organizational trauma. On the other hand, it could be seen as a rather conservative response to worries about traditional hierarchy. It also fails to unwrangle different management functions and how they might be organized, for example, as achieved by Stafford Beer (see BEER, S.). Finally, circular organization sticks with the idea of clearly definable, bounded organizations, a concept that has been severely criticized in recent literature on organizational analysis, for example, by the likes of Gibson Burrell.

The above account is abstracted from Flood and Romm (1996: 87–91) where a case study is also presented.

4 Fables and foibles

Ackoff's writings on business and management are insightful and practical; they are also irreverent and witty. *Ackoff's Fables* (1991) epitomises these last qualities. His fables are very short stories with very sharp points about personal experiences that are essentially true. According to Ackoff's mentor, Tom Cowan, they are stories that may not be true, but ought to be. The following sharp points give a flavour of Ackoff's fables and, indeed, foibles. (1) The best system designer is one who knows how to beat any system that others design. (2) The best response to an arbitrary requirement is one that is itself as arbitrary as the requirement. (3) Intelligence and creativity are producers, not products, of education, but they are often its victims. More fables and foibles are located in Ackoff's column in the first ten volumes of the journal *Systems Practice*.

5 Conclusion

Russell L. Ackoff has a career stretching six decades. His contribution has a strong practical orientation. He does not claim to be a scholar, preferring to think out his own thoughts rather than thoughts of others. Ackoff is market-led, responding in his work to current needs of his clients. These driving forces mark each stage of his work. This short piece simply acts as an introduction to the man and his work, and not covered here are, for example, applied social science and management information systems. But in each area the messages are broadly the same – encourage participation, be creative, make problems dissolve, and improve the future. If there is one resounding message Ackoff has given business and management, it is, perhaps, plan or be planned for.

ROBERT L. FLOOD
UNIVERSITY OF HULL

Further reading

*Indicates referenced in the text

Ackoff, R.L. (1978) *The Art of Problem Solving*, New York: Wiley. (Lessons for problem solvers drawn from Ackoff's experiences and reflections.)

* Ackoff, R.L. (1981) *Creating the Corporate Future*, New York: Wiley. (A full blown account of interactive planning and first mention of circular organization.)

Ackoff, R.L. (1986) *Management in Small Doses*, New York: Wiley. (A smorgasbord of insights for managers based on Ackoff's practical experiences.)

* Ackoff, R.L. (1991) *Ackoff's Fables*, New York: Wiley. (Short stories on business and management with big punch lines.)

* Ackoff, R.L. (1994) *The Democratic Organization*, New York: Oxford University Press. (A full blown account of the circular organization.)

* Ackoff, R.L. (1988–1997) 'Redesigning the Future', regular column in *Systems Practice*. (A series of vignettes that accumulate into a prism of Ackovian thought on management.)

* Ackoff, R.L. and Rivett, P. (1963) *A Manager's Guide to Operations Research*, Chichester: Wiley. (Presenting operations research in an accessible and usable form for managers.)

* Ackoff, R.L. and Sasieni, M. (1968) *Fundamentals of Operations Research*, New York: Wiley. (A concise account of Ackoff's notion of the fundamental concepts and ideas of operations research.)

Ackoff, R.L. and Emery, F.E. (1972) *On Purposeful Systems*, London: Tavistock. (The idea that management systems are purposeful, adaptive learning systems.)

* Ackoff, R.L., Vergara, E. and Gharajedaghi, J. (1984) *A Guide to Controlling Your Corporation's Future*, New York: Wiley. (An instrumental version of interactive planning.)

Ackoff, R.L., Broholm, P. and Snow, R. (1984) *Revitalizing Western Economies*, San-Francisco: Jossey-Bass. (A view of the essential ingredients needed to revitalize the economies of the developed world.)

Churchman, C.W. and Ackoff, R.L. (1950) *Methods of Inquiry*, St Louis, Missouri: Educational Publishers Inc. (Review and discussion of methods of inquiry tracing back to contrasting strands of philosophical thought.)

* Churchman, C.W., Ackoff, R.L. and Arnoff, E.L. (1957) *Introduction to Operations Research*, New York: Wiley. (Operations research conceived of in terms of applied philosophy. One third of the book is devoted to philosophical and methodological aspects of an interdisciplinary approach to real world problems. Characteristic of North American operations research.)

* Flood, R.L. and Jackson, M.C. (1991) *Creative Problem Solving: Total Systems Intervention*, Chichester: Wiley. (Provides a comprehensive account of six better known systems-based problem solving methodologies and how to use them in complementary fashion, including Ackoff's interactive planning.)

* Flood, R.L. and Romm, N.R.A. (1996) *Diversity Management: Triple Loop Learning*, Chichester: Wiley. (Sets up a discourse between the ever growing number of models, methodologies, and theories in business and management, including the relative merits of Ackoff's circular organization.)

Keys, P. (ed.) (1995) *Understanding the Process of Operational Research*, Chichester: Wiley. (Sets the scene of the historical emergence of operations research and positions Ackoff's work in this. Includes a paper by Ackoff with C. West Churchman and E.L. Arnoff.)

See also: BEER, S.; CHURCHMAN, C.W.; EMERY, F.E.; JURAN, J.M.; RIVETT, B.H.P.; VICKERS, G.; WEBER, M.

Related topics in the IEBM: DECISION MAKING; MANAGEMENT SCIENCE; OPTIMALITY AND OPTIMIZATION; ORGANIZATIONAL BEHAVIOUR; ORGANIZATIONAL BEHAVIOUR, HISTORY OF; PROBLEM SOLVING; STRATEGY, CONCEPT OF; SYSTEMS.

Nancy J. Adler (1948–)

Personal background

- born in California in 1948
- graduated from UCLA with a PhD in Management (Honours)
- executive White House intern 1969–70
- became professor at McGill University, Montreal, Canada in 1980
- named Woman of Distinction (Femme de Mérite) in 1996
- named Top University Professor in Canada in1991

Major works

International Dimensions of Organizational Behaviour (1986)
Women in Management Worldwide (1988)
Competitive frontiers: Women Managers in a Global Economy (1994)

Summary

Adler conducts research and consults on strategic international human resource management, global women leaders and managers, international negotiating, culturally synergistic problem solving and global organization development. Her books have been very popular on the international scene. For example, *International Dimensions of Organizational Behaviour* is being used in executive and management development seminars as well as in undergraduate and graduate courses worldwide in cross-cultural management.

1 Biographical data

Professor Adler took three degrees at the University of California at Los Angeles. Her initial degree was in economics followed by an MBA and finally her PhD in Human Systems Development in 1980. Her many university honours included UCLA Graduate Woman of the Year, Summa Cum Laude and graduation with honours.

Others awards throughout her career include: Woman of Distinction (Femme de Mérite) 1996, Top University Professor in Canada 1991, Executive White House Intern 1969-70.

Her current position is professor of organizational behaviour and cross cultural management at McGill University, where she has been located since 1980. Other appointments have included Bocconi University, Milan, Italy 1989–90; the University of Hong Kong, 1988–89; INSEAD, in Fontainbleau France; in the People's Republic of China 1986; the University of Hawaii 1985–86; and, from 1977–78, the American Graduate School of International Management.

Professor Adler conducts research and consults on strategic international human resource management, global women leaders and managers, international negotiating, culturally synergistic problem solving, and global organization development. She has authored more than 70 articles and produced the film *A Portable Life*. Her book *International Dimensions of Organizational Behaviour* (3rd edition, 1997) now has over 100,000 copies in print in English, French, Chinese, and Japanese. She has also published *Women in Management Worldwide* (1988) and *Competitive Frontiers: Women Managers in a Global Economy* (1994), about which James Preston, CEO of Avon Products, said '... If you're concerned about your company's success in global competition – and I don't know any executive who isn't – this book is a must-read'. The BBC, for instance, focused on her work in their television documentary on multinational teams.

Adler has consulted with major global companies and government organizations on projects in Europe, North and South America, the Middle East and Asia. She has taught

Chinese executives in the People's Republic of China, held the Citicorp Visiting Doctoral Professorship at the University of Hong Kong, and taught executive seminars at INSEAD in France and Bocconi University in Italy. She received McGill University's first Distinguished Teaching award in Management and was its recipient again in 1990.

Having served on the Board of Governors of the American Society for Training and Development (ASTD), the Canadian Social Science Advisory Committee to UNESCO, the Strategic Grants Committee of the Social Sciences and Humanities Research Council, and the executive committees of the Pacific Asian Consortium for International Business, Education and Research, the Intentional Personnel Association, and the Society for Human Resource Management's international institute. She has also held leadership positions in the Academy of International Business (AIB), the Society for Intercultural Education, Training, and Research (SIETAR), and the Academy of Management. Adler received ASTD's International Leadership award, SIETAR's Outstanding Senior Interculturalist award, the YWCA's Femme de Mérite (Woman of Distinction) award, and the Sage award for scholarly contributions to management. She was selected as a 3M teaching fellow, honouring her as one of Canada's top university professors, and elected to both the Fellows of the Academy of International Business and the Academy of Management Fellows.

2 Main contributions

Her central interests can be divided into the following three categories: cross-cultural management; strategic international human resource management; women as global leaders.

Cross-cultural management

International Dimensions of Organizational Behaviour is already in its 3rd edition (South-Western Publishing 1997 and Kent 1991 and 1986). It has been translated into Chinese, Japanese and French, and Malaysian and Korean translations are in process. One of the main themes of the book is to break down the traditional conceptual, theoretical and practical boundaries involved in understanding and managing people in countries worldwide.

Focusing on the impact of culture on organizations, it describes the ways in which cultures vary and how this affects people within organizations. In the second part of the book the concentration is on managing cultural diversity. Problem solving, organizational development, multicultural teams, leadership, motivation and decision making are all central themes. Finally, an international approach is used for conflict management and negotiating. The third part of the book deals with managing international transitions.

Adler begins with the international career as it moves across boundaries. Entry and re-entry behaviour are handled from the employee's perspective. Culture shock, how to deal with foreign culture and how to return 'home' are central themes which also include insights from the spouse's perspective. She asks in Chapter 7 'Do Russians enter bargaining sessions with the same expectations as Arabs?' 'No.' 'Are the Arab negotiating styles similar to those of Americans?' 'Again no.' All international negotiations are cross-cultural. The author goes on to point out that managers may spend more than 50% of their time negotiating. In addition, culture diversity makes effective communication more difficult. Foreigners may perceive, interpret and evaluate the world differently.

The book has a very interesting summary of the tactics used in verbal negotiating behaviours. These include: promise, threat, recommendation, warning, reward, punishment, normative appeal, commitment, self disclosure, question, command, 'no's per 30 minutes, and initial concessions. Brazilians were very high on 'no's and initial concessions while the Japanese were highest on recommendation and commitment. Americans were highest on promises. When in Rome, do as the Romans do? No, when in Rome, or Beijing or Osaka, act like an effective foreigner, Adler concludes; culture does impact organizations – in the ways people communicate, work and negotiate with other people.

Strategic international human resource management

In 1983, Adler reviewed publishing trends for the decade of the 1970s. Her survey from 24 leading management journals showed that only 4.2% had an international OB/HRM perspective. In 1990, the study was expanded and repeated. The results showed 25% were OB/HRM and 33% were international. If you intersect these two groups, 2.3% were classified as international OB/HRM.

The main trends that were found include: the importance of cross-cultural interaction, the persistence of cultural differences; and the importance of the integration of academic and industry perspectives. The first trend showed a shift from single country studies and comparative articles to publications on cross-cultural interaction. Compared with the research of the 1970s there was close to a doubling of articles focusing on interaction. Cross-cultural interaction and technological innovation are essential today and can be defined in types of organizational reactions to the need for exchange of scientific knowledge. Markets hierarchies and networks are used. Strategic networks, both of firms and individuals, are essential to the innovative capabilities of many high technology firms. Transnational firms increasingly form strategic alliances and networks. There is no longer a dominant national culture at the headquarters nor a single culture in each particular location, rather a network of alliances among equals.

Adler's second point is that culture does not go away. One group of scholars has argued that managers worldwide are converging, becoming more similar in their behaviour; others maintain divergence or dissimilarity of behaviours. The trends Adler found were that the divergence argument was winning. Finally, when academic and professional perspectives are combined, the most important and forward thinking trends

emerge. Professor Adler found that professional journals publishing academic research publish:

- more international OB/HRM articles as a proportion of all OB/HRM articles than do either purely academic or purely professional journals
- more international OB/HRM articles as a proportion of all OB/HRM articles today than was reported in the 1970s
- more research on international interaction than do either the academic or professional communities alone
- more international OB/HRM articles that include culture as a construct than do either the academic or professional communities alone
- more articles finding culture to be relevant than either of the other two communities.

Global competition requires firms and their members continually to work with and learn from people worldwide. Traditional thinking on OB/HRM requires changes when transnational dynamics and transnational firms are introduced.

Women as global leaders

Women in global leadership management has been the most recent challenge taken on by Professor Adler. In this section we will focus on one of her most recent articles, 'Global Leadership: Women Leaders'. When looking for the leaders of the future many of us continue to review men's historic patterns of success in search of models for the next century. Few have thought of looking at the equivalent patterns of historic and potential contributions of women leaders.

While there are enough problems arriving at an agreed upon definition from an American academic perspective, Adler moves on to define global leaders and leadership. In quoting Anita Roddick, founder of the highly successful global firm, The Body Shop, she shows that:

Leaders in the business world should aspire to be true planetary citizens. They have global responsibilities since their decisions affect not just the world of business, but world problems of poverty, national security and the environment. Many, sad to say, (have) duck(ed) these responsibilities, because their vision is material rather than moral.

Mary Robinson, Ireland's past president suggests:

a woman leader often has a distinctive approach as the country's chief 'storyteller' (personifying) a sense of nationhood and telling a story that also (helps) shape people's sense of their own identify'. This is leadership by 'influencing (and) inspiring' rather than by commanding.

Adler points out that no woman presidents or prime ministers came to office in the 1950s, three came to office in the 1960s, five in the 1970s, eight in the 1980s, and to date in the 1990s twenty-one have already come to office. More than half of all women who have ever served as political leaders have come into office in the last seven years. Similar increases are also happening in world businesses. Women currently own one-third of all American businesses. She goes on to suggest a global portrait of the emerging global woman leaders:

1 Diversity defines pattern
A dominant pattern in the woman leaders' background is diversity. The dominant pattern is that women are increasingly being selected to serve in senior leadership positions, not that a few countries, companies or organizations with particularly feminine cultures are choosing to select women leaders.

2 People's aspirations: hope, change and unity
Here Adler argues that women leaders' most powerful and most attractive symbolism appears to be change. In addition to symbolizing change, women leaders appear to symbolize unity. In summary, people worldwide are attracted to the symbolic message of bringing change, hope and the possibility for unity.

3 Driven by vision, not by hierarchical status
Here Adler argues that most women leaders are driven by vision, mission or cause and not by a compelling agenda. Power and the presidency are means for achieving their mission, not the mission itself.

4 Source of power: broadly based.
Women leaders tend to develop and to use broadly based popular support, rather than relying on traditional hierarchical or structural support. This support, in the case of politicians, comes direct from the people. Adler goes on to use Mary Robinson, Corazon Aquino and Benazir Bhutto as examples of this. In business the source of support and power often reflects direct support from the market place and the flattened network on many of today's modern organizations.

5 Path to power: lateral transfer
Rather than following the traditional career path up through an organization, women leaders frequently transfer into the most senior leadership position from outside the organization. For example Adler cites Gro Harlem Bruntland from Norway, a medical doctor who six years later became Prime Minister.

6 Global leadership: global visibility
International business women often receive more visibility than their male colleagues. Global business women gain access more easily to new clients, suppliers and government officials and are more frequently remembered. Similarly, women political leaders are often more visible than their male counterparts. For example, the single most frequently asked question of former British Prime Minster Thatcher was 'What is it like being a woman Prime Minister'?

Evaluation and conclusions

To sum up, Adler is considered as one of the major players in international management. She has not only worked with major global companies in projects in Europe, North and South America, the Middle East and Asia, but she has also authored more than 70 articles and produced the film *A Portable Life*. The world of organizations is no longer limited by national boundaries and Adler was one of the first to see this. Until recently, most of our understandings of management come from the American experience. However, today, we no longer have the luxury of reducing international complexity to the simplicity of assumed universality: We no longer have the luxury of assuring that there is one best way to manage.

PAT JOYNT
HENLEY MANAGEMENT COLLEGE
NORWEGIAN SCHOOL OF MANAGEMENT

Further reading

(References cited in the text marked *)

Adler, N.J. (1980) 'Re-entry: A Study of the Dynamic Coping Process Used by Repatriated Employees to Enhance Effectiveness in the Organization and Personal Learning During the Transition Back Into the Home Country'. Dissertation, Graduate School of Management, University of California at Los Angeles (UCLA), Spring. (Adler received several awards for her graduate work.)

Adler, N.J. (1983) 'A typology of management studies involving culture', *Journal of International Business Studies*, 14, 2: 29–47. (A useful typology related to Adler's main work.)

Adler, N.J. (1983) 'Organizational development in a multicultural environment', *Journal of Applied Behavioral Science*, 19, 3: 349–365.

Adler, N.J. (1984) 'Expecting international success: female managers overseas', *Columbia Journal of World Business*, 19, 3: 79–85. Reprinted in *The International Executive* 27, 2, 1985: 13–14. (A study of women managers.)

Adler, N.J. (with Susan Bartholomew) (1992) 'Managing globally competent people', *Academy of Management Executive*, 6, 3: 52–65. (A recent multi-country study of management competence.)

Adler, N.J. (1993) 'Competitive frontiers: women managers in the triad', *International Studies of Management and Organization*, 23, 2: 3–23. (A useful study of women managers.)

Adler, N.J. (1993) 'An International Perspective on the Barriers to the Advancement of Women Managers', in E. Greenglass and J. Marshall (guest eds), *Applied Psychology: An International Review*, 42, 4: 289–300. (Shows how the 'glass ceiling' works in a range of countries.)

* Adler, N.J. (1997)'Global leadership: women leaders', *Management International Review* Special Issue 1, Vol. 37. (An excellent up-to-date summary of the dynamics of women in international management.)

Adler, N.J. (1997) 'Global Leaders: A Dialogue with Future History', *International Management* 1, 2: 1–13. (A review of what and how global leaders think.)

* Adler, N.J. (1997) *International Dimensions of Organizational Behavior*, 3rd edition, Cincinnati, Ohio: South-Western Publishing (Second edition, 1991, Boston, PWS: Kent Publishing; first edition, 1986, Boston: Kent Publishing. (Probably the best book in this area – translated into several languages.)

See also: HOFSTEDE, G.; LUTHANS, F.; TUNG, R.L..

Related topics in the IEBM: CULTURE, CROSS-NATIONAL; EQUAL EMPLOYMENT OPPORTUNITIES; GLOBALIZATION; HUMAN RESOURCE MANAGEMENT; HUMAN RESOURCE MANAGEMENT, INTERNATIONAL; MANAGERIAL BEHAVIOUR; MULTINATIONALS; ORGANIZATION BEHAVIOUR; ORGANIZATION BEHAVIOUR, HISTORY OF; ORGANIZATION CULTURE; WOMEN IN MANAGEMENT AND BUSINESS.

Ansoff, H. Igor (1918–)

Personal background

- born in Vladivostock, Russia, 12 December 1918
- graduated from Stevens Institute of Technology, New Jersey (ME, MSc) and received a PhD at Brown University, Rhode Island, in 1948
- married Dorothy Webster in 1948 and has four children and three grandchildren
- held senior positions at RAND Corporation, California (1948–56) and Lockheed Aircraft Corporation (1956–63)
- held professorships at Carnegie Mellon University, Pennsylvania (1963–8) and at Vanderbilt University, Tennessee (1968–76)
- joint appointment as professor at the European Institute for Advanced Studies in Management in Brussels and at the Stockholm School of Economics (1976–83)
- organized a European network of strategic management researchers during the above tenure
- since 1983, has been Distinguished Professor of Strategic Management at United States International University, California

Major works

Corporate Strategy (1965)
Strategic Management (1979)
Implanting Strategic Management (with E.J. McDonnell) (1984)
The New Corporate Strategy (1988)

Summary

Ansoff is a prolific writer, having produced over 120 articles since 1965. He is currently working on two new books, *Optimizing Profitability in the Twenty-First Century, or How to Succeed in Business by Actually Trying* and *Multidisciplinary Managerial Theory of Strategic Behavior by Environment-Serving Organizations*. The annual Ansoff Prize for the best contribution to strategic management was established by Coopers & Lybrand, and Twente University of Technology (in The Netherlands) in 1991.

1 Introduction

Harry Igor Ansoff was born in 1918 in Vladivostock, Russia. He came with his parents to the USA when he was seventeen, with very little knowledge of English. This, however, did not stop him from graduating at the top of his class from high school. He received his ME and MSc, with honours, at the Stevens Institute of Technology, New Jersey, one of the leading educational institutions of the time, and his PhD at Brown University, Rhode Island. He joined the project management office at RAND Corporation, California, in 1948 and then joined Lockheed Aircraft Corporation in 1956. His first assignment at Lockheed was to develop a plan to enable the giant contractor to diversify its business. Diversification was a new idea at the time and there were no concepts or guidelines on how to approach the task. As a result, Ansoff and the members of the Diversification Task Force developed the basic concepts and logic of strategic analysis. His first book, *Corporate Strategy* (1965), was the outcome of this work. The book was an immediate success and resulted in worldwide recognition.

In 1968, Ansoff joined the academic community at Carnegie Mellon University, Pennsylvania, and in 1973 he moved to Vanderbilt University, Tennessee, where he was the founding dean and professor of management at the Graduate School of Management. Also in 1973, he accepted a position as professor at the European Institute for Advanced Studies in Management. Here he established a European network of researchers in strategic management. He returned to Vanderbilt University as the Distinguished Justin Potter Professor of Free American Enterprise, before returning to Europe in 1976, where, for seven years, he held a joint appointment at the Stockholm School of Economics and at the European Institute for Advanced Studies in Management. Since 1983, he has been Distinguished Professor at the United States International University in San Diego, California. He has also acted as a consultant for many leading companies, including Philips, General Electric, IBM, Gulf Oil, General Foods, Westinghouse, FN Herstal, Sterling Europa and KBB in The Netherlands.

Ansoff is often called 'the Father of Strategic Management' in recognition of his contributions to the theory and technology of optimizing the long-term profitability of environment-serving organizations. An environment-serving organization is one that, while primarily serving its extended business, also serves its social/political environment; by contrast, a firm that becomes purely self-serving soon loses track of its direction and dies. Ansoff's first pioneering contribution was *Corporate Strategy* (1965), which offered a logical systematic process for formulating firms' future strategic behaviour.

His second major contribution, which he called *Strategic Management* (1979), broadened strategic planning into a multidisciplinary process which added individual and group behaviour dynamics, political processes and organizational culture as key variables that determine the strategic behaviour and success of firms. Within the framework of strategic management, Ansoff made the following contributions:

1 he developed a 'comprehensive multidisciplinary managerial theory of strategic behaviour' by environment-serving organizations;
2 within this theory, he developed a 'theoretical contingent strategic success paradigm', which hypothesizes different success behaviours by firms on different levels of environmental turbulence;

3 he conducted extensive empirical research on the success paradigm in a cross-section of industries around the world (1983–90), which validated the paradigm (see Ansoff *et al.* 1993);
4 he provided a 'paradigmatic umbrella', which specified the domains of validity for many of the strategic success formulas proposed by other researchers;
5 using this paradigm as a cornerstone, he constructed and tested in practice a comprehensive strategic management technology (entitled 'real-time strategic management'), which can be used to optimize the future profit potential of businesses and other environment-serving organizations (Ansoff and McDonnell 1984).

2 Major contributions

Of the contributions listed in the previous section, three – the concept of environmental turbulence, the contingent strategic success paradigm and real-time strategic management – have been particularly important in shaping theories of strategic thinking.

Environmental turbulence

Ansoff constructed a model of the environment which consists of five turbulence levels, ranging from placid and predictable to highly changeable and unpredictable. For each level of turbulence, Ansoff hypothesizes a different behaviour which will optimize the profitability of the firm (Ansoff 1979). A simplified description of the levels of turbulence is shown in Figure 1.

In order for a firm to balance both the strategic and operating components, it has to look at both the external and internal environments and align its position to achieve good results. This thinking led to an awareness that analysis and interpretation of the firm's external environment is a key factor in its strategic success. Ansoff constructed a five-point scale of 'turbulence levels'. These are described by a combination of the changeability and predictability of events in the environment. The external environment then

		1	2	3	4	5
Discontinuity	Complexity of environment	National →		Regional →		Global
		Economic	+	Technological	+	Socio-political
	Novelty of change	None	Incremental– slow	Incremental– fast	Discontinuous– familiar	Discontinuous– novel
Unpredictability	Rapidity of change	Zero	Slower than response	Comparable to response	Faster than response	Supriseful
	Visibility	Total	Extrapolable	Predictable	Partially predictable	Unpredictable
Instability	Frequency of turbulence level shifts	Very low	Low	Medium	High	Very high
	Turbulence scale	1	2	3	4	5

Figure 1 Levels of turbulence
Source: Ansoff (1979)

serves as the key indicator for the firm's strategic position.

The contingent strategic success paradigm

For his second major contribution, Ansoff used the hypothesized model of turbulence to construct a theoretical strategic success paradigm based on three variables: the turbulence level in the firm's environment; the aggressiveness of the firm's strategic behaviour in the environment; and the responsiveness of the firm's management to changes in the environment. The paradigm states that the financial performance of a firm is optimized when the aggressiveness and management responsiveness of the firm both match the turbulence in the firm's environment (Ansoff 1979). A simplified graph, used for testing the alignment of a firm's strategic aggressiveness and management responsiveness with environmental turbulence, is shown in Figure 2.

The fact that a firm can be successful at one time and unsuccessful at another led Ansoff to realize that a firm's strategy has to be aligned with the level of turbulence in which it operates; otherwise its financial performance will drop. This led to the development of the contingent strategic success paradigm. A matching triplet was designed to show the link between the environment, strategy and organizational capability.

Ansoff challenges with his hypothesis the universal validity of prescriptions for firms' success which have been established in the business literature. His model does not deny the validity of such prescriptions as 'If it ain't broke don't fix it' or 'Go back to the basics'; rather it places them in a context in which each is valid under a particular set of circumstances. For instance, the prescription 'If it ain't broke don't fix it' is a prescription which is applicable and will bring success to firms operating on level one of the turbulence scale; 'Go back to the basics' is suitable for level two but dangerous for levels three and four. Similarly, strategic management is very useful on level three and vital on levels four and five. In order for companies to attain maximum profitability, they have to interpret the level of environmental turbulence and align the strategy and capability of the firm accordingly. While some maintain that there is one prescription for success, Ansoff holds that different environments call for different corporate responses.

The contingent strategic success paradigm has been empirically validated in approximately 1,000 Strategic Business Units

Level	1	2	3	4	5
Environmental turbulence	REPETITIVE No change	EXPANDING Slow incremental change	CHANGING Fast incremental change	DISCONTINUOUS Discontinuous predictable change	SUPRISEFUL Discontinuous unpredictable change
Strategy aggressiveness	STABLE Stable – based on precedents	REACTIVE Incremental – based on experience	ANTICIPATORY Incremental – based on extrapolation	ENTREPRENEURIAL Discontinuous – new strategies based on observable opportunities	CREATIVE Discontinuous – novel stategies based on creativity
Capability responsiveness	STABILITY-SEEKING Rejects change	EFFICIENCY-DRIVEN Adapts to change	MARKET-DRIVEN Seeks familiar change	ENVIRONMENT-DRIVEN Seeks related change	ENVIRONMENT-CREATING Seeks novel change

Figure 2 Hypothesized success triplets
Source: Ansoff (1979)

(SBUs), 12 industry sectors and 8 countries around the world (Ansoff *et al.* 1993) and has several applications in practice. Working managers can use a diagnostic tool derived from the paradigm (called 'strategic readiness diagnosis') to diagnose the readiness of their firms to succeed in the turbulent future. It enables a firm to identify the existence of any gap between its future environment, its current strategy and its future reactive capability. Managers can also use the paradigm to select from the many offerings from both academics and consultants the one that is most likely to optimize their firms' profitability in the future. For academics, the paradigm offers an opportunity to identify a 'place in the sun', in which their success formulas have a high probability of optimizing a firm's profitability, as well as a 'place in hell', in which these success formulas are highly unlikely to contribute to profitability.

Real-time strategic management

Ansoff's third major contribution is a practical management process called 'real-time strategic management', which is based on the contingent strategic success paradigm and which is intended to help entrepreneurial managers succeed in turbulent and unpredictable environments. The distinctive characteristics of real-time strategic management include the following:

1 use of the contingent strategic success paradigm to diagnose the firm's readiness to succeed in the future;

2 high priority attention given to ensuring that the mind-set of key managers and the firm's culture will be responsive to the future turbulence level in the environment;

3 anticipation that a strategic transformation of the firm will inevitably encounter resistance to change, accompanied by early steps to convert the resistance into organizational acceptance and support of the change;

4 recognition of the inherent unpredictability of the future during the late twentieth and early twenty-first centuries, and help for managers in estimating the risk that surrounds each major strategic decision;

5 blending entrepreneurial strategic planning, which positions the firm for success in the future, with real-time response, which helps the firm to anticipate sudden threats and opportunities;

6 timely introduction of the real-time strategic control system into the firm;

7 recognition that in turbulent environments even the best-studied strategies have a high probability of future failures. Real-time strategic management deals with this problem by using a real-time strategic control system, which revises the current strategy whenever it becomes evident that it no longer works.

Technologies of real-time strategic management

Ansoff and his associates have developed a series of procedures to guide managers through different stages of real-time strategic management. These include: (1) strategic segmentation, which segments a firm's environment into future areas of opportunity; (2) real-time issue management, which identifies and responds to novel trends, threats and opportunities; (3) strategic readiness diagnosis, which diagnoses a firm's readiness to succeed in the future; (4) design of general management, which identifies the profiles of general managers and of management organization that will be needed for success in the future; (5) entrepreneurial posture planning, which plans a firm's future posture in turbulent and unpredictable environments (where 'posture', the position that a firm takes in a strategic business area, is defined as 'strategy × capability × strategic investment'); and (6) strategic organizational transformation, which designs and guides the transformation of a firm's strategy and capability and controls resistance to change.

3 Evaluation

Igor Ansoff has been one of the leading architects of strategic management. His general contribution to this field is the holistic perspective that he brought to the study of strategic management and his focus on the strategic management of complex organizations in turbulent environments. His most important theoretical contribution is the invention and validation of the contingent strategic success paradigm, which explained the apparent contradictions among contributors to strategic management and made it possible to unify these contributions into a coherent whole. His most important contribution to practice is the real-time strategic management procedure, which helps managers to optimize firms' long-term profitability in turbulent environments.

PETER H. ANTONIOU
POMEGRANATE INTERNATIONAL

Further reading

(References cited in the text marked *)

* Ansoff, H.I. (1968) *Corporate Strategy*, New York: McGraw-Hill. (Ansoff's first book provides a logical method whereby firms can create future strategy.)

* Ansoff, H.I. (1979) *Strategic Management*, London: Macmillan. (Broadens the scope of strategic planning to take into account group, organizational, political and cultural dynamics.)

Ansoff, H.I. (1988) *The New Corporate Strategy*, New York: Wiley. (A major revision of Ansoff (1979); stresses the importance of aligning strategy with the level of environmental turbulence.)

* Ansoff, H.I. and McDonnell, E.J. (1984) *Implanting Strategic Management*, New York: Prentice Hall. (An exposition of real-time strategic management, showing how profits can be maximized in turbulent environments.)

* Ansoff, H.I. *et al.* (1993) 'Empirical support for a paradigmic theory of strategic success behaviors of environment-serving organizations', in D.E. Hussey (ed.), *International Review of Strategic Management*, vol. 4, Chichester: Wiley. (Offers empirical evidence for the validity of the strategic success paradigm.)

Lombriser, R. (1994) *Top Intrapreneurs: How Successful Senior Executives Manage Strategic Change*, London: Pitman. (Based on interviews with thirty corporate entrepreneurs, this study aims to provide a complete framework for the implementation of strategic change.)

Lombriser, R. and Ansoff, H.I. (1995) 'How successful intrapreneurs pilot firms through the turbulent 1990s', in D.E. Hussey (ed.), *International Review of Strategic Management*, vol. 6, Chichester: Wiley. (An examination of strategy at high levels of environmental turbulence.)

See also: MINTZBERG, H.; OHMAE, K.; PETTIGREW, A.M.

Related topics in the IEBM: BUSINESS HISTORY; CONTEXTS AND ENVIRONMENTS; ORGANIZATION BEHAVIOUR; ORGANIZATION BEHAVIOUR, HISTORY OF; STRATEGIC COMPETENCE; STRATEGY, CONCEPT OF; STRATEGY, IMPLEMENTATION OF; STRATEGY MAKING, POLITICS OF

Argyris, Chris (1923–)

Personal background

- born 16 July 1923 in Newark, New Jersey
- graduated from Clark University in 1947, completed Master of Science degree at Kansas University in 1949 and received his PhD from Cornell University in 1951
- married Renee Brocoum, two children
- develops what is termed a 'theory of action'
- formative influence on organizational behaviour, intervention theory, organizational learning and competence-enhancing methods of inquiry
- appointed James Bryant Conant Professor of Education and Organizational Behaviour at Harvard University

Major works

Personality and Organization (1957)
Intervention Theory and Method (1970)
Organizational Learning (with Donald Schon) (1978)
Inner Contradictions of Rigorous Research (1980)
Reasoning, Learning and Action: Individual and Organizational (1982)
Overcoming Organizational Defenses (1990)
Knowledge For Action (1993)

Summary

Chris Argyris (1923–) initiated a theory, strategy of inquiry and learning methodology known as *action science*. His approach, which is applicable to persons and organizations, enables human beings and social systems to change. Action science liberates both practitioners and researchers from the often dysfunctional grip of the status quo by generating a valid and useful knowledge of actions.

Argyris argues that people and organizations need to confront the contradictions between intentions and actual behaviours, expose the values and assumptions that govern patterned behaviours, and develop and test alternative behaviours and value systems. His ideas and methods have been applied to repetitive problems, puzzles and paradoxes in a wide range of contexts, including education, organizational development, social theorizing and management development. While his approach has often sparked controversy among conventional scholars and traditional managers, his work has been a major influence on the humanization of management and the development of grounded theories of organizational behaviour, development and social inquiry.

1 Introduction

Argyris has always been concerned with the health and effectiveness of individuals, organizations and institutions. His early research documented the ways in which budget and accounting procedures, personnel practices, executive development programmes, management style and traditional organizational structures constrain individual performance, personal growth and innovation. He demonstrated repeatedly how low-skilled, fractionated jobs carried out within pyramidal organizational structures retard individual maturity and thwart the satisfaction of higher order human needs. Argyris also showed how such effects are replicated in traditional research methods, which place subjects in top-down, unilaterally controlled situations. Both managers and researchers, he admonished, seemed to be colluding in perpetuating explanations of processes that mitigated against effectiveness and truthfulness in the organization.

As his inquiries progressed, Argyris became increasingly fascinated with what people took for granted and how unaware they seemed to be when acting upon what they took for granted. This led to a line of research which suggested that behind what is taken for granted is highly skilful behaviour, and behind this skilful behaviour is the acculturation of social virtues that foster a lack of awareness. Argyris's focus has led to a mode of inquiry involving intervention in the workplace; such interventions produce directly observable data that demonstrate how the status quo reacts when threatened.

Interventionist research methods require subjects to become 'clients' who participate in defining jointly the aims and methods of the research itself. Moreover, such methods demand that researchers have both the skill to deal with defences at several levels of analysis and the determination to explore what are often considered to be taboo subjects. In one sense, such inquiries represent a violation of culturally sanctioned avoidance strategies.

2 Biographical data

Argyris was the third son born into a middle-class family on 16 July 1923 in Newark, New Jersey, USA. Soon after his birth, his family moved to Greece for several years, returning to Irvington, New Jersey, in time for him to begin his schooling. Argyris experienced difficulty early in school because he could not speak English very well, and rejection as a minority member in the neighbourhood. His early upbringing and his experience of the disapproval of others instilled in him two enduring characteristics: a propensity to examine himself carefully to discover his deficiencies and a desire to work hard to change himself.

Towards the end of the Second World War, Argyris served as an officer in the US Signal Corps. He won awards for technical performance and efficiency while in charge of several depots in Chicago, but also discovered that his subordinates held doubts about his 'human skills'. In keeping with his early upbringing, Argyris's reaction was to endeavour to learn more about himself. Following his discharge, he continued his university education,

studying psychology, business and economics, and pursuing an academic career in organizational studies.

At an early stage in his academic career, he was influenced by the work of Roger Barker, Fritz Heider and Kurt Lewin, each of whom was revolutionizing psychology (see LEWIN, K.). Argyris then went to the School of Industrial and Labor Relations (ILR) at Cornell University to complete his PhD. ILR was a new, problem-centred school that encouraged students to question the limits of traditional disciplines. At Cornell, under the guidance of William Foote Whyte, Argyris began the value-based practices which continue to characterize his work in the 1990s: the study of everyday life as the arena in which to discover problems and from which to infer theory; the questioning of the status quo, especially with regard to the way in which it helps to perpetuate problems; making problem solving the test of any discipline; and carrying out research that is guided by concerns for external and internal validity, competence enhancement and justice.

3 Main contributions

The many significant contributions Argyris made to management thinking and practice are his responses to a number of fundamental questions. What is the impact of organizations on their members? How can organizational research be made to produce knowledge that leads to enhanced managerial practices? How can one intervene in organizations in such a way that they become more competent and effective? What inhibits individual and organizational learning and how might it be overcome?

Organizations and individuals

Early in his career, Argyris showed how traditional managers based their structures, systems and practices on inaccurate assumptions about human nature and interpersonal relationships (Argyris 1957, 1964). He noted that managers appeared to hold values such as: people are most effective when they are rational, significant human relationships have to do with the achievement of organizational objectives and human relationships are most effectively influenced through unilateral direction, coercion and control. In accordance with these values, organizations are designed using principles of task specialization, unity of direction and a clear-cut unity of command. In addition, management retains the sole right to plan work, evaluate performance and determine what information is important and may be shared, and also the right to construct reward and punishment systems that sanction its values and practices.

Argyris also summarized what is known about healthy, mature human beings in western culture. From infancy to adulthood, persons tend to demonstrate the following kinds of development: from passivity to increasing activity; from dependence on others to relative independence; from being capable of behaving in only a few ways to behaving in many different ways; from having a few, casual, short-lived interests to having many different interests; from having a short-time perspective to having a longer time perspective; from being in a subordinate position to being in an equal and/or superordinate position; and from having little self-awareness to having greater awareness of, and control over, the self. Argyris concluded that formal organizations create in healthy, mature individuals a short-time perspective and feelings of frustration, failure and conflict. Employees consequently express such feelings through such activities as absenteeism, high staff turnover, 'gold-bricking' (output restriction), psychological withdrawal, emphasizing material rewards and, in some cases, by forming trade unions. A majority of managers and organizational researchers are pessimistic, agreeing that trust and loyalty are hard to find in organizations, while conflict is common. These unintended features of organizational life are assumed somehow to be natural, rather than outcomes of the dominant but inadmissible self-fulfilling ideology of control.

At the core of Argyris's analysis of the interface between the individual and the stultifying organization is his identification of unexamined assumptions and values, including those which prohibit making implicitly held values and assumptions explicit (Argyris 1971). Faced with such prohibitions, management has a tendency to solve only symptoms and devise 'quick fix' solutions to complex problems.

Argyris makes the point that when the crucial and inadmissible are viewed simply as hypotheses and hence open to debate, new resolutions for integrating the individual and the organization will be found. In the 1960s, his own suggestions for the organization of the future – enlarged jobs, greater use of self-managed teams, leaner managerial hierarchies, feedback for learning as well as for system correction, and leadership instead of managership – clearly presaged many of the management innovations which have become popular in the 1980s and 1990s.

The collusive effect of research

Paralleling the foregoing discussion, Argyris (1982) argues that social scientists design and conduct research that colludes unwittingly with the beliefs and practices that dominate human activity. Rigorous research methods place subjects in a top-down situation that is consistent with the psychosocial structure of pyramidal organizations. To achieve internal validity, all control lies with the researchers, who make all the decisions. As a consequence, subjects become dependent and conformist. Tasks are stated explicitly and defined rigidly and norms of objectivity and rationality predominate. However, as Argyris has shown, unintended consequences result, ranging from marginal subject participation to covert hostility, from physical withdrawal to trivial responses. In other words, what people say their behaviour is seldom corresponds to their actual behaviour. Discovering valid and useful knowledge through the use of conventional scientific methods thus becomes highly problematic.

To overcome the dysfunctionality and questionable ethics of conventional, rigorous research, Argyris advocates viewing the research relationship primarily as a helping relationship in which subjects are encouraged to act naturally and be fully themselves, and where accurate feedback increases the meaningfulness of the activity for subjects. Field interventions are his mode of inquiry, where subjects become clients who participate in defining jointly the research goals, methods, participation, and research costs and rewards. For Argyris, research produces knowledge that enhances client competence first and change secondarily, as well as aiding the development of theory. He prefers, and has pioneered, rigorous theories about the way the world is, the way it should be and how to get from the one way of being to the other. He favours knowledge that is understandable, storable and retrievable under the conditions of everyday life.

Obstacles to organizational change

The work summarized above led Argyris to focus on processes of change and renewal. In his writings about management and organizational development, innovation and consultancy, he addressed the question of how an organization might move from traditional values and practices favoured by the status quo to methods that are more conducive to organizational competence and individual growth.

By the late 1960s, conditions creating the need for strategies of organizational change were increasingly in evidence. For example, rapid and unexpected environmental changes were occurring, new management knowledge and techniques were being practised and there was increasing diversity and organizational growth. At the same time, alternative management approaches based on new and very different conceptions of persons (for example, McGregor 1960) and organizations (for example, Likert 1967) were gaining widespread acceptance. Taken together, these changing practices became known as organizational development. However, the new field greatly resembled prior managerial thinking in so far as it emphasized planned change, management from the top down and the application of behavioural science. Significantly, all these aspects were rooted in unexamined ideologies of power and control. Without having developed an overall theory, organizational development has, since its inception, elaborated continuously its diagnostic models and interventional technologies and pursued system efficiency and effectiveness.

Argyris's conception of renewal differs from all other organizational development theories in two fundamental ways. One difference is his development of a generic theory of intervention that applies across all levels of social systems and in all contexts. The other is his focus on increasing competency rather than change in the interests of improving effectiveness. On the one hand, Argyris emphasizes moving attention to the values that shape problem-solving routines. On the other, he argues that real and lasting changes in organizations require more trust, more openness, more concern with feelings and greater commitment to experimenting with new ideas than is normally the case. Significantly, these are properties of interpersonal relationships, not of persons or systems. It is especially important that people in positions of authority display a high level of interpersonal competence.

According to Argyris (1970), effective interventions depend upon three centrally important processes: helping to generate valid information in order that situations and problems may be understood accurately; creating opportunities for free choice in the search for solutions; and creating conditions for internal commitment to choices and continual monitoring of actions taken. These processes require that persons, groups and organizations focus not on change but on learning (Argyris 1992). Under such conditions, attention may shift from feedback that alters actions (single-loop learning) to questioning the values that govern conventional problem-solving routines (double-loop learning). This shift is very difficult to make because organizations, and many people who work within them, develop certain deeply ingrained habits. For example, they may have a tendency to attribute blame or disguise inconsistencies in their performance. When questioned about such habits, employees often feel embarrassed or threatened and adopt defensive behaviour which prohibits double-loop learning. Both persons and organizations have theories about how to act effectively, which blind them to opportunities for real learning.

If double-loop learning leads to the competence which leads, in turn, to health, effectiveness and renewal, but defensive routines block such learning, then explaining why defensive routines persist becomes critical if one is to understand and improve management education, organizational development, social inquiry and much else. Argyris (1980) explains the persistence of defensive routines at two levels. What is easy to observe is the collusion of persons in accepting but not confronting the differences between how they justify their behaviour (their espoused theories) and how they actually behave (their theories in use). This collusion, says Argyris, is supported by culturally sanctioned, widely held positive social virtues or values, such as caring and support, respect for others, honesty, strength, integrity and so on. Implicit in such virtues, however, are rules that actually say things like: be rational and minimize emotionality; refrain from being honest with somebody if your honesty is likely to hurt his or her feelings; don't challenge the reasoning or actions of others when you disagree with them; stick to your principles at all costs; feeling vulnerable is a sign of weakness; and achieve your goals in whatever way you see fit. Overlaying these virtues is a double-bind logic, which again is widespread and culturally sanctioned and which says, in effect: act as if there are no ambiguous or inconsistent messages and act as if these are not open to discussion.

Given the existence of defensive routines, measures intended to enhance competence place considerable demands upon persons and organizations. The task of introducing into the workplace a new organizational culture – which involves learning-orientated norms, bilateral protection of others, minimal personal defensiveness, clear acceptance of responsibility for individual action and trust in processes that cannot be confirmed – is fraught with difficulties. However, such an exercise is more likely to succeed when it is based on the values which govern effective intervention, that is, valid information, free and informal choice, internal commitment to choice and constant monitoring of the effects of initiatives.

Action science

The value-based, double-loop learning cycle outlined above constitutes action science (Argyris 1982), a programme of research and intervention that is designed to understand and alter the reasoning and learning processes of individuals and organizations by exposing and examining the inner contradictions of action. Action science places considerable demands upon the intervener/researcher, who must have the necessary determination and interpersonal skill to deal with organizational and individual defensive routines (the natural response of self-sealing value systems is to reject that which threatens). In contrast to other theories of organizational behaviour and managerial thinking, perhaps the most distinctive feature of action science is that it has the potential to uncover its own contradictions and alter its own learning processes accordingly.

4 Evaluation

Argyris, in a truly large and consistent body of work, has promoted a problem-centred, value-centred approach to a valid and practical theory that examines the unintended consequences of behaviour with the aim of enhancing interpersonal competence. Action science, therefore, is a non-disciplinary theory of action in which persons and organizations are encouraged to identify and examine the values governing their problem-solving routines. At the core of the interventions which promote this kind of learning are a set of values about valid information, experimentation, choice and learning from experience. For Argyris, enhanced competence leads to the sort of change that leads, in turn, to individual and organizational health.

Action science, as strategy for both social-scientific inquiry and organizational improvement, questions conventional approaches to research and problem-solving. As Argyris's own theory predicts, his work threatens the scientific and managerial status quo and he has been criticized by scholars and managers alike. Interestingly, however, both social-scientific inquiry and management thinking is starting to reflect the principles and findings of action science – for example, various forms of collaborative inquiry are being utilized.

CRAIG LUNDBERG
SCHOOL OF HOTEL ADMINISTRATION
CORNELL UNIVERSITY

Further reading

(References cited in the text marked *)

* Argyris, C. (1957) *Personality and Organization*, New York: Harper & Row. (This book first detailed the incompatibility between mature individuals and hierarchical, mechanistic organizations.)
* Argyris, C. (1964) *Integrating the Individual and the Organization*, New York: Wiley. (An examination of ways in which organizations and managerial practices can be redesigned to provide conditions conducive to individual growth and health.)
* Argyris, C. (1970) *Intervention Theory and Method*, Reading, MA: Addison-Wesley. (A classic of organizational development which presents a normative approach to organizational change based on competency enhancement.)
* Argyris, C. (1971) *Management and Organizational Development*, New York: McGraw-Hill. (An outline of person–organization incongruency and how change agents may alter it.)
* Argyris, C. (1980) *Inner Contradictions of Rigorous Research*, New York: Academic Press. (An explanation of defensive routines and how these can serve to block double-loop learning by preventing feedback loops from functioning.)
* Argyris, C. (1982) *Reasoning, Learning and Action*, San Francisco, CA: Jossey Bass. (A description of ten years of research into the possibilities for increasing the capacity of individuals and organizations to solve difficult underlying problems by means of action science.)
* Argyris, C. (1990) *Overcoming Organizational Defenses*, Needham, MA: Allyn & Bacon. (A description of the basis for, and maintenance of, designed-in, second-order error and methods of overcoming the resulting defensive routines.)
* Argyris, C. (1992) *On Organizational Learning*, Oxford: Blackwell. (A collection of twenty-one previously published articles and chapters based on the premiss that organizational learning is an ability that organizations should develop.)
Argyris, C. (1993) 'Looking backward and inward in order to contribute to the future', in A. Bedian (ed.), *Leaders in Management Theory and Practice*, vol. 1, Greenwich, CT: JAI Press Inc. (An autobiographical essay in which Argyris describes how themes from his personal life are reflected in his scholarly work.)
Argyris, C. and Schon, D. (1978) *Organizational Learning*, Reading, MA: Addison-Wesley. (An early work on organizational learning that suggests ways in which thinking and feeling can be integrated by studying them as they exist in action.)
* Likert, R. (1967) *The Human Organization*, New York: McGraw-Hill. (Stressing process over structure, four organizational systems are described using an authoritarian-to-participative continuum.)
* McGregor, D. (1960) *The Human Side of Enterprise*, New York: McGraw-Hill. (A human relations classic that outlines contrasting sets of management assumptions and their consequences.)

See also: LEWIN, K.; MCGREGOR, D.; SCHON, D.

Related topics in the IEBM: FREUD, S.; HUMAN RELATIONS; MANAGERIAL BEHAVIOUR; OCCUPATIONAL PSYCHOLOGY; ORGANIZATION BEHAVIOUR; ORGANIZATION BEHAVIOUR, HISTORY OF; ORGANIZATION CULTURE; ORGANIZATION DEVELOPMENT; ORGANIZATIONAL LEARNING

Aston Group

Personal background

Pugh, Derek S. (1930–)

- born 1930, London
- MA, MSc (Edinburgh), Dsc (Aston), FSS, FBPsS
- research assistant, assistant lecturer, University of Edinburgh (1953–57)
- lecturer, senior research fellow, reader, Birmingham College of Technology/Aston University (1957–68)
- reader, professor of organizational behaviour, London Business School (1968–82)
- professor of systems, Open University (1983–88)
- professor of international management, Open University Buisness School (1988–95)
- visiting research professor of international management, Open University Business School (1995–)

Hickson, David J. (1931–)

- born 1931
- associate of the Chartered Institute of Secretaries (1953); MScTech UMIST, Manchester 1959; PhD (Hon) Umea, Sweden (1976)
- research fellow and lecturer, Birmingham College of Advanced Technology, subsequently University of Aston (1960–68)
- professor of organisational behaviour, University of Alberta, Canada (1968–70)
- fellow of Netherlands Institute for Advanced Study (1982–83)
- professor of organizational analysis (subsequently professor of international management and organization) University of Bradford Management Centre (1970–)

Major works

Organization Structure in its Context: Aston Programme 1 (1976)
Organizational Structure: extensions and replications: Aston Programme II (1976)
Organizational Behaviour in its Context: Aston Programme III (1977)
Organization and Nation: Aston Programme IV (1981)
Management Worldwide: the Impact of Societal Culture on Organizations around the Globe (1995)
Writers on Organizations (1996)
The Aston Programme, 3 vols (1998)

Overview

The distinctive characteristics of the Aston programme of research were its completeness (it was an attempt to identify all relevant variables for describing organizations and their context or environment), carefulness of measurement (it used multiple scales and attention to problems of reliability in what is almost the paradigm of psychometric techniques), and its variety of extensions both in terms of the kinds of organizations (business, public sector, colleges, unions, etc.) and of other levels of analysis (roles, groups and climates). The major weaknesses were its general lack of theoretical focus and an overreliance upon the use of informants and documents in collecting data on structural variables rather than use interviews. But perhaps the most important lesson to be learned from the Aston programme which is generally not the one mentioned, is the way in which the concepts were developed. All members participated in teams working in a problem-solving mode before quality work circles became popular, and produced research products that were more comprehensive and of generally higher quality than those produced by their contemporaries or even since then.

1 Historical context

Most researchers in the study of organizations would probably agree that the single most successful programme of research was the series of studies conducted at the University of Aston in Birmingham, England, during the 1960s. But to appreciate truly the magnitude of the Aston programme's achievements one has to understand the historical context and the intellectual climate of England in particular and of organizational research more generally at that time. Only one other programme of research then existed in England, that of Joan Woodward (1965) who was conducting a number of interesting case studies involving the effects of technology (see WOODWARD, J.).

The Aston Group and Woodward's research both shared the British empiricist tradition. Essentially, this means they relied heavily on inductive strategies starting with the concrete, tangible and observable, a preference that dates back to Francis Bacon and his critique of the theologians. A tradition reinforced by the greater importance of social anthropology in England than in the USA, empiricism tends to neglect the role of theory and certainly eschews deductive approaches in favour of theory-building and research.

Most articles and books on organizational research during the early 1960s were case studies frequently relying upon participant observation, the major exception being Richard Hall's attempt to operationalize Weber's model of bureaucracy in ten organizations. There was an almost total absence of what was later called comparative research, that is large numbers of organizations in which the variables or concepts were measured in standardized ways.

Meanwhile, in the USA, most of the various programmes were guided in one way or another by theory, or were at least attempting to develop organizational theory, including the work of James Thompson, Charles Perrow, Jerald Hage, and Paul Lawrence and Jay Lorsch. However, in so far as these individuals were engaged in research – not all were – they relied upon relatively small samples of organizations or comparative cases.

The only other large programme of research during the 1960s that came close to the Aston effort was the series of studies completed by Blau and his students (Blau and Schoenherr 1971). But this project differed both in research design – holding technology constant by focusing on specific kinds of organizations – and in theoretical focus, being largely concerned with the impact of size on organizational structure.

Thus, when the Aston programme began to publish its first results in the late 1960s (Pugh and Hickson 1976), collected in fifty-two quite diverse organizations and including a comprehensive list of variables – six structural and eight contextual, each of which had multiple scales – organizational research took a major step forward.

2 The Aston Group and management of research strategy

The programme of research at Aston is frequently and quite correctly referred to as the Aston Group because of the large number of people who at various times were associated with the research. Those individuals who published papers in the first three volumes are listed in Table 1 but they vary enormously in their degrees of involvement, in part because of the particular phase of the research (Pugh and Hickson 1976; Pugh and Hinings 1976; Pugh and Payne 1977). Although most of the members of the Aston Group had left the Industrial Research Unit by 1969, they continued to publish together so that the official end of the programme of research might be dated as 1973. Pugh and several colleagues went on to pursue a further phase at the London Business School in the Organization Behaviour research group. The only person to remain at Aston beyond this point was Diana

Pheysey. This list does not include the many individuals who aided in collecting the data for various studies nor does it include individuals who published some of the extensions and replications (Pugh and Hinings 1976) and especially those reported in the fourth volume (Hickson and McMillan 1981), most of whom were never at the University of Aston itself. Among others, this includes Charles McMillan, Lex Donaldson and Malcolm Warner, all of whom went on to make major contributions to the literature.

The key figure was Derek Pugh who generally conceived of the broad management of research strategy, wanted an interdisciplinary team, and adapted psychometric techniques to the problems of organizational measurement. This reflected the influences of his undergraduate degree in psychology and his Master's degree in statistics. In addition, Pugh had spent some eight years in a highly interdisciplinary group prior to arriving at Aston in 1957, an experience that shaped his choice of research strategy.

The initial funding was provided by Tom Lupton, who was a member of the Aston Group for several years. This funding allowed the Industrial Administration Unit, a fully-fledged research unit, to be established in January 1961 at the renamed University of Aston and it provided a whole year in which the group could think about what needed to be done in organizational research. The major funding was provided by a grant from the Department of Scientific and Industrial Research (1961–5), followed by a Social Science Research Council (SSRC) grant (1967–70) for the major replication (the National Study), together with support from the university itself (1965–8). The latter paid for three researchers – Payne, Pheysey and Inkson – who added the role, group and climate levels of analysis.

If the task leader was Derek Pugh, the socio-emotional leadership was provided by David Hickson who was trained in administration, had a Master's degree in research, and who continuously assailed the psychologists and sociologists with questions. Another key figure was C. Robin Hinings, a sociologist hired initially as a research assistant, who (although he moved to Birmingham in 1964) continued to be a major figure in the group and in future research with Hickson during the 1970s. These three were responsible for the largest amount of publishing, particularly during the 1960s (Pugh and Hickson 1976).

Since the Aston Group was highly successful, its management of research strategy is worth extended discussion. Four key

Table 1 Key personnel in the Aston group

Person	Training	Period in Aston
Derek S. Pugh	Psychologist, Statistics	1957–1968
David J. Hickson	Administration, Research	1960–1968
C. Robin Hinings	Sociology	1961–1964*
Tom Lupton	Anthropology	1960–1962**
Keith Macdonald	Sociology	1963–1965
Christopher Turner	Sociology	1963–1965
John Child	Sociology	1967–1968
Roy Payne	Psychology	1964–1969
Ken Inkson	Psychology	1965–1967
Diana Pheysey	Psychology	1965–1969

* moved to University of Birmingham in the same city but remained highly involved in the programme of research
** head of department and supplied first set of funds

elements were involved: (1) attempts to provide a long-term programme of research; (2) interdisciplinary involvement (see Table 1), in particular sociology and psychology; (3) high interaction (and therefore consensus) made possible because everyone worked together in a single space; and (4) everyone's name on each article unless they chose not to have it.

An important element in the success of the programme was not only the support of the SSRC but also of the University of Aston, which provided three research posts during the third stage of the project after the original grant was exhausted in 1965. By 1968, the various members had left for other universities and the industrial unit as such ceased to function, although papers continued to be published until 1973.

The combination of sociologists and psychologists in organizational research is quite rare and it explains the careful use of psychometric and advanced statistical techniques applied to collective dimensions. Another unique feature of this interdisciplinary collaboration was the attempt to unite multiple levels of analysis: role, group, organization, and context, and later even the nation (Hickson and McMillan 1981). However, the sociologists were more likely to leave the group, in part because some became involved after the first exciting stage of conceptualization, and in part because some were less interested in highly quantitative approaches to organizational measurement.

Finally, perhaps the most critical component of the Aston strategy was the use of a common room in which all the research members were located. The products were truly group efforts, more so than the order of the names might suggest (the Aston Group did not explore the advantages of rotating names on these collective products; instead the ordering was usually Pugh, Hickson, Hinings, with some variations).

3 Core study, replications and major findings

The Aston programme of research started with a random sample of forty organizations stratified on product and size, and six additional organizations. The sample excluded firms smaller than 250 employees and concentrated on large business firms and public sector organizations. In these organizations, information was obtained usually from department or division heads and from the Chief Operating Officer. This stands in contrast to the theoretically purposive design of Lawrence and Lorsch (1986) and to the panel design of Hage and Aiken (Hage 1980), where relatively large numbers of individuals were interviewed. In the sample of fifty-two organizations located in Birmingham, England, the Aston Group measured six dimensions of organizational structure (see Table 2) – specialization, standardization, formalization, centralization, configuration, and traditionalism – with sixty-four components. A critical point about these various scales was their careful grounding in the literature at the time. Thus, in measuring the concept of specialization, the Bakke activity scale was used

Table 2 Core variables

Structural dimensions	Number of primary scales
1. Specialization	21
2. Standardization	3
3. Formalization	4
4. Centralization	11
5. Configuration	24
6. Traditionalism	1
Contextual dimensions	
1. Origin and history	3
2. Ownership and control	7
3. Size	3
4. Charter	7
5. Technology	6
6. Location	1
7. Dependence	10

to generate sixteen activities found in all organizations. A similar effort was made to identify a large number of decisions.

The large number of scales was reduced with factor analysis to four major dimensions, labelled 'the structuring of activities', 'the concentration of authority', 'line control of workflow', and 'the relative size of supportive component'. Of these four, only the first three were used in subsequent publications. (It was suggested that profiles of organizations could be made employing these dimensions, but this idea has never been developed in the literature.) The three dimensions were then employed to generate a typology of organizations (Pugh and Hickson 1976). The major implication was to show that there exists more than one kind of organization, not just bureaucracy. This issue of how many kinds of organizations there are and what their constituent components are is still one of the major theoretical problems today.

The same logic of analysis was then applied to the problem of describing contexts, with some modifications. The Aston researchers isolated seven concepts of organizational context – origin and history, ownership and control, size, charter, technology, location, and dependence – and measured them with thirty-seven scales. Again, careful scale construction techniques were employed. These characterizations of the environment were less exhaustive and much more diverse than the six structural dimensions, and the measurement of the environment was consequently less complete than that of organizational structure. The extended discussion of these variables is still worth intensive reading, as many of the potential insights about organizations and their contexts have not as yet been appreciated (Pugh and Hickson 1976). Indeed, it would have been much better if the article had been published as a book in which many more of the nuances could have been explored.

The central findings were that size is the major determinant of the structuring of activities, dependence and location the major determinants of the concentration of authority, and operating variability the major determinant of the line control of workflow. The Aston Group did not attempt to construct a multidimensional view of the context as they did with organizational structure. But increasingly more and more emphasis was placed on the single variable organizational size as the key structural determinant.

During the 1960s and early 1970s, there was a continual debate about the relative merits of size versus technology as the determinant of organizational structure. The Aston Group, unlike the Blau group, operationalized what they felt was the major component of technology, namely workflow integration (Pugh and Hickson 1976). In particular, Hickson, Pugh and Pheysey in their extensive analysis argued that there was little support for Woodward's (1965) hypothesis about the importance of technology as a determinant of structure. Another component, which has since proved to be more useful, is that operating variability and diversity were included under charter, demonstrating that the major impact was on control of the workflow. At the time they developed their scales, flexible manufacturing had not emerged as a major manufacturing technology.

This first study was then replicated in several ways (Pugh and Hinings 1976). Hinings and Lee studied nine manufacturing firms in Coventry; Inkson, Pugh and Hickson developed a shorter version of the interview instrument and then replicated the research in forty more organizations chosen at random in Birmingham. Finally John Child selected a national sample of eighty-two British business organizations stratified by size in six industrial sectors. All these studies confirmed the general findings regarding the relationship between size and the structuring of activities. Of these various replications, it is primarily the paper by John Child, 'Predicting and understanding organization structure' (see Pugh and Hinings 1976) that carefully attempts to resolve the various theoretical issues associated with size and its impact on the structuring of activities, essentially arguing the same position as Blau and Schoenherr (1971), namely that size is the major determinant of complexity or number of specialists in the organizational structure (see CHILD, J.).

4 Subsequent extensions

With some minor modifications, the scales were then applied to non-business organizations including occupational interest associations, public bureaucracies, churches, and educational organizations (Pugh and Hinings 1976). These studies suggested that the concepts of specialization and centralization might be more complex than the original scales had shown, and some divergences in findings began to appear.

Equally important was the work relating the structure of the organization to the roles of the managers (Pugh and Payne 1977). There has been a relative absence of work that cuts across levels even to this day. Unfortunately, by concentrating on the top echelons, the potential variation in a number of variables that were of interest was constrained. Consistent with the earlier work of Lawrence and Lorsch, role conflict between managers was found to increase with the creation of specialized departments, standard procedures, and where role performance is recorded (see LAWRENCE, P.R. AND LORSCH, J.W.).

Besides the role studies, the structural variables were also related to studies of groups and of climate (Pugh and Payne 1977). In these studies, the research design shifted to comparative cases as the number of respondents increased. There was also a proliferation of scales, thus making it difficult to draw firm conclusions. Perhaps the major lesson from this line of research is that there was considerable variation within organizations and that climate was not strongly related to organizational structure. Finally in the fourth volume of the programme, the various scales were used in a number of international contexts, most notably Japan and other countries in the Middle East and Asia.

5 Appraisal and lessons to be drawn

Three distinct kinds of appraisal can be provided: (1) the research design and methods; (2) the conceptualization and findings; and (3) the major lessons about research management. Relative to design and methods, the intent was to obtain 'objective' measures, literally by counting documents of various kinds and obtaining the information from the top echelons. The real issue is not whether counting documents is more or less objective than interviewing people or handing out questionnaires, but which kinds of organizational variables can be accurately measured in one way or another. Since structural variables reflect distributions across the entire organization, most of these are better measured by obtaining data from some random sample of all the members, especially in organizations where there is likely to be variation across ranks or groups. For example, centralization is best measured by finding out what each level of the organization says about decision making, and not just the top participants. In contrast, many of the contextual variables can more easily be measured when information obtained is from senior management because they are in a position to know, and variations in the environment relative to particular issues are therefore less likely.

Some of the conceptualizations of the environment were brilliant and to this day have not been adequately appreciated. However, an overemphasis was placed on linear measurement, given the psychometric approach. Recent work has found that non-linear approaches provide a better conceptualization of technology. And perhaps because the sociologists tended to participate less in the entire research programme, there was not an adequate understanding that structural variables are distributional measures. In particular, centralization reflects what proportion of the people participate in decision making. Furthermore, complexity should be measured not by the Bakke list of activities but instead by what proportion of the members occupy distinct specialties and at what levels.

When these proportional measures of structure are employed in a reanalysis of the Aston and national studies, as well as some of the Blau studies and other research, a consistent pattern emerges showing that technology (particularly the dimension of variability rather than the dimension of workflow integration) is a more critical determinant of structure than of size (Hage 1980). Temporal studies indicate that the major impact of size is on the formalization or standardization of activities. Furthermore, the proportion of specialists reduces the extent of centralization. These reanalyses are in sharp contrast to the conclusions of the Aston programme and reflect how a theoretical conceptualization can lead to a quite distinct view.

But the single most important lesson to be learned from the Aston Group is how to manage research. The use of a single workroom in which everyone highly interacted and where there was considerable concern about the social relationships (Pugh and Payne 1977) demonstrates that interdisciplinary groups can deliver much higher quality products.

The best evidence for this is available in the later work of David Hickson, who continued to employ the Aston approach in studying the problem of power. His first project examines the relative power of departments in organizations (Hickson *et al.* 1971), his second the processes of decision making (Hickson *et al.* 1986). Both demonstrate the high quality and aggregative effect of having research teams make decisions jointly, being involved in *all* stages of the research, including conceptualization and analysis. In addition, the second study demonstrates the importance of long-term support for collecting enough data on a large number of critical decisions. In summary, the Aston programme represents a model of how research should be managed. The collective development of scales leads to much better measurement, and the development of teams allows for a much broader assessment of their utility.

JERALD HAGE

UNIVERSITY OF MARYLAND AT

COLLEGE PARK

Further reading

(References cited in the text marked *)

* Blau, P.M. and Schoenherr, R.A. (1971) *The Structure of Organizations*, New York: Basic Books. (The most careful exposition of the role of size on organizational structure and an example of a large-scale US research programme.)

* Hage, J. (1980) *Theories of Organizations: Form, Process, and Transformation*, New York: Wiley. (Contains the findings from a panel study and a reanalysis of some of the Aston studies especially relative to the debates on size versus technology as determinants of complexity and structure.)

* Hickson, D.J., Butler, R.J., Cray, D., Mallory, G. and Wilson, D. (1986) *Top Decisions: Strategic Decision-Making in Organizations*, San Francisco, CA: Jossey-Bass. (One of the best process studies on organizations ever completed.)

* Hickson, D.J., Hinings, C.R., Lee, C.A., Schenek, R.E. and Pennings, J.M. (1971) 'A strategic contingencies theory of intraorganizational power', *Administrative Science Quarterly* 16 (2): 216–29. (An example of the power of theory to guide research.)

* Hickson, D.J. and McMillan, C. (eds) (1981) *Organization and Nation: Aston Programme IV*, Farnborough: Gower. (The scales are used in a series of comparative and international studies.)

Hickson, D.J. and Pugh, D.S. (1995) *Management Worldwide: the Impact of Societal Culture on Organizations around the Globe*, London: Penguin Books. (An analysis of the impact of national cultures on management throughout the world, with eighteen exemplifying countries described in detail.)

* Lawrence, P.R. and Lorsch, J.W. (1986) *Organization and Environment: Managing Differentiation and Integration*, revised edn, Cambridge, MA: Harvard Business School Press. (The findings from a theoretical purposive design on the issue of how the environment determines structure.)

Pugh, D.S. (ed.) (1998) *The Aston Programme*, 3 vols, Dartmouth. (The collected research papers published between 1963 and 1997 from the Aston programme and related work.)

* Pugh, D.S. and Hickson, D.J. (1976) *Organization Structure in its Context: Aston Programme I*, Farnborough: Saxon House. (Contains the original papers published on structure and context and the major empirical findings.)

Pugh, D.S. and Hickson, D.J. (1996) *Writers on Organizations* 5th edition, London: Penguin Books; Thousand Oaks, CA: Sage. (A well-established compendium describing the principal ideas of the leading authorities on organizations and their management.)

* Pugh, D.S. and Hinings, C.R. (eds) (1976) *Organizational Structure: extensions and replications: Aston Programme II*, Farnborough: Saxon House. (The title is correct but the work

is most interesting for the divergences in findings especially relative to specialization or experts and decision making in organizations.)

* Pugh, D.S. and Payne, R.L. (eds) (1977) *Organizational Behaviour in its Context: Aston Programme III*, Farnborough: Saxon House. (Contains the analysis of the relationships between structure and role, and structure and climate.)
* Woodward, J. (1965) *Industrial Organizations: Theory and Practice*, Oxford: Oxford University Press. (The other major English programme of research, still interesting for the conceptualization of technology and how changes in it produce changes in structure.)

See also: CHILD, J.; LAWRENCE, P.R. AND LORSCH, J.W.; THOMPSON, J.; WEBER, M.; WOODWARD, J.

Related topics in the IEBM: CONTEXTS AND ENVIRONMENTS; DECISION MAKING; ORGANIZATION BEHAVIOUR, HISTORY OF; ORGANIZATION STRUCTURE; ORGANIZATIONAL CONVERGENCE; POWER; TECHNOLOGY AND ORGANIZATIONS

Barbash, Jack (1910–94)

1 Biographical data
2 Equity as a condition for efficiency
3 Institutions competing to protect employees
4 Unions
5 Conclusions

Personal background

- born on 1 August 1910 in New York
- MA in economics from New York University, 1937
- economist in the US Department of Labor, 1945–8
- economist and staff director in the US Senate Subcommittee on Labor and Labor–Management Relations, 1949–53
- worked with Arthur Goldberg in negotiating the merger of the AFL-CIO in 1955
- director of research and education, Industrial Union Department, AFL-CIO, 1955–7
- professor of economics and industrial relations, University of Wisconsin-Madison, 1957–81 (John P. Bascom Professor 1976–81)
- Professor Emeritus, University of Wisconsin-Madison, 1981–94
- died on 21 May 1994 in Madison, Wisconsin

Major works

The Practice of Unionism (1956)
American Unions: Structure Government and Politics (1967)
Trade Unions and National Economic Policy (1972)
The Elements of Industrial Relations (1984)
'Like nature, industrial relations abhors a vacuum' (1987)
'Equity as function: its rise and attributions' (1989)

Summary

Jack Barbash was a leading industrial relations scholar with roots in the US Department of Labor and the American labor movement. He played an important role in the merger of the AFL and the CIO in 1955. He also conceptualized two far-reaching concepts in industrial relations. First, that equity (the fair treatment of employees) is an indispensable condition of efficiency. Second, that three groups compete to provide or protect equity in the workplace: employers, unions and governments. Employers can be fair, but the short-run incentives to increase productivity by cost-cutting and flexibility militate against a majority of employers treating employees fairly over the long term, in the absence of a threat of unionization.

Unions discipline management to treat employees like human beings, but in doing so force management to increase efficiency more than it could have through its own internal processes. Management in turn constrains the union from making onerous claims that could bring down the enterprise and cost members their jobs. The government plays a crucial role, both in providing some equity through setting minimum standards and through the extent to which it sides with employers or unions, or attempts to maintain a balance. In the final analysis while there are opportunities for cooperation between employers and employees, Barbash (1980: 3) believes there is an inherent adversarial relationship, but '…the supreme achievement of western industrial relations has been its ability to come up with institutions that blunt the force of the adversary principle'.

1 Biographical data

Jack Barbash was born in New York in 1910, the son of a silent movie theater manager. He attended Thomas Jefferson High School in Brooklyn, and received his BA and MA degrees from New York University. After working at the Works Progress Administration, the New York Department of Labor, and the Amalgamated Clothing Workers Union, he moved with his wife Kate to Washington, DC in 1939. During the decade that included the later part of the New Deal and World War II, he worked as an economist for the recently established National Labor Relations Board, the United States Office of Education, The War Production Board and the Department of Labor. Both in New York and Washington, he was active in the Socialist Party and the presidential campaigns of Norman Thomas. He spent 1948 and 1949 in Chicago as Research and Education Director of the Amalgamated Meat Cutters and Butchers Workmen's Union. In 1949 he returned to Washington to serve as staff director of the United States Senate Subcommittee on Labor and Labor Management Relations, under the chairmanship of Senator Hubert Humphrey, and as an economist working with Arthur J. Goldberg (later United States Secretary of Labor and Supreme Court Justice) in negotiating the merger of the American Federation of Labor (AFL) and Congress of Industrial Organizations (CIO). After the merger, he joined the AFL-CIO's Industrial Union Department as director of research and education.

Beginning in 1939, he was a summer staff member of the University of Wisconsin's School for Workers, and in 1957, he joined the university as a permanent faculty member, where in 1976 he became John P. Bascom Professor of Economics and Industrial Relations, a position he held until 1981 when he retired and took Emeritus status. He authored and edited fifteen books and more than 120 articles, reports and pamphlets. In 1968, he received the first Wisconsin Student Association Award for Teaching Excellence. He continued to teach after his retirement at Penn State University, California State University at Hayward and the University of California at Davis. In addition to his teaching, he was active in professional organizations, serving in 1980 as president of both the Industrial Relations Research Association and the Association for Evolutionary Economics. In 1983, he founded and chaired to 1989 the International Industrial Relations Association (IIRA) Study Group on Industrial Relations as a Field and Industrial Relations Theory. This was the first of what have grown to be 17 study groups of the IIRA. He lectured on economics and industrial relations to groups around the country and in 55 foreign countries. He was married to Kate Barbash for 60 years, his confident, constant companion and the co-editor with him (Barbash and Barbash 1989) of a volume on industrial relations theory.

2 Equity as a condition for efficiency

Barbash conceptualized the notion that equity (fair treatment of employees) is an essential condition for efficiency in an organization. The need for equity arises from the human essence of employees. This concept is implicit in Barbash's earliest writings on unions as an institution protecting employees in the workplace, but was formalized in general terms in his book *The Elements of Industrial Relations* (1984a) and most specifically in his articles 'Like nature, industrial relations abhors a vacuum' (1987) and 'Equity as function: its rise and attribution' (1989).

In *Elements*, Barbash (1984a: 4–5) develops a framework for the relationship between employers and employees, which includes three key processes: (1) management efficiency or cost discipline; (2) a work society and union protectivism against cost discipline; (3) management's counter-protectivism on behalf of management rights or prerogatives.

In 'Like nature' Barbash (1987: 172) develops the theme that '... equity is an indispensable condition of efficiency. Unionism is the institution which has historically taken the protection of employee equity as its primary task. ... equity means fairness ...: (1) having a say in the work, (2) due process in the handling of complaints, (3) fair treatment at work, (4) meaningful work, (5) fair compensation and secure employment.'

If employees are not treated equitably then there are a variety of defenses: '... (a) through informal restriction of output, (b) through unions, (c) through state intervention, (d) through individual bargaining, (e) and management, usually under pressure, introduces its own equity by way of human relations, etc.'

Barbash is painstaking in pointing out that it is not union agitation that causes inequity but rather inherent inequities which attract union agitation.

3 Institutions competing to protect employees

A second important conceptual contribution by Barbash is the notion that in a pluralistic democracy some institutions, or a combination of institutions, will attempt to protect employees. Barbash (1987: 174) refers to this as the '"law" of equilibrium'. Writing about the void created by management's concerted union-free strategy in the later 1980s and 1990s, Barbash believed that the void would be filled somehow. With unions weak, and employee involvement approaches weakening, Barbash saw employers and the state and its institutions moving to fill this vacuum. He observed that with the unions playing a lesser role in employee protection the courts were drastically modifying the common-law doctrine of employment-at-will to impose union-like constraints on the employer's right to fire.

The historical pattern Barbash observed was waves where each of the three main institutions sought to protect employees. For Barbash the American government set the stage in the 1930s through the New Deal, and especially the Wagner Act passed in 1935 and upheld by the Supreme Court in 1937. The massive union organizing was curtailed by the Taft-Harley Act (1947) and the Landrum Griffin Act (1959). Since the mid 1950s the union share of the American workforce has declined. The high-water mark was reached at the time of the merger of the AFL and CIO, a development in which Jack Barbash played a major role working with Arthur Goldberg. At the time, he saw the merger as providing a basis for renewed growth of the American labor movement (Barbash 1956). Growth occurred

in the number of members for another two decades, but the share of unions in the workplace began what became a long decline.

The big change which occurred simultaneously with the declining union share was the increasingly open opposition by employers to unions. Barbash discussed 'Why American employers hate unions' and why American employers are different from their European counterparts (Barbash 1984b: 292):

> The notion that employees need a union to protect them from their employers had always struck employers as literally un-American ... The American tradition is more individualistic ... the state is an alien force in American ideology. It is not for most Europeans, including European employers.

Barbash believed that European management was more willing to trade off increments of efficiency for instruments of social peace. At the same time there is less active union presence in the shop floor in Europe than in the United States. Associated with this is the European view that co-determination is 'positive sum', 'cooperative' in character, whereas in the US it is viewed as 'zero-sum' (1984b: 293).

With respect to what was referred to in the 1980s and 1990s as the New Industrial Relations with active human resource management (HRM) policies, Barbash asked whether such a liberal HRM strategy can exist in the absence of the countervailing presence of unionism (1984b: 294).

4 Unions

For Barbash, 'unions do it best'; that is, unions are the best vehicle to represent and protect employees, not just from the workers' perspective but for employers as well. The cost to employers to fairly represent employees is very high. Much of Barbash's writings were concerned with describing and explaining the benefits of unions to all segments of society (1956, 1967, 1972). He also was clear from the beginning that, like all human institutions, unions could have internal problems.

But, despite possible problems, unions offer the broadest range of representation. How this works is important for business people to understand. The central perspective for Barbash is the essentially conservative nature of unions which support the economic system rather than challenge it. As Barbash observed (1987: 173): '... this "dialectic" between efficiency and equity has probably saved western capitalism from Marx's scenario of catastrophe because the western states and capitalists, contrary to Marx's assumptions, had the wit and the political insight to grasp the connection and do something about it in time.'

What does the continuing decline of the trade union movement in the United States, from a high-water mark of approximately one-third of the paid workplace in the mid 1950s to under 15 per cent in the mid 1990s mean for the workforce and for employers? Does this undermine Barbash's view that 'unions do it best'? Even in his last writings he stressed that there is an equity function to be represented in some way. If unions were doing this to a much lesser extent, then other institutions, employers and government were, at least in the shorter term, substituting for them. He foresaw some institutional need that would occur, whether or not it was unions in the forms we have known them.

In the industrial relations community there have been mixed views as to whether unions will or even can re-emerge as dominant representatives of employees, with the exception of the Scandinavian countries where there has been very high union membership. This goes back to Barbash's analysis and discussion of the structure and role of unions (1956, 1967, 1972). In the mid 1990s the view was that unions had to broaden their role beyond negotiating wages and benefits and employment security toward training, career development, mobility and transferability, together with cooperation. Barbash supported cooperation between employees and employers – but he saw this associated with unions being the voice of employees – a voice which could assist employers to improve efficiency and competitiveness.

5 Conclusions

For Jack Barbash, fair treatment of employees is required for organizations to be efficient and productive. This comes from the fact that workers are human beings. It is what sets labour markets apart from all other markets. It is inevitable that some institution, or a combination of institutions in society, will represent the equity function. Unions are an institution that supports the economic system and, Barbash asserts, benefits employers as well as employees, despite visceral American employer opposition. How unions work and how the principles of the complementarity of equity and efficiency operate was a central focus not only of Barbash's writings but also his teaching. Barbash represented the third generation of institutional economists at the University of Wisconsin-Madison following 'the father of industrial relations', John R. Commons (1934) and Selig Perlman (1928). They were labour intellectuals, combining theory with active involvement in the development of public policy to protect employees in the workplace, a tradition that became known as the 'Wisconsin School'. These were powerful scholars and teachers who were role models for their students. Barbash's former students and those influenced by his writings are now putting his ideas into practice.

NOAH M. MELTZ
UNIVERSITY OF TORONTO

Further reading

(References cited in the text marked *)

* Barbash, J. (1956) *The Practice of Unionism*, New York: Harper & Row. (Sets out the major sectors of union functioning, from the perspective of the way union people themselves look at what they are doing and why.)
* Barbash, J. (1967) *American Unions: Structure, Government and Politics*, New York: Random House. (The study of unions as a governmental system.)
* Barbash, J. (1972) *Trade Unions and National Economic Policy*, Baltimore: The Johns Hopkins Press. (Delineates the policies, institutions and environments which made trade union involvement in national economic policy feasible or unfeasible in varying degrees in Sweden,

Austria, the Netherlands, West Germany, the United Kingdom and France.)

Barbash, J. (1980) 'Values in industrial relations: the case of the adversary principle', Presidential Address, in Proceedings of the 33rd Annual Meeting of the Industrial Relations Research Association, Denver: 1–7. (Suggests that the time has come for a re-evaluation of the adversarial principle in American industrial relations.)

* Barbash, J. (1984a) *The Elements of Industrial Relations*, Madison, Wisconsin: The University of Wisconsin Press. (Sets out the logic of industrial relations as an ideology and a function including the roots of the labour problem, cost discipline, the work society, the union, and management as a bargaining organization.)

* Barbash, J. (1984b) 'Why American employers hate unions', Proceedings of the 37th Annual Meeting of the Industrial Relations Association, Dallas: 291–294. (Offers explanations of management's dislike of unions.)

* Barbash, J. (1987) 'Like nature, industrial relations abhors a vacuum', *Relations Industrielles*, 42, 1: 168–179. (Develops the notion that if unionism is not performing the equity function, management and the state act as substitutes.)

* Barbash, J. (1989) 'Equity as function: its rise and attribution', in Barbash, J. and Barbash K., (eds*) Theories and Concepts in Comparative Industrial Relations*, Columbia, SC: University of South Carolina Press: 113–122. (Sets out the reasons why equity is a necessary condition of a workable industrial society.)

Barbash, J. (1997) 'Industrial relations as problem solving', in Barbash J. and Meltz, N.M. (eds) *Theorizing in Industrial Relations: Approaches and Applications*, Sydney, Australia: Australian Centre for Industrial Relations Research and Training, University of Sydney: 17–28. (Sums up the role of industrial relations mechanisms in dealing with labour problems.)

* Barbash, J. and Barbash, K. (1989) *Theories and Concepts in Comparative Industrial Relations*, Columbia, SC: University of South Carolina Press. (A collection of articles comparing industrial relations theories and practices in general, as well as in several national contexts.)

* Commons, J.R. (1934) *Institutional Economics: Its Place in the Political Economy*, New York: Macmillan.

* Perlman, S. (1928) *A Theory of the Labor Movement*, New York: Macmillan.

Meltz, N.M. (1989) 'Industrial relations: balancing efficiency and equity', in Barbash, J. and Barbash, K. (eds) *Theories and Concepts in Comparative Industrial Relations*, Columbia, SC: University of South Carolina Press: 109–113. (Argues that equity in the treatment of employees and efficiency are primarily complementary objectives.)

See also: CLEGG, H.; DUNLOP, J.T.; KOCHAN, T.; PERLMAN, S.

Related topics in the IEBM: COLLECTIVE BARGAINING; HUMAN RESOURCE MANAGEMENT; INDUSTRIAL AND LABOUR RELATIONS; INSTITUTIONAL ECONOMICS; INDUSTRIAL RELATIONS IN THE USA; TRADE UNIONS

Barnard, Chester Irving (1886–1961)

Personal background

- born 7 November 1886, Massachusetts, into a humble family; obtained entry to Mount Hermon school in 1904 and thence to Harvard College (1906–9)
- began work in statistics department of American Telephone and Telegraph Company (AT&T) in Boston
- married Grace F. Noera
- promoted through AT&T to become president of New Jersey Bell Telephone Company 1927–47
- public service as state director of New Jersey Relief Administration during the Depression of 1930s
- continued to read widely and mix with the Harvard circle of intellectuals, developing a lifelong interest in the relationship between people and organizations
- created and became president of United Service Organizations Inc. (USO) 1942–5
- active retirement as president of Rockefeller Foundation (1948–52) and chairman of the National Science Foundation (1952–4)
- died 7 June 1961

Major works

The Functions of the Executive (1938)
Organisation and Management (1948)

Summary

Chester Barnard (1886–1961) was a successful businessman whose pioneering and influential exposition of organization theory and leadership was based on a synthesis of his own business experience and ideas drawn from a wide range of reading in the social sciences. He defined an organization as a cooperative system enabling individuals to achieve through interaction that which they would be unable to achieve on their own. The role of executive managers was to define the purpose of the organization; to establish a communication system; and to develop an appropriate system of incentives to recruit, retain and motivate employees of the organization. His contribution to ideas on leadership and decision making, and his emphasis on the values and culture of the organization as a whole have had a continuing influence on management thought up to the present time.

1 Introduction

Chester Barnard's main contribution lies in his analysis of the purpose of organizations and the role of executive managers in them. He consciously set out to counteract the predominantly 'rationalist' and 'scientific' approach to organizations with what he saw as its overemphasis on economic motivation and formal structure. He therefore gave as much importance to the informal as to the formal system, to the need for organizations to satisfy a range of human and environmental needs, and to the symbiosis between leaders and followers. His definition of organizations as 'cooperative systems' was derived from analysis, reading and his own management experience.

Very little theorizing of this nature had previously been published and Barnard commented on the fact that, unlike political theory, so little is known of the large 'formal organization as the concrete social process by which social action is largely accomplished'. His work is not easy to read – he himself said that several readings are required to understand it and Peters and Waterman (1982) have called it 'virtually unreadable'. Nevertheless, many of his ideas have been picked up and developed separately by other writers over the past fifty years, particularly those on leadership, decision making and motivation.

2 Biographical data

Barnard was born into an impecunious farming family in Malden, Massachusetts on 7 November 1886. He left school at 15 and began work as a piano tuner at the Emerson Piano Company in Boston, but felt he needed more formal education and obtained a scholarship to Mount Hermon School. After two years, he was accepted at Harvard (1906) which he left in 1909 without a degree, since he lacked a science requirement.

Barnard was offered a position as a clerk in the statistics department of AT&T, newly set up by Walter S. Gifford, a family contact from childhood who 'although a scant 22 months older acted as Barnard's mentor...throughout their 40 year tenure together within the Bell system' (Scott 1992: 61). The company was undergoing a major reorganization and expansion during this period and Barnard was promoted steadily, becoming, in 1927, president of the newly created New Jersey Bell Telephone Company. He remained there for 21 years until he retired, taking it through the difficult years of the Depression and the Second World War. Despite his paternalistic philosophy and his search for cooperation with employees, he was eventually obliged to accept union membership and collective bargaining. Barnard was not opposed to unions as such but identified with corporate policy that sought to preserve managerial freedoms as against union or government imposed restrictions. He argued strongly in favour of integrated and cooperative approaches to employee relations rather than 'adversarial' collective bargaining systems on the grounds that they were divisive and counter-productive for both employees and managers.

Throughout his managerial career, Barnard continued to read widely in several branches of the social sciences and to keep in touch with a circle of academics in and around Boston. Through L.J. Henderson, a Harvard biochemist with interdisciplinary interests, he was introduced to Pareto's writings and became stimulated by what sociology could explain that classical economic and organization theory could not. He also became acquainted, through Dean Wallace Donham of Harvard Graduate School of Business Administration, with Philip Cabot, Elton Mayo and the Roethlisberger-Dickson-Whitehead reports on the Western Electric experiments at the Hawthorne Works (see MAYO, G.E.). His theory of organization consciously set out to incorporate the insights of their research.

Barnard's main work, *The Functions of the Executive*, is a revision and expansion of eight lectures delivered at the Lowell Institute in Boston in November–December 1937. He said the invitation had stimulated him 'to arrange for orderly presentation hypotheses which I had gradually constructed through several years concerning the executive processes' (Barnard [1938] 1968: xxvii). *Organisation and Management*, first published in 1948, represents a selection from a further ten years of theorizing, lecturing and writing, drawing frequently on his public service as well as his corporate experience. The topics covered include industrial relations, leadership, management education and status systems as well as contemporary views on government.

Chester Barnard's public service activities, which were encouraged by AT&T, began with work for the War Industries Board in 1917 and continued throughout his life. He wrote up as a 'concrete sociology' case study for his presentations at Harvard, a 'riot' incident in which he was involved as director of the New Jersey Relief Administration. This showed his sympathy and fair-mindedness, and illustrated his belief that voluntary national coordination and industrial cooperation inspired by the leaders of private enterprise was both morally better and more effective than government schemes. During the Second World War, he worked as president of the United Service Organizations, a non-profit corporation that provided welfare services for the armed forces, 'the most difficult single organization and management task in my experience'. After the war Barnard helped to write the US State Department report on international control of atomic energy. These experiences led to the presidency of the

Rockefeller Foundation, followed by chairmanship of the recently created National Science Foundation, where his strong character and powerful mind again enabled him to make some major contributions.

Barnard was a very private person and his religious beliefs, musical interests and personal relationships seem to have been kept largely separate from his public life, although he was particularly upset by the death of his only child Frances in June 1951. Assessments of him vary: on the one hand, he has been 'revered as a great, humane man' and in the present New Jersey Bell Telephone Company's corporate culture his 'larger than life' reputation persists; but on the other hand, and more widely at the time, he was seen as a 'loner', 'aloof and daunting', despite the respect for his knowledge, intellect and commanding presence (Scott 1992). During his later life, although none doubted his ability as an administrator and organizer, he was also regarded as too forceful, intolerant and projecting an 'imperial image'.

Although he had been unsuccessful in obtaining the Rockefeller Foundation's support for a concrete, integrated and rigorous new 'science of behaviour' that would assist management in practical situations – an 'issue--driven' social science – Barnard was able to achieve some measure of this in his own books.

3 Main contribution

Chester Barnard's theories of organization are intricately constructed and certain key themes can be extracted which illustrate his seminal influence on management thought. His aim was to provide a comprehensive theory of cooperative behaviour in formal organizations and the theme of 'cooperation' is central. It defined an organization as a system of coordinated activities, the purpose of which is to enable individuals to achieve through combined action that which they cannot achieve alone.

The role of executive management therefore follows from this: (1) to define the purpose of the organization, taking into account the changing demands of the external and internal environment (including physical, biological and social factors) and to shape appropriately the values and culture of the organization towards achieving that purpose; (2) to establish the system of communication, that is the hierarchy and reporting structure as well as the systems for the flow of information, both up and down, between all the individuals and the units; and (3) to develop an appropriate system of incentives for recruiting and retaining staff and securing their commitment to the common purpose.

An organization was a dynamic social system combining both formal and informal processes. An organization had to be both effective (if it achieved its cooperative purpose) and efficient (if it satisfied the needs of the individuals joining it). These two aspects were complementary (Barnard [1938] 1968: 60). Barnard was also acutely aware of the need to achieve at least an equilibrium in the effort/reward bargain of the employment relationship. His theory stressed the importance of non-monetary forms of reward as well as more traditional incentives in order to recruit, retain and motivate individuals. He defined 'the executive' as all managers, but most particularly as all the senior divisional or unit heads, who thus formed the executive team. He did not regard all the tasks performed by managers as necessarily 'executive' tasks, only those necessary to maintain its key purposes. Barnard put great emphasis on the importance of leadership and distinguished between the authority of 'position' and the authority of 'personality' in understanding it. The latter he largely defined as the ability of the leader to inspire 'followership' through realization of its purpose. That is, it was the acceptance of leadership by the led that was the essential quality of a leader. Moreover, 'loyalty' (to the organization) was the essential condition of cooperative contributions of all its members (Barnard [1938] 1968: 84, 220).

Although Barnard's theories were mainly related to the individuals employed in the organization he consciously developed the wider 'stake-holder' concept, since he included shareholders, customers and even suppliers and the local community as among those involved in achieving its cooperative purpose. His recognition of the importance of the 'informal' organization and its relationship to the 'formal' not only represented a reaction against the 'classical' school and an attempt to incorporate the findings of the Hawthorne experiments, but, more importantly, reflected his own experience of the realities of organizational life and the dysfunctional effects of overemphasis on either aspect. In his discussions of decision making and its difficulties he set out many ideas which were subsequently taken up by others. These included recognition of 'incremental' decision making, the importance of 'negative' or 'non-decisions' and the 'opportunist' processes used by managers with limited information. His understanding of the role of 'intuition' as much as 'rational' thought in the processes of decision making is once again becoming more widely appreciated.

Barnard's interest in the issue of management education was also illuminated by his own lecturing experience which showed the extent to which the common understanding found among senior managers from very different backgrounds seemed 'invariably to disappear' when practical concrete problems were expressed in terms of abstract theories.

4 Evaluation

Chester Barnard's *The Functions of the Executive* was a direct outcome of his failure to find an adequate explanation of his own executive experience in classic organization or economic theory. The fact that 'so austere and difficult a book' (Andrews 1968: viii) has been reprinted so many times and has steadily increased in influence and circulation since its first appearance, is a tribute to the power and intuitive sense of the ideas Barnard developed through his combination of intellect and experience. His name appears in virtually every bibliography on organization, both academic and managerial, either as a founding father or as each age rediscovers some facet of his theory particularly appropriate to its own time.

Barnard's strength lies in the very comprehensiveness of his theory and his holistic approach so that he is not therefore easily 'classified' within any one school. Many

group him as part of the 'Human Relations' school in view of his obvious contacts with Harvard and the Western Electric researchers as well as his emphasis on cooperation. Others see him as still part of the classical 'POSDCORB' (Planning, Organizing, Staffing, Directing, Coordinating, Reporting, Budgeting) tradition (Mintzberg 1973: 10) in his emphasis on coordination, communication and the principles shaping executive action.

Since many of his ideas (including that of 'bounded rationality') were so widely developed by Herbert Simon and subsequently by March, Cyert and others, Barnard is frequently placed within the 'decision making' or 'Carnegie' tradition (see MARCH, J.G. AND CYERT, R.M.; SIMON, H.A.). This has also led to his inclusion as an 'open systems' theorist. Yet his emphasis on informal systems and the need to change in response to circumstances means that he can also be seen as a 'contingency' theorist. Barnard clearly admired the work of M.P. Follett and acknowledged several of her ideas (see FOLLETT, M.P.).

Both his critics and his admirers fault Barnard for his dense, abstract presentation and lack of concrete examples. In terms of content, more criticize his omissions than his arguments, such as his neglect of the processes of strategy formulation, of the role of the Board, of the practical problems of leadership and of a developmental approach to employee participation.

W.G. Scott (1992) claims Barnard laid the foundations of the 'managerial state' of America whereby political systems have been taken over by corporate managerial styles, processes and ethics, where whatever is 'managed', whether or not 'accountable', is seen as effective. Scott recognizes that Barnard failed to perceive that his high expectations of moral integrity from top executives, the 'managerial guardians', might not be realized in practice.

On the other hand, recent evaluations of Chester Barnard have also been highly enthusiastic. Peters and Waterman, for example, credit him chiefly for his emphasis on purpose and for sensing 'the unconventional and critical role of executives in making it all happen', for 'shaping and managing its shared values' and culture while 'ensuring that the organization simultaneously achieves its economic goals' (1982: 97). Barnard's perceptions that 'a purpose to be effective, must be accepted by all contributors to the system of efforts' and the importance of understanding the 'whole' rather than merely certain aspects are also seen by them as major strengths.

Barnard's ability to achieve a balance between academic discourse and practitioner reminiscence and to show that research and practice can be reconciled and yet be capable of development (Andrews 1968; Williamson 1990) is the quality for which he is still admired.

5 Conclusions

Chester Barnard's ideas on the role of management in large organizations were in very many respects ahead of his time. It is difficult to envisage how management literature might have developed without the originality and insights of *The Functions of the Executive* and its holistic grasp of organizational purpose and the interrelationships between formal and informal systems. Barnard was really the first to focus on the role of senior executives in large organizations and to question what they are there for. He was able to draw from but go beyond other writers of the period and their adoption of either 'classical theory', 'scientific management' or 'human relations' approaches (see HUMAN RELATIONS). His practical experience tempered and informed his own theorizing and secured recognition of his ideas by both academics and practitioners. That this has continued reflects the way in which he achieved a successful balance between the 'hard' and 'soft' approaches to organization, between the 'science' of management and the 'arts' of organizing, or to use his own metaphor for the management of organizations 'the structure of the symphony, the art of its composition and the skill of its execution' (Barnard [1938] 1968: xxxiv).

SHEILA G. ROTHWELL

Further reading

(References cited in the text marked *)

* Andrews, K.R. (1968) Introduction to 30th anniversary edition of *The Functions of the Executive*, Cambridge, MA: Harvard University Press. (A scholarly evaluation of Chester Barnard's book, interpreting his ideas and praising his insights.)
* Barnard, C.I. (1938) *The Functions of the Executive*, Cambridge, MA: Harvard University Press, 1968. (A set of papers, originally delivered as lectures at the Lowell Institute in 1937, setting out the author's influential distillation of his own experience, thinking and reading on the nature and purpose of executive management and on organization behaviour.)
* Barnard, C.I. (1948) *Organisation and Management*, Cambridge, MA: Harvard University Press. (A further set of selected papers developing ideas drawn from his public service as well as his corporate experience, covering industrial relations, leadership, management education, and status, among other topics.)
Clutterbuck, D. and Crainer, S. (1990) *Makers of Management: Men and Women who Shaped the Business World*, London: Macmillan. (Refers to Barnard as one of the 'early pioneers' who saw business organizations as the most effective means of achieving widespread social advancement, and quotes writers praising his intellect and the impact of his ideas.)
Cyert, R.M. and March, J.G. (1963) *A Behavioral Theory of the Firm*, Englewood Cliffs, NJ: Prentice Hall. (The authors build on Barnard's theories, linking classical economics to contemporary theories of decision making in large firms.)
* Mintzberg, H.M. (1973) *The Nature of Managerial Work*, New York: Harper & Row. (An empirical study of the activities of chief executives in which the author criticizes Barnard's 'classical' view of executive work, but his own list of five basic reasons why organizations need managers largely reflects Barnard's ideas on executive functions.)
* Peters, T.J. and Waterman, R.H. (1982) *In Search of Excellence*, New York: Harper & Row. (A management best seller on the key factors making for successful American companies, emphasizing the management of people and culture and praising Barnard's insights.)
Pugh, D.S. (ed.) (1971) *Organizational Theory: Selected Readings*, Harmondsworth: Penguin. (Covers structure, management and behaviour

in organizations and includes Barnard's chapter on 'the executive functions'.)

* Scott, W.G. (1992) *Chester I. Barnard and the Guardians of the Managerial State*, Lawrence, KS: University Press of Kansas. (An account of Barnard's life and writings, tracing the impact of his ideas on American institutions.)

Simon, H.A. (1957) *Administrative Behaviour*, New York: Macmillan. (Defines management in terms of decision making and builds on Barnard's ideas, developing in particular the concept of 'bounded rationality'.)

Tillett, A., Kempner, T. and Wills, G. (1970) *Management Thinkers*, Harmondsworth: Penguin. (A useful anthology of writers on management, grouped under the themes of 'efficiency', 'welfare' and 'cooperation'; Tillett's introduction to the extracts from Barnard's writings credits him as the founder of 'organizational analysis'.)

* Williamson, O.E. (ed.) (1990) *Organization Theory: From Chester Barnard to The Present or Beyond*, Oxford: Oxford University Press. (Papers contributed to a conference in honour of the 50th anniversary of the publication of *The Functions of the Executive*.)

Wolf, W.B. (1974) *The Basic Barnard*, ILR Paperback no. 14, Ithaca, NY: Cornell University. (Contains extracts from Barnard's writings and an inventory of his papers.)

See also: FAYOL, H.; FOLLETT, M.P.; KOTTER, J.; MARCH, J.G. AND CYERT, R. M.; MAYO, G.E.; MINTZBERG, H.; PETERS, T.; SIMON, H.A.

Related topics in the IEBM: COLLECTIVE BARGAINING; COMMUNICATION; CONTEXTS AND ENVIRONMENTS; DECISION MAKING; HAWTHORNE EXPERIMENTS; HUMAN RELATIONS; INCENTIVES; INDUSTRIAL RELATIONS IN THE USA; LEADERSHIP; MANAGEMENT DEVELOPMENT; MANAGEMENT IN NORTH AMERICA; MANAGEMENT SCIENCE; ORGANIZATION BEHAVIOUR; ORGANIZATION BEHAVIOUR, HISTORY OF; ORGANIZATION STRUCTURE

Bartlett, Christopher A. (1943–) and Ghoshal, Sumantra (1948–)

1 Main contribution
2 Evaluation
3 Conclusions

Christopher A. Bartlett

Personal background

- born 10 December 1943 in Brisbane, Australia
- educated at the University of Queensland, Australia (BA 1964) and Harvard Business School (MBA 1971, DBA 1979)
- before joining Harvard Business School he was a consultant for McKinsey & Company, and general manager of the French subsidiary of Baxter Travenol Laboratories
- currently professor of business administration at the Harvard Business School, Boston, Massachusetts

Sumantra Ghoshal

Personal background

- born 26 September 1948 in India
- held line and staff managerial positions with the Indian Oil Corporation
- educated at the Sloan School of Management, MIT (PhD 1985) and Harvard Business School (DBA 1986)
- associate professor and professor of business policy, INSEAD Business School, Fontainebleau, France, 1988–94
- since 1994 has been the Robert P. Bauman Professor of Strategic Leadership, London Business School

Major works

Managing Across Borders; The Transnational Solution (1989)

Transnational Management: Text, Cases and Readings in Cross Border Management (1995)

Summary

Christopher Bartlett and Sumantra Ghoshal have made an influential and significant contribution to our knowledge of the international firm and its management, strategy and structure. They argue that a powerful paradigm shift has been taking place in international business: from earlier multinational and global predispositions to a transnational strategic stance. This 'Transnational Solution' has involved the firm simultaneously seeking to achieve global efficiency and responsiveness to country/ market differences, and the maximization of innovation and organizational learning. In structural terms the transnational corporation is characterized as an integrated network organization, retaining some strategic and planning functions at the centre, but otherwise dispersing and decentralizing its activities to achieve flexibility and rapid organizational response. Critics have questioned the speed and extent to which transnational structures are being adopted, with many international firms resorting to simpler rather than more complex forms in the 1990s.

1 Main contribution

Bartlett and Ghoshal made a major contribution to the emergence of international management as a field of study in its own right – not simply a branch of international economics, but one where the strategies and decision-making of the international firm in its global environment is the central focus. Building on the work of Yves Doz, C.K. Prahalad and many others, it is in Bartlett and

43

Ghoshal's influential work (1989) that we find the fullest elaboration of the transnational corporation as a new form of international business integration which transcends frontiers. One important strength of their work is its broad, multidisciplinary sweep, linking together issues of cross border management, international strategy, organizational structure analysis and organizational psychology.

Their work was based on a five-year-long research study involving interviews with 236 managers in the worldwide operations of nine international firms: Procter and Gamble, Unilever and Kao in branded packaged goods, General Electric, Philips and Matsushita in consumer electronics, ITT, Ericsson and NEC in the telecommunications switching industry. The sample was structured as a comparative study to contrast the international strategies of firms from the United States, Europe and Japan.

Bartlett and Ghoshal's starting point is the distinction between global, multinational and international industries and their related strategies. In global industries such as consumer electronics, they argue, efficiency is the key driving force; firms like Matsushita are able to produce standardized colour TV's for a global market with massive economies of scale. In multinational industries, for example branded packaged goods such as soap powders, national responsiveness was found to be the key driving force. In international industries such as telecommunications switching, organizational learning, 'the ability to transfer knowledge and expertise from one part of the organization to others world wide' appeared to be the key to competitive advantage.

However, Bartlett and Ghoshal argue that in the intensive competitive conditions of the 1980s such 'unidimensional' competitive advantage was not enough to maintain corporate success and, instead, strategic requirements became multidimensional:

In the emerging international environment ... there are fewer and fewer examples of industries that are pure global, textbook multinational, or classic international. Instead, more and more businesses are being driven by *simultaneous* demands for global efficiency, national responsiveness, and worldwide learning. These are the characteristics of what we call a *transnational industry.*

(Bartlett and Ghoshal 1987: 12)

In their view it is the *multiple and simultaneous* nature of this imperative which characterizes transnational strategy. Bartlett and Ghoshal suggest this is a relatively recent phenomenon, responding to the complex pressures characterizing the international business environment of the late twentieth century. In structural terms the transnational corporation is characterized as an integrated network organization, retaining some strategic and planning functions at the centre, but otherwise dispersing and decentralizing its activities to achieve flexibility and rapid organizational response. Communication and coordination will often emphasize informal processes and subsidiary interdependency, in contrast to more traditional, hierarchical, headquarters/ subsidiary relationships.

The significance of this step is that since at least the late 1960s the international strategy literature had been dominated by the tension between globalization and localization pressures. The transnational concept provided a solution which transcended this conflict. In contrast to the globalizing forces emphasized by Theodore Levitt (see LEVITT, T.), Bartlett and Ghoshal argue that new localization forces were creating a further paradigm shift. Many consumers' expectations were now developing beyond a standardized 'world' product to greater levels of customization, features and quality, but still at the cost levels associated with global production. As well as more demanding customers, recessionary forces during the 1980s decade were increasing the demands host governments were making of international firms in terms of, for example, local content requirements, technology transfer and voluntary export restraints.

One important aspect of their contribution to international management as a relatively young and developing field of study was their definition of international business terminology. The terms 'multinational', 'global' and 'transnational' had been used largely interchangeably in the international business literature until the mid 1980s. For example, the United Nations used 'transnational corporation' as a generic term for the international firm. Bartlett and Ghoshal gave these concepts specific and special meanings. The renewed pressures to be flexible and responsive in their country level operations, they argued, required the return of *national* into the terminology. At the same time the continuing pressures for worldwide integration and economic efficiency was indicated by the prefix *trans*.

The transnational corporation and organizational structure

Bartlett and Ghoshal developed an organizational typology which corresponded to their strategy categories. They identified four types of organizational structure.

1 *Multinational organizational model.* This is reflected in the decentralized organizational federation of, for example, pre-war European companies with relatively autonomous subsidiaries highly responsive to local market differences. An important characteristic of these firms (for example British companies operating in Imperial markets) was the extent to which the firm was run on the basis of personal relationships and family ownership links. Often, very simple financial reporting procedures were used and the need for coordination was low.

2 *International organizational model.* Bartlett and Ghoshal argue that this type of structure became common after 1950 when 'The key task for companies that internationalized then was to transfer knowledge and expertise to overseas environments that were less advanced in technology or market development' (1989: 49). This was the organization form that best reflected the technological causes of Vernon's international product life cycle theory. In the international model some functions are centralized and others decentralized; in particular, knowledge and research and development take place at the centre and are subsequently transferred to the subsidiaries.

3 *Global organizational model.* This model emphasizes efficiency, centralization and control – a 'hub and spoke' model typical of Japanese internationalization in the 1980s – and is the organizational equivalent of global strategy, with its emphasis on efficiency and standardization.

4 *Transnational organizational model.* In Bartlett and Ghoshal's analysis the transnational corporation is a new organizational form which has developed in response to the increasingly turbulent international business environment. The transnational involves a globally integrated network structure '... in which increasingly specialized units world wide ... [are] ... linked into an integrated network that [enables] ... them to achieve their multidimensional strategic objectives of efficiency, responsiveness and innovation. The strength of this configuration springs from its fundamental characteristics: dispersion, specialization and interdependence' (1989: 89).

The features of the transnational corporation include:

a) a complex configuration of assets and capabilities in which some functions and resources are centralized and others decentralized, creating an interdependent *network* of specialized units;

b) flexibility in the role of overseas subsidiaries with differentiated contributions by national units to integrated world wide operations;

c) knowledge developed jointly and shared worldwide. This contrasts with the centralization of development and diffusion of knowledge in the global and international organization models, and its dispersal in the multinational organizational model.

Bartlett and Ghoshal's concept of the transnational corporation goes beyond the creation of a 'globally integrated network organization' and other changes in terms of the multinational corporation's (MNC's) formal structure. It also involves significant changes to informal organizational processes and the

45

'mindsets' of international managers. In their 1990 *Harvard Business Review* article they discuss two managerial 'traps' which confronted international firms in the 1980s – one strategic and one structural. The strategic trap was to adopt static, unidimensional strategies to deal with an increasingly dynamic, complex environment. The structural trap was that in responding with more complex strategies, MNC managers frequently adopted much more complex matrix style structures which were costly and cumbersome. Yet the analysis of environmental and strategy requirements was essentially correct, Bartlett and Ghoshal argue, developing an interesting biological metaphor for MNC change processes:

> ... those companies that adopted matrix structures ... correctly recognized the need for a multidimensional organization to respond to growing external complexity. The problem was that they defined their organizational objectives in purely structural terms. Yet formal structure describes only the organization's basic anatomy. Companies must also concern themselves with organizational physiology – the systems and relationships that allow the lifeblood of information to flow through the organization. And they need to develop a healthy organizational psychology – the shared norms, values and beliefs that shape the way individual managers think and act.
>
> (Bartlett and Ghoshal 1990: 140)

From their MNC interview research base, they found that the most successful companies in managing change and improving their organizational capability were those that started by trying to change organizational psychology, individual managerial attitudes and informal processes, rather than the organization's structure. The ideal starting point was 'organizational psychology and physiology' rather than 'anatomy'. They quote one of their executive interviewees as stating: 'The challenge is not so much to build a matrix structure as it is to create a matrix in the minds of our managers' (1990: 145).

2 Evaluation

Bartlett and Ghoshal discussed the emergent transnational corporation (TNC) as much in terms of management processes and mindsets as formal organizational structures. However, pursuing further their biological metaphor, their emphasis on the TNC's physiology and psychology obscured the precise nature of the organizational structure skeleton holding the international firm together.

Bartlett and Ghoshal's work excited much controversy and interest, and became a reference point for the international business strategy literature of the 1990s. A number of research studies were undertaken to test the concept of transnationality. Some critics questioned Bartlett and Ghoshal's research methodology and the validity of coming to such far-reaching conclusions about international business from such a small sample of firms. Examples of companies cited as transnational corporations (such as Electrolux, SKF or Asea Brown Boveri) in subsequent discussions, were criticized by some writers as atypical. The examples tended to involve international firms originating from one small home country – Sweden. The decentralized network which emerged, it was argued, was quite different from the more typical situation where a more centralized MNC emerged from a large home market such as the United States or Japan.

One direct piece of empirical research on the 'transnational solution' is Leong and Tan's 1993 study. This sought to test the validity of the Bartlett and Ghoshal organizational typology by a questionnaire survey of 151 MNC executives. The survey asked the respondents to categorize their own firm into one of Bartlett and Ghoshal's four organizational types, and to indicate the degree of fit with the sets of organizational characteristics summarized earlier. Leong and Tan found that multinational corporations dominated, followed by the international and global forms. The transnational form was found to be the least evident structure. One of the explanations for the findings advanced by the researchers was that most MNCs are at present operating with either multinational, international or global structures, hence the transnational represented an ideal form 'most companies are attempting to adopt' in the future. In consequence the precise characteristics of a future structure were unclear for the executives involved. A more critical stance in relation to these findings could simply conclude that there was a lack of support for the emergence of the transnational phase as proposed by Bartlett and Ghoshal.

Turner and Henry, in their 1994 study, sought to identify the extent of 'transnationalism' in a sample of ten US and European MNCs. The Bartlett and Ghoshal characteristics tested were dispersal of assets, degree of specialization and interdependence among subsidiaries. They found little evidence to support the adoption of these organizing characteristics, and even where there was some support for the geographical dispersal of assets (Unilever, Nestlé and Asea/ Brown Boveri) this was primarily the result of corporate origins and 'administrative heritage'. They concluded that most international firms had responded to the 1990s environment by simplifying their structures around worldwide product divisions.

3 Conclusions

The transnational solution is a multidimensional corporate strategy involving the simultaneous pursuit of efficiency, responsiveness and global learning. Critics suggest transnationality presents a difficult, if not impossible balancing act, the trade-offs involved insufficiently explored in the Bartlett and Ghoshal model. Empirical studies have given them relatively little support, in fact suggesting during the 1990s that multinational firms have been concerned with simplifying their organizational structures, rather than establishing more complex, network forms. In the absence of hard evidence of a paradigm shift, a number of critics have suggested transnationality is a long-term aspiration of many international firms, rather than a business reality. Bartlett and Ghoshal themselves have argued that there was no inevitability about the direction of strategic change, or that transnationality is in fact the eventual end point. Rather they

were concerned with the establishment of transnationality as one strategic mentality of worldwide companies among a number of possible predispositions, the eventual outcome depending on the complex environmental and competitive pressures international firms face.

ROBIN JOHN
SOUTH BANK UNIVERSITY BUSINESS SCHOOL

Further reading

Bartlett, C.K. and Ghoshal, S. (1987) 'Managing across borders; new strategic requirements' *Sloan Management Review*, 28, Summer: 7–18. (A succinct journal article providing an early statement of the transnational hypothesis.)

* Bartlett, C.A. and Ghoshal, S. (1989) *Managing Across Borders; The Transnational Solution*, London, Century Business. (The classic work by these authors, discussed at length in this entry.)

* Bartlett, C.A. and Ghoshal, S. (1990) 'Matrix management: not a structure, a frame of mind', *Harvard Business Review*, July–Aug: 138–145. (An important article in which the authors provide a powerful critique of global matrix organizational structures.)

* Bartlett, C.A. and Ghoshal, S. (1995) *Transnational Management: Text, Cases and Readings in Cross Border Management*, second edition, Homewood, Il: Richard D Irwin. (In this student textbook the authors provide useful summaries of the main propositions, linking these to classic readings in the international management literature and relevant case studies.)

Bartlett, C., Doz, Y. and Hedlund, G. (1990) *Managing the Global Firm*, London: Routledge. (A collection of essays providing an important discussion of cross border management and the transnational.)

* Leong, S.M. and Tan, C.T. (1993) 'Managing across borders: an empirical test of the Bartlett and Ghoshal (1989) organizational typology', *Journal of International Business Studies*, 3: 449–464. (An important research study testing the transnational model and the organizational typology.)

* Turner, I. and Henry, I. (1994) 'Managing international organizations: lessons from the field', *European Management Journal*, December 12, 4: 417–431. (An important article testing the 1989 model with a sample of ten US and European international firms.)

See also: ADLER, N.; HAMEL, G. AND PRAHA-
LAD, C.K.; LEVITT, T.; OHMAE, K.

Related topics in the IEBM: GLOBALIZA-
TION; INTERNATIONAL BUSINESS, FUTURE
TRENDS; INTERNATIONAL MARKETING;
MARKETS; MULTINATIONAL CORPORA-
TIONS; MULTINATIONAL CORPORATIONS,
HISTORY OF; MULTINATIONAL,
CORPORATIONS ORGANIZATION STRUC-
TURE IN; NETWORKS AND ORGANIZATIONS;
ORGANIZATION CULTURE; ORGANIZATION
TYPES; ORGANIZATIONAL CONVERGENCE;
TRANSFER PRICING.

Bata, Tomas (1876–1932)

Personal background

- born in Zlin, Moravia (later Czechoslovakia), 3 April 1876, the son of a shoemaker
- Founded his own compnay, in partnership with his sister and brother, in Zlin, 1894
- first of three visits to the USA in 1904, learning many of the concepts of industrial management
- during the First World War, formed a cartel of manufacturers providing shoes and boots to the Austrian army
- visited the USA again in 1919; visited the Ford factory, met and befriended Henry Ford, and began formulating the Bata system management
- killed in an air crash near Zlin, 12 July 1932

Major works

Me Zacatky (autobiography) (1924)

Summary

Tomas Bata (1876–1932) came from humble beginnings as the son of a shoemaker in a small town in Moravia to be one of the foremost entrepreneurs of the new state of Czechoslovakia. Strongly influenced by American industrial practices and the early thinking and practices of Henry Ford, Bata combined these with the cultural distinctiveness of his native Moravia to create what is still known as the 'Bata system of management'. This participative, human-oriented system was many years in advance of its time, including concepts such as empowerment, team management, worker participation and quality improvement. Unfortunately, Bata's system did not survive his premature death in 1932 and the subsequent occupation of Czechoslovakia by Nazi Germany seven years later. The company he founded still exists today, domiciled in Toronto, Canada.

1 Introduction

The Bata system of management originated from Henry Ford's ideas – before 1926 – as summarized in his seminal book *Today and Tomorrow* (Ford 1926). Ford's early view of management was based on worker autonomy, knowledge, just-in-time, waste minimization, quality and customer's involvement (customization): it was all but abandoned by Ford's turnaround embrace of mass production, Taylorism and hierarchical management in the 1930s.

In Moravia, Tomas Bata remained true to Ford's original ideas and brought them to practical fruition in the late 1920s and early 1930s. Young Tomas, who repeatedly visited, trained and worked in the USA, brought home the lessons of self-reliance, total quality management, strategic flexibility, high technology, worker participation and use of knowledge as capital. In the 1920s and early 1930s, in Moravia (in Zlin of former Czechoslovakia), Bata practised a remarkable management system which was some fifty years before its time.

2 The Bata system of management

The Bata system is a management system of extraordinary productivity and effectiveness. Its main characteristics include: integration instead of division of labour, whole-system orientation, continuous innovation and quality improvement, team and workshop self-management, profit-sharing and autonomy, workers' participation and co-determination, clearly-defined responsibilities, organizational flexibility, vigorous automation and most importantly – an uncompromisingly human-orientated capitalistic enterprise. Every employee was a partner, co-worker or associate and all workers were to become owners and capitalists.

To the contrary, mass production was based on employee disempowerment and political dependency, collective bargaining, command hierarchy of control, low quality, simplicity, extreme division of labour and disregard for the customer (see FORD, H.; TAYLOR, F.W.). This system had reigned supreme essentially from the 1930s until the 1970s. By then the Japanese-style management – with mass customization, lean production, total quality management, integrated-process management and trade-off free management – started replacing the dysfunctional hierarchies of mass production.

3 Basic principles

There are clearly identifiable principles which Tomas Bata evolved, adhered to and ultimately made to work.

His first slogan 'Thinking to the people, labor to the machines!' he proclaimed at the factory gate. He eliminated the intermediaries: a large network of Bata-run stores and outlets complemented and extended his production operations by integrating customers into the production process. He also made the consumer and the public not only the purpose, but the very foundation of his enterprise. 'Our customer – our master' and 'Service to the public' were not just slogans, but sound principles of business. Production and profits were not the ends, but the means towards improving the individual lives of all Bata employees (Bata people liked to call themselves 'associates'). Employment was stable and long term: part of each worker's earnings was reinvested in the company (the initial endowment put up by the company) – each worker became a capitalist and partial co-owner. Bata claimed that the quality of employee life was a primary concern of the employer (not of the state). He offered economic incentives to employees to stop drinking and smoking, or to lose weight. He provided family housing (with gardens) and a minimum social infrastructure: hospitals, museums, churches, swimming pools, leisure facilities, sport stadiums, roads – all part of the self-imposed responsibilities of Bata Enterprises. He also established and ran his own school of management: an institution considered too important to be left to the external and traditional providers of business education. He was seeking enhanced self-reliance, independence and vertical integration: railroads, waterways, airports, land, forests, even local government – all became connected to his enterprise. He strove to operate with no debt and with no credit: all state taxes were paid according to almost fanatical principles of integrity.

Thanks to these and similar principles, Bata's business grew and flourished even during the worldwide depression of 1929–32. He was fully aware of the qualities of his system: he knew it was a whole which could not be copied in parts – there were no 'company secrets'. Often he assured his associates that no fair competition could ever pose a threat to their performance. However, the Bata system was gravely damaged by the 'unfair competition' of politics and ideology in 1939 by the Nazis, then it was vilified and later proscribed by Marxists and communists of the post-1948 era. Bata's own family, managers and workers were forced into exile. This story is recounted in Tomas' son's book (Bata 1990), which also describes the current scope of Bata international operations. Surprisingly, after 1989 and the subsequent dissolution of Czechoslovakia, the Bata system continued to be vilified, its promoters and practitioners still ignored or ridiculed by the ex-communist regime.

4 Operational practices

Bata's symbiosis of workers' autonomy and empowerment through technology was unique and even by today's standards still remains somewhat 'futuristic'. Modern US and Japanese companies have only recently started to experiment with similar concepts. Let us consider a short sample of Bata practices:

1 the process of continuous innovation and improvement; the total system of preventive maintenance: machine shop working as 'clockwork';

2 in-house adaptation and rebuilding of all purchased machinery; 10 per cent of the engineering employees involved directly in the R&D function;

3 the assurance of continuously high-quality output with processes streamlined to eliminate breakdowns and stoppages and individual workers given quality responsibility;

4 total manufacturing flexibility achieved:
  (i) by breaking the traditional large factory plant into smaller, semi-autonomous and specialized workshops; and
  (ii) by making all machines self-contained, independently powered and motorized by electric motors (referred to as 'electric robots' by Bata);

5 changes in product styles and types were achieved quickly (in a few hours) by rearranging machine sequences and layouts, by pulling out machines temporarily ('decoupling the line') and by designing all adjustments and customization into the final stages of the production process;

6 a close personal 'ownership' relationship between workers and 'their' machine: not only was there no suspicion of the machinery but there was also no neglect, only pride of ownership, emotional involvement and total care;

7 all operators were able to stop production line conveyors at will; all waste in production was minimized (everything had to be just in time for the next step); all machines were designed to serve 'the process', not just perform individual operations;

8 dedication to automation: one of the Bata machines 'did everything but talk and sing' (the note-scribbling overseas visitors were never able to copy it; a machine called 'Union press' produced a pair of shoes in a single movement);

9 a perfect, semi-automated, rotational system of preventive maintenance of all machinery (including full overhauls and updates), carried out without ever stopping the production.

5 Human capital at Bata Enterprises

Another set of Bata's concepts is related directly to people. The need for total involvement of top management was never questioned. In order to be promoted to a top managerial position, one had to personally make a pair of shoes. All executives remained close to their product and actually had to learn how to make it themselves (compare this with top executives who have never even observed how their company's products are made or used).

Quality circles (see TOTAL QUALITY MANAGEMENT) also emerged spontaneously because they had to – the very system design of Bata management required it. More interesting is that top executives (and Bata himself) were part of the continuous quality improvement process: their suggestions ranged from company-store door design to teaching all workers statistics and profit calculations.

Many decades before the collapse of management hierarchies, Bata and his entire directorship ate in the company cafeteria (to assure proper quality of food and operations). It was insisted that each executive must be replaceable and that competent leaders must be continually trained and educated: the company-run school, the Tomas Bata School of Work and Management, was the answer. Bata was no fool: 'High wages can only be attained through human intelligence', he insisted.

Bata was also an optimist ('A day has 86,400 seconds'): he simply knew it was possible to succeed. And management by walking around? He put his office in an elevator – in order to be close to his workers. He laughed at the notion that any acquired wealth must be taken from somebody else (the 'zero-sum' fallacy): his workers were paid eight times more than the prevailing average. He projected that each worker should be able to retire at 40 and live from their accumulated capital. The best savings strategy, he taught, was the repayment of debts. He warned that producers asking for state customs and quota protections ultimately harm the public and minimize employees' gains. To beg for subsidies or bailouts was not only unworthy of a professional manager, but to Bata, any such managed competition was unacceptable.

He also dreamt, almost longingly, about the 'new machines' which would ease human mental work, computations and accounting. He had big plans for such computing machines. Bata's response to the ravages of the Depression was masterful and yet not tried anywhere else: he achieved workers' approval to reduce wages by 40 per cent; at the same time he took steps to reduce their cost of living expenditures by 50 per cent; finally, he reduced the prices of all Bata products by 50 per cent. It worked: Bata Enterprises and employees flourished even during the Depression. Bata was fond of saying: 'And how do they do things in England?' He liked to answer, rather proudly: 'Just the other way around. In England there is no understanding between managers and workers. They do not trust each other. They even have powerful adversary organizations, separately for employers and employees. Employers are not allowed to raise wages without approval ...workers cannot accept work on their own terms....' Tomas Bata was never short of courage: 'We are the pioneers. The cowards did not even start on the journey, the weak were lost on the way. Forward!'

MILAN ZELENY
FORDHAM UNIVERSITY AT LINCOLN CENTER

Further reading

(References cited in the text marked *)

Bata, T. (1992) *Knowledge in Action: Bata-System of Management*, Amsterdam: IOS Press. (First English translation of Bata's own thoughts and speeches.)

Cekota, A. (1968) *Tomas Bata: Entrepreneur Extraordinary*, Rome: EIS. (Full-length biography of Tomas Bata, concentrating on personal details but with much information on his thought and principles.)

* Bata, T.J. (1990) *Bata: Shoemaker to the World*, Toronto, ONT: Stoddart Publishing. (Describes the current scope of Bata international operations.)

* Ford, H. (1926) *Today and Tomorrow*, Garden City, NY: Doubleday, reprinted 1988, Cambridge, MA: Productivity Press. (Seminal work describing Ford's early view of management.)

Vlcek, J. (1971) 'Das Bata-Führungssystem', *Industrielle Organisation* 40 (11): 615–19. (One of the first resurrective discussions of the Bata system.)

Zeleny, M. (1987) 'The roots of modern management: Bat'a-system', *Human Systems Management* 6 (1): 4–7. Also (in Japanese) in *Standardization and Quality Control* 40 (1): 50–3. (English and Japanese discussion of the Bata system.)

Zeleny, M. (1988) 'Bat'a-system of management: managerial excellence found', *Human Systems Management* 7 (3): 213–19. (Detailed essay including statistics, quotes and excerpts for a serious student.)

Zeleny, M. 'Three men talk on Bat'a-system' (in Japanese), *Standardization and Quality Control* 41 (1): 15–24. (Discussion in Japanese of the Bata system.)

Zeleny, M. (1988) 'Practical roots of IPM', appendix to 'Integrated process management: a management technology for the new competitive era', in M.K. Starr (ed.), *Global Competitiveness: Keeping the United States on Track*, New York: W.W. Norton & Co., Inc. (The Bata system related as a case relevant to the US efforts for improved productivity.)

See also: DEMING, W.E.; FORD, H; JURAN, J.M.; MAYO, G.E.; TAYLOR, F.W.

Related topics in the IEBM: HAWTHORNE EXPERIMENTS; HUMAN RESOURCE MANAGEMENT; INDUSTRIAL DEMOCRACY; JAPANIZATION; JOB DESIGN; LABOUR PROCESS; MANAGEMENT IN JAPAN; ORGANIZATION BEHAVIOUR; ORGANIZATION BEHAVIOUR, HISTORY OF; TOTAL QUALITY MANAGEMENT

Bedaux, Charles E. (1886–1944)

1 Introduction
2 Main contribution
3 Evaluation
4 Conclusion

Personal background

- born 11 October 1886 in Paris, France
- emigrated to the USA, 1906
- worked for a furniture company in Grand Rapids, Michigan
- founded first Bedaux consultancy firm in Cleveland, 1918
- returned to France, 1927
- became advisor to the Nazis and the Vichy government after the fall of France in 1940
- captured in the Allied invasion of North Africa, 1942
- committed suicide, 18 February 1944

Major works

The Bedaux Efficiency Course for Industrial Application (1917)
Code of Standard Policy (1928, unpublished)
Code of Application Principles (undated, c.1930, unpublished)
Training Course for Field Engineers (undated, c.1930, unpublished)
Vade Mecum (1930, unpublished)

Summary

Charles E. Bedaux claimed to have found a scientific relationship between work and fatigue. This represented an important extension of the systems developed by F.W. Taylor which had failed to satisfactorily deal with the impact of strain and tiredness on performance. Bedaux's approach provided the basis for a universal measure of all work – the Bedaux or 'B' unit. This unit was used as the basis for a time-and-effort-related piecework pay system. The system spread quickly and extensively across Europe and the USA during the 1930s. However, research into the Bedaux system found that it was resisted by middle and supervisory management and it was poorly understood by many workers.

1 Introduction

Charles E. Bedaux led a bizarre life. Born in Paris, France in 1886, he emigrated to the USA at the age of 20 and had a variety of jobs, from selling life insurance to selling toothpaste which removed ink spots. Finally, he was employed by a furniture company in Grand Rapids where he developed a system for measuring worker performance which took account of fatigue. This system was the source of his fame and of a considerable fortune. He developed networks of consultancies in the USA and internationally to apply his ideas.

On returning to France in 1927 he gravitated towards fascist politics and thirteen years later when the country fell he became industrial advisor to the Nazis and the Vichy government. Bedaux's technocratic views of society held a strong appeal to the Nazis. He had a strong sense of mission, believing that poverty could be eradicated if production was organized on his methods and that an efficient society could be created if led by engineers and technocrats. In 1942 he was captured during the Allied invasion of North Africa where he was directing a scheme to build a 2,000-mile peanut-oil pipeline across the Sahara Desert. Before standing trial, he committed suicide in 1944 (Littler 1982).

This unusual life should not detract from Bedaux's significance to management thinking and practice. His system dealt with a major limitation in Taylor's work (see TAYLOR, F.W.) and as Littler states:

> Overall, it is evident that Bedaux was one of the most important figures in the international spread of scientific management in the inter-war years and crucial to the dif-

fusion of Taylorian workshop practices in Britain.

(Littler 1982: 108)

2 Main contribution

This review of Bedaux's main contribution focuses first on the central features of his system, then on how his system compares with other schemes of work measurement and payment, and finally on its diffusion.

Layton notes that 'Bedaux claimed to have solved the problem which had eluded Taylor, namely discovering the precise scientific relationship between work and fatigue' (quoted in Littler 1982: 108). Taylor had not adequately dealt with fatigue and was criticized for being unable to scientifically ground his notion of 'proper tasks'. Combining studies of fatigue and Taylorism, Bedaux sought to establish the link between elementary work motions and necessary rest periods. In so doing, Bedaux developed a 'relaxation curve' which identified the rest times necessary to offset working time with the total system based on the length of the work cycle. However, as Layton notes, there is nothing to suggest that Bedaux undertook any scientific or experimental investigations, with the result that his rest allowances were simply *ad hoc* 'guesstimates and assessments of what the local market would bear' (quoted in Littler 1982: 109).

The time taken to perform a task modified by relaxation and rest was formulated into a universal unit, the Bedaux or 'B' unit equal to 60 of these modified seconds. This has sometimes been termed the Normal Minute, the Allowed Minute or the Work Unit (Shimmin 1959: 17). It was this formulation of a universal unit which allowed for the system to be applied across very different jobs within the same factory and in so doing to create a single measuring grid, facilitating management monitoring and control.

The timing of jobs was generally based upon an organizations-and-methods procedure by which attempts were made to ensure the best layout and structure for the job. The job was broken down into component parts with each element timed by a stop watch, a simultaneous rating of the worker's speed and

effort being made against the standard 60 work units an hour. For example, an employee judged to be working at 25 per cent above normal speed would be rated 75 (60 + 15). A series of studies produced the average times and ratings for each element which were then converted into standard times – the times taken if working at the normal speed of 60 work units per hour. The total then gave the standard time for the whole operation, to which a fixed percentage was added for relaxation (Shimmin 1959).

This measure was primarily used as the basis of a reward system. The wage rate set for a '60B' performance was seen as a minimum wage whatever the actual performance: in other words, the day wage was guaranteed and formed a safety net. Any output above 60B attracted a bonus or 'premium'. Generally, the bonus calculation meant that each B point earned one-sixtieth of the base pay, but this did not produce a proportionate rate of increase in pay. This was because, Bedaux also suggested, the worker could only perform above 60B with the assistance of indirect workers. Thus, the production workers only received 75 per cent of the available bonus, the other 25 per cent going into a reserve fund for indirect staff.

In placing the Bedaux system in the context of other types of bonus scheme it is helpful to use the fourfold classification of schemes set out by Marriot (1957). First, in terms of the basic structure schemes, the Bedaux system, based upon units of output measured in time, can be contrasted with those piecework schemes which pay a price or rate per piece or unit of work. Second, with reference to the primary purpose of schemes, Marriot sees Bedaux's system as an 'inter-departmental plan', one providing equitable treatment for the frequent inter-departmental transfers occasioned by work requirements. This contrasts with systems designed to save time and 'selective plans' seeking to attract efficient workers to the plant and discourage those unable to meet work and performance targets. Third, in relation to the sharing of the bonus, Bedaux clearly shares the increase between employee and employer as well as between direct and indirect workers: this is unlike other systems where employer and employee gain or lose all and the indirect employee receives nothing. Finally, in connection with the relationship between earnings, labour costs and output, workers' earnings under Bedaux vary proportionally less than output. In other schemes, variation is in the same proportion as output or is more than output.

The Bedaux system spread rapidly and extensively across the USA and Europe during the 1930s. The impact of Taylorism on the different countries of Europe had been variable, Italy and Germany being more receptive than Britain. However, stimulated by the establishment of a permanent consultancy office in Britain, Bedaux's ideas appear to have had a broader appeal. While it is difficult to gauge the proportion of national workforces covered by the Bedaux system, Table 1 indicates that a large number of companies adopted the system, especially in the USA, France and Britain.

Table 1 Number of firms using the Bedaux system (1930–8)

USA	500
Canada	28
Britain	225
France	144
Italy	49
Belgium	22
Germany	25
Holland	39
Austria	5
Switzerland	4
Spain	2
Scandinavian countries	24
East European countries	25
Australia	17
Other countries	17
Total	1,126

Source: Littler (1982: 113)

3 Evaluation

Bedaux's contribution to management thinking and practice can be evaluated in a number of different ways. First, it can be assessed from a normative perspective. Thus the managerial advantages of the Bedaux system include the scope it provides for production planning, control and costing, and the 'points' or standard unit system reduces the various types of labour to a common denominator. The managerial disadvantages relate to the costs and complications of installing and maintaining the scheme (Marriot 1957). Moreover, these very complications make it difficult for workers to understand, which detracts from its incentive value. In a study of six factories using Bedaux, Shimmin concluded: 'Most operatives knew little of the formal structure of the scheme, nor were they familiar with the principles of time study and the calculations made by the wage office' (1959: 136). Moreover, De Man (1929) in a study of German workers concluded that one of the main factors making for dissatisfaction with Bedaux-based schemes was the workers' inability to keep track of output and wage calculations.

Second, Bedaux's contribution can be placed in the context of certain scholarly, theoretical debates. For example, it is of value to consider whether the application of the Bedaux system contributed to the craft job simplification and de-skilling central to Braverman's theories on the labour process (see BRAVERMAN, H.). On the basis of a number of factory cases from the inter-war period, Littler (1982) concludes that structural pressures exerted by Bedaux engineers did result in a divorce of 'direct' and 'indirect' labour and job simplification, as well as reducing worker autonomy initiative. However, Bedaux was not used as a direct confrontational means of *craft* de-skilling but instead was used in industries with pre-planned or semi-planned production processes, with low dependence on craft skill and knowledge.

Finally, an evaluation can made by looking at the more practically orientated studies on the operational difficulties arising with the Bedaux system. Research in the 1920s at

W&T Avery in Birmingham revealed considerable resistance to Bedaux from supervisors who opposed the centralizing tendency involved, particularly as exercised through the central time study office. In addition, Bedaux appeared to produce considerable unrest on the shop floor, with a number of strikes in the 1920s and 1930s in such companies as ICI Metal, Joseph Lucas, and Amalgamated Carburettors (Littler 1982). These strikes were related to fears of unemployment, given the goal of the Bedaux system to increase output at a reduced cost, and were also linked to concerns about de-skilling and workers being spied upon by time study engineers.

4 Conclusions

Bedaux made a major contribution to management thinking and practice through addressing a major limitation in the works of F.W.Taylor. By accounting for employee fatigue and strain, he developed a standard unit of time measurement which could be used as the basis for an incentive pay scheme. The resultant system could be applied to very different groups within the same factory, and provided a means of monitoring and controlling the labour force and related costs. The significance of the Bedaux system was reflected in its diffusion within the USA and Europe in the 1930s. Research suggests, however, that its incentive effect was weakened by the difficulties workers had in understanding the mechanics, while it also gave rise to supervisor and employee resistance.

IAN KESSLER
TEMPLETON COLLEGE, OXFORD

Further reading

(References cited in the text marked *)

Bedaux, C.E. (1917) *The Bedaux Efficiency Course for Industrial Application*, Bedaux Industrial Institute. (Setting out in detail the mechanics of the Bedaux system, this was used as a training manual by Bedaux consultants; only one copy publicly available.)
* Braverman, H. (1974) *Labor and Monopoly Capital*, New York: Monthly Review Press. (Classic work on labour process theory looking at de-skilling as a means of asserting managerial control.)
* De Man, H. (1929) *Joy in Work*, London: Allen & Unwin. (Of historical interest, providing ethnographic insights into factory work in Germany in the early twentieth century.)
* Layton, E. (1974) 'The diffusion of scientific management and mass production from the US in the twentieth century', *Proceedings of the XIVth International Congress in the History of Science, Tokyo*, 4: 377–86. (Short conference paper on the spread of Taylorism from the USA to Europe.)
* Littler, C. (1982) *The Development of the Labour Process in Capitalist Societies*, London: Heinemann Educational Books. (The most comprehensive discussion available of Bedaux's ideas, placed in strong analytical context.)
* Marriot, R. (1957) *Incentive Payment Systems*, London: Staples Press. (Dated but still useful textbook on incentive, combining prescription with some analysis.)
* Shimmin, S. (1959) *Payment by Results*, London: Staples Press. (Rare and enlightening attempt to provide empirical data on operation of bonus schemes in a number of factories.)

See also: BRAVERMAN, H; FORD, H.; GILBRETH, F.B. AND GILBRETH, L.E.M.; TAYLOR, F.W.

Related topics in the IEBM: COSTING; HUMAN RESOURCE MANAGEMENT; INDUSTRIAL AND LABOUR RELATIONS; INDUSTRIAL SABOTAGE; JOB DESIGN; JOB EVALUATION; LABOUR PROCESS; MARKETING MANAGEMENT, INTERNATIONAL; OPERATIONS MANAGEMENT; ORGANIZATION BEHAVIOUR; ORGANIZATION BEHAVIOUR, HISTORY OF; PAYMENT SYSTEMS; PRODUCTIVITY; TRADE UNIONS

Beer, Stafford (1926–)

Personal background

- born 1926 in London, England
- served in the British army, 1944–9
- production controller and founder of the Operational Research Group, Samuel Fox, within United Steel, 1949–56
- head of operational research and cybernetics, United Steel, 1956–61
- managing director of SIGMA (Science In General Management), 1961–6
- development director, International Publishing Corporation, 1966–70
- independent international consultant, 1970–

Major works

Cybernetics and Management (1959)
Decision and Control (1966)
Management Science (1968)
Brain of the Firm (1972)
Designing Freedom (1974)
Platform for Change (1975)
The Heart of the Enterprise (1979)
Diagnosing the System for Organisations (1985)
Beyond Dispute (1994)
How Many Grapes Went Into the Wine? (1994)

Summary

Stafford Beer essentially is a cybernetician working in the field of operational research and management sciences (ORMS). His career comprises senior appointments in industry and commerce, and as an international consultant. He has produced a stream of influential books and has received an array of awards and honours from professional bodies and academic institutions. Beer argues that techniques of ORMS have high utility only when employed in the light of a scientific description of the whole situation. Science for Beer is both rational and rigorous, yielding something clear and definite, testable and repeatable. It also aspires to free will through rigorous choice. Whole situation descriptions come through models built with cybernetic logic. These models must be homomorphic or isomorphic, not metaphorical or analogical. They are formulated using tools of rigorous science: mathematics, statistics and logic. Beer's most famous homomorphism, the viable system model (VSM), draws correspondence between management and organization, and human brain structure and function. The VSM stipulates rules whereby an organization (biological and social) is 'survival worthy': it is regulated, learns, adapts and evolves. Beer invented team syntegrity to complement the VSM when applied in social contexts, adding a statement of participatory democracy. Beer recognized early on that the 'analogue' of systems language has unavoidable connotations that he would rather be without; for example, the absurdity of people as deterministic and predictable thinking machines. He handles many criticisms of his work in this way. Stafford Beer might be best considered a man of cybernetic genius and within this mould, one with a recurring capacity to create and invent.

1 Biographical data

Stafford Beer was born in 1926 in London. He studied philosophy and psychology at the University of London (1943–44). He joined the British army in World War II and rose to the rank of captain. In 1949, Beer joined Samuel Fox alloy and steel makers, within United

Steel. He created and ran the operational research group and simultaneously held the management role of production controller. Here, he led the first known European application of linear programming to wire drawing, and he invented the stochastic analogue machine.

In 1956, Beer was appointed head of operational research and cybernetics for United Steel. He founded Cybor House in Sheffield. Under his leadership, it became the largest civil operational research group in the world. It was at this time that his personal interest in neurocybernetics and mathematical models of the nervous system led to the first formulation of the viable system model, for which he is best known.

In 1961, on behalf of Metra International (Paris), Beer launched SIGMA (Science In General Management) and took up the position of managing director. SIGMA was the first operational research consultancy in the UK specializing in the application of scientific management techniques to problems of policy formulation, strategic planning and the cybernetics of organization. SIGMA worked for many companies in the UK, six government departments, and on major activities abroad.

In 1966, at the personal request of the managing director and the chairman of International Publishing Corporation (IPC), Beer became IPC's development director. He created the development division and a new operating division called New Enterprises. In 1970, following a boardroom disagreement about development policy, Beer withdrew from IPC, but he was acknowledged in the *New Scientist* (15 January 1970) as a man who 'managed to deflect the course of International Publishing Corporation – the world's largest publishing empire – by some 90 degrees, but that even he could not shift it any further'.

Since 1970, Beer has operated as an independent international consultant in the sciences of management (operational research and social systems) and effective organization (organizational cybernetics). Development planning is central to his activities. He accepted a personal invitation from President Allende of Chile in 1971 to develop a new cybernetic approach to the organization and regulation of the Chilean economy. His role as scientific director occupied most of his time until the coup of 11 September 1973. Subsequently, Beer undertook cognate consultancy in the Privy Council Office and several other ministries in Ottawa, Canada, various ministries in New Delhi, India, and in the Presidential Offices of Mexico, Uruguay and Venezuela.

Beer has received many honours for his outstanding contribution as both a practitioner and a researcher. These include: Silver Medal of the Royal Swedish Academy for Engineering Sciences (1958), Invited Membership of the New York Academy of Sciences (1960), The Lanchester Prize of the Operations Research Society of America (1966), Resolution of the United States House of Representatives (1970), Freedom of the City of London (1970), The McCulloch Plaque of the American Society for Cybernetics (1970), Norbert Weiner Gold Medal of the World Organization of Systems and Cybernetics, and honorary Doctor of Laws from Concordia University in Canada (1988).

Beer's fellowships include the Royal Society for Arts and Science, the World Academy of Art and Science, the Royal Statistical Society and the Royal Economic Society. He has been president of several societies in the field of management and systems sciences. Beer has held visiting professorships and similar posts, most notably in the UK at Manchester University, the Open University, Liverpool John Moores University, University College Swansea and the University of Durham, and in North America at the University of Toronto, Canada and the University of Pennsylvania, USA.

In this most distinguished of careers, Stafford Beer made a sustained and authoritative contribution to the management and systems sciences. This is reviewed below under the headings: cybernetics, operational research and management sciences; viable system model; and team syntegrity. Also briefly touched upon, in the conclusion, is his artistic character, an essential element of his life and works.

2 Cybernetics, operational research and management sciences

Stafford Beer essentially is a cybernetician working in the field of operational research and management sciences (ORMS). His leading three books offer an appreciation of these subjects and their interrelationship – *Cybernetics and Management* (1959), *Decision and Control* (1966) and *Management Science* (1968).

ORMS, in Beer's argument, needs to be systemic to be effective. The techniques of ORMS are of high utility only when employed in the light of a scientific description of the whole situation. This means managing the whole, not just the parts. Managing the whole involves drawing together potential organizational developments, in part generated by ORMS techniques, to form new higher order plans. This mode of operating requires interdisciplinary teams since it is not possible to say in advance which branch of science is needed. ORMS, however, is not a science, rather it is doing science in a management sphere. An ORMS person does not have to be concerned with laws governing natural phenomena but must however operate across scientific disciplines being sufficiently knowledgeable and mentally agile to identify the model needed. There are laws of an interdisciplinary nature which support knowledge and agility. Cybernetics is the science of interdisciplinary laws and offers a systemic matrix through which ORMS is done and higher order plans are accomplished.

Science for Beer is both rational and rigorous. It is the precise formulation of method that yields something clear and definite, testable and repeatable. Science aspires to free will through rigorous choice (a point made in *Decision and Control*, then amplified in *Designing Freedom*). This is consistent with the original Enlightenment of the late eighteenth century. In *Decision and Control* Beer argues that ordinarily belief is fixed. He refers to three habits of fixing drawn from Charles Pierce's work: tenacity through the process of conditioning, authority when people believe they are an indivisible part of a system, and

apriority in which conclusions arise from an underlying language. Scientific fixing at least emancipates us from such uncritical patterns of 'choice' making.

In scientific mood an ORMS team begins by defining the scope of the problem. The problem does not necessarily reside where the symptoms are found, therefore the team approach must encompass the whole problem situation. This requires consultation across departmental barriers. Systemic ORMS does not reward departmental mindedness. A problem is tentatively defined, facts on this are collected and collated and suitable courses of action are examined. These are evaluated in terms of probabilities, costs, risks and potential benefits. The precise problem is pinpointed. From hereon, Beer envisages committee debates whereby well-informed, rational and rigorous decisions are made.

Clearly, Beer's notion of ORMS and subsequent decision making is that it must balance the whole. He observed in *Decision and Control* that ORMS techniques tend to maximize only one variable with one purpose in mind. This might conflict with other purposes. The way ORMS jobs 'escape' this problem is by unwittingly limiting the scope of inquiry. The old ORMS methodology cannot face extreme complexity. Beer thus declared the need for a new methodology for ORMS – one with a cybernetic orientation.

Cybernetics operates without regard to the specialized viewpoint of any one branch of science, offering the systemic capability Beer sought. Cybernetics became popularized in the mid to late 1940s through the work of Warren McCulloch and Norbert Wiener (see WIENER, N.). They described a new science of cybernetics, observing that many disciplines were saying essentially the same thing with regard to control, information, measurement and logic. Cybernetics recognized an underlying unity between control mechanisms in different sciences. Cybernetics is thus considered the general theory of control and is often called the science of communication and control.

In particular in *Cybernetics and Management*, Beer explains the concepts of cybernetics. He concludes that there are three main properties of a cybernetic system. They are exceedingly complex, probabilistic and self-regulatory. They are also purposive, meaning that from a particular viewpoint the system is seen to be organized to achieve some end. They are characterized by feedback and control that guide the purposive system. Many systems that are exceedingly complex cannot be specifically defined. Behaviour is studied by discovering the logical and statistical relationships that hold between the information that goes in and instructions that come out – the system is treated as a black box.

Beer traces cybernetics to information theory and the work of Claude Shannon. Effective operation of a system depends on an ability to store, transmit and modify information. Information kills variety (complexity) and the reduction of variety is one of the main techniques of regulation. This is not a process of simplifying the system, but making it more predictable.

The main tool of the cybernetician, Beer asserts, is 'the model'. Beer's models are logical cybernetic descriptions of a system. The change of state of a system can be represented as a transformation of the logic. Dynamic systems are thus described by a model together with a set of rules for making it change state. ORMS work is undertaken with the logic of a model in mind. The initial task, Beer observes, is coming up with logical cybernetic descriptions.

Models by definition are about comparison. For Beer, the formal scientific process begins with comparison between conceptual models. There are two conceptual models; one of the managerial situation about how the 'system really works', and one that resembles the first selected from the scientific situation by ORMS practitioners about how the 'situation really works'. The practitioners then assess to what extent does the behaviour of the one system throw light on the behaviour of another; in what ways the theories currently maintained by scientists in the one area might be transplanted into the other; whether the actual techniques of research and computation are appropriate; and whether conclusions that hold for the one system hold for the other. Ultimately, the researcher is asking under what

methodology the correspondence can be regarded as rigorously validated.

Beer recognises various ways in which comparison can be made. Metaphor offers a poetic identity relation. The research scientist wishing to be more exact may test the ideas through analogy. Yet this tends to destroy the identity relation that 'the metaphor poetically enshrines'. In any case, analogy by definition is open to dispute. The research scientist, Beer stresses, needs to formulate models precisely using tools of rigorous science – mathematics, statistics and logic. The aim is to produce two deeper level homomorphic models (that may well be isomorphic). An example used by Beer is modelling 'learning rats' and transposing this into a model for 'a learning industrial plant'. Another example is Beer's sketch for a cybernetic factory. He constructs a machine capable of adapting to its environment in the guise of an intelligence amplifier modelled on the homeostat. The result is an industrial concern looked at through cybernetic eyes as imitating functions of a living organism. The question then asked is what kind of organic control system can be proposed to pursue environmental adaptation. Beer's most famous homomorphism, the viable system model, discussed below, draws correspondence between management and organization, and human brain structure and function. The managerial situation is modelled, drawing on the science of neurophysiology (in *Brain of the Firm*), as a brain-directed organism operating in an environment. To prove his point that there are laws of an interdisciplinary nature, Beer also constructs the viable system model in *Heart of the Enterprise* from cybernetic first principles.

Appreciating Beer's views on ORMS and cybernetics, in particular those on science and modelling, is an essential prerequisite to grasping his best known invention – the viable system model.

3 Viable system model

A full exposition of the viable system model (VSM) is found in the trilogy *Brain of the Firm* (1972), *Heart of the Enterprise* (1979) and *Diagnosing the System for Organisations* (1985).

The VSM is a model that in Beer's argument encapsulates effective organization. It is a model of any viable system (biological or social). The VSM stipulates rules whereby an organization is 'survival-worthy': it is regulated, learns, adapts and evolves. It is an organization constructed around five main management functions: operations, coordination, control, intelligence and policy. Beer respectively labels these Systems One to Five. The key to their organization is the laws of interconnection in the form of a complex of information and control loops. The VSM employs amongst other things: amplifiers to increase impact of activities where needed; attenuators as activities to absorb variety; and transducers to translate information as it passes, for example, between systems. The VSM employs the law that all distinct organizations contain themselves, which Beer calls recursion. A critical principle is that each contained organization and each of the five systems which it comprises must be allowed as much autonomy as possible whilst maintaining the integrity of the whole. For business and management, it sets out details of how enterprises might work in contrast to organization charts that Beer rejects as merely devices for apportioning blame (cybernetic logic versus hierarchical logic).

The model (see Figure 1) broadly speaking separates out the main operations of an organization and specifies the relationship between these operations and the remaining four management functions that serve them: coordination, control, intelligence and policy. Operations (System One) are the primary activity of the organization, that is, what the organization is set up to do. Operations comprise a number of divisions each with operational managers. Each division is considered to be a viable system in its own right. Viability here means that each division holds a guarantee of continuity. Each division is allowed as much autonomy as possible whilst maintaining the integrity of the whole. Divisions are directly concerned with implementation. Each one connects to an operational environment, amplifying its impact on the environment and

attenuating variety entering from the environment. The divisions are serviced through four management service functions which are coupled by transducers and which attenuate variety as information flows upwards.

Coordination (System Two) ensures that there is an efficient and stable use of resources achieved in a harmonious fashion. It receives vital information about short-term problems faced in operations. It dampens uncontrolled oscillations. It also, or even primarily, manages conflict. Control (System Three) acts as an audit and control function that maintains relatively stable equilibrium between the interdependent divisions. Control deals with vital information about problems in operations that coordination is not able to cope with. Control manages resource bargaining. Control also audits the divisions in a regular and routine manner. These include operational, quality and financial audits, such as budget reviews. Control action is taken when audits show up operational problems that have not or can not be dealt with through coordination. Additionally, control interprets policy decisions and ensures that they are effectively implemented.

The intelligence and development function (System Four) captures information about the total environment. This comprises internal and external environments. Intelligence is gathered about strengths and weaknesses of internal processes. A model of the external environment is provided that identifies opportunities and threats. This information is brought together in an 'operations room', which is an environment for decision. Vital intelligence information is disseminated throughout the organization, upwards or downwards, to those who will benefit from it. Intelligence rapidly transmits urgent information upwards, alerting policy makers to serious problems in operations, coordination and control. Policy (System Five) deals with strategic decisions and issues of management style, as well as urgent information. It receives all relevant information from intelligence about strengths, weaknesses, opportunities and threats, and, on the basis of this information, reviews and modifies policy. It arbitrates between antagonistic internal

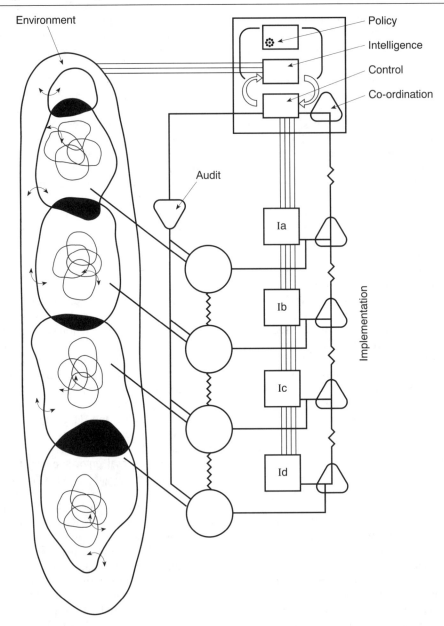

Figure 1 Viable System Model

and external demands. It represents the essential qualities of the whole just described.

Recursion means that the whole can be found in the parts. That is, whole viable systems can be found as divisions of a viable system (the divisions that make up operations or

System One). A viable system is itself a part of a larger viable system. Recursion offers a novel way in which a mission can spill-down a business or organization. A corporate mission or identity is determined by policy using a participatory method (see team syntegrity below). At higher resolution recursive levels the mission is interpreted within the identity of the whole and implemented.

A recursive design helps to avoid the negative effects of coercive structures. Recursion implements through management function whereas traditional hierarchy implements by management authority. Recursion for example promotes autonomy. The parts have as much independence as is possible given the constraints that exist when coordinating and controlling to maintain a whole. The viable system organization allows for participation (in terms of functions to be fulfilled). For example, channels for resource bargaining exist between implementation and control. Vertical loading is encouraged. This means loading down responsibility to the 'lowest level' at which it can be managed. Task formation is encouraged to reverse mechanical reductionist tendencies to produce whole jobs. People then have responsibility over their work. They can determine the needs of their customers and work out for themselves how this can be best achieved. Job grouping is encouraged to bring together efforts that are naturally related. This would bring together groups of jobs, for example, by geographical location or client type.

The central concern with the VSM expressed in the literature is that it underplays the purposeful role of individuals. For example, who in the VSM is responsible for determining the purpose of the organization? Does the VSM emphasize control at the expense of individual freedom? Does a quest for harmony and stability tend to assimilate people? Do the five management functions constitute an imposition on people? Do they mask undercurrents of resistance, difference and tension that operate informally? What is Beer's response?

Beer was aware as early as *Decision and Control* (1966) that special problems exist in maintaining a clear and distinct idea of what cybernetics is about, free from emotive and other misleading connotations of words. He is gravely concerned that the analogue of the systems language has unavoidable connotations which he would rather be without; for example, the absurdity of people as deterministic and predictable thinking machines. Although Beer rarely comments on criticisms other than in passing, a careful reading of his consistent argument strongly suggests he handles criticisms of his work in this way. He has also developed team syntegrity that might be considered Beer's ultimate statement of participatory democracy.

Extended discussions of Beer's VSM are located in Flood and Jackson (1991: 87–118) and Flood and Romm (1996: 97–104) where case studies are also presented.

4 Team syntegrity

Team syntegrity presented in *Beyond Dispute* complements the VSM. The VSM offers cybernetic principles of organization. Team syntegrity adds to this Beer's notion of people's participation. The invention seeks to organize normative, directional and strategic planning, and other creative processes. The underlying model is a regular icosahedron (it has 20 sides). This has 30 edges, each representing a person. A set of protocols creates an internal network. As debate flows around and around the network it 'reverberates and hums'. The sphere created becomes a group consciousness with no hierarchy. Beer argues that a group organized in this way is an ultimate statement of participatory democracy, since each role is indistinguishable from any other.

5 Conclusion

Stafford Beer is an exceptional person. He pursued a highly successful career in industry and commerce and as an international consultant whilst, *at the same time*, produced a stream of influential books. He defined and practiced the cybernetics of decision and control, and subsequently invented the viable system model for effective organization and the complementary team syntegrity adding participatory democracy. All of this is documented above. Beyond business and management, however, his artistic character flourishes; an essential element of his life and works. He has a lifetime interest in the classical languages Latin, Greek and Sanskrit. He practices and teaches yoga. He has published poetry and a few exhibitions of his paintings have been held. In particular, his Requiem meditation, consisting of nine interactive oil paintings, was installed in the apse of the Metropolitan Cathederal of Christ the King in Liverpool (1992 and 1993). He has broadcast frequently on radio and television. Stafford Beer, then, might be considered a man of cybernetic genius and has within this mould a recurring and indeed wide-ranging capacity to create and invent.

ROBERT L. FLOOD
UNIVERSITY OF HULL

Further reading

(References cited in the text marked *)

(† Indicates republished by Wiley, Chichester in 1994)

Beer, S. (1959) *Cybernetics and Management*, London: English Universities; New York: Wiley. Translated into Czech, Dutch, French, German, Japanese, Polish, Portuguese, Russian and Spanish. (Beer's account of cybernetic concepts and theories.)

† Beer, S. (1966) *Decision and Control: The Meaning of Operational Research and Management Cybernetics*, Chichester: Wiley. Translated into Spanish. (Awarded the Lanchester Prize for an outstanding contribution to the literature of management science in the world. Beer's account of decision making, science and modelling in operational research, from a cybernetic perspective.)

Beer, S. (1968) *Management Science: The Business Use of Operational Research*, London: Aldus. Translated into Dutch, Finnish, French, German, Japanese, Norwegian and Swedish. (An animated and easily accessible account of operational research from Beer's cybernetic perspective.)

† Beer, S. (1972) *Brain of the Firm*, London: Allan Lane and Penguin Press; New York: Herder and Herder. Translated into French, German, Italian and Swedish. Second edition (1981) Chichester and New York: Wiley. Translated into Russian. (Construction of the VSM as a homomorphic model derived from human neurocybernetics.

The second edition includes Beer's account of the Chilean experience with the VSM.)

† Beer, S. (1974) *Designing Freedom*, Toronto: Canadian Broadcasting Company. Republished (1975) Chichester and New York: Wiley. Translated into Japanese and Spanish. (A series of radio lectures captured as a set of chapters that emphasise the liberatory nature of Beer's cybernetics.)

† Beer, S. (1975) *Platform for Change*, Chichester and New York: Wiley. (A collection of Beer's important writings drawn together with a unique form of synergistic commentary.)

† Beer, S. (1979) *The Heart of the Enterprise*, Chichester and New York: Wiley. (Construction of the VSM from cybernetic first principles.)

† Beer, S. (1985) *Diagnosing the System for Organisations*, Chichester and New York: Wiley. Translated into Italian and Japanese. (Beer's operationalization of the VSM as a diagnostic tool for evaluating effectiveness of organization.)

† Beer, S. (1994) *Beyond Dispute: The Invention of Team Syntegrity*, Chichester and New York: Wiley. (Beer's model for participatory democracy that complements the VSM.)

Beer, S. (1994) *How Many Grapes Went Into the Wine? Stafford Beer on the Art and Science of Holistic Management*, Chichester: Wiley. Edited by R. Harnden and A. Leonard. (A collection of Beer's major essays on holistic management.)

Espejo, R. and Harnden, R. (eds) (1989) *The Viable System Model: Interpretations and Applications of Stafford Beer's VSM*, Chichester: Wiley. (A variety of authors present their interpretations and applications of the VSM, including a powerful critique by M.C. Jackson.)

Espejo, R. and Schwaninger, M. (1993) *Organisational Fitness: Corporate Effectiveness Through Management Cybernetics*, New York: Campus Verlag. (A range of authors discussing management cybernetics mainly from a Beerian perspective.)

* Flood, R.L. and Jackson, M.C. (1991) *Creative Problem Solving: Total Systems Intervention*, Chichester: Wiley. (Provides a comprehensive account of six better known systems-based problem solving methodologies and how to use them in complementary fashion, including Beer's VSM.)

* Flood, R.L. and Romm, N.R.A. (1996) *Diversity Management: Triple Loop Learning*, Chichester: Wiley. (Sets up a discourse between the ever growing number of models, methodolo-

gies, and theories in business and management, including the relative merits of Beer's VSM.)

See also: ACKOFF, R.L.; RIVETT, B.H.P.; SIMON, H.A.; VICKERS, G.; WIENER, N.

Related topics in the IEBM: CYBERNETICS; DECISION MAKING; GROUPS AND TEAMS; MANAGEMENT SCIENCE; OPERATIONS RESEARCH; OPTIMALITY AND OPTIMIZATION; ORGANIZATION BEHAVIOR; ORGANIZATIONAL LEARNING; SYSTEMS

Bennis, Warren (1925–)

Personal background

- born in 1925
- served in Europe as an infantry officer in the US army
- graduated in psychology and business from Antioch College, 1951
- PhD economics and social science, Massachusetts Institute of Technology (MIT), 1955
- taught at MIT, 1955–6
- taught at Boston University, 1956–9
- member of the organizational studies department at MIT, and later chairman, 1959–67
- provost and executive vice president of the State University of New York at Buffalo, 1967–71
- president, University of Cincinnati, 1971–8
- distinguished professor, University of Southern California, (USC) 1979–

Major works

Personal and Organizational Change Through Group Methods: The Laboratory Approach (with Ed Schein)(1965)
Beyond Bureaucracy (1966)
The Temporary Society (1967)
Leaders (with Burt Nanus) (1985)
Organizing Genius: The Secrets of Creative Collaboration (with P.W. Biederman)

Summary

Warren Bennis is now best known as a leadership guru. His well-written, popular books on leadership using American examples have been translated into many languages. His main academic contribution was made in the first phase of his career from 1955 to 1967. He worked first on laboratory studies of small groups, especially Tgroups, then became interested in organization development and from there in the kinds of changes taking place in society and how organizations needed to change to adapt to them. The next phase of his career was practising leadership in university administration. On returning to an academic post his main theme has been the nature of leadership and its pivotal role in organizations in the changing world: it is a messianic view and has been criticized as reviving the trait approach to leadership.

1 Biographical data

Warren Bennis was born on 8 March 1925 into a Jewish family. He sees his childhood as having been 'barren, meagre, endless'. He had a father who worked eighteen hours a day as a struggling small retailer and twin brothers who were ten years older than himself – it was the leadership flair of one of these brothers that awakened his interest in leadership. He describes himself as a boy as withdrawn, sullen and detached, removed from hope or desire and left pretty much alone. He does not remember any close friends. He did not much like school, except for one teacher. He felt marginal in his family and marginal as a Jew in a gentile community. He attributes his ability to read and respond to others to the sense of marginality that comes with Jewishness and that heightens responsiveness to the signals of the majority community. Such an analysis of his early life, which is described in *An Invented Life*, may have come from the six years he spent in Freudian analysis as a young man. From school he went into the US army for four years. In the second year he became an officer and went to Europe, where he was the youngest infantry officer in the force.

None of his family had been to university, but as an ex-serviceman he had scholarships for eight years. He went to the progressive Antioch College because an army contact had told him a lot about it. He says that the army taught him the value of organization and at Antioch College he learned to have opinions. The president, Douglas McGregor (see MCGREGOR, D.), was the most important influence on him there, and later he worked in his department at MIT.

Warren Bennis' career, after his student days, can be divided into three parts: twelve years research and teaching, mainly at MIT, when he made his main academic contribution; ten years as an university administrator; followed in 1979 by a major heart attack which stimulated a reappraisal of what he was doing; since then he has been at the USC where his main focus has been on leadership and on teaching in its broadest sense.

2 Small group dynamics and organization development

His early work was on laboratory studies of small groups. He was involved in 1955 with Tgroups at the National Training Laboratories in Bethel, Maine, and leading such a group he describes as 'a wild, exhilarating experience'. Tgroups were also called sensitivity training and aimed to encourage uninhibited discussion of the members of the groups so that the individual members could become sensitive to how others perceived them. For a time they were a popular form of human relations training, but later attracted much criticism.

In his work with Tgroups he was mainly interested in the organization of the group rather than in the development of the individual. His interest in the stages of group growth resulted in 1956 in his most widely referenced article, 'A theory of group development', which he wrote with Herbert Shepard. They described dependence and interdependence, power and love, and authority and intimacy as the central problems of group life. In most organizations and societies, they pointed out, the degree of

intimacy among members and the distribution of authority are prescribed whereas in a Tgroup they are a major area of uncertainty. Their analysis of the stages in the group and the role of the trainer are influenced by Freudian concepts.

One problem with Tgroups was that the individual members went back to the same old organizations where their newly learnt skills of openness were not acceptable. The recognition of this problem led Bennis and others to an interest in organization development; that is to ways of helping organizations to develop a culture where people were able to be more open and trusting. *Organization Development: Its Nature, Origins and Prospects* (1969) was Bennis' contribution to the Addison-Wesley series on organization development. He later abandoned organization development, complaining that it was 'intellectually kind of barren'.

He has returned to an interest in small groups in a recent book, *Organizing Genius*. This gives a lively description of the origins and development of six outstanding American groups, including the one that developed the atomic bomb, Black Mountain, the experimental college in North Carolina, and that which created Disney's *Snow White and the Seven Dwarfs*. Bennis draws some conclusions from the six groups, including his belief that all had extraordinary, visionary leaders and tended to be collegial.

3 Planning change and the changing society

In the first half of the 1960s Bennis widened his concerns from organization development. *The Planning of Change: Readings in the Applied Behavioural Sciences* (with Benne and Chin, 1962) described what we know about how to change organizations. The ills of present American society were described in *The Temporary Society* (with Slater, 1964) and the new leadership that would be required for organizations to adapt to the changing world. This book anticipated many later ideas about the future, as did *Beyond Bureaucracy* (1966), about the changing nature of organizations.

4 Leadership

Bennis's interest in and writings on leadership have a long history: he first wrote about it in the late 1950s, although his main writings on leadership date from the 1980s. Unlike most academic writers on leadership he has practised leadership – as president of the University of Cincinnati – as well as writing about it.

In some of his early studies and writing his interest in leadership was related to his interest in group dynamics: to the influence that differently structured groups had on who emerged as leader and to what complex organizational and personal variables were related to changes following laboratory training – sensitivity training, which was popular in the 1960s.

His views on leadership have evolved. In his early writings he attached great importance to trust building, openness and to encouraging participation. Later he has said that one must also recognize the importance of power relations to understand leadership. He has also become increasingly aware of the complexities of the context within which the leader is working.

Warren Bennis sees leadership as all-important at the end of the twentieth century. His best known book on leadership, *Leaders*, (1985) written with Burt Nanus, was based on a study of ninety American leaders. Despite the diversity amongst the leaders they studied, they identified four common abilities: management of attention, management of meaning, management of trust and management of self. Management of attention stems from having a vision that others are willing to share and which provides a bridge to the future. Management of meaning requires the ability to communicate the vision successfully. Management of trust is important because trust is essential to all organizations and its main component is reliability, i.e. constancy. Management of self means knowing one's skills and deploying them effectively. Bennis believes that leadership can be learnt and so has devoted part of his writing to describing how to lead.

Warren Bennis sees leadership as being embodied in an individual, and visionary, empowering leaders as being essential in the changing world. He describes leadership as transforming followers by creating visions of the goals to be pursued and by articulating ways to meet them as well as by encouraging employees' self-esteem and creativity. Coaching, he thinks, will be the model for leaders in the future. He also sees good leaders as valuing learning from others and from the environment and learning more about themselves in doing so. He calls them constant learners. Good leaders also have a strong self-regard, which appears to be related to the ability to accept people as they are. Leadership consists of three major factors: ambition or drive; competence or expertise and integrity or moral fabric. He warns against the danger in turbulent times of picking a leader with ambition and competence but little integrity.

He acknowledged, wryly, how Mary Parker Follett had said similar things about leadership forty years earlier (Bennis 1995; see FOLLETT, M.P.).

Conclusion

Warren Bennis has been unusually prolific, at all stages of his career, both in books and articles. Many of the books have been co-authored, often with colleagues. He is best known as a leadership guru, in which role he has consulted, written and lectured widely. He clearly has a mission to persuade others of what makes for a good leader and that excellent leadership is the key to tackling the rapid changes in society. He sees himself as a prophet – his Jewish inheritance – and teacher, but not one who has, or who would want to have, disciples. Those writing about Bennis emphasize the person as much as the writings. His view of leadership has been criticized as reviving the trait approach to leadership and imputing almost magical qualities to leaders.

Despite many visits abroad and periods as a visiting professor in a number of countries his approach and writings are quintessentially American and his examples of outstanding leaders and groups are drawn from the USA. However, as two of his leadership books have been widely translated his views are obviously of appeal outside the USA as well as within it. Despite his emphasis on doing away with an autocratic, command and control approach, he believes strongly in *the* leader, hence in followers.

His writings on leadership are inspirational rather than academic. This, together with his lucid, vivid style, means that he has a wider readership than those who seek to develop the academic knowledge of leadership.

ROSEMARY STEWART
TEMPLETON COLLEGE
UNIVERSITY OF OXFORD

Further reading

(References cited in the text marked *)

* Bennis, W.G. (1966) *Beyond Bureaucracy*, New York: Wiley. (Anticipated much later writing about the changes needed in the form of organizations.)
* Bennis, W.G. (1969) *Organization Development: Its Nature, Origins, and Prospects*, Reading, MA: Addison-Wesley. (One of six booklets on different aspects of organization development. This one is described as an introductory primer.)
Bennis, W.G. (1989) *On Becoming a Leader*, Reading, MA: Addison-Wesley. (Describes how people become leaders, how they lead and how organizations encourage or stifle potential leaders.)
* Bennis, W.G. (1993) *An Invented Life*, Reading, MA: Addison-Wesley. (A selection of his articles from nearly thirty years, which is a good introduction to Bennis's thinking and social concerns. The early articles start with a commentary on their current relevance. An attractive autobiographical chapter explains the rationale of the title.)
* Bennis, W. (1995) 'Thoughts on "The Essentials of Leadership"', in Graham, P. (ed.) *Mary Parker Follett – Prophet of Management*, Boston, Harvard Business School: 177–181. (Where he pays a generous tribute to Follett as having predated by forty years his writings on leadership.)
* Bennis, W. and Biederman, P. W. (1997) *Organizing Genius: The Secrets of Creative Collaboration*, Reading, MS: Addison-Wesley. (Bennis's most recent book which describes vividly the history of six great American groups, including the one that developed the atomic bomb, and the story of the making of Disney's *Snow White and the Seven Dwarfs*, and the lessons that can be drawn by comparing them.)
* Bennis, W.G. And Nanus, B. (1985) *Leaders: Five Strategies for Taking Charge*, New York: Harper & Row. (A well-known book which is a helpful guide to leadership, with a particularly good account of a leader's vision.)
* Bennis, W.G., and Shepherd, H.A. (1956) 'A theory of group development', *Human Relations*, 9, 415–457. (A frequently cited article, which argued that small groups, in their development, tend to pass through stages in which interpersonal conflicts are suppressed because they are seen as a threat to group harmony.)
* Bennis, W.G. and Slater, P.E. (1968) *The Temporary Society*, New York: Harper & Row. (Won the McKinsey Foundation Award for the best book on management that year. It is about the changes needed in America's key institutions to meet the changing world.)
* Bennis, W.G., Benne, K.D. and Chin, R. (1962) *The Planning of Change: Readings in the Applied Behavioural Sciences*, New York: Holt, Rinehart and Winston. (The aim of this volume of reading, which went into a number of editions, was to help to develop a theory about how to plan change that could be used to help train change agents. It stemmed from its editors concerns about how to plan change successfully.)
Gemmill, G. and Oakley, J. (1997) 'Leadership: an alienating social myth', in Grint, K. (ed*.) Leadership: Classical, Contemporary, and Critical Approaches*, Oxford: Oxford University Press. (Criticizes Bennis, amongst others, for presenting leadership like a myth to persuade followers that leaders are necessary, and for reviving the trait approach to leadership.)
* Schein, E.H. and Bennis, W.G. (1965) *Personal and Organizational Change Through Group Methods: The Laboratory Approach*, New York: Wiley. (A widely referenced account of the stages of development in Tgroups drawing on Freudian concepts.)

See also: ARGYRIS, C.; FOLLETT, M.P; MCGREGOR, D.; SCHEIN, E.

Related topics in the IEBM: GROUPS AND TEAMS; HUMAN RELATIONS; HUMAN RESOURCE MANAGEMENT; LEADERSHIP; MANAGEMENT GURUS; OCCUPATIONAL PSYCHOLOGY; ORGANIZATION BEHAVIOUR; ORGANIZATION BEHAVIOUR, HISTORY OF; ORGANIZATIONAL LEARNING; ORGANIZATIOON STRUCTURE

Benson, Henry (1909–95)

1 Biographical data
2 Coopers & Lybrand
3 International Accounting Standards
   Committee
4 Government adviser
5 Conclusion

Personal background

- born in 1909 in Johannesburg, South Africa
- joined Cooper Bros as an articled clerk in 1926
- became a chartered accountant in 1932
- became a partner at Cooper Bros in 1934 and remained there until 1940
- served as an officer in the Grenadier Guards, 1940–5
- became a Commander of the Order of the British Empire (CBE) in 1946
- again acted as a partner at Cooper Bros, 1946–75
- received a knighthood in 1964
- became a Knight Grand Cross of the Order of the British Empire (GBE) in 1971
- chairman of IASC, 1973–5
- adviser to the Governor of Bank of England, 1975–83
- chairman of Royal Commission on Legal Services, 1976–9
- became a life peer in 1981

Summary

Henry Benson bestrode the international accounting world after World War II and was a major part of the British business establishment for more than forty years. He was an internationalist long before 'globalization' had become a cliché, and saw clearly what were the implications of internationalization for business. He played a major role in international accounting, both as a leading player in the creation of Coopers & Lybrand as one of the select few global accounting firms, and as the person generally credited with founding the International Accounting Standards Committee (IASC). He also played a major role in British business, often behind the scenes, but also as someone frequently called on by the government, and as an adviser to the Bank of England.

1 Biographical data

Benson was born in Johannesburg on 2 August 1909. His father, who was born in Britain, emigrated to South Africa and practised as a solicitor in Johannesburg. His mother, Florence Mary Cooper, was also British: she was a daughter of Francis Cooper, one of the four Cooper brothers who founded the accounting firm in 1854. By chance, as he recounts it (Benson 1989: 8–9), Benson was taken to Cooper Bros' offices when on a visit to London at the age of 14, where a kindly uncle assured him that they would take him as an articled clerk (i.e. as a student accountant) when he left school. Two years' later, in 1926, Benson was duly dispatched from South Africa and formally entered Cooper's, a substantial but fairly staid family firm. He was to stay there, apart from war service, until his retirement in 1975, when he left an expanding international firm with more than 300 offices and 20,000 professional staff.

2 Coopers & Lybrand

Although Benson as a third generation Cooper became a partner in 1934 at the age of 25, it was not until after World War II that he took a very active role in the management of the partnership, when the older generation withdrew and John Pears became senior partner. 'We were full of enthusiasm, enjoyed good health, and had common interests … we wanted to expand both at home and overseas, to increase the clientele and to build an international organization which would hold its own with the other international firms ... we worked together on this task for the next 25 years' (Benson 1989: 43). They immediately set about opening offices in other countries (Australia, New Zealand, East Africa, Southern and West Africa, Europe) as well as building major associations with other firms (e.g. in Canada). The firm underwent a major expansion in the next ten years, and then came a major turning point in 1956 with an approach from a US firm, Lybrand, Ross Bros and Montgomery. The initial suggestion was that Coopers should represent the other firm in the UK and France, but this quickly turned into a merging of the two firms as from January 1957, although it was not until 1973 that the name Coopers & Lybrand was used worldwide.

The progression of Cooper Bros at that time can be seen from the following figures:

Year	UK firm	International firm	Offices world-wide
1945	173	239	8
1955	352	991	35
1975	2,207	18,386	332

(adapted from Benson 1989)

An openness to international influence is a major characteristic of Benson's approach. If British people of Benson's generation were international at all in their thinking, they thought normally in terms of the English-speaking world: particularly the British Commonwealth, as typified by Benson's family moving back and forth between South Africa and the UK. If they went further, it was to the US. Benson grew up in the Commonwealth ambiance, and then as an army officer spent time in the US, Egypt and Greece. In the postwar expansion of Cooper's he travelled extensively and, while the anglophone world was favoured, Europe was not forgotten. Benson was much nearer the truly international approach of the 1990s than his contemporaries. An example of this is his attitude in 1963 when sitting on a government committee looking into the possibility of introducing VAT in the UK. He went to France to ask French tax officials for the benefit of their experience of running a VAT system.

While this now seems an obvious step, at that time it was quite alien to British thinking: for example continental European countries have always borrowed and adapted company law and accounting rules from their neighbours (Walton 1995), but British company law stayed resolutely separate until entry into the EU (Napier 1995), and even in the 1970s British accountants remained stridently alarmist about the likely effects of having to adopt what they perceived as German accounting (Walton 1997). Equally, while European accountants frequently met to compare systems throughout this century, it was only in the 1970s that Anglo-American academics started to take an interest in comparative accounting (Forrester 1996).

3 International Accounting Standards Committee

It was perhaps, above all, Benson's international approach combined with his concern for technical standards, and the problems of international companies and international accounting firms, which led him to found the International Accounting Standards Committee, of which he was the first chairman. In fact the process was an incremental one. In June 1966 Benson took office as president of the Institute of Chartered Accountants of England and Wales (ICAEW): One of his first duties was to visit Canada and the US, and it was in Regina, Saskatchewan, that a meeting took place between Benson and the presidents of the Canadian Institute of Chartered Accountants and the American Institute of Certified Public Accountants (AICPA). Benson suggested that a study group should be set up to look at accounting problems and issue pronouncements.

As he explains it, he thought that if his firm were to build up a national and international practice, 'it would be quite impossible to do so without clear manuals for the guidance of partners and staff worldwide'. At the time, as he notes (Benson 1981: 27–31), after the war 'professional accountancy bodies in different parts of the world began to codify the widely differing accounting treatments which were in use in their respective countries'. He adds that although now they may look crude, at the time they were a big advance in accounting thought, but there was one serious defect: 'they were prepared without sufficient reference to what was happening in other countries so that authoritative publications were issued in different countries which conflicted, sometimes in minor ways, but sometimes on fundamental points of principle.'

After the Regina meeting, Benson went on to a meeting of the executive committee of AICPA and discussed his proposal for a three-country study group. The minutes of that meeting include the paragraph:

> It was suggested that the formation of such a group was a simple and effective way, but not the only way, of promoting international cooperation in accounting and it was agreed that similar groups might be organised with accounting organisations in other countries or that the original group might be expanded to include representatives from other countries in due course.
>
> (Benson 1981: 39)

The Accountants International Study Group (AISG) had its first meeting in February 1967 and started issuing papers.

With the benefit of hindsight, one can see that the decade from 1965 was one of considerable restructuring and tightening of regulation of accounting in the developed countries. Germany enacted a new law for listed companies in 1965 and the European Commission caused the *Groupe d'Etudes* to be set up to prepare a paper on a European accounting directive (this was to become the Fourth Directive). France had a major revision of its company law in 1966. Accounting and its regulation in both the UK and US was severely criticized, leading in the US to the Coen and the Trueblood Commissions, which in turn led to the creation of the Financial Accounting Standards Board in 1973 and its conceptual framework project. In the UK the Accounting Standards Steering Committee was set up in 1969. The first draft of the Fourth Directive was published in 1971. Benson's initiative was an early example of what became the mood of the time, with in his case the

particularity of being international. With the exception of the Fourth Directive, all the other initiatives tended to reinforce national rules and therefore potential differences, rather than aiming at international harmony.

The members of the AISG continued to meet regularly from 1967 onwards, and then at the Tenth World Congress of Accountants in Sydney, Australia, in 1972 they discussed the possibility of expanding the Group into an international body 'which would write standards for international use'. The AISG members deferred until a later meeting, in London in December 1972, the details of how to operationalize this. Benson recounts that after some discussion the accountancy bodies of Australia, France, Germany, Japan, the Netherlands and Mexico were invited to participate – 'it was felt that the number of countries would have to be restricted to nine. Anything more was felt to be unworkable and anything less would not be representative from an international point of view' (Benson 1989: 104–107). The formal inauguration of the IASC took place on 29 June 1973 when sixteen accountancy bodies from the nine countries signed the founding documents. Sir Henry Benson, as he then was, was appointed the first chairman.

The life of the IASC has not been easy and it has at different times been accused of losing its way, having no real purpose and of being a Trojan horse for the spread of Anglo-American accounting, for the greater glory of the international accounting firms. However, it has survived and, first, succeeded in making its standards a reference point used almost universally in any discussion of accounting principles. Subsequently it has grown in stature to become potentially the world's leading standard-setter. At the time of writing, IASC is on the verge of completing a programme which will provide accounting rules for financial disclosures accepted by all major stock exchanges and mandated by the International Organization of Securities Commissions.

This will be a milestone in the history of harmonization, representing a very substantial advance in comparability of financial reports between major international companies. It will very probably change the relationship between the IASC and national standard-setters, a process which has already started with countries such as France and Germany changing their statutes so that their multinationals can produce their consolidated statements in line with IASC standards.

At the same time, standard setters in emerging markets such as Singapore, Hong Kong, South America and Eastern Europe generally use IASC standards as the model from which their national rules are drawn. The IASC has come a long way since 1973 and seems likely to dominate company financial reporting in the twenty-first century.

It seems likely that the IASC either would not have been created, or would have appeared much later and in different form, without Benson's determination and initiative. Given the many other major affairs in which Benson had a hand, it is difficult to see the creation of the IASC as a central theme in his life, even if as it happens it is likely to be one of the things for which he is best remembered. It seems more likely that the IASC evolved out of his interest in professional standards in the broad sense, and his sense of the international, combined with the opportunity presented by being president of the ICAEW. He had at earlier stages of his career been involved in creating manuals, for the ordnance factories during the war and for Coopers, and it was clear that he held strongly to the view that codified rules were an essential part of guaranteeing quality in accounting. He was in a unique position as a leading member of the UK profession and a major force in an international accounting firm to understand the need for harmonization and to do something about creating the machinery which might make it possible. His involvement no doubt explains why the IASC has always been based in London, and his appointment as first chairman guaranteed it a launch with the best possible chances of success.

4 Government adviser

Benson's ability to marshal the resources and the support necessary for the foundation of the IASC can be better understood in the context of his very considerable activity as an adviser to government and business. In the war he had been involved, amongst other things, in work for the Ministry of Defence and immediately after the war for the Ministry of Housing (where he first encountered Harold Wilson). Thereafter he was involved continuously in committees, advisory boards, boards of directors and so on in all manner of areas linked to government. In the 1940s and 1950s he did work for the Ministry of Town and Country Planning, Ministry of Fuel and Power, National Coal Board and the Ministry of Transport. As already mentioned he was a member of a committee appointed by the Chancellor of the Exchequer in 1963 to look into VAT. In 1964 he was appointed an Inspector by the Board of Trade to look into the collapse of Rolls Razor Ltd., the first of the series of spectacular financial scandals which was to lead to a demand for better regulation of accounting. In 1967 he chaired an advisory committee looking into the management of the National Trust and another committee looking at the organization of the racing industry. In 1970 he headed a team investigating Rolls Royce, which was in difficulties.

Benson was an extremely busy man who had the ear of ministers, and indeed prime ministers. He recalls (Benson 1989: 155), at the time of the Rolls Royce crisis and during Edward Heath's premiership, being called into a cabinet meeting to give an oral report on Rolls Royce, and having some difficulty in concentrating because the woman who was sitting next to him, whom he assumed was a secretary, was taking copious notes and kept making *sotto voce* comments and suggestions. It was only after the meeting that he was formally introduced to Margaret Thatcher. He got to now her better when she was prime minister, even making a wooden display cabinet for her (woodwork was a life long hobby).

Of his own political views, Benson said in his autobiography: 'I have never been strongly politically orientated, though my natural leanings veer to the Right rather than the Left. I prefer to remain unfettered so that I can express my opinions … unaffected by political affiliations. One of the characteristics of an auditor is that he should at all times be independent and free to express his opinion without fear and favour' (1989: 189).

individually had such an impact on financial reporting.

PETER WALTON
UNIVERSITY OF GENEVA

5 Conclusion

Evidently Benson was a forceful personality, and those who came into contact with him did not forget him. Harold Wilson, when prime minister, met him at a reception and immediately recalled their earlier encounter more than twenty years before. Former colleagues still tell stories about him. Chris Lainé, president of the ICAEW in 1997–98 recalled in an interview (Singleton-Green 1997) that in 1971 he received an 'invitation' from Lord Benson, 'a truly formidable figure'. 'We need to open an office on the south coast, and wondered if you would like to go and do it?' Lainé recalled him saying. 'I read that as a command, which was the right interpretation'.

Benson himself was much amused by a story told by Brian Jenkins, a partner in Coopers & Lybrand, who said that when as a young accountant he went to discuss a difficult problem with Benson, the latter said: 'Jenkins, unless you agree with me we shan't make any progress.'

Benson was certainly a man who got things done and in the twenty-first century the financial reporting practices of multinational companies are going to be dominated by the rules promulgated by the body which Benson created, and nursed through its early days, just as his firm is set to become one of the biggest of the now very small group of world auditors whose attestation guarantees the credibility of financial reports. Few if any accountants have

Further reading

(References cited in the text marked*)

* Benson, H. (1981) 'Establishing standards through a voluntary professional process across national boundaries' in *Arthur Young Professors' Round Table*, Arthur Young, London 1981.
* Benson, H. (1989) *Accounting for Life*, London: Kogan Page/ICAEW.
* Forrester, D.A.R. (1996) 'European congresses of accounting: a review of their history' *European Accounting Review* 5, 1: 91–103.
* Napier, C. (1995) 'The history of financial reporting in Britain' in Walton, P. (ed) *European Financial Reporting: A History,* London: Academic Press.
* Singleton-Green, B (1997) 'Back on the front foot', *Accountancy* June: 86–87.
* Walton, P. (1995) *European Financial Reporting : A History,* London, Academic Press.
* Walton, P (1997) 'The true and fair view and the drafting of the Fourth Directive', *European Accounting Review* 6, 4.

See also: HOPWOOD, A.

Related topics in the IEBM: ACCOUNTING; ACCOUNTING, INTERNATIONAL; ACCOUNTING IN AUSTRALIA; ACCOUNTING IN FRANCE; ACCOUNTING IN GERMANY; ACCOUNTING HARMONIZATION; ACCOUNTING IN THE UNITED KINGDOM; ACCOUNTING IN THE UNITED STATES AMERICA; AUDITING; GLOBALIZATION; MULTINATIONALS; STATUTORY AUDIT

Blackett, Patrick Maynard Stuart (1897–1974)

Personal background

- born London, 18 November 1897
- served as a junior naval officer during the First World War
- attended University of Cambridge, studying mathematics and physics
- embarked upon a research career in physics at the Cavendish Laboratory under Lord Rutherford, 1921
- married Constanza Bayon, 1924
- developed an outstanding reputation for fundamental research in atomic physics, cosmic rays and rock magnetism
- pioneer of operational research techniques in military tactics and strategy in the Second World War; notable opponent of strategic bombing and critic of western nuclear policy after 1945
- Langworthy Professor of Physics at Manchester University and subsequently Professor of Physics at Imperial College
- awarded the Nobel Prize for Physics, 1948
- adviser to the Labour government 1964–70 on scientific and industrial policy
- advisor to the government of India on defence and scientific policy
- appointed president of the Royal Society, 1965
- created a Life Peer, 1969
- died 13 July 1974

Major works

Lectures on Rock Magnetism (1954)
Atomic Weapons and East–West Relations (1956)
Studies of War (1962)
Science, Technology and Aid in Developing Countries (1971)

Summary

Patrick Blackett was one of the outstanding British physicists of the twentieth century, responsible for important advances in knowledge and understanding of atomic physics, cosmic rays and rock magnetism. He was also a notable pioneer of operational research as a guide to rational decision making in military tactics and strategy. Although he remained uninterested in the application of quantitative analysis to peacetime problems in the industrial sector, he argued vigorously for the expansion of scientific and technical education as a means to national economic regeneration. This was especially the case after 1964 when he emerged as an influential policy adviser to the then Labour government. Politically, Blackett was well to the left of centre: his principled opposition to the area bombing of German towns and cities in the Second World War was a prelude to his condemnation of the spread and use of nuclear weapons. He was also concerned to reduce the problem of poverty in the Third World by enhanced provision for scientific education. In these respects the Indian sub-continent attracted his particular attention.

1 Introduction

Until the mid-1930s Blackett was a conventional, if conspicuously successful, university scientist. From that point onwards, however, and until the end of the Second World War, he became increasingly involved in military affairs, first in relation to the development of radar and second in securing the diffusion of operational research as a means to effective military planning and operations. He became a controversial figure politically as a result of his opposition to the bombing of civilians by conventional or nuclear means, a stance which led to his marginalization in public life until the 1960s. It was in this decade that his left-radical view of the world conformed closely to the ethos of the Labour Party both in opposition and government. This was especially the case in his support for State-sponsored measures to enhance the application of science and technology to private sector industry.

2 Biographical data

Patrick Maynard Stuart Blackett was born in 1897 in Kensington, London. After serving as a junior naval officer during the First World War he entered the University of Cambridge as an undergraduate, obtaining a first class degree in physics in 1921. Elected to a Magdalene College Fellowship he then embarked upon a career in fundamental research, first at the Cavendish Laboratory under Rutherford and subsequently at Birkbeck College, London, and the University of Manchester. He was elected a Fellow of the Royal Society in 1933 and was awarded the Nobel Prize for Physics in 1948. These honours were bestowed in recognition of his outstanding research contribution in the areas of atomic physics and cosmic rays.

In 1934 he was invited to join an Air Ministry committee chaired by Sir Henry Tizard to advise on the air defence of Great Britain. Tizard's efforts focused on the development of radar and in that connection considerable use was made of quantitative methods of evaluation which in this specific sphere became known as 'operational research'. After the Battle of Britain in 1940, Blackett became the most effective advocate of the use of the new discipline as an aid to military effectiveness. He was instrumental in the creation of Operational Research Sections in the Anti-Aircraft and Coastal Commands before accepting the position of Director of Naval Operational Research in January 1942, a post which he held until the end of the war (Lovell 1975).

After 1945, in addition to his scientific work, Blackett became interested in science policy as a means of enhancing British economic and industrial performance. Appointed by Attlee to an advisory committee on scientific manpower, Blackett argued strongly for the expansion of scientific and engineering education with direct reference to the civilian manufacturing sector, a theme to which he returned in the 1960s when he was appointed chief scientific adviser at the Ministry of Technology in the 1964–70 Labour government. As an advocate of governmental intervention in the private sector, Blackett was an enthusiastic supporter of the Industrial Reorganization Corporation, founded in 1966 as an official 'merger–broker' in the interests of enhanced efficiency and competitiveness. In this context, the civilian computer industry was a particular concern of Blackett's; in his view, the sector was being unreasonably starved of specialist personnel as a result of the needs of the military establishment. Blackett was created a Life Peer in 1969. He addressed the House of Lords on only four occasions before his death, confining his speeches to science policy and Third World themes (Lovell 1975).

3 Main contribution

Blackett's career embraced four themes. As a physicist he achieved national and international recognition for his achievements in fundamental research. As a scientist he made a seminal contribution to the foundation of operational research as a credible tool of analysis, albeit within the military sector. As a public figure he achieved prominence as a commentator on military and scientific policy in relation to the UK and developing countries in the Third World. As a supporter of the Labour Party he came to be regarded as 'the leading military scientist of the left' (Zuckerman 1992: 29), and in that capacity was a notably controversial figure.

In focusing on his role in operational research it is clear that Blackett was the most outstanding practitioner of the new discipline in the wartime period. Having played a major role in the application of quantitative techniques to the evaluation of radar in the period to the Battle of Britain he was then instrumental in diffusing operational research throughout the greater part of the military command structure. He achieved some spectacular results, not least at Coastal Command, where the careful application of statistical analysis to operational problems played a critical role in the defeat of the U-boat weapon in the north Atlantic (Waddington 1973). It is instructive to note, however, that despite his wartime record, Blackett took little interest in the application of operational research in peacetime. He chose instead to concentrate on his scientific activities while at the same time becoming well-known as a commentator on defence and scientific policy.

In the latter context he emerged as an inveterate opponent of nuclear weapons, a stance which reflected, in part, his principled opposition to the area bombing of Germany during the Second World War on the grounds of its military ineffectiveness and moral repugnance (Blackett 1948, 1962; Jones 1961; Snow 1961). These views dovetailed with his stance on scientific policy where he argued eloquently for increased State provision for scientific and engineering education in the belief that it was vital to Britain's industrial prospects and that the country's nuclear programme was a major drain on such qualified personnel as were available. Marginalized politically both by the post-war Labour government and succeeding Conservative administrations on account of his radical-left opinions on defence issues, Blackett returned to public influence in the mid-1960s with the election of Harold Wilson's first Labour government.

In 1964 he was appointed chief scientific advisor to the newly created Ministry of Technology. This was soon followed by his appointment to a Cabinet Office Central Advisory Council on Science and Technology, and his involvement in the creation of the Industrial Reorganization Corporation, charged with the task of reorganizing civilian industry in the national economic interest via the encouragement of mergers and the spread of best practice managerial techniques (Zuckerman 1992). In all of these respects, Blackett's views on the damaging effects on manufacturing competitiveness of a bloated military defence sector, absorbing the lion's share of the country's R&D resources, conformed closely to Harold Wilson's political rhetoric in favour of the 'white heat of the technological revolution'. This had been a well-articulated electoral slogan in 1964, denoting Wilson's own concern to cut back military R&D in favour of civilian manufacturing. It remains to be said that Blackett's interest in the problems of developing countries in the Commonwealth was also in tune with the foreign policy stance of the Labour government.

4 Evaluation

Other than in the purely scientific and operational research aspects of his career, time has not proved kind to Blackett's views. Even with respect to operational research, while there can be no doubting its military value, such evidence as exists suggests that in its peacetime civilian setting the discipline's impact has been variable. The post-war nationalized industries, for example, capitalized on the new techniques of linear programming and queuing theory, as did central and local government administration. Diffusion throughout the corporate sector, however, was slow and hesitating, at least until the 1970s when it became possible to refer meaningfully to the 'professionalization' of British management.

On the nuclear issue Blackett was clearly naïve in his assumption that atom, let alone hydrogen bombs presaged no fundamental change in the nature of warfare, while his call for British neutrality in nuclear and defence policy was similarly unrealistic in the light of prevailing international relations in the later 1940s and 1950s. Although there was real merit in his view that British industrial competitiveness was being harmed by the burgeoning human and capital needs of the defence sector, his advocacy of centralized remedial measures, focusing on new departments of State and official committees, was seriously flawed. This was well illustrated in the record of the 1964–70 Labour government which pointed to the ineffectiveness of the means in relation to the ends envisaged: the Ministry of Technology manifestly failed to rejuvenate industrial performance in the face of vested interests within the British political and economic system, while the larger-scale mergers in manufacturing industry, presided over by the Industrial Reorganization Corporation before its demise in 1970, came to be regarded as ill-advised.

5 Conclusions

Patrick Blackett was one of the most able British physicists of the twentieth century. His involvement in military affairs redounded to his country's advantage via the diffusion of quantitative techniques of evaluation under the heading of 'operational research'. He did not, however, play any significant role in the peacetime dissemination of the new discipline, preferring to concentrate on his purely scientific work together with an increasing tendency to pronounce publicly on issues of scientific and defence policy. In these respects, he achieved some recognition in his appointment as a policy advisor to the Labour government in the mid-1960s. In overall terms, however, his influence as a distinguished scientist, pontificating on issues of public concern, was severely limited by his left-wing political stance.

MAURICE KIRBY
LANCASTER UNIVERSITY

Further reading

(References cited in the text marked*)

* Blackett, P.M. (1948) *Military and Political Consequences of Atomic Energy*, London: Turnstile Press. (A work in which Blackett set out his deep scepticism about Anglo-American nuclear policy. Widely interpreted as pro-Russian, it led to his virtual exclusion from the inner circle of governmental policy advisors until the 1960s.)

Blackett, P.M. (1954) *Lectures on Rock Magnetism*, Tel Aviv: The Weizmann Press. (Published version of the Second Weizmann Memorial Lectures which sum up Blackett's key contributions as an academic physicist.)

* Blackett, P.M. (1962) *Studies of War*, Edinburgh: Oliver & Boyd. (A collection of essays on the employment of operational research techniques to determine military tactics and strategy during the Second World War. It also reflects Blackett's hostility to the concept of area bombing of civilian targets.)

Blackett, P.M. (1971) *Science, Technology and Aid in Developing Countries*, Edinburgh: Edinburgh University Press. (A work which sets out the case, in Blackett's view, for Western scientific and technological aid to developing countries.)

Clark, R.W. (1965) *Tizard*, London: Methuen. (A biography of Blackett's principal partner in criticizing Bomber Command's wartime area bombing offensive against Germany.)

* Jones, R. V. (1961) 'Scientists at war', *The Times* 6, 7, 8 April. (A sequence of letters to *The Times* commenting on Blackett's involvement in wartime controversy on area versus precision bombing.)

* Lovell, Sir Bernard (1975) 'Patrick Maynard Stuart Blackett, Baron Blackett of Chelsea', *Biographical Memoirs of Fellows of the Royal Society* 21: 1–115. (An extended resumé and commentary on Blackett's career.)

Lovell, Sir Bernard (1988) 'Blackett in war and peace: the Blackett Memorial Lecture 1987', *Journal of the Operational Research Society* 39 (3): 221–33. (A short resumé of Blackett's academic and public career from the standpoint of a sympathetic adviser.)

Slessor, J. (1956) *The Central Blue*, London: Cassell. (The autobiography of the Commander-in-Chief, Coastal Command, for the greater part of the Second World War, offering critical comment on Blackett's opposition to Bomber Command's air offensive.)

* Snow, C.P. (1961) *Science and Government*, Oxford: Oxford University Press. (A partisan account of the wartime debate on bombing policy, favourable to Blackett and portraying his principal adversary, Lord Cherwell (Professor F.A. Lindemann) as an area bombing fanatic.)

* Waddington, C.H. (1973) *OR in World War 2*, London: Paul Elek. (An in-depth evaluation of the contribution of operational research to the defeat of the U-boat weapon in the Second World War.)

* Zuckerman, Lord (1992) *Six Men Out of the Ordinary*, London: Peter Owen. (A sympathetic portrait of Blackett written from the standpoint of a wartime colleague and ardent admirer of his stand against area bombing.)

See also: ACKOFF, R.L.; BEER, S.; CHURCHMAN, C.W.; RIVETT, B.H.P.; WIENER, N.

Related topics in the IEBM: LINEAR PRO-
GRAMMING; MANAGEMENT SCIENCE; MILI-
TARY MANAGEMENT; OPERATIONS
RESEARCH; STRATEGY; SYSTEMS

Boulding, Kenneth Ewart (1910–93)

Personal background

- born 18 January 1910, Liverpool, England
- graduated BA, Oxford University, 1st class honours in philosophy, politics and economics, 1931
- Commonwealth fellowship to the University of Chicago
- assistant lecturer in economics, University of Edinburgh, 1934–7
- instructor Colgate University, New York, 1937–41, where he wrote *Economic Analysis*
- associate then full professor Iowa States College, Ames, 1943–9, where he became a labour economist
- naturalized as a US citizen, 1948
- John Bates Clark Medal of the American Economic Association, 1948
- professor of economics, University of Michigan, 1949–68
- founded the Society for the Advancement of General Systems, 1953
- professor 1968–77, distinguished professor 1977–80, University of Colorado at Boulder
- died 19 March 1993, Boulder, Colorado

Major works

Economic Analysis (1941, 4th ed 1966)
A Reconstruction of Economics (1950)
The Image (1956)
Conflict and Defense: A General Theory (1962)
Beyond Economics: Essays on Society, Religion, and Ethics (1968)
Ecodynamics: A New Theory of Societal Evolution (1978)

Summary

Boulding began his career in the 1930s as a mainstream economist writing on the leading themes of micro- and macroeconomics, with a commitment to Keynesianism. By 1950 he had broadened his view of economics to a general systems approach. He spread his interests to include the nature of knowledge, conflict, the environment and the role of grants in a national economy.

1 Biographical data

Kenneth Boulding was brought up in a strict Methodist family in Liverpool. His father had a small plumbing business which was to be bankrupt by the time of his death. Throughout his life Boulding brought a strong religious, later Quaker, tone to his economic and defence writings. Scholarships took him to Liverpool Collegiate School and New College, Oxford, where, after a year of studying chemistry, he changed to philosophy, politics and economics, initially being tutored by Lionel Robbins. Robbins introduced him to economics through making him read Marshall's *Principles of Economics*, Pigou's *Economics of Welfare*, Cassel's *The Theory of Social Economy,* and Hawtrey's *The Economic Problem*. At Oxford he also acquired an affection for the economics of Keynes and was to write several articles on investment, liquidity preference and other Keynesian themes in the 1930s (see KEYNES, J.M.). A Commonwealth Fellowship in 1932 enabled him to make his first visit to the USA, where he was to spend most of his academic career. As a graduate student he came to know leading American economists of the day, including Viner, Knight, Schultz and

Schumpeter (see SCHUMPETER, J.). Despite undertaking graduate work he never obtained a PhD. His period as an assistant lecturer in economics at the University of Edinburgh in the mid-1930s added little to his intellectual development, apart from the acquisition of a knowledge of accounting from William Baxter, later professor of accounting at the London School of Economics, which helped him to use a balance sheet approach in his later writings. Partly because of a speech defect impairing his lecturing, Edinburgh did not renew his contract.

In 1937 he returned to the USA and was appointed to Colgate University, New York State. Too poor to take a holiday he usefully spent his vacations writing up his intermediate theory notes into *Economic Analysis* (1941), a respected text for over twenty years. He married Elise Bjorn-Hansen in 1941. Under Ragnar Nurske he worked at the League of Nations' economic and financial section, (evacuated to the Institute of Advanced Study in Princeton) on European agricultural reconstruction 1913–28, which gave him his major experience of working with economic data and provided an important background study to the subsequent work of the United Nations relief and reconstruction administration.

Through taking up labour economics at Iowa State University at Ames he became convinced that for economics to contribute to the analysis of the real world it had to be studied in conjunction with political science, sociology, anthropology and psychology. He was to become more involved in the study of general systems after productively spending 1954–55 at the Center for Advanced Study in the Behavioural Sciences, Stanford in the application of social sciences to peace research. At Ames he was to write what he regarded as his finest economics book, *A Reconstruction of Economics* (1950). A sojourn at the International Christian University, Japan 1963–4 and debates there with Marxist students encouraged him to combine evolutionary theory and the social sciences. Another period of leave, in Jamaica in 1959–60, produced another strand in his thinking, distilled into his *Conflict and Defense* (1962).

His appearance was striking: a hawk-like face, surrounded by a mane of white hair but with a twinkling eye. Although a cheerful man, he admits in his autobiographical writings he was not entirely content as he believed he deserved more attention for his innovations in economics, especially his macroeconomic theory of distribution. Late in his life he expressed his philosophy as a belief in human betterment, 'a cathedral of the mind'.

2 Economic Analysis

This textbook, originally published in 1941, instead of employing the usual divisions of the subject into production, consumption, distribution and exchange, or the newer microeconomics and macroeconomics taxonomy, presented economics as a progress of analysis from demand and supply to marginal analysis, with Keynesian macroeconomics occupying an intermediate position. International trade and money were subsidiary to the main analysis. As the text was modified from edition to edition, the demand and supply analysis proved the most durable: the macroeconomics section was expanded with more space given to dynamics and growth; perfect competition became only a special case of the imperfect market. He tried to analyse the economic system as a whole by building upon a few simple assumptions about human behaviour, for example, that prices are determined by states of mind. Geometry was frequently used as a method of exposition, even to the extent of using three dimensional diagrams so that production becomes the function of three factors of production. A distinctive feature of his exposition was to view the rate of interest as a rate of growth.

3 A Reconstruction of Economics

Boulding was proud of this advanced textbook which aimed to integrate economics into social science as a whole so economics could travel down a new road. Economics is regarded as embracing the participation of all social organisms in production, consumption and the exchange of assets. The subject thus becomes a study of a set of populations which together constitute an ecosystem, which is then examined according to the extent of competition and possible equilibria within it. The 'balance sheet' is used as a tool of analysis; 'homeostasis', the state an organism is organized to maintain, is the key theory. Boulding regarded Chapter 14, in which a macroeconomic theory of distribution is presented, as his best. Influenced by Ricardo and Marx before him, he wanted to explain the relative shares of capital and labour by creating a model in which two ratios are related, of wages to gross profits and of consumption to investment. In a geometrical analysis he shows the possible consequence for output of changing the distribution of income. He concludes with the widely held view that the greatest problem of modern economies is instability of output and employment which could be tackled by a larger proportion of national income being absorbed by government. However, the book is very mechanically Keynesian in tone and does not strike the reader as possessing the originality Boulding thought.

4 *The Image*

In this ambitious general work Boulding attempted to show how the social sciences are based on knowledge. He demonstrated the importance of the image; in other words, the subjectively known knowledge structure. Events and messages determine these images; in turn these images affect behaviour. Basic similarities between human beings enable knowledge and images to become public knowledge. Through the receipt and transmission of messages images can grow, privately within individuals and publicly in organizations and society as a whole.

He applies the notion of the image to an organization by first considering an organization as composed of structures distinguished by seven different levels. The simplest level is the static level of the thing, such as a molecule, a factory or a planet. The second level is a clockwork dynamic structure consisting of repetitive movements with the parts of the structure mechanically related. Next comes the level of the homeostatic control

mechanism in which messages are received, for example, from a thermostat so that action can be taken to keep something in a constant state. Fourth, at the biological level the organization is cellular – a self-maintaining structure but also open so that it can extend its own structure. Then there is the botanical level of a society of cells which practises division of labour with different cells supporting the existence of each other: plants 'know' when to produce leaves, flowers and fruit. Sixth, there is the animal level with the characteristics of the botanical level plus awareness, mobility, a separation of sleep from waking and some self-awareness, for example, of location. The highest level is the human being. This level has the greatest capacity for the intake of information and the creation of it into large and complex images. Images of time, self-consciousness and the structure of relationships are all possible. Each level has elements of the lower levels. The higher the level the more important is the concept of the image in a theoretical model.

Images begin in the minds of single individuals but when transmitted become public images shared by the mass of its people. Public images can become fixed and used for generations. In economics latent images underlie economic theories. To understand economic dynamics, the processes of economic life, it is important to understand the process by which economic images are reorganized through the transmission of messages. Messages about the state of a national economy are received by economic agents who then influence others through their buying, spending and investing to cause swings in national economic activity. In economic development growth occurs through the rejecting of old images in favour of better ones, for example, the belief that land can only grow grass to support pastoral activities is replaced by the view that ploughing, sowing and harvesting can take place. Economic development progresses upwards through the levels of images, with each stage of development learning from the previous levels.

The fruitfulness of using image analysis impressed Boulding so much that he suggested a new science of the study of images, 'eiconomics'. In economics he admits that an eiconomical approach is not very advanced as much of it has been mechanical and the problem of information and knowledge neglected, with few exceptional pioneers, such as Friedrich von Hayek in his analysis of the price system and George Katona in his study of economic psychology. Boulding wanted his eigonomics to have a status akin to cybernetics.

Boulding's analysis of the image is very representative of his general intellectual interests. He wanted to break out of the confines of economics into an analysis applicable to all of the social sciences. But there is something tentative about his endeavour. More study of the nature of knowledge and the forms in which it are transmitted should have been attempted. Curiously, despite the long history of epistemology, he did not use the rich resources of philosophy.

5 Conflict and Defense

In this book Boulding sought to create a 'new theoretical abstraction from the general phenomenon of conflict' (1962: viii). The tools of analysis he employs are those of microeconomics, especially the theory of oligopoly. He demonstrates how the distinctions in economics between static and dynamic analysis, the insights of game theory and the notion of viability can be employed in a range of conflict situations not narrowly economic. The familiar diagrams of microeconomics of the kind he uses in his own *Economic Analysis* are repeatedly applied to the study of economic, industrial, international and ideological disputes. His lucid analysis seeks to clarify types of conflict by a detailed application of a consistent set of definitions. From the analysis follows prescription. Conflicts can be resolved in a variety of ways. There can be withdrawal from the conflict, a victory by one of the disputing parties or a procedural settlement. A disputes procedure can reconcile the disputants or achieve a compromise or accept an award by an independent arbitrator. What is most important is to catch conflicts when they are young, and to have permanent institutions on the look out for potential disputes. The attraction of the book is the

demonstration of the usefulness of established economic theory in a variety of contexts.

Opposition to war and support for peace was a central belief of Boulding's; economics was his method for putting rigour into peace research. Game theory was used to consider the conditions for a stable equilibrium between nations. Phase analysis was applied to changes in the levels of threat and integration in the international system. Just as a few simple macroeconomic models had transformed the management of national economies, clearer analysis of the international system, Boulding hoped, would produce a stable peace.

6 Environmental economics

In a famous article in 1966 on 'The Economics of the Coming Spaceship Earth' he viewed the economy of the future as being an ecological system, like a single spaceship, without unlimited reservoirs for extraction or pollution. He contrasts this with the cowboy economy, an open economy, with unlimited resources which encourages both consumption and production and attempts to maximize its throughput. As the spaceman economy is concerned with minimization, not maximization, it chiefly aims to maintain the total capital stock, including human bodies and minds, and to effect that technological change which minimizes throughput. He argued that his prediction of the limited resource economy had already occurred in the form of pollution, if not exhaustion. The problem of pollution would diminish if the price and taxation systems were changed so that people pay for the nuisances they create. The longer term question of exhaustion could be addressed by producing more durable goods so that the ratio of capital to income rises, making it easier to maintain the national stock of wealth. Boulding, who always thought much in accounting categories, preferred stocks to flows. In this context he asserted that 'well-being' is more important than the consumption which achieved it. Like John Stuart Mill (see MILL, J.S.)he was willing to approve of a stationary economy, an economy without economic growth.

7 The grants economy

Boulding made a distinction between the grants economy and the exchange economy, a contrast between economic systems with unilateral transfers and those with bilateral transfers. As a result of exchange both parties benefit but through a grant the grantor loses and the grantee gains. He argues that both national economies and the international economy have become increasingly grant-like in nature. Within economies philanthropy and government welfare programmes have increased grants; internationally foreign aid has expanded. Grants arise because of mutual recognition of persons in a community. They are uncoerced in many cases such as charity and intra-family benevolence; they are coerced through a tax-benefit system. In this analysis he wanted to change the nature of economics from being the conceptualization of an exchange economy. The exchange economy has three functions – allocation of resources and factors of production among different industries, and the promotion of economic development. Boulding argues that the grants economy supplements the exchange economy in all of these functions because taxation and subsidies can affect the working of the economy. He hopes that by explaining what the grants economy can achieve, there will be less tension between capitalist and socialist economic systems and between right and left in Western democratic societies.

However, the usefulness of this analysis is questionable. Boulding makes the distinction between unilateral and bilateral relationships, ignoring multilateral linkages in an economy. At times it seems he is attempting to force the use of his nomenclature merely to reinvent the arguments for government intervention in an economy. But to Boulding's credit, he does try to link a theory of a national economy to the notion of community.

8 Conclusions

Boulding was one of the most prolific and interdisciplinary of economists. He carefully served a long apprenticeship writing on many of the traditional branches of economic theory but increasingly was drawn to studying social systems and applying the theory economics had taught him to defence studies, a reflection of his life-long commitment to pacifism. There is also a wider ethical framework for the corpus of his writings. As a Methodist turned Quaker he could borrow theological ideas to construct a suitable ethics. 'Love', so central to Christianity, he uses to emphasize the complementarity between the market and non-market organizations such as the home, the school and the church where love can be practised. Ethics and economics both involve choice so can learn from each other.

In his lectures *The Skills of the Economist* (1958) Boulding admits that he could be described as a combination of a classical economist and a moderate Keynesian exercising, like other economists, 'his ability to abstract a system from the complex social and physical world around him' (9). The focus of attention is the world of commodities, not of the persons producing and consuming them. In looking at the relation between economics and ethics, he contrasts the 'economic ethics' of seeking a reward and economizing with the non-economic, romantic and heroic attitude. '... in the long run economics wins; ... no matter how much society is characterized by heroism and romanticism, its forms in the long run must be productive or they may not survive' (181). But there has to be an inner core of integrity, meaning and purpose.

DONALD RUTHERFORD
UNIVERSITY OF EDINBURGH

Further reading

Boulding, E. and Boulding, K.E. (1995) *The Future: Images and Processes,* Thousand Oaks, California: SAGE Publications. (A collection of essays by Boulding and his wife showing their long-standing commitment to human betterment and peace.)

* Boulding, K.E. (1950) *A Reconstruction of Economics*, New York: John Wiley & Sons.
* Boulding, K.E. (1956) *The Image,* Ann Arbor: The University of Michigan Press. (A study of the nature of knowledge structures and their application to the study of the social sciences.)

* Boulding, K.E. (1958) *The Skills of the Economist*, Ohio: Howard Allen. (A discourse on the nature of economics.)
* Boulding, K.E. (1962) *Conflict and Defense: A General Theory*, New York: Harper & Brothers. (An analysis of conflict and conflict resolution with wide applications.)
Boulding, K.E. (1962) 'The ethical perspective', in *Issues of High Moment in Our Changing Economy*, New York: National Council of Churches: 35–44. (A socialist theism based on love is outlined.)
* Boulding, K.E. (1966, 4th edition): *Economic Analysis*, New York: Harper & Row.
Boulding, K.E. (1968) *Beyond Economics: Essays on Society, Religion, and Ethics,* Ann Arbor: The University of Michigan Press. (An anthology representative of his thinking on the nature of economics, general systems, religion and the environment.)
Boulding, K.E. (1969) 'Research for peace', *Science Journal*, 5A, 4, October: 53–8.
Boulding, KE (1969) 'The grants economy', *Michigan Academician* (Papers of the Michigan Academy of Science, Arts, and Letters) 1, 1 and 2, Winter: 3–11
Boulding, K.E. (1978) *Ecodynamics; A New Theory of Societal Evolution*, London: Sage Publications. (Both biological and social evolution is a learning process with some dialectical elements.)
Boulding, K.E. (1992) 'From chemistry to economics and beyond', in M. Szenberg (ed.) *Eminent Economists. Their Life Philosophies,* Cambridge: Cambridge University Press: 69–83. (A frank account of how the events of his life affected his intellectual development.)
Glahe, F.R. and Singell, L.D. (1971–5) *Collected Papers of Kenneth Boulding*, 5 vols, Boulder, Colorado: (The essential primary source, with explanatory prefaces by Boulding and comprehensive bibliographies, consisting of 177 articles.)
Khalil, E.L. (1996) 'Kenneth Boulding: ecodynamicist or evolutionary economist ?', *Journal of Post Keynesian Economics,* 19, 1: 83–100.
Silk, L. (1978) 'The economics of Kenneth Boulding', *Journal of Economic Issues*, 12, 2: 529–34.
Troub, R.M. (1978) 'Kenneth Boulding: economics from a different perspective', *Journal of Economic Issues*, 12, 2: 501–28.
Wray, L.R. (1994) 'Kenneth Boulding's grants economics', *Journal of Economic Issues*, 28, 4: 1205–25.

See also: HAYEK, F.; KEYNES, J.M.; MARSHALL, A.; SCHUMPETER, J.

Related topics in the IEBM: BUSINESS ECONOMICS; ENVIRONMENTAL MANAGEMENT; GAME THEORY AND GAMING; MARKET STRUCTURE; ORGANIZATIONS AND TECHNOLOGY; SYSTEMS

Braverman, Harry (1922–76)

1 Introduction
2 Biographical data
3 Main contribution
4 Evaluation
5 Conclusions

Personal background

- born Brooklyn, New York, 9 December 1922, of Polish–Jewish parents
- attended City College, New York, in 1937 but left after one year without taking a degree
- married Miriam Gutman, 25 December 1941
- started apprenticeship as coppersmith in Brooklyn Navy Yard in 1938 and worked in different skilled manual occupations between 1938 and 1951
- after working as a socialist journalist and book reviewer, entered publishing, becoming in turn editor, general manager and vice president of Grove Press, 1960–7
- director of Monthly Review Press, 1967–76
- died of lymphoma, 2 August 1976

Major works

The Future of Russia (1963)
Labor and Monopoly Capital: The Degradation of Work in the Twentieth Century (1974)

Summary

Harry Braverman (1922–76) is widely regarded as developing what became known as the 'de-skilling thesis' in his classic work *Labor and Monopoly Capital* (1974). Building on Marx's writing on the 'labour process', Braverman set out to analyse critically the degrading effects of technology and scientific management on the nature of work in the twentieth century. Principally, he suggested that the drive for efficient production is also a drive for the control of workers by management. Managerial control is achieved through monopolizing judgement, knowledge and the conceptual side of work, and concomitantly excluding workers from the control and ownership of knowledge and skill acquisition. The history of work in the twentieth century is one of work degradation, as knowledge is systematically removed from direct producers and concentrated in the hands of management and their agents. This leads to the impoverishment and debasement of the quality and experience of labour for both manual and mental workers, who are condemned to execute only the routine and conceptually depleted tasks in the service of capital.

1 Introduction

Braverman's name is associated with:

1 revitalizing and expanding the Marxist analysis of work;
2 the 'degradation' or 'de-skilling' thesis which suggests that there is a underlying tendency within capitalism to substitute less or unskilled labour for skilled;
3 the representation of management as a 'control' function, legitimized by governing and excluding workers from the conceptual part of the labour process;
4 the idea that efficiency is saturated with the ideology and interests of management and is not a neutral goal.

2 Biographical data

Harry Braverman was born in Brooklyn, New York, in 1922 of Polish–Jewish parents. In 1937 he attended City College, New York, but had to leave after a year in order to find work. He later graduated in 1963 from the New School of Social Research in New York, having studied under Robert Heilbroner.

His working life falls in two parts: as a skilled manual worker (1938–51), and as journalist and publisher (from 1952 until his death in 1976). Most of his working life was spent in white-collar work, and not, as is popularly assumed, as a manual craftsman. Braverman's account of his employment history in the introduction to *Labor and Monopoly Capital* (1974) gives more weight to his early career, which may have perpetuated the idea of his writing being overly concerned with the decline in manual craftsmanship.

From 1938 to 1942 he served a four year apprenticeship as a coppersmith in the Brooklyn navy shipyard and worked there as a coppersmith for a further three years, supervising from eighteen to twenty men. He was drafted into military service in 1945 and sent to Cheyenne, Wyoming, where he worked repairing locomotives for the Union Pacific railway. After his discharge, he moved to Youngstown, Ohio, and worked in steel fabrication. He spent seven years at various trades other than that of coppersmith, including pipe fitting, sheet metal work and layout.

During this period he defined himself as 'always a moderniser' (Braverman 1974a: 6) rather than an opponent of technical change, but also as an observer of the rationalization and erosion of craft work. He also noted that 'throughout these years' he was 'an activist in the socialist movement' and a Marxist (Braverman 1974a: 6). In fact, he joined the Trokskyist Socialist Workers' Party in the 1930s, leaving with a group of other people in 1954 when he helped set up the magazine *The American Socialist*, which he edited between 1954 and 1960 when the magazine closed.

During the 1950s, in addition to socialist journalism, Braverman produced book reviews and summaries for the Book Find Club. According to his son's recollections, Braverman spent considerable time on each review, polishing his style and treating each in a 'craft' manner. The quality of his reviews stood out and attracted the attention of a New York publisher, who recruited him in 1960. Between 1960 and 1967 he worked for Grove Press as an editor. While not in any way a socialist publishing house, Grove Press had published the unexpurgated version of *Lady Chatterley's Lover* in 1959, a year before Penguin, and while at Grove Braverman was the editor in charge of *The Autobiography of Malcolm X*, which first appeared in 1964. According to his son he was a very conscientious and competent editor, manager and publisher, with considerable business acumen. When he left Grove he was a general manager and vice president, evidence of his business and managerial flair.

Between 1967 and 1976 he worked as a director at Monthly Review Press (MRP). Despite taking a considerable drop in salary to join MRP, Braverman, according to his son, moved because he wanted to 'follow the music of my youth'. The move was in fact a return to socialist publishing, and he was clearly sympathetic with the political orientation of the publishing house. It was while at MRP that Braverman wrote *Labor and Monopoly Capital*. Although he wrote another book and numerous book reviews and short articles, he is best known for that one work.

3 Main contribution

Labor and Monopoly Capital

Braverman began work on *Labor and Monopoly Capital* in the late 1960s, working in the evenings and without sabbatical leave from his job at MRP. Since its appearance the book has not been out of print and has sold over 120,000 copies in English, with the bulk of sales occurring between 1976 and 1980; average sales in English remain around 2,000 per annum. The book has been translated into Italian, Spanish, Japanese, Portuguese, French, Swedish, German, Dutch, Greek, Norwegian and Serbo-Croat, and remains in print in all these languages. It has been MRP's best-selling title.

Fame came posthumously to Braverman, as the debate on the labour process initiated by *Labor and Monopoly Capital* occurred after his death. Apart from a short reply (Braverman 1976) he was unable to respond to his numerous critics, and his premature death gave these critics a free reign in interpretation. While critical of the political and practical disengagement of university academics, ironically, *Labor and Monopoly Capital* has helped make many academic careers.

Main themes of the book

Labor and Monopoly Capital is 465 pages long, elegantly written, theoretically integrated and carefully crafted. Despite its length, the view it presents of work becoming degraded by capitalism provides a dynamic which animates the text. This view comes from Braverman's own employment experience, keen observation, research training and political outlook, informed by the conviction that:

> The ideal organization toward which the capitalist strives is one in which the worker possesses no basic skill upon which the enterprise is dependent and no historical knowledge of the past of the enterprise to serve as a fund from which to draw on in daily work, but rather where everything is codified in rules of performance or laid down in lists that may be consulted (by machines or computers, for instance), so that the worker really becomes an interchangeable part and may be exchanged for another worker with little disruption.
>
> (Braverman 1994: 24–5)

There are five parts and twenty chapters in the book, covering labour and management, science and mechanization, monopoly capital, the growth of working-class occupations and the working class itself. The substantial parts of the book concern the role and nature of the labour process in capitalism, the role of science and mechanization, the growth and effect of scientific management on the worker and the changing class structure of the USA.

A major theme of the book concerns the debunking of official statistics and quantitative US sociological classification of jobs, skills, occupations and social class. Braverman attacks the view that skills have been 'upgraded' in the twentieth century, that extended time in education equates with more skilled or knowledgeable work and that formal designations of skill equate with actual skill. Skill receives varying definitions in the book, but best equates with the idea of worker-engaged, practical–theoretical workplace systems of learning most associated with craft apprenticeships. Movement away from 'craftsmanship' generally signals skill degradation. More generally, Braverman follows Marx's view of labour as the primary attribute of human beings; as he says in his final interview in December 1975: 'What is work but the central purpose of human existence as a species, the central drive, [and] motivation of the individual as well?' (Braverman 1980: 36).

Management is considered in a primarily negative light, as an agent for controlling the worker, and the growth of management has accompanied the expansion of the workplace or detailed division of labour and dissociation of the worker from authority exercised through command of craft and technical knowledge over the labour process. Efficiency theorists such as Frederick Taylor are represented as the ideologues for management control, flourishing because they provide capital with solutions and ideas for commanding the unruly and unpredictable element of production, namely, living labour (see TAYLOR, F.W.). Scientific management as a theory is equated with capitalism as a *system*, not with the occupational aspirations of engineers or a particular moment in the industrial development of the US workplace.

Discussion of changes in the US class structure take up one-third of *Labor and Monopoly Capital*, yet these ideas have tended to get uncoupled from deliberations on 'skill' which critics have highlighted and abstracted from it. Braverman seeks to show how the US transformed itself from a population of self-employed into one of waged employees, and how these employees have been divided subsequently between manufacturing and service industries and blue-collar and white-collar occupations, engaged in officially skilled but substantially skill-deficient activities and tasks. A recently transcribed lecture given by Braverman in 1975 reinforces his primary concern with what he calls the 'making of the U.S. working class' (Braverman 1994). In both *Labor and Monopoly Capital* and this talk, 'making' is used in the structural rather than cultural sense, through the involuntary movements of Latin American and European peasant and artisan populations into waged employment in US capitalism and through the destruction of US farmers and their transformation into waged workers. Classes in this sense are made and remade through 'the powerful tendency of the capitalist mode of production to convert every form of independent work into hired or wage labour' (Braverman 1994: 19). He also documents the shrinking of employment in agriculture, and subsequently in manufacturing, as the scale and concentration of ownership leads to technical resources intensifying the labour of those that remain. Displaced workers move into the service industry as this becomes a new growth point for capital accumulation. The chapters on clerical and service occupations highlight the spread of scientific management techniques with the growth in scale of service provision.

Other class themes are Braverman's discussion of the dramatic growth of the 'new middle class' of 'intermediate employees' who stand between owners/senior managers and workers. The sexual as well as the social division of labour features in *Labor and Monopoly Capitalism*, and the work was initially praised by feminists for its treatment of female labour. However, the book's focus on waged employment downplays the role of the 'household economy' or domestic labour in capitalism, a shortcoming acknowledged by Braverman (1976). Subsequent feminist research on the workplace has also highlighted the male exclusivity of craft and skilled work which distorts the way it is produced and reproduced in capitalism (Cockburn 1983).

An important implicit theme is Braverman's methodology, which elevates the critical role of work experience in forming theory. Braverman's own employment history as craftsman, supervisor, journalist, editor, publisher and manager informs the texture of his approach to work, and he contrasts the poor quality and inaccuracies of academic and official descriptions of work with the value of reflection on lived experience by the politically engaged (Braverman 1974a). Through numerous observations on the 'de-skilling' of all forms of work, from bread-making to

printing, Braverman's confident statements on the actuality of work, on the destruction of craft skills and controls, on the inhumane reduction of people to performers of the most mindless activities, spring his working knowledge as well as his political outlook and reading. Braverman's critical comment on the ignorance of manual work on the part of the influential sociologist Daniel Bell (Braverman 1974a) is illustrative of his lifelong hostility towards ivory-tower scholasticism and politically and practically disengaged academic commentators on the world of work. Braverman was a lifelong Marxist socialist, and his working experience and writing reflects his political convictions.

4 Evaluation

Labor and Monopoly Capital continues to cast a long shadow over debates on the nature of work in the late twentieth century. From the late 1970s, a debate around the issue of the 'labour process' in capitalist society developed in all countries, especially in English-speaking countries. The labour process perspective on the ordering of work suggests that managerial action is chiefly motivated by capital–labour relations, by the strategies of employers and their agents to try to control and stabilize the 'unruly' element or factor of production, namely, living labour. Labour process analysis carries through inequality from market relations into capital–labour relations in the workplace, and suggests that the dynamics of this unequal social relationship both limit, condition and drive the structuring work. The evolution of management thought, especially around the arrangements of production, is said to follow the evolution of labour organization, with increasing sophistication, unionization, education and expectations of work challenging employers to develop ever more sophisticated control techniques and practices to maintain their power in the employment relationship.

Reactions to *Labor and Monopoly Capital* passed through different phases, from political commentary by Marxist writers to academic engagement by those both sympathetic to Braverman's Marxist epistemology and those hostile to it, who were concerned with narrowing the focus of debate to limited areas such as the nature of skill acquisition and disposal. Continued treatment of the book as a 'text' – frozen by Braverman's premature death and consequent inability to respond to critics and develop his argument through debate – was only heightened when labour process analysis in some countries (notably the UK) came under the sway of Foucauldian analysis and produced highly abstract and rarefied commentaries far removed from Braverman's desire to link the practical experience of those working for capitalism with a grounded political theory of the dynamics of the system. The 'text' has been de-politicized because the author was removed from the field of debate and response, and *Labor and Monopoly Capital* became simultaneously an icon for the faithful to seize upon and for critics to deprecate. Constructive developments within a labour process tradition, which acknowledge Braverman's contribution and sought to develop the methodology or theory, are more than outnumbered by those which pay lip service to situating the text, codify it into a few clichés and use Braverman as a straw figure who cannot answer back.

Within academic circles *Labor and Monopoly Capital* has influenced a great variety of disciplines such as labour history, labour economics, economic history, industrial relations, industrial sociology, industrial geography and organizational theory. In the USA, initial evaluation was carried out by historians and labour economists (Zimbalist 1979; Edwards 1979). These writers sought to recast the evolution of management thought through the prism of labour–capital conflict over control of the labour process. In the UK, industrial sociologists (Nichols and Beynon 1977; Nichols 1980; Thompson 1989; Littler 1982) found theoretical coherence through the work, while industrial relations writers (Kelly 1982; Wood 1982, 1989; Edwards 1986) recast the nature of conflict, the role of skilled labour and other themes through reaction and response to *Labor and Monopoly Capital*. Economists in the UK (for example, Friedman 1977) made connections between labour market, product market and labour process restructuring, which in other countries (notably France) produced theories of capitalist 'regulation' informed by crisis and transition between different labour process 'regimes'. Later, organizational theorists entered and almost monopolized ownership of the labour process debate through the annual Aston–UMIST Labour Process Conferences, which produced a stream of edited volumes on different aspects of the labour process including job design, management strategies, gender, technology, white-collar work, skill, quality and theory.

In Japan, *Labor and Monopoly Capital* fed critical debates on the nature of work which tended to expose the US basis of Braverman's assumptions and the very different reactions to and construction of scientific management and workplace struggles in Japan. In continental Europe, German engagement with the work in the early 1980s also quickly amplified its US stereotypes on skill destruction, which made little sense in the strongly institutionalized craft apprenticeship system in German manufacturing (Lane 1989).

Braverman's message of 'work degradation' therefore fitted some societies better than others. However, even in countries with intrinsic craft apprenticeship systems and an abundance of skilled labour, such as German-speaking countries, writers have confirmed parts of Braverman's thesis of 'skill polarization' or bifurcation, and have uncovered within the firm managers committed to rationalizing work through skill substitution as well as skill upgrading (Altmann *et al.* 1992).

Nevertheless, the lack of a general fit between the degradation of work thesis and particular societies reveals one important limitation of the thesis, namely, coupling to *capitalism* a universal division of labour which is more properly anchored to particular occupational and training systems. More generally, it can be said that *Labor and Monopoly Capital* undervalued the way the labour process is embedded within sociocultural contexts which lays out differing ways of putting together the employment relationship. There is just one footnote concerning Japan in the work, and writing at a time of unquestioned hegemony of US capitalism, it is not surprising that Braverman did not give sufficient attention to different national ways of putting the labour process together.

In addition to ignoring the variety between capitalist societies in the formal systems of skill acquisition and discharge, Braverman also understated the role played by 'tacit' skills, which can be necessary for the most formally unskilled activities and which provide workers with some basis of resistance to or non-compliance with the control demands of management. Skills can also be tied to workers' gender or personality in the form of 'emotional labour' – ways of looking, feeling or servicing capital in particular ways which are not necessarily part of a formalized training structure. Writers such as Hochschild (1983) developed labour process analysis by focusing on the negative consequences for workers' mental health and sense of self in servicing employers in ways which compromise their identity as individuals. Braverman anticipated much of this development in his discussion of the shift towards mass service industries, where household and other activities become subject to disciplinary and rationalizing pressures of scientific management and involve subjecting the identity of the worker to prescribed ways of being and performing.

Another theme of criticism relates to Braverman's treatment of scientific management and Taylorism as though they were the last word in management theories of work organization. Debates on the nature of work from the early 1980s are particularly associated with the rise of the Japanese economy on a international scale (together with powerful continental European economies such as Germany), and deal in post-Taylorist neologisms such as 'flexible specialization', 'innovation-mediated production' or 'lean production', where old craft or new skill structures are forged. Ideologically, these ideas suggest a break from 'de-skilling', although empirical evidence of such a move remains less convincing (Thompson 1989). Part of a labour process perspective directly offered by Braverman's methodology is that of looking 'behind' the claims of formal classifications

and management paradigms, and this still informs contemporary debates about a supposed break from Taylorism.

A major attack on *Labor and Monopoly Capital* relates to the focus in the book on the 'objective' features of skill, class and occupational structures, which neglect the theme of consciousness. Braverman justified this in terms of priorities: in his view, we need an understanding of the structural operations of the labour market and labour process prior to understanding collective or class perceptions. His view of 'subjectivity' is through the idea of class consciousness, a historical class acting for itself. Two points of criticism occur: (1) attacking this orthodox Marxist view of class structure preceding class consciousness; and (2) rejecting limiting consciousness to class: what about gender, race, occupation or identity as significant bases of action? Burawoy (1979) developed a critique of the first by demonstrating how workers use work as a space for ingenuity, games, forms of resistance which, while not challenging capitalism as a class, do offer ways of mediating and modifying managerial controls while simultaneously reproducing capitalist production values. Inserting social action into labour process would arguably have been welcomed by Braverman, who sought not to belittle or play down workers' capacity for struggle over their economic returns and for dignity in the labour process, but rather highlighted the limited effect such struggles have in preventing capitalism transforming jobs into routine activities.

5 Conclusions

The rise of the labour process perspective on management and the organization of work, particularly in English-speaking countries, owes a considerable debt to Harry Braverman. His premature death distorted development of the various hypotheses on the direction of his work as, quite simply, the prime mover of the approach was not around to debate and progress his arguments through the normal avenues of active political and intellectual discourse. Too much time was wasted in second guessing, speaking for and against *Labor and Monopoly Capital*, and too little was spent on building upon and moving on from the text. Debate moved on through a process of distortion and simplistic codification of *Labor and Monopoly Capital* into clichéd debates, such as the de-skilling thesis, often to the neglect of other major themes of the book, subtleties of disposition and argument.

CHRIS SMITH
ROYAL HOLLOWAY
UNIVERSITY OF LONDON

Further reading

(References cited in the text marked *)

* Altmann, N., Kohler, C. and Meil, P. (eds) (1992) *Technology and Work in German Industry*, London: Routledge. (A useful account of the theoretical and practical critique of Taylorism from one branch of German industrial sociology.)

Braverman, H. (1960) 'The momentum of history: review of Heilbroner', *Monthly Review* (April): 433–9. (One of Braverman's early published reviews.)

Braverman, H. (1963) *The Future of Russia*, London: Collier Macmillan. (Early book examining the future of Russia and the Soviet Union.)

Braverman, H. (1967) 'Controls and socialism', *Monthly Review* (January): 33–9. (Article which looks at the important issue of control over the workforce.)

Braverman, H. (1967) 'The successes, the failures and the prospects', *Monthly Review* (November): 22–8. (Another of Braverman's early review articles.)

Braverman, H. (1968) 'Labor and politics', *Monthly Review* (July–August): 134–45. (Another of Braverman's early review articles.)

Braverman, H. (1969) 'Lenin and Stalin: review of Lewin', *Monthly Review* (June): 45–55. (Review article of a prominent work on the Soviet Union.)

* Braverman, H. (1974a) *Labor and Monopoly Capital: The Degradation of Work in the Twentieth Century*, New York: Monthly Review Press. (The main reference for contemporary debates on the labour process. Although heavily criticized and limited by its reliance on US capitalism, the breadth and quality of the writing and analysis make the work a modern classic.)

Braverman, H. (1974b) 'Looking backward and forward', *Monthly Review* (June): 40–8. (Review article.)

Braverman, H. (1975) 'Work and unemployment', *Monthly Review* (June): 18–31. (Often cited article on unemployment.)

* Braverman, H. (1976) 'Two comments', *Monthly Review* (September): 119–24. (Response to articles provoked by *Labor and Monopoly Capital*.)

* Braverman, H. (1980) 'The last interview', *Monthly Review* (March): 34–6. (Transcript of an interview given in Toronto, in which Braverman defends *Labor and Monopoly Capital* and argues for a viable craft system of production.)

* Braverman, H. (1994) 'The making of the U.S. working class', *Monthly Review* (November): 14–35. (A transcribed lecture in which Braverman discusses the growth of waged labour in the USA, its expansion in manufacturing and services and the creation of divided occupations; one of his clearest statements on class and the labour process.)

* Burawoy, M. (1979) *Manufacturing Consent*, Chicago, IL: University of Chicago Press. (Participant observation study on piece-working on the shop floor, building on classical studies of piece-working culture and patterns of managerial indulgence towards workplace informality.)

* Cockburn, C. (1983) *Brothers: Male Dominance and Technological Change*. London: Pluto. (Shows the way men monopolize skilled work in the printing industry.)

* Edwards, R. (1979) *Contested Terrain: The Transformation of the Workplace in the Twentieth Century*, London: Heinemann. (A useful integration of labour process and labour market theory, which overviews the evolution of different management control techniques – personal, bureaucratic and technical – in US industry in the twentieth century.)

* Edwards, P. (1986) *Conflict at Work*, Oxford: Blackwell. (Develops a materialist non-Marxist interpretation of conflict within the workplace, with interesting discussion on the institutional structuring of work and the comparative formation of work cultures and their impact on labour process struggles.)

* Friedman, A.F. (1977) *Industry and Labour*, London: Macmillan. (Early and influential elaboration of labour process theory based on economic histories of two industrial sectors in the UK, hosiery and cars.)

* Hochschild, A.R. (1983) *The Managed Heart: Commercialization of Human Feeling*, Ber-

keley, CA: University of California Press. (A ground-breaking account of the development and consequence of the intervention of systematic management for the prescription of workers' behaviour and action in service sector employment.)

* Kelly, J. (1982) *Scientific Management, Job Design and Work Performance*, London: Academic Press. (A sophisticated analysis of the influences of product and labour markets on the redesign of work, suggesting that the labour process should not be privileged as an explanatory force, rather, changes in production reflect the diverse effects of the interaction of products markets, labour markets and production processes.)

* Lane, C. (1989) *Management and Labour in Europe*, Aldershot: Edward Elgar. (A useful overview of the different employment and training systems in the UK, France and Germany, and how these mediate and differentiate the nature and experience of capitalist rationalization.)

* Littler, C.R. (1982) *The Development of the Labour Process in Capitalist Societies*, London: Heinemann. (Useful for advancing labour process theory, especially by separating the procedures and processes around the systematization of the recruitment and selection of labour and its bureaucratic organization in production; and in highlighting the national peculiarities to the evolution of managerial regimes in the USA, the UK and Japan.)

* Nichols, T. (ed.) (1980) *Capital and Labour: Studies in the Capitalist Labour Process*, London: Fontana. (A largely pessimistic collection of essays on the oppression of workers under different forms of capitalism from the first wave of reaction to Braverman's work in the UK, linked by excellent introductions from the editor.)

* Nichols, T. and Benyon, H. (1977) *Living with Capitalism*, London: Routledge. (A Marxist account of work relations and experience inside a chemical company which drew considerable inspiration from *Labor and Monopoly Capitalism*.)

* Thompson, P. (1989) *The Nature of Work: An Introduction to Debates on the Labour Process*, 2nd edn, London: Macmillan. (Examines key themes which Braverman neglected or understated, such as resistance at work, consent in the employment relationship and gender relations. The second edition also evaluates post-Taylorist debates which hinges on the idea of flexible manufacturing and working.)

* Wood, S. (ed.) (1982) *The Degradation of Work? Skill, Deskilling and the Labour Process*, London: Hutchinson. (An early British critical reaction to Braverman, with useful chapters on gender, consent, skill (several) and managerial strategies.)

* Wood, S. (ed.) (1989) *The Transformation of Work? Skill, Flexibility and the Labour Process*, London: Unwin Hyman. (Ostensibly an new edition of Wood's earlier collection, this reader indicates the pace of change within the debate, revealing more attention to diverse internationalization projects, through attention to Japan and Sweden, and the new theme of flexibility which emerged in the mid-1980s.)

* Zimbalist, A. (ed.) (1979) *Case Studies on the Labor Process*, New York: Monthly Review Press. (An early American example of a case study reader, with a strong labour history bent. Worth reading for the seminal chapter by David Noble, which argues the case for managerial control rather than cost or efficiency as the motive force behind technological innovation.)

See also: BEDAUX, C.E.; FORD, H.; PERLMAN, S.; SMITH, A.; TAYLOR, F.W.

Related topics in the IEBM: COLLECTIVE BARGAINING; EQUAL EMPLOYMENT OPPORTUNITIES; HUMAN RESOURCE MANAGEMENT; INDUSTRIAL AND LABOUR RELATIONS; LABOUR PROCESS; MANAGEMENT IN GERMANY; MANAGEMENT IN JAPAN; MARX, K.H.; ORGANIZATION BEHAVIOUR, HISTORY OF; TECHNOLOGY AND ORGANIZATIONS; TRADE UNIONS; TRAINING; TRAINING, ECONOMICS OF

Burns, Tom (1913–)

Personal background

- born 16 January 1913 in London
- gained a BA from the University of Bristol
- served in the Friends Ambulance Unit, 1939–45
- prisoner of war in Germany, 1941–3
- research assistant for the West Midland Group on Post-War Reconstruction and Planning, 1945–9
- lecturer, senior lecturer, reader at the University of Edinburgh, 1949–65
- professor of sociology at the University of Edinburgh, 1965–81
- fellow of the British Academy, 1982

Major works

The Management of Innovation (Burns and Stalker) (1961)

The BBC: Public Institution and Private World (Burns) (1977)

Summary

Tom Burns was the senior author, in collaboration with George Stalker, of *The Management of Innovation*, one of the most influential books on organizational behaviour in the second half of the twentieth century. The book identified two 'ideal types' of organization structure: the mechanistic (extremely bureaucratic, hierarchical and standardized) and the organic (extremely flexible, collegiate and motivating). Mechanistic organizations are appropriate for stable environmental conditions and established products; organic organizations are appropriate for changing environments and innovative outputs. Many writers have elaborated on this distinction (cf. e.g. Drucker, Handy, Kanter, Mintzberg, q.v.), agreeing with Burns that modern environments, being fast changing, require more organic types of structure.

1 Biographical data

Tom Burns' early academic interests were in urban sociology, and he worked with the West Midland Group on Post-War Reconstruction and Planning from 1945–49. He was appointed lecturer in sociology in the University of Edinburgh in 1949, became a professor in 1965 and retired in 1981. Between 1953 and 1956, when Burns was working in the multidisciplinary Social Sciences Research Centre of the University of Edinburgh, George Stalker, a psychologist with an organization development approach, joined him as a collaborator in a research project to evaluate a government-assisted scheme intended to facilitate traditional firms in entering new, technologically advanced markets.

2 *The Management of Innovation*

Burns was first alerted to the problems which arise for firms which attempt to undertake research and development and launch innovative products, through the study of a rayon mill which was commercially successful and growing. But the research and development laboratory was regarded with suspicion and hostility by the line managers and supervisors, and it appeared not to be very effective.

The opportunity came to explore this problem further with the setting up of the Scottish Council's 'electronics scheme'. This was a government-sponsored scheme intended to help small Scottish firms who were making traditional products for which the markets were declining. Its intention was to facilitate the entry of these traditional firms into a new, expanding, science-based industry. i.e. electronics. An elaborate scheme was set up which gave financial aid, technical support from an established electronics company and initial guaranteed sales to firms prepared to enter this innovative market. Burns and Stalker studied the operation of the scheme.

In the event, most of the Scottish firms failed to realize their expectations. In no cases were the laboratory groups which were created to develop the technical innovations absorbed into the established structure of the firm and allowed to make an innovative contribution. They were always kept separate, and were the subject of considerable resentment from the established managers. In half the cases, they were disbanded or their leaders resigned. In the other cases the groups were given other jobs in testing or production etc. The firms were not able to enter the innovative markets.

In further studies with firms in England which were larger and more committed to electronics development, Burns again found that major difficulties developed between those parts of the organization which were greatly affected by technological change (e.g. sales departments, development laboratories) and those parts which were buffered from it (e.g. production, accounting departments). (Burns and Stalker 1961, Chapter 9). New departments, development teams and so on were usually placed separately so as not to disrupt the existing organization, and then had great difficulty in fitting in and making a contribution. But Burns did find firms which were better able to cope with technical innovation in products and generally were better able to tolerate continuous change. This lead to the basic distinction made in *The Management of Innovation* between mechanistic and organic organizations.

3 Mechanistic and organic organizations

The difficulties which firms face in adjusting to a situation of continuously changing technology and markets, led Burns and Stalker to describe two 'ideal types' of management organization which are the extreme points of a continuum along which most organizations can be placed (Burns and Stalker 1961, Chapter 6).

The *mechanistic* type of organization is adapted to relatively stable conditions (1961: 119–120). In it the problems and tasks of management are broken down into specialisms within which each individual carries out an assigned, precisely defined, task. The abstract nature of each individual's task means that it is pursued with techniques and purposes more or less distinct. It is not the individual's responsibility to be concerned that the task fits together with those of others, or even whether it contributes to the task of the organization as a whole or hinders it. That is the responsibility of the immediate superior. There is a clear hierarchy of control, and the responsibility for overall knowledge and coordination rests exclusively at the top of the hierarchy. Vertical communication and interaction (i.e. between superiors and subordinates) is emphasized, and there is an insistence on loyalty to the concern and obedience to superiors. This system corresponds quite closely to Weber's rational-legal bureaucracy (q.v.).

The *organic* type of organization is adapted to unstable conditions when new and unfamiliar problems continually arise (1961: 121–122). These cannot be broken down and distributed among the existing specialist roles. There is therefore a continual adjustment and redefinition of individual tasks and authority. Interactions and communication (information and advice rather than orders) may occur at any level as required by the process, and a much higher degree of commitment to the aims of the organization as a whole is generated. In an organic type of organization, the structure is always more tentative, easily changed to cope with new circumstances. Organization charts laying down the exact functions and responsibilities of each individual are not found, and indeed their use may be explicitly rejected as hampering the efficient functioning of the organization. It is therefore crucial for effective functioning for there to be an able leader. The chief executive has to have a technical vision, and the knowledge and authority to drive the organization to achieve its goals through the effective use of the internal 'political system' (as described in the next section).

Burns and Stalker's clear identification of different types of organization structure as being appropriate to particular environments made the work an important early example of what came to be called the 'contingency approach' to organizational analysis, which tied in well with the work of Woodward, Lawrence and Lorsch, and the Aston Group (see ASTON GROUP; LAWRENCE P.R. AND LORSCH, J.W.; WOODWARD, J.).

4 The three social systems of the organization

For a proper understanding of organizational functioning, Burns maintains, it is always necessary to conceive of organizations as the simultaneous working of at least three social systems (Burns 1966).

The first of these is the *formal authority system* derived from the aims of the organization, its technology and its attempts to cope with its environment. This is the overt system in terms of which all discussion about decision-making takes place. But organizations are also cooperative systems of people who have career aspirations and a *career structure*, and who compete for advancement. Thus decisions taken in the overt structure inevitably affect the differential career prospects of the members, who will therefore evaluate them in terms of the career system as well as the formal system, and will react accordingly. This leads to the third system of relationships which is part of an organization – the *political system*. Every organization is the scene of 'political' activity in which individuals and departments compete and cooperate for power. Again, all decisions in the overt

system are evaluated for their relative impact on the power structure as well as for their contribution to the achievement of the organization's goals (this analysis confirms that of Crozier, q.v.).

It is naive to consider the organization as a unitary system equated with the formal system, and any change to be successful must be acceptable in terms of the career structure and the political system as well. It is particularly so with modern, technologically based organisations which contain qualified experts who have a career structure and a technical authority which goes far beyond the organization itself and its top management. Thus the attempt to change from a mechanistic to an organismic management structure has enormous implications for the career structure (which is much less dependent on the particular organization) and the power system (which is much more diffuse, deriving from technical knowledge as much as formal position).

5 Pathological systems

The almost complete failure of the traditional Scottish firms to absorb electronics research and development engineers into their organizations lead Burns and Stalker to doubt whether a mechanistic firm can consciously change to an organic one. The problems stem from the fact that, in a mechanistic organization, individuals are not only members of the organization as a whole, but are part of the career and political systems. They have sectional interests in conflict with those of other groups. Power struggles develop between established sections to obtain control of the new functions and resources. These divert the organization from purposive adaptation and allow out-of-date mechanistic structures to be perpetuated and 'pathological' systems to develop.

Pathological systems are attempts by mechanistic organizations to cope with new problems of change, innovation and uncertainty while sticking to the formal bureaucratic structure. Burns describes three of these typical reactions.

In a mechanistic organization, the normal procedure for dealing with a matter outside an individual's sphere of responsibility is to refer it to the appropriate specialist or, failing that, to a superior. In a rapidly changing situation the need for such consultations occurs frequently, and in many instances the superior has to put the matter up higher still. A heavy load of such decisions finds its way to the chief executive, and it soon becomes apparent that many decisions can only be made by going to the top. Thus, there develops the *ambiguous figure system* of an official hierarchy and a non-officially recognized system of pair relationships between the chief executive and some dozens of people at different positions in the management structure. The head of the concern is overloaded with work, and many senior managers whose status depends on the functioning of the formal system feel frustrated at being bypassed.

Some firms attempt to cope with the problems of communication by creating more branches of the bureaucratic hierarchy, e.g. contract managers, liaison officers. This reaction leads to a system described as the *mechanistic jungle,* in which a new job or even a whole new department may be created, whose existence, paradoxically, then depends on the perpetuation of the very difficulties they were set up to overcome.

The third type of pathological response is the *super-personal* or *committee system.* A committee is the traditional way of dealing with temporary problems which cannot be solved within a single individual's role, but without upsetting the balance of power. As a permanent device it is inefficient in that it has to compete with the loyalty demanded and career structure offered by the traditional departments. This system was tried only sporadically by the firms, since it was disliked as being typical of inefficient government administration. Attempts to develop the committee as a superperson to fulfil a continuing function that no individual could carry out met with little success.

6 The British Broadcasting Corporation

Concern with the interaction of the three social systems of the organization continues in Burns' study of the British Broadcasting Corporation (Burns 1977). The BBC is a very segmented organization both horizontally, where there are a large number of departments (e.g. drama, outside broadcasts, finance) which appear to be competing as much as cooperating, and vertically, where in order to rise in the grading structure executives soon lose contact with the professional skills (e.g. journalism, engineering) which they are supposed to administer. In this situation the career and the political systems can become more important than the formal task system.

Burns charts the rise in power of the central management of the BBC at the expense of the creative and professional staff, which stems from the Corporation's financial pressures. He maintains that the BBC can only develop as a creative service dedicated to the public good if it is freed from its financial-client relationship to the government.

7 Conclusions

In spite of the fact that their book is entitled *The Management of Innovation,* Burns and Stalker's distinction has not had its major impact in the understanding of how innovative products have been developed, and then gained successful adoption (see Hage 1998). Rather, their work has been used much more generally to argue the need for organizations to be 'organic': i.e. for managements to establish a flexible structure and culture in order to be in a position to respond to the inevitably changing nature of the environment in which all organizations exist. (See HANDY, C.; KANTER, R.M.; PETERS, T.J.).

An important element contributing to the popularity and influence of the work is the fact that only a very partial reading is often given to the Burns and Stalker book. For example, 'organic' organizations are often described as though they were very open and democratic (see KANTER, R.M.). But this characterization fails to highlight that a democracy inevitably involves political processes and, indeed, political intrigue, and that a strong authority figure is required to hold the system together. Burns and Stalker describe this in the final section of the book. Again, while they propose that a mechanistic structure is appropriate for stable environmental conditions, it appears almost impossible to find such conditions in the modern world – every environment, at least as seen by the managers in it – is changing. Thus a partial rose-tinted description of the organic structure is advocated and accepted as the way forward for *all* organizations (see PETERS, T.J.). Even the term 'organic' is more attractive than the term 'mechanistic', which adds to its uncritical acceptance. (In a later paper Burns, 1963, substituted the term 'organismic' for 'organic' but this usage has not generally been taken up.) Burns and Stalker's original detailed study of management conduct still repays critical study.

DEREK PUGH
OPEN UNIVERSITY BUSINESS SCHOOL, UK

Further reading

(References cited in the text marked *)

* Burns, T. (1963) 'Industry in a new age', *New Society,* 18, 3rd January 1963; reprinted in D.S. Pugh (ed.) *Organization Theory: Selected Readings* (4th ed.) London: Penguin Books, 1997. (A concise summary by Burns himself of the two extreme types of organization, mechanistic and organic – here called 'organismic' – and the environmental situations for which they are appropriate.)

* Burns, T. (1966) 'On the plurality of social systems', in J.R. Lawrence (ed.) *Operational Research and the Social Sciences,* London: Tavistock. (A description of the three social systems – instrumental, career and political – contained within every organization).

* Burns, T. (1977) *The BBC: Public Institution and Private World,* London: Macmillan. (An expansion of the ideas developed in *The Management of Innovation* applied to the operation of the BBC.)

* Burns, T., and Stalker, G.M. (1961) *The Management of Innovation,* London: Tavistock; third edition (with new preface by Tom Burns) Oxford: Oxford University Press, 1994. (The classic book describing the studies which led to the identification of mechanistic and organic structures.)

* Hage, J. (1998) *Organizational Innovation* (The History of Management Thought series), Aldershot: Dartmouth Publishing. (Covers the work of Burns and Stalker in an overview.)

Pugh, D.S and Hickson, D.J. (1997) *Writers on Organizations* (fifth edition), London: Penguin Books; Thousand Oaks, CA: Sage Publications. (Describes the contribution of over forty organization theorists – including Burns and Stalker – whose work has a current impact on the field.)

See also: ASTON GROUP; CROZIER, M; DRUCKER, P.F.; HANDY, C.; KANTER, R,M.; LAWRENCE, P.R. AND LORSCH, J.W.; MINTZBERG, H.; PETERS, T.J.; WEBER, M.; WOODWARD, J.

Related topics in the IEBM: GROUPS AND TEAMS; ORGANIZATION BEHAVIOUR; ORGANIZATION BEHAVIOUR, HISTORY OF; ORGANIZATION STRUCTURE; ORGANIZATION TYPES; ORGANIZATIONAL PERFORMANCE; TECHNOLOGY AND ORGANIZATIONS

Chandler, Alfred Dupont, Jr (1918–)

1 **Biographical data**
2 *Strategy and Structure*
3 *The Visible Hand*
4 *Scale and Scope*
5 **Conclusions**

Personal background

- born 15 September 1918 at Guyencourt, Delaware, USA
- graduated from Harvard University, 1940
- served in US Navy during Second World War
- historian at Massachusetts Institute of Technology, 1950–63
- professor of history at Johns Hopkins University, 1963–71
- professor of business history (latterly emeritus), Harvard University, 1971 onwards
- developed central ideas on the rise of the modern diversified, multidivisional firm

Major works

Strategy and Structure (1962)
The Visible Hand (1977)
Scale and Scope (1990)

Summary

Alfred D. Chandler, Jr was the founder of modern business history and a critical early influence on the discipline of strategic management. He was the first person to document systematically the rise of modern big business, and in so doing he has heavily shaped our understanding of such important notions as 'strategy', 'organizational structure' and 'organizational capabilities'. Chandler is the author of the famous dictum 'structure follows strategy' and a strong proponent of the view that it is internal rather than external factors that are most important to competitive success. Chandler's ongoing research programme continues to influence the agenda of contemporary business thinking, as well as provoking considerable controversy.

1 Biographical data

Alfred Dupont Chandler, Jr was born at the end of the First World War into what McGraw (1988) has called a 'patrician' family in Delaware. This family background was important to his subsequent work. Chandler's great-grandfather was Henry Varnum Poor, not only founder of the Standard and Poor's Corporation but also a leading journalist in the early US railway industry. Poor's life in fact provided the subject of Chandler's doctoral dissertation, and the role of the railways in the shaping of modern business would be an important theme in the whole of his later writings. Though not related by blood, Chandler's family was also closely connected to the Du Pont chemicals family: his great grandmother had been raised by the Du Ponts, and Chandler's own middle name reflected the connection. The Du Pont corporation and General Motors (which the Du Ponts also controlled) were to form two of the four central case studies in Chandler's first great work, *Strategy and Structure*. As well as facilitating access to crucial historical materials – Chandler was also historical adviser to Alfred Sloan (see SLOAN, A.P.), the key figure at General Motors – this family background may have influenced his basically rosy view of the historical origins of modern US capitalism.

Chandler studied history as an undergraduate at Harvard, where he was a member with John F. Kennedy of the Harvard sailing team. Graduating in 1940, Chandler served as a US naval officer during the war. After a short period as a graduate student at the University of North Carolina, Chandler returned to Harvard in 1946. There he was taught by, among others, the great sociologist of the day,

Talcott Parsons: this sociological influence, particularly the interest in bureaucracy, can be seen in all his subsequent work on business organization.

In 1950, Chandler took his first job as a professional historian at the Massachusetts Institute of Technology, moving to a professorship in history at Johns Hopkins University in 1963. It was at Johns Hopkins that Chandler began the enormous task of editing the papers of former President Dwight Eisenhower. In 1971, Chandler was appointed professor of business history at Harvard Business School, where he has remained ever since. At Harvard, Chandler developed a popular second year MBA elective in business history, as well as teaching successfully on executive programmes. It is notable that Chandler's appointments at both the Massachusetts Institute of Technology and Harvard Business School were outside the conventional career tracks of a successful historian, something that may be reflected in the originality of his approach to the historical task.

It is as an academic writer rather than as a man of affairs that Chandler has had his influence, so this entry will address his contribution through considering his three main business works in turn.

2 *Strategy and Structure*

Though not in fact his first book, *Strategy and Structure: Chapters in the History of the American Industrial Enterprise* (1962) is the one which first made Alfred Chandler's reputation. It also coined several key concepts in modern management thinking, as well as spawning the first systematic research programme in strategic management.

Strategy and Structure is concerned with the strategies and organizational structures of US big business, both tracing their evolution during the first half of this century and drawing out the policy implications. Although he deals with a larger sample briefly, Chandler's focus is on the particular histories of Du Pont, General Motors, Standard Oil and Sears Roebuck as pioneers and exemplars of the general trends he finds elsewhere. Among the very first academic writers on strategic

management, Chandler needed to coin his own definition of strategy, one that is still highly influential. For him, strategy was about: 'the determination of the long-term goals and objectives of an enterprise, and the adoption of courses of action and the allocation of resources necessary for carrying out these goals' (Chandler 1962: 13). Alongside this definition, Chandler also elaborated important distinctions between 'strategy' and 'tactics', and 'strategy formulation' and 'strategy implementation'. The strategy that he was particularly concerned with was the increased product diversification observable throughout US big business during the period.

It was this strategic shift from single business to diversified business that raised the central issue of *Strategy and Structure*. Diversification typically provoked considerable problems for the traditional organizations of the first part of this century. To summarize just one of Chandler's detailed examples, Du Pont had diversified during and after the First World War to reduce dependence on its original core explosives business. However, the company soon found that it was too centralized to cope with the complexity of its new product range and plunged into losses between 1919–21. The problem was not the diversification strategy itself, but the traditional structure by which it was managed. As Chandler (1962: 314) famously put it: 'Unless structure follows strategy, inefficiency results'. The solution to Du Pont's problems was to introduce what Chandler calls the 'multidivisional structure'.

The innovation of the multidivisional was that it decentralized operating responsibilities to product divisions at the same time as keeping overall strategy firmly under the control of the headquarter's general office. In Du Pont's case, the general office was formed from the senior managers of the executive committee – none of whom had direct divisional responsibility – together with the advisory staffs of the various central departments (see Figure 1 for a simplified version of Du Pont's divisional structure). Thus, Du Pont's top general management set strategy and controlled resources detached from the operational demands of the five product divisions. This separation of responsibilities was critical:

> The basic reason for its (the multidivisional's) success was simply that it clearly removed the executives responsible for the destiny of the entire enterprise from the more routine operational responsibilities and so gave them the time, information and even psychological commitment for long-term planning and appraisal. Conversely, it placed the responsibility and the necessary authority for the operational administration in the hands of the general managers of the multifunctional divisions.
>
> (Chandler 1962: 309)

Divisional general managers got on with running the businesses, while top corporate managers concentrated on what businesses to include in the portfolio and how to coordinate the whole to maximum advantage.

Chandler's conception of the multidivisional structure had enormous and immediate influence, both practical and academic. Academically, Chandler's ideas informed Oliver Williamson's (1975) early formulation of transaction cost economics (see WILLIAMSON, O.E.) while a group of PhD students at Harvard Business School went on to analyse diversification and divisionalization in the USA and Europe in what was the first systematic programme of research in the strategic management discipline (see Scott (1973) for a summary). Practically, it was Chandler's cases that McKinsey consultants used as they promoted the new divisional form worldwide during the 1960s (at least twenty-two of the top one hundred firms in the UK used McKinsey advice on organization in this period), while Chandler's elevation of strategy to the general office provided much of the justification for the central corporate planning departments that burgeoned during the 1960s and early 1970s.

3 The Visible Hand

The Visible Hand: The Managerial Revolution in American and Business History (1977) developed and expanded many of the themes introduced in *Strategy and Structure*. While the previous book had focused on particular firms and individual managers, this book provided a more general theoretical and istorical background to the emergence of large-scale integrated capitalism and the professional managerial class that ran it (see MEANS, G.C.).

The book's title refers to the new coordinating mechanism of twentieth-century economies, the 'visible hand' of the professional manager, whose expanding organizations challenged the 'invisible hand' of the market. For Chandler, new technologies and the search for efficient use of resources explain the emergence since the middle of the last century of industrial organizations of unprecedented size and diversity. The hero in this process was the new transport technology of the railway, in which Chandler's great-grandfather had played an important reforming role. The railway played a double role: first, it made possible the geographically large markets necessary to support the mass-production systems of twentieth century big business; second, the complex and dispersed networks of the railways had required the

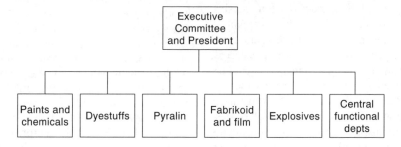

Figure 1 Du Pont's multidivisional structure, 1921
Source: Adapted from Chandler (1962: 108–9)

development for the first time of a new class of middle managers with a new systematic approach to administration and coordination.

Chandler's account of the Armour meat packaging company around the turn of the century illustrates the general process. The railway and new refrigeration technologies created the possibility of a nationwide meat-packing industry. But to take this opportunity to buy, pack and distribute highly perishable meat products across the USA required huge investment in coordination. Armour created a multi-tiered administrative hierarchy with national scope, all controlled by a clerical workforce of over 1,000, and vertically integrated forward into the ownership of its own rail-fleet. Having created this infrastructure, the search to utilize its capacity to maximum efficiency led Armour to diversify from the packing of beef, its original product, to lamb, pork and even fruit, and also to enter new markets such as fertilizer which could use its waste products.

Chandler's thesis, then, is that wherever new technologies and widened markets increase the possible volume of activity, as in meat-packing, then coordination by professional managers working through the hierarchies of large, integrated firms will supplant the uncoordinated trading processes of disintegrated chains of smaller enterprises. Once these hierarchies are created, moreover, their managers will naturally seek out other areas into which expansion will enable them to use their resources more efficiently or to create equivalent economies of coordination. So the large corporation advances. An important consequence of this process of increasing scale and complexity is the displacement of family owner-managers, typically untrained and inadequate, by a new class of salaried, professional managers. Managerial capitalism supersedes family capitalism. Chandler's claim is that it is this efficiency-seeking managerial class – with its apparatus of professional journals and associations, consultants and business schools – that coordinates the bulk of economic activity in advanced capitalist economies today.

4 Scale and Scope

Chandler's latest book extends his earlier arguments internationally, comparing the largest two hundred industrial enterprises in the USA, Britain and Germany between the First World War and the immediate post-Second World War period. British management comes out of this comparison most unfavourably, with fatal consequences for national economic performance.

In *Scale and Scope: The Dynamics of Industrial Capitalism* (1990), Chandler again emphasizes the role of new technologies, this time in creating both economies of scale (especially in capital-intensive industries amenable to mass production) and economies of scope (gained by using the same production facilities or distribution networks for many products). Economies of scale and scope gave potentially huge advantages to the large, diversified enterprises that emerged in advanced economies during the twentieth century. However, as Chandler had earlier shown at Du Pont and elsewhere, diversification and growth can create enormous problems of coordination, so he emphasizes a third source of advantage – economies of transaction costs brought about by efficient managerial hierarchies replacing market and other forms of coordination. The importance of economies of scale, scope and transactions leads Chandler to conclude that it was the readiness to make a three-pronged investment in all of manufacturing, marketing and management that distinguishes between success and failure among this international group of businesses. The combination of physical facilities and human skills brought about by this kind of three-pronged investment define each firm's 'organizational capabilities', the hard-to-imitate sources of advantage that provide the dynamics for strategic development. Those firms which early make the necessary investments in manufacturing, marketing and management seize a first mover's advantage that is hard for followers ever to catch up.

By and large, British enterprises failed to make these investments. Up until the post-war period, Britain was characterized by a personal capitalism dominated by family managers, rather than the professional managerial capitalism of the USA and Germany. Chandler cites among many examples the confectionery company Cadbury, whose seven managing directors in 1930 included five Cadburys and one cousin. The consequence for Britain of this personal capitalism was an amateurish management unable to achieve economies in transactions on the one hand and cautious investment policies that constrained economies of scale and scope on the other. Chandler compares the British Cadbury company with the German confectioner Gebrüder Stollwerck: professionally managed, Stollwerck outpaced the conservative Cadbury company by vigorous internationalization and vertical integration into distribution by vending machines. In Chandler's account this story is repeated again and again. Especially in the new industries of the twentieth century, British companies retreated as US companies – in automobiles, for example – and German companies – in chemicals – seized the first mover advantage by superior investments in all of manufacturing, marketing and management. In a pessimistic coda, however, Chandler expresses the fear that now it is US business that is failing to make the necessary investments in 'organizational capabilities' because it is distracted by a mania for takeovers and unrelated diversification.

1980). Others point to a neglect of the state and other institutional influences on the shaping of modern industrial enterprise (Fligstein 1990). Similarly underestimated perhaps are institutional influences allowing some countries to successfully abstain from the US model of diversified, multidivisional enterprise, notably in the Far East (Hamilton and Biggart 1988). Chandler may also be over-attached to the virtues of large-scale, integrated enterprise at a time when many new industries are disintegrating into networks of market-coordinated small firms (Teece 1993). The multidivisional may itself be in the act of being superseded (Bartlett and Ghoshal 1993). According to some strategy theorists, the nostrum 'structure follows strategy' simplifies the direction of causality in practice, while Chandler's separation of strategy from operations, and strategy formulation from strategy implementation, can have pernicious managerial consequences (Mintzberg 1990).

It is in the nature of founding figures to attract revisionist critiques. The continued vigour and volume of controversy surrounding Chandler's work are themselves testimony to its importance. One thing is sure: Chandler will long remain central to understanding the emergence and management of large-scale modern business.

RICHARD WHITTINGTON
UNIVERSITY OF OXFORD

5 Conclusions

By combining grand themes with rich detail, Chandler manages to convey not only insight but real excitement in exploring the origins of two of the most important phenomena of the twentieth century – the contemporary large corporation and professional management. His writings give historical context to the everyday world of the modern manager, at the same time as affording practical guidance in terms of strategy and structure. Chandler's arguments are not, however, uncontested.

The criticisms are many. Some detect a strong vein of technological determinism, combined with a highly optimistic view of managerial motives that minimizes power-seeking behaviour (Duboff and Herman

Further reading

(References cited in the text marked *)

* Bartlett, C.A. and Ghoshal, S. (1993) 'Beyond the M-Form: towards a managerial theory of the firm', *Strategic Management Journal* special issue, 4: 23–46. (Claims that Chandler's multidivisional form has now been superseded by a new highly decentralized form.)
* Chandler, A.D. (1962) *Strategy and Structure: Chapters in the History of the American Industrial Enterprise*, Cambridge, MA: MIT Press. (Chandler's classic work on the strategies and structures of US business.)
* Chandler, A.D. (1977) *The Visible Hand: The Managerial Revolution in American and Business History*, Cambridge, MA: Harvard University Press. (A broad account of both the

historical rise of large-scale enterprise in the USA and professional management.)

* Chandler, A.D. (1990) *Scale and Scope: The Dynamics of Industrial Capitalism*, Cambridge, MA: Harvard University Press. (A comparative account of the development of big business in Britain, Germany and the USA.)

Chandler, A.D. *et al* (eds) (1997) *Big Business and the Wealth of Nations*, Cambridge: CUP. (How large enterprises developed in a wide range of national settings.)

* Duboff, R.B. and Herman, E.S. (1980) 'Alfred Chandler's new business history: a review', *Politics and Society* 10: 87–110. (A wide-ranging historical and theoretical critique of Chandler's work.)

* Fligstein, N. (1990) *The Transformation of Corporate Control*, Cambridge, MA: Harvard University Press. (An alternative historical account of the rise of diversified, divisionalized business, stressing institutional factors.)

* Hamilton, G.C. and Biggart, N.W. (1988) 'Markets, cultures and authority: a comparative analysis of management and organization in the Far East', *American Journal of Sociology* supplement, 94: 52–94. (Points to the institutional limits on the overseas transfer of US theories of organization, especially to the Far East.)

* McGraw, T.K. (1988) *The Essential Alfred Chandler: Essays Towards a Historical Theory of Big Business*, Boston, MA: Harvard Business School Press. (An accessible collection of extracts from Chandler's key works, with a helpful commentary and short biography in the editor's introduction.)

* Mintzberg, H. (1990) 'The design school: reconsidering the basic premises of strategic management', *Strategic Management Journal* 11: 171–95. (A critical account of the Harvard approach to strategy and the 'structure follows strategy' idea.)

* Scott, B.R. (1973) 'The new industrial state: old myths and new realities', *Harvard Business Review* March–April: 133–48. (A summary of post-war patterns of diversification and divisionalization in Europe and the USA, supporting Chandler's thesis.)

* Teece, D.J. (1993) 'The dynamics of industrial capitalism: perspectives on Alfred Chandler's *Scale and Scope*', *Journal of Economic Literature* 31: 199–225. (An admiring but critical review of Chandler's book, arguing that his analysis may now be dated.)

Whittington, R. and Mayer, M. (1996) 'Beyond or behind the M-form? The structures of European business', in H. Thomas, D. O'Neal and M. Ghertman (eds) *Strategy, Structure and Style*, Chichester: John Wiley. (A critical discussion of both the Chandlerian and post-Chandlerian concepts of organization in the light of recent evidence from Europe.)

* Williamson, O.E. (1975) *Markets and Hierarchies: Analysis and Antitrust Implications*, New York: The Free Press. (An important theorization of Chandler's argument in terms of transaction cost economics.)

See also: MEANS, G.C; SLOAN, A.P.; WILLIAMSON, O.E.

Related topics in the IEBM: BIG BUSINESS AND CORPORATE CONTROL; BUSINESS HISTORY; CORPORATE PLANNING, PROCESS OF; MANAGEMENT IN GERMANY; MANAGEMENT IN NORTH AMERICA; MANAGEMENT IN THE UK; MERGERS, AQUISITIONS AND JOINT VENTURES; ORGANIZATION STRUCTURE; STRATEGY, CONCEPT OF; STRATEGY, IMPLEMENTATION OF; TRANSACTION COST ECONOMICS

Checkland, Peter Bernard (1930–)

Personal background

- born on 18 December 1930 in Birmingham, England, the son of a grocer's shop manager
- educated at George Dixon's Grammar School, Birmingham
- national service as a sergeant instructor in the RAF, 1948–50
- Casberd Scholar of St John's College, Oxford
- graduated with 1st class honours in chemistry, 1954
- married Glenys in 1955 and subsequently had two daughters (Glenys died in 1990)
- worked at ICI Fibres 1954–1968, latterly manager of a research group
- professor of systems, Lancaster University, 1969–1997
- visiting professorships at the University of New England, New South Wales and the University of Central Lancashire at Preston
- honorary consultant professor, North Western Polytechnical University, Xian, China
- awarded honorary DSc, City University, 1991
- awarded honorary doctorate of the Open University, 1996
- first recipient of the Most Distinguished and Outstanding Contributor Award of the Methodologies Group of the British Computer Society, 1995
- first recipient (alongside Sir Geoffrey Vickers) of the UK Systems Society Medal for Outstanding Contribution to Systems Thinking, 1997

- he has a love of English literature, jazz and rock climbing, and notes that both jazz and rock climbing involve passion and structure – a combination encouraged in his influential soft systems methodology (SSM)

Major works

Systems Thinking, Systems Practice (1981)
Soft Systems Methodology in Action (with J. Scholes)(1990)
Information, Systems and Information Systems (with S. Holwell)(1998)

Summary

Peter Checkland's fifteen years at ICI were spent successively as technical officer, team leader, section leader and group manager in ICI Fibres. During the later stages of this career, as his managerial responsibilities increased, he looked for assistance to the literature that went under the label of management science. He was horrified to find that most of what he read was irrelevant to his job. As he was later to formulate it (influenced by Vickers 1965, 1970) management science was dominated by a 'goal-seeking' paradigm exemplified in the work of the Nobel Prize winner Herbert Simon (1947) (see VICKERS, G.; SIMON, H.). Checkland regarded this as an inadequate formulation in terms of the actual practice of management which is much more about 'relationship maintaining.' A growing fascination with such matters, together with an interest in the application of systems ideas, led him to leave ICI and to join the first 'Systems' department in the UK, the postgraduate Department of Systems Engineering (later Systems then Systems and Information Management) established at Lancaster University (with a grant from ICI) by the late Professor Gwilym Jenkins.

In 1969, led by Checkland, the research began from which was to emerge SSM, his main contribution to the field of business and management. SSM is a methodology, setting out principles for the use of methods, which enables intervention in ill-structured problem situations where relationship maintaining is as least as important as goal-seeking and answering questions about 'what is required' is as significant as determining 'how to do it'. The success of SSM led to a paradigm revolution in systems thinking which liberated the discipline from the intellectual straitjacket in which it had been locked and, at the same time, made it relevant to managers. A virtuous circle of interaction between ideas and experience became possible and was fully exploited by Checkland and his co-workers at Lancaster.

The establishment of this action research programme ensured that lessons could be learned from experience and incorporated into SSM, that reflection could take place on the philosophical underpinnings of the methodology, and refinements could be made to supportive methods and techniques. Today SSM is used by both academics and practitioners, is important well beyond the confines of the systems discipline and has spread its influence to many countries outside the UK.

I Introduction

The systems idea of wholes being 'more than the sum of their parts' dates back to the Ancient Greeks. It was in the 1940s, however, that a self-conscious systems movement began to emerge closely associated with the names of Ludwig von Bertalanffy, a biologist, and Norbert Wiener, a mathematician interested in control and communication theory (see VON BERTALANFFY , L. AND WIENER, N.). Von Bertalanffy (1968) founded 'general system theory' to study the laws governing the behaviour of systems whatever their type, and Wiener (1948) founded 'cybernetics' to study control processes 'whether in the animal or the machine'. From these traditions were developed two pairs of ideas which for Checkland (1981) constitute the basic conceptual armoury of systems thinking: emergence and hierarchy; and communication and control. Bringing these ideas together yields the notion of a whole system demonstrating emergent properties and capable of adapting in the face of disturbances from its environment. Checkland (1981) embraced a particular use of this 'adaptive whole system' metaphor as offering a better vehicle for making progress in tackling management problems than did the traditional scientific method.

In the decades following the birth of the systems movement the discipline developed in a number of directions. Checkland's sympathies lay with those interested in applying systems ideas to help with real-world problems. In this camp he recognized three categories – work in 'hard' systems thinking, e.g. systems engineering; systems ideas used as an aid to decision-making, e.g. RAND style systems analysis; and work in soft systems thinking, e.g. his own development of SSM. For understanding his contribution it is essential to know how he differentiates his work from systems engineering (SE) and systems analysis (SA). In fact, for Checkland (1981), SE and SA are underpinned by a similar shared belief. That belief is that real-world problems can be formulated in the following way:

- there is a desired state, S_1
- there is a present state, S_0
- there are alternative ways of getting from $S_0 - S_1$
- problem-solving consists of defining S_1 and S_0 and selecting the means of reducing the difference between them.

Checkland sees these 'systematic' approaches as embodying a poverty-stricken goal-seeking model with a concentration on 'how to do it.' What was needed, if systems ideas were to become relevant to managers, was a systemic methodology capable of operating in 'soft' problem situations where goals and objectives, as well as the means of reaching them, are problematical.

2 Main contribution

Emergence of SSM

The SE methodology employed at Lancaster University at the time of Checkland's arrival was of its type in demanding well-structured problems with clearly defined objectives and measures of performance. The research strategy he adopted was to use it to tackle management problems and learn from the results. During the course of this action research the methodology had to be radically changed to make it appropriate for dealing with the greater complexity and ambiguity of managerial situations.

It is possible to see three intellectual breakthroughs as crucial to the emergence of SSM. The first was the delineation of the notion of 'human activity system' for exploring human affairs. Previous systems thinkers had sought to model physical systems, designed systems and even social systems, but they had not treated purposeful human activity systemically. A human activity system is a systems model of the activities people need to undertake in order to pursue a particular purpose. Second, it was realized that the models employed in SSM could not be attempts to model the real-world, rather they needed to be epistemological devices used to find out about the real world. This is because if, as is usually the case in managerial situations, there is lack of agreement about goals or about the nature of the system to be engineered, any number of models of human activity can be constructed which have resonance for those involved and are therefore relevant to intervention. It follows also that, in order to have sensible debate, it is necessary to be explicit about the world view taken as given in each of the models used. Third, while the models produced in hard systems thinking are blueprints for design, human activity system models are contributions to a debate about possible change. They explicitly set out what activities are necessary to achieve a purpose meaningful from a particular point of view. On the basis of such models participants in the problem situation, aided by a facilitator if necessary, are able to learn their way to what changes are systemically desirable and culturally feasible given the meanings and relationships that currently pertain in the situation. Thus SSM is a learning system.

These three breakthroughs allowed Checkland to propose a fully developed soft systems methodology premised on a fundamental shift of 'systemicity from the world to the process of enquiry into the world' (Checkland 1989).

Mode 1 SSM

Although Checkland no longer uses it, the representation of SSM as a seven-stage learning system which appeared in 1981 in *Systems Thinking, Systems Practice*, is still the best known today. It is shown in Figure 1. In the first and second stages a problem situation is entered and expressed. The aim is to gain and disseminate an understanding of a situation with which various participants feel a degree of unease. Often, expression takes the form of 'rich pictures': pictorial, cartoon-like representations of the problem situation which highlight significant and contentious aspects in a manner likely to lead to original thinking at Stage 3. The drawing of rich pictures is one of the most successful and frequently used of the methods that have come to be associated with SSM.

The third stage involves choosing relevant human activity systems offering insight into the problem situation and preparing root definitions from these relevant systems. A root definition should capture the essence of the relevant system and, to ensure that it does, should be constructed giving consideration to all the elements brought to mind by the mnemonic CATWOE (customers, actors, transformation process, world-view, owners, environmental constraints). As the 'W' indicates, each root definition reflects a different way of conceiving of the problem situation. For example, in considering a prison, it might be helpful to consider it as a punishment system, a rehabilitation system, a system for taking revenge, a system to protect society, and as a system that constitutes a 'university of crime' (Checkland 1987). In Stage 4 these root definitions are used to build conceptual models. Conceptual models consist initially of seven or so verbs, structured in a logical sequence and representing those minimum activities that are necessary to achieve the purpose enshrined in the root definition.

Conceptual models, developed if necessary to a higher level of resolution, are then

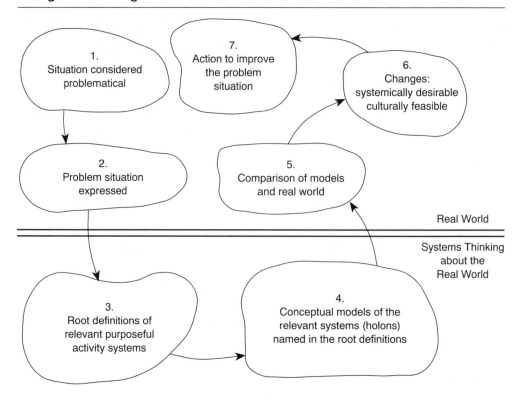

Figure 1

brought back 'above the line', (see Figure 1) to be compared with what is perceived to exist in the real world. This constitutes Stage 5 of SSM. The aim is to provide material for debate about possible change among those concerned with the problem situation. Thus SSM facilitates a social process in which Ws are held up for examination and their implications, in terms of human activities, are made explicit and discussed. Stage 6 should see an accommodation developing over changes that are both desirable and feasible – desirable in terms of the systems models and feasible given the history of the situation, the power structure, and prevailing attitudes. When accomodations are found, action can be taken to improve the problem situation (Stage 7). The conclusion of the methodological cycle does not see a 'solution' to the original problem but merely the emergence of another, different problem situation. Problem resolving, for Checkland, is a never-ending process in which participants' attitudes and perceptions are continually tested and changed and they come to entertain new conceptions of desirability and feasibility.

A significant feature of SSM, emphasized by Checkland (1985), is that it is doubly systemic; combining a cyclic learning process with the use of systems models within that process. The cyclic learning process articulates natural processes of management that occur in organizations; worrying about the present situation, postulating alternatives, and seeking accommodations which allow change to happen. Theoretically it draws upon Vickers' (1970) account of the way appreciative systems originate, develop and change. The systems models employed by the methodology are, as we know, human activity system models of purposeful activity each expressing explicitly a particular viewpoint.

As experience of using SSM accumulated, Checkland began to find the original seven-stage representation too limiting. It had always been stressed that the learning cycle could be commenced at any stage and that SSM was to be used flexibly and iteratively, but the seven-stage model still seemed to contribute to a systematic (rather than systemic) step-by-step understanding of the process and one, moreover, in which use of the methodology appeared cut off from the ordinary day-to-day activities of an organization. In an attempt to overcome this, and to demonstrate that SSM in use required constant attention to the interrelationships between situational logic and situational culture, a new representation of the methodology was developed (Checkland and Scholes 1990; see Figure 2). This 'two strands model' gives equal space to the cultural stream of analysis as to the logic-based stream and indicates some enhancements to the former which were added during the 1980s. The cultural stream is seen to depend on three types of inquiry – referred to as Analysis 1, 2 and 3. Analysis 1 considers the intervention itself and the roles of client(s),

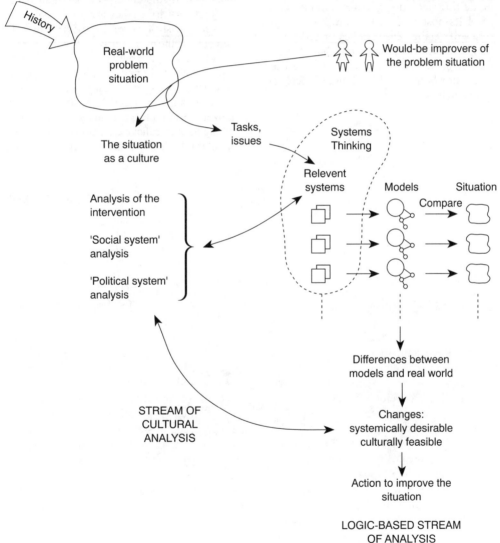

Figure 2

problem solver(s) and problem owners. Analysis 2, 'social system analysis', looks at social roles, norms of behaviour, and what values are used in judging role performance. Analysis 3 (a response to criticisms made of SSM's lack of attention to issues of power – see Evaluation) examines the politics of the problem situation and how power is obtained and used.

Checkland's second major work on SSM (with Scholes, 1990) presented this 'two strands model' of the methodology together with some modifications to the methods, modelling techniques etc., supportive of SSM. Its most important feature, however, is a series of detailed case studies of SSM in action, and its most original contribution the reflection on those case studies, including a new distinction between Mode 1 and Mode 2 uses of the methodology.

Mode 2 SSM

The concept of Mode 2 SSM arises from reflection on how SSM is most easily and productively used by managers in their daily working lives. In practice Checkland and Scholes (1990) reasoned, managers are absorbed by the pressures and concerns of their immediate environments. They act and react according to their personalities, knowledge, instincts and so on and are unlikely, on an everyday basis, to operate according to the rules of a methodology. Rather than being methodology driven they are situation driven. They may wish however, from time to time, to step outside the hurly-burly of ongoing events to try to make sense of what is happening or to apply some structured thinking to proposals for change. In these circumstances, if SSM's procedures and methods have become internalized sufficiently, a manager or group of managers can refer to the approach to help them think through the situation they are

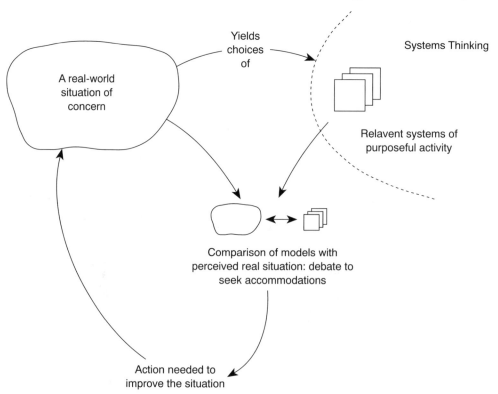

Figure 3

experiencing and the possibilities that it opens up. This, Checkland and Scholes would call a Mode 2 use of SSM.

As set out in *Soft Systems Methodology in Action*, Mode 2 SSM is not meant to replace Mode 1. Rather they represent a spectrum of possible uses. Mode 1 interventions are methodology driven and prescribe certain activities that need to be carried out. Mode 2 'interactions' are situation driven and allow managers to make sense of what is going on. In Mode 1, SSM is external and dominates proceedings. In Mode 2 it is internalized and only occasionally breaks the surface of ongoing events. It is not easy to capture SSM in a way that does justice to both Mode 1 and Mode 2, and the rather sparse representation of Figure 3 is the currently preferred diagram for this purpose.

SSM and information systems

The field of study in which SSM has made its greatest impact, outside systems itself, is information systems (IS). The idea that Checkland's methodology could help with some of the problems (failure to deliver on objectives, resistance from end-users) which plagued the design and implementation of such systems, was attractive to some of his collaborators at Lancaster (e.g. Wilson 1984) as well as many concerned with information technology applications elsewhere. Checkland has now turned his own attention to the field of information systems and regards the insight that purposeful activity models can be used in IS work as crucial to the recent history of SSM.

A third Checkland book appeared (1998), written with Sue Holwell who worked in both IS and IT in the Australian Government Service for twenty years. The book, *Information, Systems and Information Systems*, is an ambitious attempt to 'initiate conceptual cleansing in the IS area'. This involves trying to bring intellectual clarity to confusions about such concepts as 'data', 'information' and 'knowledge', and replacing the out-dated model of the organization as a machine which has traditionally been used to underpin work in information systems. In the authors' view

experience demonstrates the inadequacy of such a model. The book endeavours, as did its two predecessors, to provide a more adequate match between theory and actual experience so that the two can be brought into a mutually informing relationship. A set of case studies of SSM at work show how this can be realized and the effect it could have on the more productive employment of information technology.

3 Evaluation

In an early paper, Checkland (1972) declared his intention to take systems thinking beyond the abstractions of general system theory and the constraints of specialized technique. The story of SSM reveals the success of this enterprise. Contemporary SSM is based on some clearly stated principles or 'constitutive rules' (Checkland 1981; Checkland and Scholes 1990) which guide the process of intervention (or 'interaction' in Mode 2). It is these rules which make research on the methodology possible and allow the methods and techniques which support SSM to be continually improved. At the same time as SSM sets out principles for method use it does not determine that use. It provides a different response in each situation depending on the user and the nature of the situation. It is this flexibility which ensures its relevance in so many managerial situations.

Checkland was not the only systems thinker to see the need for a change in direction in the discipline. Colleagues at Lancaster University, such as Brian Wilson (1984) and the late Ron Anderton, helped shape the development of SSM and, in the US, Ackoff (1981) and Churchman (1971), created 'softer' systems approaches in reaction to the road that operations research had taken (see ACKOFF, R.L. AND CHURCHMAN, C.W.). More recently, Senge (1990) has become something of a guru by 'softening' system dynamics (see SENGE, P.). None of these, however, has achieved the clarity of thought necessary to work through the implications of shifting 'systemicity from the world to the process of enquiry into the world'. Checkland claims to have made his intellectual revolution on the basis of practical experience using SSM. There is no doubt, however, that the development of SSM has also benefited from being theoretically informed: early on by the work of Churchman and Vickers, later by the writings of such as Dilthey, Weber and Habermas (see WEBER, M.). It was this theory that enabled Checkland to conceptualize so clearly the break with functionalist, 'hard', systems thinking and to consciously construct SSM on new, interpretive theoretical foundations.

Checkland has attracted most criticism on the very issue of the theoretical alignment of the principles underpinning SSM. The constitutive rules openly embrace an interpretive position which provokes those coming from functionalist or more radical philosophical and sociological paradigms (see Jackson 1991). To put it at its simplest, functionalists believe that there is something in the various models produced by experts in management science and organization theory which make it worthwhile managers taking account of them. To Checkland such models may merit a place at the debating table but they certainly cannot provide any objective truth about how organizations should be designed and managed. Radicals argue that the context in which the methodology is most often used, serving managers in hierarchical organizations, means that the participative debate upon which its success depends is constrained. Checkland is largely silent on how power effects the 'neutrality' of SSM. He feels that his experiences with SSM support an interpretive account of the social world. Others wonder whether his research programme has been sufficiently well designed to justify properly this conclusion.

4 Conclusion

Checkland's break with the predominant goal-seeking tradition in management science, and his recognition of the significance of relationship-maintaining as an alternative, have led to a revolution in systems thinking. The research programme based on SSM, and linking ideas and experience so directly, operationalized this and enabled the continual development of the methodology. SSM is an achievement which has hugely increased the relevance of systems thinking to business and management.

MIKE C. JACKSON
LINCOLN SCHOOL OF MANAGEMENT
UNIVERSITY OF LINCOLNSHIRE AND
HUMBERSIDE

Further reading

(References cited in the text marked *)

* Ackoff, R.L. (1981) *Creating the Corporate Future*, New York: Wiley. (An account of Ackoff's Interactive Planning.)
* Checkland, P.B. (1972) 'Towards a systems-based methodology for real-world problem-solving', *Journal of Systems Engineering*, 3, 2. (First full account of SSM.)
* Checkland, P.B. (1981) *Systems Thinking, Systems Practice*, Chichester: Wiley. (Charts the development of systems thinking and explains SSM.)
* Checkland, P.B. (1985) 'From optimising to learning: A development of systems thinking for the 1990s', *Journal of the Operational Research Society*, 36: 757–767. (Details of the shift from hard systems thinking to soft systems thinking.)
* Checkland, P.B. (1987) 'The application of systems thinking in real-world problem-situations: The emergence of SSM', in M.C. Jackson and P. Keys (eds) *New Directions in Management Science*, Aldershot: Gower: 87–96. (The emergence of SSM with illustrations of key ideas.)
* Checkland, P.B. (1989) 'Soft Systems Methodology', in J. Rosenhead (ed.) *Rational Analysis for a Problematic World*, Chichester: Wiley: 71–100 (Good account of the thinking underpinning SSM.)
* Checkland, P.B. and Scholes, J. (1990) *Soft Systems Methodology in Action*, Chichester: Wiley. (Developments in SSM, case studies and explanations of Mode 1 and Mode 2.)
* Checkland, P.B. and Holwell, S. (1998) *Information, Systems and Information Systems*, Chichester: Wiley. (Applications of SSM to information systems design and implementation.)
* Churchman, C.W. (1971) *The Design of Inquiring Systems*, New York: Basic Books. (Philosophers looked at as designers of inquiring systems.)
* Jackson, M.C. (1991) *Systems Methodology for the Management Sciences*, New York: Plenum.

(Review of systems methodologies with particular reference to their theoretical underpinnings.)

* Senge, P. (1990) *The Fifth Discipline*, London: Random House. (Hugely popular development of system dynamics in a soft direction.)
* Simon, H.A. (1947) *Administrative Behaviour*, New York: Macmillan. (Classic account of how to improve rationality in organisations.)
* Vickers, G. (1965) *The Art of Judgement*, London: Chapman and Hall. (Argues the importance of relationship maintaining in management.)
* Vickers, G. (1970) *Freedom in a Rocking Boat*, London: Allen Lane. (Fullest account of Vickers' notion of appreciative systems.)
* Von Bertalanffy, L. (1968) *General System Theory*, Harmondsworth: Penguin. (Essays on the development of general system theory.)

* Wiener, N. (1948) *Cybernetics*, New York: Wiley. (Introduced cybernetics, the science of communication and control.)
* Wilson, B. (1984) *Systems : Concepts, Methodologies and Applications*, Chichester, Wiley. (Another rendition of SSM from a colleague of Checkland's.)

See also: ACKOFF, R.L.; CHURCHMAN, C.W.; SENGE, P.; SIMON, H.; VICKERS, G.; VON BERTALANFFY, L.;WIENER, N.; WEBER, M.

Related topics in the IEBM: CYBERNETICS; DECISION MAKING; INFORMATION AND KNOWLEDGE INDUSTRY; INFORMATION REVOLUTION; MANAGEMENT SCIENCE; OPTIMALITY; ORGANIZATION BEHAVIOUR; ORGANIZATION STRUCTURE; ORGANIZATIONAL LEARNING; PROBLEM SOLVING

Child, John (1940–)

Personal background

- born 10 November 1940 in Manchester, England
- spent childhood and youth in South London and Surrey, England
- graduated in economics from the University of Cambridge, 1962 with double first class honours
- obtained PhD from St Johns College, Cambridge, 1967
- systems analyst, Rolls Royce 1965–6
- research fellow, Aston University, Industrial Administration Research Unit, 1966–8
- senior research fellow, London Business School, 1968–73
- professor of organizational behaviour, Aston University, 1973–91
- professor, China–EC management programme, Beijing, People's Republic of China, 1985–9
- dean and director, China–EC Management Institute, Beijing, 1989–90
- Guinness professor of management studies, Judge Institute of Management, University of Cambridge 1991–
- fellow of St Johns College, Cambridge, 1991–

Major works

British Management Thought (1969)
'Organisational structure, environment and performance: the role of strategic choice' (1972)
'Price to pay? Professionalism and work organisation in Britain and West Germany' (with M. Fores, I. Glover and P. Lawrence)(1982)
'Information technology, organisation and the responses to strategic challenges' (1987)
Information Technology in European Services (with R. Loveridge)(1990)
Management in China during the Age of Reform (1994)
'From fiefs to clans and network capitalism: explaining China's emerging economic order' (with M. Boisot)(1996)

Summary

John Child is one of the handful of contemporary European scholars whose work is acknowledged by North American audiences as contributing to the emergence of the scholarly discipline of organizational behaviour (OB). In part this is because of his early association with the Aston School and with its attempt to measure organizational structures. However, it is through one article written in 1972 that he became one of the most quoted management theorists of the late twentieth century. In it he critiqued the Aston approach to contingency analysis and, more broadly, the deterministic nature of current thinking in OB. The article synthesized arguments for the existence of scope for strategic choice by corporate executives. It contributed to the Chandlerian position on the influences of the strategic agent in shaping business performance. Coming as it did from a leading positivistic researcher, its effect among North American scholars has been seen to be seminal.

However, Child went on to become one of the most prolific of European writers on management and has researched a wide range of issues. It is indeed difficult to speak of his work as constituting a single oeuvre. He himself describes his approach as theoretically eclectic. His research agenda has been almost entirely shaped by current concerns in business policy. It moves from the design of the workplace to the institutional structuring of national economic development. In approaching each succeeding level of organizational structure Child generally attributes significance to a wider range of socio-political variables than would be normal in the more functionally oriented North American mode of OB analysis. There remains however a tension in much of his analysis. The design imperatives demanded of structural prescription must necessarily remain open-ended as a result of the political process which he places at the centre of his analytical frame.

I Biographical data

John Child is the elder of two sons born during World War II to a British father working as a senior civil servant and a German mother. After the war, the family moved south from Manchester to London when his father was appointed an official historian to the Foreign Office, later moving to HM Cabinet Office in the same role. Child obtained entry to St Johns College Cambridge on a state scholarship from Purley Grammar School. At Cambridge, he obtained a college scholarship while reading for an Economics Tripos, majoring in the recently introduced papers in sociology. He obtained one of the rarely awarded Double Firsts and remained at St Johns to write a doctoral thesis on the twentieth century emergence of British management thought, with John Goldthorpe as his supervisor. Before the final acceptance of his thesis he had left to take up a management traineeship and a job as systems analyst with Rolls Royce Ltd based in Shrewsbury. In the same year, 1965, he married Elizabeth Mitchener whom he had known since undergraduate days. Late in the following year he was attracted back to academe and to the nearby University of Aston in

Birmingham by an offer from Derek Pugh and David Hickson, leaders of the team later known as the Aston Programme (see ASTON GROUP). When, two years later, Pugh moved to a chair at London Business School, Child accompanied him as a senior research fellow.

Over the following four years Child played a leading role in the design and operationalization of the second stage or national sample of the Aston Programme. In a series of single and jointly authored papers, Child both critiqued and extended the measures and methodology of the earlier programme. While these articles published in the *Administrative Science Quarterly* served to establish his reputation in North America, it was a contemporaneous (1972) paper in the British journal *Sociology* that was to become his more cited work. Finkelstein and Hambuck (1996) describe it as a major influence in redirecting American research on organizational behaviour (OB) away from contextual determinism to a renewed concern for the effects of executive leadership.

While at London, Child began the first of a wider range of collaborative relationships that were to mark much of his later work. With Lex Donaldson, Malcolm Warner and Ray Loveridge, he extended the work of the Aston Programme to take in occupational interest associations. In 1973 he returned to Aston as professor in OB. In the next years, he collaborated with others on a series of empirical research projects on supervisory management, on professionalization and on the growth of the firm; all the time continuing to explore the implications of the original Aston findings on size and complexity in organization form. Collaboration with Alfred Keiser, at the University of Mannheim in the late 1970s brought the beginning of a new phase in his research on comparative management. This work was extended in a six-country, six-university comparison of the effects of information technology on the service sectors undertaken over the 1980s. Concurrently, Child acted as director of the ESRC Work Organisation Research Centre based at Aston jointly with Ray Loveridge and Peter Clark.

In 1985, he became a visiting professor at the China–EC Management Institute and in

1989 succeeded Max Boisot, on secondment, as the dean. In this position he steered the Institute through the tumultuous events of that year. Shortly after returning to England in 1991, he was appointed to the Guinness chair of management studies in the newly created Judge Institute of Management at Cambridge and returned to St John's College as a fellow.

His empirical work in the 1990s has focused almost entirely on the study of Western joint ventures in Eastern European countries and the People's Republic of China, studies undertaken with a number of collaborators in those regions as well as with Max Boisot and David Faulkner.

While primarily regarded as a leading empirical researcher Child has occupied a number of administrative and editorial roles with distinction including the editor-in-chief of *Organization Studies* and has gained a reputation for his personal contributions to the development of scholarly professional bodies in the UK and Europe. Like his former mentors Pugh and Hickson, he has remained essentially part of the European scholarly community in spite of his high reputation in North America. His family home remains in the English Midlands, though his son and daughter with Elizabeth are both married and pursue their professional careers elsewhere.

2 British Management Thought

Child's first major work derived from his doctoral thesis and shows clear signs of the contemporary concern with the need to justify management authority in the context of mid-century Britain. Child distinguished his analysis from that of the already famous Bendix (1956) comparative study of management ideology by suggesting that his aim was to emphasize the importance of technical effectiveness in managerial discourse as well as the purely legitimatory function (1969: 23). The aim of the book was to trace the historical search for a generally applicable body of knowledge that would provide the basis for claims to professional status by British management. This work was seen to have two major thrusts: the first related to the need to gain employee commitment and, in particular,

to attempt at consensual control through the application of human relations precepts; the second to the search for the 'optimal' principles of organizational design. Both were treated by Child from the stand-point of manufacturing or industrial management.

His narrative account opens with the disquiet felt by employers professing Christian principles at mounting class struggle at the beginning of the twentieth century. The role of Quaker employers, particularly the Rowntrees and Cadburys, in mobilizing concern about health and safety in the workplace was complemented by growing attempts at professionalism in pursuit of technical efficiency. World War I and its aftermath brought support from central government and of Fabian thinkers such as Sidney Webb for both of these concerns. This cycle of government interventionism was to be repeated under the conditions of central planning and coordination during World War II and its aftermath. Between the wars, associations such as the Institute of Industrial Administration and Institute of Labour Management (or Personnel from 1947) were conduits for the twin streams of American management thinking in scientific management and in what became known as human relations. However, as late as 1954 only a minute proportion of British management were attempting the examinations of these and other would-be qualifying associations. Only one distinctively professional school existed between the wars at Manchester Technical College (the second, established in 1947, was at the Birmingham Central Technical College or Aston, where Child was later to be employed).

Child traced the development of managerial thought through the rising number of text books written and public addresses given by senior executives and management consultants: the latter being largely educated in USA, the former most often coming from firms within the 'new' sectors such as telecommunications, chemicals and processed foods. The emphasis remained, however, on the traditional importance of 'leadership of men' and on 'teamwork', as demonstrated in the wartime experiences of ex-office managers. This approach was applied to both corporate management and to the supervision of operatives. Management concern for situational factors such as labour market pressures and working conditions abated between the wars. The findings of Mayo and the Harvard school of human relations tended to be taken as endorsing a paternalism present in most public pronouncements by senior management (see MAYO, G.E.). The human relations rhetoric could not disguise the tension that existed between the 'disinterested professionalism' contained in the universalistic principles of scientific management and the concern for the social welfare of labour present in traditional paternalism.

Child saw a potential resolution in this conflict in Mary Parker Folletts' notion of 'the laws of the situation'(see FOLLETT, M.P.). The latter had been mistakenly taken to endorse a Mayoite manipulation of group sentiments. Child, however, perceived it as opening new perspectives on the dynamic processes of management. His assessment of the post-World War II 'challenge of social science', with its reliance on more generalizable structural laws is guarded. He concludes on a note of tempered optimism about the extent to which social science can provide a basis for education within the new British business schools of the 1960s. While social science had discredited much of the established body of management thought, it had not, thus far, substantiated a new and equivalent set of prescriptions for administrative practice. 'Indeed, to the extent that social science is concerned with the comparative analysis of complex, varied and changing situations, it is difficult to see how it can ever be expected to produce exact prescriptions rather than probabilitarian assessments for those who wish to apply its insights to practical purposes' (1969: 245). In this eventuality, Child agrees with a quoted article by Joan Woodward in suggesting that managers are likely to follow the more principled edicts of ideology in choosing and justifying particular decision choices (see WOODWARD, J.). However 'progress towards an organisational science will be more rapid if the academic training of managers encourages them to be more receptive to researchers' (259).

3 'Organisational structure, environment and performance'

At the time of writing this article, Child had already published two books offering a historically interpretative view of management control and decision making. The tension that existed between this view and that of the contextual determinism represented in the Aston studies was to be resolved in this paper. Essentially, Child continued to attach significance to the level of environmental variability present in the Aston approach, and to complexity in terms of heterogeneity, dispersion and turbulence within the organizational context. A third characteristic was, however, of overriding importance. It was what Child describes as the 'illiberality', or the amount of threat experienced from the environment. Put simply, Child, like Chandler and many critics of free-market economics, pointed to the fact that strategic decision makers often believed themselves to have some degree of monopoly over a particular contextual domain or market place. Furthermore, Child hypothesized that, 'The design of organisational structure only has a limited effect on performance levels achieved, and this is perceived to be the case by a dominant coalition' (1972: 16)

The formulation of strategy and its implementation are, then, to be seen as part of a political process by which a coalition of managerial interests within any organization gains and retains authority. The scope for strategic choice is determined only in part by 'objective' externalities. Of equal importance is the need to satisfy the expectations of resource providers in the light of their perceptions of the firm's performance and the congeniality of its present structural configuration. Their prior ideology is assumed to colour this 'evaluation to some degree' (17).

In a later (1997) re-evaluation of this article, Child emphasizes the relative stability of the basic beliefs or mindset of strategic actors and the constraints set by these cognitive preconceptions. Learning is seen to be time-related and located within events and along social networks conjoining the firm or organization to its contexts. These conditions can be seen as contributing to what are described as 'inner' and 'outer' cycles of structuration. These cycles appear to refer to the process of reconceptualization in the actors' frame of reference in determining what the organization is about, in the context of what is believed to be the likely needs and demands to be met within its socio-economic context.

4 'Price to pay?'

Through the 1970s Child published a number of articles in *Administrative Science Quarterly* and elsewhere based on the Aston Programme findings of the relationship between size of organization and specialization of task functions. The relationship is particularly identified in what was described as indirect or non-productive tasks. These findings chimed with current policy concerns about the rapid increase in service employment which appeared to be related to a low growth in overall productivity in Western countries. Two other themes appear in Child's writing over the 1970s. The first is his exploration of the literature on professionalization undertaken with Janet Fulk (née Schreisheim) the second is a similar review of the literature on national cultures leading to his collaboration with Alfred Keiser in cross-national studies of British and German management.

The 'Price to pay?' article, again in *Sociology*, can be regarded as the culminating commentary on these various bodies of research. It represents a severe critique of the historical strategies of professionalization adopted by specialized groups of administrative management in Britain. It is a tendency seen to accentuate the effects of the growth in size of employing firms. Large-scale bureaucracies were seen to fragment responsibility for the design of value-adding operations: attempts to form professional interest groups by British middle managers segmented information flows still further. By contrast, hierarchical status and authority in German organizations is seen to derive from a mixture of their meritocratic basis in formal qualifications and a longevity of experience within the internal market of a single organization.

5 'Information technology, organisation and the response to strategic challenges'

In the 1980s, Child's work moved away from the use of survey techniques to the adoption of case studies and, in keeping with European trends, to a new focus on workplace restructuring and labour process analysis. Much of his approach is summarized in 'Managerial strategies, new technology and the labour process' (1985). In this latter paper, Child extends his use of 'bounded rationality' in explaining the manner in which operational tasks are restructured and/or relocated within the market place as a result of radical changes in market demand and technological innovation. In a later paper, 'Information technology, organisation and the response to strategic challenges', he addresses the way in which corporate decision makers select modes of governance or 'steering devices' in a risk-effective manner.

The need to respond to radical contextual change is compounded for the executive by the risks entailed in implementing changes in workplace operations. Corporate management in the West had sought to minimize these risks by devolving and 'spinning off' operational units. The resulting 'loose linked' chain of value adding operations had been *enabled* by the emergence of information technology (IT) as a *means* to the centralization of control through the remote monitoring of tasks and through the ability to integrate performance data for the purposes of strategic planning.

Analytically, two characteristics of the resulting situation were seen to be important in shaping executive choices. Together they circumscribe what, after Boisot (1979, 1996), Child describes as C-space or cultural space. The first is the degree to which the knowledge or information embodied in the core competencies of their firms or organizations ('task related technological attributes') is codified in a standardized, formalized and specific way. The second is the extent of knowledge sharing or the *diffusion* of information across a given population of organizations. The position chosen in the area oblineated by these two dimensions is based on a desire to economize on transaction costs. These adhere closely to the ideal types put forward by Williamson (1985) moving along the market to hierarchy continuum by way of the holding group and coordinated contracting.

A concurrent paper (1987) written with Chris Smith offers greater insight into what Child considered the nature of cultural space. This paper describes the attempts of Cadbury management to change their corporate culture and, in particular, that of the work place. This is seen as a long drawn-out process of reconceptualization, or 're-cognition' on the part of senior management and its transmission to other internal actors. The initial movement derived from intellectual energizing by strategic agents, who themselves have learnt from significant external referents among competitors making up their sectoral set. The new paradigm emerges both from technically successful experimentation and new best-practice within the sector. It has, however, to be justified and legitimated by reference to a traditional ideology.

6 'From fiefs to clans and network capitalism'

Child's use of the C-space concept has extended over a series of case study analyses of corporate joint-ventures undertaken by Western firms in Eastern Europe and in the People's Republic of China (PRC). His most significant work on the socio-economic transformation of the PRC was contained in a book published in 1994, *Management in China During the Age of Reform*, again based on case histories of firms within the context of sector and state. However, in an article written jointly with Max Boisot he provides the clearest exposition of the C-space approach as applied to the PRC. The economic development of Western countries (including pre-Soviet European states) in seen to have moved from feudal fiefdoms (uncodified: undiffused information) to the development of national bureaucracies (high codification: low diffusion) and, finally, to increased reliance on market mechanisms (high codification: high

diffusion). The leaders of the Chinese communist party attempted such a route, before reverting to an attempt to regenerate radical fervour in the Cultural Revolution. After 1979 they slowly became aware of the need to build on a clan-like localized structure (low codification: high diffusion) in order to coordinate and, loosely, to control economic transformation in a politically viable way.

Boisot and Child (1996) describe the resultant system as 'network capitalism'. They, rather tellingly, distinguish it from attempts by Anglo-Saxon firms to collaborate on the basis of short-term risk spreading of a purely instrumental kind. The relationships between the Chinese state and the economic actor is seen to be mediated by a range of community relationships which have gained or retained an economic functionality that is non-imitatable and may well be permanent.

7 Conclusion

Child's work might be presented as focusing upon succeeding levels of collective social closure from occupational associations, to the organization of the firm, to the emergence of sectoral sets and onwards up to the development of national business systems. Its purpose has been to open explanation of the structure of each of these collective forms to the incorporation of political process. Over much of his writing it might be said that the nature of that process and, therefore, the underlying basis for social closure, has been left open to a number of competing or complementary explanations of possible goals, attitudes and beliefs of managerial actors. As Child suggests in his own re-evaluation of his 1972 article, its publication was indubitably instrumental in unlocking a diverse range of interpretative approaches to the study of organizational structures among OB scholars.

In much of his own later work he appears to adopt the notion of 'bounded rationality' in 'strategic choice'. Decisions are seen as being based on the actors' intention to maximise personal satisfactions relating to a relatively stable ordering of preferences. This order is created by a pre-determined mind-set of action-orientation (see Whittington1988).

Learning involves the testing of such shared orientations or recipes against the perceived constraints of political process and exogenous or 'objective' contingencies. In his empirical analysis of this process contained in such studies as those of Cadbury Ltd and in corporate joint-ventures, Child advances our understanding of organizational learning as an interpretative but structurally located management activity. It might seem that these presentations owe more to his earlier association with the Cambridge action-orientation perspective (see Goldthorpe *et al.* 1968) than to the stylized comparative static framework provided by the C-space taxonomy.

RAY LOVERIDGE
ASTON BUSINESS SCHOOL

Further reading

(References cited in the text marked *)

* Bendix, R. (1956) *Work and Authority in Industry: Ideologies of Management in the Course of Industrialization*, New York NY: John Wiley & Sons. (One of a group of studies financed by the Ford Foundation in the 1950s to investigate key dimensions in comparative management structure and styles across modern nation states. Bendix traces the historical evolution of management ideas over the industrialization of England, Russia and USA.)

Boisot, M. (1995) *Information Space. A Framework for Learning in Organisations, Institutions and Cultures*, London: International Thomson Business Press. (An extended attempt to develop the anthropological concept of 'cultural space'. Crudely speaking this may be seen as meaning any population using a common language. As suggested above Boisot isolates two dimensions in order to elucidate his analysis of barriers to communication between different communities in organizations and organized societies. Possibly the concepts explored in this work are best approached through Boisot's earlier case study analysis.)

* Boisot, M and Child, J. (1996) 'From fiefs to clans and network capitalism: explaining China's emerging economic order', *Administrative Science Quarterly*, 41: 600–628. (An analysis of the economic development of mainland China which suggests that its continued evolution will take the form of loosely linked local networks within the formally centralized framework of state bureaucracy. Its adopted mode of capitalism will thus be distinctively different from that in the West.)

* Child, J. (1969) *British Management Thought – a Critical Analysis*, London: Allen & Unwin. (An account of the twentieth century development of professionalization within British management and the complementary evolution of social science – see summary above.)

* Child, J. (1972) 'Organisational structure, environment and performance: the role of strategic choice', *Sociology*, 6, 1: 1–22. (A critique of the assumptions underlying the determinant value attributed to contextual factors, or so-called 'contingencies', in shaping organizational structure and strategy. Points to the scope for choice in real-life decision making and the loose relationship between choices made and actual corporate performance.)

Child, J. (1977) *Organisation: A Guide to Problems and Practice* (second edition 1984), London: Harper & Row. (A comprehensive and clearly written text on organizational design written for 'practising management and administration'. The second edition is extensively rewritten to take in many contemporaneous case examples from Child's research and consultancy.)

* Child, J. (1985) 'Managerial strategies, new technology and the labour process', in D. Knights et al (eds) *Job Redesign: Critical Perspectives on the Labour Process)* Aldershot: Gower. (A commentary on the marxiant de-skilling or degradation of labour thesis. It suggests that managerial orientations can lead to their adoption of a variety of steering devices. These, in turn, may relate to a range of modes of laying-off risk among which de-skilling is only one.)

* Child, J. (1987) 'Information technology, organisation and the response to strategic challenges', *California Management Review*, XXX, 1, Fall. (A lucid account of corporate responses to market, organizational and technological change in the 1980s with explanation provided through Williamson's general theory of transaction costs – see below.)

* Child, J. (1994) *Management in China During the Age of Reform,* Cambridge: Cambridge University Press. (A significant attempt at 'bottom-up' analysis of the macro-shifts in the regime's strategy towards industrialization in the PCR over the 1980s. Based on case study evidence drawn from privatized Chinese enterprises Child develops his notion of localized strategic choice within a contractual environment shaped by the initiatives taken by managers

themselves in the face of ambiguity and complexity.)

Child, J. (1997) 'Structural choice in the analysis of action, structure, organisations and environment: retrospect and prospect' *Organisation Studies*, 18/1, 43–76. (An interesting retrospective interpretation of his own work in which Child shapes its implications around the currently relevant notion of learning organizations.)

Child, J. and Keiser, A. (1979)'Organisational and managerial roles in British and West German companies: an examination of the culture thesis', in C.J. Lammers and D.J. Hickson (eds) *Organisations Alike and Unlike*, London: Routledge and Kegan Paul. (A pioneering empirical study of strategic attitudes and beliefs among similarly positioned senior executives in a sample of large British and German firms. It suggested that recipes for success were, indeed, 'culture-bound'. Teaching based on imported prescriptions from American business schools should therefore be questioned.)

* Child, J. and Loveridge, R. (1990*) Information Technology in European Services: Towards a Microelectronic Future,* Oxford: Blackwell. (A comparative study of the introduction of IT at the point-of-service in three sectors, banking, health care and retailing. It is based on case studies located in six European countries: the UK, Belgium, Sweden, Germany, Italy and Hungary. It also contains extensive summaries of the theoretical literature on technological innovation, cross-cultural comparisons and direct service occupations. It concludes by relating an apparent 'organizational conservatism' to 'the politics of learning' which, in turn, are related to the institutional and ideological context present in each country.)

* Child, J. and Smith, C. (1987) 'The content and process of organisational transformation – Cadbury Limited in its sector', *Journal of Management Studies*, 24/6, November, 565–593. (The 'firm-in-sector' perspective is seen as relating the firm to an 'organizational-set'. This is defined in terms of three elements: 1) a set of unique objective conditions; 2) a cognitive arena which provides a subjective frame for adjudging performance and recipes for success; 3) a network of potential and actual collaborators and/or competitors.)

* Finkelstein, S. and Hambuck, D.C. (1996) *Strategic Leadership*, St. Paul MN: West. (A comprehensive text on corporate leadership which contains one of the few critiques of Child's (1972) thesis on strategic choice. It praises the

work for shifting the focus of OB explanation away from structural causation but sees 'equivocality' in Child's focus on 'dominant coalition' as the location of strategic decision making.)

Goldthorpe, J.H., Lockwood, D., Bechhofer, F. and Platt, J. (1968) *The Affluent Worker: Industrial Attitudes and Behaviour,*Cambridge: Cambridge University Press. (One of three books drawn from an attitude survey of automobile workers at GM's plant at Luton, UK. Theoretically significant for its development of Weber's notion of verstehen or action-orientation. The personal goals and related sources of job commitment within the workforce had to be seen in terms of their personal perception of the job. This was shaped by their personal experience of social mobility in career and their choices of social referents. Objective conditions provided by work-place technology or by a shared market (class) positioning had to be seen through 'the eyes of the beholder'.)

* Whittington, R. (1988) 'Environmental structure and theories of strategic choice', *Journal of Management Studies*, 25, 521–536. (A seminal review of the literature stemming from Child's (1972) article which concludes by adopting a view of the strategist's mind-set not unlike that described above in Goldthorpe *et al.'s*analysis of orientation-to-work – see above.)

* Williamson, O.E. (1985*) The Economic Institutions of Capitalism,* New York NY: Free Press. (One of a series of books and articles in which Williamson elaborates and extends his claim that transaction costs are the prime shaper of governance structures ie modes of organization and contracting. This volume includes consideration of relational contracting based on trust built on experience of the other party. This is a theme addressed by Child in his 1990s work on joint ventures particularly in the Chinese context.)

See also: ASTON GROUP; FOLLETT, M.P.; MAYO, G.E.; WOODWARD, J.

Related topics in the IEBM: INFORMATION TECHNOLOGY; MANAGEMENT IN CHINA; MANAGEMENT EDUCATION IN CHINA; MANAGEMENT IN GERMANY; ORGANIZATION BEHAVIOUR; ORGANIZATION BEHAVIOUR, HISTORY OF; ORGANIZATION STRUCTURE; ORGANIZATION TYPES; ORGANIZATIONAL LEARNING; STRATEGIC CHOICE; TECHNOLOGY AND ORGANIZATIONS

Churchman, C. West (1913–)

1 Biographical data
2 Moral commitment
3 Operations research
4 Systemic thinking
5 Conclusion

Personal background

- born 1913, Mount Airy, Pennsylvania, USA
- assistant professor, University of Pennsylvania, 1939–42
- head of statistical section, Frankford Arsenal, 1942–6
- professor at the University of Pennsylvania, 1946–7
- professor at Wayne University, Detroit, 1947–51
- professor and director of the Operations Research Group, Case Institute of Technology, 1951–58
- professor and director, Centre for Research in Management Sciences, Business School of the University of California at Berkeley, 1958–81
- Professor Emeritus, Business School of the University of California at Berkeley, 1981–
- nominated for the Nobel Prize award in the field of social systems, 1984

Major works

Elements of Logic and Formal Science (1940)
Theory of Experimental Inference (1948)
Methods of Inquiry (with R.L. Ackoff)(1950)
Introduction to Operations Research (with R.L. Ackoff and E.L. Arnoff)(1957)
Prediction and Optimal Decision (1960)
The Systems Approach (1968)
Challenge to Reason (1968)
The Design of Inquiring Systems (1971)
The Systems Approach and its Enemies (1979)
Thought and Wisdom (1982)

Summary

C. West Churchman is a philosopher with an intense moral commitment to employ systemic thinking for the betterment of humanity. He co-defined operations research and might be considered the main founder of the modern systems approach. For Churchman, operations research was always a systemic activity. Employing mixed teams in operations research practice was an expression of this, as was his interest in parts of organizations and how they might interact. Churchman subsequently developed a caravan of systemic concepts and concerns. Seven of the more important ones are summarized below (marked by italics). He formulated an anatomy of system *teleology* – nine conditions that must be fulfilled for 'a system' to demonstrate purposefulness. He established ways of exploring and bounding problem contexts: *sweep in* – developing knowledge of the totality of relevant conditions; *unfolding* – adding structure and meaning to people's experiences; and *boundary setting* – defining an action area for improvement through the counterparts 'sweep in' and 'unfolding'. He argued that improvement, say in terms of efficiency and/or effectiveness, is primarily about ethics. He also stressed the importance of *securing* improvement and in connection with this was amongst the first to note the importance of sustainability and the central role of measurement. More broadly, he developed a vision of systemic *wisdom*. Churchman's work can be criticized as esoteric, yet he still impressed on many researcher's minds the recurrent question of whether they can justify their choices and actions. Churchman thus earned himself a reputation as the moral conscience of operations research, management sciences, systems sciences and, indeed, all other fields of business and management that dare to consult his work. In so doing he emphasizes his concern for *hope*.

1 Biographical data

C. West Churchman was born in 1913 at Mount Airy, Pennsylvania, USA. His moral grounding and early education was under the guidance of Quakers. At university he trained as a philosopher and logician. In 1936, he was awarded by the University of Pennsylvania a PhD in statistical inference for a thesis entitled *Towards a Logic of Propositions*. In 1939, he joined the faculty of the university as assistant professor. It was shortly afterwards that he published *Elements of Logic and Formal Science* (1940).

The 1940s was a defining period for Churchman, in particular because it brought him close to two figures who made a lasting impact on his life. The first of these was his mentor Edgar A. Singer of the American pragmatism tradition. The second figure was his life long friend Russell L. Ackoff. In 1939, Ackoff joined a course offered by Churchman entitled 'modern philosophy'. In Ackoff's words, the two of them 'hit it off'. Over the next twenty years they worked closely together and in large part co-defined operations research.

In 1942 Ackoff was drafted and Churchman, who was not eligible because of dependent parents, became head of a statistical section of the Frankford Arsenal. Churchman and Ackoff continued to collaborate by mail. After World War II, in 1946, they rented a small house together, resumed their university positions and worked intensely in partnership. Churchman and Ackoff then moved to Wayne University, Detroit, in 1947. The two published *Methods of Inquiry* (1950). In 1951, Churchman and Ackoff moved together to Case Institute of Technology, where they formed the Operations Research Group under Churchman's directorship and professorship. Churchman, in his time at Case, played a pivotal role in co-defining operations research as a discipline and a practice. Churchman collaborated with Ackoff and Arnoff in producing the path-breaking *Introduction to Operations Research* (1957). He also served as the first editor-in-chief of *Management Science* (1954–1961) and as editor-in-chief of *Philosophy of Science* (1949–1959).

After nearly twenty years in partnership with Ackoff, Churchman in 1958 left Case and launched a new and lasting era of his intellectual life at the University of California, Berkeley. In a professorial role he founded and directed the Centre for Research in Management Science (later renamed the Centre for Research in Management). Churchman labelled the next decade 'the dreary '60s' as he saw operations research become systematically mathematized. He resigned editorship of *Management Science* because submissions increasingly became mathematics for mathematics sake, and were doing little for humanity. Meanwhile, Churchman's '60s was scintillating.

Churchman took along to Berkeley a deep interest in systemic thinking that had already surfaced, for example, in *Introduction to Operations Research*. He thought through management as a philosophical challenge, testing people's capacity to appreciate the ethics of whole systems. Churchman's passion for systemic thinking and ethical alertness runs through four of his most important texts: *The Systems Approach* (1968), *Challenge to Reason* (1968), *The Design of Inquiring Systems* (1971), and *The Systems Approach and Its Enemies* (1979). These four books raised questions that operations research and management sciences are still grappling with today. They are also forerunners of two recent movements in systemic thinking: soft systems thinking, spearheaded in the UK by Peter Checkland since the 1970s; and critical systems thinking, launched from the University of Hull, UK, in the mid-1980s.

The extent and impact of Churchman's work is marked by his nomination in 1984 for the Nobel Prize award in the field of social systems. Whilst Ludwig von Bertalanffy might be considered the main founder of the systems movement (see VON BERTALANFFY, L.), C. West Churchman might be considered co-definer of operations research and main founder of the modern systems approach. Sections 3 and 4 look in more detail at those two seminal contributions, with greater emphasis placed on systemic thinking where his most important contributions are located. To set the scene, however, we must look first at Churchman's moral commitment.

2 Moral commitment

It is simply not possible to appreciate C. West Churchman's contributions without grasping, indeed *feeling*, the intensity of his moral commitment. A deep ethical concern is rooted in his early Quaker education. Since then, Churchman has spent his life dedicated to humanity. His work begins and ends with humanity in scientific research. He insists that scientists must take responsibility for the social consequences of their work. Science, as well as philosophy, should be employed to study serious problems like hunger, poverty and war. This is why Churchman became fed-up with life in philosophy departments who, in his words, asked 'silly questions'. It is why he became fed-up with the large number of mathematical submissions to *Management Science* that were never applied. Churchman, inspired by his mentor Edgar A. Singer, called for increasing human purposefulness and participation in systems design in a never ending cycle that entertains attack from its worst enemies. (Singer's influence is evident in each of Churchman's main publications.) Churchman is thus relentless in his quest for critically reflective and moral practice. He does this by raising questions. There are no answers, he states, just more questions. For example, ask Churchman if a value-free society is possible and he will question if a value-free science is moral. Ethical alertness, then, comes from this form of critical systemic thinking. Now let us turn to Churchman's contribution to operations research.

3 Operations research

When, in 1951, Churchman and Ackoff formed the Operations Research Group at the Case Institute of Technology , their purpose was to apply philosophy, through operations research, to industrial and governmental issues. Churchman had concluded that to apply philosophy he had to find a home outside of a philosophy department. In that period, the two largely co-defined operations research. *Introduction to Operations Research* (1957) was the first international textbook in the field. One third of the book is devoted to philosophical and methodological aspects of an interdisciplinary approach to real world problems. The remainder of the text covers techniques such as linear programming, inventory control, production scheduling, queuing problems, and sequencing.

Distinguishing North American operations research from operational research in the UK, Churchman emphasized the importance of mixed teams that bring to bear a range of expertise on diverse problem situations. Teams might comprise people from any or all functions of the organization depending on context. A team approach is an early expression of systemic thinking in Churchman's work, in its recognition of the diverse nature of the whole problem situation. It reflects an interest in parts of organizations, how they might interact together and with their environment. Churchman developed his ideas in relation to operations research in *Prediction and Optimal Decision* (1960), focusing on scientific consideration of value judgments in applied science.

Churchman, however, grew increasingly unhappy about developments in operations research in the 'dreary '60s'. He had no issue with techniques in themselves as long as they demonstrated practical utility *and* were employed in a systemic manner. He employed systemic awareness to show limitations in what is now labelled traditional operations research. The following optimal inventory policy is a classic, well-cited example (e.g., see *The Design of Inquiring Systems* 1971).

It is not feasible, Churchman declares, to design an optimal (efficient and effective) inventory policy without considering all conceivable alternatives to holding an inventory. The best of the foregone opportunities represents an inventory's opportunity cost. He asks, how can we judge whether an inventory policy is sound without knowing the opportunity cost? Beyond any technique, then, there is a need to investigate the larger system of an organization's opportunities. There is no rational design for improvement without knowledge about the total relevant system. Operations research, then, was always a systemic activity for Churchman.

4 Systemic thinking

The case for Churchman's systemic thinking is made in the last two sections. First, ethical alertness comes from thinking systemically. Second, efficiency and effectiveness comes from thinking about the total relevant system. Churchman's systemic thinking is about ethics, efficiency and effectiveness, and it is captured in seven central concepts chosen for review below: teleology, sweep in, unfolding, boundary setting, securing, wisdom and hope. There are many others.

Teleology

(As in *Design of Inquiring Systems* 1971, and *The Systems Approach and Its Enemies* 1979). Churchman, in his anatomy of system teleology, set out nine conditions that must be fulfilled for 'a system' (S) to demonstrate purposefulness. These conditions are:

- S is teleological
- S has a measure of performance
- there is a client whose interests are served
- S has teleological components
- S has an environment
- there is a decision maker who can produce changes in the measure of performance of S
- there is a designer whose design of S influences the decision maker leading to changes in the measure of performance of S
- the designer aims to maximize S's value to the client
- there is a built in guarantee that the purpose of S defined by the measure of performance of S can be achieved and secured.

Any such appreciation of S, however, raises questions of system identification that Churchman addressed through 'sweep in'.

Sweep in

(As in *Systems Approach and Its Enemies* 1979). For Churchman, systems are not real entities existing 'out there' waiting to be identified. Rather, systems are whole system judgements, that is, judgements made in the knowledge of the totality of relevant conditions. This suggests, following Singer, a sweep in process, that is, sweeping in ever more features of the problem context. Sweeping in helps participants become more aware and increasingly able to appreciate contrasting systems of meaning. This is an attempt to raise understanding rather than realize absolute knowledge. Sweep in is a process of critical self-reflection that helps people think or debate their way out of 'mind traps' (borrowing Geoffrey Vickers' terminology, see VICKERS, G.). However, the sweep in process in isolation suggests ever expanding boundaries which is not realistic if things are to get done. Churchman thus recognized a need for unfolding.

Unfolding

(As in *Systems Approach and Its Enemies* 1979). The process of unfolding is brought to light by Ulrich (1988). Unfolding draws upon the nine conditions of Churchman's anatomy of system teleology. The conditions help people to add structure and meaning to their experiences. People may employ them to surface plausible interpretations of events. This aids them to identify possible clients, designers, decision makers, and other affected people. It helps people to consider measures of performance and who might gain or suffer from a design. Unfolding is therefore the critical counterpart to sweep in. Sweep in and unfolding culminate for Churchman in boundary setting.

Boundary setting

(As in *Systems Approach and Its Enemies* 1979). Defining an action area from the problem context through sweep in and unfolding centres on drawing boundaries around possible clients and consequently surfacing issues and dilemmas for discussion. Put succinctly, the linked questions are who is in, who is out, what are the possible consequences, and how might we feel about this? Boundary setting thus raises questions of ethics, efficiency and effectiveness in a search for improvement and shows them to be inextricably linked. Boundaries are always open to further debate through sweep in and are thus temporary. Boundaries are the result of choice. For each choice located by unfolding there are always other possible options that will arise by sweeping in. Boundaries are therefore partial. The temporary and partial nature of boundary setting is suggestive of improvements to make, for now, but raises the question of how improvement is to be secured.

Securing

(As in *The Design of Inquiring Systems* 1971). According to Churchman, to secure improvement means that over time improvement persists, i.e., improvement must be sustainable. Systems of measurement are central to knowing that improvement has been secured. As Ulrich (1994) notes, this means considering choices for improvement by critically taking into account and tracking long-term environmental and developmental implications. The aim is to make choices that deliver ecologically viable in addition to socio-economically and socio-culturally desirable future improvements. So, the sweep in process, for example, must embrace our children's future. Our children, some yet to be born, must be recognized as possible clients of today's decision processes. This leads us to Churchman's two motivators, wisdom and hope.

Wisdom

(As in *Thought and Wisdom* 1982). Wisdom is thought combined with a concern for ethics.

Hope

(As in 'In search of an ethical science' 1997). Hope is the spiritual belief in an ethical future.

The simplicity of Churchman's notions of wisdom and hope belies their potency. Now to conclude.

5 Conclusion

C. West Churchman has made a giant-sized contribution to intellectual thought in operations research, management sciences and systems sciences. This plays second role only to the intensity of feeling about a moral commitment to human betterment that his writing demands. Churchman's work can be criticized as esoteric, yet he still impressed on many researcher's minds the recurrent question of whether they can justify their choices and actions. Churchman thus earned himself a reputation as the moral conscience of operations research, management sciences, systems sciences and, indeed, all other fields of business and management that dare to consult his work. Research in the management field must accept the significance of wisdom and the need for hope. The importance of this visionary and influential work is marked by Churchman's nomination in 1984 for the Nobel Prize award in the field of social systems.

ROBERT L. FLOOD
UNIVERSITY OF HULL

Further reading

(References cited in the text marked *)

Ackoff, R.L. (1988) 'C. West Churchman', *Systems Practice* 1: 351–356. (An account of a friendship with Churchman by the friend.)

* Churchman, C.W. (1940) *Elements of Logic and Formal Science*, New York: Lippincott. (Investigation into logic as the basis of science.)

Churchman, C.W. (1948) *Theory of Experimental Inference*, New York: Macmillan. (Philosophical foundation for later pioneering work in operations research, emphasizing North American pragmatism.)

Churchman, C.W. (1960) *Prediction and Optimal Decision*, Englewood Cliffs, New Jersey: Prentice Hall. (Scientific consideration of value judgements in applied science.)

* Churchman, C.W. (1968) *The Systems Approach*, New York: Delta. (Churchman's vision of the systems approach as a continuing debate between various attitudes of mind with respect to society. Updated in 1979 relating it to its sequel, *The Systems Approach and Its Enemies*.)

* Churchman, C.W. (1968) *Challenge to Reason*, New York: McGraw-Hill. (A philosophical discussion about the need for whole system understanding in the process of designing improvement.)
* Churchman, C.W. (1971) *The Design of Inquiring Systems: Basic Concepts of Systems and Organizations*, New York: Basic Books. (Examines inquiring systems that constitute modern science. Reinterprets the work of great philosophers in this context. It reflects upon our attempts to know and better our world through management science, social engineering and information systems. To secure betterment, it is argued, systems must be capable of learning.)
* Churchman, C.W. (1979) *The Systems Approach and Its Enemies*, New York: Basic Books. (Argues that we must not treat as 'irrational' citizens who contest the rationality of a design. Rather, we need a dialectic framework to help enter into a discourse with other rationalities. In this way the systems approach becomes truly self-reflective.)
* Churchman, C.W. (1982) *Thought and Wisdom*, Seaside, California: Intersystems. (Self-reflective account of how Churchman is continuing today to deal with major concerns such as environmental protection, future generations and peace.)
* Churchman, C.W. (1997) 'In search of an ethical science: an interview with C. West Churchman', *Journal of Business Ethics*, 16: 731-744. (An interview with J.P. van Gigch, E. Koenigsberg and B. Dean, discussing Churchman's central concerns and concepts.)
* Churchman, C.W. and Ackoff, R.L. (1950) *Methods of Inquiry*, St. Louis, Missouri: Educational Publishers Inc. (Review and discussion of methods of inquiry tracing back to contrasting strands of philosophical thought.)
* Churchman, C.W., Ackoff, R.L. and Arnoff, E.L. (1957) *Introduction to Operations Research*, New York: Wiley. (Operations research conceived of in terms of applied philosophy. One third devoted to philosophical and methodological aspects of an interdisciplinary approach to real world problems. Characteristic of North American operations research with a focus on mixed teams.)

Flood, R.L. and Jackson, M.C. (1991) *Critical Systems Thinking: Directed Readings*, Chichester: Wiley. (Roots the emergence of critical systems thinking particularly in the work of Churchman. Includes a classic paper by Churchman.)

Keys, P. (ed.) (1995) *Understanding The Process of Operational Research*, Chichester: Wiley. (Sets the scene of the historical emergence of operations research and positions Churchman's work in this. Includes a paper by Churchman with R.L. Ackoff and E.L. Arnoff.)

* Ulrich, W. (1988) 'Churchman's "process of unfolding" – Its significance for policy analysis and evaluation', *Systems Practice* 1: 415-428. (An incisive account of the process of unfolding from a disciple of Churchman.)
* Ulrich, W. (1994) 'Can we secure future responsive management through systems thinking and design?', *Interfaces*, 24: 26-37. (A discussion of cognitive and methodological difficulties in future responsive management based on Churchman's thinking.)

75th Birthday Festschrift for Churchman (1989) *Systems Practice* 1, 4 (W. Ulrich, ed.).

80th Birthday Festschrift for Churchman (1994) *Interfaces* 24, 4 (E. Koenigsberg, and J.P. van Gigch, J.P., eds).

See also: ACKOFF, R.L.; BEER, S.; CHECKLAND, P.; RIVETT, B.H.P.; VON BERTALANFFY, L.; VICKERS, G.

Related topics in the IEBM: BUSINESS ETHICS; CYBERNETICS; DECISION MAKING; ENVIRONMENTAL MANAGEMENT; MANAGEMENT SCIENCE; OPTIMALITY AND OPTIMIZATION; ORGANIZATION BEHAVIOUR; SYSTEMS

Clegg, Hugh Armstrong (1920–1995)

1 Biography
2 Philosophical underpinnings
3 The emerging themes
4 Conclusion

Career summary

- born 22 May 1920
- educated at Kingswood School, Bath and then Magdalen College, University of Oxford
- fellow of Nuffield College, University of Oxford (1949–66)
- member of Royal Commission on Trade Unions and Employers' Associations (1965–68)
- member of National Board for Prices and Incomes (1966–68)
- professor of industrial relations, University of Warwick (1967–79)
- member of Council of Advisory, Conciliation and Arbitration Service (1974–79)
- director of the Industrial Relations Research Unit of the Social Science Research Council (1970–74)
- chairman of the Standing Commission on Pay Comparability (1979–80)
- died 9 December 1995

Major works

The System of Industrial Relations in Great Britain (1954), (edited with A. Flanders)
General Union (1954)
A New Approach to Industrial Democracy (1960)
A History of British Trade Unions Vol 1 (1964) (with A. Fox and A. F. Thompson); *Vol 2* (1985), *Vol 3* (1994)
The System of Industrial Relations in Great Britain (1970)
Trade Unionism under Collective Bargaining (1976)

The Changing System of Industrial Relations in Great Britain (1976)

Overview

Hugh Clegg was the most influential British scholar of industrial relations in the latter half of the twentieth century. At a time when the subject dominated economic and political life he was also centrally involved in public policy formulation. He wrote the definitive history of British trade unionism as well as contemporary studies of, *inter alia*, industrial democracy, incomes policy, trade union government and collective bargaining. He established a tradition of empirical research, and also an internationally distinguished centre of industrial relations research and teaching, at Warwick University, which were to continue to flourish after his death.

1 Biography

The son of a Methodist minister, Hugh Clegg demonstrated a rebellious spirit from an early age, joining the Communist Party while head boy of his school. He went to Oxford for one year before the Second World War began and then served five years in the ranks as a telephone engineer. Having battled across Europe with the liberating forces, he returned to Oxford where in due course he took the best degree of his year. It was the labour scholar G.D.H. Cole who there introduced him to the study of industrial relations, which appealed to Clegg's egalitarian and insubordinate instincts. He joined the newly founded Nuffield College and worked on a history of the General and Municipal Workers' Union as a doctoral student. Although he never submitted his thesis for examination, it was to be published as *General Union* in 1954, and he was elected a fellow of Nuffield College in 1949.

At Oxford Clegg started a twenty-year partnership with Allan Flanders (see FLANDERS, A.D.), a pre-War trade union activist who had played a central role in the recreation of the German trade union movement under the Allied Control Commission. Leaving the Communist Party, Clegg committed his remarkable intelligence to the factual analysis of organized labour, leaving the more theoretical aspects to Flanders in a close division of effort which, after Flanders' death in 1973, he was to have difficulty shaking off. They started a weekly seminar series which provided an unparalleled stimulus to British industrial relations scholarship and gave rise to what was retrospectively to be called the 'Oxford School' of research (Bugler 1968). They edited, and took the major part in writing, the first edition of *The System of Industrial Relations in Great Britain* which, when published in 1954, broke new ground as a research-based, multi-disciplinary analysis of the subject. During his time at Oxford, Clegg was to publish authoritative studies on a wide range of hitherto largely neglected subjects, including industrial relations in the newly nationalized industries and in public transport, employer organization, trade union administration and industrial democracy. He also wrote, with Alan Fox and A. F. Thompson, the first volume of the definitive *History of British Trade Unions*, the final two volumes of which he was to complete on his own after his retirement (see FOX, A.).

The growing industrial unrest of the 1960s led to Clegg increasingly being called to serve on the many official enquiries and arbitrations which were then the favoured means of resolving disputes. His involvement in conflicts in railways, docks, shipping and the car industry revealed unusually subtle political judgement which made him a natural candidate when in 1965 a Labour government set up both a Royal Commission on Trade Unions and Employers' Associations concerned with industrial relations reform, and a National Board for Prices and Incomes, concerned with managing an incomes policy. His contribution to both was substantial, partly because he had considerable drafting skills, and partly because he insisted that both bodies

should have very substantial research backing. He initiated unprecedented programmes of surveys and case studies whereby both Commission and Board broke from the traditional mould of passively receiving evidence, adopting instead a far more pro-active and investigative form of enquiry.

He built on this appetite for empirical fieldwork when he moved to the newly founded University of Warwick in 1967, winning in 1970 a substantial research unit funded by the (then) Social Science Research Council, which was to provide a financially secure basis for industrial relations research for the next 30 years. At the same time he established a multi-disciplinary post-graduate course in industrial relations which has remained internationally outstanding and a fertile source of doctoral students and industrial relations academics. His own research while at Warwick resulted in books on incomes policy, trade union government, and the international comparative study *Trade Unionism under Collective Bargaining*. He also produced two complete rewrites of *The System of Industrial Relations in Great Britain* which drew on his encyclopaedic knowledge and became the widely accepted textbook on the then politically controversial subject. Clegg took early retirement in 1979 to return to his *History*. In that year, in the wake of substantial disputes in the public services, he was persuaded to become chair of a Standing Commission on Pay Comparability, which was successful in establishing a public service pay policy until wound up by the new government of Margaret Thatcher in the following year. Clegg thus ended his active involvement with both the analysis and the practice of contemporary trade unionism just as it was about to suffer the ignominy of its long retreat.

2 Philosophical underpinnings

A view once expressed by Clegg was that 'an ounce of fact is worth a pound of theory', and there can be no doubting that his published life's work amounted to a great weight of books containing little discussion of theory and a vast amount of sparely expressed fact. It was not, as we shall see, that he was unaware of the theoretical underpinnings of his work; it was rather that he was painfully aware that the study of organized labour has long been awash with, in varying degrees, plausible and optimistic theories, which have usually been sustained by little more than myth and ignorance. His primary purpose in both his historical and contemporary research was therefore to get as close as possible to establishing the facts of what happened when, and to understanding the perceptions and motives of the men and women involved. For some readers this made his writing dull, with too much description and not enough story. But that would not have bothered Clegg. As both a teacher and as a manager of research he was unusually open minded about how others interpreted the facts. His prime concern was that they did so with comprehensive knowledge and complete honesty.

Here we shall not discuss Clegg's historical work, nor his monographs on particular events and industries. Instead we shall focus on those studies in which, as a somewhat reluctant theorist, he distilled out of his empirical broth those particular understandings of industrial relations which have altered the course of subsequent thinking. As a preliminary, however, it is instructive to outline the philosophical and ideological positions that underpinned this work.

Perhaps as a result of his rebellion against both Christianity and Marxism, Clegg exhibited both an antipathy to dogma and a strong sense of morality. It was a feature of most of those scholars who were in at the start of the Oxford School, doubtless reinforced by their bitter youthful experience of fighting against or fleeing from totalitarianism. Forty years later, in a retrospective essay, Clegg was to spell out very clearly what he thought was common to the Oxford School:

> we were pluralists, believing that a free society consists of a large number of overlapping groups, each with its own interests and objectives which its members are entitled to pursue so long as they do so with reasonable regard to the rights and interests

of others. But that did not distinguish us from most other social and political theorists of that time, except Marxists, and today only from Marxists and Thatcherites. We were also egalitarians, wishing to see a shift in the distribution of wealth towards those with lower incomes, and a shift of power over the conduct of their working lives and environment towards working men and women; and, for both these reasons, emphasising the importance of trade unions in industry, in the economy, and in society. We therefore attached special importance to collective bargaining as the means whereby trade unions pursue their objectives.

(Clegg 1990)

This commitment to collective bargaining as, if not the only valid means of industrial governance, at least the optimal one, was a recurring theme in Clegg's work. This was reflected in the ringing and unanimous endorsement (which he had himself drafted) of the Report of the Royal Commission:

> Properly conducted, collective bargaining is the most effective means of giving workers the right to representation in decisions affecting their working lives, a right which is or should be the prerogative of every worker in a democratic society. While therefore the first task in the reform of British industrial relations is to bring greater order into collective bargaining in the company or plant, the second is to extend the coverage of collective bargaining and the organization of workers on which it depends.

(Donovan 1968: para 212)

Seven years after that Report, Clegg felt obliged to defend this position and its commitment to pluralism against the attacks of Marxist critics who argued that reformism served managerial interests (Clegg 1975). His defence made plain his view that pluralism was a normative philosophy rather than a simple description of a political process. But the climate of criticism was to change. Another seven years later, it was a sign of how sharply the direction of attack had shifted that Clegg was obliged to defend himself against charges of political bias from the then Conservative government. A year-long official inquiry, initiated by the Secretary of State in 1982, was held into the charges that the Industrial Relations Research Unit which he had created was biased because it 'was dominated by a particular philosophy of collective bargaining, favoured by the 1968 Royal Commission, which played down the potential use of legal regulation and led to undue emphasis on trade unions'(Brown 1998). Although his Unit was exonerated of all the charges of bias, a succession of hostile new laws over the next decade was to make plain just how far official opinion had swung against collective bargaining.

3 The emerging themes

If any book was the founding text of the Oxford School it was Flanders and Clegg's *The System of Industrial Relations in Great Britain* (1954). Written at what in retrospect can be seen to have been the high tide of consensus over the British 'system' of industry-based collective bargaining, it far excelled other contemporary texts in its analysis of the contextual circumstances and informal characteristics (Brown 1997). There was a heavy emphasis on the historical origins of institutions, and a sensitivity to economic influences, but a neglect of explicitly sociological analyses, and a frank disdain of personnel management. The legal chapter by Otto Kahn-Freund, arguably the most sophisticated analysis of British labour law that had yet been written was, however, rich in sociological insight.

The System was to influence a generation of British industrial relations scholars, including those involved in a most active period of public policy concern with the subject. But it was also seminal for much of the subsequent work of both Clegg and Flanders. For Clegg, three strands deserve to be followed. The first is the issue of industrial democracy. The second is the optimal level of collective bargaining. The third strand is that of the determinants of collective bargaining structures.

A target of Clegg's criticism in *The System* was the practice of joint consultation, which had blossomed during the war and the immediate post-war years. Having scoured the empirical evidence he asked why it should be that a 'device' which was given almost universal public approval should appear to have such limited success. He concluded that it is because it is based upon the mistaken belief of an identity of interest between employers and employees – what later would be called by Fox a 'unitary' view (Fox 1966) – and that employers only resorted to it when full employment placed them on the defensive. He argued that 'the need to establish channels of communication in large-scale enterprises is not dependent on the state of employment; and the desire for greater industrial democracy has not been completely destroyed even during slumps. . . . Joint consultation may help to reduce antagonism, and to solve difficulties before they become disputes; but antagonisms and difficulties will remain. They are inherent in a free society' (Flanders and Clegg 1954: 364).

This argument was developed in *A New Approach to Industrial Democracy* (1960), which he described in the preface as a 'rather hasty' essay provoked by his being rapporteur at a conference in 1958 in Vienna on 'Workers' Participation in Management'. More than anything else that Clegg wrote, this was an exercise in political science, reviewing the history and theory of industrial democracy, surveying contemporary international experience and, with hitherto uncharacteristic panache, arguing out his 'new theory'. It is surely of significance that his most fulsome thanks in the preface went to Tony Crosland MP 'who has given me more help with this book than I have received before in any book that I have written. I can only hope that it is worthy of him'. Crosland's influential *The Future of Socialism* (Crosland 1956) had argued a non-Marxist, egalitarian and strongly pluralist political philosophy. When in 1977 Crosland, who was by then Foreign Secretary, died unexpectedly at the age of only 59, Clegg was to confess to being dismayed by the scale of his sense of personal loss. Certainly the similarity in their personal philosophy was very evident in *A New Approach*, with its unequivocal conclusion that strong trade unions, independent of and capable of bargaining with management, were the best vehicle for the furtherance of the democratic rights of employees. It was a view which, as we have seen, was to reappear in the words of the Royal Commission in 1968 and, though barely challenged at the time, was subsequently to fall sharply from favour and be officially repudiated after 1979.

Paradoxically, a second strand of Clegg's thinking, which surfaced clearly for the first time with the Royal Commission's report, was controversial at the time but has subsequently been rendered indisputable by the course of events. This concerns the optimal level of bargaining, and in particular, the necessity for what would now be called 'enterprise bargaining' to replace industrial agreements for much of the private sector. There had been a general expectation that the Royal Commission would propose new legislative measures which would curb the capacity of shop stewards, bargaining at the workplace, to subvert industry-wide collective bargaining. Supported by the legal analysis of his fellow commissioner Kahn-Freund, and the written evidence of Flanders, Clegg succeeded in winning the Commission over to a contrary view. This was that the central malaise was one of bargaining structure, with a formal system of industrial agreements in conflict with an informal system of workplace bargaining in which employers were heavily implicated. The law could play little part in the procedural reform that was necessary. It was up to employers to decide which system they could best work with and, if it was one of enterprise-based bargaining, to provide the appropriate union representatives with uncompromised authority to conclude agreements. Over the following quarter century, enterprise-based bargaining was largely to displace industrial bargaining in a conclusive vindication of this argument.

The third strand of Clegg's theoretical innovation built on the primacy he gave to employers in determining collective bargaining structures. In *Trade Unionism under Collective Bargaining* he developed a general theory of trade union behaviour on the basis of a comparison of six different countries. His preface made clear the extent to which he felt he was building on the work of Flanders. 'That does not mean he would have agreed with what I have written, had he been able to see it. For, although we usually came to the same conclusion during the twenty-odd years we worked together, more often than not it was by very different routes. The architecture of his theory would have been nobler and more substantial' (Clegg 1976). This was a short and vigorously argued book, deliberately stripped of references and what he called 'the apparatus of scholarship'. It sketched out an overview of union behaviour in the different countries and accounted for variations in terms of a number of distinct dimensions of national bargaining structure. It then explained variations in bargaining structure in terms of employer strategy and the role of legal intervention at particular critical political junctures. Despite twenty intervening years which have seen many trade union movements in severe decline, the theory stands up surprisingly well, still having considerable explanatory power with regard to, among other things, strike behaviour, industrial democracy and wage determination. The major loose end to which Clegg confessed, his inability to deal with trade unions' political role, has been effectively tackled by subsequent scholars. (Martin 1989; Crouch 1993).

4 Conclusion

This brief account of Hugh Clegg's scholarly contribution has deliberately emphasized its strong theoretical content. At a time when industrial relations was at the centre of public concern his work had a major influence on policy formulation. By his emphasis upon the empirical analysis of all aspects of the subject both in what he wrote and in what he caused others to write, he placed it on a firm academic foundation. As a result he sidelined or defused many traditional areas of theoretical debate. But in their place he provided an alternative theoretical approach to the analysis of collective bargaining, organized labour, and the role of management which shows every sign of dominating the study of industrial relations, at least in Britain, for the foreseeable future.

WILLIAM BROWN
UNIVERSITY OF CAMBRIDGE

Further reading

(References cited in the text marked *)

* Bugler, J. (1968) 'The New Oxford Group', *New Society*, 15 February. (A contemporary account of the Oxford School of industrial relations.)
* Brown, W. A.(1997) 'The High Tide of Consensus', *Historical Studies in Industrial Relations*, No 4. (A retrospective review of the first edition of The System.)
* Brown, W. A. (1998) Funders and Research: the Vulnerability of the Subject, in G. Strauss and K. Whitfield (eds.) *Researching the World of Work*, ILR Press, Cornell: Cornell University Press. (An account of the official enquiry into allegations that the work of the research Unit that Clegg founded was 'politically biased'.)
  Clegg, H. A. (1954) *General Union*, Oxford: Blackwell. (Clegg's unsubmitted doctoral thesis.)
* Clegg, H. A. (1960) *A New Approach to Industrial Democracy*, Oxford: Blackwell. (A major essay in political science analysis.)
* Clegg, H. A. (1964) *A History of British Trade Unions Vol 1* (with A. Fox and A. F. Thompson); *Vol 2* (1985); *Vol 3* (1994). Oxford: Oxford University Press. (The definitive study of the subject.)
* Clegg, H. A. (1970) *The System of Industrial Relations in Great Britain*. Oxford: Blackwell. (Clegg's first comprehensive textbook; having no text in common with its predecessor of the same name.)
* Clegg, H. A. (1975) 'Pluralism in Industrial Relations', *British Journal of Industrial Relations*, 13 (3). (A defence of the philosophy of pluralism in industrial relations.)
* Clegg, H. A. (1976) *Trade Unionism under Collective Bargaining*. Oxford: Blackwell. (A theory of trade union behaviour derived from international comparison.)
* Clegg, H. A. (1976) *The Changing System of Industrial Relations in Great Britain*. Oxford: Blackwell. (A complete rewrite of the 1970 textbook at a time of rapid institutional change.)
* Clegg, H. A.(1990) 'The Oxford School of Industrial Relations', Warwick Papers in Industrial Relations, No. 31, IRRU, University of Warwick, Coventry. (A reflective retrospective essay on the rise and dispersal of the Oxford School.)
* Crosland, C. A. R. (1956) *The Future of Socialism*. London: Jonathan Cape. (An influential account of non-Marxian Fabian socialist thinking.)
* Crouch, C. (1993) *Industrial Relations and European State Traditions*. Oxford: Clarendon Press. (An ambitious attempt to explain international institutional differences in terms of historical and sociological development.)
* Donovan (1968) *Report of the Royal Commission on Trade Unions and Employers' Associations 1965–1968*. Cmnd 3623, London: HMSO. (An important analysis of contemporary industrial relations, heavily influenced by the Oxford School.)
* Flanders, A. and Clegg, H. A. (1954) *The System of Industrial Relations in Great Britain*. Oxford: Blackwell. (The founding publication of the Oxford School.)
* Fox, A. (1966) *Industrial Sociology and Industrial Relations*. Royal Commission Research Paper No 3, London: HMSO. (A particularly influential contribution to Donovan and subsequent analysis.)
* Martin, R.M. (1989) *Trade Unionism: Purposes and Forms*. Oxford: Clarendon Press. (An attempt to explain the political behaviour of trade union by one of Clegg's close colleagues.)

See also: FLANDERS, A.D.; FOX, A.

Related topics in the IEBM: COLLECTIVE BARGAINING; CORPORATISM; EMPLOYEE RELATIONS; EMPLOYERS ASSOCIATIONS; HUMAN RESOURCE MANAGEMENT; INDUSTRIAL AND LABOUR RELATIONS; INDUSTRIAL CONFLICT; INDUSTRIAL DEMOCRACY; TRADE UNIONS

Coase, Ronald (1910–)

Personal background

- born 29 December 1910, Willesden, UK
- studied at the London School of Economics
- greatly influenced by Arnold Plant
- Applied economic analysis to the structure of business
- worked in the USA after 1951
- Used economics to analyse legal institutions
- joined the University of Chicago Law School in 1964
- developed work on economic regulation
- awarded the Nobel Prize for economics in 1991

Major works

'The nature of the firm' (1937)
'The problem of social cost' (1960)

Summary

Coase used economics to analyse the structure of institutions. He was the first economist explicitly to propose that the structure of business was determined by transactions costs. The organization of production within a firm saves on the costs of contracting with outsiders but it substitutes problems of internal control. This trade-off between external transactions costs and internal organization costs determines the size and scope of the enterprise. Coase also applied transactions cost analysis to problems of pollution and social costs more generally. He noted that systems of regulation or taxation which prevented people from coming to agreements with each other might be disadvantageous for society as a whole. From this insight flowed the modern economic analysis of tort law and of government regulation.

1 Introduction

The theme running through Coase's work is that institutional arrangements affect transactions costs and that these play an important part in determining economic results. Without transactions costs the structure of institutions would not matter. In practice, the way property rights are assigned and the costs of trading them matter a great deal.

2 Biographical data

Born in Willesden, North London, in 1910, Coase studied commerce at the London School of Economics (LSE), where he was influenced by Arnold Plant. He travelled to the USA in 1931 on a scholarship to study why the structure of firms varied across industries. The resulting paper was eventually published in 1937. Coase taught at the LSE until 1951 and worked at the offices of the War Cabinet (1941–6). Thereafter Coase left for the USA and worked at the State University of New York at Buffalo (1951–8), Stanford University (1958), the University of Virginia (1959) and finally the University of Chicago Law School (1964–81). In Chicago, Coase edited the *Journal of Law and Economics*. He was awarded the Nobel Prize for Economics in 1991.

3 Main contribution

In the early 1930s, there was no established theory to explain why some firms were highly vertically integrated – making their own components, distributing their own products and developing their own supplies of raw materials – while others were more specialized – using market contracts with other firms to obtain supplies and sell their output. Similarly, no explanation existed for the fact that some firms produced a wide range of different goods while others were much more specialized. A descriptive taxonomy of firms existed – a set of boxes labelled 'vertically', 'horizontally' or 'laterally' integrated – but no explanation of the forces which might determine why firms adopt one form of organization rather than another .

Coase's answer to this question, formulated on his trip to the USA and published in his 1937 paper 'The nature of the firm', was couched in very general terms and was ultimately to prove very fruitful. Activities were undertaken within firms rather than across markets when this was the less costly option. There is a cost of using the price mechanism which organization within the firm can avoid. Within the firm, resources are allocated by the conscious decision and authority of an entrepreneur or manager. People, when they join a firm, agree to be 'organized'. The use of market contracts requires the investment of time and resources in information gathering and contract negotiation and renegotiation, which can be cut down within the firm. Relations within the firm are characterized by durable contracts whose terms do not attempt to establish what is required of the parties in every detail. Coase sees the entrepreneur as the centre of a set of such contracts. Other people in the firm have contracts with the entrepreneur rather than with each other and this reduces the number of contractual links that have to be negotiated.

In his 1937 paper, Coase thus set out the modern 'nexus of contracts' view of the firm. In the process, he applied the most basic economic concepts of opportunity cost and substitution at the margin. The whole economy was not organized as a single firm because the costs of internal organization would rise with size and scope. The market and the firm were substitute mechanisms for achieving the coordination of resources. Some activities would be much less costly to organize internally, while in the case of others the market might have clear advantages. With some activities,

the decision would be finely judged and these marginal cases would be located at the boundary of the firm and the market.

There are close connections between Coase's early work on the firm and his later work on social costs. Indeed, the impact of the latter in 1960 encouraged a reappraisal of the former, which had been, until that point, admired but not used as the basis of further research. His 1960 paper, 'The problem of social cost', had a profound influence on the way economists thought about spill-over effects or 'externalities' (see MARSHALL, A.). The standard approach at the time was that the existence of some harmful effect associated with an activity – such as noise or air pollution – required the government to impose a tax on the offending activity equal at the margin to the value of the damage caused. This policy was linked to the economist A.C. Pigou.

Coase pointed out that this type of policy recommendation entirely ignored the possibility that people could come to voluntary agreements about such harmful activities. A person suffering from the noise of a neighbour might bribe the neighbour to reduce it, to confine it to certain times of the day or to erect sound-insulating barriers. These abatement activities would be carried to the point at which the marginal benefit of further peace and quiet to the purchaser was just equal to the extra cost of achieving it. Alternatively, the noisy person could purchase the consent of the sensitive neighbour to tolerate the noise. He or she might start by simply bribing the neighbour to accept small amounts of noise and then continue by erecting sound-insulating screens when these become cheaper than further bribes to the neighbour. Eventually, the benefit of making more noise will be less than the cost of compensating the neighbour (either by screens or money bribes) and the noisy activity will be pursued no further.

By formulating the problem in this way, Coase was able to clarify some major issues. First, Coase emphasized the reciprocal nature of external harm. The presence of a noise-sensitive neighbour might be as inhibiting and inconvenient to a noisy one as the other way round. Second, if there existed mutual advantages in coming to some agreement about noise, the parties would have an incentive to bargain to a point at which no further joint advantage was derivable. Third, this agreement would not depend upon the initial assignment of property rights (a point later disputed by theorists). Whether the noisy neighbour had to buy rights to make noise from the quiet one or the quiet neighbour had to buy rights to peace and quiet from the noisy one, the amount of noise that was eventually made or the size and effectiveness of the sound-insulating screens would be unaffected. Fourth, these results would only apply in a world in which transactions costs were negligible and property rights were clear. Where agreements were costly to negotiate and enforce it would not follow that the assignment of rights left the final allocation of resources unaffected or that people could always bargain to an efficient agreement. The structure of legal rules and institutions would therefore be important in determining how resources were allocated in areas where markets were missing.

4 Evaluation

The significance of Coase's analysis of the effect of transactions costs on economic organization was not immediately appreciated. By the late 1960s, however, researchers began to build on his foundations. Armen Alchian and Harold Demsetz (1972) and Oliver Williamson (1975, 1985) openly acknowledged Coase's influence on their work on the organization of firms (see WIL-LIAMSON, O.E.). These economists began to ask what factors determine the level of transactions costs. Williamson argues that firms form when transactions are frequent, where the environment is uncertain and where the transactors are vulnerable to 'opportunism'. Alchian and Demsetz emphasize the problems that arise where output comes from many team members and where the value of the individual contribution of each person cannot be observed.

Other economic theorists of the late 1970s and 1980s began to look more closely at the incentive properties of contracts. Instead of the stark choice between market and firm, this modern literature presents the world as a spectrum of contractual possibilities. The general problem is characterized as one of principal and agent, with the principal attempting to elicit effort from the agent in conditions of poor or non-existent information. This approach has been influential in the theory of the finance of the firm (for example, Jensen and Meckling 1976), where bond finance and equity finance are arranged to minimize agency costs, in the field of managerial incentive contracts (for example Jensen and Murphy 1990), where shareholders attempt to align managers' interests with their own, and in the analysis of the structure of the firm. Rubin (1978), for example, considers the franchise chain as a method of eliciting effort from the franchisee while giving the franchiser an incentive to maintain the value of the brand name.

Developments in the world of business have made the questions posed in Coase's paper ever more pertinent. The growth of multinational enterprise prompts the Coasian question of why activities located in many different countries should be coordinated in a single firm – a question investigated by Dunning (1973) and Buckley and Casson (1976). The use of joint ventures raises the issue of why such market-like agreements are sometimes preferred over a full merger. The observation that in some countries the same industries are more vertically integrated than in others, for example the motor industry in the USA compared with Japan, suggests that transactions costs must be lower in the less integrated environment. The reasons for this have been sought by economists and management theorists (see INDUSTRIAL ECONOMICS).

In the field of public policy, the 1980s and 1990s are forcing Coasian analysis to the fore. Whether to privatize an industry in a vertically integrated form or to break it down into smaller components is a quintessentially Coasian question. To divide train companies from the owner of the track, or to insist on the division between the production of gas and its distribution, or the generation of electricity and its transmission is to insist on the use of market contracts at certain points in place of internal organization. Transactions costs and economic incentives are at the heart of these issues along with the idea that transactional inefficiencies may be worth incurring in order to achieve the benefits of greater competition.

Coase's 1937 paper forms the foundation stone of much of the modern economics and management literature on the structure of firms. Over time, however, modifications to his conception have become accepted. It is no longer assumed that the exercise of authority is the main characteristic which separates firm from market. Within the firm, people will often have a wide area of discretion and will act as agents rather than passive takers of instructions from the management. Similarly, recent thinking has tended to emphasize the generation of specialized capabilities within the firm – competitive advantages – which can only be exploited internally and cannot be traded directly using the market mechanism. The possibility of substitution between firm and market is thereby thrown into question in some circumstances. In the face of sudden and substantial innovation, for example, organization within the firm may be necessary to force through the necessary changes (Silver 1984).

Coase's work on social cost has been equally influential. His 1960 paper gave rise to much technical discussion about the so-called 'Coase theorem' and the precise circumstances in which it would hold. Economic theorists pointed out that even in a world of zero transactions costs the final allocation of resources would not be entirely independent of the initial assignment of property rights if a person's willingness to pay for a beneficial change or to avoid a harmful one varied with wealth. Although much of the subsequent discussion concerned the properties of Coase's system in conditions of zero transactions costs and a 'Coasian world' has come, paradoxically, to be understood in the economics profession as one without transactions costs, the long-term importance of Coase's contribution will be found in his insistence that transacting inevitably involves costs and that these affect economic behaviour and the efficiency of economic systems.

The growth of the study of law and economics, especially in the USA, was stimulated directly by Coase's work on social cost. Posner (1973) drew on it directly in his analysis of legal institutions. Where transactions are costly, the question of how rights should be allocated becomes a central one for economic students of the law. Posner advanced the proposition that if agreements are prevented by excessive transactions costs, rights should be assigned to the party that would value them most highly (and would hence purchase them), were transactions costs negligible. In other words, the law should mimic the market. More recently, free market environmentalists such as Anderson and Leal (1991) have emphasized the importance of establishing clear property rights in environmental resources so that a Coasian process of agreement can occur. In general, however, Coase's work cannot be used to assert the universal supremacy of market solutions over regulatory solutions to environmental and other problems. Sometimes transactions costs will be low enough to favour markets, whereas at other times some form of regulation may be preferred. The direct comparison of available institutions in realistic circumstances is ultimately the only way of adjudicating on these issues.

Although Coase's intellectual contribution is founded on two extremely influential scientific papers of a conceptual and theoretical nature, the corpus of his work more generally is based upon close observation of practical circumstances. It was, for example, his work on the allocation of radio frequencies by the Federal Communications Commission (Coase 1959) that led to the idea that a market in rights to frequencies would produce superior results. Similarly, his objections to marginal cost pricing in the public sector (Coase 1946) were based on very practical observations. If setting prices equal to marginal cost necessitated a subsidy, the costs of raising this revenue by increased taxation should be taken into consideration. Further, once subsidies are permitted, the incentive to maintain technical efficiency in the industry is undermined. Average cost pricing at least provides a rudimentary way of testing that total benefits exceed total costs. Coase's article on the lighthouse (1974) provides another example of this way of thinking. Students of economics would, from reading the textbooks, have reasonably assumed that no lighthouses could possibly have been provided before the state became involved. Coase shows this to be completely wrong historically and discusses the mechanisms by which lighthouse builders managed to overcome the transactions cost problem and gather lighthouse dues.

5 Conclusion

Transactions costs provide the leitmotif which runs through Coase's career. His influence has been profound within the economics profession, but it has also spread out more widely to management thinkers, who may be Coasians without knowing it. Although Coase has been honoured for theoretical work, his background in commerce has given him a common-sense approach to problems that has an appeal outside the economics profession narrowly construed.

MARTIN RICKETTS
UNIVERSITY OF BUCKINGHAM

Further reading

(References cited in the text marked *)

* Alchian, A. and Demsetz, H. (1972) 'Production, information costs and economic organization', *American Economic Review* 62 (5): 777–95. (Emphasizes information costs as the factor explaining organization within the firm.)
* Anderson, T.L. and Leal, D.R. (1991) *Free Market Environmentalism*, San Francisco, CA: Pacific Research Institute for Public Policy. (Recommends the greater use of property rights and legal remedies instead of regulation for environmental problems.)
* Buckley, P.J. and Casson, M. (1976) *The Future of Multinational Enterprise*, London: Macmillan. (Discusses the reasons for organizing multinational operations within a single firm instead of across markets.)
* Coase, R.H. (1937) 'The nature of the firm', *Economica* (new series) 4 (16): 386–405. (One of the two main papers mentioned in Coase's Nobel Prize citation.)
* Coase, R.H. (1946) 'The marginal cost controversy', *Economica* (new series) 13 (51): 169–82. (A paper which indicates Coase's distrust of 'theoretical' economics, that is, economics which ignores transactions costs.)
* Coase, R.H. (1959) 'The Federal Communications Commission', *Journal of Law and Economics* 2: 1–40. (Coase criticizes the Federal Communications Commission's method of allocating radio frequencies.)
* Coase, R.H. (1960) 'The problem of social cost', *Journal of Law and Economics* 3: 1–44. (An influential paper showing that the problem of social cost was a problem of transacting and property rights.)
* Coase, R.H. (1974) 'The lighthouse in economics', *Journal of Law and Economics* 17 (2): 357–76. (Coase shows how entrepreneurs can often think of ways to overcome transactions costs.)
* Dunning, J.H. (1973) 'The determinants of international production', *Oxford Economic Papers* 25 (3): 289. (Argues that multinational expansion occurs to make use of non-tradeable enterprise-specific advantages.)
* Jensen, M.C. and Meckling, W.H. (1976) 'Theory of the firm: managerial behaviour, agency costs and ownership structure', *Journal of Financial Economics* 3 (4): 305–60. (Established the 'agency cost' approach to corporate finance.)
* Jensen, M.C. and Murphy, K.J. (1990) 'Performance pay and top management incentives', *Journal of Political Economy* 98 (2): 225–64. (Discusses the compatibility of Chief Executive Officer incentive contracts with the theory of principal and agent.)
  Medema, S.G. (1994) *Ronald H. Coase*, New York: St Martin's Press. (An overview of Coase's life and an assessment of his work.)
* Posner, R.A. (1973) *Economic Analysis of Law*, Boston, MA: Little, Brown. (The application of Coasian economic analysis to the study of law.)
* Rubin, P.H. (1978) 'The theory of the firm and the structure of the franchise contract', *Journal of Law and Economics* 21 (1): 223–33. (Rubin sees the franchise chain as an alternative to full integration – a very Coasian perspective.)
* Silver, M. (1984) *Enterprise and the Scope of the Firm*, Oxford: Martin Robertson. (Vertical integration is seen as a means used by entrepreneurs to force through change that market contracts could not handle.)
* Williamson, O.E. (1975) *Markets and Hierarchies: Analysis and Antitrust Implications*, New York: The Free Press. (The title clearly declares Coase's influence – hierarchies or firms as an alternative to markets.)
* Williamson, O.E. (1985) *The Economic Institutions of Capitalism: Firms, Markets, Relational Contracting* New York: The Free Press.

(A major work analysing the governance of transactional relations).

See also: MARSHALL, A.; WILLIAMSON, O.E.

Related topics in the IEBM: BUSINESS ECONOMICS; COMPETITIVE STRATEGIES, DEVELOPMENT OF; ENVIRONMENTAL MANAGEMENT; EVOLUTIONARY THEORY OF THE FIRM; GROWTH OF THE FIRM AND NETWORKING; INSTITUTIONAL ECONOMICS; MANAGERIAL THEORIES OF THE FIRM; MARKET STRUCTURE AND CONDUCT; MULTINATIONAL CORPORATIONS; NEOCLASSICAL ECONOMICS; TRANSACTION COST ECONOMICS

Crozier, Michel (1922–)

Personal background

- born on 5 November 1922 in Sainte-Menehould, France
- business studies (Hautes Études Commerciales, Paris)
- doctorate degrees in law and in literature (La Sorbonne, Paris)
- spent his career as a research fellow in sociology at the Centre National de la Recherche Scientifique (Paris)
- developed a theory of bureaucracy and a methodology enabling the analysis of organized systems of collective action
- founder of the Centre de Sociologie des Organisations (Paris)

Major works

The Bureaucratic Phenomenon (1963)
The World of the Office Worker (1965)
Actors and Systems (with E. Friedberg) (1977)

Summary

Michel Crozier (1922–) is a respected influence on the development of bureaucratization as a subject of the sociology of organizations. He also invented a methodology called 'strategic analysis' of behaviours using power relationships, which gives an entry point to understanding and managing collective action in organized settings. He considers sociology of organizations as a way of reasoning and a tool for social engineering applicable to industrial and post-industrial societies. Crozier aims at a cultural and mental revolution in order to overcome scientific management as well as human relations approaches in the governance of societies and in the management of organizations. In his role as a sociologist, an essayist and an advocate for reforms he has worldwide influence in fields such as the modernization of the public sector.

1 Introduction

Can sociological research be the key to a new culture in organizations and in polities which would be based upon the understanding of human situations in their specific social context? Crozier believes that a scientific approach to social systems and organizations can liberate social relations and management policies from emotional and mechanistic perspectives. Change processes can occur and have a lasting effect when organizations help their members to play open games, allowing power relationships to fulfil their own individual goals as well as to include collective action into their own stakes. Sociology of organizations is for Crozier a part of a more general theory of human freedom, which in turn is a prerequisite of participation and investment people make to solve collective problems in modern societies.

The Crozier approach is a combination of the frequent penchant of French intellectuals to change society and the empirical rigour of American sociology in its quest to discover scientific laws. At a time when Europe was still struggling with Taylorism and paternalism, he was influenced by the most prominent American sociologists, from A. Kardiner to J. March. Empirical data could and should help organizations to be less order-centred and more action-oriented. His style of research is based upon a very detailed in-depth observation of organizations in their daily functioning and a clinical analysis through monographs on single cases. Organizations as such are social constructs, showing specific inside characteristics and some fitting with societal cultural norms and values.

Crozier's best-known book remains *The Bureaucratic Phenomenon.*

2 Biographical data

Crozier was born on 5 November 1922 in Sainte-Menehould, a city in eastern France. His family was in the hardware business. He moved to Paris where he received his academic training. He graduated from HEC (Hautes Études Commerciales), a leading business school. At La Sorbonne, he studied literature and law. He became what was known at the time as a Parisian leftist intellectual. He published poems under a pseudonym and was committed to political ideals. He stood very close to anarchism, at a time when the Communist Party dominated the Left Bank circles in Paris.

At the end of 1947, Crozier left France and spent a year in the USA. He travelled around the country and interviewed about 600 people at the grassroots level. He wanted to learn how the leftist arm of the American trade unions, the American Federation of Labour (AFL), which was influenced by leaders close to Trotskyism, could successfully fight big business. In 1951, he published a book on plants and trade unions in the USA, which reported his observations (Crozier 1951b).

During these Cold War years, Crozier experienced mixed feelings towards the social sciences and the USA. Despite the fact that he witnessed at close hand the daily practices of the American labour movement, he did not consider himself a professional sociologist. His goal was clearly ideological and political, namely to change the world. He wanted, for example, to help French workers to understand and thus adapt to the AFL bargaining tactics so that they could increase their own negotiation power. This stance was clearly illustrated by his article on 'Human engineering', published by *Les Temps Modernes*, a critical, left-wing magazine directed by the philosopher Jean-Paul Sartre (Crozier 1951a). Crozier developed a very aggressive critique of how applied social sciences were being used by management in order to manipulate their employers. French scholars, artists and writers, he maintained, need not accept how

sciences like psychoanalysis and sociology in the USA were developing tools for big business.

In 1952, Crozier became a sociologist. He joined the CNRS (Centre National de la Recherche Scientifique) where he stayed for forty-one years, up to retirement. He was interested in the class awareness of the middle classes. Gradually, his scientific focus moved towards the organization as a social construct. He launched an impressive number of research projects, throwing himself into empirical studies and fieldwork. Within a ten-year period, he studied a financial agency of the Post Office, the state tobacco enterprise, a large bank, insurance companies and the ministry of war veterans.

In 1963, he received a doctoral degree at The Sorbonne. Two books offered a synthesis of his field research: *The Bureaucratic Phenomenon* and *The World of the Office Worker.* The former, which developed major new theories about organizations, quickly made his name famous in France and in the USA.

Crozier founded his own research centre, the Centre de Sociologie des Organisations, which became in the late 1960s a major reference in his field, attracting scholars such as E. Friedberg, P. Grémion and J.-C. Thoenig. Its long-term programme was devoted to public administration, organizational change and organized collective action. Crozier gave a synthesis of it in *Actors and Systems*, which he published in 1977 with Friedberg. A significant contribution was made to the field in 1976 when he and Thoenig urged the study of interorganizational network as specific social systems in *The regulation of complex organized systems.*

Crozier also invested time and energy in building 'bridges' between France and the USA. Visiting Harvard University as a professor or joining the Trilateral Commission as an expert, he was interested in understanding the fundamental patterns of the functioning of both countries. In 1973 *The Stalled Society* was published in English, a diagnosis of why France is unable to modernize. In 1980, he wrote *The Trouble with America*, which underlines rigidities and dysfunctioning in contemporary US society.

He emphasized the role of intellectuals as agents of change in society and became an advocate of social reforms in France, trying to find an alternative to socialism and conservatism on issues such as the modernization of companies, the reform of elite education or the decentralization of public affairs. He set up an active and innovative postgraduate school of sociology at the Institut d'Études Politiques of Paris which trained students as well as practitioners to become social engineers and social scientists.

3 Main contributions

Crozier has made a contribution to the theory of bureaucracy and bureaucratization. His fieldwork on how French public agencies function daily as social systems allowed him to go beyond the classic work of R. Merton, P. Selznick and A. Gouldner on bureaucracies as dysfunctioning organizations. A bureaucracy is characterized by four scientific properties (Crozier 1963: chapter 7):

1 Decision making is centralized and isolated in an artificial way from implementation. Those who make decisions sit at the top of the hierarchy of authority and do not themselves implement their own decisions. Those at the bottom who face local problems do not make the decision themselves, show no interest in doing so, but in turn develop an expertise in implementing the decisions. Such a social and functional distance between the two groups allows each of them to protect themselves from the other.

2 Universal and impersonal rules are extensively used. No room is left for particularistic and discretionary problem solving. General principles, standardized procedures, whether formal or informal, cover all situations, tasks and problems. The acceptance of rules by the participants enable them to build up niches of autonomy.

3 Strong peer-group pressure implies that each hierarchical level is quite isolated from the others and that a high degree of social stratification is present inside the organization. By conforming to their group

interests, individuals may lower their personal dependence on their superiors.

4 In a world of rigid structures and low communication capacity, power relations develop in a parallel and informal way between different hierarchical levels and groups. Superiors do not talk to their subordinates. But information processes nevertheless occur between the top and the bottom which are mediated through structures such as the trade unions.

Crozier underlines the basic dilemma in which a bureaucracy is caught. Bureaucratization is a self-sustaining process fuelled by a vicious circle. The more an organization is centralized, stratified and adopting impersonal rules, the more it uses these properties as a solution to the problems they induce. A bureaucracy is a social system which is unable to correct itself whenever it has to deal with errors. It does not learn and adapt itself to a changing environment, except through a global shake-up. Some problems may, for instance, occur at a local level and at the bottom echelon of the organization. Instead of decentralizing authority and making use of flexibility, the organization shall reinforce the role of the top and design more general principles for action, even if this means delaying its reaction and losing its fine-tuning capacity. Bureaucracy functions as a system which generates many inside advantages for its members, including the subordinate levels, despite the errors and rigidities it generates. Impersonal rules or centralization of decision making allow subordinates to minimize the discretionary intervention of their superiors on their own situation. They also allocate to the superiors formal authority and social status without being personally exposed to the consequences of action.

Power as a central concept and as an analytical tool represents another relevant contribution made by Crozier (1963: chapters 5 and 6). Influenced by H. Simon's approach of bounded rationality and by R. Dahl's operational definition of power as the ability of actor A to get actor B to adopt a behaviour B would not adopt if A were absent, Crozier deals with an explanation of human relations and causes of behaviour in organized collective action. Organization as such is characterized by interdependence between different actors. Cooperation is not a natural or spontaneous pattern of behaviour. Actors behave in a cooperative or in a cooperation-avoidance way according to the stakes or goals they try to fulfil wherever they are. Stakes and goals are short-term oriented, contingent and more or less stable. The behaviour adopted by an actor in his relationship with the organization is called a strategy, which means that the actor makes a rational calculation in order to fulfil his goals and, by taking into account the resources, he controls the actors and in turn the constraints he faces from other actors. Hence the more an actor himself controls uncertainties which are relevant for other actors, the more he has power over them, which means that he can set the conditions and terms of their behaviours and exchanges and make them dependent on his own good will.

Such a strategic analysis of behaviour has been developed in what remains one of the classic monographs of organization: the study of the tobacco plant. In a highly bureaucratic context, the only actors who are capable of unpredictable behaviour are the maintenance workers. The ways in which they repair the machines have consequences for the bonus of their fellow workers, the production workers. Power in the plant is controlled by them. Even the hierarchy, which holds the formal authority, does not exert any role in the way the plant is governed as a social system. In his subsequent books, Crozier has developed an approach he calls systems of action in order to explain collective behaviours in organized settings, whether they are institutionally designed or informally structured. In other words, the rationality of collective behaviours in organized settings is bounded by the way various inside groups adjust themselves to the power relationship which structures their interactions.

Crozier analyses the cultural lag which may exist between institutions and their environment. Such is the case with France. The bureaucratic model of organization and action is no longer able to fulfil the needs for cooperation and innovation through experimentation that industrial rationality and mass culture require. Bureaucratization is also a cultural phenomenon which carries specific norms and values. In France, Crozier shows that bureaucratic organizations satisfy patterns such as the fear of face to face relationships and the search for formal equality between peers. Organizations are culturally embedded in national contexts.

JEAN-CLAUDE THOENIG
CENTRE NATIONAL DE LA RECHERCHE
SCIENTIFIQUE, PARIS

Further reading

(References cited in the text marked *)

* Crozier, M. (1951a) 'Human engineering', *Les Temps Modernes* 69 (July): 44–75. (A leftist critique of the methods American big business has used to control the working class and the role of academics.)

* Crozier, M. (1951b) *Syndicats et ouvriers d'Amérique*, Paris: Editions Ouvriéres. (A report on AFL bargaining and negotiation practices as an example of how trade unions can gain power in their struggle with business.)

Crozier, M. (1957) 'Recherche sociologique et société industrielle', *L'Education Nationale* 3: 1–2. (The first presentation by Crozier of how he considers sociology of organizations as a cultural input and an agent of change for industrial societies.)

* Crozier, M. (1963) *The Bureaucratic Phenomenon*, Chicago, IL: University of Chicago Press, 1964. (Crozier's exposition of sociology of organizations which has become internationally known as one of the classics about power, bureaucracy, and culture.)

* Crozier, M. (1965) *The World of the Office Worker*, Chicago, IL: University of Chicago Press, 1971. (Deals with the group identity of lower white-collar workers, their cultural and social homogeneity.)

* Crozier, M. (1970) *The Stalled Society*, New York: Viking Press, 1973. (A global diagnosis of the factors of resistance to change and modernization faced by the organizational and cultural infrastructures of French society.)

* Crozier, M. (1980) *The Trouble with America*, Berkeley, CA: University of California Press, 1985. (A diagnosis of the cultural, organizational and political problems which American society faces.)

Crozier, M. (1987) *Etat modeste, Etat moderne*, Paris: Fayard. (Suggests basic reforms in the way a modern industrial and democratic state apparatus should govern and manage public policies.)

Crozier, M. (1995) *La Crise de l'intelligence: Essai sur l'impuissance, des élites à se réformer*, Paris: Inteséditions. (Explores the question of why social élites are a major obstacle to the modernization of society.)

* Crozier, M. and Friedberg, E. (1977) *Actors and Systems*, Chicago, IL: University of Chicago Press, 1980. (A presentation of the major research projects achieved between 1964 and 1976 by Crozier and his associates of the Centre de Sociologie des Organisations.)

* Crozier, M. and Thoenig, J.-C. (1976), 'The regulation of complex organized systems', *Administrative Science Quarterly* 21 (4): 547–70. (A seminal paper about the study of interorganizational networks, and its application to the case of French Public Administration.)

Pavé, F. (ed.) (1994) *L'analyse stratégique: sa genése, ses applications et ses problémes actuels. Autour de Michel Crozier*, Paris: Le Seuil. (A report on a colloquium about Crozier with contributions by P. Grémion and Crozier.)

See also: GOULDNER, A.W.; MARCH, J.G. AND CYERT, R.M.; TAYLOR, F.W.; WEBER, M.

Related topics in the IEBM: DECISION MAKING; MANAGEMENT IN FRANCE; ORGANIZATION BEHAVIOUR; ORGANIZATION BEHAVIOUR, HISTORY OF; ORGANIZATION CULTURE; ORGANIZATION DEVELOPMENT; POWER; TRADE UNIONS; WORK SYSTEMS

Deming, William Edwards (1900–93)

Personal background

- born 14 October 1900, in Sioux City, Iowa, the son of a lawyer and land developer
- studied at Wyoming and Colorado Universities, then gained a doctorate in mathematical physics from Yale University in 1928
- first wife, Agnes Bell, died in 1930; second wife, Lola Shupe, died in 1986
- developed an interest in statistical methods after joining the US Department of Agriculture
- joined the National Bureau of Census in 1939, where his methods were credited for major productivity improvements
- taught managers and engineers in the USA during the Second World War and invited by General MacArthur to Japan after the war to help advise on the Japanese census
- in 1950 asked by JUSE (the Union of Japanese Scientists and Engineers) to lecture on statistical methods for industry
- first American to be awarded the Order of the Sacred Treasure by the Japanese Emperor (1960)
- most of the rest of his life was spent preaching the Deming philosophy in Japan and the USA; Deming was still conducting seminars until a month before his death, on 20 December 1993, at the age of 93

Major works

Sample Design in Business Research (1960)
Out of Crisis: Quality, Productivity and Competitive Position (1986)
The New Economics for Industry, Government and Education (1993)

Summary

W. Edwards Deming (1900–93) was one of the most famous and influential advocates of total quality management. His words are now being carried by thousands of 'Deming disciples' around the world. It is possible that history may credit him as the most important management guru of the late twentieth century.

Deming blamed the problems of industry on management's failure to eliminate waste and establish control over variation in production processes, and advocated the use of rigorous statistical methods to reduce scrap and improve quality (Deming 1960, 1986). His methods depended on a customer orientation and on eliminating waste and improving quality at the point of production or service delivery. Teamwork, cooperation and giving workers the tools to do a good job ought to replace competition, fear and incompetent management. Deming's ideas were embraced by Japanese industry in the post-war period and since then Japanese companies have competed fiercely for the Deming Prize. Only in the 1980s did Deming become a prophet in his own country, although his ideas have rapidly come to be seen by many as the answer to the ills of Western industry.

1 Introduction

In his early working life Deming developed his ideas about the application of statistical methods for the improvement of organizational performance. Largely unknown in his own country of the USA, he rapidly became a folk hero in Japan during the 1950s. The award of the Sacred Treasure by the Japanese Emperor in 1960 is one indication of the high esteem he enjoyed. Deming's experiences in Japan helped him develop the philosophy which he propagated in the USA as well as Japan for the remainder of his life. Only in the early 1980s was Deming taken seriously in the Western World. Ten years later, Deming was arguably the most influential business guru across the world.

2 Main contributions

Deming is widely seen as the founder of total quality management (TQM), though he was heavily influenced during his early working life by other experts in applied statistical methods, particularly Joseph Juran and Walter Shewart (Oliver and Wilkinson 1992) (see JURAN, J.M.). Deming's contribution to management and organization stemmed from his belief that quality and customer satisfaction should be built into products rather than dependent on an army of quality inspectors who would detect errors after the event. In order to achieve this, workers would have to be given the training and the tools to 'get it right first time'. Eliminating defects and continually improving processes at the point of production would not only reduce the costs of waste materials, scrap product and quality specialists' employment, it would lead to a new approach to the management of organizations. Workers would no longer be treated as commodities; instead, resources would be devoted to the development of their capabilities and they would be more fully involved in the organization. Deming called for a management philosophy based on cooperative problem solving and asked managers to 'drive out fear' from the workplace, for instance, by eliminating performance-related pay systems which he referred to as 'fear schemes'. 'Competition is our ruination', he said, 'the decline will continue until we learn'. In these respects, the 'Deming way' may have more in common with the human relations than the scientific management movement.

During his time working in the USA until the end of the Second World War, Deming was largely unknown and the enthusiasm with which his ideas were embraced in Japan must have come as something of a surprise. At that time, Japanese industry was devastated and the country had to begin rebuilding from the basis of an established reputation for shoddy quality. Deming visited Japan to speak to industrialists on several occasions during the early 1950s and the Deming Prize was created as early as 1951. (Only 36 years later was the US equivalent – the Baldridge Prize – established.) During the 1950s and 1960s statistical quality control and quality management more generally became widely established throughout Japanese industry. Methods such as statistical process control, the 'Deming Wheel' and quality circles were widely adopted (Warner 1994).

The extent to which Deming can be credited with the post-war Japanese economic miracle is difficult to assess. In an interview with *The Financial Times* (30 December 1993) Juran maintained that 'If neither I nor Deming had gone to Japan in the early 1950s, the Japanese would still have established world quality leadership'. This raises the debated question of the extent to which Japanese industry was simply open to new ideas because of the post-war crisis (whereas the Americans could be complacent in their world dominance). At the turn of the 1990s, Deming himself commented that 'Americans have still not learned it, nor the Western World... Some people have said that you have to be in a crisis before you pay attention. The Japanese were in trouble. We're in worse trouble, because we don't know it'. The rapid diffusion of total quality management in Japan also raises the question of the extent to which Deming's ideas fitted easily with Japanese employment practices and organizational traditions. Teamwork, consensus decision making, employee involvement and close paternalistic relationships between employer and employee had been established in Japan in the earlier part of the twentieth century, and an emphasis on customer satisfaction rather than short-term profits, fits more easily in a country where companies are less dependent on the stock market and can take long-term growth as the primary objective.

The ideas of the mature Deming may indeed have been influenced by his own experience of Japan. His now famous 'fourteen points' were formulated only in the 1970s and are suggestive of a philosophical approach which, for many Westerners, might demand something of a revolution in thinking. The fourteen points are:

1 create constancy of purpose;
2 adopt the new philosophy;
3 cease dependence on inspection to achieve quality;
4 end the practice of awarding business on the basis of price tag;
5 improve constantly and forever the system of production and service;
6 institute training on the job;
7 institute leadership;
8 drive out fear;
9 break down barriers between departments;
10 eliminate slogans, exhortations and targets;
11a eliminate work standards (quotas) on the factory floor;
11b eliminate management by objectives;
12a remove the barriers that rob the hourly worker of his right to pride of workmanship;
12b remove the barriers that rob people in management and in engineering of their right to pride of workmanship;
13 institute a rigorous programme of education and self-improvement;
14 put everybody in the company to work to accomplish the transformation.

Only in 1980, following a documentary broadcast on US television entitled *If Japan Can, Why Can't We?* did Deming become widely known outside Japan. Deming appeared for nine minutes at the end of the ninety-minute programme and at once he was in great demand. The context was a crisis of competitiveness of US industry, which was losing market share to Japan in an increasing number of sectors. Here was the American who had advised the managements of the most successful economy in the world, eager to spread the gospel to his fellow natives from his modest office in Washington. Company presidents formed a queue to seek his advice. One of the first was Don Peterson, the Chief Executive of Ford. Peterson later said he was 'proud to be a Deming disciple' and attributed Ford's revival in the 1980s to the quality management transformation prompted by Deming. Hundreds of other major organizations, including the armed forces and government,

sought Deming's counsel and by the end of the 1980s his ideas were prominent throughout the Western World. A plethora of books on total quality were published as practitioners and academics jumped on the bandwagon. In the 1990s 'total quality', 'customer service', 'teamwork' and 'continuous improvement' have become established in the vocabularies of managers and leaders everywhere. Quality had become the panacea for all the ills of any organization.

3 Evaluation

The implications of Deming's ideas for management and organizational behaviour are debatable, as reflected in a whole series of scholarly articles in the late 1980s and early 1990s. At one extreme, TQM has been contrasted favourably with 'Taylorism' or 'Fordism' (see TAYLOR, F.W.; FORD, H.). From this perspective TQM is a revolutionary development in management which replaces the separation of mental and manual labour characteristic of Taylorism with employee involvement and development, teamwork and giving workers the tools to do the job. Deming is presented as a humanist and management–worker relations are based on a high degree of trust and reciprocity. At the other extreme, TQM has been characterized as a means of extending management control over workers (Delbridge *et al.* 1992). From this perspective, the stopwatch of the industrial engineer remains central, and additional mechanisms for ensuring that employees conform to the standards set by management are introduced. In particular, waste elimination, which is central to Deming's philosophy, entails the elimination of *human* as well as material waste, leading to the pressure to get 60 seconds of work for every minute the worker is paid. Also, variation in production processes, which must be rigorously controlled, depends on frequent or constant performance measurement and the tracing of all faults to source – often the individual workers. Hence, TQM has been related to work intensification and heightened surveillance of individual behaviour and appeals to humanism are ideological gloss.

Deming's own writings would suggest, if anything, that he would have placed himself firmly in the humanist school (he advocated 'working smarter, not harder'), though he never commented on suggestions that the application of his methods could lead to totalitarian work regimes. This should not be surprising, since Deming's audience was a practitioner one whose concerns were primarily how to achieve organizational success. In any case, like all sacred texts, those of Deming are open to selective interpretation by those who apply the ideas and a range of other social, political and economic forces come to bear on the form of management and organization which emerges in the real world. In other words, it may be possible that applications of the Deming philosophy could lead to different outcomes for management and organizational behaviour.

4 Conclusions

Deming was one of the founders of the total quality movement, which first took hold in Japan in the 1950s and was exported back to the USA and the Western World only in the 1980s. Central to the Deming philosophy is an obsession with waste elimination, continuous improvement and control over variation, and the application of the methods to achieve these objectives have important, but debated, consequences for management and organization. Deming is already a hero in the world of management and his place in the history books is assured. Exactly how his contribution to management will come to be characterized, however, remains to be seen.

BARRY WILKINSON
SCHOOL OF MANAGEMENT
UNIVERSITY OF BATH

Further reading

(References cited in the text marked *)

* Delbridge, R., Turnbull, P. and Wilkinson, B. (1992) 'Pushing back the frontiers', *New Technology, Work and Employment* 7 (2): 97–106. (A critical discussion of the effects on workers of the implementation of TQM.)

* Deming, W.E. (1960) *Sample Design in Business Research*, New York: Wiley. (An account of the application of statistical methods in business processes which can reduce waste and improve quality.)

* Deming, W.E. (1986) *Out of Crisis: Quality, Productivity and Competitive Position*, Cambridge: Cambridge University Press. (The mature Deming's most famous work on the nature and application of TQM.)

* Deming, W.E. (1993) *The New Economics for Industry, Government and Education*, Cambridge, MA: MIT. (Deming's last work, ambitiously attempting to apply his philosophy at a broad institutional level.)

* Oliver, N. and Wilkinson, B. (1992) *The Japanisation of British Industry*, Oxford: Blackwell. (Discusses the organizational and management implications of applying TQM in Japanese and other companies in the UK.)

Scherkenbach, W.H. (1991) *The Deming Route to Quality and Productivity*, London: Mercury. (A practitioner guide to the application of the Deming philosophy in business.)

* Warner, M. (1994) 'Japanese culture, western management: Taylorism and human resources in Japan', *Organization Studies* 15 (4): 509–33. (Provides a historical account of the adoption of Taylorism and, subsequently, TQM in Japan.)

See also: FORD, H.; ISHIKAWA, K.; JURAN, J.M.; OHNO, T.; TAYLOR, F.W.; TOYODA FAMILY

Related topics in the IEBM: COMMITMENT IN JAPAN; GROUPS AND TEAMS; GURU CONCEPT; HUMAN RELATIONS; HUMAN RESOURCE MANAGEMENT; JAPANIZATION; JUST-IN-TIME PHILOSOPHIES; MANAGEMENT IN JAPAN; MOTIVATION AND SATISFACTION; ORGANIZATION BEHAVIOUR; PAYMENT SYSTEMS; TOTAL QUALITY MANAGEMENT

DiMaggio, Paul (1951–) and Powell, Walter W (1951–)

1 Biographical data
2 The iron cage revisited
3 *The New Institutionalism in Organization Analysis*
4 Observation and critical evaluation

Personal background

Paul DiMaggio

- born in Philadelphia, USA in 1951
- graduated from Swarthmore College in 1971
- PhD in sociology from Harvard University, 1979
- Yale University (1979–92), School of Organization and Management and the Institution for Social and Policy Studies; director of the Yale Program on Non-Profit Organizations, 1982–7
- professor of sociology and co-director of the Center for Arts and Cultural Policy Studies at Princeton University, 1992–

Walter Powell

- born in Raleigh, North Carolina, USA in 1951
- graduated from Florida State University in 1971
- received an MA (1975) and PhD (1978) from the department of sociology, State University of New York at Stony Brook, where he was also a lecturer and assistant professor
- Yale University (1979–87), becoming professor of organization and management
- associate professor at the Sloan School, MIT, 1985
- fellow at the Center for Advanced Study in the Behavioral Sciences, 1986–7
- professor of sociology at the University of Arizona, 1991–

Major works

'The iron cage revisited: institutional isomorphism and collective rationality in organizational fields' (1983)
The New Institutionalism in Organizational Analysis (1991)

Summary

DiMaggio and Powell focus analytic attention outside the firm on the institutional context and those institutional mechanisms through which firms might be induced, coerced and regulated to adopt structures and cultures which do not necessarily enhance economic performance. There is a propensity within fields of organizations that are inter-related to possess similar patterns of structure, action and outputs. This is institutional isomorphism and occurs because organizations seek legitimacy from the state, from professional associations and from other key organizations on which they are dependent. Legitimacy is granted only if organizations conform to certain requirements. Once innovations achieve legitimacy in a field then many organizations accept their validity and adopt the innovation. These institutional processes of isomorphism unfold and take hold even in the absence of evidence that organizational performance is improved. The level of analysis is intrasocietal rather than societal. The approach leads to major revisions in orthodox organization analysis and to explanations of the diffusion and adoption of innovations.

1 Biographical data

Paul DiMaggio was born in 1951, graduated in 1971 and completed his doctorate in sociology at Harvard University in 1979. He spent from 1979 to 1992 at Yale University in the School of Organization and Management and the Program on Non-Profit Organizations, of which he was director. In 1992 he joined Princeton University as professor of sociology and co-director of the Center for Arts and Cultural Policy Studies. He is married to Carol Mason, professor of biology at the Columbia University and has two sons. He has published work on country music and its changing locus and its centre: Opry; and on popular culture, social class and the consumption of arts, the structure of audiences and the approach of Bourdieu. His publications in this field combines work on organizational analysis, social stratification, non-profit organizations and the sociology of culture.

Walter (Woody) Powell was also born in 1951 and graduated in 1971. He joined the department of sociology at the State University of New York at Stony Brook, where he completed his masters, doctorate (1978) and lectured. From 1979–87 he worked at Yale as assistant and associate professor of sociology, organization and management. In 1986–87 he was a fellow at the internally famous Center for Advanced Study in the Behavioral Sciences in California. Since 1988 he has been at the University of Arizona as professor of sociology and director of the Social and Behavioral Sciences Research Institute. His earliest publications are on the publishing industry (competition, concentration and the shift from craft forms to corporations) and then television and non-profit organizations. His current publishing includes network forms, the arms race, Schumpeter and the locus of innovation and learning in the biotechnology industry.

2 'The iron cage revisited' (1983)

This bold article, published in 1983, sets out the new institutional approach and explains how organizational fields tend to homogenize organizations. In it DiMaggio and Powell discuss the major mechanisms involved and then rework Weber's account of the iron cage (see WEBER, M.). They argue that new institutionalism locates firms of all kinds in a sociological frame of analysis with institutions at the core, and thereby criticize orthodox organizational analysis for its shallow contextualism and its pre-occupation with efficiency.

There are three major elements to their argument.

1 Organizations facing similar environmental conditions are becoming more homogeneous in their structure, culture and actions. Such similarities arise from advanced bureaucratization. Organizations are becoming similar without becoming more efficient, and this process of becoming similar is referred to as isomorphism. An pervasive cluster of processes outside organizations and inside institutions create mechanisms which constrain and enable organizations. The role of the market mechanism is slight in well-established fields. Consequently, the ritual, ceremonial and political features of organizational life overwhelm the narrow pursuit of efficiency.

2 The concept of organizational fields as a middle-level concept is crucial. Organizational fields are situations where firms and organizational units face similar environmental conditions which are created by other organizations (including key suppliers, regulatory agencies, consultancies and customers) the state and professionals. Organization fields emerge over time and they are recognized by increasing interaction and connectedness amongst the units within the field. There are common information loads and shared inter-organizational patterns of coalition and domination as well as mutual awareness of issues through trade associations. Organizational fields will be most homogeneous when certain conditions apply:

- organizations are very dependent (e.g. centralization of resource supply);

- in high uncertainty there is a tendency to copy legitimate alternatives ;

- the firms rely most on sectoral and professional associations;

- when state transactions are high there will be few visible alternative templates .

3 Isomorphism – the process of becoming similar – in organizational fields is of two main types: competitive and institutional. Competitive isomorphism has been explored in population ecology and evolu-

tionary theories, but requires supplementing by institutional isomorphism. At the birth of a new field, the market mechanism is the most influential. Once the field is established the professions, other organizations and the state become pre-eminent. Institutional isomorphism is examined through three mechanisms which shape homogenization processes within specific organization fields: coercive, mimetic and normative.

- Coercive processes can range from the imposition of templates and rules (e.g. legal requirements for audits) to the equally influential though more subtle inducement to adopt rituals of conformity in order to gain legitimacy. Coercive and regulative processes arise from the cultural expectations in the host society and from the state (central and local), and from dependence upon powerful organizations.

- Mimetic processes arise from uncertainty, the sources of which are extensive. Copying enhances legitimacy and there is a relatively small pool of variations to be selected from. Even international firms purchase new templates from a small set of consulting firms. The history of management reform is dominated by instances of isomorphic modelling. The selection process for innovations is more influenced by isomorphic tendencies than by evidence that efficiency will improve.

- Normative processes of isomorphism largely arise from the collective struggle of professionals to define the conditions and methods of their working and to control other parties. Professionals typically seek to establish areas of jurisdiction around a cognitive base which provides legitimacy (e.g. the audit) and occupational autonomy (e.g. accountancy). Of course, professionals are subject to various coercive and mimetic pressures, yet it is the growth of their networks which provide the channels down which homogenizing tendencies can travel (e.g. adoption of computer-based integration). Professions filter and socialize their personnel thereby enabling and privileging normative isomorphism.

The theory of institutional isomorphism is analytically powerful. The genesis of legitimated models and the structuring of organization fields provide an equal role for direct, coercive power and for normative power to set the rules of the game. Thus, Weber's original invocation of the iron cage as a configuration of pressures requires revision, and orthodox organizational analysis has to be radically altered.

3 *The New Institutionalism in Organization Analysis* (1991)

This edited collection draws together new institutional approaches and provides empirical illustrations and exemplars.

There is a striking combining of elements from different theoretical approaches. At the micro-level the rational actor approach is replaced by theorizing of practical action as cognitive guidance systems (March and Simon 1958). Ethnomethodology and Bourdieu's (1977) notion of habitus and structuration theory are included; a longitudinal dimension is encouraged. The empirical studies are organized around the issues of how organizational fields are constructed and how the interplay of institutional and competitive forces leads into problem of institutional change. Many of the empirical examples are drawn from the public sector (e.g. museums) and the role of the state at different levels (e.g. regulating corporate competition).

Powell and DiMaggio emphasize four themes:

1 The new institutionalism locates the firm in a wide array of inter-organizational networks and national propensities and the symbolic role of the formal structure is highlighted. Organizational fields are typified by slow alteration: inertia is explained by the imperative of maintaining legitimacy. Cognitions are primarily explored through routines, scripts, classifications and schemas. The firm's strategic agenda is disciplining the members rather than the policy relevance. Conflicts and struggles are located more in the organizational field than inside the organization.

2 Institutions are theorized as stable templates (designs) for sequences of activity which are recursively reproduced. The templates and their discourse provide a grammar of strategic action rooted in the past. For example, American football provides a template of activity sequences and discourse which reproduces national predispositions and provides taken-for-grated solutions to organizational problems (Clark 1987). It is these taken-for-granted elements of action, especially the classification schemes and the situated, practical consciousness – knowledge without concepts – which is embodied in the reproduction of social and organizational structures. The basic insight is that within organizations its members continuously utilize and improvise on generative rules which are pre-existing and have been internalized through shared typifications of past experience. There is regulated improvisation on the templates.

3 The rejection of the orthodox conceptualization of the environment–organization relationship in organizational analysis is central. The isolated firm is refocalized into the societal institutions where the state is a major source of rules and legitimacy. Market processes are shown to be more like networks of rules with a strong institutional signature. The state often plays a key role in the position of sectors as part of national priorities (e.g. Japan). There is a society-wide system of interorganizational networks with cultures, roles and rules which are nationally specific. Organizational structures are externally authored, imposed, imprinted and induced. This embedding of organizations affects the content and form of innovations imported from outside. So, American college males in the 1870s imported association football and rugby union and the emergent outcome became American football (Clark 1987). Consequently, the importation by American organizations of Japanese innovations might also be anticipated to lead to hybrid and novel outcomes.

4 Issues are listed for attention and are addressed in current work:

- institutional change and power
- explaining the origins, reproduction and disappearance of institutionalized forms
- the role of interorganizational networks in innovation
- economic sociology: the market as a social-cultural system in reconstruction
- the linkages from social science analysis into policy
- patterns of interorganizational competition, influence and co-ordination
- the autonomy of levels and the role of the central state.

Economic sociology becomes a major line of development.

4 Observation and critical evaluation

DiMaggio and Powell are giving impetus and direction to the re-focalizing of the firm into its context (Scott 1995) and are making a significant examination of economic sociology. Their approach is also transforming thinking about the diffusion and adoption of innovations. In evaluating their approach six points should be emphasized. First, it is necessary to situate institutions and organizations fields within multi-level frameworks which extend through the societal level into the world economy (Scott 1995). Each level possesses important elements of autonomy. Second, more linking should be made with the approaches to national systems of innovation, especially to the claims that there is competition between contexts. This requires more historical and comparative research. For example, the distinctive features of the American market – its size, composition, speed of saturation – have been neglected. Third, most sectors, and hence organization fields, are experiencing market competition arising from international trade and there are many examples of de-institutionalization. These range from core sectors such as automobiles to the professions (e.g. in accounting). The life-course of fields contains several key moments of transition (Oliver 1992). Studies of the dynamics and politics reveal emergent potentials arising from contradictions, competition and conflicts. There is an important bridge to be crossed between these developments and studies of the life course of major sectors, especially with respect to the role of design capabilities. Fourth, at the organizational level there are strategic responses of varying kinds to institutional processes of isomorphism (Oliver 1991). Differentiated organizations develop specialized, protective (cosmetic) capacities for dealing with the context. Intra-organizational dynamics shape the zones of manoeuvre available to organizations within particular fields. Fifth, the new institutionalism is certainly social constructionist, yet there is a revival of interest in causal processes which is becoming known as the realist turn. The implications of this development need to be accommodated. Will the realist turn in organizational analysis influence further developments? Sixth, DiMaggio and Powell have loosened the earlier rejection of efficiency at the level of firm. A more significant attempt should be made to develop their approach to the study of organizational performance.

The approach of DiMaggio and Powell is developing and the implications for organizational analysis are still unfolding.

PETER CLARK
UNIVERSITY OF BIRMINGHAM

Further reading

(References cited in text marked *)

Abrahamson, E. and Fombrum, C. J. (1992) 'Forging the iron cage: interorganizational networks and the production of macro-culture', *Journal of Management Studies* 29: 175–194. (How organizational fields participate in shaping the cultural context they inhabit.)

* Bourdieu, P. (1977) *Outline of a Theory of Practice*, Cambridge: Cambridge University Press. (A complex and essential explanation of habitus.)

* Clark, P.A. (1987) *Anglo-American Innovation*, Berlin: de Gruyter. (How the cluster of organization fields in a nation shapes the constitution and transfer of innovations.)

* DiMaggio, P. J. and Powell, W.W. (1983) 'The iron cage revisited: institutional isomorphism and collective rationality in organization fields', *American Sociological Review* 48: 147–160. (The breakthrough article.)

Fligstein, N. (1996) 'Markets as politics: a political-cultural approach to market institutions', *American Sociological Review* 61: 656–673. (A sociological approach to markets.)

* March, J. G. and Simon, H.A. (1958) *Organizations*, New York: Wiley.

* Oliver, C. (1991) 'Strategic responses to institutional processes', *Academy of Management Review* 16: 145–179. (Typology of strategic responses.)

* Oliver, C. (1992) 'The antecedents of deinstitutionalization', *Organization Studies* 13/14: 653–588. (Presents a 'four moments' framework for analyzing organization fields, especially moments of de-institutionalization.)

* Powell, W.W. and DiMaggio, P.J. (1991) *The New Institutionalism in Organizational Analysis*, Chicago: University of Chicago Press. (Defines the main tenets, scope and achievements of institutional approaches.)

Powell, W.W. Koput, K. W. and Smith-Doerr, L. (1996), 'Interorganizational collaboration and the locus of innovation: networks of learning in biotechnology', *Administrative Science Quarterly* 41: 116–145. (Organization fields in biotechnology as interfirm networks of learning and of the locus of innovation.)

* Scott, W.R. (1995) *Institutions and Organisations*, London: Sage. (A clear statement of the new institutionalization and constructive account of strengths and research issues.)

See also: HANNAN, M. AND FREEMAN, J.; MARCH, J.G. AND CYERT, R.M.; SIMON, H.A.; WEBER, M.

Related topics in the IEBM: BUSINESS ECONOMICS; INSTITUTIONAL ECONOMICS; INTER-ORGANIZATIONAL RELATIONS; MARKETS; ORGANIZATION BEHAVIOUR; ORGANIZATION BEHAVIOUR, HISTORY OF; ORGANIZATION STRUCTURE; ORGANIZATION TYPES

Downs, Anthony (1930–)

Personal background

- graduated from Carleton College (Minnesota), BA in political theory and international relations, *summa cum laude*, 1952
- graduated from Stanford University, MA and PhD in economics, 1956
- employed by Real Estate Research Corporation, 1959–77 including period as chairman for four years
- acted as consultant to many large corporations including IBM, Standard Oil of Indiana, Shell Oil Corporation and J.C. Penney
- on faculty of University of Chicago, economic and political science departments, 1959–62
- economic consultant at Rand Corporation, Santa Monica, 1963–65
- appointed by President Johnson to National Commission on Urban Problems, 1967
- served as consultant to Department of Housing and Urban Development, 1967–89
- currently senior fellow, Brookings Institute, which he joined in June 1977
- continues on boards of directors of eight organizations, many connected with real estate and urban development
- has given over 1000 speeches to hundreds of organizations and continues as a speaker on real estate economics, housing and urban policies
- has developed ideas at the interface between public and private policies

Major works

An Economic Theory of Democracy (1957)
Inside Bureacracy (1967)
'Contrasting strategies for the economic development of metropolitan areas in the United States and Western Europe' (1993)

Summary

Anthony Downs is not usually seen as a major author in the field of management yet his work is invaluable in understanding the increasingly important relationship between the private and public sectors. He has published extensively, with over 400 publications to his name, in the areas of the economic theory of democracy, the economic theory of bureaucracy, and on public and urban affairs. It is for his book *Inside Bureaucracy,* published in 1967, that he remains best known in the management field. This book analyses in considerable depth the internal processes and life cycle of bureaucracies and he proposes 'Downs' law of increasing conservatism'. This law states that bureaucracies become more rigid and less able to change as they get older. The thinking underlying this work concerns the boundary between political, bureaucratic and market mechanisms for the allocation of resources and the coordination of economies. This theme runs through Downs' work and is the main reason that it retains a relevance to the broader problems of business and management when issues of regulation and of managing within highly regulated environments arise.

1 Biographical data

Downs has not followed a conventional university academic career. In 1959, soon after his university education, for 18 years he became a member and then chairman of the Real Estate Corporation, a nationwide consulting firm advising private and public decision-makers on real estate investment, housing policies, and urban affairs. He then joined the Brookings Institution in Washington DC in 1977 where he is a senior fellow. Brookings is a private, non-profit research organization specializing in public policy studies.

Downs read political theory and international relations at Carleton College and then went to Stanford to take a PhD in economics. This combination of political theory and economics shines through his earlier writings on the economic theories of democracy and bureaucracy. For three years he served on the faculty of the economic and political science departments at the University of Chicago, initially intermeshing this position with work at the Real Estate Corporation.

The practical bent which this career pattern indicates also shows in the many consultancies held, both in the private and public sectors. Of particular relevance to writing on urban affairs was his membership of the Department of Housing and Urban Development. In 1967 President Johnson appointed Downs to the National Commission on Urban Problems and in 1989 he was appointed to the Advisory Commission on Regulatory Barriers to Affordable Housing. He also maintains a number of directorships and frequently speaks to audiences on real estate economics, housing and urban policies

2 The economics of democracy

In his first book, *An Economic Theory of Democracy* (1957), Downs made a pioneering contribution to the theory of collective choice. Since the 1950s, the question of how public preferences could accurately be reflected in government policies had exercised the minds of economists. The theory of collective choice up to that time had rested, to a high degree, upon the notion that public officials could be relied upon correctly to assess public preferences and that as a matter of duty they would honestly implement policies to fulfil those preferences. Instead of this rather altruistic view of public officials, Downs viewed politicians as utility pursuers where their utility functions contain a considerable element of

calculative self interest and where the chances of re-election and pursuit of their own ideologies play an important part. In order to pursue their self-interest politicians, therefore, have to compete for votes.

The development of this kind of hard-headed economic model was aimed at trying to improve the understanding of public choice and its implementation into governments' policies. These theoretical developments also helped to understand collective choice as an alternative to a market mechanism. They introduced the notion of discretion into the process in the same way that firms have discretion in their market environments. This kind of thinking lays the ground for a view of public bureaucracies as businesses selling products to customers.

The model requires three principle actors: the voter with a utility function, the self-interested politician trying attract votes and making policies, and the self-interested bureaucrat who implements policies. Voters are assumed to have preferences periodically expressed as votes, which politicians try to capture; politicians then make decisions with an eye to gaining future votes. For politicians, votes play a similar role to money for the entrepreneur in the theory of the firm. The difference is that the utility function of voters is complex and that in order to implement policies politicians have to rely upon bureaucrats. In going from voters' preferences to implementation there is, therefore, considerable scope for distortions to occur. It is the process by which this distortion occurs, and its consequences, that provide the central questions for the economic theory of democracy.

The effect of a two-party political system in this model is for politicians to focus on the 'median voter' with a consequent two sources of distortion: the first, in the relationship between the voter and politician, the second in the relationship between politician and bureaucrat. The first distortion leads to a fiscal illusion. Downs (1960) sees this illusion as generally going in the direction of the allocated public expenditure budget being too small because the benefits of public expenditure are diffuse and not appropriable to individuals, whereas the tax burden has a direct impact upon voters (Heald 1983: 110–111).

Downs' conclusion on public expenditure, however, is at variance with the conclusion that became more fashionable in the 1980s under Reagan and Thatcher type economics. According to theorists such as Buchanan and Tullock (1962), who gained ascendancy at that time, the distortions between voter and politician lead to an overestimate of public expenditure because politicians are rewarded by paying off interest groups who demand special favours. Because of the difficulty of measuring costs and benefits there is no way of systematically testing the truth of the two positions

3 The economics of bureaucracy

As explained above, application of economic rationality to the analysis of political behaviour also requires an understanding of how bureaucracy works. Downs' best-known work, *Inside Bureaucracy* (1967a), asks what a bureaucracy looks like if we assume that officials are motivated by self-interest. He, and others working in the same genre, therefore departs from Weber's (1968) notion of how bureaucrats work (see WEBER, M.). Weber emphasizes bureaucracy as a rational form of organization in the sense that it is an efficient means of reaching given ends; his theory emphasizes obedience to impersonal legal authority, lack of appropriation of positions, appointment by technical competence, and a whole series of measures which are designed to attenuate the effects of self-interest. In contrast, the economic theory of bureaucracy is concerned with deviations that the assumption of the self-interested official would bring to Weber's ideal type. The result is a book which is a series of propositions, presented as, laws but which are essentially untestable, and which can appear as truisms, unless we remember that the wider purpose is to understand how the economic theory of bureaucracy fits in with the economic theory of democracy.

A lead up to the economic theory of bureaucracy can be seen in the paper 'A theory of large managerial firms' (Monsen and Downs 1965). The model here is quite similar to that of the economic theory of democracy with, in large corporations, external shareholders replacing voters, top managers replacing politicians, and middle managers replacing bureaucrats. At the level of the firm the model rejects the profit maximization assumption of classical economics which, Downs states, is only of significance in small firms. The main hypotheses in the theory of large managerial firms are: (1) owners desire firms to be managed to provide a steady income and appreciation of market value; (2) managers act so as to manage their lifetime income; (3) bureaucratic structures are biased towards the desires of top management when facing shareholders; (4) middle and lower management only partially carry out the orders of top management. Hence, in (3) and (4) we see similar contradictory biases referred to under the economics of democracy. Shareholders (voters) utilities are not faithfully pursued by the directors (the politicians) they vote into office because the directors (politicians) have their own utilities which stress continuity of office, while at the same time middle and lower management (bureaucrats) have their own utilities which tend to stress persistence of existing routines. In this sense, organization could be seen less as a hierarchy but more as a three-cornered tussle between these gropus, a point that is never really brought out, although Cyert and March's (1963) *Behavioral Theory of the Firm*, with its emphasis upon the firm as a coalition, had been published (see MARCH, J.G. AND CYERT, R.M.).

Inside Bureaucracy examines these questions of organizational distortion more closely for their implications for the internal operation of bureaus. The book introduces a more dynamic aspect by discussing the life cycle of bureaus and then deriving a series of 16 'laws'. Perhaps the most central of these laws is Downs' 'law of increasing conservatism' ,which states that 'all organizations tend to become more conservative as they become older, unless they experience periods of very rapid growth or internal turnover'. This tendency can be explained in terms of the persistence of routines which are developed to increase efficiency but which also become reasons for maintaining office holders in their positions. However, the motivation to expand can also provide a countervailing force towards change and which is likely to be induced by a performance gap. Top officials in a bureau are particularly likely to benefit from a growth in size since they can gain an increased budget, power, prestige and salary.

The self-interest axiom has the danger of becoming a tautology but Downs emphasizes that self-interest is not the same as utility maximization (1967a: 83) and tries to explain the origin of interests in terms of a hierarchy of goals covering goals such as money, power, prestige and the like. Following from this Downs identifies a number of specific types of official behaviour, such as the climber, the conserver, the advocate, the zealot, and the statesman.

The way in which bureaus introduce distortions in communication is also analysed, as is how these may be overcome by several devices. Redundancy of information sources, while adding cost, allow more people to be informed about a subject; this can be achieved by the use of external sources or by internal duplication. Recipients of information also need to be aware of possible biases and biases can be reduced by using methods of precise coding, as in quantitative statements, although the dangers of trying to impose false accuracy on complex information is also recognized.

Inside Bureaucracy also outlines the processes of decision making and notes the inherent asymmetry of search due to problems of goal divergence, economies of delegation, individual biases and the impact of time pressures. As part of the process of reducing search costs, budgets tend to continue from one year to the next at more or less the same level unless there is a marked performance gap in a bureau.

Inside Bureaucracy provides a series of valuable insights into the operation of internal organizations. Starting from a background of economics Downs tends to overplay the notion of 'distortion' since it is difficult to know which way distortion will go, but his work

bears comparison with contemporaneous sociological work on the 'dysfunctions' of formal organization (Blau and Scott 1963). Whereas Downs took Weber's ideal type of bureaucracy and examined its distortions, the contemporaneous work of the Aston Group set about empirically measuring the dimensions of bureaucratic structure but without concerning themselves with internal distortions or dysfunctions (see ASTON GROUP). This was indeed an era of growth of theorizing about bureaucracy and organizations in general and Downs can be said to have made a significant contribution through *Inside Bureaucracy*.

4 Urban affairs

Downs' early work in the broad area of urban affairs is surveyed in *Urban Problems and Prospects* (1976). One contribution of relevance to management is his paper 'A realistic look at the final payoffs from urban data systems' (1967b) which provides a warning not to let automated data systems take over from administrators in city governments. The other managerially relevant paper 'Competition and community schools' (1970) is quite prophetic in view of its time of publication. Here one finds a programme for introducing competition, means of evaluating outputs, allocating discretion, and freedom of consumer choice in public schools. Many of these policies are now becoming conventional wisdom in schools and leading an associated managerial revolution.

Downs' book *Stuck in Traffic: Coping With Peak-Hour Traffic Congestion* (1992) also indicates his concern with the wider practical problems of urban society by advocating a number of measures which could be used to attenuate the considerable problems that modern societies experience in controlling the motor car. He does not dogmatically advocate marketer type road pricing solutions but favours mixed solutions combining market and regulatory mechanisms. Nevertheless, he is not optimistic about the efficacy of such measures and ends suggesting that drivers learn to enjoy congestion by getting an air conditioned car equipped with all the home comforts.

5 Conclusions

In the sense that Downs set out to challenge neo-classical assumptions about the profit motive in firms he could be said to have taken a radical stance in his early work. Such theories no longer appear as particularly radical but there does remain, however, a paradox in the economic theories of politics and bureaucracy as Heald (1983: 111) points out. When facing customers or voters officials and bureaucrats are assumed to behave as rational economic people and to pursue self-interest. When facing in the other direction, internally to lower level officials, they are subject to distortions of information and hence cannot behave rationally. This paradox seems to underlie the problem that this kind of theorizing has in understanding which direction bureaucracies will go. For instance, in the economic theory of democracy, will bureaucratic distortions inflate or deflate the budget?

Scholars such as Buchanan and Tullock (IEA 1979) have been used in the UK to bolster arguments for the reduction of public spending during the privatization era of the 1980s and early 1990s. Downs appears as less dogmatic and more pragmatic in favouring more mixed solutions to the question of the boundary between public and private sectors. He seems to appreciate the real problems of ever being able to scientifically test hypotheses that try to choose between politics, bureaucracies and markets. Even if, however, his work may lack the apparent certainties of a definitive theory, *Inside Bureaucracy* and the economic theory of democracy still provides a rich vein of ideas of relevance to managerial issues at the border of the private and public sectors.

RICHARD BUTLER
UNIVERSITY OF BRADFORD

Further reading

(References cited in the text marked *)

* Blau, P. M. and Scott, W. R. (1963) *Formal Organizations: A Comparative Approach*, London: Routledge & Kegan Paul. (A source book on organizational theory and the dysfunctions of organizations.)

* Buchanan, J. M. and Tullock, G. (1962) *The Calculus of Consent,* Ann Arbor: University of Michigan Press. (A seminal work on the failures of government and of making rational collective choices.)

* Cyert, R. and March, J. G. (1963) *A Behavioral Theory of the Firm*, Englewood Cliffs: Prentice-Hall. (A classic work which provides both complementary and alternative perspectives on the behaviour of firms.)

* Downs, A. (1957) *An Economic Theory of Democracy*, New York: Harper and Row. (A pioneering contribution to the economic theory of democracy describing politicians as utility maxmizers where the utility function includes both vote catching, ideology and social welfare.)

* Downs, A. (1960) 'Why the government budget is too small in a democracy', *World Politics* 12, 4: 541–563.

* Monsen Jr., R. J. and Downs, A. (1965) 'A theory of large managerial firms', *Journal of Political Economy*, LXXIII, 3: 221-236. (Outlines the conflict between the desire of owners or large firms to provide a steady income and appreciation of share value, and the desire of managers to maximize lifetime earnings.)

* Downs, A. (1967a) *Inside Bureaucracy* (a RAND Corporation research study), Boston: Little Brown and Company. (Downs' best-known work from a managerial perspective. Outlines a series of propositions about how bureaus and their officials actually work rather than how the theory of bureaucracy suggests they should behave.)

* Downs, A. (1967b) 'A realistic look at the final payoffs from urban data systems', *Public Administration Review*, XXVII, 3: 204-210.

* Downs, A. (1970) 'Competition and community schools', in H.M. Levin (ed.) *Community Control of Schools,* Washington, DC: The Brooking Institute: 219–249.

* Downs, A. (1976) *Urban Problems and Prospects*, second edition, Chicago: Rand McNally. (Brings together thirteen papers on Downs' work in connection with urban problems, including Downs (1967a) and (1970) above.)

* Downs, A. (1992) *Stuck in Traffic: Coping With Peak-Hour Traffic Congestion*, Washington, DC: The Brookings Institution, and Cambridge, Mass.: The Lincoln Institute of Land Policy. (Sees car commuters as not paying true social costs of their behaviour thereby encouraging excessive spread of metropolitan areas with consequent increases in energy consumption and pollution.)

Downs, A. (1993) 'Contrasting strategies for the economic development of metropolitan areas in the United States and Western Europe', in A.A. Summers, P.C. Cheshire and L. Senn (eds) *Urban Change in the United States and Western Europe: Comparative Analysis and Policy'*, Washington D. C.: The Urban Institute Press: 15-54. (A comparison of American and European urban development strategies.)

* Heald, D. (1983) *Public Expenditure: Its Defence and Reform*, Oxford: Basil Blackwell. (Provides a balanced discussion about public spending and political versus market.)

* IEA (1979) *The Taming of Government*, London: The Institute of Economic Affairs. (A number of prominent pro-market scholars – including Tullock – discuss the inadequacies of public spending and bureaucracies.)

* Pugh, D.S. and Hickson, D.J. (eds) (1978) *Organizational Structure in its Context: The Aston Programme I,* Farnborough, Hants.: Saxon House. (A collection of the Aston papers going back to their 1963 paper outlining the dimensions of bureaucracy through to the empirical papers.)

* Weber, M. (1968) *Economy and Society: An Outline of Interpretive Sociology*, G. Roth and G. Wittick (eds) New York: Bedminster Press. (The classic work defining the main characteristics of bureaucracy and the associated legal form of authority, and its place in history. See especially pp. 217–227.)

See also: ASTON GROUP; MARCH, J.G. AND CYERT, R.M.; SIMON, H.A.; WEBER, M.

Related topics in the IEBM: BUSINESS ECONOMICS; MARKETS AND PUBLIC POLICY; NEO-CLASSICAL ECONOMICS; ORGANIZATION BEHAVIOUR; ORGANIZATION STRUCTURE; PUBLIC SECTOR ORGANIZATIONS

Drucker, Peter F. (1909–)

Personal background

- born in Vienna, 13 May 1909
- settled permanently in the USA in 1937, working as an economist and consultant
- professor of philosophy and politics, Bennington College, Vermont 1942
- professor of management, New York University, 1952
- published *Management: Tasks, Responsibilities, Practices*, 1974
- published his first novel, *The Last of All Possible Worlds*, 1982

Major works

The End of Economic Man (1936)
The Future of Industrial Man (1942)
The Concept of the Corporation (1946)
The Practice of Management (1954)
Managing for Results (1964)
The Effective Executive (1967)
People and Performance (1973)
Management: Tasks, Responsibilities, Practices (1974)
The Unseen Revolution (1976)
Adventures of a Bystander (1979)
Towards the Next Economics (1981)
Innovation and Entrepreneurship (1985)
The Frontiers of Management (1987)

Summary

Peter Drucker is one of the most prominent writers and thinkers on management this century. His works span a wide range of political and economic issues, but it is his writings on management that have made him famous. He coined the term 'management by objectives' and is considered largely responsible for changing attitudes away from scientific management towards a more philosophical approach in which management can be reduced to a series of generic tasks and in which goals are of greater importance than functions.

1 Introduction

Drucker can perhaps best be described as emphasizing a humanistic approach to management. He sees business enterprises as playing a crucial role in modern society and places the manager at the heart of the enterprise in a role which emphasizes both dynamism and control. Managers guide and direct organizations in order to achieve economic performance, and hence social good. A far-sighted thinker and philosopher, Drucker is also a superb writer and communicator, owing much of his success to his fluent writing style and his ability to capture the imagination of his audience. He has been criticized for promoting of an overgeneralized view of management, particularly the concept of the 'transferable manager', but his overall approach to the subject of management has won almost universal acceptance.

2 Biographical data

Peter Ferdinand Drucker was born in Vienna in 1909. His father, Adolph Drucker, was a leading Viennese lawyer and prominent Austrian liberal, a co-founder of Salzburg Music Festival who emigrated to the USA in 1938 after the *Anschluss* (the annexation of Austria by Nazi Germany). In his autobiography, *Adventures of a Bystander* (1979), Drucker recalls vividly growing up in Vienna during the First World War and the familial and cultural influences which helped shape his thinking in later life.

In the 1930s Drucker worked as a journalist and an economist in Europe before making his permanent base in the USA in 1937. In 1942 he took up an academic post at Bennington College, Vermont, moving to New York University ten years later to become professor of management. Teaching, writing and consulting for some of the USA's leading companies have occupied his time ever since.

Drucker is a prolific writer, and through his writing is possible to see how his ideas have developed and changed over time. In 1936, still not yet 30 years old, he published his first book, *The End of Economic Man*, a study of the economic origins of fascism. Coherent and beautifully written, it remains one of the best attempts at understanding the success of fascism and how it was able to take root in Europe. His second book, *The Future of Industrial Man* (1942), published while the Second World War was at its height, looked forward to the post-war world and anticipated with considerable accuracy the nature of that world. Already by this time, however, he was moving away from studies of politics and society towards more specific studies of organizations. In this third book, *The Concept of the Corporation* (1946), he identified the organizational type that he believed would dominate the future of society, politics and economics.

From here, it became necessary to understand how corporations function and what makes the difference between success and failure. Drucker's belief was that the mainspring of the corporation was the manager, and he proceeded to focus on the nature of managerial work. Over the next twenty years he produced five books which remain among the most influential ever written on this subject, beginning with *The Practice of Management* in 1954 and ending with *Management: Tasks, Responsibilities, Practices* in 1974. It is the latter book which sums up his philosophy to the fullest, defining the nature of the corporation and the manager, defining the parameters of managerial work and goals, and defining the impacts of the corporation on its social environment.

At around this time, however, the focus of Drucker's own work began to broaden once more. The three most influential of his later books, *Towards the Next Economics* (1981), *Innovation and Entrepreneurship* (1985) and *The Frontiers of Management* (1987) continue to look at the task and role of the manager but in an increasingly broad perspective, taking into account social, political, macroeconomic and – increasingly – technological change. His later books argue that managers should learn not only how to understand their own role but also how to adapt that role in order to become more effective in their work.

3 Main contribution

Before the Second World War, management in the USA was dominated by the principles laid down by Taylor and Ford who viewed management as a science. Drucker, coming from a liberal humanist background, chose instead to see management as a philosophy. Instead of analysing each task in detail, he looked for general principles of management which underlie all managerial tasks. By shifting the emphasis of these tasks to output rather than throughput, he created the concept of management by objectives. Instead of simply managing processes, managers should set goals and then work towards them.

Tasks

The key element in the business enterprise is the manager, who plays a central role in pulling disparate resources together and creating products. Although he sometimes refers to managers as 'the basic human resource of the enterprise' (Drucker 1973: 3), it is clear that management is not so much a resource as a catalyst: 'The manager is the dynamic, life-giving element in every business. Without his leadership, the "resources of production" remain resources and never become production' (Drucker 1954: 3). He even foresaw a time when workers would become redundant, having been replaced by automation, but managers would remain, with the effect that all employment would be managerial; we would then have progressed from a society of labour to a society of management (Drucker 1973).

As well as harnessing resources and creating production, the manager is also responsible for guidance and control. In Drucker's view, this role is almost entirely pro-active: 'Economic forces set limits to what a manager can do. They create opportunities for management's action. But they do not by themselves dictate what a business is or what it does' (Drucker 1973: 88). He then goes further, assigning to managers the primary role for not only managing enterprise but creating markets:

> There is only one valid definition of business purpose: *to create a customer*. Markets are not created by God, nature or economic forces, but by the people who manage a business. The want a business satisfies may have been felt by customers … but it remained a potential want until business people converted it into effective action. Only then are there customers and a market.
>
> (Drucker 1973: 89)

On managers, therefore, fall the tasks of harnessing labour and resources to create production and of developing markets into which these products can be sold. The managerial dimension is what gives the enterprise its strengths; managers must add value, striving to create something that is greater than the sum of the resources put in. Here Drucker departs from scientific management, which stressed the use of resources in the most *efficient* manner. Drucker instead stresses a creative element in which managers use resources in the most *effective* manner in order to achieve the goals of the enterprise.

This combination of catalyst and proactive control comes very close to a direct identification of the enterprise with its managers. Drucker does not go so far as to say that the managers *are* the enterprise, but he repeatedly stresses their paramount role: 'The enterprise can decide, act and behave only as its managers do – by itself the enterprise has no effective existence' (Drucker 1954: 7).

Responsibilities

In Drucker's view, all institutions exist in order to achieve some specific aim; for business enterprises, that aim is economic performance (Drucker 1974). Within that enterprise, the manager has three responsibilities: (1) to achieve economic performance; (2) to make work productive so that performance can be achieved more easily; and (3) to manage the social impacts which the enterprise as an organization has on its environment.

Although a leadership role is obviously indicated, Drucker stops short of defining the task of management as leadership. He prefers instead to use the term 'responsibility'; managers are 'responsible' for contribution, both their own and those of their employees. As such, management is a function, not a power, and he urges managers to avoid the perception that they are at the top and the workers are below them. His view is rather of managers as the pivot of the organization around which all else – labour, resources, markets, environment – revolves.

An important dimension in all of Drucker's work is the need for managers to consider the social impacts which they and their organizations have on their environment. Managers must be more than technocrats; they need to recognize the social dimension to their work (Drucker 1974). The larger and more powerful the business becomes, the greater the impact and hence the greater the need to consider the social dimension: 'The demand for social responsibility is, in large measure, the price of success' (Drucker 1973: 289). As Tarrant (1976) comments:

> Drucker never loses sight of the public good that rests within the organization in general and the corporation in particular. Corporations must be managed, not only according to a set of pragmatic rules, but within a philosophical framework that conforms to the role of the organization in the industrial society.
>
> (Tarrant 1976: 84)

In Drucker's philosophy, the ultimate purpose of the enterprise is to create social benefit. The organization serves to transform human strength into production, and 'personal strengths make social benefits' (Drucker 1974: 810). This belief lies at the core of Drucker's entire philosophy of management.

Practices

From this background, Drucker (1973) sets out to define practices and how managers can become more effective. He begins by listing the key dimensions of management:

- as a craft and tool for achievement
- as an intellectual discipline in its own right
- as people working, alone and together
- as society's organ for the performance of vital tasks
- as an integrating, synthesizing function in a complex and changing world.

He insists that managers must be involved in their work, and speaks often of the 'thrill' of management. Involvement, however, does not mean there is any lack of discipline or rigour. In *The Effective Executive* (1967), Drucker maintains that effectiveness consists of a set of practices, which can be learned. His definition of effectiveness is founded on five principles:

1 effective executives know where their time goes
2 they focus on results, not work
3 they build on strengths, not weaknesses
4 they concentrate on areas where superior performance will produce outstanding results
5 they make effective decisions, taking the right steps in the right sequence.

Following on from his assertion that the ultimate function of the manager is to create a customer, Drucker asserts that the two basic functions of management are innovation and marketing. He devotes relatively little attention to marketing, but the need to understand and manage innovation is a constant theme running through most of his later books. He strongly criticizes companies that believe that 'innovation is inspiration and entrepreneurship is good luck' (Drucker 1985: ix) and argues that innovation is a discipline that can be learned. Again, he believes that innovation is primarily a *management* function, and stresses that managers should rely on technology, not the other way around: one of his most often-quoted statements, 'the computer is a moron', refers to the need to use technology as a tool for innovation, not as a substitute for it.

4 Evaluation

Drucker is not without his critics, and the paradigm he has created does have its flaws. Tarrant (1976) notes an excessive emphasis on economic performance and meeting the bottom line, a criticism which could be seen as unjustified in light of Drucker's constant stress on the need for social responsibility. At the same time, the latter idea never quite seems to meld with the rest of his work. Chapters on the need for social responsibility often sit uncomfortably apart from the rest of the books in which they appear. For someone from Drucker's background, the need for social responsibility is apparent; to the generations of managers in the post-war USA, there is no obvious link.

One outgrowth of Drucker's theories has been the concept of the transferable manager. By positing management as a set of fundamental practices, he may have unwittingly encouraged the belief that any trained manager can manage any business, regardless of its nature and function. Drucker himself has never believed this and has argued that managers must know the business they are in (Tarrant 1976), but the perception that management skills are generic and effortlessly transferable remains strong.

Against these objections, however, there remains the fact that Drucker has done more than probably any other individual to define the nature of management in the period after the Second World War. It is commonly said that before this time managers did not know they were managers; Drucker showed them that they were. Drucker's philosophy of management has pervaded management thinking at all levels, from the highest reaches of business academia to the lowest levels of even small companies. Management by objectives remains a commonly-used concept, even if it now sometimes goes by other names.

5 Conclusions

The following samples from Drucker's writing are among those collected by Tarrant (1976) and included in an appendix entitled 'The Sayings of Chairman Peter'. They reflect not only the general tenor of Peter Drucker's philosophy of management, but also the inimitable style with which he expressed that philosophy:

> Most sales training is totally unjustified. At best it makes an incompetent salesman out of a moron.
>
> If you have too many problems, maybe you should go out of business. There is no law that says a company has to last forever.
>
> Management by objectives works if you know the objective. Ninety per cent of the time you don't.
>
> We subordinate economics to politics; but we examine moral and political issues in economic terms.
>
> We must stop talking of profit as a reward. It is a cost. There are no rewards; only the costs of yesterday and tomorrow.
> (Tarrant 1976: 255–60)
> MORGEN WITZEL
> LONDON BUSINESS SCHOOL

Further reading

(References cited in the text marked *)

* Drucker, P.F. (1946) *The Concept of the Corporation*, London: John Day. (An analysis of the corporation as an organization from a social and political standpoint, using General Motors as a principal example; useful for showing the development of Drucker's thought.)
* Drucker, P.F. (1954) *The Practice of Management*, London: Heinemann. (Drucker's first, influential work on management, which introduces the concept of management by objectives.)
Drucker, P.F. (1964) *Managing for Results: Economic Tasks and Risk-taking Decisions*, Oxford: Heinemann. (Revisits many of the themes in *The Practice of Management*, arguing that change makes new approaches to management an imperative.)
* Drucker, P.F. (1965) *The Future of Industrial Man*, London: New Executive Library. (Reprint of Drucker's second book, originally published in 1942, which looked forward to the future of the capitalist world in the post-Second World War era.)
* Drucker, P.F. (1967) *The Effective Executive*, London: Heinemann. (One of Drucker's most important books on management which sets out to describe the nature and sources of managerial effectiveness.)
* Drucker, P.F. (1969) *The End of Economic Man: The Origins of Totalitarianism*, 2nd edn, New York: Harper & Row. (Reprint of Drucker's first book, first published in 1936, which sets forth his views on the economic origins of fascism.)
* Drucker, P.F. (1973) *People and Performance: The Best of Peter Drucker on Management*, London: Heinemann. (A series of articles and essays, some previously published. There is a particular focus on the human element in management.)
* Drucker, P.F. (1974) *Management: Tasks, Responsibilities, Practices*, London: Heinemann. (Perhaps Drucker's best-known book, this is a comprehensive distillation of Drucker's views on the practice of management.)
Drucker, P.F. (1976) *The Unseen Revolution: How Pension Fund Socialism Came to America*, London: Heinemann. (The book that launched the now-familiar argument that pension funds are in the process of acquiring greater and greater control over capital in western countries.)
* Drucker, P.F. (1979) *Adventures of a Bystander*, London: Heinemann. (Autobiography, essential reading for those interested in knowing more about the man and the context in which he formulated his ideas.)
* Drucker, P.F. (1981) *Towards the Next Economics, and Other Essays*, London: Heinemann. (A collection of essays, many of which move away from purely managerial issues and focus once more on broader economic issues.)
Drucker, P.F. (1982) *The Last of All Possible Worlds*, London: Heinemann. (Drucker's first novel, set in Europe in 1906; strongly reflective of the author's own background.)
* Drucker, P.F. (1985) *Innovation and Entrepreneurship: Practices and Principles*, Oxford: Butterworth Heinemann. (This book attempts to define the fundamental principles of innovation and entrepreneurship and provide definitions of each.)

* Drucker, P.F. (1987) *The Frontiers of Management*, Oxford: Butterworth Heinemann. (A collection of essays which examines the challenges of the future which face business people today.)

  Drucker, P.F. (1993) *Post-Capitalist Society*, Oxford: Butterworth Heinemann. (A return to social and political analysis, looking at themes such as the knowledge society, beyond the nation-state and the organization as society.)

* Tarrant, J.J. (1976) *Drucker: The Man Who Invented Corporate Society*, London: Barrie & Jenkins. (The best review of Drucker and his work so far attempted.)

See also: BARNARD, C.I..; FAYOL, H.; FORD, H.; TAYLOR, F.W.

Related topics in the IEBM: BUSINESS CULTURE, NORTH AMERICAN; BUSINESS ECONOMICS; BUSINESS ETHICS; BUSINESS HISTORY; BUSINESS AND SOCIETY; ENTREPRENEURSHIP; ENVIRONMENTAL REPORTING; GENERAL MANAGEMENT; GURU CONCEPT; HUMAN RELATIONS; INNOVATION MANAGEMENT; INNOVATION AND TECHNOLOGICAL CHANGE; MARKETING

Dunlop, John Thomas (1914–)

Personal background

- born 15 July 1914, Placerville, California, USA
- early academic career, University of California at Berkeley; also at Stanford University, USA, and Cambridge, UK
- main academic career spent at Cambridge, Massachusetts (Harvard University)
- extensive practical experience starting with War Labor Board (1943–5)
- Chairman of Construction Industry Stabilization Commission (1971–4); also served on stabilization agencies with informal dispute settlement procedures, boards of inquiry, disputes at critical installations with a special focus on railways, airlines and construction; extensive arbitration experience
- helped greatly to establish industrial relations as a distinctive academic discipline
- focal contribution in the areas of wage determination, industrial relations systems and dispute settlement

Major works

Wage Determination Under Trade Unions (1944)
Industrial Relations Systems (1958)
Dispute Resolution: Negotiation and Consensus Building (1984)

Summary

J.T. Dunlop (1914–) substantially shaped the development of industrial relations as an academic discipline and in a way which was interlinked with his own extensive practical experiences. His *Industrial Relations Systems* helped to isolate the main contours of a subject area. He has also contributed significantly to the study of wage determination under trade unionism; to the theory of practice of dispute settlement; and to the identification of the significance of human resource development for international competitive advantage.

1 Introduction

John Dunlop has exerted a significant influence on theory, policy and practice in the sphere of industrial relations. The analysis which follows addresses five themes: (1) the establishment of the elements in the discipline of industrial relations; (2) the theory and analysis of wage determination (with a focus on the impact of trade unionism); (3) the contribution to the area of dispute resolution; (4) the later focus on human resource development; and (5) the practical aspects of Dunlop's contribution.

So far as his academic career is concerned, Dunlop has set this out in an autobiographical note (Kaufman 1988). The earliest point in his career was spent at the University of California in Berkeley (1933–6) where he was taught by, among others, Charles A. Gulick, Jr. In his second graduate year (1936–7) he moved to Stanford University, followed by a period at Cambridge University, UK (1937–8). In 1938, following the suggestion of John Kenneth Galbraith, he arrived at Cambridge, Massachusetts, as a teaching fellow and Harvard became his main base thereafter.

2 The discipline of industrial relations

Arguably the most important legacy of John Dunlop (at least in the assessment of the worldwide academic community) has been in his contribution to the establishment of a distinctive discipline of industrial relations. Prior to the publication of *Industrial Relations Systems* in 1958 there had of course been very many analyses of labour theory and practice. But critical to John Dunlop's contribution was the establishment of the core elements of a subject area and the attempt to argue that the discipline was fundamentally different from, say, economics or politics.

At the time of writing *Industrial Relations Systems* Dunlop was influenced by the work of Talcott Parsons. Dunlop did not seek a general theory of all social action (as had been the objective of Parsons), but he did attempt to provide an analysis of social action in industrial societies that applied to its industrial relations aspects and which possessed a level of generality greater than that for particular industries or countries. Above all, the need for a far greater 'theoretical structure and orientation' to industrial relations was recognized and as Dunlop (1958: vi) in a famous passage argued: 'Facts have outrun ideas. Integrating theory has lagged far behind expanding experience. The many worlds of industrial relations have been changing more rapidly than the ideas to interpret, to explain, and to relate to them.'

In *Industrial Relations Systems*, Dunlop thus sought to establish a general theory of industrial relations that would: (1) enable analysis and interpretation of the 'widest possible range of industrial relations facts and practices'; (2) facilitate comparative studies of industrial relations among different countries and industries; and (3) link direct experience with the realm of ideas. In every industrial society, Dunlop argued that distinctive groups of workers and managers were created and an industrial relations system could thus be identified in all such countries. Six main propositions were central to Dunlop's formulation:

1 the industrial relations system is an analytical subsystem of industrial society and is on the *same* logical plane as the economic system
2 the industrial relations system is a separate and distinctive subsystem of society
3 there are relationships and boundary lines between a society and the industrial relations system
4 the industrial relations system is logically an abstraction
5 there is a distinctive analytical and theoretical subject matter to industrial relations
6 three separate analytical problems include the relation of the industrial relations system to the society as a whole, the relation to the economic system and the inner structure and characteristics of the industrial relations system itself.

This forms the basis of Dunlop's more detailed specification of the structure of the industrial relations system itself. As he argued, 'an industrial relations system at any one time in its development is regarded as comprised of certain actors, certain contexts, an ideology which binds the industrial relations system together, and a body of rules created to govern the actors at the workplace and work community' (Dunlop 1958: 7).

The 'actors' (note again the effect of the language of Talcott Parsons) comprised: (1) a hierarchy of managers and their representatives in supervision; (2) a hierarchy of workers (non-managerial) and any spokesmen; and (3) specialized governmental agencies (and specialized private agencies created by the first two actors) concerned with workers, enterprises and their relationships. The contexts comprised significant aspects of the environment and encompassed: (1) the technological characteristics of the workplace and work community; (2) the market or budgetary constraints which impinge on the actors; and (3) the locus and distribution of power in the wider society. The 'actors' were seen as establishing rules for the workplace and work community (these cover procedures for establishing rules, substantive rules and the procedures for deciding their application to particular situations). And finally, the ideology of the industrial relations system is 'a set of ideas and beliefs commonly held by the actors that helps to bind or to integrate the system together as an entity' (Dunlop 1958: 26).

In terms of mapping the field of industrial relations, much of what was set out by Dunlop is still broadly accepted. However, there have been several improvements to the original conception. This has applied particularly to the development of environmental contexts to include legal and cultural elements. Moreover, the processes of industrial relations have been subsequently refined.

The substantial corpus of critical writings which have also emerged have been testimony to the vigour and relevance of the original Dunlopian conception. The main criticisms have been the absence of testable theories (indeed the industrial relations system conception is a model rather than a theory), the focus on comparative *statics* not dynamics, the consensual nature of the formulation (ideologies are *not* necessary shared) and the absence of a proper treatment of conflict and power (within the industrial relations system) in the original formulation. But none of this diminishes the vital importance of Dunlop's conception in establishing the central constituents of the discipline of industrial relations itself.

3 The theory of wage determination under trade unions

Dunlop's (1944) early work (and for which he is most noted in the USA) was linked with an analysis of wage determination under trade unions. In his classic book with this title, he articulated the central views that: (1) wage determination under collective bargaining was indeed different from wage fixing under non-economic conditions, but the differences were not as great as had sometimes been supposed; and (2) although trade unions were not solely concerned with the maximization of income of their members, they certainly could not be construed as essentially political agents.

In *Wage Determination Under Trade Unions*, then, a variety of themes were covered, including: the development of an economic model of a trade union; wage policies of trade unions, 'bargaining power' and inter-market relations; trade unions' interest in related markets; cyclical patterns of industrial wage variation; cyclical variation in labour's share in the national income; labour's return as a cost and the price mechanism and collective bargaining.

Two particularly lasting themes were the analysis of the wage policies of trade unions and the analysis of 'bargaining power'. In the first place, then, a number of non-income objectives of wage policy were identified that encompassed: (1) the promotion of union membership; (2) work allocation; (3) leisure; (4) controlling the rate of introduction of technical innovations; (5) improvements in working conditions; and (6) control of entry to the trade. But even the income objectives of wage policies were viewed as complex. There could be the national pronouncements of national organization, justification within a bargaining unit and the elements of a wages policy (including differentials, product market conditions, employment effects and method of wage payment). Above all, from an analytical point of view, specific wage policies included: (1) a more cyclical relationship between wage rates and employment; and (2) cyclical fluctuations in wage structure. Finally, wage differentials among enterprises and wage differentials among local unions were assessed.

The interpretation of 'bargaining power' was firmly grounded in the recognition of inequalities between 'buyers' and 'sellers' in the marketplace and was rooted in economic analysis. The factors influencing bargaining power included the tastes of workers and employees, market conditions and so-called 'pure bargaining power' (or the ability to get favourable bargains apart from market conditions). Bargaining power consists of the relative abilities of the two contracting parties to influence the wage; that can be analysed in terms of various types of competition.

Part of Dunlop's heritage has been that he stimulated a great deal of further analysis and debate on trade union wage policies and collective bargaining. In particular, the 'political school' took him to task for his one-sided economic interpretation and preferred a conception of trade unions as political agencies. But against his critics, in the preface to the 1950 edition, Dunlop argued:

1 political wage setting is most likely to occur in newer unions experiencing acute factional struggles but not in mature collective bargaining relations
2 the political focus tends to apply best to the short run; the longer the time scale the less valuable the emphasis on political considerations
3 labour leaders are acutely aware of economic and technological considerations and these temper any effects of union politics
4 the 'stubborn facts' of the external world are avoided even though in reality changes in prices, profits and employment in related markets all affect wage rates and wages rate movements.

4 Dispute resolution

No analysis of John Dunlop would be complete without reference to his work on dispute resolution. Indeed, he has had a long-standing theoretical and practical focus on labour peace and a strong preference for regulations in industrial relations to be jointly negotiated between labour and management. This is a perennial theme in a spectrum of Dunlop's work, including not least his *Industrial Relations Systems*, where the network or 'web of rules' was seen as the primary 'centre of attention' of the industrial relations system.

Throughout his career, Dunlop has been concerned to establish a negotiations alternative in dispute resolution. Broadly speaking, as he argued, it is possible in western societies to discern two major approaches to the resolution of conflicts; 'the give and take' of the market place and governmental regulations. What he preferred, however, was negotiation coupled with a variety of specialized mediation and arbitration services for securing labour peace. Indeed, quoting George Simmel

(1955: 115) he noted that 'on the whole, compromise, especially that brought about through exchange, no matter how much we think it is an everyday technique we take for granted, is one of mankind's greatest inventions'.

This focus of interest led John Dunlop to develop abstract as well as practical approaches to negotiations. He thus noted at least four approaches to negotiation: (1) formal models linked with the notion of bargaining power; (2) the use of experimental or simulated bargaining games; (3) the deployment of econometric methods to measure aspects of arbitration or collective bargaining; and (4) verbatim accounts of exchanges from the earliest stages of negotiations to the achievement of a settlement. Dunlop preferred a somewhat different approach: 'to limit' the types of negotiations considered and then to outline a number of key principles central to an understanding of the negotiation 'process' (Dunlop 1984: 9).

Labour–management negotiations thus had certain interesting characteristics: (1) the parties and organizations expect to continue to be engaged to interact over a future period; (2) the parties to the negotiations are not monolithic; and (3) the negotiators are concerned with more than one single issue. The development of a framework for analysing negotiations thus requires the analyst first to account for diverse internal interests. Acknowledgement then must be made of the initial proposals for agreement, the changing positions in negotiations, the role of a deadline, end-play, a judgement, overt conflict, going public, implementing the settlement and the personal ingredient.

In the event of problems in this process, the role of mediation was seen as fundamental. Moreover, the mediation process was itself capable of analytical interpretation. First, mediation relates fundamentally to the communications flow. Second, the mediator function often involves the development of mutually acceptable factual data. Third, the mediator serves as a private, informal adviser to both sides. Fourth, the mediator can formulate a distinctive and imaginative package. Fifth, the mediator has a special opportunity in the 'end game' of negotiations. Sixth, a critical factor affecting the role of the mediator is the circumstances at the point of entry into a dispute. Seventh, the mediator may be asked to serve as an arbitrator. And finally, mediators may play a role in settlement of some disputes by asserting a moral authority or assuming a role in the public interest.

Overall, too, Dunlop envisaged substantial advantages of the negotiation process, including the likelihood of a successful enforcement of any agreement, the level of detail facilitated, the 'basic' superiority of a genuinely settled controversy and the creative, problem solving nature of negotiations as opposed to litigation or governmental fiat. Moreover, he argued that negotiation would play an increasingly important role in conflict resolution.

An extension of Dunlop's interest in negotiation was obviously, too, a general endorsement of trade unions and a long-standing interest in labour issues. This spanned a variety of contributions (including wage determination). But his contribution here is particularly linked with his work with Derek Bok entitled *Labour and the American Community* (1970). This covered such issues as trade unions and public opinion, a profile of the labour movement, democracy and union government, the protection of minority interests, the administration of unions and collective bargaining. But despite the interest in unions and collective bargaining, Bok and Dunlop had a deep-seated concern for the future of these organizations and their activities which broadly proved to be accurate at least in the USA:

The dangers for the labor movement lie in very different fields. Unions face evident risks that they will be taken more and more for granted by their members, that they will function at a growing disadvantage in dealing with institutions possessing greater knowledge and superior techniques, and that their social role will be preempted increasingly by other groups. Should these risks materialize, the prospects are that unions will become progressively duller bureaucracies, more fractious at times to arouse an indifferent membership, but

largely ignored in the major developments of the society and rather widely disliked as a necessary evil and a source of periodic inconvenience.

(Bok and Dunlop 1970: 486)

5 The challenge of human resource development

A latter-day concern of John Dunlop has been with the emergent issue of human resource development. There has been globally an increasing awareness of these matters. Indeed, alongside technology and knowledge, it is recognized that a key resource in the competitive advantage of nations has become the quality of workforces (their abilities, skills, motivation and education levels).

The backcloth for John Dunlop's interest has been the relatively poor performance of countries like the USA in terms of productivity. For Dunlop economic growth and productivity advance depend on four basic factors: research and development, investment in plant and equipment, investment in infrastructure and investment in human resource development. Furthermore, on his testimony, the 'creation of a more productive, skilled and adaptable workforce in turn depends on: (1) the educational system; (2) health care; (3) training and retraining; (4) family policy; (5) labour–management policies at the workplace; and (6) the general growth of public services' (Dunlop 1992: 52).

The more detailed case of John Dunlop is as follows. Despite a growing educational attainment of the workforce in the USA there are significant educational problems for a substantial percentage of the population. This is compounded by high absenteeism and school dropout rates. Healthcare and housing are also a problem for significant numbers of the American population. There is a bias in US national labour policy towards conflict and against cooperation. And finally, morale in the public service sector is at a low ebb. In essence, then, as he offered the following argument:

It is my sincere conviction that it is the failure to develop appropriate institutions to educate, to train and retrain to maintain health, to manage and elicit productive and cooperative services from its workforce that is our country's most critical failure. Our poor performance with human resources cannot in the longterm be offset or compensated for the test of international competition by location, national resources, history, capital structure or our political democracy.

(Dunlop 1992: 53)

Fundamentally, John Dunlop has articulated a series of issues of vital consequence for the human resources of modern nations. Above all, he has added weight to the conviction that the development of trained, productive and adaptable human resources is at the very heart of competitive advantage and not simply a desirable but non-essential goal of labour, government and business alike.

6 Practical activities

Another important aspect of John Dunlop's contribution to the field of industrial relations has been his major practical activities. He has been particularly noted for his work on arbitration. For years he chaired the National Joint Board for Jurisdictional Disputes, a construction panel. He was dean of faculty at Harvard University and served on many joint union–management commissions. He has also been chair of the commissions on the Future of Worker–Management Relations (which is primarily concerned with making suggestions for labour law reform). He was a Secretary of Labor in the Ford Administration and had a drive to simplify the number of industrial relations related regulations which, in his view, overburdened the parties. But, dramatically, in an effort to check a wage–price spiral in the construction industry he worked out a deal to centralize bargaining (the impending bill was vetoed and John Dunlop, in consequence, resigned).

More systematically, his enormous breadth of experience and accomplishment in dispute resolution and problem solving in industrial relations may be set out under the following nine heads: (1) stabilization agencies concerned with dispute settlement; (2) stabilization agencies concerned with informal dispute settlement; (3) Boards of Inquiry under the Taft–Hartley Act; (4) disputes at critical installations; (5) railways and airlines; (6) construction; (7) private umpire arbitration; (8) private labour–management committees: neutral member or umpire; and (9) public sector committees.

In more detail, his work with dispute settlement commenced with the War Labor Board (1943–5). He was also a public member of the Wage Stabilization Board (1950–3) and Chairman of the Construction Industry Stabilization Commission (1971–4). Informal Dispute Settlement Bodies included the Cost of Living Council (1973–4) and the Tripartite Pay Advisory Committee (1979–80) of which he was Chairman. Under the provisions of the Taft–Hartley Act, he was a member of the boards of inquiry into, for example, the General Electric Company (1966).

So far as disputes at critical installations are concerned, these included the President's Commission on Labour Relations in the Atomic Energy Installations (1948–9), the Missile Sites Labour Commissions (1961–7) and the Nevada Test Site Committee (1965–7). But he is particularly noted for his work in the main industrial groupings of railways and airlines, and construction. For instance, he was a member of the Presidential Railroad Commission (1960–2) and Chairman of Emergency Board 167 American Airlines and Transport workers Union of America. But above all, he is noted for his close attention to the construction industry and its various labour problems. These activities are too extensive to develop in detail but include the Wage Adjustment Board (1943–7), the Construction Industry Joint Conference (1959–68), the Appeals Board (Jurisdictional Disputes) (1965–8) and being arbitrator on jurisdictional issues (1981–) (Alaskan Oilfields Construction Agreements).

Other industries were also covered in his role as private umpire in arbitration including the Pittsburgh Plate Glass Company and Eastern Airlines. In private labour management committees he was a neutral member or umpire in groups that included the Kaiser Steel Company (1959–67), the Tailored Clothing companies (1977–) and the *ad hoc* maritime committee (1977–80).

Finally, his activities in public sector committees included: the Governors' Committee on Public Employee Relations, New York State (1965–9); the Joint Labour–Management Committee for Municipal Police and Fire, Commonwealth of Massachusetts (1977–); and the Task Force in Public Pensions and Disability, Commonwealth of Massachusetts (1982).

7 Conclusions

John Dunlop has thus contributed in a major way to the theory and practice of industrial relations. He was substantially responsible for establishing one of the key theoretical contributions to the discipline. He charted a major theory of wage determination under trade unions. He theoretically developed the area of negotiations and collective bargaining behaviour and had a long-standing interest in trade unions. Latterly he has been concerned with the importance of human resource development. And he has had a most impressive and influential public role in arbitration and dispute settlement and in his work for the Dunlop Commission. His contribution to theory and practice in a key area of business and management has thus been impressive, comprehensive and long-lasting.

MICHAEL POOLE
CARDIFF BUSINESS SCHOOL

Note

The author is grateful to Professor George Strauss for his valuable help in preparing this entry.

Further reading

(References cited in the text marked *)

* Bok, D. and Dunlop, J.T. (1970) *Labor and the American Community*, New York: Simon & Schuster. (Develops a detailed account of labour in US society, its public image, practices and future role.)
* Dunlop, J.T. (1944) *Wage Determination under Trade Unions*, New York: Macmillan. (An early classic setting out Dunlop's influential theories on wage determination.)
* Dunlop, J.T. (1958) *Industrial Relations Systems*, New York: Holt, Rinehart and Winston. (Dunlop's classic theoretical work outlining the systems approach to industrial relations and establishing the 'contours' of the discipline.)
* Dunlop, J.T. (1984) *Dispute Resolution: Negotiation and Consensus Building*, Dover, MA: Auburn House. (Details Dunlop's theory of negotiation and outlines the importance he attaches to negotiation and mediation as means of dispute settlement rather than markets or governmental fiat.)
* Dunlop, J.T. (1992) 'The challenge of human resources development', *Industrial Relations* 31 (1): 50–5. (Sets out the importance of human resources development for the competitive advantage of nations and the problems faced by the USA in these respects.)
* Kaufman, B. (ed.) (1988) *How Labor Markets Work*, Lexington, MA: D.C. Heath & Co. (Incorporates an autobiographical account and is a vital source for understanding the extent of Dunlop's overall contribution to the theory and practice of industrial relations.)
* Kochan, T.A. (1995) 'Using the Dunlop report to achieve mutual gains', Industrial Relations 34 (3): 350–66. (Summarizes the major conclusions and recommendations of the Dunlop Commission report and analyses the potential benefits.)
* Simmel, G. (1955) *Conflict and the Web of Group Affiliations*, Glencoe, IL: The Free Press. (Sets out the theory of groups and the importance of processes of negotiation in reaching successful outcomes.)

See also: BARBASH, J.; CLEGG, H.A.; KOCHAN, T.; PERLMAN, S.; STRAUSS, G.

Related topics in the IEBM: COLLECTIVE BARGAINING; EMPLOYEE DEVELOPMENT; HUMAN RESOURCE MANAGEMENT; HUMAN RESOURCE MANAGEMENT, INTERNATIONAL; INDUSTRIAL AND LABOUR RELATIONS; LABOUR MARKETS; TRADE UNIONS

Emery, Frederick Edmund (1925–97)

Personal background

- born to a sheep shearing family in Western Australia, 27 August 1925
- left school at 14 and worked as a junior draughtsman in a Western Australian mining office
- enrolled in Western Australia's University in 1943, doing science and first year psychology, and finished his BSc in 1945
- enrolled at the University of Melbourne and took a doctorate in psychology , 1953
- first visited the Tavistock Institute of Human Relations briefly in 1949, in 1951–2 and for an extensive period in the 1960s during which he spent a year as a fellow at the Stanford Center for Advanced Studies in Behavioral Science
- visiting Busch Professor at the Wharton School of Business, University of Pennsylvania, 1982–4
- won the Australian Psychological Association's inaugural Elton Mayo Award, 1988
- received a DSc from Macquarrie University in 1992
- died in Canberra on 10 April 1997

Major works

Many of Fred Emery's most important contributions are contained in two volumes:

The Social Engagement of Science: A Tavistock Anthology (E. Trist and H. Murray, eds) Volume II (1993), Volume III (1997)

Summary

Fred Emery was a theorist who made several very practical contributions to organizational design and management thinking. He used an 'open systems' model derived from biology to describe various forms of environmental pressures and their impact on organizational structure and leadership. With colleagues at the Tavistock Institute in London, he developed the important socio-technical model which has been widely used and applied in manufacturing as well as in service industries. It was found that democratic leadership using 'semi-autonomous' teams of multi-skilled operators achieved superior results to designs using a division of labour and a hierarchic system of control. Democratic methods of decision making in search conferences are being used by organizations to make changes in anticipation of future events.

1 Overview

To an unusual degree Fred Emery combined original theory with practical application and in this way, as well as in several others, he followed and developed the work of Kurt Lewin (see LEWIN, K.). Emery was a visionary and idealist, but every one of his contributions to the effective development of organizational life was intended to be of use to ordinary people in ordinary workplaces. Most of the ideas and practices described in this entry were carried out during his long association with the Tavistock Institute in London and in collaboration with several colleagues, but principally Eric Trist (see TRIST, E.) with whom he developed a long lasting symbiotic intellectual relationship.

His very considerable output, much of it only published in accessible form in the 1990s, can be grouped into four areas: (1) treating the internal as well as the external environment of organizations as systems. This approach led to the description of several

173

types of environmental texture and their consequences for the design of enterprises; (2) developing, with Eric Trist, a profound understanding of the optimal design relationships between technology and people, now called sociotechnology; (3) conceptualizing and implementing organizational democracy, including important demonstration projects in Scandinavia; (4) developing searching methodologies for organizational learning and planning the future.

These four developments are deeply intertwined and derive from Emery's profound belief in the goodness of humankind. It is only by seeing people, organizations and the environment in which they operate as open systems in constant interaction, that important human as well as effectiveness objectives can be fulfilled. For instance there is a relation between organizational democracy operating in an enterprise as a whole and autonomous work teams in individual sub-units. Similarly, optimum job design cannot be achieved if new technology is based exclusively on engineering considerations. Furthermore, turbulence of the external organizational environment leads to pressures that can be appropriately met by involving employees in relevant aspects of the decision process.

For Emery and his colleagues, concepts like team working, participation, semi-autonomy, job design and multi-skilling are treated within an open system perspective, but many social scientists and consultants are content to use these concepts as isolated events in a closed system. It is therefore important to distinguish between 'tinkering' and 'holistic' system design.

2 Organizations as systems

Emery's approach to systems thinking is derived from the study of biology. Although, as we shall see, there are practical applications to management and organizations, the theory is abstract, complex, and still evolving. In the two volumes on systems thinking edited by Emery, no definition of 'system' is offered (Emery 1969, 1981). However, the term derives from the Greek, meaning an organized whole, and Emery and others often use the German term 'gestalt', signifying a shape or whole constellation to differentiate it from the more traditional scientific approach which investigates individual parts or sub-systems. Emery claims that 'gestalten' have properties that characterize the higher levels of organization which can be called 'living systems'. From this one derives a number of system characteristics, for instance its openness to the environment.

Within an open system, the primary task of senior management is to handle the boundary conditions of an enterprise and management should not be distracted from this by the more usual secondary task of concentrating on intra-organizational issues. Since the objectives of an enterprise cannot be adequately formulated without including its relationship to the environment, the task of management is governed by the need to match the capacities of the enterprise to the requirements of the environment. In a widely quoted article, Emery and Trist (1965) developed a four stage typology of 'causal textures' through which the environment affects organizations and requires different decision making structures to achieve a successful accommodation. The first and mildest form of environmental pressure derives from the economist's classical market and can usually be handled by trial and error. The second type corresponds to the economist's imperfect competition as a consequence of which organizations tend to grow and develop a more hierarchical centralized control system. Type three occurs in what the economist calls an oligopolistic market. To deal successfully with a small number of tactically agile competitors requires a decentralized, flexible organization with a premium on speed of decision making and effective implementation.

While these three types of environment are well known, the fourth type, called 'turbulent fields', does not appear to have previously received attention. Its dynamic property involves a significant increase in uncertainty and unpredictability so that not only the different components of the field (i.e. organizations) are changing, but the field itself (legal requirements, value systems, public regulations, technology etc.) is in a state of flux and constantly threatens to undermine stability. Coping with this type of complex environmental turbulence requires non-traditional organizational forms, such as matrix structures using flexible influence, sharing work methods and a corresponding shift in values from McGregor's mechanistic theory X assumptions to his humanistic theory Y (see MCGREGOR, D.). This accommodation in organizational culture is congruent with democratic practices (see Section 5 below).

To achieve a 'steady state' for the system in a human organization, leadership and commitment are necessary with clearly formulated and agreed goals. For members of the organization to respond to constantly changing challenges, even to emergencies, the system has to be based on self-regulation. Within such a constantly self-adjusting system of semi-autonomous units, regulatory mechanisms, like cost control, are acceptable and make a valuable contribution to continuing the 'steady state' of the whole configuration and its progressive movement towards agreed goals. A purposive progressive human system recognizes the interdependence of its constituent parts and consequently the limits to democratic self-determination implied by the prefix 'semi' in relation to the term 'autonomy', but it must include participative mechanisms to allow for the exercise of choice (see Section 4).

This complex balance between freedom and constraint, which requires some sacrifice to autonomy, may threaten commitment unless it is carefully structured and communicated through a flexible leadership style. From this perspective, it is important to recognize that an enterprise, as a socio-technical system, can increase the value of the 'gestalt' only if the parts of the system can do something together that they cannot accomplish alone.

3 The socio-technical model

The socio-technical model is an outcome of systems thinking and has become an important, widely recognized and used paradigm in the social sciences. It was 'discovered' during a research project carried out by a team from the Tavistock Institute in British coal mines in the 1950s. Fred Emery was not part of the original field team but contributed to the development of the emerging model, particularly by describing the relationship between open and closed systems and the implication of this difference for the notion of a 'steady state' which in turn could be related to Kurt Lewin's theories (see LEWIN, K.).

Like most important theories, it is quite simple. Whenever a technology interacts with people it is not possible to maximize the utility (or the theoretical potential) of either the technology or the social dimension on its own. The best benefit from the interacting system of people and technology depends on finding a joint optimization solution. The optimum fit of technology and people will discover a relationship between the competence of the human operator and the skill potential of the technology.

Emery makes an important distinction between purely technical requirements and socio-technical requirements. In relation to the former he gives the example of the speed of a conveyor which feeds a particular machine at the highest possible rate as an illustration which falls outside the scope of socio-technical analysis because there is no direct human intervention (Emery 1993)

Emery also makes a distinction between two forms of alienation. One is the alienation of a person from the activity of producing goods or services. The usual example of this form of alienation is the repetitive short cycle soul-destroying job immortalized by Charlie Chaplin in the film *Modern Times*. The second form identified by Emery is the alienation of a person from the product of his or her labour. This type of alienation is a function of an individual's relationship to the enterprise or even to society. It results from a lack of identification with the product or the goals of the enterprise and a passive inability to exert influence in the work system.

4 Democratizing organizations

Fred Emery's most important and long-lasting contribution to management thinking and practice is likely to be his work on democratizing organizations. His idealism naturally led him to champion the disenfranchised and powerless and his study of organizations persuaded him that new structural arrangements could make dull jobs more interesting. At the same time through participation the experience of people at the shop floor could significantly improve the effectiveness of organizations. We saw in Section 3 that organizations subjected to turbulent field environments were required to adjust by using flexible participative methods. In addition, the coal studies demonstrated the superior productivity of multi-skilled, semi- autonomous groups over a more traditional division of labour without employee participation. This research was also one of the first British studies to show the negative effect of job stress on performance. Since this work in the 1950s the literature on team working and semi-autonomy has grown spectacularly and has influenced organizational design. While the National Coal Board was not prepared to learn from the experience of the Tavistock studies, Emery found enthusiastic interest in Norway, a country with a long-established democratic tradition and fairly progressive trade unions. He was able to start up a life-long collaboration with Einar Thorsrud and the Norwegian Work Research Centre which has had far-reaching repercussions in both Norway and Sweden; it has lasted over thirty-five years and is set to continue well into the twenty-first century. Emery and Thorsrud were influenced by the coal board studies as well as Kurt Lewin's work on democratic leadership (see LEWIN, K.) and the post-World War II growth of legally supported organizational democracy measures in many continental countries, but particularly in West Germany.

With the support of the Norwegian employers' organisation and the trade unions they started a series of action oriented studies to demonstrate the effect of direct employee participation at the lowest level of organization (Emery and Thorsrud 1976). They had looked at formal representative participation on boards of directors in Norway and West Germany and came to believe that these

changes at the top of the organizational pyramid had no effect on what was going on further down, did not make ordinary jobs more interesting and did not give employees more direct influence (Emery and Thorsrud 1969). It is interesting to note that although Scandinavian politicians listened to Emery and Thorsrud they nevertheless went ahead and passed legislation which gave workers representation and certain rights at board room level. Later, Emery changed his mind and admitted that legislation and even board representation, when suitably linked to lower levels, could be an effective support system for democratizing organizational life. He was pleased to see that the Norwegian Parliament had passed work design legislation which supported his work design criteria and he observed that the German 1972 Work Constitution Act required the 'tailoring of jobs to meet human needs' (Emery 1993).

The Scandinavian demonstration studies on participation and socio-technical work design were enormously influential among social scientists and progressive managers in different parts of the world; they have affected consultancy practice, inspired pioneering developments in many countries, and also led to large-scale applied research projects in Norway and Sweden in the 1990s. Some of these will continue into the next century. (Heller, Pusic, Strauss and Wilpert 1998).

Nevertheless, in spite of demonstrating various and often substantial improvements to organizational effectiveness and job satisfaction, there was resistance and diffusion was quite limited. Consequently, new methods to facilitate change and anticipate the future had to be developed.

5 Learning and the future

The various theories and practical experiences Emery accumulated over many years led to a variety of schemas to communicate knowledge, facilitate learning and introduce changes based on the available evidence. Pervasive resistance to change was a weakness that had become particularly obvious in the various action research projects in Norway. Although these projects had been successful in demonstrating the effectiveness of semi-autonomous working and a variety of changes in job design, they failed to achieve a satisfactory follow-through or diffusion between organizations or even within the organization that hosted the successful experiment.

It was felt that perhaps over-enthusiastic researchers played too active a part in the implementation process. Consequently, the researchers used more indirect and client-centred designs and registered some successes. Sometimes the poor implementation results could be attributed to a critical change in the economic climate which altered the organization's priorities. In one well-known action project in Shell UK with which Emery was associated, the Suez crisis in 1956 and a change of managing director ended a successful programme which had included a self-generated new company philosophy accepted at board level and several successful socio-technical designs at lower levels of the organization. Perhaps one should recognize that nothing lasts for ever and that, in any case, changing priorities based on different environmental conditions would lead to adjustments in the dynamic conditions characterizing the 'steady state'. However, adjustment is different from abandonment and, in a rational world, success in one organization should lead to diffusion to other organizations. It is clear, however, that rationality is not the only motive for organizational decision making (see SIMON, H.A.).

Emery's dynamic personality did not allow him to contemplate failure. Nor was he satisfied with the widely known achievements in democratizing organizations, gained during his collaboration in Norway and the later successful diffusion to Sweden (Qvale 1996). He and his colleagues were constantly trying out new approaches and were increasingly concerned to devise methods beyond the *status quo* which would stimulate managers and other employees to anticipate future developments. This meant adjusting enterprise policy within a systems thinking framework to achieve a 'steady state' relationship with its environment over time.

What emerged is known as the 'search conference', which has quite different dynamic characteristics from traditional conferences, seminar, or committee meetings (M. Emery 1997). Search conferences look for a shared understanding and mutual acceptance of a diversity of interpretations and values. This will lead to a search for communalities based on ideals and a penetrating diagnosis of current realities and future opportunities and threats.

The social scientist acts as facilitator, not as expert, so that the diagnosis as well as the outcomes are group-generated and, if successful, create a commitment which carries the process forward into implementation. Search conferences assemble people from different levels of experience and status who have some common interest, a minimum basis of trust, and a desire to explore options and learning opportunities. They start by asking people to suspend judgement and get off their favourite hobbyhorses. They are expected to assume that the future is not immutable but can be influenced to a considerable extent by suitable human intervention. Hence the aim is to look some years ahead and this almost invariably means discarding current preoccupations and favourite short-term remedies.

The search conferences usually start by charting current beliefs, values and perceptions of the external social fields in an atmosphere which discourages evaluation and criticism. The group then builds up a picture of how and why they have arrived at their present position and the likely influences and changes they anticipate over the next decade or beyond. How do they perceive the past, current and future environments and to what extent is there a match or mismatch between their analysis of organizational reality and environmental conditions?

This kind of analysis usually leads to an agreement that some kind of change is required to achieve congruence between different system level needs, including the current and anticipated external environment. The next stage explores 'ideal' but realizable options and attempts generating a common or at least acceptable vision of a desirable future. Such a vision tends to motivate people to explore and accept a range of agreed actions. The final stage of most search conferences will form a number of task groups to design the detailed pathways leading to the future.

Search conferences need time – usually two days and two nights. Fred Emery and Merrelyn have collaborated actively in the development of these conferences over several years and with Eric Trist, encouraged many people to apply open systems analysis as a theoretical vehicle to achieve viable organizational adjustment to changing circumstances.

6 Conclusions

Fred Emery's contribution to management thinking and practice revolves around two main concepts: open system theory and democratic practices. Open system theory draws attention to the importance of analyzing the socio-economic environment and concentrating management's task on supervising and managing the boundary between the external conditions and internal organizational structures, culture and behaviour.

The socio-technical model is another aspect of systems thinking and has become an important social science paradigm. The blending of the human and technical systems is accomplished by a process called joint optimization. This matching procedure between different systems or parts of a system involves choices. There is not a single solution, but some choices are superior to others in terms of overall effectiveness. However, over time, as the environment, the technology and or the competence of people changes, so must the choices and the optimizing solutions.

Emery's experience with field work in Britain, Australia and Scandinavia convinced him that in modern organizations, in most cases, participative structures and democratic behaviour produces better overall results than bureaucratic structures and autocratic behaviour. He illustrated this at the open systems level of organizations which require democratic values and structures to cope with turbulent fields and at the socio-technical level where semi-autonomous, multi-skilled teams could be shown to be superior to the traditional routine short cycle operations based on a detailed division of labour.

The same two concepts, open system thinking and democratic procedures, were also applied to the challenging task of implementing findings into practical solutions through search conferences. Search conferences start by scanning the past and present environment then built up a series of choices based on the collective experience of the people involved and finished with a democratically arrived consensus and a procedure for converting it into practice.

FRANK HELLER
THE TAVISTOCK INSTITUTE, LONDON

Further reading

(References cited in the text marked *)

* Emery, F.E. (ed.)(1969) *Systems Thinking*, Volume 1, Harmondsworth: Penguin Modern Management Readings.
* Emery, F.E. (ed.)(1981) *Systems Thinking*, Volume 2, Harmondsworth: Penguin Modern Management Readings. (The 1969 and 1981 edited volumes contain 45 contributions on systems thinking by authors from different scientific fields. Seven articles are by Emery.)
* Emery, F.E. (1993) 'The characteristics of socio-technical systems', in E. Trist and H. Murray (eds) *The Social Engagement of Social Science,Volume II. The socio-technical perspective. A Tavistock Anthology*, Philadelphia: University of Pennsylvania Press: 157–186. (One of Emery's more important descriptions of the socio-technical model.)
* Emery, F.E. and Thorsrud, E. (1969) *Form and Content in Industrial Democracy*, London: Tavistock Publications. (Stems from the early collaboration of Emery and Thorsrud and describes events in different countries.)
* Emery, F.E. and Thorsrud, Einar (1976) *Democracy At Work. A Report of the Norwegian Industrial Democracy Program*. Leiden: Martinus Nijhoff. (Describes four pioneering action research projects in Norway.)
* Emery, F.E. and Trist, E.L. (1965) 'The causal texture of organisational environments', *Human Relations* 18: 21–33. Reprinted in: Emery 1969 and in Trist, Emery and Murray 1997. (Describes four different critical environmental pressures and the necessary organizational adaptation.)
* Emery, M. (1997) 'The search conference', in E. Trist, F. Emery and H. Murray (eds) *The Social Engagement of Social Science: A Tavistock An-*

thology. Volume III. The Socio-ecological Perspective, Philadelphia: University of Pennsylvania Press. (A detailed theoretical and descriptive account of search conferences.)

* Heller, F., Pusic, E.; Wilpert, B. and Strauss, G. (1998) *Organizational Participation: Myth and Reality*, Oxford: Oxford University Press. (Provides an overview and evaluation of organizational participation research and experience in many countries since 1945.)

* Qvale, T. (1996) 'Local development and institutional change: Experience from a "Fifth Generation" National programme for the democratization of working life', in P. Drenth, P. Koopman and B. Wilpert (eds) *Organizational Decision Making under Different Economic and Political Conditions,* Amsterdam: North Holland. (An account of five generations of work design projects in Norway.)

* Trist, E., Emery, F. and Murray, H. (1997) *The Social Engagement of Social Science: A Tavistock Anthology. Volume III. The Socio-ecological Perspective,* Philadelphia: University of Pennsylvania Press. (Contains 34 contributions on the work of the Tavistock Institute, 17 with Fred Emery as author or co-author.)

See also: ACKOFF, R.L.; LEWIN, K.; MCGREGOR, D.; TRIST, E.; SIMON, H.A.

Related topics in the IEBM: CONTEXTS AND ENVIRONMENTS; DECISION MAKING; INDUSTRIAL DEMOCRACY; MANAGEMENT IN SCANDINAVIA; ORGANIZATION BEHAVIOUR; ORGANIZATION BEHAVIOUR, HISTORY OF; SYSTEMS; WORK SYSTEMS

Etzioni, Amitai Werner (1929–)

Personal background

- born 4 January 1929 in Cologne, Germany
- married Minerva Morales, 14 September 1965 (died 20 September 1985); they had five sons
- received a BA from the Hebrew University of Jerusalem in 1954, and an MA in 1956
- received a PhD in sociology from the University of California, Berkeley in 1958
- member of faculty in the department of sociology, Columbia University, New York, 1958–80
- research associate (part-time) at the Institute of War and Peace Studies, Columbia University, 1961–71
- professor of sociology, Columbia University, from 1967, chair of department 1969–78, senior staff member of Bureau of Applied Social Research, Columbia University, 1961–71 (associate director, 1969–70), director of Centre for Policy Research, 1968–89
- guest scholar, Brookings Institution, 1978–9
- senior adviser to Richard Harden, special assistant to the President, White House 1979–80
- professor, The George Washington University, 1980–7
- Thomas Henry Carroll Ford Foundation Professor at Graduate School of Business, Harvard, 1987–9

Major works

A Comparative Analysis of Complex Organizations (1961)
Modern Organizations (1964)
The Active Society: A Theory of Societal and Political Processes (1968)
Social Problems (1976)
The Moral Dimension: Towards a New Economics (1988)

Summary

Amitai Etzioni has had a highly successful career both as leading organizational sociologist and as an engaged academic campaigner. He has been able to bridge the worlds of theory and socio-political activism, without compromising on either side. He has also shown an unusual ability to link sociology and neo-classical economics, providing the ideas of a moral dimension and a concept of communitarianism as a means of linking the two in the interests of social regeneration. In organizational theory Etzioni is best known for the work he published in the early 1960s on compliance theory, introducing a normative element into organizational theory which was to prove itself to be far ahead of the work of contemporaries operating in the more superficial human relations or systems traditions.

1 Background

Amitai Etzioni was born into a German Jewish family in Cologne in 1929. Following Hitler's rise to power the family emigrated to Palestine, and the family name hebraized from Falk to Etzioni. The society in which Etzioni spent his formative years, that of Israel in the years before and after independence in 1948, was characterized by strongly cohesive social collectivities, based on a hard-edged practical version of German–Russian social utopianism. This was particularly true of the kibbutzim (the management style and structures of which were among the areas covered by Etzioni's early research) and the various other types of collectively-managed enterprise, but also the then Israeli army (Etzioni's first book was *Diary of a Common Soldier*, published in Hebrew in 1952). As a sociology student in the Hebrew University of Jerusalem (1950–54), his teachers included the social philosopher Martin Buber, who emphasized the existential fulfilment of the individual in society (the latter being 'I and Thou', later amended by Etzioni to 'I and We'). If this background, in terms of Etzioni's own socialization and his early research, is taken into account, it may serve to explain the intensity with which Etzioni has been preoccupied by the inadequacy of American-style individualism as a stable foundation for liberal society, and the concomitant need to develop a disciplined communitarian alternative. His background in what was then a society held together by strong normative discipline also helps explain the importance he has given to normative elements, never apparently being tempted by the non-normative approaches of pure systems theory or models based purely on rational calculation and/or conflict. Indeed, the insight which first projected Etzioni into the academic limelight, that of the different sources of compliance (coercion, economic/pecumiary, normative) is arguably much clearer if one imagines normative-based compliance in the type of organization with which Etzioni was acquainted in his youth in Israel, than the religious organizations (by definition relatively removed from the practical or economic sphere) usually cited as examples.

2 Academic career

Etzioni left Israel to join the PhD programme at Berkeley, from which he graduated in 1958. He joined the staff at Columbia University, New York, where he was to spend most of the next twenty-two years. He was already demonstrating his ability to be prolific across the whole range of academic and journalistic publishing, which by the 1990s had seen him publish fifteen single-author books, over two hundred journal articles and chapters, and more than four hundred newspaper articles, columns and short pieces, covering a vast range of topics from organization theory, public administration, political theory, politics, social theory, social problems, economics, war and peace studies, health, ethics, industry, and all manner of contemporary issues in American politics, business, culture and society.

This range of interests found expression through the different institutional umbrellas under which Etzioni operated at Columbia – the Bureau of Applied Social Research, the Institute of War and Peace Studies, the Center for Policy Research. Following the publication of *A Comparative Analysis of Complex Organization* (1961) and *Modern Organization* (1964), plus a substantial number of related articles in the *Administrative Science Quarterly*, Etzioni became a leading name in organizational sociology. He received his professorship in 1967 and became chair of the department the following year.

Etzioni's early work was grounded in the role of normative bases for compliance and social stability within organizations. Gradually he was to pursue this idea into the wider social arena, particularly from 1967/8 onwards. Here his concerns reflected the turbulence in US society and politics during the period, although (unlike perhaps other leading management thinkers such as Abraham Maslow; see MASLOW, A.H.) his engagement with contemporary concerns retained a hard critical edge – he was not carried away by the excitement of what was going on; even a book of its time like *Demonstration Democracy* (1971) was a very sober evaluation of the utility of protest as a means of regulation in a democracy. Etzioni's major work of the period, and his most ambitious of all, *The Active Society* (1968), an attempt to revitalize the notion of 'community' in both practical and theoretical terms via organizational theory (this finding a middle path between the determinism of much sociological theory, and the voluntarism of political thought) was however, not the success he had expected, and in the years that followed he became preoccupied with another area of potential synthesis – his attempt to find a workable bridge between sociology and economics, a concern that could be traced back to his undergraduate days, when (neoclassical) economics was the minor subject to his sociology major. This was to culminate in his very influential socio-economics tract, *The Moral Dimension*, in 1988. This, however, came after one of the greatest disappointments of his life – his failure to successfully influence the Carter administration (as opposed to the second-level advisers) in the direction of 'reindustrialization' (his plans for economic regeneration arose out of his work at the Brookings Institution in the late 1970s and were to be the subject of his *Immodest Agenda – Rebuilding America for the 21st Century* of 1983). Etzioni appears to have blamed his lack of mastery of economics for this (one would have thought unsurprising) failure, and his later work was strengthened theoretically by his determination to correct the shortcoming. Finally, in the 1990s, Etzioni began to win a wider audience again for his theoretical championing of communitarianism.

3 Main contribution

In organization theory Etzioni is primarily known for his early work on 'compliance', expounded *in A Comparative Analysis of Complex Organizations* (1961) and subsequent work in the early 1960s. The focus on compliance allowed a more subtle two-way approach to the study of control and leadership. Etzioni argued that compliance could be based on coercion (as in total institutions), on economic or pecuniary interest (as under Taylorism; see TAYLOR F.W.), or it could be based in acceptance of normative values (associated typically with religious groups, although it is argued in the previous section that Etzioni may, from his own experience, have had a wider range of organizations in mind). Etzioni added to this the useful (although disputable) insight that these bases of compliance could only be used one at a time, and, once established, could not be successfully exchanged for each other or combined.

Etzioni's work in this area appears to have led him towards something of a life's mission to mitigate the effects of an ideology of individualism operating in a moral vacuum, which he saw as leading to chaos or the imposition of coercion. His thinking in this area

remains far from naive idealism, and his best works on this issues, such as *The Moral Dimension* (1988) are powerful both as theoretical works, synthesizing economic and social theory, and as tracts seeking to inspire greater social cohesion. Although his work from the mid-1960s onwards gradually removed Etzioni from the fields of organization or management studies, his career can in retrospect be seen to have anticipated many of the developments in organizational theory since 1980 (culture, postmodernism, ethics), his chosen field of theory, the interaction between rational calculation and communitarian values is of continuing relevance for organization theory.

4 Evaluation and conclusion

Etzioni's achievement looks far more impressive if his career is taken as a whole. After the considerable success of his early works, he was never again to have the same sureness of touch – his works would receive considerable praise, but would never quite become the dominant works in their area of study. Despite his consistently high level of scholarship and theoretical strength, his work was too often operating between disciplines to guarantee him the solid reputation he may be seen as deserving (although he has always been among the most heavily cited US social scientists). Despite his substantial later achievements, and a very substantial catalogue of publications, much of his reputation still stands on the early work on complex organizations. These are however, works that have dated surprisingly little, and just as they inspired a whole idiosyncratic line of theoretical development on Etzioni's part, so their use of the normative base of compliance moved organizational sociology far beyond the debates generated from Weber, Parsons and critical theory, towards an altogether more complex view of organizations, which anticipated much of the later more eclectic developments in organization theory.

Etzioni has in many respects been the exception among organization theorists. Where others have borrowed from other disciplines to try to strengthen organizational theory,

Etzioni brought greater depth to the study of organizations, and then used the concepts thus generated to enrich economics and social theory.

ADRIAN CAMPBELL
SCHOOL OF PUBLIC POLICY
UNIVERSITY OF BIRMINGHAM

Further reading

(References cited in the text marked *)

Antonides, G., Arts, W. and van Raaij, W.F. (eds) (1991) *The Consumption of Time and the Timing of Consumption: Towards a New Behavioural and Socio-Economics; Contributions in Honor of Amitai Etzioni*, Amsterdam: North-Holland. (A festschrift/symposium, with a brief autobiography by Etzioni 'Autobiographical notes of a socio-economist', an exhaustive bibliography of Etzioni's work up until 1990, and full details of editorial and related posts held by Etzioni throughout his career.)

* Etzioni, A. (1961) *A Comparative Analysis of Complex Organizations*, Glencoe, Illinois: Free Press (revised and enlarged edition, Free Press, 1975). (This first major work shows Etzioni's debt to Parsonian Structural Functionalism, but his ability to move beyond via his, subsequently highly influential, concept of power/compliance.)

* Etzioni, A.(1964) *Modern Organizations* , Englewood Cliffs, New Jersey: Prentice-Hall. (A concisely argued review of the post-Weberian bureaucracy in modern society, with a particular focus on the relationship between professional status, information and power.)

* Etzioni, A.(1968) *The Active Society: A Theory of Societal and Political Processes*, New York: Free Press. (A large-scale attempt to reassert the potential of the social for cohesive rational action and progress, against individualist chaos.)

* Etzioni, A. (1988) *The Moral Dimension: Towards a New Economics*, New York: Free Press. (Etzioni draws on the thinking of his mentor Martin Buber to mount an impressive and thoroughgoing challenge to neo-classical economics in its role as an increasingly dominant paradigm in the social sciences.)

Etzioni, A (1993) *The Spirit of Community: Rights, Responsibilities and the Communitarian Agenda*, New York: Crown. (Aimed at a popular audience, the book is to some extent a manifesto for communitarianism. Etzioni calls for a reassertion of the social, but with a more effective balance between rights and responsibilities.)

Sciulli, D. (ed.) (1996) *Macro Socio-Economics: from Theory to Activism*, London: M.E.Sharpe. (An extremely useful set of appraisals and applications of Etzioni's work and concepts. The contributions deal with Etzioni's work both as a whole and in terms of its main phases/themes.)

See also: MASLOW, A.H.; TAYLOR F.W.; WEBER, M.

Related topics in the IEBM: INDUSTRIAL DEMOCRACY; MANAGEMENT IN ISRAEL; MANAGEMENT IN NORTH AMERICA; MARKETS AND PUBLIC POLICY; MOTIVATION AND SATISFACTION; NEO-CLASSICAL ECONOMICS; ORGANIZATION BEHAVIOUR; ORGANIZATION BEHAVIOUR, HISTORY OF; ORGANIZATION STRUCTURE

Fayol, Henri (1841–1925)

1 Background
2 Main contribution
3 Evaluation

Personal background

- born in Constantinople, 29 July 1841
- trained as mining engineer, appointed manager of Commentry collieries in 1866; carried out widely acclaimed research on coal strata
- general manager (managing director) of the Compagnie Commentry, Fourchambault and Decazeville, 1888–1918
- author of many publications on mining, engineering and administration
- adviser to French government on administration after 1918
- founder of Centre d'Études Administratives, Paris, 1920
- a major formative influence on classical management thought
- died in Paris, November 1925

Major works

General and Industrial Management (1916)

Summary

Henri Fayol was one of the most influential management thinkers of the early twentieth century. His work complemented that of F.W. Taylor and represents one of the most important contributions to classical management theory (see TAYLOR, F.W.). Fayol's work contained the first significant attempt to develop principles of top-level management, and his work also represents one of the first attempts to analyse the different activities that make up the managerial role.

Fayol's reputation has suffered on account of his being widely perceived by subsequent generations as a technocrat developing mechanistic abstract laws of administration.

This has partly been the result of some of his statements being taken too literally, and the difficulty involved in translating his terminology into English.

1 Background

Henri Fayol studied at the Lycée at Lyon and the École Nationale des Mines at St Étienne, from which he graduated in 1860 at the unusually early age of 19. He then joined the Commentry-Fourchambault mining company (later Commentry, Forchambault and Decazeville), with which he was to be associated for the next sixty-five years. As a middle manager he was to achieve distinction for his published research into geological problems, and as managing director of the company from 1888 to 1918, he was acclaimed for his rescue of this large and strategically important firm from the threat of bankruptcy, turning it into a sustained commercial and technical success. He remained on the board of directors of the firm until his death in 1925 (Fayol 1984; Dale 1970).

Fayol attributed his success as managing director to his administrative approach rather than his technical knowledge; during his tenure there were dramatic improvements in the company's metallurgical interests, the technicalities of which he, as a mining engineer, understood little. The ideas he applied were those he was later to recommend in more detail in his later work: command, coordination, control, organization charts, ten-year forecasts and plans (Dale 1970). Fayol had developed these methods over twenty years in the company before taking charge.

That a mining engineer such as Fayol should be the first to develop such a model of management is not surprising given the nature of the work involved. Pollard (1965) has shown how and why the mining industry of the period went far further than other sectors in the development of extended and formalized structures of management. The mining context also calls into question the popular image of Fayol as a naive designer of abstract principles. Fayol would of necessity have been aware of the degree to which all manner of physical, geological and human contingencies could affect the implementation of plans. His approach did not assume uncertainty to be absent; rather, it sought ways of minimizing that uncertainty.

From 1900 onwards, Fayol's contributions to the proceedings of professional societies began to focus on administrative rather than technical issues. One such paper, presented to the Jubilee Congress of the Société de l'Industrie Minérale in 1908, was to form the basis of his main work on administration, *Administration industrielle et générale*, which was published in 1916. This work sufficed to guarantee Fayol's fame in management circles throughout Europe and North America, particularly after the English translations of 1925 and 1949.

Retiring from the private sector in 1918, Fayol turned his energies towards public administration. He lectured at the École Nationale de Guerre, and established the Centre d'Études Administratives to act as forum to publicize his ideas on administration. In particular he aimed to de-politicize and professionalize the administration of public utilities in a way that anticipated the Haldane reforms in the UK and many subsequent initiatives in public administration (Baker 1972). Initially he had more success with the Belgian government, which applied his approach in successive ministerial reorganizations. In July 1922, however, the French government presented an act to parliament which called for the Department of Posts, Telegraphs and Telephones to be reorganized according to Fayol's theories (his polemic of 1921 had focused on this Department).

Fayol remained sceptical of the state's ability to manage effectively without fundamental reorganization. It is ironic that at the time of his death he was working on the reorganization of the state tobacco monopoly, later to be immortalized by Crozier (1964).

Fayol took an active part in the first International Congress of Administrative Science in Brussels in 1910. There, he argued against the then prevailing view of administration as being confined to governmental activities, preferring to define 'administration' in terms of the activities necessary to run any large enterprise. At the second Congress (also in Brussels) in 1923, Fayol played a leading part, and was this time more specifically concerned with public administration. He argued boldly that administrative theory should focus first on how well the highest levels of government were structured rather than how well their decisions were carried out at middle levels (Urwick 1937). It was this preoccupation with the highest level of the organization, whether in government or in industry, that most distinguished Fayol's work from that of his contemporaries.

2 Main contribution

Fayol and Taylor

Some useful comparisons may be drawn between Fayol and Taylor (see TAYLOR, F.W.). Both were longstanding practitioners in heavy industry; both had distinguished themselves in technical research and experimentation before focusing on theories of management. Both have been seen as typifying the mechanistic approach to organization, although in both cases this is at best a simplification of their analyses and recommendations. However, Fayol escaped the controversy, contradictions, social unease and early demise that beset Taylor. Fayol's ideas are also more attractive in that they are more abstract, more amenable to adaptation and less atomistic than those of Taylor.

Fayol and Taylor tend to be lumped together by more recent management theorists, and are seen as having an overly rational or 'mechanistic' approach to management (Morgan 1986; Scott 1992). Although this view accurately reflects the way the work of both was interpreted by their successors, in Fayol's case it is not entirely just. Fayol saw the organization in quasi-biological terms as a 'body corporate' (*corps social*), rather than a smooth-running machine. The rules he put forward were intended as guidelines to limit and contain uncertainty, but not to eliminate it altogether.

The main difference between Fayol and Taylor, however, lies in the level of analysis. Fayol's prime concern is with the effectiveness of the 'high command' and how this affects the functioning of the organization as a whole. Taylor, on the other hand, is concerned primarily with labour productivity and the individual task:

> Fayol showed beyond question what Taylor himself appreciated, but what many of his imitators have failed to emphasize, that better management is not merely a question of improving the output of labour and the planning of subordinate units of organisation, it is above all a matter of closer study and more administrative training for (managers) at the top. Seldom in history can two men working in an identical field have differed so sharply in methods and in the details of their careers and yet have produced work which was so complementary.
>
> (Urwick 1937: 129)

Fayol on administration

The term 'administration' in Fayol's writing is often translated into English as 'management'. This does not entirely fit with Fayol's own use of the term. While he helped to widen the usage of the term 'administration' beyond the public sector, he saw administration as only one of six functions of management, the others being technical operations, commercial operations, financial operations, security and accounting.

Despite the importance of the other five functions, Fayol took the view, derived from his own experience, that administration was the most crucial in terms of the success or failure of an organization. In particular, Fayol was convinced that technical knowledge was not sufficient to make effective managers, and that while technical knowledge was the main quality required at lower levels, administrative ability became more important than technical ability as managers rose to higher ranks. This should not be taken to mean that Fayol was in favour of managers with only administrative skills, but rather that technical knowledge without administrative skill could only lead to failure.

Fayol may be credited with being among the first to see management or administration as a process rather than just a set of rules or structures, although he believed the latter were also necessary. The administrative role, in his view, consisted of five processes or activities: planning/forecasting, organizing, co-ordinating, commanding and controlling. These activities were seen as being part of all of the work of the administrator, not as specific actions in themselves.

Here one should bear in mind that the French words used for three of these terms do not entirely coincide with their English equivalents. *Prévoyance* implies more general forward thinking and anticipation and does not necessarily imply formal planning, although Fayol was an advocate of a ten-year planning horizon, with frequent revisions. *Commander* could be translated as 'giving instructions' rather than 'commanding' with its military overtones. *Contrôler* can be taken simply to mean checking or inspection, rather than control. Similarly, coordination was intended to mean not some rigid system of control but rather the process by which top management ensured a balance between different functions and priorities, while organizing was seen as consisting of sixteen duties (Fayol 1925), most of which could be summarized in more modern terms under the heading of human resources responsibilities of line management.

The five activities of management and the sixteen organizational duties are to be carried out in accordance with what Fayol puts forward as his fourteen principles of administration, themselves a precursor of other such lists such as Deming's fourteen points. It is significant that Fayol restrained himself from over-systematizing his theory: the five activities of administration and the sixteen duties of organization are not made to tie in with the fourteen principles in any integrated schema, although Urwick (1937) showed that this could be done. This restraint on Fayol's part belies the popular view of him as an oversystematic seeker after clear abstract laws.

The fourteen principles are clearly pre-scriptive but almost all are open to flexible interpretation, and this appears to have been Fayol's intention. They are as follows:

1 Division of work: Fayol believed division of labour to be efficient, but subject to certain limits beyond which it would bring diminishing returns.

2 Authority: Fayol believed official authority should be legitimized by personal authority and aligned with responsibility.

3 Discipline: this refers primarily to the honouring of agreements and rules.

4 Unity of command: employees should not be subject to orders from two different and potentially contradictory sources.

5 Unity of direction: Fayol consistently uses the biological analogy, seeing the organization as an organism which should not have two heads.

6 Subordination of individual interest: Fayol saw it as essential that the interests of one group should not be advanced at the expense of the others or of the organization as a whole.

7 Remuneration: Fayol argued that remuneration should be fair and should be enough to motivate but should not be excessive; he was sceptical of profit sharing as a means of solving conflict between capital and labour, and believed instead in the need for judgement and experience in finding the right rate of pay.

8 Centralization: although Fayol appears to see top management in the role of the brain of the organization, he states clearly that employees are not cogs in a machine, and that they affect the way decisions are put in practice. He appears to favour a pragmatic approach where an appropriate level exists for each type of decision. There is less emphasis on the separation of concept and execution than in Taylor's thinking.

9 Scalar chain: all personnel are to be arranged in a clear hierarchical structure. Fayol was aware of problems of communication across the hierarchy and therefore advocated the use of lateral 'bridges' where appropriate, although he appears to have preferred this to be agreed formally;

10 Order: everyone and everything must have its appointed place, although this may be seen as an ideal rather than an injunction to organize every last detail.

11 Equity: all levels should treat their staff equitably. Here Fayol is clearly thinking in terms of employees' perceptions rather than any hard and fast statutes.

12 Stability of tenure of personnel: this refers to the high costs of developing managers who know the organization and those in it. Fayol goes so far as to state that mediocre managers who stay are better than outstanding managers who leave.

13 Initiative: allowing initiative is seen as a means of motivating staff, and managers are expected to allow this at the expense of their own 'vanity'.

14 *Esprit de corps*: Fayol was an advocate of what might be termed an integrated culture. Interestingly for one often seen as the epitome of bureaucratic management, Fayol argued against the culture of memo-writing (as opposed to verbal communication) which he saw as necessarily divisive.

3 Evaluation

Fayol's work contains a number of finely balanced concepts which may give rise to misundertanding. Although a proponent of clear hierarchical divisions ('bridges' across the hierarchy are recommended, but only if superiors are continually kept informed), Fayol nonetheless clearly states that: 'Management … is neither an exclusive privilege nor a particular responsibility of the head of the organisation … it is an activity spread across all members of the body corporate' (Fayol 1984: 13).

On the one hand he believed in a universal science of management, applicable to all sectors; on the other hand, as a practitioner he was aware that: 'There is nothing absolute in management affairs… Seldom do we apply the same principle twice in identical conditions; allowance must be made for changing circumstances' (Fayol 1949: 19). Part of the interest of Fayol's work derives from the way in which he himself seems not to have been entirely clear whether he was a universalist or a pragmatist, a codifier or an interpreter of organizational reality.

ADRIAN CAMPBELL
UNIVERSITY OF BIRMINGHAM

Further reading

(References cited in the text marked *)

* Baker, R. (1972) *Administrative Theory and Public Administration*, London: Hutchinson. (Contains a concise critical review of Fayol's thinking, particularly as applied to public administration.)

Brodie, M. (1962) 'Henri Fayol: *Administration industrielle et générale*, a re-interpretation', *Public Administration* 40: 311–17. (A useful guide to the way in which non-francophone commentators misunderstood Fayol's ideas on account of the ambiguities of the English translations.)

Brodie, M. (1967) *Fayol on Administration*, London: Lyon, Grant & Green. (Perhaps the most substantial and balanced summary and interpretation of Fayol's work, emphasizing the process of managing and the universal principles.)

* Crozier, M. (1964) *The Bureaucratic Phenomenon*, London: Tavistock Publications. (Highly influential study of power in bureaucracies with case material drawn primarily from the French state sector, which was the focus of Fayol's interests in his last years.)

* Dale, E. (1970) *Readings in Management: Landmarks and New Frontiers*, 2nd edn, New York: McGraw-Hill. (Contains a brief discussion of the degree to which Fayol really believed in universal principles of management, and a translation of an extract from his 'L'Éveil de l'esprit profond' (1927), detailing administrative techniques used to reverse the declining the fortunes of the mining company Commentry, Fourchambault and Decazeville.)

Fayol, H. (1921) *L'incapacité industrielle de l'État: les P.T.T.*, Paris, Dunod. (A polemic on the need to apply administrative rather than political principles to the management of public sector organisations, via the example of the state Department of Posts, Telegraph and Telephones.)

* Fayol, H. (1925) *Administration industrielle et générale* (General and Industrial Management), Paris: Dunod. (Fayol's best-known work, originally published in 1916 in *Bulletin de la Société de l'Industrie Minérale*.)

Fayol, H. (1937) 'The administrative theory in the state', in L. Gulick and L. Urwick (eds), *Papers on the Science of Administration*, New York: Institute of Public Administration, Columbia University. (A translation of Fayol's paper to the 2nd International Congress on Administrative Science, 1923.)

* Fayol, H. (1949) *General and Industrial Management*, trans. C. Storrs, London: Pitman. (This is the best known translation; there is an earlier translation by J.A. Couborough, entitled *Industrial and General Administration*, published in 1925 by The International Management Institute, Geneva.)

* Fayol, H. (1984) *General and Industrial Management*, trans. I. Gray, New York: David S. Lake. (Complete retranslation of original, with extensive revisions. Aimed at a wide readership, it minimizes 'archaic language' and references to obsolete contemporary debates and provides biographical and interpretative guidance.)

Lepawski, A. (1949) *Administration: the Art and Science of Organisation and Management*, New York: Alfred A. Knopf. (Demonstrates the degree to which Fayol was not the first to attempt to set out universal principles of administration; provides some useful contextual material on French administrative traditions and practices.)

* Morgan, G. (1986) *Images of Organization*, London: Sage Publications. (The chapter entitled 'Mechanization takes command' provides one of the best summaries of the case against Fayol and Taylor as examples of 'mechanistic' management thought.)

* Pollard, S. (1965) *The Genesis of Modern Management*, London: Arnold. (Useful as general background for the context in which Fayol worked, showing the reasons why more elaborate and formalized management structures appeared first in the mining industry of the nineteenth century.)

* Scott, W.R. (1992) *Organizations: Rational, Natural and Open Systems*, Englewood Cliffs, NJ: Prentice Hall. (Provides one of the best analyses of the 'rational' approach to organizations, drawing together the work of Fayol, Taylor, Weber and their successors.)

Sofer, C. (1972) *Organizations in Theory and Practice*, London: Heinemann. (A brief discussion of the contribution and limitations of Fayol's work, alongside that of comparable figures such as Babbage and Lee.)

* Urwick, L. (1937) 'The function of administration: with special reference to the work of Henri Fayol', in L. Gulick and L. Urwick (eds), *Papers on the Science of Administration*, New York: Institute of Public Administration, Columbia University. (A detailed review of

Fayol's thinking, showing it to have anticipated later work in the USA such as that of Mooney and Reiley.)

See also: CROZIER, M.; DEMING, W.E.; FORD, H.; GULICK, L.H.; TAYLOR, F.W.; URWICK, L.F.; WEBER, M.

Related topics in the IEBM: GENERAL MANAGEMENT; HUMAN CAPITAL; HUMAN RELATIONS; HUMAN RESOURCE MANAGEMENT; LEADERSHIP; ORGANIZATION BEHAVIOUR; ORGANIZATION BEHAVIOUR, HISTORY OF; ORGANIZATION TYPES; PUBLIC SECTOR MANAGEMENT

Fiedler, Fred E. (1923–)

Personal background

- born in Vienna in 1923; left for America in 1938
- studied at University of Chicago gaining a masters degree in clinical psychology (working with Carl Rogers) and a PhD on the therapeutic relationship, 1946–9,
- moved to Illinois to work with Lee Cronbach in 1951 and, two years later, established the Group Effectiveness Research Laboratory
- became professor of psychology at the University of Washington in 1969
- retired in 1992, though continues to be active, primarily in the leadership training area
- developed the notion that leadership effectiveness was contingent on the relationship between the leader and situational factors; produced training programmes to put the 'contingency model' into practice

Major works

A Theory of Leadership Effectiveness (1967)
Improving Leadership Effectiveness: The Leader Match Concept (with M.M. Chemers and L. Mahar)(1976)
New Approaches to Effective Leadership: Cognitive Resources and Human Performance (with J.E. Garcia)(1987)

Summary

Without doubt Fiedler is best known for his 'contingency model' of leadership effectiveness. This provided a new way forward in the leadership area – an area where researchers had failed to show that effectiveness was predictable solely on the basis of leader characteristics – be they personal traits or behaviours. His original contribution was the provision of a metric for measuring and classifying leadership situations, a way of distinguishing between two sorts of leader, and a way of combining these with data about leadership effectiveness. He also is well known for his work on leadership training, promoting the view that leadership effectiveness could be improved, not by trying to change the leader but by changing the situation; he has produced training materials for just this purpose. Contingency models came to be the norm and not just in the leadership area; some now think they have outlived their usefulness.

1 History of work and ideas

Fiedler's early work experience was extremely varied, including over twenty jobs such as selling, repairing trucks, debt collecting and book keeping. This was followed by four years as a soldier after which he returned to his studies, got married, and within four years had a masters degree in clinical psychology and a PhD. It was during this time that he began his life-long interest in aspects of interpersonal relations and their connection with different sorts of effectiveness criteria. So, for example, early work on diagnostic competence suggested that reputedly superior therapists described their own self-concept and that of their client in very similar ways. Out of this work evolved the 'assumed similarity of opposites' (ASO) measure, along with the 'least preferred co-worker' (LPC) questionnaire. Both measures obtained information on some aspects of a person's perceptions of others and were examined in relation to a wide variety of individual and group performance measures.

In 1951 he moved to the University of Illinois, first to work with Lee Cronbach and later to join the psychology department and establish the Group Effectiveness Research Laboratory. There he continued his earlier interests, investigating for example, connections between group members' relations with their group (group cohesiveness) and other individual issues such as personal adjustment, leadership and group performance. A programme of research was begun on cross-cultural relations resulting in the development and application of the 'culture assimilator' – a training programme for improving relations.

By far his best known work concerns leadership effectiveness. The first and seminal publications described his 'contingency model'. For a long time after Fiedler and a great many co-workers attempted to validate and to extend the original model and to 'explain' the meaning of the predictor measures of leadership effectiveness. This line of work developed into a programme of leadership training called 'leadermatch', and finally into 'cognitive resource theory' where he shifted his focus to leader intelligence and experience and their relations with leader performance.

2 A contingency model of leadership effectiveness

Research into leadership has been directed towards two questions: what kind of person achieves leadership status, and what factors influence their effectiveness. Early studies, and there were hundreds of them, failed to support the notion that people in leadership positions had personal traits that set them apart from non-leaders. And so attention shifted to leaders' behaviours: to ways of measuring them, and to their relations with group performance – viewed as an indicator of the leader's effectiveness. By the late 1950s and early 1960s it became clear that leadership effectiveness could not be predicted on the basis of behavioural data alone. Then, in 1964, came the 'contingency model'. The basic argument was that leadership effectiveness was 'contingent' (dependent) on both aspects of a leader and aspects of their

situation. The general contingency line of argument, now so commonplace, then was an innovation and certainly was Fiedler's major contribution, both in its specifics and as a way of thinking about person–context relations.

In his early studies Fiedler obtained ASO and LPC scores from leaders (inputs from person) and correlated these with data about group productivity – regarded as effectiveness data (outputs). To his surprise, sometimes the correlations were positive and sometimes they were negative. The contingency hypothesis emerged from attempts to make sense of this. Post hoc analyses were run on existing studies, sorting them according to likely differences between leadership contexts ('inputs from the situation') and systematic relations seemed to result. It seemed to Fiedler that correlations between LPC/ASO and group effectiveness were positive or negative depending on the type of group (good or poor group atmosphere), the type of task (structured or unstructured), and the type of leader position (high or low position power). He combined these to produce eight (2×2×2) leadership situations, ordered them from 'very favourable' to 'very unfavourable' – a reference to how much control the situation seemed to afford leaders in their attempts to lead – and argued that low LPC leaders were more effective in very favourable and very unfavourable situations whilst high LPC leaders were effective in situations of moderate favourableness (see Fiedler 1964, 1967).

This was the beginning of many years of further investigation and controversy. Following his 1971 paper 'Validation and extension of the contingency model of leadership effectiveness: a review of empirical findings', Fiedler concluded that his initial hypothesis had been validated and turned his attention to explanation and generalization. Others continued to investigate the validity of his hypothesis (had studies indeed shown it to be predictive and could further evidence of this sort be obtained?); the stability and meaning of LPC scores (just what were they telling us about leaders and how did this relate to the meaning of the claimed relationships?); and methodological and statistical issues. Fiedler's model provoked interesting questions in all these areas, questions that seemed answerable through research and analysis. As to the answers, they remain very controversial. Fiedler himself believes the contingency hypothesis has 'substantial support', regards the LPC measure as adequate, and views explanation of the meaning of these (established) relationships as all that is lacking (see e.g. Fiedler 1992); some agree (e.g. Strube and Garcia 1981), some do not (e.g. Hosking 1981), others have moved on to different conceptions of leadership (see e.g. Grint 1997)

3 Explaining, extending, and applying the contingency model

From the 1970s onwards Fiedler turned his attention to understanding the meaning of LPC scores and to developing the practical implications of his model; leadership training became a central theme, as did the role of experience and intelligence. In 1976 he joined with Marty Chemers and Linda Mahar to publish a training manual entitled *Improving Leadership Effectiveness: The Leader Match Concept*. This manual introduces the concept of leadership style and readers complete the LPC. They then are provided with the 'tools for accurately diagnosing and classifying leadership situations' (1974: 4) along with practice in using those tools. Finally, the leader match concept is described and leaders are instructed in how to manipulate group atmosphere, task structure and position power so that they can change the situation to obtain a 'match' with their style and, as a result, improve their effectiveness.

In Fiedler's view, leader match training has been validated, is cost effective and has long lasting effects (e.g. Fiedler 1992, 1996). Others argue that since leader match depends on the contingency model it rests on very shaky foundations (Hosking and Schriesheim 1978). This said, once again Fiedler's work has generated interesting and important questions. One such question concerns the pros and cons of applying a 'micro' theory that deals with only a small 'part of the world', so to speak. What might be the usefulness,

possible unanticipated and negative consequences, and the ethical issues involved in such an application?

Cognitive resource theory, like leader match, emerged as a part of Fiedler's continuing interest in the relationships described by the original model – what did LPC mean, why did it predict, and how could it be applied? He argues that leaders may or may not be able to use their 'cognitive resources' depending on their leadership context. In his view stress is a key moderator – under low stress conditions leaders tend to use their 'intelligence' and misuse their 'experience' whilst the reverse is true in situations of high stress. This leads him to consider how leaders may be helped to make effective use of their cognitive resources and so improve their leadership performance. He argues that organizations should continue to select for experience, intelligence and job-related knowledge but should manipulate stress levels so that leaders may use effectively their cognitive resources.

4 Commentary

One of the ways in which a research area moves on ('progresses'?) is that the questions change. Some leadership researchers and trainers now have serious doubts about the focus on individuals as leaders and the treatment of group performance as a signifier of a leader's effectiveness. The doubts arise for many reasons, some of which concern trends in work settings and the way work is done. For example, given current trends such as 'flattening' hierarchies, teamworking, and enabling, does it make sense to single out one individual as a leader and to make that person individually responsible for a group's performance? In addition, there now are good theoretical reasons to set aside the assumption that individuals (e.g. leaders) and contexts (e.g. leadership situations) each can be treated as if they had a separate existence and their own defining characteristics. Yet without this assumption the contingency way of thinking about person – context relations loses its necessary pre-theoretical foundations. So, those with a continuing interest in 'leadership' will need to find another way to avoid individualistic and culturalist separations of person and setting.

Another contingency model assumption that some would like to abandon is that leadership, leadership situations and leadership effectiveness usefully may be defined from a single perspective. A variety of recent developments invite us to assume, theorize and investigate multiple perspectives, or 'voices', each of which might radically differ in their constructions of a situation and e.g. what they would regard as 'effective'. Important amongst such changes are, for example, increasing globalization, new communication technologies, teamworking, and the management of diversity, all of which invite attention to multiple and contrasting local realities and to relations between different realities. This, in turn, invites reconceptualization of the two key ways in which relations have been theorized in terms of power and knowledge. Both are being theorized in ways that move away from individualistic conceptions and locate them in ongoing, collective processes. So, for example, 'power over' is being exposed as a limiting conception of relations and notions of 'power to' and 'power with' are being developed. Similar things are happening with knowledge where 'knowing how' – knowing in action – is receiving more attention. To conclude, there are reasons to argue that the contingency model has outlived its usefulness – but it was useful. If the term 'leadership' continues to attract interest then it may have to be very differently understood (see e.g. Calas and Smircich, 1997; Dachler and Hosking 1995; Hosking, in press).

DIAN MARIE HOSKING
ASTON UNIVERSITY BUSINESS SCHOOL

Further reading

(References cited in the text marked *)

* Calas, M. and Smircich, L. (1997) 'Voicing seduction to silence leadership', in K. Grint (ed.) *Leadership: Classical, Contemporary, and Critical Approaches*, Oxford: OUP
* Dachler, H.P. and Hosking, D.M. (1995) 'The primacy of relations in socially constructing organizational realities', in D.M. Hosking, H.P. Dachler and K.J. Gergen *Management and Organisation: Relational Alternatives to Individualism*, Aldershot: Avebury. (Theorizes social processes from a social constructionist perspective using leadership to illustrate the arguments.)
* Fiedler, F.E. (1964) 'A contingency model of leadership effectiveness', in L. Berkowitz (ed.) *Advances in Experimental Social Psychology* 1: 149–190, New York: Academic Press. (First statement of the contingency hypothesis.)
* Fiedler, F.E. (1967) *A Theory of Leadership Effectiveness*, New York: McGraw Hill. (Outlines contingency hypotheses, some validation studies, and the emerging theory of the relations described.)
* Fiedler,F.E. (1971) 'Validation and extension of the contingency model of leadership effectiveness: a review of empirical findings', *Psychological Bulletin* 76: 128–148. (As its title suggests.)
* Fiedler, F.E. (1992) 'Life in a pretzel-shaped universe', in A.G. Bedeian (ed.) *Management Laureates: A Collection of Autobiographical Essays,* Volume 1, Conn: JAI Press. (Fiedler talks about his life and work.)
* Fiedler, F.E. (1996) 'Research on leadership selection and training: one view of the future', *Administrative Science Quarterly* 41: 241–250.
* Fiedler, F.E., Chemers. M.M. and Mahar, L. (1976) *Improving Leadership Effectiveness: The Leader Match Concept,* New York: Wiley. (A training manual instructing the reader in how to apply the model.)
* Fiedler, F.E. and Garcia, J.E. (1987) *New Approaches to Effective Leadership: Cognitive Resources and Human Performance*, New York: John Wiley. (Further extensions of the original model, now includes stress, leader intelligence, and experience.)
* Grint, K. (ed.) (1997) *Leadership: Classical, Contemporary, and Critical Approaches*, Oxford: OUP. (As the title says; includes three critical pieces.)
* Hosking, D.M. (1981) 'A critical evaluation of Fiedler's contingency hypothesis', in G.M. Stephenson and J.M. Davis (eds) *Progress in Applied Social Psychology* Volume 1: 103–154. (Detailed analysis of methodologies, data, predictor measures, and explanations; conclusions generally negative.)
* Hosking, D.M. (in press) 'Leadership and leadership training: a relational constructionist perspective', *The European Journal of Occupational and Organisational Psychology.* (Takes a social constructionist approach to leadership and leadership training.)

* Hosking, D.M. and Schriesheim, C. A. (1978). 'Improving leadership effectiveness: The leader match concept', *Administrative Science Quarterly*, 23: 496–505. (Summarises leader match, argues that application of the model is not justified and could be dysfunctional.)
* Strube,M.J. and Garcia, J.E. (1981) 'A meta-analytical investigation of Fiedler's contingency model of leadership effectiveness', *Psychological Bulletin* 85, 1199–1237 (Statistical analysis of aggregated findings, concludes there are small but significant effects.)

See also: KOTTER, J.; MCGREGOR, D.; WEBER, M.

Related topics in the IEBM: COMMITMENT IN JAPAN; GENERAL MANAGEMENT; GROUPS AND TEAMS; LEADERSHIP; OCCUPATIONAL PSYCHOLOGY; ORGANIZATION BEHAVIOUR; ORGANIZATION BEHAVIOUR, HISTORY OF; ORGANIZATION STRUCTURE; ORGANIZATIONAL PERFORMANCE; POWER

Flanders, Allan David (1910–73)

1 Introduction
2 Main contribution
3 Evaluation
4 Conclusions

Personal background

- born 27 July 1910
- educated at Latymer Upper School; Landerziehungsheim Walkemuhle, Germany
- various jobs, including draughtsman
- research Assistant, TUC (1943–46)
- head of Political Branch, British Control Commission, Germany (1946–47)
- senior lecturer in Industrial Relations, University of Oxford (1949–69; MA 1950)
- faculty fellow, Nuffield College Oxford (1964–69)
- member, Secretary of State's Colonial Advisory Committee (1954–62)
- industrial relations adviser, National Board for Prices and Incomes (1965–68)
- full time member, Commission on Industrial Relations (1969–71)
- reader in Industrial Relations, University of Warwick (1971–73; CBE 1971)
- early writer and theorist of industrial relations, a key member of the influential 'Oxford School of Industrial Relations' and also involved in policy
- died 29 September 1973

Major works

The Fawley Productivity Agreements (1964)
Management and Unions (1970)

Summary

Allan Flanders was an inquiring and influential theorist of industrial relations, a management area hitherto renowned for its empiricism and focus on 'facts' and practical problems. He was also the principal theoretical architect of an important group of academics whose reformist pluralism became so influential in the UK in the 1960s and 1970s. Flanders wrote general and specialized texts and chapters on various aspects of industrial relations, including some early comparative analysis. He continually expounded the panacea of social partnership (as via collective bargaining), which underpinned much of his work. Furthermore, Flanders' relatively late starting and short academic career was interspersed (and perhaps distracted to some extent) with involvement in political and active policy debates when industrial relations was the focus of heated controversy and analysis mixed with prescription, administration and reform. His untimely death robbed the academic community of a perceptive thinker on management with work experience and diverse policy involvement. In short, Flanders was a 'guru' of the 'Oxford School' and industrial relations of the 1960s and 1970s, and one who, unlike contemporary versions, had the ear of politicians and policy makers.

1 Introduction

The coverage of the broad canvas on which such a multi-faceted thinker as Flanders worked is constrained given the nature of this publication. Therefore, his more obviously political work, sympathy for social democracy and hostility of the Marxist and communist left, are not detailed. Flanders' unusual personal background (see Clegg 1990) included an education in Germany at the adult school run by the International Socialist Kampfbund, founded by the socialist philosopher Leonard Nelson. After Hitler came to power, he returned to Britain and sustained ideas of ethical socialism via the Socialist Vanguard/Union group and its *Socialist Commentary*. During the Second World War

Flanders joined the TUC to help prepare its 'Report on Postwar Reconstruction' and returned to Germany with the British Control Commission in 1946. He played a key part in setting up the structure of industrial unionism (see TRADE UNIONS), which many saw as a central feature of the political economy of post-war Germany. In 1949 he took up a lectureship at Oxford, where he spent virtually his entire academic career (with a stint at the same college as Clegg and Fox) (see CLEGG, H.A.), while also serving on several important government committees. These diverse experiences helped fertilize, incubate and mature Flanders' thoughts and ideas.

Flanders produced early texts on industrial relations matters, those of major importance being, for example, Flanders (1952) and Flanders and Clegg (1954). Many industrial relations scholars were brought up on, and influenced by, this work. He wrote on a range of topics, such as incomes policy, wages, pay systems, conflict and 'normative systems', and union–state relations (Flanders 1970, 1974). Importantly, Flanders was the first British industrial relations scholar since the Webbs to endeavour to write about theory.

2 Main contribution

A single volume of the more important of Flanders' work exists (Flanders 1970). This collection displays both the evolution and unity of his thought on the changing roles and responsibilities of unions, management and government, and at a theoretical level reflects his concern to analyse industrial relations and the institution of collective bargaining in terms of job regulation and his belief in social partnership. His other seminal work (Flanders 1964) includes many of these themes within a case study of an oil refinery, and which contained lessons of wider application. Flanders' main contributions will be analysed via; his definition of industrial relations; trade unions; management; collective bargaining and productivity bargaining; and the influential 'Oxford School of Industrial Relations' and the

public bodies it swayed, although all these are often interlinked (see FOX, A.; CLEGG, H.A.).

First, industrial relations was famously defined by Flanders as 'a system of rules' and the 'study of the institutions of job regulation'. Even his critics registered that this was of great significance and an influential pioneering attempt to give theoretical unity, precision and meaning to the notion of industrial relations and its study (Hyman 1975). Its centrality was that it helped give some substance to what industrial relations actually 'was', what to research (and reform), and had some universal applicability.

Second, Flanders wrote about trade unions. Unions had 'two faces' ('sword of justice' and 'vested interest'), and gave priority to their industrial over political methods, which had lower and upper limits. The purpose of unions was participation in job regulation as a means for worker development. Unions were involved in the 'force of tradition' and attachment to 'voluntarism'. However, precisely formulated models of trade union action and behaviour seldom appeared in his writings, although Poole (1981) outlines Flanders' principal explanatory dimensions.

Third, management often felt Flanders' ire. For instance, under-employment, overtime and restrictive labour practices were the 'sign of managerial lethargy and incompetence' (Flanders 1964: 235). The roots of such 'irresponsibility' were within management itself and its frame of mind – to have as little to do with industrial relations as possible, to default to personnel and unions, and to give nothing away unless pressured. Such attitudes prevailed as management had neither the knowledge nor confidence to act differently due to a lack of training and the inherent uncertainties of industrial relations matters. Also, for Flanders (1964: 255) treating management as a 'profession' was invalid 'as long as it has no accepted standards of conduct which fully define its moral responsibilities'. Similar ideas flowed through Flanders' (1970: 147) work on industry's 'social responsibilities', which were based on the 'simple yet overriding consideration' of workers' dignity and respect for the intrinsic worth of the human personality.

Fourth, Flanders developed an influential understanding of collective bargaining. This is an explicitly collective way of managing employment with a role for unions. A spectrum of outcomes result, from collective agreements through to common understandings of varying degrees of formality and precision and levels, from national to factory. Originating in his criticism of the Webbs' classical conception, for Flanders collective bargaining had less economic significance, as simply a device for gaining 'rewards', and was more a political process giving workers 'voice', a participative form of decision making, enhancing self-respect and dignity, and an expression of industrial and pluralist democracy. Workers needed opportunities for making their own choices and decisions, not autocratic nor even paternalistic management. Such notions appear in his interest in industrial democracy, as in the John Lewis Partnership study (Flanders *et al.* 1968).

Similar views appear in Flanders' (1964) seminal work on productivity bargaining. Acceptance of Esso's suggestion to study their Fawley refinery experiment was crucial as the task refreshed and stimulated Flanders and the book established his reputation at home and abroad (Clegg 1990). Flanders believed productivity bargaining could revise 'inefficient' work practices. Importantly, it would reconstruct and democratize workplace relations by negotiation and joint agreement and responsibility, extend collective bargaining and integrate trade union shop stewards into the heart of management decision making processes, while marching management to a 'higher ground' and new 'moral order' as the process produced regard and respect for workplace democracy (Ahlstrand 1990). Flanders' work struck a 'chord' at the time and continued to reverberate. For instance, 'Industrial Relations: What is Wrong with the System?' drew on Fawley's general conclusions and posed questions for the bright new hope for reforming industrial relations – the governmental enquiry into trade unions and employers' associations. Flanders' evidence to the Donovan Commission was revised for publication as 'Collective Bargaining: Prescription for

Change', indicating where reform must begin to improve industrial relations. In particular, he criticized the 'drift' and 'chaotic state' of relations between management and trade union shop stewards, with largely informal, fragmented and autonomous collective bargaining resulting in a litany of problems: unofficial strikes; earnings drift; labour under-utilization and resistance to change; overtime and demoralization of incentive pay schemes; inequitable and unstable pay structures; decline in industrial discipline; undermining of external regulation by industry-wide and other agreements; and weakening of membership control by trade unions and employers' associations. This led to Flanders' (1970: 172) famous dictum that management 'can only regain control by sharing it'.

Fifth, Flanders was a key member of the 'Oxford School of Industrial Relations', whose impact was enhanced by governmental interventions. The group, whose composition and unity are contested, assumed 'progressive' employers and 'pragmatic' governments would cooperate under the influence of 'reason' and 'goodwill', and mixed systems theory (i.e. concern for rule making), with epistemological and theoretical origins grounded in the historiographical researches and substantive theories of the Webbs coupled with Durkheimian sociological precepts (Poole 1981). The group's influence flowed powerfully not only to governmental levels, but also through institutional (e.g. with members serving as arbitrators and on pay boards) and academic (e.g the moulding of students and researchers and development of the Industrial Relations Research Unit) waters. The methods, analysis and prescriptions of this group continued to echo down the years, acting almost as a touchstone for much subsequent thought and work.

3 Evaluation

There can be two views of Flanders' work. First, Flanders was far too narrow, naive, simplistic and overly-focused on collectives, institutions and formality. Yet, industrial relations developed along a more individualistic, unregulated trajectory, with the erosion of collective bargaining and spread of non-collective pay and employment. These developments were not foreseen. Flanders' work was criticized. This included his industrial relations definition (see Hyman 1975, 1989) due to its perceived interest in 'order' and how patterns of social relations are stabilized rather than in the significance of challenges to prevailing structures. This 'conservative' tendency appeared in the words he used: 'institutions', directing attention to formal, rather than informal, organizations, the more likely sources of challenges; 'regulation', which is too restrictive, focusing on how conflict is controlled rather than on processes through which disputes are generated; and 'system' as a Dunlopian set of rules, putting undue emphasis on stability maintenance. Indeed, pluralism was criticized for accepting 'the master institutions, principles and assumptions of the *status quo* as non-problematical' (Fox 1973: 219), thus reinforcing views that these are legitimate, inevitable and unchangeable. The Flanderite underpinnings of Donovan were also attacked for over-emphasis on collective bargaining and methodological and theoretical paucity and even 'total ignorance' of collective bargaining history in those industries where it first extensively developed and for following the 'Oxford Line's' 'short-term rule of thumb over the broader generalization, a rather low awareness of those disciplines ... which illuminate the field with normative observations, and a variety of propagandist mini-reformism which consists partly in leading people boldly in the direction they appear to be going anyway' (Turner 1968: 358).

There were also critiques of Flanders' conception of, and belief in, collective bargaining, often incorrectly seen as almost a magic elixir for workplace ills. This contained a 'basic error at the heart' (Fox 1975: 154) because its anti-Webbsian foundations and distinctions – as between individual and collective bargaining and its implications and results – were flawed. Flanders' evaluation of productivity bargaining was blurred by his vision of what 'ought' to be and his own

personal philosophy and ideological beliefs (Ahlstrand 1990). Tellingly, productivity bargaining even failed in its Fawley heartland, being used to minimize rather than enhance the collective role of unions, with remaining hostility to union participation as management operated in a unitarist manner and even withdrew collective bargaining (Ahlstrand 1990). In short, pluralist, reformist ideas were not really useful for the realities of workplace employment relations and became even less so over time – as seen when the unitarist assumptions of human resource management gathered pace and penetrated businesses. Thus, at first glance, Flanders has seemingly not 'weathered well' and while of historical significance, his work is of less contemporary relevance.

On the other hand, Flanders was in many ways a path-breaking and far-sighted thinker and despite operating within a particular socio-economic and political milieux, has retained his importance and relevance and has stood the test of time. For instance, Flanders' industrial relations definition was acceptable as, for example, 'institutions' covers both formal and informal organizations, as used in his Fawley study (Clegg 1979). Criticisms of the pluralist Donovanites were unfair given their diversity and that many later produced theoretical work (Poole 1981). Indeed, Flanders' thoughts contributed to more systematic explanations for union growth and the nature of trade unionism under collective bargaining (Clegg 1976), the notable analytical advances of the 1970s. Flanders' research on productivity bargaining was important as it was a managerial attempt to seize the initiative and sent widespread shock waves as it opened lengthy debate about endemic problems and solutions and it also contained antecedence for 'strategy', often seen as an almost paradigmatic development in industrial relations (Ahlstrand 1990). It explored the world of informal bargaining and how it might be contained by formal structures, emphasized the central priority of management initiative and control systems and was the first academic study to argue for the replacement of multi- by single-employer bargaining.

Other precursors of debates of contemporary relevance can be seen. Flanders (1964: 247) noted management's use of 'every method available for the direct communication of information', all too often mistakenly presented as a panacea for creating co-operation and resolving problems. Indeed, as Flanders' (1970: 172) warned, co-operation could not be fostered by 'propaganda and exhortation, by preaching its benefits', nor communication, which was often 'auxiliary to the system of control'. Debates on differences between human resource management and personnel management were previewed when Flanders (1964: 255) argued that 'the success of personnel management as a specialized function has to be judged by the extent to which the need for it declines, and that there is a need to integrate into line management decisions on labour relations'. Flanders' robust and visionary views on management's failings and weaknesses have remained poignant.

Nevertheless, Flanders' clarion calls were often ignored. We must not overlook his over-optimism concerning reform and behavioural change. Rapacious management, the collapse of the public sector and the state as the model 'good employer' and the increasing fragmentation and diversity of the workforce in a world of increasingly marginalized and flexible labour, are difficult terrain for Flanderite analysis and solutions. He seemed to focus less on the messy, murky world of individual employment relations which are less receptive to universal panaceas. To be sure some of these caveats are based on hindsight, and apply to many of his contemporaries, but they temper any wholly positive evaluation of Flanders' work.

4 Conclusions

Flanders' writings have had a mixed history but his place in management thought is secure. His often carefully crafted work contains important perceptions which often emerge on re-reading. While it is true that Flanders' policy prescriptions and his theory of collective bargaining were partial and are now somewhat dated; he still advanced this theory further than anyone else at the time;

and his sharp observations about managerial failings are as pertinent as they ever were. The pluralist ideal of collective bargaining, which looked moribund by the 1980s, is re-emerging in a different (European and Blairite) guise. Flanders' analysis of collective bargaining as a political process and the non-economic objectives of trade unionists still holds. Also, pluralism seemed conservative to the 1970s radicals, but in the light of contemporary managerial unitarism and beliefs in new nostrums, a Flanders who warned about managers believing their own rhetorics and who demonstrated the values of sharing control could play a major role. Current interests in social partnership are definitely Flanders' style. In sum, Flanders made key contributions to many areas of industrial relations and initiated and encouraged important debates and advances. He was also a 'guru' in his day with public influence. Flanders' work was of significance for its relatively rare comparative analysis and theoretical unity, and has continued to have resonance down the years.

CHRIS ROWLEY
ROYAL HOLLOWAY COLLEGE
UNIVERSITY OF LONDON

Note

Many thanks to Nuffield College's peerless library and librarians, Arthur Marsh, Malcolm Warner and especially Pat McGovern, Rod Martin, Willy Brown, Paul Edwards and John Kelly for insightful comments and suggestions on an earlier draft. The normal disclaimers apply.

Further Reading

(References cited in the text marked *)

* Ahlstrand, B. (1990) *The Quest for Productivity: A Case Study of Fawley after Flanders*. Cambridge: Cambridge University Press. (An interesting follow-up analysis of Flanders' key work.)
* Clegg, H. (1976) *Trade Unionism under Collective Bargaining: A Theory Based on Comparisons of Six Countries*. Oxford: Blackwell. (Acknowledges the importance and influence of Flanders' ideas.)

* Clegg, H. (1979) *The Changing System of Industrial Relations in Great Britain.* Oxford: Blackwell. (Standard text whose antecedence was Flanders and Clegg 1954.)

* Clegg, (1990) 'The Oxford School of Industrial Relations', *Warwick Papers in Industrial Relations*, IRRU, University of Warwick No.31 January. (Fascinating outline of origins, membership, role and characteristics of the Oxford School.)

* Flanders, A. (1952) *Trade Unions.* London: Hutchinson's University Library. (Standard text on trade unions which had gone through seven editions by 1968.)

* Flanders, A. (1964) *The Fawley Productivity Agreements: A Case Study of Management and Collective Bargaining.* London: Faber and Faber. (Seminal work on productivity bargaining and seen as one of his key contributions.)

* Flanders, A. (1970) *Management and Unions: The Theory and Reform of Industrial Relations.* London: Faber and Faber. (The key collection of much of his most important work.)

* Flanders, A. (1974) 'The Tradition of Voluntarism', *British Journal of Industrial Relations* xii (3): 352–370. (Appearing after his death, displays his increasing interest in the role of the state.)

* Flanders, A. and Clegg, H. (eds) (1954) *The System of Industrial Relations in Great Britain: Its History, Law and Institutions.* Oxford: Blackwell. (A path-breaking, but almost exclusively institutional, formative text.)

* Flanders, A.; Pomeranz, R. and Woodward, J. (1968) *Experiment in Industrial Democracy: A Study of the John Lewis Partnership.* London: Faber and Faber. (An analysis of industrial democracy in the major retailer and its wider implications.)

* Fox, A. (1973) 'Industrial Relations: A Social Critique of Pluralist Ideology' in J. Child (ed) *Man and Organization: The Search for Explanation and Social Relevance.* (pp.185–231). London: Allen and Unwin. (An influential critique of pluralism and its proponents.)

* Fox, A. (1975) 'Collective Bargaining, Flanders and the Webbs', *British Journal of Industrial Relations* xiii (2): 151–174. (An important attack on Flanders' analysis and work on collective bargaining.)

* Hyman, R. (1975) *Industrial Relations: A Marxist Introduction.* London: Macmillan. (An alternative theoretical view of industrial relations.)

* Hyman, R. (1989) *The Political Economy of Industrial Relations: Theory and Practice in a Cold Climate.* London: Macmillan. (A useful collection providing different perspectives to Flanders.)

* Poole, M. (1981) *Theories of Trade Unionism: A Sociology of Industrial Relations.* London: Routledge and Keegan Paul. (A comprehensive study of trade unionism, with an excellent section on Flanders.)

* Turner, H.A. (1968) 'The Royal Commission's Research Papers', *British Journal of Industrial Relations* vi (3): 346–359. (A withering attack on Donovan and its contributors, including Flanders.)

See also: CLEGG, H.A.; DUNLOP, J.T.; FOX, A.

Related topics in the IEBM: COLLECTIVE BARGAINING; CORPORATISM; EMPLOYEE RELATIONS, MANAGEMENT OF; EMPLOYERS' ASSOCIATIONS; GURU CONCEPT; HUMAN RESOURCE MANAGEMENT; INDUSTRIAL AND LABOUR RELATIONS; INDUSTRIAL DEMOCRACY; MANAGERIAL BEHAVIOUR; MANAGEMENT DEVELOPMENT; PRODUCTIVITY; TRADE UNION; WORK SYSTEMSS

Follett, Mary Parker (1868–1933)

Personal background

- born 3 September 1868 in Quincy, near Boston, Massachusetts
- graduated *summa cum laude* from Radcliffe College, Cambridge, Massachusetts, in economics, government, law and philosophy in 1898
- introduced the concept of the business as a social agency and economic unit; advocated group-work and democratic governance in the workplace for most effective performance
- died Boston, 18 December 1933

Major works

The Speaker of the House of Representatives (1896)

The New State–Group Organization: The Solution for Popular Government (1918)

Creative Experience (1924)

Summary

Mary Parker Follett (1868–1933) was primarily a political scientist who advocated the establishment of neighbourhood groups as primary units of self-governance and as the most effective means of achieving true citizenship and the fairer and more productive society. She was also active, and an innovator, in the field of social work. She brought to business organization and management her knowledge and experience from these other fields. As in government and in social work, so in the business: group-work and self-governance through the group would ensure most satisfying and productive results.

Follett dealt with the basic questions which underlie all relations: conflict, power, authority, leadership, control. She applied the findings of both the physical and social sciences to the business organization and demonstrated the need to create unity of action out of diversity of interests and to foster good human relations in the workplace. Her teachings, widely acclaimed in her lifetime, lost favour after her death. However, their underlying importance and value have been gaining ground and, at the onset of the twenty-first century, Follett is coming into her own: she is now considered to be the 'Prophet of Management' (Graham 1995a).

1 Introduction

Follett brought to the study of business organization and management the concepts she had developed as a political scientist and the hands-on experience she acquired as a manager in the social work field. She held that the unit of society was not the individual in isolation but the 'group-individual' (Child 1969). It is through the groups to which they belong that individuals derive their identity and fulfil their potential.

Managers and managed are basically of the same ilk. For Follett, thinking and doing are not separate activities, but parts of the same process, in which either part may precede and have greater weight than the other. To structure the work organization on a strict hierarchical order does not reflect the realities and the needs of everyday life, and to resolve conflict constructively, domination and compromise do not work in the long run. The parties in conflict must themselves find their own solution, the solution that meets their mutual, underlying real demands.

As against the concept of 'power-over' which is reductionist and wasteful of resources, Follett introduced the concept of 'power-with', also found in nature, which is co-active and increases the total power of the group. Follett demonstrated that there is no need for personal order-giving or order-taking. Each situation has its own law and it is this law which dictates the order, to be obeyed by both manager and managed. Within the group, Follett held that the followers' responsibility is to keep their leader in full charge by actively participating in the ongoing decision-making process, and not merely complying with direction.

It is difficult to encapsulate Follett's teaching but the following two quotations give an idea of the comprehensiveness and the modernity of her thought: 'The form of [business] organization should be such as to allow or induce the continuous coordination of the experience of men' (Metcalf and Urwick 1941: 121); 'If we want harmony between labor and capital, we must make labor and capital into one group: we must have an integration of interests and motives, of standards and ideals of justice' (Follett 1918: 117).

Follett's teachings failed to make headway after her death. In the USA, the difficult social conditions of the Depression years in the 1930s and the ensuing conflicting relations between labour and capital meant that her concepts of partnership and participation in the workplace went against the grain of the ideology of the times. Further, she had come to management late in life and *Dynamic Administration*, the collection of her lectures on business organization, was not published until 1941, some years after her death. However, her philosophy started to gain ground in the 1950s and gathered momentum by the 1990s. Follett's ideas, based on connecting, coordinating and integrating, are better attuned to the latest open systems thinking.

2 Biographical data

Mary Parker Follett was born in Quincy, near Boston, Massachusetts, in September 1868. Her parents came from old-established Quincy stock. Her mother was an invalid and her father died when she was in her teens. The domestic manager from very early on, Follett, on her father's death, had also to take charge of the family's financial affairs. Money, on her mother's side, in due course made her financially independent.

Follett was a brilliant scholar, first at the Thayer Academy in Braintree, then at the Society for the College Instruction of Women (now Radcliffe College), with a year spent at Newnham College, Cambridge, England, and finally returning to Radcliffe College to graduate from there in 1898 *summa cum laude* in economics, government, law and philosophy. She was fluent in French and German and kept herself informed in her fields of interest of what was new on both sides of the Atlantic.

Even before her graduation, Follett gained recognition as an original and serious historian with her book *The Speaker of the House of Representatives* which was published in 1896. Here, she detailed the intricate workings of the legislative process and pioneered the twin-pronged approach she would later use in all her work: studying meticulously the records and, in addition, interviewing the people involved to get directly from them their views and reactions.

Follett was 32 years old when she completed her formal studies. In 1891 she had met a Miss Isobel Briggs, an Englishwoman some twenty years her senior and, by 1896, they had set up house together; theirs was 'one of the closest, most fertile and noble friendships I have known' a friend wrote. Through Miss Briggs and her own connections and interests, Follett became an integral part of the sparkling intellectual and social Boston/Harvard milieu of those days.

After her studies, Follett went into social work. She started in a men's club, in a very rough district of Boston. With her cast of mind, it was perhaps inevitable that she would be an innovator. Very quickly, recognizing the environment as of the essence, she visualized that the local schoolhouse, if used in the evenings as a club, would be more congenial than the institutional settlement house.

Under her leadership and with her unremitting attention to detail, evening centres in the schools were started and soon prospered. Recreation was important, but even more so was work. 'Why not use the evening centres additionally as placement bureaux?' she asked herself. The Boston centres in due course became models for other cities to copy. In 1917, they were incorporated into Boston's public school system and, a tribute to Follett's organizing ability, continued to be run for many years on the same structures she had set up.

During those years in social work, Follett was learning at first-hand the workings and the potential of the group-process: how people working together could evolve, develop and carry out their own plans. She saw the local group as the political base for self-government. Always the scholar, she recorded her experiences and crystallized her new thinking in her next book: *The New State–Group Organization: The Solution for Popular Government* (1918).

This book had a favourable reception, nationally and internationally, and established her as a public figure on both sides of the Atlantic. At home in Massachusetts, she began to represent the public on arbitration boards, minimum wage boards and public tribunals. As a member of these committees, Follett now experienced at first hand the politics of industrial relations. Many of the examples in her next book *Creative Experience* (1924) came from these new activities and situations.

Creative Experience brought her a new career and a different audience: businessmen, many of whom asked for her help with their management problems. She investigated specific situations in their factories, studied their organizations and suggested improvements. The Bureau of Personnel Administration, in New York, which held annual conferences for business executives and invited prestigious speakers for these occasions set the seal of approval upon Follett as a front-rank management thinker. Its director, Henry C. Metcalf, who had worked with her in the early 1900s and knew the range of her interests, invited her to give a series of lectures on 'The psychological foundations of business administration' at the 1925 conference and continued to ask her to lecture at this annual event over the years.

In England, Seebohm Rowntree, both a businessman and a management pioneer, asked her, first in 1926 and then in later years, to address his annual conferences on

management themes at Balliol College, Oxford. It was here that she met Lyndall Urwick (see URWICK, L.F.), who became her greatest admirer and worked unremittingly to spread her teaching. From her Newnham College days, Follett had developed close ties with England. Her books and activities now connected her with the top academics, politicians and businessmen in England. After Miss Briggs's death, Follett came in 1928 to live in England and shared a house with Dame Katharine Furse in Chelsea, London.

In early 1933, Follett was invited to give the inaugural lectures at the Department of Business Administration (later to become the Department of Industrial Relations) of the London School of Economics – a distinct honour. Lyndall Urwick later collected and published them, under the title of *Freedom and Coordination*. In December 1933, Follett went to Boston to sort out her financial affairs. While there, she was taken ill and died on 18 December 1933.

3 Main contribution

Follett's work, especially in the field of management, was in many ways seminal. She came to the subject when American industrial expansion was proceeding at a phenomenal rate, with an inevitable impact on social conditions. The problems of management were of course growing in parallel. Frederick W. Taylor (see TAYLOR, F.W.) had established the *rationale* of management. Follett came on the scene to establish its *philosophy*, although this role has not escaped criticism (for example, Pugh *et al.* 1975).

Not engaged in business management herself, she was frequently taxed by industrialists about their growing problems. To these, she brought the insights and the disciplines of the social scientist she was. Each problem, she held, was *sui generis* and had to be examined in its component parts and also as a whole. The relevant technology, the complexities of human nature and the demand of the market had to be understood in their dynamic interaction. It was from this analysis as a whole that the solution had to be propounded and then tested against the realities of life in the workplace.

It follows that Follett could be no believer in set systems, for she knew that no system could encompass all the richness and contingency of life. One of the foundations of Follett's philosophy was her belief in the unity of knowledge. She once said:

> I do wish that, when a principle has been worked out, say in ethics, it did not have to be discovered all over again in psychology, in economics, in government, in business, in biology and in sociology. It's such a waste of time.

In expanding this view and seeing clearly the interconnectedness of things, she wrote:

> I think we should undepartmentalize our thinking in regard to every problem that comes to us. I do not think that we have psychological and ethical and economic problems. We have human problems, with psychological, ethical and economic aspects, and as many others as you like.
> (Metcalf and Urwick 1941: 184)

As a dedicated social scientist, Follett was no sentimentalist. She appealed not to men's better nature but to their common sense and their long-term interest.

No small part of Follett's main contribution was in her laying down the four fundamental principles of organization:

1 coordination as the reciprocal relating of all the factors in a situation
2 coordination by direct contact of the responsible persons concerned
3 coordinating in the early stages
4 coordination as a continuing process.

These principles for effective organization, she held, can be applied to any set-up, not merely to those in commerce or industry.

4 Evaluation

Apart from her work as a political scientist and innovator in the social work field, Mary Parker Follett is chiefly remembered for her contribution to management thinking. She has not been uniformly appreciated since her death in 1933, as her teachings lost favour in the struggling Depression years. In her day, she was in considerable demand as a lecturer and counsellor on management, but she died before she could consolidate and publish her lectures. So, she left no definitive account of her work in the management field. It was Lyndall Urwick and Henry C. Metcalf who rescued it for posterity and published her lectures in 1941 in *Dynamic Administration: The Collected Papers of Mary Parker Follett*. It was Lyndall Urwick who, in 1949, published under the title of *Freedom and Coordination* the lectures she had given at the London School of Economics. And it is from these two works that the generations since her death have gradually come to value her teachings in administration and management.

Follett's strength derives from the combination of three factors. The first is the knowledge and skills she brought from her mastery of much of the social science field – she had studied deeply across the whole gamut from economics to psychology to jurisprudence; the second was her profound empathy with people; and the third was her own practical experience and her shrewd assessment of the ways of the world. It was thus that she brought a new look at the problems of society in general and those of industry in particular. This new look is now becoming established practice in forward-looking management thinking and practice.

5 Conclusion

Follett made a major contribution to the management thinking of her day, emphasizing good human relations in the workplace. She added a new dimension to the study of management by applying to it the findings of the social sciences, in particular of psychology. Her teaching is as valid today as it was when she was developing it in the mid-1920s. Her work will be further developed with the changing social, economic and technological scene but it is unlikely to be superseded.

PAULINE GRAHAM
UNIVERSITY OF BRADFORD

Further reading

(References cited in the text marked *)

* Child, J. (1969) *British Management Thought*, London: Allen & Unwin. (A review and a critical analysis of British management thought.)
* Follett, M.P. (1896) *The Speaker of the House of Representatives*, New York: Longmans Green. (Gives a detailed analysis of the legislative process involved in the work of the Speaker of the House of Representatives.)
* Follett, M.P. (1918) *The New State–Group Organization: The Solution for Popular Government*, New York: Longmans Green. (Gives Follett's basic tenets on the place of the individual in society and the importance of the group for effective self-governance and democracy.)
* Follett, M.P. (1924) *Creative Experience*, New York: Longmans Green. (Uses Gestalt psychology to explain relationships and to show how shared experience can be used to bring about democratic governance.)
Fox, E.M and Urwick, L.F (eds) (1973) *Dynamic Administration: The Collected Papers of Mary Parker Follett*, London: Pitman. (Gives the most comprehensive collection of Follett's lectures and an up-to-date assessment of Follett's work.)
Graham, P. (1987) *Dynamic Managing – The Follett Way*, London: Professional Publishing and British Institute of Management. (Looks at the value of Follett's concepts for effective management.)
Graham, P. (1991) *Integrative Management: Creating Unity from Diversity*, Oxford: Blackwell. (Uses Follett's concepts to ensure that a business is recognized both as a social agency and an economic unit.)
* Graham, P. (ed.) (1995a) *Mary Parker Follett: Prophet of Management*, Boston, MA: Harvard Business School Press. (Offers Follett's writings on key concepts with commentaries on them by experts.)
Graham, P. (1995b) 'The mother of management', *European Quality Journal* 2 (4): 21–3. (Gives an overview of some of Follett's concepts.)
* Metcalf, H.C. and Urwick, L.F. (eds) (1941) *Dynamic Administration: The Collected Papers of Mary Parker Follett*, Bath: Management Publications Trust. (The first edition of Follett's collection of lectures, bringing Follett's teachings to the attention of the discerning reader of management literature.)
* Pugh, D., Mansfield, R. and Warner, M. (1975) *Research in Organizational Behaviour*, London: Heinemann. (Gives a short summary of organizational behaviour as a subject.)
Shadovitz, D. (1995) 'Back to the present', *Human Resource Executive Journal* (June): 71–3. (Quotes Follett on authority, partnership, collective bargaining, etc.)
* Urwick, L.F. (ed.) (1949) *Freedom and Coordination*, London: Management Publications Trust. (A collection of Follett's lectures given in early 1933 at the London School of Economics.)
Urwick, L. and Brech, E.F.L. (1945) *The Making of Scientific Management: Thirteen Pioneers*, London: Management Publications Trust. (Covers studies of thirteen pioneers in management and includes a chapter on Follett.)
Wood, S. (1995) 'Ideas with a contemporary ring', *European Quality Journal* 2 (4): 23–4. (Shows the relevance of Follett's insights on total quality management.)

See also: MCGREGOR, D.; TAYLOR, F.W.; URWICK, L. F.

Related topics in the IEBM: BUSINESS SCHOOLS; HUMAN RELATIONS; HUMAN RESOURCE MANAGEMENT; INDUSTRIAL AND LABOUR RELATIONS; MANAGEMENT IN NORTH AMERICA; ORGANIZATION BEHAVIOUR; ORGANIZATION BEHAVIOUR, HISTORY OF; POWER

Ford, Henry (1863–1947)

Personal background

- born of Irish immigrant farmers near Dearborn, Michigan, on 30 July 1863
- attended school intermittently for eight years
- trained as machinist in Detroit, and built first experimental car in 1896
- married Clara Bryant, 1888
- built up Ford Motor Company from 1903
- successfully pursued vision of motoring for the masses, rather than as a hobby for the rich
- main single architect of high-volume, highly efficient assembly-line production
- died Dearborn, Michigan, on 7 April 1947

Major works

My Life and Work (1922)*
Today and Tomorrow (1926)*
My Philosophy of Industry (1929)
Moving Forward (1931)*

* Ford was the nominal co-author of these, with Samuel Crowther

Summary

Henry Ford (1863–1947) was a major creative force behind the twentieth-century growth of very large-scale assembly-line production in general, and of the car industry and motoring for the masses in particular. He helped to free the nascent motor industry in the USA from Eastern financial interests, and combined highly efficient, high-volume and vertically integrated production with high wages and low pricing. These innovations were copied widely in many industries and countries, although Ford cars were rarely famous for being technically advanced. Ford's achievements helped to stimulate urbanization, large-scale road building and important developments in agriculture and services, as well as in manufacturing. Ford was an eccentric philanthropist and a not always benevolent autocrat. He and his work are still controversial.

1 Introduction

Ford is generally regarded as the prime mover of the twentieth century's 'industry of industries', and as having brought the industrial revolution to its culmination. His company combined the manufacture and assembly of virtually all of the parts that went into making a car, using perpetual directed motion in the form of the moving assembly line with numerous moving sub-assembly lines feeding into the main one, and applying the principle of vertical integration through a complex of interdependent units. Money and human effort were expended in ways designed to sustain high levels of output: Ford workers were paid, from 1914, exceptionally high wages; prices were kept low; sales were maintained at a high level; and company expansion was internally financed.

Although Ford is often credited with inventing the assembly line and highly efficient high-volume mass production, most of the inventions and ideas that enabled him to become successful and famous had existed for decades, or in some cases for centuries. Apart from the internal combustion engine and the motor car itself, such inventions and ideas included scientific management, with its development of time study, motion study and the planned use of pay as an incentive; interchangeable parts; the use of planning and standardized procedures in stock control, production, accounting and so on; assembly lines and production lines; and even continuously moving assembly-line production.

However, Ford did develop a system of production, assembly and transport which was unprecedented in its mobility and extent, and which anticipated late twentieth-century just-in-time practice. Ford's main ambition, to bring motoring to the masses, was quintessentially American, with his belief in equality, movement, change, realism, straightforwardness and simplicity. The way in which Ford's genius for self-publicity dramatized and facilitated his achievement, his neglect of organization for the long term, and the weaknesses in the Ford company's management after its early success were also very American. Ford is now often associated with rigid patterns of production and with exploitation of employees (Galbraith 1960; Beynon 1973), but there are grounds, too, for calling him a remarkable innovator and philanthropist (Ford 1991).

2 Biographical data

Henry Ford was born on his father's farm near Dearborn, Michigan, eight miles west of Detroit, on 30 July 1863. He was one of eight children of William and Mary Ford. He attended a one-room rural school when not helping on the family farm or tinkering with watches and farm machinery. He learned some basic arithmetic and reading and writing and was barely literate.

For three years from the age of 16 Ford served an apprenticeship as a machinist in James Flower's Machine Shop in Detroit. He learned about the internal combustion engine, and he supplemented his income by repairing watches, toying with the idea of mass-producing them. He worked as a qualified machinist at the Detroit Drydock Company, but soon returned to the family farm, where he set up a small machine shop and worked part-time for the Westinghouse Engine Company. He built a tractor with a home-made steam engine and an old mowing machine chassis.

Ford returned to Detroit to become an engineer for the Edison Illuminating Company and became its chief engineer in 1893. He had married Clara Bryant in 1888, and in 1893 she gave birth to Ford's only son, Edsel. As chief engineer with the Edison Company, Ford was responsible for maintaining electrical services in Detroit and on call for twenty-four hours a day. Without regular hours, he could experiment at length with his ideas of making a petrol-powered vehicle. He had made his first internal combustion engine in 1893. He finished the 'quadricycle', his first car, in 1896. The lightest of the pioneer cars, with a buggy frame mounted on four bicycle wheels, it possibly foreshadowed Ford's later emphasis on low price. He sold it to help finance the building of his second car, which he also sold in due course to finance the third. In this way he was also different from many other pioneer car inventors, who kept their creations, and he was foreshadowing his later strong reliance on expansion through growth of sales to a mass market, as opposed to reliance on external finance of sales to the wealthy.

Between 1896 and 1903 Ford built several new cars and had various backers, including those who, in 1899, formed the Detroit Automobile Company. This had Ford as its superintendent and failed mainly because of his inexperience in organizing production. It was dissolved after just over a year and replaced by the Henry Ford Company with the same main financial backer, William Murphy, a Detroit lumber dealer. During these years Ford enhanced his reputation by building and driving several successful racing cars, and he also acquired Childe Harold Wills, a brilliant engineer who was to be crucial in developing Ford cars.

At this time, however, Ford felt that his passenger cars were not yet ready for customers and insisted on improving whatever car he was working on, whereas his backers wanted more, and more profitable, cars to put on the market. In 1902 he left the Henry Ford Company, which was later to become the Cadillac Motor Car Company. Although he had offended many of Detroit's wealthiest citizens by his dealings with his former backers, Ford found other partners in a group headed by Alexander Malcomson, a Detroit coal dealer, and the Ford Motor Company was founded in June 1903 with Ford and Malcomson as the main stockholders. Others included John and

Horace Dodge, who made the chassis, engines and transmissions for Ford's cars, and James Couzens, who was to become Ford's business agent. In 1905 Ford bought Malcomson out after a quarrel, which Ford won, over whether to build high-priced cars or cars for the masses. Thus, by 1905 Ford was in almost complete financial and operational control of his own company.

In the first decade of the twentieth century the American car industry became independent, no longer an experimental sideline of companies with other interests, but one made up of companies solely dedicated to making cars. It was relatively easy to sell cars, but production methods were still in their infancy. However, cars were beginning to drop their buggy and bicycle ancestry, with steering wheels replacing tillers, engines moving from under the driver's seat to the front, and metal starting to replace wood in construction. Ford was pursuing his aim of making a car that was tough, cheap and easy to run. By the time that Ford's Model T appeared in 1908, the Ford Motor Company was already established as a leader in the industry.

The years from 1908 to 1914 saw Ford start to establish himself as a popular hero through the production of the Model T, the successful fight against the Selden patent, and through the development by 1914 of the most advanced and widely publicized system of production yet devised. The Model T, 'Tin Lizzie', was made for 19 years from October 1908, and nearly 17,000,000 were sold, as many as all other cars made worldwide in that period, mainly in the USA but with 250,000 going to the UK and nearly 1,000,000 to Canada. The Model T was a major force for change in the USA, stimulating large-scale highway building, urbanization and the growth of suburbs, ending the physical isolation of many farmers and the reign of the horse in farm transport, and enabling millions of people to travel widely and independently for the first time.

Ford's fight against the Selden patent, which covered the production of all petrol-powered cars and supposedly reserved it for members of the Association of Licensed Automobile Manufacturers (ALAM), lasted six years. The victory apparently set the industry free from Eastern financial power and industrial combinations and added to Ford's burgeoning status as a popular hero. However, the ALAM did not in fact operate as a monopoly; it was mainly the fact that the suit against the ALAM was mounted at the height of the campaign against trusts in the USA that allowed Ford to derive so much favourable publicity from it.

The construction of Ford's new plant at Highland Park, Detroit, with the constantly moving chassis assembly line installed in January 1914, made possible the delivery of parts, assemblies and subassemblies to the main line at precise times. Where it had previously taken over twelve hours to produce a complete chassis, it now took only a fraction over one and one-half. This was one part of a series of developments which made Ford world famous. In 1914 the average daily wage in the US car industry was $2.34. In that year Ford decided to pay eligible workers at least $5 per day and to cut the working day by one hour to eight hours, enabling a three-shift system to be worked. Ford was portrayed as either a naive socialist or great humanitarian. Most firms tried to pay the lowest wages and to seek the highest prices that they could get away with. However, Ford priced the Model T as low as possible (over its lifetime, its price went down from $950 in 1908 to $290 by 1927) so as to sell as many as he could, meeting the price by efficiency and volume. He foresaw that if this philosophy were applied extensively, workers would be able to buy things which had hitherto been luxuries, such as cars, in ways which would profit everyone, not least employers, leading to the mass US affluence of the 1950s.

Ford relied on several strong personalities to help him realize his ambitions. His business genius was James Couzens, and William Knudsen and Charles Sorensen were his production ones, and the industrial architect Albert Kahn designed the epoch-making Highland Park plant. John Lee was his industrial and human relations expert and the creator of the company's sociological department, which made the first attempt, a little eccentric and crude like its ultimate author, at a systematic personnel and industrial relations policy in the motor industry. Between 1903 and 1913 Couzens was a major force in the company, organizing its sales and controlling its spending while driving it to expand and develop its production.

In the decade spanning 1920 Henry Ford's career was at its height. For the company it was an era of financially secure expansion. Until the USA entered the First World War in 1917 its motor industry did little to gear itself up for war. Ford had made a naive effort to get the combatants to stop fighting in 1915. In 1917 he announced that his company would be at the US Government's disposal and that he would return all profits on war contracts to it. This was merely a publicity stunt but the company did make many aeroplane engines, military vehicles and a number of submarine chasers. During the same period the enormous new River Rouge plant began to be built in Detroit and Ford's production of cars reached its highest level. In 1919 the Ford family became the sole owners of the Ford Motor Company, buying the shares held by others. By 1920 several other companies were starting to compete in the mass car market, mainly by trying to build a slightly better car than the Model T for an only marginally higher price.

When, in 1920, the Ford Motor Company was reorganized under Ford and his family co-owners, no single person had ever controlled so enormous an enterprise so completely. In 1927 the company moved its main centre from the Highland Park to the River Rouge plant. The latter finally embodied all of Ford's ideas about self-sufficiency, with its supplies coming from Ford-owned ore and coal mines, timberland, rubber plantations, a sawmill, a glassworks, foundries and steelworks, on Ford-owned railways and ships. All this was done with profits from the Model T, without a cent being borrowed.

The Ford Motor Company diversified in 1922 when it acquired the up-market Lincoln car company. It ventured quite promisingly into aviation for a few years from 1926 and later, during the Second World War, produced large numbers of bomber aircraft and tanks, and aircraft and tank engines.

The very scale of Ford's domination of both his own business and the car industry in general, combined with the growth of competitor companies, products and industries, and Ford's own slowly diminishing energy pointed the way towards relative decline. His famous statement about customers being able to buy any car 'as long as it is black' is illustrative of Ford's mixture of democratic and creative, and autocratic and egotistical, impulses.

Ford, having achieved by 1920 most of what he had originally set out to do, became increasingly complacent and erratic. He manipulated his managers, often ruthlessly, and fired or otherwise drove out many of the best ones. His cars were increasingly technically conservative, with their brakes, four-cylinder engines and transmissions often conspicuously dated in the 1920s and 1930s. The company lost its industry leadership, coming third in the US motor industry in terms of sales in 1936, behind General Motors and Chrysler, although a V-8 engine was introduced in 1932. The Model A, which had at last replaced the popular but obsolete Model T in 1927, was a reasonable success, but it was only made for four years. Ford resisted trade union organization by using worker spies, company police and violence, and cut wages to below the industry norms (to $4 a day) in 1932. He first signed a union contract in 1941, several years after GM and Chrysler had first recognized the Union of Automobile Workers.

In the Second World War the company was largely devoted to war production. Henry Ford had a stroke and his son Edsel became fatally ill, worn down by the intrigues which his father had fostered. Indeed from around 1925 onwards Henry Ford had lost much of his interest in the details of the Ford Motor Company's affairs, and Edsel was largely an administrator. 'Cast Iron Charlie' Sorensen ran the plant and was increasingly responsible for maintaining the company as an organization until his retirement early in 1944. Ford's grandson, Henry II, became a director in 1943, Executive Vice-President in 1944, and President in September 1945, two years before his grandfather died. At the age of 27,

Henry Ford II began converting the company from wartime to peacetime production.

Under the terms of Henry Ford's will 95 per cent of the company's common stock went to the Ford Foundation. This philanthropic trust had been set up in 1936 as a way of keeping family control of the company. In 1956 most of its securities were sold to the public and the Ford Motor Company became much more like a typical large American corporation. The Ford Foundation became the wealthiest private foundation in the world.

As an engineer and manager of a kind, Ford was untutored, often highly original, and above all an enthusiast, an experimenter and an empiricist. His often highly naive and idealistic enthusiasms exposed him to ridicule from time to time, as when he chartered an ocean liner in 1915, the 'Peace Ship', to take himself and a number of pacifists to Europe to try to end the First World War by persuasion. In 1918 he was almost elected to the US Senate, and in the same year he began publicizing a number of anti-Semitic views (eventually withdrawn) in a newspaper that he had bought. He established schools, a mainly rural museum, a restored rural town and village factories. He socialized publicly with fellow innovators like Thomas Edison and through the old-fashioned dances which he had organized in opposition to jazz. In much of what Ford did in his later years there was a strong element of didacticism concerned with teaching people about that which, for Ford, was worth retaining from the slower-moving world which his efforts had done and were doing so much, so dramatically, to transform.

3 Main contribution

According to Chandler (1990), Ford's key strength as the 'first mover' of the US motor industry was his understanding of 'throughput'. One key aspect of this was Ford's desire for his company to be as self-contained as possible. Another was his belief in 'plenty for all', as expressed in his slogan 'high wages to create large markets'. He did not invent (although he certainly did symbolize) mass production, just-in-time inventory control, vertical integration, a slightly crude but quite

effective version of the marketing concept, the large motor company as a multinational, human resource management or corporate philanthropy, but he brought several of these to fruition, added significantly to the development of others, and integrated most of them with considerable effectiveness. His major achievements were, however, to bring motoring to the US masses and, in the process, to help generate mass affluence and to liberate millions of people from hard physical labour. He was also ahead of his time when he put the needs of customers and workers before those of shareholders.

In spite of all these achievements, Ford had a markedly happy-go-lucky attitude towards the development of techniques and theories of management and organization. He was prejudiced against college-trained engineers and his company organized and ran in a very haphazard way what would now be called research and development activities. Little if anything was done to organize accounting along systematic lines, advertising was also badly neglected, and his approach to personnel management oscillated between advanced forms of empowerment and enlightened paternalism on the one hand and the large-scale mobilization of paranoia on the other.

Although he has often been associated with scientific management (see TAYLOR, F.W.), there is little if any evidence to show that Ford was directly affected by any of the advanced management thinking of the eras that he lived and worked through. While he did develop a highly rational and organized system of production before 1920 his personal control of it from then into the 1940s was more or less disastrous. From the early 1930s to the death of his son Edsel in 1943, the management of the Ford Motor Company was split inefficiently between Ford himself, a fading autocrat whose occasional interventions usually came through Harry Bennett, the near-criminal boss of the 'Service Department', which was responsible for 'personnel', and Charlie Sorensen, who managed production and who tried to hold the company together with the administrative help of Edsel, its president since 1919, who was able and popular but much abused by his father.

Ford's philosophy and attitudes were moulded by the tension between the simplicities of his early life and the complexities of his business in the USA in the late nineteenth and early twentieth century. Very American, a pure Yankee with a strong belief in equality and an acceptance of social flux built into him, he attracted adjectives like homely, original, pragmatic, optimistic, unconventional, democratic and empirical. He was certainly a simplifier of issues and tasks whose love of efficiency came from his austere rural background. Such qualities hardened as he did, with age, into stubbornness and authoritarianism. The strength of his approach to management was his tough-minded 'can-do' innovativeness, but its corresponding weakness was a lack of respect for orderly planning and rational ways of dividing labour. Ford largely achieved his aim of using machinery to make jobs easy and to create new ones on a very large scale, developing a system of employment, production and marketing which brought mass affluence into being because the strengths outweighed the weaknesses for most of his career.

A utilitarian belief in the greatest good for the greatest number and a deep sense of responsibility clearly underpinned much of what Ford did. He valued affluence and mobility, and his attitude towards his workers, a combination of *laissez-faire* and paternalism, and his very American aim of turning luxuries into necessities, were all associated with his faith in the notion that moral development is most likely to follow material progress.

Typically of the Midwest farm boys of his generation, who had left the land to seek work in the rapidly growing US cities, Ford believed that the country was natural and good, and the city artificial and evil. He also felt that industrialization was destroying cities and making it possible for everyone to live in the country. Like Frederick Taylor (see TAYLOR, F.W.) of the scientific management movement, and Thorstein Veblen, the Norwegian-US economist and sociologist (see VEBLEN, T.B.), Ford thought that industrialization would help replace corrupt and parasitical Eastern aristocrats and finance capitalists with a new class of producers. All three were typical of the Progressive thinkers of the USA between the late nineteenth and early twentieth centuries. The Progressive movement acquired an ideal of a community which was mobile and continually expanding, although in the same era the term 'backwash' was being used to describe how the US dream of infinite land and the continually moving frontier had ended, with people more concerned with settling down than before.

Like many outstandingly successful individuals, Ford is more easily understood when a few important facts about him are remembered. One is his unsophisticated background and lack of formal education, another is the context of extraordinary change and opportunity through which he grew from youth to middle-aged success, and a third is his considerable age and reduced physical and mental capacities in the last fifteen or so often erratic and sad years of his life. Both at and away from the Ford Motor Company his life and behaviour were often dramatically complex and contradictory. As an employer, for example, he was highly enlightened and progressive in some ways and at some times, and a repressive and capricious autocrat in and at others. However, there is evidence of a pattern of a lengthy struggle to succeed, followed by dramatic success, followed by long and only partially concealed decline, all interwoven with and influencing many aspects of his life.

Ford's anti-Semitism was an unfortunate product of his strong penchant for self-publicity and his often startling parochialism and ignorance. More loutish than malicious, it was common among his generation, before the Second World War, and foolishly misdepicted Jews as international capitalists, overly commercial and decadent. Ford also believed, benevolently in this case, in rural production, in bringing factories and farming close together, rather than in having them located apart and in mutual opposition. His many contradictions were exemplified further by his apparent belief, in late middle age, that people were happier when deprived of choice.

4 Evaluation

The essence of Ford's work and of his vision was to define mass production and to bring the industrialization process to a kind of maturity. Mechanization, moving inventories and vertical integration were central to the achievement of his vision. So, too, was Ford's use of his power, material and personal, to inspire. He defined morality as 'the law of right action', as more than just trying to be good, as the exercise of will in order to accelerate the inevitable and the positive. He advocated money-making as a service to others, not as exploitation. To 'find a way or to make one' of liberating people from back-breaking toil was another major strand of his ideal.

One of the main criticisms of Ford was that of inadequate organization. It was a justified criticism. Thus, as Ford himself wrote in 1926:

> a business, in my way of thinking, is not a machine. It is a collection of people who are brought together to do work and not to write letters to one another. It is not necessary for any one department to know what any other department is doing . . . It is not necessary to have meetings to establish good feelings between individuals or departments. It is not necessary for people to love each other in order to work together.
> (Ford and Crowther 1926: 91–2)

There is a lot that is didactic and written for effect in this brief quotation from Ford's book with Samuel Crowther, *My Life and Work*, but it certainly reflects much of Ford's way of working. There is no doubt that Ford was far better at building a team in 1910 than in 1925, that he had become an autocrat unable to relinquish power, an omnipotent, selfish dictator professing humanitarian objectives. In the 1930s the weaknesses of his methods were being highlighted by hard times. Thus, the very integrated nature of the Ford Motor Company's production in the USA became overly expensive because as demand and output decreased, unit costs rose much faster for Ford than for other companies.

Also, as Ford grew older and more inflexible the weaknesses of his management of people, always apparent, became dramatically obvious. Increasingly after the 1910s he drove the most able people away and half-destroyed his organization in the process. He had always treated some of his managers badly but in the 1930s especially, such treatment became the norm. His erratic judgements of people were also more obvious. His tendency to work by hunch, his impulsiveness and lack of thoroughness were central both to his success and his decline.

At least from the standpoint of the late twentieth century, Ford was no very great engineer or business person, and much more of a coordinator, exploiter and publicity-seeking impresario of a number of powerful existing trends. He was someone whose flaws were increasingly apparent, both in his generally deteriorating attitudes and behaviour, and more specifically in the growing commercial and technical conservatism of his last twenty-five years. Much of his early success, up to 1915, has also been attributed, with considerable justification, to his early business genius James Couzens.

Ford's lack of system and his prejudices, his often small-minded, suspicious, jealous, opinionated, malicious and insincere behaviour were widely documented, even by those who praised him the most. Yet so, too, were his many often major innovations, his flexibility when seriously challenged, as by trade unions in his later years, and the fact that he was a pioneer and major achiever.

From a reading of Ford's life and of the work of many critics of assembly-line mass production, it is clear that while popular portrayals of Ford as a high priest of modernism and of rationalist exploitation of employees contain important grains of truth, the real picture is more complicated. It is clear that a great deal of very flexible thinking went into the creation of 'inflexible' Fordist methods of production, and into the partly self-regarding publicizing of them and of their wider ramifications. Also, Ford himself was plainly a very idiosyncratic person and not merely understandable as a farm boy made good. Thus, although his methods were central to a great many of the changes of his life and times, they were often unique to him and his company and not always typical of the motor industry in particular or to mass production in general. Much of what Ford did was strictly technology- and/or market-driven, and unconnected in any direct way with scientific management.

His paternalism was much more inspired by commercial foresight and self-interest and by vanity than by human relations-style thinking, which it largely pre-dated, in any case. Perhaps the two main effects of Ford's work on subsequent management thinking were through the conflation and stereotyping of his treatment of workers and of the supposedly 'alienating' character of assembly-line mass production, which fuelled negative perceptions and portrayals of manufacturing; and the awful example of mismanagement and disorganization that the Ford Motor Company presented in the last quarter century of his life, which almost certainly helped to stimulate creative and rational forms of work organization into being at General Motors and elsewhere.

In spite of all of his errors, Ford's life offers a very great example of bold and broadly positive change. He was admired more in developing, or in what were then developing countries, than in those with abundant supplies of mechanical skill, such as Germany and the UK. There was much that was courageous as well as much that was venal in his use of publicity. His practice of working and innovating by hunch, widely criticized in the years after his death, has increasingly been recognized as an integral feature of effective behaviour by management researchers. Nevins and Hill (1962: 269–70) regarded his career as 'perhaps the most impressive and certainly the most spectacular of American industrial history', and wrote of Ford as being 'before 1915 ... on the whole an attractive figure', whose early idealism and ignorance caused him to suffer, harden and then inflict suffering in later life and in the face of powerfully changing times and cynical, spiteful and hurtful attacks and distortions from lesser people. It was only as a schoolboy that he thought that 'history is bunk'. As a mature man he expressed considerable respect for and interest in it, because he had grown to be so keen to retain and cherish what had been positive in his past.

5 Conclusion

The main elements of Ford's work were: (1) large-scale mechanization of a major, epoch-defining, industry; (2) large-scale vertical integration; (3) continually moving inventory; and (4) the worker as consumer, developing mass markets through mass production and high wages. Ford's work included the temporary culmination of many technical and commercial trends. The reactions to it that it provoked, in the form of more varied and more rational divisions of labour and forms of human resource management, in many organizations and sectors, were probably just as important as its direct ones of bringing motoring to the multitude and of developing mass affluence.

IAN GLOVER
UNIVERSITY OF STIRLING

Further reading

(References in the text marked*)

* Beynon, H. (1973) *Working for Ford*, London: Allen Lane. (A very critical account of assembly line work for Ford UK c.1970.)
Burlingame, R. (1949) *Backgrounds of Power: the Human Story of Mass Production*, London and New York: Charles Scribner's Sons. (Very wide-ranging and readable history of mass production which contains an invaluable account of what was original in Ford's achievements, and what was not.)
Burlingame, R. (1954) *Henry Ford*, New York: Knopf. (An excellent short biography.)
Chandler, A.D., Jr (1964) *Giant Enterprise: Ford, General Motors and the Automobile Industry*, New York: Harcourt, Brace and World. (A very useful collection of edited readings covering most aspects of Ford's history until the 1960s.)
* Chandler, A.D., Jr (1990) *Scale and Scope: The Dynamics of Industrial Capitalism*, Cambridge, MA: Belknap Press, Harvard University Press. (General account of growth of large-scale industry in the twentieth century with many useful references to Ford, including ones about Ford's activities in Germany and the UK.)

Dale, E. (1960) *The Great Organizers*, New York: McGraw-Hill. (On the development of systematic organization in American management, with useful references to the apparent lack of it at Ford.)

Ford, H. (1929) *My Philosophy of Industry*, London: Harrap. (Ninety short pages of often homespun, often original thoughts which need to be appraised with historical empathy. Foreword by Ronnie Lessem emphasizes Ford's visionary qualities.)

* Ford, H. (1991) *Ford on Management*, Oxford: Blackwell. (Contains material from Ford's *My Life and Work* and *My Philosophy of Industry*.)

* Ford, H. and Crowther, S. (1926) *My Life and Work*, New York: Doubleday. (Reprint of the 1922 work. Lively account, written by Crowther but relies on material from Ford and is widely regarded as authoritative.)

Ford, H. and Crowther, S. (1926) *Today and Tomorrow*, New York: Garden City. (Second of three accounts, written by Crowther but based on material from and inspired by Ford, on Ford's work and philosophy, which sold all over the world.)

Ford, H. and Crowther, S. (1931) *Moving Forward*, New York: Garden City. (Covers production, technology, management, wages and other issues, offering constructive and imaginative advice to business around the beginning of the inter-war Depression.)

* Galbraith, J.K. (1960) *The Liberal Hour*, New York: Hamish Hamilton. (Contains a coherent but not altogether convincing attack on 'the Ford myth', and other related essays.)

Gelderman, C.W. (1989) *Henry Ford: The Wayward Capitalist*, New York: St Martin's Press. (Comprehensive, respected biography.)

McKinlay, A. and Starkey, K. (1994) 'After Henry: continuity and change in the Ford Motor Company', *Business History* 36 (1): 184–206. (Briefly builds on and continues the story of Ford after the first Henry Ford and his grandson, the Henry in the title.)

Nevins, A. and Hill, F.E. (1954) *Ford: The Times, The Man, The Company*, New York: Charles Scribner's Sons. (Very detailed, authoritative overview.)

Nevins, A. and Hill, F.E. (1957) *Ford: Expansion and Challenge, 1925–1933*, New York: Charles Scribner's Sons. (Heavyweight, very detailed and wide-ranging, very well written, balanced classic account of Ford's heyday, expansion and first serious problems.)

* Nevins, A. and Hill, F.E. (1962) *Ford: Decline and Rebirth, 1933–1962*, New York: Charles Scribner's Sons. (Takes the story of Henry Ford and the Ford Motor Company from the 1930's Depression through the Second World War, Ford's death, and post-war recovery and expansion.)

Noble, D.W. (1981) *The Progressive Mind: 1890–1917*, Minneapolis, MN: Burgess. (Deals with the collective identity of middle class Americans in the years when Ford was establishing himself, paying specific attention to his values and influence.)

Rae, J.B. (1959) *American Automobile Manufacturers: The First Forty Years*, Philadelphia, PA: Chilton. (Covers the history of the industry's companies until the mid-1930s; contains a history of Ford and his company up until then, and includes many helpful comparisons with competitors.)

Rae, J.B. (1965) *The American Automobile: A Brief History*, Chicago, IL: University of Chicago Press. (Covers the industry from the 1890s to the 1960s; includes a balanced account of Ford's role.)

Sorensen, C.E. (1957) *Forty years with Ford*, London: Jonathan Cape. (Ford's tough production boss's vivid and ultimately sympathetic (and unwittingly self-revealing) account of 'What ... Henry Ford [was] really like'.)

Starkey K. and McKinlay, A. (1990) 'Managing for Ford', *Sociology* 28 (4): 975–90. (How management in Ford became very autocratic around 1920, its history since then, and how it has recently been changing under pressure from foreign competition.)

Sward, K. (1948) *The Legend of Henry Ford*, New York: Rinehart. (Hostile account by a former Union of Automobile Workers organizer; a useful antidote to the hero-worship of Ford.)

Wik, R.M. (1972) *Henry Ford and Grass-Roots America*, Ann Arbor, MI: University of Michigan Press. (A catalogue of the fan letters sent to Ford, mainly by the US public.)

See also: CHANDLER, A. D.; OHNO, T.; SLOAN, A. P.; TAYLOR, F.W.; TOYODA FAMILY; VEBLEN, T. B.

Related topics in the IEBM: ADVERTISING CAMPAIGNS; BIG BUSINESS AND CORPORATE CONTROL; BUSINESS HISTORY; HUMAN RESOURCES MANAGEMENT; JUST-IN-TIME PHILOSOPHIES; LABOUR PROCESS; MANAGEMENT IN NORTH AMERICA; MANAGEMENT SCIENCE; MANUFACTURING SYSTEMS, DESIGN OF; MULTINATIONAL CORPORATIONS; PERSONEL MANAGEMENT; TRADE UNIONS

Forrester, Jay Wright (1918–)

Personal background

- born 14 July 1918 near Arnold, Nebraska, USA
- studied electrical engineering at the University of Nebraska, 1935–39
- became research assistant at MIT in 1939; worked with Gordon Brown on servo-mechanism control for radar antennae and guns
- received masters degree from MIT, 1945
- became director of MIT Digital Computer Laboratory, 1946
- married Susan Swett, 27 July 1946
- worked on development of aircraft flight simulators, Whirlwind digital computer and SAGE air defence system, 1946–56
- head of Digital Computer Division in MIT's Lincoln Laboratory, 1952–56
- received patent for magnetic core memory, 1956
- appointed professor of management at Sloan School, 1956
- developed and applied the System Dynamics approach
- inducted into the National Inventors' Hall of Fame, 1979

Major works

Industrial Dynamics (1961)
Principles of Systems (1968)
Urban Dynamics (1969)
World Dynamics (1971)
Collected Papers of Jay W. Forrester (1975)

Summary

Forrester is the inventor of System Dynamics, a form of computer simulation modelling which uses the concept of information feedback to model social systems, including companies and economies. The aim is to work with managers to support debate regarding long term policy. The approach has been applied by Forrester to business problems, to the growth of cities and to global development. Today, his ideas are supported by a network of university researchers and are practised globally by corporations and consulting firms.

1 Introduction

Everything converged for Forrester when he moved to MIT's Sloan School of Management. He brought his training in servomechanisms and his belief in the educational benefits of computers (for which he had created a vital component). He also had a practical bent, having been brought up on a cattle ranch and trained as an engineer. And he had boundless confidence.

Forrester worked with General Electric who had a problem of unwanted oscillations in inventory levels and staff numbers. In an attempt to guide the system, their managers collected information on inventory and staff levels and took what they judged to be the appropriate corrective actions. The state of each level, the action taken by managers to influence it and its result could be seen as components of a 'feedback loop'. Forrester diagnosed that there were many feedback loops in operation. As a result, actions produced unexpected results in unexpected quarters. These would produce further actions which would have unexpected results of their own, calling for yet further action and so forth. By aggregating together in a model the various actions and feedback loops, Forrester showed that the managers' interventions in the system produced counter-intuitive effects.

Policies aimed at holding the system at pre-determined levels instead combined to amplify oscillations. The oscillations were not generated by external, market noise; the causes were internal, or endogenous. With only a paper model, Forrester was able to begin re-designing the operating policies and stabilize the system.

Forrester concluded that servomechanistic ideas could be applied to systems with human actors and that taking an aggregated view would help managers to understand the behaviour over time of systems which they sought to steer but which defied their intuition. His approach responded to Alfred Sloan's call for a management school in a technical institution. Forrester called it 'Industrial Dynamics'; later it became 'System Dynamics'.

2 Main contribution

The field of management studies in the late 1950s seemed to Forrester to be only a loose assembly of empirical observations. With *Industrial Dynamics* (1961), his aim was therefore nothing less than a revolution in management science. This book advances a new way to understand management problems. Forrester proposes that feedback concepts can provide a sound theoretical foundation and integrating framework for diverse observations on the behaviour of social systems. Companies, economies, all social systems, should be modelled as flow rates and accumulations linked by information feedback loops. The purpose is to learn about modes of behaviour and design policies which improve performance. With this book, System Dynamics was created.

There are three distinguishing features of System Dynamics. First, the use of 'feedback loops'. These involve the collection of information, followed by controlling action based on policies, followed by new information collection. These closed loops of causal links involve delays and non-linear relationships. Computer simulation, the second feature, follows: humans can conceptualize such complex models but they do not have the cognitive capacity to calculate the dynamic behaviour

unassisted. But simulation rigorously calculates the consequences over time. The interplay of loops and non-linear relationships means that different parts of a system become important – dominant – at different times. Counter-intuitive behaviour results and may be explored in a creative and compelling way using simulation. The third feature is engagement with mental models. Forrester believes that the most important information about social systems is not written down but is held as 'mental models'. These contain our assumptions about what causes what. They are complex and subtle, involving hard, quantitative variables and softer, more qualitative aspects. And they are the basis for decision making. The only way to deal with a problematic situation is to grasp and change the mental models of the managers running that system. Modelling must therefore stay close to managers and help them to see their mental models represented in a computer model. By experimenting with such models the managers learn, develop their intuition and create a shared mental model. Subsequent policy-making is informed by a rigorous and comprehensive use of their own knowledge of the system.

Industrial Dynamics contains the grounding ideas of System Dynamics, rules for model creation and a string of examples. Forrester's integrative aspirations are clear. Case studies can be brought to life by the use of models which are causal theories. These models become flight simulators for managers, acting as laboratories for scientific experiments in support of management education. Forrester's subsequent books have added detail to this theory and shown its application.

Principles of Systems (1968) draws on a decade's work by Forrester and his co-researchers. It is essentially a tutorial, containing examples of model formulation and analysis. By the late 1960s many fine modelling studies had been done and this book uses some in exercises. Forrester's two subsequent books demonstrate further the ambition of System Dynamics.

Urban Dynamics (1969) is Forrester's attempt to understand the forces that produce the growth, stagnation, decline and revival of a city. He presents a generic model of a city and studies the types of behaviour that can result and the policies which might reverse decline. It is a characteristically Forrestian undertaking; audacious and courageous. It provides some powerful insights into the structural causes behind urban stagnation. Chapter 6, 'Notes on complex systems', is particularly noteworthy, providing a set of qualitative insights regarding the counter-intuitive behaviour of social systems. The insights are applicable across a wide range of settings, demonstrating the ability of System Dynamics to act as an integrating framework.

World Dynamics (1971) is an account of Forrester's work with the Club of Rome. It is an attempt to understand the dynamics of aggregate global development. Forrester uses a System Dynamics model to study the interaction of population, agricultural and industrial production, pollution, quality of life, capital investment and natural resources. His policy conclusions raise serious questions about the interaction of growth and human dignity in a world of finite resources. Despite the pages of equations and graphs, the public response was extraordinary: sales were huge and the book was the subject of world-wide comment and debate. Forrester's ideas on the problems associated with caring for the environment whilst making long-term versus short-term trade-offs have entered the core of modern environmentalist thinking. Further studies have extended this founding work of global modelling.

The range of Forrester's ideas is seen in *Collected Papers of Jay W. Forrester* (1975). This book contains various applications of System Dynamics, including advertising strategy and the growth management of a start-up company and papers on the principles of the approach, including part of a session given by Forrester to the US House of Representatives.

To judge Forrester's work we must also consider his institutional contribution, that is, the work of his co-researchers and of the global membership of the International System Dynamics Society (ISDS), created in 1986. A longer bibliography is available (

Sastry and Sterman 1993) and a sample is given in the further reading section below.

Despite formally retiring from Sloan in 1989, Forrester has continued his work. He has long engaged in the project of bringing feedback analysis into classical economics to study non-equilibrium states. The 'National Model' project at MIT aims to provide a causal theory for many of the macro phenomena seen in the US economy. Various pieces have appeared which indicate that system dynamicists are asking fundamental questions about the assumptions behind economic orthodoxy (Forrester 1989 and also Sterman in Richardson 1996, Radzicki and Sterman 1994). Forrester's other major interest is the 'K-12' project which aims to bring System Dynamics-based learning to children. Work has centred on creating materials to help teachers and students from kindergarten age upwards to adopt 'learner-directed learning' approaches across a wide curriculum (Forrester 1990).

3 Evaluation

Forrester's ideas have various connections and antecedents, including Wiener's work and Tustin's 1953 feedback study of economic systems. Forrester's use of computer simulation is the major advance over the latter. Richardson argues that although feedback thinking had been used widely before, Forrester catalyzed an evolutionary leap in the form of feedback thinking called the 'servomechanistic thread', in which prime importance is attached to the study of policies and the resultant patterns of behaviour of feedback systems (Richardson 1991). Forrester's concept of shared mental models has connections with Ackoff's 'organizational memory' and his ideas are also related to the problem structuring methods of 'soft' OR (Lane 1994)(see ACKOFF, R.L.).

A frequent criticism of System Dynamics is that it is nothing more than a naive, hyper-rationalist attempt to engineer social systems as if they were natural systems. This 'hard modelling' attitude is observable in some practitioners but is probably less prevalent in System Dynamics than in the world of OR.

Furthermore, the criticism only applies if the focus is solely on models. But if a model is used to play a creative and reflective role in a group seeking only qualitative insights then the criticism is inappropriate.

The relevance and success of Forrester's ideas may be assessed by the number and quality of academic researchers and by corporate interest in System Dynamics. By the mid 1990s the ISDS had more than 500 members in every continent and an annual conference. Research has covered the intellectual roots of System Dynamics (Richardson 1991), the management of large software projects (Abdel-Hamid and Madnick 1990) and a Third World perspective on global development (Saeed 1991). Further work appears in the *System Dynamics Review*, a journal founded in 1985 and now published by John Wiley & Sons. Business relevance has built steadily and recently Senge's popularizing description of the use of 'micro-worlds' to deliver experiential learning attracted considerable management attention (Senge 1990). This attention has been cemented by further high quality model-based studies (Sterman, Repenning and Kofman 1997) and demand has lead to many books in the field – including all of Forrester's – being republished by Productivity Press.

4 Conclusions

Jay W. Forrester has created a compelling means of modelling social systems whilst involving senior decision makers. His own work established the principles of System Dynamics and demonstrated some high profile applications. He added to his previous considerable achievements a method of strategic modelling which enjoys strong business interest. Growing academic support, combined with his sponsorship of innovative school teaching approaches, would seem to guarantee continued interest in the rigorous application of his ideas to important problems.

DAVID LANE
LONDON SCHOOL OF ECONOMICS AND
POLITICAL SCIENCE

Further reading

(References cited in the text marked *)

* Abdel-Hamid, T.K. and Madnick, S. (1990) *Software Project Dynamics, An Integrated Approach*, Englewood Cliffs, NJ: Prentice Hall. (Application to the management of software development.)

* Forrester, J.W. (1961) *Industrial Dynamics*, Portland, OR: Productivity Press (re-publication). (Core text for Forrester's work; aspirations, guidelines and examples of System Dynamics.)

* Forrester, J.W. (1968) *Principles of Systems*, Portland, OR: Productivity Press (re-publication). (Study guide for the technical aspects of model analysis)

* Forrester, J.W. (1969) *Urban Dynamics*, Portland, OR: Productivity Press (re-publication). (Application to urban stagnation.)

* Forrester, J.W. (1971) *World Dynamics*, Portland, OR: Productivity Press (re-publication). (Application to global development.)

* Forrester, J.W. (1975) *Collected Papers of Jay W. Forrester*, Portland, OR: Productivity Press (re-publication). (Survey of examples and theory across two decades.)

* Forrester, J.W. (1989) 'The System Dynamics National Model: Macrobehaviour from microstructure', in: P.M. Milling and E.O.K. Zahn (eds) *Computer-based Management of Complex Systems*, Berlin: Springer. (Report on Forrester's economic work.)

* Forrester, J.W. (1990) 'System dynamics – adding structure and relevance to pre-college education', in K.R. Manning (ed.) *Shaping the Future* Cambridge, MA: MIT Press. (Description of the contribution made by System Dynamics to learner-directed learning in schools.)

* Lane, D.C. (1994) 'With a little help from our friends: how system dynamics and soft OR can learn from each other', *System Dynamics Review 10(2–3): Systems Thinkers, Systems Thinking*, Chichester: Wiley. (Introduces a collection linking Forrester's ideas to system science and 'Soft' OR.)

Morecroft, J.D.W. and Sterman, J.D. (eds) (1994) *Modeling for Learning Organizations*, Portland, OR: Productivity Press. (Contemporary theory and application examples.)

* Radzicki, M.J. and Sterman, J.D. (1994) 'Evolutionary economics and system dynamics', in R.W. England (ed.) *Evolutionary Concepts in Contemporary Economics*, Ann Arbor, USA: University of Michigan Press. (An agenda for the

contribution that System Dynamics can make to evolutionary economics.)

Randers, J. (ed.) (1980) *Elements of the System Dynamics Method*, Portland, OR: Productivity Press (re-publication). (Papers on theory and application.)

* Richardson, G.P. (1991) *Feedback Thought in Social Science and Systems Theory*, Philadelphia: Univ. Pennsylvania. (Traces the use of feedback ideas by previous social thinkers.)

* Richardson, G.P. (ed.) (1996) *Modelling for Management*, Aldershot, UK: Dartmouth. (Wide-ranging collection of pieces on many applications as well as theoretical pieces.)

Richardson, G.P. and Pugh, A.L. (1981) *Introduction to System Dynamics Modelling with DYNAMO*, Portland, OR: Productivity Press (re-publication). (Describes in detail the principles of model conceptualization, formulation and use.)

* Saeed, K. (1991) *Towards Sustainable Development*, Lahore: Progressive Publishers. (Computer-supported exploration of policies for a developing country.)

* Sastry, M.A. and Sterman, J.D. (1993) 'Desert island dynamics: an annotated survey of the essential system dynamics literature', downloadable from: http://web.mit.edu/jsterman/www/DID.html (More than 100 useful texts.)

* Senge, P. (1990) *The Fifth Discipline*, New York: Doubleday/Currency. (Explores the links between System Dynamics and the 'learning organization' concept.)

* Sterman, J., Repenning, N. and Kofman, F. (1997) 'Unanticipated side effects of successful quality improvement programs', *Management Science* 43 (4): 503–521. (Analysis of problems experienced by companies attempting TQM implementation.)

Vennix, J.A.M. (1996) *Group Model-building: Facilitating Team Learning Using System Dynamics*, Chichester: Wiley. (Links Forrester's work with group decision support and 'Soft' OR.)

See also: ACKOFF, R.L.; BOULDING, K.; CHECKLAND, P.; VON BERTALAMFFY, L.; WIENER, N.

Related topics in the IEBM: CYBERNETICS; ENVIRONMENTAL MANAGEMENT; MANAGEMENT SCIENCE; NON-LINEAR PROGRAMMING; OPTIMAL DESIGN MODELS; OPTIMALITY AND OPTIMIZATION; ORGANIZATIONAL LEARNING; SYSTEMS

Foucault, Michel (1926–1984)

Personal background

- born 15 October 1926 in Poitiers, the son of a surgeon; attended the local Catholic school before becoming a boarder at the Lycee Henri IV in Paris
- graduated from the Ecole Normale Superieure and the Sorbonne (where he studied under Althusser) in 1948; began work in psychopathology at the Clinic Hospital Saint-Anne; joined the Communist Party
- received agregation in philosophy (1951) and a diploma in psychopathology (1952); broke with the Communist Party (1951).
- held lectureships at the University of Lille (department of psychology, 1951–5) and Uppsala (French literature and culture 1955–8), and directorship of the French Institute in Hamburg (1959)
- professor of philosophy at the University of Clermont-Ferrand (1960–6) and at the University of Tunis (1966–8)
- professor and dean at the University of Paris VIII at Vincennes (1968–70).
- professor of history of systems of thought, College de France (1970–84).
- early death in Paris, Salpetriere Hospital, 25 June 1984, from AIDS/cerebral tumour

Major works

Madness and Civilization (doctoral thesis)(1961)

The Archaeology of Knowledge (1969)

Discipline and Punish: Birth of the Prison (1975)

The History of Sexuality (Volume 1 1976, Volume 2 1984)

Summary

Michel Foucault (1926–84) was the best known and most influential French philosopher of the late twentieth century, becoming internationally known in the last years of his life, and particularly following his tragic early death. His works were diverse in terms of their subject matter – the history of attitudes to madness, sexuality, punishment, historical methodology – but there was a unifying theme: the idea that the Enlightenment's and liberal humanism's emphasis on the individual subject, and on progress and civilization, was misplaced and concealed the real nature of social changes over the last two centuries – the extension of the normalizing society supported by the technology and architecture of surveillance, the modernist project. This led Foucault to preoccupations with power, which he saw as increasingly all-pervasive and intangible, and 'governmentality' (governmental rationality), which he saw as involving increasingly total discipline over apparently individual subjects both of which have had an influence on contemporary organizational theory.

1 Introduction

Michel Foucault was perhaps the last and, with the exception of Sartre, the greatest (in terms of popular reputation at least) of the literary hero-philosophers that have been a feature of French cultural and political life during the twentieth century. As one of the leading figures associated with postmodernism, perhaps it is also fitting that one of his most abiding achievements was to resist categorization, even as a postmodernist. His thought has much in common with that of Derrida, and he has often been regarded as a poststructuralist, although his proximity to Nietzsche's thought could place him in the ranks of the literary modernists of an earlier generation. He shares Sartre's nihilistic view of human destiny, but, like the poststructuralists, he cannot accept the idea of the individual as agent. It is social processes that interest him, not the thoughts, action or intentions of individuals.

Whilst this brings him closer to the Marxists, he cannot share their debt to eighteenth-century enlightenment and the idea of history as progress – his strongest critics have been Marxist theorists loyal to the modernist principles of the Frankfurt School, notably Jurgen Habermas. Such critics have attacked his abandonment of any emphasis on repression of the individual subject (indeed he came close to arguing that repression/power was the means by which individuals and their 'souls' were constituted), although, on the other hand, his work on asylums drew early plaudits from those such as R.D.Laing, concerned with liberation of the individual.

It is difficult to find in Foucault's work one major original idea to account for his fame. There are unifying themes, arguments and leitmotivs, but no stable set of concepts. The ideas seem to emerge differently each time – in parallel with his major works, themselves replete with rhetorical devices, he published a wide range of lectures and interviews, in which the overall effect is one of indeterminacy. It may be argued that this is fitting and consistent for a post-structuralist or a postmodernist, but Foucault claimed to have been neither of these. However, he is clearly no mere literary jester either, since his works and statements are generally imbued with a moralizing tone, of which the target is usually the Bourgeoisie and its protective camouflage, the philosophy of the Enlightenment. It is one of the curiosities of Foucault's thought that he was able to leave Marxian theory behind, but not the hate-construct of the bourgeoisie, although the idea of an unseen bourgeois conspiracy to maximize surveilliance and 'normalize' an unsuspecting world is an absurdity from any postmodern (or Marxian?) standpoint – on the contrary it appears like a nightmarish caricature of modernism.

To a large extent this may not matter – Foucault's fame ultimately may rest on his style, both as a personality and as a speaker and writer. Unlike Derrida, Foucault's prose, and his speech, are arresting and force their way through dense thickets of paradox and ambiguity whilst preserving the surface appearance of pure lucidity. It is perhaps his unrivalled ability to live out the role of the radical philosopher hero and to connect with the post-1968 public in France and the post-socialist/post-politics public elsewhere, that assured Foucault of his enduring popularity.

2 Biographical data

Michel Foucault was born on 15 October, 1926, to a middle-class family in Poitier. His father was a surgeon (hence, it was later claimed, his detached 'anatomical' view of mutually separate historical processes). He attended the local Catholic School before being sent to the prestigious Lycee Henri IV in Paris. From there it was natural progression to enter one of the Grandes Ecoles, in this case the Ecole Normale Superieure, alongside which he studied philosophy under Althusser at the Sorbonne. It is curious that after his promising start in philosophy, he moved towards a more medical discipline, psychpathology. One senses that the area of madness, that where he was first break into the public consciousness in 1961 with the published success of his doctoral thesis *Folie et Deraison* (*Madness and Civilization*), was one where Foucault's already impressive abilities as literary philosophical were complemented by practical knowledge and experience. Although in retrospect the book contains many of the themes of later works (the Enlightenment leading to the liberation of the insane, after their confinement, only because it was now possible to replace physical restraint by psychological restraint), it reached across to specialists of very different political or philosophical orientations. It has often been commented that although the historical aspects of the work have been found to be unsound by historians (this has usually been the case with Foucault's work, although not necessarily to their detriment), the conventional histories of caring for the insane were never to be the same again. The same combination of nihilistic theory (destruction but not replacement of Enlightenment principles) and literary brilliance was then applied to the medical and other professions from the renaissance to the nineteenth century.

It may appear curious that, despite his early success, Foucault chose to occupy relatively obscure academic posts – Lille, Uppsala, Clermont-Ferrand, Tunis – although this may be a misreading of French academic career progression. Certainly his return to Paris in 1968 and, arguably, the beginning of his most productive period, could not have been better timed. As dean of the new Paris VIII University at Vincennes (from 1968–70), he was the natural leader for what was a radical ghetto, laid waste by the failure of the events of '68, but at the same time (it may be argued) intoxicated by the liberation from politics which had occurred as a result of this failure. Although his activities in this period – editing of radical journals, endless interviews and ideological disputes – appeared characteristic of a radical leader, one may interpret Foucault's role as being precisely that: to keep alive the appearance, the myth of revolution, whilst allowing the intelligentsia to withdraw from politics into literary and cultural concerns (which could of course be argued to be political in their own way). Little in Foucault's thought, apart from the attacks on the bourgeoisie, had any radical or political content in terms of prescription (see discussion of power below), and his radicalism appeared to be reduced to gestures (such as his much criticized support for the Khomeiniite Revolution in Iran). In retrospect the collapse of the far Left and the Communist Party in the late 1970s looks a foregone conclusion, culminating in the victory of Mitterand's socialists in 1981, which forced the intelligentsia to accept social democracy. Foucault's ability to carry the appearance of radicalism into this new era (not least through new forms of radicalism such as his openness about his homosexuality) earned him a continuing stream of criticism from the Left traditionalists.

In 1970 Foucault received his final and most prestigious post – chair in systems of thought at the College de France, which he was to occupy until his death from AIDS in 1984

3 Main contribution

Foucault's reputation rests largely on four major works: *Madness and Civilization* (1961); *The Archaeology of Knowledge* (1969); *Discipline and Punish: Birth of the Prison* (1975); *The History of Sexuality* (Volume 1 1976, Volume 2 1984). Given considerations of space, those concepts most cited in respect of organizational theory are focused on here.

Foucault's contribution to organizational theory may be summarized in terms of two concepts – power and surveillance. Pursuing his earlier view that liberal treatment of the insane reflected an increased propensity for psychological rather than physical control, Foucault broadened this idea (through his study of prisons) such that he perceived an expansion of surveillance from the eighteenth century onwards (an outgrowth of liberal rationalism) which would gradually lead to a totalized form of social control. The bourgeoisie would seek to eliminate uncertainty and 'normalize' all society. Foucault 's presented this view by means of popularizing Bentham's nineteenth century architectural decision of the 'Panopticon', a prison whose design incorporated maximum surveillance.

Related to this was Foucault's view of power. He moved increasingly farther from Marxist concerns with repression of individuals or groups by other individuals or groups. Power was not simply an attribute of conflict situations, or an instrument possessed, or lacked, by social actors. Instead it operated throughout the social system. All social relations were mediated by power. Far from being crushed by power, individuals were actually shaped and constituted by the exercise of power throughout society.

Foucault remained true to the post-structuralist principle of not recognizing individual agency – he believed that in studies of government the king's head (the concern with the motives and actions of the powerful) had yet to be cut of. He still, however, appeared to require a conspiracy of a (somewhat ill-defined) bourgeoisie to stand in the background and provide the impetus for the rise in surveillance, rather than entrust this to faceless social processes. This reflected a long-standing Foucauldian principle that rational-legal institutions were nothing more than a camouflage, although he argued also (more interestingly) that the technology of surveillance was more important than the use or motive to which it was applied.

4 Evaluation

From the point of view of organization theory Foucault's contribution on the topics on which he is most often cited, power and the Panopticon, seems to have symbolic rather than actual analytical importance. Organization theorists clearly have a need to cite someone like Foucault, the personification of radicalism. The ideas themselves would appear to have limited usefulness. Whilst the Panopticon clearly does reflect certain aspects of its age, and of our own – the desire to eliminate uncertainty via ruthless application of administrative order – it is perhaps best understood as an unrealizable aspiration of a certain type of person, whereas Foucault appears to imply that the project is available to be realized on a grand scale.

He also seems to regard discipline and surveillance as negative, whereas in different contexts this may not be the case (although it would be necessary to believe in human agency and motive to develop this view).

The idea of power as a pervasive social phenomenon is at first sight a refreshing change from the simplicities of 'A has power over B' and its many variants in organizational theory, as is the idea of power shaping the personality and society in ways that are not unidirectional. This broader, more fluid picture is however spoiled by the re-insertion of the evil bourgeoisie into the picture, which makes an absurdity of the whole approach – why should the bourgeoisie be an active agent and no one else? On this point a more traditional approach of exploiting elites would make more sense.

More important, the theory has little explanatory power. If power is everywhere all the time, working in all directions at once, one might as well say it is nowhere (as Baudrillard and others have noted). We are unable to reconstruct events in any organization from the point of view of power, because we cannot, according to this view, distinguish one person's power (or strategy) from another's. The concept closes many doors (empirical and theoretical). It is not clear whether it opens any in exchange – rather the idea of power seems to lose all meaning.

Finally, the concepts involved are not really as original as is believed – the idea of power existing in relationships between persons rather than being possessed by an individual emerged long ago in much duller surrounding, as did Foucault's related idea regarding Power as Knowledge and Knowledge as Power. This had surely been grasped decades ago by even the most plodding contingency theorist.

As for the underlying theme of the regimentation of working life, was this not far better handled by the likes of Reinhard Bendix in the 1950s, precisely because distinctions and comparison were made between different traditions of capitalism and management, rather than seek a grand unifying conspiracy?

5 Conclusion

As an individual Michel Foucault's achievement was immense, as is his continuing fame. As with Derrida, it could be argued that his success owes as much to his style, in Foucault's case a strongly individual and persuasive voice, rather than any major idea or school of thought (one speaks of a Foucault 'effect' not a Foucault School).

Whilst his place in the philosophical pantheon is secure, his contribution to organization theory seems more questionable, not least because it has often been taken as read. Foucault's work is a primarily literary rather than analytical exercise. The concepts raised and developed within it are buoyed up and protected from their contradictions by the sheer brilliance and pace of Foucault's style. Extracted from the context of his work, and the literary style associated with it, they tend to lose their lustre.

ADRIAN CAMPBELL
UNIVERSITY OF BIRMINGHAM

Further reading

(References cited in the text marked *)

Burchell, G., Gordon, C. and Miller, P. (eds)(1991) *The Foucault Effect: Studies in Governmentality*, Brighton: Harvester Wheatsheaf. (This collection brings together a range of international contributions which build on Foucault's governmentality concept both in theoretical terms and in analyses of contemporary state policies.)

Burke, P. (ed)(1992) *Critical Essays on Michel Foucault*, Aldershot: Scolar Press. (A well-chosen collection, structured to cover each of Foucault's major works, with Foucault's contributions included alongside those of his critics.)

Callinicos, A. (1989) *Against Postmodernism: A Marxist Critique,* London: Polity. (Provides a comparative analysis of Foucault and Derrida placing both in the tradition of literary modernism, and reinforcing the Marxist charge that their work is apolitical and essentially conservative.)

Daudi, P. (1986) *Power in the Organization: The Discourse of Power in Managerial Praxis*, Oxford: Blackwell. (A relatively early example of an empirical organizational study built on a theoretical base strongly influenced by Foucault.)

* Foucault, M. (1971) *Madness and Civilization: A History of Insanity in the Age of Reason*, London: Tavistock (translation by Richard Howard of the *Folie et Deraison: Histoire de la Folie a l'Age Classique*, Paris: Plon, 1961). (Much criticized on grounds of historical accuracy, this is the first major work in which Foucault seeks to undermine the ideas of Progress, the Enlightenment and liberal humanism.)

* Foucault, M. (1972) *The Archaeology of Knowledge*, New York: Harper and Row (translation by A.Sheridan of *L'Archeologie du Savoir*, Paris: Gallimard, 1969). (In pursuit of a more fragmented and less progress-oriented view of history, the methodological concept of 'archaeology' is applied to emphasize the degree to which knowledge(s) – or epistemes, as Foucault terms them – are formed and develop within cognitive limits, which change over time, such that they cannot simply be traced or assumed by later researchers, but rather they have to be 'unearthed'.)

* Foucault, M. (1977) *Discipline and Punish: Birth of the Prison*, (translation by A. Sheridan of *Surveiller et Punir: Naissance de la Prison*, Paris: Gallimard, 1975). (Perhaps the best-known and most influential of Foucault's writings, it presents the idea of bourgeois society being availed of the technology of surveillance which allows a creeping 'normalization' of all social occur, increasing control but making punishment or direct coercion less necessary.)

Gordon, C. (1980) *Michel Foucault. Power/Knowledge: Selected interviews and other writing 1972–77*, Brighton: Harvester Wheatsheaf. (A well-edited introduction to the most influential lines of Foucault's thinking – the afterword makes an extended case for Foucault the radical, in response to criticism from elsewhere on the Left.)

McKinley, A. And Starkey, K. (1998) *Foucault, Management and Organization Theory*, London: Sage; New Delhi; Thousand Oaks. (This collection is the most up-to-date compilation of critical assessments of his contribution to organization theory.)

Merquior, J.G. (1985) *Foucault*, London: Fontana/Harper Collins. (The degree to which Foucault's version of history – notably in Discipline and Punish – has been rejected and is fundamentally inaccurate and over-generalized by historians is made clear.)

Miller, P. (1987) *Domination and Power*, London: Routledge. (Sets out Foucault's work on power as being in clear opposition to that of Marxian critical theorists, notably the Frankfurt School.)

Rabinow, P. (1984) *The Foucault Reader*, London, Penguin. (The selection emphasizes the social and political aspects of Foucault's thought, rather than his historical/archaeological works, but giving pride of place to the anti-Enlightenment stance, which serves to provide the context for the other writings.)

Smart, B. (ed)(1995) *Michel Foucault: Critical Assessments* (seven volumes), London, Routledge. (An impressive collection, which by its sheer scale and comprehensiveness conveys the importance of the 'Foucault effect'. Contains a wide range of contributions, some building on Foucault's ideas, others questioning their validity.)

See also: CROZIER, M.; PFEFFER, J. AND SALANCIK, G.R.; MORGAN, G.; WEBER, M.

Related topics in the IEBM: DECONSTRUCTION ANALYSIS AND MANAGEMENT; ORGANIZATION BEHAVIOUR; ORGANIZATION BEHAVIOUR, HISTORY OF; ORGANIZATION PARADIGMS; ORGANIZATION STRUCTURE; POWER; SYSTEMS

Fox, Alan (1920–)

Personal background

- born in London, England, 23 January 1920
- married Margaret Dow in 1950; two children
- lecturer at Ruskin College, Oxford (1951–7)
- research fellow, at Nuffield College, Oxford (1957–63)
- lecturer in industrial sociology, University of Oxford (1963–79)

Major works

Industrial Sociology and Industrial Relations (1966)
Beyond Contract (1974)
History and Heritage (1985)

Summary

Alan Fox is best-known for his identification of the 'unitary', 'pluralist' and 'radical' perspectives on the employment relationship. His own work moved from the pluralist to the radical view, and he subsequently developed an analysis of trust which has enjoyed growing recognition as later workers have taken up this concept. Yet his own account of trust placed it firmly within an analysis of power and inequality, and he provided an extended critique of managerial nostrums which became perhaps even more pertinent than when it was first written. His later work pursued these concerns through an exploration of the 'social origins' of British industrial relations in which he connected the management of the employment relationship to an account of the distinctive pattern of class and labour relations in Britain.

1 Biographical data

Alan Fox was born in 1920 to a poor London family. After leaving school at the age of fourteen, he worked as an office clerk, a semi-skilled factory worker and a forestry labourer. Following six years' wartime service in the Royal Air Force, during which he was awarded the Distinguished Flying Medal, he went in 1947 to Ruskin College, Oxford, and later Exeter College to study philosophy, politics and economics. Oxford was to be his home for the rest of his career. He became a lecturer at Ruskin, a research fellow at Nuffield and, from 1963 to 1979, university lecturer in industrial sociology.

Fox's autobiography (Fox 1990) presents his intellectual development with candour and self-deprecation. Fox was always something of a shy outsider and he was uncomfortable with public affairs. He established close personal relationships, of which the most important for his academic work were those with Allan Flanders and Hugh Clegg (see CLEGG, H. AND FLANDERS, A.D.); the three are the scholars most closely associated with what was later termed the 'Oxford school' of industrial relations. Though retiring and non-assertive, Fox possesses strong intellectual determination, illustrated most sharply by his vigorous critique of the 'pluralist' underpinnings of the Oxford School, a critique which involved him in attacking the ideas of close friends and colleagues. Fox's development has been that of an unrelenting search for intellectual understanding of society. As he puts it, he was driven by a need to 'understand not simply *how* I differed from others but precisely *why*' (Fox 1990: 236), and he feels that his work slowly attained a unity.

2 Frames of reference in employment relations

Industrial Sociology and Industrial Relations, Fox's short (33-page) research paper for the Royal Commission into British industrial relations, the Donovan Commission, has had a lasting impact for its identification of two 'frames of reference' (Fox 1966). The 'unitary' view is based on the analogy of a team and stresses the common purpose of the enterprise. It has one source of authority and one focus of loyalty. But such a view is unrealistic because work organizations comprise many groups with divergent interests. Fox quotes Peter Drucker as saying that the goal of management is to maximize economic performance, so that authority cannot be discharged 'primarily in the interest of those over whom the enterprise rules' (see DRUCKER, P.F.). 'It follows', says Fox, that management 'must sometimes act against the interests of workpeople as they see them, and that this is incompatible with the concept of common purpose' (1966: 5).

Fox goes on to advocate a 'pluralistic' approach based on the acceptance of the idea of divergent interests. In this view, trade unions have a legitimate place in the enterprise because they reflect the interests of particular groups. Because of the various sources of authority and differing goals, conflict is endemic. Those adopting a unitary view, by contrast, are unlikely ever to be reconciled to unions and to insist on managerial prerogative, with the result that expressions of conflict are seen as pathological. The common result was that managements asserted their rights while having to deal with the facts of work group independence, so that management 'connives at the extension of unilateral regulation by work-groups' (Fox 1966: 14). The solution was for managements to recognize instances of conflict as rational responses by workers pursuing their interests as they saw them, and to develop regulatory institutions based on this reality rather than the pretence of a single source of authority. This analysis underlay the recommendations of the Donovan Commission, which advocated the reform of collective bargaining institutions so as to deal with the 'challenge from below' which had grown up unacknowledged.

Pluralism rapidly came under attack (see especially Hyman 1978): institutional reform was mere tinkering with problems of conflict which reflected fundamental inequalities of power. Some of Fox's colleagues defended the pluralist view but he became convinced of the value of a more 'radical' frame of reference and in a series of publications culminating in *Beyond Contract* (Fox 1974) he laid out his views. He became convinced that a 'liberal reformist' approach carried an 'unavowed bias' (Fox 1990: 232): though order might appear to be in the interests of all, could it not simply mean that the interests of one side were being promoted? Whatever the intention of reformers perhaps they were 'favouring management by helping them the better to manipulate their workforce'. A more radical account of the nature of power and inequality was required.

A key feature of Fox's radicalism was that it was not Marxist. Fox made a clear distinction between analysis and prescription. Analysis is needed to identify the systematic sources of inequality and the ways in which the powerful can manipulate institutions such as the law. But it does not follow that the solution is to reject all forms of law or to hope that an undefined revolution will dissolve all the problems of conflict and inequality. Radicalism for Fox did not mean a celebration of conflict or an endorsement of a particular political programme. Fox thus contributes to the very English radical tradition of exposing class-based forms of power and inequality while remaining sceptical about any permanent solution: a tradition which in many ways is critical of all forms of authority. As he writes, 'I find great appeal in that long radical tradition, adorned by such names as William Morris, R. H. Tawney, George Orwell and Edward Thompson, which seeks to reduce the abundant inequalities in British society ... while retaining what is best in a country which still cherishes, though now more precariously, many social decencies' (Fox 1985b: 205).

3 Trust and power

Beyond Contract was significant for two reasons. First, it contained a developed statement of Fox's radical model. A pluralist view rests on the 'crucial' working assumption that 'there exists between the parties [in workplace relations] something approximating to a balance of power' (Fox 1974: 265). The radical alternative was to explore deeper sources of inequality and the imbalances of power.

Second, and crucially, Fox did not lock himself into a rigid radicalism, in which all forms of workplace government were dismissed as variants of exploitation. Instead, he developed models of two forms of relationship, those based on low and high trust. He is focusing here on trust, not in the sense of personal relationships between individuals, but at the level of what he calls institutionalized trust. This is embodied in, to use Fox's words, 'the social arrangements, decisions and policies' which people try to impose on each other (Fox 1985b: 109), notably 'the regulation of people in their task activities; the rewards and punishments brought to bear on them; and their relations with others in terms of interdependence, communication, inspection, supervision and authority' (Fox 1974: 68). *Beyond Contract* lays out detailed illustrations of low and high trust 'syndromes'. The logic of a radical view stresses power and tendencies towards problems of low trust. High-trust relations are pursued not because of shared interests but because 'they are thought to evoke commitment to managerial ends, improve performance, promote adaptability and receptivity to change, [and] stabilize the labour force' (Fox 1974: 363). However, high-trust relations could be sustained under certain conditions, notably where technical and organizational change encouraged efforts at serious dialogue.

This work anticipated later concerns in two main ways. First, high-trust models became a central focus of the 1980s and 1990s, with talk of high commitment though new devices such as total quality management. Yet Fox's analysis, together with the accompanying account aimed at a more managerial audience *Man Mismanagement* (1985b, second edition),

places such enthusiasm in context. The history of job redesign experiments, for example, was one of limited ambitions and the frequent abandonment of experiments that were hailed as truly innovative. There are always pressures towards low trust relationships, and policies of high trust still rest on relationships of power.

The second aspect of *Beyond Contract* is more analytical. Since the book was written, numerous authors have begun to analyse trust as a key component of bargaining relationships. Societies such as the Japanese and the German have been described as high trust, reflecting the institutionalization of long-term relationships in the commercial field as well as in employment. In more market-driven economies such as those of Britain and North America, the concern has been to find the conditions which will permit long-term relationships, and with them high trust, to emerge. The interest in 'productivity coalitions' is one example. Fox's analysis thus continues to inform major debates.

4 *History and Heritage*

Apart from a few forays into comparative analysis, Fox retained his focus on Britain. His last major work, *History and Heritage* (1985a), explored the historical evolution of industrial relations. It is a much more wide-ranging work than the term 'a history of British industrial relations' might imply. Traditionally, a volume on this subject would focus on trade unions and collective bargaining as institutions. Fox's book differs in several respects.

First, it analyses industrial relations in terms of patterns of class compromise. The behaviour of companies and of the state is given central attention, and this behaviour is analysed in relation to the problem of regulating class inequality. The central paradox of Britain is the development of a labour movement which was capable of resistance to management within the workplace but which was profoundly politically conservative. The answer lies in the series of compromises made by employers and the state at times of crisis. They eschewed both (pluralist) recognition of labour organizations and (unitarist) authoritarianism. They thus helped to create a labour movement with a strongly 'restrictivist' mentality in the workplace but without wider ambitions.

Second, Fox addresses many analytical debates. He makes no effort to take on such debates directly, and theoretically-oriented scholars may have failed to identify his contribution, but it is there for those willing to seek it. A key example is the theory of the state. At the time when Fox was writing, debate on the state was emerging from highly abstract discussion of 'relative autonomy', with writers identifying the need to consider the state historically as an actor in the negotiation of class compromise. Fox's analysis of the British case offers much pertinent material. In particular, it explains the logic of the situation as it appeared to key actors at certain crucial junctures, the reasons for particular choices, and the ways in which choices reflected but were not determined by previous policies. Such an analysis, which might now be labelled as a 'strategic choice approach', reveals how a particular approach to the management of labour slowly evolved and how each stage of development reflected the past.

Third, though this is an account of Britain, there is a strong comparative thread which surfaces in, for example, Fox's consideration of why the British state took a less authoritarian line than its German counterpart. The evolution of British industrial relations reflected a distinctive pattern of class forces, in particular the deeply entrenched workplace focus of the labour movement. Studies of other countries (notably Fulcher's 1991 comparison of Sweden and Britain) have begun to pursue the same logic of exploring the policies of governments, employers and worker organizations and the ways in which these interacted..

5 Evaluation

Fox's work on frames of reference is perhaps his most famous contribution. It might also be viewed as the most dated, since the decline of unions and the rise of human resource management might indicate that a unitary approach is not as outmoded as was suggested. Yet even at a time when non-union firms might have been viewed as relics of the past, Fox (1966: 5) was careful to indicate why a unitary view might be retained. He identified three roles of such an ideology: self-reassurance, persuasion, and the legitimization of authority. Such roles may continue to exist. The task at the time, moreover, was not to explain why managers believe in unitarism but to offer them a more realistic pluralist view. None the less, Fox may have given insufficient attention to the ability of unitary ideas to survive. His later work would have been strengthened by further analysis of how employers defend and sustain unitary views.

To evaluate the frames of reference, we need to distinguish between an analytical perspective and a purported description of social actors' beliefs. Many treatments confuse these aspects. For example, it is often noted that the radical view is unlikely to describe many workers' beliefs as though this is a criticism of the view as an intellectual perspective. As for the differences between the perspectives, some pluralists, notably Hugh Clegg (1979; see CLEGG, H.), retorted that they had been saying much the same thing as the radicals without the rhetorical flourishes. In retrospect, the need for radicals to distance themselves from pluralism is understandable, though later debates have moved on from seeking sharp distinctions.

As with many social science perspectives, the test is not whether they can prove themselves better than others at the abstract level, for Clegg was right to the extent that pluralism and radicalism may be hard to separate. It is whether an approach offers a constructive research programme. The radical view has done so in encouraging research which looks at the fundamentals of the employment relationship: the bases of conflict, the negotiation of consent, and the need to see managerial strategies not as unitary solutions, but as partial responses to continuing problems of control and order. In this approach, it merged with accounts from the 'labour process' tradition. *Beyond Contract* was published in the same year (1974) as Braverman's celebrated *Labor and Monopoly Capital* (see BRAVERMAN, H.). Yet those attracted to a critique of managerial labour strategies tended to focus on the latter work rather than Fox's more subtle account. Unlike Braverman, it did not focus on one logic driving the capitalist enterprise, and it drew out differing dimensions of labour control policy based on low and high trust. The latter feature has much in common with other theories of the labour process, notably Friedman's (1977). Fox did not, however, directly engage with the labour process debate, and discussion of his ideas has been limited. Yet his account of low and high trust and of coercion and consent suggests a research programme which explores the different ways in which these principles are used in practice. Later work has begun to address this issue, and some detours might have been avoided had Fox's analysis of the tensions between conflict and consent been given fuller attention. Where his own work could have been strengthened was more attention to the economic and social conditions which led to low or high trust syndromes.

A broadly radical view underpins much current debate. But in many respects unitary views are more prevalent than in the 1960s, as managers commonly speak of 'empowerment' and assume that shared visions of organizational goals can be attained. Fox's work thus contains a dual legacy of a framework to understand such developments and a means of questioning them. Such questioning does not mean rejection, still less a celebration of conflict. It means exposing their assumptions and inconsistencies. Fox's own attempts in this regard continue to be relevant to any manager who believes that trust and consent are readily generated.

PAUL EDWARDS
UNIVERSITY OF WARWICK

The advice of Alan Fox and also Chris Rowley is gratefully acknowledged.

Further reading

(References cited in the text marked *)

* Clegg, H.A. (1979) *The Changing System of Industrial Relations in Great Britain*, Oxford: Blackwell. (Standard treatment of the subject, containing Clegg's defence of pluralism.)

* Fox, A. (1966) *Industrial Sociology and Industrial Relations*, Research Paper 3, Royal Commission on Trade Unions and Employers' Associations. London: HMSO. (Fox's statement of frames of reference, with detailed examples from contemporary industrial sociology.)

* Fox, A. (1974) *Beyond Contract: Work, Power and Trust Relations*, London: Faber and Faber. (Analytical treatment of a radical perspective and trust relations.)

* Fox, A. (1985a) *History and Heritage: the Social Origins of the British Industrial Relations System*, London: Allen and Unwin. (Richly detailed account of British class relations from the 1700s to the 1980s.)

* Fox, A. (1985b) *Man Mismanagement*, London: Hutchinson. (Second edition of a text aimed at managers, drawing on the theories of *Beyond Contract*.)

* Fox, A. (1990) *A Very Late Development: An Autobiography*, Coventry: Industrial Relations Research Unit. (Exposition of Fox's intellectual journey through the class system, with particular reference to his wartime experiences.)

* Friedman, A. L. (1977) *Industry and Labour*, London: Macmillan. (Study of two management strategies, direct control and responsible autonomy, with strong parallels with models of low and high trust.)

* Fulcher, J. (1991) *Labour Movements, Employers and the State*, Oxford: Clarendon. (Comparative analysis of the regulation of the employment relationship in Britain and Sweden, using methods similar to Fox's.)

* Hyman, R. (1978) 'Pluralism, procedural consensus and collective bargaining', *British Journal of Industrial Relations* 16 (1): 16–40. (Extended critique of pluralism, relating its industrial relations exponents to political theory.)

See also: BRAVERMAN, H; CLEGG, H.; FLANDERS, A.D.; DRUCKER, P.F.

Related topics in the IEBM: COLLECTIVE BARGAINING; EMPLOYEE RELATIONS, MANAGEMENT OF; EMPLOYERS' ASSOCIATIONS; GENERAL MANAGEMENT; INDUSTRIAL DEMOCRACY; INDUSTRIAL AND LABOUR RELATIONS; MANAGEMENT IN GERMANY; MANAGEMENT IN THE UNITED KINGDOM; TRADE UNIONS

Friedman, Milton (1912–)

1 Introduction
2 Major contributions
3 Conclusion

Personal background

- born 31 July 1912, New York City
- educated at Rutgers and Chicago; PhD from Columbia, 1946
- worked for the US National Resources Committee 1935–7
- worked for the division of tax research, US Treasury, 1941
- research staff with the National Bureau of Economic Research, 1937–81
- associate director at the division of war research, Columbia University, 1943–5
- awarded the Nobel Prize for Economics, 1976
- taught at the University of Chicago, 1948–77
- Paul Snowdon Russell Distinguished Service Professor of Economics, University of Chicago
- has lectured extensively at universities in Europe, Japan and Latin America; holds numerous degrees
- fellow at the Hoover Institute, Stanford University since 1977

Major works

The Methodology of Positive Economics (1953)
A Theory of Consumption Function (1957)
A Monetary History of the United States, 1867–1960 (with Anna J. Schwartz) (1963)
Monetary Statistics of the United States (with Anna J. Schwartz) (1970)

Summary

Milton Friedman, the 1976 Nobel Prize winner for excellence in economics, is widely regarded as the leader of the Chicago School of Monetary Economics. This school stresses the importance of the Quantity Theory of Money as the key instrument of government policy. His contributions to the development of economics are extensive, ranging from economic methods to economic history to international economics.

1 Introduction

Throughout his long and distinguished career, Milton Friedman has made major contributions to economic analysis and the conduct of economic policy. This significant work encompasses economic methodology, money, economic history, micro- and macroeconomics, economic policy and international economics.

Friedman was awarded the Nobel Prize in Economics in 1976 for his achievements in the fields of consumption analysis, monetary history and theory and for his demonstration of the complexity of stabilization policy.

As early as 1950 Friedman was a major critic of the dominance of Keynesian economics (see KEYNES, J.M.). He led the intellectual and public charge for a major re-evaluation of the role of the central bank in the conduct of monetary policy. However his contribution was not limited to the role of money in economic theory and policy and his challenging work in methodology, flexible exchange rates, the permanent income hypothesis and the issue of an inflation–unemployment trade-off were all significant contributions to knowledge.

Friedman's influence was not limited to the economic profession. His ideas with their forceful verbal and written presentation were known by political leaders in the USA and overseas, the press and to readers of his weekly column in *Newsweek*.

2 Major contributions

During his long and distinguished career Friedman has made major contributions in the key areas of economic analysis, including methodology, money, consumption, economic policy, inflation and unemployment, and debates over exchange rate policy.

In *The Methodology of Positive Economics*, Friedman made a powerful case for using implications rather than assumptions as a testing ground for economic theory. Indeed, his notion of the 'as if' hypothesis is crucial to understanding his extensive empirical works, especially in the fields of money. Friedman's first and major significant empirical work was undertaken with his associates in the Workshop in Money and Banking at the University of Chicago and in the National Bureau of Economic Research. This work culminated in three major publications: *A Monetary History of the United States, 1867–1960* co-authored with Anna J. Schwartz; an accompanying volume by Philip Cagan, *Determinants and Effects of Changes in the Stock of Money, 1875–1960*; and *Monetary Statistics of the United States*, co-authored again with Schwartz.

In these and subsequent works, Friedman led the charge of the Chicago School in its cry that 'money matters'. He attacked the way many economists had ignored the significance of money and monetary policy when analysing business cycles and inflation. Drawing upon his detailed historical analysis of money, Friedman re-formulated a new theory of the demand for money. His detailed empirical findings and analysis of the relationship between increases in money supply and the resulting changes in income and prices led him to argue that the demand for money is in fact very stable.

Friedman's pioneering work on money led him to a re-statement of the quantity theory of money in which the distinctive feature is a theory of the demand for real balances. He argued that while it was the case that monetary authorities controlled the nominal stock of money, what really mattered to the holders of money was the real quantity of money. He concluded that in a sense, the goal of monetary policy should be to ensure a long-term stable growth in the supply of money.

In his criticism of the approaches and support of Keynesians to economic policy, Friedman distinguished between three forms of lags which appeared in economic policy: the observation lag, the decision lag and the effect lag. He argued that these lags had major destabilizing effects and the challenge should be to simplify monetary policy to achieve stable growth in supply.

In the debates which raged in the economic profession, especially in the 1970s, it was Friedman who was the first to demonstrate that the assumption of a simple trade-off between inflation and unemployment was only a temporary phenomenon. Moreover, he argued that in the long run, no such trade-off existed.

Interrelated to Friedman's analysis of inflation and unemployment, was his pioneering work in international economics. In a 1950 essay, Friedman was an advocate for freely fluctuating exchange rates. His paper was written at a time when the Bretton Woods agreement, and the subsequent creation of the International Monetary Fund and the World Bank with its position of fixing exchange rates, was the prevailing wisdom. Friedman's analysis of how a movement to flexible exchange rates would improve the balance of payments adjustment was truly pioneering. He critically tore apart the arguments that flexible exchange rates would encourage destabilization and his position was vindicated some twenty years later when the world moved to a flexible exchange rate regime.

Friedman's work on consumption constitutes another example of his contribution to the development of economic analysis. He extended and refined the absolute income hypothesis to create a theory of consumption based on the hypothesis that permanent income, not annual income, is the *key* determinant factor when assessing total consumption expenditure. In his detailed work, *A Theory of the Consumption Function* (1957) he surveyed a large amount of empirical evidence with which the permanent income hypothesis is consistent and distinguished between temporary and permanent income – he concluded that a greater proportion of temporary income is saved than in the latter.

3 Conclusion

Friedman's contribution to the development and refinement of numerous areas of economic analysis has been significant, provocative, pathbreaking, public and challenging. His work on money, consumption, exchange rates and economic methodology have been major contributions. His work in economic history has led to a re-evaluation of the important linkages between money, monetary policy and growth in a nation's path of economic development. His role in the re-interpretation of the scope for discretionary action in monetary and fiscal policy in economic management have had significant impacts on how governments have conducted economic policy, especially since 1970.

JOHN CUNNINGHAM WOOD
UNIVERSITY OF NOTRE DAME
AUSTRALIA

Further reading

(References cited in the text marked *)

Cagan, P. (1965) *Determiants and Effects of Changes in the Stock of Money, 1875-1960*, Ann Arbor, MI: University MicroFilms International. (Companion work to that of Friedman with the Workshop in Money and Banking.)

Friedman, M. (1953) *Essays in Positive Economics*, Chicago, IL: University of Chicago Press. (Provides a detailed account of Friedman's methodology and places an overriding stress on economics as a predictable science.)

* Friedman, M. (1957) *A Theory of the Consumption Function*, Princeton, NJ: Princeton University Press. (Re-assesses J.M. Keynes's consumption function analysis and argues that people adjust their consumption with respect to variations in their permanent income.)

Friedman, M. (1962) *Capitalism and Freedom*, Chicago, IL: University of Chicago Press. (A provocative work which embodies many of his liberal and political views.)

* Friedman, M. and Schwartz, A.J. (1963) *A Monetary History of the United States, 1867–1960*, Princeton, NJ: Princeton University Press. (An in-depth study of the topic, produced for the National Bureau of Economic Research.)

* Friedman, M. and Schwartz, A.J. (1970) *Monetary Statistics of the United States*, New York: Columbia University Press. (The result of the same period of empirical work as the 1963 publication, again produced for the National Bureau of Economic Research.)

See also: HAYEK, F.; KEYNES, J.M.

Related topics in the IEBM: BUSINESS CYCLES; EMPLOYMENT AND UNEMPLOYMENT, ECONOMICS OF; EXCHANGE RATE ECONOMICS; INFLATION; MONETARISM; NEOCLASSICAL ECONOMICS

Fukuzawa, Yukichi (1835–1901)

Personal background

- born in Osaka, Japan, on 10 January 1835, the second son of a lower-ranking samurai
- studied Dutch and then English in the late 1850s
- travelled to the USA and Europe in the 1860s in the Shogunate envoy and mission
- married O'Kin Toki, 1861
- inaugurated his school in 1858, ten years later named Keio gijuku (college) and, since 1890, Keio University
- founded a newspaper, *Jiji shimpo*, in 1882
- was an educator and a journalist throughout his life
- died on 3 February 1901

Major works

Book Keeping, vol. 1 (1873), vol. 2 (1874)
Political Economy for Citizens part 1 (1877), part 2 (1880)
Discourse on Industry and Business (1893)

Summary

Fukuzawa is known as the most prominent of a group of advocates of Western civilization at the onset of modern Japan. He introduced the joint stock company and Western-type bookkeeping into commercial trade and business while he tried to demolish the traditional contempt of merchant and money. Fukuzawa founded both Keio University and a newspaper, the *Jiji shimpo*. Through his writings and speeches he encouraged his students and other audiences to participate in industry and trade with not only a practical knowledge of economics but also a dedication, integrity and frugality rooted deeply in traditional samurai ethos.

1 Introduction

Yukichi Fukuzawa (1835–1901) was the most prominent of a group of intellectuals who advocated the adoption of Western civilization at the onset of modern Japan (see IBUKA, M.; IWASAKI, Y.; MATSUSHITA, K.; OHNO, T.; TOYODA FAMILY; UENO, Y.). He perceived that two elements in Western society were necessary for Japan to become a civilized nation: science in the material sphere and a sense of self-reliance in the spiritual sphere. He believed that individual self-reliance could be attained with economic independence, which in turn could bring economic growth and national independence. Therefore, he earnestly introduced modern institutions such as the joint stock company along with practices such as Western-type book-keeping. He established a commercial college in order to diffuse the latter practice.

Both Keio University and the *Jiji shimpo*, a newspaper, were founded by Fukuzawa. He tried to demolish his students' traditional distrust of commerce and encouraged them to participate in industry and trade – especially international trade – as well as the traditionally more respectable profession of politics. In fact, the university produced many leading businessmen. As a prolific writer with a plain and lucid style, he untiringly endeavoured to persuade his readers to apply scientific knowledge and thinking in business and commerce.

Fukuzawa was doing more than a mere wholesaling of Western ideas. He recognized that domestic infant industries should be protected until mature, and did not hesitate to admire and recommend the traditional samurai virtues of dedication, integrity and so forth, even after he had discarded his stipend and privilege of samurai (warrior vassal).

2 Biographical data

Fukuzawa was born the second son of a lower-ranking samurai on 10 January 1835 in the city of Osaka. His father had been stationed there for fourteen years to work for his lord's treasury. When Fukuzawa was only 18 months years old, his father died of a sudden illness and his family was forced to return together to their home town of Nakatsu in northern Kyushu. He grew up there and started his education late because of family poverty. In 1854, a year after US Commodore M.A. Perry had knocked on the closed doors of Japan, Fukuzawa's elder brother, who had inherited his father's office, suggested that he should learn Dutch in order to master Western gunnery. Fukuzawa immediately went to Nagasaki, the only port opened to the limited trade with the Netherlands and China. The next year he moved to Osaka for more intensive study in the Academy of Physician K. Ogata, where he studied not only Dutch but also science for three years, and became the top student.

In the autumn of 1858 Fukuzawa was summoned to the lord's house in Edo (now Tokyo) to teach Dutch studies to a small class there. A year later he visited Yokohama, the main port opened for trade by the 1858 Treaty of Friendship and Commerce. There he found neither a signboard nor a label in Dutch, and learned that English was the common language. Undaunted, he began to learn English by himself. In early 1860 he volunteered to be a servant of Admiral Y. Kimura of the *Kanrin maru*, the vessel venturing a trans-Pacific voyage on the occasion of the Shogunate envoy to the USA for the ratification of the 1858 Treaty. He went to San Francisco and stayed less than two months. On his return, Fukuzawa was hired in the translation office of the Shogunate. In 1862 he again had the opportunity to join a year-long journey around Europe as a translator in the Shogunate envoy to the treaty countries. In 1867 he visited Washington and New York as the secretary of the mission for purchasing a warship.

After those travels Fukuzawa published *Seiyo jijo* (Conditions in the West) in three volumes (1866–70). All the material consisted of both his observations and translations from the source books obtained during his travels. Volume 1 in particular, in which his knowledge about joint stock companies and managerial information of the railway and postal service were incorporated, sold so well that he became known as a leading advocate of Western civilization. Just before the Meiji Restoration he named his school Keio gijuku (college). Immediately after the Restoration Fukuzawa refused the offer to work in the new government, since he determined to take the task of educating his countrymen, both young and adult. Thus, he became exclusively engaged in teaching at Keio, and in writing and translating a variety of textbooks for the pupils and pamphlets for the people at large.

In the mid-1870s Fukuzawa switched from these activities to concentrating on writing original works. He lectured occasionally to the students in Keio, which became a university in 1890. After the publication of the *Jiji shimpo* (meaning 'Timely News') in 1882, he devoted himself to writing articles about every aspect of society, including history, politics, international relations, political economy, business and industry, education, family and women's rights. Thus, Fukuzawa contributed to the modernization of Japan not only as an educator but also as a journalist. He died on 3 February 1901.

3 Main contribution

Fukuzawa obtained a full understanding of the structure and working of competitive society from J.H. Burton's *Political Economy* (Anon. 1852). He was so fascinated with the principles of political economy that he even continued his lecture on F. Wayland, *The Elements of Political Economy* (1841), on 4 July 1868, the day the Battle at the Hill of Ueno took place not far from the Keio campus. Also, he used parts of these two textbooks in his own books, *Conditions in the West* and *An Encouragement of Learning* (1872–76). The latter was widely read as well as the former.

Fukuzawa himself wrote one elementary textbook, namely *Political Economy for Citizens* (1877, 1880), which covered both elementary knowledge and simple laws of economics useful for civil life in a market economy. He apparently wrote it for school pupils, but he hoped (in the preface to part 1) that boys and girls could tell or read the text to their parents at home. This expectation reveals his imagination in his attempt to enlighten the public.

The book also put forward the theory of what Fukuzawa was actually doing: leading an independent life. In practice, Fukuzawa joined the publisher's association of Tokyo in 1869 and worked as a writer/publisher for next three years. Then Fukuzawa developed this business, with a few of his former students, into the Keio gijuku Press, a joint stock company. The press earned handsome profits until the Ministry of Education began to consider both Fukuzawa's and the Keio fellows' books too liberal to be on the list of recommended school textbooks.

Fukuzawa also encouraged his disciples and friends to start the trading companies, the Maruya (now Maruzen) Company and the Morimura Company. He held some shares in the former, which was, according to him, an experimental school of importation practices. The latter was engaged in exporting silk and other domestic products, and opened a branch office in New York. The Yokohama Specie Bank (now the Bank of Tokyo) and the Meiji Life Insurance were financial corporations established in the early 1880s on Fukuzawa's suggestion. His disciples, N. Koizumi, T. Abe and others worked as the president or directors in these corporations.

Fukuzawa's other contribution to the field of commerce was a scientific one: the introduction of Western-style book-keeping. He realized the necessity and usefulness of this 'practical science' when he read *Bryant and Stratton's Common School Book keeping* (1861: 1), and then used the book to teach the subject and decided to translate it. The translation (*Choai no ho* (1873–4)) proved to be more difficult than any other one Fukuzawa had previously done as he was unfamiliar with the trade. He had to create new words for technical terms that did not exist in the Japanese language. In today's terminology many of the translated terms have become obsolete;

nevertheless, some of the basic ones are still used as Fukuzawa coined them more than a century ago.

It is not a digression to mention here that Fukuzawa taught his wife, O'Kin, book-keeping in the early 1870s. She kept a monthly cash book for the household, collaborating with her husband to obtain the annual sum and balance by adding the accounts he managed, every year throughout his life.

Fukuzawa's endeavours to introduce book-keeping extended even further. In 1874 he sent a few of his disciples who had mastered the original text to Osaka to start a new school, Keio gijuku, Osaka. As the city was the national centre of commerce and trade, Fukuzawa reasoned that the merchants in Osaka should be equipped with this new art for their future participation in international trade. The school, however, closed in a few years. This was because merchants were conventionally trained through apprenticeship, and consequently most could not see the significance of school education and a strange method of book-keeping for their clerks.

None the less, his efforts were not in vain. One of the dispatched disciples, H. Shoda, was employed by the Mitsubishi Company and began the new accounting system in the company in 1877. Moreover, Fukuzawa helped to start the Tokyo Commercial College (today Hitotsubashi University) in 1875 and placed a course in book-keeping in the Keio curriculum in 1878. He also ran, at his own expense, a school of book-keeping in the business centre of Tokyo from 1879 to 1882. Meanwhile, some 500 students were trained in this school. Eventually these endeavours urged the establishment of commercial colleges in Kobe, Osaka and elsewhere.

In 1893, Fukuzawa pushed his 'encouragement' of business forwards in *Discourse on Industry and Business*, which was a series of articles once published in the *Jiji shimpo*. By this time he saw that Japan's infant industries, particularly the cotton industry, had developed sufficiently to compete with its Indian counterpart in the Asian market, provided that the government removed tariff barriers on both imported raw cotton and exported cotton products. However, he argued that Japanese business and trade were not yet well prepared for world competition as they continued to carry over their conservative attitude and traditional practices. Fukuzawa claimed that an investment in human capital should be an integral component in the field of industry and business.

Nevertheless, he argued that Japanese businessmen had to preserve such virtues as dedication and integrity, which, he deemed, had been embedded well in the samurai tradition. This contradicting recommendation of his is not surprising, for Fukuzawa always took a pragmatic and selective approach to an actual problem. He had one foot in Western studies and the other one in Japanese history.

4 Conclusion

Fukuzawa advocated Western institutions and practices in every field. In business he introduced the joint stock company, book-keeping, and commercial colleges. His main aim was to 'revolutionize' the mentality of the people – from the traditional conservatism of merchants to a dynamic industrialism of businessmen.

Some of his contemporaries denounced him as a Mammonist. However, he tried not only to demolish the traditional distrust of merchant held by samurai but also to remove Mammonism and conventionalism in the traditional merchant. He emphasized samurai puritanism. An American scholar, Kinmonth (1978), interprets Fukuzawa's *Encouragement of Learning* as urging *shizoku* (former samurai) to learn Western studies in order to get higher positions and wealthy life. But Fukuzawa was hardly concerned with a (traditional) class interest either. He proclaimed that economic independence was the material base of self-reliance, which in turn was the foundation of national independence and wealth. In fact, the number of commoners and their sons in Keio and in his audiences well exceeded those of shizoku and their sons in the 1880s. Thus, his ideal businessman was a samurai-like person, regardless of the premodern status, with practical, scientific knowledge in economics and accounting.

As regards to women's participation in industry and business, Fukuzawa introduced the fact that American women worked as telephone operators, business clerks, physicians and so on, and he expected Japanese women to undertake similar and other appropriate professions in the near future; he declared that no one proved Japanese women alone were incapable while those of the West were capable (1988). He also recommended that both wives and daughters acquire knowledge of economics and of the civil code as their 'pocket daggers' (1988: 223) to protect themselves and to make themselves independent.

SHUNSAKU NISHIKAWA
KEIO UNIVERSITY

Further reading

(References cited in the text marked *)

* Anon. (1852) *Political Economy, for Use in Schools and for Private Instruction*, London: W & R Chambers. (Author identified by Craig as J.H. Burton; Fukuzawa translated the first half of this book for vol. 2 of *Conditions*.)

Blacker, C. (1964) *The Japanese Enlightenment*, Cambridge: Cambridge University Press. (A classic study of Fukuzawa, discussing Fukuzawa's life, enlightenment activity and philosophy.)

* Bryant, H.B., Stratton, H.D. and Packard, S.S. (1861) *Bryant and Stratton's Common School Book Keeping*, New York: Ivison Blakeman Taylor & Co. (The original book of Fukuzawa's *Choai no ho*.)

Craig, A.M. (1984) 'John Hill Burton and Fukuzawa Yukichi', *Annals of Modern Japanese Studies* 1: 218–38. (Identifies Burton as the author of *Political Economy*, and discusses how Fukuzawa accepted Scottish ideas, 'creatively' translating them into Japanese.)

* Fukuzawa, Y. (1866–70) *Seiyo jijo* (Conditions in the West), vol. 1, Tokyo: Shokodo, 1866; vol. 2, Tokyo: Keio gijuku, 1868; vol. 3, Tokyo: Keio gijuku, 1870. (Discusses social institutions, technical innovations, history, political systems, military power and fiscal and economic strengths in the West.)

* Fukuzawa, Y. (1872–6) *An Encouragement of Learning*, trans. D.A. Dilworth and U. Hirano, Tokyo: Sophia University, 1969. (A collection of essays written for enlightenment, originally published under the title *Gakumon no susume*.)

* Fukuzawa, Y. (1873–4) *Choai no ho* (Book keeping), Tokyo: Keio gijuku Press. (Translation of Bryant *et al.*; vol. 1 entitled *Single Entry* and vol. 2 *Double Entry*.)

Fukuzawa, Y. (1875) *An Outline of a Theory of Civilization*, trans. D.A. Dilworth and G. Cameron Hurst, Tokyo: Sophia University, 1970. (Fukuzawa's opus discussing the evolution of Japanese history as compared with that of the West.)

* Fukuzawa, Y. (1877; 1880) *Minkan keizai roku* (Political Economy for Citizens), Tokyo: Keio gijuku Press. (Discusses household and moral economy in part 1 and social economy in part 2.)

* Fukuzawa, Y. (1893) *Jitsugyo ron* (Discourse on Industry and Business), Tokyo: Jiji shimpo sha. (Proposes first proceeding into free trade, and emphasizes more active human investment in business in order to achieve 'business revolution'.)

Fukuzawa, Y. (1899) *The Autobiography of Fukuzawa Yukichi*, trans. E. Kiyooka, Lanham, MA., New York and London: Madison Books, 1992. (A candid narrative of his life, originally published by *Jiji shimpo sha*.)

* Fukuzawa, Y. (1988) *Fukuzawa Yukichi on Japanese Women, Selected Works*, trans. and ed. E. Kiyooka, Tokyo: University of Tokyo Press. (Includes Fukuzawa's *On Japanese Women* (1885), *The New Greater Learnings for Women* (1899) and other writings on women's equality.)

* Kinmonth, E.H. (1978) 'Fukuzawa reconsidered: *Gakumon no susume* and its audience', *Journal of Asian Studies*, 37 (4): 677–96. (Finds no more novelty in *Gakumon no susume* other than an 'encouragement' of learning by jobless shizoku aiming at higher posts and richer lives.)

Nishikawa, S. (1988) 'The historical legacy in "modern" Japan: competition, paper currency, and benevolence', *Japan Foundation Newsletter*, 16 (1): 1–8. (Discusses Fukuzawa's pragmatic approach to economic problems and selective use of the historical legacies in political economy.)

Sugiyama, C. (1988) 'Fukuzawa Yukichi', in C. Sugiyama and H. Mizuta (eds), *Enlightenment and Beyond: Political Economy Comes to Japan*, Tokyo: University of Tokyo Press. (Appreciates Fukuzawa's leading role in introducing political economy.)

Trescott, P.B. (1989) 'Scottish political economy comes to the Far East: the Burton Chambers *Political Economy* and the introduction of Western ideas in Japan and China', *History of Political Economy*, 21 (3): 481–502. (Discusses both the translation and acceptance of Burton's textbook in Japan and China.)

* Wayland, F. (1841) *The Elements of Political Economy*, 4th edn, Boston, MA: Gould and Lincoln. (Fukuzawa purchased copies on his visit to New York and Washington; used as a textbook in Keio during the 1870s.)

See also: IBUKA, M.; IWASAKI, Y.; MATSUSHITA, K.; OHNO, T.; TOYODA FAMILY; UENO, Y.

Related topics in the IEBM: ACCOUNTING IN JAPAN; BUSINESS HISTORY, JAPANESE; MANAGEMENT EDUCATION IN JAPAN; MANAGEMENT IN JAPAN ; MANAGEMENT IN PACIFIC ASIA

Galbraith, John Kenneth (1908–)

Personal background

- born 15 October 1908 at Iona Station, Ontario, Canada, the son of a farmer and liberal politician
- educated in all branches of agriculture at Ontario Agricultural College, now the University of Guelph, 1926–31, graduating with distinction
- PhD student at Berkeley, University of California 1931–4
- instructor at Harvard University 1934–7
- acquires US citizenship and marries Kitty (Catherine Merriam) Atwater, 1937
- Social Science Council fellowship at University of Cambridge, 1937
- assistant professor at Princeton University, 1939–40
- head of economic research of the American Farm Bureau Federation, Chicago, 1940
- US price controller at the Office of Price Administration and Civilian Supply, 1941–3
- journalist then an editor of *Fortune* magazine, 1943 and 1946–8
- director of the US Strategic Bombing Survey 1943–6
- professor of economics, Harvard University 1948–75; Paul M. Warburg Professor of Economics 1960–75
- US Ambassador to India, 1961–3
- president of the American Economic Association, 1972

Major works

A Theory of Price Control (1952)
American Capitalism: The Concept of Countervailing Power (1952)
The Affluent Society (1958)
Economic Development (1964)
The New Industrial State (1967)
Economics and the Public Purpose (1973)
A Life in Our Times (1981)
A History of Economics: The Past as the Present (1987)

Summary

John Kenneth Galbraith, who was born in 1908, is the most famous of twentieth-century American institutionalist economists. One of the first American converts to Keynesianism, he has consistently argued that governments should control the level of aggregate demand, using a mixture of fiscal policy and price and income controls. Much of his work, like that of an earlier institutionalist Thorstein Veblen (1857–1929), has attempted to explore the implications of the dominant role of corporations in modern economies. Surrounding the core of his work has been a study of economic development and the history of economic thought. The fluency of his pen has given him the status of a modern economic guru.

1 Introduction

Galbraith grew up in Ontario where his father, of Scottish descent, farmed, managed an insurance company and participated in the local Liberal Party. He was educated at the local Ontario Agricultural College (later Guelph University), studying a wide range of theoretical and practical agricultural subjects. It was there he discovered his major talent – writing – by contributing columns on agriculture to the local press.

His long career in economics took off when he became a PhD student at Berkeley, California, in 1931. He broadened his interests by researching into the structure of California's county government and by taking graduate courses in economics. In his first academic position, as an assistant to the professor of agricultural economics at Harvard in 1934, he again reached out into a wider study of economics, espousing the new macroeconomics of John Maynard Keynes (see KEYNES, J.M.). In 1937, he took up a Social Sciences Research Council fellowship at Cambridge where, unable to work with Keynes who was then recuperating from a heart attack, he gained from association with other leading macroeconomists there, including Michel Kalecki (1899–1970), Richard Kahn (1905–89) and Piero Sraffa (1898–1983). Much of his time in Cambridge, Galbraith spent in private reading: 'I penetrated the thicket of the technical controversy surrounding Keynes's work and became one of the acknowledged oracles' (Galbraith 1981: 77). After Cambridge the Galbraiths travelled extensively in Europe and in 1939, he took up an assistant professorship at Princeton, soon to be interrupted by the demands of war work.

With the experience of price control work for the US National Defense Advisory Council in 1940, he was appointed to the powerful position of controller of prices in the USA at the Office of Production Management, occupying that key position from 1940 to 1943. His work on price control made possible his most theoretical work, *A Theory of Price Control* (1952) and led him thereafter to recommend prices and incomes policies. For the rest of the Second World War, he put to good use his growing literary talents, first as a journalist, then editor at *Fortune* magazine. His period in journalism was interrupted by his work in 1945 for the US Strategic Bombing Survey in Germany and Japan. He interviewed leading Germans, including Albert Speer, and concluded that bombing had been less successful than claimed in bringing the war to a conclusion.

He departed from *Fortune* in 1948. Back at Harvard, he resumed his academic career as an economics lecturer and director of agricultural and marketing research; after a year, he became a professor in economics, in 1960 he moved to the endowed Paul M. Warburg chair and retired in 1975. He has been a generous benefactor to Harvard giving the royalties of the second edition of *The Affluent Society* for the establishment of the Galbraith Teaching Prize and to the Fogg Art Museum a collection of miniatures. Although Harvard remained his base for decades, he developed his twin interests of Democratic Party politics and commentating on modern economies.

Before the Second World War he had campaigned for Franklin Roosevelt and had become a friend of the Kennedys through being tutor to Jack Kennedy at Harvard. Galbraith's talents as a speech writer were used in presidential campaigns by both Adlai Stevenson in 1952 and by John Kennedy in 1960. In 1961, Galbraith was appointed US Ambassador to India. This led to a new interest, economic development, which he explained to his Indian hosts and wrote about in many subsequent works. Opposed to growing involvement in the Vietnam War, Galbraith returned to Harvard in 1963. Subsequently he continued to work in presidential elections for the Democrats, even speaking for Clinton in 1992.

Galbraith's dissatisfaction with the working of market economies and his devotion to Keynesianism formed the basis for a series of highly successful books. At the core of his distinctive contribution to economics was his trilogy *The Affluent Society* (1958), *The New Industrial State* (1967) and *Economics and the Public Purpose* (1973). But his influence has not been limited to his writings. For decades he has been a popular lecturer throughout the world and the confidant of many leading politicians.

2 Main contribution to economics

Although he began his career as an agricultural economist, he quickly appreciated the significance of Keynesian macroeconomics. As early as 1939 in a discussion of farm income he emphasized the importance of the level of national income. His preference for fiscal policy over monetary policy and the efficacy of public works as a means of achieving full employment was stated as early as 1940.

His experience as a price controller in 1941–3 led to his reflections on the theoretical basis for price controls. In 1952 in *A Theory of Price Control*, Galbraith argued that price controls are needed to supplement the incentives and compulsions of an unplanned, disequilibrium economy. Not only is inflation checked, but unused resources are employed if direct price controls are used. However, Galbraith asserted that these controls must be used in conjunction with other macroeconomic policies.

In *American Capitalism* (1952) his controversial analysis of the modern corporation began. He claimed that oligopoly had replaced the competitive environment true of the nineteenth century. With the growth of industrial concentration, the only check to corporations was the 'countervailing power' of trade unions and major purchasers of intermediate products, for example, car firms buying steel. This countervailing power, Galbraith claims, has given the economy the capacity for autonomous self-regulation. In such a decentralized economy the State is left with the roles of influencing the level of demand and restraining inflation through price controls. In *The New Industrial State* (1967) he claimed that the large corporations of the USA constitute the 'new industrial system'. The corporations are run by their managers, not their owners, who have created a 'technostructure' based on modern technology and planning. Through vertical integration, corporations are able to plan: this planning supersedes the market and eliminates uncertainty. Instead of seeking to maximize profits, modern corporations are concerned primarily with their survival and expansion. Consumer sovereignty is replaced by market control by corporations. To make the planning of corporations possible, the State has to control the level of aggregate demand through maintaining an adequate level of government expenditure. Galbraith modified this corporate view of the US economy in *Economics and the Public Purpose* (1973) by integrating small businesses into his analysis. Recognizing that smaller firms have little control over prices, Galbraith recommended exemption of the small business

sector from anti-trust laws so that they could combine to stabilize prices and output.

His most famous work, *The Affluent Society* (1958), which long remained a best seller, argued that Keynesianism had wrongly developed into the philosophy of attempting to cure all social ills by the expansion of production. To maintain growth in production, firms have to create wants through advertising and marketing techniques; to maintain purchasing power, consumer debt has to rise, unchecked by monetary and fiscal policies. The promotion of private production is at the expense of the public sector, creating the social imbalance of private affluence and public squalor. In a vivid passage Galbraith describes the fate of a family taking their new automobile out for a picnic:

> They picnic on exquisitely packaged food from a portable icebox by a polluted stream and go on to spend the night at a park which is a menace to public health and morals. Just before dozing off on an air-mattress, beneath a nylon tent, amid the stench of decaying refuse, they may reflect vaguely on the curious unevenness of their blessings.
>
> (Galbraith 1958: 197)

The imbalance could be removed only by a change in the taxation system which keeps the growth in public revenues in line with the expansion of private incomes.

In *The Culture of Contentment* (1992), Galbraith returns to a broad social theme. He argues that the majority of the population consists of the economically and socially fortunate and it is under threat from the short-termism of economic policy, unpopular military action and the possibility of a revolt by the urban underclass. Only a return to strong Keynesian fiscal policy to keep recessions at bay and to improve cities can solve current problems.

Galbraith's experiences in India in the early 1960s gave him an interest in economic development. In *Economic Development in Perspective* (1962) and in its revised version *Economic Development* (1964) he argued for the formation of national plans which are appropriate to a particular stage of economic development with a balanced increase in the capital stock and technical development. A good plan has a strategy which combines the visible (capital plant), the invisible (sound management methods) and a theory of consumption (which determines the appropriate range of consumer goods to be available).

From the time of his postgraduate studies, Galbraith has maintained an interest in the history of economic thought, attempting to make sense of the Marshallian economics in which he was trained and of the Keynesian revolution which he lived through (see MARSHALL, A.). In his late work, *A History of Economics: The Past as the Present* (1987) Galbraith interweaves economic history and economic thought to demonstrate: 'Economic ideas, as Keynes averred, do guide policy. But the ideas are also the offspring of policy and of the interests which it serves' (Galbraith 1987: 299). To some extent in these words Galbraith is summarizing much of his own work.

3 Conclusions

The frequent generalizations and absence of modern analysis of data have inevitably exposed Galbraith to considerable criticism from both economists and business leaders. The air of authority which permeates Galbraith's work soon disperses when more detailed empirical works are considered alongside. The most authoritative critique of Galbraith is Friedman's (1977). He aims blow after blow at the central ideas of the Galbraithian system. *The Affluent Society* is attacked for denigrating the tastes of ordinary people and ignoring the huge expansion of government expenditure. The propositions of *American Capitalism* are ruthlessly dissected: big business and unions are often allies rather than opponents generating countervailing power, as Galbraith claims; concentrations of power are in fact often unstable, as has happened with cartels. The empirical finding that the profits of large corporations are often more variable than the average for all quoted corporations is stated to refute much of *The New Industrial State*. The concept of 'countervailing power' has also been mercilessly dissected by other authors so that Galbraith has

been forced to bow to his critics. Sharpe (1973), for example, argued that countervailing power is a feeble substitute for the market as it does not allocate property, regulate prices optimally, eliminate poverty or provide amenities and public services.

Allen (1967) uses his knowledge as an industrial economist to refute Galbraith's generalizations about the working of the US economy. In particular, the ideas that large firms are more innovative than small and medium-sized firms, that large companies are immune from external pressures on their profits and that consumers are passive are contradicted. Galbraith's view that corporate planning succeeds in prescribing the future volume of production, demand and prices of particular goods is without evidence.

Galbraith scores highly in the Social Science Citation Index but is not widely taught in graduate schools, perhaps because he has been too multidisciplinary in his approach to economics and at odds with the formal economic model building dominating modern economic theorizing. But despite being unanalytical and often careless in his judgements, he has within his great readership some academic followers, especially among institutionalist, radical and post-Keynesian economists – and even a hostile mainstream critic, Friedman, praises Galbraith for being the only person to write a theory of price control. Arthur M. Schlesinger, Jr, the US historian, sums up Galbraith as 'the great economist, social philosopher, politician, diplomat, satirist, novelist, wit, bon vivant, and generous-hearted friend at work and at play'.

DONALD RUTHERFORD
UNIVERSITY OF EDINBURGH

Further reading

(References cited in the text marked *)

* Allen, G.C. (1967) *Economic Fact and Fantasy*, occasional paper 14, London: Institute of Economic Affairs. (A detailed refutation of the assumptions Galbraith makes about business behaviour.)

Breit, W. (1984) 'Galbraith and Friedman: two versions of economic reality', *Journal of Post-Keynesian Economics* 7: 18–29. (The artistry of

Galbraith is contrasted with Friedman's monetarist methodology.)

Colander, D. (1984) 'Galbraith and the theory of price control', *Journal of Post-Keynesian Economics* 7: 30–42. (Galbraith's theory is too classical and ignores the permanence of excess supply.)

* Friedman, M. (1977) *From Galbraith to Economic Freedom*, occasional paper 49, London: Institute of Economic Affairs. (Critical of the weak empiricism of Galbraith's works but appreciative of his price control analysis.)

* Galbraith, J.K. (1952) *A Theory of Price Control*, Cambridge, MA: Harvard University Press. (Argued that price controls are needed to supplement the incentives and compulsions of an unplanned, disequilibrium economy.)

* Galbraith, J.K. (1952) *American Capitalism: The Concept of Countervailing Power*, Boston, MA: Houghton Mifflin. (Controversial analysis of the modern corporation. Claimed that oligopoly had replaced the competitive environment true of the nineteenth century.)

* Galbraith, J.K. (1958) *The Affluent Society*, Boston, MA: Houghton Mifflin. (Argued that Keynesianism had wrongly developed into the philosophy of attempting to cure all social ills by the expansion of production.)

* Galbraith, J.K. (1962) *Economic Development in Perspective*, Cambridge, MA: Harvard University Press. (Argued for the formation of national plans which are appropriate to a particular stage of economic development with a balanced increase in the capital stock and technical development.

* Galbraith, J.K. (1964) *Economic Development*, Cambridge, MA: Harvard University Press. (Revision of *Economic Development in Perspective*.)

* Galbraith, J.K. (1967) *The New Industrial State*, Boston, MA: Houghton Mifflin. (Claimed that the large corporations of the USA constitute the 'new industrial system'.)

* Galbraith, J.K. (1973) *Economics and the Public Purpose*, Boston, MA: Houghton Mifflin. (Recommended the exemption of the small business sector from anti-trust laws so that they could combine to stabilize prices and output.)

* Galbraith, J.K. (1981) *A Life in Our Times*, Boston, MA: Houghton Mifflin.

* Galbraith, J.K. (1987) *A History of Economics: The Past as the Present*, London: Hamish Hamilton. (Uses economic history and economic thought to demonstrate how economic ideas guide policy.)

* Galbraith, J.K. (1992) *The Culture of Contentment*, Boston, MA: Houghton Mifflin. (Describes the modern phenomenon of the contented wealthy: a large class of affluent people who have no short-term interest in using their resources to help the poorer classes.)

Galbraith, J.K. (1994) *The World Economy Since The Wars: A Personal View*, Boston, MA: Houghton Mifflin. (Traces the economic history of the twentieth century.)

Hession, C.H. (1972) *John Kenneth Galbraith and His Critics*, New York: W.W. Norton & Co. Inc. (A review of the principal criticisms of Galbraithian notions of countervailing power and competition.)

Lamson, P. (1991) *Speaking of Galbraith: A Personal Portrait*, New York: Ticknor & Fields. (A sympathetic account of his life, main books and their reception.)

McFadzean, Sir F. (1977) *The Economics of John Kenneth Galbraith: A Study in Fantasy*, London: Centre for Policy Studies. (An attack on the methodology of his analysis of the corporation.)

Reisman, D. (1980) *Galbraith and Market Capitalism*, London: Macmillan. (This demonstrates that Galbraith's contribution to economics is modest, apart from work on price control.)

Samuels, W.J. (1984) 'Galbraith on economics as a system of professional belief', *Journal of Post-Keynesian Economic* 7: 61–76. (Galbraithian economics is based on beliefs not empirical truths, as a shield for power.)

* Sharpe, M.E. (1973) *John Kenneth Galbraith and the Lower Economics*, London: Macmillan. (This emphasizes that Galbraith is influential as a social critic but erroneous in much of his economics.)

See also: KEYNES, J.M.; MARSHALL, A.; VEBLEN, T. B.

Related topics in the IEBM: BIG BUSINESS AND CORPORATE CONTROL; BUSINESS AND SOCIETY; CORPORATE GOVERNANCE; ECONOMICS OF DEVELOPING COUNTRIES; EMPLOYMENT AND UNEMPLOYMENT, ECONOMICS OF; GOVERNMENT, INDUSTRY AND THE PUBLIC SECTOR; INFLATION; INSTITUTIONAL ECONOMICS; SRAFFA, P.

Gilbreth, Frank Bunker (1868–1924) and Gilbreth, Lillian Evelyn Moller (1878–1972)

Gilbreth, Frank Bunker

Personal background

- born 7 July 1868 in Fairfield, Maine, USA
- family background of New England settlers, with strong Puritan and Pilgrim traditions
- on leaving school worked as a bricklayer's apprentice, learning the building industry trade, and set about devising means of saving wasteful labour; became a highly successful building contractor
- married Lillian Evelyn Moller in 1904
- from 1907 to 1913, collaborated with Taylor and Gantt in the development of 'scientific management', his contribution being in 'motion study'
- in 1912, opened his own consultancy business to concentrate on 'management engineering'
- died suddenly on 14 June 1924

Major works

Bricklaying System (1909)
Motion Study (1911)
Primer of Scientific Management (1912)
Fatigue Study (with Lillian M. Gilbreth) (1916)
Applied Motion Study (with Lillian M. Gilbreth) (1917)
Motion Study for the Handicapped (with Lillian M. Gilbreth) (1920)

Gilbreth, Lillian Evelyn Moller

Personal background

- born 24 May 1878 in Oakland, California, USA into a prosperous family of German extraction
- studied at the University of California
- married Frank Bunker Gilbreth in 1904
- completed doctoral thesis on *The Psychology of Management* in 1911
- joined her husband's management consultancy business in 1912, becoming a fully-fledged partner in the quest for 'the one best way to do work'
- on Frank Gilbreth's sudden death in June 1924, went in his place to the First International Management Congress in Prague
- continued running the business, extended her writing and lecturing and did volunteer work for various organizations
- received more than twenty honorary degrees and special commendations from universities and professional societies
- died 2 February 1972 at the age of ninety-three

Major works

The Psychology of Management (1914)
The Quest of the One Best Way: A Sketch of the Life of Frank Bunker Gilbreth (1924)
The Home-Maker and Her Job (1927)
Normal Lives for the Disabled (with Edna Yost) (1944)
Management in the Home: Happier Living through Saving Time and Energy (1954)

Summary

Frank Bunker Gilbreth (1868–1924) pioneered the field of 'motion study' and is recognized as one of the founders of 'scientific management'. His constant quest, and on marriage in partnership with his wife, was to eliminate waste by finding the 'one best way to do work'. Lillian M. Gilbreth (1878–1972), a teacher and industrial psychologist, was among the first to appreciate the need of good human relations in the workplace. She had a profound influence on her husband in alerting him to the dynamic aspects of management.

Together, they formed a most successful partnership, each complementing the other's abilities and experience. In their quest for the 'one best way', they studied task, worker, tools and working environment in 'scientific detail' to adjust and integrate them for highest productivity. The process charts and other techniques they devised remain essentially unchanged in modern systems analysis. They were also interested in the human aspect of industry and emphasized the need for training and worker involvement.

Lillian Gilbreth, after her husband's death in 1924, continued to run the business, lectured on management and on home economics at different universities and worked on applying motion study principles to help the handicapped. She also made time for voluntary work with local and national organizations. She has been called the 'First Lady of Management'.

I Early lives

Frank Bunker Gilbreth

Gilbreth was born on 7 July 1868 in Fairfield, Maine, into a family deeply rooted in the strong Puritan and Pilgrim traditions of the New England settler. This background greatly influenced his character and outlook. His father died when he was 3 years old, but his mother spared no effort to give the children a good education and the best training available. Frank Gilbreth was educated at Phillips Academy, Andover, where his feeling for mechanics first appeared; and at the Rice Grammar School, Boston, where this developed into an interest in mathematics and mechanical drawing. He succeeded in qualifying for entry to the Massachusetts Institute

of Technology but decided instead to start work immediately after school.

At 17, he became a bricklayer's apprentice. His progress was rapid. He went, with great success, through trade after trade of the construction company in which he worked and took evening classes to complement his knowledge of the building industry. By the age of 27, he was chief superintendent of his employing company.

From the beginning, Gilbreth was struck by the waste involved in the methods and practices existing in the construction industry and he set out to eliminate or at least reduce it. He developed 'the best ways' of laying bricks and handling materials; of rigging scaffolding and training apprentices: generally improving methods, while lowering costs and paying higher wages.

In April 1895, Gilbreth decided to open his own contracting business in Boston, Massachusetts. Working on the basic principles of good workmanship and sound materials, he was successful from the start. His business quickly grew. Always a keen observer, he learnt a great deal from his client firms. His business journeys abroad kept him abreast of what was new outside the USA. He gradually moved from being the contractor carrying out the full job with his own plant and men to the construction consultant, advising the client on all aspects of the work required. As the business grew, he was able to run not only a busy New York office with branches throughout the USA but also a London office with contracts for the Admiralty and the War Office.

In October 1904, he married Lillian Evelyn Moller. Together, they became 'partners for life' in marriage and in a most successful working partnership, in which each was able to complement the other's knowledge, abilities and experience.

Lillian Evelyn Moller

Lillian Moller was born in Oakland, California on 24 May 1878, to one of the leading families in the town. After being tutored at home and attending public elementary and high schools in Oakland, she studied at the University of California, where she received a

B.Litt. degree in 1900 and, later, a Master's degree in English, on a thesis on Ben Jonson's *Bartholomew Fair*. Studying for a doctorate, she took leave in 1903 to tour Europe. In Boston, prior to her departure, she met Frank Gilbreth, a cousin of her chaperone. They married in 1904.

2 Frank and Lillian Gilbreth: the partnership

From the outset, they were determined to work together but with a growing family (there were to be twelve children, six boys and six girls), Lillian's contribution to the joint enterprise was somewhat restricted in the early days. However, she worked at home in editing her husband's many publications and on her own researches where, the better to complement his field of knowledge, she took up the subject of industrial psychology.

Gilbreth became closely associated with Frederick W. Taylor (see TAYLOR, F.W.) in 1907. They admired each other's work and became firm allies in the development of scientific management. In *Primer of Scientific Management* (1912), Gilbreth answered some of the questions in the hundreds of letters Taylor was receiving from all over the world. The answers ranged from definition of terms to the laws of scientific management and their application; from the effect on the worker of scientific management to its relation to other lines of activity; and always extolled the virtues of 'scientific management' as a 'square deal' for both worker and employer.

Taylor, on his side, admired Gilbreth's work, constantly quoting his work on bricklaying as an outstanding example of the principles he was seeking to popularize. Together, they came to England in 1910 on a formal visit to the Institution of Mechanical Engineers to put before them the concepts developed through 'scientific management'. However, the happy relationship ended, somewhat abruptly, in 1913. By then, the Gilbreths were established as management consultants. This development brought them into direct competition not with Taylor himself but with the circle of men round Taylor whom he assigned to

firms who asked for his help. Taylor recommended one of these friends to a firm while Gilbreth was still there acting as a consultant. The Gilbreths were incensed. Relations between the two men cooled considerably and Lillian Gilbreth was to hold thereafter that Taylor 'was not a nice person'.

In his 'management engineering' consultancy, Gilbreth extended the application of motion study to the general field of manufacturing and turned his focus to the study of fatigue. He isolated forty-two variables causing fatigue, fifteen relating to the worker himself, fourteen to the surroundings and thirteen to the motions required for the job itself. He developed two techniques to study a movement in the required precision. He subdivided it into basic motions – such as search, select, lift, load, position and so on – which he called 'therbligs' (a variation on the spelling of Gilbreth) and he placed a large-faced clock calibrated in fractions of minutes in the field of vision of the camera as it filmed the worker. These two innovations enabled him to catch and time the smallest motion and was the beginning of his micromotion study.

Gilbreth also developed the 'cyclegraphic' technique by attaching small electric light bulbs to the hands or other moving parts of the worker. As the worker moved, the paths of lights appeared, giving the direction of all the movements made. The cyclegraph grew into the 'chronocyclegraph', where a flashing bulb showed acceleration and deceleration of movements by appearing on the screen as a series of dots and dashes.

As a major in the US Army in 1917, Gilbreth successfully applied his motion study methods to the training of recruits. He also applied them in work for the rehabilitation of the injured. In the article he wrote in December 1915 for the *Journal of the American Society of Mechanical Engineers* entitled 'Motion study for the crippled soldier', he explained how motion study could help the handicapped.

The Gilbreths knew that he had developed a heart condition during the War but this did not make him reduce his activities in any way. He continued his very busy professional life. He went from factory to factory, installing time-saving systems; he wrote; he spoke at conferences and seminars; he worked in his laboratories at his home. The strain would have been tremendous. The end came suddenly. He died on 14 June 1924, just before he was due to sail for Europe.

Lillian Gilbreth was his active partner in all this work and together they published *Fatigue Study* (1916), *Applied Motion Study* (1917) and *Motion Study for the Handicapped* (1920). On marriage, she had changed the focus of her studies to psychology, the better to complement his work. In 1911, she produced a doctoral thesis on *The Psychology of Management* which was serialized in *The Industrial Engineering Magazine* in 1912–13 and published in book form in 1914. The publishers, reflecting the times, insisted that she be listed by her initials only, to avoid indicating the author was a woman.

She lectured at the private laboratory in their home and at schools of engineering and business. She became a full working partner in the consultancy business. It was her special contribution to insist on the importance of good human relations and training in the workplace and she did much to humanize her husband's views and widen the outlook of their clients.

In her letter of 10 April 1925 to the Editor of *The National Cyclopedia of American Biography*, Lillian Gilbreth wrote about their work on motion study:

When we started this work, we had at our command Mr Gilbreth's technical training, and his many years' experience through every stage from apprentice to contracting engineer in erecting buildings, dams and so forth, my own theoretical training in education and psychology and some practical experience in teaching. It is really impossible and it seems to me unnecessary, and I am sure that you will agree with this, to try to separate our work. If it is worth anything, it is as a demonstration of what can be done by a cooperation founded on mutual interests and desires, and a training on the one hand for leadership, in the case of Mr Gilbreth, and on the other hand for 'tending' in my own case.
(Urwick and Brech 1945: 126–7)

3 Lillian Gilbreth

The partnership ended dramatically. In June 1924, three days before he was due to leave for conferences in England and Czechoslovakia, Frank Gilbreth died in a telephone booth as he was calling Lillian to tell her of 'an idea I had about saving motions on packing those soapflakes for Lever Brothers' (Gilbreth and Carey 1949: 137).

On his death, she was left with eleven children (one had died) ranging in age from 2 to 19. Showing her indomitable spirit, she called a family conference and told them:

I am going on that boat tomorrow, the one your father planned to take. He had the tickets. I am going to give those speeches for him in London and Prague, by jingo. I think that's the way your father wants it.
(Gilbreth and Carey 1949: 236)

She was not long in redirecting her energies. Purdue University, where her husband had been a visiting lecturer, asked her on his death to take his place. This she did until 1935 when she was appointed professor of management, a chair she continued to occupy until 1948.

This pursuit was not her only activity. She started to use motion study to analyse work in the home, studies which she continued, on and off, for some twenty years. The results appeared from time to time in popular periodicals like *Good Housekeeping* and *Better Homes and Gardens* and in two major publications, *The Home-Maker and Her Job* (1927) and *Management in the Home* (1954). Apart from her work at Purdue University, she also acted as consultant to university departments on home economics, and here she exercised considerable influence on the development of home management courses throughout the country.

As an extension of her husband's work for disabled soldiers, Lillian Gilbreth used the techniques of motion study analysis to design special equipment and routines to make housework possible for handicapped people. She reported this in *Normal Lives for the Disabled* (1944), co-authored by Edna Yost.

Lillian Gilbreth was extraordinarily energetic and public-spirited and responded wholeheartedly to all the calls that were made upon her. She became a member of the President's Emergency Committee for Unemployment Relief in 1930, an educational adviser during the Second World War and joined the Civil Defense Advisory Commission in 1951. She also found time to do volunteer work for the Girl Scouts of America, for various organizations helping the handicapped and for churches and libraries in her community.

Lillian Gilbreth continued her research work beyond the age of 70 and was in fact still lecturing and writing in her eighties. Honours were showered on her. In all, she received more than twenty honorary degrees and special commendations from professional societies. She has been called 'The First Lady of Management'. She died in 1972.

4 Contributions

Gilbreth's early work in the construction industry was original. He pioneered what became known as the 'Science of Motion Study'. He simplified the work of bricklaying so well that the eighteen motions thought necessary to place a brick were reduced to at most five, thus increasing the daily output per man, after some training and without additional strain, from 1,000 to 2,700 bricks. Through detailed analysis and study of the movements involved in the performance of operations and of the environment in which they were taking place, he laid the foundations of effective production management.

In due course, the Gilbreths also devised process charts to map out the flow of work as it moved through the shop. This technique and the various symbols used to show the various stages of the task remain essentially the same in modern systems analysis. The Gilbreths were as interested in understanding the psychological bases of organized human activity as they were in developing the physical 'one best way' to do a task.

To begin with, they enthusiastically promoted scientific management. In the *Primer of Scientific Management* (1912) Frank Gilbreth explains it in detail and supports it unreservedly. In *The Psychology of Management* (1914) Lillian Gilbreth distinguishes three types of management: traditional, transitory and scientific, this last type being 'a science, i.e., which operates according to known, formulated, and applied laws' (Gilbreth 1914: 8), this last being the one to aim for.

However, they had a more *inclusive* view of management than Taylor. Over time, they began to disagree with some of his methods, as for example that of secretly recording the workers' activities. They wanted to show the workers how to improve productivity not by working *faster*, but by working *better*; to show them not only *how* to change or improve their methods of work but also *why*.

Their interest in scientific management was but a part of their overall social vision to help individuals lead a fuller life. In *Cheaper by the Dozen* (the best-selling non-fiction book in 1949, later made into a film) his children, reminiscing about their home life, recorded that:

> Someone once asked Dad: 'But what do you want to save time *for*? What are you going to do with it?' 'For work, if you love that best,' said Dad. 'For education, for beauty, for art, for pleasure.' He looked over the top of his pince-nez. 'For mumblety-peg, if that's where your heart lies.'
>
> (Gilbreth and Carey 1949: 237)

5 Critique

'Motion study' has not been used in production management as much as the Gilbreths would have wished. Misunderstood, it has been suspected of being a means of controlling workers in their every movement. The battle lines between capital and labour were drawn in the decades (the 1920s to the 1940s) following the introduction of 'scientific management' and attempts to measure and standardize the workers' productivity brought trade union accusations of 'unfair labor practices' and of dehumanizing the workers. For this, perhaps the Gilbreths were partly responsible. By defining their search for 'the one best way', their work could be interpreted as seeking to robotize workers by limiting them to a strict sequence of steps in carrying out their tasks.

It cannot be denied, also, that specialization and shorter job cycles de-skill the worker. To some extent, Gilbreth himself in part recognized this by saying that, in any case, it should not cause the worker any unhappiness. More liberal than Taylor in his views, Gilbreth nevertheless, in his writings, treats the worker in the main as a fairly *static* factor.

Lillian Gilbreth, writing some fifty years later, could see the limitations of the early work of the pioneers:

> The people who started the scientific management movement did not have the advantage of an arts and letters background or training in philosophy, and they did not read or speak other languages fluently or travel a great deal. They were mechanical engineers, trained in the fashion of their time. They went into industry and devoted their lives to making the best use of their own and other people's time, energy and money. They did not realize that management was something that had come down through the ages and was being practiced in some form or other in every country in the world.

She was also able to recognize that her husband's work was not as unique as they had thought:

> As it turned out, many things which were done quite independently in the United States proved to have been done previously in other countries. For example, my husband found, after he spent a long time developing the cyclegraph method, that Marey had done it in France.
>
> (Gilbreth 1963: 119)

Lillian Gilbreth herself, by inclination and training, understood the dynamic of relationships and the contribution that the workers could make, if involved and committed to the common task. After her husband's death, and over time, she worked hard to promote the use of 'motion study'; and she also worked hard to bring about effective cooperation in the workplace.

PAULINE GRAHAM
UNIVERSITY OF BRADFORD

Further reading

(References cited in the text marked *)

Gilbreth, F.B. (1908) *Concrete System*, New York: Engineering News Publishing. (Detailed advice to concrete contractors on how best to direct the workers.)

Gilbreth, F.B. (1908) *Field System*, New York: Myron C. Clark Publishing. (An accounting system, without a set of books, for construction contractors to see weekly the total cost of the job.)

Gilbreth, F.B. (1909) *Bricklaying System*, New York: Myron C. Clark Publishing. (Technical book showing the best way of laying bricks through motion study.)

Gilbreth, F.B. (1911) *Motion Study*, New York: D. van Nostrand. (Shows how the efficiency of the worker can be improved using illustrations of motion study in bricklaying.)

* Gilbreth, F.B. (1912) *Primer of Scientific Management*, New York: D. van Nostrand. (Explains scientific management by means of questions and answers, with a foreword by Louis D. Brandeis.)

* Gilbreth, F.B. (1915) 'Motion study for the crippled soldier', *Journal of the American Society of Mechanical Engineers* 37: 669. (Shows how motion study can help the crippled soldier.)

* Gilbreth, F.B. and Gilbreth, L.M. (1916) *Fatigue Study*, New York: Sturgis & Walton. (A meticulous analysis of the variables that cause fatigue and the means to be used to avoid or reduce it.)

* Gilbreth, F.B. and Gilbreth, L.M. (1917) *Applied Motion Study*, New York: Sturgis & Walton. (Covers applications of motion study analysis.)

* Gilbreth, F.B. and Gilbreth, L.M. (1920) *Motion Study for the Handicapped*, New York: Macmillan. (Explains how motion study can be used to help the handicapped.)

Gilbreth, F.B., Jr (1970) *Time out for Happiness*, New York: Thomas Y. Crowell. (The third sequel of the Gilbreth story, this time written by F.B. Gilbreth on his own.)

* Gilbreth, F.B., Jr and Carey, E.G. (1949) *Cheaper by the Dozen*, New York: Thomas Y. Crowell. (Written by two of the Gilbreth children, this is an affectionate memoir of life in the Gilbreth household.)

Gilbreth, F.B., Jr and Carey, E.G. (1950) *Belles on Their Toes*, New York: Thomas Y. Crowell. (The sequel to *Cheaper by the Dozen*.)

* Gilbreth, L.M. (1914) *The Psychology of Management*, New York: Sturgis & Walton. (Analyses the different typologies of management.)

Gilbreth, L.M. (1924) *The Quest of the One Best Way: A Sketch of the Life of Frank Bunker Gilbreth*, Chicago, IL: Society of Industrial Engineers. (A reprint of Lillian Gilbreth's biography of her husband, republished in 1973 by Hive Publishing, Easton, PA.)

* Gilbreth, L.M. (1927) *The Home-Maker and Her Job*, New York: D. Appleton. (Shows how motion study can be used in the home for the highest efficiency.)

* Gilbreth, L.M. (1954) *Management in the Home: Happier Living through Saving Time and Energy*, New York: Dodd, Mead. (Applies scientific management principles and techniques to home management.)

* Gilbreth, L.M. (1963) 'Work and management', *Advanced Management Journal* September: 119. (Gilbreth's later reflections on the topic.)

* Gilbreth, L.M. and Yost, E. (1944) *Normal Lives for the Disabled*, NY: Appleton & Co. (Shows how, using motion study analysis, special equipment can be designed to help the disabled lead normal lives.)

Spriegel, W.R. and Meyers, C.E. (eds) (1953) *The Writings of the Gilbreths*, Homewood, IL: Irwin. (Comprehensive coverage of the writings of the Gilbreths.)

* Urwick L. and Brech, E.F.L. (1945) *The Making of Scientific Management: Thirteen Pioneers*, London: Management Publications Trust. (An overview of the early European and US pioneers in management thinking.)

Yost, E. (1949) *Frank and Lillian Gilbreth: Partners for Life*, New Brunswick, NJ: Rutgers University Press. (An affectionate biography of the Gilbreths, by a close friend of Lillian Gilbreth.)

See also: BEDAUX, C.E.; FORD, H.; TAYLOR, F.W.

Related topics in the IEBM: HUMAN RELATIONS; INDUSTRIAL AND LABOUR RELATIONS; OCCUPATIONAL PSYCHOLOGY; ORGANIZATION BEHAVIOUR; ORGANIZATION BEHAVIOUR, HISTORY OF; SYSTEMS ANALYSIS AND DESIGN; TRADE UNIONS; WORK SYSTEMS

Gouldner, Alvin W. (1920–80)

1 Gouldner's contribution to industrial sociology
2 Gouldner's approach to critical theory

Personal background

- born in New York City, 29 July 1920
- studied sociology at the University of Columbia, New York, 1943–7
- taught sociology at the University of Buffalo, New York, 1947–52
- obtained a doctorate from Columbia, 1952
- taught at the University of Antioch, Ohio, 1952–4
- associate professor in the department of sociology, University of Illinois, 1954–9
- appointed Max Weber Research Professor in Social Theory at Washington University, St Louis, 1959
- spent a year at the Center for Advanced Studies in the Behavioural Sciences, Palo Alto, 1961–2
- served as president of the Society for the Study of Social Problems, 1962
- received the Russell Sage Foundation Research Award, 1965–6
- appointed professor of sociology at the University of Amsterdam, 1969
- while in Europe, founded and edited the journal *Theory and Society*
- died 15 December 1980 in Madrid, aged 60

Major works

Studies in Leadership (ed.) (1950)
Patterns of Industrial Bureaucracy (1954a)
Wildcat Strike (1954b)
Applied Sociology: Opportunities and Problems (edited with S.M. Miller) (1965)
Enter Plato: Classical Greece and the Origins of Social Theory (1965)
The Coming Crisis of Western Sociology (1971)

For Sociology. Renewal and Critique in Sociology Today (1975)
The Dialectic of Ideology and Technology (1976)
The Future of Intellectuals and the Rise of the New Class (1979)
The Two Marxisms: Contradictions and Anomalies in the Development of Theory (1980)
Against Fragmentation. The Origins of Marxism and the Sociology of Intellectuals (1985)

Summary

Gouldner's formative training in the discipline of sociology took place at the University of Columbia, New York, where he came into contact with a teaching staff of the highest calibre including Robert Lynd, Robert MacIver, Charles Page, Paul Lazersfeld and Robert Merton. With Merton he sustained a lifelong intellectual friendship. Before leaving Columbia he was to have research experience with members of the Frankfurt School in exile. He worked under the direction of Marie Jahoda, who was collaborating with Max Horkheimer and others on the Studies in Prejudice project, which was to develop the concept of 'the authoritarian personality'. He taught sociology for five years at the University of Buffalo and conducted fieldwork in the gypsum plant near by, work which formed the basis of his doctorate, which the examiners saw as a piece of original research and scholarship. It led to the publication of two books, *Patterns of Industrial Bureaucracy* and *Wildcat Strike*. Later, teaching at Illinois, he had special responsibility for the teaching of social theory thus, in effect, succeeding the great cultural theorist, Florian Znaniecki. *Theory and Society*, the journal he founded and edited while living in Europe, quickly and deservedly established an international reputation for the high quality of its contributions to social theory.

1 Gouldner's contribution to industrial sociology

Alvin Gouldner was an US sociologist in the radical tradition of Thorstein Veblen (see VEBLEN, T.B.), Robert Lynd and C. Wright Mills. His political radicalism expressed itself in membership of the Communist Party in the USA for a short time in the 1940s but he was scarcely cut out to be a Party man. By the end of his life he called himself an Marxist outlaw. His early contacts with members of the Frankfurt School were important. As late as 1976, in *The Dialectic of Ideology and Technology*, he was giving serious but not uncritical attention to the work of the School, especially their treatment of the mass media and the cultural apparatus in capitalist societies. Even so, his own intellectual orientation was shaped by significant non-Marxist sources. Mannheim's influence is plain and acknowledged and has to be negotiated in any discussion of the role of the intelligentsia. Weber is there and announced from the beginning of his work in industrial sociology (see WEBER, M.). Merton, although it was not always realized at the time, was there as guide, mentor and friendly critic and the lifelong correspondence that took place between them is both moving and revealing. Merton thought very highly of Gouldner's 1959 essay 'Reciprocity and autonomy in functional theory' (reproduced in *For Sociology* 1975). Although not persuaded by it, Gouldner also found the work of Talcott Parsons a challenge. Thus it was that a great part of *The Coming Crisis of Western Sociology* (1971) involved a critical exposition of Parsons' work since its functionalism represented the dominant sociological paradigm of the 1950s and 1960s in the USA.

2 Gouldner's approach to critical theory

Patterns of Industrial Bureaucracy, published in 1954, is widely recognized as a classic of industrial sociology. Gouldner used Weber's ideal type approach to the study of bureaucracy whilst showing originality in reformulating the typology in the light of his research experience (see WEBER, M.). Thus he distinguishes between punishment-centred, representative and 'mock' bureaucracy as he seeks to show how and why rules are sometimes obeyed and sometimes not. He shows how the succession from one plant manager to another, in the context of wider changes in the market, led to changes in the nature of rule making and enforcement from an indulgency to a stringency pattern. This allowed him to give central consideration to the ways in which the legitimacy of managerial behaviour in relation to employees came to be seriously questioned and of the ways in which this was reinforced by the nature of the local community. The changing expectations and conflicts to which this gave rise were further explored in *Wildcat Strike* (1954b), a subject which he sought to elucidate within a general theory of group tensions. This kind of theorizing he saw as a strategic bridge between 'pure' and 'applied' sociology. If the first was concerned with prediction and understanding the second was seen as a guide for action in time of trouble. There is, in *Patterns of Industrial Bureaucracy* a valuable appendix on fieldwork procedures which gives us a clue to the exercise of the sociological imagination in ways in which Wright Mills would most certainly have approved. It shows how theory and method can come together in research practice. There was a value concern written in to this work, namely, how far can we move to more representative forms of bureaucracy in modern industry, and thus to industrial democracy. In this Gouldner was resisting what he was to term 'metaphysical pathos' in Weber's treatment of bureaucracy and Michel's 'iron law of oligarchy' (see MICHELS, R.).

Gouldner returned to the relation between pure and applied sociology in the course of a very different study, *Enter Plato*, published in 1965. There he explored different kinds of knowledge – knowledge for its own sake contrasted with technical knowledge – and the significance of the dialectical method in approaching and critiquing truth claims. In particular, he examined the adequacy of Plato's approach to planned social change. Gouldner argued that sociologists today have to balance optimism and pessimism within themselves when approaching social problems. They should be aware of their own limitations while doing all they can to relieve human suffering, without glossing over the difficulties. Sociologists should, nevertheless, play with, formulate and entertain various solutions to social problems rather than simply describe and explain them:

> They need a constructive quality of the imagination which can sense what might be. If some of their proposals turn out to be extravagant, needless, wasteful, outrageous, or even utopian, no one needs to buy them: but let them be freely available on the market place of ideas – rather than be self-inhibited – where they can be compared with the shopworn social worlds that are presently up for sale.
>
> (Gouldner 1965: 295–6)

Gouldner saw sociology as having both a repressive and a liberating potential. *The Coming Crisis of Western Sociology*, published in 1971, was a fierce attack on the practice of sociology in the USA and the former Soviet Union, which, in both cases, albeit for different reasons and in different ways, had become repressive. But there was one similarity: they were both grounded in functionalist theories of the social system. Sociologists became integrated into the liberal establishment of US welfarism or into the state Marxism of the Soviet Union and in each case lost their critical independence. Appearing to be neutral, they were in practice acting in ways which were supportive of the status quo. Gouldner argued for the development of what he termed a reflexive sociology. This involved examining the domain assumptions and sentiments on which theories are grounded, including our own, and being seriously prepared to amend work in the face of hostile information (rather than ignore or smother it). Such an emancipatory sociology could not just return to 'pure' sociology since it was now 'in' the world and not 'above' it, but it had to be historically sensitive. We have

to be prepared to see the ways in which yesterday's good news, say of Freudianism, the scientific revolution or Marxism, can become part of today's bad news, the dark side of the dialectic. This study, reminiscent in some ways of Wright Mills' *The Power Elite* (1956) and *The Sociological Imagination* (1959), attracted a barrage of criticism from some of his US colleagues.

Gouldner did not flinch from contest and controversy. This is memorably captured in the book of essays *For Sociology* (1975). The advocacy of the title was itself a side-swipe at Althusser's *For Marx* (1969). Unlike Althusser, who dealt in ahistorical analysis with no place for agency, Gouldner was preoccupied with the relationship between agency and structure, constraint and human action, and sought to apprehend ways in which human beings could recover their own society and culture. In this collection are included an extended reply to critics of *The Coming Crisis*; 'The politics of the mind', a much published and cited essay on value-freedom; 'Anti-minotaur: the myth of a value-free sociology'; and 'The sociologist as partisan: sociology and the welfare state'. This last was a response to Howard Becker's Presidential Address to the Society for the Study of Social Problems, 'Whose side are we on?'. First published in 1968 it can be seen as a forerunner to *The Coming Crisis*. His interest in the relationship between sociology and Marxism is evident in part three of the book. In particular, 'The two Marxisms' gives us a sense of the argument to be taken up in great detail in the book of that title. He is concerned to distinguish between scientific and critical Marxism and is unconvinced by the first and not finally satisfied by the second (Gouldner 1980).

It is significant that the book ends with a chapter entitled 'Nightmare Marxism'. Every theoretical system, he argued, has another system inside struggling to get out. The nightmare is that the caged system will break out. In the case of Marxism the nightmare is that it is just another religion of the oppressed:

> In the nightmare, socialism does not mean that the proletariat becomes the ruling class, but that the state becomes the

dominant force; this new collectivist state brings a new stagnation to the economy, rather than a new productivity; . . . the expropriation of the bourgeoisie is not the basis of a new emancipation, but of a new, many times worse domination.

(Gouldner 1980: 382)

Since the nightmare had become reality in some forms of existing socialism, and especially Stalinism, Gouldner recognized that Marxism itself not only had to be seen as a critique of bourgeois societies but itself had to be open to critique. It also had to be demystified by showing the limits of Marxist consciousness. This, after all, is part of the practice of the dialectic and the exercise of reflexivity. It helps to explain why he advocated the development of a culture of critical discourse in which there is nothing in principle that speakers will permanently refuse to discuss or make problematic. This is treated extensively in *The Dialectic of Ideology and Technology* (1976) and *The Future of Intellectuals and the Rise of the New Class* (1979). No system can capture this kind of critical thinking as it seeks, in an open-ended way, to understand itself and the world.

JOHN ELDRIDGE
UNIVERSITY OF GLASGOW

Further reading

(References cited in the text marked *)

* Althusser, L. (1969) *For Marx*, London: Allen Lane. (Offers a version of Marxist structuralism that severely plays down the role of agency in social explanation.)
Burawoy, M. (1982) 'The written and the repressed in Gouldner's industrial sociology', *Theory and Society* 11: 831–51. (Excellent overview of Gouldner's sociology; crisp and true.)
Gouldner, A.W. (ed.) (1950) *Studies in Leadership*, New York: Harper & Row. (One of the first, and still best, studies of leadership.)
* Gouldner, A.W. (1954a) *Patterns of Industrial Bureaucracy*, Glencoe, IL: The Free Press. (Groundbreaking study of the ways in which a US gypsum mine changed its social organization and the consequences for social relations in the plant and community.)

* Gouldner, A.W. (1954b) *Wildcat Strike*, New York: Antioch Press. (Much-cited case study of a US gypsum mine. A companion volume to *Patterns of Industrial Bureaucracy*.)
* Gouldner, A.W. (1965) *Enter Plato: Classical Greece and the Origins of Social Theory*, London: Routledge & Kegan Paul. (Study offering a sociological account of the structure and culture of ancient Greece. Covers the continuing significance of the Socratic method for critical theory.)
* Gouldner, A.W. (1971) *The Coming Crisis of Western Sociology*, London: Routledge & Kegan Paul. (Account of the state of sociology in the USA and former Soviet Union. Critiques the functionalist orientation and advocates a reflexive sociology.)
* Gouldner, A.W. (1975) *For Sociology. Renewal and Critique in Sociology Today*, Harmondsworth: Penguin. (A collection of essays on themes related to sociological and Marxist theory, with contributions to the value debate in sociology.)
* Gouldner, A.W. (1976) *The Dialectic of Ideology and Technology*, London: Macmillan. (A study about ideology as a form of discourse, with a valuable discussion on the communications revolution.)
* Gouldner, A.W. (1979) *The Future of Intellectuals and the Rise of the New Class*, London: Macmillan. (Discussion of the role of intellectuals and technical intelligentsia in the modern world, and in what sense they constitute a new class.)
* Gouldner, A.W. (1980) *The Two Marxisms: Contradictions and Anomalies in the Development of Theory*, London: Macmillan. (Review of the varieties of Marxism and their role in the development of social theory. Pivots on the distinction between 'scientific' and 'critical' Marxism.)
Gouldner, A.W. (1985) *Against Fragmentation. The Origins of Marxism and the Sociology of Intellectuals*, Oxford: Oxford University Press. (Posthumous publication developing themes discussed in *The Future of Intellectuals* and *The Two Marxisms*.)
Gouldner, A.W. and Miller, S.M. (1965) *Applied Sociology: Opportunities and Problems*, New York: The Free Press. (Basic textbook covering the fundamentals of sociology.)
Jay, M. (1982) 'For Gouldner: reflections on an outlaw Marxist', *Theory and Society* 11: 759–78. (Sophisticated discussion of Gouldner's critical theory.)

Lemert, C. and Piccone, P. (1982) 'Gouldner's theoretical method and reflexive sociology', *Theory and Society* 11: 733–57. (Thoughtful account of Gouldner's approach to the relationship between theory and method in sociology.)

Merton, R.K. (1982) 'Alvin W. Gouldner: genesis and growth of a friendship', *Theory and Society* 11: 915–38. (Account of his lifelong intellectual debates and correspondence with his former student.)

* Wright Mills, C. (1956) *The Power Elite*, New York: Oxford University Press. (A study of the role of elites, especially political, military and economic, in the mid-twentieth century, within the framework of mass society theory.)

* Wright Mills, C. (1959) *The Sociological Imagination*, New York: Oxford University Press. (A critical discussion of the state of US sociology in the mid-twentieth century and a claim that sociology should be grounded in historical and comparative study.)

See also: MICHELS, R.; VEBLEN, T.B.; WEBER, M.

Related topics in the IEBM: LEADERSHIP; MARX, K.H.; ORGANIZATION BEHAVIOUR; ORGANIZATION BEHAVIOUR, HISTORY OF; ORGANIZATION PARADIGMS; ORGANIZATION STRUCTURE; ORGANIZATION TYPES; POWER

Gulick, Luther Halsey (1892–1993)

Personal background

- born in Osaka, Japan in 1892
- president of the National Institute for Public Administration (later Institute for Public Administration), 1921
- chaired Regents Inquiry into public education in New York, 1935–8
- member of the Brownlow Committee for reorganization of the office of the President of the USA, 1930s
- consultant to President Nasser of Egypt on Egyptian constitution, 1962
- delivered the William W. Cook Foundation lectures at the University of Michigan, 1961
- died in New York, January 1993

Major works

Education for American Life: Report of the Regent's Inquiry (1936)
Papers on the Science of Administration (ed. with L.F. Urwick)(1937)
Administrative Reflections from World War II (1948)
The Metropolitan Problem and American Ideas (1962)

Summary

Gulick wrote on and practised the 'science' of administration throughout his long career. He sought to render administration as a discipline, to make it more effective by harnessing it to a handful of simple principles. He believed effective administration had to be simple and durable, able to withstand the toughest internal and environmental stresses, and believed that organizations were tools to achieve ends. His ideas at times approach a philosophy of administration, though he is rarely less than practical; the how and the why of management always go together. Systematic purpose and clear policy, he believed, would always achieve desired ends.

1 Introduction

One of the most remarkable figures in the history of public administration in the USA, Gulick is today rarely studied outside that country. This is unfortunate, as through his long career he was exposed perhaps more than any other thinker and writer on management to non-American influences and ideas. A collaborator of Lyndall Urwick and Henri Fayol (see FAYOL, H.; URWICK, L.F.), he merges (with varying degrees of success) European 'humanistic' views of management with Taylorite scientism in an effective fusion, most notably in *Papers on the Science of Administration* (1937) which he co-edited with Urwick. Gulick was active at a time when there was much less difference between the concepts of public and private sector management than is commonly assumed today. Certainly Gulick himself drew few such distinctions; he repeatedly comments that his principles are equally valid for both sectors; his work shows the influence of management thinkers such as Urwick and Follett, as well as writers on public administration such as Dimock and Litchfield (see FOLLET, M.P.).

2 Biographical data

Gulick was born in Osaka, Japan, into an exceptional family. His grandparents were among the first Western missionaries to visit Hawai'i, and later travelled to Japan (where Gulick's grandfather translated the Bible into Japanese) and China. Gulick's father was a noted physical fitness expert and is sometimes credited, along with James Naismith, with the invention of basketball.

In 1919, at the age of 27, Gulick was named head of the training school at the Bureau of Municipal Research. Two years later, the Bureau was reorganized as the National Institute for Public Administration (which in 1931 became the Institute of Public Administration), and Gulick became its president. This was the beginning of a remarkable career spanning some seventy years. In 1922, under Gulick's leadership, the Institute began international work; it served as the model for the Institute for Municipal Research in Tokyo, and later worked with the government of Yugoslavia and advised the Chinese government of Chiang Kai-Shek on financial reform. In the 1930s, Gulick joined the Brownlow Committee to reorganize the office of the President, and helped establish the Public Administration Clearinghouse.

In 1937, Gulick co-edited *Papers on the Science of Administration* with Lyndall Urwick. This seminal work represents most of the major strains of management thinking in the first half of the twentieth century. Contributors included many of the major names in management and administration theory of the time: as well as Gulick and Urwick, leading figures in private and public sector thinking, there were essays by Henry Dennison, Henri Fayol, Mary Parker Follett, John Lee and James Mooney (see FAYOL, H.; FOLLETT, M.P.). With contributions from the USA, UK and France, this remains one of the most international works on management thinking ever published, all the more impressive because the participants were not conscious of being 'international' in focus.

Following World War II Gulick produced an analysis of the effectiveness of administration in the USA under the stresses of wartime. He continued to work internationally and, in the early 1960s, served as consultant to President Nasser regarding new constitution for Egypt. He wrote or co-authored fifteen books and around two hundred articles, the first in 1920 and the last 70 years later, at the age of 97. He died in New York in 1993, a week short of his 101st birthday.

3 Main contribution

In the opening paper of *Papers on the Science of Administration* (Gulick and Urwick 1937), Gulick sets out his own philosophy of administration. This is perhaps the clearest and most detailed expression of his overall views, and is interesting in that the influences of Taylorism and then-contemporary European management thinking are both evident (see TAYLOR, F.W.). On the one hand, there is the emphasis on control that stems from the scientific revolution and the experiences of business in America; on the other, there is the focus on leadership and guidance that comes straight from Fayol and a European humanist tradition that grew out of government and military administration rather than from 'pure' business experience.

There is also, perhaps more clearly than anywhere else in Gulick's writings, the emphasis on ends, not means. He begins with the classical concept of the division of labour, and sees this as the root of organization: 'Work division is the foundation of organization; indeed, the reason for organization' (1937: 3). His concepts of the division of labour echo those found in the classical economists such as Smith, Mill and Say. There are, he says, clear limits beyond which the division of work cannot go: if the subdivision creates tasks which result in less than one person's labour; the limits of technology and custom, and, most importantly, if the division of labour passes beyond physical division into organic division; 'it might seem far more efficient to have the front half of the cow in the pasture grazing and the rear half in the barn being milked all the time, but this organic division would fail' (1937: 5). The whole is greater than the sum of its parts: 'a piece of work to be done cannot be subdivided into the obvious component parts without great danger that the central design, the operating relationships, the imprisoned idea, will be lost' (1937: 5). Although Gulick believed in decentralization, there were limits beyond which decentralization could not go.

What makes the whole greater than the sum of its parts, he says, is the architect, the leader, the person who coordinates the activities of the specialists. The coordinator is a form of specialist called in when the subdivision of work is no longer possible. Coordination can be achieved in two primary ways: by organizing people, subdividing them into groups allotted to particular tasks, and by 'the dominance of an idea, that is, the development of intelligent singleness of purpose in the minds and wills of those who are working together as a group, so that each worker will of his own accord fit his task into the whole with skill and enthusiasm' (1937: 6). These two principles of organization are co-dependent, and the successful enterprise requires both in equal measure. It is important to note that Gulick believed organization is necessary to co-ordination, not vice versa.

Although Gulick believes in the power of experts, he warns against giving them too much power: experts should be 'on tap, not on top'. It is dangerous to give anyone authority outside their own realm of expertise:

In this particular, educators, lawyers, priests, admirals, doctors, scientists, engineers, accountants, merchants and bankers are all the same – having achieved technical competence or 'success' in one field, they come to think this competence is a general quality detachable from the field and inherent in themselves. They step without embarrassment into other areas. They do not remember that the robes of authority in one kingdom confer no sovereignty in another; but that there are merely a masquerade.

(Gulick 1937: 11)

The people at the top of the organization need to take a broad focus. He adapts his view of the role of the chief executive from Fayol, using the acronym POSDCORB: planning, organizing, staffing, directing, coordinating, reporting and budgeting. The role of the chief executive is to maintain the structure and network of the organization and keep it pointed towards its goals. In a passage which prefigures much later organization thinking, Gulick proposes that work units can be aggregated according to four criteria: by purpose (that is, by the aims of the work unit), by process (what they are actually doing, such

as engineering or accounting), by the persons or things dealt with or served (products made, customer group served) and by place or location (1937: 33–4). Each of these four principles has a different impact on the coordinating function:

If all of the departments are set up on the basis of purpose, then the task of the chief executive will be to see that the major purposes are not in conflict and that the various processes which are used are consistent ... If all the departments are set up on the basis of process, the work methods will be well standardized on professional lines, and the chief executive will have to see that these are co-ordinated and timed to produce the results and render the services ... If place be the basis of departmentalization, that is, if the services be decentralized, then the task of the chief executive is ... to see that each of these services makes use of standard techniques and that the work in each area is part of a general programme and policy.

(Gulick 1937: 33–4)

If departments within an organization are ordered by more than one of the above – as is often the case – then the task of the chief executive becomes even more complex. There is particularly a danger of friction between departments where they intersect or overlap. A critical management function is the reduction of this friction to ensure the smooth functioning of the organization.

This friction can be reduced or overcome, Gulick says, by the introduction of a fifth co-ordinating element, coordination by ideas:

Any large and complicated enterprise would be incapable of effective organization if reliance for co-ordination were placed in organization alone. Organization is necessary; in a large enterprise it is essential, but it does not take the place of a dominant central idea as the foundation of action and self-co-ordination in the daily operation of all parts of the enterprise. Accordingly, the most difficult task of the chief executive is not command, it is leadership, that is, the development of the desire and will to work together for a purpose in the minds of those who are associated in any activity.

(Gulick 1937: 37)

Gulick points out that people do not respond to the same rules as machines: 'Human beings are compounded of cogitation and emotion and do not function well when treated as though they were merely cogs in motion (1937: 38). People will perform far better and sacrifice much more if they are motivated by loyalty, if their minds as well as their bodies are engaged in their task. To ensure this happens, organizations require a management structure which includes personnel management, structure which can develop creative effort, proper reporting not only for control but to enhance morale, the development of professional associations among employees, research to overcome problems in the workplace, honour and awards for achievement, and an organization which allows people to work to their potential. He uses the example of a nation at war to show how an idea can prove more powerful than any leader or organizational principle.

Finally, Gulick is keen to stress the limits of coordination. Five factors combine to limit the ability of leaders to coordinate organizations: the uncertainty of the future, the lack of knowledge on the part of the leaders themselves, the lack of administrative skill and technique on the part of the same leaders, the more general lack of ordered and scientifically based skills and programmes, and 'the vast number of variables involved and the incompleteness of human knowledge, particularly with regard to man and life' (1937: 40).

In his later writings, Gulick continued to press for the recognition and acceptance of principles of management. He saw life, particularly after the World War II, as being increasingly complex and change-laden, and he felt that management could 'bring some order out of chaos along the path of human purpose' (Gulick 1948: 16). Again, he repeats, the task of management is the same whether one is involved in business, government, education or warfare. Organizations are not holy things;

they are tools directed towards an end. Nowhere is this more apparent than in his writings on organization for war: 'Organizations and the men who direct them are expendable. In a world of unprecedented emergencies and uncharted experiences, many things must be tried. When some fail to meet the situation, or when they have served their immediate purpose, they must be superseded. They are casualties, sacrificed in the process of institutional running' (1948: 31). This same view, taken to extremes, led him to advocate the sacrifice of individuals in the organization to preserve the integrity of the whole:

> … the prestige of top management must be maintained even though this involves a certain shifting of responsibility for individual failures and successes to subordinate organizations and men. This is cruel to these organizations and men, but it preserves the integrity of total management in a world of trial and error. In administration, as in baseball, it is the batting average that counts, not the occasional strikeout. Top management must be held accountable for the total record, not each segment.
>
> (Gulick 1948: 32)

He continued also to develop his theme of the importance of a guiding idea. A clear statement of purpose, he says, which is universally understood throughout the organization, is the most important single success factor. The crucial step is the 'translation from purpose to programme' (Gulick 1948: 78). Missions or objectives also had to be limited. One consequence of this was an emphasis on decentralization; organizations ought to be free to pursue their objectives with minimal interference or contact with others. Too many external influences and 'the sense of purpose and dedication may well be lost, and a great deal of friction generated through internal conflicts and rivalries' (Gulick 1961: 85).

His analysis of the effectiveness of American public administration during World War II led him to conclude that planning is an essential component of management; he advised continuous planning, both before a project and during it as a source of self-reflection and analysis. Planning, research and operations go hand in hand; they are simultaneous and interdependent activities. Planning also must be flexible, and must be enabling not inhibiting; one should not overplan, as this closes off options now and in the future (Gulick 1961).

Although he spent most of his life pursuing this goal, Gulick concluded that a fully developed 'theory' of administration remained out of reach; what had evolved instead were 'more or less valid and partially tested assumptions' rather than proven theory (Gulick 1961: 85). At the same time he was highly critical of much 'new' management thinking, which he saw as reinventing the wheel, and particularly of new and obfuscating jargon: 'those who work with these vocabularies run the risk of finding that, like Hamlet in the grave scene, they are deep in soliloquy but without benefit of footlights' (Gulick 1961: 81).

4 Evaluation

Gulick was clearly a powerful thinker who exerted an influence over the science of administration for many years. The simplicity and directness of his views makes for refreshing reading, and the combined influence of American and European theories comes as something as a surprise; only in the 1990s in the work of people like Charles Handy are we beginning to find our way back towards some kind of theoretical synthesis (see HANDY, C.).

Gulick's authoritarian views on organization, with their emphasis on the strong leader and their willingness to sacrifice individual members in pursuit of the common good are not fashionable today (although it could be argued that they are nonetheless widely practised). Leadership, he said, is a fundamental necessity. Although he believed in decentralization, he called for strong hierarchy, with the leader having primary responsibility for both the structure of the organization and the dissemination of the 'guiding idea'.

Although he stated plainly that 'It is the men and not the organization chart that do the work' (1937: 38), Gulick never really came to grips with the human element in

organizations. He recognized its importance but could never systematize it in the way he could other elements: the unpredictability of human nature ultimately baffled him, as it has many other management thinkers since. In Gulick's organization, where men and women can be sacrificed without thought to cover up the failures of others for the common good of the organization, it is difficult to see how one can at the same expect the kind of loyalty and body-and-mind devotion which he hopes will be inspired. Such self-sacrifice happens in wartime; in the field of commerce, where the stakes are lower, such behaviour is more rare.

On balance, Gulick seems determined at times to fit people into the organization view. The emphasis on science, and the influence of the military experience, all led to a doctrine of necessity in the face of change, of order against the onset of chaos. Similarly, he recognized the importance of leadership, but gave no definitions of it; like the earlier classical economists, he assumed its presence but gave no leads on how it could be built or identified.

Despite these criticisms, Gulick deserves to be recognized as one of the leading thinkers on organization, some of whose ideas ahead of their time. His views on the importance of mission, of the 'guiding idea' which inspire members of the organization and lead them to greater than normal efforts, have now become part of received wisdom. His attitude to planning, and his view that organizations are but ends to means, deserve closer attention by management scholars.

5 Conclusion

To sum up, over the course of a long and distinguished career, Gulick made many contributions to public administration, in the USA and around the world. He felt that administration was a generic concept which could be applied equally to business and government, and that it ought to be founded on firm scientific principles; he dedicated much of his life to attempts to define and refine those principles. Although his writings are now out of fashion, they continue to offer much valuable food for thought for today's manager.

MORGEN WITZEL
LONDON BUSINESS SCHOOL
DURHAM UNIVERSITY BUSINESS SCHOOL

The author would like to thank the staff of the Institute of Public Administration in New York for providing information on Gulick's life and times.

Further reading

(References cited in the text are marked *)

Barnard, C. (1938) *The Functions of the Executive*, Cambridge, MA: Harvard University Press. (Contemporary work on management and leadership, whose influence Gulick acknowledged.)

Dimock, M.E. (1958) *A Philosophy of Administration: Towards Creative Growth*, New York: Harper & Bros. (A strongly philosophical work on management, the influence of which can be seen in Gulick's writings on administration.)

Fayol, H. (1930) *Industrial and General Administration*, trans. J.A. Coubrough, Geneva: International Management Association. (Gulick was clearly influenced by Fayol, and often cites this particular translation.)

Fitch, L.C. (1997) *Make Democracy Work: The Life and Letters of Luther Halsey Gulick, 1892–1993*, Berkeley, CA: Institute of Governmental Studies. (Full-length study of one the most remarkable figures in US public administration.)

* Gulick, L.H. (1936) *Education for American Life: Report of the Regent's Inquiry*, New York: McGraw-Hill. (The report of a commission of inquiry into public education in New York, which Gulick chaired.)

* Gulick, L.H. and Urwick, L.F. (eds) (1937) *Papers on the Science of Administration*, New York: Institute of Public Administration. (Collection of seminal papers on administration, with contributions from Gulick, Urwick, Fayol, Follett and Mooney, among others.)

* Gulick, L.H. (1948) *Administrative Reflections from World War II*, University, AL: University of Alabama Press, 1948.

* Gulick, L.H. (1962) *The Metropolitan Problem and American Ideas*, New York: Alfred A. Knopf. (Transcript of five lectures on government and administration, delivered at the University of Michigan in 1961.)

'Timeline of events in IPA's history', at http://www.theipa.org (Short history of the Institute of Public Administration, an organization which Gulick led for many years.)

See also: FAYOL, H.; FOLLETT, M.P.; HANDY, C.; MILL, J.S.; SMITH, A.; TAYLOR, F.E.; URWICK, L.F.

Related topics in the IEBM: GENERAL MANAGEMENT; HUMAN RELATIONS; HUMAN RESOURCE MANAGEMENT; MARKETS AND PUBLIC POLICY; ORGANIZATION BEHAVIOUR; ORGANIZATION BEHAVIOUR, HISTORY OF; ORGANIZATION STRUCTURE

Hamel, Gary (1954–) and Prahalad, C.K. (1941–)

1 Biographical data
2 *Harvard Business Review* and thesis
3 *Competing for the Future*
4 Strategy as revolution
5 Evaluation

Personal background

Gary Hamel

- born in 1954
- received a Bsc from Andrews University in 1975 and an MBA from the University of Michigan in 1976
- graduated from the University of Michigan with a PhD in business in 1990
- joined the London Business School in 1983, teaching global strategy whilst completing his thesis
- founded Strategos in 1994
- currently visiting professor of strategy and international management at the London Business School
- chairman of Strategos and serves on the board of governors of the Strategic Management Society

C.K. Prahalad

- born 1941
- Harvard University, 1975; International Teachers Program (ITP), Harvard University, 1972; Indian Institute of Management, Ahmedabad, 1966; BSc, Loyola College, University of Madras, 1960
- worked in industry 1960–71
- visiting research fellow at Harvard Business School, 1975
- professor and chairman of the Management Education Program, Indian Institute of Management, Ahmedabad, 1975–77
- visiting professor, INSEAD, France, Summer 1981

- joined University of Michigan Business School as associate professor, 1978–86
- currently Harvey C. Fruehauf Professor of Business Administration and professor of corporate strategy and international business, University of Michigan Business School

Major works

Competing for the Future: Breakthrough Strategies (1994)

Summary

Gary Hamel's renown is inseparable from his highly successful collaboration with C.K. Prahalad. Together, they developed managerial-oriented ideas on strategy that ran counter to the prevailing spirit of downsizing and financial control prevailing in the 1980s. As many corporations thought through the complexity of restructuring, Hamel and Prahalad provided a window for top-management decision making on possible future alternatives. Their ideas have been more powerful in the world of practice than in research. However, in changing practice, they have influenced the phenomena studied by academics.

1 Biographical data

Gary Hamel attended Andrews University in Berrien Springs, Michigan. Andrews University was founded by Seventh Day Adventists and maintains the goal of providing a 'high quality Christian education'. Subsequently, he pursued an MBA and later PhD in business at the University of Michigan. While finishing this thesis, Hamel joined the faculty of the London Business School where he taught global strategy for a number of years.

At the University of Michigan, he studied international business and strategy and also started his partnership with Professor C.K. Prahalad, who exercised a powerful influence on his early thinking. Prahalad had received a DBA in 1975 from the Harvard University Business School and was already renowned for his incisive articles on the organization and strategy of multinational corporations. Prahalad's work often has a Cartesian precision in the development of a few principles, backed with rich business examples. The analytical but grounded quality of his thinking is clearly evident in his article on 'dominant logic' (developed with Richard Bettis and Stephen Bradley) that describes a firm's implied strategic orientation. Their article published in the *Strategic Management Review* (Prahalad and Bettis 1986) won a retrospective prize for best paper. Contrary to the broader academic conventions, Prahalad openly advocated the importance of contributing to managerial practice as the critical benchmark for successful research.

No doubt, Prahalad's views shaped Hamel's revealed preference for publishing in management-oriented publications, primarily the *Harvard Business Review*, and his criticism of conventional academic approaches. He wrote, for example, in his thesis on collaboration:

> Practitioners – and if research is not for their benefit, for whose benefit is it – are likely to find little value in causality statements, however iron-clad, that are dependent on a precise and rarely occurring admixture of qualifying conditions. What the practitioner wants is theory which recognizes, and synthesizes the contingencies, trade-offs, and inter-relationships which so frustrate the traditional researcher.
>
> (102)

Hamel has published several key articles in the *Harvard Business Review*, most with Prahalad. A number have won the McKinsey Award for best publications of the year in the review, more prizes than won by any other author. These articles developed the notions of strategic intent, core competence, and expeditionary marketing. Much of this success was earned while Hamel was still preparing his thesis. The disparity between his status as a lecturer and later untenured professor and his growing fame as a management thinker and consultant enhanced his criticism of the bias of academic research towards empirically and theoretically reasoned study. He was awarded his PhD in 1990.

Prahalad and Hamel sold their consulting firm for an undisclosed sum believed to be for several millions of dollars. While retaining a position at the London Business School, he moved to northern California. In 1994, he founded the consulting firm of Strategos a company, in his words, which 'help companies imagine the future, and having imagined it, create it'. During this later years and independent of Prahalad, Hamel proposed a distinctly anti-Cartesian call for creativity and revolutionary strategy.

2 *Harvard Business Review* and thesis

The articles co-authored by Gary Hamel and C.K. Prahalad and published in the *Harvard Business Review* show a filtering of early initiatives into a coherent strategy doctrine. Their initial article on global strategy was an influential, though not distinctly original article. Prahalad had in his Harvard thesis applied the Lawrence and Lorsch framework of integration and differentiation to the multinational firm; integration represented the forces that pushed the firm toward recognizing interdependence among country subsidiaries; differentiation reflected the diversity of cultural, consumer, and political factors across countries (see LAWRENCE, P.R. AND LORSCH J.W.). The Prahalad and Hamel article made a few distinctions among strategies before proposing that the success of a global strategy rested in cross-subsidization across countries. A manager could apply the cash flows earned in one country to building a position in another. This framework had a distinctly cash flow matrix imprint, and was in large a Boston Consulting Group cash cow concept applied to international markets.

Later joint work focused on the role of collaboration and joint ventures in international strategy. In this work, Prahalad and Hamel (and co-author Yves Doz; Prahalad, Hamel and Doz 1989) were quick to stress the importance of learning in the context of these ventures. It is important to recall the debate at this time frequently centered on the belief that Japanese firms used joint ventures to acquire the technology of Western partners who they then discarded; a point of view which was expressed strongly in an article by a future Secretary of Labor, Robert Reich, published in the *Harvard Business Review* (Reich and Mankin 1986) (see REICH, R.). This belief of a Japanese intent to absorb foreign technology is not entirely absent in the writings of Prahalad and Hamel at this time. Hamel's emphasis on joint ventures as 'learning races' reflects a refined concern over the dangers of losing 'core technologies' to Japanese partners.

As seen in his thesis completed in 1990, this perspective later shed its overtones of Japanese competitive threats to a broad framework on how to create value in joint ventures through enhancing a firm's 'receptivity' to learning. This thesis took a grounded-theory approach to propose an eclectic approach to collaboration:

> Researchers who tie themselves to a particular stanchion limit the range of their insights … (These researchers) all seem to have devoted more attention to demonstrating the applicability of pre-existing theory to the emerging collaborative phenomenon than to developing a theory of collaborative behavior that grew out of the phenomenon itself. With their allegiance to existing theoretical constructs, each of these researchers has taken hold of a different part of the elephant and has a different story to tell. It's not clear that anyone knows what the elephant looks like in its entirety.
>
> (99)

Rather than delineate his contribution to existing theory, Hamel instead detailed in greater depth many of the points made in his previous publications. Using extensive interviews with top managers in several countries, he illustrated from business practice how successful firms are more receptive to learning.

Through their growing exposure to Japanese firms due to their field research and other activities, Prahalad and Hamel developed a more nuanced interpretation of Japanese strategy as reflecting a long-term strategy based around a defined set of core competencies. This interpretation is to be found, partially, in Japanese writings, especially the book written by Imai, Kagono, and Nonaka which compared the long-term evolutionary focus of Japanese firms to the revolutionary strategies of American companies. It is also again strongly reflective of the highly publicized strategies of some Japanese firms who boldly stated their global intentions in terms of core technologies. A prominent example is NEC who announced their ambition to lead in the '2 Cs' of communications and computers.

In comparison, many American firms during the 1980s underwent radical restructuring built around divisionalization with tight financial objectives. High technology firms such as Corning and AT&T sought repeatedly the appropriate organizational form by which to provide financial incentives and controls to guide managers' decisions. The prevailing corpus of strategic thinking, as taught in business schools and in consulting, was strongly influenced by the writings and consulting practice of Michael Porter, a professor at the Harvard Business School and founder of the consulting firm Monitor. Porter (see PORTER, M.) advocated an 'industry structure' approach to market definition and to identifying the sources of competitive advantage. He stressed the importance of understanding the forces that erode profitability and the factors that lead to excessive rivalry in well-defined industries. His frameworks of industry structure and the value chain provided a set of heuristics drawn from economic theory and that could, in more sophisticated extensions, bridge to the evolving body of work on game theory and strategy.

Hamel and Prahalad wrote three original articles that expressed a view of strategy that was radically distinct from the industry structure approach. Initially, they claimed their view was in greater accordance with the emergent success of Japanese firms than the downsizing and divisionalization strategies of American firms. The most successful of these articles was the 1990 publication 'The core competence of the corporation', which became the most redistributed article in the *Review*'s history. Drawing on a comparison between NEC and GTE, the article expressed an important trademark of their approach: their willingness to commend and to criticize firms. The article proposed that successful firms such as NEC focus on core competencies that become realized through the creation of core products. They defined a core competence as a skill that is difficult to imitate, that consumers value, and that can be applied to multiple markets. This definition reflects their explicit reasoning that an orientation to consumers is a hallmark of a successful strategy. Defining a core competence *in vacuo* leads to faulty analysis that pinpoints non-strategic skills as core. A core competence can only be defined in terms of the customer. The other two articles described the importance of long-term orientation of a 'strategic intent' and of searching for new areas of exploration by looking for 'white spaces' that fall between the market strategies of divisions and strategic groups.

3 Competing for the Future

Hamel and Prahalad distilled their writings in one of the most successful business books ever published entitled *Competing for the Future* (1994). This book is the Harvard Business School Press's most successful publication. The book presents their ideas already published as articles, with a greater focus on the importance of competing for the long-run. Without explicitly criticizing other strategic approaches, they briefly assail the industry structure approach as fighting last year's battles. Instead, corporations should build long-term competencies that exploit the white spaces by creating positions of leverage.

They make explicit that they 'start with a pro-bigness bias'. The book is oriented to giving advice to managers of large corporations and is directed towards finding the sources of strategic renewal. These sources are found by

linking core competencies to 'gateways' for new opportunities. The role of strategy is to 'stretch' the resources of a company. A strategy should not fit a company to its environment, but create gaps between their current capabilities and aspirations. By creating this dynamic, managers motivate their firms to realize their aspirations.

4 Strategy as revolution

In his first clear departure from his intellectual partnership with Prahalad, Hamel built upon the idea of stretch to argue that strategy is revolution. Much like Tom Peters (see PETERS, T.J.) who moved from the analysis of 'excellent' firms to strategy as guerilla warfare, Hamel chose to develop the emotive implications of his thinking. Strategy is no longer the province of top management, but is the expression of democratic sentiments in a firm. Everyone makes strategy. In this new role, top managers often find themselves quickly moving to take leadership of bandwagons that have bubbled up from below. The consulting firm of Strategos, headed by Hamel, takes this notion of strategy as a creative democratic process as its mission.

5 Evaluation

The writing and career of Hamel are too recent to evaluate for their historic contribution to management thought. However, it is apparent that Hamel and Prahalad's success is surely driven by a counter-trend insistence on long-term commitment to a strategy and to investment in capabilities as opposed to the financial emphasis on quarterly justification of economic value added. Clearly influenced by what they perceived in Japan, they filtered these observations into a honed statement as to what should drive the strategic process in the firm.

While attentive to learning across countries, Hamel and Prahalad are not interested in the institutional and contextual explanations for these differences. They take the large firm as the unit of analysis. The strength of the US in growing small firms to industrial giants in a few years plays little acknowledged role in their analysis. Their writings imply the position that European firms are paradigms of globalized companies, and Japanese firms epitomize the ability of large companies to renew their innovative potential. Hamel, however, too quickly wrote off the American computer industry (see his article with Bettis and Bradley; Bettis, Bradley and Hamel 1992), and did not acknowledge the institutional strengths in the American system of allowing small firms to grow and large firms, such as Motorola, to shed older technologies by divesting and outsourcing.

Despite their hostility to academic conventions, Hamel and Prahalad espoused a set of ideas to which a new body of academics could point to as legitimizing their recent theorizing on competitive advantage as derived from an evolutionary development of unique resources. Yet, they did not themselves seek to link their ideas to these and affiliated developments. As a result, their writings often are deficient in suggesting too hastily that competitive and quantitative assessments are misdirected. Their emphasis on consumer value implies the need for a way to identify what consumers prefer. The value of competencies must, by logic, be party determined by the capabilities of other firms to offer competing products; yet competitive assessment is largely ignored. Though right in their evaluation of the bias of financial criteria, Hamel and Prahalad ignore recent efforts in financial economics that support their insights. Core competence and white spaces imply a 'real option' thinking, in which a firm explores new markets by making investment bets on new capabilities. The notion of strategy as revolution suggests the need for some refined criteria by which choice among competing petitions might be made: majority vote,

Hamel and Prahalad offer rarely more than logic and insightful cases as evidence for the accuracy of their ideas; statistics and even numerical facts do not populate their pages. In this regard, they implicitly embrace Popper and Campbell's view of academic ideas as arising out of an evolutionary epistemology in which 'good ideas' survive. But this presumption raises the intriguing issue of what is the relevant community that selects. Prahalad and

Hamel, as indicated in the above quotation, are quite clear that business practice is the ultimate test. The face validation of ideas is their acceptance by practitioners. The two authors are not shy in popular articles to identify this validation in the extent to which their ideas enjoy commercial success.

Hamel's epistemology challenges the rationalistic conventions of an academy that cannot accept him without contradicting their own principles. American business schools desperately raised themselves from their lowly miasma as described in the devastating Howell report of the 1950s. Their gain of academic success rode on the explicit and ideological programme to install science and method into business curriculum. Operations research, management science, finance and economic mathematics became taken as paradigmatic of the new business school. Two rounds of Nobel prizes went to achievements in financial economics (portfolio and derivative theories); an earlier Nobel Prize went to Herbert Simon for his formal analysis of bounded rationality (see SIMON, H.). The resolution of the institutional insecurity of the professional school in the university was to imitate the sciences through functional specialization and increasing formalization. By the 1980s, these efforts had largely succeeded in organizational behavior, marketing, operations, accounting, and belatedly in business policy and strategy.

Hamel and Prahalad found inimical the constraints imposed by functional and scientific aspirations of business research. However, unlike his mentor Prahalad, Hamel has developed even further a non-Cartesian emphasis on revolutionary strategy as expressive of a creative democracy. He does not rely upon any studies on participative management, creativity, or innovation. In this latest appeal, he is openly provocative in calling for the freeing of imagination from the strictures of business schools. Even if they appreciate his contributions, he recognizes that they cannot easily accept him.

Hamel and Prahalad are not interdisciplinary; they are non-disciplinary, holistic thinkers. They drove consciously a stake into the wound of professional schools seeking academic validation from their universities. To succeed in changing business school education, Hamel's natural allies are the humanities and theology. Neither of these fields has made an in-road to the business school but both express important values for many business people. Whether the premise of strategy as revolution can be sustained over the interim is contingent on the direction of the future development of the culture of business and their schools of professional training.

BRUCE KOGUT
THE WHARTON SCHOOL
UNIVERSITY OF PENNSYLVANIA

Further reading

(References cited in the text marked*)

* Bettis, R.A. Bradley, S.P. and Hamel, G. (1992) 'Outsourcing and industrial decline', *Academy of Management Executive* 6 (1): 7–22. (A useful analysis of outsourcing and competitiveness.)

Hamel, G. (1991) 'Competition and inter-partner learning within international strategic alliances', *Strategic Management Journal* Summer, 12: 83–103. (A key article on international strategic alliances.)

Hamel, G. (1996), 'Strategy as revolution', *Harvard Business Review*, 74 (4): 69–71. (Another key article on the strategy as a concept.)

Hamel, G. and Prahalad, C.K. (1989) 'Strategic Intent', *Harvard Business Review,* (Won coveted McKinsey Award.)

* Hamel, G. and Prahalad, C.K. (1985) 'Do you really have a global strategy?' *Harvard Business Review,* July/August, 63(4): 139–148. (An early example of their pathbreaking analysis.)

Hamel, G. and Prahalad, C.K. (1990) 'The core competence of the corporation', *Harvard Business Review,* (Won coveted McKinsey Award and is the most reprinted article in Harvard Business Review's history.)

Hamel, G. and Prahalad, C.K. (1991) 'Corporate imagination and expeditionary marketing', *Harvard Business Review*, July/August. (This article places a greater emphasis on the marketing element.)

Hamel, G. and Prahalad, C.K. (1993) 'Strategy as stretch and leverage', *Harvard Business Review*, March/April, 71 (2) 75–84. (Explains how to develop strategies to create leverage.)

* Hamel, G. and Prahalad, C.K. (1994) *Competing for the Future: Breakthrough Strategies*, Boston, MA: Harvard Business School Press. (Offers an innovative blueprint for what your company must be doing today if it is to occupy the competitive high ground of tomorrow.)

Hamel, G. and Prahalad, C.K. (1994) 'Competing for the future', *Harvard Business Review*, July/August. (A seminal article now regarded as a classic.)

Hamel, G. and Prahalad, C.K. (1994) 'Strategy as a field of study: why search for a new paradigm?', *Strategic Management Journal* 15, Summer Special Issue. (An overview of strategy as a field of study.)

* Hamel, G., Doz, Y.L. and Prahalad, C.K. (1989) 'Collaborate with your competitors – and win', *Harvard Business Review* Jan/Feb, 67 (1): 133–139. (This article is now a classic.)

Prahalad, C.K. and Bettis, R.A. (1986) 'The dominant logic: a new linkage between diversity and performance', *Strategic Management Journal*, 7: 485–501. (An important early contribution by Prahalad.)

Reich, R.B. and Mankin, E.D., (1986), 'Joint ventures with Japan give away our future', *Harvard Business Review*, March/April 64 (2): 78–86. (Critical article on how joint ventures with Japanese firms lead to possible loss of competitive advantage.)

Note: Strategos can be visited at www.strategos-net.com

See also: LAWRENCE, P.R. AND LORSCH J.W; NONAKA, I.; PETERS, T.J.; REICH, R.; SIMON, H.A.

Related topics in the IEBM: BUSINESS ECONOMICS; DOWNSIZING; MULTINATIONAL ORGANIZATION, STRUCTURE IN; ORGANIZATIONAL INFORMATION AND KNOWLEDGE; STRATEGIC CHOICE; STRATEGY

Hammer, Michael (1948–)

Personal background

- born in 1948
- bachelors, masters and PhD from Massachussets Institute of Technology
- software engineer, IBM
- professor of computer science, Massachussets Institute of Technology
- PRISM research project with Index Consulting Group
- president, Hammer and Company

Major works

Reengineering the Corporation (1993)
The Reengineering Revolution (1995)
Beyond Reengineering (1997)

Summary

Michael Hammer invented the term 'reengineering' in the late 1980s to describe the use of information technology to radically redesign business processes to achieve dramatic improvements in performance. The concept first came to public attention in an article in the *Harvard Business Review* (Hammer 1990) and was subsequently promoted through a series of best-selling books which established Hammer as one of the most influential management thinkers of the early 1990s. While Hammer would argue that reengineering's success was attributable to the novelty of the concept and its ability to deliver results, others have suggested that this may also have been due to reengineering's attunement to the spirit of the times and to the effectiveness of Hammer's rhetoric. A more serious criticism of Hammer's work has been its neglect of people, as Hammer himself belatedly acknowledged. This omission may help to account for evidence that by 1997 the popularity of reengineering was in decline.

1 Introduction

Michael Hammer, a former computer science professor from MIT, rose to prominence in the early 1990s as the progenitor and leading protagonist of 'reengineering'. The concept was developed through a consultancy research project in the late 1980s directed by Thomas Davenport. Although Davenport was the first to report on this work in the *Sloan Management Review* (Davenport and Short 1990) it was Hammer's article in the July 1990 *Harvard Business Review* (Hammer 1990) that attracted the greater attention. In this, he argued that companies should 'reengineer' their businesses: using the power of modern information technology to radically redesign business processes to achieve dramatic improvements in performance. His ideas were expanded in a book *Reengineering the Corporation* (1993) which he co-authored with James Champy, chairman of the CSC Index consultancy. The book became an international bestseller and spawned a market for reengineering consultancy and related services which was estimated as amounting to $51 billion by 1995 (Davenport 1995). Growing criticisms of reengineering were answered by Hammer in his second book, *The Reengineering Revolution* (1995, co-authored with Steven Stanton). By late 1996, however, there were signs that the concept was losing its appeal and Hammer's 1997 book was entitled *Beyond Reengineering*. Although this acknowledged some mistakes in the practice, and to a lesser extent theory, of reengineering it was largely a reaffirmation of the original ideas.

2 Main contribution

Hammer's 1990 article is entitled 'Reengineering work: don't automate, obliterate' and carries the heading 'Managers can release the real power of computers by challenging centuries-old notions about work'. In many ways, this captures the spirit of his contribution: a simple and robust solution to problems of business performance through the use of modern information technology. This approach is presented, moreover, as a radical over-turning of established wisdom; a theme picked up in the subtitle of *Reengineering the Corporation*, which describes itself as 'a manifesto for business revolution' and in the title of the second book.

Throughout his writings, Hammer has been remarkably consistent in adopting a standard definition of reengineering as 'the fundamental rethinking and radical redesign of business processes to achieve dramatic improvements in contemporary measures of business performance'. The key words of this definition, that are identified as central to the reengineering concept, are 'radical', 'dramatic' and 'process' (although fundamental and redesign also feature in some versions). 'Radical' is taken to indicate that redesign should start with a blank slate – throw out all the old processes and assumptions and start again; reengineering is a new beginning. 'Dramatic' refers to reengineering's performance improvement targets. In contrast to the incremental approach of Total Quality Management, reengineering aims for quantum leaps in performance, achieving breakthroughs rather than marginal improvements.

Process, however, has latterly been identified by Hammer as the principal aspect of reengineering. He argues that since the time of Adam Smith, the division of labour has encouraged the proliferation of functional divisions in organisations and that modern management practices have developed to improve the task-centred structures that this gives rise to. Hammer proposes, however, that organisations are fundamentally comprised of processes: collections of activities that take various kinds of input and create an output that is of value to a customer. Identifying and fundamentally redesigning the processes of an organisation to make them simpler and able to deliver value to the customer more effectively is seen as the only way for companies to survive in the future.

While Hammer's arguments have, broadly speaking, revolved around these themes in all his writings, it is also possible to detect some shifts over time. Thus, the *Harvard Business Review* article set out *seven* principles of reengineering which may be seen as being based on a particular information-processing view of organisations, and this is reinforced by the article's emphasis on the contribution of IT to organisational transformation. *Reengineering the Corporation* also identified a significant role for IT, devoting a whole chapter to discussing examples of the way in which it breaks the rules that limit how work is conducted. Although IT is mentioned in *The Reengineering Revolution* and *Beyond Reengineering* as one of the elements used by companies in their redesigned processes, it is no longer afforded particular significance (and is not specifically identified in the index).

Two other significant shifts have been in the claims for the novelty and distinctiveness of the concept and for the scope of its relevance. In *Reengineering the Corporation*, Hammer is insistent that reengineering is a new concept and this is endorsed on the cover by Peter Drucker (see DRUCKER, P.). In particular Hammer argues that reengineering differs fundamentally from quality improvement and is at pains to distance himself from the perceived failures of the Total Quality Management movement. These claims are repeated in *The Reengineering Revolution* . By the time of *Beyond Reengineering*, however, TQM and reengineering are being presented as complementary.

The examples of successful reengineering cited in the early works are almost exclusively large American corporations, often major multinationals. In *The Reengineering Revolution*, however, Hammer is keen to emphasise its relevance to small companies, to countries outside the USA and even to the public/nonprofit sector (described as 'mission-driven' organisations). Reengineering has thus become a universal solution.

In addition to making the case for reengineering and defining its key elements, a significant proportion of each of Hammer's three books is devoted to explanation of how to manage a (successful) reengineering project and of the organisational implications of reengineering. In *Reengineering the Corporation*, the various roles involved in implementing reengineering are discussed with particular emphasis on the need for strong and visionary leadership. The 'new world of work' created by reengineering is also described. Reengineering, it is suggested, will require a shift from: functional departments to process teams; simple tasks to multidimensional work; control to empowerment; training to education; payment for activity to compensation by results; promotion by performance to advancement based on ability; protective to productive values; managers as supervisors to managers as coaches; hierarchical to flat organisational structures; and executives as scorekeepers to executive leadership.

In *The Reengineering Revolution* , which decribes itself as a 'handbook', there is discussion of: the use of consultants; how to overcome resistance and 'counter-revolutionary' arguments; and the art of selling change. *Beyond Reengineering* addresses a broader picture, arguing that reengineering involves a fundamental transformation of work, management, enterprise and ultimately of society. All workers, it is argued, need to become self-managing professionals, managers must become process owners, coaches and leaders. Organisations will thus become *flexible*, *boundaryless* and *wholly dedicated to efficient delivery of value to customers*. Only in this way can businesses and national economies continue to prosper and economic growth be sustained.

A final important feature of all Hammer's work has been his use of examples of companies who have successfully, and in some cases unsuccessfully, undertaken reengineering to illustrate his argument. Such tales of reengineering practice support Hammer's contention that the concept is firmly based on consultancy experience rather than academic theorising. As with Tom Peters (see PETERS, T.J.), however, Hammer has not always been lucky in his choice of reengineering exemplars. As his critics have joyfully noted, a number of the companies he has profiled have subsequently encountered serious problems. In *Reengineering the Corporation*, Hammer also gave a hostage to fortune in reporting that 50–70% of organizations that undertake reengineering fail to achieve the dramatic results they intended and this 'myth of reengineering failure' has continued to haunt his later writings. Hammer's response has been to argue that reengineering is not inherently risky, indeed success is guaranteed for those who follow its principles correctly. Rather, failure can be traced to readily identifiable, and hence potentially avoidable, deficiencies of reengineering practice.

3 Evaluation

As Grint (1994) and many other authors have suggested, the components of reengineering, such as process orientation, work redesign, or multi-skilled teamworking, are not particularly novel. Each has featured in influential management ideas, some of which date back to the nineteenth century. While it could be argued, as some reengineering proponents do, that it is the particular combination of elements that makes reengineering distinctive, in *The Reengineering Revolution* Hammer specifically rejects the claim that 'reengineering is nothing new', drawing attention to differences between reengineering and other approaches such as industrial engineering or quality management. As if recognising the weakness of his position, however, Hammer also offers the more pragmatic response: 'who cares'. The only thing that matters is that reengineering works.

This concession is further compounded by Hammer's willingness, most openly acknowledged in *Beyond Reengineering*, to claim credit for successful change initiatives which he identifies as reengineering even if they did not call themselves that, or even occured before the concept was invented. Equally, many unsuccessful projects are discounted because, it is argued, they were not really reengineering after all. Thus, even if it were possible to identify a specific set of practices based on common principles which constituted reengineering, they would not all be associated with that specific term.

This step creates a particular problem in assessing the importance of Hammer's contribution to management thinking. His major achievement is the popularization of a concept, which on closer examination appears not to have a single, universally-accepted meaning. This situation is not unique to reengineering, but it does raise the question of why the concept became so immensely successful; to the extent, Hammer claims in *The Reengineering Revolution*, that more than three-quarters of America's largest companies were said to be undertaking reengineering projects in 1994. If reengineering was a new label rather than a revolutionary new concept, then what made it so popular?

Grint (1994) has attributed reengineering's attraction to its 'resonance' with a number of aspects of popular opinion in the early 1990s. For example Grint identifies resonances with American culture and symbolism. In *Reengineering the Corporation* Hammer specifically argues that reengineering was 'made in the USA', in contrast to foreign imports such as quality management, and that it exemplifies and capitalizes on what is seen as the American entrepreneurial spirit. The same theme is still present in *Beyond Reengineering*, which invokes American patriotism at the time of the Gulf War and devotes a whole chapter to the lessons that reengineering projects can learn from American football. Although this raises the question of why reengineering has achieved such international success, it does suggest that Hammer may have been successful in tapping into a spirit of resurgent national confidence.

Grint also draws attention to political and temporal resonances. Hammer's frequent and high profile descriptions of reengineering as revolutionary, with its overtones of communist thinking, would not seem a natural feature of American business language. As Grint, points out, however, the rise of reengineering coincided with the collapse of the former Soviet Union, enabling a rehabilitation of such language. Indeed, *Beyond Reengineering* cites both Marx and Trotsky without apparent irony.

This leads to another significant aspect of Hammer's work, his rhetoric. There are frequent quotations from business leaders, and American cultural, sporting and political figures as well as classic writers to support and illuminate the ideas. The writing is studded with catchphrases, such as 'paving the cowpaths', 'rearranging the deckchairs on the Titanic', 'dusting the furniture at Pompeii'. There are alliterative lists of 'mechanisms for overcoming resistance' or 'tools of reengineering leadership', as well as numbered lists of 'principles' and 'ways to fail at reengineering'. The language is simple, direct and supremely self-confident: reengineering is the most important management concept since Adam Smith's *Wealth of Nations*; it is the only means of ensuring an organisations survival; it always works if people do it right (see SMITH, A.).

As Jones (1994) notes, Hammer's rhetoric also frequently has a specifically religious flavour; many popular reports of Hammer's presentational style refer to his 'evangelism', and he himself has described it as 'a theology' (Byrne 1992). It is evident not just in his use of biblical references and in quotations from religious authorities such as Talmudic scholars or Pope John Paul II, but in the underlying message of redemption through suffering and rebirth. In *The Reengineering Revolution* this is made explicit in a discussion of the 'The case of the road to the promised land' which analyses the change management lessons in the story of the Israelites exodus from Egypt. This religious aspect may be seen as another cultural and symbolic resonance of Hammer's work.

Highlighting Hammer's rhetoric, however, does not imply a criticism of his contribution. As Eccles and Nohria (1992) argue, powerful rhetoric is an important feature of succesful management and Hammer's writings contain many examples of the techniques they identify as effective. What would seem more questionable though is the violence of the language and the implications this has for the approach to organisational change. The original *Harvard Business Review* article, for example, proposed the obliteration of old processes. In an interview with *Business Week*, Hammer argued that the 'fat' in organisations 'is not waiting around on top to be cut. It's marbled in and the only way you get it out is by grinding it out and frying it out' (Byrne 1992). Elsewhere Hammer has likened reengineering to a neutron bomb which kills the people and leaves the structures standing, and there are numerous other references in his writings to violent solutions to resistance. Combined with a rather crude economism – Hammer argues that economic rewards are ultimately the only real motivator – this produces a narrow, relentlessly competitive and aggressive vision of organizations and society. While Hammer recognizes that people may have other concerns, such as solidarity, intangible rewards, and a balance of work and personal life, and that a reengineered society risks becoming rootless and alienated, excluding those who are unable or unwilling to embrace its principles, he is happy to defend his vision on the basis that it is simply 'realistic'. In *Beyond Reengineering*, he also acknowledges the stress and personal costs of work in a reengineered organization, but argues that this is redeemed by the 'substance, meaning and value' that the survivors of reengineering find in their work.

The effect of reengineering on people and the nature of the organizations it creates has been a long-standing criticism and became a source of disagreement between Hammer and other early collaborators such as Champy and Davenport (Davenport 1995). Although Hammer sought to refute accusations of reengineering's 'inhumanity' and its association with downsizing in *The Reengineering Revolution*, this did not appear to be effective in stilling concerns and by late 1996 Hammer was conceding that reengineering had been 'insufficiently appreciative of the human dimension', a fault that he attributed to his engineering background (White 1996). That this was associated with reports that the appeal of reengineering was in significant decline may not be entirely coincidental. Thus, as the title of *Beyond Reengineering* suggests, although Hammer appears to remain convinced of his concept's enduring importance, it may be that its best days are past.

MATTHEW JONES
UNIVERSITY OF CAMBRIDGE

Further reading

(References cited in the text are marked *)

* Byrne, J. (1992) 'Management's new gurus', *Business Week* 31 August: 42–50. (A review of leading management thinkers in the early 1990s.)
* Davenport, T.H. and Short, J.E. (1990) 'The new industrial engineering: information technology and business process redesign', *Sloan Management Review* Summer: 11–27. (An alternative description of reengineering which marginally preceded Hammer's 1990 article.)
  Davenport, T.H. and Stoddard, D.B. (1994) 'Reengineering: business change of mythic proportions', *MIS Quarterly* 18 (2): 121–127. (A discussion of the myths of reengineering – implicitly criticizing Hammer's ideas.)
* Davenport, T.H. (1995) 'The fad that forgot people', *Fast Company* November. (A critique of reengineering's neglect of people and the hype that grew up around the concept.)
* Eccles, R.G. and Nohria, N. (1992) *Beyond the Hype*, Boston: Harvard Business School Press. (A discussion of the role of rhetoric in management.)
* Grint, K. (1994) 'Reengineering history: social resonances and business process reengineering', *Organization* 1 (1): 179–201. (A critical analysis of re-engineering's novelty and popularity.)
* Hammer, M. (1990) 'Reengineering work: don't automate, obliterate', *Harvard Business Review* July/August: 104-112. (Widely-cited as the article which launched the reengineering bandwagon.)
* Jones, M.R. (1994) 'Don't emancipate, exaggerate: rhetoric, "reality" and re-engineering', in R. Baskerville; S. Smithson, and J. DeGross (eds) *Information Technology and New Emergent Forms of Organizations*. Amsterdam: North-Holland. (A critical review of the reengineering literature, with particular attention to the rhetoric employed.)
  Jones, M.R. (1996) 'Reengineering', in M. Warner (ed.) *International Encyclopedia of Business and Management*. London: International Thomson. (A critical review of the key aspects of reengineering.)

Strassman, P.A. (1994) 'The hocus-pocus of reengineering', *Across the Board* 31, 35-38. (An early critique of Hammer's ideas.)

* White, J.B. (1996) 'Reengineering gurus take steps to remodel their stalling vehicles', *Wall Street Journal* 26 November: A1. (A report of Hammer's acknowledgement of reengineering's neglect of people.)

See also: DRUCKER, P.; PETERS, T.J.; SMITH, A.

Related topics in the IEBM: DOWNSIZING; GROUPS AND TEAMS; INFORMATION REVOLUTION; LABOUR PROCESS; ORGANIZATIONAL LEARNING; ORGANIZATIONAL PERFORMANCE; REENGINEERING; TOTAL QUALITY MANAGEMENT; WORK SYSTEMS

Handy, Charles (1932–)

1 Introduction
2 Biographical data
3 Main contribution
4 Evaluation
5 Conclusion

Personal background

- born 1932 in Kildare, Ireland, the son of a clergyman
- worked for Shell International and Anglo-American
- founder and director of the Sloan Management Programme, London Business School, in 1967
- professor, 1972, and governor of London Business School, 1974
- warden of St. George's House, Windsor, 1977

Major works

Understanding Organizations (1976)
Gods of Management: The Changing Work of Organisations (1979)
The Future of Work (1984)
The Age of Unreason (1989)
Waiting for the Mountain to Move: And Other Reflections on Life (1991)
The Empty Raincoat (1994)
Beyond Certainty: The Changing World of Organizations (1996)

Summary

Charles Handy is a writer on organizations with a psychological and philosophical focus. He couples a call for a radical change in the way organizations exist and function with a deep concern for the welfare of the individuals caught up in these changing times. A management guru whose thought evinces considerable complexity, Handy tries to bring to management a spiritual and ethical dimension. He offers such concepts as the 'gods of management', archetypes drawn from the classical past of Europe which seek to serve as metaphors for organizational culture, and the 'shamrock organization', which describes the new decentralized or 'federal' organization of the future.

1 Introduction

Kennedy (1994: 7) calls Handy 'Britain's only world-class business guru, whose writings can be compared to those of Peter Drucker on economic and social change'. Handy originally made his mark with his text *Understanding Organizations* in 1976. Recent books such as *The Age of Unreason* and *The Empty Raincoat* have been best-sellers, and have turned the focus onto the individuals making up organizations. His writings are rich and at times complex. He draws on a variety of metaphors, illustrating his work with quotes from sources as varied as the Bible and Gilbert and Sullivan. He focuses on themes such as discontinuity and human dynamics, and sees the organization of the future as being smaller and more networked, with core teams handling essential functions and contracting out work to skilled employees. Like Drucker, he believes that all work will eventually come to depend on knowledge (see DRUCKER, P.F.). To replace the corporate ladder, which will die along with the structured corporation, Handy proposes the portfolio career, in which managers will seek to acquire a variety of skills and will move from different parts of the 'shamrock organization' to others, or to other organizations.

2 Biographical data

Born in the Republic of Ireland in 1932, the son of an archdeacon, Charles Handy was educated at Oriel College, Oxford, and the Sloan School of Management at the Massachusetts Institute of Technology. He was an executive with Shell International and an economist with the Anglo-American Corporation before joining London Business School in 1967. There he taught managerial psychology and development for a number of years, but his enduring legacy to the institution is the Sloan Management Programme, which he helped to found and directed for some years. He was made a full professor in 1972 and joined London Business School's board of governors in 1974. In 1977 he was appointed warden of St. George's House, Windsor, a private conference and study centre, and he has since been appointed chairman of the Royal Society for the Encouragement of Arts, Manufacture and Commerce. Since leaving London Business School (where he remained a visiting professor for some years), he has focused on writing and broadcasting. As well as managerial writing and consulting, Handy is a regular contributor to 'Thought for the Day', a religious-philosophical opinion programme broadcast by the BBC. He is married and lives in Norfolk.

3 Main contribution

In *Understanding Organizations*, the work which first brought him to public notice, Handy concludes that the study of people in organizations is not to do with predictive certainty. Organizations are highly complex, and learning about them can be slow and painful (Handy 1976: 219). There are simply too many variables – he identifies over sixty – which can affect what happens in organizations. He goes on to discuss these variables under six basic headings: motivation, roles and interactions, leadership, power and influence, the internal dynamics of groups, and organization cultures. In the course of this discussion he rehearses, summarizes and analyses a very wide variety of previous and current thought on these subjects and, in those areas closest to his own heart, adds his own interpretation.

His discussion of the motivation to work (Handy 1976: 29–59) centres around the concept of the 'motivation calculus': each individual, in the context of his or her needs and in the context of the likely result of any action,

calculates how much effort he or she will expend in order to achieve this result. However, this calculation is not made in isolation; each individual also operates in the context of one or more psychological contracts with organizations to which he or she belongs, which in turn can be of different types:

1 *coercive*, where the individual has no choice but to perform the actions on behalf of the organization
2 *calculative*, where the individual performs the actions on the basis of personal gain or reward
3 *cooperative*, where the individual identifies with the organization's goals and seeks to maximize the reward for both organization and self.

The above gives some idea of the richness and complexity of Handy's levels of analysis. He sees organizations primarily, if not solely, in terms of human dynamics. Motivation interacts with power and influence. It is important to recognize that complete individual freedom does not exist; all of us are bounded in some way, and the moment we accept membership of any organization, even society as a whole, we surrender parts of our freedom and accept the authority of others over us. In turn, we adopt various coping mechanisms for securing as much of our freedom as we can, and are subjected to stress when we are unable to do so.

Organizations in turn subdivide themselves into groups. Groups have many names and many functions, and organizations rely on them for a variety of purposes: to distribute, manage and control work, to solve problems and take decisions, to collect and process information and ideas, to coordinate activities within the organization, to increase commitment and involvement, and to negotiate and resolve conflicts. However, says Handy, it is equally important to recognize the purposes for which individuals use groups: as a means of satisfying social or affiliation needs, as a means of defining a concept of self, as means of acquiring support for their own personal objectives, and as a means for sharing or taking part in a common purpose.

The effectiveness of groups, then, depends on a variety of factors. Handy divides these into three classifications:

1 *givens*, including the size and composition of the group itself, the task it has been set and the environment within which it is working
2 *intervening factors*, which include the style of leadership of the group, the processes and procedures it uses to carry out its tasks, and the motivation of its members
3 *outcomes*, including both the productivity of the group and the satisfaction of its members.

All these factors and influence coalesce in Handy's concept of organization culture. To explain his framework, he creates organizational metaphors based on the culture of classical Greece. The Greeks, he says, believed in gods as personae of various human characteristics, and identified personally with those gods whom they believed most closely resembled themselves and satisfied their personal needs. The Greek gods were in fact social and personal archetypes; and it follows that if individuals can be affiliated with them, so can organizations. Handy here acknowledges the influence of Gareth Morgan, who describes the explanatory power of metaphor for understanding and analyzing organizations (see MORGAN, G.).

In *Understanding Organizations* and again in *Gods of Management*, Handy develops four types of organization, each of which can be associated with a particular Greek deity (see Figure 1).

The *power culture* (called the *club culture* in *Gods of Management*), is ruled by a single dominant individual. Power cultures are typically found where the organization is led by the founding entrepreneur. All power flows from one central source in the organization through a web-like network of influence and communication. Control is exercised on a personal level rather than through rules or procedures. These cultures, Handy says, 'are proud but strong'. They judge by results, not means, and are tolerant of individuals. They are often very flexible and able to react quickly,

The Culture	The Picture	The God
Club		Zeus
Role		Apollo
Task		Athena
Existential		Dionysus

Figure 1

particularly while they remain small. The problem, however, is that they depend very much on the nature of the dominant individual, who can be capricious. Thus Handy assigns this archetype to Zeus, the chief of the gods, who dispensed favours and thunderbolts from his seat high on Olympus seemingly on the basis of personal whim.

The *role culture*, by contrast, is hierarchical and bureaucratized. The organization tends to be divided up by functions into distinct finance, marketing, production and other departments. Handy likens these to the pillars supporting a Greek temple – ordered, stable, supporting the top of the organization but not mutually interdependent – and assigns this archetype to Apollo, the god of logic and reason. The strength of this organization rests on strong definitions of jobs and authority, on strictly defined and focused roles. Coordination of roles takes place by a narrow band of senior managers at the top of the organization.

The *task culture* is one where the primary orientation is on the job or project. Handy represents this a net, though he says that some strands of the net are likely to be stronger and thicker than others. This is a flexible and highly adaptive culture; within the organization, groups and teams can be formed and

275

reformed as and when they are needed to meet specific challenges or overcome particular problems. The major difficulty in this culture is control; there is no centre to the network, and therefore it is difficult to find people taking responsibility for issues such as resource allocation. Handy notes that this is the current fashionable model but cautions against too-ready acceptance of it:

> It is the culture most in tune with current ideologies of change and adaptation, individual freedom and low status differentials. But ... it is not always the appropriate culture for the climate and technology. If organizations do not all embrace this culture, it may be that they are not just out-of-date and old-fashioned – but right.
>
> (Handy 1976: 189)

Somewhat curiously, Handy assigns this archetype to the goddess Athena in her role as war leader, though in fact her persona as goddess of craftsmen and weavers might be more appropriate.

Finally, there is the *person culture*, which 'exists only to serve and assist the individuals within it' (Handy 1976: 189). Handy describes this as a cluster, and uses a scatter diagram to represent it. These are organizations drawn together solely on the basis of mutual self-interest, and Handy acknowledges that not many organizations fit this model; examples of those that do include barristers' chambers and hippie communes. He assigns this archetype to the self-interested god Dionysos, who some might say is a singularly appropriate patron for both the examples given.

Handy does not assert the primacy of one archetype over the others. Just as the Greeks worshipped many gods, so there is room for many cultures in the organizational pantheon. Handy's ideal-type organization would have room for all these cultures within it, reflecting the diverse nature of the groups and individuals involved. His solution to the problem of controlling this diversity is decentralization, which he characterizes in *Gods of Management* as 'federalism' or 'organizational villages'. Small organizational sub-units working relatively free from central interference would be free to develop the cultures that best suited their own group and individual needs.

In *The Age of Unreason*, Handy reinvents the 'organizational village' as the 'shamrock organization'. This is essentially a tripartite structure. The first part is composed of core workers – qualified professionals, managers and technicians – whose work is essential to the organization. They are the prime repositories of organizational knowledge, and it is they who serve to distinguish the organization and give it its character and direction. The workers in the core are well paid with large salaries and benefits, for which they are expected to work long hours and give commitment.

The second part is composed of the non-essential work which needs doing, but which is contracted out rather than being done in the company. Contracting out to specialists means that work can be done, in theory at least, better and more cheaply. The third part is the flexible labour force, a band of part-time and temporary workers whom the organization uses to fill in gaps between the other two parts when required. Here, Handy says, the organization must be careful and resist the temptation to try to pay the least possible wage and squeeze the most possible output from the part-time and temporary labour. These workers, with no security and little loyalty, are unlikely to respond to this kind of pressure. Good wages must be paid in order to ensure good quality output.

The problem of managing these different cultures and, in particular, adjusting to different management styles as one moves around the organization, is one which Handy addresses here at some length. His major concern is for managerial adaptability and flexibility: not just to enhance organizational and group effectiveness, but for the sake of the managers themselves, who are being placed under increasingly high levels of stress. Forced to manage conflicts between different cultures over time, often without clear objectives, managers are caught between the need to generate trust and exercise control. In *Gods of Management*, Handy is optimistic about our ability solve these problems and create new organizational forms, but he acknowledges there are major problems. He asks several key questions. If traditional patterns of organization break down, how will people continue to earn a living? How will they be educated? And most important of all, how will they acquire personal security in an increasingly insecure age?

These conflicts are not easily resolvable, and it is to these that Handy returns in his later works, most notably *The Age of Unreason* and *The Empty Raincoat*. In the latter, he advises us to accept the inevitability of change and flux; paradox is here to stay. His advice is to pick out those thing which are constant: continuity, who we are and where we are coming from; connectedness, our relationships with others and the world around us; and most difficult of all, direction, a cause to work for in an age of seeming randomness. Ultimately, Handy believes, the ethical and spiritual dimensions of who we are will give us our guidance.

4 Evaluation

Carol Kennedy's (1994) comparison of Handy with Peter Drucker is a valid one (see DRUCKER, P.F.). Both write of the onset of change and flux, and urge organizations to become more responsive; both stress the human dynamic of organizations, treating management more as a philosophy than a science. Both, influenced by European humanist ideals, discuss the necessity of personal development and fulfilment within organizations, though Handy takes this rather further than Drucker.

The comparison with Drucker also works on another level. Both seek ultimately to be inspirational, to give people confidence in facing the future. In terms of the practical problems involved in confronting the future, however, their guidance is limited. Handy is, ultimately, an optimist, and he believes most people will ultimately come to terms with flux, paradox and insecurity. What will happen if they do not, he does not say. This is not to deny his genuine concern for the problems these trends raise; unlike contemporaries such as Tom Peters, who see the new business age solely as a frontier full of excitement, Handy is aware of the social and spiritual costs of change (see PETERS, T.J.). His major premise, expressed very clearly in his latest book, *The Hungry Spirit*, is that human beings have the innate ability and desire to make the world a better place, and that they will use a combination of reason and faith to do so. *The Hungry Spirit* is an important book in that it squarely confronts the empty space that exists between economic values and moral values in Western society; but while the reader is left in no doubt about the nature of the problem, the solution seems as elusive as ever.

Perhaps the most important lesson to be drawn from Handy is the need to see organizations and economies as, first and foremost, interactions of human beings. His delving into the European historical past to find archetypes which can describe our ways of thinking about organization is a theme which ought to be pursued still further, and the intimation that European culture still has something to offer to the study of business ought likewise to be investigated. By treating organizations as mental constructs rather than physical facts, he has opened the door to a better understanding of how we can learn about organizations and, ultimately, shape them to our needs. Perhaps by doing so, we will get closer to solving the larger societal problems to which Handy's own attention is increasingly turning.

5 Conclusion

Handy writes about the future of organizations and work in a time of conflict, change and flux. Of all the leading management gurus, his is the work which is most human-centred and least 'scientific'. He provides a valuable palliative to both the formal rationalism still inherent in much of the business world, and the drive towards change at any cost evident in the writings of some of his colleagues. Handy's search is a search for a world in which change and flux are normal and accepted. He believes that continuity and paradox can be reconciled, and harmony can ultimately be achieved, in organizations, economies and societies alike.

MORGEN WITZEL
LONDON BUSINESS SCHOOL
DURHAM UNIVERSITY BUSINESS SCHOOL

Further reading

(References cited in the text are marked *)

* Handy, C. (1976) *Understanding Organizations*, London: Penguin.
* Handy, C. (1979) *Gods of Management: The Changing Work of Organisations*, London: Arrow.
* Handy, C. (1984) *The Future of Work*, Oxford: Blackwell. (Introduces some of the themes concerning the changing nature of work that would appear in his later books.)
  Handy, C., Gordon, C., Gow, I. and Randlesome, C. (1988) *Making Managers*, London: Pitman. (On the nature of the managerial task and on how managers are 'created'.)
* Handy, C. (1989) *The Age of Unreason*, London: Business Books. (The work which first brought Handy to prominence as a management thinker and philosopher.)
* Handy, C. (1991) *Waiting for the Mountain to Move: And Other Reflections on Life*, London: Hutchinson. (Philosophical reflections.)
* Handy, C. (1994b) *The Empty Raincoat: Making Sense of the Future*, London: Hutchinson. (Handy's most philosophical work, exploring the social, ethical and even spiritual dimensions of organization and work; published in the USA under the title *The Age of Paradox*.)
* Handy, C. (1995a) *The Changing World of Organizations*, London: Arrow. (Collection of essays on the changing nature of the world and the future of organizations and work.)
* Handy, C. (1997) *The Hungry Spirit*, London: Random House. (Handy's most philosophical and ethical works, in which he explores the limits of capitalism and argues for a new order of business and social values.)
* Kennedy, C. (1994) *Managing With the Gurus*, London: Century. (One of the few surveys of management gurus to discuss Handy in any detail.)

See also: DRUCKER, P.F.; MORGAN, G.; PETERS, T.J.

Related topics in the IEBM: BUSINESS ETHICS; DOWNSIZING; FUTUROLOGY; GENERAL MANAGEMENT; GLOBALIZATION; GLOBALIZATION AND SOCIETY; HUMAN RESOURCE MANAGEMENT; ORGANIZATION BEHAVIOUR; ORGANIZATION BEHAVIOUR, HISTORY OF; ORGANIZATION DEVELOPMENT; ORGANIZATIONAL STRUCTURE; ORGANIZING, PROCESS OF; WORK ETHIC; WORK AND LEISURE

Hannan, Michael (1943–) and Freeman, John (1945–)

Personal background

Michael Hannan

- born 14 July 1943
- BA in sociology, College of the Holy Cross, 1965
- MA in sociology, University of North Carolina, Chapel Hill, 1968
- PhD in sociology, University of North Carolina, Chapel Hill, 1970
- currently professor of organizational behavior and human resources, Graduate School of Business, Stanford University at Stanford, 1969–84, 1991–

John Freeman

- born 1945
- received Max Weber Award from American Sociological Association in 1992 for the book *Organizational Ecology* with Michael Hannan
- currently Leo B. and Florence Hetzel Professor of Entrepreneurship and Innovation at Haas School of Business, University of California at Berkeley

Major works

'The population ecology of organizations' in *American Journal of Sociology* (1977)
Organizational Ecology (1989)

Summary

Michael Hannan and John Freeman entered the hall of fame of organization sciences in 1977 with their thought provoking article 'The population ecology of organizations' in the *American Journal of Sociology*. Population ecology, or organizational ecology (OE), is a sociological theory of what happens to and within populations of organizations with the aim to give an answer to the simple but fundamental question: why are there so many different kinds of organizations? The key elements of the theory involve Darwinian selection, organizational inertia, density-dependent founding and mortality rates, and niche-width strategies. OE has produced an impressive and still rapidly increasing number of empirical studies. There is no doubt that the empirical tradition that has been established by OE is an important enrichment of organization sciences, notwithstanding the critique that has been raised against the theory's assumptions. In recent years, a cry for increased theoretical precision has emerged, particularly through enriching the theory's selection argument. OE clearly is a vital and still progressing subbranch of the organizational sciences.

1 Organizational ecology

The world of organizations is characterized by a tremendous variety in organizational forms: large companies coexist with numerous small ones; some have a bureaucratic structure whereas others are 'lean and mean'; and although many companies are diversified, their competitors might be highly specialized. Where does this diversity come from and how does it evolve over time? Which organizational forms proliferate? Why and how do certain organizational forms disappear? These questions are at the core of what is called organization science or theory. Michael Hannan and John Freeman entered the hall of fame of organization sciences in

1977 with their thought-provoking article 'The population ecology of organizations' in the *American Journal of Sociology*, which comprehensively deals with the questions posed above. Population ecology, or organizational ecology (OE), is a sociological theory of what happens to and within populations of organizations. The publication of Michael Hannan's and John Freeman's *Organizational Ecology* in 1989 marked a transition from adolescence to maturity in the development of a then twelve-year old population of organization studies. More than any other organization theory, OE focuses on the dynamics in and of the world of organizations. As said, the aim of understanding changes in organizational forms is to give an answer to the simple but fundamental question: why are there so many different kinds of organizations? (Hannan and Freeman 1977).

OE was and is a frame-breaking perspective as its assumptions deviate from more traditional theoretical accounts of the functioning of organizations. To get a first grasp of the theory it is therefore essential to introduce the key building blocks of Hannan and Freeman's OE, and to contrast it with other organizational theories. In addition, we will briefly take stock of the theory's achievements. Subsequently, we will introduce the concepts of selection (versus adaptation), relative inertia (versus flexibility), competition and legitimation, density dependence and niche width which are so central to OE. This contribution focuses on theoretical issues in particular. For extensive reviews of OE and its offsprings, including the empirical studies, we refer to Baum (1996), Hannan and Carroll (1992) and Hannan and Freeman (1989). In advance, a remark as to OE's nature is needed. OE is a truly *academic* theory, in which virtually no attention at all is paid to possible applications in the real world of firm managers or policy makers. So, in this contribution we respect OE's nature by ignoring the issue of practical applicability.

Selection (versus adaptation)

Basically, organizational change can come about in two ways: Darwinian selection and Lamarckian adaptation. Darwinian selection implies that change results from the replacement of incumbent organizations, which do not fit with the requirements of the environment and are thus selected out, by new organizational forms. OE, which is inspired by careful analogies from biological population theories, stresses the importance of selection to understand the dynamics of organizations. This contrasts sharply with the more traditional Lamarckian view, arguing that change is the result of adaptation processes at the individual level of organizations. That is, organizations continuously adapt their strategies and structures to the requirements of the environment. The emphasis of OE on selection processes has two implications for the theory. First, what differentiates OE from its companions in the field of organization studies, is the focus on the *population* or industry as the prime level of analysis. It is not so much the (behaviour in and of) individual organization that matters, but rather the interaction among groups of (adjacent) organizational forms. Indeed, many developments in the world of organizations cannot be explained by looking at the strategy of individual firms only. For instance, 2,300 firms operated in the Swiss watch industry in the 1950s. In 1984, only 632 firms still remained in business (Carroll and Hannan 1995). Similarly, the postwar Dutch newspaper industry witnessed a large decrease in the number of daily newspapers, with the entry rate virtually dropping to zero all together. Clearly, it is too simplistic to refer to managerial incompetence and bad strategy to account for this dramatic shift. Second, as OE assumes that change is the result of replacement, the dynamics of populations can be understood by analyzing the vital rates of populations: that is, founding (birth or entry) and mortality (death or exit). The interest is not so much in explaining the vital rates *per se*, but rather in tracing aggregate rates at the population level and understanding the implications of mortality and founding processes for the dynamics of the distribution of organizational characteristics (i.e. diversity) over time.

Relative inertia (versus flexibility)

Darwinian selection will only work if, and only if, the target of selection – i.e. organizations – is sufficiently inert. Otherwise timely adaptation of organizations would change the selection target before the Darwinian processes have materialized. As mentioned above, the central tenet in mainstream organization theory is that incumbent firms are and should be flexible enough to continuously change their strategies and structures. Broadly speaking, two important assumptions are (implicitly) made by adherents of the adaptation (or strategic choice) model of organizational change: (1) organizations are able to implement transformations with success; (2) flexibility increases profitability and ultimately survival chances. This typical twin of assumptions is clear from standard text books in strategic management. The validity of both strategic choice assumptions, however, is questioned by OE. Here, Hannan and Freeman's classic article 'Structural inertia and organizational change' in the 1984 issue of the *American Sociological Review* has set the tone.

The first assumption is not realistic according to OE, as organizations are hard pressed to adjust their 'blueprint' (Hannan and Freeman 1977). They feature relative inertia: that is, they lag behind changes in the environment (Hannan and Freeman 1984). This is not to say that organizations never change, but rather that adjustments are rare and appear only after significant delays. So, organizations tend to be inert relative to environmental turbulence. Additionally, OE suggests that organizational change, if possible at all, does increase the failure rate. The reason is that the impact of changing the core features of an organization is equivalent to creating a new organization. Indeed, a number of scholars observed that failure rates increased after organizations implemented major structural changes (Amburgey, Kelley and Barnett 1993). For example, Finnish newspapers that introduced radical changes in their product's political profile or circulation frequency in the 1771–1963 period, were characterized by higher failure rates than their 'conservative'

counterparts (Amburgey, Kelly and Barnett 1993). The bottom line is that 'as the large number of regularly occurring organizational failures indicates, adaptation models are limited in their abilities to explain organizational change' (Carroll and Harrison 1993: 93).

OE opposes the simplistic second assumption that flexibility is the only key to efficiency and (thus) to organizational survival. As already mentioned, relative inertia (i.e. the opposite of flexibility) is a central concept in the Darwinian selection theory of OE. OE posits that inertia is not only a precondition for Darwinian selection, but – even more important – also a *consequence* (Hannan and Freeman 1984). In other words, selection favours organizational forms characterized by relatively inert structures. The underlying logic runs as follows (Hannan and Freeman 1984). First, organizations have to be *reliable*: organizations can only be reliable suppliers of goods and services if they operate on the basis of routines that guide their functioning. Second, organizations have to be *accountable* for their activities and performance. Accountability also requires stable rules and procedures. Third, organizational reliability and accountability can only be guaranteed if organizational structures are highly *reproducible*. The routines, rules and procedures determining reliability and accountability must stay in place over time. Selection pressures will work in this direction: hence, rigid and viable blueprints are selected (Boeker 1988). The effects of reliability, accountability and reproducibility cumulate into the argument that 'the modern world favors collective actors that can demonstrate or at least reasonably claim a capacity for reliable performance and can account rationally for their actions. So it favors organizations over other kinds of collectives and favors certain kinds of organizations over others, since not all organizations have these properties in equal measure. Selection within organizational populations tends to eliminate organizations with low reliability and accountability … Thus we assume that selection in populations of organizations in modern societies favors forms with high reliability of performance and high levels of accountability' (Hannan and Freeman 1989: 74). For instance, a *conditio sine qua non* for the viability of a newspaper are a reproducible layout and reliable circulation.

Competition and legitimation

OE's focus on selection goes together with its emphasis on the analysis of the population-level founding and mortality rates. These vital rates determine the growth trajectories of populations. Until now, most theoretical and empirical work has focused on explaining the striking similarity of the growth trajectories of very (if not radically) different organizational populations, varying from banks and breweries to labour unions and voluntary social service organizations. The number of organizations in a population typically grows slowly initially, and then increases rapidly to a peak. Once the peak is reached, there is usually a sharp decline and occasionally stabilization (Carroll and Hannan 1989). (The development of) the number of organizations within a population depends on various factors according to OE. First of all, the *niche* in which the population resides, is crucial. A niche expresses the population's role and function in a community. For example, the newspaper industry's role in Western societies is to inform the reader audience about whatever the journalist profession considers of interest. An important feature of a niche is its *carrying capacity* (that is, its maximum size). Social and material restrictions limit the extent to which particular roles and functions are needed. For example, the aggregate circulation size of newspapers is limited by the number of potential readers. The carrying capacity of a niche only represents an upper bound on aggregate activity performed by a particular organizational form. Exogenous factors determine the carrying capacity of populations. For instance, the carrying capacity of the newspaper industry in many developing countries is severely limited by bad economic conditions and malfunctioning educational systems.

The striking similarity of growth trajectories of populations, however, suggests that there is an intrinsic dynamic of contraction and expansion (Carroll 1984). This growth pattern can be explained by two forces: *competition* and *legitimation*. Competition within a population or among populations occurs if resources within the niche are scarce. Legitimation refers to the social acceptance of the organizational form, new forms having low legitimacy. As they perform reliably and accountably over time, they may acquire higher legitimacy. Shifts in the relative importance of competition and legitimation induce dynamics in the constellation of a population: the number of organizations in a population changes over time. OE assumes that both competition and legitimation increases with the aging of the organizational form. On the one hand, a new form has to acquire legitimacy over time. Hence, the expectation is that the founding rates increase with age. On the other hand, as more organizations come to inhabit the niche, competition within the population will increase. So, competition is expected to be negatively associated with founding rates. Analoguous reasoning predicts that the mortality rate is high at first (liability of newness and insufficient legitimacy), then falls with increasing legitimation up to a point (in the neighbourhood of the carrying capacity) and then rises due to intensified competition.

Density dependence

OE's theory of selection focuses on the influence of the mere number of organizations on entry and exit events. In the language of OE: competition and legitimation cause nonmonotonic density dependence in the vital rates. That is, the relationship between density and the founding rate has the form of an inverted U. The relationship, however, between density and the mortality rate has a U-shape (Hannan and Carroll 1992). The combined result of both density-dependent forces of competition and legitimation over time is a logistic curve of the development of a population's density over its entire history. The appropriate time frame is population specific, and may run over a number of centuries. The nonmonotonic density dependence in vital rates has been confirmed by a still increasing number of empirical studies in a diversity of populations, for example, breweries, labour unions, newspapers, semiconductor producers, life insurance companies and banks (Carroll 1988; Hannan and Carroll 1992). The density-dependence patterns have also been reported for the newspaper industries in Argentina, Ireland and the San Francisco Bay Area (Hannan and Carroll 1992).

To explain the apparent drop in the density of populations after reaching a peak, OE introduces another mechanism: density delay. That is, density at the time of founding has a persistent positive effect on mortality rates (Carroll and Hannan 1989). Density delay causes mortality rates to be particularly high after a population has reached its peak: therefore, the number of organizations then starts to drop. Empirical research indeed shows that building a new organization in tightly-packed niches results in the so-called 'liability of resource scarcity'. For instance, a new newspaper will face higher failure chances now and in the future if its market niche at the date of entry is already occupied by a large number of established competitors because the potential to distract readers from the incumbents is anything but high. Contemporaneous density and density at founding are not the only independent variables used by OE to explain the vital rates. Other variables that are normally incorporated into the empirical models are exogenous factors reflecting economic conditions, institutional changes, political turmoils, organization size (liability of smallness), organization age (liability of newness), et cetera. The effects of density remain significant after controlling for those covariates. Furthermore, the mortality rates are higher for smaller and younger as opposed to larger and older organizations, as expected.

The niche width argument

In 1983, Freeman and Hannan supplemented OE with what became known as 'niche width theory' in their article 'Niche width and the dynamics of organizational populations' in the *American Journal of Sociology*. Carroll (1985), following Freeman and Hannan (1983), distinguishes two ideal-typical types of organizational strategy profiles: generalists and specialists. Generalists focus on the centre of the market, making an appeal to a wide spectrum of resources in their environment so as to survive. Conversely, specialists attempt to survive in specific niches within the market, exploiting a limited set of environmental resources. In the newspaper industry, for example, national newspapers operate as generalists whilst regional newspapers are positioned as specialists. Processes of resource partitioning generate a dual market structure in those industries that are characterized by scale economies. Whenever scale economies are important (e.g. in order to realize wide circulation), firms will be inclined to focus on the centre of the market (e.g. the average newspaper reader). This process produces a concentration of generalists in the centre of the market, which creates opportunities for specialists to supply those segments of the market that generalists, by necessity, cannot deliver what they want (e.g. the non-average newspaper reader). Carroll (1985, 1987) indeed concludes that in the US newspaper industry a rise in the degree of concentration (i.e., the cumulated market share of the top four newspapers) was associated with an increased failure rate of national newspapers (generalists) *and* a decreased failure rate of regional newspapers (specialists).

The theory embraces the fundamental 'universal law' as to the evolution of competitive processes in the social world in general. Competition may well produce heterogeneity rather than homogeneity within industries. In Western newspaper industries, for instance, competition for attractive market niches has produced considerable heterogeneity in terms of reader profiles and circulation areas. Firms can at any moment be confronted with the fundamental dilemma that is central to niche width theory: a firm either opts for a growth strategy of fighting for the center of the market or prefers to avoid tough competition by moving into the market's periphery. Both options may be associated with above-normal profitability and higher survival rates, though for different reasons. Clearly, the nature of the resources that permit firms to grow large, depends upon the underlying features of the industry in question. In the newspaper industry, for example, growth-enhancing resources may derive from investments in productive capacity.

2 A key critique

OE has been heavily pushed by its proponents as a new and innovative paradigm. No wonder that it induced a recurrent response by opponents. By way of illustration, we summarize an ongoing key debate as to OE's fundamentals. This debate pertains to OE's fundamental claim that relative inertia is the rule rather than the exception in organizational life. OE has frequently been criticized by strategic management scholars for being overly deterministic and neglecting the free will of managers (Bourgeois 1994). However, Hannan and Freeman (1989) argue that determinism is not at all the opposite of voluntarism. Indeed, it is not because OE assumes that natural selection causes diversity in organizational forms that managers do not make choices, change strategies and even try to adapt their organizations to changing environmental conditions. As Hannan and Freeman (1989: 22) put it, 'even when actors strive to cope with their environments, action may be random with respect to adaptation as long as the environments are highly uncertain or the connections between means and ends are not well understood. It is the *match* between action and environmental outcomes that must be random on the average for selection models to apply'. So, OE is only 'deterministic' in the sense that long-run organizational survival is mainly determined by environmental conditions. This implies that OE questions the 'great man' theories of organizational history.

A more fundamental issue is therefore which assumption is more valid: relative inertia (OE), which is a prerequisite for Darwinian selection to occur, or relative flexibility (strategic management), reflecting the Lamarckian view. The OE-assumption of relative inertia has not, as yet, been seriously verified. However, this is also the case for relative flexibility, which has been taken for granted by many strategic management scholars, assuming that managers scan the environment, being able to continuously fine-tune the strategy and structure of their organizations in accordance with environmental changes. The latter implies that organizational diversity is mainly the consequence of organizational change. Although the views of both 'camps' differ substantially at first glance, considerable overlap can be observed when looking at the behavioural theory of strategic decision-making processes.

In our view, however, a frequently neglected possibility is that inertia and flexibility are not necessarily the opposites on a continuum. In an insightful paper, Burgelman (1991) argues that organizations can consistently remain successful by a carefully balanced strategy-making approach consisting of inertia *and* flexibility (cf. Van Witteloostuijn 1998). Burgelman uses an intra-organizational ecological perspective on strategy making. He distinguishes two kinds of strategic processes: induced and autonomous. Induced strategic initiatives fit within the current strategy, routines and goals of the organization and are compatible with the current distinctive competence. The internal selection of such initiatives by top managers reflects current external selection pressures. This process, however, only allows an organization to adapt to incremental environmental change and is therefore tantamount to relative inertia. Burgelman argues that induced processes are necessary to build on past success and to exploit the opportunities associated with the current domain. To achieve long-run survival, however, induced processes should be balanced with autonomous strategic processes. The latter refer to the internal selection of strategic initiatives outside the scope of the current strategy. An important task of top management is to nurture such operational-level strategic initiatives. Autonomous processes, when funded and supported by top management, allow continuous strategic renewal and offer organizations possibilities for anticipatory adaptation. The point is that long-run survival of firms is enhanced by 'balancing of variation-reduction and variation-increasing mechanisms. It suggests that one process leads to relative inertia and incremental adjustments, while the other expands the firm's domain and renews the organization's distinctive competence base, countering inertia and serving some of the functions of reorientation' (Burgelman 1991: 257). For example, a national newspaper may experiment away from its inert core by introducing changes in local chain papers. If successful, local experiments may be transferred to the national level.

3 Beyond organizational ecology

OE has produced an impressive and still rapidly increasing number of empirical studies (Baum 1996). For example, the number of studies that have tested density-dependence hypotheses reaches infinity. No doubt, the empirical tradition that has been established by OE is an important enrichment of organization sciences, notwithstanding the critique that has been raised against the theory's assumptions. In recent years, a cry for increased theoretical precision has emerged, however. For example, Baum (1996: 107–108) concludes his impressive review of OE with a plea for such precision with reference to the need for 'asking new kinds of research questions that develop links with other streams in organization theory'. We believe that the organizational subdisciplines within economics, particularly industrial organization, are specifically promising in this respect (Boone and Van Witteloostuijn 1995).

Hannan and Freeman started an ambitious and impressive research programme in 1977 with the purpose to find answers to fundamental questions such as 'why are there so many different kinds of organizations?' (Hannan and Freeman 1977) and 'what are the dynamics of modern economies, states, and societies?' (Hannan and Carroll 1992). As a start, the research strategy of mainstream OE has logically been one of searching for 'general laws'. For instance, concerning density dependence and its resources, Hannan and Carroll (1992: 18) argue that 'our primary argument – is intended to apply to all kinds of organizational populations. That is, the theory applies to populations of all types, in any time period, and in any society'. The same stance can be witnessed for other aspects of the theory such as the 'liability of smallness' and 'liability of newness' hypotheses. This search for generality implies that very little attention has been given to *differences between* and *within* populations or industries. This observation relates, of course, to the criticism raised in the strategic management literature discussed above. In our view, OE can therefore be classified as a general theory of *similarities*. We would like to stress that there is nothing wrong with such a research strategy. Moreover, despite some inconsistent findings mentioned above, the research findings of OE are impressive indeed. However, OE only represents one side of the coin. We agree with Carroll (1984: 90) that 'the future development of organizational theory depends not on the dominance of one perspective, but on the welding of the most important insights from various perspectives'. It is in this respect that we think that both industrial organization and the economically-inspired subfield of strategic management (e.g. game theory and competitor analysis, respectively) are important candidates for cross-fertilization.

ARJEN VAN WITTELOOSTUIJN AND
CHRISTOPHE BOONE
UNIVERSITY MAASTRICHT

Further reading

(References cited in the text are marked *)

* Amburgey, T.L., Kelly, D. and Barnett, W.P. (1993) 'Resetting the clock: the dynamics of organizational change and failure', *Administrative Science Quarterly* 38: 51–73. (This paper deals with the liability of newness argument, indicating which organizational changes increase mortality rates under what circumstances.)

Barnett, W.P. and Amburgey, T.L. (1990) 'Do larger organizations generate stronger competition?', in J.V. Singh (ed.) *Organizational Evolution: New Directions*, Newbury Park, CA: Sage, 78–102. (This chapter reports the results of an empirical OE study that deviate from the orthodox density-dependence hypotheses.)

* Baum, J.A.C. (1996), 'Organizational ecology', in S.R. Clegg, C. Hardy and W.R. Nord (eds) *Handbook of Organization Studies*, London: Sage, 77–114. (This chapter is an in-depth re-

view of the OE literature with an emphasis on the robustness of the empirical findings.)

* Boeker, W.P. (1988) 'Organizational origins: entrepreneurial and environmental imprinting at the time of founding', in G.R. Carroll (ed.) *Ecological Models of Organizations*, Cambridge, MA: Ballinger, 33–52. (This paper explains why organizational relative inertia may be the outcome of selection processes.)

* Boone, C. and Witteloostuijn, A. van (1995) 'Industrial organization and organizational ecology: the potentials for cross-fertilization', *Organization Studies* 16: 265–298. (This paper is an in-depth plea for cross-fertilizing OE and industrial organization, which is the economic theory of competition.)

* Bourgeois, L.J. III (1984) 'Strategic management and determinism', *Academy of Management Review* 9: 586–596. (This paper is a review of the literature on organizational change with a focus on the determinism versus voluntarism dilemma.)

* Burgelman, R.A. (1991) 'Intraorganizational ecology of strategy making and organizational adaptation: theory and field research', *Organization Science* 2: 239–262. (This paper applies OE reasoning to the internal processes of organizations, so developing an OE-inspired theory of organizational learning.)

* Carroll, G.R. (1984) 'Organizational ecology', *Annual Review of Sociology* 10: 71–93. (This paper reviews the contribution of organizational ecology, and points to avenues for future research.)

* Carroll, G.R. (1985) 'Concentration and specialization: dynamics of niche width in populations of organizations', *American Journal of Sociology* 90: 1262–1283. (This paper is an empirical test of the niche width and resource-partitioning theories.)

* Carroll, G.R. (1987) *Publish and Perish: the Organizational Ecology of Newspaper Industries*, Greenwich, CT: JAI Press. (This book reports the results of in-depth empirical studies into newspaper industries with a focus on testing niche width and resource-partitioning hypotheses.)

* Carroll, G.R. (ed.) (1988) *Ecological Models of Organizations*, Cambridge, MA: Ballinger. (This book includes a number of papers that reflect the potential of the OE framework in studying selection processes.)

* Carroll, G.R. and Hannan, M.T. (1989) 'Density delay in the evolution of organizational populations: a model and five empirical tests', *Administrative Science Quarterly* 34: 411–430. (This paper reports the results of five empirical studies into the density-delay hypothesis.)

* Carroll, G.R. and Harrison, J.R. (1993) 'Evolution among competing organizational forms', *World Futures* 37: 91–110. (This paper describes the results of a simulation experiment that derives macro processes in organizational populations from micro events at the organizational level.)

* Carroll, G.R. and Hannan, M.T. (eds)(1995) *Organizations in Industry: Strategy, Structure and Selection*, New York: Oxford University Press. (This book explores the applicability of OE to real-world issues of organizational strategy, structure and selection.)

* Freeman, J. and Hannan, M.T. (1983) 'Niche width and the dynamics of organizational populations', *American Journal of Sociology* 88: 1116–1145. (This paper introduces OE's niche width theory, including the generalism–specialism typology.)

* Hannan, M.T. and Carroll, G.R. (1992) *Dynamics of Organizational Populations: Density, Legitimation and Competition*, New York: Oxford University Press. (This book is an in-depth treatment of OE's density-dependence arguments, including an overview of the empirical results.)

* Hannan, M.T. and Freeman J. (1977) 'The population ecology of organizations', *American Journal of Sociology* 82: 929–964. (This paper introduces the fundamentals of OE by exploring the deterministic perspective of Darwinian selection processes in organizational populations.)

* Hannan, M.T. and Freeman J. (1984) 'Structural inertia and organizational change', *American Sociological Review* 49: 149–164. (This paper explores the theoretical underpinning of OE's central assumption of relative inertia.)

* Hannan, M.T. and Freeman J. (1989), *Organizational Ecology*, Cambridge, MA: Harvard University Press. (This book takes stock of the achievements of the then twelve-year-old OE tradition, and introduces the theory's essentials.)

* Witteloostuijn, A. van (1998) 'Bridging behavioral and economic theories of decline: organizational inertia, strategic competition and chronic failure', *Management Science*, 44: forthcoming. (This paper explores the impact of relative inertia on firm performance in a game-theoretic model, including preliminary evidence from the chemical industry.)

See also: COASE, R.; DIMAGGIO, P. AND POW-
ELL, W.W.; LAWRENCE, P.R. AND LORSCH,
J.W.; MARSHALL, A.; MINTZBERG, H.; PE-
TERS, T.J.; PORTER, M.E.

Related topics in the IEBM: BUSINESS ECO-
NOMICS; CONTEXTS AND ENVIRONMENTS;
ORGANIZATION BEHAVIOUR; ORGANIZA-
TION BEHAVIOUR, HISTORY OF; ORGANIZA-
TIONAL DECLINE AND FAILURE; ORGANIZA-
TION PARADIGMS; ORGANIZATIONAL
PERFORMANCE; ORGANIZATION STRUC-
TURE; ORGANIZATIONAL POPULATIONS;
TRADE UNIONS

Hayek, Friedrich August von (1899–1992)

Personal background

- born 8 May 1899, Vienna, Austria
- served in the Austro-Hungarian army on the Italian front, 1917–18
- studied law and economics at the University of Vienna, 1918–23
- developed his theory of the business cycle and capital theory between 1928 and 1941
- became a British citizen, 1938
- developed his methodology of the social sciences and his evolutionary theory of social institutions from the 1940s
- founded the Mont Pèlerin Society, 1947
- was awarded the Nobel Prize for Economics, 1974
- made a Companion of Honour by Queen Elizabeth II in 1984 'for his services to the study of economics'
- died Freiburg, Germany, 23 March 1992

Major works

Prices and Production (1931)
Profits, Interest, and Investment (1939)
The Pure Theory of Capital (1941)
The Road to Serfdom (1944)
The Sensory Order (1952)
The Counter-Revolution of Science (1955)
The Constitution of Liberty (1960)
Law, Legislation and Liberty (1973, 1976, 1979)

Summary

F.A. von Hayek's business cycle theory was the main rival of J.M. Keynes' theory during the 1930s. He made major contributions to capital theory, monetary theory, the study of the feasibility of socialism, the methodology of social science, cognitive psychology, the evolutionary theory of social institutions, social and legal philosophy, intellectual history, and political theory. In all of these fields, the central unifying themes in Hayek's thought are spontaneous evolution, coordination, and the limitations of human knowledge.

1 Introduction

Hayek was a major contributor to the great economic debates of the 1930s. During this period, the London School of Economics (LSE) became the centre of organized opposition to the ideas of John Maynard Keynes (see KEYNES, J.M.). Hayek, who held a chair at the LSE, was Keynes' major opponent in the controversy about the causes and remedies of economic crises. In the debate on the foundations of capital theory, Hayek criticized the ideas of Frank Knight. He was also a major critic of Oskar Lange, F.M. Taylor and H.D. Dickinson, who defended the economic feasibility of a socialist centrally planned system. The debates of the 1930s continue to influence economics in the 1990s.

From the early 1920s to the 1980s, Hayek wrote repeatedly on the reorganization of the international monetary system as a means of fighting inflation and furthering monetary stability. After his defeat against Keynes, he generalized his economic theory into a comprehensive theory of social institutions. The generalized theory is based on the recognition that most institutions are spontaneously evolved, unintended consequences of individual human decisions.

2 Biographical data

Hayek was born on 8 May 1899 in Vienna, Austria. In 1917 he was drafted into the Austro–Hungarian army and served at the Italian front. After demobilization, he studied law, and later economics, at the University of

Vienna. During this period he came under the intellectual influence of Friedrich von Wieser and Ludwig von Mises. He received a doctorate in law in 1921 and economics in 1923. He spent the next year and a half in the USA where he studied the latest developments in business cycle research. In 1926 he married Helene von Frisch and the following year he was made the first director (and the sole employee) of the Austrian Institute for Business Cycle Research, founded by Mises in 1927.

In 1929, Hayek obtained his *Habilitation* (licence to teach at the university) and his *Habilitationsschrift* was published that same year under the title *Geldtheorie und Konjunkturtheorie* (published as *Monetary Theory and the Trade Cycle* in 1933). From this time until 1931 he was *Privatdozent* in political economy at the University of Vienna. At this time Lionel Robbins, who saw in Hayek an ally against the rising influence of Keynes, invited him to deliver a series of guest lectures at the London School of Economics (LSE). These made such an impression that Hayek was offered the Tooke Chair of Economic Science and Statistics at LSE, a position which he held until 1950.

Hayek became a British citizen in 1938 and was elected a Fellow of the British Academy six year later. In 1945, the year after the publication of *The Road to Serfdom* (his immensely successful critique of totalitarianism – which for Hayek included both Socialism and Nazism), Hayek went on a well-attended lecture tour of the USA. Two years afterwards he founded the Mont Pèlerin Society in order to stimulate thought about the liberal market society: membership of the society has kept growing and today includes many prominent conservative thinkers, including several Nobel Prize winners and politicians.

Hayek moved to the University of Chicago in 1950, where he occupied the specially-created chair of Social and Moral Sciences, a post which he held for twelve years. Having divorced his first wife, he married Helene Bitterlich in 1960 and, two years later, the couple moved back to Europe, Hayek accepting the Chair of Economic policy at the University of Freiburg, Germany. He held an honorary professorship at the University of Salzburg in Austria from 1969 until 1974, the year he was awarded the Nobel Prize for Economic Science. In the years following this he travelled extensively and was awarded many honorary titles, including that of 'Companion of Honour' by Queen Elizabeth in 1984 'for his services to the study of economics'. His last years were spent in Freiburg where his health deteriorated and where he died on 23 March 1992. He was given a State funeral in Vienna.

3 Main contributions

Economic theory

The counter-revolution of 1989 in eastern Europe can be seen to vindicate Hayek's arguments of the 1930s against central economic planning. In subsequent decades, he generalized these arguments into a critique of all forms of centralized and deliberate organization of society. In the 1990s, Hayek's work became the subject of much interest in the former communist countries. Ironically, this had not been the case in the West when the problems that Keynesian theories could not solve were rediscovered beginning in the 1960s. Nor did the controversy in capital theory, about re-switching of production techniques and reversals in capital intensity (fought out in the professional journals during the 1960s and 1970s), lead economists to study Hayek's work. Yet in both cases this would have been natural, as Hayek's early work discusses these problems.

The reason why economists failed to rediscover Hayek's economics lies in the outcome of Hayek's controversy with Keynes. When Keynes published his *General Theory* in 1936, economists had turned away from Hayek almost unanimously. Whereas Hayek had been one of the most influential economists of the 1930s, memories of his economics started to fade rapidly. His sophisticated, detailed and highly technical elaborations of his economic theory, published in *Profits, Interest and Investment* (1939) and *The Pure Theory of Capital* (1941), came too late. It was not until 1974, when Hayek was awarded

289

the Nobel Prize for Economics, that his work began to be rediscovered.

The concept of planning is central to Hayek's economic theory. This is not as surprising as it may seem in view of his criticism of socialism. At the basis of all of Hayek's economic analysis is the idea that individuals make plans, which have to be adapted in response to unexpected changes. This individualistic concept of a plan introduces the concepts of time and expectations. Both concepts are crucial tools in Hayek's generalization, in 1927 and 1928, of Walrasian static general equilibrium theory into an intertemporal general equilibrium theory.

The theory explains the relationships among all markets both contemporaneously and through time. Business cycles (disequilibrium growth) are explained as caused by a factor which disturbs these relationships: the elastic money supply in a modern fractional reserve (or credit) monetary system. Money is not neutral, in that changes in the quantity of money distort the real relative prices that correspond to real relative scarcities of goods and services through time. Because entrepreneurs base their expectations on the only prices they are capable of perceiving, money prices, these non-neutral changes in the money supply cause them to take the wrong investment decisions. The resulting changes in the production structure are not reversed until entrepreneurs discover that the supply of the goods they produce is not matched by a corresponding demand. Thus, inflation, a growth of the money supply that is not justified by a growth of real production, causes stagnation. It was precisely this phenomenon of 'stagflation' which, much later, in the 1970s, marked the decline of Keynesianism.

Hayek's emphasis on perceived relative prices is consistent with a criticism found in his first published work: that an aggregate construct such as the price level is not a causal factor because it is not what decision makers perceive. A constant price level may hide wildly fluctuating relative prices. Therefore, theories that recommend stabilizing the general price level as a remedy against cyclical fluctuations in output and employment are mistaken.

Social theory and methodology

When Hayek's career as an economist seemed to have come to an end, he moved to other disciplines. He started devoting himself to the theory of knowledge, the methodology of the social sciences and the study of the institutional framework of a market economy. The first result of this reorientation was *The Road to Serfdom* (1944), which found an immense popular audience. In 1950, Hayek was appointed professor of Social and Moral Sciences at the University of Chicago, where he remained until 1962. During this period, he developed his ideas on a liberal market society, which were published in *The Constitution of Liberty* (1960), one of his best works.

Although Hayek switched disciplines, he did not deviate from the general course of development his thought had taken. His social and political philosophy, his philosophy of law and his methodology of social science are united by one central theme, which had also become more and more explicit in his economics: the limitations of human knowledge. This theme makes its appearance in Hayek's thought as early as 1920, during his student years, when he developed a theory of cognitive psychology in reaction to Ernst Mach's theory of perception. Much later, in 1952, Hayek published his cognitive psychology in *The Sensory Order*.

The limitations of human knowledge are at the basis of Hayek's criticism of centrally directed economies. He argued that no central organization is capable of gathering or processing all the information that is needed to coordinate all economic activities. This critique is also the starting point of a series of publications in which Hayek attempts to explain the functioning of markets, starting with 'Economics and knowledge' in 1937 (now also recognized as the start of the economics of information). The core idea is that the price mechanism is a means for coordinating the dispersed, specific knowledge of individual decision makers. Competition complements the price system, in that it is a dynamic process through which new knowledge and opportunities are discovered.

Hayek's methodology, too, is based on the recognition that human knowledge of a complex environment is necessarily limited. Hayek criticizes the use of quantitative methods in so far as they suggest a degree of exactness that is not attainable. Economists and econometricians pretend to know much more and to have much more detailed knowledge than their subject matter allows for. This pseudo-exactness is dangerous as it leads to wrong decisions that affect the lives of millions. In his Nobel address, Hayek rejected modern, Keynesian macroeconomics for adhering to this fallacy. This tradition derives from a mistaken, positivistic methodology, which Hayek criticized in *The Counter-Revolution of Science* (1955).

Hayek did not reject the use of mathematics or empirical economic research as such. He had travelled to the USA, in 1923–4, to acquaint himself with the latest methods in empirical business cycle research. In 1927 he became the first director of the Austrian Institute for Business Cycle Research, founded by Ludwig von Mises. Hayek had also prepared a mathematical appendix (which for reasons beyond his influence was not published) to his *The Pure Theory of Capital* and, immediately before the war, he took the initiative in founding an international institute for business cycle research that was to have involved the major researchers of the period, including Jan Tinbergen. (Due to the Second World War, the project never got off the ground and was not revived after the war.) He proved himself to be a master of the art of empirical research in a report (compiled at the request of the British Colonial Office during a six-week holiday in 1947) on the economic state of Gibraltar. In his later work, he recommended mathematics as an important tool for coming to grips with complexity.

Evolution and coordination

In Hayek's social, political and legal philosophy, the theme of limited knowledge is combined with an evolutionary analysis of social institutions. Hayek distinguishes between *organizations* (or *taxeis*, singular: *taxis*) and *spontaneous orders* (or *cosmoi*, singular: *cosmos*). The former are defined as purposive human creations and the latter as institutions that have evolved spontaneously as the unintended consequences of individual actions. Spontaneous orders include such phenomena as the market and the historically evolved systems of law. Whereas organizations contain only the explicit knowledge that went into their making, spontaneous orders embody the accumulated and largely tacit knowledge of many generations. This is one of the reasons why the detailed explanation of the functioning of spontaneous orders transcends the capacities of human reason, and why deliberate interventions in spontaneously grown institutions have unintended consequences that may lead to their destruction.

The relative stability of social institutions that can be observed in reality raises the question of how such institutions coordinate the enormous number of individual decisions and actions taken by their members. This is another central theme in Hayek's work. In Hayek's evolutionary approach to coordination problems, history (or 'path dependency' as it is now called) plays a crucial part. Hayek's interest in historical developments is reflected in his voluminous work on the history of ideas and on economic history. Starting with his earliest publication, he introduces every problem that he addresses by giving an account of how it has arisen in the history of thought.

Following his retirement in 1969, Hayek resumed his earlier work in business cycle theory and the theory of money. More importantly, he developed new evolutionary insights into the *Rechtsstaat* (rule of law) as the legal and political framework for a liberal market society. Published in the three volumes of *Law, Legislation and Liberty* (1973, 1976 and 1979), this body of thought was the rather more conservative successor to *The Constitution of Liberty*. It was this work in particular that began to attract a large readership in eastern Europe in the early 1990s, when the lack of an adequate legal and political framework made itself painfully felt.

Monetary theory and non-interventionism

In 1937 Hayek had advocated the re-introduction of the gold standard as an international means of exchange. He saw as its main advantage its ability to be independent of the whims of a monetary authority. This idea evolved via an international commodity standard into the proposal, in the 1970s, to subject the issuing of money to the discipline of the market. Known as *free banking*, Hayek's proposal for free competition in issuing money was motivated by the idea that governments are always subject to the influences of interest groups and hence cannot conduct an independent and neutral monetary policy. This is one aspect of Hayek's offensive against the arbitrariness of an interventionist government.

Hayek also advocated a conservative brand of liberalism that is opposed to any kind of intervention, notably the interventions by governments and by organized labour in the spontaneous order of a market society. To stimulate thought about the intellectual foundations of a liberal society, he founded the Mont Pèlerin Society in 1947.

4 Evaluation and conclusion

Despite the exceptional many-sidedness and the high level of intellectual sophistication of Hayek's work, his influence remained limited until the late 1980s, particularly among economists. However, this started to change with the emergence of evolutionary theorizing in social science. Although Hayek's early work rarely influenced early developments in this field (unlike in neural network theory, where Hayek's *The Sensory Order* was one of the sources of inspiration), his ideas are now being rediscovered. For example, interest in spontaneous, non-formal organizations began to enjoy a revival during the 1990s.

Oliver Williamson's analysis of coordination problems in markets and organizations is intellectually (although not historically) a descendant of Hayek's work (see WILLIAMSON, O.E.). Other issues that are of relevance to management science are Hayek's analysis of competition as a discovery process and of the institutional environment of the business organization. In the 1990s, the latter proved to be of great relevance to the transformation processes in eastern Europe. However, economists and organization theorists studying capitalist economies in the West will find that they, too, stand to learn from Hayek's work.

The following is just one example of an area in which Hayek's ideas may stimulate future research in management science. Herbert Simon's analysis of complexity bears close parallels to Hayek's. While Simon has applied his ideas about complexity much more explicitly to the organizational environment, Hayek's ideas on complexity are linked to an evolutionary approach to social institutions. Nevertheless, the closeness of Simon's and Hayek's analyses of complexity points to the value of a study of the implications of an evolutionary approach to organizational complexity.

JACK BIRNER
UNIVERSITY OF MAASTRICHT

Further reading

(References cited in the text marked *)

Barry, N.P. (1979) *Hayek's Social and Economic Philosophy*, London: Macmillan. (Popular introduction to all the main components of Hayek's work except his psychology.)

Birner, J. and Zijp, R. van (eds) (1994) *Hayek, Coordination and Evolution; His Legacy in Philosophy, Politics, Economics and the History of Ideas*, London and New York: Routledge. (Hayek's work – except capital theory – critically discussed and placed in a contemporary framework.)

Butler, E. (1983) *Hayek, His Contribution to the Political and Economic Thought of Our Time*, London: Temple Smith. (An alternative popular introduction to all the main components of Hayek's work except his psychology.)

Hayek, F.A. von (1928) 'Intertemporal price equilibrium and movements in the value of money', in F.A. Hayek (1984) *Money, Capital and Fluctuations, Early Essays*, London: Routledge & Kegan Paul. (The first intertemporal general equilibrium theory ever to be developed in economics; this chapter is central to Hayek's economic theory.)

Hayek, F.A. von (1931) *Prices and Production*, London: Routledge. (The four guest lectures at the LSE describing the changes in the structure of production which comprises the business cycle.)

Hayek, F.A. von (1937) *Monetary Nationalism and International Stability*, London: Longmans Green. (Reprint (1970) New York: August M. Kelley. Unduly neglected series of five lectures on international monetary coordination.)

* Hayek, F.A. von (1939) *Profits, Interest, and Investment*, 2nd edn, Clifton, NJ: Augustus M. Kelley, 1975. (Collection of essays on capital theory, including a microeconomic restatement of Hayek's business cycle theory that answers a number of critics.)

* Hayek, F.A. von (1941) *The Pure Theory of Capital*, London: Routledge & Kegan Paul. (Sophisticated technical elaboration of Hayek's earlier economic theory.)

* Hayek, F.A. von (1944) *The Road to Serfdom*, London: Routledge & Kegan Paul. (Hayek's first integrated historical analysis and criticism of socialism.)

Hayek, F.A. von (1949) *Individualism and Economic Order*, London: Routledge & Kegan Paul. (Collection of key articles on spontaneous orders, coordination, the price system, competition and socialism; includes the seminal article 'Economics and knowledge', a discussion of the economics of information and the literature on coordination.)

* Hayek, F.A. von (1952) *The Sensory Order*, Chicago, IL: University of Chicago Press. (Elaboration of a 1920 manuscript on cognitive psychology, one of the sources of inspiration of neural network theory.)

* Hayek, F.A. von (1955) *The Counter-Revolution of Science*, Glencoe, IL: The Free Press. (Hayek's arguments against the positivistic methodology in social science.)

* Hayek, F.A. von (1960) *The Constitution of Liberty*, London: Routledge & Kegan Paul. (Well-balanced *magnum opus* on the foundations of a liberal market society.)

* Hayek, F.A. von (1973, 1976, 1979) *Law, Legislation and Liberty*: vol. 1 *Rules and Order*; vol. 2 *The Mirage of Social Justice*; vol. 3 *The Political Order of a Free People*, London: Routledge & Kegan Paul. (Elaboration in an evolutionary and conservative direction of *The Constitution of Liberty*.)

Hayek, F.A. von (1978) *New Studies in Philosophy, Politics, Economics and the History of Ideas*, part 1, London: Routledge & Kegan Paul. (Essays on complexity, spontaneous evolution of rules, and institutions as unintended consequences of individual actions.)

Hayek, F.A. von (1988) *The Fatal Conceit. The Errors of Socialism*, in W.W. Bartley III (ed.), *The Collected Works of Friedrich August von Hayek*, vol. I, London: Routledge. (Last conservative restatement of Hayek's theory of society, containing passages on cultural evolution.)

* Keynes. J.M. (1936) *The General Theory of Employment, Interest and Money*, New York: Harcourt Brace. (Reprinted in volume 7 of Keynes' *Collected Works*.)

Schreuder H. (1993) 'Coase, Hayek, and hierarchy', in S.M. Lindenberg and H. Schreuder (eds), *Interdisciplinary Perspectives on Organization Studies*, Oxford: Pergamon Press. (Links the coordination theme in Williamson's and Mintzberg's organizational economics to Coase and Hayek.)

Weimer W.B. (1982) 'Hayek's approach to the problems of complex phenomena: an introduction to the theoretical psychology of *The Sensory Order*, in W.B. Weimer and D.S. Palermo (eds), *Cognition and the Symbolic Processes*, vol. 2, Hillsdale, NJ: Lawrence Erlbaum Associates. (Summary of Hayek's psychology and analysis of its place in the whole of his thought.)

See also: COASE, R.; FRIEDMAN, M.; KEYNES, J.M.; SCHUMPETER, J.; SIMON, H.E.; WILLIAMSON, O.E.

Related topics in the IEBM: BUSINESS CYCLES; BUSINESS ECONOMICS; KNIGHT, F.H.; INFLATION; MARKETS; MARKET STRUCTURE; MARX, K.H.; MANAGEMENT SCIENCE; MONETARISM; NEO-CLASSICAL ECONOMICS

Herzberg, Frederick (1923–)

Personal background

- born 18 April 1923, USA
- trained first in psychology, he studied mental health in the industrial world
- his research focused on human motivation in the work situation, its effects on the individual's satisfaction at work and on mental health
- extremely influenced by his Judaeo-Christian roots, which explains his frequent and lengthy references to the Bible
- Professor of Management at a Utah University
- gained an international reputation and was a well-known consultant in the 1960s and 1970s

Major works

The Motivation to Work (with B. Mausner and B. Snyderman) (1959)
Work and the Nature of Man (1966)

Summary

Frederick Herzberg, psychologist by training and a university professor, studied motivation at work in companies where he was also involved as a consultant. His theory of motivation at work, also called 'actualization–atmosphere' factors, is based on the hierarchical human needs approach, as well as on the study of the great biblical myths of Adam and Abraham. The actualization factors are work and all forms of gratitude achieved through work. Acting upon these factors allows one to modify individual behaviour at work in a deep and long-lasting manner. The atmosphere factors are remuneration, job security, management policy in the company and relations between colleagues. Acting on these factors only gives temporary satisfaction and does not modify behaviour on a long-term basis. The implicit hypothesis in Herzberg's work – that a person should grow through their work – and its applications in the organization of companies had considerable success in the 1970s. The management of companies puts in place policies of job enrichment and enlargement of tasks, polyvalency and job rotation, of which he was the instigator. He criticized the idea of the individual at work, central to Taylorism. Today, society has considerably evolved, and his arguments seem very far from contemporary preoccupations, which underlines even more the theoretical weaknesses in his hypothesis.

1 Theoretical foundations

Frederick Herzberg is a social psychologist who deals specifically with the field of work and the company. His work is inspired by the theory of human needs: he finds the source both in psychology and Darwinism, and also in great Christian myths. Psychology and the comparison of humans with animals taught him that the human organism is comparable to the animal's in so far as they must both submit to their needs. For humans, however, the needs are in hierarchical order: at the top lies the need of self-accomplishment which can be achieved through work. On the other hand, the study of certain great Judaeo-Christian myths shows that they express motivations common to all humanity.

The myth of Adam tells us that the first man was created with all the attributes of perfection, but that God chased him from Paradise on Earth when he ate the fruit from the tree of knowledge:

Two thousand years of teaching convinced multitudes that when Adam was thrown out of Paradise, humanity was condemned, perverted, chained to a life of suffering. From that notion of human guilt, life has to be expiated by the suffering of the fall of Adam. His first aim is, therefore, to escape the multiple situations which generate pain, which he encounters in his new world of alienation.

(Herzberg 1966: chapter 2)

There is, therefore, in every human an aspiration to flee the pains of this world. One can see it in the world of work, when the individual seeks to improve their work conditions. But this improvement does not correspond to the dynamic approach of the individual at work and does not satisfy the need for fulfilment and self-realization.

The second myth, expressing a universal vision of man, is that of Abraham. This perspective is radically different. Herzberg recalls the passage from the Bible in which God promises Abraham descendants as innumerable as the grains of sand by the sea, as long as Adam obeys Him, and rises and travels to the Promised Land. Herzberg's lesson: 'The second definition of man, as explained by Abraham, is that man is a resourceful being, has received inborn virtualities, such that God has chosen him to be His emissary here on earth' (Herzberg 1966: chapter 2). This is a dynamic and positive perspective, where man is considered a being full of potential who needs help in accomplishing his goal.

The biblical myth teaches us that two coexisting natures in man correspond to two outlooks on humanity. The first one is the pessimistic tradition of human nature, eighteenth century Jansenism, where man is first and foremost subjected to the consequences of his original sin. He needs to be supervised and guided, he seeks protection from the pain caused by the environment he has been in since his fall – 'you'll earn your bread with the sweat of your brow', the valley of tears where the man's days drift away awaiting death. The other outlook, an optimistic one, is where man, having been created in the image of God, is a being full of virtue and resources, so long as he is given the power to exercise them.

2 The application in the world of work

These myths, transposed into the world of work, are interpreted as an escape from the suffering and the aspiration to grow. The motivation at work must rely on the second tendency. Herzberg finds confirmation of the second theory of motivation in several empirical inquiries that he directed. These allowed him to discover and define the factors of satisfaction or discontent at work. The first ones – the satisfaction factors – correspond to Abraham's nature and are called actualization factors. The second ones – the factors of discontent – are called atmosphere or 'hygiene' factors and correspond to Adam's nature. There are five actualization factors: achievement, recognition for achievement, work itself, responsibility, and the possibility of development or growth. Atmosphere factors are more numerous: management policy in the company, management (its qualities and defects), remuneration, work conditions, relations between people (management, employees, equals), prestige, job security, factors from personal life (when work affects one's personal life, like a transfer to a new place.)

Actualization factors provide individuals with a sense of long-term satisfaction. Carrying out tasks which lead to accomplishment at work (and not to humdrum and uninteresting work), recognizing the work accomplished, changing the job itself, being given responsibility at work – all these actions lead to long-term and positive changes in attitude because they rely on Abraham's nature, the only one capable of encouraging motivation. Atmosphere factors such as rising salaries, changing management, altering the management of personnel, improving work conditions, job guarantee, acting upon relations between people, however, all tend towards a decline in tension, which may be significant but their influence is only temporary and does not modify in-depth behaviour.

In order to confirm the theoretical foundations and generalize the applications of such factors, Herzberg relies on the results of his empirical enquiries, carried out in companies around the world (the USA; industrial, rural, and hospital environments; all professional categories in Europe, Finland and Hungary). When he asks individuals to recall their best and worst memories, they always remember positively actions concerning actualization factors ('I had a more interesting job', or 'My boss congratulated me on this job') and remember negatively actions concerning atmosphere factors ('I had a rise in salary, it's better, but it does not correspond at all to what the company could have done', etc).

Two of Herzberg's examples remain famous. The first concerns the work organization of secretaries at the Bell Telephone Company. These secretaries had to answer the letters from the shareholders of the company. The results were programmed according to pre-established formulas and verified twice by supervisors. The morale of the secretaries was low, absenteeism high and errors numerous. Several atmosphere factors (rise in salary, changes and development of hierarchies, planning of the work environment) failed to change anything. The organization of work was changed. Each secretary was put in charge of a specific area, where they became an expert, and in which they advised their colleagues. Supervision was reduced. Each wrote and signed the letters themselves. Among themselves they organized the workload for the day. After a decline in productivity in the first weeks, there was a considerable rise in productivity and a level of response quality never reached before.

The other example is the installation of telephone lines at the same Bell Telephone Company. As before, work for the same client was divided between several departments: departments for orders, connection and installation, and of verification. The overall outfit did not work well, with delays and mediocre quality. All tasks were then merged, one person being in charge of the ordering, connection, verification and ultimate contacts with the client. The results were phenomenal in terms of productivity, quality and employee satisfaction.

3 Changes introduced in the company

In terms of personnel management policies in companies, the influence of Frederick Herzberg's theories was important and was followed by immediate effects, although these differed from country to country.

There is no doubt that managerial policies on task enrichment and enlargement, as well as policies on job rotation which expanded rapidly in the 1960s and 1970s, owe much to Herzberg. The ideas which had prevailed until then on human nature and human needs at work were those of Taylorism and Fordism, where individuals at work demanded high salaries that ensured them a standard of living which previous generations could not even have imagined (see FORD, H.; TAYLOR, F.W.). Following that idea, the nature of work took second place to the preoccupations of managers. The fact that workers asked for a high salary so that their essential needs were more or less met acknowledged the assumption that they could work without being interested in the work itself – which is what Taylorism results in when the workload is organized by the manager and not by the workers. The disastrous consequences of this vision of the organization of work came at the time Herzberg was carrying out his research. After the boom of the post-war years, the period between the second half of the 1960s and the beginning of the 1980s was the time when disaffection with work and the rejection of unskilled work appeared to be important developments in the world of work. In a number of large companies in all the industrialized countries, the results were the same: the absenteeism rate among unskilled workers reached an all-time high, a lack of concern for quality sometimes stretched as far as sabotage, and there was a rejection of work due to lack of interest. All these factors became important concerns for managers and politicians. Movements like those of the hippies of the West Coast of the USA, or those of 1968 in Europe, appeared to threaten the society built on industrial order. Métro, boulot, dodo (tube, work, sleep) the famous French slogan of the student revolution of 1968, illustrates the rejection of a society which is supposed to confer well-being but which alienates those who serve it.

Several explanations for this crisis seem plausible. For instance, the absence of any consideration of the fundamental needs of human nature, the dislike of hard working conditions, the rejection of constraints linked to industrial production, are all explanations given in Herzberg's works. Many managers, political figures and trade union officials accepted this explanation and sought remedies at this level, introducing changes in the policies of government in industrialized countries to improve work conditions. Meanwhile many companies instigated concrete reforms, especially for unskilled or semi-skilled workers in large firms.

Two theoretical movements guided these changes. The first one can be directly linked to the works of Herzberg, as mentioned above – and is concerned with task enrichment and enlargement, and with job rotation. If the rejection of work comes from the fact that the job is not interesting, all possible measures must be taken to change the situation. Increasing the responsibility of those who supervise machinery, allowing them to carry out extra tasks, such as minor adjustments, maintenance, cleaning or customer despatch – by identifying the team or the worker in charge of that task – implementing job rotation between workers instead of the same people always doing the same job, all are designed to make work more attractive and to motivate the workers. This can be carried over to office work. The main point is to re-examine work stations and work content in order to give employees responsibilities, which Taylor's over-emphasized division of work removed.

The success of the application of Herzberg's theory of motivation cannot be understood without considering the contribution from another theoretical movement, which consolidates these principles and adds nuances. This is the sociocultural movement which was based on the pioneer works of the Tavistock Institute of London. These had started before the Second World War and were orientated towards psychology and psychoanalysis. The main idea developed in this group was that, in order to modify individual behaviour, one must act on the group. Members of a small work group, when given autonomy and confidence in its own organization, will behave more productively than under the old system. Work in small self-organized groups is much superior to the traditional model of work organized and run by a hierarchy. This idea is translated into practice by the introduction of semi-autonomous groups.

In 1950, a famous experiment on work organization in coal mines was interpreted as the demonstration of the importance of the connection between the type of work and the organization of that work (Trist and Bamforth 1951). In certain technical conditions, the organization of specialized tasks discouraged people. Morale and collective output were considerably improved by giving teams of miners more autonomy in the organization of their work, by creating semi-autonomous groups. Spectacular results were obtained in connection with clocking-in, absenteeism and work accidents. Other experiments confirm these results. The idea of the semi-autonomous group was very successful, at a time when the influence of Herzberg's ideas was expanding. The influence of these two currents became conjoined.

The two theories have in common the principle of behaviour dictated by the individual – either the individual themselves, as in Herzberg, or the influence of the group on the individual, as in the movements that have grown from the work of the Tavistock Institute. The reforms introduced into companies as a result of these movements almost always combine work enrichment and enlargement with autonomous or semi-autonomous groups.

4 The great reforms

In line with Herzberg and the Tavistock group, a certain number of steps were taken following the difficulties experienced by companies and industrial society. Some of the most famous cases are discussed below.

First are the changes introduced by the Volvo factories in Kalmar, Sweden, at the beginning of the 1970s. Following the development of a bad social climate, which translated into a very high absenteeism rate in the assembly workshop and a lack of quality that damaged Volvo's brand image and thus the sales of its cars, the management decided to remove the assembly line for cars and to replace it with production organized by units. Car parts were brought to the reduced workshops, where a team of workers was in charge of the assembly. This team (the same size as the old one) organized itself to share out the work, carry it out in the given time and control the quality. The job was thus expanded and enriched, and the workers gained versatility. They received extra training for their new maintenance and control tasks, as well as gaining the experience of teamwork. The results were extremely positive according to those involved – employees, management and trade unions. There was a better social climate, a significant fall in absenteeism, and a spectacular rise in quality. Its success attracted observers from around the world.

Many other measures were taken at the same time in other European countries, often by governmental and official bodies. In Germany, the *Humanisierung der Arbeit* programme, launched at the beginning of the 1970s by the Social Democratic government, carried out important research and encouraged changes in German factories similar to those at Volvo. These changes centred on the reorganization of the job, in accord with Herzberg's theories mentioned above. In France, in 1974, the government created *l'Agence Nationale pour l'Amélioration des Conditions de Travail* to encourage social innovations and to launch research programmes. Many innovations aimed at improvement of the conditions and organization of work in companies were encouraged, followed through and later given as examples in publications circulated by the agency.

It seems that the movement was less important in the UK, for reasons such as the long history of industrialization, the absence of sociopolitical upheaval which was important in countries like Germany and France, and especially the emphasis given to professional abilities and skilled workers. The result was the constant presence of a high degree of autonomy and control within workshops. Nevertheless, many new forms of work organization were introduced in UK companies, in the shape of enriched and enlarged work and autonomous groups. Traces of this are found in two reports: the Donovan Report, *Report of the Royal Commission on Trade Unions and Employers' Associations* (1968), which centred especially on changes in professional relations; and the Bullock Report, *Report of the Committee of Inquiry on Industrial Democracy* (1977), which was orientated more towards the idea of industrial democracy.

In the USA it seems the movement was slowed down because of the tradition of collective bargaining, in which trade union officials and management negotiate on a basis of rules which are supposed to be unchangeable, or very difficult to alter (such as the seniority rule and job descriptions) and which make the workers feel they own their work rights, so to speak (see COLLECTIVE BARGAINING). New reforms in the organization of work were introduced by management, not without great resistance from trade unions. Quantitative evaluation is difficult, but Herzberg's homeland did not value his ideas as highly as did other nations.

In sum, Herzberg's ideas contributed to the launch of an important movement in favour of work reorganization and changes within companies and in industrial relations in most of the industrialized countries which operated on the Taylor/Ford system of the division of labour and offered a limited outlook on the idea of people at work, their motivations and their expectations.

5 Twenty years later

Re-reading Herzberg's written work twenty years on and re-evaluating the impact of the reforms initiated by his theories, one is struck by the gap between the problems of that period and the problems today, and by the fate of the changes he promulgated. What is also striking is the compartmentalization of the world of ideas. At a time when Herzberg's ideas were triumphing in the world of management and industrial relations, the great theoretical movements which were to impose themselves in later years (the analysis of organizations in particular) were entirely ignored by supporters of Herzberg's theories.

The undoubted contribution of Herzberg is his rejection of the basic ideas of Taylor and Ford on human nature, ideas which had previously prevailed. 'Good' salaries, given by the management to workers, seemed to be a sufficient reason to make them accept the job, and the work conditions, and to sufficiently motivate them to work. Against that, Herzberg reminded us strongly that the worker is motivated by his interest in what he does and by his involvement in work, that he is not a machine, and that he tolerates with great difficulty an organization which distances itself from his work. Herzberg made possible a new way of thinking about the work itself and the organization of that work as a function of the interest workers or employees have in what they do – and not as a function of the salary alone. He reminded managers that the worker and the employee can be interested in their work. A late piece of evidence, perhaps, but an important one.

Another contribution made by Herzberg is in the modification of the division of labour and the omnipotent power of overall command management. Autonomy was given back to specialized and less-qualified workers. So, beyond work conditions as such, the organization of work itself was rethought. Giving the workers more room to organize, through machine control and maintenance, was a way of weakening the traditional division of labour, of ending the slogan 'work and shut up' of Taylor – and of rethinking the radical division of labour which prevailed until then. In this sense, Herzberg was the instigator of more flexible, supple organizations, and of network companies as we know them today.

Despite all this, Herzberg's theories appear very remote from today's analysis of work behaviour. There are several reasons for this. The first is the theoretical weakness in his argument – especially in his theory about needs. That the individual has needs is a way of presenting human nature in an acceptable form. What is not acceptable is the hierarchy of these needs, regardless of the work situation and discussion of the actual individual. Herzberg introduces a behavioural determination which removes all freedom from the individual. In order to achieve this, he adopts an implicit hypothesis whereby man must fulfil himself through work – his book could have been entitled 'Work is the nature of man', replacing 'and' by 'is'. This implicit assumption was never demonstrated or proved by him, and neither has anybody subsequently managed to offer sufficient proof that fulfilment through work is a universal and permanent motivation. Every individual chooses their own path to self-fulfilment, but that path can change course throughout a lifetime and nobody but the person involved is able to know how. Furthermore, there are a thousand forms of fulfilment at work: for example, strikes, sabotage and industrial action. Absenteeism is another form of behaviour where the individual prefers other options to work, even if it is interesting. The theory of needs has limits in its universal claim to explain human behaviour beyond specific situations and individual judgements.

When one analyses Herzberg's experiments closely, one can see that he essentially concentrated on the reorganization of work. His advice was to propose a better organization, a simplification of the communication structure. A good consultant in an organization would have probably come to the same conclusions. That the new form of organization makes some individuals momentarily 'happier' in their work, and shows an improvement in productivity, does not demonstrate the validity of the theory of needs. All organizational changes seen as managerial action in favour of the employees are always greeted well by them. Fulfilment of oneself is not the point. But this is what Herzberg tried to demonstrate, with his biblical references. Man is fulfilled by developing his creative abilities and work is the ideal place for human fulfilment, according to Herzberg. This argument, central to Herzberg's theory, is what makes it weak.

Unemployment and the precarious situation of today's industrial world has radically changed things since Herzberg's time. This makes his arguments remote from today's problems and renders his work obsolete. The outdated character of his argument does not come from the socio-economic context, but from the weaknesses in his theoretical foundations. Nobody, today, supports seriously his theory of needs. A theory which lasts is a theory whose basic elements are solid enough to acknowledge reality, even years after it was formulated.

Since Frederick Herzberg, theories on work motivation have leant more towards the idea of work satisfaction rather than company incentives, where motivations seem to be linked to organizational structure rather than to human nature. The most progressive work has been that of March and Simon (1958) and after that the work of Aoki (1984), or with a more managerial perspective, the works of Mintzberg, especially his *The Structuring of Organizations*.

PHILIPPE BERNOUX
UNIVERSITÉ LUMIÈRE LYON II

Further reading

(References cited in the text marked *)

* Aoki, M. (1984) *The Co-operative Game Theory of the Firm*. Oxford: Clarendon Press.
* Bullock Committee (1977) *Report of the Committee of Inquiry on Industrial Democracy*, London: HMSO.
* Donovan Commission (1968) *Report of the Royal Commission on Trade Unions and Employers' Associations*, London: HMSO.
  Herzberg, F. (1959) *Managerial Choice: To Be Efficient and To Be Human*, New York: Dow-Jones Irwin.
* Herzberg, F. (1966) *Work and the Nature of Man*, Cleveland, OH: The World Publishing Company. (Herzberg's main work in which he exposes his theory of needs and the biblical roots in his 'actualization–atmosphere' theory.)
  Herzberg, F., Mausner, B. and Snyderman, B. (1959) *The Motivation to Work* New York: Wiley. (Presentation of his enquiry into the feelings humans have towards their work. This enquiry led to his theory put forward in *Work and the Nature of Man*.)
  Grootings, P., Gustavsen, B. and Hethy, L. (eds) (1989) *New Forms of Work Organization in Europe*, New Brunswick, NJ, and Oxford: Transaction Publishers. (Presentation and critical analysis of the main changes in the organization of work in European countries, whether influenced by Herzberg or not.)
* March, J.G. and Simon, R.M. (1958) *Organizations*. New York: Wiley.
* Mintzberg, H. (1979) *The Structuring of Organizations*. Englewood Cliffs, NJ: Prentice-Hall. (The first, now famous, book by Mintzberg.)
  Paul, W.J., Jr, Robertson, K.B. and Herzberg, F. (1969) 'Job enrichment pays off', *Harvard Business Review* 47: 61–78.
* Trist, E.L. and Bamforth, K.W. (1951) 'Some social and psychological consequences of the longwall method of coal-getting', *Human Relations* 4 (1): 6–24, 37–8. (Report of the famous 1950 experiment, demonstrating the connection between the type of work and the organization of that work.)

See also: MASLOW, A.H.; MAYO, G.E.; TAYLOR, F.W.; TRIST, E.

Related topics in the IEBM: FREUD, S.; GROUPS AND TEAMS; HUMAN RELATIONS; HUMAN RESOURCE MANAGEMENT; HUMAN RESOURCE MANAGEMENT, INTERNATIONAL; INDUSTRIAL DEMOCRACY; INDUSTRIAL AND LABOUR RELATIONS; MOTIVATION AND SATISFACTION; OCCUPATIONAL PSYCHOLOGY; ORGANIZATION BEHAVIOUR, HISTORY OF; WORK ETHIC

Hofstede, Geert (1928–)

1 Introduction
2 Main contribution
3 Evaluation
4 Conclusions

Personal background

- born in Haarlem, The Netherlands, 2 October 1928
- married with four sons
- holds an MSc in mechanical engineering and a PhD in social psychology
- early work experience includes posts as worker, foreman, plant manager in numerous Dutch companies, and chief psychologist in an American multinational company
- founder and first director of the Institute for Research on Intercultural Cooperation
- has held senior positions in both industry and academic establishments
- has advised government organizations in Europe, Asia and North America
- has taught and researched in Europe's top business schools and institutes
- held the Chair of Organizational Anthropology and International Management at the University of Maastricht prior to retirement in 1993.

Major works

The Game of Budget Control (1967)
Culture's Consequences (1980)
Cultures and Organizations: Software of the Mind (1991)
Uncommon Sense About Organizations (1994)

Summary

Hofstede has made a significant contribution to our understanding of organizations. He argues that, and in many cases demonstrates how, national cultures might systematically influence organizations largely through the values that employees hold and bring with them to their workplace. That organizations are to a great extent 'creatures' of their national setting was not totally in dispute by the time Hofstede's work became known, but he provided researchers with a theoretical framework within which the relationship between organizations and culture could be explained. He also enhanced awareness among managers in multinational firms of the diversity of their employees' cultural background and its implications for leadership styles.

1 Introduction

As a discipline, academic research into organizations is essentially a twentieth-century phenomenon. For decades researchers had been in search of the best way to manage firms and it was not until the late 1950s and early 1960s that a contingency model was developed. This model suggested that situational factors such as production technology and market conditions might call for different management styles and work organizations. But it was still flawed in a fundamental way as it ignored the cultural predispositions of employees, managers and indeed of the societies within which organizations operated. A seminal work by Michel Crozier discussing French bureaucracy in relation to French national culture (Crozier 1964) paved the way for a totally new perspective, which was later followed by many other researchers the world over (see CROZIER, M.). Within this new cultural perspective one of the most significant studies, which had enormous implications for the understanding of organizations, was carried out by Geert Hofstede (1980).

2 Main contribution

Hofstede's early contributions to the study of organizations were in the area of the effects of formal control systems on organizations and on the people in them. His PhD thesis *The Game of Budget Control* in 1967 focuses on what is now known as 'behavioral accounting'. On the basis of extensive in-depth interviews in five manufacturing plants in the Netherlands and the correlations between subjective opinions and objective accounting data, he concluded that the key issue in the effectiveness of a control system was not so much the amount of participation in standard-setting (as was the common belief), but management's ability to maintain a 'game spirit' around the achievement of the budget's objectives. This was a study of what later would be called 'organization culture'. In the 1970s Hofstede's research focus moved to differences in national cultures and their impact on organizations, and later in the 1980s to differences in organization cultures within the same nation.

The empirical research base for Hofstede's main study was found in a body of attitude-survey response data obtained within subsidiaries of one large US multinational corporation, to which the author had access. At the time, Hofstede was a member of a team that conducted the in-house company surveys, the results of which were not intended as a contribution to academia but as an aid to the company's own internal aims. When the surveys were conducted, the company was perhaps at the height of its power as a multinational firm and had subsidiaries in about 100 countries. Further related data were subsequently collected at a business school in Switzerland, where managers from various countries attended executive courses.

The multinational company-based data were collected twice, around 1968 and around 1972, and covered over 116,000 completed questionnaires from employees in fifty different occupations and sixty-six different nationalities. Each questionnaire contained about 150 questions dealing with values, perceptions and satisfactions. Twenty different language versions were used. For technical reasons, the analysis of the data which led to Hofstede's main propositions centred around the questionnaire responses from employees in forty countries. Of the organizations surveyed, thirty-nine were subsidiaries of the same large US-based multinational company. The fortieth was a Yugoslav worker-managed organization which, among other activities, imported and serviced the US firm's products in Yugoslavia.

Analysis of the data at country level, using only twenty of the 150 items on the questionnaire, led to a grouping of the work-related value items into four 'ecological dimensions' on the basis of theoretical relevance and the statistical relationship of individual country mean scores for forty countries. Four such dimensions of national culture were identified which Hofstede labelled: (1) power distance; (2) uncertainty avoidance; (3) individualism/collectivism; and (4) masculinity/femininity.

Comparing and cross-analysing his findings with those of other researchers, Hofstede sought to demonstrate the origins of these dimensions in primary social institutions such as religion and family, and their consequences for secondary institutions such as economy, politics and, of course, business organizations. He argued that these cultural dimensions determine the ways in which organizations are structured and managed. *Power distance* is conceptually related to 'concentration of authority' (centralization). It indicates the extent to which a society accepts that power in institutions and organizations is distributed unequally. This is reflected just as much in the values of the less powerful members of the society as in the values of the more powerful ones. Some national and regional cultures are characterized by large inequality, with power concentrated in the hands of small and permanent elites, centralized organizations with tall hierarchical pyramids, and restricted upward communication. Others are characterized by less inequality, more social mobility, less concentration of power in the hands of a small elite, decentralized organizations with flatter hierarchies, and upward communication that is relatively free.

Uncertainty avoidance is related to 'structuring of activities' (formalization, specialization, standardization) and indicates a society's lack of tolerance for uncertainty and ambiguity. This expresses itself in higher levels of anxiety and energy releases, a greater need for formal rules and absolute truth, and less tolerance for people or groups with deviant ideas or behaviours. Some cultures represent higher levels of activity and personal energy. The more active cultures tend to apply more specialization, formalization, and standardization in their organizations. They put a higher value on uniformity and are less tolerant of, and interested in, deviant ideas. They tend to avoid risky decisions. The less active cultures attach less importance to formal rules and specialization, they are not interested in uniformity and are able to tolerate a large variety of different ideas. They more easily take risks in personal decisions.

Individualism refers to a loosely-knit social framework in society where people are supposed to take care of themselves and of their immediate families only, *collectivism* to one in which they can expect their relatives, clan or work organization to look after them. More collectivist societies call for greater emotional dependence of members on their organizations. In a society in equilibrium the organizations in turn assume a broad responsibility for their members.

The predominant pattern of socialization in almost all societies is for men to be more assertive and for women to be more nurturing. Various data on the importance of work goals show near consistency on men scoring advancement and earnings as more important, women scoring quality of life and people. With respect to work goals, some societies are nearer the masculinity end of the *masculinity/femininity* dimension, others nearer the femininity end.

In a collaborative study with researchers working in southeast Asia, Hofstede and his colleagues identified a fifth dimension, *time orientation* (Hofstede and Bond 1988). This dimension is argued to distinguish 'short-term oriented' cultures from the 'long-term oriented' ones. On the basis of these five cultural dimensions, national cultures around the world could in general be mapped out into clusters among which differences can be observed. For instance, nations such as those in Latin parts of America and Europe as well as Asia and Africa score higher on power distance than those in non-Latin America and those in Europe with Germanic traditions. This means that in the former group of countries the distribution of power among people at various levels is less equal than is the case in the latter nations.

People in Western and developed countries appear to be more individualistic than their counterparts in Eastern and less developed ones, with Japan taking a unique position in the middle. A long-term orientation is mostly found in east Asian countries, in particular in China, Hong Kong, Taiwan, Japan and South Korea. Hofstede's colleagues, King and Bond (1985) argue that this has something to do with the Confucian traditions in these countries, which emphasize thrift and perseverance – virtues associated with long-term orientation. These virtues, as Hofstede (1994) rightly points out, are not of course unique to the countries with a Confucian heritage. The extent to which people can tolerate ambiguity and cope with uncertainty also varies from nation to nation, with Anglo, Nordic and Chinese people more at ease with uncertainty than those who come from Japan, Latin countries and German-speaking nations. As a consequence of this trait, a more structured and organized way of life may have more appeal to the latter group of peoples than it may to the former.

Disentanglement of national culture from organizational culture is an issue which has posed a formidable challenge to the researchers of comparative organizations, a challenge which has not yet been fully met. Hofstede's study is a major exception here because the organizational subculture was to some extent held constant. The employees in the thirty-nine subsidiaries of the US corporation whose responses were analyzed in the exercise had all no doubt to some extent been socialized to the company's subculture: they shared the same superstructure and policies, they were selected to belong to the same occupational categories, so they did very much the same kind of work, they were of the same education level and varied only marginally in age and sex composition. However, this still does not demonstrate in a concrete manner to what extent what we observe to be the respondents' values and attitudes have their roots in national or organizational cultures.

In a recent project Hofstede sought to address this issue more directly (Hofstede *et al.* 1990). The study was conducted in Holland and Denmark. Comparing otherwise similar people, the authors found considerable differences in *values* (in the sense of broad, nonspecific feelings such as good and evil) between the two national cultures. Among organizational cultures, they found considerable differences in *practices* for people who held about the same values. The study appears not to have quite succeeded in separating the influences of organizational culture from that of national culture on employees' work-related values and attitudes. As the authors themselves point out:

> All in all, having gone out to study organizational value differences and having done this in two countries for reasons of convenience, we seem to have mainly caught national value differences.
>
> (Hofstede *et al.* 1990: 300)

3 Evaluation

The impact of Hofstede's work is not limited to the field of management. His work has been cited in the fields of cross-cultural psychology, communications, marketing, psychiatry, education, organization sociology, political science, anthropology, philosophy and history.

Over the years a large number of researchers have replicated Hofstede's study, using his framework and his questionnaire items in one form or another, and many teachers and managers with international experience have learned a great deal from his work (Sondergaard 1994). However, the findings and conclusions of Hofstede's study should be treated with caution on methodological grounds.

The research was entirely based on an attitude-survey questionnaire which is certainly the least appropriate, least desirable way of studying culture. Moreover, the respondents, employees of a multinational corporation's subsidiaries, were an extremely narrow and specific sample of their countries' populations. They belonged to the middle class of their society rather than to the upper, working or rural classes. The company was a US one with a well-known strong organizational culture, which might well have 'ironed out' certain manifestations of local national cultures.

Confining national culture to a handful of dimensions gives only a simplistic and unidimensional picture of reality. National culture is too vibrant and complex a phenomenon to be treated like this. It is too simple, for instance, to say that country A is lower on uncertainty avoidance compared to country B. Country A may in fact be higher on the uncertainty avoidance index (UAI) when it comes to driving habits, but lower on sexual conduct expected of the young, in comparison with country B (Chapman and Antoniou 1994). Power distance, to give another example, is also highly situation-based: an Indian man might feel more powerful than his wife at home, but less so at work if he happens to be the director of a firm of which she is the owner-chairperson. There may in fact be a whole host of complicated reasons why some people behave one way under one condition, and a different way under another. It is therefore arguable that Hofstede's findings reflect the values and attitudes of a large sample of employees in relation to their specific work environment at the time the study was conducted.

The causal linkages which Hofstede believes to exist between cultural dimensions on the one hand, and employees' behaviour in work-related contexts or national performance of various countries as a whole on the other, are problematical. For instance, in one country uncertainty avoidance may be the cause of low labour turnover; in another the economic downturn and high unemployment may be the culprit. In some countries individualism and masculinity might be related to economic advancement while in others collectivism and patriotism might be behind their progress. If organizations in one country do not use very many written rules and regulations this may have nothing to do with their employees' low uncertainty avoidance; it may be because of a high rate of illiteracy among the employees, especially among manual workers (Tayeb 1988).

There is some inconsistency in the ways in which the core items of the questionnaire have been formed into indices. For power distance and uncertainty avoidance indices we have percentages added up, subtracted and multiplied by constant numbers; for individualism and masculinity indices it is the factor analysis which decides what items are included in each index. The indices themselves, moreover, are argued to be 'ecological' and, as such, are unsuitable for use in comparative studies where less than ten countries are investigated.

Finally, the relationships between the four dimensions of work-related values and attitudes and the structures of the organizations whose employees participated in the study were not empirically investigated. The relationships are conceptual and speculative. Conclusions about the overwhelming influence of cultural factors on organizational structure were based on speculations and subsequent 'after-event' corroboration with the findings of other studies, rather than 'hard' evidence (Tayeb 1994). We do not know, for instance, how each of the subsidiaries of the multinational corporation whose employees' attitudes and values were measured was organized.

4 Conclusions

We live in an increasingly shrinking world, where internationalization is bringing us into closer contacts with one another. Understanding other peoples and fostering sensitivity to their ways of life are very crucial to the success of our social and business interactions. Researchers who have compared and studied organizations cross-culturally have in the main enhanced our recognition of: (1) the fact that cultural values and attitudes are different in degree at least, if not in absolute terms in

some cases, from one society to another; (2) the fact that different cultural groups behave differently under similar circumstances because of the differences in their underlying values and attitudes; and (3) the important role that culture plays in shaping work organizations and other social institutions. Hofstede's immense role in this enhanced recognition is indisputable. He opened up the way and gave researchers a theoretical framework which could help them explain their findings in a new perspective. Managers of multinational firms are now better-equipped to understand the diversity of their employees.

MONIR TAYEB
HERIOT-WATT UNIVERSITY

Further reading

(References cited in the text marked*)

* Chapman, M. and Antoniou, C. (1994) 'Uncertainty avoidance in Greece: an ethnographic illustration', paper presented to the annual Academy of International Business (UK) Conference, Bradford, April. (An excellent and extensive analysis of the multifaceted nature of national culture.)
* Crozier, M. (1964) *The Bureaucratic Phenomenon*, London: Tavistock Publications. (A seminal investigation into French culture and French organizations.)
* Hofstede, G. (1967) *The Game of Budget Control*, Assen: Netherlands: Van Gorcum and (1968) London: Tavistock Publications. (An assessment of behavioural accounting, and a cultural approach to organizational control.)
* Hofstede, G. (1980) *Culture's Consequences*, Newbury Park, CA: Sage Publications. (A detailed analysis of Hofstede's major work.)
Hofstede, G. (1991) *Cultures and Organizations: Software of the Mind*, London: McGraw-Hill. (A major part of the book concerns the study already analysed in the 1988 work; there is a chapter which deals with organizational culture.)
* Hofstede, G. (1994) 'The business of international business is culture', *International Business Review* 3 (1): 114. (A useful summary of Hofstede's research findings.)
Hofstede, G. (1994) *Uncommon Sense About Organizations: Cases, Studies and Field Observations,* Thousand Oaks CA: Sage Publications.

(A collection of studies revealing uneasy truths about organizational life.)

* Hofstede, G. and Bond, M.H. (1988) 'Confucius and economic growth: new trends in culture's consequences', *Organizational Dynamics* 16 (4): 421. (A discussion of the time orientation dimension.)

* Hofstede, G., Neuijen, B. and Ohavy, D. (1990) 'Measuring organizational cultures: a qualitative and quantitative study across twenty cases', *Administrative Science Quarterly* 35 (June): 286316. (Presents the main findings of a study into organizational culture.)

* King, A.Y.C. and Bond, M.H. (1985) 'The confucian paradigm of man: a sociological view', in W. Tseng and D. Wu (eds), *Chinese Culture and Mental Health*, New York: Columbia University Press. (A discussion of Confucian precepts.)

* Sondergaard, M. (1994) 'Research note: Hofstede's consequences: a study of reviews, citations and replications', *Organization Studies* 15: 44756. (Lists various studies which discussed and/or replicated Hofstede's work.)

* Tayeb, M.H. (1988) *Organizations and National Culture,* London: Sage Publications. (A comparative study of Indian and English cultures and organizations.)

* Tayeb, M.H. (1994) 'Organizations and national culture: methodology considered', *Organization Studies* 15 (3): 42946. (A critique of methodologies employed in cross-cultural studies.)

See also: ADLER, N; CROZIER, M.; LUTHANS, F.; TUNG, R.L.

Related topics in the IEBM: CULTURE, CROSS-NATIONAL; GLOBALIZATION; HUMAN RESOURCE MANAGEMENT; HUMAN RESOURCE MANAGEMENT, INTERNATIONAL; ORGANIZATION BEHAVIOUR; ORGANIZATION BEHAVIOUR, HISTORY OF; ORGANIZATION STRUCTURE; POWER

Hopwood, Anthony (1944–)

Personal background

- born 18 May 1944 in Stoke-on-Trent, UK
- graduated in economics and accounting in 1965 with first class honours from the London School of Economics and Political Science (LSE), and went to Chicago as a Fulbright Scholar
- graduated with an MBA from Chicago in 1967, and with a PhD in 1971
- lecturer at the Manchester Business School, UK, 197–73
- in 1972 became visiting professor of management at the European Institute for Advanced Studies in Management (EIASM), a position still held
- member of senior staff at the Administrative Staff College, Henley-on-Thames, 1973–75
- founded the journal *Accounting, Organizations and Society* in 1976, continuing as editor to the present day
- professorial fellow at the Oxford Centre for Management Studies, 1976–78
- Institute of Chartered Accountants Professor of Accounting and Financial Reporting at the London Business School (LBS), 1978–85
- was the 1981 American Accounting Association's Distinguished International Visiting Lecturer
- Ernst and Young Professor of International Accounting and Financial Management at the LSE, 1985–95
- awarded a honorary doctorate from the Turku School of Economics, Finland in 1989 and from the University of Gothenburg in 1992
- professor of management studies at the University of Oxford, fellow of Templeton College, 1995–97
- president of EIASM, 1995–
- deputy director of the School of Management Studies, University of Oxford, 1995–98
- American Standard Companies Professor of Operations Management at the University of Oxford and Student of Christ Church, 1997–

Major works

An Accounting System and Managerial Behaviour (1973)
'The roles of accounting in organizations and society '(1980)
'Accounting in its social context: towards a history of value added in the United Kingdom' (1985)
'The archaeology of accounting systems' (1987)
Accounting from the Outside (1988)
'Accounting and organisational change' (1990)
'Some reflections on "the harmonization of accounting in the EU"' (1994)

Summary

Anthony Hopwood has had a profound influence on the accounting thought of the last 30 years. Through his work an awareness has developed that accounting is not just about figures, but needs to be seen in the wider context of management practices and management thought. Accounting, argues Hopwood, is both shaped by this wider context, and itself shapes our understanding of what the enterprise is and does.

His contribution has not just been in terms of additions to our knowledge about accounting; he has also enabled and promoted research in accounting in several different ways. First, through opening up new agendas for the study of accounting, bringing in insights from organizational studies and later from the wider field of social theory. The agendas which he has created for research have provided valuable themes to be taken up by other researchers. Second, beyond opening up new agendas for research in accounting, he has also created a successful academic journal, *Accounting, Organizations and Society*, which has provided a place for the new research on the organizational and social aspects of accounting to be published and thus brought to a wider audience. Third, through his institution-building activities, in particular his contribution to building up the European Accounting Association (EAA) which has provided an important arena for furthering European research in accounting. Additionally, in his role as professor at the European Institute for Advanced Studies in Management (EIASM), and as its current president, he has more generally encouraged the development of management thought in a European context. Thus he has not only influenced management thought, but also opened up many opportunities for others to do so.

I Introduction: the early years

Anthony Hopwood was born towards the end of World War II in Stoke-on-Trent, an area in the north Midlands known for its long tradition of pottery manufacture. At the age of 11 he gained a place at the local grammar school, Hanley High School, where outstanding examination results gave him the chance to study at university. His decision to choose accountancy as his field of study grew out of an interest in the subject stimulated by a family member who was an accountant. On several occasions he had even considered leaving school to become a professional accountant, however the opportunity to study at The London School of Economics and Political Studies (LSE) was irresistible. It was an exciting place in the early 1960s, with an active research environment under the leadership of professors William Baxter, Harold Edey and Basil Yamey.

Having gained a first class honours degree in economics and accounting, he decided that he wanted to do research in the area of finance. The limited possibility for doctoral study in the UK led him to decide to enrol on an American doctoral programme. He obtained a Fulbright Scholarship to study at the University of Chicago which by this time was one of the top universities for the study of accounting and finance. As part of his studies, he was obliged to take some optional courses. One which he took in organization theory inspired him to change his focus from finance to the behavioural aspects of accounting systems. This was a change that was to prove decisive for his future career.

In the 1960s most studies of the effects of accounting data on decision behaviour were based on laboratory studies. Reports based on different accounting methods were presented to samples of financial analysts, managers and students, and it was observed whether their decision behaviours were dependent on the type of data received. Not convinced that this was the most fruitful way to study accounting in action, he decided that he would carry out field research on accounting in an organization. This was controversial as it created a new precedent for accounting research in Chicago; it was also difficult to find a research site, but eventually access was gained to a major steel company. There he observed and studied the role of accounting, becoming fascinated by how managerial processes gave accounting data an organizational meaning and significance.

In 1971 his PhD thesis was accepted, and in 1973 it appeared as a book under the title *An Accounting System and Managerial Behaviour*. The major results also appeared as articles in the *Journal of Accounting Research* and in the *Accounting Review*. In the latter article he concluded that: 'the relationship between accounting data and decision behaviour is moderated by the leadership style and social context of the decision maker'. This was an indirect but powerful challenge to the results of laboratory studies on accounting and decision making, which did not go unnoticed. Some of the more radical and wide ranging ideas which he had developed during his PhD studies did not appear in the thesis itself, but eventually were published in a monograph, *Accounting and Human Behaviour* (1974). All in all these were insightful presentations of the way in which accounting was integral to activity in the enterprise, and ones which were to be influential in the ensuing years.

2 Main contributions

Accounting in its organisational context

In 1970 Hopwood returned to the UK, and to a position at the Manchester Business School. There he became part of the group of young academics who were actively exploring management thought using insights from sociology and anthropology, as well as from organisational studies. From examining accounting in action in the organization, Hopwood began to be interested in how accounting got caught up in wider transformations of enterprises, and to consider how accounting itself might be influenced by organizational changes. This work ultimately proved to be very influential: it changed the agenda of management accounting by introducing the idea of a two-way interaction between accounting and organizations. This not only spawned a great amount of research, but also affected the way management accounting is taught and perceived by practitioners.

While his early work was developed to some extent as a reaction and critique of the American research traditions he had met at Chicago, during the 1970s he began to situate himself more as a European academic. This was stimulated, amongst other things, by his growing involvement with European accounting ideas and institutions. In 1971 he and a French academic, Edmund Marques, were appointed as visiting members of the faculty of the European Institute of Advanced Studies in Management (EIASM) with the aim of developing a series of European accounting research workshops. These soon became successful events, and contributed to the exchange of ideas and to the recognition of the varied and rich traditions of accounting in

different European countries. It marked the beginning of the development of an invisible college of accounting academics in Europe, which was later to manifest itself visibly in the formation of the European Accounting Association (EAA). The EAA has held annual conferences since 1978 in which Hopwood has played an important role, and their contribution to the development of an accounting research community in Europe cannot be underestimated. Hopwood's openness towards and interest in the accounting institutions, knowledge and practice of other countries has been important in developing an appreciation of these other traditions which can enrich our understanding of accounting as a social practice.

This was not the only important institutional development in which he was involved during these years. Identifying that the editorial policies and concerns of existing academic journals were not particularly facilitative to the new work being done on accounting in organizations, when the opportunity arose Hopwood started a new journal *Accounting Organizations and Society*, the first issue of which was published in 1976. The title represented his vision for a journal which would reflect an agenda for research which would involve openly exploring the ways in which accounting functions in organizational and social settings.

After a brief period at the Administrative Staff College at Henley, in 1976 Hopwood was appointed to the Oxford Centre for Management Studies (now Templeton College, Oxford) as professorial fellow. He gathered together a research team with the explicit aim of understanding what might be at stake in an organizational and social analysis of accounting. They soon began to focus on the study of accounting change in various different settings, arguing that the ruptures associated with change could reveal aspects of accounting which were normally not visible.

Accounting, institutions and society

In 1978 Hopwood took up an appointment at the London Business School as professor. The analysis of accounting being developed in collaboration with his research team was clearly now including 'society' as well as 'organization'. One of their first pieces to be published was an article entitled 'The roles of accounting in organizations and society' (Burchell *et al.* 1980). In some sense this can be seen as filling out the agenda which had been laid down through the first editorials of *Accounting, Organizations and Society*. It was a very influential article, in particular because it opened up a wide agenda for research; creating an intellectual space for others could explore.

The research team worked on several topics around the theme of accounting change. The most cited of these studies has been that entitled: 'Accounting in its social context: towards a history of value added in the United Kingdom' (Burchell, Clubb and Hopwood 1985). It clearly expressed the importance of the social to accounting, opening with the words 'Accounting is coming to be seen as a social rather than a purely technical phenomenon … Albeit slowly, the ways in which accounting both emerges from and itself gives rise to the wider contexts in which it operates are starting to be appreciated' (1985: 381). Inspired by the notion that studying accounting change provides an important means of opening up accounting to social analysis, the paper traces the emergence of a new form of accounting in the UK in the 1970s, namely value added accounting. The complexity of the process which is revealed clearly illustrates the poverty of simplistic approaches to the study of accounting change.

This interest in accounting change was put to action on a more practical level when he was appointed in 1984 as convenor of a committee established by the research board of the Institute of Chartered Accountants in England and Wales (ICAEW) to look at the ways in which the accounting environment might change over the next twenty years. He brought together a wide group of scholars and practitioners to discuss the issues. The final report, published as a book in 1990 (Hopwood, Page and Turley 1990), was an insightful contribution to debate both within the profession and outside.

The complex intertwining of the accounting and the social has formed the theme of many of Hopwood's works from the early 1980s onwards. One particular aspect of this which has concerned him is the enormous growth of knowledge around accounting; from textbooks and manuals to professional pronouncements and, more recently, research. As a result of this process of knowledge creation we can talk rather than merely do accounting, an 'accounting-speak' that can have an autonomy from accounting practice. In other words, the doing of accounting can be confronted with our ability to talk accounting and changed as a result. Thus accounting knowledge has played a role in making accounting what it was not.

Accounting research can be seen as a specialized form of 'accounting speak'; this is explored in a lecture entitled 'Accounting research and accounting practice: the ambiguous relationship between the two' (Hopwood 1988). Here some of the different ways in which accounting research has been called upon to play a role in the accounting standard setting process are examined. While it is claimed that research fulfils a technical function, research knowledge in accountancy has, in practice, often played more of a strategic than the technical role; one prominent example being that of the American accounting standard-setting body's project to establish a conceptual framework for accounting. Rather than radically changing the craft of accounting in practice, it was called upon to serve institutional roles in legitimating actions of the profession.

This use of accounting to serve institutional roles was also taken up in a public lecture held at Leeds University in 1985 entitled 'Accounting and the domain of the public: some observations on current developments', which dealt with the introduction of accounting in the public sector in the UK (Hopwood 1988). In the mid-1980s the Tory government were pushing to make public sector organizations justify their existence in economic terms. Not surprisingly, accounting began to be appealed to in this process; not only just as a means of giving 'an account', but also demonstrating a commitment to the newly introduced economic rationales. However, to see it as having symbolic effects must not lead us to ignore that it can have very particular effects in particular organizations. Entering into an organization, accounting creates a particular kind of visibility of events which may lead to transference of power and resources; however not necessarily in accordance with the arguments originally advanced for its introduction. Returning to an earlier theme, Hopwood ends with an appeal for more effort to be placed on studying the specific manifestations of accounting in specific organizations.

Accounting and the politics of accounting change

The appointment of Hopwood as professor at the LSE in 1985, together with his student colleague, Michael Bromwich, brought an academic revolution. As one of the current professors of accounting at the LSE, Michael Power, writes, at this period the LSE established itself as an international focus for research into the social and institutional character of accounting practice. The recruiting of a number of continental European PhD students, and academic staff with an international orientation made the department exceptional in the UK.

Hopwood's interest in accounting regulation moved into the political sphere when he agreed in 1989 to produce a consultative report for the European Commission on the harmonization of accounting standards within the EC (Hopwood 1990b). In the report, he analyses the consequences of the regulatory initiatives taken in the community up to that time, and discusses possible future initiatives. Arguing the need for furthering accounting harmonization within the Community, but being conscious of the ponderous nature of the process of producing accounting directives he suggests a new organizational form, a 'European Accounting Forum'. The Forum would aim not to be a regulator of accounting itself, but to strive to improve communication between national standard setters. Taken up in practice, the Accounting Forum was established in 1991, but due to various reasons, some predicted by Hopwood in his original report, it has not been particularly influential. In an article critically analyzing developments in accounting harmonization in the EU, he remarks how constellations of power and influence around the large accounting firms, the profession, and their supranational organizations shape international developments (Hopwood 1994).

After a decade at the LSE he moved back to Oxford University, and at the same time took on the challenging job of being president of European Institute of Advanced Studies in Management (EIASM). At a time when the academic study of management studies is becoming more internationalized in all European countries, the very European perspective and meeting place which this organization can provide is more important now than ever.

3 Conclusion

Anthony Hopwood's career as an accounting academic has spanned a quarter century of exciting times in a subject whose proverbial dullness, he would argue, has helped to cover up its important role in modern society; a role which is far more complex than indicated by the glowing statements of mission which grace the openings of textbooks. He has influenced both academia in accounting and accounting in practice through his insightful analyses of the way in which accounting and organisations interact with one another. That changing an enterprise's management accounting system may have other and different consequences than those intended can no longer be a surprise.

As a prominent academic his activities and writings have not always been met by agreement. There has been inevitable critique, some of which has come from the mainstream, who argue that his work diminishes and confuses the true path of progress for accountancy. A rather different critique has come from the radical left, who have argued that his writings have not gone as far as they could have in revealing accounting's true nature as a tool of capitalism. He has not been afraid to take up the debate, both verbally and in print. It has precisely been one of his aims to challenge simple images of accounting which claim for it some kind of 'true' essence and purpose.

Institutional developments and activities have played an important part in his academic life, especially since the mid-1980s. These have been of crucial importance to other scholars, opening up possibilities which might not otherwise have existed for the exploration of accounting as a social phenomenon.

ANNE LOFT
COPENHAGEN BUSINESS SCHOOL

Further reading

(References cited in the text marked *)

* Burchell, S., Clubb, C. and Hopwood, A.G. (1985) 'Accounting in its social context: towards a history of value added in the United Kingdom', *Accounting, Organizations and Society* 10 (4): 381–413. (An accounting classic, dealing with the interaction between accounting and society.)
* Burchell, S., Clubb, C., Hopwood, A., Hughes, J. and Nahapiet, J. (1980) 'The roles of accounting in organizations and society', *Accounting, Organizations and Society* 5 (1): 5–27. (An accounting classic; introduces and explores the many roles of accounting.)
* Hopwood, A.G. (1973) *An Accounting System and Managerial Behavior*, Mass. USA: Lexington Books. (His PhD thesis.)
* Hopwood, A.G. (1974) *Accounting and Human Behaviour*, London: Accountancy Age Books. (Extends and explores more widely the themes in his PhD thesis.)
  Hopwood, A.G. (1987) 'The archaeology of accounting systems', *Accounting, Organizations and Society* 12 (3): 207–234. (An analysis of several case studies of accounting change, and theoretical discussion of the issues.)

* Hopwood, A.G. (1988) *Accounting from the Outside*, New York: Garland Publishing, Inc. (This contains his collected works up to that date, including published articles cited here. There are many interesting articles either previously unpublished or published in obscure journals which deserve further reading. Two worth special mention are the lectures: 'Accounting research and accounting practice: the ambiguous relationship between the two' (549–578) and Accounting and the domain of the public: some observations on current developments' (259–277).)
  Hopwood A.G. (1990a) 'Accounting and organisational change', *Accounting, Auditing and Accountability Journal* 3 (1): 7–17. (A short but insightful article.)
* Hopwood, A.G. (1990b) 'Harmonisation of accounting standards within the EC: a perspective for the future', in Commission of the European Communities *The Future of Harmonisation of Accounting Standards within the European Communities*, Brussels: CEC. (A valuable discussion of harmonization issues.)
* Hopwood, A.G. (1994) 'Some reflections on 'the harmonization of accounting in the EU', *The European Accounting Review* 3 (2): 241–253. (A critical analysis of the received wisdom about accounting harmonization.)
* Hopwood, A.G., Page, M. and Turley, S. (1990) *Understanding Accounting in a Changing Environment*, Hemel Hempstead: Prentice Hall/ICAEW. (A project for the ICAEW on what the future might bring to accounting and accountants.)

See also: BENSON, H.; CHANDLER, A.D.; MINTZBERG, H.; PATON, W.A.

Related topics in the IEBM: ACCOUNTING; ACCOUNTING AND ORGANIZATIONS; ACCOUTING HARMONIZATION; ACCOUNTING IN UNITED KINGDOM; AUDITING; CREATIVE ACCOUNTING; ORGANIZATION BEHAVIOUR; ORGANIZATION CULTURE

Ibuka, Masaru (1908–97)

Personal background

- born Nikko, Tochigi, on 11 April 1908
- attended Faculty of Science and Engineering, Waseda University
- married Sekiko Maeda, 1926
- founded Tokyo Tsushin Kogyo (Tokyo Telecommunication Engineering – the forerunner of Sony), 1946
- became president of Tokyo Tsushin Kogyo, 1950
- changed the company name to Sony, 1958
- became chairman of Sony, 1971
- retired from active work and took up the honorary chairmanship of Sony, 1976
- died of heart failure in Tokyo on 17 December 1997

Major works

Watashino Rirekisho (My Personal History) (1962)
Sozo Eno Tabi (Journey to Creation) (1985)
Ibuka Masaru no Sekai: Erekutoronikusu ni Chosen Shite (The World of Masaru Ibuka: The Challenge of Electronics) (1993)

Summary

Masaru Ibuka is a famous entrepreneur who founded Sony, the worldwide electronics company. He was an innovative engineer and also a capable manager. Sony grew from a small firm, numbering tens of employees in 1946, to an electronics giant. In post-war Japan, Ibuka became a figure symbolic of mass consumption, and also of peace, because Sony was a producer of consumer products, not military ones: the firm is famous for making such things as tape recorders, transistor radios, television sets, video cassette recorders and Walkman personal stereos. His attitude, stressing originality, is different from typical Japanese firms' behaviour, which has a tendency to follow suit and imitate the inventions of others. After leaving active involvement in Sony, he has spent much time in the activity of *zaikai* (Japan's big business circle) and in studying the educational problems of children to expand their potentials.

1 Introduction

Ibuka is renowned for his unique inventiveness, business strategy and innovative flair. His inventions have brought him about seventy patents. His strategy, which attaches importance to differentiating, brought him fame as an entrepreneur, along with Soichiro Honda, Akio Morita (see MORITA, A.) and others. Their vivid entrepreneurship represented one aspect of post-war Japan. This tendency to respect originality and not to follow courses laid down by others, is quite different from the group-orientated characteristics seen in trade associations and *keiretsu*. Why and how did Ibuka follow such policies, and what was the result?

2 Biographical data

Ibuka was born in Nikko; his father worked for a medium-sized *zaibatsu*, Furukawa, and died when Ibuka was a child. After a complex childhood as regards his family life, he entered Waseda University and studied electrical engineering. During his time as a university student, he made some remarkable inventions and became known as a student inventor. Around the same time, he became a Christian, though not a passionate one. After graduation, he began to work for Photo Chemical Laboratory in 1933, which was then making recording machines and films.

Not fully satisfied with this firm, he moved into Nihon Ko-on Kogyo (Japan Light and Sound Engineering), and then in 1940, he started a new company, Nihon Sokutei Ki (Japan Measuring Tools) which manufactured relay machines used for searching for submarines. Through this work, Ibuka came to be connected with the navy, where he met Akio Morita, a technical sub-lieutenant. Immediately after the war, Ibuka began again with a new organization called Tokyo Tsushin Kenkyujo, whose main product was voltmeters. Six months later, this was incorporated as Tokyo Telecommunication Engineering, which was renamed Sony in 1958.

Ibuka became president of the firm in 1950 and chairman in 1971, with Morita succeeding as president. In 1976, Ibuka became honorary chairman, with Morita taking the chairmanship as chief executive officer.

3 Main contribution

Ibuka showed brilliant leadership in developing Sony, especially from 1945 to 1976 as president and chairman. His hallmark as an entrepreneur is a scientific-mindedness and interest in innovation. His background in engineering is likely to have been the source of his liking for innovation. During the turbulent years between 1945 and 1950, Sony tried out a variety of products and eventually succeeded in making Japan's first tape recorders, after painstaking trials and errors, in 1950. Ibuka provided strong technical guidance for this project. To achieve his goal, Ibuka recruited many university graduates, including those with doctorates and master's degrees, and even a later Nobel prize laureate, Leona Esaki. A third of Sony's employees were highly educated people. This top-heavy structure, which is related to Ibuka's scientific-minded policy, contributed to the development of tape recorders.

Another example of Ibuka's technological orientation stems from a three-month visit he made to the USA in 1952, where he realized the potential of transistors. After returning to Japan, he pushed research on transistors. In 1953 Sony obtained non-exclusive rights from Western Electric for its 1948 transistor

technology. This did not, however, bring technical know-how, so Sony had to develop its own applications technology. Finally, Sony succeeded in mass-producing transistors. At the outset, the yield ratio of transistor production was so low (5 per cent) that it was thought too risky to launch. Yet Ibuka thought that even if the yield ratio was only 5 per cent, it would have a huge potential for improvement.

Ibuka expanded R&D activity to new fields such as transistor radios, the first transistor television sets, the first home video recorders, integrated circuit-based radios, Trinitron colour television tubes, U-matic videotape recorders and Betamax video cassette recorders. These innovative products were realized through the resolute driving force of Ibuka.

Ibuka's inclination was always toward consumer products, not industrial ones and particularly not military ones. The excellence of Sony's niche strategy is demonstrated by the fact that transistors were used for radios, which a great many consumers wanted at that time. Everyone hoped to have a radio because it was a symbol of affluence. In 1955, one of the first transistor radios in the world was made by Sony. Ibuka was consumer-orientated to the core, and preferred to develop products for direct use by individuals. Almost all products were for private use, although some goods were made for radio and television stations. Transistor radios and transistor television sets, home video recorders, colour television sets and Betamax recorders exemplify this tendency.

The surge of private consumer demand was so enormous that this strategy tied in perfectly with post-war development. Ibuka's emphasis on the civil use of transistors was also conducive to development, since the demand for military use was negligible in Japan. The cost constraints imposed by the civil market facilitated the rapid development of the transistor. In the USA, on the other hand, the military market was dominant which impeded the development of transistor production.

However, there were some mistakes which stemmed from sticking to consumer demand. For instance, in 1963 Ibuka ordered the cessation of production of special audio machinery for broadcasting stations because it was too costly and troublesome. The person in charge of the operation objected, as he thought that if television stations were seen to be using Sony's products, this would engender trust in general users. But Ibuka did not change his view that Sony should concentrate on mass consumer products. More importantly, Sony never fully developed IC (integrated circuits) although some trials were done. Because of failures at the early stage, Sony too promptly abandoned the development of IC, in spite of Ibuka's tenacity in transistor development. It was the same with the development of a magnetic scale to measure materials for machine tools.

One aspect of products particularly favoured by Ibuka is compactness. Accordingly, Sony continually developed smaller and lighter products, going from tube to transistor, to IC-based to pocket-sized radios. Microtelevisions, Walkmans and video Walkmans are also sold by Sony. This is well suited to the post-war trend whereby many products have been getting smaller. This enabled Sony to grow fast by capturing the market.

To give an example of this concern with size, the first tape recorder weighed about 100 pounds, but a few years later this went down to only 30 pounds as a result of improvements. Nowadays pocket-sized radios and the Walkman continue the trend. These factors – innovation and consumer orientation, and the smallness of products – were instrumental in developing Sony from a small local factory to a multinational enterprise with many thousands of employees.

4 Evaluation

The Sony spirit is expressed, among other things, as 'not liking to do the same thing as others do' (Sony 1986). Profits as a result of cost reduction through simple mass production and mass marketing are not part of the strategy. By aggressive investment in R&D, and making ingenious products, Sony can produce what others cannot, and continuous production of such products is Sony's cornerstone.

Ibuka has never lost his innovative stance, although occasional mistakes have been made. His commitment to consumer products and inclination to compactness were quite effective for the development of Sony. His innovative and challenging mind is illuminated in the following passage:

> While we should make less risky decisions based on scientific data, it is vitally important to keep the sharp and bold spirit which enables us to challenge. If we become frightened and do nothing, Sony will come to be an old-fashioned firm. If you judge that it is good for Sony, you should daringly try it. Responsibility implies the boldness to fulfil it.
>
> (Sony 1986)

The Ibuka spirit is still the backbone of Sony, in spite of his retirement from the front. The heavy weighting, however, towards technology and consumer products was changed after Ibuka's retirement. It is well known that Betamax video cassette recorders were defeated by VHS. Some argued that Betamax was technically superior to VHS, but commercially VHS won the video cassette recorder war. Faced with this situation, Sony responded by restructuring its organization, introducing a multidivisional structure and reinforcing the mass production system and especially its marketing organization. Manufacturing of audio and visual machinery for broadcasting stations was reintroduced. Fortunately, the production of the magnetic scale, which had continued as the business of a subsidiary, became helpful to the parent company's profitability in bleak years.

In terms of corporate culture, Sony has a unique atmosphere, thanks to Ibuka's intellectual and practical influence. It does not have the company song and motto that are almost obligatory for Japanese firms. Relatively speaking, Sony emphasizes individuality. It is said that Ibuka and Morita address their employees as (for example) 'Smith-san' or 'Jones-kun'. These polite expressions reveal the less authoritative and more egalitarian character of Sony, which probably derives from Ibuka's gentle and imaginative influence.

5 Conclusion

Ibuka is a legendary and highly respected entrepreneur in Japan. He provides a contrast with many top managers of large firms in Japan. If the organization-orientated culture is typical of Japanese firms, Ibuka might be considered an exception in the Japanese business world, along with Soichiro Honda and Akio Morita. Ibuka's brand of ingenuity is urgently needed in today's competitive world.

ETSUO ABE
MEIJI UNIVERSITY

Further reading

(References cited in the text marked *)

Ibuka, M. (1980) *Watashino Rirekisho* (My Personal History), Tokyo: Nihon Keizai Shinbunsha . (Ibuka's own description of the first half of his life, first published in 1962.)

Ibuka, M. (1985) *Sozo Eno Tabi* (Journey to Creation), Tokyo: Kosei Shuppansha.

Ibuka, M. (1993) *Ibuka Masaru no Sekai: Erekutoronikusu ni Chosen Shite* (The World of Masaru Ibuka: The Challenge of Electronics), Tokyo: Mainichi Shinbunsha. (Records of interviews.)

Morita, A. (1987) *Made in Japan: Akio Morita and Sony*, London: Collins. (Interesting self-portrait of Morita and Sony; provides an accurate explanation of Japanese business behaviour.)

Nakagawa, Y. (1993) *Sozo no Jinsei: Ibuka Masaru* (Life of Creation), Tokyo: Kodansha. (Biography of Masaru Ibuka, using personal interviews as sources.)

Noda, K. (1963) 'Sony', *Ekonomisuto* (11 June): 72–6.

* Sony Koho Shitsu (ed.) (1986) *Kaisha no Yuki* (*The Boldness of a Company*), Tokyo: Kodansha. (The only official company history of Sony.)

See also: ISHIKAWA, K.; MORITA, A.; NONAKA, I.; OHMAE, K.

Related topics in the IEBM: BUSINESS CULTURE, JAPANESE; BUSINESS HISTORY, JAPANESE; BUSINESS STRATEGY, JAPANESE; COMMITMENT IN JAPAN; GLOBALIZATION; INDUSTRIAL RELATIONS IN JAPAN; INTERNATIONAL MARKETING; JAPANIZATION; MANAGEMENT IN JAPAN; MANAGEMENT IN PACIFIC ASIA; NEW PRODUCT DEVELOPMENT; TECHNOLOGY DIFFUSION IN JAPAN

Ishikawa, Kaoru (1915–89)

Personal background

- born in 1915 into a family of prominent industrialists
- graduated in applied chemistry from University of Tokyo (1939)
- technical officer in the Japanese Navy (1939–41)
- worked in industry until 1947 when he joined the University of Tokyo, developing a keen interest in the study of statistical techniques
- developed the Ishikawa diagram in 1943
- invited by the Japanese Union of Scientists and Engineers (JUSE) in 1949 to join the QC Research Group
- became Director of the Chemical Society in Japan (1952), promoting quality control
- a member of the International Standards Organization (ISO) from 1969, becoming its chairman in 1977 and encouraging standardization of quality
- became a member of the ISO's executive committee in 1981
- was constantly in demand worldwide to give seminars and advice on Japanese quality control techniques until his death in 1989

Major works

Introduction to Quality Control (1954)
What is Total Quality Control? The Japanese Way (1985)

Summary

Kaoru Ishikawa will always be recognized as a major contributor to the concept of total quality control or the management of quality. He maintained that the management of quality necessitates the company-wide involvement of employees and managers through quality circles, a focus on the process rather than the individual when a problem is investigated through the use of the Ishikawa diagram, and a reliance on statistical techniques for company-wide quality control. Ishikawa believed that Japanese success in dominating world markets comes from their dedication and belief in the power of quality control.

1 Biographical data

Kaoru Ishikawa was born in 1915 in Japan. On graduating from the Department of Applied Chemistry at the University of Tokyo in March 1939, he took up employment with a company in the utilities sector. A few months later he had to join the Japanese Navy where he spent two years as a technical officer and was involved in education and training. After that he returned to work in industry.

In 1947 he joined the University of Tokyo to carry out research. As a scientist he realized the difficulties in analysing scattered data and being able to interpret it. This drove him to take a keen interest in statistics and in the study of statistical techniques. In 1949 he was invited by the Japanese Union of Scientists and Engineers (JUSE) to join a task force called QC Research Group to conduct pioneering work in the area of quality control (QC) and the use of statistical methods. For the next forty years or so Ishikawa dedicated himself entirely to this field and tried to help professional associations, academic institutions and industrial organizations worldwide in the application of QC principles.

Ishikawa promoted the slogan 'The next process is your customer' in the 1950s to resolve conflict between departments and to encourage teamwork between the various functions. In 1952 he became director of the

Chemical Society in Japan and encouraged networks and joint projects with academic institutions in the field of QC and the co-sponsorship of annual conferences on QC activities. These annual conferences started to focus on the needs of various groups in employment, including managers, supervisors and workers. This led to the birth of quality circles in 1962 and the acknowledgement that QC has to involve everyone in the organization and that it should focus on the process and the end customer.

This great period of QC revolution in Japan was marked by intensive programmes of education and training on QC and quality circles, the publication of various journals on the subject and the development of case studies about the application of these concepts and their related benefits. Ishikawa was heavily involved in the setting up of quality standards and was closely involved in the Japanese Industrial Standards body (JIS) and the International Standards Organization (ISO). In 1969 he became a member of the ISO chapter in Japan and its chairman in 1977. He became a member of the ISO's executive committee in 1981 and this gave him the opportunity to influence international cooperation through standardization of quality. Although Ishikawa believed that standards were essential in determining minimum and acceptable levels of quality, he did not consider they were enough in themselves or that their implementation would necessarily lead to customer satisfaction. He believed that while taking into account standards, the challenge for QC was also to set higher goals and avoid complacency through continuous improvement and a commitment to satisfying customer requirements time and time again.

Until his death in 1989, Ishikawa travelled extensively and was constantly in demand by governments, universities and industrial organizations to give seminars and advice on Japanese QC techniques. He worked closely with the other gurus of quality including Deming and Juran whom he met in the 1950s when they were invited to give seminars on QC to Japanese managers (see DEMING, W.E.; JURAN, J.M.). He served as president of the Musashi

Institute of Technology and in great demand as a consultant in Japan and other countries.

2 Main contribution

Ishikawa's major contribution can perhaps be highlighted by focusing on his role in the development of the Japanese total quality control (TQC) approach, the introduction of the Ishikawa diagram (cause-and-effect analysis) and the promotion of QC circles. These are now examined in turn.

Total quality control in Japan

Japan's post-war economic success is often regarded as being mainly due to the way that the Japanese have recognized human potential. This is shown in a commitment to harnessing employees' creativity and a determination to optimize quality and eliminate waste. Ishikawa and others are recognized for their efforts in bringing about this so-called 'miracle' by insisting that QC becomes everybody's responsibility. During his worldwide travels Ishikawa urged his audiences to purchase Japanese products and services because the quality would be guaranteed.

Controlling quality effectively involves, argued Ishikawa, integrating various elements:

1 the control of the quality of the product/service *per se*
2 the integrated control of cost, price and profit
3 the control of a reliable supply chain and delivery system.

Ishikawa stated that 'to practice quality control is to develop, design, produce and service a quality product which is most economical, most useful, and always satisfactory to the consumer' (Ishikawa 1985).

Ishikawa strongly believed that organizations had no choice but to control quality for as long as they had a desire to compete in the marketplace with products and services. He often warned that 'total quality control consists of doing what should be done as a matter of course' (Ishikawa 1989a). Ishikawa also maintained that TQC is not a fast-acting drug like penicillin, but a slow-acting herbal remedy that will gradually improve a company's constitution if taken over a long period (Ishikawa 1989a). The evolution process of TQC in Japan was recognized as being successful due to ten critical factors:

1 QC activities that represent a company-wide approach with the full participation and involvement of everyone
2 a senior management commitment not to compromise on quality and a belief in the quality-first principle
3 the development and sharing of a company vision and achieving desired objectives by implementing a quality policy
4 QC audits through self-assessment using the Deming prize framework, first introduced in 1951
5 quality assurance and process management using facts and a continuous improvement approach in all the various functions
6 the positive encouragement of teamwork and quality circles throughout the organization
7 insistence on QC training and education on a regular basis
8 the use of statistical techniques at elementary and advanced levels
9 appreciation of the relevance of QC at all levels and in all industrial sectors and the need for it to be spread throughout Japanese industry and commerce
10 governmental support and national QC promotion through such means as Quality Month, various QC symposia and the establishment of QC circle headquarters.

The Ishikawa diagram

Ishikawa advocated the use of statistical techniques in company-wide quality control (CWQC). He classified them into three categories (elemental, intermediate and advanced) and argued that 90 to 95 per cent of all problems can be solved using the elemental statistical techniques, which do not require specialist knowledge.

The Ishikawa diagram, also referred to as cause-and-effect (C&E) analysis or the fishbone diagram, is one of the most basic and important tools of quality improvement. It was introduced by Ishikawa in 1943 and represents a structured approach to problem solving. It is used to organize the information generated by brainstorming sessions in order to consider potential causes of problems. All possibilities are scrutinized until a cause-and-effect relationship is established.

The diagram provides a comprehensive view of the quality process and its surrounding environment. Ishikawa developed this technique (not a truly statistical technique) to help Japanese managers analyse problems associated with the processes that they were responsible for. He believed that causes can be associated with any of the following factors in a manufacturing/service environment: (1) methods; (2) materials; (3) manpower; (4) machines; and (5) environment. In addition to determining the impact of individual causes, the Ishikawa diagram can establish the interrelationships between various causes. It is highly compatible with brainstorming techniques and encourages the involvement of different people, all of whom are encouraged to participate in isolating key sources of problems.

The following steps should be observed when using cause-and-effect diagrams:

1 identify the is
2 build major causes around the problem structure
3 use team effort to brainstorm sub-causes under each cause
4 allow for an incubation period before revisiting and re-examining these sub-cause
5 highlight the vital few/most likely causes
6 check the most likely causes through data collection and analysis to determine the level of impact on the problem under study.

Quality control circles

During the early stages of promoting TQC in Japan it became very clear to Ishikawa and others that education and training on QC principles should not simply be limited to management and engineering levels, but had to be spread downwards to all other employees too. It was therefore considered very important to involve both shop-floor supervisors and employees in QC activities since they are more closely associated with the various processes than anyone else. They possess all the facts and information needed by senior managers in order to make the right decision. The effectiveness of senior managers can only be measured by their success in involving all employees.

A journal, referred to as *Gemba-to-QC*, was issued for the first time in April 1962 and marked the big launch of the quality circles movement. The QC circle headquarters was established in 1963, with nine QC circle regional chapters in 1964 and others after that. Quality circles are promoted through journals, books, videos, case studies, conferences, seminars and courses.

The notion of voluntarism is at the heart of QC circles. Unlike project teams, people decide whether they want to join without any coercion from senior managers. The following points compare quality circles with other teamwork approaches for tackling improvement projects:

1 QC circles deal with local issues only, while other teamwork deals with problem solving and the control of organizational problems
2 a bottom-up approach is used for QC circles and a top-down, project-based approach for other teamwork
3 quality circles allow free choice to determine areas for improvement, whereas project teams are specifically allocated tasks from the top
4 quality circles constitute a continuous process while project teams are dismantled once the project is finished
5 quality circles do not have to formally report to senior managers while project teams have to keep senior managers informed on a regular basis.

The major premise behind the role of quality circles, according to Ishikawa, is encouraging all employees to contribute to the value-added process for the benefit of the end customer. He also realized the need to show respect for people by allowing employees to decide on the setting up and management of their work environment. More importantly, he allowed individual employees to contribute to their best ability in terms of creativity and innovation and encouraged the harnessing of their ideas.

3 Evaluation

The concept of TQC was first introduced by Armand V. Feigenbaum in his book entitled *Total Quality Control: Engineering and Management*, in 1961. His definition of TQC is functionally based since he recommends that one specific function should have the task of controlling quality. This suggests specialism rather than encouraging company-wide involvement.

The benefits of involving all employees

In contrast to Feigenbaum, Ishikawa argued that TQC had to depend on contributions from all employees and that individuals alone would be unable to deliver quality to the end customers. He believed that TQC was not just a mere set of tools or specialist skills, but that it was also about education, training and altering employees' behaviour so that they would continuously strive to improve quality and eliminate waste. He considered it to be about respect for others and appreciating the valuable contributions of everyone concerned. TQC, in Japanese terms, is about pursuing one process where particular goals and the means to achieve them cannot be separated. Performance management and measurement are thus heavily dependant on the ability of senior managers to deploy organizational objectives effectively at all levels.

Total quality control compared with the zero defects movement

Ishikawa believed that TQC 'starts and finishes with education'. He criticized the zero defects (ZD) movement which was introduced in the West and which was considered to have failed for the following reasons:

1 The emphasis of the ZD movement was on encouraging people to do their best and to work harder rather than teaching them to work in a more intelligent way.
2 People were not educated or trained to use tools and techniques for controlling quality. The ZD principle was not regarded as a scientific approach to the management of quality.
3 In the ZD approach people were strongly encouraged to comply with the standard and to observe the written rules. This contrasts with Ishikawa's approach where people are strongly encouraged to challenge existing standards and continuously improve on them so that quality is optimized and performance greatly enhanced. Quality circles are, according to Ishikawa, the ideal tool for enhancing quality since they are created with a long-term objective in mind and are based on 'voluntarism'. Quality is likely to be sustainable since people's attitudes and behaviour are geared towards improving quality.
4 Taylorism and scientific management principles inherent in many organizations in the West are thought to be more detrimental to human potential since creativity and innovation are suppressed and human dignity can often be disregarded (see TAYLOR, F.W.).
5 Participation and close involvement were not included in the zero defects movement. People were asked to agree to initiatives often instigated by senior managers.
6 Employees were often held responsible for mistakes, since the ZD movement focuses on the individual and the task rather than the process and its immediate environment.

The so-called Japanese 'miracle'

Many people, including gurus such as Deming and Juran (see DEMING, W.E.; JURAN, J.M.), have questioned whether there is 'a Japanese miracle'. QC ideas were introduced in several countries, but none of these attained the quality improvement results achieved by the Japanese. Juran, like Deming, blames this failure on attitudes and a lack of commitment from management (Lake 1988; Wild 1985). The core of the Japanese miracle is perhaps the ability to recognize the power of the human potential. It is people who control and manage processes and their continuous creativity and innovation will determine the standards of quality, and not the other way round. The contribution of Ishikawa was to highlight the following features:

1 All work is a process and therefore it is important to understand who the customers and suppliers are and determine their true requirements.
2 The management of quality requires an integrated approach, taking into consideration cost, quality *per se*, productivity and reliable delivery.
3 Work is a horizontal process which involves all the key functions; quality improvements therefore can only happen if all key areas are involved using both a team-based approach and quality circles.
4 QC is very much about behaviour and attitude rather than a set of tools and techniques: continuous education and training is essential for effective QC and management.
5 Quality circles are the real way to improve quality and they are a means of establishing respect for people and harnessing their creative and innovative potential.

4 Conclusion

Ishikawa's legacy is apparent in the many organizations around the world that are now using the principles of CWQC and total quality management. Worldwide, thousands of quality circles strive for continuous improvement and help enhance the degree of competitiveness of their organizations. Newly emerging industrial nations and global companies are using the TQC approach based on Japanese principles. South Korea, Singapore, Malaysia and the Republic of China make extensive use of quality circles and have benefited from the early teachings of Ishikawa.

In the West, in addition to a fresh approach which focuses more on people and human dignity at work, other principles have now evolved which have been used in Japan for many years. For instance, the use of auditing systems of QC and its management through self-assessment is an important development. In the USA the Malcolm Baldrige National Quality Award (MBNQA), introduced in 1987, is a framework for auditing quality which is extensively used in American firms. In Europe the European Foundation for Quality Management, created in 1988, introduced the European Quality Award (EQA) which is increasingly used in European organizations.

Ishikawa always believed that if other nations had the courage to imitate the Japanese and look at the 'soft issues' of people and how they work, they could also perform miracles. This has already started to happen: many non-Japanese competitors are now achieving superiority in the marketplace and have even superseded the standards of Japan.

MOHAMED ZAIRI
UNIVERSITY OF BRADFORD

Further reading

(References cited in the text marked *)

Cocheu, T. (1992) 'Training with quality', *Training and Development* 46 (5): 22–32. (Details a quality improvement strategy and a training strategy for organizations.)

Gitlow, H., Gitlow, S. and Oppenheim, A. (1989) *Tools and Methods for the Improvement of Quality*, Boston, MA: Irwin. (A reference for process improvement techniques which covers the fishbone diagram technique.)

Ishikawa, K. (1985) *What is Total Quality Control?: The Japanese Way* Englewood Cliffs, NJ: Prentice Hall. (A complete reference guide to the introduction of TQC.)

Ishikawa, K. (1988) 'Group wide quality control', *Journal for Quality and Participation*, 11 (March): 4–6. (Describes how the concept of group wide QC, an extension of CWQC, is used in Japan.)

* Ishikawa, K. (1989a) *Introduction to Quality Control*, 3rd edn, Tokyo: Chapman and Hall. (Covers basic principles of QC as well as TQC and its implementation; first edition in 1954)

Ishikawa, K. (1989b) 'How to apply company-wide quality control in foreign countries', *Quality Progress*, 12 (September): 70–4. (Discusses the problems encountered in countries that have attempted to introduce the Japanese approach to total quality management.)

* Lake, M. (1988) 'Re-examining the role for industrial engineering', proceedings of IIE Integrated Systems Conference, 30 October–2 November, St Louis, MO.

* Wild, R. (1985) 'The education and training of engineers and managers for manufacture', *Industrial and Commercial Training* (September–October): 17–19.

Zairi, M. (1991) *Total Quality Management for Engineers*, Cambridge: Woodhead Publishing. (Covers the evolution of the quality philosophy and describes the work of all the gurus including Ishikawa.)

See also: DEMING, W.E.; JURAN, J.M.; OHNO, T.; SHINGO, S.; TAYLOR, F.W.

Related topics in the IEBM: COMMITMENT IN JAPAN; JAPANIZATION; JUST-IN-TIME PHILOSOPHIES; MANAGEMENT IN JAPAN; MANAGEMENT IN PACIFIC ASIA; PROBLEM SOLVING; TEAMS IN MANUFACTURING; TOTAL QUALITY MANAGEMENT

Iwasaki, Yataro (1834–85)

Personal background

- born Inokuchi, Kochi Aki-gun, Tosa, on 11 December 1834
- student at Koyusha, Kochi, 1848
- studied in Edo, 1854-5
- student at Shorin Juku, Nagahama-mura, Tosa 1858
- became a servant of the Tosa Han, 1859
- married Kise, Takashiba, 1862
- established the Mitsubishi Shokai, 1873
- died, from stomach cancer, on 7 February 1885

Major works

Iwasaki Yataro Nikki (Diaries of Yataro Iwasaki) (1975)

Summary

Yataro Iwasaki was a founder of the Mitsubishi *zaibatsu*, now known as the Mitsubishi group, the most powerful *keiretsu* (company group, based on family ties) in Japan. Iwasaki was a very energetic, tough and shrewd entrepreneur who succeeded in accumulating great personal wealth in less than twenty years. Starting as a servant of the Tosa Han (Tosa clan), he built a huge shipping empire and diversified into ship repairing, coal and copper mining, warehousing and finance. As a result of this diversification, Mitsubishi was able to lay the foundations for later development. The group's achievements are due largely to Iwasaki's boldness, meticulousness and insight, which took advantage of the rapidly changing times.

1 Introduction

Yataro Iwasaki is known as a *seisho* ('political merchant'), since he had a close relationship with the government. At the same time, he was a man who could defy authority and order. He was a fervent nationalist, but sometimes the pursuit of personal wealth overshadowed his politics. He made it a rule to maintain one-man leadership, not sharing his authority and power with others. He was far from being an 'organization man', and was even rather dictatorial. However, he hired many able university graduates and evaluated their abilities, placing them in cardinal positions.

The characteristic of the Mitsubishi *zaibatsu* is said to be the concept of 'strength of organization'. This may seem to contradict the one-man rule set by Iwasaki and which also became the basic principle in later management of Mitsubishi, but these aspects will be clarified in the course of the discussion.

2 Biographical data

Iwasaki was born in Inokuchi-mura, of the Tosa Han. The Tosa Han was a powerful clan, one of four great Hans. Iwasaki's family belonged to a semi-*samurai* (warrior) class with the character of farmers. His family was not very wealthy, but some of his mother's relatives were educated. Accordingly, he was raised in quite an academic atmosphere. He moved to Kochi, which was a central town in Tosa, in 1848 and there learned Confucianism as an academic subject. Six years later he went to Edo (the former name of Tokyo) as a student, but he was obliged to return because his father had quarrelled, while drunk, with a high-ranking official, and was subsequently imprisoned, whereas the official was not. Yataro, believing the situation to be unfair, protested violently and was also incarcerated. He and his father were in prison for some time, and after his release, Yataro was required to stay in a remote part of the country.

This misfortune, however, turned into a blessing, because in 1858 it provided him with the opportunity to become acquainted with Toyo Yoshida and Shojiro Goto, who were influential *samurai* in the Tosa Han. He was hired as a bureaucrat and was allowed to become a *samurai*. In those days, the Tosa Han tried to encourage industries such as paper, camphor and so on. By means of money thus earned, the Han, who had the right to official military power, purchased armaments and ships from foreign countries. Iwasaki was engaged in this field and was highly valued as a manager: he was promoted from a lower official to a high-ranking bureaucrat responsible for this business.

The new Meiji government, formed in 1868, discouraged business by local governments (that is, Han). The Tosa Han therefore had to separate off its business by transferring it to a person or persons. This was not a simple process: first, the Tsukumo Shokai (company) was established in 1870, with Iwasaki at its head. Then this was reorganized into the Mitsukawa Shokai in 1872 and finally the Mitsubishi Shokai was set up in 1873 as a completely private firm belonging to Iwasaki. He declared to employees and friends that, from then on, he would concentrate on the shipping business, leaving behind any interest in a position in the bureaucratic world.

Following his declaration of interest in shipping, Iwasaki demonstrated outstanding entrepreneurial ability, building up a shipping empire, as well as related businesses such as insurance, warehousing, financing, mining and ship repairing. In February 1885, in the midst of Mitsubishi's fierce struggle with Kyodo Unyu Kaisha (Joint Transportation Company), he died. His successor, his younger brother Yanosuke, weathered the storm and developed Mitsubishi into a big *zaibatsu*, second only to Mitsui.

3 Main contribution

Yataro Iwasaki concentrated mainly on shipping. He took over ships and offices from the Tosa Han and managed them effectively, competing with Yubin Jokisen Kaisha (the mail steamship company) which had been formed as a half-governmental, half-private firm. Red tape dogged the efficiency of that company and it hesitated to help the government in sending troops to Taiwan in 1874 on account of some political problems. The mainstream government politicians Toshimichi Okubo and Shigenobu Okuma became indignant and enlisted Mitsubishi's support instead. Iwasaki was willing to undertake the transportation of troops to Taiwan. This cooperation gained the government's trust, and Iwasaki later formed a close relationship with the government, especially with the two politicians mentioned above. Thus, he came to be called a 'political merchant'.

Okubo, the leader of the government, decided to make Mitsubishi a national flagship company, even though it was a private firm. With the support of the government, in 1874 Mitsubishi challenged the Pacific Mail Steamship Company, an American firm which ran the line from Shanghai to Yokohama. Iwasaki succeeded in defeating Pacific Mail but, shortly after this victory, P&O Steam Navigation Company appeared as a new competitor. P&O forged links with influential Japanese trade associations in the sugar and cotton industries and so forth, defying Mitsubishi's monopoly of the Shanghai and Yokohama line. The government backed Mitsubishi, issuing a 'Foreign Ship Boarding Regulation' which designated complex procedures and charges aimed at discouraging the use of P&O ships. In addition, Mitsubishi devised the exchange credit system that financed shippers by using cargo as security. This strategy was effective in recapturing business from P&O, and after fierce price wars, Mitsubishi succeeded in defeating P&O.

The decisive incident that brought about Mitsubishi's monopoly in shipping was the Satsuma Rebellion of 1877. This rebellion was on such a significant scale that the government sent large numbers of troops to Satsuma (a clan). Consequently, Iwasaki earned huge profits transporting soldiers and materials by sea. Mitsubishi's monopoly was thus completed and it began to demand high monopolistic prices. As a result, there was extensive criticism of Mitsubishi's monopoly, but Iwasaki rejected it arrogantly.

Following the assassination of Okubo, another patron, Okuma, lost political power in 1881. Thereafter, Iwasaki lost supporters in the government. Mitsui, a large *zaibatsu*, joined forces with Eiichi Shibusawa (an influential leader in the business world and with Yajiro Shinagawa (a bureaucrat backed by the mainstream political group Saccho, the successor to the Satsuma and Choshu clans). The resulting company, Kyodo Unyu Kaisha, challenged Mitsubishi's shipping monopoly and began waging a harsh price-cutting war. During the struggle, Iwasaki died. As a consequence, both parties reached a compromise. However, the compromise favoured Mitsubishi, since Mitsubishi still had the power to continue the fight. In September 1885, Nihon Yusen was formed as a merger of both firms. Later on, Mitsubishi moved the bulk of its business from shipping to coal and copper mines, marine and life insurance, shipbuilding, banking and warehousing.

Mitsubishi's new businesses were all closely related to shipping. For example, marine insurance was indispensable for shippers, so it was natural that Iwasaki should set up a marine insurance company, Tokyo Kaijo Hoken Kaisha. Although this company was promoted by Shibusawa and nobles from 1878, Iwasaki was the largest shareholder. From the exchange credit system started during the rivalry with P&O, Mitsubishi's banking business accrued. In 1881, aiming to sell coal to shipping firms, Mitsubishi bought a well known Takashima mine from Shojiro Goto, whose daughter was married to Yanosuke. This mine later proved very profitable. Such diversifications, however, were carried out on a far greater scale under the leadership of Yanosuke Iwasaki, although the foundations had been laid by Iwasaki.

4 Evaluation

Yataro Iwasaki believed that the concept of sole leadership was superior to joint management or joint ownership (as in the *gappon shugi* – literally, joint stock company – praised by Shibusawa). Ownership was never dispersed and was held steadfastly in the Iwasaki family, which always made the most important business decisions. Yataro Iwasaki was a genuine owner-entrepreneur, pursuing a top-down decision making style. The effectiveness of his approach was attested to in the development of the shipping industry and in the defeats of some governmental firms. Nevertheless, Iwasaki employed many university graduates from Tokyo Imperial University and Keio University (whose head was Yukichi Fukuzawa, a close friend of Iwasaki – see FUKUZAWA, Y.). Shoda and Kondo from Keio, Takaaki Kato from Imperial and Kagami from Tokyo Kosho all entered Mitsubishi in important positions: Iwasaki preferred university graduates to *banto* (managers), in the traditional style.

A further feature of Mitsubishi is Iwasaki's use of kinship. Shoda, Kondo, Kato and Kagami had all married women of the Iwasaki family. Availing himself of family ties and employing able university graduates, Iwasaki constructed a solid organization, a quality that Mitsubishi subsequently became famous for. Iwasaki's sons-in-law both became prime ministers, stretching ties of kinship into the political world.

Iwasaki was occasionally called a '*samurai* capitalist' or '*samurai* entrepreneur', as a result of his personality and family background. However, his political interest was not very strong, as the following comment on Iwasaki by his superior during the Tosa Shokai period (1867-70) reveals: 'Iwasaki pays attention only to business, and never knows the importance of the nation'(Miwa 1947: 30–1). On the other hand, it is also said that Iwasaki was strong on nationalism. Compared to Mitsui and Sumitomo, who derived from old merchant houses, Iwasaki, an entrepreneur, had a distinct nationalistic outlook.

5 Conclusion

As a 'political merchant' and the creator of a shipping monopoly, Yataro Iwasaki attracted notoriety during his lifetime. He was a target of jealousy on account of his tremendous wealth, his position being comparable to that of Rockefeller in the USA. After the fall of

Okuma, who was a great patron of Mitsubishi, Iwasaki clarified his policy of non-involvement in politics, realizing the dangers of political ties. Hereafter, this principle became the basic rule for Mitsubishi.

Iwasaki was powerful and pushy, sometimes arrogant. He was a person of action and a quick decision maker who always made the final decisions, never delegating authority and power. At the same time, however, he employed a large number of university graduates, recognizing the usefulness of higher education. He never went to the West, but sent his brother and sons to such institutions as Pennsylvania University and Cambridge University, appreciating fully the significance of Western knowledge. Despite rigorous one-man leadership, he succeeded in building a great organization, and it is such principles and policies that formed the foundation of the strength of the Mitsubishi group today.

ETSUO ABE
MEIJI UNIVERSITY

Further reading

Iwasaki, Y. (1967) *Iwasaki Yataro Den* (Biography of Yataro Iwasaki), 2 vols, Tokyo: Iwasaki Yataro Yanosuke Denki Hensan Iinkai. (An authoritative biography of Yataro Iwasaki.)

Iwasaki, Y. (1975) *Iwasaki Yataro Nikki* (The Diaries of Yataro Iwasaki) (1975), Tokyo: Iwasaki Yataro Yanosuke Denki Hensan Iinkai. (Provides insight into the life and work of Yataro Iwasaki.)

Mishima, Y. (1989) *The Mitsubishi: Its Challenge and Strategy*, Greenwich, CT: JAI Press Inc. (A study of the Mitsubishi conglomerate, covering four generations: Yataro, Yanosuke, Hisaya and Koyata.)

Miwa, R. (1974) 'Mitsubishi no Hassei to Iwasaki Yataro' (The rise of Mitsubishi and Yataro Iwasaki), in K. Nakagawa, H Monikawa and T. Yui (eds) *Kindai Nihon Keieishi no Kiso Chishiki* (Basic Knowledge of Modern Japanese Business History), Tokyo: Yuhikaku. (A brief but to-the-point explanation of Mitsubishi's success.)

Ohshima, K., Kato, T. and Ouchi, T. (1976) 'Iwasaki Yataro', in *Meiji Shokino Kigyoka* (Entrepreneurs in the Early Meiji Era), Tokyo: University of Tokyo Press. (An analysis of Yataro Iwasaki as a 'political merchant'.)

Wray, W.D. (1984) *Mitsubishi and the N.Y.K., 1870–1914*, Cambridge, MA.: Harvard University Press. (Discusses the main force behind the development of the Mitsubishi *zaibatsu*.)

Yamamura, K. (1967) 'Founding of Mitsubishi: a case study in Japanese business history', *Business History Review* 46 (2): 141–60. (A study of the origins of the Mitsubishi group.)

See also: FUKUZAWA, Y.

Related topics in the IEBM: BUSINESS HISTORY, JAPANESE; MANAGEMENT IN JAPAN; SHIBUSAWA, E.; *ZAIBATSU (KEIRETSU)*.

Jaques, Elliott (1917–)

Personal background

- born 18 January 1917
- educated at the University of Toronto (BA, MA) and Johns Hopkins Medical School (MD)
- served as a major in the Royal Canadian Army Medical Corps, 1941–5
- Harvard University (PhD)
- founder member of the Tavistock Institute of Human Relations, 1946–51
- qualified as a psychoanalyst (British Psychoanalytic Society), 1951
- director of the Institute of Organization and Social Studies, Brunel University (1970–85) now Professor Emeritus of Social Sciences
- visiting research professor in management sciences, George Washington University, 1989–

Major works

The Changing Culture of a Factory (1951)
Measurement of Responsibility (1956)
Equitable Payment (1961)
A General Theory of Bureaucracy (1976)
The Form of Time (1982)
Requisite Organization (1988)
Creativity and Work (1990)
Requisite Organization: A Total System for Effective Managerial Organization and Managerial Leadership for the 21st Century (1997)

Summary

Jaques' thinking about management and his concept of 'the requisite organization' is best understood in the light of his profound concern for the design of social institutions which make it possible for people to live together, to work together, to *be* together in ethical ways. He maintains that the importance of work in modern societies is such that the achievement of liberty, freedom, trust and justice in the wider society is dependent on the way employing organizations are designed.

For the Kantian moral imperative 'act as if the maxim from which you were to act were to become through your will a universal law of nature', we may substitute the principle of acting in such a way as to increase, by however little, the amount of faith and confidence which people may have in one another. Individual goodwill must be supported and encouraged by social mechanisms and institutions which channel and direct behaviour within confidence-inducing limits.

(Jaques 1976: 374)

Requisite organizations respond to the nature of work and to the nature of people as they work as individuals and together. The outcome is that people can work together in ways that strengthen bonds of mutual trust and fairness, enhance imagination and innovation, and reduce suspicion and mistrust; the organization achieves its purposes and contributes to the health of the wider society. 'Antirequisite' organizations support autocratic coercion and destructive anxiety, and thus inhibit creativity. Although they may appear to be effective for some years, they eventually flounder.

At the core of a requisite organization lies Jaques' definition of work as 'the exercise of discretion within prescribed limits to reach a goal within a stated completion time' (Jaques 1956: 85). Jaques' profound insight into the significance of time for human behaviour led to a commitment to 'breathing life back into the social sciences' by using time to achieve equal ratio scale measurement in them. For him the form of time is the form of living, episodes – suffused with intention, meaning and hope – are the fundamental things that can be explored in the human sciences (Jaques 1982).

1 Introduction

Jaques came to his views about requisite organization through a highly empirical process shaped by early work with colleagues at the Tavistock Institute in the United Kingdom. The fundamental principle of 'social analysis' was that the consultants offered analyses, made no recommendations and never arrogated to themselves the responsibilities of the people in the organization who had initiated the study. At the heart of the process lay 'listening to the music behind the words' with acute sensitivity to every aspect of what each person said and to every hint of what could, with encouragement, be articulated (Rowbottom 1977).

This attentive listening created a climate in which people could voice the subtleties of experience they lived but had not articulated – the tacit knowledge of which Polanyi (1958) speaks. They found themselves able to say how they *felt* about the process of their work, about the decisions they were called upon to make and the anxiety of waiting to see how they turned out, about the reward they felt would be fair for the level of responsibility they were asked to carry, about their working relationships with others and how they felt about the fairness of their working conditions.

A requisite organization is felt to be fair in that it provides for the major needs of the normal individual: to use his or her full capacities in work, to participate in policy-making; to have recourse to appeal against the judgement of a manager; and to receive equitable reward ('felt-fair' pay, Jaques 1961).

2 Biographical data

Jaques is a prolific writer of books and articles. He originally trained as a medical practitioner and psychiatrist, and later as a psychoanalyst, his psychoanalytic work being particularly influenced by Melanie Klein. He came to work at the Tavistock during World War II and was involved in the selection of officers after Dunkirk. Soon after the war he and his colleagues began what was to become a 30-year social analytic project with the Glacier Metal Company in the UK (Jaques and Brown 1965). In 1967, he founded the Brunel Institute of Organization and Social Studies (BIOSS) and was its director until 1981. His ideas continue to be elaborated and applied through the work of BIOSS in the private and public sector across the world. His work has been an important influence on the work of the Centre for Voluntary Organization at the London School of Economics. He has worked extensively in the USA, Australia and Canada. His work has had a significant impact on the US Military. He is Professor Emeritus at Brunel University in the UK and since 1989 has been Visiting Professor of Management Science at George Washington University, Washington DC.

3 Major contributions

His most significant contribution is to draw attention to the significance of time for human behaviour and, in particular, for people at work (Jaques 1982). He described three aspects of time: *time of intention*, set by a manager, agreed with direct reports and expressed in a target completion time for a project; *fruition* time, as the person waits for decisions to ripen; *time of achievement*, when the outcome of decisions can be evaluated – this may or may not be the same as the target completion time.

Associations and executive hierarchies

In a requisite organization there is a clear distinction between the association which initiates and defines purpose – to increase shareholder value, to provide a public service, to defend a nation, to run a club for example – and the executives accountable for realizing that purpose. Jaques has always been clear about the importance of distinguishing between the role of the chairman which represents the founding association (in corporations this will be composed largely of institutional investors) and the role of the chief executive accountable for realizing their purposes (Jaques 1976, 1997).

Levels of work

Clarity about accountability underlies Jaques' model of qualitatively distinct levels of work. He discovered this systematic structure in 1957 when consistent setting of target completion times revealed clear cut-off points at three months, one year, two, five, ten and twenty years (see Figure 1). Since then time-span measurements have been used widely to define level of work and design requisite organizations. The purpose of the levels is to distribute accountability and authority in such a way that managers can fairly be held to account for achieving (or not) the purposes of the organization. The essential, frequently misunderstood point is that these are levels of *work* and not of status and grading.

There is a widely held intuitive feel for timescales, seen for instance in the ubiquity of three- to five-year plans, annual budgets and so on. The point about *time-span* is that it defines the level of work and provides an important element of the relationship between a manager and his or her direct reports. Time-span allows them to honour one of the most significant and often neglected parts of their relationship – the sharing of intention by the manager, the taking on of that intention by the direct report and the synchronizing of their intentions in a target completion time. Thus prepared, they can work together until the actual time of achievement (or not) and can review the work in a clear and consistent manner. Time of intention is an essential prerequisite of performance management and of 'the learning organization'.

Definition of work

Jaques definition of work as 'the exercise of discretion and the application of knowledge within prescribed limits in order to achieve a goal within a stated completion time' emerged from his attentive listening to how it *feels* for the person to make a decision and

then to live – for weeks, even years – with the uncertainty and anxiety of not knowing for sure that it was good enough while continuing to make decisions to meet changing circumstances as work progresses. The way the accompanying anxiety is managed is a good indication of the requisiteness of the organization.

The *prescribed limits* are the objectively set rules in the form of policies (written and unwritten), procedures, and physical controls which must be obeyed. By defining the field, these limits free the person to use his or her discretion in coping with uncertainties, vicissitudes, unknowns as they feel towards the wisest way of forwarding the work for which they are responsible (Jaques 1956; Evans 1979).

The *discretionary content* feels completely different: it is about the fine judgements the person makes for him or herself – the 'judgement calls' when we do not and cannot know what to do. As Jaques put it, this is a 'sphere of psychological activity which, although extremely familiar, remains … ill-defined. There is no satisfactory … language for it. We speak about judgement, intuition, nous … We cannot put into words what it is that we are taking into account in doing what we are doing, and in that sense we do not know that what we are doing will get us where we want to go, will achieve the result we want to achieve. We judge that it will, we think it will, but we are not sure *and only time will tell*' (Jaques 1988: 156).

Characteristic of Jaques is his sensitivity to how it *feels* to adhere to prescribed limits: the person is responding to choices someone else has made and can assess and control their contribution by reference to objective standards. Appraisal and control of discretion is through reference to intuitively sensed internal standards within each of us until completion time when the effect of our decisions can be externally reviewed.

The work, capacity, pay nexus

The fundamental building block of a requisite organization is the work, capacity, pay nexus: alignment between the work the person is

Levels of work	Time-span		Description	Typical Organizational Titles
VII	50 yrs	Strategic	Strategic design; development; deployment of complex systems	Corporation
	20 yrs			
VI			Direct deployment of complex systems	Group
	10 yrs			
V		Comprehensive	Complex system; encompassing operating systems and modifying context	Subsidiary
	5 yrs			
IV			Alternative operating systems - management of mutual recognition unit	Unit
	2 yrs			
III		Operational	Direct operating systems - management of mutual knowledge system	General Management
	1 yrs			
II			Direct operating methods - supervision of a mutual knowledge system	Section
I	3 mths		Direct operating tasks	Shop floor

Figure 1

responsible for and his or her capacity to do it with grace and consistency, while ensuring an equitable reward that feels fair (Jaques 1976, 1997). The key concept is levels of work measured in time-span. The longer the time during which discretion has to be exercised without the results being evaluated, the greater the psychological effort required for the work. The longer you have to tolerate uncertainty and yet keep on with your work, the greater is the responsibility. The longer the organization leaves an employee to carry on exercising discretion, making decisions and committing resources, the greater is the reliance upon that person and the greater the responsibility allocated.

The sharing of intention by a manager with direct reports thus includes responsibility for ensuring that each is able to use his or her capacity to exercise discretion to the full; and that none should be so overwhelmed by the attendant uncertainty that they can no longer make decisions but can only gamble, or so under-challenged by their work that they withdraw their energies. The exercise of discretion through time is directly connected with felt weight of responsibility and with the person's intuitive sense of the total reward that he or she feels to be fair – their 'felt-fair pay'.

Earning progression and growth of capacity

Jaques' extensive studies of individual earnings made it possible for him to construct an array of progression curves (See Figure 2; Jaques 1956, 1961).

As Jaques realized that people made consistent links between their earnings, their responsibilities and exercising discretion, it occurred to him that the progression curves might also reflect a consistent pattern of

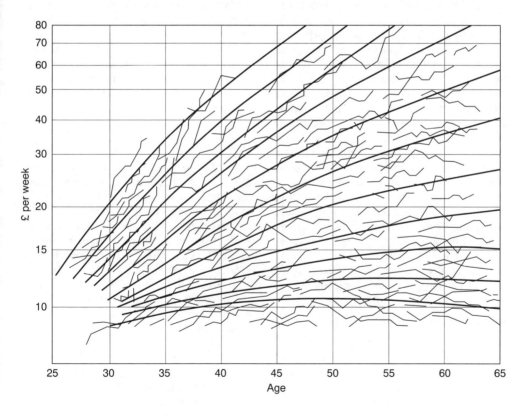

Figure 2

growth in the capacity to exercise discretion – 'capability'. This hypothesis has been systematically tested over the last 18 years in longitudinal studies of 'capability' in a wide range of organizations and cultures. These studies demonstrate that capability grows at broadly predictable rates, and that, if each individual is to use it to the full, this growth must be paced with growth in responsibility. To be prevented from working at full capacity by being asked to carry too much or too little responsibility is constricting, degrading and finally persecuting. The studies make it clear that there are no differences in distribution of capability with regard to gender, race or educational opportunity (Stamp 1986).

Evaluation of potential capability

Jaques considers that one of his most important findings is a precise connection between the pattern of human capability and widespread organizational form. On the basis of work with the US army it was concluded that there are four methods that people use in processing information when they are deeply engrossed in work (Jaques, Gibson and Isaac 1978; Jaques and Cason 1994). These processes increase in complexity from 'declarative' (the use of discrete, unconnected pieces of information) to 'parallel' (building two or more series and connecting them), and can be observed in the way people muster their case when fully engaged in arguing a position.

Because each of the levels that he discovered in the 1950s requires one type of mental processing, Jaques sees this finding as an explanation of the ubiquity of managerial hierarchies with a regular pattern of levels of work. The finding also makes it possible to match individual capability to role complexity.

Working relationships

Jaques describes this as 'one of the really untidy areas of life in organizations' (Jaques 1988: 59). He points out that the failure to specify accountability and authority is one of the major sources of conflict between people as they try to work together. It makes it easy for people to arrogate authority or to deny

accountability and pass the buck. These conflicts are frequently interpreted as issues of 'personality' and not seen as the consequence of anti-requisite design. They lead inexorably to mistrust, manoeuvring, and loss of creativity.

One example is the precise specification of the differences between the roles of manager and supervisor (Jaques 1988). The supervisor has authority to recommend or veto appointment of a particular person to a team, the manager has the authority to decide; the supervisor has authority to assign specific tasks, the manager decides the types of task; the supervisor has authority to recommend on appraisal of effectiveness, the manager decides; the supervisor has authority to recommend initiation of transfer of the person to another team, the manager decides.

Jaques makes many other precise distinctions – between monitoring, advising and service providing for example, and between work which is delegated to a direct report and work where the output is to support the higher level output of a manager. These clarifications of working relationships are not niceties but the foundation for the mutual trust and effective cooperation of a requisite organization.

Review of work

Time of achievement is the actual time taken to complete a project; it may or may not be the same as the time of intention. The moment of completion is filled with the way the person *feels* when decision outcomes are evaluated – directly by customers for the self-employed, directly by a manager and indirectly by the market or the public for employees. It is essential that the person should feel that the output of his or her judgements is fairly evaluated by someone whose views they respect.

The key point is that completion time is the moment when it is possible to evaluate and review the exercise of discretion throughout the project. While this is unlikely to be confined to a single individual, the reality is that someone has to be held accountable if purposes are to be realized. In the light of the vulnerability to evaluation of the person who has been exercising their discretion, this is a sensitive moment which can bring to the fore either the opportunity to learn, or the experience of feeling misunderstood, persecuted, undervalued. The handling of time of achievement is thus crucial for the requisite organization.

Employment

Once you get a job you find yourself in one of the most significant of modern human relationships: between a superior and a subordinate. This is a relationship of great psychological subtlety and complexity in which economic security, recognition and self-esteem are all enwrapped. The objective is set in defined terms by the employer who inspects the final outcome at the time of completion and who must be satisfied if the employment is to continue. There is always an external framework to guide and assess the exercise of discretion and there is thus greater potential for the emergence of destructive anxieties if authorities and rights of appeal have not been clarified. In a requisite organization, the relationships between a manager and direct reports and with the manager-once-removed are clearly defined in order to make the most of the opportunity for review and learning provided by *time of achievement* and to minimize the potential for power play, denial of responsibility and persecution.

Self-employment

Jaques points to important differences between employment and self-employment. The primary task in running a business lies in discovering what consumer needs may be satisfied at a profit. The self-employed person has an external reference for the work, but it is not given by a manager: discovering it requires a particular kind of sensitivity to the needs of others. Failure to discover this external reference – to understand the market – results in a gradual loss of business and not in direct personal evaluation as from an employer.

4 Evaluation

Jaques offers a comprehensive system for designing organizations that enhance the constructive and minimize the destructive elements of people working together – as full- or part-time employees, or self-employed. Much of his thinking has become common currency in organizations – 'discretion', 'judgement calls' and 'time-horizons' are widely used. 'Flattening' of organizations more often than not leads to a pattern of the levels as defined by him, and when 'downsizing' removes a level of work that is necessary, it soon creeps back in. Interest in 'empowering' people at work is an attempt to gain access to the discretionary energy of people. In a requisite organization each person will be 'empowered' to use their discretion within a framework of prescribed limits: one of the fundamental tenets of such an organization being that each person is able to use his or her capability to exercise discretion to the full.

Research into the cognitive unconscious (Reber 1993) provides support for Jaques' emphasis on the direct connection between the processes involved in work and unconscious mental activity.

> Industrial society ... has overvalued ... the critical, the conscious, the verbal, the brain ... everything to do with knowledge ... It has lost its ability sufficiently to value and to feel secure in relying upon the other side of the human equation – the side that contains intuition, judgement, flowing unverbalised sense, the feel of the situation, the deeper sense of simply understanding what is right and wrong or fair or just, the sense of the reasonable, the ability to sit back and reflect and remember and to feel a part of one's past and present, and to identify with other human beings, to feel empathy and sensitivity ... what Keats has called 'negative capability' ... being in uncertainties, mysteries, doubts without any irritable reaching after facts and reason.
>
> (Jaques 1982: 221)

GILLIAN STAMP
BRUNEL INSTITUTE OF ORGANISATION AND
SOCIAL STUDIES (BIOSS)

Further reading

(References cited in the text marked *)

* Evans, J. (1979) *The Management of Human Capacity*, UK: MCB Publications. (A thoughtful and thorough critique of Jaques' fundamental ideas.)

Jaques, E. (1951) *The Changing Culture of a Factory*, London: Tavistock Publications. (The attention given to institutional, structural issues gives it a unique place in the literature.)

* Jaques, E. (1956) *Measurement of Responsibility*, London: Tavistock Publications. (A clear, simple exposition of the pattern of ideas elaborated in Jaques' later work.)

* Jaques, E. (1961) *Equitable Payment*, London: Heinemann. (A full discussion of the significant concept of 'felt-fair' pay.)

* Jaques, E. and Brown W. (1965) *Glacier Project Papers*, London: Heinemann. (A full account of the fruitful collaboration between Jaques the social analyst and Brown the managing director.)

* Jaques, E. (1976) *A General Theory of Bureaucracy*, London: Heinemann. (A full account of the interconnection of all the elements of Jaques' theory and its application.)

* Jaques, E. Gibson, R. and Isaac, J. (1978) *Levels of Abstraction in Logic and Human Action: A Theory of Discontinuity in the Structure of Mathematical Logic, Psychological Behaviour and Social Organization*, London: Heinemann. (A collection of essays about levels of complexity in formal logic, organization and human capability.)

* Jaques, E. (1982) *The Form of Time*, US: Crane Russak and Co. Inc; London: Heinemann. (A powerful and sensitive exposition of Jaques' philosophy of the role of time in human affairs.)

* Jaques, E. (1988) *Requisite Organization*, Falls Church: Cason Hall and Co. Publishers. (Also second edition 1997, see below).

Jaques, E. (1990) *Creativity and Work*, International Universities Press. (A collection of essays about psychoanalysis, work, uncertainty and knowledge.)

Jaques, E. and Clement S. (1991) *Executive Leadership*, Falls Church: Cason Hall and Co. Publishers. (A study of the implications and practice of leadership at different levels in organizations.)

Jaques, E. and Cason K. (1994) *Human Capability*, Falls Church: Cason Hall and Co. Publishers. (A study of findings about the evaluation of potential capability.)

* Jaques, E. (1997) *Requisite Organization: A Total System for Effective Managerial Organization and Managerial Leadership for the 21st Century*, Falls Church: Cason Hall and Co. Publishers.

* Polanyi, M. (1958) *Personal Knowledge: Toward a Post-Critical Philosophy*, Chicago: University of Chicago Press. (A philosophical study of tacit knowledge.)

* Reber, A. (1993) *Implicit Learning and Tacit Knowledge: An Essay on the Cognitive Unconscious*, Oxford: Oxford University Press. (An account of 30 years of experiments and an evolutionary explanation of implicit learning.)

* Rowbottom, R. (1977) *Social Analysis*, London: Heinemann. (A study, critique and description of collaborative analysis of organizational issues.)

Rowbottom, R. and Billis, D. (1977) 'The stratification of work and organizational design', *Human Relations* 30, 1.

* Stamp, G. (1986) 'Some observations on the career paths of women', *Journal of Applied Behavioural Science* 22, 4: 385–396.

Stamp, G. (1992) *Day of Judgement – in Festschrift for Elliott Jaques*, Falls Church: Cason Hall and Co. Publishers.

Stamp, G. and Stamp, C. (1993) 'Well-being at work: aligning purposes, people, strategies and structures', *The International Journal of Career Management* 5, .3.

See also: ANSOFF, I.; EMERY, F.; TRIST, E.

Related topics in the IEBM: CULTURE; GENERAL MANAGEMENT; HUMAN RESOURCE MANAGEMENT; HUMAN RELATIONS; ORGANIZATION BEHAVIOUR; ORGANIZATION BEHAVIOUR, HISTORY OF; ORGANIZATION CULTURE; ORGANIZATION DEVELOPMENT; ORGANIZATIONAL LEARNING; ORGANIZATIONAL PERFORMANCE; PERFORMANCE APPRAISAL

Juran, Joseph M. (1904–)

Personal background

- born 24 December 1904 in Braila, Romania
- emigrated to the USA in 1912
- gained a BS in electrical engineering from the University of Minnesota and a doctorate in jurisprudence (JD) from Loyola University in Chicago
- married in 1926 and has four children
- worked as an engineer, industrial executive, government administrator, university professor, impartial labour arbitrator, corporate director and management consultant
- became one of the major gurus on the quality revolution
- *Juran's Quality Control Handbook*, first published in 1951, inspired many quality professionals worldwide, and is still the international reference work on the subject
- Chairman Emeritus of Juran Institute Inc., which he founded in 1979
- awarded Japan's Order of the Sacred Treasure in 1981 by Emperor Hirohito

Major works

Juran's Quality Control Handbook (1951)
Managerial Breakthrough (1964)
The Corporate Director (with J.K. Londen) (1966)
Upper Management and Quality, 4th edn (1982)
Juran on Planning for Quality (1988)
Juran on Leadership for Quality: An Executive Handbook (1989)
Juran on Quality by Design (1992)

Summary

Juran has had a considerable influence as a quality guru on the senior manager's role in introducing quality to their business. He argues that although over the past one hundred years Taylor's scientific management has become obsolete, very little has been suggested to replace it. Companies tend to spend time replanning microprocesses which have little bearing on the macroprocesses.

The quality revolution is, according to Juran, an integrated management system which can replace Taylorism, as proved by the Japanese, and assist organizations to make great strides and achieve superior levels of competitiveness. However, it is important, he maintains, that the introduction of quality becomes the ultimate responsibility of senior managers. Effective quality introduction can only take place with proper *planning* and *execution*.

Juran argues that the quality revolution in Japan has been succeeding since the 1950s because of the close involvement of chief executive officers (CEOs) and chairmen of companies, while in the USA, CEOs concentrated their efforts on financial reports instead. He proposes that the Japanese miracle was not due to his and Dr Edwards Deming's teachings as claimed but rather to Japanese commitment and dedication at all levels to make quality work. He believes that organizations that take time to get their managers involved in quality improvement will almost definitely get ahead of their competitors.

1 Biographical data

Joseph M. Juran was born on 24 December 1904 in Braila, Romania. He lived in a city called Carpathia and was the son of a shoemaker. He emigrated to the USA in 1912 and was married in 1926. He has four children, nine grandchildren and five great-grandchildren. Juran holds a BS in electrical engineering from the University of Minnesota and a doctorate in jurisprudence (JD) from Loyola University in Chicago (Ettorre 1994).

Juran's career has taken him through various paths: he worked as an engineer, industrial executive, government administrator, university professor, impartial labour arbitrator, corporate director and management consultant (Juran 1988a). His breakthrough came when he decided to break away from industry. His last job was that of a manager at Western Electric. He started to work as a freelance at the age of 40 and for the following fifty years he became one of the leading proponents of quality, alongside, for example, Deming, Ishikawa and Crosby (see DEMING, W.E.; ISHIKAWA, K.).

During his career Juran has written several works that are used as universal references on the subject of quality; his book *Quality Control Handbook*, first published in 1951, is still the major international reference work on the subject. He has conducted seminars, workshops and advisory projects for thousands of companies and has produced international training courses with support materials such as training books and video cassettes. Consulting and lecturing around the world, Juran has advised both industrialists and governments. He has received more than thirty medals, fellowships and honorary memberships, the most prestigious being Japan's Order of the Sacred Treasure. This award was conferred in 1981 by Emperor Hirohito for his contribution to the development of quality control in Japan and the facilitation of US and Japanese friendship. Juran also holds the position of Chairman Emeritus of Juran Institute Inc., which he founded in 1979.

2 Main contribution

It may be useful to present Juran's main contribution by focusing on three main areas: (1) quality from the customer's perspective; (2) the Pareto principle; and (3) quality as a management responsibility.

Defining quality from the customer's perspective

The phrase 'fitness for use' was first introduced by Juran, who applied the expression for both product and service characteristics. He argues that fitness for use has to be judged by the user and not by the manufacturer. Job titles mean less than the realization that each person is a supplier of products and services to other internal and even external customers. In the same way, everyone is a true customer to upstream suppliers in the product's value added chain (Ruark 1991). Juran insists on identifying customer needs first. He describes the quality planning road map as the 'interlocking input–output chain' and insists that every activity has a triple role of customer, processor and supplier.

The father of the Pareto principle

The 'Pareto principle' represents a phenomenon whereby in any population that contributes to a common effect, a relative few of the contributors account for the bulk of the effect (Juran 1992a). It is a state of nature (the way things happen) as well as a process (a way of thinking about problems) (Burr 1990). According to this principle there is a maldistribution of quality losses. It suggests that most effects come from relatively few causes. Since it helps people focus on areas with the biggest impact, the Pareto principle is one of the most powerful tools of quality improvement. It can be used on a regular basis for identifying causes of problems and attempting to eliminate or greatly reduce those with the largest impact.

Concerned by comments that the Pareto principle is attributable to Vilfredo Pareto, Juran writes:

> Years ago I gave the name 'Pareto' to this principle of the 'vital few and trivial many'. On subsequent challenge, I was forced to confess that I had mistakenly applied the wrong name to the principle … The Pareto principle as a universal was not original with Pareto. Where then did the universal originate? To my knowledge, the first exposition was by myself. Had I been

structured along different lines, assuredly I would have called it the Juran principle. However, I was not structured that way. Yet I did need a shorthand designation, and I had no qualm about Pareto's name. Hence the Pareto principle.

(Juran 1992a: 68)

The full story of the Pareto principle may be summarized as follows: the vital few and trivial many concept has always existed in our everyday life. Vilfredo Pareto observed this phenomenon in relation to wealth distribution. His major contribution was the advancement of a logarithmic law of income distribution to fit the vital few and trivial many phenomena. In the 1950s, Juran was the first person to realize that the Pareto principle can be applied in most activities of work. He coined the phrase 'vital few and trivial many' to the principle.

Quality – a management responsibility

Juran is perhaps the quality guru who explicitly places the responsibility for quality with senior managers. He blames American CEOs for abdicating responsibility for quality and delegating it to lower levels as a less important challenge. He refers to the responsibility for quality as non-delegable roles by explaining that: 'American CEOs didn't understand that quality was no longer one problem among many. It was now the problem. They didn't realize that fixing quality meant fixing whole companies, a task that can't be delegated' (Juran 1993: 45).

Juran dispels the myth that Japan's success is largely due to him and Dr Edwards Deming (see DEMING, W.E.) for their efforts in the 1950s. He explains:

In my view, there is not a shred of truth in such assertions. Had Deming and I stayed at home, the Japanese would have achieved World quality leadership all the same. We did provide a jump start, without which the Japanese would have been put to more work and the job might have taken longer, but they would still be ahead of the United States in the quality revolution.

(Juran 1993: 42)

The Japanese were very keen to listen and learn from quality experts all over the world. When Juran was invited in 1954 by the Japanese Federation of Economic Organizations (the *Keidanren*) and the Japanese Union for Scientists and Engineers to give seminars, the same opportunities were provided for US senior managers. The latter, however, decided not to take any advice on board, as Juran explains: 'What I told them was what I have been telling audiences in the United states for years. The difference was not what I said but whose ears heard it'(Juran 1993: 45).

Juran claims that the reason why the Japanese were successful was because they attentively listened to all his advice and really understood what he was driving at. They realized early on that to create a competitive advantage through quality, attention has to be given not just to product defects and producing goods according to customer specification, but quality has to represent the business itself, it has to be represented strategically. In essence, the Japanese succeed with quality because they observe the following critical factors:

- quality is a senior management responsibility
- it is compulsory for all managers to be trained on quality issues
- continuous improvement is not project related but introduced as a culture of work
- all engineers are trained in the use of statistical tools
- employee involvement has been introduced systematically and in a sustainable manner through the quality control circles (QCC) movement
- quality improvement targets are integrated into business performance and driven by quality strategic planning and deployment processes.

The Japanese have taken quality seriously and developed attitudes and behaviours which represent a work culture where quality is part of the job and not a separate activity. This is perhaps the major reason for their success. In the West, however, companies tended to focus on what Juran calls 'the wrong indicators', those which measure financial gains and not quality improvements.

Juran recommends seven steps that any CEO must subscribe to in order to bring about the quality revolution:

1 CEOs must create a steering committee or a quality council and they must chair all the meetings.
2 CEOs must realize that quality management is the management of business operations. As such, they must have clear quality targets as part of the business plan.
3 They need to encourage education and training for quality throughout the whole organization so that people start to believe that quality is part of the job and not a separate activity.
4 CEOs must move away from just looking at financial indicators; they have to develop measures for quality.
5 Quality improvements have to be measured continuously and progress monitored against the set corporate targets.
6 Efforts for quality improvements, problem solving, creativity and innovation have to be recognized.
7 Reward systems have to be compatible with customer quality excellence standards and not necessarily productivity standards and a 'working hard' type of approach. Customer quality excellence standards require frequent changes and new innovation and this must be recognized by senior managers.

3 Evaluation

In his quality crusade Juran has played a significant role in teaching all of us that the notion of quality which is related to improvements of products and services only is a naïve and very simplistic one. Juran argues that there are three universal processes for managing quality:

1 Quality planning (establish goals for quality, know customers and their demands, translate the needs into physical/tangible outputs by developing processes that are capable and consistent).

2 Quality control (using Plan-Do-Check-Act, monitor the performance of the process to optimize quality output).
3 Quality improvement (identify and solve problems, use a team approach to continuously search for better ways to optimize quality, maintain high standards of quality performance).

These three steps are referred to as the Juran Trilogy which represents quality as a corporate-wide approach, where products and services are only one element.

Juran has also contributed significantly by insisting that quality can only be delivered through a series of incremental contributions, through the creation of a value chain (customer–supplier chain). He argues that every employee is both a supplier and a customer. Juran describes what he calls the *triple role concept* by arguing that everything takes place through *a process* which has customers and suppliers.

Juran's suggested quality planning road map produces an integrated management system where goals and corporate targets are developed and deployed from a top-down approach and performance improvement and innovation from a bottom-up approach. Juran argues that by starting with a planning stage for quality, senior managers *have* to be involved and they cannot choose to delegate to lower levels. The triple role approach also secures employee involvement and participation because it introduces a discipline of focusing on the end customer, goal congruence and ignores the notion of 'super-heroes and prima donnas'.

Juran predicts that the twenty-first century is going to be the era of a quality revolution. He clearly distinguishes the quality revolution from the technological revolution which took place in the 1980s. He explains that the role of technology is to use the forces of nature and the utilization of matter to benefit man and to meet the needs of humanity. The case is, however, different for quality which is more specifically concerned with identifying customer needs and designing ways of meeting those needs. Juran urges senior managers to rise to the challenge of a quality revolution by 'quantifying the return on investment of quality'(Stratton 1993: 65).

Juran taught us that there is nothing called 'the quality miracle' and that a number of lessons should be learned from the Japanese. First, quality is a senior management responsibility. Second, quality is not product or service productivity related; it is about people, flexibility, change, creativity and innovation, and therefore education and training on quality issues are fundamentally important. Third, quality improvement needs to focus on *the process*, a concern for every employee since everyone is both a supplier and a customer. Finally, quality is not an act of faith; it has to be measured, improved and monitored against corporate targets.

4 Conclusions

Juran's lifelong contribution to the quality revolution cannot be specifically pinned down. He taught us the quality concept from an integrated, corporate-wide perspective. His frustration was with senior managers who failed to grasp his vision that quality is not a local, operational, small activity which seeks to inspect, identify defects and eliminate them before they reach the customer. He has also tried to preach the message that quality improvement is not a *mechanistic* process for meeting requirements through fulfilling demands according to predetermined specifications, but quality improvement is about big leaps, breakthroughs and innovation aimed at creating a competitive advantage.

Juran believes that the quality revolution has just started: 'This century has really been the century of productivity. I think we can safely say that we're headed into the century of quality' (Ettorre 1994: 12). He maintains that in the coming years even more attention will be given to partnerships with suppliers and customers, and partnerships with the workforce. The latter will involve more empowerment and self-managed teams working in a multi-functional and team-based approach to project management. Juran predicts a move from management for *control* to leadership through *coaching* and *supporting*. Increasingly, managing will involve both

learning to handle changes on a frequent basis and developing effective strategies to cope with changes.

Juran does not agree with the word 'retirement', tirelessly working on unfinished projects. He says (about dying): 'When I go, please let me go at my word processor' (Stratton 1993: 65).

MOHAMED ZAIRI
UNIVERSITY OF BRADFORD

Further reading

(References cited in the text marked *)

Bryce, G.R. (1991) 'Quality management theories and their application, *Quality* 30 (1): 15–18. (Discusses the various quality approaches adopted by management theorists and consultants, and where they emphasize the need to control and manage quality.)

* Burr, J.T. (1990) 'The tools of quality – part VI: Pareto charts', *Quality Progress* 23 (11): 59–61. (This paper discusses the Pareto principle which is one of the most powerful decision tools available. It also presents it as a way of thinking about problems and motivating people for problem solving.)

Caudron, S. (1993) 'Just what is total quality management?', *Personnel Journal* 72 (2): 32. (This article discusses TQM as a way of transforming organizations and how it links to business results. It also presents reasons of why TQM programmes tend to not succeed and fail.)

Delsanter, J.M. (1993) 'Rewarding technology', *TQM Magazine* 5 (2): 31–3. (An interview with Juran discussing the compatibility of technology and quality as a result of him winning the 1992 US National Medal of Technology.)

* Ettorre, B. (1994) 'Juran on quality', *Management Review* January: 10–13. (This is an interview with Joseph Juran on quality evolution and its future challenges.)

Heinzlmeir, L.A. (1991) 'Under the spell of the quality gurus', *Canadian Manager* 16 (1): 22–3. (Discusses the contribution of the various gurus such as Deming, Juran, Crosby and Taguchi and their different styles.)

Juran, J.M. (1964) *Managerial Breakthrough*, New York: McGraw-Hill. (Discusses the implementation of change in general management.)

Juran, J.M. (1982) *Upper Management and Quality*, 4th edn, New York: McGraw-Hill. (The ideal training guide for senior managers.)

* Juran, J.M. (1988a) *Juran on Planning for Quality*, New York: The Free Press. (Presents a revised approach to quality planning to overcome all problems associated with quality.)

Juran, J.M. (1951, 1988b) *Juran's Quality Control Handbook*, 4th edn, New York: McGraw-Hill. (A classic in the quality field, first published in 1951.)

Juran, J.M. (1989) *Juran on Leadership for Quality: An Executive Handbook*, New York: The Free Press. (In this book Juran explains with precision how quality can be made to be an 'obsession' in every single organization from top management to employees at all levels. This is the only way to become competitive. Juran provides a set of necessary steps for top managers to follow in order that quality implementation can lead to effective business results.)

Juran, J. M. (1991) 'The evolution of Japanese leadership in quality', *Journal of Quality and Participation* 14 (4): 72–7. (Discusses how the Japanese have changed attitudes towards quality and the various factors which led them to sustain their commitment over the years.)

* Juran, J.M. (1992a) *Juran on Quality by Design*, New York: The Free Press. (Aims to assist companies to achieve quality leadership through mastery of how to plan for quality.)

Juran, J.M. (1992b) 'Departmental quality planning', *National Productivity Review* 11 (3): 287–300. (Discusses the redesign of jobs, F.W. Taylor's work and worker participation in quality planning.)

* Juran, J.M. (1993) 'Made in the USA: a renaissance in quality', *Harvard Business Review* 71 (4): 42–50. (This is a paper which presents the views of Joseph Juran about how Japanese and American CEOs view quality and why in the past Americans did not get the message of quality and the positive developments of the 1990s which are creating a new American revolution.)

* Juran, J.M. and Londen, J.K. (1966) *The Corporate Director*, New York: American Management Association. (Discusses the role and tasks of a board of directors.)

* Ruark, B. (1991) 'Globalization of fitness for use', *Journal for Quality and Participation* March: 68–72. (This paper presents the quality philosophy based on 'fitness for use', the meaning of customers and the key parameters of FIT (Flexibility, Innovation and Time).)

* Stratton, B. (1993) 'A few words about the last word', *Quality Progress* October: 63–5. (This is an article based on material from Joseph M. Juran's March 1993 presentation in Milwaukee, USA, 'The Last Word'.)

See also: DEMING, W.E.; ISHIKAWA, K; OHNO, T.; SHINGO, S.; TAYLOR, F.W.; UENO, Y.

Related topics in the IEBM: JAPANIZATION; JUST-IN-TIME PHILOSOPHIES; MANAGEMENT IN JAPAN; MANUFACTURING MANAGEMENT; OPERATIONS MANAGEMENT; ORGANIZATION BEHAVIOUR; ORGANIZATIONAL LEARNING; PAYMENT SYSTEMS; TOTAL QUALITY MANAGEMENT; WORK SYSTEMS

Kanter, Rosabeth Moss (1943–)

Personal background

- born 15 March 1943 in Cleveland, Ohio, USA
- BA (sociology) Bryn Mawr College, MA, PhD University of Michigan
- assistant professor of sociology, Brandeis University, 1967–73
- visiting associate professor of administration, Harvard University, 1973–4
- associate professor of sociology, Brandeis University, 1974–7
- associate professor of sociology, Yale University, 1977–8; professor of sociology, 1978–86
- professor of management, Harvard University, 1986–
- editor, *Harvard Business Review*, 1989–92
- founding committee member, International Women's Forum

Major works

Work and Family in the United States (1976)
Another Voice: Feminist Perspectives on Social Life and Social Science (1977)
Men and Women of the Corporation (1977)
A Tale of 'O' (with Barry A. Stein) (1980)
The Change Masters (1983)
Creating the Future (with Michael S. Dukakis) (1988)
When Giants Learn to Dance (1989)

Summary

Rosabeth Moss Kanter is a well-known writer, academic and consultant in the USA. A sociologist by training, she has long been interested in the dynamics of organizations and has written eleven books and more than 150 articles setting out her views. Her most famous work, *When Giants Learn to Dance*, prescribes strategies and calls on corporations to become more flexible and better at communicating. She is one of the few women who can legitimately be called a management 'guru'.

1 Introduction

Coming from a background of sociology, Kanter has made the organization her primary field of study. Her expressed aim is to not only understand and explain the corporation but also to make it both more effective and a better place to work. Her view, based on her work as an academic and consultant, is that most corporate structures impede innovation and communication; she has proposed a number of steps which corporations (particularly corporations in the USA) need to take if they are to compete more effectively and if the USA is to remain a world economic force.

2 Biographical data

Born in Ohio in 1943, Kanter was educated at Bryn Mawr College and then the University of Michigan. Her first husband died in 1969, shortly after she began her academic career at Brandeis University; her second, Barry Stein, is also an occasional colleague and co-author. Her background was in sociology, but she became interested from an early period in the sociology of corporations. As she told the Chicago *Tribune* (6 May 1979), 'I realized very early in college that corporations are among the most powerful entities in society, and if you care about how the world is run, you have to find out about them. My interest has always been in how a complex world is put together.'

Kanter taught sociology at Brandeis for ten years, with a one-year break as a visiting professor at Harvard University. Her early writing centred on work and family and was characterized by a feminist perspective. Later, at Yale University and then as a professor of management at Harvard, she began focusing on what she saw as the dominant organizational structure in modern society, the corporation. Her two major works, *The Change Masters* and *When Giants Learn to Dance*, have made her among the most respected writers and thinkers on management in the USA today. She is also one of the most prominent women in business in the world, and has played a leading role in organizations such as the International Women's Forum.

3 Main contribution

In *The Change Masters*, Kanter laid down a challenge to corporations in the USA: 'we face social and economic changes of unexpected magnitude and variety, which past processes cannot accommodate, which require instead innovative responses' (Kanter 1983: 19). In her view, innovation is the only way forward. The organizational response must be to create a climate in which innovation can flourish.

The problem, she states, is that corporations are inherently unused to managing innovation. Innovation was traditionally a process that happens outside the corporation, and was traditionally an activity carried out by talented individuals or entrepreneurs. Today the need is to 'create conditions, even inside larger organizations, that make it possible for individuals to get the power to experiment, to create, to develop, to test – to innovate' (Kanter 1983: 23). Some corporations manage to do this; in others, the climate is such that innovation is actually impeded and retarded.

Kanter's view of this problem is essentially a sociological one. She believes that climate and communication within the organization are the keys to creating a situation where innovation can flourish. Lack of communication is a critical problem. Workers feel cut off from the prime decision makers at executive level, and lack power; their responses are either to

try to achieve promotion and therefore power, or slip into a static state in which they perform less and less productively. Managers are caught in the middle; in the eyes of workers they have power, but in reality all they have to do is enforce decisions made at a higher level. The result is bureaucratic and demotivating.

Her solution is to break down these barriers and create an organizational atmosphere where executives know, and can communicate with, their employees, both formally and informally. There is a strong emphasis on employee participation, coalitions and teamwork, themes she was to continue in her later work; one of the central foci of Kanter's writing is the need for cooperation, whether between employees within a corporation, between corporations, or between corporations and government. Her belief is that the era of the 'lone wolf' entrepreneur is over; we are now in the 'post-entrepreneurial era' where the economic future (of the USA at least) depends on large corporations. In 1988 she collaborated with Massachusetts governor Michael Dukakis to write *Creating the Future*, an analysis of the 'Massachusetts miracle' in which local economic regeneration had been achieved through a combination of state and private effort. The book, which also showed the influence of Robert Reich (see REICH, R.M.), Kanter's colleague at Harvard, was part of Dukakis' ultimately unsuccessful presidential campaign that year; the victor, George Bush, instead espoused a policy of competition and non-intervention.

The logical extension of the quasi-sociological ideas in *The Change Masters* was to explain not only how but why corporations need to become more innovative, and to provide a model for future development. This extension can be found in *When Giants Learn to Dance*, Kanter's most popular and successful book. Here, Kanter begins by bluntly spelling out the challenge to corporations in the 1990s – the need to do more with less. 'This constitutes the great corporate balancing act. Cut back and grow. Trim down and build. Accomplish more, and do it in new areas, with fewer resources' (Kanter 1989: 31).

Kanter accepts the prevailing view that corporations needed to become 'leaner and fitter' in an attempt to become more flexible, but she attacks what she called 'slashing' of organizational structures and spending without regard for consequences. She warns that there are no quick solutions. She develops what she calls 'the post-entrepreneurial principles' of management, which should:

- Minimize objectives and maximize options. Keep fixed costs low and as often as possible use 'variable' or 'contingent' means to achieve corporate goals.
- Find leverage through influence and combination. Derive power from access and involvement, rather than from full control or total ownership.
- Encourage 'churn'. Keep things moving. Encourage continuous regrouping of people and functions and products to produce unexpected, creative new combinations. Redefine turnover as positive (a source of renewal) rather than negative.

(Kanter 1989: 354)

The corporation of the future, Kanter believes, will be a much more flexible place, where jobs are designed around projects rather than schedules. There is an obvious consequence in human terms, and Kanter acknowledges the tension between the corporate need for flexibility and the needs of employees and managers for security. The solution, she believes, is for employees to find security not through association with a specific job or company but through employability, the knowledge that they can always find employment. Work structures also need to be more flexible; employees may need to spend more time at work, but at the same time corporations need to provide more time for families to spend together. For the flexible, responsive corporation, Kanter describes three strategies:

1 the development of greater synergy, with more internal cooperation and better integrated organization
2 the establishment of alliances with other organizations
3 the development of 'newstreams', new business possibilities to take the organization into the future.

The result, says Kanter, will be the demise of bureaucracies and the emergence of more cooperative, interactive organizations able to meet the challenges of the future. 'These three post-entrepreneurial strategies can change sluggish organizations into agile athletic champions in the global corporate Olympics. They can show bloated, elephantine corpocracies how to dance' (Kanter 1989: 35).

4 Evaluation

Kanter has much in common with other management gurus of the 1980s such as Tom Peters (see PETERS, T.J.). Like many in the generation following Drucker (see DRUCKER, P.F.), she emphasizes innovation, flexibility and responsiveness and warns that corporations need to break down their rigid structures and become better at adapting to change. Again like other writers of her generation, she identifies the human component as crucial in this change process; this is management as art, rather than science, where human creativity is the crucial element in maintaining competitive strength.

Several factors, however, set Kanter apart. The first is her recognition of the human needs of employees, a result of her background as a sociologist and also perhaps of the feminist perspective of some of her work. Her emphasis on the need for changing work patterns is not one-way operation; corporations too need to be flexible, and recognize the importance of family life. Kanter understands not only organizations but the feelings and attitudes of the individuals who comprise them.

Second, she believes more emphatically than most in collaboration and cooperation, to the extent that she envisages a strong role for government in business. People and organizations, government and business, all have a collaborative role to play. Finally, there is her strong patriotism. Kanter's work is aimed specifically at US companies; behind all her writing is the understanding that unless US corporations can maintain their competitive position, the economy and thence the society of the USA will suffer. Some have maintained that Kanter's views are simplistic, but none can deny the conviction with which she holds those views.

5 Conclusion

Rosabeth Moss Kanter is one of the most notable writers on management to emerge in the USA in the past two decades. Her work focuses on the sociology of organizations, including both the need of organizations to adapt to change and the role of the individual in creating change. She advocates an organizational atmosphere where innovation and flux are encouraged and seen as positive forces.

MORGEN WITZEL
LONDON BUSINESS SCHOOL
AND DURHAM UNIVERSITY BUSINESS SCHOOL

Further reading

(References cited in the text marked *)

* Chicago *Tribune* (1979) 6 May interview with Rosabeth Moss Kanter.
Hodgetts, R.M. (1995) 'A conversation with Rosabeth Moss Kanter', *Organizational Dynamics* 24 (1). (Interview with Kanter in which she sums up her views on globalization.)
Kanter, R.M. (1976) *Work and Family in the United States: A Critical Review and Research and Policy Agenda*, New York: Russell Sage Foundation. (Kanter's first book, a call for greater attention to the effects of work on family life.)
Kanter, R.M. (1977a) *Another Voice: Feminist Perspectives on Social Life and Social Science*, New York: Doubleday. (Primarily a sociological work but it shows the beginnings of her ideas on organization thinking.)
Kanter, R.M. (1977b) *Men and Women of the Corporation*, New York: Basic Books. (An important and useful work on human dynamics in organizations.)
* Kanter, R.M. (1983) *The Change Masters: Innovation for Productivity in the American Corporation*, New York: Simon & Schuster. (A call to arms, urging American corporations to embrace innovation and create a climate in which it can flourish.)
* Kanter, R.M. (1989) *When Giants Learn to Dance: Mastering the Challenge of Strategy, Management in Careers in the 1990s*, New York: Simon & Schuster. (Kanter's most famous work, which describes the challenges facing US corporations in the 'post-entrepreneurial' era.)
Kanter, R.M. (1995) *World Class*, New York: Simon & Schuster. (Kanter's most important recent work in which she describes the importance of globalization for the modern buisness and the need for a sustainable corporate response.)
* Kanter, R.M. and Dukakis, M.S. (1988) *Creating the Future: The Massachusetts Comeback and Its Promise for America*, New York: Summit Books. (An analysis of the so-called 'Massachusetts miracle' of the 1980s, written with state governor Michael Dukakis who was also the Democratic presidential candidate in that year.)
Kanter, R.M. and Stein, B.A. (1980) *A Tale of 'O': On Being Different in an Organization*, New York: Harper & Row. (A humorous, yet thought-provoking look at human behaviour in organizations: the hero, a solitary 'O' must work with and compete with a crowd of 'X's.)

See also: DRUCKER, P.F.; PETERS, T.J.; REICH, R.M.;

Related topics in the IEBM: COMMUNICATION; CREATIVITY MANAGEMENT; CULTURE; DIVERSITY; DOWNSIZING; EMPLOYEE DEVELOPMENT; ENTREPRENEURSHIP; EQUAL EMPLOYMENT OPPORTUNITIES; FLEXIBILITY; GOVERNMENT, INDUSTRY AND THE PUBLIC SECTOR; GURU CONCEPT; HUMAN RESOURCE MANAGEMENT; HUMAN RESOURCE MANAGEMENT, INTERNATIONAL; INNOVATION AND CHANGE; INNOVATION MANAGEMENT; INNOVATION AND TECHNOLOGICAL CHANGE; MANAGEMENT IN NORTH AMERICA; ORGANIZATION BEHAVIOUR; ORGANIZATION DEVELOPMENT; STRATEGY, CONCEPT OF; WOMEN IN MANAGEMENT AND BUSINESS

Keynes, John Maynard (1883–1946)

Personal background

- born 5 June 1883, Cambridge, England
- educated at Eton and Cambridge
- combined careers of civil servant, financial speculator and academic with a strong appreciation of the arts
- chief representative of HM Treasury at the Paris peace conference, 1918
- married Lydia Lopokova of the Ballets Russes, 1925
- elevated to the peerage, 1942
- British representative at Bretton Woods conference, 1944
- died 21 April 1946

Major works

The Economic Consequences of the Peace (1919)
Treatise on Probability (1921)
A Tract on Monetary Reform (1923)
A Treatise on Money (1930)
The General Theory of Employment, Interest and Money (1936)

Summary

J.M. Keynes is not only the greatest economist of the twentieth century, he is also, still, the most controversial. He has been called the father of macroeconomics, but there had been others before him who had concerned themselves with analysis at the aggregate level. His achievement as a theorist was to appreciate the non-neutrality of monetary factors in the economy, fully integrating them into an explanation of how the economy works. Previous doctrines maintained that the role of money was to serve only as a convenient intermediary in exchanges of commodities: at best it had no effect, at worst it was responsible for fluctuations in prices which were expected to be temporary, and in the long run the economy would right itself and return to full employment.

Keynes' analysis explained for the first time why unemployment was not a mistake or due to a failure of entrepreneurial nerve but could result from rational choice. The costs incurred in achieving an expansion of employment, he pointed out, rise faster than the resulting sales of output; thus it becomes unprofitable to expand output and employment beyond a point which may be short of full employment. Since this situation will persist until some external force operates to change it, we have *unemployment equilibrium*, despite the fact that all agents are doing the best for themselves ('maximizing') within the constraints they face. Perhaps the most important point for the business and management is that there are consequences of individual actions which cannot be foreseen: an investment may not pay the return which was expected, not because it was a bad idea but because it was implemented at the 'wrong' time – when, for example, others were not also investing and thereby boosting demand for the product as well as for their own.

1 Beginnings

John Maynard Keynes was born in Cambridge, England, the eldest of three children. His father, John Neville Keynes, was a Cambridge don (and later Registrar of the University) lecturing in logic and political economy. Political economy is the older name for economics and literally means the housekeeping of the State. It was perceived not as a technical discipline, but as a moral science, along with politics and philosophy. J.N. Keynes' work on the scope and method of political economy remains a classic. Maynard's mother, Florence Ada Keynes, was unusual for her time. Educated at Newnham College in the pioneering days of women's education at Cambridge, she was active in progressive social projects and became the first woman mayor of Cambridge. The family was Congregationalist.

Maynard's instruction in economics, along with the other essential subjects, began at home; his father supervised his studies and they worked together in the father's study. Maynard was perceived as exceptionally intelligent from an early age and was pushed rather hard, but where a lesser child might have found this onerous or have rebelled, he revelled in the work and excelled. He won a scholarship to Eton where he developed his knowledge of philosophy and began to cultivate an interest in and to collect rare books (he later collected Newton's alchemical papers). He went from there to King's College, Cambridge, where philosophy and ethics claimed his attention more than the subject he was reading, mathematics.

Keynes obtained a first class degree in 1905 and then, with Alfred Marshall's encouragement and supervision, stayed on in Cambridge to study for the economics examinations but elected to sit the Civil Service Examinations instead (see MARSHALL, A.). He came second and joined the India Office where he spent just two years. From 1908 to the outbreak of the First World War Keynes was back in Cambridge, lecturing in economics and revising his fellowship dissertation.

2 Emergent philosophy

Keynes and his Cambridge circle, especially the members of the exclusive group 'The Apostles', were much influenced by the philosophy of G.E. Moore. For Moore, the contemplation of beauty and the enjoyment of friendship were the true purposes of life, a view deeply subversive of Victorian values.

His artistic interests spanned theatre, ballet, painting and rare books (he founded the Arts Council and the Arts Theatre at Cambridge). In Keynes these goals were balanced by the acceptance of a duty to contribute to public life, which he did in abundance. He was also keenly interested in the political philosophy of Edmund Burke. Keynes developed his Ideal, but was also prepared to develop the art of the possible (Fitzgibbons 1988; Helburn 1992; O'Donnell 1989; Skidelsky 1983).

While at the India Office, Keynes transformed an early critique of Moore into a pioneering work on the philosophy of probability, which he submitted to King's College as a fellowship dissertation in 1908. He was not elected until the following year (one of Keynes' few setbacks), after the thesis had been revised. It was not published until 1921, as *Treatise on Probability*.

The purpose of *Probability* is to derive principles of rational behaviour when there is true uncertainty. True uncertainty is to be distinguished from the type of uncertainty for which appropriate behaviour can be derived from classical probability. Classical probability pertains to experiments whose outcomes must be independent of time, both the time at which the experiment is conducted (context) and the sequence of the events within the experiment. The problem of decision making in the face of an uncertain future is qualitatively different from the controlled experiment – history does not repeat itself.

The rules of classical probability offer no insight into appropriate action under true uncertainty. Nevertheless, true uncertainty need not paralyse us or reduce us to pure guesswork. Clues exist to the probable relation between actions and their consequences in some cases. Repeated evidence from these clues, while not definitive, add to what Keynes called the 'degree of rational belief' in the probable connection between an action and the outcome. These probabilities provide a guide to rational action (Carabelli 1988; O'Donnell 1989). When, much later, Keynes wrote *The General Theory*, a central concept is behaviour under this kind of irreducible uncertainty.

3 Early economics

While at the India Office, Keynes closely examined India's monetary system and in 1913 published *Indian Currency and Finance*. Although the mode of analysis used is traditional, the book shows two features which characterize Keynes' work throughout his life and which would provoke the evolution of his thought: his thorough knowledge of economic institutions and his pragmatic approach to policy recommendations to improve those institutions. He strongly supports the use of discretion over rule-following in monetary matters and expresses a scepticism about the gold standard. When he came to oppose Britain's exchange rate policy after the 1914–18 war he had even more ammunition against the gold standard, but in this work his scepticism was based on his understanding that the success of the standard was not due to the standard itself but was contingent on the existence of a single, strong financial centre, which was London at that time. This understanding of the institutional and historical context was not at all part of the conventional wisdom of the day, which regarded the gold standard as self-evidently the source of monetary order.

Keynes entered the Treasury in January 1915 to work on wartime internal and external finance, and at the end of the war he was the Treasury's chief representative at the Paris peace conference. Keynes did not accept the implicit limitations of his brief but took the perspective of a highly placed statesman/politician. He bitterly opposed the settlement France was trying to impose on Germany, arguing that Germany could not pay what France was asking; the attempt would first bankrupt and then embitter her, and that was dangerous (and so it proved).

When his view did not prevail, Keynes resigned in protest and published his views as *The Economic Consequences of the Peace* (1919). The book was a sensation, both for the depth of its analysis of the economic causes of the war and the consequences of the proposed peace, but also for its vivid depiction of the way strong political forces were being played out at the conference and its devastating characterization of the chief participants. Keynes was now famous, not as an academic but in the world of affairs (he became a subject of David Low's cartoons). But in official circles the book was (understandably) considered deeply offensive. The Treasury sent Keynes into outer darkness – until they needed him again.

In the 1920s, Keynes returned to a life of lecturing at Cambridge (unpaid, in order to leave time for writing), journalism, financial dealings, academic writing and the fulfilment of Moore's goals of the enjoyment of friendship and of beauty. He spent part of each week at King's and at Gordon Square in London's Bloomsbury. Eventually he also took a lease on a house in Sussex. The academic was balanced by the man of affairs, the manager by the aesthete (Skidelsky 1992).

4 The gold standard debate

After the *Treatise on Probability* was revised for publication in 1921, Keynes the political economist employed his powers of persuasion in vigorous opposition to Britain's return to the gold standard. Keynes the academic put his ideas together as *A Tract on Monetary Reform* (1923). His position on the gold standard began where his *Indian Currency and Finance* had left off. The international context had changed. London's position as the world's sole, well-developed, strong financial centre could now be challenged by New York. Added to this was the fact that the debate entirely revolved around going back to the gold standard at the pre-war parity, despite the fact that prices in Britain had risen far higher than in the countries which constituted the competition – most notably America. Thus Britain would have to deflate, which she duly did. To those who understood monetary factors as creators of only temporary disruption this was perhaps not a daunting prospect, but to Keynes the personal tragedy and the social waste of the unemployment which would inevitably follow far outweighed the potential benefits of the standard.

Keynes was almost alone in his opposition, and it was an argument he lost. The gold standard was perceived as the only right arrangement, and the return to pre-war parity as the only honourable course, because to establish a lower parity would be to default in part to one's creditors. Britain had, of course, entered heavily into debt to fight the war, and a substantial portion of that debt was held abroad.

In the first two years after the war, Britain experienced one of the sharpest price fluctuations of her modern peacetime history. The retail price index rose 16 per cent in 1920, then fell by 28 per cent over the next two years. Still this fall was not enough to achieve parity and it had already had the effects Keynes feared: unemployment rose to 14 per cent in 1922 and continued to be high for the entire inter-war period, never falling below 10 per cent. The deflation in preparation for the return to gold was continued after the return (1925) to support the standard. Labour rebelled in 1926 with the General Strike, but it took the world recession provoked by the Wall Street crash and the collapse of world trade to make the gold standard finally untenable. Britain eventually came off in 1931.

In the face of all this upheaval, one can understand the impatience Keynes felt with the traditional methodology of the long run, disturbed by transitory monetary factors. In the *Tract on Monetary Reform* there is a famous statement, often taken out of context:

> But the *long run* is a misleading guide to current affairs. *In the long run* we are all dead. Economists set themselves too easy, too useless a task if in tempestuous seasons they can only tell us that when the storm is long past the ocean is flat again.
>
> (*CW* IV: 65)

In the tempestuous season associated with the return to gold, Keynes also displayed his distinct preference for avoiding unemployment, at the expense of profits if necessary (in *The General Theory* it was *rentier* income he was happier to see cut). In the *Tract* he argued for high interest rates to engineer a deflation of profits rather than a demand deflation which would cause incomes to fall and layoffs to rise. The contribution of that work to the Keynesian Revolution lies in its rejection of the long run as the foundation of economic

analysis. This rejection was later to form the basis of the transition from *A Treatise on Money* to *The General Theory*.

5 From *A Treatise on Money* to *The General Theory*

Post-war events had emphasized the influence of banking and monetary policy on the economy (see FRIEDMAN, M.). Some economists, however, persisted in the misconception that money is neutral, affecting only 'nominal' variables. Keynes, who was always prepared to accept the evidence of his own eyes, could not sustain such a belief. He determined to write a treatise on money, consolidating his accumulated knowledge of the working of money markets and the role of money in the economy. What resulted is a scholarly work, somewhat ponderous in style, in two volumes following the traditional separation of the 'pure theory' of money from applied theory. The definitive treatise was not the medium for someone like Keynes, whose restless mind was constantly being stimulated by active participation in public affairs, who was learning all the time. Keynes' thinking developed in conjunction with his work for the Macmillan Committee on the Finance of Industry (Clarke 1988).

The *Treatise on Money* (1930) is an important work, both for the wealth of institutional and historical detail it contains and for its development of an approach towards the 'deviations' from the long run in which monetary and 'real' factors are integrated. It takes up the challenge of the *Tract* to discover what processes of adjustment are provoked by variations in demand, which result in unexpected ('windfall') profits and losses. Windfalls are defined as deviations from the 'flat sea' of a long-period equilibrium. This long-period equilibrium is completely traditional: just-normal profits and normal real wages, with equilibrium prices determined by the quantity of money. Departures from long-period (full) employment are attributed to a lack of entrepreneurial nerve (if entrepreneurs would produce more they would discover they could sell it) and assumed to be temporary.

Within the theory, wages must fall to cure unemployment.

These are thoroughly classical conclusions, but the *Treatise* contained an important step towards *The General Theory* in arguing that the rate of interest (the price of securities), instead of being determined by flows of saving and the demand for funds to finance investment, was set by the activities of optimistic and pessimistic speculators ('bulls' and 'bears'). These activities involved the deployment of the stock of financial wealth, not just flows. In modern terms, Keynes took a portfolio approach. The effect of concentrating on the activities of bulls and bears is to break the traditional link between the rate of interest and the rate of profit and thus the link to 'fundamentals'. Speculators are not interested in fundamentals but in a quick profit on their financial dealings. (Keynes should know; he earned his living that way.)

When Keynes published the *Treatise* in 1930, the British economy had been depressed since 1922, and the slide to the bottom of the depression caused by the collapse first of American economic activity and then of world trade had begun. Could anyone really believe that eight years of unemployment of over 10 per cent (nine more years were to come) were due to 'transitory monetary factors'? There are those who, faced with a conflict between their theory and the evidence, will defend their theory, finding 'imperfections' in the world's performance. When Keynes perceived that the world and theory were out of line, he looked for a new theory.

In Cambridge, there emerged a group of brilliant younger colleagues (known as the 'Circus') who met to discuss the *Treatise*; they provided criticism, particularly of the inability of the work to explain variations in output except as random variation. Thus employment also was random. That was no explanation, and explanation was urgent. In mid-1931, with work for the Macmillan Committee out of the way, Keynes therefore began to revise his ideas to provide the needed explanation. In the course of doing so he produced his greatest work, which resulted in a radically altered structure for economic theory: *The General Theory of Employment, Interest and Money* (1936).

6 The Keynesian Revolution

The Keynesian Revolution is popularly understood to be the policy conclusion associated with *The General Theory*: governments should run deficits to counteract a slump. But others had advocated this policy long before Keynes. His complaint, indeed, was that this policy recommendation could not be supported by existing theory. The purpose of the work was to provide the theory which justifies that policy and outlines the circumstances in which it should be pursued. It is the theory, and even more, the method which underlies it, which is truly revolutionary.

The key concept of *The General Theory* is the 'principle of effective demand'. This principle states that employment is determined by aggregate demand, given prevailing wages and technical conditions of supply. Demand determines the level of output which it is profitable for firms to supply, as well as appropriate prices. This is true even for small firms, who in traditional theory are said to take prices as given. Keynes here made two obvious points: prices cannot be taken as given, for the market in which the goods are to be sold is in the (inherently uncertain) future; and prices facing an individual firm are conditional on the aggregate level of economic activity. Therefore there is no way that firms, even those too small to influence the market by their actions, can determine appropriate output and hiring policy without first taking a view ('forming an expectation') of aggregate demand. This is necessary because aggregate demand can vary, perhaps suddenly and unexpectedly but (in contrast to the 1930 work) not only randomly. *The General Theory* explores the reasons for explicable, if not predictable, variation.

If demand is not adequate to justify full employment, there is 'involuntary unemployment' and there is no mechanism by which an adequate level of demand can be brought about by the actions of. If producers' expectations of demand are met at a level of production which does not absorb all the labour willing to work at the going wage, unemployment can continue indefinitely. Equilibrium will be a position of full employment only by accident, and equilibrium with unemployment is just as likely. It is not a mistake – expectations are fulfilled.

Where the 1930 work posits a long period with only one level of output (normal output) supplemented by random fluctuations, *The General Theory* explores the determination of output in the context where it actually takes place (when the capital stock is given and output can only be expanded by hiring more labour), hence the direct link between output and employment. Technically, this is known as the short period, but it can last a long or a short length of actual time depending on how quickly new capital comes on stream and begins to contribute to production. The classical sheet anchor of the long run has finally been abandoned and with it the 'classical dichotomy', whereby the quantity of money determined prices and 'real variables' were determined by 'real factors'. Aggregate demand is a monetary variable; there are no elements determined by purely 'real' forces. Monetary factors are neither neutral nor transitory.

The elements of aggregate demand are consumption and investment. Consumption is mainly determined by income and thus responds when aggregate income rises, but consumption cannot initiate such a rise. Investment, on the other hand, is free of current income, for two reasons: the purpose of investment is to expand the capacity to meet future, not current, demand; and at least some investment is not financed by current cash flow but by bank loans. Since banks can make loans which correspond to no prior saving, this source of lending makes possible an excess of investment over current saving, in contrast to the classical story where investment is constrained by the amount of saving. Saving is now adjusted to investment through increased income, not the other way round.

Both by reason of the potential volatility of entrepreneurs' expectations of future demand and the lack of any financial constraint other than bankers' evaluations, investment is the unpredictable element of demand. This is not all bad, for it is investment which can lift the economy out of recession in the short run and provide capacity and improved competitiveness in the longer term. Investment not only provides additional income equal to itself but also initiates further rounds of induced consumption expenditure such that the income generated will be a multiple of the original investment. This is the famous 'multiplier', an idea first mooted by Keynes and Hubert Henderson (*Can Lloyd George Do It?* 1929) and developed by Keynes' colleague Richard Kahn (1931).

The rate of interest is the price to be paid for borrowing to finance investment. The general level of the rate of interest, Keynes argued, is determined by the same forces as those described in the *Treatise* : the speculative expectations and activities of 'bulls' and 'bears'. If they, and bankers, share the same ups and downs of optimism as the investing producers, investment will be still more volatile.

It had been believed that if employers as a whole simply decided to produce more, they would find that they would sell the increased output, since employment and income would have risen (this is known as Say's Law – supply creates its own demand). An important part of Keynes' story is the 'fundamental psychological law' (as he called it) that less than the whole of a rise in income would be consumed (the marginal propensity to consume is less than one). Thus as income rises there is a gap to be filled if producers are to sell all their output. If investment is not forthcoming to fill that gap, there are two possibilities: give encouragement to investment or find some other way to fill the gap. Investment depends on expectations of the further future and the rate of interest. It is difficult to 'talk up' the future prospects of an economy to affect expectations (though some governments have tried this), and in time of recession it is extremely difficult to push interest rates down, because they are so low already. This is where the famous policy recommendation of government expenditure enters the picture – to fill a gap left by depressed investment in a time of high unemployment. The multiplier analysis shows that the resulting improvement in economic activity would go a long way towards financing the policy through lower unemployment benefit and higher tax yields.

The alternative 'cure' for unemployment proposed at the time (and by many others subsequently) was to lower wages. *The General Theory* shows that this proposition assumes that wages are only a cost, whereas they are both a cost and a source of demand. It is therefore impossible to argue that a cut in wages would leave demand unaffected. It is difficult to predict what would actually happen, but one certainly cannot assert that an unambiguous improvement would follow. Keynes was of the view that a cut in wages might actually damage employment.

7 The Second World War and after

The General Theory brought to fruition the long struggle to escape from established modes of thought which had begun in the dissatisfaction with long-period analysis expressed in the *Tract on Monetary Reform*. But Keynes was never solely a theorist. In the political context of the time the book's message was urgent. In the ten years between the General Strike and the 1936 work, the plight of the worker had worsened, and alternative systems were claiming to have the answer to unemployment and poverty, namely communism and fascism. But it was to be rearmament, not Keynes' ideas, which came to the rescue.

In 1937, Keynes suffered his first heart attack, with other complications. His activities were sharply reduced for the next two years, and when war broke out he planned to spend the duration in Cambridge, thus releasing those more fit for government or military service. But his urge to action and his expertise resulted in publications and speeches and quite soon a pamphlet on the pressing subject, *How to Pay for the War* (1940). Then he joined the Chancellor of the Exchequer's Consultative Council, and soon a room was found for him in the Treasury, where he concerned himself not only with the financing of the war but also with preparing to shape postwar trade and especially payments.

The *Treatise on Money* had ended with a plan for a supranational bank, an idea which Keynes had mooted even in his very first book. His proposal for an international clearing union, which became known as the Keynes Plan, formed the British starting point at the negotiations which culminated at Bretton Woods, where the framework for the international monetary system was agreed. The clearing union represented a complete break with any automaticity in international monetary mechanisms in favour of discretionary monetary management, albeit with a limited brief on this international scale. Keynes' concern was to prevent creditor countries from building up idle balances. This is a direct generalization to the international sphere of the concern in *The General Theory* that, especially in a recession, people would prefer liquidity, with the result that the rate of interest would remain high and exert a deflationary influence.

The Americans could not be persuaded to go as far as the Keynes Plan, not least because they knew that they were already a chief creditor and they feared a further outpouring of dollar loans. The resulting International Monetary Fund corresponded more closely to the less far-reaching plan of the American representative, Harry Dexter White. Keynes was in a weak bargaining position: he would soon have to negotiate an American loan to Britain. He dared not walk out, as he had done in Paris. The terms of the subsequent loan were quite onerous but the best Keynes could do. Despite his reservations, he argued passionately for its acceptance, most notably in a moving speech in the House of Lords, to which he had been elevated in 1942. The loan agreement was signed just in time for Parliament, which had been waiting for the outcome to ratify the Bretton Woods Articles of Agreement. Three months later, Keynes went to the inaugural meeting of the Bretton Woods institutions (the International Monetary Fund and World Bank) at Savannah, Georgia in March 1946. It was not, as Keynes expected, a pleasant party; there was an agenda of final details, but in these, all the old conflicts surfaced.

On the train back to New York, Keynes collapsed from exhaustion. A few weeks later, at his Sussex home on Easter Sunday, he suffered another heart attack. This time it was fatal.

8 Evaluation

Keynes' contribution can be evaluated at two levels: the contribution of his entire career as an economist and the contribution of the source-book of the Keynesian Revolution. This entry has stressed the continuous evolution of his thought and the application of his theoretical framework, as it evolved, to important social and political questions at the highest level.

Keynes' life as an economist was of a piece, even as his ideas evolved. This is something we are just beginning to realize as the result of extensive scholarship. It is often said that an economist must also be a philosopher, an historian, a politician. Keynes was all these and more, especially a polemicist and persuader, and he wielded a mighty pen. Skidelsky (1992) has argued that there was no centre to the man, that he was a follower of events. The view expressed here is that his ethics, political philosophy and mathematical philosophy all influenced the shape of his economic ideas until finally, in *The General Theory*, there was a unity between theory and policy which expressed his philosophical beliefs.

Keynes' economics was founded on his own observation both of institutions and psychology. This is not the usual way; economics has developed as a logical system based on what are asserted to be self-evident axioms – it is deductive. Keynes' economics was both deductive and inductive, the latter often the product of intuition and thus left implicit. There are examples in the above text: the evolution of the banking system to the point where credit requires no prior saving is the foundation of the shift from investment being determined by savings to its leading position in the determination of income; the psychology of consumption stops the economy from necessarily reaching full employment; the psychology of optimism and pessimism drives both investment and the securities markets.

Keynes' masterwork, *The General Theory of Employment, Interest and Money*, was perhaps too radical for its time, or even for today. It has only recently become appreciated how radical the work really is. Consider the psychological barriers to assimilating its message. It says that:

1 when there is widespread unemployment, workers have no ability to improve their employment prospects, as employment is determined by what employers expect demand to be, and the main element which alters demand from one period to the next is investment, which is also a decision of 'capital'

2 workers can bargain for a money wage, but the price level, and hence their real wage, is determined also by aggregate demand

3 producers determine investment independently of saving, and households have no control over that element of aggregate demand through the provision of finance

4 finance is in the hands of bankers, who can create credit with the stroke of a pen and who are as subject to waves of optimism and pessimism as the entrepreneurs

5 the price of borrowing (the rate of interest) is determined in the market for securities, where speculators care little for the economic fundamentals (productivity or the profit of productive firms) but aim only to make money by outwitting each other and the central bank

6 the lending which bankers do results in changes in the money supply, over which the public at large has no control, yet the willingness to lend determines employment, output and even future competitiveness.

All these things are true because production is organized along capitalist lines, where the ownership of the means of production is in the hands of a few. These producers must commit themselves to hiring labour at contractual wages in order to produce for market sale in the future. By definition, the future, and thus the market, is uncertain. The producers therefore take the risk that their decisions will not be profitable – or not as profitable as they had expected. The workers, on the other hand, have uncertain employment and also have no bargaining power over their real wage: 'the market', in aggregate, determines prices and thus the real wage.

The monetary side of Keynes' story also pertains to a specific stage of institutional development. Unlike the classical theory of the rate of interest, which depends on flows of saving and investment, this theory recognizes the importance in advanced economies of markets for secondhand financial assets. This was a gradual but highly significant development. It allows the individual to hold a claim on the profits of business without the risks which are run by the entrepreneurs, who are 'locked in' to their investments and who must run them for profit and, if profits are disappointing, face the risk of bankruptcy. Financial claims are liquid to the individual, though of course they are not liquid for their holders collectively. The advantage to the individual is balanced by the divorce this market creates between long-term profits expected from running the business and the rate of return to the financial players.

The theory also recognizes, albeit implicitly, that bankers have the power to create money and thus to determine, at least in part, both the composition and the level of aggregate income. *The General Theory*, in other words, faces up to the world as it actually is, even if some of its power relations are unpleasant to acknowledge. It is not surprising that a theory which both goes against the established way of doing economics and recognizes some unpleasant facts should have a difficult passage. Almost as soon as the book was published the upholders of tradition began the process of bringing its message back into the fold. Eventually a system of simultaneous equations with past and future obliterated (and therefore uncertainty and expectations) came to represent Keynes' system: this was 'Keynesian economics', with its emphasis on government expenditure, even 'fine tuning', forgetting all of Keynes' caveats. The recovery of Keynes' economics can be said to begin in earnest with Leijonhufvud's 1968 work *On Keynesian Economics and the Economics of Keynes* – they are not at all the same.

9 Conclusion

Keynes demonstrated that in a modern monetary, capitalist economy, the economic system left to itself can produce long-standing unemployment. He concluded that the economic system needs some help if it is to produce the highest level of efficiency while preserving a liberal society. He favoured conscious monetary management, at both the national and the international levels, and some management also of investment, which tended to be short-sighted and capricious if left entirely in private hands. It has to be said that he was unduly optimistic about the selfless motivation of governments.

In the hands of his interpreters, 'Keynesianism' became formulaic. Keynes never relinquished the role of interpretation and judgement in economic affairs.

VICTORIA CHICK
UNIVERSITY COLLEGE LONDON

Further reading

(References cited in the text marked *)

Amadeo, E.J. (1989) *Keynes's Principle of Effective Demand*, Aldershot: Edward Elgar. (Exposition of the economics of *The General Theory* which pays special attention to the relation between that work and the *Treatise on Money*.)

Bryce, R.B. (1977) 'Keynes as seen by his students in the 1930s (i)', in D. Patinkin and J.C. Leith (eds), *Keynes, Cambridge and The General Theory*, London: Macmillan. (Best simple exposition of the basic ideas of *The General Theory*.)

* Carabelli, A.M. (1988) *On Keynes's Method*, London: Macmillan. (Traces influence of the *Treatise on Probability* on Keynes' method, especially that of *The General Theory*.)

Chick, V. (1983) *Macroeconomics After Keynes: A Reconsideration of the General Theory*, Cambridge, MA: MIT Press. (A reconstruction of the economics of *The General Theory*. Technical but not mathematical.)

* Clarke, P. (1988) *The Keynesian Revolution in the Making*, Oxford: Clarendon Press. (Traces the interplay of Keynes' participation in the Macmillan Committee and the development of the *Treatise on Money*.)

* Fitzgibbons, A. (1988) *Keynes's Vision*, Oxford: Oxford University Press. (Explores Keynes' fundamental philosophy.)

Harcourt, G.C. and Riach, P. (eds) (1996) *Maynard Keynes' General Theory*, 2nd edn, London: Routledge. (Articles commissioned from many Keynes scholars; each has a chapter or topic of *The General Theory* to 'update'. Full bibliography of debates since *The General Theory* was published.)

Harrod, R.F. (1951) *The Life of John Maynard Keynes*, London: Macmillan. (Biography by a distinguished economist, a contemporary of Keynes.)

* Helburn, S.W. (1992) 'On Keynes's Ethics', in P. Arestis and V. Chick (eds), *Recent Developments in Post-Keynesian Economics*, Aldershot: Edward Elgar. (Shows the relationship between Keynes' ethics, political philosophy and economics.)

* Kahn, R.F. (1931) 'The relation of home investment to unemployment', *Economic Journal* 41 (162): 173–98. (Original exposition of the multiplier.)

* Keynes, J.M. *The Collected Writings of J. M. Keynes*, 30 vols, eds. D.E. Moggridge and E.A.G. Robinson, London: Macmillan. (Published 1971–1989. Works cited in this entry are contained in the volumes listed: *Indian Currency and Finance*, CW I; *The Economic Consequences of the Peace*, CW II; *A Tract on Monetary Reform*, CW IV; *A Treatise on Money*, CW V *The General Theory of Employment, Interest and Money*, CW VII; *Treatise on Probability*, CW VIII; *Can Lloyd George Do It?*, CW IX; *How to Pay for the War*, CW IX.)

* Leijonhufvud, A. (1968) *On Keynesian Economics and the Economics of Keynes*, Oxford: Oxford University Press. (Throws Keynesian economics and Leijonhufvud's interpretation of Keynes in sharp relief. Controversial interpretation.)

Moggridge, D.E. (1980) *Keynes*, 2nd edn, London: Macmillan. (Shorter biography and exposition of the development of Keynes' thought.)

Moggridge, D.E. (1992) *Maynard Keynes: An Economist's Biography*, London: Routledge. (Full, modern biography by the chief editor of Keynes' *Collected Writings*. Strongly based on original sources.)

* O'Donnell, R.M. (1989) *Keynes: Philosophy, Economics and Politics*, London: Macmillan. (Its basic proposition is that Keynes' thought can be perceived as a unity over these three fields of thought.)

* Skidelsky, R. (1983, 1992) *John Maynard Keynes*, 3 vols, London: Macmillan. (Extensive, modern biography.)

See also: FRIEDMAN, M.; HAYEK, F.A. VON; MARSHALL, A.; SAMUELSON, P.A.

Related topics in the IEBM: ARROW, K.J.; BIG BUSINESS AND CORPORATE CONTROL; BUSINESS CYCLES; BUSINESS ECONOMICS; COLLECTIVE BARGAINING; EMPLOYMENT AND UNEMPLOYMENT, ECONOMICS OF; FINANCE, INTERNATIONAL; INFLATION; INSTITUTIONAL ECONOMICS; INTEREST RATE RISK; KNIGHT, F.H.; LABOUR MARKETS; MARKETS; MARKETS AND PUBLIC POLICY; MARKET STRUCTURE AND CONDUCT; MONETARISM; NEO-CLASSICAL ECONOMICS

Kochan, Thomas A. (1947–)

Personal background

- born 28 September 1947 in Wisconsin, USA
- graduated from the University of Wisconsin-Madison with a BBA (1969), MS (1971), PhD (1973)
- assistant professor then associate professor, School of Industrial and Labor Relations, Cornell University, 1973–80
- on leave to the US Department of Labor, Washington DC, 1979–80
- professor at the Sloan School of Management, Massachusetts Institute of Technology (MIT), 1980–
- president of the International Industrial Relations Association, 1992–95
- member of the (Dunlop) Commission for the Future of Worker–Management Relations, 1993–95
- president of the Industrial Relations Research Association, 1999–2000

Major works

The Transformation of American Industrial Relations (with H.C. Katz and R.B. McKersie)(1986)

Collective Bargaining and Industrial Relations (1980, 1987, 1991)

Transforming Organizations (with M. Useem)(1992)

The Mutual Gains Enterprise (with P. Osterman)(1994)

Employment Relations in the Growing Asian Economies (with A. Verma and R. Lansbury)(1995)

Employment Relations in a Changing World Economy (with R. Locke and M. Piore)(1995)

Managing for the Future (with D. Ancona, M. Scully, M. Van Maanen and D.E. Westney)(1996)

After Lean Production (with R.D. Lansbury and J.P. MacDuffie)(1997)

Summary

Thomas A. Kochan is the George M. Bunker Professor of Management at MIT's Sloan School of Management. He began at MIT in 1980 as a professor of industrial relations (IR) and from 1988 to 1991 he was head of the behavioral and policy sciences area in the Sloan School. He was also a member of the MIT Commission on Industrial Productivity. He was previously at Cornell University where he worked at the School of Industrial and Labor Relations from 1973 to 1980. He was on leave as a consultant for a year to the Secretary of Labor in the Department of Labor's Office of Policy Evaluation and Research, Washington. He has been a third-party mediator, fact finder, and arbitrator and a consultant to a variety of government and private-sector organizations and labour-management groups.

He has conducted research on a range of topics related to IR/human relations (HR). In 1996, Kochan received the Heneman Career Achievement Award; he was a centennial visiting professor at the London School of Economics in 1995; in 1997 he was elected a fellow of the National Academy of Human Resources.

Kochan has been recognized in the USA as one of the leaders of research, scholarship, teaching, consulting and advisory work in employment relations (IR and HR) since the mid-1970s. One of his most important contributions was to revive an interdisciplinary approach to IR/HR, integrating IR with aspects of human resource management (HRM) and organizational behaviour, drawing particularly on quantitative research methods used hitherto more in such other social sciences, economics, sociology and psychology. Since the mid-1980s he has also played a prominent role internationally and published widely on comparative IR and HR. While president of the International IR Association (1992–95), he helped to introduce more rigorous research activities into the Association.

1 Biographical data

Kochan was born in rural Wisconsin into a Catholic family. His father was a small farmer whose family had migrated to Wisconsin from Prussia. Kochan helped on the farm as a young man. He has a brother and three sisters. In 1969 he married Kathy Otis, a nurse practitioner, in Wisconsin and they have five children, the first four of whom they adopted; two of them from Korea. Baseball is one of Kochan's non-work interests, and despite a hectic work schedule for years he has made time to coach a 'little league' baseball team.

Kochan studied for all of his degrees at the University of Wisconsin, one of America's best land-grant state universities, which has long held an enviable reputation in industrial relations. Some of the leading US industrial relations (IR) scholars have been associated with Wisconsin, including Jack Barbash, John Commons, Solomon Levine, Selig Perlman and James Stern (see BARBASH, J.; PERLMAN, S.), and it hosts the secretariat of the Industrial Relations Research Association. Kochan's PhD thesis examined multi-lateral bargaining in the public sector. His classmates at Wisconsin included others who have gone on to

become well-known scholars in similar fields including Roy Adams, Lee Dyer, Haruo Shimada, and Hoyt Wheeler.

2 Collective Bargaining and Industrial Relations

Much of Kochan's work in the 1970s focused on the public sector and examined the impact of various procedures under the Taylor Law (a New York State statute) to reach agreements without resorting to strike action. This made an important contribution. Nonetheless, it was the publication of his book, *Collective Bargaining and Industrial Relations* (1980), that established Kochan's reputation as a leading scholar in the USA. Most earlier books in the field had adopted an 'historical-institutional' approach that had tended to emphasize detailed *descriptions* of the legal framework, labour history and current issues being faced by practitioners.

Kochan aimed to develop a 'more *analytical* approach to the study of collective bargaining' (1980: vii). His central purpose was to 'integrate the advances in theory building and empirical research from the behavioural sciences and economics with the strong institutional base from which the study of collective bargaining and union management relations has evolved' (1980: viii). The importance of this book was illustrated by the prestigious journal *Industrial Relations* publishing a review symposium devoted to it. The contributors to this review included leading scholars from the USA and the UK.

3 The Transformation of American Industrial Relations

His leading role flourished after he moved to MIT, where, together with Harry Katz and Bob McKersie, Kochan researched and wrote *The Transformation of American Industrial Relations* (1986), which received the annual award from the US Academy of Management for the best scholarly book on management. This work examined the development of new management approaches to IR and sought to explain the decline of unionism and the 'New

Deal' model of IR in the USA. *Transformation* developed a 'strategic choice' framework to explain the changing nature of US IR. To an extent Kochan *et al.* (1986) extend and build on the influential IR systems model developed by Dunlop (1958). They argued that the systems model was no longer adequate since one of its key assumptions, a shared ideology among the major actors (employers, unions, and government), no longer applied in the USA. With the decline of unions, management strategies had become more dominant. The consequent changes to IR had resulted in a two-fold transformation. First, there was a shift away from traditional IR based on collective bargaining; second, there were new workplace arrangements and HRM systems that mostly originated in the non-union sector.

Although *Transformation* was widely acclaimed, it fuelled considerable debate (e.g. Chelius and Dworkin 1990). Four main questions were raised by critics of the book: is there sufficient evidence of transformation? Is strategic choice sufficient to explain the nature of change in IR? How extensive has been the implementation of sophisticated HRM practices? How applicable are the concepts of transformation and strategic choice to the international scene? In response to their critics, Kochan *et al.* (1986) argued that subsequent events had further substantiated their claims. *Transformation* provided evidence that the locus of activity in American IR had shifted to the strategic and workplace levels. They claimed that unions found it difficult to decide whether and how they should fit into the new IR system. Indeed, the emergence of an alternative non-union system (embracing the majority of the workforce) was one of the key developments contributing to the perceptions of a transformation of American IR during the 1980s.

In association with the *Transformation* project, Kochan also led many sub-projects including: examinations of quality of working life (QWL) experiments; health and safety committees; high-performance work systems (e.g. at the General Motors Saturn plant); and other elements of what have become known as world-class manufacturing (WCM).

4 Employment Relations in a Changing World Economy

Following the debates over the *Transformation* book, particularly about its possible international applicability, Kochan and his colleagues at MIT initiated a series of international and comparative studies. These originated partly from interest in whether IR systems in other countries were being transformed in a similar manner to their US analysis. An international team of researchers, coordinated by the MIT group, undertook studies in a range of Organization of Economic Co-operation and Development (OECD) countries to ascertain the changing nature of employment relations in several key industries including: airlines, banking, car manufacturing, steel and telecommunications. The focus of the studies were on IR/HR practices, which included changes in work organization, patterns of skill formation and training, compensation (remuneration) arrangements, employment and staffing practices including job security.

Several common patterns emerged from the research. A transformation process appeared to be underway internationally that included the following features: first, increased importance of the role of enterprise-specific strategies and decisions, which required some decentralization of IR activities in these countries with traditions of national or industry-wide collective bargaining; second, increased emphasis on flexibility, teamwork and communications within enterprises as firms sought to empower workers to improve productivity and product quality; third, a strong emphasis on skill development and training to enable workers to contribute to the enterprise; and fourth, as membership in unions declined, there was growing interest in new models of representation and decision making. Finally, a new role for government emerged as a facilitator of innovation at the workplace (Locke, Kochan and Piore, 1995).

The international project spawned a number of other studies based on the key industries such as telecommunications (Katz 1997), car manufacturing (Kochan, Lansbury and MacDuffie 1997), as well as subsequent volumes on banking and steel. In Australia, a book was published which included studies from all of the key industries (Kitay and Lansbury 1997).

5 Employment Relations in the Growing Asian Economies

The conceptual framework which the MIT team used for researching employment relations in OECD countries was subsequently extended to newly industrializing economies in Asia (Verma, Kochan and Lansbury 1995). This project sought to understand better the interaction between employment relations policies and economic development. The study showed such economies began the process of development by creating some initial conditions conducive to investment. This often translated to low wages and low unionization. However, as investment increased over time, the initial labour market conditions inevitably changed. As demands for unionization and collective bargaining grew there were pressures for wage increases. These could be termed secondary conditions of the labour market because they followed the initial spate of investment.

The response of business and public policies to secondary conditions in the labour market appeared to influence the trajectory of economic growth. Some governments responded to rising wages and growing demands for worker 'voice' with suppressive measures. Others, however, responded in more measured ways to accommodate the secondary conditions. While no single 'Asian model' had emerged, in all the cases where growth was sustained, governments sought to accommodate secondary changes in the labour market rather than try to regain the initial conditions. As in the OECD study, the Asian countries that were most successful in the long run were those which were willing and able to learn from innovation and to adopt employment relations practices which provided a 'best fit' for their particular situation.

6 After Lean Production: Changing Employment Practices in the World Auto Industry

Through his key role in the MIT-initiated International Motor Vehicle Program (IMVP), Kochan has made a significant contribution to research on the interaction between production systems and employment relations. In their best-selling book, which reported IMVP results, Womack, Jones and Roos (1990) argued that lean production (essentially the Toyota production system) was the most effective way to manufacture cars and that companies which failed to adopt this approach would be less competitive (see WOMACK, J.P. AND JONES, D.T.). Kochan subsequently led an international research project, within the aegis of the IMVP, which showed that employment practices are shaped not in a deterministic fashion by methods of production or some singular technological or economic imperative, but by a multiplicity of factors (Kochan, Lansbury and MacDuffie 1997). This project concluded that while there was a general trend towards the adoption of lean production across the world car industry, the extent and rate of adoption and diffusion would be the result of interaction between global competitive pressures and the strategies chosen by firms, governments and the workforce.

7 The Dunlop Commission and other professional activities

Kochan strives to relate theory to practice and vice versa. He is committed to the need for academics and public policy makers to play a constructive role in reforming employment relations and work systems. In the early 1990s he undertook a significant study of the increasing use of subcontracting in the petrochemicals industry and its impact on safety and union density.

He has been involved in significant public policy inquiries. He was a member of the Commission on the Future of Worker–Management Relations established by President Clinton in 1993 and chaired by John Dunlop.

The Commission investigated methods to improve the productivity and global competitiveness of the American workplace. The final report by the Commission in 1995 recommended restructuring national labour and employment policies. Given that there was only a minority of the legislature that was interested in reforming US labor law, the report was not implemented by the government. Although Kochan supported the Commission's findings and recommendations, he advocated that they should have been bolder. Kochan's own proposals built upon his work with Paul Osterman in *The Mutual Gains Enterprise* (1994) and called for a coalition for mutual gains. This sought to promote experiments with new approaches to participation, representation and workplace governance and thereby improve the climate for employment relations at national and workplace levels.

8 Conclusions

By combining new conceptual approaches to the broad field of employment relations (IR and HRM) with a strong empirical focus on changing practices and policies, Kochan has made significant contributions to theory and practice. His use of strategic choice as a means of analysing the changing nature of employment relations has provided a useful interdisciplinary approach to his writings. He has maintained the traditions established by his predecessors at Wisconsin of being engaged in key policy debates and contributing to improvements in the practice of IR and management, whilst also analysing underlying causes of change. While he has remained a public intellectual in the USA, his later work has also adopted an international perspective. Through his comparative research Kochan has achieved an influence which extends well beyond the USA and Europe to emerging and newly industrializing economies.

GREG J. BAMBER,
GRIFFITH UNVERSITY, QUEENSLAND,
AUSTRALIA

RUSSELL D. LANSBURY,
SYDNEY UNIVERSITY, NEW SOUTH WALES,
AUSTRALIA.

Further reading

(References cited in the text are marked *)

* Ancona, D., Kochan, T., Scully, M., Van Maanen, J. and Westney, D.E., (1996) *Managing for the Future: Organizational Behavior and Processes*, Cincinnati: South-Western College Publishing. (Examines the organization of the future; networked, flat, flexible and made up of a diverse workforce, viewing change through three lenses: strategic; political; and cultural.)

Bamber, G.J. and Lansbury, R.D. (eds) (1998) (forthcoming) *International and Comparative Employment Relations: A Study of Industrialised Market Economies,* third edition, Allen & Unwin/Sage: Sydney/London. (A discussion of ten key industrialized economies. He wrote the foreword. The strategic choice approach developed by Kochan *et al.* is a point of departure for a comparative analysis of changing patterns of employment relations.)

* Chelius, J. and Dworkin, J. (1990) *Reflections on the Transformation of Industrial Relations*, New Jersey: Institute of Management and Labor Readings, Rutgers, State University of New Jersey. (A collection of essays by leading researchers which analyse the book: Kochan, Katz and McKersie (1986). Contributors include: Richard Block, George Strauss, James Begin, John Fossum and Jacques Rojot. The editors argue that although Kochan *et al.* have not created a new paradigm in industrial relations, their work raises important issues for future research.)

* Dunlop, J. (1958) *Industrial Relations Systems*, New York: Holt, Rinehart & Winston. (This important book offers a definition of an 'industrial relations system' and compares a number of national systems.)

* Katz, H.C. (ed) (1997) *Telecommunications: Restructuring Work and Employment Relations Worldwide*, Ithaca: Cornell University Press. (Examines the effects of deregulation and globalization on corporate strategies and structure in the global telecommunications industry, and how this has altered the nature of work. The authors use a common framework inspired by Kochan *et al.* (1986) to analyse changes in employment relations in ten countries.)

* Kitay, J and Lansbury, R.D. (eds)(1997) *Changing Employment Relations in Australia*, Melbourne: Oxford University Press. (An analysis of in six industries: airlines, autos, banking, information technology, steel and telecommunications. The conceptual framework for the

study was adapted from the work of Locke, Kochan and Piore (1995).)

* Kochan, T. (1980) *Collective Bargaining and Industrial Relations: From Theory to Policy and Practice*, Homewood: Irwin. (An analytical approach which integrates theoretical and empirical research as well as providing a strong institutional base. This book is the subject of a review symposium in *Industrial Relations: A Journal of Economy and Society*, Vol. 21, No. 1, Winter. 1982.)

* Kochan, T. and Osterman, P. (1994) *The Mutual Gains Enterprise*, Boston: Harvard Business School Press. (An analysis of new approaches to participation, representation and workplace governance which provide opportunities for a 'coalition of mutual gains' between employees and employers.)

* Kochan, T., and Useem, M. (1992) *Transforming Organizations*, New York: Oxford University Press. (Discusses how organizations should adapt to global markets. It argues that changing parts of an organization will not be successful as systemic changes across whole organizations will be required.)

* Kochan, T., Katz, H.C. and McKersie, R.B. (1986) *The Transformation of American Industrial Relations*, New York: Basic Books. (Explains the decline of unionism and the 'New Deal' model in the USA using a 'strategic choice' framework, which emphasized the importance of new management strategies; includes an analysis of new workplace arrangements and HRM systems in the expanding non-union sector.)

* Kochan, T., Lansbury R.D. and MacDuffie, J.P. (1997) *After Lean Production: Changing Employment Practices in the World Auto Industry*, Ithaca: Cornell University Press. (Research based on car assembly plants in eleven countries includes the way work is organized, how workers and managers interact, the way in which worker representatives respond to lean production strategies and the nature of the adaptation and innovation process.)

* Locke, R., Kochan, T. and Piore, M. (eds) (1995) *Employment Relations in a Changing World Economy*, Cambridge: MIT Press. (An analysis of industrial economies in the context of increased global competition and changing technologies. While a general transformation process appears to be underway, there are differences in the way different countries have adapted to change.)

* Womack, J.P., Jones, D.T. and Roos, D. (1990) *The Machine that Changed the World*, New York: Rawson/Macmillan. (Examines the differences between mass production and lean production in the automotive industry in Japan, North America and western Europe. Reports the results and implications of MIT's IMVP.)

* Verma, A., Kochan, T. and Lansbury, D. (eds) (1995) *Employment Relations in the Growing Asian Economies*, London: Routledge. (An analysis of the role of IR/HR in the context of economic development in: China, Hong Kong, India, Malaysia, the Philippines, Singapore, Korea and Taiwan. It is argued that unless a synergy is created between firm-level and state-level employment relations policies, economic growth is unlikely to be sustainable.)

See also: BARBASH, J.; DUNLOP, J.D.; PERLMAN, S.; REICH, R.; WOMACK, J.P. AND JONES, D.T.

Related topics in the IEBM: COLLECTIVE BARGAINING; EMPLOYEE RELATIONS, MANAGEMENT OF; GLOBALIZATION; HUMAN RESOURCE MANAGEMENT; INDUSTRIAL AND LABOUR RELATIONS; INDUSTRIAL RELATIONS IN THE UNITED STATES AMERICA; JAPANIZATION; MANAGEMENT IN NORTH AMERICA; MANAGEMENT IN PACIFIC ASIA; MANUFACTURING STRATEGY; ORGANIZATION BEHAVIOUR; PAYMENT SYSTEMS; PROFIT-SHARING; WORK SYSTEMS

Kotler, Philip (1931–)

Personal background

- born 27 May 1931 in Chicago, USA
- undergraduate at De Paul University, 1948–50
- graduated with an MA in economics from the University of Chicago, 1953
- received a PhD in economics at Massachusetts Institute of Technology, 1956
- post doctorate researcher at Harvard University, 1960–1
- associate professor of economics, Roosevelt University, 1957–61
- assistant professor of marketing, Kellogg Graduate School of Management, Northwestern University 1962–4
- associate professor of marketing, Kellogg Graduate School of Management, Northwestern University, 1965–8
- Montgomery Ward Professor of Marketing, Kellogg Graduate School of Management, Northwestern University, 1969–72
- Harold T. Martin Professor of Marketing, Kellogg Graduate School of Management, Northwestern University, 1973–87
- Johnson & Son Distinguished Professor of International Marketing, Kellogg Graduate School of Management, Northwestern University, 1988–

Major works

Marketing for Health Care Organizations (with R.N. Clarke) (1987)
Social Marketing: Strategies for Changing Public Behaviour (1989)
Principles of Marketing (1996)
Principles of Marketing, The European Edition (with G. Armstrong, J. Saunders and V. Wong) (1996)
Strategic Marketing for Nonprofit Organizations (with A. Andreasen) (1996)
Marketing Management: Analysis, Planning, Implementation and Control (1997)

Summary

Philip Kotler is the founder of modern marketing management. His legendary text *Marketing Management: Analysis, Planning, Implementation and Control* has significantly influenced and developed worldwide understanding of the concept of marketing and its managerial role in 'fulfilling needs profitably'. In the late 1960s Kotler thought that academic approaches to marketing lacked theoretical grounding and analytical quality, and subsequently the first edition of *Marketing Management* marked the evolution of scientific rigour in the discipline of marketing. During his long-standing career as a marketing professor, Kotler has consulted with the captains of multitudinous industries, lectured to inexhaustible audiences, written 15 books (available in 27 languages), and influenced the thinking of tens of thousands of the world's top marketing executives. As a result he has been christened the 'Father of Modern Marketing' by his peers, students, supporters and critics worldwide.

1 Biographical data

Who's Who in America describes Philip Kotler as a marketing educator, consultant and writer, a son, a husband and father of three daughters – an indication of a sonorous man who values all spheres of life equally. He entered the discipline of marketing from an economics perspective, having studied economics in order to understand how the economy works and what forces determine the size, growth and distribution of the commercial environment.

He graduated with an MA in economics from the University of Chicago in 1953; having studied under Milton Friedman he became a 'free enterpriser'. He went on to receive a PhD in economics at Massachusetts Institute of Technology in 1956 under Paul Samuelson, subsequently developing a Keynesian perspective and an overwhelming dissonance as a result. This dissonance was resolved after an informal introduction to marketing from friends (including Bob Buzzell and Jerome McCarthy) made whilst he studied on a one-year Ford Foundation sponsored post-doctorate research programme at Harvard University (1960–61). This unorthodox path into marketing is reflected in his work which applies social, behavioural, economic and quantitative sciences to marketing management, emulating the analytical characteristics he cultivated from his early economic background.

Whilst teaching economics at Roosevelt University, in 1962 Kotler was invited to join the School of Business at Northwestern University to teach either managerial economics *or* marketing. He chose marketing and began his esteemed career as assistant professor of marketing at the distinguished Kellogg School of Management. He was promoted to an associate professor in 1965, to a full professor in 1969, to Chair in 1973, and to Distinguished Professor in 1988, where he continues to pursue his vocation.

Kotler holds honorary doctorate degrees from DePaul University (1988), the International Management Centre (1989), the University of Zurich (1990) and Athens University of Economics and Business (1995). In 1985 he was named the first recipient of two major awards: the Distinguished Marketing Educator of the Year Award of the American Marketing Association and the Philip Kotler Award for Excellence in Health Care Marketing of the Academy of Health Care Services Marketing. In 1989 he also received the Charles Coolidge Parlin National Marketing Award and the Victor Mataja Medal.

Kotler's theoretical and education work has been implemented in his manifold consulting activities: beneficiaries of his expertise include IBM, Apple, General Electric, Ford, AT&T, Motorola, Bank of America, DuPont and Ciba Geigy.

2 Modern marketing management

Philip Kotler's inaugural contribution to marketing was to bring the discipline to the forefront of business management. On taking up the position at the School of Business at Northwestern University, he examined existing marketing textbooks determining there was an inadequacy of quality theoretical texts in the field and as a result decided to write his own text book, *Marketing Management: Analysis, Planning, Implementation and Control*, a groundbreaking text which changed perceptions of marketing from exclusively selling, advertising and market research to the more expansive cognition of marketing as a science. This text, first adopted by the University of Chicago on their introduction to marketing course, has become the world's most recommended marketing text; its visibility and notoriety is present in students work at undergraduate and postgraduate levels on a global scale.

Kotler developed the concept of modern marketing management as the process which takes the specialists in marketing – planners, researchers, advertising, customer service and sales people – away from their individual role towards a collective interactive endeavour with the objective of achieving a marketing orientation throughout the company. Kotler gave credence to the belief that marketing management is not simply the collective effort of specialists to produce marketing strategies, but an axiom constituting the driving force behind the achievement of an organization-wide marketing driven customer orientation, a philosophy which is guided by marketing specialists but implemented by all departments with the interactive goal of performance optimization. In Kotler's opinion, *Marketing Management:*

Analysis, Planning, Implementation and Control introduced a strong systemization of marketing by establishing it on a foundation of economic, behavioural, organizational and quantitative science, and giving it the academic and managerial credibility it had previously strived to achieve.

Kotler's deliberation of the infusion of managerial, behavioural, political, international and economic concepts lead to further development of marketing thought. He argued that if the fundamental concept of economics is scarcity, of politics is power, of sociology is the group, and of anthropology is culture, then the core concept of marketing is *exchange*. The essence of marketing is the transaction – the exchange between two or more parties – as a consequence marketing is seen as a discipline of human behaviour, a social process.

Social marketing is concerned with social change, and focuses on the use of resources in modern industrial nations and in the developing regions of the world. The foundation of the social marketing concept lies with the premise that a profitable business does not have to adopt a philosophy of unfettered capitalism, Keynesian-neoclassical focus on growth, an over-specialization in the search for competitive advantage, or monopoly power. This economically dominated approach to business management and capitalist society emphasizes growth rather than development, unlike the concept of social marketing; the paradigm of social marketing seeks to pursue growth and equity within the context of social awareness, resource stability and the achievement of the interlinking objectives of economic *and* social advantage, so deepening the concept of marketing.

3 Deepening the marketing concept

Kotler's second major contribution to the discipline of marketing is his conceptualization of how marketing can be implemented to precipitate social causes.

Until the early 1970s marketing was viewed as a discipline for business organizations exchanging products and services to satisfy needs profitably, however, based on the premise that marketing is a social process and not simply a business function of the profit-orientated firm, Kotler 'deepened' the paradigm of marketing science to incorporate social causes.

Influenced by events of social protest and countercultural experimentation in the early 1970s, alongside Gerald Zaltman at Northwestern University, Kotler decided to widen the application of marketing to social causes such as US Aid, the World Health Organization and the World Bank, arguing that marketing can be a highly effective management technology for social change. The societal marketing concept works on the view that marketing is exchange in differing contexts, and applies marketing principles to ecology, political advertising and social responsibility.

4 Broadening the concept of marketing

As Kotler himself says (Kotler 1987), he has taken marketing into new sectors of society and shown its potential contribution to non-profit organizations. In 1969 Kotler and Levy suggested that the concept of marketing can be broadened to include non-business organizations such as churches, police departments, hospitals and schools. Developing the limits of marketing was the message of 'Broadening the concept of marketing' (Kotler and Levy 1969) which boldly embraced non-business organizations into the realm of marketing. The balance of objectives and resources against needs and opportunities is required in non-business organizations and, for example, Kotler has influenced a generation of health professionals on how to market causes such as anti-smoking, Aids awareness and anti-drugs campaigns.

The broadening of the marketing concept is based on the same core principle of marketing – *exchange* – which states that marketing occurs when people want to satisfy needs and desires through exchange: the act of obtaining a desired object or service by giving something in return (Kotler, Jatusripitak and

Maesincee 1997). This principle does not have to be profitable in economic terms, however. It is Kotler's opinion that 'marketing is a pervasive societal activity that goes considerably beyond the selling of toothpaste, soap and steel' (Kotler and Levy 1972: 10): there are after all reflective needs to be satisfied and demands target audiences are asked to exchange something they value for something beneficial (Kotler and Andreasen 1996).

Beyond developing marketing's conceptual and practical applicability to non-profit organizations and social causes, Kotler has broadened marketing to the marketing of people and places including cities, states and nations – and the focus of his book *High Visibility* (Kotler, Rein and Stoller 1998*).* He argues that offering suggestions of the understanding of the 'place buyer', tourists, new residents, factories, investors, though the marketing concept can benefit a place's economy.

Broadening the concept of marketing to non-profit sectors requires the development of a systematic approach to solving marketing problems, and an awareness and understanding of the key tools and procedures necessary for an effective marketing orientation (Kotler and Andreasen 1996). Kotler inaugurated the marketing paradigm which concentrates on the exchange of social, medical and psychological benefit other than profit maximization, and by doing so has lead to a worldwide implementation of marketing on non-profit organizations and a global research agenda with far reaching consequences.

5 Conclusions

Students are educated to perform roles in international and global business, and already millions of students have studied Kotler's *Marketing Management* text book. In addition many academics and practising managers have been inspired by his developing, deepening and broadening of the marketing concept and the traditional boundaries of marketing science. The skill of customer acquisition, activation and retention, the selection and focus on satisfying needs in a exceptional manner, no matter what type of business you are in – detergents, confectionery, health care,

ecology, tourism – has become the Kotler marketing management of the twentieth century.

However, critics of Kotler's philosophy are well documented, and it is debated by his peers world wide. Animadversion of Kotler's contribution to marketing centres around this broadening and deepening of the marketing concept, with his work being criticized for simplifying the market domain, and contributing little more than the formulation of matrix's and boxes that can be applied to almost any organization's services and products no matter what need they satisfy.

This view is not, however, held by many academics and professionals, as most agree that Kotler's worldwide success is based on the belief that theoretical evolution must have its practical uses and that those uses should not be obscured by the research tools or the technical vocabulary of the academic (Zaltman 1972): his proficiency in communicating with students, academics and practising managers separately and on aggregate is the key to his sustained success in the marketing domain. At the 1989 Charles Coolidge Parlin National Marketing Award ceremony, Kotler was presented the award with the words:

> Dr. Kotler is one of the world's leading distinguished scholars of our time. His extensive contributions to marketing literature, and his innovative consulting work for leading corporations worldwide has made him a leader in marketing.
>
> (Krulis-Randa 1990)

CAROLYN STRONG
CARDIFF BUSINESS SCHOOL
UNIVERSITY OF WALES

Further reading

(References cited in text marked *)

Beck, U. (1989) *From Industrialised Society to the Risk Society: Questions of Survival, Social Structure and Ecological Enlightenment. Theory, Culture & Society,* London: Sage.

* Kotler, P. and Levy, S.J. (1969) 'Broadening the concept of marketing', *Journal of Marketing,* January: 10–15.

* Kotler, P. (1997) *Marketing Management: Analysis, Planning, Implementation and Control*, Englewood Cliffs, NJ: Prentice Hall.
* Kotler, P. and Clarke, R.N. (1987) *Marketing for Health Care Organizations*, Englewood Cliffs, NJ: Prentice Hall.
* Kotler, P. and Andreasen, A. (1996) *Strategic Marketing for Nonprofit Organizations,* Englewood Cliffs, NJ: Prentice Hall.
* Kotler, P., Armstrong, G., Saunders, J. and Wong, V. (1996) *Principles of Marketing, The European Edition.* Englewood Cliffs, NJ: Prentice Hall.
* Kotler, P., Jatusripitak, S. and Maesincee, S. (1997) *The Marketing of Nations: A Strategic Approach to Building National Wealth*, New York, NY: The Free Press.
* Kotler, P., Rein, I. and Stoller, M. (1998) *High Visibility*, USA: NTC.
* Krulis-Randa (1990) Speech delivered by Dr. Jan S. Krulis-Randa upon awarding an honorary degree to Philip Kotler form University of Zurich.
* Zaltman, G. (1972), 'Leaders in marketing', *Journal of Marketing* 36, October: 60–61.

Further resources

Web site – http://www.kellogg.nwu.edu/faculty/bio/KOTLER.HTM
Letter to Robert Bartles, 27 May 1987
Speech delivered by Dr Jan S. Krulis-Randa upon awarding an Honorary Degree to Philip Kotter from University of Zurich, 1990.

See also: LEVIIT, T.

Related topics in the IEBM: GLOBALIZATION; HEALTH MANAGEMENT; INTERNATIONAL MARKETING; MARKETING; MARKETING MANAGEMENT, INTERNATIONAL; NOT-FOR-PROFIT MARKETING; NOT-FOR-PROFIT MANAGEMENT; STRATEGY

Kotter, John P. (1947–)

Personal background

- born in San Diego, USA, in 1947
- received a BSc in electrical engineering, from the Massachusetts Institute of Technology (MIT), 1968
- received an MS in management from the Sloan School of Management, MIT, 1970
- received a PhD in organizational behaviour from the Graduate School of Business Administration, Harvard University, 1972
- from 1972 has had a career at the Graduate School of Business Administration, Harvard University, where he received tenure and full professorship in 1980
- he is the Konosuke Matsushita Professor of leadership, organizational behaviour and human resource management

Major works

Mayors in Action: Five Approaches to Urban Governance (with P.R.Lawrence) (1974)
The General Managers (1982)
A Force for Change: How Leadership Differs From Management (1990)
Corporate Culture and Performance (with J. Heskett)(1992)
The New Rules: How to Succeed in Today's Post-Corporate World (1995)

Summary

The importance of good leadership in modern business and what should be done to develop good leaders and to help them to become yet more effective has become the major theme of Kotter's work. In his early writings, he contributed to studies of managerial behaviour.

He has been following the careers of the MBA class of 1974 from the Harvard Business School and in 1995 published his findings and conclusions about the nature of successful careers today. He has also studied the effects of corporate culture upon business performance. Most of Kotter's books are based on extensive research and the conclusions and their implications are presented succinctly and attractively in books, articles and videos for executives and as an aid to teaching executives.

1 Managerial behaviour

John Kotter first made his name and is most frequently referenced for his research into managerial behaviour, a sparsely researched area compared with those of leadership and careers that he researched later. In *Mayors in Action* (1974), which he wrote with Paul Lawrence and which is based on his doctoral work, two key ideas, agenda setting and network building, were developed: these then formed part of the framework for analysis in his next book, *The General Managers* (1982). In these books he argues that the managers he researched developed an agenda during the first six months to a year in the job. These agendas were composed of loosely connected goals and plans, and were therefore more personal, more strategic and longer term than formal company plans. To achieve their agendas, the mayors and the general managers developed a network of contacts who could be of help and took time to keep this network up to date and hopefully supportive.

In *The General Managers*, Kotter observes, as previous researchers had done, that the managers' time was characterized by brief and disjointed conversations. He stresses the importance of relationships outside the straight line hierarchy. One of the most important contributions of this book, apart from the concepts of agenda and network building, is his analysis of the differences as well as the similarities in the behaviour of the fifteen general managers whom he studied and his emphasis on the differences in the context within which they worked, making it, he argues, unlikely that they could move successfully to a general manager's job in a different setting. Here, he was attacking the idea of general management as a common set of knowledge and skills that was transferable across companies and industries.

2 Leadership

A question that should be asked when there are so many leadership pundits and so much research on leadership, especially in the USA, is: what is distinctive about Kotter's contribution? He is not a major researcher on leadership such as Fiedler or Bass, although he has done a lot of research related to leadership; his distinctive contribution is that he is the relatively unusual combination of someone who uses his research to provide the basis for his advice to businessmen. The often extensive and prolonged research background is described briefly in a preface to his books, with some details of research methods at the back, while his findings are used to give clear, short pointers on successful leadership illustrated by vivid examples.

Many writers have pontificated about the difference between leadership and management, while others have exalted leadership and disparaged management. Kotter has done neither, but sought unusually to research what others see to be the differences and to collect critical incidents that illustrate leadership in action. He reports the results in *A Force for Change: How Leadership Differs from Management* (1990) and argues that both are essential but that business today needs more leadership. Some of these arguments are foreshadowed in an earlier book, *The Leadership Factor* (1988). He identified four major differences between management and leadership. The first is in the approach to what he calls 'creating an agenda' – the concept which he first used in *Mayors in Action* and developed as a major concept in *The General Managers*. Managers plan and budget within

specific time frames whereas leaders, as many other writers have said, develop a vision for the future and strategies for achieving the vision. The second difference he calls 'developing a human network for achieving the agenda': managers are concerned with organizing and staffing while leaders aim to align people by communicating the vision. The third difference is in the approach to execution: managers are monitoring results and problem solving and leaders are motivating and inspiring people so that they are energized. Traditional writers on management might object to this distinction because motivating has long been called one of the functions of management; the difference lies in inspiring and energizing that Kotter, like other modern writers on leadership, see as a leadership function. The fourth difference is in the outcomes: management produces a degree of predictability and order whereas leaders produce change. How much leadership is needed in a firm will therefore depend upon the amount of change that is required and how much management upon the amount of complexity that the firm faces.

One of Kotter's ongoing concerns is the greater need today for leaders at all levels of management to meet current competitive challenges, a concern which developed during the course of research in the 1970s. The views on, and practice in, attracting, developing and retaining leadership talent were explored in four subsequent and related studies, and the conclusions of all the research are discussed in *The Leadership Factor* (1988), which is about the greater need for leadership in companies today and about how they should, and often fail, to provide adequately for leadership and management succession.

Discussions about providing adequately for future managers have a long history: some companies recognized this need before World War II, and *Management Succession* (1956), a survey of what the fifty largest manufacturing companies in Britain were doing to recruit, select, train and develop their managers, covered similar ground and similarly found that many companies were not doing all they should, especially when compared with the best practice. The major difference between the two books, published over thirty years apart, is the focus on leadership, although the prescriptions for how to develop leaders are similar to what a few of the best companies on both sides of the Atlantic were doing to develop good managers in the 1950s and even earlier.

The studies that Kotter undertook with James Heskett into the relation between corporate cultures and economic performance, (Kotter and Heskett 1992) also identified the importance of good leadership. They calculated 'culture strength indices' for over 200 big US companies and tried to correlate the strength of the company's culture with its economic performance. They did find that there was a positive correlation, but it was weaker than many management theorists would have expected. They concluded that only cultures that encourage flexibility and adaptive behaviour are associated with superior long-term business performance. They studied companies in which there had been successful cultural change and said that there were one or two unusually capable leaders at the top.

Until *Matsushita Leadership* (1997) Kotter had reported on American leaders, but this new book was a departure in that it is both a biography and about a famous Japanese businessman. The link with his other work relates to the leadership lessons that he draws upon.

3 Careers in a changing world

The New Rules: How to Succeed in Today's Post-Corporate World (1995) are the practical conclusions that he draws from his twenty-year tracer study of 115 Harvard MBAs from the class of 1974, supplemented by other studies of 85 executives, most of whom did not have MBA degrees. All but 7 per cent of the 1974 Harvard MBAs studied were men, so the study started too early to provide information about how women MBAs fared and indeed 'women' or 'gender' is not indexed. However, Kotter's key messages from the research are about the ways in which careers are changing and the implications of this for those who want successful careers. He emphasizes the opportunities and hazards afforded by globalization, and argues that traditional careers in large companies are providing fewer opportunities for success than work in small, entrepreneurial companies or by acting as a consultant or other service provider to large companies. Another advantage he found of working for a small company for the MBAs was greater work satisfaction than for those working in large or medium-sized firms.

The entrepreneurs in the group started their businesses in the service sector because, Kotter says, the entry barriers are lower and there are more opportunities. Only 9 per cent started manufacturing businesses. The entrepreneurs were like the rest of the class of 1974 except that they had a greater desire for independence, were more hardworking, needed more autonomy and had less need for security.

The book is mainly about what it takes to succeed. High standards are important, though dealers, even unscrupulous ones, can do well financially; a strong desire to win is required, as is lifelong learning; and it is essential to move quickly if the environment is not stretching you. Overall, Kotter paints an encouraging picture of MBAs' satisfaction with their work and with their families.

4 Improving executive performance

Improving executive performance is an aspect of all Kotter's books since the findings of his research are always related to their implications for more effective management and leadership. His 1985 work *Power and Influence: Beyond Formal Authority* was based on his course on the successful influencing of people, which arose out of the lessons he drew from earlier research. In it he examined the changing nature of managerial and professional work, the relational context of work – examining relations with subordinates, bosses and those outside the chain of command – and different stages in careers, and discussed the implications of each section for personal effectiveness and leadership. His later research on careers resulted in a course on the selection and management of a career

Kotter has become increasingly concerned about the need for good leaders and the importance of helping people to be effective leaders. He has contributed to this by his books – which are always written so that they are an easy read for executives – by his Harvard Business School teaching, his lectures to company groups and, unusually, by his video interviews of leaders, which he uses as an important teaching tool. His writing, video presentations and lectures are acclaimed for their usefulness, and he is legendary for the time and care that he gives to visual presentations. His articles in *the Harvard Business Review* over twenty years have sold more reprints than any other author during that time.

5 Conclusions

John Kotter has followed an unusually consistent development of ideas. Each research project and book developed naturally from the previous one. What is not foreshadowed in *Mayors in Action* and in *The General Managers* is his interest in leadership and in corporate culture: neither appear in the appendix of either book.

His career, once he had switched to studying organizational behaviour from electrical engineering, is however the antithesis of the careers that he advocates for success in business. It has been steady and consistent: promotion within the same organization, the Harvard Graduate School of Business; pursuing a series of related research projects and using their findings to offer advice to executives and to contribute to teaching. He has retained his interest in research and most of his books are the conclusions from one, often a number, of research projects – it is not clear how big a role doctoral students may have had in some of these. However, he has chosen to present these conclusions in books and articles addressed to executives and not in academic articles, and has used the findings of his research to offer lessons for improving executive effectiveness rather than to contribute to the development of academic knowledge. This explains why his work, after his early studies of managerial behaviour, is not as frequently referenced in academic writing as the extent of his research would have suggested and should have merited if he had been interested in developing its academic implications. His plaudits, after his early work in managerial behaviour, have come from awards for his executive writing and teaching rather than for his academic contributions.

ROSEMARY STEWART
TEMPLETON COLLEGE
UNIVERSITY OF OXFORD

Further reading

(References cited in the text marked *)

* Acton Society Trust (1956) *Management Succession: The Recruitment, Selection, Training and Promotion of Managers*, London, The Acton Society Trust. (A study of what the fifty largest manufacturing companies in Britain were doing in the early 1950s to provide for management development and succession.)
* Kotter, J.P. (1982) *The General Managers*, New York: Free Press. (His major contribution to studies of managerial behaviour.)
* Kotter, J.P. (1985) *Power and Influence: Beyond Formal Authority*, New York: Free Press. (Based on his Harvard Business School course aimed at helping executives to influence people more effectively and deriving from his research into managerial behaviour.)
* Kotter, J.P. (1988) *The Leadership Factor*, New York: Free Press. (About the importance of leadership today and what should be done to provide for future leaders.)
* Kotter, J.P. (1990) *A Force for Change: How Leadership Differs from Management*, New York: Free Press. (Based on a research study, it discusses the nature of leadership and how it differs from management, and argues that both are essential but that leadership is becoming more important.)
* Kotter, J.P. (1995) *The New Rules: How to Succeed in Today's Post-Corporate World*, New York: Free Press. (Report of a twenty-year study of the careers of Harvard Business School MBAs of 1974 with advice about how to be successful today.)
* Kotter, J.P. (1996) *Leading Change,* Boston, MA: Harvard Business School Press. (The development of a successful Harvard Business School article, which describes how to lead change successfully.)

* Kotter, J.P. (1997) *Matsushita Leadership*, New York, Free Press. (A biography of an outstandingly successful Japanese businessman and the leadership lessons that it offers.)
* Kotter, J.P. and Heskett, J. (1992) *Corporate Culture and Performance*, New York: Free Press. (A study of the relation between a strong corporate culture and company performance, concluding that the culture must be adaptive.)
* Kotter, J.P. and Lawrence, P.R. (1974) *Mayors in Action: Five Approaches to Urban Governance*, New York: John Wiley. (First introduces concepts of agendas and network building and lays the foundation for much of Kotter's subsequent work.)

See also: BARNARD, C.I.; DRUCKER, P.F.; FAYOL, H.; MATSUSHITA, K.

Related topics in the IEBM: CORPORATE GOVERNANCE; CORPORATE STRATEGIC CHANGE; CULTURE; GENERAL MANAGEMENT; GLOBALIZATION; HUMAN RESOURCE MANAGEMENT; LEADERSHIP; MANAGERIAL BEHAVIOUR; MANAGEMENT IN JAPAN; ORGANIZATION BEHAVIOUR; ORGANIZATION CULTURE; POWER

Lawler, Edward E. III (1938–)

Personal background

- born 16 June 1938
- graduated from Brown University, 1960
- received a PhD from the University of California at Berkeley, 1964
- professor of administrative science and psychology at Yale, 1964–72
- professor of psychology at the University of Michigan, and programme director at their Institute for Social Research, 1972–80
- professor of research at the University of Southern California, and director of the Center for Effective Organizations in the School of Business Administration, 1978–

Major works

Pay and Organizational Effectiveness (1971)
Pay and Organizational Development (1981)
High Involvement Management (1986)

Summary

Edward E. Lawler III is widely recognized in the academic community for his seminal thinking and research on the psychology of pay, expectancy theory, equity theory, and the effects of job characteristics on employee motivation. Among executives and professionals in the business community he is recognized as the leading expert on pay and, more recently, for his writing on increasing organizational effectiveness through different forms of employee participation. At the core of his thinking and research has been a focus on pay. Beginning in the 1960s he was one of the first to study systematically the effects of pay on the motivation of employees. Beginning around 1980 and continuing to the present, his focus on pay has expanded to include many different forms of compensation. His focus has also expanded into how alternative forms of employee participation, in conjunction with pay, can be used to create high involvement organizations that have a distinct competitive advantage.

1 Biographical data

Edward Emmett Lawler III, known to many as 'Ed', grew up in Virginia and graduated from the St Stephens School in Alexandria, Virginia in 1956. He graduated from Brown University in 1960, where he was on both the football and track teams. In football he was named to the Scholastic All-Ivy Team. He then moved to California where he studied under Lyman Porter (his mentor), Edwin Ghiselli and Mason Haire at Berkeley. It was at Berkeley that his interest in industrial and organizational psychology first developed.

After receiving a PhD in psychology from Berkeley in 1964, he was recruited by Chris Argyris to join a growing group of young organizational behavior scholars at Yale University's department of Industrial Administration, later re-named as Administrative Sciences in 1967. In 1971, many of his valued Yale colleagues left the university (Chris Argyris, Benjamin Schneider, Douglas T. (Tim) Hall, Andrew Pettigrew and Roy Lewicki) and, in 1972, Ed Lawler moved to the University of Michigan where he joined their organizational psychology programme and, until 1980, served as a programme director in the Institute for Social Research. During this period, he was also affiliated with the Battelle Memorial Institute as a visiting scientist in their human affairs research centre in Seattle, WA. In 1978, he took a position as professor of research in the School of Business

Administration at the University of Southern California and founded the Center for Effective Organizations (CEO). He has been at CEO ever since.

2 Pay and Organizational Effectiveness

Pay and Organizational Effectiveness was Lawler's third book, but the first written by himself. It was the integration of two streams of research he had pursued since graduate school: the expectancy theory of motivation and the effects of pay on employee motivation, and was encyclopedic in its coverage of these two topics. Lawler's focus at this stage of his career was on the individual psychology of people in work organizations.

The book was concerned with three main topics: the importance of pay versus other rewards; the effectiveness of pay in motivating performance and job attendance; and what determines one's satisfaction with pay. Each of these topics is discussed in depth, based on the accumulated academic research available at that time. It should be noted that Lawler was a major contributor to the research on expectancy theory, equity theory, and pay as a motivator. Over twenty of his scholarly works are cited in the references section.

The theoretical framework used by Lawler to examine pay is expectancy theory. Although Victor Vroom (1964) is credited with the development of expectancy theory, Lyman Porter and Edward Lawler (1968) expanded and refined Vroom's work. This theory has three basic components: valence (V), instrumentality (I), and expectancy (E). Valence refers to the degree of desirability of a reward for a particular individual. Different people attach different levels of valence depending on their own unique situation. Instrumentality refers to an individual's perception of the link between successful job performance and the receipt of various rewards (or its converse, i.e. the connection between poor performance and receiving certain punishments). By multiplying the valence of each reward by the probability of its being a consequence of good performance, one

estimates the amount of desire a person has to be good at their own job. However, the desire to be very good is an insufficient explanation of motivation, because a person's expectation of actually being successful must also be considered. Stated in a formula:

$$\text{effort devoted to performing well} = [E \times (V \times I)]$$

the effect of pay on motivation was analyzed primarily in terms of valence and instrumentality. In the case of valence, Lawler reviewed the research into the importance of pay as compared with other rewards, e.g., job security, recognition and so on. He also considered what makes the valence of pay increase or decrease for an individual. In the case of instrumentality, Lawler examined what affects the strength of association between job performance and pay. One important comparison in this regard is between piece-rate versus hourly pay. In the former there is a much clearer and stronger connection than in the latter. Lawler clearly shows that *both* the importance of pay and the closeness of its link to performance are necessary in order for pay to be an important motivating factor. Although this might sound self-evident, surveys of organizational leaders indicated that pay was assumed by most of them to be a potent motivator in most situations. Lawler, however, contradicted this by specifying the conditions that will maximize the motivating potential of pay, as well as those that will minimize it.

Lawler's work on the effects of 'pay secrecy' was quite distinctive and contradicted the typical practice in most organizations. He showed that pay secrecy led to lower motivation than would be the case if pay policy and the actual pay of personnel were more openly shared with all employees.

The final chapter, titled 'The role of pay in organizations', had a different focus. It was concerned with the role of pay as just one factor in the complex set of systems that compose work organizations. It is in this chapter that one can see the direction for his future work – his future writing would be much less concerned with individual psychology, focusing instead on the use of pay as one way to effect organizational change. This may be clearly seen in the next book to be discussed.

3 Pay and Organizational Development

Pay and Organizational Development was published by Addison-Wesley in their well-known and highly regarded Organizational Development (OD) Series. This series is read by many who are academics as well as those in business. As a result, this book led to greater visibility among consultants to organizations and internal staff members responsible for OD activities.

The treatment of pay is quite broad in this book. Lawler covers topics such as the all-salaried workforce, skill-based compensation, cafeteria benefits and gainsharing (also known as Scanlon Plans). Besides expanding the scope of compensation, he devotes considerable space to 'process issues' of how pay is determined. The process of making pay-related decisions is discussed in relation to fundamental strategic issues, to performance-based pay, and a chapter on performance appraisal relates process to the pay for a particular individual. (It is this emphasis on process that will become dominant in his later work where the role of employee participation eclipses that of compensation.)

Pay and Organizational Development is written from the perspective of the organization itself, or those responsible for making key strategic decisions with respect to compensation. This is in stark contrast to *Pay and Organizational Effectiveness*, which was primarily focused on the individual employee, as indicated in its subtitle, *A Psychological View.*

An important theme in Lawler's writing for this and subsequent books emerges here: the concern with the 'fit' of pay systems with other systems in an organization. For example, the optimal pay system for a company that is a traditional, steep hierarchy operating in a relatively stable market is going to be quite different from its opposite. Organizations that are flatter, more participative, and that operate in more fluid markets need pay systems that

will support their type of organization. In this latter situation, highly participative management styles should be matched with compensation systems with which they are compatible. This would mean getting rid of time-clocks and making all rank-and-file employees paid on a salary basis. It would mean basing a significant portion of an employee's compensation on something other than the job that is performed.

Alternative ways to determine an employee's compensation in the highly participative organization include the following. First, some portion of pay can be based on the skills that the employee has acquired. This encourages learning, but must also be supported by a training system. Second, some portion of an employee's compensation can be based on the success of the organization as a whole. 'Gain-sharing' is the preferred method for an organization-based reward, in contrast to either profit-sharing or to employee stock ownership programmes. Gain-sharing is a system for paying bonuses to employees based on cutting costs. Because cost control is something that employees at all levels can influence, it is the preferred method. Only the most senior level managers have a direct impact on profits, and the price of a company's stock is influenced by many factors outside the control of even the chief executive officer of the organization.

Finally, Lawler argues persuasively that compensation systems should be the *lead* system in organizational development efforts. Because pay is so important to employees, switching to a more participative compensation plan will be more convincing than trying to become participative through employee training and workshops. This step is a strong message to corporate management, because of the fears associated with changing compensation systems. Lawler bolsters his argument by noting that no matter what system is used as the lead system, compensation must be changed anyway in order to fit with a different management style. By starting with compensation, however, change efforts are more credible to the lower-level employee.

4 *High Involvement Management*

High Involvement Management completes three transitions from *Pay and Organizational Effectiveness*: (a) from an emphasis on the individual to that of the total organization; (b) from an emphasis on compensation to employee participation in which compensation is just one factor; and (c) from addressing a primarily academic readership to one that is primarily corporate.

Lawler argues persuasively that most of today's organizations operate in such dynamic environments that they can only succeed with a highly flexible and involved workforce. A number of participative mechanisms are discussed here: quality circles, regular employee surveys, job enrichment, work teams, involvement of unions and gain-sharing. As can be seen from this list, compensation systems such as gain-sharing recede into the background in comparison with these other forms of participation.

The prototypes for high involvement organizations are to be found for example in the newest manufacturing plants being built in the USA. New plant start-ups provide top management and organizational planners the opportunity to begin with an entire new set of systems, rather than having to replace existing systems, and resistance to change is therefore minimized. Lawler names specific examples, such as General Motors' Saturn Corporation, and contrasts them with older plants within the same organization.

The new plant prototype as a model of high involvement management has employee participation at its core. In such a plant, top management assumes that employees are competent and motivated, rather than incompetent and lazy. Respect for individuals is of critical importance. The organizational structure is flat, forcing decisions to be made at lower levels where they are to be implemented. Employees work on enriched jobs with more variety and much more autonomy. Work is done in groups rather than solely by an individual, and workers may rotate jobs within their group. Computer controlled information systems are used to give information to lower level employees rather than to control them. The physical layout of work areas de-emphasizes status differences among employees and facilitates socializing. Compensation is partly based on the skills one has, partly based on gain-sharing (or at least profit-sharing), and there are cafeteria fringe benefits. Employees are involved in the performance appraisal process and in pay determination. Personnel policies recognize differences among individuals and are supportive of tensions between work and off-the-job issues. New employees are recruited with a 'realistic job preview' so that they do not experience unpleasant surprises when work begins. Personnel selection emphasizes assessment of both personality and interpersonal skills, as much as the more traditional physical and mental skills. If the company is unionized, the adversarial relationship is muted in favor of partnership.

5 Conclusions

Edward E. Lawler III is clearly one of the most influential management scholars of the second half of the twentieth century. Beginning as a traditionally trained industrial and organizational psychologist, his early career was intensely focused on the individual psychology of people at work. His emphasis on pay distinguished him from other scholars of his time and led directly to his receiving the Distinguished Scientific Award from the American Compensation Association in 1972. In 1990 he won the Career Research Excellence Award from the Society for Industrial and Organizational Psychology for his contributions throughout the field of motivation.

Among fellow academicians, Ed Lawler will be remembered for his seminal contributions to motivation theory in general. More specifically his contributions include the effect of pay on motivation, expectancy theory, equity theory and job design theory. Among corporate leaders, he will be remembered as a forceful spokesman for much greater employee involvement at work.

JOHN P. WANOUS
OHIO STATE UNIVERSITY

Further reading

(References cited in the text marked *)

Hackman, J.R. and Lawler, E.E. III (1971) 'Employee reactions to job characteristics', *Journal of Applied Psychology* 55: 259–286. (This is the seminal work for the job characteristics model of how jobs influence employee attitudes and behaviour.)

Lawler, E.E., III (1968) 'Equity theory as a predictor of productivity and work quality', *Psychological Bulletin* 70: 596–610. (Review of this body of work that was very popular in the 1960s.)

* Lawler, E.E. III (1971) *Pay and Organizational Effectiveness: A Psychological View*, New York: McGraw-Hill. (Detailed account of how pay affects individual motivation.)

* Lawler, E.E. III (1981) *Pay and Organizational Development,* Reading, MA: Addison-Wesley. (The role of pay in changing organizations is touted as the way to begin change in order to have maximum impact.)

* Lawler, E.E. III (1986) *High-Involvement Management,* San Francisco: Jossey-Bass. (Advocacy of a broad array of participative practices in order to get high employee involvement and commitment.)

* Porter, L.W. and Lawler, E.E. III (1968) *Managerial Attitudes and Performance*, Homewood, IL: Irwin-Dorsey. (Takes the expectancy theory of motivation and adds several refinements. Data from a large survey of managers are used to test the theory.)

* Vroom, V.H. (1964) *Work and Motivation*, New York: Wiley. (This is the original statement of applying expectancy theory to the behaviour of people at work. This was the dominant paradigm for studying motivation for at least 15 years.)

See also: ARGYRIS, C.; HERZBERG, F.; MASLOW, A.H.

Related topics in the IEBM: COLLECTIVE BARGAINING; EMPLOYEE, RELATIONS, MANAGEMENT OF; JOB DESIGN; MOTIVATION AND SATISFACTION; OCCUPATIONAL PSYCHOLOGY; ORGANIZATION BEHAVIOUR; ORGANIZATION BEHAVIOUR, HISTORY OF; ORGANIZATION STRUCTURE; ORGANIZATIONAL PERFORMANCE; PAYMENT SYSTEMS; PROFIT-SHARING; TRADE UNIONS; TRAINING; TRAINING, ECONOMICS OF; WORK SYSTEMS

Lawrence, Paul Roger (1922–) and Lorsch, Jay William (1932–)

1 Main contribution
2 Evaluation
3 Conclusions

Personal background

Paul Roger Lawrence

* Paul Lawrence born Rochelle, Illinois, 26 April 1922
* educated at Albion College and then at Harvard University (MBA 1947, DCS 1950)
* appointed Donham Professor of Organization Behaviour at Harvard, 1961

Jay William Lorsch

* Jay Lorsch born St. Joseph, Missouri, 8 October 1932
* educated at Antioch College and Columbia University, then took DBA in organization behaviour at Harvard University in 1964
* taught at Harvard Business School since 1965; currently Louis E. Kirstein Professor of Human Relations

Major works

Organization and Environment: Managing Differentiation and Integration, Lawrence and Lorsch (1967)

Organizations and Their Members: A Contingency Approach, Lorsch (with J.J. Morse) (1969)

Matrix, Lawrence (with S.M. Davis) (1983)

Summary

Paul Lawrence and Jay Lorsch can be regarded as the first researchers (perhaps along with Fiedler) to explicitly use the term 'contingency theory' in their writings. At the time of the publication of *Organization and Environment* in 1967, several other researchers on both sides of the Atlantic were following similar lines of enquiry that were beginning to converge on the notion that there was no one universalist 'best way' to manage an organization, but rather a 'best way' for managing in a particular context. The idea of contingency became a label for the fit between internal organization, individual predisposition and the external context. The work of Lawrence and Lorsch focused particularly on the impact that the environment, characterized by uncertainty and rapid rates of change, had on internal organization characteristics. Their subsequent and separate works have built on from these early ideas and findings.

1 Main contribution

The fundamental question which drove the research of Lawrence and Lorsch can be stated basically as follows: 'what kind of organization is necessary to cope with various economic and market conditions?' This question in itself recognized something that managers had long experienced, that different environments have particular technical and economic characteristics each of which demands a different competitive strategy if the organization is to survive and prosper. At the time they began their work, however, such ideas had not been explored. This research was important not only for the then emerging body of organization theory, but also for practising managers who were having to make decisions about very real organizational issues. Lawrence and Lorsch felt that these decisions were being informed by research that sought the 'one best way' or by imitating competitors. Furthermore, this situation was being exacerbated by the constant change and diversity of the environmental circumstances that managers faced.

In dealing with this complex topic, Lawrence and Lorsch tried very hard to be parsimonious in their use of concepts, believing that it is too difficult for managers mentally to manipulate a large number of relationships amongst variables. To develop their ideas, they used a concept of the organization as an open system in which the behaviours of the members are interrelated and interdependent with the task, the personalities of other members and the written and unwritten rules which guide behaviour. Thus the behaviour of managers is determined not only by their own personalities but also by the ways in which they interact with their colleagues. Lawrence and Lorsch's main interest, however, was not with the individual manager but with understanding the behaviour of a large number of such managers. This required them to consider two ways in which organizations function as systems.

First, as systems grow they become differentiated into parts and the whole task becomes broken down into sub-tasks. However, these differentiated parts have to be integrated if the system is to be viable. Second, systems adapt to the outside world. These concepts of differentiation, integration and adaptation had been present in earlier works as well, but Lawrence and Lorsch suggested that earlier writers had not recognized the systemic properties of differentiation, in that managers would develop different goals, working styles and mental processes, and would exhibit differences in both attitude and behaviour. This in itself was not new; but Lawrence and Lorsch went further and identified three dimensions along which these differences develop. These dimensions are orientation towards particular goals (different objectives), time orientation (the immediacy of problems) and interpersonal orientation. They also suggest that earlier theorists did not take into account how functional units in particular might have developed different formal reporting and control mechanisms and reward systems; this became the fourth dimension of differentiation, defined as 'the difference in cognitive and

emotional orientation among managers in different functional departments' (Lawrence and Lorsch 1967: 11).

The orientations, if they differ markedly, may also be a source of difficulty in the integration process, which essentially becomes one of how such potential diversity of interest is dealt with in order to gain benefit from effective transactions with the environment. Integration is thus 'the quality of the state of collaboration that exists among departments that are required to achieve unity of effort by the demands of the environment' (Lawrence and Lorsch 1967: 11). This basic theory can be elaborated into the proposition that, in order to be effective, organizations need not only appropriate differentiation but also adequate integration.

In order to explore this theory further, Lawrence and Lorsch carried out an empirical study of organizations. The study, carried out in two phases, was driven initially by observations on cases that had been gathered for teaching purposes, but the first part of the main study was based on six organizations operating in the plastics industry. This provided a context that was changing quite quickly in terms of both products and processes, driven by a continually emerging body of knowledge. The second phase involved the study of two firms, one highly effective and the other less so, in each of two sectors, food and containers. Effectiveness was measured by 'conventional economic and commercial standards' (Lawrence and Lorsch 1967: 19).

The studies found that all ten firms segmented their environments, and that the greater the degree of uncertainty within each environment and the greater the diversity between the segments, the greater the need for the firms to differentiate their internal organization. A comparison of the organizations in the plastics and container industries reflected this, in that the effective plastics firm which was found to have high diversity in its environment exhibited a highly differentiated structure. In the container industry the opposite was found.

However, as was suggested earlier, differentiation brings in its wake potential integration problems. Lawrence and Lorsch found that effective organizations in the plastics and food industries used different combinations of devices or mechanisms to achieve integration. All used paper systems, formal hierarchy and direct contacts between members of different departments, at least to some extent. In the container firm, the least differentiated, these three proved sufficient. In the effective food firm there was evidence of temporary teams being set up and some functional managers were also assigned an integrative role; the plastics company also had established a special integrating department and a set of well-established integrating teams.

The effective performers in the plastics and food industries exhibited both high differentiation and high integration. Behaviourally, conflicts were dealt with by managers who were prepared to face the issues and work through them rather than letting one party impose a solution on the other. Conflicts were not smoothed over but confronted. Lawrence and Lorsch also found that individuals were more effective in this role if they had knowledge of the issues and not just formal authority to deal with them; the power to effect decisions should thus be located where the knowledge to arrive at a solution also exists.

Given these latter comments, it is easy to see how later work (Davis and Lawrence 1983) developed on matrix forms of organization in which power balances and decision making are crucially located within integrating roles such as project managers. They also provide the spur for Lorsch's further work (Lorsch and Morse 1969) that looked at the fit between individual predispositions, organizational characteristics and performance. This, the authors suggested, made it possible for individuals to feel competent, consequently enabling them to be motivated. However, it is the clear unambiguous message that organizations are most effective when they are designed or aligned to their chosen environments which emerges most strongly from their work. The two concepts – differentiation and integration – remain the underpinning of many ideas on organization design.

Since their initial collaboration, Lawrence and Lorsch have diverged in terms of their research interests. Lorsch's more recent work has focused on decision making and corporate governance, while Lawrence has investigated issues of industry regeneration.

2 Evaluation

The results of the 1967 study create feelings of both assurance and to some extent unease. They are stunningly and elegantly simple to comprehend by both academic and practitioner audiences, but while they have been incorporated in much subsequent work and writings on organizations by academics and thus taught to managers, how easy they would be for practitioners to actually implement is open to question. Indeed, in a commentary on their own work, Lawrence and Lorsch themselves pick up on this theme and note that 'it would have been wise to have provided more guidance for managers interested in our ideas' (Lawrence and Lorsch 1991: 493). This seems to be a very real problem for many plausible and thorough research findings; in achieving the aim of using very few concepts, the application may have been made too difficult. Few managers will have had the opportunity to read Lawrence and Lorsch (1967), or even their practitioner-oriented work (Lawrence and Lorsch 1969), in any depth or to understand the thoughts underpinning the operationalization of the concepts, thus being able to make truly informed decisions on implementation issues.

In common with most pieces of social research, especially those exposed to wide reading, debate and critical acclaim, there has been close and serious scrutiny of the methods and instruments employed by Lawrence and Lorsch to generate their data and findings. Most of the criticism has focused on the reliability of the questionnaire used as one of the three ways to generate data on environmental uncertainty. However, Lawrence and Lorsch did find that their judgement of uncertainty in the three industries was reflected in their empirical results, and to be fair they did draw attention in the book to the 'crudity' of the instrument and 'slipperiness' of the variable itself. These are not easy concepts to operationalize, and others with the benefit of hindsight have perhaps done better.

Finally, there are those that take more fundamental issue with the notion of contingency theory itself. The theory may be thought to be overly deterministic when there is in reality a large area of discretion in organization design, as the elements of such theory (Lawrence and Lorsch's work being one element) are not at all unified or even particularly well integrated. More fundamental is the question as to whether the only purpose of organization design is to achieve efficiency. A counter view would be that design is based on how well it reflects the political realities within an organization; existing structures may actually preclude change, as it will disturb the existing structure. The existing structure arguably provides the framework upon which the power structure is based, so that in effect a political rationality rather than a task rationality may in fact drive structural design. While Lawrence and Lorsch do discuss power and influence, the discussion is based around the task rather than the political system.

3 Conclusions

Lawrence and Lorsch's initial work on the differentiation of organization and environments and the integration of the differentiated functions within an organization produced some seemingly simple and robust conclusions to guide both management academics and practitioners. Their findings, which have stood the test of time, cast very serious doubt on whether there is a 'one best way' of organizing, a thesis that was already under serious investigation by researchers on both sides of the Atlantic. The resultant body of research became known as contingency theory, a theory or set of ideas which has guided (some would say pervaded) much of the organizational research that followed.

GEOFF MALLORY
OPEN UNIVERSITY BUSINESS SCHOOL

Further reading

(References cited in the text marked *)

* Davis, S.M. and Lawrence, P.R. (1983) *Matrix*, New York: Basic Books. (Important work on matrix forms of organizations.)
* Lawrence, P.R. and Lorsch, J.W. (1967) *Organization and Environment: Managing Differentiation and Integration*, Boston, MA: Harvard University Press. (The classic work by these authors, described in detail in the text of this entry.)
* Lawrence, P.R. and Lorsch, J.W. (1969) *Developing Organizations: Diagnosis and Action*, Wokingham: Addison-Wesley. (A practitioner oriented book on contingency theory in the Addison-Wesley series on organization development.)
* Lawrence, P.R. and Lorsch, J.W. (1991) 'Review of organization and environment: managing differentiation and integration', *Journal of Management* 17 (2): 491–3. (A review by the authors of the contribution that the original study has made to our understanding of organizations.)
Lorsch, J.W. and Lawrence, P.R. (eds) (1970) *Studies in Organization Design*, Homewood, IL: Irwin Dorsey. (A collection of follow up papers to the 1967 study mainly authored by the editors' doctoral students.)
* Lorsch, J.W. and Morse, J.J. (1969) *Organizations and Their Members: A Contingency Approach*, Wokingham: Addison-Wesley. (Later work by Lorsch which looks at the relationship between individual and organizational characteristics.)

See also: ASTON GROUP; BURNS, T. AND STALKER, G.M.; FIEDLER, F.E.; HANNAN, M. AND FREEMAN, J.

Related topics in the IEBM: CORPORATE GOVERNANCE; CONTEXTS AND ENVIRONMENTS; MANAGERIAL BEHAVIOUR; OCCUPATIONAL PSYCHOLOGY; ORGANIZATION BEHAVIOUR; ORGANIZATION BEHAVIOUR, HISTORY OF; ORGANIZATION STRUCTURE; ORGANIZATION DEVELOPMENT; ORGANIZATIONAL LEARNING; SYSTEMS

Levitt, Theodore (1925–)

Personal background

- born in 1925
- graduated with an AB from Antioch College in 1949 and a PhD in economics from Ohio State University in 1951
- assistant professor of economics at the University of North Dakota, 1951–5
- full-time consultant and on the board of directors to a large number of US and global corporations in a variety of consumer, industrial, and financial services businesses, including Saatchi & Saatchi Company PLC, Consolidated Natural Gas Company and Landmark Graphics Corporation
- lecturer of business at Harvard Business School, 1959–64
- four-time winner of McKinsey Awards for best articles in the *Harvard Business Review*; winner of Academy of Management Award for outstanding business book of the year, 1962, for *Innovation in Marketing*; winner of John Hancock Award for Excellence in Business Journalism in 1969; recipient of the Charles Coolidge Parlin Award as 'Marketing Man of the Year', 1970; recipient of the George Gallup Award for Marketing Excellence, 1976; recipient of the 1978 Paul D. Converse Award of the American Marketing Association for Outstanding Contributions to Marketing Theory and Science; recipient of the 1989 William M. McFeely Award of the International Management Council for major contributions to management; recipient of a Fulbright Senior Research Fellowship, awarded in 1953
- editor of the *Harvard Business Review*, 1985–9
- Edward W. Carter Professor of Business Administration, Emeritus, Harvard University Graduate School of Administration 1964–90

Major works

Innovation in Marketing (1962)
Industrial Purchasing Behavior: A Study in Communication Effects (1965)
The Marketing Mode: Pathways to Corporate Growth (1969)
The Third Sector: New Tactics for a Responsive Society (1973)
Marketing for Business Growth (1976)
The Marketing Imagination (1983)
Thinking About Management (1990)

Summary

Levitt had a major influence on marketing philosophy, on how services and products are conceptualized, and on our notions of differentiation, globalization and industrialization. He presaged much of the work on service quality and benchmarking. His work was seldom neutral – he expressed an opinion, and consequently provoked many debates. Many of his ideas have become central to marketing thinking.

1 Introduction

As a neophitic MBA student, for me the reading of the Levitt's (1960) 'Marketing myopia' was a revelation. Suddenly business was not merely about managing, making profits and controlling things, it was about imagination and potential. Indeed, the theme that characterizes much of Levitt's work is the imaginative questioning and transformation of received wisdom. His vision was expansive, seeing through and beyond accepted boundaries, his legacy to marketing proximal. It is fair to say that Levitt was one of the key intellectual catalysts behind the late twentieth century's efflorescence of marketing. Although time may have not been kind to many of Levitt's early predictions (rocket powered cars, ultrasonics, fuel cells, and the end of oil by 1985), the promethean spirit which infused his writing lives on: Levitt made marketing interesting – he was marketing's marketer. We bought his ideas, not because they were true, definitive or even consistent, but because they inspired us.

For most of his academic life Theodore Levitt was professor of marketing at Harvard Business School. Editor of the *Harvard Business Review* for many years, he won the McKinsey award for the best article in HBR no less than four times. Levitt made an impact on marketing thinking early in his career. 'Marketing myopia' (Levitt, 1960/1975), one of the most requested HBR reprints, was written while he was a junior faculty member at Harvard. His influence continued throughout his career, with a stream of articles and books that on the one hand cogently evangelized his marketing philosophy and on the other challenged the discipline's boundaries. In the following paragraphs we explore various themes that link some of Levitt's most seminal ideas, ideas which have become central to many people's cannon of modern marketing thought.

2 A marketing philosophy

Levitt's marketing philosophy is characterized by a central theme: customers first. The purpose of a business is to serve the customer; products are only means to serving customers, not ends in themselves; and customers are assets to be cultivated in ongoing relationships. Specifically, in 'Marketing and the corporate purpose' Levitt (1977) challenges the oft heard and finance-inspired claim that the purpose of a business is to make a profit. He argues that this view is misguided, and that profit is a *by-product* of serving customers. Indeed, the customer can be the only true purpose of a business. No business function can operate effectively without a clear understanding of how to get customers and what their needs and wants are. Marketing is everyone's business, serving the customers the only corporate purpose.

The theme of customer first underpins the ineluctable Levitt (1960/1975) article, 'Marketing myopia'. Here, he propounds the view that products are only means to ends. The ends are meeting customer needs and wants. Companies, which focus on products rather then the needs they meet, are doomed to anachronism and ultimate failure. Finally, in 'After the sale is over', Levitt (1983) put forward the thesis that when you have a customer you have an asset, and just like any asset, customer relationships need to be managed. The shift from discrete transaction to ongoing relationships changes how an organization views and interacts with its customers. Here Levitt re-introduces time back into the notion of exchange, and helps lay the foundations for an extensive subsequent body of work on relationship marketing. In summary, Levitt's marketing philosophy argues that organizations need to switch their focus from profits to people (customers), from products to people, and from transactions to ongoing relationships with people.

3 Differentiation

The second theme that can be discerned in Levitt's writings concerns differentiation. He explores the differentiation of nominally generic products, and expands this notion by focusing on the intangible aspects of products. For example, in 'Marketing success through the differentiation – of anything' (1980) Levitt confronts the enduring belief that a generic product cannot be differentiated. He argues that differentiation is the essence of competition and that anything can be differentiated. Introducing the total product concept he argues that one can differentiate a product on the dimensions of expectation the expected product), augmentation (the augmented product), and potentiality (the potential product). In 'Marketing intangible products and product intangibles' (1981) Levitt extends and explores the notion of differentiation with specific reference to services. He argues that the intangible (e.g. service) is an integral part of the most tangible of products (like stainless steel), and thus the most generic product can be differentiated through its intangible components. He also argues that the process can usefully be applied in reverse. Thus even the most intangible of services can productively be tangiblized – to provide a reified reminder to the customer.

4 Globalization and industrialization

For Levitt two forces which are changing business around the world are globalization and industrialization. Specifically, he reinterprets these themes from a marketing perspective. For example, in 'The globalization of markets' (1983) Levitt argues that people have essentially the same needs, and that technology is homogenizing people's wants and behaviour. For Levitt, the inhabitants of the global village are becoming more and more alike, with their value systems becoming increasingly homogenized. This phenomenon is creating true global markets, rendering the multinational company concept obsolete, and the local market player evermore exposed to competition from true global corporations.

In two important articles, 'The industrialization of service' (1976) and 'Production-line approach to service' (1972) Levitt confronts assumptions about the nature of service and explores the increasing ability to industrialize services previously though to be the unique products of humans. Levitt argues that by taking the human element out of service, people will actually prefer them. Thus, just as Fordism transformed manufacturing (products), so will it transform services. For Levitt, the underlying sub-component of the forces of globalization and industrialization is technology and its homogenizing ability. On the one hand, technology is making markets global by driving a convergence of peoples' needs and wants and, on the other, it is making it possible to homogenize services.

5 Rethinking products

Although Levitt is wary of becoming fixated with products (marketing myopia), he also wrote perspicaciously about products and their management. For example, in 'Exploiting the product life cycle' (1965) Levitt challenges the notion that certain products are doomed to old age and death. By finding new uses and new users product life is limited more by the marketers imagination than the inherent product. In 'Imitation innovation' (1966) he argues that although creativity is central to the function of marketing, it is not something that can be monopolized. Thus, presaging more recent ideas on benchmarking, Levitt urges companies to be good imitators as well as good innovators. Few products, services or ideas are inimitable; companies that realize this will on the one hand incorporate the best features of competitors offerings and, on the other, not rest on the assumption of an enduring product superiority.

6 Marketing as imagination

Probably the quintessential theme that permeates and concatenates many of Levitt's articles is that of imagination. He argues the case for a shift in emphasis in marketing, a shift from marketing as a science to marketing as an art; a discipline where the Dionysean powers of the imagination are valued as much as Apollean rigour and rationality. Levitt's marketing imagination, his ability to see the world afresh, is amply illustrated in one of his latest HBR articles. In an article on advertising and ethics, Levitt (1993) explores the paradoxical relationship we have with adverts and throws into question the notion that adverts are manipulative and unethical. He argues that in a world of mistrust, advertising is one of the few honest forms of symbolic exchange. Advertising acts on behalf of whoever is paying, hides no agenda but openly seeks your money. Advertising is ethical in the sense that it is explicit and transparent in its objectives – unlike may other late twentieth century phenomena.

7 Critique and conclusion

Levitt's work is not without inconsistencies, ironies or paradoxes. A few examples will suffice. Consider his arguments on differentiation and globalization. On the one hand he argues that any generic product or service can be made different, yet on the other that the people who buy them are becoming increasingly similar (i.e. generic), a process which ultimately would negate the point of differentiation. Similar conceptual circularities can be found in his arguments on services. Thus he proposes that the generic tangible can be differentiated through the intangible (service) and that the intangible service should be industrialized. The irony here is that if we follow Levitt's advice we have an ever-increasing homogenization of services – services will become generic (e.g. bank teller machines) – again negating the initial rational for differentiation through service. His views on products and customer vacillated throughout his writing – he oscillated between extreme customer and product orientations. In 'Marketing myopia' he championed customer orientation and lambasted the product-focus as myopic. Yet in his writings on globalization and the industrialization of services he championed standardization – playing down differences in customers in favour of homogenization and the concomitant economies of scale that could be realized in the creation of standardized products and services. Finally, Levitt's argument that products are merely means to ends, to be discarded when a better means appears, contrasts sharply with his assertion that products need not follow a life cycle, but can endure and thrive long after 'marketing myopia' would suggest. Buggy whips are still made, as are railroads, and petroleum is still the dominant energy source for transport.

Yet to focus on the ironies and paradoxes in Levitt's thinking is in a sense to miss the point. Levitt's contribution was the creation of a space so that a dialogue could be established. His thesis was the seed for other's antithesis and years of debate. His vision was so wide, it was perhaps inevitable he suffered hyperopia, a legacy which is still alive and well within the catholic church of marketing. As a somewhat older academic, the re-reading of the Levitt's 'Marketing myopia' is still a revelation. Not because it is 'true' or erudite (though it is rhetorically beguiling), but because it invites one to think. No higher accolade can be paid to an academic – as a cursory glance at the vast majority of enervating marketing articles and texts will attest.

PIERRE BERTHON
UNIVERSITY OF WALES

Further reading

(References cited in the text are marked *)

* Levitt, T. (1960) 'Marketing myopia', *Harvard Business Review* July–August: 45–56. (Quintessential Levitt – quintessential marketing: read it.)
* Levitt, T. (1965) 'Exploit the product life cycle', *Harvard Business Review* November–December: 43–54. (Questions the notion that products inevitably mature, decline and die: the product life cycle concept meets the end of its life cycle.)
* Levitt, T. (1966) 'Innovation Imitation', *Harvard Business Review*, September–October: 42–55. (Imitation is not only the sincerest form of flattery – it makes good business sense.)
* Levitt, T. (1972) 'Production-line approach to service', *Harvard Business Review* September–October: 41–52. (Henry Ford comes to service.)
* Levitt, T. (1975) 'Marketing myopia', *Harvard Business Review* September–October: 23–34. (A reprint of the 1960 article with a retrospective commentary – re-read it.)
* Levitt, T. (1976) 'The industrialization of service', *Harvard Business Review* September–October: 63–74. (Enduring, obsolete notions of service – one human serving another – mask a revolution: technology does it better.)
* Levitt, T. (1977) 'Marketing and the corporate purpose', in Backman, J. (ed.) *Changing Marketing Strategies in a New Economy*, New York: Bobbs-Merrill. (There are many business remedies, only one panacea: create and keep a customer – all else is derivative.)
* Levitt, T. (1980) 'Marketing success through the differentiation – of anything', *Harvard Business Review* January–February: 83–91. (When is a commodity not an commodity? When Levitt is your marketer.)

* Levitt, T. (1981) 'Marketing intangible products and product intangibles', *Harvard Business Review* May–June: 94–104. (Often customers don't know what they are getting until they don't – so remind them.)
* Levitt, T. (1983) 'After the sale is over', *Harvard Business Review*, September–October: 87–93. (A sale consummates a courtship: then one has to get down to the real job of living – and staying – together.)
* Levitt, T. (1983) 'The globalization of markets', *Harvard Business Review* May–June: 92–102. (Technology standardizes products – and people: the world is not only becoming smaller it's becoming more homogeneous. Global markets necessitate global players.)
* Levitt, T. (1993) 'Advertising: the poetry of becoming', *Harvard Business Review,* September–October: 87–93. ('ad' – diction?)

See also: KOTLER, P.; MCLUHAN, H.M.; OHMAE, K.

Related topics in the IEBM: ADVERTISING CAMPAIGNS; ADVERTISING STRATEGY, INTERNATIONAL; GLOBALIZATION; INFORMATION REVOLUTION; INTERNATIONAL MARKETING; MARKETING; MARKETING, CULTURAL DIFFERENCES IN; MARKETS; MULTINATIONAL CORPORATIONS; NEW PRODUCT DEVELOPMENT; PRICING ISSUES IN MARKETING; RETAILING; STRATEGY, CONCEPT OF

Lewin, Kurt (1890–1947)

Personal background

- born on 9 September 1890 in Moligno, Prussia; educated in a Gymnasium in Berlin, later in universities of Freiburg, Munich and Berlin, where he received his doctorate in 1914
- from 1922 to 1931 taught philosophy and psychology in Berlin, but from 1932 onwards spent nearly all his time in the United States, starting with a visiting professorship to Stanford (1932–3)
- during the 1930s he taught at Cornell, the State University of Iowa, the University of California, and at Harvard
- during the 1940s he was professor and director of the Research Centre for Group Dynamics at MIT and consultant to various government departments; he was also the chief consultant to the Commission on Community Interrelations of the American Jewish Congress; vice president, Institute of Ethnic Affairs; and a member and chair of all major psychological bodies, including the French Psychological Society
- died on 12 February 1947 at Newtonville, Massachusetts

Major works

Patterns of aggressive behavior in experimentally created social climates (with Lippitt and White) (1939)
Studies in group decisions (1954)
The solution of a chronic conflict in industry (1948)

Summary

Kurt Lewin was one of the most versatile and innovative social scientists of the twentieth century. His work is particularly relevant for several areas of management theory and practice – for instance, organizational change, conflict management, motivation and leadership – and he was one of the first to attempt to build a bridge between different social science disciplines, including economics.

1 Practice through theory

Perhaps Lewin's major contribution was in developing a theory and a methodology for relating knowledge to action. Managers working at the 'sharp end' of problem solving have frequently failed to appreciate the contribution of behavioural social scientists, even when they contribute to the analysis and solution of practical issues. Part of the critique relates to managers' scepticism of theory, which, particularly in the Anglo-Saxon world, is frequently associated with something *sui generis* different from practice; something vague, lofty and pretentious. Lewin tackled this controversy head-on by arguing and demonstrating that there is nothing so practical as a good theory. Without a theory, our observation of events is likely to be haphazard, random and therefore unrepresentative. This important truth is still not appreciated by managers and a large number of consultants, and, in particular, by writers of popular 'how to do it' books on management, like the various prescriptions for seeking out 'excellence'. Checklists and diagrams connecting up circles and rectangles with lines or arrows are of little value unless they are derived from clearly stated assumptions (hypotheses) and tested.

There is no one best way of testing hypotheses. Occasionally, however, systematic controlled research with careful statistical measurement is appropriate, at least as a beginning (see the description of leadership research below). In general, Lewin believed that the best way to validate one's assumptions is to test the theory in the process of implementation. This is often called 'action research'. However, the sequence of these two terms has given the impression that action should precede research. This is possible only in a limited number of circumstances – for instance, if the action is based on previously validated knowledge. More usually, some systematic fact-finding, based on appropriate assumptions, has to precede implementation and action. To avoid this confusion, Argyris, whose methodology in stressing the role of action as a validating procedure is similar to Lewin's, has coined the term 'action science' to describe his approach (Argyris and Schn 1991: 86) (see ARGYRIS, C.). Heller has used the term 'research action' and claims that this is an appropriate way to describe Lewin's own work (Heller 1993: 1238).

2 Lewin on change

One way or another, nearly all social science is concerned with change. Theoreticians analyse the phenomenon of change and in particular they try to discover the antecedent circumstances and the conditions under which change in attitudes, values or behaviour is successful. Practitioners are concerned with techniques or routines that help to produce change in people and/or organizations. Here the symbiosis between theory and practice is particularly obvious and its frequent absence especially dysfunctional.

Lewin (1954) put forward a three-phase theory of change that has become very influential. Whatever the current situation from which a change is sought as desirable, the first step is to 'unfreeze' that situation. For instance, a well-established consumption pattern will need unfreezing before new buyer choices can be established (see below). Unfreezing behaviour or habits is extremely difficult, particularly if they have existed for a long time and have been reinforced by approval or success. Unfreezing is facilitated during periods of crisis or catharsis, which may puncture the boundaries that hold together the existing sys-

tem of beliefs, values and behaviour. If the existing boundaries have been dismantled, the next step is called 'moving'. The person or group has to be induced to move away from the previous position of beliefs, values and behaviour towards some apparently better or more desirable alternative. Finally, if the shift has been successful, it has to be 'frozen', that is to say, embedded in an equilibrium of pros and cons – Lewin calls them forces – that are likely to ensure a continuation over time of the newly embraced beliefs, values and behaviour.

The three-phase approach to change requires a considerable investment of resources, as well as research-based knowledge of the conditions that facilitate unfreezing, moving and freezing. Lewin contributed evidence in support of his theory by a series of experiments to change the behaviour of US housewives, Red Cross workers and young mothers during the Second World War. In the tradition of action research, a variety of experiments were conducted to test the different power of lectures versus group-decision methods in changing consumer behaviour. The two methods were carefully matched for content, expert delivery, size of group and length of time (about forty-five minutes). In one of the experiments, small groups of thirteen or seventeen Red Cross volunteers engaged in home nursing were organized with the objective of increasing the consumption of beef hearts, sweetbreads and kidneys as substitutes for meat, which was scarce. Offal was very unpopular, often associated with dog food, and disliked for the odour given off during cooking. So it was not anticipated that change in consumption behaviour could easily be achieved. The lecture, as well as the group discussion, presented the nutritional, vitamin and mineral value of offal, giving detailed explanations, stressing economic and health advantages and explaining ways of cooking to minimize the usual objections to odour, texture and appearance. In the group-decision setting, the presenter soon encouraged discussion and introduced the factual information in response to various points brought up by the women volunteers. At the end of the meeting, participants were asked whether they were prepared to make a decision on using offal and if they were, to show this by raising their hands.

Data on consumption before and after these two change methods show that only 3 per cent of the women who attended the lecture served offal, while 30 per cent did so after the group-decision method. Similar results were achieved with other groups, for instance mothers asked to give their children cod-liver oil or orange juice (Lewin 1954: chapter 21). Group decisions were always much more effective and in several cases the change in behaviour was greater after four weeks than after two weeks. A related piece of research with operators and supervisors in a manufacturing plant found similar differences between lectures and group discussions (Levine and Butler 1954).

These experiments were used to illustrate the three-phase change sequence, with the raising of hands signifying commitment, by illustrating the use of refreezing as a way of consolidating the positive forces for change. The theoretical explanation of this work also points to the motivating power of involvement and active participation compared with the passivity of a group during lectures.

Lewin also experimented with another potentially very powerful learning and motivating method called 'levels of aspiration'. This method can be used with groups or individuals and uses goal-setting in four stages. The first stage asks what a person or group expects to achieve: this is the first level of aspiration. The second stage assesses the actual performance of the individual or group. In stage three, the results of this performance are fed back as information. The final stage is to get another estimate of expected performance (this is the second level of aspiration). This sequence can be followed several times. The level of aspiration procedure allows people to learn and assess their own potential in a given activity and it gives an indication of the strength of motivation. Highly motivated, successful people set their level of aspiration consistently above their achievement, though not by a large margin. In other words, they set themselves high but realistic targets. Unsuccessful, less motivated people tend to set targets equal to or below achievement, or unrealistically high. This

aspect of Lewin's work has been somewhat neglected in recent years, though it can be seen to be close to the important area of target-setting research, which has been shown to have a very powerful effect on motivation and performance (Locke 1978).

3 Lewin on leadership

Leadership straddles disciplines from political theory to psychology and, in the twentieth century, has been extensively researched and debated in management-related subjects. In spite of the enormous volume of literature, our knowledge and conceptualization are very distant from the status of paradigms and this limits the practical application of this area of study.

However, there is one large segment of the leadership literature that has benefited from Lewin's ability to combine a simple experimental design with a practical preoccupation. During the 1930s, the world witnessed the rise of two important political autocracies, in Nazi Germany and Soviet Russia. Lewin, as a German Jew, had experienced this at first hand and was grateful to have found shelter in the USA. Typically, he did not assume that he knew enough about the effects and behavioural consequences of autocratic, democratic and *laissez-faire* leadership to guide social policy. He therefore planned a classic series of controlled semi-experimental situations in a number of boys' clubs, in which the behavioural consequences of the deliberately contrived variations of the three leadership styles could be assessed (Lewin *et al.* 1939).

Adult leaders of boys' clubs were instructed to use three clearly defined styles of leadership on different groups of boys so that each leader would demonstrate autocratic, democratic and *laissez-faire* behaviour on different groups. This design was chosen to eliminate bias due to the personality or popularity of a given leader. The three styles were carefully described and elaborate recordings of behaviour in all sessions allowed the researchers to test whether the instructions were followed. The recordings also enabled the researchers to discover what happened in each session and the experimental design produced groups of boys matched for intelligence, social participation and other characteristics.

The autocratic leadership style produced two distinctly different reactions. One club demonstrated considerable frustration and some aggression towards the autocratic leader, as well as some dependency on him. By contrast, three clubs reacted to autocracy by showing marked dependency on the leader and no capacity for initiating group action, but relatively low levels of frustration and tension. The children's work activity dropped to a minimum when the autocratic leader was absent, but was high in both democratic and *laissez-faire* groups.

The democratic leader stimulated the boys' independence eight times more frequently than the autocratic leader and twice as often as the *laissez-faire* leader. There was a considerable amount of group-mindedness and interpersonal friendliness and there was significantly more work-related conversation. There was more confiding in each other, very little aggression and very little discontent. Hostility occurred only six times in the democratic groups, but 186 times in the autocratic groups.

In the *laissez-faire* situation, group achievement was far lower than under any of the other leadership situations. This applied to quantity as well as quality of work. There was also a significant tendency to concentrate on play. Under this leadership, children felt it necessary to ask a large number of questions, while activity was less organized, less efficient and less satisfying than under democracy.

While a great many more detailed observations are available, the overall results clearly point towards the superiority of democratic leadership.

4 Lewin's scientific approach

Lewin's three decades of scientific work are an example of successful bridge-building between disciplines and, on that score alone, he remains a pioneer who has few imitators. The connection between theory and practice has already been mentioned and will have long-lasting consequences. A fundamental aspect of this is action research and its variant, research action. The leadership studies in

boys' clubs are an example of the latter because, before these studies, no firm empirical evidence of the behavioural consequences of autocratic, democratic and *laissez-faire* styles was established. As a consequence, research had to precede policy recommendations and their application to boys' clubs or manufacturing situations (Levine and Butler 1954). The studies on changing US consumer behaviour are somewhere between research action and action research because the three-phase change theory had already been developed and was supported by evidence. However, the efficacy of the different attempts to introduce new behaviour and commitment had to be systematically researched.

Problem solving where action takes precedence over research comes in Lewin's work on social planning and action. He noted that planning usually starts with a general idea and the aim of reaching some objective. This is followed by taking the first step towards the execution of the plan, for instance to improve inter-group relations and reduce discrimination and prejudice (see GROUPS AND TEAMS). This first step is followed by fact-finding to evaluate the action and to help the planners gain more insight into the situation, thus helping them to plan correctly for the next step. Action research related to social management therefore takes the form of a sequence of planning, action, fact-finding, further planning and action, more research and so on (Lewin 1948: chapter 13).

Another important aspect of Lewin's bridge-building is the way he connected psychology, his own social discipline, with other areas of social science, principally sociology. He criticized psychologists who are so preoccupied with studying an individual's mental processes that they forget to assess the social and environmental conditions which constrain, facilitate or even determine the individual's thinking and action. His advocacy is similar to what we now call an 'open systems approach', in which the environment receives full consideration. This philosophy determined his design of the leadership studies in boys' clubs and, from the results, he concluded that the difference in people's behaviour in autocratic or democratic situations is not the result of different individual personality traits, but is a consequence of the social environment within which people operate.

The relevance of Lewin's work to modern business and management gains in strength when we see the relationship between his approach to change, leadership and motivation. A democratic participative leadership style seems to be more motivating and consequently more effective than alternative methods. In the change experiments, the group-decision procedure involved greater member participation than the lecture method and was more successful. The autonomy for the decision, by raising hands in a gesture of commitment, was left to each individual – though this was undoubtedly reinforced by seeing how the group had reacted. In the boys' clubs, the democratic leaders achieved their effectiveness by motivating individuals and encouraging them to use their competence and initiative within a framework provided by the leader. Without the leader's framework, the autonomy of the *laissez-faire* group failed to provide the motivation for coherent action. At the same time, autocratic, centralized decision-making failed to tap the initiative and skills of individuals and consequently lowered their level of achievement. The resolution of social conflict seems to benefit from skilled democratic leaders.

Lewin's work is relevant for problems facing management in the areas of leadership, motivation and the introduction of change. He has also made a major contribution to social science by demonstrating the practicality of theory and the effectiveness of combining research with action.

FRANK HELLER
THE TAVISTOCK INSTITUTE, LONDON

Further reading

(References cited in the text marked *)

* Argyris, C. and Schon, D.A. (1991) 'Participatory action research and action science compared: a commentary', in William Foote Whyte (ed.), *Participatory Action Research*, London: Sage Publications. (In line with Lewin's philosophy, the article criticizes current action research approaches that neglect fact-finding and research informed by analytical theory.)

* Heller, F.A. (1993) 'Another look at action research', *Human Relations* 46 (10): 1235–42. (Explains the Lewin-initiated tradition of conceptually-based, rigorous research as an antecedent to action and criticizes policy and action based on inadequate data.)

* Levine, J. and Butler, J. (1954) 'Lecture versus group decision in changing behaviour', *Journal of Applied Psychology* 36: 29–33. (A detailed account of a follow-up of Lewin's famous group-decision and consensus method, using 395 workers and 29 supervisors. Also reprinted in D. Cartwright and A. Zander (eds) *Group Dynamics: Research and Theory*, London: Tavistock Publications, 1954.)

* Lewin, K., Lippitt, R. and White, R.K. (1939) 'Patterns of aggressive behavior in experimentally created social climates', *Journal of Social Psychology* 10: 271–301. (This is one of the classic theory-informed, semi-laboratory experimental studies that Lewin pioneered.)

* Lewin, K. (1948) 'The solution of a chronic conflict in industry', in K. Lewin, *Resolving Social Conflicts: Selected Papers in Group Dynamics*, New York: Harper Brothers. (A classic description of Lewin's dynamic approach to handling social conflicts with a method applicable to many different situations.)

* Lewin, K. (1954) 'Studies in group decision', in D. Cartwright and A. Zander (eds), *Group Dynamics: Research and Theory*, London: Tavistock Publications. (This is an account of Lewin's group-consensus method of changing attitudes and behaviour.)

* Locke, E.A. (1978) 'The ubiquity of the technique of goal-setting in theories of and approaches to employee motivation', *Academy of Management Review* 3: 594–601. (This important work on the potential for change derived from goal-setting behaviour is closely related to Lewin's work on levels of aspiration and supports its theory.)

See also: ARGYRIS, C.; MAYO, G.E.

Related topics in the IEBM: CONSUMER BEHAVIOUR; GROUPS AND TEAMS; HUMAN RELATIONS; INDUSTRIAL DEMOCRACY; INNOVATION AND CHANGE; LEADERSHIP; MOTIVATION AND SATISFACTION; OCCUPATIONAL PSYCHOLOGY; ORGANIZATION BEHAVIOUR; ORGANIZATION BEHAVIOUR, HISTORY OF; ORGANIZATIONAL LEARNING

Limperg, Theodore (1879–1961)

Personal background

- born Amsterdam, The Netherlands, 21 December 1879
- practised as an auditor, 1901–22, and was a major influence on the Dutch auditing profession during its formative years
- professor at Municipal University of Amsterdam, where he developed a theory of current cost accounting and a theory of auditing, 1922–50
- died 6 December 1961 in Amsterdam

Major works

'Consequences of depreciation of the guilder for enterprise value and profit determination of the enterprise' (1937)

Bedrijfseconomie (Business Economics) (1964–8)

Summary

Theodore Limperg, Jr (1879–1961) initiated the scientific study of accounting and auditing in The Netherlands. While his theoretical work was wide-ranging, demonstrating a comprehensive and practical approach to business economics, Limperg is best known outside The Netherlands for his advocacy of current cost accounting. In order to establish a basis for his cost accounting theories, he made the development of value theory a particular focus of study – accounting practices derived from this theory are especially pertinent in times of high inflation. In the 1990s, Limperg's contributions continue to have an recognizable influence on accounting practices in The Netherlands.

1 Introduction

Limperg's influence on the development of accounting practice and theory in The Netherlands has been pervasive, despite the fact that little of his scientific work was published during his lifetime. His students established a comparatively extensive practice of current cost accounting in The Netherlands, making that country a key point of reference in the international discussions on accounting for inflation during the 1960s and 1970s. In this way, Limperg's views have had considerable international influence, even though direct access to his work by foreign researchers has been hindered by linguistic difficulties.

Although Limperg had not been educated at a university, he showed himself dedicated to the establishment of business economics as an academic discipline. In his opinion, the scientific nature of business economics implied that its precepts should be based on deductive reasoning from economic principles, rather than on codification of business practice. Yet his ample experience of business life as an auditor meant that his deduced norms, which he presented with great authority, never became detached from reality.

2 Biographical data

Limperg was born in 1879 in Amsterdam, into a middle-class family. His father was an engineer in the service of the public works department of the city of Amsterdam. Limperg did not go to university, but attended a select practice-oriented school for commercial training. He joined an audit firm in 1900 and became a partner in 1901. Until 1922, he was to continue the practice of auditing in a succession of different partnerships.

During this period, he played an active role in the organized Dutch auditing profession. The first organization of auditors in The Netherlands had been founded in 1895, and Limperg used every opportunity to shape the still young profession according to his views. According to Limperg's vision, auditors should not confine themselves to a superficial checking of accounting records. Rather, they should develop a high level of theoretical and practical economic expertise in order to gain insight into the economic situation of the enterprise. This comprehensive understanding of the enterprise should form the basis of the opinion on financial statements and should make the auditor a valued advisor to business. Through his editorship of a professional journal and his involvement with professional education, Limperg was able to leave the imprint of his views on the practices and attitudes of Dutch auditors.

In 1922, when he was well established as one of the leaders of the auditing profession, Limperg was made a professor in the newly established faculty of economics at the Municipal University of Amsterdam. His teaching assignment reflected the wide area of knowledge he considered was necessary for auditors to master. In The Netherlands, the various areas of business administration, such as organization, finance, marketing and accounting, tend to be viewed collectively as one subject area, known as business economics, which derives a certain unity from a strong reliance on economics. Limperg was one of the first professors of *bedrijfseconomie* (literally, business or enterprise economics) in his country.

After being made a professor, Limperg gave up the practice of auditing, but remained closely involved with the organizational and theoretical development of the Dutch auditing profession. In keeping with the wide scope of his chair, he was also active in a number of areas other than accounting and auditing. First among these was his work on efficiency and scientific management. He did much to spread the knowledge of foreign ideas on this subject in The Netherlands. He was president of the Conseil International de l'Organisation Scientifique from 1932 to 1935 and honorary president of that body until 1953. Limperg retired as professor in 1950, after receiving an honorary doctorate from the University of Rotterdam. He married in 1906 and had three children.

3 Main contribution

Outside The Netherlands, Limperg is known chiefly for his advocacy of current cost accounting. Although the remainder of this article deals only with this aspect of his thinking, it should be kept in mind that his theoretical work had a far wider scope. In accounting, his contributions included valuable work in cost accounting, including standard costing and budgeting. Limperg's views, as outlined here, were developed during the 1920s and were substantially complete by the end of that decade.

Limperg did not aim directly at developing an accounting theory. In keeping with the notion of a comprehensive approach to business economics, he attempted to put forward an economic theory of the firm that would be the common starting point for more specific theories, such as income measurement. In order to develop a basis for his theoretical structure, he devoted much attention to developing a value theory. Limperg defined a concept of value that would be applicable in the context of a business, as opposed to the subjective value concepts of contemporary mainstream economics that were based on individual preferences and assessments of utility. He based his value concept on the notion of hypothetical deprival: the value of an asset could be determined by calculating what the loss to the enterprise would be if it were to be deprived of the asset.

In the simple case of a trading firm, assets are bought for resale at higher prices. It is economically rational for the firm to continue the process of buying and selling as long as there is a positive difference between buying and selling prices. If the firm were to lose one item of inventory, it could restore its former position by replacing the lost asset with a new one. It would be rational to do so if the purchase price of the replacement was lower than its current selling price. In this case, then, 'value' is equal to current, or replacement, cost.

If the selling price of the asset fell below its replacement cost, it would no longer be rational to replace the asset when lost. Its value would therefore be equal to the revenue lost, that is, equal to the realizable value of the asset net of selling costs.

Thus, as a general rule, Limperg established that value is equal to either current cost or net realizable value, whichever is the smallest figure.

In the case of productive assets, net realizable value is usually not relevant for valuation, since these assets are not held for resale, but for the production of other goods intended for sale. The relevant quantity is the present value of the income generated by the sale of the products, and it is this present value that should be compared to current cost. However, productive assets will only be employed so long as the income they generate through production exceeds the revenue to be gained simply by selling them. Therefore, when present value falls below net realizable value, the latter will indicate the value of the asset to the firm.

The general rule of valuation established by Limperg can then be stated as: value is the *lowest* of (1) current cost and (2) the *highest* of (a) present value or (b) net realizable value.

It is evident that in an enterprise where continuous production is rational, the present value of an asset is higher than its net realizable value, and current or replacement cost is lower than present value. In ordinary circumstances of continuity, value is therefore equal to current cost.

It is this logical conclusion that led Limperg to advocating the use of current cost accounting. Almost as an axiom, he stated that accounts should be based on the theoretically correct measure of value. The propagation of current cost accounting could be supported by demonstrating that use of current cost was not merely the result of applying a correct value theory, but that it also led to beneficial results in practice.

In times of inflation, the calculation of income as the difference between revenue and historical cost of goods sold may lead to a financing problem if all income is distributed to the owners. In this case, the enterprise may not be able to finance the higher replacement cost of the goods sold, and its continuity may be threatened. When cost of goods sold as reported in the income statement is determined by the current rather than by the historical cost, this problem is evaded. Any remaining income can then be distributed safely without impairing the continuity of the enterprise.

To implement his theory of current cost accounting, Limperg proposed that companies create a 'reserve for price differences', which would be credited with the excess of current cost over historical cost of goods sold. Negative differences could be debited to this account, but only to the extent that the account had previously been credited with positive differences. Otherwise, according to Limperg, prudence would dictate that inventory be marked down and a loss taken when current costs fell below historical costs.

4 Dissemination and influence

Limperg began to teach his value theory, and its implications for accounting, in his classes at the Municipal University of Amsterdam during the 1920s. After a few years, he and his students began to introduce his ideas into the courses and professional examinations of the Dutch Institute of Auditors. Limperg's stature within the auditing profession, of which he had been one of the leaders since the first decade of the century, ensured that his ideas received due attention.

Unlike Germany, with its hyper-inflation following the First World War, The Netherlands experienced fairly stable prices through most of the 1920s and 1930s. During this period, therefore, Limperg advocated current cost accounting not as a practical solution to a pressing problem, but as the theoretically correct method of accounting, irrespective of actual price changes. Within the academic community, his ideas were received and debated on their theoretical merits.

When price changes did occur, at first with the 1936 devaluation of the guilder, and more severely in the late 1940s and early 1950s, Limperg's current cost accounting proposals suddenly acquired considerable practical significance. The educational efforts of Limperg and his students had made a large number of auditors and accounting staff familiar with current cost accounting, and when inflation increased, voices from within the business community began to advocate the use of current cost data for tax purposes, financial reporting and price controls. From the early 1950s onwards, a number of large Dutch companies began to use current cost data in their published financial statements. Since financial reporting was largely unregulated at the time, there were no legal impediments to companies experimenting with current cost accounting in this way. The Dutch tax authorities, however, never accepted the use of current cost accounting for taxation purposes.

Most notable among the companies practising current cost accounting was the electronics group Philips, whose financial statements were based on current cost from 1951 until 1992. Officers from the Philips group propagated current cost accounting at home and abroad, and the company became a standard example in English-language discussions on the practical nature of such methods.

Although the accounting practices of Dutch companies using current cost methods did not always coincide in every detail with Limperg's ideas, the fact that current cost accounting was used in practice at all in The Netherlands can be traced directly to Limperg's considerable influence on accounting education. This influence extended to the field of company law. In 1983, for example, Limperg's tripartite value concept was used to adapt the provisions of the Fourth European Community Directive on Company Law to Dutch law.

Regarding the acceptance of current cost accounting in practice, developments in The Netherlands differed markedly from those in Germany. Accounting theoreticians in the latter country, notably Fritz Schmidt (1882–1950), were ahead of Limperg in proposing current cost accounting during the hyper-inflation of the early 1920s. However, partly owing to the more restrictive nature of German company law, current cost accounting has never gained a lasting foothold in Germany.

Limperg published many polemical articles in professional literature while he was active as an auditor, but he published little of the scientific work he developed since 1922.

While only the outline of his theories on current cost accounting was published in Dutch in 1936 and 1937, the details of his views were transmitted readily enough in his lectures and by his students. In the 1960s, Limperg's collected lecture notes containing his views on all areas of business economics were published posthumously. Yet the absence of a full statement of Limperg's current cost accounting proposals by his own hand has made it difficult for accounting researchers in the English-speaking world to develop a clear perception of Limperg's significance.

In the English-speaking world, the origins of current cost accounting are often traced to US and UK publications of the 1930s, disregarding developments on the mainland of Europe. Limperg's tripartite value concept is therefore often encountered in the English literature as 'value to the owner' or 'deprival value', and as such it is traced to the work of the American, James C. Bonbright of 1937. Although the Dutch and Anglo-American concepts are identical, they have, in fact, been developed independently, showing that developments in accounting theory could occur in relative isolation until the latter part of the twentieth century. It was only during the 1960s and 1970s, when there was growing international interest in accounting for inflation developments, that the English-language literature began to appreciate developments in continental Europe.

By the 1960s and 1970s, the practice of current cost accounting was well established in The Netherlands, and could serve as an example to others. For example, in developing its favourable stance to current cost accounting, the UK Sandilands Committee report of 1975 was based in part on the fact that forms of current cost accounting were practised on a substantial scale in The Netherlands.

5 Conclusion

Whether or not Limperg's proposals on current cost accounting will continue to have direct practical relevance depends on the recurrence and severity of inflation. In a more general sense, his permanent contribution, which he shares with other accounting theoreticians of the twentieth century, consists of a wider perspective on accounting. By suggesting that accounting does not have to restrict itself to continued applications of received practice, Limperg helped invest the discipline, at least potentially, with the flexibility to respond to changing circumstances and needs.

KEES CAMFFERMAN
VRIJE UNIVERSITEIT, AMSTERDAM

Further reading

Brink, H. (1992) 'A history of Philips' accounting policies on the basis of its annual reports', *The European Accounting Review* 1 (2): 255–75. (An annotated chronology of Philips' current cost accounting practices with a good bibliography.)

Burgert, R. (1972) 'Reservations about "replacement value" accounting in The Netherlands', *Abacus* 8 (2): 111–26. (Written by a leading Dutch academic, this is a critical review of Limperg's theory which remains relevant to accounting practice in the 1990s.)

Camfferman, K. and Zeff, S.A. (1994) 'The contributions of Th. Limperg Jr (1879–1961) to Dutch accounting and auditing', in J.R. Edwards (ed.), *Twentieth Century Accounting Thinkers*, London: Routledge. (One of the longer introductory articles extant, with an extensive bibliography.)

Clarke, F.L. and Dean, G.W. (1990) *Contributions of Limperg and Schmidt to the Replacement Cost Debate in the 1920s*, New York: Garland. (Contains full-length English translations of key texts by Limperg and his students plus translated excerpts from Limperg's *Bedrijfseconomie* (1964–68).)

Flint, D. (1985) 'Professor Limperg's audit philosophy: the theory of inspired confidence', in J.W. Schoonderbeek (ed.), *The Social Respon-* *sibility of the Auditor*, Amsterdam: Limperg Institute. (An introduction to Limperg's views on auditing, which have not been covered in this entry.)

Limperg, T. (1937) 'Consequences of depreciation of the guilder for enterprise value and profit determination of the enterprise', in F.L. Clarke and G.W. Dean (eds) (1990), *Contributions of Limperg and Schmidt to the Replacement Cost Debate in the 1920s*, New York: Garland. (A translation of the most important published statement of Limperg's current cost accounting theory made during his lifetime.)

Seventer, A. van (1975) 'Replacement value theory in modern Dutch accounting', *The International Journal of Accounting*, 11 (1): 67–94. (A less complete, but more readily available alternative to van Sloten (1987).)

Sloten, P.J. van (1987) 'The Dutch contribution to replacement value accounting theory and practice', ICRA Occasional Paper 21, Lancaster: International Centre for Research in Accounting, University of Lancaster. (An extensive discussion of Limperg's theory, later modifications by his students and practical application in The Netherlands.)

Whittington, G. (1981) 'The British contribution to income theory', in M. Bromwich and A. Hopwood (eds), *Essays in British Accounting Research*, London: Pitman. (A comprehensive review of theory development from a British point of view, with an attempt to position Limperg.)

See also: HOPWOOD, A.; PACIOLI, L.; SCHUMACHER, E.F.

Related topics in the IEBM: ACCOUTING; ASSET VALUATION, DEPRECIATION AND PROVISIONS; AUDITING; COSTING; COST–VOLUME–PROFIT RELATIONSHIPS; INFLATION ACCOUNTING

Lindblom, Charles Edward (1917–)

Personal background

- born in Turlock, California, on 22 March 1917
- educated at Stanford University and Chicago
- taught at the University of Minnesota and Yale University
- director of the Institute for Policy Studies

Major works

The Science of Muddling Through (1959)
The Policy Making Process, second edition (1980)

Summary

Lindblom's enduring legacy for both public policy makers and managers making strategy was to expand on and develop the notion of incrementalism in decision making processes. This represented a movement from what Hickson *et al.* (1986) later characterized as prescriptive theories of decision making towards more descriptive theory. He described what decision makers actually do when faced with complex problems and argued that while they do intend to be 'rational', the processes themselves do not follow the trajectories of rational decision making as described in the decision making literature. This development has its roots in the limitations of policy makers to comprehend and process not only the data for a comprehensive review of alternatives but also in their limitations in clarifying the range of objectives to be achieved. In these respects his work not only mirrors but adds to the work of others such as Herbert Simon, James March and Richard Cyert (see SIMON, H.; MARCH, J.G. AND CYERT, R.M.) on decision making in organizations, as it highlights the interplay of both politics and rationality in decision making processes. The notion of incrementalism also provided a significant input into later work on strategic management from such authors such as Quinn (1980) and Johnson (1988).

1 Main contribution

In the development of his ideas, Lindblom (1959) drew contrasts between two decision making processes by using the image of a tree. Thus the first type of process he called the 'root', or rational comprehensive methodology, and the second a 'branch', or successive limited comparisons methodology. In the former the decision maker starts from fundamentals, the roots of the problem, each time they are called to make a decision. Past experience is used only to the extent that it is embodied in some sort of theory, for example in determining policy on inflation an administrator would probably compare alternatives by using some theory of prices. In the second process, the decision maker continually builds out (branches) from the current situation step by step, in small stages (increments). It is this type of process that he set out to formalize in the 1959 paper as 'the science of muddling through'.

He found it difficult to find examples of the root method in practice. It is perhaps more an ideal type rather than a reality as it fails to adapt to two crucial characteristics of decision making: decision makers and the problems they face. As with all ideal type constructions it is, however, useful as a framework to reflect upon actual situations and events.

How then do managers and policy makers actually cope with complex problems in the context of the lack of information and their own cognitive limitations? The root method requires that the values and objectives be clarified in advance of any development and examination of alternative courses of action. While this is a laudable goal, according to Lindblom what actually happens is that interested parties or stakeholders disagree on many of the critical values and objectives. This situation may lead decision makers down various pathways. They may follow their own values for example, but each does not result in the uncertainty being eliminated and thus has to accommodate the many values without necessarily being able to rank them. In addition, preferences change so any process needs to be flexible and responsive enough to accommodate this additional source of uncertainty. Lindblom poses the question of how the relative importance of these conflicting values can be stated without reference to trade-offs between alternatives for solving the problem. The decision maker thus looks at how much of each of the set of objectives is satisfied by an alternative. It is thus impossible to consider objectives without considering the alternatives. In his terms 'one simultaneously chooses a policy to attain certain objectives and chooses the objectives themselves' (1959: 82). This, he goes on to suggest, focuses attention on marginal or incremental changes in values or objectives, which reduces the need for information on values and objectives compared with the root methodology and does not strain cognitive limits.

How then is the 'best' alternative chosen? The root method demands thorough analysis and choice based on which alternative is the most appropriate to achieve the desired ends but, as alternatives, objectives and values are so intertwined, discussion becomes focused on agreement on a policy (alternative). This becomes the only real test of correctness. Trying to ensure agreement on ends as well as means is not productive. Is this an inferior method to the root method of test against objective? Lindblom argues no, as the objectives themselves 'have no ultimate validity other than they are agreed upon. Hence, agreement is the test of best policy in both methods' (1959: 84). In his eyes, it is not irrational for a decision maker to argue that a decision is good

without being able to fully specify what it is good for.

The root method should leave out no important factor, but limits to decision makers intellectual capacity set very finite limits to this process. This allied to the complexity of problems means that decision makers must use simplification routines. Lindblom found that simplification is achieved by limiting consideration to those alternatives that differ only in a relatively small degree from those decisions already in effect. This results in the reduction of both the number of alternatives to be considered and the amount of analysis needed. Analysis is accomplished by investigating to what extent the consequences of an alternative differ from the status quo. This is the counterpart to the marginal (or incremental) comparison of values and objectives discussed above. In this way ends, or objectives, become adjusted to the means for achieving them. Thus they are changed as they are considered. This means that decision making is a serial activity. Problems are addressed but rarely solved and themselves become transformed in the process. It may then be argued that decision making involves a movement away from a series of situations or issues rather than towards a well-defined goal. Small improvements to a situation are made rather than major shifts in direction. In this way, complex problems can be coped with, information collection is limited, choice is restricted and time horizons short. Action can then actually be taken. The diverse values that participants might hold are recognized but the iterative nature of the process circumvents parties taking firm stands on principles as decisions may change their nature.

The result is a practical and elegant description of the way that decision making can proceed given the impossibility of attaining the ideals of a pure rational model of process. It is a working methodology which on the face of it looks conservative. Small changes which do not have major consequences are made may be inappropriate for a situation needing radical movement. Yet Lindblom points out that it could be just as effective to make many small rapid movements. Each incremental step may be easy as it is not accompanied by major consequences. At the very least, it is a step that can be taken by decision makers who are not then overwhelmed with the enormity of following a more difficult route.

2 Evaluation

Although Lindblom developed his ideas within a framework of public administration and policy making they have gained currency, as evidenced by their frequent citations, in work on strategy making in other forms of organization. They do provide managers with practical ways of coping with complex issues from whatever sector they operate in. That rationality becomes tempered by problem complexity and the views of interested parties has been refined, empirically explored and developed by others. Some examples are summarized in the following paragraphs.

Hickson *et al.* (1986), in their empirical investigation of strategic decision making in UK organizations from both public and private sectors, found that what they termed 'controls decisions' – those that involved planning and budgeting, funds allocations and data processing – 'were the prototype for incrementalism'. These decisions were not particularly novel, but had serious consequences and were subject to the political pressure of diverse interests. Yet the processes led to less change than most of the other topic types. They tend to mirror the locked-in balance of power between interests rather than reflect any sense of direction of activity. They accommodate interests.

Quinn (1980) also tested and developed the idea of incrementalism into what he terms logical incrementalism. In this view or process, strategy does not emerge from a stream of small muddling through decisions but has a more deliberate intent. In this view the strategist has an idea for a suitable course of action but has neither the information nor the political support to realize it. Planning becomes very important as it allows information to be collected and to hold discussion with the various interests to build some form of consensus. During this process the strategy is shaped and reshaped and subsequently emerges. After many iterations and usually much time,

implementation finally occurs. The key difference to Lindblom's original idea seems to be that throughout this process the broad view, if a good one, remains fairly constant and consistent. There is thus an overall strategic logic to the strategy making process which probably does involve incremental steps.

Johnson (1988) in his study of strategy making processes in a menswear retail group noted that as both forms of incrementalism rely on discussion and on negotiating an accommodation with the involved interests, managers may lose sight of any changes in the external environment. Thus strategic drift, the deviation between managers' decisions and environmental changes, is likely to occur. The internal focus, a source of strength in an incremental approach to decision making, may too easily become a comfort zone for managers. Johnson suggests that managers may be reluctant to break their thinking out of this zone. If drift persists then radical strategic change may be required if an organization is to survive. The managerial group will become forced to confront their views, or their paradigm, of how things work. Incrementalist methodologies may thus provide managers with an inappropriate and narrowly focused 'mental model' of the world .

By explicitly recognizing the evolutionary rather than revolutionary nature of policy making the idea of incrementalism is also a way of helping us to understand behaviour in other organizations and social groupings, such as countries. We do not become solely focused on major discontinuities but on the evolution of institutions and systems which proscribe the behaviour rather than on describing differences in the behaviour and ascribing that difference to 'culture'. Locating international comparisons on such things as educational attainment in a policy making framework makes them meaningful rather than just empty reporting of empirical data and reflections.

3 Conclusions

Lindblom's work on policy making had proved to be a significant and enduring contribution to our understanding of public policy making in particular, and strategy processes in all organizations in general. The practical and descriptive orientation of the methodology or 'the science of muddling through' has not only informed managers but has provided a base from which scholars have developed further understandings of this complex managerial process. The recognition of the interaction between means, ends and values, the limited search and evaluation of alternative course of action and the evolutionary rather than revolutionary nature of process provide insights of rare clarity and relevance.

GEOFF MALLORY
OPEN UNIVERSITY BUSINESS SCHOOL

Further reading

(References cited in the text marked *)

* Hickson, D.J., Butler, R.J., Cray, D., Mallory, G.R. and Wilson, D.C. (1986) *Top Decisions: Strategic Decision Making in Organizations*, San Francisco: Jossey-Bass,. (A major empirical study of strategic decison making behavoiur in UK organizations which develops a taxonomy of process based on the complexity of problems and political interest.)
* Johnson, G. (1988) 'Rethinking incrementalism', *Strategic Management Journal* 9: 313–327. (Examines the implications of using incrementalism as a process of strategy formation. Builds on the problems of strategic drift and the development of strong paradigms of management thought and action.)

* Lindblom, C.E. (1959) 'The science of muddling through', *Public Administration Review*, 19: 79–88. (Outlines the development of the root and branch methodologies discused at length in the body of this entry.)
* Lindblom, C.E.(1980) *The Policy Making Process*, second edition, Englewood Cliffs, New Jersey: Prentice-Hall. (A more detailed exposition of policy making and the interaction of politics with decision making.)
Lindblom, C.E. and Braybrooke, D. (1963) *A Strategy of Decision*, New York: Free Press. (Unites Lindlom's work with Braybrookes on utilitarianism and how these converge on the notion of census functions in the policy making context.)
Morgan, G. (1997) *Images of Organization*, second edition, London: Sage. (Develops the use of metaphor to characterize organizations. Lindblom's work appears in the organizations as brains metaphor.)
Pugh, D.S. and Hickson, D.J. (1993) *Great Writers on Organization*, Aldershot: Dartmouth. (An extensive collection of short summaries of the work of writers. Includes a discussion of Lindblom in the decision making section.)
* Quinn, J.B. (1980) *Strategies for Change: Logical Incrementalism*, Homewood, Ill: Homewood. (Discussion of strategy making in ten organizations using incrementalism as a base reference.)

See also: MARCH, J.G. AND CYERT, R.M.; SIMON, H; WEBER, M..

Related topics in the IEBM: DECISION MAKING; ORGANIZATION BEHAVIOUR; ORGANIZATION BEHAVIOUR, HISTORY OF; PROBLEM SOLVING; POWER; PUBLIC SECTOR MANAGEMENT; SYSTEMS

Luthans, Fred (1939–)

Personal background

- born in Clinton Iowa, 1939
- graduated from the University of Iowa, 1965
- served in the US Army at West Point, 1965–7
- professor at the University of Nebraska, Lincoln, 1967–
- president of the Academy of Management, 1986

Major works

Organizational Behavior (1973)

Organizational Behavior Modification (with R. Kreitner)(1975)

Real Managers (with R.M. Hodgetts and S. Rosenkrantz)(1988)

International Management (with R.M. Hodgetts)(1991)

Summary

Luthans has published a number of major books including the widely used *Organizational Behavior*, now in its eighth edition, and the more specialized *Organizational Behavior Modification* (written with Robert Kreitner), which won the American Society of Personnel Administration award for outstanding contribution to human resources management. His book *Real Managers* resulted from a four-year research study which has been recently replicated with a large sample of managers in Russia and the resulting papers have been published in academic journals. His most recent book is *International Management* which was published by McGraw-Hill, and is now in its third edition. He has well over a hundred refereed journal articles, the latest being a meta-analysis of his research studies over the past 20 years on organizational behaviour modification to be published in the *Academy of Management Journal*. The consulting editor for the McGraw-Hill Management Series for 22 years, Professor Luthans also serves on a number of editorial boards and is currently the editor of *Organizational Dynamics*, the major journal of the American Management Association and is editor-in-chief of the *Journal of World Business* (formerly the *Columbia Journal of World Business*).

1 Introduction

Luthans is the George Holmes Distinguished Professor of Management at the University of Nebraska, Lincoln. He has been a visiting scholar at a number of colleges and universities and has lectured in most European and Pacific Rim countries. He has taught entire international management courses as a visiting faculty member at the Universities of Hawaii, Macau, Chemnitz in the former East Germany, and Tirane in Albania. He was president of the Midwest Academy of Management in 1981–82 and in 1985–86 he served as the 41st president of the Academy of Management and chairman of the board of governors. Currently, he is editor of *Organizational Dynamics* and the author of numerous books, including *Organizational Behavior* and *International Management*. He is one of a very few management scholars who is a fellow of the Academy of Management (in 1997 he received the 10,000 member academy's Distinguished Educator Award), the Decision Sciences Institute and the Pan Pacific Business Association, and he has been a member of the executive committee for the Pan Pacific Conference – which helps to organise the annual meeting held in Pacific Rim countries – since its beginning 15 years ago. He has been involved with some of the premier empirical studies on motivation and behavioural management techniques and the analysis of managerial activities in Russia; these articles have been published in the *Academy of Management Journal*, the *Journal of International Business Studies*, and the *Journal of Organizational Behaviour Management*. Since the very beginning of the transition to a market economy after the fall of communism in Eastern Europe, he has been actively involved in management education programmes sponsored by the US Agency for International Development in Albania (over a dozen trips) and Macedonia, and US Information Agency programmes involving the Central Asian countries of Kazakhstan, Kyrgyzstan, and Tajikstan. Professor Luthans' most recent international research involves the use of meta-analytic techniques to cluster countries for cross-cultural, comparative management. He is also involved in meta-analytic studies of the impact of behavioural management and self-efficacy on task performance.

2 Main contributions

Professor Luthans' work can be divided into the following categories:

- organizational behaviour
- social learning theory
- real managers
- international management.

Organizational behaviour

Early in his career, Luthans published several articles with his mentors and peers as co-authors. This early period started in 1964 and includes a two-year stint in the army teaching at West Point, where he also met Chris Argyris (see ARGYRIS, C.).

Organizational Behavior was published by McGraw-Hill in 1973. Luthans began writing the text in the evenings in 1968 as a more behavioural science based text seemed to be needed, and since there was no benchmark he used the psychology and management education he had earlier received at the University of Iowa. According to Luthans the conceptual framework at that time involved a historical and behavioural science framework with separate sections on anthropology, sociology and psychology along with a scientific methodology foundation. Major areas of the first edition also covered 'the formal organization system' with three chapters on classical, neoclassical and modern organization theory, two chapters on decision making and an additional three chapters on communication, control and technology.

The 'human behaviour' part of the book had chapters on basic behavioural analysis, perception, learning, motivation and personality. The last part of the book dealt with the outcome(s) of the formal organization. There were chapters on groups dynamics, conflict and change, motivation and leadership and behavioural applications for management. The book has been revised over the years and the present eighth edition (1998) retains the basic conceptual framework but in a different order. The historical and foundation part is much shorter, and there are two chapters on emerging organization and diversity and ethics. Essentially the macro to micro orientation from the earlier editions has been revised, with less weight now given to the macro and more weight given to items like attitudes, commitment, social cognitive variables, applications in motivation/job design, leadership and behavioural management. New to the scene from 25 years ago are social learning theory, goal setting, teams, negotiating skills, stress, organization culture and international organizational behaviour.

Social learning theory

Throughout Professor Luthans' life he has also credited his doctorate students in his own learning. When Tim Davis emerged on the scene in the 1970s he was able to move Luthans from his radical behaviourism plateau into a more social learning paradigm. Although he remains a Skinnerian behaviourist he has a great deal of sympathy for the Banduraian social learning approach.

The importance he gave to the social learning approach led Luthans to integrate it into organizational behaviour modification in an article for *Organizational Dynamics* titled

'Radical behaviourists mellowing out'. The Luthans–Kreitner book (*Organizational Behavior Modification*, 1975) was revised and retitled *Organizational Behavior Modification and Beyond* (1985) This expansion of organizational behaviour modification (OB Mod) recognised overt and covert antecedents and consequences, which Luthans called the SOBC (situation–organism–behaviour–consequence) contingency framework, recognising the need for cognitive mediating processes.

Real managers

Professor Luthans has written his autobiography in *Management Laureates* (Volume 4, 1996). This autobiography is especially important in analyzing his reasons for his classic study *Real Managers* (Luthans, Hodgetts and Rosenkrantz 1988). Mintzberg had cracked the door with his work on five chief executives (see MINTZBERG, H.), but there was a lingering question in Luthans mind primarily based on his own experiences with 'real managers'.

Along came another doctorate student, Nancy Morey, with her emphasis on the emic approach (let the subjects and the setting define the research). Observation and rigorous qualitative methodologies were now on the agenda. But the concerns about generality and having a large enough sample to perform some type of statistics remained; time, money and cooperation by the sample were the requirements. The office of Naval Research provided a large grant, procedures, measures and data were developed and an initial study was done with a sample of 44. The second phase involved observation and checklists generated from the initial study to observe 248 real managers. In terms of frequency of occurrence the activities found were: traditional management (32%); routine communication (29%); HRM (20%); networking (19%).

The next phase involved the study of successful and effective managers. An index of level over tenure was used to measure success, and an index combining subordinate satisfaction and commitment and perceived quantity and quality of the unit was used for effectiveness.

The results showed that the relative contribution to successful managers were networking (48%), routine communication (28%), traditional management (13%) and HRM (11%). By contrast, the relative contributions made to effective managers were routine communications (44%), HRM (26%), traditional management (19%) and networking (11%). Newspapers across the US picked up the results of this study which showed such a disparity between successful and effective managers.

Luthans reports that next to his organizational behaviour modification research he considers the 1980s real manager project as the most important work he has done. Following that, the next challenge on the horizon was international management.

International management

In many of the areas of his previous work, Luthans was a pioneer, but in international business and strategy the textbooks were already well established. However, if one redefines the area as moving from international business and strategy to international management then there were only a few in the area. Luthans' colleague Richard Hodgetts had moved to Florida International University and called upon Fred to 'cooperate'. The first main line international management text was signed with McGraw-Hill. *International Management* covers five main areas: the perspective and environment of international management; the strategies and functions of international management; international HRM; the human side of international management; international management horizons. The recent completion of the third edition attests to the book's success.

3 Evaluation and conclusions

Luthans completed his PhD in 1962 just as the mainstream management field was starting to emerge. With his grounding in human relations, organization theory and psychology he used this basis as a framework for his work in organizational behaviour modification (OB Mod) His first book was published in 1973 and was followed in 1975 by the OB Mod book. His next critical breakthrough came in the late 1970s and 1980s with the social learning approach, and he has recently expanded into the international management area. His textbooks are probably the greatest contribution he has made to the study of management.

PAT JOYNT

HENLEY MANAGEMENT COLLEGE

NORWEGIAN SCHOOL OF MANAGEMENT

Further readings

(References cited in the text are marked *)

Luthans, F. (1972) *Contemporary Readings in Organizational Behavior*, third edition 1981, New York: McGraw-Hill Book Company.

* Luthans, F. (1973) *Organizational Behavior*, eighth edition 1998, New York: McGraw-Hill Book Company. (This is one of the classics in management and organization theory, and has sold worldwide. An excellent reference book.)

Luthans, F. (1976) *Introduction to Management: A Contingency Approach*, New York: McGraw-Hill Book Company. (A well-known book in the contingency area.)

Luthans, F. and Hodgetts, R.M. (1973) *Cases and Study Guide for Organizational Behavior*, second edition 1977, New York: McGraw-Hill Book Company.

* Luthans, F. and Hodgetts, R.M. (1975) *International Management*, third edition 1994, New York: McGraw-Hill Book Company. (One of the first texts on international management.)

Luthans, F. and Hodgetts, R.M. (1996) 'North American management', in M. Warner (ed.) *International Encyclopaedia of Business and Management*, London: International Thomson Business Press. (A concise overview of mainly US management.)

Luthans, F. and Hodgetts, R.M. (1996) 'Managing in America', in M. Warner and P. Joynt (eds) *Managing Across Cultures*. London: International Thomson Business Press. (A modified version of the above chapter.)

* Luthans, F. and Kreitner, R. (1985) *Organizational Behavior Modification and Beyond*, Glenview, IL: Scott Foresman.Publishers. (This book formed the basis for the ASPA award for the 'outstanding contribution to human resource management'. It was originally published in 1975 as *Organizational Behavior Modification*.)

* Luthans, F., Hodgetts, R.M. and Rosenkrantz, S. (1988) *Real Managers*, Cambridge, MA: Ballinger Publishing Company. (An excellent reader for both the practitioner and the academic.)

Luthans, F., Patrick, R. and Luthans, B.C. (1995) 'Doing business in Eastern Europe: Political, economic, and cultural diversity', *Business Horizons*, September–October: 9–16. (A practical guide to doing business in this area.)

Luthans, F. Sommer, S. and Bae, S.H. (1995) 'The structure–climate relationship in Korean organizations', *Asia Pacific Journal of Management*, 12 (2): 23–36. (One of the few papers on Korean organizational climate in the field.)

See also: ADLER, N.; ARGYRIS, C.; HOFSTEDE, G.; MINTZBERG, H.; TUNG, R.L.

Related topics in the IEBM: CULTURE; CULTURE, CROSS-NATIONAL; GLOBALIZATION; HUMAN RESOURCE MANAGEMENT; INTERNATIONAL BUSINESS ELITES; MANAGERIAL BEHAVIOUR; MULTINATIONAL CORPORATIONS; ORGANIZATION BEHAVIOUR; ORGANIZATION BEHAVIOUR, HISTORY OF; ORGANIZATION CULTURE; ORGANIZATIONAL LEARNING; ORGANIZING, PROCESS OF

McClelland, David C. (1917–)

Personal background

- born 20 May 1917, USA
- married first, Mary Sharpless, 1938, five children; second, Marian Adams, 1984, two children
- completed PhD in psychology, Yale University, 1941
- professor at Wesleyan University, Connecticut; American Friends Service Committee, Bryn Mawr College, Pennsylvania, 1942–6
- Wesleyan University, Connecticut, 1946–9, 1950–2, 19536, professor and chairman in department of psychology
- programme director, Ford Foundation, 1952–3
- Harvard University, 1949–50, 1956–87, professor and chairman in department of social relations
- founded the business that became McBer & Company, 1963
- Boston University, professor since 1987

Major works

Personality (1951)

The Achievement Motive (with J.W. Atkinson, R.A. Clark and E.L. Lowell) (1953)

Talent and Society (with A.L. Baldwin, U. Bronfenbrenner and F.L. Strodbeck) (1958)

The Achieving Society (1961)

The Roots of Consciousness (1964)

The Drinking Man: Alcohol and Human Motivation (with W.N. Davis, R. Kalin and E. Wanner) (1972)

Power: The Inner Experience (1975)

Motives, Personality and Society: Selected Papers (1984)

Human Motivation (1985)

Summary

Few scholars have had as much impact on the research literature on the practice of management as David C. McClelland. In his work, there have been four major themes directly related to management. One has been the creation of a theory of human motives and a supporting and enlightening empirical base, most notably addressing the needs for achievement, affiliation, power and the leadership motive profile. A second theme has been the definition of motivational change, establishment of empirical support for this theory and the inspiration, coaching and perseverance in application projects at individual, organizational, community and national levels around the world. A third theme has been the development of tests and operant methods such as the thematic apperception test, behavioural event interview and the test of thematic analysis, which have been used in research and applications. A fourth theme has been the development of job competency studies, methods and applications as a way to link human capabilities to performance at work in many occupations, from scientists to social workers, secretaries to executives, and priests to admirals.

1 A theory of human motives

Human motivation, in McClelland's perspective, is the arousal of particular motives in a specific setting. A motive is 'a recurrent concern for a goal state or condition as measured in fantasy which drives, directs and selects the behavior of the individual' (McClelland 1985). Building on the work of Henry Murray (1938), he further stipulated that three particular motives are useful in understanding most work-related behaviour. They are the need for achievement (N Ach), the need for affiliation (N Aff) and the need for power (N Pow). Although most of his work focused on N Ach from the late 1940s through the 1960s (McClelland et al. 1953; McClelland 1961; McClelland and Winter 1969), N Pow emerged as a focal point of research in the late 1960s and through to the 1990s (McClelland et al. 1972; McClelland 1975, 1985).

The need for achievement is an unconscious drive to do better and to aspire to a standard of excellence (see MASLOW, A.H.). People with strong N Ach often assess themselves as a way to measure progress towards various ends. They set goals; strive to take moderate risks (that is to say challenging but realistic); prefer individual activities; prefer recreational activities during which a person can get a 'score' (like golf or bowling); and prefer occupations where performance data are clearly available (such as sales positions or owners/managers of small businesses).

The need for power is an unconscious drive to have impact on others. People with strong N Pow often assert themselves against or in the presence of others in various ways. They seek and obtain leadership positions in social groups, professional associations, and work; they gamble, drink alcoholic beverages and commit aggressive acts; they tend to have high blood pressure and prefer interpersonally competitive sports such as tennis or football; they like to collect prestige possessions and prefer occupations in which they can help or have an impact on others, such as teaching, religious ministry and management positions.

The need for affiliation is an unconscious drive to be a part of warm, close relationships and friendships (see MAYO, G.E.; HERZBERG, F.). People with strong N Aff often choose to spend time with close friends or significant others rather than be in any other setting. They regularly write letters or make long-distance telephone calls to friends or family; they prefer to work in groups and are sensitive to others' reactions to them; they prefer

collaborative, non-competitive activities (such as picnics) and occupations in which they work closely with others, such as teaching young children and counselling.

The work of McClelland and his colleagues established the importance of a person's 'pattern' of these motives – everyone has some level of each motive, but the relative dominance varies. It is the pattern of a person's motive strength that is often the most indicative of occupational performance and success. For example, high N Ach, low N Aff, and moderate N Pow is characteristic of successful entrepreneurs throughout the world. High N Pow, moderate to low N Aff, moderate N Ach and high activity inhibition (a measure of self-control) is characteristic of effective leaders and of middle-level and executive managers (McClelland and Boyatzis 1982). Moderate N Ach, N Aff and N Pow is characteristic of effective helpers (Kolb and Boyatzis 1970) and integrators (Lawrence and Lorsch 1967).

In addition to studying motives at the individual level, McClelland initiated a series of studies on motivational trends at national and societal levels. He established an empirical link between motivational themes in cultural modes of expression (such as literature, hymns, ballads, myths, children's books and art), national events (the rise and fall of an economy, social movements, wars) and national biomedical norms (for example, high blood pressure, heart attacks, alcohol use and abuse) (McClelland 1961, 1975; McClelland et al. 1972).

This approach to motivation has appealed to practitioners and scholars of management, human resources and organizational development. McClelland's definitions, data and applications were cited as the most useful approach to motivation in a study by the accounting and consulting firm Touche Ross (Miller 1981). The initial attraction to the approach often comes from what McClelland would label the wrong reason – to discover ways to get people to work harder or ways to deal with problem employees. The charm of the theory is the ease of remembering the tripartite division. It is also quite seductive, with people remembering their own motive profiles for decades, even if they forget everything else about the workshop or seminar in which it was addressed: it probes the unconscious and helps to get beneath the rational arguments we build to make us look good to others or feel justified in our actions. Also, it helps that almost any distribution of the motives is related to effectiveness in some occupation. Lastly, it organizes human behaviour into a set of reasonable categories, so if a person does not like their motive distribution or thinks it will make a desired future difficult to achieve they can simply change their motives.

2 Changing motives and motivational environments

What began as a casual conversation between McClelland and several colleagues led to multiple efforts to explore the possibility of a person changing their own motives. The concept was amazingly simple: if you know how people with certain motives think and act, can a person change their motives simply by changing their thoughts and actions? The simple answer was yes. After years of experiments in countries throughout the world, several observations can be made: (1) people can change the relative weighting of their motives (the shape of their motive profile); (2) people will only change if they want to change (you cannot change someone else); (3) change cannot occur without a change in environmental supports such as the norms and values of the person's reference groups or work setting; and (4) any attempts at motivational change increase a person's sense of efficacy.

The earliest attempts by McClelland were to stimulate business and economic development by training small business owners and managers in achievement thinking and behaviour. This was successful in India and other countries (McClelland and Winter 1969) and subsequently with minority owner-operated small businesses in the USA (Miron and McClelland 1979). The method was extended to the power motive in efforts to help alcoholics (McClelland et al. 1972), then to help executives and middle-level managers in industry (McClelland and Burnham 1976),

and was even used even within the context of community development (McClelland et al. 1975).

The approach was summarized by McClelland (1965): give people feedback about their current thinking patterns (motives) and behaviour, help them to understand the research on the relationship between motives and successful performance, encourage them to set goals and plan for experimentation with new thought patterns and behaviours, attempt to create supportive systems (what we would now call support groups, learning teams or self-designing study groups) and ask them to periodically re-evaluate progress toward their goals. It was an empowering message, but many sceptics doubted the efficacy of the programmes. McClelland then set out to study the effects. Longitudinal studies were conducted in companies, communities and schools in India and the USA. The resulting data have always been open to dispute concerning the size of the effect, but the upshot was clear: it worked. People felt more in control of their lives following most of these programmes and when the desired changes did not occur, it was typically found that some of the elements proposed in the 1965 theory of motive change were missing.

3 Tests, measures and operant methods

The discoveries about motives and motivational change would not have been possible without operant measures, and McClelland has been an advocate of operant methods (tests where a person must operate and generate thoughts or actions in response to a stimulus) for decades. He contrasts their rich data to the more traditional scores a person gets from 'respondent' tests (tests calling for a true/false rating, or ranking response to each item typically in a large set of items).

A person demonstrates thought, emotion, action and choices through operant measures. For example, in the thematic apperception test, a person creates and tells a story about what is happening after looking at a picture for about a minute. The pictures are selected to be somewhat ambiguous, thus allowing the person to project a wide variety of responses. In the behavioural event interview (a variation of the critical incident interview), a person is asked to tell about a recent time when they felt effective in their job. The thematic analysis test asks people to compare and contrast two sets of stories as a way to sample the complexity of their thought processes (Winter and McClelland 1978). Often, the person's response is audiotaped and, as many operant methods do not involve paper-and-pencil responses, they are often referred to as measures rather than as tests.

McClelland developed compelling evidence to show that operant methods, as compared to respondent methods, consistently show: (1) more criterion validity; (2) less test–retest reliability; (3) greater sensitivity (in being able to discriminate mood changes, style differences and other somewhat subtle, dynamic aspects of human thought and behaviour); (4) more uniqueness, being less likely to suffer from multicollinearity; and (5) increased utility in applications to human or organizational development (McClelland 1985).

The key to rigorous research and ethical use of operant methods is in the process of coding the raw information. McClelland extended thematic analysis from a highly unreliable, clinical art form to a legitimate research method (Smith *et al.* 1992; Boyatzis 1996). To achieve validity, the coding of the raw information requires consistency of judgment, or inter-rater reliability. It is difficult, if not impossible, to achieve reliability without a clear, explicit codebook. The use of codebooks and reliable coding opened the doors to many new measures, which in turn allowed creative inquiry into people's motives (McClelland 1985), skills (McClelland 1973; McClelland and Boyatzis 1980; Boyatzis 1982) and the effect of college on students' development (Winter *et al.* 1981).

Training in this approach to code development has typically been available only as a tutorial from a researcher who actually uses operant methods. Many of McClelland's former students had the opportunity to attend a graduate seminar in thematic analysis which

he taught at Harvard. Some have created seminars or doctoral courses, for example at Boston University and University of Michigan (Abigail Stewart), Wesleyan University and University of Michigan (David Winter), and Case Western Reserve University (Richard Boyatzis).

It would have been difficult to discover the thought processes and behaviour related to motives without these methods. In the rowing boat across the intellectual river from the bank of research to the bank of application, these operant methods were the oars.

4 Job competencies and human resource development

Operant methods also revealed a level of insight, definition and precision in assessment of aspects of a person's talent. Building on earlier work on motives, McClelland *et al.* (1958) conceptualized a broad array of skills as a reflection of a person's capability. Reviving his earlier personality theory (McClelland 1951), McClelland and his colleagues at McBer & Company expanded the search for competencies in the early 1970s (skills, self-image, traits and motives) in many occupations (Boyatzis 1982; Spencer and Spencer 1993). On this approach, the definition of job competency differs from many behaviouristic approaches to skills identification in that the job competency definition requires the person's intent to be understood, thereby going beyond merely observing the person's actions. In this way there is an emphasis on characteristics of the 'person' rather than just the tasks involved in the job.

Using operant methods to explore the differences in thoughts, feelings and behaviour of superior performers when compared to average or poor performers, competency models were developed and validated against performance in a job (or job family) in a specific organization. Studies were completed on bank tellers, social workers, police, priests, generals and admirals, executives, sales representatives, scientists, programmers, consultants, marketing managers, project managers and so forth. The competency assessment methods developed a picture of how the superior performer thinks, feels and acts in his work setting. This contextual and concrete picture provided case studies and models which help anyone in a job, or aspiring to one, to develop their capability. The focus was always on the 'superior' or outstanding performer, not because others were not valuable and able to contribute to the organization, but because this rarefied group (often about 5 per cent and never more than 10 per cent of the people in a job family in any organization) provided guidance as role models and hope to their co-workers.

As professionals in organizations were trained in the techniques of job competency assessment, they developed competency-based training programmes, career-pathing systems (that went beyond succession planning), developmental assessment programmes, coaching and guidance programmes, recruiting, selection and promotion systems, and even incentive compensation methods. The goal was to increase the percentage of people in each job family who could demonstrate (that is to say use) the competencies related to superior performance. While helping the organization, competency models and applications also offered guidance, encouragement and methods for people to develop their own capabilities in whatever directions they desired.

5 Conclusion

The impressive contribution of the four themes outlined are but a small part of David McClelland's impact on management. He has personally trained and developed legions of scholars, consultants and leaders, stimulating their curiosity, guiding and often provoking them to contribute to the field and practice of management. He has also been a founder or influential director of over fourteen for-profit and not-for-profit consulting companies, the most notable of which has been McBer & Company (now a part of The Hay/McBer Group).

There are numerous messages running consistently through his career and contributions. One is that good research is a multidisciplinary effort, combining insights from psychology, sociology, anthropology, medicine and other disciplines: research is the link between theory and practice. A second message is that phenomena are complex and therefore require many perspectives to be understood: measurement requires creativity, ingenuity and hard work. Finally, and above all, is the McClelland optimism that if we can measure something operantly, we can actually change it.

RICHARD E. BOYATZIS
CASE WESTERN RESERVE UNIVERSITY

Further reading

(References cited in the text marked *)

* Boyatzis, R.E. (1982) *The Competent Manager: A Model for Effective Performance*, New York: Wiley. (Research on performance-based competencies and a competency model of over 2,000 managers)
* Boyatzis, R.E. (1996) *Thematic Analysis: A Method for Transforming Qualitative Information into Quantitative Data*, Cleveland, OH: Case Western Reserve University. (A methodology book for identifying themes or patterns in qualitative information.)
* Kolb, D.A. and Boyatzis, R.E. (1970) 'On the dynamics of the helping relationship', *Journal of Applied Behavioral Sciences* 6 (3): 267–90. (Research on effective versus ineffective helpers.)
* Lawrence, P.R. and Lorsch, J.W. (1967) 'New management job: the integrator', *Harvard Business Review* 45 (6): 142–51. (Research on managers in 'integrative jobs'.)
* McClelland, D.C. (1951) *Personality*, New York: William Sloane Associates. (A comprehensive personality theory.)
* McClelland, D.C. (1961) *The Achieving Society*, New York: Van Nostrand Reinhold. (Multidisciplinary research on the effects of achievement motivation on individual behaviour (for example, risks and goals), entrepreneurial success, and cultures.)
  McClelland, D.C. (1964) *The Roots of Consciousness*, New York: Van Nostrand Reinhold. (Collected papers.)
* McClelland, D.C. (1965) 'Toward a theory of motive acquisition', *American Psychologist* 20: 321–33. (A theory and framework of how individuals can change their motives.)

* McClelland, D.C. (1973) 'Testing for competence rather than intelligence', *American Psychologist* 28: 1–14. (Review of research showing that competencies, in addition to intelligence, are important to occupational success.)

* McClelland, D.C. (1975) *Power: The Inner Experience*, New York: Irvington. (Multidisciplinary research on the effects of power motivation on individual behaviour (for example, aggression and drinking), organizational leadership, and cultures (for example, predicting US entry into war, heart attacks in various countries around the world).)

McClelland, D.C. (1979) 'Inhibited power motivation and high blood pressure in men', *Journal of Abnormal Psychology* 88: 182–90. (Research on the relationship between high blood pressure and power motives.)

McClelland, D.C. (1984) *Motives, Personality and Society: Selected Papers*, New York: Praeger. (A collection of his papers by his colleagues about topics of continuing interest to McClelland.)

* McClelland, D.C. (1985) *Human Motivation*, New York: Cambridge University Press. (An integrated review of his own work and others regarding human motivation.)

* McClelland, D.C. and Boyatzis, R.E. (1980) 'Opportunities for counselors from the competency assessment movement', *Personnel and Guidance Journal* 58: 368–72. (Review of potential applications of competency testing for counselling.)

* McClelland, D.C. and Boyatzis, R.E. (1982) 'The leadership motive pattern and long-term success in management', *Journal of Applied Psychology* 67 (6): 737–43. (Longitudinal research on the leadership motive profile.)

* McClelland, D.C. and Burnham, D.H. (1976) 'Power is the great motivator', *Harvard Business Review* 54: 100–11. (Case study of application of the motivation concepts to a company.)

* McClelland, D.C. and Winter, D.G. (1969) *Motivating Economic Achievement*, NY: The Free Press. (Application of achievement motivation training in India.)

* McClelland, D.C., Rhinesmith, S. and Kristensen, R. (1975) 'The effects of power training on community action agencies', *Journal of Applied Behavioral Sciences* 11: 92–115. (Application of power motivation training in community development.)

* McClelland, D.C., Atkinson, J.W., Clark, R.A. and Lowell, E.L. (1953) *The Achievement Motive*, NY: Appleton Century-Crofts. (The original research on the achievement motive.)

* McClelland, D.C., Baldwin, A.L., Bronfenbrenner, U. and Strodbeck, F.L. (1958) *Talent and Society*, NY: Van Nostrand Reinhold. (Conceptual ground work for later work on competencies.)

* McClelland, D.C., Davis, W.N., Kalin, R. and Wanner, E. (1972) *The Drinking Man: Alcohol and Human Motivation*, NY: The Free Press. (Multidisciplinary research on the relationship of power motives and drinking.)

* Miller, W.B. (1981) 'Motivation techniques: does one work best?', *Management Review* February: 47–52. (Study of companies as to the most useful theories and work on motivation.)

* Miron, D. and McClelland, D.C. (1979) 'The impact of achievement motivation training on small business', *California Management Review* 21 (4): 13–28. (Research on the effect of achievement motivation training on minority, small businesses.)

* Murray, H.A. (1938) *Explorations in Personality*, NY: Oxford University Press. (A comprehensive personality theory.)

* Smith, C.P., Atkinson, J.W., McClelland, D.C. and Veroff, J. (eds) (1992) *Motivation and Personality: Handbook of Thematic Content Analysis*, New York: Cambridge University Press. (Examples of codes used with the Thematic Apperception Test.)

* Spencer, L.M., Jr and Spencer, S. (1993) *Competence at Work: Models for Superior Performance*, New York: Wiley. (Competency models of various occupations.)

Stewart, A.J. (ed.) (1982) *Motivation and Society: A Volume in Honor of David C. McClelland*, San Francisco, CA: Jossey Bass. (A collection of papers by his colleagues about topics of continuing interest to McClelland.)

* Winter, D.G. and McClelland, D.C. (1978) 'Thematic analysis: an empirically derived measure of the effects of liberal arts education', *Journal of Educational Psychology* 70: 8–16. (A code and test for pattern-recognition ability.)

* Winter, D.G., McClelland D.G. and Stewart, A.J. (1981) *A New Case for the Liberal Arts: Assessing Institutional Goals and Student Development*, San Francisco, CA: Jossey Bass. (Impact of undergraduate college or university on competencies.)

See also: ARGYRIS, C.; HERZBERG, F.; MASLOW, A.H.; MAYO, G.E.

Related topics in the IEBM: CULTURE, CROSS-NATIONAL; ECONOMICS OF DEVELOPING COUNTRIES; HUMAN RESOURCE MANAGEMENT; MOTIVATION AND SATISFACTION; OCCUPATIONAL PSYCHOLOGY; ORGANIZATION BEHAVIOUR; ORGANIZATION BEHAVIOUR, HISTORY OF; ORGANIZATION CULTURE; ORGANIZATION DEVELOPMENT; ORGANIZATION STRUCTURE; POWER; RECRUITMENT AND SELECTION; SMALL BUSINESS STRATEGY

McGregor, Douglas (1906–64)

Personal background

- born in 1906
- trained at the City College of Detroit and the Graduate School of Arts and Sciences at Harvard, reading social psychology
- president of Antioch College, 1948–54
- professor of management at MIT, 1954–64
- died 1964

Major works

The Human Side of the Enterprise (1960)
Leadership and Motivation (1966)
The Professional Manager (1967)

Summary

Douglas McGregor was an American social psychologist who became influential as a management guru after World War II. He is best known for his proposal of Theory Y (based on assumptions of 'support') which he contrasts with Theory X (based on assumptions of 'control'.) Together with organizational theorists like Argyris and Herzberg (see ARGYRIS, C.; HERZBERG, F.), McGregor showed how organization, leadership and job design could create more enriched, motivating jobs to boost employee's autonomy and possibly creativity.

Introduction

Douglas McGregor was trained at the City College of Detroit and at the Graduate School of Arts and Sciences at Harvard where he studied social psychology. His career as a psychologist was not notably successful and he switched to university administration in which he so distinguished himself as to become president of Antioch College in 1948, where he stayed six years. Antioch, long in the vanguard of progressive and student-centred education, was a beacon for educators during the 1950s. In the USA, business has tended to be conservative and highly disciplined, while child-rearing perspectives and education have been liberal and permissive extolling the self-expression of the learner.

When McGregor became a professor of management at MIT's Sloan School in 1954, it was therefore for his experience of university administration that he was best known. This experience had *preceded* his exposure to management studies and he was always more interested in this experience than in the then conservative orthodoxies of command and control. Nor was McGregor particularly intellectual. Instead of starting with concepts and trying to deduce experience, his approach was inductive, generalizing from his own relationships and experiences into a set of highly lucid propositions which made him famous. For, at heart, McGregor was ahead of his time by several decades. He saw both managers and workers as *learners,* a view only recently accepted as businesses have become more and more complex. He also treated businesses as the self-expression of managers and subordinates. In the years since he died he has gained in stature, and the systems dynamics department at MIT sees its work under first Jay Forrester and now Peter Senge (see FORRESTER, J.W.; SENGE, P.) as the vindication of his legacy.

2 The Human Side of the Enterprise

Very few business writers are as beholden to a single work as is McGregor. Owing to his early death at the age of 57 McGregor has left us only this one example of his thinking and a few essays. But for this book he would hardly be known in the field of management studies at all, yet because of it his place is assured and honoured.

He begins by considering the nature of social science. All science, he argues, is an *adaption* to the nature of the phenomena being studied. We can't make water flow uphill, nor can we make the most important things that people do predictable and controllable. Ironically we can control routinized behaviours – when someone shows up for work, what meetings they will attend – but the more vital the aspects of their work become, the less control we can exercise.

All managerial conduct is based on 'theory', a loosely connected set of assumptions about the human nature with which we are dealing. It behoves us to examine carefully the assumptions we make, since these are partly self-fulfilling. Physical objects do not change their appearance and conduct when we invent theories about them, but human beings do. We get our belief in authority from three principle sources; the military, the church – especially the Roman Catholic church – and the physical sciences which require unilateral control over dead objects for experiments to be conducted. All these are special cases of extreme dependence on authority. None illumine a world that is increasingly *interdependent*. The human side of the enterprise allows a wide latitude of initiatives from highly unpredictable and uncontrollable sources. Moreover satisfaction at work relies on the exercise of such initiatives.

Nor do the roles of people stand still in some fixity. A manager can be a boss, an observer, a consultant, a facilitator, a friend, a resource, a teacher and so on. The more flexibly s/he behaves the more s/he adjusts to the situation, the less predictable s/he will be. Yet this capacity to play multiple roles is a vital part of adaptation to the nature of human enterprise.

McGregor distinguishes two underlying 'theorie' – really sets of working assumptions. He calls these 'Theory X' and 'Theory Y'. Theory X is the traditional view of direction and control. It is to McGregor's credit that he spells out in detail what would have to be true were such control necessary:

Theory X assumes …
– The average human being has an inherent dislike of work and will avoid it if he can.
Therefore:
– Most people must be coerced, controlled, directed, threatened with punishment to get them to put forth adequate effort …
This is because he …
– Prefers to be directed, wishes to avoid responsibility, has relatively little ambition, wants security above all.

McGregor is careful to avoid suggesting that senior managers go about proclaiming so dour a philosophy. His argument is rather that they would *necessarily* have to assume this to carry out the policies they do, for example piecework incentives, punching time-cloaks and so on. He does suggest that Theory X may be less driven by misanthropy than by eagerness to don the mantle of 'science'. If only human beings could emulate Newton's laws of motion the 'scientific' nature of administration would be assured. McGregor also makes it clear that his objectives are to the unilateralism of sanctions, not to whether such sanctions punish employees or reward employees.

Theory Y is *not* a preference for 'soft' over 'hard'. McGregor rejects the human relations school's doctrine that 'kindness pays'. Rather, Theory Y is a set of assumptions contrasting with Theory X:

Theory Y assumes …
– The expenditure of physical and mental effort in work is as natural as play or rest.
– External controls are not the sole means … [of motivation] since man will exercise self-direction and self-control in the service of objectives to which he is committed.
– Commitment to objectives is a function of the rewards associated with their achievement (which can take the form of actualizing both the self and organizational objectives).
– The average human being learns under proper conditions not only to accept but to seek responsibility.
– The capacity to exercise a relatively high degree of imagination, ingenuity and creativity in the solution of organizational problems is widely, not narrowly, distributed in the population.

– Under the conditions of modern industrial life, the intellectual potentialities of the average human being are only partially utilized.

It follows from this that the major task of the organization is to integrate personal goals with its own policy objectives.

It is fairly clear where the major influences on McGregor's work come from. As someone coming to management studies only in his fifties, he looked for the scholars who most clarified his own experience at Antioch. Foremost among these is Abraham Maslow (see MASLOW, A.H.), who published his need hierarchy in his 1954 book *Motivation and Personality,* the year McGregor left Antioch. Maslow theorized that human beings grow through a sequence of stages of need: (1) physiological needs; (2) safety needs; (3) social needs; (4) self-esteem needs; (5) self-actualization. Theory Y is clearly predicted on needs for esteem and self-actualization, while Theory X assumes a physiological need for security under a boss on whom one is dependent. The church and the army are both concerned with enabling members to be saved and to survive battle. A second major influence, often cited by McGregor, is Peter Drucker (see DRUCKER, P.F.), whose 'management by objectives' could only work in a manner which upheld human development if in fact the objectives of the organization and that of the individual manager were integratable (Drucker 1954). A third major influence was Chris Argyris (see ARGYRIS, C.) and his 1957 book *Personality and Organization,* which argued that personality development could be achieved through organization development. In the two cases the relevant principles of organization overlapped. McGregor was also very much an advocate of the human relations school, which had started with the studies of Elton Mayo at the Hawthorne works (see MAYO, G.E.)

3 A champion of the Scanlon Plan

Perhaps for this reason McGregor became a major champion of the Scanlon Plan, writing the introduction to the book of that name by

Frederick C. Lesieur. Joseph Scanlon was a trades unionist who invented an ingenious plan of worker–management collaboration now operated in over 5,000 units across the USA, thanks in part to its being adopted by Japanese companies in the late 1970s. Without McGregor's endorsement, it is unlikely the plan could have survived, given its origins on the union side of industry. It was operating in 50 US companies by McGregor's death in 1964.

The plan extolled in *The Human Side of the Enterprise* consists of calculating a ration of input–output costs for a given production unit. Workers contribute half an hour a day of 'their' time and are 'given' half an hour of 'the company's' time. In this hour, they meet to discuss and invent ways of producing the same as before for less cost, and/or producing more for the same cost. Fifty per cent of these savings go to employees, and 50 per cent go to the shareholders. As in the Hawthorne experiment the process of doing the work and *learning how it might better be done,* proceeds in phases.

The plan utilizes groups or teams, and McGregor was also involved in the National Training Laboratories and the T-Group (Training Group) movement. It was not simply employees who developed up the need hierarchy but groups that grew more dynamic and effective as members learned more about each other's capacities. The Scanlon Plan harnessed group development, individual development and organizational development in a single process, in which 'everyone could be an entrepreneur' devising ways to improve the ratio and sharing the gains.

4 Evaluation

It is not difficult to criticize McGregor. Early objections to his work was that it was 'normative' not objective, an issue of faith in others, not genuine social science. You could not employ Theory Y unless you really believed in it and once you believed in it, you had sacrificed scientific detachment. A more discerning criticism saw it as the heir to 'spiritual technology' to which Americans have long been prey. Was this not a variation on Dale

Carnegie's *How to Win Friends and Influence People* and Norman Vincent Peale's *The Power of Positive Thinking*? Did it not come down to Pollyanna's 'Glad Game', where you pretended to be glad and *became* glad as others responded to your cheerfulness? Who has not encountered the coercive good cheer of American glad-handing?

Moreover, the effectiveness of Theory Y depends upon a crucial misunderstanding. The employee who is so generously thought about, mistakes these complementary views for judgements about his or her *unique* character: 'My boss really appreciates me!' But the boss is, in fact, in thrall to a formula, approving of the employee because this is effective human relations policy. The more conscious one is of Theory Y as a set of operating assumptions the less attention one pays to the actual employee and his or her humanity.

Moreover, employees will soon note that Theory Y and its universalized generosity of spirit is being applied to *everyone* and therefore has little significance to anyone in particular including each of those employees. As a *New Yorker* cartoon put it: 'Well done and carry on – whoever you are!' said by a boss to an anonymous employee. However, we should not hold McGregor responsible for popular folklore in American culture. If you aim to write a bestseller, as this book certainly was, you are bound to evole the currents aboard in that culture. Douglas McGregor was saying something profoundly important and new, which since his death has risen to being an issue of major importance.

5 McGregor's lasting legacy: living systems are self-organizing

What McGregor taught us is that human systems, and hence living systems in general, are *spontaneously alive.* They do not have to be *motivated.* They *are* motivated. If we have the patience to learn about the form this takes, we can facilitate it, develop it and harness it to the goals of the corporation and the developing group. There is increasing evidence from chemistry, biology, evolution, sub-atomic physics, mathematics, ecology and brain-research that life is a *self-organizing system* far from equilibrium, with an energy and momentum of its own. We cannot *cause* others to behave or otherwise 'motivate' them, we can only educe from them and trigger their autonomous activities, which unfold through their own rules. McGregor was among the first to insist that this was so, to urge us to *look for* this potential in human enterprise, or it would pass us by. If we accuse him of trying to manipulate others by coercive optimism then we wilfully miss his basic point, that *all* manipulative sanctions, threatening or kindly intended, will blind us to the reality of human potential.

CHARLES HAMPDEN-TURNER
JUDGE INSTITUTE OF MANAGEMENT STUDIES
UNIVERSITY OF CAMBRIDGE

Further reading

(References cited in the text marked *)

* Argyris, C. (1957) *Personality and Organization*, New York: Harper & Row. (This book first detailed the incompatibility between mature individuals and hierarchical, mechanistic organizations.)
* Drucker, P.F. (1954) *The Practice of Management*, London: Heinemann. (Drucker's first, influential work on management, which introduces the concept of management by objectives.)
  Kennedy, Carol (1996) *Managing With the Gurus*, London: Century. (Summarizes 'Theory X' and 'Theory Y' and McGregor's work on motivation.)
* McGregor, D. (1960) *The Human Side of the Enterprise*, New York: McGraw-Hill. (Probably his best-know publication.)
* McGregor, D. (1966) *Leadership and Motivation*, New York: MIT Press. (In this book, he argues for supportive relationships-organization.)
* McGregor, D. (1967) *The Professional Manager*, New York: McGraw-Hill. (Posthumous publication of McGregor's final development of his ideas.)
* Maslow, A.H. ([1954] 1970) *Motivation and Personality*, New York: Harper & Bros. (Maslow's most important work, in which he sets out to integrate into psychological theory the main idea underlying his work on motivation, that 'higher needs' were an essential 'instinctoid' part of

human nature and that psychopathologies were the result of thwarting such needs.)

Morgan, G. (1997) *Images of Organization*, London: Sage. (Discusses McGregor's work in his chapter on organizations and organisms.)

Pugh, D. S., Hickson, D.J. and Hinings, C.R. (1964) *Writers on Organizations*, London: Penguin Books. (Contains a succinct comparison of McGregor's work with Likerts.)

See also: ARYGRIS. C.; BENNIS, W.; DRUCKER, P.F.; FORRESTER, J.W.; MASLOW. A.H.; MAYO, G.E.; SENGE, P.

Related topics in the IEBM: HAWTHORNE EXPERIMENTS; HUMAN RELATIONS; HUMAN RESOURCE MANAGEMENT; MANAGERIAL BEHAVIOUR; MOTIVATION AND SATISFACTION; OCCUPATIONAL PSYCHOLOGY; ORGANIZATION BEHAVIOUR; ORGANIZATION BEHAVIOUR, HISTORY OF; ORGANIZATION STRUCTURE; ORGANIZATIONAL LEARNING; PAYMENT SYSTEMS; PROFIT-SHARING; SYSTEMS

McLuhan, Herbert Marshall (1911–80)

Personal background

- born Edmonton, Alberta, 21 July 1911
- attended University of Manitoba (BA, MA) and took his PhD at Cambridge
- married Corinne Lewis, 1939
- took up a teaching post at University of Toronto in 1946 and given a full professorship in 1952
- chairman of the Ford Foundation Seminar on Culture and Communication, 1953–5
- founded the Centre for Culture and Technology at University of Toronto in 1963
- appeared in the Woody Allen film *Annie Hall* as himself, 1977
- died 31 December 1980, after a severe stroke

Major works

The Mechanical Bride: Folklore of Industrial Man (1951)
The Gutenberg Galaxy (1962)
Understanding Media: The Extensions of Man (1964)
War and Peace in the Global Village (with Q. Fiore) (1968)
Through the Vanishing Point: Space in Poetry and Painting (with H. Parker) (1968)
Culture is Our Business (1970)
Laws of Media: The New Science (with E. McLuhan) (1988, published posthumously)

Summary

Marshall McLuhan (1911–80) is widely regarded as one of the greatest thinkers on communication and culture of the twentieth century. He was himself a superb and innovative communicator, easily bridging the gap between academia and popular culture, and his work at the Centre for Culture and Technology in Toronto both made his academic reputation and turned him into a pop icon in the 1960s. His works on the relationship between culture and communication have had considerable influence on the advertising profession; two of his most noted books, *The Mechanical Bride* and *Culture is Our Business*, focused specifically on the advertising industry. His work has also had and continues to have an influence on the ongoing debate over globalization.

1 Introduction

McLuhan became famous for two phrases: 'the global village', which referred to the increasing trend towards worldwide cultural convergence, and 'the medium is the message', referring to the impact of technology on communications. He attempted to communicate these ideas through a variety of forms. His books are often illustrations of the 'medium is the message' theme; illustrations, different typefaces and unusual layouts are mixed with quotes from psychologists, sociologists and writers such as James Joyce and T.S. Eliot. Critics have argued that his work is not new and that his principal themes had already been developed by others. However, as one critic says:

> McLuhan added very little in a conceptual sense. He did not need to, for the elements of the paradigm had already received consensus. McLuhan did two things: he synthesized the previously disparate elements, and he applied them, with great wit and imagination, to the immediate data of consciousness.
>
> (Curtis 1978: 79)

It is for the latter in particular that McLuhan will be remembered.

2 Biographical data

Herbert Marshall McLuhan was born in 1911 in Edmonton, Alberta. After taking his BA and MA at the University of Manitoba, he studied for his PhD at Cambridge and in 1936 took up his first teaching position at the University of Wisconsin. He later taught at the University of St Louis and Assumption University, before returning to Canada in 1946. He taught at the University of Toronto from that year until his death.

He first came to prominence with the publication of *The Mechanical Bride*, a study of the American advertising industry, in 1951. In 1952 he was made a full professor, and he chaired the Ford Foundation Seminar on Culture and Communication from 1953 to 1955. His interests then turned towards the influence of technology on the media; the result was the publication of *The Gutenberg Galaxy* in 1962, and in 1963 McLuhan established the Centre for Culture and Technology at the University of Toronto.

The publication of *Understanding Media* in 1964 brought him international status, and through the 1960s and 1970s he became an increasingly influential writer and thinker on the relationship between culture, media and technology. More than a dozen books and hundreds of articles focused on subjects such as technology (*War and Peace in the Global Village*), art (*Through the Vanishing Point*) and advertising (*Culture is Our Business*). He was widely consulted by world leaders including Jimmy Carter and Pierre Trudeau, and was appointed by the Vatican in 1973 as consultant to the Pontifical Commission for Social Communication. He received more than twenty major awards, including Fellow of the Royal Society of Canada (1964) and Companion of the Order of Canada (1970). He died in 1980, while working on several books and preparing to speak at a major conference in the USA.

3 Main contribution

McLuhan's work was characterized by three principal themes. The first is the concept of art as cognition, referring to the symbolic meanings to be found in visual messages ranging from art to advertising. The second is that technology is an extension of man; the content of any message is inevitably affected by the technology used to communicate it. Third, McLuhan believed that human development had passed through two ages, the primitive and the industrial or 'typographical', and had now entered a third age, the technological.

That McLuhan should have chosen to focus on advertising in his first major discussion of art as cognition is typical of his approach to the relationship between art and popular culture. In *The Mechanical Bride*, McLuhan deconstructed a series of print advertisements, showing the symbolic elements present in each. His conclusion was that advertisements are a kind of folklore; he returned to this theme in *Culture is Our Business*, in which he described advertisements as 'the cave art of the twentieth century' (McLuhan 1970: 7). His views on advertising were, however, not entirely benevolent:

> Ours is the first age in which many thousands of the best-trained individual minds have made it a full-time business to get inside the collective public mind. To get inside in order to manipulate, exploit, control is the object now. And to generate heat not light is the intention. To keep everybody in the helpless state engendered by prolonged mental rutting is the effect of many ads and much entertainment alike.
>
> (McLuhan 1951: v)

Understanding Media marked McLuhan's first major exploration of the second theme, the impact of technology on media. The text of this book begins:

> In a culture like ours, long accustomed to splitting and dividing all things as a means of control, it is sometimes a bit of a shock to be reminded that, in operational and practical fact, the medium is the message. This is merely to say that the personal and social consequences of any medium – that

is, any extension of ourselves – result from the new scale that is introduced into our affairs by each extension of ourselves, or by any new technology.

(McLuhan 1964: 7)

McLuhan went on to describe the negative and positive effects of this principle. Automation, for example, eliminates jobs; it also, he claims, creates new roles for people in relation to their work, replacing associations destroyed by the immediately preceding mechanical revolution. The same point is made with relation to media; humankind graduated from an oral to a written culture through the introduction of the printing press, but television and radio were now returning people to an oral culture.

This concept of a circular process, or of humanity returning to an earlier way of life through technology, is the third major theme in McLuhan's work. 'If Gutenberg technology retrieved the ancient world and dumped it in the lap of the Renaissance,' he wrote, 'electric technology has retrieved the primal, archaic worlds, past and present, private and corporate, and dumped them on the western doorstep for processing' (McLuhan 1970: 7).

The best summary of the fundamentals of McLuhan's thought can probably be found in *Laws of Media*, published some years after his death. The original intention was to produce a second edition of *Understanding Media*, but the analysis goes far deeper than the original book. In this work, McLuhan posits four fundamental principles with ramifications for communicators in every field, including advertising. They are:

1 every technology extends some organ or faculty of the user
2 when one area of experience is heightened or intensified, another is diminished or numbed
3 every form, pushed to the limit of its potential, changes its characteristics
4 the content of any medium is an older medium (that is new media subsume all older forms of media).

Typically, when formulating these 'laws', McLuhan insisted that the definition of 'law'

be that given by Popper: a scientific law is one so stated as to be capable of falsification. McLuhan understood only too well how time could alter perceptions and make his own theories obsolete.

4 Evaluation

Neill (1993) has commented that it is difficult to offer a critique of McLuhan's ideas, as his reputation is so great that it affects people's perceptions of his thought. To a certain extent, McLuhan was living proof that the medium is the message; it became difficult to separate the man from his ideas. Neill himself has strongly attacked a number of McLuhan's theories as being scientifically unproven and possibly unprovable. He argues that *Laws of Media* is probably McLuhan's best book, as there is evidence of the thought processes behind the theories.

Curtis (1978) points out that many of McLuhan's theories had already been propounded by other authors. Certainly the idea of the global village had already been set out by Mumford (1961) with his concept of 'one world man', while George Lukács and Franco Fortini had published theories of art and meaning which resembled those of McLuhan. His historical theories go back directly to Henri Bergson's model of history as process.

Like most modernists, McLuhan greatly overestimated the immediate impact of the printing press, and greatly underestimated the penetration of the written word before Gutenberg; as a result, he placed more emphasis on the technology and less on the education required to use it. Education, not technology, has always been the key barrier to assimilation of written words. His strong focus on media meant that at times McLuhan also ignored the impact of other forms of technology; the revolution in travel may have done as much to create a global village as the revolution in communication. Interestingly as well, McLuhan failed to foresee how the computer revolution would develop, giving people the ability to manipulate and control the media before and as it reached them. From the medium is the message, we are moving towards a paradigm where the viewer is the medium.

That having been said, McLuhan's articulation of the impact of communication on culture and vice versa remains a powerful one. His views continue to inform the debate on globalization, and proponents of globalization such as Levitt remain indebted to him. His impact on the advertising industry is summed up by Day (1967: 1): 'McLuhan is saying something that every good advertising man senses for himself, though rarely crystallizes or formalizes to anything like this extent'. That the medium used can have greater impact than the message is clearly a concept of vital importance for advertisers. Day spells out five points from McLuhan's work which advertisers need to take into account:

1 advertising must be alive to its environment
2 advertisers must try to predict the environment
3 each medium should be used for what it can do best
4 the audience should participate as far as possible
5 the picture should always tell the 'real' story.

McLuhan's views on the importance of language and symbol are less well known but equally significant. The impact of technological media in the 1990s, as satellite television girdles the globe, is easy to see, but McLuhan defined media as any 'extension of self' and thus by definition included pictures and words in more mundane forms of communication. Language, he felt, was the most powerful metaphor of all. In one of his last letters, to Canadian Prime Minister Pierre Trudeau, McLuhan wrote:

The speaker of any language assumes it as a medium or a mask by which he experiences the world in a special way, and by which he relates to people in a very special way ... A language in the hands of a lawyer or a judge or a bureaucrat has a quite different significance from the same language used by friends or enemies ... the *effects* of

language as media are quite different from the input or intended meanings. All inputs have side effects which are usually considered irrelevant by the speaker or sender.

(Molinaro *et al.* 1987: 542)

5 Conclusion

Marshall McLuhan was one of the best-known and most articulate commentators on the changes in communications, culture and society in the latter half of the twentieth century. His observations on technology, media and communication are of importance to psychologists and sociologists, and equally to businesses, especially those involved in advertising and marketing. At a deeper level, however, McLuhan's comments on language and symbol are important to all forms of human interaction. The phrase 'the medium is the message' has itself become part of popular folklore, and remains as a symbol of his theories and his achievement.

MORGEN WITZEL
LONDON BUSINESS SCHOOL
DURHAM UNIVERSITY BUSINESS SCHOOL

Further reading

(References cited in the text marked *)

* Curtis, J.M. (1978) *Culture as Polyphony: An Essay on the Nature of Paradigms*, Columbia, MO: University of Missouri Press. (Includes a good summary of McLuhan, placing his theories in the context of similar work by contemporaries.)
* Day, B. (1967) *The Message of Marshall McLuhan*, London: Lintas. (An assessment of the importance of McLuhan from the perspective of the advertising industry.)
  Levitt, T. 'The globalization of markets', *Harvard Business Review* 61 (May–June): 3. (A controversial article arguing that global media have brought about a global convergence of markets.)
* McLuhan, M. (1951) *The Mechanical Bride: Folklore of Industrial Man*, New York: Vanguard. (McLuhan's first work on advertising, which is highly critical of the uses to which advertising is put.)
* McLuhan, M. (1962) *The Gutenberg Galaxy*, New York: McGraw-Hill. Looks at how changing

scientific and technological paradigms affect our view of the world.)

* McLuhan, M. (1964) *Understanding Media: The Extensions of Man*, London: Routledge & Kegan Paul. (The classic work on media, exploring the concept of the medium as the message.)

* McLuhan, M. (1970) *Culture is Our Business*, New York: McGraw-Hill. (McLuhan's second look at advertising, in which he maintains that it is a reversion to primitive art forms.)

McLuhan, M. and Fiore, Q. (1968) *War and Peace in the Global Village*, New York: McGraw-Hill. (Discussion of the impact of technology on humanity; new technologies create space, but they also create pain.)

* McLuhan, M. and McLuhan, E. (1988) *Laws of Media: The New Science*, Toronto: University of Toronto Press. (The last and possibly the best summary of McLuhan's ideas.)

McLuhan, M. and Parker, H. (1968) *Through the Vanishing Point: Space in Poetry and Painting*, New York: Harper & Row. (Explores the use of symbol and metaphor in both visual arts and the written word.)

* Molinaro, M., McLuhan, C. and Boyd, W. (eds) (1987) *Letters of Marshall McLuhan*, Toronto: Oxford University Press. (Selected letters of McLuhan to a variety of people, including President Jimmy Carter and Prime Minister Pierre Trudeau.)

* Mumford, L. (1961) *The City in History*, New York: Harcourt, Brace & World. (Articulates another version of the concept of the global village, called 'one world man'.)

* Neill, S.D. (1993) *Clarifying McLuhan: An Assessment of Process and Product*, Westport, CN: Greenwood Press. (An analysis and critique of McLuhan's works, from a former associate and colleague.)

Sanderson, G. and Macdonald, F. (eds) (1989) *Marshall McLuhan, the Man and His Message*, Golden, CL: Fulcrum. (A selection of articles on McLuhan and his work.)

See also: LEVITT, T.; KOTLER, P.

Related topics in the IEBM: ADVERTISING CAMPAIGNS; ADVERTISING STRATEGY, INTERNATIONAL; COMMUNICATION; COMMUNICATION, CROSS-CULTURAL; GLOBALIZATION; INFORMATION REVOLUTION; MARKETING; MARKETING COMMUNICATIONS; MARKETING MANAGEMENT, INTERNATIONAL; MARKETING STRATEGY; TECHNOLOGY AND ORGANIZATIONS

March, James Gardner (1928–) and Cyert, Richard Michael (1921–)

1 Main contribution
2 Evaluation
3 Conclusions

Personal background

James Gardner March

- James March born Cleveland, Ohio, 15 January 1928
- educated at University of Wisconsin and Yale University (PhD in political science, 1953)
- taught at Carnegie Institute of Technology and University of California, Irvine; professor at Stanford University from 1970

Richard Michael Cyert

- Richard Cyert born Winona, Minnesota, 22 July 1921
- educated at University of Minnesota and Columbia University (PhD in economics, 1951)
- professor at Carnegie-Mellon University from 1972

Major works

A Behavioral Theory of the Firm (1963)
A Behavioral Theory of the Firm, 2nd edn (1992)

Summary

The impetus behind *A Behavioral Theory of the Firm*, one of the most significant writings on decision making within organizations, was the belief that better understanding of contemporary decision making required that existing studies of market factors be supplemented by an examination of the internal operation of the firm: a fusion of economics and research on
organizations. These ideas and associated research agenda were at that time a fairly significant deviation from the then dominant ideas in both fields, but in later years their work has become, in the words of the preface to the second edition: 'part of a received doctrine. In particular the perspective that sees firms as coalitions of multiple, conflicting interests using standard rules and procedures to operate under conditions of bounded rationality.'

1 Main contribution

Decision making was, at least prior to the work of Cyert and March and that of Simon (see SIMON, H.A.), traditionally portrayed and theorized around concepts such as intentionality, consequentiality and optimization. It was assumed that decisions were in some way based on preferences such as wants and needs, and on expectations surrounding outcomes associated with different alternatives. It was also assumed that the 'best possible' alternative (in terms of preferences and consequences) is the one that will be chosen. This set of assumptions also carried with it notions of a unitary decision maker, and thus could be questioned as to how far they could explain and/or predict human behaviour at the aggregate level of organization.

This view of aggregates displaying human attributes is still problematic; in particular the attribute of the possession of a coherent well-defined set of preferences is perhaps most difficult to cope with. The counter view is that decision making in organizations involves multiple actors with inconsistent preferences or goals, a result of the basic division of labour (see LAWRENCE, P.R. AND LORSCH, J.W.). Thus there is a political system to cope with as well as the other, more cognitive limits to rationality.

Allied to this is the notion that preferences may not be stable, but may change as decision makers become influenced in different ways. Thus a model of the firm becomes one of a shifting multiple-goal coalition of interests in which the views and preferences of the currently dominant group hold sway. Following this view, the goals of the firm are not a given but are the result of negotiations and bargaining among and between different interests. In any situation a coalition could include interests both inside and outside the firm; it could include managers, shareholders and agents of the state as well as all the sub-units inside the organization.

These limits to rational action are thus bound to impact on decision-making processes in several ways. Cyert and March developed four concepts to portray their theory of decision making:

- quasi-resolution of conflict
- uncertainty avoidance
- problemistic search
- organizational learning

Quasi-resolution of conflict describes a state of affairs that is prevalent in most organizations most of the time and which, as was suggested above, characterizes a situation in which the organization is seen as a coalition of members having different goals. Such conflicts obviously need resolving in some way. Cyert and March believe that most organizations both exist and thrive with conflicting goals, and procedures for resolving conflicts do not reduce goals to a common dimension or even make them consistent, but posit that conflicts are resolved by using local rationality, acceptable-level decision rules and sequential attention to goals.

Local rationality assumes that as organizations are broken down into sub-units each will face local problems, and thus each will deal with a limited set of problems and have a limited set of goals. Thus sales or marketing departments, for example, are primarily responsible for sales-related goals and strategy. Each can try and be rational within these local parameters, but of course these local rationalities, as with goals, will probably be mutually inconsistent. It is questionable whether this idea of factoring complex problems into sub-problems does in fact resolve conflicts and generate decisions that are consistent both with each other and with the external environment. This, Cyert and March suggest, depends on or is facilitated by the other two characteristics, decision rules on an acceptable level and sequential attention to goals.

The first of these has to do with the level of consistency that is tolerable for the organization; if this is low, then divergence is tolerable. An outcome may only need to be acceptable rather than optimal. Cyert and March suggest that organizations do have weak rules of consistency and are thus able to tolerate local rationality in decision making. There are two reasons for this: first, a large number of local decisions would be consistent anyway, and second, the system will in fact under-exploit the environment and thus there will be resources to cover any potential inconsistency. Finally, sequential attention to goals describes the situation when organizations attend to different goals at different points in time. The authors give as an example a firm which is subject to the pressures of smoothing production and then satisfying customers by offering more product variation, solving one before the other. Setting up this 'time buffer' is an important way of handling problems.

Uncertainty is a feature of all organizational decision making and is something with which organizations must live. The behaviour of the market, attitudes of stakeholders and future legislation all create and maintain uncertain states for decision makers, and much of the body of knowledge on decision making is concerned with finding certainty for such decision makers. Cyert and March find that organizations pursue a different strategy, that of uncertainty avoidance. They avoid having to fully anticipate future events by using decision rules which emphasize short-term reaction to short-term feedback; they solve short-term pressing problems rather than make projections of future states. They also avoid uncertainty in the future states of their environment by negotiating stability into that environment. In their words: 'they impose plans, standard operating procedures, industry tradition and uncertainty absorbing contracts on that environment' (Cyert and March 1992: 167).

In a similar way, organizations also seek to manage their internal environment; a plan or budget can be seen as a series of contracts between sub-units. As with industry conventions governing price setting, for example, internal conventions are stable during the life of such internal contracts and therefore provide a way for each unit to avoid the uncertainties which would have been inherent in the behaviour of others.

Problemistic search relates to the notion of bounded rationality. If organizations do adopt acceptable goals and select the first option that meets those goals, then search is stimulated by the problem and is not the far-sighted regular search which is unrelated to specific problems. If the problem drives search behaviour then, in their terms, it is motivated search. Search is also simple-minded; it operates with a simple causal model unless driven to a more complex one.

Search in these circumstances follows two simple rules. First, search is conducted near to the problem symptom or near the current solution. This suggests that problem cause will be near its effect and the solution will be near an old one. This may of course inhibit radical solutions. If these rules do not generate solutions, then there may be two further developments. The models of causality may become more complex; second search may enter into areas where there is some slack that can be taken up or into politically weak areas by renegotiating the coalition to disadvantage those areas.

Search is also biased; the ways in which environments are viewed is a reflection of variations in the training, experience and goals of the participants in the process. Cyert and March's final concept is that of organizational learning. While it is nave to assume that organizations learn in the ways that individuals do, they found that organizations do exhibit adaptive behaviour over time, and adapt at all three stages of the decision process, in goals, attention rules and search rules. Goals can change in response to experience in reaching previous goals, and also by looking at how other organizations are performing; organiza-

tions also learn to focus their attention on parts of their environment and ignore others. Finally, if search is problem oriented it could be assumed that search rules will adapt; this is a result of failures of problemistic search.

Cyert and March suggest that these concepts will prove more useful in investigating organizational decision making than those associated with traditional and more economics-based models of decision-making behaviour. Such work has led students of decision making into many and varied modes of enquiry and writing on decision-making behaviour. It later led March *et al.* (1972) to notions of decision-making behaviour as a 'garbage can'.

2 Evaluation

The study of modern organization and its contribution to social and economic progress has generated a vast amount of empirical observation and literature. The study of decision-making behaviour is a significant and crucial part of that corpus because knowledge can, through the decisions that managers and administrators make, have a profound impact on the nature of the goods and services that we demand, acquire and ultimately consume. It is through decision making that we see organizational actions or inactions and the interplay of multiple interests and rationalities.

It is in developing our understanding of this complex phenomenon and historical context that we must evaluate the work of Cyert and March. It was their recognition that studies of decision making had somehow ignored the internal context, the structural properties of the modern organization based on division of labour which creates sub-units facing a different task and task environment, and the subsequent problem of integrating and coordinating action among them. It was an understanding of this that they undertook, together with a knowledge and understanding of the limitations of traditional economic theories, in building their behavioural theory of the firm. This was an immense scholastic achievement, as it built new ideas which have developed, broadened and complicated our ideas on decision making. In their own terms, simple-minded search was proving ineffective in the quest for an understanding of observed behaviour, and thus more learning and a more complex model was both needed and provided.

The concepts Cyert and March developed have guided most subsequent organizational decision-making work and have entered the language and consciousness of both academics and practitioners. These developments later led March to wonder, in the introductory chapter of *Decisions and Organizations* (March 1988), whether if scientific progress is measured by simplification, is the subsequent work on decision making stimulated by the original book (Cyert and March 1963) actually a retrogression? Decision-making research has certainly moved towards the recognition that rationality is limited, conflicts do occur and search is simple-minded, and away from the simple view of a world populated by rational economic actors. Both economic and behavioural theories have benefited from the work done in this tradition by scholars throughout the world. In many respects the early work of Cyert and March set the standard and direction of that enquiry.

3 Conclusions

In some way a conclusion is neither necessary or particularly appropriate, as further work to understand the complex modern organization proceeds apace. March has continued to work on and develop these ideas throughout his professional career, and will no doubt go on even though he has officially retired.

GEOFF MALLORY
SCHOOL OF MANAGEMENT
THE OPEN UNIVERSITY

Further reading

(References cited in the text marked *)

* Cohen, M.D., March, J.G. and Olsen, J.P. (1972) 'A garbage can model of organizational choice', *Administrative Science Quarterly* 17: 1–25. (Outlines the development of a model of choice in organized anarchies, that is, organizations in which preferences are problematic, the technology is unclear and participation in decision making is fluid.)

* Cyert, R.M. and March, J.G. (1963) *A Behavioral Theory of the Firm*, New York: Prentice Hall. (Leading work on organization behaviour, discussed at length in the body of this entry.)

* Cyert, R.M. and March, J.G. (1992) *A Behavioral Theory of the Firm*, 2nd edn, New York: Prentice Hall. (Updated edition of Cyert and March (1963), the contents of which are also discussed at length in the body of the entry.)

* March, J.G. (1988) *Decisions and Organizations*, Oxford: Blackwell. (A collection of March's publications with various co-authors, including Cyert. The introduction succinctly sets out the development of a whole series of ideas on decision making.)

March, J.G. and Olsen, J.P. (1976) *Ambiguity and Choice in Organizations*, Bergen: Universitetsfrlaget. (A collection of selected readings reflecting work done in Scandinavia and elsewhere.)

March, J.G. and Olsen, J.P. (1989) *Rediscovering Institutions: The Organizational Basis of Politics*, New York: The Free Press. (A collection of previously published and original work which builds on the notion that political institutions determine the context of political action. It examines how they function, how they affect politics and how they might be improved.)

See also: LAWRENCE, P.R. AND LORSCH, J.W.; SIMON, H.A.

Related topics in the IEBM: BUSINESS ECONOMICS; DECISION MAKING; OCCUPATIONAL PSYCHOLOGY; ORGANIZATION BEHAVIOUR; ORGANIZATION BEHAVIOUR, HISTORY OF; ORGANIZATIONAL LEARNING

Marshall, Alfred (1842–1924)

Personal background

- born 26 July 1842 in London
- educated at Merchant Taylors' School and entered St John's College, Cambridge University, in 1862 to prepare for the mathematical tripos
- 'Second Wrangler' in 1865 and elected fellow of his college
- appointed in 1868 as college lecturer in moral science at St John's
- by 1870 adopted economics as his life's work
- married Mary Paley (1850–1944) in 1877, forcing him to resign his fellowship
- moved to the new University College at Bristol and in 1883 moved to Balliol College, Oxford
- professor of political economy at Cambridge University, 1885–1908
- *Principles of Economics* published in 1890
- voluntary retirement in 1908, bringing a last opportunity for sustained literary work
- died 13 July 1924 at Balliol Croft, his Cambridge home of many years

Major works

Economics of Industry (with M.P. Marshall) (1879)
Principles of Economics (1890)
Industry and Trade (1919)
Money, Credit and Commerce (1923)

Summary

Alfred Marshall was the effective founder of the Cambridge School of Economics which rose to worldwide prominence in the interwar years. His *Principles of Economics* (1890) exercised considerable influence on the development of economics, especially in English-speaking countries, and popularized tools still important in the working economist's toolbox. Marshall was an inspiring teacher, his most prominent students being John Maynard Keynes (1883–1946), the most famous economist of the twentieth century, and Arthur Cecil Pigou (1877–1959), pioneer of welfare economics, who was to succeed Marshall as professor at Cambridge. Among the leading economists of his era, Marshall was notable for his strong interest in industrial and labour questions and his persistent attempts to familiarize himself with the realities of business life and the concerns of labour. The new degree course in economics and related studies adopted at Cambridge in 1903 at Marshall's urging was an early attempt to provide for management education in conjunction with the training of economists. Marshall's *Industry and Trade* (1919) contains his most detailed and realistic discussion of business organization and management.

1 Biographical data

Marshall, whose father was an employee of the Bank of England, was born and spent his formative years in London. Educated at the venerable Merchant Taylors' School, he entered St John's College, Cambridge, in 1862 to prepare for Cambridge University's prestigious mathematical tripos. Emerging in the elevated position of 'Second Wrangler' in 1865, he was soon elected fellow of his college. Leaving mathematics and physical science behind, he embarked upon an intensive exploration of the moral and philosophical bases of human behaviour and society. Appointed in 1868 as college lecturer in moral science at St John's, he rapidly concentrated on economics which he had by 1870 adopted as his life's work. He soon established himself as Cambridge's leading teacher of the subject, but published little.

Marriage in 1877 to Mary Paley (1850–1944), an early student at what was to become Newnham College, forced Marshall to resign his fellowship. He left Cambridge for the new University College at Bristol, where illness soon restricted his activities, inducing chronic valetudinairianism, and in 1883 moved to Balliol College, Oxford. However, the unexpected death of the previous incumbent brought Marshall back to Cambridge at the beginning of 1885 as professor of political economy. He held this chair until his voluntary retirement in 1908. The appearance of *Principles of Economics* in 1890 augmented notably his published output and cemented his international reputation and his standing as the UK's leading economist.

The years of professorship were onerous, with heavy teaching responsibilities, taken seriously, and substantial public service. Marshall struggled persistently, and not always diplomatically, to increase the provisions and resources for his subject within the university and to attract students capable of advancing economic science. The institution of the new economics tripos in 1903 secured growing room for his subject and planted the seed from which the Cambridge School was to develop, but resources and students continued to be scarce until after his retirement. Retirement brought a last opportunity for the sustained literary work that the busy years after 1890 had precluded, and Marshall's long labours were eventually, if incompletely, rewarded by the appearance of *Industry and Trade* in 1919 and *Money, Credit and Commerce* in 1923. He died in 1924 at Balliol Croft, his Cambridge home of many years.

2 Background to Marshall's economics

Economics in 1870 was settled into a rather quiescent state, still dominated in the UK by the ideas of the classical economists, especially John Stuart Mill (1806–73) (see MILL, J.S.). But stirrings of change were evident. The publication in 1871 of the *Theory of Political Economy* by William Stanley Jevons (1835–82) was a notable harbinger of the coming 'neo-classical revolution', an approach which was to emphasize demand, optimizing behaviour and mathematical formalization, while continuing the deductive tradition of the classical school. This tradition itself was under attack, especially in Germany, by an increasingly aggressive historical school, emphasizing induction and case studies. More generally, Darwinian ideas were challenging traditional certainties in fundamental ways and social concern with the plight of the poor was rising.

Marshall was strongly influenced by this intellectual milieu. Although prone later to exaggerate his subjective originality, it is clear that he did independently develop some key ideas of neo-classical economics. But he was always to remain critical of extended deduction based on extreme formalization, urging that deduction be guided by a close observation of history and context and make full allowance for non-quantitative aspects. He could follow the historical school only so far, emphasizing that observation without a guiding analytical framework could yield no knowledge of causes.

Influenced by Darwinian ideas, and especially the views of Herbert Spencer (1820–1903), Marshall placed considerable emphasis on the evolution of human character. Traits were seen as strongly dependent upon an individual's environment and upbringing. The improvement of humankind was to Marshall a more important aspect of economic growth than was humankind's increased command over nature, although the latter was to some extent a precondition for the former. Concern over those in poverty, over the enlightenment of the working classes, and over threats to the UK's continued economic progress from developments abroad and misguided policies at home, all underlay Marshall's strong desire to make economics relevant to practical concerns. While recognizing that economists as such had no special authority to speak on normative matters, he was not always careful to observe the positive–normative distinction. For him, economic issues and ethical concerns were intricately interrelated.

3 Early work and *Principles of Economics*

Marshall largely completed in the 1870s a book on foreign trade and protection but eventually chose not to publish it, although some of its theoretical appendices were printed for private circulation in 1879 as the *Pure Theory of Foreign Trade* and the *Pure Theory of Domestic Values*. These remarkable pieces, although not widely circulated, were sufficiently impressive to mark him as a major economic theorist. The year 1879 also saw the publication of *Economics of Industry* written by Marshall and his wife. Ostensibly an introductory textbook, this put forward a theory of factor pricing and income distribution along marginal-productivity lines which helps justify Marshall's claim to objective as well as subjective originality in the development of the marginalist neo-classical programme. This theory together with the *Pure Theory of Domestic Values* was the core from which Marshall developed his *Principles of Economics*, composition of which began in 1881. The 1880s also saw a steady flow of occasional publications and his important monetary evidence to the Gold and Silver Commission, 1887–8.

Upon its appearance in 1890, *Principles* was widely acknowledged as an important addition to the literature of economics. Its impact came not so much from the theoretical advances it embodied, although there were some, as from its breadth and humanity of outlook and its weaving of the new ideas developed since 1870 into a larger tapestry, preserving what was best in the classical tradition (and in the process exaggerating

somewhat the extent of continuity) while acknowledging to a degree the claims of historicism and evolutionism.

On a theoretical level, *Principles* is most noteworthy for its reliance on what has come to be termed a partial-equilibrium approach. This involves the analysis of interactions within a single market on the approximative assumption that surrounding circumstances are unaffected by what happens there. This approach sacrifices theoretical precision for ready applicability and remains prominent in applied economics. An extension of the partial-equilibrium approach is found in Marshall's period analysis, which analyses market equilibrium by ignoring those forces within the market that move slowly, or average out rapidly, compared with the length of the period whose ruling circumstances are to be explained. Associated with this period analysis is Marshall's concept of quasi-rent: the income of any productive factor in fixed supply for the length of period being considered can be regarded as a rent, determined by price rather than price determining. But this residual character of the factor return may not be preserved for longer periods. For sufficiently long periods, any payments necessary to maintain supply of the factor intact become price determining. Only if factor supply is truly exogenous (the Ricardian case) is the factor return always a pure rent.

Marshall's treatment of consumer demand for a commodity relied heavily on the assumption that the commodity was a negligible element in expenditure. His popularization and refinement of the consumer surplus concept relied on a similar condition. The powerful application of this concept to problems of welfare economics under both competition and monopoly was an important feature of his work.

In analysing supply conditions for a manufactured product, Marshall laid stress on scale economies and imperfect competition. The latter presumed that each firm must establish a particular clientele and supply network whose gradual acquisition is a form of investment, embodied in 'good will'. Rapid increase in sales would thus be difficult, necessitating large price reductions. Hence, rapid exploitation of internal economies of scale would be precluded, while over long periods a management life cycle would diminish entrepreneurial drive and eventually terminate the business. This economics of the mid-Victorian family business could not accommodate satisfactorily the rise of the modern corporation. Although suggestive of later developments in imperfect competition theory, it has failed the survival test. On the other hand, the adjunct notion of external economies due to increased subdivision of function and osmosis of expertise as the *industry's* output increases has remained seminal, if elusive.

Principles closed with an extended discussion of income distribution among productive factors. Here a more aggregative approach was adopted. National income was viewed as the joint product of all factors, each of which received its marginal product. Marshall integrated a neo-classical marginal productivity approach to factor demand with a treatment of factor supply on classical lines. The economy-of-high-wages idea that increased wages might boost worker productivity and efficiency (partly through better diet and living conditions and eventually through broadened horizons and greater opportunities for self-improvement) was a prominent and complicating aspect of his presentation.

Marshall – always sensitive to criticism – spent much time and effort in revising the eight editions of *Principles* appearing in his lifetime, especially the first five. The substance of his views does not seem to have altered, however. He also worked for over a decade on a planned second volume to deal with money, foreign trade, industry, labour, government, and so on, a project eventually abandoned as unmanageable. In the sixth edition of 1910 the appellation 'Volume One' was replaced by 'An Introductory Volume'.

4 Industry and Trade

At the height of the tariff controversy in the UK in 1903 Marshall commenced a short book on the issue of the day. Its scope soon grew into a major study of national industries

in relation to international trade, treating industrial, labour market and commercial developments and policies in the UK, France, Germany, the USA, etc. as the source of changes in international trade. When *Industry and Trade* at last appeared in 1919 it was an imperfect realization of this grandiose plan, while *Money, Credit and Commerce* of 1923 was less a continuation than an attempt to rescue early work that should have been developed in the abandoned second volume of *Principles*.

Despite a failure to apply to international trade the studies of national industry, and despite a selective consideration of individual industries, *Industry and Trade* remains a rich source of information and insight into managerial and commercial policies and possibilities for government guidance. The book's analytical focus is not on atomistic competition or entrenched monopoly (the cases dealt with in *Principles*) but on group action by trusts, pools, organized labour, etc. and on monopolies that are 'conditional' and subject to the ever-present threat of entry. The lack of a clear theoretical skeleton has caused the book to be slighted by economists, but it offers much of interest to students of management and business practice as well as to business historians.

5 Beyond the academy

Marshall strove persistently to glean first-hand knowledge of economic reality, visiting factories and working-class quarters. He spent the summer of 1876 in the USA studying the realities of protectionism. He was also an avid reader of factual economic literature and studies. He took every opportunity to question those from other walks of life who crossed his path or stayed with him in Cambridge. Despite this curiosity, he was hardly an extroverted man-of-the-world, and a lack of robustness served to narrow further the circle of his acquaintances and contacts outside Cambridge.

Before 1890 his outside contacts seem to have been mainly with trade unionists, cooperators and social reformers. Service on the Royal Commission on Labour, 1891–4, together with the rise of militant 'new union-ism', appears to have dampened his enthusi-asm for labour movements. Increasingly, the enterprising and chivalrous captain of indus-try, fearlessly pioneering new paths and driven by the desire for constructive achieve-ment rather than mere wealth, became the he-roic figure in Marshall's world view – a figure threatened by the dragons of government con-trol and the sirens of enervating protection-ism. It is doubtful whether this figure was drawn fully from life. Marshall's acquain-tance with leading businessmen seems to have been slight. Charles Booth (1840–1916), shi-powner, is perhaps an exception, but the link here was Booth's pioneering studies of Lon-don poverty. Sir David Dale (1829–1906), ironmaster and a fellow member of the Labour Commission, was someone Marshall knew and admired, and the years in Bristol had ac-quainted him with a few local businessmen active in the affairs of the local college. But the letters secured from businessmen and other public figures to support Marshall's 1903 campaign for a new economics tripos in Cambridge suggest that the circle of his busi-ness acquaintances remained small. His views of the business world combined penetration and acuteness with an element of naivety.

The new economics tripos, although pri-marily designed to train economists, promised relevant alternatives for those intending to en-ter the higher ranks of business. Marshall's goal here was to provide a broad, flexible and knowledgeable outlook rather than a technical command of current business practice. His hopes in this direction were hardly met, but they did help garner outside support to counter Cambridge's curricular conservatism.

JOHN K. WHITAKER
UNIVERSITY OF VIRGINIA

Further reading

(References cited in the text marked *)

Groenewegen, p. (1996) *A Soaring Eagle: Alfred Marshall 1942–1924*, Aldershot: Edward El-gar. (A full-scale biography.)

Guillebaud, C.W. (ed.) (1961) *Alfred Marshall's Principles of Economics*, 9th (variorum) edn, 2 vols, London: Macmillan. (The first volume re-prints the eighth edition of this book; the second provides variant passages from earlier editions and supporting documents.)

* Jevons, W.S. (1871) *The Theory of Political Econ-omy*, London: Macmillan. (Pioneering work in neo-classical economics.)

Keynes, J.M. (ed.) (1926) *Official Papers of Alfred Marshall*, London: Macmillan. (Reproduces Marshall's important evidence to government enquiries.)

McWilliams Tullberg, R. (1990) *Alfred Marshall in Retrospect*, Aldershot: Edward Elgar. (Es-says on Marshall's work and life by various authors, including 'Marshall on business' by J. Maloney.)

* Marshall, A. (1890) *Principles of Economics*, Lon-don: Macmillan. (First edition of his magnum opus, in which Marshall expounds his theories of value and distribution. Revised editions in 1891, 1895, 1898, 1907, 1919, 1916 and 1920.)

* Marshall, A. (1919) *Industry and Trade*, London: Macmillan. (A major treatment of applied eco-nomics and business history from a cosmopoli-tan perspective.)

* Marshall, A. (1923) *Money, Credit and Com-merce*, London: Macmillan. (Expounds his theories of money and international trade.)

* Marshall, A. and Marshall, M.P. (1879) *Economics of Industry*, London: Macmillan. (First general statement of Marshall's theories of value and distribution, disguised as an elementary text-book.)

O'Brien, D.P. (1981) 'Alfred Marshall, 1842–1924', in D.P. O'Brien and J.R. Presley (eds), *Pioneers of Modern Economics in Brit-ain*, London: Macmillan. (A scholarly survey of Marshall's work.)

Pigou, A.C. (ed.) (1925) *Memorials of Alfred Mar-shall*, London: Macmillan. (Reproduces many of Marshall's occasional writings and some correspondence; prefaced by J.M. Keynes' re-markable memoir.)

Whitaker, J.K. (ed.) (1975) *Early Economic Writ-ings of Alfred Marshall, 1867–1890*, London: Macmillan. (Reproduces with commentary Marshall's early manuscripts, including the *Pure Theory* pieces.)

Whitaker, J.K. (1987) 'Alfred Marshall (1842–1924)', in J. Eatwell, M. Milgate and P. Newman (eds), *The New Palgrave: A Diction-ary of Economics*, London: Macmillan. (An ex-tended review and assessment with a comprehensive bibliography.)

Whitaker, J.K. (ed.) (1990) *Centenary Essays on Alfred Marshall*, Cambridge: Cambridge

University Press. (Essays by different authors on various aspects of Marshall's work and life.)

Whitaker, J.K. (ed.) (1996) *The Correspondence of Alfred Marshall, Economist*, 3 vols, Cambridge: Cambridge University Press. (A comprehensive edition of Marshall's correspondence.)

See also: KEYNES, J.M.; MILL, J.S.

Related topics in the IEBM: CONSUMER BEHAVIOUR; INDUSTRIAL ECONOMICS; INTERNATIONAL TRADE AND FOREIGN DIRECT INVESTMENT; NEO-CLASSICAL ECONOMICS; RICARDO, D.

Maslow, Abraham H. (1908–70)

Personal background

- born Brooklyn, New York 1 April 1908
- trained as behavioural psychologist, specializing initially in primate social behaviour
- professor of social psychology at Brandeis University and president of the American Psychological Association (1967–8); previously taught at Brooklyn College and the Western Behavioural Sciences Institute
- developed the theory of a 'hierarchy of needs'
- was a formative influence on the development of motivation theory
- died 8 June 1970

Major works

The Principles of Abnormal Psychology (with Bela Mittelman) (1941)
'A theory of human motivation' (1943)
Motivation and Personality (1954)
Towards a Psychology of Being (1962)
Eupsychian Management: A Journal (1965)
The Psychology of Science (1967)
The Farther Reaches of Human Nature (1971)

Summary

Maslow was a formative influence on motivation theory. Through clinical research, he developed an idea whereby human needs could be classified in terms of a hierarchy of five steps: physiological needs, safety needs, social or love needs, ego or self-esteem needs and self-fulfilment or 'self-actualization' needs.

Maslow's ideas took motivation theory beyond the simpler models of scientific management and behaviourist practitioners. He developed a more dynamic model of changing needs and wants, one which gave new emphasis to the role of unconscious motives. From 1943 when the theory was first published, until his death in 1970, Maslow dominated the field of motivation. Many later theories of motivation, such as those of McGregor (1960), Herzberg (1966) and Alderfer (1972), were direct descendants of those of Maslow, and his theory forms the starting point for most subsequent reviews of the subject.

1 Introduction

Maslow's theories arise from a diverse range of influences, including biology, anthropology, clinical psychology and psychoanalysis. The last was perhaps the most enduring. Maslow clearly linked his concept of love needs with the work of Freud (although he saw his work as contradicting several of Freud's main precepts), the concept of self-esteem needs with that of Adler, and the concept of self-actualization (and its implications at the level of society as a whole) with that of Fromm (although his main debt was to Goldstein 1939).

Prior to Maslow, motivation theory took as its starting point the need to satisfy physiological drives such as hunger, sex and thirst. Maslow argued that although these drives or needs could be used as 'channels' for other higher or more complex needs, they were relatively isolated and localized.

Maslow's first crucial insight was that because physiological needs dominated when they were unsatisfied it did not mean that they continued to dominate once they had been satisfied. On the contrary, once satisfied a need continues to exist only potentially, with the emphasis moving ahead to 'higher needs'.

This led to a shift in the focus of motivation theory, from deprivation to gratification. Maslow was influenced by medical research findings of the 1930s concerning homeostasis and also the discovery that human appetites for different foodstuffs could be taken as reliable indicators of actual (unconscious) bodily needs. The logic of this process, whereby the gratification of each successive need served to activate another, drew Maslow inexorably towards the idea with which his name is associated, that of the 'hierarchy of needs'.

2 The hierarchy of needs

Maslow identified five main categories of needs, as follows:

1 *Physiological needs.* These include hunger, thirst, sex (which Maslow distinguished from love or self-esteem) and sleep. Maslow ascribed to these needs greater power than any of the higher needs, but only when deprivation occurs.

2 *Safety needs.* Safety needs present a more complex picture in that there is greater potential for subjectivity. Children, according to Maslow, openly express strong needs for safety and security, needs which are more muted in adults. Neurotic individuals, however, are unable to suspend their fear of potential danger, even when it is remote, and construct elaborate rituals and procedures to limit the uncertainty of their environment.

3 *Social or love needs.* Initially Maslow referred to the third level of needs in terms of love only. Later he broadened the concept to cover what he termed 'social needs'. In his early work, he had demonstrated the close association between the sexual instinct and aggression in primates (Maslow 1971), and he saw love as being based on reciprocal feelings rather than aggression, and analogous to wider social bonding.

4 *Ego or self-esteem needs.* Maslow had researched the effects of a collapse of self-confidence in traumatized individuals, and believed that, in a healthy individual, self-esteem was based on real capacity rather than wishful thinking. Maslow's theory was able to explain why employees who were adequately paid, secure in their positions and with reasonably good social relationships might still be discontented.

5 *Self-actualization or fulfilment needs.* Maslow believed that negative emotions and psychological characteristics were linked to the blocking or distorting of higher qualities, which he saw as an essential and universal feature of human nature. He became increasingly preoccupied with the nature of transcendental or 'peak' experiences, and with whether self-actualization was necessarily a transient phenomenon.

3 Evaluation

Maslow's theory of the hierarchy of needs has long been a standard feature of textbooks, and has suffered through being applied too literally. The theory has attracted increasing criticism over the years, particularly regarding the idea that a need did not act as a motivator until all lower needs had been satisfied. The theory may also be criticized for failing to take individual differences sufficiently into account or to allow for wider organizational, political, social or economic factors.

Some of these later criticisms were allowed for or raised by Maslow himself at the outset. He was aware, for example, that people could deprive themselves in terms of lower needs in order to satisfy higher ones. This he attempted to explain, not entirely convincingly, through the idea that individuals who had traditionally been satisfied in terms of particular needs were more likely to withstand deprivation of these in order to concentrate on higher needs. He accepted the possibility that not all human beings could potentially be motivated by self-fulfilment, or even self-esteem, and believed that sustained deprivation could neutralize the three higher categories of needs.

The most serious criticism, however, is that there has been found no empirical support for the hierarchy of needs model, or of the mechanisms that were claimed to operate between each level of need (see Wahba and Bridwell 1976; Rauschenberger *et al.* 1980).

Maslow's own response to this reflects his holistic concept of psychological science:

> It is fair to say that this theory has been quite successful in a clinical, social and personological way, but not in a laboratory and experimental way. It has fitted very well with the personal experience of most people and has often given them a structured theory that has helped them to make better sense of their inner lives. It seems for most people to have a direct, personal, subjective plausibility. And yet it still lacks experimental verification and support. I have not yet been able to think of a good way to put it to test in the laboratory.
>
> (Maslow 1970: xii)

4 Conclusion

Overall, Maslow's thinking was more subtle, flexible and wide-ranging than the popularized form in which his theory has become famous might suggest. To that extent, his ideas have been a victim of their own success. He almost certainly did not intend to be seen as a purveyor of panaceas for management problems, and probably did not intend either that his theory should be used to solve problems of motivation in a simple categorizing fashion. Maslow loathed simple categories and dichotomies, believing instead in a unified and integrated human nature. His main concern was not with motivation in the organization sense, but with ethical psychology, seeking to find the link between the universality of higher aspirations and values and the prevalence of their opposite in practice.

ADRIAN CAMPBELL
UNIVERSITY OF BIRMINGHAM

Further reading

(References cited in the text marked *)

* Alderfer, C.P. (1972) *Existence Relatedness and Growth: Human Needs in Organizational Settings* New York: The Free Press. (Alderfer moved away from the hierarchy of needs idea, but the categorization of needs is strongly influenced by Maslow.)

* Goldstein, K. (1939) *The Organism*, New York: American Book Company. (The work which first developed the concept of self-actualization, and which was to have a major influence on Maslow's thinking.)

* Herzberg, F. (1966) *Work the Nature of Man*, Cleveland, OH: World Publishing Co. (Herzberg put forward the 'hygiene' factors theory of motivation which develops further Maslow's idea that once a need is met it ceases to count.)

Lee, R. and Lawrence, P. (1991) *Politics at Work*, Cheltenham: Stanley Thornes. (A very useful textbook which provides a detailed overview of motivation theory, contrasting post-Maslow theories with more recent politics-based approaches.)

* McGregor, D. (1960) *The Human Side of Enterprise*, New York: McGraw-Hill. (Maslow's theory of needs and the concept of self-actualization provide the starting point for McGregor's development of his famous 'theory X and theory Y' formulation. Although Maslow in his later writings used the concept of theory Y, he was also critical of McGregor (see Maslow 1965).)

Maslow, A.H. (1943) 'A theory of human motivation', *Psychological Review* 50: 370–96. (The original and most succinct exposition of the hierarchy of needs theory. Reprinted in Vroom, V. and Deci, E. (eds) (1970) *Management and Motivation: Selected Readings*, London: Penguin.)

* Maslow, A.H. ([1954] 1970) *Motivation and Personality*, New York: Harper & Bros. (Maslow's most important work, in which he sets out to integrate into psychological theory the main idea underlying his work on motivation, that 'higher needs' were an essential 'instinctoid' part of human nature and that psychopathologies were the result of thwarting such needs. Closely linked to this was a polemic against a dissecting/dichotomizing approach to psychology. Maslow was insistent that human nature was a unified essence that could only be understood as an integrated whole, not the sum of its parts. In a substantially revised edition of 1970, Maslow noted and celebrated the advance of a more humanistic conception of psychology and human science in general.)

Maslow, A.H. (1962) *Towards a Psychology of Being*, Princeton, NJ: Van Nostrand. (This book provides Maslow's clearest and most detailed statement of his concept of 'psychological health' (the original intended title of the book) and its relationship to psychological illness

(Maslow preferred to use the terms 'growth' and 'diminution or stunting' instead of health and illness). It is argued that the two opposites are closely linked to each other and need to be understood as part of a holistic human nature.)

Maslow, A.H. (1965) *Eupsychian Management: A Journal*, Homewood, IL: Richard D. Irwin and the Dorsey Press. (Part of the journal represents a friendly critique of management theory, notably that of Drucker for being too idealistic. The journal brings out one of the paradoxes of Maslow, his belief in the universality of good or higher intentions and his recognition of the degree to which these will be absent in practice. The journal seeks to define enlightened management practices, and the concern with holistic psychology is evident throughout.)

Maslow, A.H. (1967) *The Psychology of Science: A Reconnaissance*, New York: Harper & Row. (Maslow presents a critique of mechanistic as opposed to humanistic science, and defends his concept of 'personology', the study of the whole person.)

* Maslow, A.H. (1971) *The Farther Reaches of Human Nature*, New York: Viking. (A very useful compilation of Maslow's articles, chosen by the author in 1969 and published after his death; it also contains a full bibliography of Maslow's work. The articles chosen range through all Maslow's themes from humanistic biology through creativity and peak experiences to motivation and education, science and society, being and transcendence. The format brings out the nature of Maslow's work as a whole made up of highly varied by interconnected parts.)

Maslow, A.H. and Mittelman, B. (1941) *The Principles of Abnormal Psychology*, New York: Harper & Row. (An ambitious attempt to create a 'dynamic' psychology. This meant an emphasis on the motivating aspects of psychic states, and how they influence action consciously or unconsciously. The work shows the thinking that underlay aspects of Maslow's motivation theory, and his overall concern with the nature of the relationship between states of mind and

their environment, and between positive and negative states of mind.)

* Rauschenberger, J., Schmitt, N. and Hunter, J. (1980) 'A test of the need hierarchy concept by a Markov model of change in need strength', *Administrative Science Quarterly* (December): 654–70. (Report of a study testing the idea that needs trigger a higher need as they become satisfied. The study found no basis for Maslow's idea.)

Robbins, S. (1989) *Organizational Behaviour: Concepts, Controversies and Applications*, 4th edn, Englewood Cliffs, NJ: Prentice Hall. (Chapter 6 provides a very useful and concise review of the motivation theories of Maslow and his successors, and a summary of the criticism that may be made of them.)

Rose, M. (1978) *Industrial Behaviour: Theoretical Development Since Taylor*, London: Penguin. (Chapter 19 provides a well-researched and well-argued critique of Maslow's successors (Likert, McGregor, Herzberg, Argyris). In particular, the latter are seen to ignore Maslow's own reservations about the universal applicability of the hierarchy of needs model.)

* Wahba. M. and Bridwell, L. (1976) 'Maslow reconsidered: a review of research on the need hierarchy theory', *Organizational Behaviour and Human Performance* (April): 212–40. (A very useful and thorough review detailing the degree to which the key concepts of Maslow's theory lack empirical support.)

See also: ARGYRIS, C.; HERZBERG, F; MCLELLAND, D..

Related topics in the IEBM: COMMITMENT IN JAPAN; FREUD, S.; GROUPS AND TEAMS; MOTIVATION AND SATISFACTION; OCCUPATIONAL PSYCHOLOGY; ORGANIZATION BEHAVIOUR; ORGANIZATION BEHAVIOUR, HISTORY OF; ORGANIZATIONAL LEARNING

Matsushita, Konosuke (1894–1989)

Personal background

- born 27 November 1894 in Japan at Aza Sendanno-ki, Wasamura, Kaiso-gun, Wakayama Prefecture into an impoverished farm family
- father lost home and farmlands in rice market speculation, 1899
- left school, aged 9, to take an apprenticeship in a *hibachi* (charcoal grill) shop
- joined Osaka Electric Light company as an interior wiring assistant in 1910
- opened a small electrical fixture shop in Osaka in 1918
- invented bullet-shaped, battery-operated bicycle lamps in 1923
- his home electrical appliance plant becomes the Matsushita Electrical Industrial Company, 1932
- founded Peace and Happiness through Prosperity (PHP) Institute, 1946
- first visits to the USA and Europe in 1951
- established contractual ties with Philips, 1952
- resigned as chairman of Matsushita Electric in 1973 and took up post of executive advisor
- died of pneumonia, aged 94, on 27 April 1989

Major works

Quest for Prosperity: The Life of a Japanese Industrialist (1988)

Summary

Konosuke Matsushita (1894–1989) is famed for two major contributions to the

development of Japanese business and management – for the founding, development and direction of Matsushita Denki Sangyo (Matsushita Electric Industrial Company), which has become one of the world's largest consumer electronics companies, and for a stream of writings and reflections which contributed to philosophies of management. His business career had relatively humble beginnings in inter-war Japan, but blossomed in the postwar recovery, and Matsushita Electric Company's market shares in 'the three treasures' (washing machines, refrigerators and television) made it synonymous with the mass production, mass consumption and rising living standards of Japan's high-growth years. Konosuke Matsushita was closely identified with many of the features of business organization and management which underpinned this prosperity and he championed a humanistic philosophy of business and management in his writings and practice. Thus he is widely seen as the patriarch of the Japanese consumer electronics industry and a 'god of business management'.

I Biographical data

Konosuke Matsushita was born in Wakayama Prefecture in 1894, the youngest of three boys and five girls in a comfortable landlord family which drew its income from tenant farmers. His carefree early childhood was interrupted by loss of the family farmlands and home after his father's unsuccessful speculation on the rice market in 1898. The move to a cramped town apartment and the family vulnerabilities and vicissitudes were compounded by the young Matsushita's own frail health and the deaths of the three oldest children (including the two brothers) by 1901 from infectious ailments. So, at the age of 9, Konosuke Matsushita left school and boarded a train to take an apprenticeship in a *hibachi* (charcoal stove) maker's shop, followed by an apprenticeship in a newly fashionable bicycle shop, which introduced him to lathes and repair work. At the age of 15, the fascination of electricity, seen in the trains of Osaka, beckoned him to join the Osaka Electric Light Company as a wiring assistant.

Still troubled by his own poor health but emboldened by his promotion to inspector, the 23-year-old Matsushita decided to form his own business, the Matsushita Electric Company, which manufactured electric sockets. In 1918, he started a business manufacturing electrical fixtures in a two-room apartment with less than ¥100 capital. In the early 1920s, he diversified his activities by developing a new battery-powered bicycle lamp to replace the candle lamps which had been vulnerable to even the slightest winds.

During the depression of 1929 stock lay unsold in warehouses, but the company weathered the storm when Matsushita determined that he would not lay off employees but allow them to work half time on full pay, and urge employees, relatives and friends to sell the company's goods (Matsushita 1984: 129). Despite recession, the company made steady progress and Matsushita selected 5 May (Boys' Day) 1932 as the official founding day to re-launch the company with its corporate mission to society. The fifth day of the fifth month had historic significance as one of the traditional seasonal festivals in the 'Tokugawa period' (1600-1868) and usually celebrated as 'boys' day' until it was designated children's day in 1948. As 'boys' day', it was customary to hang long streamers from house poles depicting the carp to celebrate the courage and bravery of the fish in its swim (and the courage of young males in life). Thus, it seemed an auspicious day to launch the new beginning for the Matsushita Electric company. The company song 'Ai to Hikari to Yume de' (With Love and Light and Dream), introduced in 1933, was another of Matsushita's innovations designed to build the corporate spirit of the company.

As the militarist governments took direct control over the economy in the late 1930s, the Matsushita Electric Company was increasingly mobilized for state purposes and drawn into war production. While Konosuke Matsushita later commented that companies had little option but to comply at the time, the company's commitment reaped the advantages of domestic prosperity and the widening markets in Korea, Taiwan and Manchuria.

The end of the Second World War marked a bleak period for Matsushita and his company. His earlier involvement in industrial production earned the family a citation as a *zaibatsu* family and the company was marked for dissolution. The *zaibatsu* were financial and industrial combines that operated as units under the control of families through holding companies used as the command centres for the group. They limited shareholding, controlled the appointment of officers and used a variety of additional measures to maintain control. Because they came to assume a dominant position in the Japanese economy after the turn of the century, the US Occupation authorities determined that the *zaibatsu* should be dissolved to democratize the economy and prevent the re-emergence of Japanese militarism. Yet in the middle of the turbulence of a wage demand pursued vigorously by the company union, the union and employees paused to deliver 15,000 signatures on a petition to 'save the linchpin' of the company. Surprised to learn that this was a labour union petition to retain and not remove a company president, the administration relented. The family was removed from the list, Konosuke Matsushita remained head of the enterprise, and the company was not broken down.

Finally freed from Allied Occupation restrictions, Matsushita made visits to the USA and Europe in 1951 and determined that the USA would become a major market for the company. But Matsushita personally selected the European company, Philips, for close links and technology licence arrangements in 1952. By 1953, the company was proving its product lines in Japan with the successful introduction of washing machines, televisions and refrigerators, with vacuum cleaners added in 1954. By 1957, the company had moved into high-quality FM radio receivers and developed a colour television receiver in 1958. Successful domestic sales provided a springboard for an ambitious international strategy, independent from the trading companies which dominated the trading system in Japan. Matsushita was one of the first companies to take advantage of low labour costs and stable dollar relations for overseas production in the less-developed countries of East Asia.

The 1970s were marked by the battle between JVC (in which Matsushita had a 50 per cent shareholding since the early 1950s) and its allies against Sony over the standard for the video cassette recorder (VCR). Matsushita had been developing a system, but on hearing of a superior 'VHS' system being developed in JVC, Akio Tanii (Head of Matsushita VCR development) argued for a delay in order to refine the JVC VHS system. This delay in launching a Matsushita company product until it could be based on the new JVC VHS system meant that Sony, determined not to share its technology, could enjoy a one-year monopoly in the market for its 'Betamax' system. Yet Konosuke Matsushita argued rightly that Sony had insufficient production capacity and the JVC-Matsushita allies were able to enter the marketplace and establish VHS as the industry standard through their production and marketing strengths.

Konosuke Matsushita remained head of the company until 1973 when he retired from direct management, but he retained considerable influence as a special adviser. He devoted much of his time in retirement to writing on business philosophy. He died in 1989 aged 94. His estate was recorded at ¥244.9 billion, the highest figure in Japan's history (Rafferty 1995: 186).

2 Main contribution

Matsushita learned from the biography of Henry Ford the importance of broadening demand by mass production and lowering the product price (Matsushita 1984: 21) (see FORD, H.). Within his company, he broadened and developed the mass-production ideas into strategies which became the epitome of Japanese management. Yet to achieve this position, Matsushita had to adopt and develop many novel business practices unfamiliar to the traditions of the larger companies such as the *zaibatsu* and trading companies.

He set the company in its place in society with a quasi-religious mission: 'The real mission of Matsushita Electric is to produce an inexhaustible supply of goods, thus creating peace and prosperity throughout the land' (Matsushita 1984: 22). His promotion of a 'good fit' between company strategy and structure and the culture of the wider society have attracted much admiration (Pascale and Athos 1982). In the midst of the uncertainties of 1946, Matsushita established the Peace and Happiness through Prosperity (PHP) Institute, as a response to the war. Later, it became a vehicle for publishing his homilies on management and for training. In 1980, he added the Matsushita School of Government and Management, the aim of which was to develop leaders for Japan in the 1980s and 1990s.

In 1933, The Matsushita Electric Company was among the pioneers in adopting a divisional management structure in order to clarify the achievements and responsibilities of the various divisions and in order to give a better idea of company strengths and weaknesses (Matsushita 1988: 223–4; Suzuki 1991: 305–8). The centrifugal tendencies of divisionalization were countered by linking methods in successive programmes of divisionalization (Pascale and Athos 1982: 33). Further innovatory organizational features in a Japanese company were the five-year business plan and profit centres, both introduced by Matsushita.

Matsushita set great store by effective distribution, going directly to retailers to create a strong system of single-channel retail outlets, and reinforcing relationships with trade financing (Pascale and Athos 1982: 30). Success in this field enabled the increase in market shares which financed the cost cutting and the virtuous circle of a consumer goods company aiming at mass consumption through mass production.

Eager to re-establish the company as quickly as possible after the relaxation of constraints, Matsushita was an early adopter of assembly line production, which he observed in Toyota's car production in 1951–2 (Matsushita 1992: 146–7). He directed his managers to visit Toyota and learn from their practice (see TOYODA FAMILY).

The advantages of 'just-in-time' production and low stock holdings were borne in on Konosuke Matsushita when he reviewed the level of losses through excess stockholding in company plants after a large earthquake struck Niigata on the Sea of Japan coast in 1964 (Matsushita 1984: 98–9). Yet Matsushita himself had already developed an important ingredient of the just-in-time system in the 1930s by building strong relations with suppliers, surprising suppliers with visits and advice to secure the cost-cutting which Matsushita sought.

Good industrial relations were an important feature stressed and secured by Matsushita. His determination to maintain stable employment in the depression and the support of the company union against the occupation directives were two examples of the rapport with employees. The Matsushita enterprise union was one of the biggest members of the industrial union federation, the Japanese Federation of Electrical Machine Workers' Unions (*Denki Roren*). The Federation has supported the Social Democratic Party. Through these links, Matsushita was able to sustain a cooperative rather than a conflictual model of union-management relations. Against the background of declining unionism in most industrial countries, Matsushita still supported labour unions and thought that the Japanese enterprise union could serve as a model in developing countries (Matsushita 1989: 76–8; Whitehill 1991: 247–8).

The successful battle with Sony over the VHS standard demonstrated the importance of a comprehensive approach to innovation and the need to ally technical virtuosity to marketing and production strengths.

3 Evaluation

As a major industrialist featuring in Japan's post-war economic success, Matsushita promoted many of the features of organization and management now thought to be distinctive of Japanese business. Moreover, he added a philosophy of business which emphasized the interdependence of the various stakeholders in the enterprise – customers, employees and suppliers.

Matsushita's character revealed in his home-spun writings has been likened to that of 'a kindly, but elderly clergyman of the conservative school' (Rafferty 1995: 187). He conceded that he made little mention of his wife and family in his writings, but asked for his readers' understanding as he was a man of the nineteenth century (Matsushita 1988: ix).

Konosuke Matsushita founded and developed a major company in spite of his lack of family connections and advantages. It has grown from his small workshop into a giant multinational corporate group with over 200,000 employees, more than 100 subsidiaries and plants, and aggregate annual sales of US$35 billion. Despite a lack of formal education, he both managed the company and was an influence on a much wider audience through his writings: these were remarkable achievements. Today, the debate is whether the framework which he built has become a cage inhibiting further development and whether the company can adapt to changing business conditions in the 1990s. Throughout the long years under his personal direction the company built a reputation based on following the technical innovations of rivals with superior production engineering and marketing. The relatively low level of research and development (R&D) spending has raised questions about the company's ability to secure the more creative individuals and relationships thought necessary for the 1990s.

4 Conclusion

In the mid-1980s, Tanii, the new president, concluded that the traditional consumer electronics markets were saturated. He urged entry into new markets, but feared difficulties in attracting the most able engineers to advance the company's R&D effort, and complained that the company's 600 subsidiaries and group companies were weakly harnessed to pull in the new directions. One signal policy revision was directed toward achieving a new relationship with the network of 25,000 corner stores, which had served Matsushita well in the past but were now threatened by discount stores. However, Tanii resigned in 1993, taking responsibility for increasing difficulties such as widely publicized refrigerator faults, a financial scandal and sluggish company performance. Underlying these difficulties were problematic relations with the Matsushita family and Tanii's attempt to fashion a new style and structure for the company. Chairman Masaharu Matsushita, son-in-law of the founder, was a strong critic of the scheme (Rafferty 1995: 189). The new president, Morishita, abandoned the Tanii plans and put in place new proposals to renew the company, taking care to show the continuities with Konosuke Matsushita:

> Our basic philosophy of the company inherited from our founder has not changed at all. We must contribute to society and contribute to the well-being of people, and this is immutable and we will follow it eternally. But our founder was a very flexible person, very innovative. I shall be as innovative as he was. Times are changing and the society and economy are changing rapidly, so we must change to meet new challenges.
>
> (Rafferty 1995: 202)

KEVIN MCCORMICK
UNIVERSITY OF SUSSEX

Further reading

(References cited in the text marked *)

Gould, R. (1970) *The Matsushita Phenomenon*, Tokyo: Diamond Sha (The Diamond Publishing Company). (This study attempts to explain the success of the Matsushita Electric Industrial Company through an examination of the influence of Konosuke Matsushita's personal business philosophy and rested on secondary materials and interviews with Konosuke Matsushita.)

Kono, T. (1984) *Strategy and Structure of Japanese Enterprises*, London: Macmillan. (This study gives a view of similarities and differences among some of the major Japanese companies in their development of strategy and structure.)

* Matsushita, K. (1984) *Not for Bread Alone: A Business Ethos, a Management Ethic*, Tokyo: PHP Institute. (This volume draws on four books written in Japanese by Konosuke Matsushita between 1973 and 1980. It contains the short essays 'Earthquake shakeup' and 'Clear the warehouses'.)

* Matsushita, K. (1988) *Quest for Prosperity: The Life of a Japanese Industrialist*, Tokyo: PHP Institute.

* Matsushita, K. (1989) *As I See It*, Tokyo: PHP Institute. (This collection of fifty-six essays comes from Matsushita's column in the monthly magazine *PHP Intersect* over the years 1985 to 1989. They include 'Labour and management: Yin and Yang', a 1988 essay in which he praised labour unions and their enterprise form.)

Matsushita, K. (1991) *Velvet Glove: Iron Fist*, Tokyo: PHP Institute. (Originally published in Japanese in 1973 as *Shidosha no Joken: Jinshin no myomi ni omou* (Prerequisites of Leadership: The Secrets of Charisma).)

* Matsushita, K. (1992) *People Before Products*, Tokyo: PHP Institute. (Contains material from two books written in Japanese, *Jinjimagekyo: watashi no mikata sodatekata* (My approach to Personnel Management) and *Oriori no ki-Jinsey de deatta hitotachi* (Accounts of Memorable Encounters).)

Matsushita, K. (1993) *A Piece of the Action*, Tokyo: PHP Institute. (This volume is based on *Shain kokoroecho* (Precepts for Employees) (1981) and *Jinsei kokoroecho* (Precepts of Life) (1984).)

* Pascale, R. T. and Athos, A. G. (1982) *The Art of Japanese Management*, Harmondsworth: Penguin. (This study looks closely at the management system – strategy, organizational structure, financial controls, etc. – in the Matsushita Electric Company.)

* Rafferty, K. I. (1995) *Inside Japan's Power Houses: The Culture, Mystique and Future of Japan's Greatest Corporations*, London: Weidenfeld & Nicolson. (This volume reviews the history and future prospects of several major Japanese corporations including the Matsushita Electric Company.)

* Suzuki, Y. (1991) *Japanese Management Structures, 1920–80*, Basingstoke: Macmillan. (This book examines the organization structure of the 100 largest Japanese industrial companies over the period since 1920, and includes Matsushita.)

* Whitehill, A. (1991) *Japanese Management: Tradition and Transition*, London: Routledge. (This overview of Japanese management provides a context for studying aspects of Mat-

sushita's contributions to the development of his company and management in Japan.)

See also: FORD, H.; KOTTER, J.; MORITA, A.; OHNO, T.; SHINGO, S.; TOYODA FAMILY

Related topics in the IEBM: BUSINESS HISTORY, JAPANESE; ECONOMY OF JAPAN; GLOBALIZATION; INDUSTRIAL RELATIONS IN JAPAN; JAPANIZATION; JUST-IN-TIME PHILOSOPHIES; MANAGEMENT EDUCATION IN JAPAN; MANAGEMENT IN JAPAN; TOTAL QUALITY MANAGEMENT; *ZAIBATSU* (*KEIRETSU*)

Mayo, George Elton (1880–1949)

1 Main contribution
2 Evaluation
3 Conclusion

Personal background

- born 26 December 1880, Adelaide, Australia
- studied philosophy and psychology at the University of Adelaide
- lecturer and later professor of philosophy and psychology, University of Queensland, Australia, 1911–23
- married Dorothea McConnel, 1913
- conducted research programme in industrial psychiatry at the University of Pennsylvania, 1923–6
- appointed to a research position at Harvard Business School, 1926
- commenced involvement in Hawthorne experiments, 1928
- developed human relations theory of management
- conducted research on human relations in wartime industries during the Second World War
- retired and moved to England to write and continue consulting work, 1947
- died 1 September 1949, Guildford, England

Major works

The Human Problems of an Industrial Civilization (1933)
The Social Problems of an Industrial Civilization (1945)

Summary

Elton Mayo sought to apply the insights of psychiatry and the social sciences to the organization of work and to management practice. He criticized engineers and management theorists, such as F.W. Taylor, for focusing solely on the technical organization of work and for believing that workers were solely motivated by economic incentives. Using the findings of the Hawthorne experiments, in which he was the pivotal figure, Mayo argued that managers needed to take account of the social organization of the workplace and the human needs of the workers. The writings of Mayo and his colleagues at the Harvard Business School formed the basis of human relations theory and had a significant impact on management theory and practice in the 1940s and 1950s.

1 Main contribution

Research at Hawthorne

In 1928, Mayo was invited by the Western Electric Company to inspect some experiments being undertaken at the company's Hawthorne Works on the outskirts of Chicago. Mayo's name has since become synonymous with the Hawthorne experiments, both because of his influence on the experiments and because the Hawthorne experiments dominated and defined his career (see TAYLOR, F.W.).

The Western Electric factory was a prime example of the principles of scientific management espoused by Frederick Winslow Taylor and of the mass production techniques of Henry Ford. When Mayo first visited, it was a huge factory of almost 25,000 workers, the main manufacturing plant for the Bell telephone system in the USA. Engineers controlled every stage of the production process, time and motion studies were made of every task and, wherever possible, work was fragmented into simple tasks performed by machine operatives and assemblers. But the company was also a leader in the implementation of personnel management. Its senior managers constantly emphasized the importance of gaining the enthusiasm and loyalty of the workers, not just their obedience.

Two sets of experiments had already been undertaken. Tests on the effects of lighting on worker productivity had been conducted from 1924–7, as part of a national research programme instigated by the electrical industry. The study at Hawthorne involved measuring the impact of different levels of lighting on the output of several groups of workers. From the start, the engineers in charge of the study recognised that it would be difficult to control other factors such as changes in supervision associated with the tests and the workers' knowledge that lighting levels were being changed, and indeed the results seemed to show that these factors were more important than changes in lighting levels. Hawthorne's senior managers decided to use similar techniques to explore the effects of personnel practices such as the level of supervision and wage payment systems.

Relay assembly test room

Using the test room built for the lighting experiments, production engineers instigated a new experiment to test the effect of rest periods and changes in the hours of work on production and on workers' attitudes. The five workers in the 'relay assembly test room' were engaged in the assembly of small electrical relays, a repetitive task requiring speed and manual dexterity. Detailed records were compiled of individual production rates, temperature and humidity in the test room, workers' family lives and medical conditions and even the conversations that the workers had among themselves.

Conditions in the test room were then systematically altered, primarily by introducing a separate group payment scheme for the test-room workers and then by introducing various combinations of rest periods and shortened working hours. The output of the workers climbed steadily, and climbed even higher when two of the workers were replaced because they were restricting their production and encouraging the others to do the same. When the rest periods were removed and

hours of work returned to the normal forty-eight hours per week, production remained some 20 per cent higher than at the start of the test over a year earlier.

Later, writers on the experiments have referred to this marked increase in production despite the return to the original test-room conditions as the Hawthorne Effect; arguments have raged ever since as to how to explain it. At the time, the company researchers were unsure whether it was due to fewer relay types, changes in supervision, economic incentives due to the small group payment scheme or psychological factors triggered by the special attention received by the workers.

Interpreting the relay assembly test

Mayo initially looked at the relay assembly test room as the opportunity to continue the research he had pursued in textile mills in Philadelphia and factories in Boston. He had left Australia for the USA in order to pursue his interest in explaining and preventing industrial unrest by applying theories and techniques drawn from psychiatry and physiology. His thesis was that poor working conditions, long hours and awkward postures led to industrial fatigue and, most importantly, to mild psychiatric disturbances, which in turn could collectively lead to industrial unrest. He was convinced that the relay test showed that rest periods would reduce fatigue and result in increased production. Mayo's interpretations added further layers of explanation rather than simplifying the explanations of the data. But he reconciled the Hawthorne engineers to the fact that they would not find easy answers and encouraged them to use the experiments to explore deeper into the complex question of worker motivation and productivity.

Although the relay test continued for another four years, the focus of the industrial research at Hawthorne shifted to other projects. Mayo played a central role in all of these as advisor and interpreter, although the company researchers did not always agree with his views or follow his advice. Equally important, Mayo gave his academic imprimatur to the experiments, ensured that senior company executives understood and supported the work and kept social scientists in North America and the UK fully informed of the latest developments.

In the next stage of the experiments, the company researchers commenced a massive programme of interviewing all the workers at the plant, with the intention of providing an insight into the workers' likes and dislikes, attitudes and morale. Under Mayo's guidance, the interviewers were trained in clinical techniques borrowed from psychiatry; he suggested that the interviews should be seen as a way for the workers to 'let off steam' rather than a mechanism for identifying legitimate grievances. In practice, the company researchers used the interviews in both ways. The interviews also became the basis for a new supervisory training programme, which stressed the need for supervisors to understand the personal needs of their subordinates.

Bank wiring test

In the final major study, the bank wiring test, the focus shifted to a study of the social structures and social relationships among a group of male workers and their influence on production. It was quickly recognized that the workers were restricting their output, with the knowledge and tacit agreement of their immediate supervisor. Explanations for this differed. The company researchers and Mayo's student, Fritz Roethlisberger, were initially inclined to see the workers' behaviour as a rational, economic response, for the workers anticipated that if they worked consistently faster, their payment rate would be cut. Mayo firmly rejected such an interpretation, arguing instead that the restriction of output was an unconscious reaction by the workers to a system that did not provide them with an incentive to work harder. The workers' desire to be part of a group, in this case based around the restriction of output, was overwhelming the technical and managerial organization of the workplace, in which workers were meant to produce as much as possible.

Human relations in industry

The research at the Hawthorne Works ceased in 1932, a victim of the Depression, but the Hawthorne experiments entered a new phase at the Harvard Business School, where under Mayo's direction they were written up for publication in three books and numerous articles. At Harvard, many of the differences in interpretation that had been evident during the experiments themselves were ironed out and the major work, Roethlisberger and Dickson's *Management and the Worker* (1939), provided a definitive official account that accorded closely with Mayo's theoretical perspectives. A less significant work, *The Industrial Worker* by Mayo's colleague Thomas North Whitehead (1938), provided an exhaustive statistical analysis of the relay assembly test room data.

Mayo much preferred giving informal talks about the experiments and his publications on them consisted of short essays and a collection of lectures published as *The Human Problems of an Industrial Civilization* (1933). This book captures neatly Mayo's strengths and weaknesses and gives a flavour of the informal communication style that the Western Electric managers, corporate executives and Rockefeller Foundation officials found so refreshing. (Between 1923 and 1943, Mayo and his colleagues received grants totalling $1,520,000 from the Rockefeller Foundation – a huge sum even by Rockefeller standards.) The breadth of Mayo's interests and reading leaps off the page: the theories and research findings of psychiatry, psychology, physiology, political theory, social anthropology, biochemistry, economics and sociology surround the three central chapters on the Hawthorne experiments.

Mayo argued that the social collaboration found in traditional societies and small communities was due to the individual's unconscious adherence to social codes. Modern society had broken down traditional social codes and collaboration, resulting in a mass society of maladjusted individuals. The solution lay not in mass democracy, unions or industrial democracy, but in the emergence of a properly trained administrative elite that would develop techniques to promote social collaboration. He pursued this argument further in *The Social Problems of an Industrial Civilization* (1945), suggesting that the real threat to civilization was not the atomic bomb, but business and political leaders' lack of skill in managing human relations.

Mayo thus saw the relay assembly and bank wiring test rooms as exemplars of the choices that lay before society. The relay test room was an industrial utopia, in which the workers were content and well adapted and production rose, because managers had inadvertently created a positive environment that forged a social group. The bank wiring test room, by contrast, was an industrial dystopia, its workers discontented and maladjusted and restriction of output the result. For the remainder of his career, Mayo would seek ways to encourage industrial managers to understand the human dimensions and needs of the people in their organization, although always within a framework that emphasized the irrationality and emotionalism of workers.

2 Evaluation

The work of Mayo and his colleagues had a significant impact on management theory and practice from the late 1930s into the 1950s, especially in North America. *Management and the Worker* was widely quoted and summarized, while Fritz Roethlisberger published a large number of articles that popularized the new human relations approach. Mayo had visited Britain every year during the summer, keeping researchers there informed of his work, and worked there briefly as a consultant after his retirement from Harvard. In post-war Europe, information about human relations and the Hawthorne experiments was widely disseminated through productivity councils and training programmes sponsored by the US Marshall Plan.

The term 'human relations' quickly came to embrace a diversity of views and practices, many of them far removed from Mayo's conservative ideas. Thus, while Mayo opposed, the emergence of powerful industrial unions in the USA in the late 1930s, Roethlisberger

and other human relations researchers readily accepted the new system of collective bargaining. Indeed, they argued that the presence of organized labour made it all the more important that managers and supervisors should understand the human dynamics of the shop floor. As other centres of research into human relations were established, Mayo's theoretical approach was set aside. For example, research at the Tavistock Institute of Human Relations in Britain emphasized the impact of technology on the organization of work and on worker satisfaction (see TRIST, E.L.).

Human relations became so successful that by the late 1940s it was starting to attract a steady stream of criticism. Sociologist Daniel Bell criticized Mayo and his associates for psychologizing the worker while ignoring the institutional and power relationships of industry and for seeing industrial relations as a problem of communication and leadership rather than the accommodation of conflicting interests.

Many commentators have subsequently dismissed Mayo and his colleagues as being simply servants of powerful corporate interests, creating an ideology of human relations that dismissed workers' views and providing new manipulative techniques for managers. Certainly Mayo can be criticized on these grounds: thus he readily used increases in production as a measure of worker contentment with working conditions and management. But he saw himself as a reformer setting out to reduce the conflict of industrial capitalism by changing the attitude of workers and employers alike and reshaping the workplace culture.

3 Conclusion

Elton Mayo can be credited with two major achievements. First, he stressed that managers had to take into account the human and social dimensions of the workplace, not simply maintain their obsession with the technical organization of work. Mayo was not alone in making this point in the 1920s and 1930s, but in the Hawthorne experiments he was able to link his arguments to a large-scale research project that seemed to provide scientific proof.

Second, Mayo showed the benefits of being able to undertake long-term research in the workplace. In contrast to the frustrating experiences of many other researchers, Mayo was able to persuade Western Electric to continue to expand its research programme at Hawthorne without the company becoming overly concerned about immediate benefits or that the research would show up deficiencies in the organization. Mayo and the Hawthorne researchers opened up a space for research in the workplace that many other social scientists later explored. Ever since Mayo, managers and social scientists have been trying to find new ways of creating Hawthorne Effects.

RICHARD GILLESPIE
MUSEUM OF VICTORIA

Further Reading

(References cited in the text marked *)

Baritz, L. (1960) *The Servants of Power: A History of the Use of Social Sciences in American Industry*, Middletown, CT: Wesleyan University Press. (An early and influential radical history of industrial psychology and sociology in America.)

Bourke, H. (1982) 'Industrial unrest as social pathology: the Australian writings of Elton Mayo', *Historical Studies* 20 (79): 217–33. (An analysis of Mayo's early social and political views.)

Carey, A. (1967) 'The Hawthorne studies: a radical criticism', *American Sociological Review* 32 (3): 403–16. (The first major critical analysis of the Hawthorne experiments, based simply on a rereading of the official accounts.)

Franke, R.H. (1980) 'Worker productivity at Hawthorne', *American Sociological Review* 45 (6): 1006–27. (An example of one of the many statistical reworkings of the relay assembly test room data.)

Gillespie, R. (1991) *Manufacturing Knowledge: A History of the Hawthorne Experiments*, Cambridge: Cambridge University Press. (A detailed account of the Hawthorne experiments based on a close analysis of the original records of the experiments.)

* Mayo, G.E. (1933) *The Human Problems of an Industrial Civilization*, New York: Macmillan. (A collection of lectures that interprets the Hawthorne experiments in the context of Mayo's broader psychological theories and social thought.)

Mayo, G.E. (1945) *The Social Problems of an Industrial Civilization*, Boston, MA: Graduate School of Business Administration, Harvard University. (Mayo argues that the future of civilization depends on managers and social administrators acquiring human relations skills.)

Roethlisberger, F.J. (1977) *The Elusive Phenomena*, Boston, MA: Harvard Business School Press. (Includes chapters on Mayo and the Hawthorne experiments, written by Mayo's closest colleague.)

* Roethlisberger, F.J. and Dickson, W.J. (1939) *Management and the Worker*, Cambridge, MA: Harvard University Press. (The official account of the Hawthorne experiments, written under Mayo's supervision.)

Rose, M. (1978) *Industrial Behaviour: Theoretical Development Since Taylor*, Harmondsworth: Penguin. (Analyses Mayo's thought and the Hawthorne experiments in the context of subsequent research on industrial behaviour in Britain and the USA.)

Smith, J.H. (1975) 'The significance of Elton Mayo', in G.E. Mayo, *The Social Problems of an Industrial Civilization*, London: Routledge & Kegan Paul: ix–xiii. (A spirited defence of the value of Mayo's work for contemporary industrial sociology.)

Trahair, R.C.S. (1984) *The Humanist Temper: The Life and Work of Elton Mayo*, New Brunswick, NJ: Transaction Publishers. (The most detailed account of Mayo's career, based on his personal papers.)

* Whitehead, T.N. (1938) *The Industrial Worker*, Cambridge, MA: Harvard University Press. (A statistical analysis of the data by one of Mayo's colleagues, seeking to prove the role of personal and social relationships in the relay assembly room).

See also: FOLLETT, M.P.; LEWIN, K.; TRIST, E.L.

Related topics in the IEBM: COLLECTIVE BARGAINING; GROUPS AND TEAMS; HAWTHORNE EXPERIMENTS; HUMAN RELATIONS; HUMAN RESOURCE MANAGEMENT; MOTIVATION AND SATISFACTION; OCCUPATIONAL PSYCHOLOGY; ORGANIZATION BEHAVIOUR, HISTORY OF; ORGANIZATION STRUCTURE; PRODUCTIVITY; TRADE UNIONS

Means, Gardiner Coit (1896–1988)

Personal background

- born on 8 June 1896 in Windham, Connecticut, USA
- obtained a BA degree in chemistry and a PhD in economics from Harvard University in 1918 and 1933 respectively
- married Caroline F. Ware, 1927
- developed the doctrine of administered prices
- influenced the development of national economic planning
- formative influence on post-Keynesian economics
- quietly died at home on 15 February 1988

Major works

The Modern Corporation and Private Property (with Adolf A. Berle) (1933)
Industrial Prices and Their Relative Inflexibility (1935)
The Structure of the American Economy, part I: *Basic Characteristics* (1939)
Pricing Power and the Public Interest (1962)

Summary

Means developed the doctrine of administered prices as an alternative theory to orthodox economic theory. His primary contributions within the doctrine were administered prices, administrative inflation, the modern corporation and the necessity for government guidance of economic activity. He also contributed significantly to the development of indicative national economic planning.

1 Introduction

Means was born on 8 June 1896 in Windham, Connecticut. He entered Harvard at the age of eighteen, majoring in chemistry. With the outbreak of war in 1917, Means left Harvard to enlist in the Army and was eventually assigned to the Aviation Section of the Signals Corps where he spent his time learning how to fly aeroplanes. Upon his discharge in January 1919, he joined the Near East Relief, an organization dealing with Armenian refugees, and went off to Turkey. As part of his job in Turkey, Means had to obtain supplies from local markets which required him to engage in price and quantity bargaining with the merchants. Thus, he experienced at first hand a market situation in which prices were determined in the course of carrying out the transaction itself. Returning to the USA in 1920, Means entered Lowell Textile School to study wool manufacturing. After two years of study, he left and set up Means Weave Shop to make a high-quality (and high-priced) handwoven blanket of his own design. Through running the enterprise, Means became well acquainted with the Boston wool market and the textile machinery market; he quickly surmised that US industrial life was very different from what he had experienced in Turkey.

While still managing his textile enterprise, Means enrolled as a graduate student in Harvard's Department of Economics in 1924. His subsequent exposure to economic theory convinced him that it had little relevance to the modern corporatist economy of the USA in the twentieth century. After receiving his MA in 1927, Adolf Berle recruited him to work on his research project on the modern corporation. The outcome of the collaboration was *The Modern Corporation and Private Property* (1933) in which Means contributed the tripartite distinction between ownership, control and management and the economic arguments regarding the implications of:

1 the separation of ownership from control for the traditional theoretical roles of private property, wealth and the profit motive in directing economic activity and increasing social welfare
2 enterprise size for costs
3 enterprise size for the coordination of economic activities by the forces of supply and demand in the marketplace.

His work on the modern corporation also became the basis of his doctoral dissertation which he was awarded by Harvard in 1933.

Shortly after President Franklin D. Roosevelt took office in 1933, Means was recruited to a position of Economic Advisor on Finance to Henry Wallace, the Secretary of Agriculture. In taking the position, Means took it for granted that he would be trying to develop policies and instruments that would make the economy work more effectively. However, he found that his suggestions were not taken seriously by the policy makers. Therefore, he undertook an empirical study of wholesale prices and used the results to explain why Roosevelt's economic policies failed to produce economic recovery. The study was published in 1935 as *Industrial Prices and their Relative Inflexibility*. The impact of the study on the thinking of economists and policy makers was significant and Means used this fame to get transferred to the National Resources Committee, which had been set up to engage in indicative national economic planning. While at the committee he initiated a research project to develop a model of the US economy that could be used for economic planning. The fruits of the project were published in *The Structure of the American Economy*, part I: *Basic Characteristics* (1939). However, the rise in popularity of US Keynesianism resulted in the project being closed down before Means was able to fully develop the model (see KEYNES, J.M.).

After leaving the National Resources Committee, Means obtained the position of Associate Director of Research for the Committee for Economic Development, a business-sponsored, private research group originally concerned with government policies to ensure a full-employment transition to a peacetime economy. While at the Committee he instigated the collection of statistical series on money flows, now regularly published by the Federal Reserve Board in its flow of funds accounts. Means retired from the Committee in 1958 and spent his remaining years writing and lecturing on the modern corporate enterprise, its impact upon the economy and public welfare and its destructive implications for orthodox economic theory (Means 1962a; 1962b). He also testified before congressional committees on administered prices and administrative inflation. Means died quietly at home on 15 February 1988.

2 Main contributions

Means believed that the advent of the large modern corporation rendered many of the fundamental concepts of orthodox economics obsolete, with the result that new concepts had to be forged and a new picture of economic relationships created. In pursuing this agenda he developed the concepts of administered prices and administrative inflation and developed an alternative theory to orthodox economics, his doctrine of administered prices. The doctrine delineated the forces that affect the coordination of economic activity and determined the actual manner in which the modern corporate economy operated. In particular, instead of having all prices in the economy determined in their particular markets, Means had some determined in the market and the rest of the prices in the economy determined by corporate management and administered to the market. Consequently, when deficient demand shocks hit the economy, prices in the market sector would fall, thereby, in principle, maintaining output levels, whereas prices in the administered sector would remain relatively stable while output fell. Since the US corporate economy contained both sectors, Means argued that their interaction with regard to a deficient demand shock would produce a striking decline of prices in the market sector and a striking decline in production and hence unemployment in the administered sector. Thus, for Means, the stability of non-market-determined administered market prices was the primary reason for the breakdown in the coordination of economic activities which turned business fluctuations from being the dance-of-prices to a production and employment phenomenon.

Given the economic relationships embodied in the doctrine – such as administered prices, administrative inflation, target rate of return pricing, market power and non-market control of economic activity – Means emphasized their human and institutional nature and hence their amenability by social action. For example, given the existence of administered prices, Means argued that a serious deficiency of buying was unlikely to be corrected by any of the economic forces inherent in a modern economy in such a way as to bring about the full use of resources. Thus he concluded that the under-utilization of economic resources was a problem of social organization which could only be corrected through social or government industrial policy making.

The need for government involvement in guiding economic activity in order to avoid unemployment and thereby enhancing the quality of human life comes out clearly in Means' advocation of indicative national economic planning. The call for economic planning was frequently heard during the inter-war period, in part because of the apparent success of the five-year plans in the Soviet Union. Means also called for national economic planning, but with a democratic twist. Economic planning involved, he argued, the development of a range of different plans, each of which would bring about and maintain the full employment of the nation's economic resources; and the elected representatives would choose the plan which best fulfilled their political objectives. To back up his methodological approach to planning, Means endeavoured to develop a model of the US economy which could, for example, be used to determine the pattern of consumption, resource use and labour employment at different levels of national income. Although Means was unable to develop the model fully, he did develop the first multi-sector statistical model of the US economy, which also had the distinction of actually being used for planning

purposes to determine the amount of capital equipment required by the iron and steel industry over the existing equipment at various levels of consumer income.

3 Evaluation

Orthodox economists' evaluations of Means' contributions to economics centre on administered prices, administrative inflation and the separation of ownership from control. Generally, orthodox economists question the empirical existence of administered prices and administrative inflation. The most noted attack on the former came from George Stigler and James Kindahl in their book *The Behavior of Industrial Prices* (1970). Upon examining the transaction price data which was collected especially for their study, Stigler and Kindahl claimed that it did not support the existence of administered prices. Means, and much later Denis Carlton (1986), analysed the same price data and came to the opposite conclusion. As for the latter, various economists produced econometric studies which purported to show that price increases were weakly if at all correlated with industrial concentration and therefore claimed that administrative inflation did not exist. However, none of them realized that what they were testing was not Means' administrative inflation thesis, but something quite different.

For many years after Means had introduced the possibility that the separation of ownership from control might have an impact on the motivation of business leaders, it was commonly argued that where the separation did not exist, the owner attempted to maximize its profits, while for enterprises where it did exist the business leaders attempted to maximize growth, pursue satisfactory profit or engage in some other non-profit-maximizing behaviour. Means actually did not think that the separation of ownership from control had any impact upon the motivation of business leaders; so for him, whether business leaders attempted to maximize their profits or not depended more on empirical observation and the social and institutional nature of the corporate enterprise. Yet, since the 1970s orthodox economists have sought to refute Means' supposed claim, utilizing agency theory and thereby dismissing this contribution to economics. Thus, while orthodox economists grudgingly admit that Means had something interesting to say in a historical sense, they do not believe that he made any really important contributions to economics.

Non-orthodox economists such as post-Keynesians and institutionalists have a more positive evaluation of Means' contributions to economics. At a general level, they consider his analysis of the modern corporation as seminal and relevant as long as corporate capitalism exists; and accept the existence of administered prices and administrative inflation and Means' analysis of their impact on the coordination of economic activity. Moreover, they accept Means' dictum that the existence of the modern corporation requires a complete restructuring of economic theory and consider his doctrine of administered prices as contributing significantly to the reconstruction process. The post-Keynesians and institutionalists fully accept Means' economic arguments for the necessity of government involvement in guiding economic activity if full employment is to be achieved; they also fully accept his ethical position that opposing government involvement in the economy is immoral in that by doing so many members of society would be condemned to a life of misery (Samuels and Medema 1990).

At a more particular level, the institutionalists found Means' ideas on the corporation (specifically, concentration and size, the dispersion of stock ownership and the separation of control), the corporate system, the changing meaning of private property, the economy as a system of power and the corporation as private government very important and useful. His analysis of administered prices and the role of inflexible, administered prices in macroeconomic coordination failures, while somewhat in conflict with Keynes, has been readily accepted by post-Keynesians.

4 Conclusions

Means developed the doctrine of administered prices as an alternative theory to orthodox economic theory. His primary contributions within the doctrine were administered prices, administrative inflation, the modern corporation and the necessity for government guidance of economic activity. He also contributed significantly to the development of indicative national economic planning.

While Means' contributions to economics have been depreciated by orthodox economists, they have, conversely, been well received by post-Keynesians and institutionalists. By reason of his iconoclastic personality, Means developed his doctrine without attempting to create a school of followers; yet his ideas have influenced and affected the theories and arguments of economists, orthodox or not, for over fifty years.

FREDERIC S. LEE
DE MONTFORT UNIVERSITY

Further reading

(References cited in the text marked *)

* Berle, A.A. and Means, G.C. (1933) *The Modern Corporation and Private Property*, New York: Macmillan. (Means' classical study of the modern corporation and its consequences for economic theory.)

* Carlton, D.W. (1986) 'The rigidity of prices', *American Economic Review* 76 (4): 637–58. (Re-examines the Stigler and Kindahl price data and concludes that administered prices exist.)

Lee, F.S. (1988) 'A new dealer in agriculture: G.C. Means and the writing of *Industrial Prices*', *Review of Social Economy* 46 (2): 180–202. (Covers Means' work as an advisor to Wallace and his writing of *Industrial Prices*.)

Lee, F.S. (1990) 'From multi-industry planning to Keynesian planning: Gardiner Means, the American Keynesians, and national economic planning at the National Resources Committee', *Journal of Policy History* 2 (2): 186–212. (Covers Means' work at the National Resources Committee and his model of the US economy.)

Lee, F.S. (1998) 'Administered price hyposthesis and the dominance of Neoclassical price theory: the case of the Industrial Prices dispute', *History of Political Economy* 30. (Covers the controversy between Means and Stigler over administered prices.)

* Means, G.C. (1935) *Industrial Prices and their Relative Inflexibility*, Washington, DC: GPO. (In this work Means first introduced the concept of administered prices; reprinted in *The Heterodox Economics of Gardiner C. Means: A Collection*.)

* Means, G.C. (1939) *The Structure of the American Economy*, part I: *Basic Characteristics*, Washington, DC: GPO. (Means' most articulate conception of the US economy.)

* Means, G.C. (1962a) *The Corporate Revolution in America*, New York: Crowell-Collier Press. (Contains mostly essays on administered prices, administrative inflation and economic policy.)

* Means, G.C. (1962b) *Pricing Power and the Public Interest*, New York: Harper & Brothers. (Means' best theoretical analysis of the corporate enterprise and its impact on the public interest.)

Means, G.C. (1991) *The Heterodox Economics of Gardiner C. Means: A Collection*, F.S. Lee and W.J. Samuels (eds), Armonk, NY: M.E. Sharpe. (A collection of Means' published and unpublished articles and papers.)

Means, G.C. (1994) *A Monetary Theory of Employment*, W.J. Samuels and F.S. Lee (eds), Armonk, NY: M.E. Sharpe. (An anti-Keynesian theory of employment written in 1947.)

* Samuels, W.J. and Medema, S.G. (1990) *Gardiner C. Means' Institutional and Post-Keynesian Economics: An Interpretation and Assessment*, Armonk, NY: M.E. Sharpe. (An interpretative survey of Means' contributions to economics.)

* Stigler, G.J. and Kindahl, J.K. (1970) *The Behavior of Industrial Prices*, New York: National Bureau of Economic Research. (A well-known empirical study, which concluded that administered prices did not exist.)

See also: GALBRAITH, J.K.; KEYNES, J.M.

Related topics in the IEBM: AGENCY, MARKETS AND HIERARCHIES; BIG BUSINESS AND CORPORATE CONTROL; EMPLOYMENT AND UNEMPLOYMENT, ECONOMICS OF; GROWTH OF THE FIRM AND NETWORKING; INSTITUTIONAL ECONOMICS; MANAGEMENT IN NORTH AMERICA; MANAGERIAL BEHAVIOUR; NEO-CLASSICAL ECONOMICS; ORGANIZATION BEHAVIOUR; ORGANIZATION BEHAVIOUR, HISTORY OF

Michels, Roberto (1876–1936)

Personal background

- born Cologne, Germany, 1876, into a German-French-Belgian, Catholic bourgeois family
- attended *Gymnasium* in Berlin and then studied at the Sorbonne, Munich, Leipzig and Halle
- became heavily involved in socialist politics 1900–7: unable to follow a conventional academic career in Germany
- close associate of Max Weber throughout his life, but especially during the period 1900–10
- moved to Turin, Italy, in 1907
- opposed the German position in the First World War
- appointed professor of economics, Perugia University, 1928
- died in Rome, 1936

Major works

Political Parties (1911)
Lectures on Political Sociology (1927)

Summary

Roberto Michels (1876–1936) was the author of the aphorism 'who says organization says oligarchy'. A politically committed intellectual, he was active in the international revolutionary socialist movement before the First World War. This experience provided the basis for his major work, *Political Parties*, published in 1911. Michels became increasingly pessimistic about the prospects for revolutionary democratic socialism, *Political Parties* translating his democratic pessimism into psychological and sociological terms. His ideas have provided the basis for subsequent research both in elite theory in political science and in the sociology of organizational behaviour. Subsequent research has undermined many of Michels' original assumptions, but *Political Parties* remains a key work.

1 Introduction

Michels' 'iron law of oligarchy' states that parties and organizations which aim to be democratic inevitably become oligarchic because the very fact of organization requires control and coordination by a minority, and the minority inevitably develops interests separate from the majority. Michels based his conclusions partly on his own experience as an intellectual involved in socialist politics and trade unionism and partly upon extensive reading, rather than systematic academic research. His pessimism about democracy was to eventually lead him to support Fascism in Italy after the First World War. Subsequent research has shown that Michels operated with a simplified conception of democracy, especially as regards trade unions, and that his pessimism was exaggerated. Although Michels' specific vision and hypotheses have been heavily modified, his emphasis on the link between organizational principles, leadership interests, group psychology and democratic performance has been very fruitful for understanding the operation of voluntary membership organizations, especially trade unions.

2 Biographical data

Roberto Michels was one of a highly influential group of social scientists active in the socialist movement before the First World War. He came from an affluent Rhineland

Catholic family, but deviated from convention by going away to *Gymnasium* in Berlin for his education and subsequently joining the German army. His army career was brief, and he became an itinerant student in England, France and Germany before completing his dissertation in history at Halle University in 1900. He became involved in socialist politics, becoming particularly friendly with Max Weber (see WEBER, M.). However, Michels' upper-class background, sympathy for syndicalism and commitment to academic scholarship meant that he made little progress in the Socialist Party. At the same time his political beliefs made a conventional academic career impossible in Germany. He therefore took up a post in Italy in 1907. He then moved to Switzerland in 1914, before returning to Italy after the First World War. He ended his academic career as a professor at Perugia University, and he died in Rome in 1936.

Michels' writings were profoundly influenced by his experiences and *Political Parties* is a lively read. His accounts of meetings in Germany, France and Italy are sharply observed and characteristic:

> the regular attendants at public meetings and committees are by no means always proletarians … [The proletarian's] place at meetings is taken by petty bourgeois, by those who come to sell newspapers and picture post cards, by clerks, by young intellectuals who have not yet got a place in their own circle, people who are glad to hear themselves spoken of as authentic proletarians and to be glorified as the class of the future.
>
> (Michels [1911] 1959: 52)

Michels' work reflects experience in the European international socialist movement, especially in Germany, more than British or US experience, although Michels visited Britain and the USA and his work has been given great prominence in the English-speaking world.

3 Main contribution

Michels' work has been highly influential in political science as well as in understanding

business and management, but this entry concentrates on his contribution to understanding economic organizations, especially trade unions. Michels believed that trade union executive committees inevitably dominated rank and file union members. 'The principal cause of oligarchy in [unions] is to be found in the technical indispensability of leadership' (Michels [1911] 1959: 400). He continued:

> … oligarchy depends upon … *the psychology of the organization itself* … upon the tactical and technical necessities which result from the consolidation of every disciplined political aggregate … The fundamental sociological law of political parties … may be formulated in the following terms: It is organization which gives birth to the dominion of the elected over the electors, of the mandatories over the mandators, of the delegates over the delegators. Who says organization says oligarchy.
>
> (Michels [1911] 1959: 401;
> original emphasis)

To be effective, organizations need a division of labour between leaders and followers. The division inevitably leads to increased power for the leaders, with the role of followers being to agree, as they usually do, or disagree, as a minority occasionally do. Organizational need is reinforced by the individual interests of union leaders in maintaining a middle-class way of life and by the ability of the leading group to ensure its re-election. Greater knowledge, control over the means of communication within the union and the deference usually given by the rank and file to their leaders mean that leaders are usually able to maintain control. Elections become occasions for reinforcing the position of the leadership, not for changing it: 'leaders become transformed into a closed caste' (Michels [1911] 1959: 156). Michels believed that these conclusions were valid for both political parties and trade unions.

4 Evaluation

One reason for the popularity of Michels' iron law is academic; it is one of the few propositions in social science that has a plausible claim to being a universal proposition. Two other reasons are political. From a right-wing perspective the 'iron law' provides a rationale for the belief that unions do not serve the interests of their members effectively; the iron law explains why union leaders, normally left-wing in this scenario, are able to use unions for their own ends. At the other end of the political spectrum, one strand of Marxist writing sees trade unions as indissolubly linked with the structure of capitalism. Union leaders are a counter-revolutionary force, who collude with employers to prevent rank and file union members from exerting pressure on employers for a fundamental transformation of society (Hyman 1975). But the most important reason for the law's influence is that it suggests an important universal organizational tendency.

Michels' iron law has been the starting point for almost all subsequent discussions of union democracy. The most famous remains the 1956 US study of the International Typographical Union by Lipset and his colleagues (Lipset *et al.* 1956). The ITU was seen as unique because it contained an organized opposition, capable of defeating the incumbent union leadership on a number of occasions. This was due to several factors. First, the high status of the occupation covered by the union made it acceptable for former leaders to return to their craft. Second, strong commitment to the craft led to high levels of involvement in union affairs. Third, union members were able to communicate with each other outside the formal structures of the union because of the way work was organized and the high level of interest in matters affecting the craft. Finally, the union's bargaining structure was relatively decentralized, thus providing independent bases for power within the union. By studying the exceptional conditions underlying the 'deviant case' Lipset and his colleagues believed that they had confirmed Michels' iron law.

Scepticism about Michels' views has grown since the 1950s. The relationship between leaders and followers has been shown to be more complex, with unions differing in the extent to which they approximate the Michelsian norm. Some unions in some countries – for example, IG Metall, the German metal workers union, in the early 1960s under Otto Brenner, or the Transport and General Workers Union under Arthur Deakin in Britain in the 1950s – operated in the way Michels outlined, with a dominant leader and little involvement by rank and file members. However, unions operated in quite different ways in other situations.

A less simple picture developed in the 1970s, with closer empirical research into the intricacies of union politics. Two features were particularly important: first, the role of elections; and second, the development of the role of unofficial leaders within structures of decentralized collective bargaining.

Edelstein and Warner (1975) show how elections maintain union democracy. The degree of leadership domination over the rank and file is shown by the closeness of election results and the frequency of defeat for incumbent or heir apparent candidates. Close election results are possible where the union structure allows for independent substructures, and where union members are able to communicate amongst themselves outside union channels. However, union leaders are defeated in elections on only relatively rare occasions, usually when the union has been defeated in a particularly bitter industrial conflict. Moreover, changes in union organization in the 1990s have made it less likely that union leaders will be defeated in elections, particularly in Britain; the legal requirement that national union leaders should be elected by postal ballot has favoured leadership influence over elections, by reducing the influence of rank and file activists. This has increased oligarchical tendencies, whether the leadership is right-wing or left-wing (Smith *et al.* 1993).

The second factor limiting the relevance of Michels' law is the significance of lay union members, especially in decentralized systems of collective bargaining. Administering unions requires the unpaid work of union members, especially in Britain; leaders ignoring their views are likely to lose commitment. Moreover, union leaders are recruited from rank and file trade union activists, and retain many of the beliefs with which they entered union politics. The structure of collective bargaining is also important. If collective bargaining is centralized, external pressures increase the relevance of Michels' conclusions; pressure from the employer is exercised on a broad front and national solidarity may be necessary to respond effectively. Hence unions operating on a national scale, such as public sector unions in Britain or the Swedish national trade union centre, the LO, especially in the 1970s, are likely to be oligarchic. Unions operating in environments with decentralized collective bargaining are more likely to operate according to democratic procedures. The changes in bargaining structures in the British engineering industry in the 1970s represent an extreme example of external pressures reducing oligarchical tendencies in this matter.

Changes in union environments in the 1980s and 1990s have given new impetus to Michels' ideas. Michels was discussing the internal workings of political parties and radical unions facing conflicts with governments or strong employers. His conclusions depend partly on relations between the union or political party and its opponents; organizations in a hostile environment require discipline more than organizations operating in a more benign environment. In the English-speaking world unions are operating in an increasingly hostile environment requiring internal discipline. In the UK specifically, legislation has made it important for union leaders to exercise control over industrial action, to prevent legal proceedings being taken against the union. Elsewhere, both at the European Union level and at the national level, the close links between union leaders and major national political parties have contributed to leaders being increasingly associated with the political elite, with the danger of divorce from the views of union members.

The potential for manipulation of rank and file opinion by the leadership has been increased by technological changes making direct vertical communication between leaders and members easier. The dispersal of employees in smaller enterprises and establishments has made horizontal organization between rank and file groups more difficult. The conception of unions as service organizations designed to satisfy the needs of individual union members through the provision of specialized services, such as legal advice (the 'Automobile Association' view of trade unions), has increased the influence of a central professionalized bureaucracy at the expense of local lay leadership. As unions rely more on national organization and professionalized provision of services and less on local shop floor activists, tendencies towards oligarchy are likely to increase.

Michels' work has also been highly influential in the study of political parties, especially in Britain and in France (Mackenzie 1955; Duverger 1954) and voluntary organizations, for example, religious organizations. Mackenzie's study showed how the Party machine was the major influence in the British Labour Party in the 1960s, despite the rhetoric of democratic participation; the differences between the Labour Party and the Conservative Party were much less than the Party's rhetoric suggested. Duverger's research showed the same tendencies in France.

The most famous study in organizational behaviour directly influenced by Michels remains Philip Selznick's study of the conservation agency, the Tennessee Valley Authority, originally published in 1949 and republished in 1966 (Selznick 1966). Selznick rephrased the 'iron law' in terms of unanticipated consequences primarily arising from 'commitments' made by the organization: most relevantly, commitments generated by the process of institutionalization and by the creation of interest groupings through the process of delegating (or consolidating) responsibility for particular organizational objectives – the interests of the part become transmuted into the interests of the whole (not the other way round).

5 Conclusion

Michels' aphorism 'who says organization says oligarchy' provides the basis for the analysis of government in trade unions, political parties and voluntary organizations. He saw oligarchy as an inevitable result of the need for organizations to have leaders. The separation between leaders and followers inevitably led leaders to develop interests separate from their followers, a difference that was reinforced by the higher education level of leaders and by the psychological deference given by the followers. Michels based his views on the experience of the German Social Democratic Party in the early years of the twentieth century, but his law has provided the basis for subsequent empirical social research. The initial universal law has been qualified, to show that organization does not inevitably result in oligarchy, but that it depends on the precise structure of the organization and the environment in which it is operating. In particular, for trade unions it depends upon the extent and form of collective bargaining. However, trends in industrial relations are making it more likely that Michels' hypothesis will be confirmed in the future than it has been in the recent past, due to developments in union organization and the economic, political and social environments in which unions operate.

RODERICK MARTIN
UNIVERSITY OF GLASGOW

Further reading

(References cited in the text marked *)

Allen, V.L. (1954) *Power in Trade Unions: A Study of Their Organization in Great Britain*, London: Longman, Green & Co. (A detailed study of union government in Britain, primarily based on union formal constitutions.)

Duverger, M. (1954) *Political Parties: their Organization and Activity in the Modern State*, London: Methuen. (An international comparative analysis of party structures and party systems.)

* Edelstein, J.D. and Warner, M. (1975) *Comparative Union Democracy: Organization and Opposition in British and American Unions*, London: Allen & Unwin. (A thorough comparative study of formal organization.)

* Hyman, R. (1975) *Industrial Relations: A Marxist Introduction*, London: Macmillan. (A clear general account of union democracy from a Marxist perspective. See also later editions of the same work.)

Linz, J. (1968) 'Roberto Michels', in *International Encyclopedia of the Social Sciences*, New York: The Free Press. (An analysis of Michels' thought, concentrating on political aspects.)

* Lipset, S.M., Trow, M.A. and Coleman, J.S. (1956) *Union Democracy: The Internal Politics of the International Typographical Union*, Glencoe, IL: The Free Press. (The classic study of democratic US trade unionism.)

Mackenzie, R.T. (1955) *British Political Parties: The Distribution of Power Within the Conservative and Labour Parties*, London: Macmillan. (The standard comparative study of the British Conservative and Labour parties.)

Martin, R. (1985) 'Union democracy: an explanatory framework', in W.E.J. McCarthy (ed.), *Trade Unions*, 2nd edn, Harmondsworth: Penguin. (A comparative sociological analysis of the factors influencing union democracy.)

* Michels, R. (1911) *Political Parties: A Sociological Study of the Oligarchical Tendencies of Modern Democracy*, New York: Dover Publications, 1959. (Re-publication of the first English translation, 1915.)

Michels, R. (1949) *First Lectures in Political Sociology*, Minneapolis: University of Minnesota Press. (A late exposition of Michels' basic approach to politics.)

* Selznick, P. (1966) *TVA and the Grass Roots: A Study in the Sociology of Formal Organization*, New York: Harper Torchbooks. (A detailed exposition of the US Tennessee Valley Authority, its internal working and relations with government.)

* Smith, P., Fosh, P., Martin, R., Morris, H. and Undy, R. (1993) 'Ballots and union government in the 1980s', *British Journal of Industrial Relations* vol. 31: 365–82. (A study of the effects of government policy on union politics.)

Undy, R. and Martin, R. (1984) *Ballots and Trade Union Democracy*, Oxford: Blackwell. (An examination of union government in Britain in the early 1980s.)

See also: BARBASH, J.; CLEGG, H.; PERLMAN, S.; STRAUSS, G.; WEBER, M.

Related topics in the IEBM: COLLECTIVE BARGAINING; CORPORATISM; INDUSTRIAL DEMOCRACY; INDUSTRIAL AND LABOUR RELATIONS; INDUSTRIAL DEMOCRACY; LEADERSHIP; ORGANIZATION BEHAVIOUR; ORGANIZATION BEHAVIOUR, HISTORY OF; ORGANIZATION STRUCTURE; POWER; TRADE UNIONS

Miles, Raymond E. (1932–) and Snow, Charles C. (1945–)

Personal background

Raymond E. Miles

- born 2 November 1932
- received a BA from North Texas State University in 1954
- received an MBA in 1958 and a PhD in 1963 from Stanford University
- joined the faculty at the University of California, Berkeley in 1963 and became a professor in 1971
- dean of the school of business administration , Berkeley, 1983–90
- Professor Emeritus of business administration, Berkeley

Charles C. Snow

- born in San Diego, California, in 1945
- received a BSc in business management from San Diego University in 1967
- received a PhD from the University of California, Berkeley, in 1972
- currently Mellon Bank Professor of Organizational Behavior, College of Business Administration, Pennsylvania State University

Major works

Organizational Strategy, Structure and Process (Miles and Snow) (1978)
Theories of Management: Implications for Organization Behavior (Miles) (1975)
Strategies for Corporate Success (Snow and R.A. Pitts) (1986)
Strategy, Organization Design and Human Resource Management (Snow) (1989)

Summary

Miles and Snow have brought together a number of diverse strands of theory about organizations and attempted to relate the ways in which organizations formulate strategy, structure and process. They see organizations as working to solve a set of three problems: the entrepreneurial problem, the engineering problem and the administrative problem. These together form the adaptive cycle. Although responses to the adaptive cycle are unique to each organization, they can be sorted into various classifications. Based on their own research, Miles and Snow define four basic archetypes: defenders, prospectors, analysers and reactors. In later work, they argue that an organization's success is dependent on the tightness of fit between the various elements of strategy, structure and process.

1 Introduction

Raymond Miles and Charles Snow are noted American academics; Miles with the University of California at Berkeley and Snow at Pennsylvania State University. Both specialize in organization behaviour, though their work takes in other disciplines as well, notably strategy. They have produced only one book together, the highly influential *Organizational Strategy, Structure and Process* (Miles and Snow 1978), though both have written other works alone and with other collaborators. Raymond Miles earlier confessed that he had little taste for writing books, as his dedication and enthusiasm 'tended to drop off after about twenty pages' (Miles 1975: 2). However, the small volume of work they have produced is a significant contribution to the field of organization structure.

2 Main contribution

In *Organizational Strategy, Structure and Process*, Miles and Snow begin by defining an organization as 'both an articulated purpose and an established mechanism for achieving it' (Miles and Snow 1978: 3). This bridge between aim and action is a fundamental theme throughout their work, the primary purpose of which is to examine the concept of organizational fit – that is, how well adapted are the organization's structure and process to the strategy they are meant to implement?

Earlier, Miles (1975) had identified goals, technology and structure as the key variables in organization. Miles and Snow posed questions about why organizations, even very similar organizations operating in the same market, differ in these key areas. They conclude that these differences stem from inside organizations themselves. Organizations act to create their own environment; they are not merely reactive. The decisions made by organizations can and do change the environment within which they operate. Miles and Snow see the environment as: 'not a homogeneous entity but rather ... a complex combination of factors such as product and labour market conditions, industry customs and practices, governmental regulations, and relations with financial and raw materials suppliers. Each of these factors tends to influence the organization in its own unique way' (1978: 18). Environmental variables have to be aligned with each other, and also with internal variables within the organization, such as its product-market domain, its technology, its structure and its processes.

How does this alignment occur? Miles and Snow reject the idea of natural selection, 'within a given group of organizations, some by chance alone will develop characteristics more compatible with emerging environmental conditions than will their counterparts' (1978: 19) and rational selection, whereby 'the managers of successful organizations efficiently select, adopt and discard structural and process components to

maintain the organization's equilibrium with its environment' (1978: 19). Their research suggests neither is the case, and they opt instead for the strategic choice model first formulated by Child (1972), which emphasizes the role of top decision makers and leaders as the primary link between the organization and its environment. They refer to these decision makers as the 'dominant coalition'; 'every organization has a group of decision makers whose influence on the system is greatest. This group of executives has problem-finding as well as problem-solving capabilities' (1978: 20).

The dominant coalition is responsible for defining the company's attitude to and relations with its environment in several ways. First, it sets perceptions; organizations respond to what their management perceives is important, and tend to ignore that which is perceived as unimportant. As the coalition is also largely responsible for scanning the environment and determining which elements are to be considered at all, this is doubly important. The dominant coalition is responsible for segmenting the environment and assigning work activities accordingly. Finally, it makes the decisions which set the boundaries for strategy, structure and performance. Management's strategic choices shape the organization's structure and process. At the same time structure and process constrain strategy: once a structure and process are in place, these define strategic bounds, which cannot be exceeded without alterations to structure and process.

To sum up, 'the strategic-choice approach essentially argues that the effectiveness of organizational adaptation hinges on the dominant coalition's perception of environmental conditions and the decisions it makes concerning how the organization will cope with these conditions ... this complex and dynamic process can be broken apart into three major problems: entrepreneurial, engineering and administrative' (1978: 21). These three problems together form the adaptive cycle (see Figure 1). The entrepreneurial problem involves the adaptation of ideas into specific products or services; the engineering problem creates a system or set of processes for the

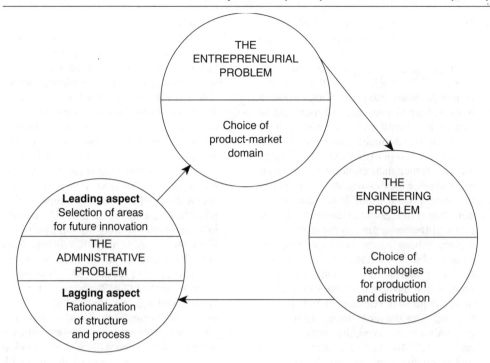

Figure 1

production of these; and the administrative problem seeks to rationalize and stabilize these activities so as to reduce uncertainty within the system.

The adaptive cycle, say Miles and Snow, is a complex and dynamic process, constantly ongoing; they characterize it as 'a general physiology of organizational behaviour. By dealing with the organization as a whole, the adaptive cycle provides a means of conceptualizing the major elements of adaptation and of visualizing the relationships among them' (1978: 27). In the words of Pugh and Hickson (1989: 63), the adaptive cycle shows how 'the entrepreneurial, engineering and administrative problems are tackled in coherent, mutually complementary ways which enable the organization as a whole to survive'. Tackling one issue alone is not enough; the interdependence of all three must be recognized and the firm must be prepared to deal with them all. Miles and Snow cite a case of a publisher who solved the engineering problem by coming up with a radical new way of producing a

particular book, but failed to solve the administration problem by implementing this solution on a wider basis, thus losing their potential competitive advantage.

The adaptive cycle is common to all firms, but they respond to it in different ways: 'Since organizations enact their own environments, it is at least theoretically possible that no two organizational strategies will be the same. That is, every organization will choose its own target market and develop its own set of products and services, and these domain decisions will then be supported by appropriate decisions concerning the organization's technology, structure, and process' (1978: 28). Based on their research into several different industries, Miles and Snow define four alternative ways of moving through the adaptive cycle, each responding to the three problems in different ways. These four responses are characterized as archetypes: they are the defender, the analyser, the prospector and the reactor.

1 *Defenders* are organizations which are established in fairly narrow product or market domains and choose to defend this territory rather than expanding into new domains. Their solution to the entrepreneurial problem is to take a strong position in these narrow domains and then seek to sustain that position by competing from strengths such as quality and price. Any expansion is a deeper penetration of existing markets rather than exploration into new ones. Having established strong bounds to the entrepreneurial problem, managers in defender organizations tend to devote much of their attention to the engineering problem; these managers are often experts in particular fields, and they turn their expertise to matters such as quality and cost control, inventory management and scheduling. Pugh and Hickson (1989) remark that defender solutions to the administrative problem are typically administrative and strongly focused on control. Finance and production functions dominate. While this system is efficient, however, there is a risk that it may not be placed to exploit new opportunities.

2 *Prospectors* are the opposite of defenders. Instead of remaining entrenched in a narrow domain, they constantly seek for new opportunities in other fields. They are willing to take risks and experiment, and they tend to value innovation above profitability, which means that they can be less than efficient. They emphasize 'doing the right things' rather than 'doing things right'. This approach dominates their attitude to the entrepreneurial problem; they focus heavily on research and development and on new market research and are constantly scanning their environment for new opportunities. This attitude requires that the solution to the engineering problem must achieve organizational flexibility, including the ability to use and adapt many different technologies, often simultaneously. The workforce too must be flexible and adaptable. The administrative problem is one of ensuring facilitation and encouraging innovation, rather than control which would inhibit the other two functions. The administrative solution usually focuses on devices such as work in small groups, product teams and close communication. Decentralization is usually one result. The prospector tends to be flexible and adaptable but can be less efficient and incurs greater risk when launching new products.

3 *Analysers* are crossovers between defenders and prospectors. Typically, they operate in two types of product-market domain: one, as with defenders, is narrow and stable, while the other type, as with analysers, is in a state of flux. Correspondingly, analysers use defender-time formal structures in their stable markets and analyser-type loose structures in their fluctuating markets. This solution to the entrepreneurial problem aims to reduce risk while maximizing profits; as Pugh and Hickson (1989) comment, analysers tend to be followers of change, not leaders. with the engineering problem too, analysers adopt a mixed approach and will probably develop a technical core capable of dealing with both stable and flexible workloads. The administrative response will likewise be a mixture of centralized functions and autonomous work groups.

4 *Reactors* are organizations who do not in fact have a viable strategy. Unlike defenders, prospectors and analysers, who take a particular approach to the adaptive cycle, reactors perceive change and uncertainty but are unable to formulate an adequate response. Accordingly, they do not make adjustments at all until adjustments are forced on them. Miles and Snow give three reasons why organizations might assume a reactor posture:

a) there may be a strategy but this has not been properly articulated, so that too few managers understand the strategy and what is expected of them;

b) perhaps there is a recognized strategy, but the technology and structure do not fit it, hampering effective responses;

c) perhaps strategy and structure actually contradict one another, as when a firm with a defender-type structure requires a prospector-type strategy in order to adapt and survive.

It was from the reactor concept that Miles and Snow went on to produce their concept of organizational fit (Miles and Snow 1984). They argue that organizational success can be determined by the quality of the 'fit' between an organization's strategy, structure, and management processes. Those organizations which succeed are those that achieve a 'strategic fit' with their environment, and support their strategies with appropriate structures and processes. Fit is essential; at least some fit, what they describe as 'minimal fit', is required if the organization is to survive at all. Lack of fit is likely to be demonstrated by slow but marked decline, rather than catastrophic failure, so it is important to be able to recognize the signs of fit.

However, true excellence requires what Miles and Snow call 'tight fit'; when strategy, structure and management process all mesh together smoothly and simply, without elaborate coordinating mechanisms. They suggest that most of the characteristics of good management, such as focus, leanness, involvement and so on, are products of tight fit, particularly when the resulting strategy has been clearly articulated. Achieving tight fit, particularly when it can be achieved early, can result in companies reaching a 'Hall of Fame', becoming leaders in their fields over the long term.

3 Evaluation

Miles and Snow's work on the adaptive cycle and organizational responses is interesting in that they are basing their work on real practice rather than best practice. The result is a fairly clinical survey of organizational approaches to strategy, structure and process. The important lesson they draw is that companies can make a choice; they are not constrained by their environment, and they can adapt provided the will and the direction are there.

The concept of fit is a particularly useful one for organizations. Making it work requires a holistic view of the organization, its goals and its environment, and the ability and the will to adapt organizational elements to achieve fit. Providing these are present, there seems no reason why fit cannot be achieved.

In their primary work, Miles and Snow do not deal with the reasons why firms adopt particular perspectives. It might be useful, for example, to know what influencing factors drive some firms to become defenders and others to become prospectors. If, as they suggest, top managers, the dominant coalition, influence and determine the direction the organization takes, then the personal attributes of the members of the dominant coalition must play some role. Miles and Snow do explore the human dimension in separate works (Miles 1975; Snow 1989), but this element is lacking in their study of the adaptive cycle.

4 Conclusion

Miles and Snow demonstrate how organizations are capable of determining their own environments and the kinds of strategic, technical and operational choices they can make. They describe the challenge facing organizations as an adaptive cycle composed of three problems, entrepreneurial (or market), engineering (or technical) and administrative (or managerial). They classify firms' responses to the cycle as falling into one of four categories:

1 Defenders, who concentrate on existing markets and emphasize the engineering problem;
2 Prospectors, who concentrate on new opportunities and emphasize the entrepreneurial problem;
3 Analysers, who adopt a mixed approach and stress the administrative problem, insofar as they stress any one of the three over the others;
4 Reactors, who fail to develop a strategic approach at all.

They argue that reactors are often created because of a lack of fit between strategy, structure and process, and urge firms to ensure that all three elements are firmly aligned.

MORGEN WITZEL
LONDON BUSINESS SCHOOL
DURHAM UNIVERSITY BUSINESS SCHOOL

Further reading

(references cited in the text marked *)

Burns, T. and Stalker, G.M. (1961) *The Management Innovation*, London: Tavistock. (Early work which suggests the concept of fit, later explored by Miles and Snow.)

* Miles, R.E. (1975) *Theories of Management: Implications for Organization Behaviour and Development*, New York: McGraw-Hill. (Miles' synthesis of theories of management.)

* Miles, R.E. and Snow, C.C. (1978) *Organizational Strategy, Structure and Process*, New York: McGraw-Hill. (Miles and Snow's best-known work, which develops a typology of organizational strategies.)

* Miles, R.E. and Snow, C.C. (1984) 'Fit, failure and the hall of fame', *California Management Review* 26 (3): 10–28. (An examination of the concept of organization fit among strategy, structure and management processes.)

* Pitts, R.A. and Snow, C.C. (1986) *Strategies for Corporate Success*, New York: Wiley. (Standard entry-level text on corporate strategy.)

Pugh, D.S. (ed.)(1990) *Organisation Theory: Selected Readings*, third edition, London: Penguin. (Contains a reprint of Miles and Snow 1984.)

Pugh, D.S. and Hickson, D. (1989) *Writers on Organisations*, fourth edition, London: Penguin. (Includes a short synopsis of Miles and Snow 1978; a good introduction to the key points of their work.)

* Snow, C.C. (ed.) (1989) *Strategy, Organization Design and Human Resource Management*, New York: JAI Press. (Charles Snow's more recent work, which introduces human resource management into the earlier concepts.)

See also: ASTON GROUP; BURNS, T.; CHANDLER, A.D.; CHILD, J.; HANNAN, M. AND FREEMAN, J.; LAWRENCE, P.R. AND LORSCH, J.W.

Related topics in the IEBM: BUSINESS ECONOMICS; CONTEXTS AND ENVIRONMENTS; INDUSTRIAL ECONOMICS; MANAGERIAL BEHAVIOUR; MANAGERIAL THEORIES OF THE FIRM; ORGANIZATION BEHAVIOUR; ORGANIZATION BEHAVIOUR, HISTORY OF; ORGANIZATION STRUCTURE; STRATEGY, CONCEPT OF; STRATEGIC CHOICE

Mill, John Stuart (1806–73)

Personal background

- born in London, 20 May 1806
- educated at home by his father, James Mill, and by Jeremy Bentham
- joined the East India Company as a clerk at the company's London offices, 1823
- arrested for distributing pamphlets in favour of birth control, 1823
- suffered nervous breakdown, 1826–7
- publication of his first major work, *A System of Logic*, 1843
- retired from East India Company, 1858
- MP for Westminster, 1865–8
- died 7 May 1873 at Avignon, France

Major works

A System of Logic (1843)
Principles of Political Economy (1848)
On Liberty (1859)
Utilitarianism (1862)
Auguste Comte and Positivism (1865)
Autobiography (1873)

Summary

John Stuart Mill was a leading political economist of the mid-nineteenth century. An intellectual descendant of the utilitarian school, he quickly evolved his own methodology and philosophy. While he did not reject utilitarian principles, he argued that people often behave in ways not associated with self-interest. Although his economics were mostly of an orthodox nature, his insistence that there were no universally valid laws and that economics was a subject requiring empirical study place
him in an important position, linking the classical economists of the early nineteenth century with the neo-classicists of the twentieth century.

1 Introduction

Mill's economic theories are strongly influenced by his own beliefs about the nature of individuals and agencies. He had a strong personal dislike of conflict and debate, and seldom chose to attack other thinkers; instead, he examined their thought using a methodology he himself had developed and then incorporated it into his own work. A radical, he believed very strongly in subjects such as free will, liberty and the emancipation of women; in economic terms he was influenced by Adam Smith, Ricardo and Malthus as well as his own father (see SMITH, A.). For many thinkers both contemporary and modern Mill has remained something of an enigma, a fierce critic of both *laissez-faire* capitalism and socialism, a staunch defender of the free market and yet a believer in the role of government. His enduring contribution, however, was the establishment of economics as a discipline; he may be seen as both the last classical economist and the first modern economist.

2 Biographical data

It might almost be said that John Stuart Mill was destined from the moment of his birth to become a philosopher and political economist. His father, James Mill, was a noted thinker in his own right, a cobbler's son from a small village in Scotland who had risen to prominence as a writer and economist; among his circle of friends were Jeremy Bentham and David Ricardo. It was James Mill and Bentham who decided that, given the deficiencies of public education, they would educate Mill's son privately, and John Stuart Mill records in his *Autobiography* (Mill 1979) that

461

he began studying Greek at the age of three, Latin at eight and chemistry at twelve.

After informally studying law he took a post as clerk with the East India Company (then charged with the civil administration of India, which was not technically part of the British Empire) in London, remaining with the Company for thirty-five years. A convinced utilitarian thanks to his education, he was close to Bentham and even served as the latter's secretary for several years. He helped found the London Debating Society in 1825; he also adopted a strong position in favour of the emancipation of women.

In 1826–7, however, Mill suffered a nervous breakdown. As he recovered, he began to change his views substantially on a number of issues. In particular he turned largely against the mechanical materialism of Bentham; more generally, he began searching for broader perspectives on logic, science and economics. He also developed a dislike of conflict and adversarial discussion, possibly as a result of the poor health which he suffered for much of his life; in the words of Halliday (1976: 31): 'He was bound to assert the truth whenever and wherever he could, but truth would neither be conceived nor quickened in conditions of conflict, nor would it be arrived at by means of narrow commitment'.

Mill rejected the notion that economic activity was governed by immutable laws. An admirer of Adam Smith, Mill believed that many of the political economists writing since Smith's time were wrong in their attempts to systematize Smith's views along rational lines. 'It became apparent to him . . . that the key methodological issues with which all moral sciences had to contend was that their phenomena were of human origin' (Oakley 1994: x). This outlook pervades all Mill's writing, particularly *Principles of Political Economy* which first appeared in 1848.

The rejection of immutable laws in economics divided Mill from the utilitarians; at the same time his staunch defence of free will and civil liberty, along with his dislike of conflict, divided him from the socialists. He wrote articles defending the revolutionaries of 1848, but he abhorred the idea of revolution and he attacked the authoritarianism implicit in the socialism of Saint-Simon and Comte. The same dislike of authoritarianism led him to retire from the East India Company in 1858 when the British government took control of India from the Company in the aftermath of the Indian Mutiny (1857–8). In 1865 Mill was elected MP for Westminster; in parliament, his most notable achievement was to lead an attack on the Governor of Jamaica, who had used troops to quell civil unrest in the colony and caused the deaths of several hundred people. He failed to be re-elected in 1868. He died in Avignon, France, in 1873.

3 Main contribution

Mill's main contribution must be his insistence that there are no self-evident, universally applicable laws in economics and that empirical study is essential. He was one of the first writers to take this view, and his pragmatism and intellectual rigour make his work stand out even today among the many dogmatic, ideological tracts that have appeared both before and since.

In order to understand Mill's political economy, it is first necessary to understand his view that economic activity was governed by human nature. Further, human nature, was not as the utilitarians assumed, entirely governed by self-interest; people could and did behave in such a way as to benefit society as a whole. Mill did not reject the doctrine of necessity entirely, but he believed that free will and its expression were of fundamental importance in understanding economics. Because human behaviour did not always remain within the bounds associated with 'economic man', human economic behaviour was not always rational. In his *Autobiography* he wrote that while self-interest is often paramount, this is only because society makes it so; remove the pressures for survival and the common good will re-emerge as a motive. 'Education, habit and the cultivation of sentiments will make a common man dig or weave for his country as readily as fight for his country' (Mill 1979: 176).

In his writings on economic theory, Mill examined the thinking of conventional political economists since Adam Smith using the empirical standards he had laid down in his own work, *A System of Logic*. He found himself in broad agreement with most of them; the rational models they had worked out were valid. A professed admirer of David Ricardo, Mill followed the latter's thinking on the determination of value and price; his views on economic cycles are similar to those of Malthus. Production is distributed through the means of exchange and distribution takes place to three classes – labourers, capitalists and landlords. The latter were separated from capitalists by the nature of property; while Mill believed that individuals had a right to private property which they had made or earned, they did not have an automatic right to land, which had not been made by human agency. In this, at least, Mill remained strongly influenced by the views of his father.

In some areas his thinking is entirely in line with that of Bentham and Ricardo. On labour, for example, he rejected state intervention and 'argued that the labourer must get what he can, though subject to the general interest' (Williams 1976: 9); utility should prevail. He also accepted that, although the poor should be encouraged to better themselves through education in order to achieve a better standard of living, assisting the poor through redistribution of wealth could be likened to slavery.

Mill's contribution did not so much reject the utilitarian view as modify it. Mill believed that 'under the rule of individual property, the division of the produce is the result of two determining agencies: competition and custom' (Mill 1994: 50). The non-rational (custom) and the rational (competition) co-exist in economics, depending on the behaviour of the individuals involved. In other words, the radical utilitarian views are valid, but they are not *solely* valid: non-rational influences must be taken into account as well.

It is thus Mill's philosophy which forms his economics. The existence of competition and custom requires that both individual and public agency have a role to play in society. Free will is essential, but so is social reform by agencies. Government, in Mill's view, came in two forms: authoritative, which controlled people through force and sanctions, and non-

authoritative, which encouraged them to govern themselves through voluntary participation. He was strongly in favour of local government, being influenced in this respect by the views of democracy espoused by de Tocqueville.

These views come through in his writings on public utilities such as water and the railways, which Mill described as 'natural monopolies'. He did not believe that capitalists should be allowed to control these utilities as this was tantamount to allowing companies to levy a tax on the people, but neither did he believe that they should be controlled by government, with all its manifest inefficiencies:

> The inferiority of government agency, for example, in any of the common operations of industry or commerce, is proved by the fact, that it is hardly ever able to maintain itself in equal competition with individual agency, where the individuals possess the requisite degree of industrial enterprise, and can command the necessary assemblage of means.
>
> (Mill 1994: 331)

His argument was that utilities should as far as possible be decentralized and localized, with government maintaining what would today be called a strategic role but local enterprises providing day to day management of operations.

Mill was strongly critical of both capitalism and socialism. Capitalism, he argued, created inequalities; it was a selfish and egotistical doctrine, a source of class conflict and oppressive in that it did not allow wage labourers to develop and progress. Socialism offered the chance to redress these wrongs, but socialism had its own problems; among these Mill listed the disincentive to work, the loss of liberty, excessive stimulation of population growth and the disincentive to technological progress. Principally, however, Mill simply did not feel that any of the forms of socialism then being developed, including Marxian communism, were feasible. Socialism implied a static society, which Mill believed to be incompatible with human nature. Mill's answer to the problem drew from both doctrines; he argued for capitalism with worker involvement, including profit sharing and worker participation in management.

4 Evaluation

Reactions to Mill, in both his own lifetime and since, have been strongly mixed. Williams (1976: 9) comments that Mill has been seen variously as 'a brave noble spirit championing freedom in the face of a hostile environment, or as a mere representative thinker of mid-Victorian England, or as a crude individualist, or as a secret and intolerant dogmatist'.

More measured views see Mill as an important link in the chain of development of economic thought from Adam Smith through to the modern period. Riley, in his introduction to *Principles of Political Economy*, sums up Mill thus:

> Mill's philosophy is a superior version of utilitarian radicalism in which the basic tenets of the old school are retained yet integrated with a broader perspective on human nature, a perspective that goes well beyond self-interest (enlightened or otherwise) and takes account of the possibility that individuals might develop higher moral and aesthetic sentiments.
>
> (Riley in Mill 1994: xiv)

From an economic perspective, Mill was one of the first economists to argue the need 'to balance history and theory, induction and deduction' (Williams 1976: 25) and take a pragmatic view of economics and markets.

Mill died in 1873, by which time communism was becoming a powerful force and winning many converts. In the century of political and economic polarization which followed, Mill's 'radical' views do not at first sight seem to have had much of a following. Belief in liberty and free will pervaded his economic thinking, set him against the doctrinaire socialists, yet his insistence on the role of government, even in its non-authoritarian form, won him few friends on the political right. However, his influence has remained considerable. Ryan (1987) points out that the Fabian socialist movement in the UK followed Mill to some degree, and Hollander (1985) notes the continuities between Mill's classical economics and modern neo-classical theory. In practical terms, the experiments with a mixture of free markets and socialism during the 'New Deal' in the USA in the 1930s, and in the UK from the 1930s through to the 1970s reflect something of Mill's own search for a middle ground; though it is doubtful if Mill himself would have approved of any of these policies.

For modern businesses, the key point to take from Mill is probably his belief that humans do not always act according to the principles of economic self-interest. That most will do so most of the time is undoubted but, as Mill points out, once the pressures of daily survival are lifted, people sometimes show a tendency to consider the common good as well, and make decisions accordingly. Most marketing by charities and not-for-profit agencies is based on this very premise, but in many consumer goods and service sectors as well marketers must wrestle with the fact that consumers do not always act in their own best interests. Further, Mill's belief that workers can be motivated to work for their country as they might fight for it is an issue that could be usefully explored by human resource managers; it is likely that Mill would have approved, in theory at least, of post-war Japan where workers did indeed mobilize to work for both country and company, often quite against their own perceived self-interest.

5 Conclusions

Perhaps Mill's most important contribution lies in his insistence that economics needed to be treated as a discipline in its own right, requiring its own methodology and empirical study. In this he anticipated twentieth-century neo-classical economics. It can be argued that the study of economics has in some quarters gone too far down this road and is insufficiently related to factors such as politics and environment, and the human element that Mill stressed so strongly does not always receive the attention it deserves. Nevertheless, by separating economics from general political theory and giving it the beginnings of a methodology, Mill made a valuable contribution to modern economic science.

MORGEN WITZEL
LONDON BUSINESS SCHOOL
DURHAM UNIVERSITY BUSINESS SCHOOL

Further reading

(References cited in the text marked *)

* Halliday, R.J. (1976) *John Stuart Mill*, London: Allen & Unwin. (Examination of Mill and his work, emphasizing the change in Mill's thinking after 1826–7.)

* Hollander, S. (1985) *The Economics of John Stuart Mill*, 2 vols, Oxford: Blackwell. (A complete and authoritative examination of Mill's economics by one of the leading scholars in this field.)

Kurer, O. (1991) *John Stuart Mill: The Politics of Progress*, New York: Garland. (A good examination of Mill's political beliefs, including a clear account of his criticisms of capitalism and socialism.)

* Mill, J.S. (1979) *Autobiography*, Harmondsworth: Penguin. (A popular edition of the final 1873 edition of Mill's autobiography.)

* Mill, J.S. (1973) *A System of Logic*, Buffalo, NY: University of Toronto Press. (The classic work which established Mill as a distinguished thinker and logician.)

Mill, J.S. (1991) *On Liberty and Other Essays*, J. Gray, (ed.), Oxford: Oxford University Press. (Modern volume contains four of Mill's best known essays, 'On Liberty', 'Utilitarianism', 'Considerations of Representative Government' and 'The Subjection of Women'.)

Mill, J.S. (1993) *Auguste Comte and Positivism*, Bristol: Thoemmes Press. (Reprint of the 1865 edition; an attack on Comte and positivist doctrines which influenced early socialist thinking.)

* Mill, J.S. (1994) *Principles of Political Economy and Chapters on Socialism*, J. Riley (ed.), Oxford: Oxford University Press. (Mill's major work on political economy, along with the chapters from his unfinished book on socialism.)

* Oakley, A. (1994) *Classical Economic Man: Human Agency and Methodology in the Political Economy of Adam Smith and John Stuart Mill*, Aldershot: Edward Elgar. (A useful work which sets Mill in context with other political economists after Smith.)

* Ryan, A. (1987) *The Philosophy of John Stuart Mill*, 2nd edn, London: Macmillan. (A more general philosophical examination of Mill, including his work on logic and ethics.)

Schwartz, Pedro (1972) *The New Political Economy of J.S. Mill*, London: London School of Economics and Political Science. (Looks at Mill and Malthus together; an appendix reproduces some early nineteenth century pamphlets concerning birth control.)

* Williams, G.L. (ed.) (1976) *John Stuart Mill on Politics and Society*, London: Fontana. (A good introductory selection of Mill's writings, in paperback form.)

See also: SMITH, A.

Related topics in the IEBM: HUMAN RESOURCE MANAGEMENT; MALTHUS, T.R.; MARKET STRUCTURE; MARKET STRUCTURE AND CONTENT; MOTIVATION AND SATISFACTION; NEO-CLASSICAL ECONOMICS; ORGANIZATION BEHAVIOUR, HISTORY OF; RICARDO, D.

Mintzberg, Henry (1939–)

1 Introduction
2 Biographical data
3 Main contribution
4 Evaluation

Personal background

- born Toronto, 2 September 1939
- received degree in mechanical engineering from McGill University (1961), BA from George Williams College (1962), SM in management from Massachusetts Institute of Technology (1965) and PhD from Sloan School of Management (1968)
- took up teaching post at McGill University, 1972
- won McKinsey Award for best article in *Harvard Business Review*, 1975, 1987
- appointed Bronfman Professor of Management at McGill University, 1978
- president of the Strategic Management Association, 1988–9

Major works

The Nature of Managerial Work (1973)
Mintzberg on Management: Inside the Strange World of Organisations (1989)
The Strategy Process (with J.B. Quinn) (1991)
The Rise and Fall of Strategic Planning (1994)

Summary

Mintzberg was the first scholar in management studies to be elected to Canada's Royal Society and has the rare distinction of publishing four articles in *Harvard Business Review* since 1975, twice winning the McKinsey Award. It is perhaps typical of Mintzberg that, with thousands of eager strategists acknowledging his leadership of the Strategic Management Society in 1989, he then announced 'the fall' of strategic management as a concept.

1 Introduction

Henry Mintzberg became famous by casting a jaundiced eye at the posturing of academics in the field known first as business policy and later by the more elevated title of strategy. By studying what business managers actually did, Mintzberg found that there was less 'command and control' than *ad hoc* improvisation and adjustment to change. He likened the pretensions of those managers who behaved like battlefield commanders to the disastrous advance of Allied soldiers in the Battle of Passchendaele, in which 20,000 died while senior commanders remained largely ignorant of the waterlogged terrain. In Mintzberg's view, what was needed was a less 'heroic' view of strategy as something that emerges from the actual experience of those in the front lines, which may not have been 'planned' at all but has instead grown from real engagements.

2 Biographical data

Mintzberg's personal history foreshadowed in a number of ways his distinctive views on strategy. His early education was not out of the ordinary, and although he studied engineering he was not particularly committed to it as a discipline. His first job was in operations research with Canadian Pacific Railways. This gave him an interesting view of a system in its entirety, but two years proved to be enough to satisfy his curiosity. His attitude was later summed up in the dedication to his book *Mintzberg on Management*: 'To those who spend our public lives working for organisations and our private lives escaping from them' (Mintzberg 1989).

He first applied to the Massachusetts Institute of Technology (MIT) expecting to be rejected, but was accepted. He quickly gravitated to the softer ends of his studies because they were more practical: 'Engineers think analogically. They are not afraid of getting their hands dirty. . . I can't say that for economists and other advocates of the Rational Model.' Pushed by his own preferences, he found himself as a doctoral candidate in a non-existent department of business policy at MIT's Sloan School of Management, where there were no professors to supervise him and no orthodoxy to receive. Immersed in unplanned opportunities and a rich mixture of unusual people in contiguous subjects, Mintzberg, as he would say of organizations similarly situated, emerged. The opening lines of his first published article reveal a liking for paradox and for patterns which emerge from contrasting pressures:

> Man's beginnings were described in the Bible in terms of conscious planning and grand strategy. The opposing theory developed by Darwin suggested that no such grand design existed but that environmental forces gradually shaped man's evolution.
>
> (Mintzberg 1989)

Mintzberg was destined to become the 'Darwin' haunting the 'Established Church' at Harvard Business School, although increasingly he went beyond mere opposition to uncover the interplay between plans and outcomes.

3 Main contribution

A synthesis of Mintzberg's conclusions after more than sixteen years of research may be found in 'Crafting strategy' (Mintzberg 1987), an article in which he uses a metaphor from the work of his ex-wife, a well-known potter. Just as the potter shapes her clay by allowing it to emerge from between her hands which work intuitively and aesthetically to incorporate any happy accident or inspired touch, so strategists shape the evolving patterns of their policy. According to Mintzberg:

> Craft evokes traditional skill, dedication, perfection through the mastery of detail.

What springs to mind is not so much thinking and reason as involvement, a feeling of intimacy and harmony with the materials at hand, developed through long experience and commitment. Formulation and implementation merge into a process of learning through which creative strategies evolve.

> (Mintzberg 1987)

The hands shape the clay yet, as the wheel turns, the clay shapes the hands which preserve what is valued while remoulding the rest of an endlessly iterative process:

> Her mind is on the clay, but she is also aware of sitting between her past experience and her future prospects. She knows exactly what has and has not worked for her in the past. She has intimate knowledge of her work, her capabilities and her markets. As a craftsman she senses rather than analyses these things; her knowledge is tacit.
>
> (Mintzberg 1987)

In order to grasp what Mintzberg is advocating, it is first necessary to recognize the orthodoxy with which he is contending. His objection is to the concept of strategy as a plan which has been worked out in advance in the head of the strategist. Rather, he sees strategy as a pattern of activities over time which include observations of what has actually occurred. He is not saying that plans are irrelevant, only that actions speak louder than intentions and often subsume them.

The orthodox school sees strategy springing fully armed like Athena from the head of the strategist who 'sees it all'; a dogma of immaculate perception. The design is deliberate, conscious and articulated; it is first formulated from on high and is then implemented in detail by other members of the organization. Mintzberg contends that strategy need not be deliberate but can emerge. Thus Honda executives, camping on the floor of a Los Angeles apartment, discovered that it was their small 50 cc motorbikes that Americans wanted, not the powerful machines that won races. Nor does strategy need to be conscious; the Honda handlebars were inspired by

Buddha's eyebrows in a culturally-influenced design. Finally, strategy may be not so much articulated beforehand by MBA graduates as learned after the act by anyone in the organization in touch with the environment. In this event it is the 'implementation' that forms strategy, and the two fuse rather than becoming dichotomized. Of course one can always attribute conscious artifice to individuals, and doubtless they are flattered to be seen as contriving an event which they actually stumbled over; but this 'reconstructed logic' should not be confused with the genuine 'logic of discovery', or what actually happens.

In his doctoral thesis, Mintzberg traced the activities of samples of senior managers. He found that the best of them spent a negligible proportion of their time in academically acclaimed activities such as planning, organizing, coordinating and controlling, nor did they speed-read the organizational equivalent of the business school case study and make incisive decisions from abstracted information. On the contrary, they found themselves responding endlessly to inputs they could not have anticipated and accumulating personal judgements based on face-to-face or telephone communications.

The orthodox view of strategy is clearly somewhat idealized and prescriptive: 'We know that managers muddle through but they would do better to design strategy more carefully in advance.' Mintzberg's objection, however, extends not simply to the unrealistic idealizations of grand strategy but to the ideal itself. While strategy is being designed, the environment is changing much as the battlefield at Passchendaele in 1917 was turned by rain into a sea of mud even as the General Staff, far behind the lines, designed their 'great plan' in which one-quarter of a million Allied soldiers died or were wounded. The separation of formulation from implementation proved highly inflexible. The conscious articulation of the strategy narrowed awareness, allowing the donkeys to lead the lions to disaster. Lost in the process is peripheral vision, rapid reaction and the capacity to learn before the quagmire sets in. Strategy presupposes some stability, and can seriously mislead when the environment is subject to unanticipated change.

It is for this reason that Mintzberg has resigned from all teaching of MBAs. In his view, judgement about human behaviour cannot be taught, nor can nuances or aesthetic appreciation be conveyed, to those with little prior experience of real management. The human relations practices by which Japanese and other Asian firms achieve such cohesion and unity of purpose have long been known; indeed, they themselves learned these practices from the West in the 1950s. The reason why Western firms themselves have not absorbed and valued such lessons is that these are concepts with organized, lived experience, and to students without experience they appear only as techniques of low efficacy and precision. The attempt to know before we act is not simply a defect in business policy; it relegates personal knowledge and emergent strategy to a subordinate level. It is the major structural flaw in the edifice of US management education and helps explain why the 'world's teacher' of business is itself in deepening crisis. The error is fundamental, because it confuses cause with effect.

The proper design of strategy in Mintzberg's view is the effect of having studied emergent plans, improvisations, adaptations and strategies at the grass roots. One of his favourite quotations is from Einstein: 'The confusion of means and ends characterizes our age.'

4 Evaluation

What makes Mintzberg such an intriguing controversialist may in part be a weakness; he almost never stops attacking. The position he attacks, that of the 'the design school' of strategy, retains an important part in overall strategy formation. Mintzberg champions the 'emergent strategy' school of thought, and this perspective has its contribution to make. Yet it can still be argued that management have to design strategy in accordance with the accomplishments emerging from the grass roots. The two schools can in fact be combined to achieve a synthesis: the best the firm's employees have accomplished can be organized by the vision of those at the top. Mintzberg's adversarialism is in danger of generating yet another schism in the organization.

None the less, Mintzberg's intellectual clarity and incisive criticism have made for a masterly and finely detailed integration not only of the organizations that he has patiently researched for many years, but also of his own life and intellectual development. He exemplifies the need for personal integrity to understand and to reflect the process of integration in social systems.

CHARLES HAMPDEN-TURNER
JUDGE INSTITUTE OF MANAGEMENT STUDIES,
UNIVERSITY OF CAMBRIDGE

Further reading

(References cited in the text marked *)

Mintzberg, H. (1972) *The Nature of Managerial Work*, New York: HarperCollins. (Early and important contribution to the definition of the managerial task.)

Mintzberg, H. (1975) 'The manager's job: folklore and fact', *Harvard Business Review* (July–August). (Cuts through some of the myths around management and offers plain definitions of the managerial task.)

Mintzberg, H. (1976) 'Planning on the left side and managing on the right', *Harvard Business Re-view* (July–August). (Classic article in which Mintzberg looks at the differences between planning and managing.)

* Mintzberg, H. (1987) 'Crafting strategy', *Harvard Business Review* (July–August). (Another classic article, this one on the strategy-making process.)

* Mintzberg, H. (1989) *Mintzberg on Management: Inside the Strange World of Organisations*, New York: The Free Press. (Often-cited work which combines organization behaviour with a fine understanding of human behaviour.)

Mintzberg, H. (1994) *The Rise and Fall of Strategic Planning*, New York: The Free Press. (Still-controversial work in which Mintzberg pursues his thesis that strategic management is more or less dead as a concept.)

Mintzberg, H. and Quinn, J.B. (eds) (1991) *The Strategy Process*, Englewood Cliffs, NJ: Prentice Hall. (Contains reprints of nearly all of Mintzberg's earlier work.)

See also: ANSOFF, H.I.; DRUCKER, P.F.

Related topics in the IEBM: MANAGERIAL BEHAVIOUR; MANAGERIAL THEORIES OF THE FIRM; MILITARY MANAGEMENT; ORGANIZATION BEHAVIOUR; ORGANIZATION BEHAVIOUR, HISTORY OF; STRATEGY, CONCEPT OF; ; STRATEGY, IMPLEMENTATION OF; STRATEGY AND RATIONALITY; STRATEGY AND TECHNOLOGICAL DEVELOPMENT

Morgan, Gareth (1943–)

Personal background

- born in Wales, 22 December 1943
- studied at London School of Economics (BSc in economics, 1965), University of Texas (MA in public administration, 1970) and University of Lancaster (PhD in organization theory, 1980)
- worked as a professional accountant in local government in the UK, later taught at University of Texas and University of Lancaster
- became professor of administrative studies at York University, Ontario
- made Life Fellow of the International Academy of Management, 1987

Major works

Sociological Paradigms and Organizational Analyses (with G. Burrell) (1979)
Beyond Method: Strategies for Social Research (1983)
Images of Organization (1986)
Riding the Waves of Change: Developing Managerial Competences for a Turbulent World (1988)
Imaginization: The Art of Creative Management (1993)

Summary

Gareth Morgan is professor of administrative studies at York University in Ontario. He has become well-known for his studies of organizations, in particular for his book *Images of Organization* (1986) which is one of the most influential and original works on organizations in recent years. In a rich and original synthesis, Morgan captures much of the history of organizational studies, human resource management and critical theory in eight powerful metaphors. These metaphors, whether pure or mixed, represent the patterns of strategy, policy and conduct of various corporations. Indeed, in Morgan's view, whole economies and business cultures are the hostages of a few mixed metaphors, often used without awareness or examination of their consequences.

1 Introduction

Morgan begins with the problem of partial rationalities. Organizations, he believes, enact metaphors and live them out with fateful consequences. To manage an organization as if operating a machine, steering a ship or wielding a weapon is to embody that metaphor in action. It is self-fulfilling in the sense that both the advantages and perils of the metaphor are realized. Managers may unwittingly construct a reality they dread through an incapacity to reflect upon the metaphor in use.

In Morgan's view, metaphors are a tool for understanding, not to be confused with reality itself. At the heart of his work lie eight metaphors of organizations: they can be seen as machines, organisms, brains, cultures, political systems, psychic prisons, flux and transformation or instruments of domination. However, these metaphors are not exclusive, and each has its drawbacks as well as its advantages. It is crucial to remember that Morgan believes all organizations partake of several or even all of these metaphors. Through combining metaphors, one can gain different perspectives on an organization and thus greater insight into the ways in which it functions, both internally and in relation to its environment.

2 Biographical data

Born in Wales, Gareth Morgan trained as an economist at the London School of Economics and worked as a professional accountant in local government. In the late 1960s he went to the University of Texas, but courses in organizational studies left him with doubts about what was being accounted for.

His next move was to a post at the University of Lancaster, where he was able to pursue his interests in organizations and management. The further he delved into this subject, however, the more he came to realize that there was no fundamental agreement as to what an organization entailed. He began a deeper study of sociology and the philosophy of the social sciences, researches which resulted in his co-authorship of *Sociological Paradigms and Organizational Analyses* (Morgan and Burrell 1979). This book challenged the foundations of organizational theory and had widespread repercussions.

While this book was successful, it was also highly theoretical. Morgan (possibly still influenced by his background in accounting) was more interested in the practical aspects of his research. His next book, *Beyond Method: Strategies for Social Research* (1983b) went beyond methodological disputes to study the reality and images of organizations. The image an organization had of itself, Morgan argued, was of paramount importance. Accounting, for example, could be a history of transactions, a branch of economics, a form of information, a disciplined control, or a methodology.

This same approach characterizes his best-known and most influential book, *Images of Organization* (1986). In this work he elaborates his eight metaphors of organization, metaphors in which all businesses and even business cultures participate. Organizations are by their nature paradoxical, combining many different and sometimes incompatible dimensions at once. Metaphors are contingent on particular circumstances: the more images we have, the more versatile are our ways of understanding both organization and action. Tension between metaphors creates flux, flow, transformation, loops and self-renewal. Morgan uses the term 'imaginization' to describe the process of breaking free from the grip of the mechanistic view to unite thought and action creatively and productively. The more angles and frames we employ, without becoming obsessed by any one view, the more sophisticated will be our understanding; conscious that we are using metaphor, we avoid mistaking it for the absolute truth.

Morgan uses these metaphors in his own research and consulting, most recently in *Riding the Waves of Change* (1988), a study of executives in Canada. In this study he worked with executives, showing them how metaphors can be used to describe new and necessary forms of managerial competence. Metaphors could also be used to help executives understand the dynamics of their organizations, both internally and externally.

3 Main contribution

Morgan has developed eight key metaphors (or rather clusters of metaphors, as each has a host of possible images and themes within it) for organizations. These images include the 'inside' view of managers as well as the 'outside' view of social critics and observers. All have relevance in certain circumstances, while any single metaphor, even if successful in the short term, will ultimately prove inadequate and blinker managers from recognizing particular threats. There is therefore no one 'best' metaphor. Morgan's favourite metaphor is metaphor itself, the process of recognizing the new as like yet unlike the images at hand. Even the eight metaphors explored below are no substitute for the metaphorical process itself.

Organizations as machines

The word 'organization' comes from the Greek *organ*, meaning tool, and it was perhaps inevitable that organizations would begin to think of themselves in the image of their most powerful tools and adopt the perspectives of their members who had the most professional education, the engineers and accountants. Weber (see WEBER, M.) has

471

shown that the mechanization of industry was accompanied by a bureaucratic form of organization, while the classical management theory of Fayol and Mooney stressed the unity and chain of command within the organization (see FAYOL, H.). With the scientific management theories of Taylor, the metaphor of organization as machine reached its highest point of development (see TAYLOR, F.W.). Although the machine metaphor is indispensable (if for no other reason than that modern organizations themselves contain a great number of machines), it also has its drawbacks; it is inflexible and slow to adapt to changes in the environment, it is poor at processing new ideas and learning, and the hierarchical structures can lead to inefficiency and slow responses. Morgan's strongest objection, however, is that machines have only 'technical rationality' and cannot process double-loop learning.

Organizations as organisms

An obvious counterpoint to the machine image is that of the organism or living system, drawing on biology where the mechanists had drawn on physics. This metaphor is based strongly on the concept of organizations as responses to social needs. Variants can be seen in the work of Argyris and McGregor, who argued for the need to integrate personality with the organization (see ARGYRIS, C.); Trist and Bamforth who developed the concept of a socio-technical system (see TRIST, E.L.); Burns and Stalker who discovered that 'mechanistic' organizations could not respond to turbulent environments as fast as 'organic' ones (see Lawrence and Lorsch who used the concepts of differentiation and integration, borrowed from biology, to develop contingency theory (see LAWRENCE, P.R. AND LORSCH, J.W.); and Mintzberg, who developed the notion of organizations as species which must fit within their environments (see MINTZBERG, H.). The organic metaphor has a number of advantages, including the ability to respond quickly to changing environments; it supplements parts with processes and things with relationships, stressing change, variety, creativity and flexibility. Business is seen in

the context of enhancing life forms, a highly inclusive perspective. Yet, any way of seeing is also a way of not seeing. Organicism misses those forms held together by ideas, norms and visions, and almost certainly over-emphasizes the unity of the whole.

Organizations as brains

If an organization is not simply a living system but a self-organizing system, then the more appropriate metaphor is that of the brain. This should not be confused with the brains of individuals within the organization; rather, the organization as a whole is designed to process information, to act on it, and to learn from the consequences. Approaches to the brain metaphor include Simon's concept of bounded rationality, in which organizations choose among alternatives which are limited by time, knowledge and rationality, and Wiener's theory of cybernetics (see SIMON, H.A.; WIENER, N.). The latter is concerned with circular feedback loops, which receive positive or negative feedback from the environment; negative feedback detects and corrects deviation, while positive feedback keeps the system on track. The next stage beyond cybernetics is the concept of the 'holographic organization' in which information and learning combine in a process of constant improvement and improvisation. The advent of desktop computers and networks has gone some way towards making the holographic organization a reality, as managers are linked to one another and can share information in a matter of seconds. However, this metaphor too has its dangers; learning is not the only objective, no matter how broadly defined. Not all organizations are able to find the flexibility and openness to adopt this frame.

Organizations as cultures

Culture refers to the pattern of a society or an organization's knowledge, values, ideologies, laws, rituals and mutual expectations. Cultures can both limit strategies and enhance them. Morgan holds culture to be important because it represents the enactment of our ideas and values; it is the ongoing, proactive process of reality construction. Internally, the holographic organization depends on culture to convey to each member a vision of the network or 'game plan'; externally, cultures pattern the outputs of the organization to the extent that they go beyond reacting to their environment and begin a process of enculturation among their customers, drawing them into a web of mutual enthusiasm or hostility, trust or suspicion. The latter variables draw attention to the fact that attempts to construct reality through culture do not always succeed; indeed, sometimes they fail disastrously. The problem with the culture metaphor is its tendency to ignore the very unequal powers of pattern making; it requires a political dimension.

Organizations as political systems

Morgan conceives of organizations as mini-states which are either unitary (with all employees striving for a common objective), pluralist (featuring a collection of diverse interests in a loose coalition around formal goals) or radical (a battleground in which rival classes or sectors are opposed). It is often a political matter as to who controls scarce resources, who gets knowledge and information first, who has access to information networks, who gets to speak publicly, or where decisions are made. Intertwined with other metaphors of the organization are the needs of key actors, departments and interests all seeking to further their own powers. It is important to understand political considerations and motivations, but the dangers of this metaphor lie in its potential to encourage confrontation. Too often power is seen as power *over* people, not power *through* them.

Organizations as psychic prisons

Not all images of organizations are necessarily positive; in some cases organizations collude to perpetuate fantasies, like the US car manufacturers who denied the market inroads being made by Japanese makers until it was almost too late. It is possible to create certainties within the organization which

successfully deny the uncertainties outside, and many organizational cultures are created by the need to deny and defend. Here Morgan again cites the example of Taylor; the discipline of scientific management was largely shaped by Taylor's own needs to control and discipline himself against illness. There are many views on the psychological drives behind organization building, and Morgan uses these to challenge the 'rational model' of organizations, suggesting that a test of the pathology of organizations is their level of resistance to innovation and change.

Organizations as flux and transformation

The Greek philosopher Heraclitus conceived of the world as a continuous flux, a 'liquid reality'. According to this view, organizations replicate themselves and grow by an unfolding of their own codes which are potentially readable in their self-images, myths, metaphors and structures. Thus to some extent, at least, the pattern of the organization reflects the pattern of its environment, and the manner in which the organization interacts with its environment is partly predetermined. Changes come from random variations which are then incorporated into the organization's identity. How firms deal with these changes has implications for their operations. Some firms can be described as egocentric, forever studying themselves and missing changes in the environment, while others are capable of systemic wisdom, discovering the developmental logics which they share with other systems. This process, also known as 'autopoiesis', involves loops rather than lines, with complex systems and feedback maintaining the balance. The question posed by Morgan here is to what extent are organizations in the business of managing contradiction, paradox and dilemma.

Organizations as instruments of domination

The self-centred variety of autopoiesis leads to Morgan's final metaphor, that of the organization which serves as a system for simply overpowering the environment in which it functions. There is a tension here between what is possible and what has too often happened in the past; historically, organizations have exploited slave labour, polluted their physical surroundings and offered unsafe products on the market. Others use their power less ruthlessly but dominate through sheer physical size; Exxon, for example, has a gross national product (GNP) larger than that of most countries. However, Morgan points out that not all domination is involuntary; a partnership eagerly sought may be 'unfair' in that the weaker partner may languish while the other grows stronger, but this situation may be acceptable to both.

While each of these eight successive images has added insight to the ways organizations act, the result is dilemma or paradox; the planned mechanism is the counterpoint to the spontaneous organism, the line of cause and effect is opposed to the loop and the open system is in conflict with the self-renewing one. Morgan's view is that there is no one right metaphor; all organizations partake to some degree of all these metaphors, and all allow access to greater understanding of organizations and how they function.

4 Evaluation

Morgan is particularly concerned to promote double-loop learning. Single-loop learning is when an organization first notes and then reduces any deviations from a standard it has set; for example, full machine utilization is a standard and firms can learn to reduce downtime by a single feedback loop. A second or double loop is introduced when the firm begins to experiment not only with downtime itself but with the objective of manipulating it downwards. Where full machine utilization has been achieved by piling up inventory, investing in spares, increasing maintenance and supervision and creating organizational slack, then this objective may need modification and qualification. In double learning the firm studies the feedback from its objectives (first loop) in order to evaluate how those objectives are feeding back on its strategy (second loop). Morgan's view is that double-

loop learning is crucial to understanding strategy, and to understanding and approaching the tasks of organizations, in order to challenge the assumptions that bind them into ineffective modes of operation.

Morgan's crucial insight, however, is that corporate objectives and the processes of management are embedded in dominant metaphors. To continue with the example above, full machine utilization is likely to be one of several objectives derived from the metaphor of the organization as machine. To reflect upon these metaphors is to re-examine basic objectives and critique not only corporate strategy but also the basis of the company's approach to organization and management. In the absence of an articulated strategy, the dominant metaphors are the strategy; in the presence of an articulated strategy, the dominant metaphors will distort or facilitate it.

Morgan's excursus into the processes by which we organize, enquire and learn has convinced him that we make sense of the world by juxtaposing the familiar with the unfamiliar. We learn by successfully integrating the like with the unlike, mind with reality, by means of metaphorical understanding. Thus an organization may be compared to a mechanism but it may also be compared to an organism; the more subtle and comprehensive our understanding, the more versatile and flexible the organization can become.

If Morgan's work has a failing, it is in not being clear enough about how we are to overcome the paradox of opposing metaphors. There is not enough explanation as to how we could make these more coherent, for example, by subsuming organism and mechanism under brain and mind. Clearly, this is the next necessary step in the research process.

5 Conclusion

Morgan's metaphors, which condense over one thousand books and eight scholarly paradigms into an action-orientated thesis, are a marked achievement and an invaluable exercise for the reflective strategist. By bringing the richness of a wide variety of sciences into organization studies and making explicit the links between other forms and forms of organization, he has given us a different view of organizations themselves; a sometimes contradictory view, to be sure, but one whose contradictions are mirrored in real life.

CHARLES HAMPDEN-TURNER
JUDGE INSTITUTE OF MANAGEMENT STUDIES,
UNIVERSITY OF CAMBRIDGE

Further reading

(References cited in the text marked *)

Morgan, G. (1983a) 'Rethinking corporate strategy: a cybernetic perspective', *Human Relations* 36: 345–60. (Article which links strategy to systems thinking.)

* Morgan, G. (1983b) *Beyond Method: Strategies for Social Research*, Newbury Park, CA: Sage Publications. (A look at new paradigms for social research.)

* Morgan, G. (1986) *Images of Organization*, Newbury Park, CA: Sage Publications. (Morgan's most famous work outlining the paradigms described in this entry.)

Morgan, G. (1987) *Creative Organization Theory*, Newbury Park, CA: Sage Publications. (Following from the previous work, Morgan describes new theories of organization.)

* Morgan, G. (1988) *Riding the Waves of Change: Developing Managerial Competences for a Turbulent World*, San Francisco, CA: Jossey Bass. (A more practitioner-orientated work, Morgan looks here at managerial skills.)

Morgan, G. (1993) *Imaginization: The Art of Creative Management*, Newbury Park, CA: Sage Publications. (Argues for more intuition and a break from strict, confining methodologies.)

* Morgan, G. and Burrell, G. (eds) (1979) *Sociological Paradigms and Organizational Analyses*, London: Heinemann. (Links the theories of sociology to organizations.)

See also: ARGYRIS, C.; FAYOL, H.; LAWRENCE, P.R. AND LORSCH, J.W.; MINTZBERG, HSIMON, H.A.; TAYLOR, F.W.; TRIST, E.L.; WEBER, M.;WIENER, N.

Related topics in the IEBM: ACCOUNTING; ACCOUNTING AND ORGANIZATIONS; BUSINESS CULTURE, EUROPEAN; BUSINESS CULTURE, JAPANESE; BUSINESS CULTURE, NORTH AMERICAN; CONTEXTS AND ENVIRONMENTS; CYBERNETICS; HUMAN RESOURCE MANAGEMENT; INFORMATION TECHNOLOGY; MANAGEMENT SCIENCE; ORGANIZATION BEHAVIOUR; ORGANIZATION BEHAVIOUR, HISTORY OF; ORGANIZATION CULTURE; ORGANIZATION DEVELOPMENT; ORGANIZATION PARADIGMS; ORGANIZATION TYPES; ORGANIZATIONAL LEARNING; POWER; STRATEGIC CHOICE; STRATEGY, CONCEPT OF

Morita, Akio (1921–)

Personal background

- born in Nagoya, on 26 January 1921, the eldest son of a wealthy *sake-brewing family*
- studied physics at Osaka Imperial University
- wartime service in the Imperial Japanese Navy as a technical officer
- joined Masaru Ibuka in Tokyo Tsushin Kogyo (Tokyo Telecommunications Engineering Company) (TTK) in 1946
- first international success when TTK began mass production of the world's smallest transistor radio in 1955
- TTK renamed as Sony Corporation in 1958
- became president of Sony Corporation in 1971 and chairman in 1976
- awarded the Albert Medal by the Royal Society of Arts and Manufactures in the UK, 1982
- Sony acquired CBS Records, 1987
- Sony acquired Columbia Pictures Entertainment Group from Coca-Cola, 1989
- knighted for services to Anglo-Japanese relations, 1992
- retired as chairman due to ill health at the age of 73, 1994

Major works

Made in Japan: Akio Morita and Sony (with E.M. Reingold and M. Shimomura) (1987)

Summary

The name of Akio Morita has become almost synonymous with the Sony Corporation, one of the foremost brand names in consumer electronics. The company has become renowned worldwide for a flood of innovatory products, including the transistor radio, the 'Trinitron' television tube and screen, the 'Betamax' video cassette recorder, and the 'Walkman' portable cassette player. Morita will always be remembered as the 'product champion' for the development of the Walkman cassette recorder. His success as co-founder and chairman of Sony in post-1945 Japan has marked him out as one of the outstanding businessmen of his generation. Ibuka and Morita determined to develop a company based on innovation. While Ibuka (the engineer) focused on the technical side, Morita (the physicist) gave much attention to marketing. They made innovations in managerial style too, to try to create an organizational structure and culture to foster innovation. Morita coined terms such as 'global localization' to characterize his company's approach to overseas operations. In addition to his prominent role in representative business organizations, such as the Keidanren, his excellent command of the English language, his forthright manner and his readiness to engage with a variety of audiences and media enabled him to play a wide role in the dissemination of business philosophies and in the representation of Japanese industry in overseas relations.

1 Biographical data

Akio Morita was born in 1921 into a rich and privileged *sake*-brewing family which traced its history back over fifteen generations (Morita *et al.* 1987: 4–5, 9). Morita's early determination to overturn tradition and strike out on his own path was evident in his decision to become an engineer rather than follow in the family footsteps as eldest son and take charge of one of Japan's oldest brewing businesses. His own father had given up his business studies course at Keio University to discharge his duty as eldest son and rescue the business from a decline triggered by one or two generations of aesthetic Morita art collectors. Yet Morita evaded his father's preferred course of economics and entered Osaka Imperial University to study physics under Professor Tsunesaburo Asada, an outstanding applied physicist.

By 1940, Asada was engaged on research work for the Imperial Japanese Navy and the young Morita helped with projects. Through this connection, Morita gained a commission as a technical officer. On graduation, he was assigned to the navy to work on thermal guidance weapons and night-vision gun sights. Here he met a brilliant electronics engineer, Masaru Ibuka, whose amplifier was critical for work on submarine detection (see IBUKA, M.). Thirteen years older than Morita, Ibuka was to become a friend, colleague, partner and co-founder of the Sony Corporation.

At the end of the war, Ibuka, with seven of his former colleagues, formed a small company, Tokyo Tsushin Kenkyusho (Tokyo Telecommunications Laboratory), to make short-wave radio adapters in a gutted department store in downtown Tokyo. Morita became a part-time employee of Ibuka's company and a part-time teacher at the Tokyo Institute of Technology (TIT). However, he took the opportunity of the purge of former military personnel from teaching to leave TIT and also negotiated his release from obligations to the Morita family business. By 1946, he was free to join Ibuka in a new company, Tokyo Tsushin Kogyo (Tokyo Telecommunications Engineering Company, abbreviated as TTK). The blessing of the Morita family was made evident in a series of loans to the fledgling company.

Morita and Ibuka had an initial vision for an innovative company: 'a clever company that would make new high technology products in ingenious ways' (Morita et al. 1987: 50). Yet the basic survival of the company rested on supplying new motors and magnetic pickups for the growing interest in popular music recordings in occupied Japan. An opportunity for innovation arose with Ibuka's inspection of an American tape recorder (and the need to adopt a paper tape as an alternative

to magnetic tape). Despite the technical virtuosity of the product, disappointing sales led Morita to the realization that they would need to identify, educate and even create a market for a product that was new to Japan. Using demonstrations in law courts on how to solve the shortage of stenographers, as well as visits to schools, Morita worked successfully to secure a market.

Morita was impressed by a music student's detailed and constructive criticism of the sound quality of the tape recorder and invited the student, Norio Ohga, to join the company as a consultant on the development of a new tape recorder. Meanwhile, Ibuka was exploring the potential for a small valveless radio using the transistor developed by the Bell Laboratories of the Western Electric Company in the USA. TTK began mass production of the radios in 1955. Morita learned from his first trip to the USA that the company was unlikely to excite interest in this potentially huge market, and so Morita and Ibuka renamed their TTK radio company Sony, derived from the Latin word *sonus* (meaning 'sound'), an appropriate name for a company preoccupied with audio technology.

The celebration of Sony's fifteenth anniversary in May 1961 brought Morita into sharp conflict with the labour union. Morita saw the original union as left-dominated and considered that it was using the celebration as a bargaining counter in its demand for a union shop. Resisting this demand as an infringement of individual liberties, Morita outflanked the union demonstration planned for the anniversary celebration by donning a morning coat at the headquarters building, thus giving the impression that that was where the celebration would take place; meanwhile Ibuka addressed guests, including prime minister Ikeda, at another venue. Subsequently, Morita went on the offensive by responding positively to the formation of a rival union by engineering staff. Nearly three decades later, Morita observed that the Sony parent company had two unions, one of which still caused occasional difficulty, but a majority of the employees were non-unionized (Morita et al. 1987: 141–3).

Motivated by Ibuka's complaints about the headphones of recorders, Morita set a specification for Sony engineers which led to the development of the Walkman. Morita set the engineers to strip out the recording features of a tape recorder, to lighten the resulting playback-only machine, to produce lightweight headphones and to achieve a target price within the budget range of a teenager. In the face of scepticism from engineers and salesmen, Morita persisted and added that the project time-scale should be six, rather than twelve, months. The Walkman machine that appeared in 1979 has become the stuff of legend in terms of its impact on sales and lifestyles.

In 1989, Morita's co-authorship, with an ebullient right-of-centre politician, of a book entitled *The Japan That Can Say 'No'* brought sharply mixed reactions. Washington policy makers tended to focus on the more strident notes of co-author, Shintaro Ishihara: for example, his claim that Japan could tip the balance of strategic power by selling semiconductors to the USSR. Although some Japanese thought that Japan should re-examine its national interests in the post cold-war era, Morita was deeply embarrassed by the affair and refused permission for his own contributions to be included in the US edition. Morita's own strictures had been directed at American society, which he believed had come to devalue manufacturing, and at American management, which had often abandoned high-quality manufacturing in favour of making money by manipulating financial markets. However, the more nationalistic overtones of his co-author were a liability for Morita, who was prominent as a constructive spokesperson in trade friction talks and also for Sony, with its large presence in the US market.

Morita achieved even greater prominence in the USA through the Sony Corporation's purchase of the US cultural icons CBS Records and Columbia pictures, and by 1990 he had arrived in *Fortune*'s list of 'The Year's Twenty-five Most Fascinating People'. This followed a rather different kind of recognition accorded him by the UK in 1982, when the Royal Society of Arts and Manufactures presented him with the Albert Medal 'for outstanding contributions to technological innovation and management, industrial design, industrial relations and video systems, and the growth of world trade relations'. In 1992, Queen Elizabeth II granted Morita an honorary knighthood in recognition of his contributions to Anglo-Japanese relations.

During the speculation between the July elections in 1993 and the formation of the new Japanese cabinet, Morita, despite being politically unattached, was widely tipped for the post of minister in the Ministry of International Trade and Industry. However, the possibility of Morita's further participation in public life was cut short by a stroke in 1993. Morita announced his retirement as the Sony Chairman in November 1994 after a disappointingly slow recovery.

2 Main contribution

Some commentators emphasize that Morita was not the creator of new technology but someone with the vision and skill to package it and create markets. Such commentaries should not underestimate the importance of his own technical background in appreciating new technology or in motivating teams of engineers to achieve technological breakthroughs.

Morita built Sony's reputation for high-quality technology through a firm insistence on controlling the distribution of company products (Morita 1986: 98–102). The company's forerunner, TTK, avoided using the traditional trading companies, despite their familiarity with the USA, on the grounds that they were unfamiliar with TTK products and did not necessarily share the TTK business philosophy. In the mid-1950s, the Bulova company offered to purchase a large order of radios, provided that they carried the Bulova name, but Morita refused to put another company's name on a TTK product. In 1959, Morita determined that Sony's first transistorized television set should not be discounted or marketed cheaply, and risk damage to its image. Although this strategy of tight control over the technology proved successful in the early years, it came into serious difficulties with the development of the video recorder and the market failure of Sony's Betamax system. If Sony had been willing to share its technology then it might have built an alliance to secure sufficient market share to withstand the arrival of JVC and its allies with the VHS system.

Morita commented that he and his colleagues had little formal business training, and much of their activity was developed through experience. As an innovative company, they did relatively little market research but pinned their efforts on refining their product development and then educating and communicating with the public.

Few companies have matched the track record for innovative products from the Sony Corporation. The company has kept faith with the original vision of Morita and Ibuka of a company where teamwork and creativity could flourish. Yet it has been a demanding strategy. Sony has poured much greater resources into research and development (R&D) than its rivals: for example, the annual R&D budget as a proportion of sales has often been double that of a company such as Matsushita (see MATSUSHITA, K.). Moreover, Sony has had to keep on innovating as the rivals have moved into the Sony slipstream with effective manufacturing capabilities and cheaper versions of Sony innovations. The profit record comparisons suggest that the followers often make a better return for their shareholders (Rafferty 1995).

Under Morita's leadership, Sony has not been innovative in technology alone. Morita has tried to secure organizational structures which motivate engineers and, even with a company of 6,000 employees in 1965, Sony had not established a formal organizational structure (Suzuki 1991: 312). However by 1970, Sony had adopted a divisional structure, which was further developed into a division headquarters structure through the 1970s. In 1970, Sony became the first Japanese company to appear on the New York Stock Exchange and the first to raise capital in the USA. The company has pioneered new business practices and developments in human resource management. In the early years, because of rapid growth and technology

intensiveness, Sony breached the tradition of 'lifetime employment' by attracting experienced staff from other companies (Kono 1984: 31). As Sony became established as a larger company itself, it was less easy to play the maverick with vigorous mid-career recruitment. Yet, even in the 1990s, Sony is still regarded as an innovative company and watched as a key to new developments in personnel policy in Japan, for example in its policies and practices for graduate recruitment.

Morita coined the term 'global localization' to describe the Sony Corporation's strategy in response to global competition as a combination of local management style and marketing with an overall corporate philosophy and a high standard of technology. With over 70 per cent of its sales outside Japan and an increasing proportion of its manufacturing overseas, Sony has built a network of factories to serve each of its main markets. By 1991, 475 of the 500 overseas subsidiaries were headed by non-Japanese staff, whereas in 1994, only thirteen of Matsushita's 158 subsidiaries were headed by a person who was not Japanese (Rafferty 1995: 197; Kono 1984: 164). Regional managers have been given considerable scope for investment and product decisions and senior managers from the worldwide subsidiaries hold a twice-yearly policy meeting to facilitate more rapid responses to market changes and new product launches. Thus, Morita's concept has become a guide for policy and practice.

Morita's retirement meant not only the loss of a colourful chairman for the Sony Corporation, but the loss to public life of the chair elect of the Keidanren, the very influential Japan Federation of Economic Organizations. Throughout the 1980s, Morita had acted as an important mediator in trade negotiations – someone who could urge Americans to put their house in order and strengthen their manufacturing industry while telling the Japanese to reduce their working hours and simplify distribution systems.

3 Evaluation

The Walkman has become one of the most successful products of the century, frequently appearing in popular listings of the top-ten technological innovations, and so successful that rival companies have adopted the name 'Walkman' as a generic term for portable cassette players. By 1993, over 100 million Walkmans had been sold worldwide. The outstanding success of this one product could mean that Akio Morita figures more in the public imagination as 'Mr Walkman' than as the founder and chairman of a major electronics company or as an international industrialist.

From its early years, Morita's company had a strong international outlook. This orientation was driven partly by its constrained situation in Japan where Matsushita had built a huge network of over 20,000 retail outlets which sold mainly Matsushita products. By 1965, over half Sony's sales were to overseas markets, especially to North America. Morita's personal commitment to an international orientation was signalled by the move of his family to the USA in the 1960s and the education of his children in Europe. His keen advocacy of Japanese staff going out beyond the Japanese community in overseas locations was reflected in his decision to locate the German subsidiary away from the Japanese community in Düsseldorf.

Morita has conceded that a creative company is likely to make mistakes and he has admitted his responsibility in the Betamax débâcle, in that he failed to build alliances and share technology. The US$3.4 billion takeover of Columbia Pictures in 1989 has remained controversial. Many argue that the financial and management problems of the acquisition have illustrated the wide gulf between US and Japanese business practice, even in Japan's most Westernized company.

Succession can be a major problem bequeathed by any charismatic leader to an organization. Yet Sony has continued to select presidents who have broken the anticipated organizational mould, reflecting a determination to develop along new paths and select leaders fit to grapple with novel problems. Ohga, the musician and opera singer who became president in 1982, had been Morita's direct nominee. Nobuyuki Idei, who became president in 1995 (as Ohga moved to

chairman), moved from head of Sony's product design strategy, past several more senior front-runner candidates, to become president. With a background in politics and economics, his strengths are said to lie in his understanding of both the hardware and the software aspects of Sony's business. Approaching its fiftieth anniversary in 1996, Sony is no longer the small, entrepreneurial company that was led by the charismatic Morita. Yet the vision of its founders remains a powerful talisman for a company with one of the most famous brand names in the world.

4 Conclusion

Morita has sometimes been regarded as a maverick, applauded for his courage and outspoken views and contrasted with the massed ranks of more reticent and self-effacing Japanese businessmen. Some even comment on the non-Japanese conduct of Morita and Sony. Yet Morita has served as an exemplar for a post-war generation in Japanese business. Morita *et al.*'s book, *Made in Japan* (1987), carries the sub-text 'self-made', for it describes the growth of a company whose founders, lacking substantial advantage, but with skill and technological resourcefulness in the post-war era, anticipated and responded to worldwide consumer demand. Moreover, the name Morita has always carried a strong sense of tradition in the 300-year-old family business which prepared such staples of the Japanese diet as *sake*, soy sauce and *miso* paste. His own public role in Japan and overseas has written a family tradition of public service in a modern idiom: 'Being in a business so central to the life of the community (*sake* brewing), the Morita family has taken a position of civic leadership as well' (Morita *et al.* 1987: 4–5).

KEVIN MCCORMICK
UNIVERSITY OF SUSSEX

Further reading

(References cited in the text marked *)

* Ishihara, S. (1991) *The Japan that Can Say 'No'*, New York: Simon & Schuster. (This English-

language version of the book was published without Morita's contribution. Its bold assertion of Japan's capacity to influence relations between the superpowers struck some sensitive nerves among its US readers.)

* Ishihara, S. and Morita, A. (1989) *'No' to ieru Nippon* (The Japan That Can Say 'No'), Tokyo: Kobunsha. (This controversial book sold more than one million copies in 1989 and 1990. Morita gave an account of industrial relations in Japan as essentially cooperative and a contributory factor in Japan's post-war economic development and outlined his view of the shortcomings of American management.)

* Kono, T. (1984) *Strategy and Structure of Japanese Enterprises*, London: Macmillan. (This account of strategy and structure among Japanese companies gives particular insights into the multinational aspects of management and organization in Sony Corporation.)

* Morita, A. (1986) 'When Sony was an up-and-comer', *Forbes* 138 (7): 98–102. (This paper offers insights into the early years of the Sony Corporation.)

Morita, A. (1992) 'Partnering for competitiveness: the role of Japanese business', *Harvard Business Review* 70 (3): 76–83. (This paper discusses the international role of Japanese corporations.)

* Morita, A., Reingold, E.M. and Shimomura, M. (1987) *Made in Japan: Akio Morita and Sony*, London: Collins. (This autobiography covers the development of Morita and Sony and the context of Japan's post-war development.)

Pascale, R.T. and Athos, A.G. (1982) *The Art of Japanese Management*, Harmondsworth: Penguin. (This study of Japanese management is based on a close analysis of Konosuke Matsushita and the Matsushita Electric company: comparisons with Morita and Sony are often made.)

* Rafferty, K.I. (1995) *Inside Japan's Power Houses: The Culture, Mystique and Future of Japan's Greatest Corporations*, London: Weidenfeld & Nicolson. (This study of some major corporations provides illustrative comparisons of strategies and performance between the Sony Corporation and the Matsushita Electric Company.)

* Suzuki, Y. (1991) *Japanese Management Structures, 1920–80*, Basingstoke: Macmillan. (This study gives an account of the adoption of the divisional organizational form in the Sony Corporation.)

Whitehill, A. (1991) *Japanese Management: Tradition and Transition*, London: Routledge. (This overview of Japanese management provides a context for Morita's own distinctive approach to management.)

See also: IBUKA, M.; MATSUSHITA, K.; OHMAE, K.; OHNO, T.

Related topics in the IEBH: GLOBALIZATION; INDUSTRIAL RELATIONS IN JAPAN; JAPANIZATION; JUST-IN-TIME; MANAGEMENT EDUCATION IN JAPAN; MANAGEMENT IN JAPAN; NEW PRODUCT DEVELOPMENT; TOTAL QUALITY MANAGEMENT

Nonaka, Ikujiro (1935–)

1 Biographical data
2 Strategy and organization
3 Self-renewal and innovation
4 Knowledge creation
5 Conclusions

Personal background

- born in Tokyo, Japan, 10 May 1935
- received a BS in political science from Waseda University, Japan, 1958
- member of the corporate staff at Fuji Electric Company, Japan,1958–70
- received an MBA (1968) and a PhD (1972) from the University of California, Berkeley, USA
- professor in the department of business administration, Nanzan University, Japan, 1978–9
- professor in the department of social sciences, National Defence Academy, Japan, 1979–82
- professor at the Institute of Business Research, Hitotsubashi University, Japan, 1982–
- director of research at the National Institute of Science and Technology Policy, Japan, 1991–5
- director of the Institute of Business Research, Hitotsubashi University, Japan, 1995–7
- professor and director of the department of knowledge science, Japan Advanced Institute of Science and Technology, Hokuriku, Japan, 1997–
- professor at the Innovation Research Centre, Hitotsubashi University, Japan, 1997–
- Xerox Distinguished Professor of Knowledge, Haas School of Business, University of California, Berkeley, USA, 1997–

Major works

The Knowledge-Creating Company (1995)
Managing Organizational Knowledge Creation (1991) (in Japanese)
Strategic vs. Evolutionary Management: A US–Japan Comparison of Strategy and Organization (1985).
Organization and Market: A Contingency Theory (1974) (in Japanese)

Summary

Ikujiro Nonaka is recognized as a leading figure in management studies in both Japan and the West and has played a key role in the bringing insights from Japanese management practice to a wider audience. His research, whilst spanning international boundaries, transcends them by dealing with common issues of strategy and organization, self renewal, innovation and knowledge creation processes. The main themes running throughout his work relate to information and knowledge and their role in business strategy and organization. His work includes a balance between practical case studies and creative theory development. He is best known for his work on organizational knowledge creation.

1 Biographical data

Ikujiro Nonaka was born in Tokyo, Japan in 1935. He graduated in political science in 1958 from Waseda University and entered the Fuji Electric Company where he worked as a staff member for over ten years. In the late 1960s he graduated from the University of California at Berkeley MBA course. Following this he continued to pursue an academic career by carrying out doctoral research at Berkeley. He has said that this combination of work in industry and training in research based on theory development enabled him to combine a compulsion to be 'practical and seek reality in business' with his interest in theory development.

He completed his PhD thesis entitled 'Organization and market: exploratory study of centralization vs. decentralization' in the autumn of 1972. His subsequent book *Organization and Market: A Contingency Theory* (published in Japanese) won the 1974 Nikkei Award in Economics and Business. In 1978 he returned to Japan and a post as professor in the department of business administration at Nanzan University before moving to a post in the department of social sciences at the National Defence Academy. There he carried out research on contingency theory based on the information processing paradigm. In 1982 he moved to the Institute of Business Research at Hitotsubashi University, becoming director in 1995.

His book *Strategic vs. Evolutionary Management: A US–Japan Comparison of Strategy and Organization* written jointly with Kagono *et al.* was published in 1985. The Japanese version won the 1984 Book of the Year Award of the Academic Association of Organizational Science in Japan. In 1988, his *Sloan Management Review* article 'Toward middle-up-down management: accelerating information creation' won the fouth annual Richard Beckhard Prize. His 1991 *Harvard Business Review* article on 'The knowledge creating company' has also been frequently cited and his related book in Japanese entitled *Managing Organizational Knowledge Creation* won the 1991 Nippon Administrative Management Association prize.

From 1991–5, he combined his work at Hitotsubashi with being a research director of the National Institute of Science and Technology Policy, the Japanese Science and Technology Agency's Policy Research Centre based in the centre of Tokyo. 1995 saw the publication of his most influential work *The Knowledge-Creating Company* which was awarded the 1996 Best Book of the Year Award in Business and Management by the Association of American Publishers.

In 1997, whilst remaining a professor at Hitotsubashi University's Innovation Research Centre, he took up an appointment as professor at the Japan Advanced Institute of Science and Technology (JAIST) in Tatsunokuchi, Ishikawa Prefecture, in the Hokuriku region of Japan, where he is research director of the newly created department of knowledge science. In 1997, he also became the first Xerox Distinguished Professor of Knowledge at the University of California, Berkeley, a chair jointly funded by Fuji Xerox in Japan and Xerox Corporation in the USA.

The long period of time that Nonaka has spent in the USA, combined with education both there and in Japan, has contributed to his unusual ability to bridge the two cultures and write equally successfully for both a Japanese and US readership; something evidenced by the prizes and critical acclaim his work has received in both Japan and the USA. His work has ranged widely over the areas of business strategy and organization studies. However, it is for his work in connection with the establishment of knowledge as an area of specialist study within the field of management studies that he is best known.

Since his work can be divided into three main areas – strategy and organization studies, self-renewal and innovation management and organizational knowledge creation – these will each be considered in turn. Nonaka, it should be said, has published widely in both English and Japanese. Whilst most of his work in Japanese has been published in English in some form this summary is necessarily limited in referring to just his publications in English.

2 Strategy and organization

Though not his first book, one which summarizes much of his earlier post-doctoral work and contains the seeds of his later work is his *Strategic vs. Evolutionary Management: A US–Japan Comparison of Strategy and Organization* (Nonaka *et al.* 1985). This book describes research carried out between 1976 and the early 1980s. It forms the first attempt to compare systematically the strategy and organization of US and Japanese companies. It also shows the development of his thinking from comparing US and Japanese management using a contingency based approach to the consideration of an evolutionary theory of organization and the use of a self-organizing organizational paradigm.

The work identifies four types of environmental adaption comprising either an operations or a product orientation to strategy combined with either a group dynamics or a bureaucratic dynamics approach to organization. Japanese companies are identified as adapting primarily via a group dynamics/operations approach whilst US firms are characterized by a bureaucratic dynamics /product orientation. A move towards a more group dynamics/product orientation is advocated for both. A key factor in the adaption process is identified as the accumulation of information and transfer of knowledge and the information orientation of the company. Another feature of the group dynamics/operations approach is exemplified by the case study of Matsushita where the feature of redundancy in product development is seen as a benefit, an idea that Nonaka develops in his later work. The book concludes with a discussion of an evolutionary view of strategy as a self-organizing paradigm. Knowledge is seen as a key element in this process and companies with a group dynamics approach are seen to have an advantage in that they can 'generate, select and retain new variations and thereby continually renew themselves'. This concept of the self-renewing organization is another which Nonaka develops further in his later writing.

The main emphasis in this work is on comparative study. A contingency-based approach is used because it is consistent with both information processing and resource dependency models. However, there are references to Nonaka's earlier doctoral work and a wish to develop the information processing paradigm and it is this theme of information, leading on to what he calls the 'similar but different' concept of knowledge that runs throughout his work.

3 Self-renewal and innovation

Nonaka's subsequent writing has developed the themes of information and organization and highlighted the role of product development and innovation in the self-renewal of a company's organization.

In writing about innovation, Nonaka is largely concerned with innovation processes involved in major projects in large companies which helps emphasize the relevance to the organization as a whole. In the article 'The new new product development game', (1986) Nonaka and Takeuchi advocate a 'rugby' based approach to product development. Traditional sequential approaches to new product development are seen as more limited than one that involves constant interaction among multidisciplinary team members who move through the development process in overlapping stages. Case studies involving the development of the Honda City, Canon and Fuji-Xerox copiers and Canon cameras are used to identify six characteristics of leading product development processes: 1) built-in stability; 2) self-organizing project teams; 3) overlapping product development phases; 4) multilevel and multifunction learning; 5) subtle control; 6) learning transfer.

In a further article 'Creating organizational order out of chaos: self-renewal in Japanese firms' (1988), Nonaka argues that the essence of self-organization lies in information creation and that self-renewal depends on an organization's ability to control the consequent creation and dissolution of organizational order. The self-renewing process is described as comprising four steps: 1) the creation of chaos or fluctuation in a company; 2) the amplification of that chaos and a focusing on contradictions; 3) a dynamic cooperation through the formation of self-organizing teams acting in a rugby-like manner; 4) the restructuring of the accumulated information into knowledge. The first three steps in this process are identified as information creation processes and the fourth as an integrative process by which a learning organization transforms information into knowledge stock to be distributed around the organization.

Whilst Nonaka's earlier comparative work was based on contingency theory, in his work on self-renewal and innovation he goes beyond the contingency theory/information processing view in which organizations are seen as adopting a structure which can best process information generated by the environment. Instead, he takes the view that human beings are not just processors but creators of information and that this creation of information is an essential part of organizational self-renewal.

A further development from Nonaka's study of the innovation and product development process in large companies occurs in his discussion of the development of the Honda City in his article 'Toward middle-up-down management: accelerating information creation' (1988). Here, Nonaka develops the idea of information creation as a source of innovation and renewal involving self-organizing teams. He does this by highlighting the key role of middle management in Japanese companies' information creation processes. In doing so he identifies three modes of information creation involving: deductive, inductive and 'compressive' management. The latter of these involves an emphasis on time, self-organizing teams and a 'middle-up-down management' approach involving both articulate and tacit knowledge. Middle managers are thus identified as being in a key position to act as an agent for change. This change process, involving contradictions and their resolution, comprises a spiral process of lower hypothesis testing, middle range theory and top level theory creation which in turn leads to the creation of further contradictions, thus continuing the self-renewal process.

Nonaka sums up many of his ideas relating to innovation in his article concerning information redundancy in the innovation process 'Redundant, overlapping organization : a Japanese approach to managing the innovation process' (1990). He re-emphasizes that the innovation process in Japanese companies follows an information-creating, not an information-processing, model. He also defines 'information redundancy', as a condition where excess or supplemental information is shared among a group in addition to the basic information that each individual, department, or organization needs to perform its assigned functions. This increases the possibility of loyalty and trust forming within the organization and of generating problems and solutions. This 'information

redundancy', thus directly affects the information and knowledge-creating characteristics of a company.

4 Knowledge creation

The most recent trend in Nonaka's writing is from consideration of information creation to a concentration on the subsequent process of knowledge creation identified earlier as the final stage in the self-renewal process followed by many companies. This draws on a number of Nonaka's books and articles in both Japanese and English (e.g. Nonaka 1991, 1994) as well as Nonaka's earlier work on innovation and organizational self-renewal.

The key work which summarizes Nonaka's thinking on this issue is his book *The Knowledge-Creating Company* (Nonaka and Takeuchi 1995). The focus of this book is on organizational knowledge creation , not on knowledge per se. It draws on a long line of philosophers' considerations of the nature of knowledge. Though not listed amongst the foremost of these philosophers, the key one for Nonaka's approach is Michael Polanyi, whose distinction between tacit and explicit knowledge is central to much of Nonaka's writing. Within this scheme, Western knowledge creation is seen as individual-based and explicit knowledge-oriented with an emphasis on the firm as an information processing machine. In contrast, Japanese knowledge creation is seen as group-based and tacit knowledge-oriented depending not on information processing but on tapping the tacit and sometimes subjective insights of employees.

The dynamic process by which new knowledge is created within the organization – in the form of new products, services or systems – is put forward as the cornerstone of innovation. Japanese companies' organizational knowledge creation is identified as resulting from the interaction between tacit knowledge and explicit knowledge. Four knowledge creating conversion modes are proposed : tacit to tacit (socialization), tacit to explicit (externalization), explicit to explicit (combination) and explicit to tacit (internalization). Externalization is the key step in creating new knowledge and in achieving this the role of metaphors, analogies and modelling is emphasized.

Amongst a number of others, two case studies involving international collaboration in product development are discussed. These emphasize the particular importance of prolonged socialization and externalization, which leads to the interesting observation that both of these processes take time to achieve since it takes time to build trust and share tacit knowledge across cultural and linguistic barriers.

At the heart of Nonaka and Takeuchi's theory of organizational knowledge creation there is an interaction over time between an epistemological (knowledge conversion) spiral and an ontological (organizational level) spiral process from one organizational level of aggregation to another. The former spiral, involving interaction between tacit and explicit forms, and the latter spiral interaction, between individual, group and organizational levels, in part reminiscent of the spiral process involved in 'middle-up-down' management referred to above. These three dimensions form the framework for the dynamic knowledge creation process that fuels innovation.

Two further important aspects are that neither Japanese nor Western models and neither hierarchical nor task force-oriented structures are proposed as ideal for knowledge creation. Instead, a 'hypertext' organization which facilitates the process allied with an integration of both Western and Japanese methodologies. Nonaka's view of the developing 'knowledge society' is thus one where knowledge creation skills are crucial and nationality irrelevant.

5 Conclusions

Ikujiro Nonaka is acknowledged by many to be Japan's leading management scholar. The record of well-respected, indeed prize-winning publications, and what is universally acknowledged as creative theory development supports this. This success might be said to be based on two bridges. First, a bridge between theory and practice through a combination of creative theory generation and interesting case studies. Second, a bridge over the linguistic and cultural gap which so often hinders learning from Japan, but one involving a balanced view of the advantages and disadvantages of both Western and Japanese approaches.

The majority of Nonaka's work concentrates on the management of large Japanese companies with a well-established middle management layer. Some have questioned whether a theory of organizational knowledge creation which emphasizes the role of middle management can apply to small companies. However, it seems likely that senior small company managers have in many senses similar micro and macro management roles to large company middle managers. Furthermore, Nonaka's spirals of knowledge creation begin at an individual level and involve greater and greater organizational units eventually crossing organizational boundaries. Thus Nonaka's theory of organizational knowledge creation would seem to be independent of organization size, though as the case studies on international collaboration show, the greater the cultural or organizational barriers involved the more they can affect the process of knowledge creation.

The issue of barriers is also the source of another potential criticizm which some have raised. Barriers to learning often occur within Western organizations due to internal political considerations. Organizational knowledge creation as proposed by Nonaka and Takeuchi depends on a lack of internal barriers to knowledge creating interactions and a beneficial lack of such barriers is evident in the Japanese firms studied.

However, Nonaka and Takeuchi's theory is proposed not as a model for Japanese Organizational Knowledge Creation but as a generic model. This begs the question as to how the model will fare outside a Japanese context where Western employees may be more self-centred than organization-centred and where the integrative abilities of Western organizations may not match those of Japanese organizations. Against such criticism, it must be said that even if cultural and institutional issues can affect organizational knowledge creation processes they do not necessarily contradict the theory that Nonaka and Takeuchi propose.

As Japan approaches the twenty-first century it is moving from being an information-based to a knowledge-based society and many aspects of its economy are shifting towards promoting creativity and originality. Management of knowledge and of other intellectual assets are without doubt major issues in business today, whether nationally or globally. However, without knowledge creation skills there will be no new knowledge or new intellectual assets to manage and thus Nonaka's leading research and creative thinking in this field will continue to be a significant contribution to understanding this important aspect of management.

ROBERT PITKETHLY
UNIVERSITY OF OXFORD

Further reading

(References cited in the text marked *)

Nonaka, I. (1974) *Organization and Market: A Contingency Theory*, Tokyo: Chikura Shobo, (An early statement of his original work in Japanese).

* Nonaka, I. (1988) 'Toward middle-up-down management: accelerating information creation', *Sloan Management Review* 29: 9–18. (The Honda City case is used to propose 'middle-up--down management' as a method of information creation.)

* Nonaka, I. (1988) 'Creating organizational order out of chaos: self-renewal in Japanese firms', *California Management Review* 30: 57–73. (Argues that self-organization involves information creation and that self-renewal additionally comprises restructuring of that information into knowledge.)

* Nonaka, I. (1990) 'Redundant, overlapping organization: a Japanese approach to managing the innovation process' *California Management Review* 32: 27-38. (Discusses 'information redundancy' and suggests that Japanese innovation follows an information-creating, not information-processing, model.)

Nonaka, I. (1991) *Managing Organizational Knowledge Creation*, Tokyo: Nihon Keizai Shimbun-sha, (Sets out his theory of Organizational Knowledge creation processes in Japanese).

* Nonaka, I. (1991) 'The knowledge-creating company', *Harvard Business Review* 69: 96–104. (Contrasts Western views of knowledge and information processing with Japanese company thinking.)

* Nonaka, I. (1994) 'A dynamic theory of organizational knowledge creation', *Organization Science* 5 : 14–37. (Discusses four key knowledge creating interactions between tacit and explicit knowledge.)

* Nonaka, I. and Takeuchi, H. (1986), 'The new new product development game', *Harvard Business Review* 64: 137–146. (Advocates constant interaction between multidisciplinary teams involved in overlapping development stages.)

* Nonaka, I.. and Takeuchi, H. (1995) *The Knowledge-Creating Company*, New York : Oxford University Press. (Nonaka's key work on his theory of Organizational Knowledge Creation).

* Nonaka, I. and Yamanouchi, T. (1989) 'Managing innovation as a self-renewing process', *Journal of Business Venturing* 4: 299–315. (Development of Canon's Mini Copier shows how self-renewal of an organization involves a process of information creation.)

* Nonaka, I. *et al.* (1985) *Strategic vs. Evolutionary Management: A US–Japan Comparison of Strategy and Organization*, Amsterdam: North-Holland. (A broad but detailed questionnaire and contingency theory based comparative study of US and Japanese management.)

See also: OHMAE, K.; STARBUCK, W.

Related topics in the IEBM: GROUPS AND TEAMS; INFORMATION AND KNOWLEDGE INDUSTRY; INNOVATION AND CHANGE; JAPANIZATION; MANAGEMENT IN JAPAN; NEW PRODUCT DEVELOPMENT; ORGANIZATION BEHAVIOUR; ORGANIZATION STRUCTURE; ORGANIZATIONAL INFORMATION AND KNOWLEDGE; ORGANIZATIONAL LEARNING

Ohmae, Kenichi (1943–)

1 Introduction
2 Biographical data
3 Main contribution
4 Evaluation
5 Conclusions

Personal background

- born Kyushu, Japan, in 1943
- trained as a concert flautist and nuclear physicist at Japan's Waseda University and at the Tokyo Institute of Technology; PhD in Nuclear Engineering from Massachusetts Institute of Technology
- joined McKinsey in 1972; managing director of its Tokyo office
- advisor to Japanese former prime minister Nakasone
- writes frequently for *The Wall Street Journal* and the *Harvard Business Review*

Major works

The Mind of the Strategist (1982)
Triad Power: The Coming Shape of Global Competition (1985)
Beyond National Borders: Reflections on Japan and the World (1987)
The Borderless World: Power and Strategy in the Interlinked Economy (1990)

Summary

Ohmae is one of Japan's most influential thinkers and the best-known Japanese business consultant in the West. His original and probing mind tries to get below the surface of issues. He has written over thirty books, principally in Japanese, exploring issues of business strategy and economic theory, and social as well as political questions.

1 Introduction

Although Ohmae had written five books on strategy (three of them best sellers) in Japanese, he came to the West's attention through his first book in English, *The Mind of the Strategist* (1982). The book gained instant popularity partly because, as a result of the astonishing rise in Japan's fortunes, many in the West were seeking to understand 'how the Japanese do it'. However, the book was essentially a re-examination of the fundamentals of logic and intuition in relation to strategy from a Japanese perspective. The book is still one of the most straightforward, easy to read and inspiring works on the subject. With each subsequent book, however, Ohmae has become more and more of an enthusiast for global free trade, berating governments and bureaucracies for getting in the way. The *Financial Times* once described him as 'a personality in a land where outspoken personalities are rare. And while most Japanese are anxious not to offend, Ohmae is blunt and often downright rude'.

2 Biographical data

Kenichi Ohmae was born in Kyushu, Japan, in 1943. After studying as a concert flautist and then as a nuclear physicist at Japan's Waseda University and at The Tokyo Institute of Technology, he chose to continue his interest in nuclear physics at the Massachusetts Institute of Technology, completing a PhD there before being recruited by the management consultancy firm McKinsey. He rose rapidly within the ranks, writing along the way, and becoming managing director of McKinsey in Japan. He is married and has two daughters.

3 Main contribution

Ohmae's main contribution has been to the debate about the globalization of business. In *Triad Power* (1985), he argues that companies in international markets need to establish a strong presence in each of the three main economic zones in the world: the USA, Europe, and Japan and the Pacific. If a company fails to do this it becomes vulnerable, in Ohmae's view, because its global competitors can use their strengths in the other major markets to fuel attacks on that company.

Ohmae points out that the triad, with its population of some 630 million customers, has a triple key to success: commitment, creativity and competitiveness. The last two depend on several factors, notably the level and quantity of education/training and the willingness and adaptability to find a work with good joint venture partners.

Such ideas were received favourably, but there was less congratulation when Ohmae proposed moving all of Japan's rice producers to Alabama, where they could buy the land cheaply, using the proceeds from their farm lands in Japan which could be vacated and sold in order to make room for buildings: 'The heavy subsidies to Japanese farmers are holding back development and making the cost of rice artificially high' (Ohmae 1990: 142–3). Ohmae's solution would, he believed, cut the price of rice by two-thirds and stimulate the economy at the same time.

Ohmae's world view strips economics down to first principles. He feels that interdependence is the key to making our world work. Among his most controversial claims was that there was no trade imbalance between the USA and Japan: 'the sales of US companies in Japan plus imports from the United States equal the sales of Japanese companies in the United States plus exports to that country' (Ohmae 1990: 142–3).

In *Beyond National Borders* (1987), Ohmae proposes a common community (cultural, monetary and political) for Japan, Europe and the USA, and argues that the three zones ought to share political power – a political arrangement similar to the Treaty of Rome, which established the European Economic Community in 1957. In 1990 Ohmae published the *The Borderless World* in which he argues that global strategy is 'almost a matter of survival' because competition in most fields is increasingly global. Ohmae divides global strategy into five phases. In the first phase, a company needs a strong product concept as well as an orientation to export. In the second, the company needs to establish branches in the target country to handle sales and marketing. The third phase is marked by the replication of the manufacturing operation in key markets. The fourth phase, 'insiderization', aims to create a clone of the entire parent company in those locations, complete with research and development, engineering, finance, personnel and other headquarters functions; such an approach enables products to be developed for those markets, and enables the development of those markets as well as the building of strong local management. Finally, the complete 'global company' can emerge, which involves transferring some corporate functions, such as brand management or research and development, either back to the old centre or to new centres which develop excellence in that area of activity. The global company survives and flourishes on the basis of shared values and on the basis of an effective communication network right across the organization.

Ohmae believes that the globalization of the world economy may lead to the disintegration of the nation-state as we have understood it. 'The nation is an unnatural unit' he said in a speech in Tokyo in 1992, 'every time I try to define it, I'm baffled'. In his view, individuals belong first to the earth and secondly to their immediate community. One day, he believes, the availability of consumer goods will be the yardstick by which all governments will be judged. 'Information is changing the world. Its power is so strong that it is impossible to hold it back. The emerging new reality is that consumers will decide for themselves what they want'. As the tide of human knowledge rises, it will submerge nationalism to produce a world of loose federations and affiliations of local regions and 'region-states'. He believes that there is:

no longer such a thing as the US versus Japan. In fact, we sometimes cannot even distinguish between them or any other countries, because we have an increasing amount of cross-investment between countries. But, even though we have been brought up thinking in terms of nation-states, efforts in the EC and trade pacts in the ASEAN countries, North America and Latin America, demonstrate a trend whereby people are already thinking along the radical lines of lowering trade barriers and forming greater economic units. This is a move away from trade based on the political agenda of parochial governments. It is actually a step toward allowing trade to take place freely on a regional scale and then on a world scale which is in the interest of consumers The world economy is already interlinked, with consumer wants and consumer needs becoming increasingly similar. As this happens, consumers will eventually take the upper hand in deciding the policies of their nation. Sovereignty has shifted from the central national government to the consumer.

(Ohmae 1987)

4 Evaluation

Ohmae has timed his contributions right, picking up key themes which exercised readers at the time of publication. However, the books also have the status of contemporary classics. In the long run, *The Mind of the Strategist* (1982) is his only book to date which will continue to be read, because most of the arguments of the other books are time-bound and will either have happened or be seen to be unrealistic.

However, *The Borderless World* (1990) is an implicit attack on macroeconomic theory in the form in which it is still taught and studied in university and business school courses, even though the world has moved on. In Ohmae's view, power has passed out of the hands of governments and business magnates into the hands of customers who are driving multinationals to operate and sell 'in many countries at once and who in the process are helping to create a borderless economy where trade statistics are meaningless'. This is because the statistics are skewed by the fact that the total exports or imports from any country do not have any way of indicating the individual companies which are exporting or importing products, and because companies are increasingly owned by shareholders from other countries. While making the wider point, Ohmae was also turning the free trade argument of the USA's Japan-bashers against themselves.

Ohmae's attack on government is also noteworthy: attempts to control organic currency fluctuation can discourage investment: the US trade deficit as well as the Japanese surplus are both illusions (as long as US dollars are used as the international currency of settlement, the US technically has no foreign trade). 'Artificially expensive dollars during the Reagan years forced quite a few American companies towards offshore production. Artificially cheaper dollars have not pulled them back but rather have made the US itself inexpensive for foreigners to buy'. Currency fluctuations have simply given chief executive officers and their companies wider options in global strategy. Their actions are now beyond government control.

For the first time in human history, Ohmae believes, nations no longer derive their wealth only from such physical resources such as gold mines, but also from intellectual property and education. This is the only area where governments can play a proper role, providing for and encouraging education and creating the right infrastructure, both physical and legal, in which global trade can enrich us all.

5 Conclusions

This view is all very well for approximately 10 per cent of the world's population who will benefit, compared to the 90 per cent who will lose out in comparative terms, in the unbridled *laissez-faire* capitalism which Ohmae advocates. Although proponents of that viewpoint like to emphasize that, in absolute terms, most people have benefited from the varieties of *laissez-faire* capitalism which have held sway since the Second World War, they neglect to observe that the achievement has been at a certain cost to the environment and to future generations, and that continuing down the same path is unsustainable because the world simply cannot give to every family on earth the American dream of two cars and a detached house with its own swimming pool. And if we do so for anything less than 100 per cent of the world, we will have to find ways of controlling the jealousy and capacity for theft, violence and destruction of those who are left out. So far, religion and government have performed that role. It is not at all clear that 'the invisible hand of the market' is capable of doing this by itself, if the experience of Anglo-American-style economies is anything to go by.

PRABHU S. GUPTARA
ADVANCE: MANAGEMENT TRAINING LTD
UNION BANK OF SWITZERLAND

Further reading

(References cited in the text marked*)

* Ohmae, K. (1982) *The Mind of the Strategist*, New York: McGraw-Hill. (Leans against the tendency, in the Anglo-American business world, to focus on numbers and 'facts'; urges a balance between these and intuitive knowledge of the market as well as of customers in developing strategy.)
* Ohmae, K. (1985) *Triad Power: The Coming Shape of Global Competition*, New York: Free Press. (Argues that there are three principal areas of the world where the battle for global business domination is fought: the USA, Japan and Europe.)
* Ohmae, K. (1987) *Beyond National Borders: Reflections on Japan and the World*, Homewood, IL: Dow Jones-Irwin. (Responds to the US accusation that Japan dumps its products abroad and has tariff as well as non-tariff barriers which make it, in effect, a protected economy; also ponders Japan's new position in the world, socially and politically.)
* Ohmae, K. (1990) *The Borderless World: Power and Strategy in the Interlinked Economy*, New York: Collins. (Develops his idea of the Triad beyond the three countries, to suggest that the rich people of the world, wherever they may be, form an Interlinked Economy; considers the implications for strategy, economics, government and business.)

See also: LEVITT, T.; MORITA, A.; SUN TZU

Related topics in the IEBM: BUSINESS CULTURE, JAPANESE; BUSINESS STRATEGY, JAPANESE; ECONOMIC INTEGRATION, INTERNATIONAL; GLOBALIZATION; INFORMATION REVOLUTION; JAPANIZATION; MANAGEMENT IN JAPAN; MANAGEMENT IN NORTH AMERICA; MULTINATIONAL CORPORATIONS, ORGANIZATION STRUCTURE IN; STRATEGIC CHOICE; STRATEGY; STRATEGY, CONCEPT OF

Ohno, Taiichi (1912–1990)

Personal background

- born at Port Arthur, Manchuria, China, in February 1912
- graduated from Department of Mechanical Engineering of Nagoya Technical High School in Nagoya, Japan in 1932
- joined Toyoda Spinning and Weaving Company in 1932
- transferred to Toyota Motor Company 1942
- named machine shop manager 1949
- appointed managing director of Toyota Motor Company in 1964
- promoted to executive vice president in 1975
- retired from Toyota Motor Company in 1978
- became chairman of Toyoda Gosei, a Toyota Motor Company supplier, in 1978
- resided in Toyota-shi, Aichi-ken, until his death in 1990

Major works

Toyota Production System: Beyond Large-Scale Production (1988)
Just-in-Time For Today and Tomorrow (1988)

Summary

Taiichi Ohno is generally regarded as the 'father' of the Toyota Production System (TPS). This innovative approach to production can simultaneously reduce costs, improve quality, and reduce lead times. It played a major role in the growth of the Toyota Motor Company, and has spread throughout the world as 'just-in-time' (JIT) manufacturing.

Ohno combined missionary zeal with engineering pragmatism in developing the Toyota System. He had an idealized, Platonic vision of manufacturing, with products flowing continuously through the factory, from work station to work station, eliminating completely what he called 'waste'. He considered all activities that did not add value to the product a form of waste. Non-value activities include product moves, inspections, and, particularly, the accumulation of inventory. For a period of thirty years, from 1945 to 1975, Ohno systematically pursued the elimination of production 'waste'. The collection of techniques that he used evolved into an effective and integrated system – the TPS.

1 Introduction

Taiichi Ohno's transfer to the Toyota Motor Company in 1942 was a fortuitous move. He was the right man, in the right place, at the right time. In post-war Japan automobile demand was low, raw material costs were high, and productivity was very low. In 1945, Toyota's President, Kiichiro Toyoda, launched a bold 'Catch Up With America' campaign. This was a formidable challenge, since the productivity of the US car manufacturers was ten times that of Japanese producers like Toyota. Ohno realized that this productivity gap could not be explained by differences in physical effort. He concluded that the reason had to be wasteful practices in Japanese manufacturing and for him, the elimination of this waste at Toyota became an obsession.

2 Biographical data

Taiichi Ohno was born in 1912 in Manchuria, China. He attended school in Japan, graduating from the mechanical engineering department of Nagoya Technical High School in the spring of 1932. Jobs were scarce, but fortunately Ohno's father was an acquaintance of Kiichiro Toyoda, President of the Toyoda Spinning and Weaving Company (see TOYODA FAMILY). Ohno joined Toyoda shortly after graduation. He worked as a textile engineer for ten years, gaining valuable experience during a period in which the Japanese textile industry made great strides in global competitiveness by improving production methods and reducing costs. In 1942 Ohno moved to another part of the Toyoda organization, the Toyota Motor Company – a marketing consultant had recommended that the family name be modified.

Ohno's textile experience proved to be a valuable asset, since the automotive industry, including Toyota, was lagging behind the textile industry in manufacturing effectiveness. Ohno started developing the Toyota System while he was foreman of the machine shop. He was greatly influenced by what he considered two 'pillars of wisdom', developed by Kiichiro Toyoda as part of his 'Catch Up With America' campaign. First, just-in-time production flow: parts should arrive at each work station at the exact time and in the exact quantity needed. Second, 'autonomation', or automation with a human touch: machines should be equipped with an automatic checking device to ensure that every piece produced is acceptable. If not, the machine should shut itself off and activate a trouble signal.

Toyoda's 'pillars of wisdom' meshed well with Ohno's desire to eliminate waste, and they became cornerstones of his production system. His success in dramatically increasing Toyota's productivity gained him a series of promotions. He became a director in 1954, managing director in 1964 and executive vice president in 1975. He retired from Toyota in 1978 and assumed the chairmanship of a member of the Toyota *keiretsu* (family of suppliers), Toyoda Gosei. He resided in Toyota-shi, Aichi-ken until his death, 28 May 1990.

3 Main contributions

Ohno 'stood on Henry Ford's shoulders' (see FORD, H.). The Ford system of mass production, developed in the early 1900s, was a dramatic break with the prevailing craft-based production. Ford eliminated the need for craft skills by the use of interchangeable parts. He capitalized on this advantage by linking together an army of unskilled workers, each performing a short, standardized portion of the total process. The emphasis on flow was enhanced by the development of the moving assembly line.

The Ford system was the standard of competitiveness in the post-war auto industry, but it had to be modified to suit the conditions at Toyota. The need for long production runs of a single model at Ford was incompatible with the low volume of the Japanese automobile market and the severe shortage of resources in Japan made it impractical to adopt the Ford system of using large inventories of parts. The Toyota Production System (TPS) evolved out of the need to adapt Ford mass production to the economic realities of post-war Japan.

The challenge facing Ohno was to overcome Ford's economies of scale with greater flexibility, or 'economies of scope'. This had to be done without the large buffer inventories needed by Ford to keep the assembly line going in the face of problems such as late part deliveries, machine breakdowns and defective parts. Ohno's major contribution is the manner in which he met this challenge.

By dramatically reducing machine and assembly set-up times, it became feasible for Toyota to produce a continuous stream of small quantities of a variety of models. This 'mixed model production' decreased inventories, increased model flexibility and shortened delivery times. To ensure continuity of product flow without large buffers, support programmes were developed to eliminate production problems systematically. These programmes included 'Total Preventative Maintenance', 'Total Quality Management', 'Continuous Improvement',

'Autonomation', and 'Just-in-Time supplier deliveries'.

Ohno's innovative solution improved the Ford system for mass production by making it more efficient and more flexible. But it also improved the low volume production of repetitively built products. Because the TPS reduces inventories, and because it does not require major capital investment, it can be implemented by smaller producers to realize the benefits of continuous flow production. This is a major contribution, since about 75 per cent of manufacturing companies have insufficient volume to qualify as mass producers.

Ohno's philosophy in developing the TPS has changed the way in which production system designers approach their task. His relentless pursuit of perfection, striving for the 'wasteless' manufacturing of 'zero defect' products, is a powerful model for improving established manufacturing practices. There inevitably are obstacles to attaining perfection. Ohno's philosophy is to systematically remove as many of these obstacles as possible, by identifying and eliminating their root causes:

> Underneath the 'cause' of a problem, the *real cause* is hidden. In every case, we must dig up the real cause by asking *why, why, why, why, why?*. Otherwise countermeasures cannot be taken and the problems will not be truly solved.
>
> (Ohno 1988b: 126)

In Ohno's view, asking the five 'whys' leads to the 'how' of the real cause. His emphasis on finding fundamental solutions contrasted with the prevailing notion of providing short term relief for symptoms – to 'keep the line going'. It resulted in one of his most famous contributions – giving workers the authority to shut down production in the face of a problem, until the cause is identified and corrected. Ohno recognized that keeping the line going by the use of contingency resources removed much of the incentive for management to address the root causes of problems. Shutting down production is a very effective way to attract management's attention and gain their commitment to finding long-term solutions.

4 Evaluation

The TPS has spread throughout the industrialized world, setting new standards of product quality and cost, benefiting consumers and contributing to higher living standards. The TPS sharply reduces inventories in the production process. This has dampened the impact of inventory swings on the amplitude of business cycles, promoting economic stability. Ohno's innovative thinking has influenced a generation of manufacturing theorists and practitioners, providing them with both an effective method of organizing production and a proved philosophy for continual improvement.

For the workers, the TPS provides an orderly and organized workplace, relative freedom from frustrating production problems, and the opportunity to participate in continuous improvement efforts. There is, however, a negative side. There is considerable anecdotal evidence of high stress levels among just-in-time (JIT) workers, especially in automotive plants. The use of stressful practices in the design and operation of JIT appears to run counter to Ohno's stated philosophy. For example, he questioned the practice of 'speeding up' a production line: 'Ford never intended to cause workers to work harder and harder, to feel driven by their machines, and alienated from their work . . . however, an idea does not always evolve in a direction hoped for by its creator' (Ohno 1988b: 100).

Ironically, there is evidence of a conflict between Ohno's enlightened human resource philosophy and his passion for eliminating waste. Horseley and Buckley claim that at Toyota 'the workers lived in fear of Taiichi Ohno. . . . He seemed to his juniors like a man with a special mission' (1990: 156). Apparently, that mission caused him to engage in stressful practices such as removing some of the workers from a smoothly operating line, to force further improvements. The potential for stressful practices in JIT appears to be high. However, managers implementing JIT according to Ohno's stated philosophy should reject the use of stressful tactics that yield marginal returns at the expense of worker safety and well-being.

5 Conclusion

It is likely that Taiichi Ohno will have a place in manufacturing history alongside giants like Henry Ford and Frederick Taylor (see TAYLOR, F.W.). Like Ford's 'mass production' and Taylor's 'scientific management', Ohno's Toyota Production System is a significant break with prevailing manufacturing practice. In Thomas Kuhn's terms, Ohno's work represents a 'paradigm shift' – a new standard for the organization of production that makes it possible to achieve dramatic increases in productivity and quality (Kuhn 1970).

Like the systems of Ford and Taylor, however, Ohno's TPS also has the potential for a negative effect on workers. Managers, trade unions and workers should be collectively concerned that Ohno's innovative approach to producing high quality, low cost products be implemented with due concern for the welfare of the work force.

ROBERT F. CONTI
BRYANT COLLEGE, SMITHFIELD, RI

Further reading

(References cited in the text marked *)

* Horsley, W. and Buckley, R. (1990) *Nippon, New Superpower*, London: BBC Books. (Places the TPS in the context of the history of Japan's emergence as a post-Second World War economic superpower.)

Klein, J. (1989) 'The human costs of manufacturing reform', *Harvard Business Review* March–April: 60–6. (Excellent coverage of the causes of JIT worker stress, with some practical prescriptions for minimizing the problem.)

* Kuhn, T.S. (1970) *The Structure of Scientific Revolutions*, Chicago, IL: Chicago University Press. (The classic treatment of scientific revolution as a process of change in the accepted 'paradigm', or conceptual foundation, in a given discipline.)

Monden, Y. (1993) *Toyota Management System, Linking the Seven Key Functional Areas*, Portland, OR: Productivity Press. (Description of how the TPS is integrated into a total management system that links the major functional areas at Toyota.)

Ohno, T. (1988a) *Just-in-Time For Today and Tomorrow*, Cambridge, MA: Productivity Press. (Development of the theme that the biggest waste is a product that doesn't sell. Emphasizes the use of market information to avoid speculative production.)

* Ohno, T. (1988b) *Toyota Production System, Beyond Large-Scale Production*, Cambridge, MA: Productivity Press. (Discussion of the evolution and operation of the Toyota Production System by the person most responsible for its success.)

Shingo, S. (1989) *A Study of the Toyota Production System From an Industrial Engineering Viewpoint*, Cambridge, MA: Productivity Press. (Excellent technical coverage of the details of the Toyota System by an associate of Ohno.)

Shonberger, R. (1982) *Japanese Manufacturing Techniques*, New York: The Free Press. (Very readable introduction to the concepts and techniques of JIT manufacturing.)

Toyoda, E. and Toyoda, S. (1988) *Toyota – A History of the First 50 Years*, Toyota City: Toyota Motor Corporation. (Fascinating history of the growth of Toyota, beginning with the decision to build cars in 1933. Excellent coverage of the role of the Toyota Production System in the company's success.)

Whitehall, A. (1991) *Japanese Management, Tradition and Transition*, London: Routledge. (Comprehensive coverage of aspects of the management process unique to the Japanese. Discusses the Toyota System in the context of a national focus on 'getting the most from the least' in manufacturing.)

Womack, J.P., Jones, D.T., and Roos, D. (1990) *The Machine That Changed the World*, New York: Rawson/Macmillan. (Major worldwide study of the automobile industry which concludes that the use of 'lean production' – a generic version of the Toyota Production System – is a competitive necessity for car manufacturers.)

See also: FORD, H.; SHINGO, S.; TAYLOR, F.W.; TOYODA FAMILY

Related topics in the IEBM: INVENTORY AND JUST-IN-TIME MODELS; JAPANIZATION; JUST-IN-TIME PHILOSOPHIES; MANAGEMENT IN JAPAN; MANUFACTURING SYSTEMS, DESIGN OF; OPERATIONS MANAGEMENT; PRODUCTIVITY; TEAMS IN MANUFACTURING; TOTAL QUALITY MANAGEMENT

Pacioli, Luca (c. 1445–1517)

Personal background

- born Sansepolcro, Tuscany
- became tutor to the sons of a wealthy Venetian merchant
- entered the Franciscan order while continuing his academic career
- professor at several major Italian universities
- returned to live in Sansepolcro after 1509
- died in 1517, reportedly at the age of seventy

Major works

Summa de arithmetica geometria proportioni & proportionalita (Encyclopedia of arithmetic, geometry, proportion and proportionality) (1494)

De divina proportione (Of divine proportion) (1509)

Summary

Pacioli was the leading Italian mathematician of his period. His *Summa de arithmetica geometria proportioni & proportionalita*, published in Venice in 1494, was a compendium of mathematics which emphasized the use of mathematics in the solution of business and other practical problems. It included the first printed exposition of double-entry book-keeping.

1 Introduction

Luca Pacioli was the best-known mathematician of the Italian Renaissance. His two major works, the *Summa de arithmetica* and the *De divina proportione*, secured his fame. Today, he is most widely known for the inclusion in the *Summa* of the first published exposition of double-entry book-keeping, a system or method that originated in Italy around 1300 and is in general use today. It has proved to be an adaptable method for the organization of financial data of business enterprises, regardless of their size or type of economic activity. It has also been suitable for the structuring of national income accounts.

2 Biographical data

Of modest family background, Pacioli was educated in his native Sansepolcro (also known as San Sepolcro or Borgo San Sepolcro), near Arezzo in Tuscany. In 1464, he went to Venice as tutor of the sons of a wealthy merchant. At some time between 1470 and 1477 he entered the Franciscan Order. He was allowed to continue his career as teacher of mathematical subjects, and over the next three decades he served as professor, for short periods, at major Italian universities. His professorships brought him into contact with many of his most famous contemporaries, including popes, rulers and artists. In 1496, he became a friend of Leonardo da Vinci. After the publication in Venice of both his *Euclid* and the *De divina proportione* in 1509, Pacioli spent most of his time in and near Sansepolcro, where he rose in the Franciscan hierarchy. He died in 1517, his death notice recording his age as seventy.

3 Main contribution

The *Summa de arithmetica* was published in Venice in November 1494, and reprinted in Toscolano on Lake Garda in 1523. It has been described as the first mathematical encyclopedia of the Renaissance, its contents covering arithmetic, algebra and geometry. In major respects, it was a lineal descendant of the manuscript *Liber abaci* of 1202. This work, by Leonard of Pisa (also known as Leonardo Fibonacci), was an encyclopedia of medieval mathematics that played an important role in promoting the use of Hindu-Arabic numerals and methods of reckoning in western Europe. Pacioli acknowledged his great debt to Fibonacci, and his *Summa* helped to disseminate knowledge of his work, which itself did not appear in print until the nineteenth century.

The *Summa* also owes much to the large number of so-called *abaci* (abacus books) that were written in Italy during the three centuries between the time of Leonardo Fibonacci and Pacioli. In order to understand fully the nature and origins of the *Summa*, it is necessary to explore further the history of abacus books in Italy.

Background to the *Summa*

Abacus books were written for use by merchants, teachers and the self-taught. They were also used by the *maestri d'abaco* (teachers of arithmetic), who gave private tuition or taught in *scuole d'abaco* (also known as *botteghe d'abaco*), which were established in the leading Italian commercial centres for youths intent on mercantile careers – these were early, albeit modest, forerunners of modern institutions of business education.

Although the abacus books differed considerably in scope and detail, their common element was to show how arithmetic, algebra and geometry could be used to solve problems encountered by merchants and others involved in business affairs. Such problems included: conversion of amounts from one currency into another; division of partnership profits; calculation of interest; gauging the contents of a pyramidical heap of corn or a cylindrical barrel of wine; calculating the height of a wall; and calculating the number of bricks for building a wall. Some of the surviving manuscripts also include non-mathematical material useful to merchants, such as: nomenclature and descriptions of commodities; weights, measures and currencies in different cities; dates of fairs and markets; and rates of exchange. Material of this kind constituted the

contents of another category of manuscript, known in Italy as *pratiche di mercatura*, some of which circulated widely.

None of the surviving abacus books includes instruction in book-keeping, which youths were evidently expected to learn mainly during their apprenticeships. Book-keeping was taught by some *maestri d'abaco*, their private pupils being youths and others aspiring to mastery of the subject. Their students included young men sent from Germany and other countries to Italy to study commercial practices and techniques. Matthäus Schwarz, who became the head book-keeper of Jakob Fugger, the wealthy and influential Augsburg financier and merchant, was taught double-entry book-keeping in Venice by one of these teachers. Although no example has survived, manuscripts explaining double-entry book-keeping were probably in circulation. One historian has argued, on insecure grounds, that Pacioli took the bulk of his exposition on book-keeping in the *Summa* from such a manuscript, presumed to be Venetian (Besta 1929).

Despite the derivation of their name from the abacus (a counting board or frame on which calculations were made with counters or beads), the Italian abacus books taught the use of Hindu-Arabic numerals and reckoning methods. They are often referred to as 'arithmetics'. The first printed arithmetic was published in Treviso, Italy, in 1478. Its unknown author explained that he wrote it in response to requests by certain youths who intended to follow commercial careers.

Pacioli's exposition

Pacioli's *Summa* is an encyclopedic abacus book. It is far bigger and more comprehensive than any of its predecessors. Pacioli was an excellent compiler and presenter, although no innovator as mathematician. He wrote in Italian rather than in Latin so as to reach a larger readership (most of the surviving abacus books are in Italian), and his treatment of most subjects is compendious. For example, he presents eight different procedures for multiplication, while at the same time he inserted occasional small diversions, one of which tries to reconcile the multiplication of fractions with the biblical injunction to increase and multiply.

In addition to the arithmetical and mathematical material that makes up the majority of this bulky book, Pacioli, like many abacus book authors, included non-mathematical material. This material is collected together in the final major section of the *Summa's* first and larger part (the second part is on geometry). Pacioli's non-mathematical material includes no procedures, rules or analysis that are not dealt with in the preceding sections on arithmetic and algebra. There are discussions of partnerships, barter, bills of exchange, interest calculations and a *Tariffa* of lists of weights and measures, commodities, exchange rates and so on. The *Tariffa* is taken without acknowledgement from a manuscript ascribed to Lorenzo Chiarini, which was first published as a printed book in Florence in 1481.

Pacioli's exposition of book-keeping, *Particularis de computis & scripturis* (Of bookkeeping and writings), comes immediately before the *Tariffa*. It takes up only a small part of the massive *Summa*, which was the first printed book to include an exposition of book-keeping. (A manuscript addressed to merchants, dated 1458, includes a short chapter on double-entry book-keeping. Written by a merchant Benedetto Cotrugli, the manuscript is not an *abaco*: it instructs how a merchant should conduct himself, and includes material on such topics as barter, bills of exchange and insurance.)

Pacioli dedicated the *Summa* to the Duke of Urbino. He writes that he included a section on book-keeping because the Duke's subjects needed to know about this in the running of their business affairs. Pacioli suggests that without detailed and orderly accounting records, the merchant is confused and has no peace of mind; he conducts his business as if blind, and suffers losses. He explains his intention to describe step by step a method for keeping account books which he recommends as being the best available. The section is evidently addressed to merchants rather than to students.

Although Pacioli did not use any of the various terms in Italian that came to be used for 'double-entry book-keeping', that is the system he expounded. He emphasizes the duality of entries, one debit, the other credit, for each transaction; he includes personal accounts, asset accounts, revenue and expenditure accounts and a capital account; and he shows how the accounts are inter-related. Pacioli does not claim to have invented the system. Indeed, historians have been able to trace examples of the use of the system as early as AD 1300.

Pacioli explains that he will be following the (*modo*) (method or manner) of Venice, which of all methods is to be most commended. There are three principal account books: the waste-book or memorial; the journal; and the ledger. He shows how the merchant takes an inventory when he begins his accounting. He then traces the items in the inventory through the journal to the accounts in the ledger. This exposition is followed first by the treatment of various classes of transaction, and then by three chapters on the closing of the ledger. A summary chapter, which introduces some new material, is followed by three addenda which are not integrated with the rest of the section.

Pacioli's exposition does not include any discussion of two related topics that are central to the concerns of accountants today – the valuation of assets and liabilities for balance sheet purposes, and the accounting measurement of periodic profits. In this respect, he did not differ from the great majority of authors of book-keeping texts up to, say, 1840. He cannot be faulted for this omission, since these topics did not matter to the merchants and others who studied or used double-entry book-keeping.

4 Evaluation

In many ways, Pacioli's exposition is commendable. The inelegance of his language is compensated for by lively asides and incidental bits of information. The topics are introduced systematically and in logical sequence, though there are occasional distracting digressions. Nevertheless, for all its merits, it is unlikely that a reader would have been able to acquire a mastery of the subject from Pacioli's text unless he or she already had a good grounding in it, had access to a competent book-keeper, or had a well-kept set of account books to follow as a model.

In some places the text is marred by faulty printing and poor editing: a serious example is the discussion and illustration of the characteristic form of Venetian-style journal entries, which is almost incomprehensible. What is more, Pacioli does not give specimen rulings of the various account books, nor does he show how a set of inter-connected transactions should be entered in them. There is also no attempt either to explain the logic or cohesion of the double-entry system or to provide an ordered guide as to which accounts are to be debited and credited for each of a comprehensive range of transactions – the latter omission was far more serious for those who had to keep accounts. Finally, a key chapter dealing with the process of balancing and closing a ledger and opening its successor is inadequate as well as confusing.

The book-keeping section in the *Summa* might not therefore have been of much use to merchants in their counting-houses or to students trying to teach themselves. The weight and bulk of the book also militated against its use as a reference work. Moreover, Pacioli's exposition is limited to the basic essentials of the subject. While this stress on essentials was appropriate in a general text, it made the work less useful to any merchant who may have needed guidance on more complex topics. There is, for instance, no consideration of book-keeping questions raised by fluctuations in the rate of exchange. Yet merchants of Venice and of other Italian cities often had dealings with foreign agents or correspondents. There is also no discussion of accounting designed for the needs of manufacturing enterprises. The sub-division of the ledger into two or more inter-locking ledgers, which was a practice of several large enterprises in fifteenth-century Florence, is also not discussed. However, the last two subjects were rarely included in book-keeping texts before the nineteenth century.

The influence of Pacioli's pioneering text on double-entry book-keeping was indirect, but important. The first two effective printed books on book-keeping were to a considerable extent based on Pacioli's work. Domenico Manzoni's *Quaderno doppio* (Double-entry ledger) was first published in 1540 in Venice, and there were several later editions. Manzoni, a book-keeper, took much from Pacioli, without acknowledgement. He improved upon his model, including new material and adding a specimen set of account books, with entries in them for three hundred transactions, the whole made convenient for users by a detailed classified list of transactions. As Manzoni's book dealt only with book-keeping, it was light and easy to handle. As an exposition and extended illustration of double-entry book-keeping, Manzoni's work can be faulted only where he followed Pacioli too closely.

Jam Ympyn, an Antwerp mercer who had spent several years in Italy, completed his *Nieuwe instructie* (New instruction) before he died in 1540. It was published by his widow in Antwerp in 1543. The original Dutch version was translated into French that same year, and an English version appeared in London in 1547. Like Manzoni, Ympyn made extensive use of Pacioli's *Summa*, but introduced many improvements. He also provided a written-up set of specimen account books, the illustrative transactions perhaps based on his own business experience.

Both the Manzoni and Ympyn works would have been useful for students and merchants. The same is not true of Hugh Oldcastle's *A Profitable Treatyce*, published in London in 1543. It was much more faithful to Pacioli's text than Manzoni's or Ympyn's books. Oldcastle simply excised various parts of the *Summa*, including whole chapters, such as the chapter on the closing of the ledger. When the Oldcastle book was re-issued in 1588 by John Mellis, the latter 'beautified' the text, supplemented it with a model set of account books and tried unsuccessfully to graft passages taken from later works on to the Paciolian text. His efforts were undistinguished.

By the end of the sixteenth century, books on book-keeping seldom included references to Pacioli or passages that can be traced to Pacioli or his two followers, Manzoni and Ympyn. Pacioli's arrangement of topics and style of exposition are rarely evident after 1600, by which time the 'father of book-keeping' might have had difficulty in recognizing his distant progeny.

Pacioli intended his *Summa de arithmetica* to be a repository of information and instruction useful for merchants and other practical people. His second major work, *De divina proportione* – published in Venice in 1509 – is quite different. In it, Pacioli developed metaphysical ideas about mathematics, the five regular geometrical bodies, proportion (notably the 'divine proportion' or golden section), the cube and the circle. These topics had no relevance to the practical concerns of merchants, although some were of interest to architects. In *De divina proportione*, Pacioli was able to give free rein to his preoccupation with speculative, even mystical, ideas. Of this preoccupation, there is only the occasional trace in the utilitarian *Summa*: Pacioli did not associate double-entry book-keeping with the mathematics of the cosmos or the music of the spheres.

BASIL S. YAMEY
LONDON SCHOOL OF ECONOMICS

Further reading

(References cited in the text marked*)

* Besta, F. (1929) *La Ragioneria* (Book-keeping), vol. 3, 2nd edn, Milan.

Egmond, W. van (1976) *The Commercial Revolution and the Beginnings of Western Mathematics in Renaissance Florence, 1300–1500*, Ann Arbor, MI: University Microfilm International. (A detailed study of Italian *abaci* manuscripts.)

Jaywardene, S.A. (1974) 'Luca Pacioli', *Dictionary of Scientific Biography* vol 10, New York.

Swetz, F.J. (1987) *Capitalism and Arithmetic: The New Math of the 15th Century*, La Salle, IL: Open Court. (Includes a translation of the first printed arithmetic book in Italian.)

Yamey, B.S. (ed.) (1994) *Luca Pacioli: Exposition of Double Entry Bookkeeping Venice 1494*, Venice: Albrizzi Editore. (Includes a translation by Antonia von Gebsattel of Pacioli's text, and introduction and commentary by Yamey.)

See also: LIMPERG, T.; PATON, W.; SCHMALENBACH, E.

Related topics in the IEBM: ACCOUNTING; CASH FLOW ACCOUNTING; FINANCIAL ACCOUNTING

Parasuraman, A. (1948–), Zeithaml, Valarie (1948–) and Berry, Leonard L. (1942–)

Personal background

A. Parasuraman

- born in India in 1948
- educated at the Indian Institute of Management (Ahmedabad), and earned a DBA from the University of Indiana
- taught at Texas A&M University, where he was the Federated Professor of Marketing
- currently professor and the James McLamore Chair in Marketing at the University of Miami

Valarie Zeithaml

- born in Baltimore, Maryland in 1948
- received a PhD in marketing from the University of Maryland
- taught at Texas A&M University, the Fuqua School of Business at Duke University and the University of North Carolina at Chapel Hill
- also worked as a director of Partners in Service Excellence
- currently a member of the marketing faculty at the Kenan-Flagler School of Business at the University of North Carolina, Chapel Hill

Berry, Leonard L.

- born in 1942
- awarded a PhD from Arizona State University in 1968
- member of the board of directors of CompUSA and Hastings Entertainment, Inc.
- elected as a public member of the board of directors for the Council of Better Business Bureaus in 1995
- won the Faculty Distinguished Achievement Award in Teaching at Texas A&M University, and in May 1996 he won the Faculty Distinguished Award in Research
- currently holds the J.C. Penny Chair of Retailing Studies, and is professor of marketing and director of the Centre for Retailing Studies in the College of Business Administration at Texas A&M University
- editor of the *Arthur Anderson Retailing Issues Letter* and a member of the American Marketing Association

Major works

'A conceptual model of service quality and its implications for future research' (1985)
'SERVQUAL: a multiple-item scale for measuring customer perceptions of service quality' (1988)

Summary

Few streams of academic research in marketing have led to a more prolific ensuing flow of endeavour than that begun in the mid-1980s by a team now known simply, but very well, in the academic journals of the discipline as 'PZB'. Their work on service quality has spawned a large number of replications, many efforts aimed at rigorously testing its reliability and validity, and an abundance of research in other management disciplines such as human resources, purchasing and information systems directed at applying their thinking in these functions.

Introduction

A. 'Parsu' Parasuraman, Valarie Zeithaml and Leonard Berry were all members of the marketing faculty at the Texas A&M University in the mid-1980s when they attracted significant research funding from the Marketing Science Institute (MSI) to study the quality of service. The MSI is a body established and financed by major corporations in the USA (most of the Fortune 500 are members today), with the purpose of funding high level research into the issues in marketing which are of greatest concern to member companies. In the early 1980s the members and trustees of the MSI identified the quality of service provided by service firms, or manufacturers where service constituted a major portion of their offering, as their issue of greatest concern. This in itself represented a major advance. Until this time the marketing of services had not received a great deal of attention in the literature, nor was services marketing much taught in business school programmes, despite the fact that services were already accounting for a major portion of output in most advanced economies. Service quality had been paid almost no attention at all.

PZB's first effort was directed at an understanding of what constituted service quality from a customer perspective. The team conducted extensive focus groups among customers of a range of service businesses. This led them to define service quality as the 'gap' between the customer's *expectation* of what he or she would receive from an excellent service provider, and the customer's *perception* of what he or she would actually receive from a particular service provider. Simply, if the customer perceived himself or herself to have received what they expected they would be technically 'satisfied'; if expectations exceeded perceptions the customer would be dissatisfied, frustrated and angry; and likewise, delighted, excited and more than satisfied if the opposite situation prevailed. Their operationalization of this service quality gap as an attitude is different to simple customer satisfaction. The latter is seen by PZB to be more dynamic by nature, and something that exists on an incident-for-incident basis.

Service quality is a learned predisposition that is more stable over time, which is consistently favourable or unfavourable, and is constructed by a series of discrete 'satisfaction' encounters with a service provider. The customer's expectations of service quality were in turn learned from personal experience, the customer's needs at the time, word of mouth communication and the external communication of services providers.

PZB then turned their attention to what was occurring within services firms in order to identify the barriers that might prohibit them from delivering service of a quality that the customer expected. This led to the description of four internal 'gaps' within organizations that would cause service quality not to meet customer expectations unless addressed. These internal gaps, in order of sequence, were:

- managers not understanding customer expectations;
- managers not setting service quality standards to meet these expectations;
- the firm not delivering service of a quality to meet the set standards;
- the firm's external communication to customers not matching what was actually delivered to them.

This work resulted in a series of MSI working papers, and culminated in 1985 in a paper by the team entitled 'A conceptual model of service quality and its implications for future research', in the *Journal of Marketing* (PZB 1995), the discipline's major journal. The service model rapidly became known as the 'Gaps' model among marketing academics and researchers.

PZB next considered the development of an instrument for the measurement of service quality – the customer's gap in their model – namely, that between expectations and perceptions. This work is described in their 1988 paper, 'SERVQUAL: a multiple-item scale for measuring customer perceptions of service quality' (PZB 1988), which appeared in the *Journal of Retailing*. Their concern was that the measure of service quality should be a generic one, that is, it could be applied across a wide range of service firms with only minimal adaptation. Developed following very rigorous psychometric guidelines, SERVQUAL is a 22-item scale that requires a respondent to indicate their expectations of an excellent provider of a particular service, then their perceptions of the service quality offered by a particular provider. Service quality for that respondent is calculated simply by subtracting the expectation statement score from the matching perception statement score, in order to gain an indication of the 'gap'. When this is done for a sample of a firm's customers, the firm is able to gauge the extent of gaps on the various items constituting SERVQUAL, as well as an overall service quality index, or 'SQI'. PZB also point out that customers have expectations and perceptions along a number of dimensions of service quality, which they define as follows:

- *Tangibles* – Physical facilities, equipment, and appearance of personnel;
- *Reliability* – Ability to perform the promised service dependably and accurately;
- *Responsiveness* – Willingness to help customers and provide prompt service;
- *Assurance* – Knowledge and courtesy of employees and their ability to inspire trust and confidence;
- *Empathy* – Caring, individualized attention the firm provides its customers.

It would not be unrealistic to say that this instrument has spurred more survey research in marketing than just about any other. Undergraduate and masters level students have used it to assess service quality in a vast range of situations at universities and colleges across the globe. The instrument also began to be used by commercial marketing research firms, and in addition immediately attracted the attention of the academic community, who were concerned with two issues of measurement, namely reliability and validity, and who began to subject SERVQUAL to rigorous testing in this regard. Needless to say, this resulted in a flood of papers in the academic journals, and to many responses and rejoinders from PZB.

2 Criticizm of SERVQUAL in the marketing literature

The difficulties with the SERVQUAL instrument identified in the literature can be grouped into two main categories: a) conceptual and b) empirical; although the boundary between them blurs because they are closely inter-related. The conceptual problems centre on:

1 the use of two separate instruments to measure perceptions and expectations in order to operationalize a third conceptually distinct construct of service quality, as a 'gap'
2 the ambiguity of the expectations construct
3 the suitability of using a single instrument to measure service quality across different industries, organizations and situations

The empirical problems are, by and large, the result of these conceptual difficulties, most notably the use of difference scores. Difficulties that have most often been attributed to the SERVQUAL instrument include low reliability, unstable dimensionality and poor convergent validity.

Conceptual difficulties with SERVQUAL

The use of difference scores
Teas (1994) criticises the SERVQUAL expectations that are variously defined as desires, wants, what a service provider should possess, normative expectations, and the level of service a customer hopes to receive. He says that these multiple definitions of 'expectations' in the SERVQUAL literature result in a concept that is open to multiple interpretations, which can result in potentially serious measurement validity problems.

Applicability of SERVQUAL across industries
Another often mentioned conceptual problem with SERVQUAL concerns the applicability of a single instrument for measuring service quality across different industries. Carman (1990) in a study of SERVQUAL across four different industries, found it necessary to add

items to the instrument in order to adequately capture the service quality construct in various settings. Brown, Churchill and Peter (1993) concluded that it takes more than simple adaptation of the SERVQUAL items to effectively address service quality across diverse settings.

The SERVQUAL instrument – empirical difficulties

A difference score is created by subtracting the measure of one construct from the measure of another in an attempt to create a measure of a third distinct construct thus, an expectation score is subtracted from a perception score to create such a 'gap' measure of service quality. Among the difficulties related to the use of difference measures discussed in the literature are low reliability, unstable dimensionality, and poor predictive and convergent validity.

Low reliability
A number of researchers have criticized the fact that the use of a difference score results in a lower reliability of the SERVQUAL instrument, and have furthermore suggested that the wrong formula has consistently been used to calculate the instrument's reliability.

Predictive and convergent validity
The superior predictive and convergent validity of perception-only scores was the major focus of work by Cronin and Taylor (1992). Their results indicated higher adjusted r-squared values for perception-only scores across four different industries. The perception component of the perception-minus-expectation score consistently performs better as a predictor of overall service quality than the difference score itself (Parasuraman, Zeithaml and Berry1991; Cronin and Taylor 1992).

Unstable dimensionality of the SERVQUAL instrument

The results of several studies have argued that the five dimensions claimed for the SERVQUAL instrument are unstable.

3 Counter-arguments to the criticizms

The SERVQUAL debate has certainly not been one-sided. PZB have responded in full with sound and solid arguments regarding the conceptual and empirical aspects of their conceptualization of service quality.

Subtraction as simulation

The gap formulation was not merely suggested or implied as a convenient simplification; it was derived and conceptualized from extensive focus group research (PZB 1985). While performance-only approaches are well known in the marketing literature (cf. Cronin and Taylor 1992) and might result in marginally better predictive validity, one might question the diagnostic insights they provide to the manager.

Is the expectations construct ambiguous?

First, PZB (Parasuraman, Berry and Zeithaml 1994) state that it is likely that customers consider most of the 22 items in the SERVQUAL instrument to be vector attributes (a point also acknowledged by Teas). Second, in their response to Brown, Churchill and Peter (1993), who also noted the variability problem in a similar fashion, PZB (Parasuraman, Berry and Zeithaml 1993) argue that this will only be really problematic when the SERVQUAL gaps are used as dependent variables in analysis.

Applicability of SERVQUAL across industries and settings

PBZ (1991) balance this argument by asserting that the SERVQUAL items represent core evaluation criteria that transcend specific companies and industries, providing a basic skeleton underlying service quality that can be supplemented with context-specific items when necessary.

Three reasons merit the use of a generic measure:

- few service organizations have truly unique features that make the standard SERVQUAL dimensions inappropriate;
- it is difficult to discern any unique features in a domain that have been excluded from SERVQUAL, although that does not mean this is impossible;
- there is a good diagnostic reason for using a generic measure of service quality. While managers may want to know how they compare with other similar organizations, nowadays many want to compare themselves with other excellent service providers.

Reliability of difference scores

Most researchers, including PZB, have used the standard formula for the calculation of coefficient alpha (Cronbach 1951), to calculate the reliability coefficients for the SERVQUAL dimensions. While this may be inappropriate, the real question is, of course, whether the effect of this is serious? The reliability of a scale operationalized as the difference between two measures will be low to the extent that: a) the correlation between the component measures is high (in this instance, perceptions and expectations); b) the reliabilities of the component measures (perceptions and expectations) is low. PZB (Parasuraman, Berry and Zeithaml 1993) argue strongly that these conditions (a) and (b) are not likely to be serious problems in the case of SERVQUAL.

Predictive and convergent validity of SERVQUAL

It has been contended that performance-based, or perceptions-only measures of service quality have: a) higher correlations with other measures of the same construct (convergent validity); and b) higher correlations with other conceptually related constructs. PZB (Parasuraman, Berry and Zeithaml 1994) argue convincingly that service quality measurements that incorporate customer expectations provide richer diagnostic information than those that merely use perceptions. Managers find the concept of a gap most useful, for

it indicates a shortfall, something which needs to be closed. Just as important, managers want to know and should know what their customers expect. In summary, without wishing to sacrifice statistical rigour, one might nevertheless be reluctant to 'throw the baby out with the bath water' – managers benefit from the additional diagnostics which a gap measure and its components provide.

4 Evaluation

SERVQUAL and the Gaps model have focused the particular attention of the academic marketing community, researchers in other areas of management in general (cf. Pitt, Watson and Kavan 1995), and practising managers as well, on the issues of service quality and management. A 'gap' suggests a difference between an existing and a more ideal situation, and as such is a simple but powerful way of concentrating the attention on both deficiencies and areas of outstanding performance. SERVQUAL is a generic measure of service quality that has been, and can be used across a wide range of organizationional settings in many countries. The Gaps model enables one to identify not only what the customer's expectations and perceptions of service quality are, but to come within the organization and detect what internal barriers exist that prohibit the organization from delivering quality of service that the customer expects.

5 Conclusion

While PZB has been one of the most durable teams in the major marketing literature, it should be pointed out that each of the team have been prolific researchers and writers in their own right. Parasuraman has made major contributions in such areas as sales force management, promotion and marketing research. Zeithaml has written extensively on marketing communication strategy, pricing, and understanding the marketing environment. Berry has worked in financial services, retailing and services pricing. Two members of the team have also moved on from Texas A&M – Parasuraman holds the James MacLamore

Chair in Marketing at the University of Miami, while Zeithaml has moved from full-time management consulting to a chair at the University of North Carolina. Nevertheless, the impact of PZB's contributions to our understanding of service quality will be felt for a long time to come.

LEYLAND PITT
CARDIFF BUSINESS SCHOOL
UNIVERSITY OF WALES

Further reading

(References cited in the text marked *)

* Brown, T.J., Churchill, G.A., Jr. and Peter, J.P. (1993) 'Research note: improving the measurement of service quality', *Journal of Retailing* 69, 1: 127–139. (Criticizes the SERVQUAL conceptualization of service quality, primarily because of its use of 'difference scores'.)
* Carman, J M. (1990) 'Consumer perceptions of service quality: an assessment of the SERVQUAL dimensions', *Journal of Retailing* 66, 1: 33 – 55. (The first major empirical test of SERVQUAL; generally complimentary, but criticizes nomological and discriminant validity, primarily because of inability to reproduce distinct factor sructures.)
* Cronbach, L.J. (1951) 'Coefficient alpha and the internal structure of tests', *Psychometrika* 16, 3: 297–333. (Classic and fundamental work still used to consider internal consistency and reliability of psychometric tests.)
* Cronin, J.J. and Taylor, S.A. (1992) 'Measuring service quality: a reexamination and extension', *Journal of Marketing* 56, 3: 55-68. (Questions the SERVQUAL conceptualization, and argues that performance-only measures of service quality produce stronger statistical properties.)
* Parasuraman, A., Berry, L.L. and Zeithaml, V.A. (1994) 'Reassessment of expectations as a comparison standard in measuring service quality: implications for further research', *Journal of Marketing* 58, January: 111–124. (Refutes much of the criticizm of Teas, and Cronin and Taylor.)
* Parasuraman, A., Berry, L.L. and Zeithaml, V.A. (1993) 'Research note: More on improving quality measurement', *Journal of Retailing* 69, 1: 140–147. (Counters the arguments of Brown et al., particulalry regarding the reliability of 'gaps' scores.)
* Parasuraman, A., Zeithaml, V.A. and Berry, L L. (1985) 'A conceptual model of service quality and its implications for future research', *Journal of Marketing* 41–55. (Seminal work which describes the 'gaps' approach to the measurement and management of service quality.)
* Parasuraman, A., Zeithaml, V.A. and Berry, L L. (1988) 'SERVQUAL: a multiple-item scale for measuring customer perceptions of service quality', *Journal of Retailing* 64, Spring: 12–40. (Major technical paper which describes the psychometric development and validation of SERVQUAL as a generic instrument for the measurement of service quality.)
* Parasuraman, A., Zeithaml, V.A. and Berry, L.L. (1991) 'Refinement and reassessment of the SERVQUAL scale', *Journal of Retailing* 67, 4: 420–450. (Further refinement of SERVQUAL, with particular reference to the expectations components.)
* Pitt, L.F., Watson, R.T. and Kavan, B.C. (1995) 'Service quality – a measure of information systems effectiveness', *MIS Quarterly* 19, 2: 173–187. (Demonstrates the reliability and validity of SERVQUAL in the measurement of information systems effectiveness in three large information systems departments within major organizations across three countries.)
* Teas, R.K. (1994) 'Expectations as a comparison standard in measuring service quality: an assessment of a reassessment', *Journal of Marketing* 58, 1, 132–139. (Questions several aspects of SERVQUAL and the 'gaps' approach, with particular emphasis on the conceptualisation of the expectations components.)

See also: KOTLER, P.; LEVITT, T.

Related topics in the IEBM: CONSUMER BEHAVIOUR; INTERNATIONAL MARKETING; MARKETING; MARKETING, FOUNDATIONS OF; MARKETING STRATEGY; RELATIONSHIP MARKETING; SERVICES, MARKETING OF

Parkinson, Cyril Northcote (1909–93)

Personal background

- born in Barnard Castle, County Durham, England, 30 July 1909, the second son of an art teacher
- educated at St Peter's School, York, Emmanuel College, Cambridge (MA), and King's College, London (PhD)
- master, Britannia Royal Naval College, Dartmouth, 1939; military service, 1940–5; Lecturer in History, University of Liverpool, 1946; Raffles Professor of History, University of Malaya, Singapore, 1950–8
- lived in Singapore (1950–8) and the Channel Islands (1960–89)
- married first, 1943, Ethelwyn Edith Graves (marriage dissolved); second, 1952, Elizabeth Ann Fry (died 1983); third, 1985, Iris (Ingrid) Hilda Waters
- helped to found and develop the National Maritime Museum and the University of Malaya
- Fellow of the Royal Historical Society and member of the French Académie de Marine, the US Naval Institute and the Archives Commission of the Government of India
- died at Canterbury, England, 9 March 1993

Major works

Trade in the Eastern Seas, 1793–1813 (1937)
The Trade Winds (1948)
The Evolution of Political Thought (1958a)
Parkinson's Law (1958b)
British Intervention in Malaya 1861–1877 (1964)

Left Luggage from Marx to Wilson (1967)
Industrial Disruption (1973)
Communicate: Parkinson's Formula for Business Survival (1977)
The Law, or Still in Pursuit (1979)

Summary

C. Northcote Parkinson (1909–93), author, playwright, journalist, biographer and historian, is perhaps best remembered for the satirical *Parkinson's Law* which, among other things, stated that: 'Work expands to fill the time available for its completion' (1958b: 4). Parkinson's contribution to business and management is as a co-author and editor of several satirical and factual books on general business and management topics. As a naval historian his work remains authoritative; his books on British naval supremacy and maritime trade in the Napoleonic era are still regarded as important works. Indeed, these historical analyses, published before and immediately after the Second World War, also identify and discuss many of the key influences on international trade which are to be found listed in today's business texts.

1 Introduction

Parkinson is generally remembered as a writer of popular books on business and management, and especially for the satire of perhaps his most famous book *Parkinson's Law* (1958b). He is less well-known as a serious scholar, whose work on the trade and maritime history of the Napoleonic era is still highly regarded. His work was not restricted to business, management and history, but included books on political science and a large number of fictional books, novels and plays, as well as contributions to encyclopedias and journals. Regardless of the topic, however, Parkinson's work is always characterized by a clarity of expression and presentation that is often lacking in contemporary writing.

Parkinson's standards of writing and thinking range from the simple and commonsense to the very complex and erudite. This breadth of thought, combined with an ability to identify the main issues in any subject and convey them effectively to the reader, enabled him to make a major contribution to each of the disciplines in which he worked. Nevertheless, his contribution to business and management literature is often thought of as being restricted to the role of co-author, using his writing ability to convey major business issues discussed in the academic literature to a more general audience. Although the vast majority of his business and management writing is in the form of co-authored prescriptive books, his satirical writing on bureaucracy, describing not so much the failure of bureaucracy itself but the effects of the mismanagement of bureaucracy, contains much for the serious student of business and management. In this respect, Parkinson may be seen as a background influence on a number of contemporary lay and academic business and management writers.

2 Biographical data

Cyril Northcote Parkinson was born at Barnard Castle in County Durham, England. The second son of an art teacher, Parkinson spent his school years at St Peter's School, York, before going on to Emmanuel College, Cambridge to study history. After receiving an MA in history, he moved to King's College, London to study for a PhD under A.P. Newton. This was unusual because the inter-war years had seen a decline in the popularity of history, with its emphasis on war and conflict, as a subject of study at the highest university level. Parkinson's doctoral thesis, entitled *Trade in the Eastern Seas, 1803–1910*, illustrated the inextricable link between commerce and conflict, and was to provide the basis for much of his later work as an historian.

While studying for his PhD, Parkinson worked with Sir Geoffrey Callander to establish the National Maritime Museum in London before briefly returning to Cambridge to conduct research and write. There was, however, little call for the maritime history in which he specialized, so he left, taking a post as senior history master at Blundell's School in Tiverton in 1938. The following year he took a post at Britannia Royal Naval College, Dartmouth, as lecturer in naval history, which he held until 1940 when he was commissioned with the rank of Captain into the Queen's Royal Regiment. He remained in the British Army throughout the Second World War, and was involved in the organization and training of the RAF Regiment before being promoted to the rank of Major in 1943 and moving to the War Office (General Staff) the following year, where he served until he was demobilized in 1945.

Parkinson became a lecturer at the University of Liverpool in 1946 with the intention of developing a historical centre based around the city's seafaring and trading histories. Although he lived to see his vision fulfilled with the opening of the Merseyside Maritime Museum in 1980, it proved to be an impossible task in the austere post-war years, and Parkinson emigrated to Singapore in 1950 where, from 1950–8, he was Raffles Professor of History at the University of Malaya. He was then a visiting professor at the University of Harvard in 1958 and at the Universities of Illinois and California in 1959–60.

Towards the end of his time in Singapore he had written *Parkinson's Law* (1958b) and, with its success, increasingly devoted time to the lecture circuit. This involved him writing in the winter and lecturing in the UK and the USA in the summer. Although less and less involved with academic life he was, from 1970 until his death, Professor Emeritus and Honorary President of Troy State University, Alabama. His achievements were recognized further by the awards of an Honorary LLD (Doctor of Law) from the University of Maryland in 1974 and of an Honorary DLitt (Doctor of Literature) from Troy State University in 1976.

After his retirement from full-time academic life in 1960, Parkinson settled in the Channel Islands and spent his time painting, sailing and writing. As an academic, his writing had been somewhat restricted to naval history, but he was now free to explore other areas, and his published output was remarkable. He contributed articles to seven different daily and weekly newspapers, and published two plays and a number of books on business and management, as well as fictional books including the Delancey series of novels and the acclaimed spoof *The Life and Times of Horatio Hornblower* (1970). So accurate was this as an account of an admiral in the Royal Navy at the time of Nelson that archivists at the National Maritime Museum were often hard put to pacify irate and insistent researchers, hunting in vain for Hornblower papers and records which, of course, did not exist.

Parkinson was especially prolific during his sixties and early seventies. He wrote four books and a novel in a single year (1977), and a total of fourteen books (of which seven were novels) in the eight years to 1983. Coincident with the death of his second wife in 1983, however, his output decreased until he remarried and moved to the Isle of Man in 1987. His time there was to provide the inspiration for his final novel, *Manhunt: Wartime Adventure on the Isle of Man* (1990). Parkinson moved to Canterbury in 1989 and began work on his autobiography. This was to have been a development of *A Law unto Themselves* (1966), a biographical review of the lives of a number of people he claimed to have been driving influences in his own life. Entitled *'A Law unto Myself'*, the autobiography unfortunately remained unpublished.

Despite an apparently well-planned career, Parkinson himself admitted that, when young, he was torn first between becoming an artist or a schoolteacher. Once at Cambridge, however, his interest in history was nurtured by Edward Welbourne, master of Emmanuel College, who gave Parkinson a preference for plain facts. His time at Cambridge taught him to form his own ideas and opinions on a subject, rather than rely on the those of his supervisors. In particular, Parkinson credited Welbourne for giving him an interest in economic history and the history of technology, both of which may be seen to underpin many of his historical and business works.

Apart from Welbourne, a major influence on Parkinson's early writing career was the historical biographer Hilaire Belloc. He learned the high standard of English prose, which is characteristic of his writing, from the Poet Laureate John Masefield. It was perhaps from G.K. Chesterton, however, that Parkinson learned his method of analysis and presentation. Chesterton, he claimed, always went back to first principles, argued them from the strictest logic, reached a sensible but unexpected conclusion and then put it forward as a laughable paradox.

Parkinson also enjoyed the challenge of physical accomplishments, believing firmly that scholarship was only one element in a well-rounded individual. A fencer, amateur dramatist and gifted painter, he rode a bicycle from York to Penzance and back in the summer of 1934, travelled throughout Europe in the summer of 1936 and, as a Lieutenant in the 22nd London Regiment, played an active part in the funeral procession of King George V.

3 Main contribution

Parkinson's main literary contributions are in the fields of history, political science, and business and management. With regard to maritime history and the history of international trade, *Trade in the Eastern Seas, 1793–1813* (1937), *The Trade Winds* (1948) and *British Intervention in Malaya 1861–1877* (1964), for example, make major contributions. This is because they each provide not only outstanding illustrations of the effects such issues as politics, economics, sociocultural differences and technological advances had on the early development of international business, but they also detail the critical role Britain played in that development. *East and West* (1963), meanwhile, sets international trade in a broader context, by providing a thesis of world history in terms of the cyclical movement of power balances and conflict between dynamic Eastern and Western civilizations over time.

In terms of Parkinson's contribution to political science, two books stand out. The first, entitled *The Evolution of Political Thought* (1958a), sets out to dispel a number of fallacies that had built up in the existing literature. These include the fallacies that political theory has its origins in ancient Greece and that the progress of political thought has been an unbroken procession of exclusively Western achievement. Recognizing that an idea expressed in speech or action may be at least as original and powerful as that expressed in writing, Parkinson illustrates his argument by discussing four forms of government (monarchy, oligarchy, democracy and dictatorship), showing their origin, nature, relative success, theoretical justification, decline and decay. The result is a bold historical analysis of the evolution of political thought, which proposes that the sequence of political institutions falls within the life cycle of different civilizations.

As a history of the labour movement in the UK, *Left Luggage from Marx to Wilson* (1967) was unremarkable. Its contribution, however, is in the analysis that is made of the history, and the conclusions that result from it. Parkinson argued that the visions of the labour movement's pioneers had degenerated into dogma; that the trade unions, cooperatives and professional institutions had brought about an erosion of democracy within the movement; that its attempts to create a classless society had been converted into an acceptance that privilege was inescapable as a means of generating public wealth; and that ownership was of marginal importance, since both public and private enterprise had come under much the same sort of professional management. Thus, Parkinson had, by the late 1960s, identified issues which were to be at the centre of the political debate in the UK during the 1980s and 1990s.

Parkinson's Law (1958b) was perhaps his most successful contribution to business and management. This had its genesis in a short critique (entitled 'The Educationists and the Pyramid') (Parkinson 1966: 127) of an assurance given in 1951 by a Malayan Government politician as to the efficiency of his departments. In it, and in the series of articles written for *The Economist* that followed it, as well as the resulting *Parkinson's Law*, Parkinson based his arguments on the observations of military, government and business bureaucracies. These observations led him to include in *Parkinson's Law* the law that: 'Work expands to fill the time available' (1958b: 4). The converse of this was 'it is the busiest man who has time to spare'. The reasons for work expanding lay in the desire of officials 'to multiply subordinates, not rivals', and 'to make work for each other' (1958b: 5). Parkinson used, as a major example of these axioms, the considerable expansion of Admiralty and dockyard officials, clerks and workers, which he claimed occurred at the same time as the inter-war reduction in warships and serving officers. He also showed how the staff of the Colonial Office more than quadrupled between 1935 and 1954, despite this being a period of imperial decline. *Parkinson's Law* also deals with the principles and practice of selection for employment; the staffing of committees from cabinets of ministers downwards; how meetings function; the function and organization of social gatherings; the ways in which committees handle money; how the grandiosity of buildings and the achievements of their owners are often inversely related; 'injelitance' (incompetence combined with jealousy) and its effects; and the process of deciding when people should retire.

Parkinson's term 'injelitance' covers a major phenomenon of employment in all but the smallest organizations, one which official social science has, for obvious reasons, conspicuously ignored. Parkinson light-heartedly describes the phenomenon as diverse, beginning whenever someone is employed who 'combines in himself a high concentration of incompetence and jealousy' (Parkinson 1958b: 96). When such people achieve positions of power, he claims, they 'eject all those abler than themselves' (1958b: 97), gradually eliminating intelligence from the organization, and thereby increasing the levels of smugness and apathy, with the result that the organization becomes useless. According to Parkinson, a highly intolerant hatchet person may be only a temporary solution, with ridicule and castigation only slightly more effective; in extreme cases Parkinson himself, 'the greatest living authority' (1958b: 105) may be hired as a consultant at great expense. Alternatively, the organization's establishments should be completely evacuated and thoroughly disinfected, and all files and equipment destroyed. Lastly, it may be necessary to: 'insure [the buildings] heavily against fire, and then set them alight' (1958b: 108).

The sequels to *Parkinson's Law*, entitled *The Law and the Profits* (1960), *In-laws and Outlaws* (1962), *Mrs Parkinson's Law* (1969), *The Law of Delay, or Playing for Time* (1970), *The Law, or Still in Pursuit* (1979) and *The Law Complete* (1983), developed the theme of *Parkinson's Law* further. In this way, and from his continuing observations of public, private, corporate and domestic life, Parkinson derived such laws as 'Expenditure rises to meet income' (Parkinson 1960: 3), and 'Action expands to fill the void created by human failure' (Parkinson 1970: 4).

In each of the books in the series, as well as the preceding *Economist* articles, Parkinson adopted a partly Weberian approach to argue that modern rational bureaucracies, dependent as they are upon the development of a money economy, a free market, legal codification and the expansion of the administration, are inevitable, inefficient and formally irrational (Weber 1922) (see WEBER, M.). *Parkinson's Law* and its sequels also showed what other, more academic, studies had shown (for example, Merton 1949; Selznick 1966). This was that government officials can act in self-interested ways and that the dysfunctionality of some bureaucratic rules can lead to the unintended consequence of the rules becoming ends in themselves.

Industrial Disruption (1973) and *Communicate: Parkinson's Formula for Business Survival* (1977) were both examples of his later contributions to the business and management literature, many of which were co-authored or edited by him. *Industrial Disruption* brings together a number of distinguished writers to illustrate the value of effective industrial relations. In it, Parkinson identifies origins and prevailing trends of industrial conflict in different industries and, using selected case studies as illustration, suggests four general rules for its cure: (1) offer security of employment; (2) achieve higher levels of efficiency in the firm; (3) employ a higher proportion of women; and (4) negotiate with honesty.

Communicate builds on this last rule and provides a comprehensive illustration of the need for business leaders to communicate effectively with the numerous business stakeholders. Described in its foreword by Peter Drucker as a book which for the first time tackles all four elements of communication (knowing when, how and what to say, and to whom), it also shows the influence that both operating and remote environments have on business success (see DRUCKER, P.). Other business and management books included *All About Balance Sheets* (1978), one of two co-authored books on practical business finance, and a complementary nine-book series on management, including *How to Get to the Top: Without Ulcers, Tranquillisers or Heart Attacks* (1976).

Apart from his writing, Parkinson's main professional contribution was perhaps to the University of Malaya which, as Raffles Professor of History, he helped found and develop. Against the 1950s background of Malaya's civil war (during which he was also the local war correspondent), Singapore's move to independence and its consequently intense political activity, Parkinson's mission was to establish a historical background for the country which its varied peoples might then share. This involved, among other things, a study of the rubber industry, which had given the colony its early wealth, and the sponsorship of a number of archaeological expeditions to unearth the Malayan peninsula's early history.

4 Evaluation

As a historian, Parkinson's interests in Napoleonic maritime trade coincided happily with gaps in the naval literature, gaps which he successfully set about filling. He is regarded as one of the pioneers of the study of naval history in the Napoleonic era, and is acknowledged as being one of the most rigorous of scholars of his time in the discipline. History, being less than popular during the inter-war years and immediately after the Second World War, tended to encourage a focused approach, with certain scholars concentrating on the economic impact of maritime trade while others concentrated on navies and war at sea. Parkinson, however, brought a range of perspectives to his subject which the often very focused research of even the contemporary scholar lacks. As a result, he was able to analyse the impact of trade, war and foreign policy on each other in a way in which other writers on the subject could not.

As a writer of books on business and politics, much of Parkinson's sharp criticism of public expenditure was, at least in part, derived from an upbringing which made him acutely aware of both the advantages of economy and thrift and, as a firm believer in public school education, of both the positive and negative effects of the class system. The success of *Parkinson's Law* perhaps came not so much from the lessons its author taught, for he wrote nothing in it that was not already known to experienced people, but from the lesson G.K. Chesterton taught its author. This was that a sane and logical argument can be disguised in a joke and so be doubly effective.

Much of Parkinson's writing was therefore laced with a dry, dead-pan wit. The strength of his work lay, arguably, in an outstanding analytical ability which, combined with humour, enabled him to identify the driving forces in any topic and convey them effectively to the reader. This can be seen most clearly in his works on business and management, which focused on issues he had often observed and found stimulating, and on which he could offer both controversial and highly original comment, often with the help of writers more academically qualified to write about those issues than himself. As such, he was the provider of empirical and anecdotal evidence for writers in the subject with whom he collaborated, as well as being a catalyst for their ideas. At first glance, Parkinson's main contribution to business and management might therefore be as a conduit through which major business issues, sometimes well discussed in the academic literature, could be brought successfully to the attention of a wider audience. As a result, despite the fact that his name and the associated 'Law' have passed into the English language, Parkinson is rarely quoted in the business and management literature.

Yet Parkinson's writing was often far more insightful, and as a consequence contained far more wisdom, than the contemporary management guru and business recipe books of the 1980s and 1990s. His books, written with enormous verve and clarity of argument, as well as with a masterly command of the English language, also far outclass more recent writings in terms of their readability. What they have in common is a certain disregard for rational bureaucracy. In Parkinson's case this is funny and stimulating, but in some later works it is disturbing because the alternative seems to be anarchy, chaos, the war of all against all, and a rising tide of overt nepotism as one of the least worrying possibilities.

Parkinson's thought may have lent a certain legitimacy to such recent critics of mechanistic bureaucratic organizations, but it would be a little dangerous to associate him with those who foster the belief that all rational divisions of labour are bad. On the contrary, Parkinson argued for bureaucracy as an essential and valuable feature of contemporary life, reserving his ultimate criticism, and interest, not for bureaucracy itself but for its mismanagement. His insights are relevant to social and organizational psychologists involved in group behaviour (social power, social perception, impression management and the relationship between role and identity); to the thinking of other witty and popular, but realistic (as opposed to prescriptive) gurus, and ultimately serious management writers like Anthony Jay and Robert Heller; and to the thinking of such heavyweight sociological students of organizational life as Melville Dalton, Robert Jackall and Andrew Pettigrew.

5 Conclusions

The main elements of Parkinson's work fall into five categories:

1 his writings on management, most of which were insightful and humorously sceptical, and all of which had solid practical ramifications

2 a small number of serious books on business

3   a small number of books about politics and
    political thought
4   several books on maritime history
5   diverse works of fiction, and of general and
    military history.

Although Parkinson did not possess the
singlemindedness of purpose of the truly
dedicated scholar, but rather the broader ideal
of a balanced range of accomplishments, it
would be very unfair to criticize him, in the
ways fashionable in the later years of his life,
for a 'lack of focus'. This is because he wrote
so successfully on a wide range of subjects. A
gentleman scholar, and a moral and serious
man, Parkinson described himself as an artist.
He combined considerable breadth of vision
and depth of understanding with a lightness of
touch in his writing. This is perhaps one reason why his work, although serious and generally illuminating, is too often only admired
from a distance.

MARK DIBBEN
UNIVERSITY OF ABERDEEN

IAN GLOVER
UNIVERSITY OF STIRLING

Further reading

(References cited in the text marked *)

Dalton, M. (1959) *Men Who Manage: Fusions of
Feeling and Theory in Administration*, New
York: Wiley. (Investigates the co-existence of
formal and informal management systems and
their combined effect on the management of
business problems.)

Drucker, P. (1966) *The Effective Executive*, London: Heinemann. (Discusses the improvements
in managerial effectiveness which may be
achieved by the management of time, by individual contributions, by prioritizing and by decision making.)

Heller, R. (1990) *Culture Shock: The Office Revolution*, London: Hodder & Stoughton. (Discusses the role that information technology may
play in creating competitive advantage in business.)

Jackall, R. (1988) *Moral Mazes: The World of Corporate Managers*, New York: Oxford University Press. (A detailed historical and
sociological study of the social and ethical aspects of corporate life.)

Jay, A. (1967) *Management and Machiavelli*, London: Hodder & Stoughton. (Sets numerous important elements of management thinking and
practice in the context of history and political
science to explore the character of management
down the ages.)

* Merton, R. (1949) *Social Theory and Social Structure*, 3rd edn, Glencoe, IL: The Free Press.
(Compares theories of social structure and reference groups using an empirical investigation
of public bureaucracies.)

* Parkinson, C.N. (1934) *Edward Pellew Viscount
Exmouth, Admiral of the Red*, London: Me-
thuen. (An authorized biography of Admiral Sir
Edward Pellew, distinguished contemporary of
Admiral Lord Nelson. Parkinson's first pub-
lished work.)

* Parkinson, C.N. (1937) *Trade in the Eastern Seas,
1793–1813*, Cambridge: Cambridge University
Press. (An account of the extensive British and
French trading and foreign direct investment
interests in Africa, India and the Far East during
the period, illustrating how the naval wars of
1793–1815, recognized as the Classic Age of
British Sea Power, are only rendered meaningful when seen within their commercial context.)

* Parkinson, C.N. (1948) *The Trade Winds*, London:
Allen & Unwin. (A joint-authored volume describing the main aspects of British overseas
trade during the period 1793–1815, including
essays on the development of the ports of London, Liverpool and Bristol.)

* Parkinson, C.N. (1958a) *The Evolution of Political
Thought*, London: University of London Press.
(An historical analysis of the development of
political thought, illustrating the separate influences of both Oriental and Western civilizations on different forms of government.)

* Parkinson, C.N. (1958b) *Parkinson's Law*, London: John Murray. (An archetypal satirical illustration of the effects of the mismanagement
of bureaucracies.)

* Parkinson, C.N. (1960) *The Law and the Profits*,
London: John Murray.

* Parkinson, C.N. (1962) *In-laws and Outlaws*, London: John Murray.

* Parkinson, C.N. (1964a) *British Intervention in
Malaya 1861–1877*, Singapore: Malaya University Press. (Illustrates the impact of commercial, political and military interests on
British Government policy during 1867–77,
and shows how these interests led to the absorp-
tion of much of Malaya into the British Empire.)

* Parkinson, C.N. (1964b) *East and West*, London:
John Murray.

* Parkinson, C.N. (1966) *A Law unto Themselves*, London: John Murray.
* Parkinson, C.N. (1967) *Left Luggage from Marx to Wilson*, London: John Murray. (A broad historical survey of the development of the Labour Movement in the UK.)
* Parkinson, C.N. (1969) *Mrs Parkinson's Law*, London: John Murray.
* Parkinson, C.N. (1970) *The Law of Delay, or Playing for Time*, London: John Murray.
* Parkinson, C.N. (ed.) *et al.* (1973) *Industrial Disruption*, London: Leviathan. (A joint-authored prescriptive illustration of the origins and trends of industrial conflict in different societies.)
* Parkinson, C.N. (1976) *How to get to the Top: Without Ulcers, Tranquillisers or Heart Attacks*, McMillan India Ltd.
* Parkinson, C.N. (1977) *Communicate: Parkinson's Formula for Business Survival*, London: Prentice Hall. (A prescriptive examination of the need for effective communication in business.)
* Parkinson, C.N. (1978) *All about Balance Sheets*, McMillan India Ltd.
* Parkinson, C.N. (1979) *The Law, or Still in Pursuit*, London: John Murray. (One of six sequels to *Parkinson's Law* (1958), providing a satirical illustration on the continuing impact of administrative bodies on everyday life.)
* Parkinson, C.N. (1983) *The Law Complete*, Ballantine Books Incorporated.
  Pettigrew, A. (1985) *The Awakening Giant*, London: Blackwell. (A comprehensive longitudinal study of changes in management, organization and business strategy at ICI, the UK chemicals manufacturer.)
  Pugh, D.S. *et al.* (1971) *Writers on Organisations*, 2nd edn, Harmondsworth: Penguin. (A broad introductory selection of edited writings on different aspects of organizations, including key excerpts from the work of, for example, Barnard, Drucker, Mayo, Simon and Weber.)
* Selznick, P. (1966) *TVA and the Grass Roots*, New York: Harper Torch Books. (A study of the workings of a bureaucracy (the Tennessee Valley Authority), highlighting recurrent conflicts between power, ideology and policy requirements.)
* Weber, M. (1922) *Wirtschaft und Gesellschaft*, trans. as *Economy and Society: An Outline of Interpretative Sociology*, (trans.) G. Roth and G. Wittich, New York: Bedminster Press, 1968. (An archetypal empirical comparison of social structures and normative orders, examining the influences of such phenomena as class, power and status on the workings of, for example, the law, bureaucracy, the city and politics.)

See also: DRUCKER, P. F.; WEBER, M.

Related topics in the IEBM: BUSINESS HISTORY; COMMUNICATION; GURU CONCEPT; INDUSTRIAL AND LABOUR RELATIONS; MACHIAVELLI, N.; MANAGEMENT IN THE UNITED KINGDOM; MEETINGS AND CHAIRING; ORGANIZATION BEHAVIOUR; ORGANIZATION BEHAVIOUR: HISTORY OF; ORGANIZATION STRUCTURE; PUBLIC SECTOR MANAGEMENT; TRADE UNIONS

Paton, William Andrew (1889–1991)

Personal background

- born 19 July 1889 in Calumet, Michigan, USA
- grew up on a farm in difficult economic times
- had little formal schooling prior to university
- majored in economics but was drawn into accounting
- married Mary K. Sleator in 1914
- became one of the foremost US accounting academics
- died 26 April 1991 in Ann Arbor, Michigan

Major works

Principles of Accounting (with R.A. Stevenson) (1918)

Accounting Theory – With Special Reference to the Corporate Enterprise (1922)

Accountants' Handbook (1932, 1943)

An Introduction to Corporate Accounting Standards (with A.C. Littleton) (1940)

Asset Accounting (with William A. Paton, Jr) (1952)

Corporation Accounts and Statements (with William A. Paton, Jr) (1955)

Summary

William A. Paton (1889–1991) was a persistent advocate of the use of economic reasoning in the discourse on accounting principles. He was the author of innovative textbooks that reflected his advocacy of the use of current values in financial statements and the proper recognition of interest in accounting reckonings. He was co-author of the most influential monograph in the US accounting literature, *An Introduction to Corporate Accounting Standards*.

1 Introduction

During an academic accounting career spanning more than forty years, Paton argued eloquently that economic reasoning should be the guiding principle in company financial reporting. In books and articles, he was a strong advocate of bringing current replacement costs into the accounts and of giving proper recognition to the interest element in accounting reckonings. He was a leading figure in the American Accounting Association, was the founder and first editor of its research journal, *The Accounting Review*, and served for twelve years on the Committee on Accounting Procedure of the American Institute of (Certified Public) Accountants (AICPA), which was charged with issuing authoritative pronouncements on 'generally accepted accounting principles' (GAAP) between 1939 and 1959. Together with A.C. Littleton, he wrote the most influential monograph in the US accounting literature, *An Introduction to Corporate Accounting Standards* (1940).

2 Biographical data

Paton was born on 19 July 1889 in Calumet, Michigan. His father, Andrew Paton, had immigrated from Scotland in 1851 as a child, and his mother, Mary Nowlin, was of Yankee stock. Most of his youth was spent in the copper country of Michigan, working on the family farm during trying economic times.

Although his formal schooling was minimal, Paton was an avid reader. By age sixteen, when he passed the eighth grade examination, he had attended school for only three years. Seven years later, following a year of high school and nearly three years at Michigan State Normal College (now Eastern Michigan University), Paton enrolled at the University of Michigan. He financed his studies through part-time jobs and by selling books from house to house during vacations. In 1915, he received a BA degree in economics from the university, and, with remarkable dispatch, he obtained an MA in 1916 and the PhD in 1917, both degrees also in economics. His doctoral dissertation was entitled 'The theory of accounts', which formed the basis for his celebrated treatise, *Accounting Theory – With Special Reference to the Corporate Enterprise*, published in 1922. In 1927, he became a Certified Public Accountant in the State of Michigan.

He married Mary K. Sleator in 1914, and they had three children, one of whom, William A. Paton, Jr, became an accounting and finance academic and was a junior author of two of Paton's textbooks. Paton died on 26 April 1991 in Ann Arbor, Michigan, in his 102nd year.

3 Main contribution

Paton attributed the origin of his interest in accounting to the appearance of Charles E. Sprague's *The Philosophy of Accounts* and Henry Rand Hatfield's *Modern Accounting*, published in 1908 and 1909, respectively. Prior to that, most accounting textbooks dispensed rules and practices to be memorized rather than theories and analysis to challenge the intellect. In his first year at Michigan, Paton took an accounting course from David Friday, an economist who, Paton later said, knew nothing of accounting. The class plodded through a dull textbook until, one day, Friday announced the arrival of the path-breaking works by Sprague and Hatfield, which he recommended to the class and placed on library reserve. Paton has written that, 'I don't believe I would ever have gone further in accounting if it hadn't been' for the stimulation provided by those two books (Paton 1978: 3).

In 1917, Paton accepted an assistant professorship at the University of Michigan. He was promoted to associate professor in 1919 and to full professor in 1921, and in 1947 he was one of twelve Michigan faculty members honoured by the designation 'university professor'. His dual faculty title became Edwin Francis Gay University Professor of Accounting and Professor of Economics. He became Professor Emeritus in 1959.

In 1916, a year before he completed his doctoral thesis, Paton and Russell A. Stevenson published a slender textbook, *Principles of Accounting*. They issued a revised and expanded version of the book a year later, and in 1918 they produced a 685-page tome that represented a bold challenge to accounting orthodoxy, especially from two authors who had not yet reached their thirtieth birthdays. Articles published contemporaneously by Paton alone, as well as his doctoral thesis completed in 1917, provide ample evidence that he was the one principally responsible for the radicalism in the book. Departing from the traditional characterization of the balance sheet as assets = liabilities + proprietorship, Paton instead proposed assets = equities. He recommended that the 'net revenue' from operations be drawn without showing interest and taxes as expenses. Instead, they would be shown as distributions of income. In this way, the operating result would not be affected by whether the company had been financed by debt or equity capital and by 'coerced' payments to government. Paton was to become known as the principal US advocate of the entity theory of accounting, under which the enterprise is the central focus of accounting. According to the proprietorship theory, which Sprague and Hatfield, among others, had championed, the proprietor was the focal point in accounting for an enterprise. Although it is not clear that it makes much difference whether one adopts one theory or the other in deciding how to account for an enterprise, the two theories and their comparative merits have commanded considerable attention in the literature.

In *Principles of Accounting*, Paton and Stevenson joined Sprague in classifying bond discount as a subtraction from the face value of bonds payable, and not as a 'deferred charge' among the assets, as most authors recommended and continued to recommend until 1971, when Paton's preference became accepted practice. This was one of several reforms proposed by Paton that did not become accepted practice until decades later.

In a policy recommendation that was associated with Paton during the remainder of his long career, he and Stevenson argued that the periodic appreciation in the replacement cost of fixed assets should be recorded in the accounts, but in a way so as not to obscure the original costs. In *Principles of Accounting*, they also contended that this appreciation should be included in net revenue, but Paton retreated from this position in the 1920s and instead preferred to credit the appreciation to a capital revaluation account. In this respect, he departed from what has come to be called 'financial capital maintenance' in favour of 'physical capital maintenance'.

By any standard, *Principles of Accounting* was more than just a textbook. As a work of full-throated advocacy, it represented the beginning of Paton's long crusade to inject economic thinking into accounting debates that were typically burdened by conservatism and appeals to precedent and legal form. Paton described himself as a 'value man', and not one to worship at the altar of historical cost. In his early years, he held the view that managers, in making decisions about the most efficient use of economic resources, depended, in large measure, on the accounts for relevant information. Hence, it was essential that the accounts show current values, and not be confined to outdated historical costs. By the end of the 1930s, he began to emphasize the informational needs of shareholders.

In a 1920 article and in his 1922 treatise, *Accounting Theory*, Paton modified his earlier position somewhat. Perhaps because he judged that much of the recent run-up in the replacement cost of fixed assets may have been traceable to the doubling of the general price level between 1915 and 1920, he was reluctant to recognize it in the accounts. Referring to an article by Livingston Middleditch Jr, Paton, for the first time, conceded

the usefulness of preparing supplementary statements to show the effects on the comparative financial statements of the changing purchasing power of the monetary unit. From 1938 onwards, he drew on Henry W. Sweeney's famous book, *Stabilized Accounting* (1936), to argue forcefully that the impact on the financial statements of movements in the general price level should be displayed in supplementary statements, and he was the first textbook author to illustrate how such a set of supplementary statements might be prepared. He never recommended that such effects be recorded in the accounts or reflected in the basic financial statements themselves.

One of the salient features of *Accounting Theory* was a chapter devoted to explicating 'The basic postulates of accounting', which was the first systematic treatment of the important assumptions underlying the reasoning process used by accountants.

In later works, written in the 1930s and 1940s, Paton reverted to his earlier advocacy that the replacement cost of fixed assets be reflected in the accounts, and devised a 'compromise procedure' by which the periodic depreciation on the excess of the replacement cost over the historical cost of fixed assets would appear in the income statement but would be added back before determining net income and be charged directly against the revaluation capital account. Paton had been troubled for some time that replacement cost had no standing either in income tax law or dividend law, raising questions about its legitimacy in accounting. This compromise allowed him to avoid the issue of its effect on net income, while still reporting its amount in the financial statements.

Another Patonian device to bring current values into the accounts was his 'even deal' interpretation of a corporation's decision to acquire a significant fraction of its outstanding common stock at a price considerably higher (or lower) than the recorded issue price. Paton interpreted such a transaction as an occasion for revaluing the corporation's assets. He would book an upward (or downward) revaluation of the corporation's assets by grossing up to the 100 per cent level the differential between the acquisition price and the recorded issue price for the fraction of the equity that was acquired.

Both of these devices were developed at a time, in the late 1930s, when Paton's confidence in the supremacy of current values in the determination of income was at its lowest point.

While Paton's specific policy recommendations to reflect current values in the financial statements underwent modifications over the years, in the end he reasserted his belief that historical costs could not stand alone in the basic financial statements, and should be accompanied (or, in some instances, supplanted) by current values.

4 Role in the American Accounting Association

Paton was the only member of the American Accounting Association (which was known as the American Association of University Instructors in Accounting from its founding in 1916 until 1936) to have occupied all of the elected offices on the executive committee. He served as its president in 1922, and played a major part in founding the Association's research journal, *The Accounting Review*, in 1926. He served as editor from 1926 to 1928.

Paton was also a driving force in the movement to broaden the Association's membership base and expand its objectives to include an aggressive programme of publishing research monographs and of promoting the development of accounting principles. The Association was reorganized along these lines in January 1936, following which its executive committee, with Paton as a member, gave notice to the American Institute of Accountants, the practitioner body, that the Association would be a major player in the formulation of accounting principles for acceptance by the recently established Securities and Exchange Commission. The executive committee's first salvo was the issue of a policy statement entitled 'A tentative statement of accounting principles affecting corporate reports' (1936), which was, in the main, a strong defence of historical cost accounting and which was intended to advance the dialogue on accounting principles. Three members of the executive committee, Eric L. Kohler (president), A.C. Littleton and Howard C. Greer, were arch historical costers and evidently dominated the committee discussions.

Four years later, the Association published Paton and Littleton's *An Introduction to Corporate Accounting Standards*, which elaborated upon the 1936 statement and effectively set the terms for discourse on financial accounting for decades to come. The authors adopted an income-statement approach to analysing financial accounting issues, and their vivid construct, the 'matching of costs and revenues', has become one of the most commonly invoked criteria for resolving disagreements over accounting principles.

In the first six chapters of the 1940 monograph, the authors supplied a conceptual framework to fit the historical cost design of the 1936 statement, yet in the final chapter, written chiefly by Paton, sympathy was expressed for the showing of current values as supplemental information. However, it is for the historical cost elaboration that the monograph is universally known, not for the discursive treatment of a number of current value issues in the last chapter.

5 Other activities and honours

Paton published a succession of accounting textbooks spanning the period from 1916 to 1971. Unlike the ordinary run of US accounting textbooks, which have largely been catalogues of extant practice, his texts were crusades for accounting reform. They challenged the intellect and obliged teacher and student alike to define and redefine the role of accounting in society.

Paton edited and was the principal contributor to the second and third editions of the encyclopedic *Accountants' Handbook* (1932, 1943), and he wrote scores of articles in professional and academic journals. As with his textbooks, his articles were not bland dissertations on accounting practice. He exposed weaknesses in theories and practice and argued vigorously (and colourfully) for accounting reports built on a sound economic foundation.

Paton was a spellbinding teacher, whether in heavily populated undergraduate accounting lectures or in doctoral seminars. Many of his doctoral students went on to become leading accounting academics.

From 1938 to 1950, Paton was a member of the American Institute's Committee on Accounting Procedure, whose Accounting Research Bulletins constituted the authoritative expression of US GAAP. His name appeared on more Bulletins, thirty-three in all, than any other member in the Committee's twenty-one-year history.

Paton frequently gave expert testimony in public utility rate cases, and he was an outspoken critic of the Federal Power Commission's 'original cost' doctrine. He also appeared several times before Congressional committees on matters of economic policy and pending tax legislation.

In 1944, Paton was the recipient of the AICPA's gold medal for distinguished service to the profession, and in 1950 he was the first accounting academic inducted into the 'accounting hall of fame'. In 1987, the AICPA recognized him as 'accounting educator of the century'.

Among Paton's many writings were staunch defences of the free enterprise system. In virtually all matters, Paton was a political conservative.

6 Evaluation

Among his colleagues and students at the University of Michigan, as well as others who were exposed to the fire of his oratory or who followed his vigorous writings, Paton was known as an eloquent exponent of the use of economic reasoning in accounting determinations. At the policy level, he argued during most of his career for the inclusion of current values in financial statements. Yet it is ironic that Paton's lasting impact on several generations of practitioners and educators was through a single work: the 1940 monograph with Littleton, which has played a powerful

role in implanting a historical cost tradition in US accounting.

STEPHEN ZEFF
RICE UNIVERSITY

Further reading

(References cited in the text marked *)

* American Accounting Association (1936) 'A tentative statement of accounting principles affecting corporate reports', *The Accounting Review* 11 (2): 187–91. (A policy statement on accounting principles by the executive committee of the American Accounting Association.)

Edwards, J. and Salmonson, R. (1961) *Contributions of Four Accounting Pioneers*, East Lansing, MI: Bureau of Business and Economic Research, Graduate School of Business Administration, Michigan State University. (A compilation of abstracts of Paton's periodical writings.)

* Hatfield, H. (1909) *Modern Accounting: Its Principles and Some of Its Problems*, New York: D. Appleton & Company. (Reprinted by Arno Press. A comprehensive and insightful textbook on the state of modern accounting and the literature.)

Ijiri, Y. (1980) 'An introduction to corporate accounting standards: a review', *The Accounting Review* 55 (4): 620–8. (A retrospective examination of Paton and Littleton's 1940 monograph.)

* Paton, W. (1922) *Accounting Theory – With Special Reference to the Corporate Enterprise*, New York: Ronald Press. (Reprinted by Scholars Book Co. The work that best embodies Paton's accounting thought.)

* Paton, W. (1932) *Accountants' Handbook*, New York: Ronald Press. (This book and its successor, published in 1943, were encyclopedic surveys of the field.)

* Paton, W. (1943) *Accountants' Handbook*, New York: Ronald Press.

* Paton, W. (1978) 'Wandering into accounting: notes on [a] writing career', *The Accounting Historians Journal* 5 (2): 1–10. (An autobiographical account.)

* Paton, W. and Littleton, A. (1940) *An Introduction to Corporate Accounting Standards*, American Accounting Association.

* Paton, W. and Paton, W., Jr (1952) *Asset Accounting*, New York: Macmillan. (A textbook bearing the imprint of senior Paton's crusading views.)

Paton, W. and Paton, W., Jr (1955) *Corporation Accounts and Statements*, New York: Macmillan. (A textbook in the same vein as 'Asset Accounting'.)

* Paton, W. and Stevenson, R. (1918) *Principles of Accounting*, New York: Macmillan. (Reprinted by Arno Press. A work of radical advocacy by the two young authors.)

Previts, G. and Robinson, T. (1994) 'William A. Paton (1889–1991): theorist and educator', in J.R. Edwards (ed.), *Twentieth-Century Accounting Thinkers*, London: Routledge. (An essay on Paton's contributions to accounting theory and practice.)

* Sprague, C. (1908) *The Philosophy of Accounts*, New York: C. Sprague. (A pioneering treatise on accounting.)

* Sweeney, H. (1936) *Stabilized Accounting*, New York: Harper & Brothers. (Reprinted by Holt, Rinehart and Winston and by Arno Press. The first explication and illustration of accounting for the effects of inflation.)

Taggart, H. (ed.) (1964) *Paton on Accounting: Selected Writings of William A. Paton*, Ann Arbor, MI: Bureau of Business Research, Graduate School of Business Administration, University of Michigan. (Contains notes by the editor, Paton's colleague, on each of the forty-six articles.)

Taggart, H. *et al.* (1992) 'A tribute to William A. Paton', *The Accounting Review* 67 (1): 1–16. (A set of encomiums published shortly after Paton's death.)

Zeff, S. (1979) 'Paton on the effects of changing prices on accounting, 1916–55', in S.A. Zeff, J. Demski and N. Dopuch (eds), *Essays in Honor of William A. Paton: Pioneer Accounting Theorist*, Ann Arbor, MI: Division of Research, Graduate School of Business Administration, University of Michigan. (The author traces the evolution of Paton's thinking on a subject central to his work.)

See also: BENSON, H.; HOPWOOD, A.; LIMPERG, T.; PACIOLI, L.; SCHMALENBACH, E.

Related topics in the IEBM: ACCOUNTING IN THE UNITED STATES OF AMERICA; ASSET VALUATION, DEPRECIATION AND PROVISIONS; FINANCIAL ACCOUNTING; INFLATION ACCOUNTING

Perlman, Selig (1888–1959)

Personal background

- born in 1888 in Bialystok, Poland, then a part of Russia
- after briefly studying in Italy, emigrated to the US in 1908
- received a PhD from the University of Wisconsin, 1915
- assistant, associate and full professor of economics at the University of Wisconsin from 1915–59
- developed a fundamental theory of worker collective action and provided a noteworthy defence of American labour exceptionalism.

Major works

A History of Trade Unionism in the United States (1922)
A Theory of the Labor Movement (1928)

Summary

Selig Perlman is most well known for his book *A Theory of the Labor Movement* published in 1928. In it he developed the proposition that working people throughout history, when left to their own devices, have formed organizations designed to protect their short-term working interests. Contrary to Marx, Perlman argued that over time, as they matured, worker's organizations would tend to focus on the accomplishment of better terms and conditions of employment rather than on radical social change. Perlman applied the theory comparatively in order to offer an explanation for the apparently exceptional non-radical character of the American labour movement. Many consider *A Theory of the Labor Movement* to be an apologetic for American labour's choice of business unionism over socialist unionism.

1 Biographical data

Selig Perlman was born in 1888 in Poland, which at that time was an integral part of Czarist Russia. As a student Perlman was very much influenced by the writings of Karl Marx. Because of limited opportunities available to Jews for further education in his home country, Perlman went to Italy to study at the University of Naples. There he met the American socialist William English Walling who sponsored his emigration to the US. In America Perlman went to the University of Wisconsin where, after completing his baccalaureate thesis on socialism in Milwaukee from 1893–1910, he became part of the research group of John R. Commons. That group went on to produce the multi-volume *History of Labour in the United States*, of which Perlman submitted his section as his PhD thesis.

After World War I Perlman was commissioned to rewrite Richard T. Ely's *The Labor Movement in America* but after disagreements with Ely, the book was published under Perlman's name alone as *A History of Trade Unionism in the United States*. Reflecting on lessons learned as a student, colleague and research associate of Commons and other members of the Wisconsin team as well as his knowledge of labour developments in Europe, Perlman in 1928 published his very influential *A Theory of the Labor Movement*. That book attracted considerable attention at the time and continues to be mandatory reading for students of labour movement theory to this day. In 1935 he co-authored, along with Philip Taft, the fourth volume of Commons and Associates' *History of Labour in the United States* covering the years 1893–1932.

In addition to his scholarly work Perlman was a member of the Wisconsin Human Rights Commission for many years. Unlike his mentor John Commons, however, he was not strongly involved in practical work outside of the university. He is said to have accepted one assignment as an arbitrator after which he did no more because the case required that he uphold a dismissal. According to friends and colleagues, he was a conscientious teacher who took a personal interest in his students. He was not, however, very involved in professional associations having to do with his specialty and spent most of his time in Madison. After retiring from the University of Wisconsin in 1959, he accepted an offer to teach at the University of Pennsylvania but died before being able to take up that post.

2 The Theory of the Labor Movement

Perlman's theory of the labour movement was written as a direct response to the ideas of Karl Marx that dominated thinking about the nature and development of labour movements. Marxian theory held that economic evolution followed a predictable path leading inevitably to socialism. As capitalist society evolved, workers eventually would begin to realize the class based, exploitative nature of that society. As they became more class conscious, workers would create trade unions and political parties that would tend to become more radical over time.

Perlman argued that this Marxian prediction was wrong. Worker organizations would not inevitably become more radical under capitalism. Instead, Perlman claimed to have identified a tendency among 'manual groups' throughout history to have had their economic attitudes shaped by a 'consciousness of scarcity of opportunity' which is distinctly different from the 'abundance conscious' outlook of the business community. This common trait among manualists has led them to design institutions such as trade unions with a view towards controlling jobs and the conditions associated with jobs. Contrary to Marxian

theory, labour movements which reflect this 'organic' philosophy of labour are likely to be unresponsive to calls for revolution. However, this 'home grown' philosophy of labour competes for worker allegiance both with the 'abundance consciousness' of the capitalist and with the philosophy and programme of the 'intellectual,' a term used by Perlman to refer almost exclusively to socialist thinkers and activists. Because workers lack confidence in their native instincts immature unions may very well be attracted to the programmes of the intellectuals. They may also be weak and unstable if workers are attracted to the individualistic philosophy of business. However, as unions mature, they should become more stable and more 'job conscious.'

Perlman's essential proposition is that three factors are:

> 'basic in any modern labour situation: first, the resistance power of capitalism, determined by its own historical development; second, the degree of dominance over the labor movements by the intellectual's 'mentality,' which regularly underestimates capitalism's resistance power and overestimates labor's will to radical change; and, third, the degree of maturity of trade union 'mentality.
>
> (Perlman 1928: x)

With reference to the three factors, Perlman attempts to explain developments in Russia, Germany, Britain and the United States.

In Russia there was a capitalist class that was dominated by the state and thus, without government support, was very weak. The trade union movement that had begun to develop in the 1890s was ruthlessly suppressed in the first two decades of the twentieth century. There was also a thriving intellectual community bent on revolution. According to Perlman's analysis, when the Russian state was destabilized in the course of World War I, the revolution succeeded because there were no strong business or labour institutions to stand in its way.

In Germany, on the other hand, the capitalist class had developed a character and independent strength of its own and by the first world war the trade unions had become a very important factor in their own right separate from the intellectual-dominated Social Democratic Party. Although the German labour movement had initially embraced a radical creed that considered revolution its primary goal, by the turn of the century the trade unions had become strong enough to assert their own more conservative 'job conscious' interests. As a result, when the government collapsed during World War I, the combination of a strong, independent capitalist class and a 'job conscious' trade union movement prevented the intellectuals from abolishing capitalism as had happened in Russia.

Noting that British labour developments are often put forth as support for Marxist theory, Perlman argues that detailed study of the situation leads to a different conclusion. Even though workplace-focused craft unions were followed by socialist industrial unions in the 1890s British workers did not really reject 'pure and simple' unionism in favour of revolutionary unionism. Instead the 'New Unionism' was successful not because its leaders were socialists but rather because of their aggressiveness during a time when the older unionism had lost it militancy. Moreover, Perlman argues, British socialism had more to do with religious messianism than with revolutionary fervour. Intellectuals associated with the Fabian Society did attempt to 'make the labor movement into a draft horse for their socialism.' However, by the late 1920s, according to Perlman, most British unions were still focused primarily on jobs and working conditions.

Although Perlman put forth a theory that he claimed to be capable of explaining developments in many countries, his thesis is most well known for its explanation and defence of American Exceptionalism. By the 1920s, the mainstream of nearly all European labour movements had adopted some variant of socialism as its guiding philosophy. The US was exceptional in that by that time the dominant institution of the movement was the American Federation of Labor. The AFL had explicitly rejected socialism and proclaimed itself firmly committed to 'pure and simple'

unionism – a development that led intellectuals to pronounce it 'reactionary, hopeless and badly in need of new ideas and new blood'. Socialism had attracted some unionists in the late nineteenth and early twentieth centuries and it had resulted in the formation of a political party that had some initial success in attracting electoral support. However, by the mid 1920s most trade union leaders had turned away from socialism and the socialist party was in disarray. Accounting for this failure of socialism in the US has been a favourite subject of historians and social theorists ever since (see e.g. Lipset 1977; Goldfield 1990; Forbath 1991; Voss 1993).

Drawing on the work of Sombart (1906/1976) Perlman's explanation was that, due to conditions peculiar to the US, socialism had an almost impossible time taking root. Because of the pioneering character of the country, the institution of private property was very strong. Given this condition American workers for much of the nineteenth century were attracted, along with other members of the 'producing classes' such as farmers and small businessmen, not to the socialistic theories of the intellectuals but rather to 'the philosophy of 'anti-monopoly'. The main impediment of worker advancement, according to this perspective, was not capitalist exploitation but rather monopolistic practices that interfered with the 'producer's free and abundant opportunities'. Labour leaders associated with this movement sought to make both land and capital more readily available. These conditions would allow workers to form producer's cooperatives in order to take advantage of the abundant opportunities. Continued failures of cooperatives led to the demise of this tendency by the mid 1880s, however.

Another factor that separated America from Europe was the lack of cohesiveness of the working class resulting from successive waves of immigration. Each generation of workers saw in the next wave a 'competitive menace' to be fought off rather than an ally in the struggle for worker advancement. This ethnic, linguistic, religious and cultural heterogeneity made it nearly impossible to find a basis for unity other than 'job consciousness' with its limited object of 'wage and job control.'

Perlman also argued that the programme of socialism, at least of reform socialism, did not 'fit' American circumstances because of the nature of the political system. Not only is the federal, congressional system diverse but also both major American parties are very pragmatic and thus are willing to 'steal the thunder' from any new party that might put forth a popular plank. Additionally because the right to vote and broad access to education were established relatively early in the nineteenth century it was not necessary for the American movement, as it had been necessary for European movements, to struggle in order to win these rights.

Why had the 'job conscious' approach of the American Federation of Labor succeeded in the establishment of a stable form of unionism by the 1920s? According to Perlman, it did so because it 'fitted' both the external environment and the American worker's 'psychology'. It fitted because it recognized the conservatism of American society with respect to private property and private initiative, because it understood the limitations of the political instrument under American conditions, because it appreciated the constraints placed on labour solidarity by the heterogeneity of the American working class, and because it was under no delusion with respect to the 'true psychology of the workingman'.

But the 'fittness' of the AFL brand of job conscious unionism did not mean, Perlman went on to argue, that its long-term survival was assured. Instead it would have to fight a continuing battle with capital. Because of American conditions capitalism in the US was very strong not only in its resistance by force to unionism but also because of its will to win over workers to its individualistic philosophy by the use of devices such as company unions and the provision of good working conditions and fair treatment.

3 Conclusions

Even though *A Theory of the Labor Movement* is considered by many to be one of the 'great books' about trade unions in the twentieth

century it has attracted a good deal of criticism. Most of Perlman's observations about the reasons for the absence of socialism in the United States were not new or unique (see e.g. Sombart 1906/1976). Moreover, Gulick and Bers (1953) in the most heated attack on the theory argue that the three-concept system is merely definitional and as such does not amount to an adequate theory. Along with other critics they also argue that the 'psychology' of the working person and the business person are not, in practice, so starkly different. Nor, it has been suggested, is the distinction between the nature and approach of the intellectual and the manualist entirely appropriate. In many countries, for example, labour movements led by leaders up from the ranks continue to support a combination of political and economistic methods to achieve gains for workers. Recent work into nineteenth century labour history in the US has also resulted in criticism of Perlman's findings. Rather than a simple struggle between the ideas of capitalism, socialism and business unionism, in fact labour activity during the period was more complex and nuanced (Perlman 1976; Lipset 1977; Voss 1993; Forbath 1991; Goldfield 1990). Despite these criticisms Perlman's essential insight, that workers and organizations which faithfully reflect core worker values tend to place priority on jobs and immediate conditions of employment rather than on larger political aims, continues to attract strong adherents.

ROY J. ADAMS
DEGROOTE SCHOOL OF BUSINESS
MCMASTER UNIVERSITY, CANADA

Further reading

(References cited in the text marked *)

* Forbath, W.E. (1991) *Law and the Shaping of the American Labor Movement*, Cambridge, Mass.: Harvard University Press. (Review of recent work on American Exceptionalism and analysis of the effects of court decisions on union political strategy in the US.)
* Goldfield, M. (1990) 'Class, race and politics in the United States: white supremacy as the main explanation for the peculiarities of American politics from colonial times to the present',

Research in Political Economy 12: 83–127. (Argument for the influence of white supremacy on American Exceptionalism).

* Gulick, C.A. and Bers, M.K. (1953) 'Insight and illusion in Perlman's theory of the labor movement', *Industrial and Labor Relations Review* 6 (1): 510–531. (The major critique of *A Theory of the Labor Movement.*)

* Lipset, S.M. (1977) 'Why no socialism in the United States?', in S. Bialer and S. Sluzar (eds) *Radicalism in the Contemporary Age*, Boulder, Colorado: Westview, 31–150. (Extensive review of explanations of American Exceptionalism.)

* Perlman, M. (1976) *Labor Union Theories in America, Background and Development*, Westport, Connecticut: Greenwood Press, (originally published in 1958 by Row, Peterson and Company, Evanston). (The principal book on labour union theories in the US.)

* Sombart, W. (1976) *Why is there no Socialism in the United States?* White Plains, NY: International Arts and Sciences Press (originally published in 1906 by the Verlag van J.C.B. Mohr of Tübingen under the title *Warum gibt es I den Vereinigten Staaten keinen Sozialismus?*). (Early analysis of American Exceptionalism.)

Taft, P. (1976) 'Reflections on Selig Perlman as teacher and writer', *Industrial and Labor Relations Review* 29 (2): 249–257. (Background on Perlman's life and career.)

* Voss, K. (1993) *The Making of American Exceptionalism*, Ithaca, N.Y.: Cornell University Press. (Reanalysis of the Knights of Labor as a class-based movement and a critique of prevailing explanations of American Exceptionalism.)

See also: BARBASH, J.; BRAVERMAN, H.; DUNLOP, J.D.; KOCHAN, T.; MICHELS, R.; STRAUSS, G.

Related topics in the IEBM: EMPLOYEE RELATIONS, MANAGEMENT; HUMAN RESOURCE MANAGEMENT; INDUSTRIAL AND LABOUR RELATIONS; INDUSTRIAL DEMOCRACY; INDUSTRIAL RELATIONS IN THE UNITED STATES AMERICA; LABOUR PROCESS; MARX, K.H.; PROFIT-SHARING; TRADE UNIONS; WORK SYSTEMS

Peters, Thomas J. (1942–)

1 Introduction
2 Biographical data
3 Main contribution
4 Evaluation
5 Conclusions

Personal background

- born Baltimore, Maryland, 7 November 1942
- served in the US Navy, 1966–70
- BCE, MCE Cornell University, MBA Stanford University (1972), PhD (1977)
- consultant with Peate Marwick Mitchell in Washington, DC, 1970–3
- worked for the US government in Washington, 1973–4
- joined McKinsey & Co. in San Francisco, 1974, becoming principal practice leader on organizational effectiveness, 1976
- left McKinsey & Co. in 1981 to set up his own firm, the Tom Peters Group, based in Palo Alto, California
- widely quoted and cited commentator on business in the USA, appearing frequently in US newspapers and on television
- married with family, lives in California and Vermont

Major works

In Search of Excellence: Lessons from America's Best-run Companies (with Robert H. Waterman, Jr) (1982)

A Passion for Excellence: The Leadership Difference (with Nancy Austin) (1985)

Thriving on Chaos: Handbook for a Management Revolution (1987)

Liberation Management: Necessary Disorganization for the Nanosecond Nineties (1992)

Summary

Tom Peters (1942–) is possibly the most popular and widely read management 'guru' of the 1980s and 1990s. Unlike contemporaries such as Michael Porter, Peter Drucker and Charles Handy, (q.v.) Peters does not have a strongly academic background; his theories on management are derived from his own personal experiences as a consultant. Peters has come to believe that many of the fundamental principles on which management in the USA is based are wrong, and he speaks increasingly of the need for 'revolution' and 'liberation' from old, outmoded management techniques and styles. He has been criticized for an allegedly superficial approach in his writings, but many of the concepts he has called for, such as looser structures, broader perspectives and the ability to manage ambiguity, are now part of the accepted canon of management thinking.

1 Introduction

Peters entered the world of management consultancy in the 1970s at a time when business in the USA was increasingly being seen (not least by himself) as moribund, lacking in imagination and suffering more and more from foreign competition. His work with the consulting firm McKinsey & Co. led him to believe that some US companies could be described as 'excellent', and further, that there were certain identifiable features which all these companies had in common. His determination to identify those features led to his first and best-known book, *In Search of Excellence* (1982), co-written with Richard H. Waterman.

Peters' later books, as well as his articles, television appearances and consulting work, have expanded on these earlier themes. He continues to believe that excellence is both possible and achievable, and he continues to advocate, more strongly than ever, the need for a fundamentally new approach to business and management, based on organizational culture, quality, customer focus and – perhaps most controversially – decentralized organizations with strongly empowered employees. In Peters' view, management should be about decentralization and deliberate lack of focus and control, fostering an atmosphere of 'intentional chaos' where creativity and dynamism can be nurtured. His books are phenomenally popular, especially with younger and middle managers, and many of his ideas are now part of modern management thinking.

2 Biographical data

Tom Peters was born in 1942. After attending university he served for four years in the US Navy, from 1966 to 1970 at the height of the Vietnam War. He refers to the war later in *In Search of Excellence*, where he is highly critical of the 'rationalist' approach of US military leaders during the war.

Leaving the navy, he first joined the consulting firm Peate Marwick Mitchell in Washington, DC. In 1973, he joined the US Government Office of Management and Budget, also in Washington, first as director of a cabinet committee on international narcotics control and then as assistant to the director for federal drug abuse policy. Leaving government service in 1974, he moved to San Francisco where he became an associate with the international management consulting firm McKinsey & Co.

It was at McKinsey that Peters began to develop his concepts of organizational effectiveness and excellence. In 1976, he became the firm's principal practice leader on organizational effectiveness, and also began to become known as a writer and speaker. His team at McKinsey began investigating the nature of organizational and business excellence, ultimately conducting a survey of leading US businesses and creating the frameworks which were later distilled into *In Search of Excellence*.

In Search of Excellence sold over one million copies around the world and became one of the most popular management books of all time. It also made Peters himself a highly visible figure. He became known as a pundit; his media credits include a weekly column syndicated in US newspapers and a television series on the PBS network. In 1981, he left McKinsey to set up his own firm, the Tom Peters Group, through which he manages his media work and also seminars and consulting sessions for a variety of clients. Few other figures in management have reached such a wide audience.

Peters continues to write and develop his theories, paying particular attention to changes in the business environment. In *Thriving on Chaos* (1987), he warned that the recommendations spelled out in *In Search of Excellence* were no longer 'nice-to-do' but 'must-do' concepts. In *Liberation Management* (1992), he described his own view of a management revolution, the principles of which were a complete rethinking of organizational scale and control with a greater emphasis on decentralized units and flexibility. The concept of managing ambiguity, which he discussed as a key feature of managerial excellence in *In Search of Excellence*, is now a major theme running through all his work.

3 Main contribution

In *In Search of Excellence*, Peters asked what it is that companies can do to achieve excellence. He chose to examine the subject not by using academic models, but by using his own experiences and those of his colleagues, selecting real-life examples of companies which had achieved excellence and then seeking common factors.

Peters' '7–S' model consists of seven organizational variables: structure, strategy, systems, skills, staff, style and shared values. The latter is at the centre of the model and is obviously most important. In Peters' view, excellence is a cultural factor, with companies working hard to make sure employees buy into that culture; he quotes psychologist Ernest Becker to the effect that people are driven by a dualism: a need to conform and a simultaneous need to be seen as individuals. Companies which achieve excellence will meet both these needs on the part of their employees. Peters accepts that this is a paradox, and continues: 'If there is one striking feature of the excellent companies, it is this ability to manage ambiguity and paradox. What our rational economist friends tell us ought not to be possible the excellent companies do routinely' (1982: xxiv).

Quality and customer orientation are also important hallmarks, but Peters' other strongest emphases are on streamlining and simplifying organizations. *In Search of Excellence* claimed that excellent companies were those which were 'brilliant on basics': 'Tools didn't substitute for thinking... those companies worked hard to keep things simple in a complex world' (Peters and Waterman 1982: 13). His later books attack this theme more strongly. In *Thriving on Chaos*, he attacks the cult of 'giantism' and, by implication, Taylorism and the whole concept of specialized labour, calling for greater empowerment of employees and fewer controls (Peters 1987: 13 ff.) (see TAYLOR, F.W.). In *Liberation Management*, he cites the German *mittelstand* system which encourages many small to medium enterprises to establish themselves in niche markets, limiting growth but managing innovation and customer service through small, focused units (Peters 1992). He has consistently attacked large, inflexible organizations and in 1992 claimed that: 'Middle management, as we have known it since the railroads invented it right after the Civil War, is dead' (Peters 1992: 758).

Most of all, however, Peters has argued for a revolution in outlook on the part of management. He believes that the notion of management as a science has come close to eclipsing the notion of management as an art and:

Professionalism in management is regularly equated with hard-headed rationality.... The numerative, rationalist approach to management dominates the business schools. It teaches us that well-trained professional managers can manage anything. It seeks detached, analytical justification for all decisions. It is right enough to be dangerously wrong, and it has arguably led us seriously astray.
(Peters and Waterman 1982: 29)

He attacks concepts such as economy of scale and low-cost production which are often believed to be the only ways to success: 'The numerative, analytical component has an in-built conservative bias. Cost reduction becomes priority number one and revenue enhancement takes a back seat' (Peters and Waterman 1982: 44). He encourages 'overspending' on product development and quality control, and customer service, arguing that even if these do not yield value for money in the classical sense, encouraging innovation and focusing on customers are powerful marketing tools and will help the company achieve excellence.

His commitment to the need for a management revolution is as strong as Taylor's and, like Taylor, Peters believes that success depends on people. Unlike Taylor, however, he believes that successful management of people depends on removing controls, encouraging individuality and promoting 'stars'. In the Peters revolution, small, responsive, flexible management units which stay close to both their customers and their employees represent the way of the future.

4 Evaluation

It is difficult to evaluate the impact which Peters' work has had on management in the USA. His books are read around the world, and many of his themes have universal applicability, but there is a strong cultural bias throughout on US management and its environment. Within that parameter, it can be seen that a number of US companies and organizations have been adapting themselves and their operations along the lines Peters suggests; but whether they did so as a result of reading his work cannot be proven. Nor should it be ignored that not all of the companies that Peters cites as examples of excellence have been successful over the long term; IBM, for example, has run into repeated problems since the publication of *In Search of Excellence*.

In Search of Excellence drew favourable attention from business schools and business leaders, and many of the former put it on their reading syllabus for students. The later works have sometimes been criticized but have more often been ignored by academics. The increasingly radical tone of the books may have offended many scholars, and his criticisms of business schools and their apparent dedication to excessive rationality has also won him few friends. One criticism of Peters' work is that it is too superficial, concentrating on a handful of examples and lacking academic rigour. However, Peters himself is strongly influenced by academic thinking; his comment that 'organization falls out of strategy' is drawn from Chandler, and his theories on organizational culture owe something to the work of Mayo and Barnard at Harvard Business School in the 1930s (see CHANDLER, A.D.; MAYO, G.E.; BARNARD, C.I.). In *Liberation Management*, Peters acknowledges the influence of Charles Handy.

Peters has made a considerable contribution to the debate about the future of management, especially in the USA but elsewhere in the world as well. He has sometimes been criticized for too prescriptive an approach, offering a 'cookbook' of 'recipes' for success; yet those same recipes have proven to be popular and enduring. Phrases like 'managing ambiguity' have now passed into the management lexicon, and his call for a more holistic view of management with less specialization and more attention to general themes has been widely taken up by business schools, especially in Europe.

The influence of his ideas can be seen indirectly in academic thinking as well. Service industries, with their special operations and marketing problems of managing a product which is consumed at the same time as it is produced, were quick to see the applicability of Peters' theories. Textbooks on services marketing such as Bateson (1988) speak of empowering employees and promoting 'stars' as one of the key aspects of a successful service organization. Production industries were perhaps slower to come to the same view, but Hill (1989) has pushed the idea that manufacturing companies needed to pay more attention to the marketing–operations interface, get closer to their customers and look to smaller, more focused units as ways of improving profitability. The view that cost control is the bottom line is no longer as prevalent as it once was.

What Peters has undeniably done is make a contribution to the debate about how companies should be run and open it up to a broad audience. This was not necessarily his primary or his only goal:

> Am I a middle management basher? Yes. Are most of the people who come to my seminars middle managers? Yes. Why do they come? Beats me.
>
> (Peters 1992: 715)

In fact, middle managers follow Peters because, in an era when the role and value of the middle manager are increasingly uncertain, he offers them a chance to at least discuss how they might make a greater contribution. His books, which have now sold over four million copies, and his other writings have given many managers greater enthusiasm for and interest in the complexities and ambiguities of their jobs; in the revolution, he himself has been a catalyst in bringing managers closer to the fundamentals of excellence.

5 Conclusion

In *In Search of Excellence* (1982: 13–16), Peters defined eight attributes as distinctive of the excellent company:

1 a bias for action (taking the initiative)
2 close to the customer
3 autonomy and entrepreneurship
4 productivity through people
5 hands-on, value-driven leadership
6 stick to the knitting (stay close to the business you know)
7 simple form, lean staff
8 simultaneous tight-loose properties (central core values combined with decentralized organization)

His arguments for simplicity, meaning and action are powerful ones, and have struck a chord with many managers around the world; he is one of the most popular management gurus of his generation precisely because he offers managers and companies the prospect of hope and an exciting future. While many of his prescriptions are radical and his work contains a strong cultural bias towards the USA, the fundamentals about which Peters writes have universal applicability.

MORGEN WITZEL
LONDON BUSINESS SCHOOL
DURHAM UNIVERSITY BUSINESS SCHOOL

Further reading

(References cited in the text marked *)

Barnard, C.I. (1968) *The Functions of the Executive*, Cambridge, MA: Harvard University Press. (Summary of Barnard's theories, including the experimental work referred to in the text.)

* Bateson, J.E.G. (1988) *Managing Services Marketing*, Chicago, IL: Dryden. (A standard textbook on services marketing.)

Chandler, A.D., Jr (1962) *Strategy and Structure: Chapters in the History of American Industrial Enterprise*, Cambridge, MA: MIT Press. (Classic work of business history, which tries to make past business practices appear relevant to modern conditions.)

* Hill, T. (1989) *Manufacturing Strategy: Text and Cases*, Homewood, IL: Irwin. (A standard textbook on operations strategy.)

* Peters, T.J. (1987) *Thriving on Chaos: Handbook for a Management Revolution*, New York: Knopf. (Urges companies to adopt a more radical approach to management, with five key strategic focal points.)

Peters, T.J. (1991) *Beyond Hierarchy: Organizations in the 1990s*, New York: Knopf. (Study of organizations and how breaking down hierarchies can lead to competitive freedom.)

* Peters, T.J. (1992) *Liberation Management: Necessary Disorganization for the Nanosecond Nineties*, New York: Knopf. (Peters' most recent and most radical work, calling for greater decentralization and freedom.)

* Peters, T.J. (1994) *The Pursuit of Wow! Every Person's Guide to Topsy Turvy-Times*. New York: Vintage. (Urges managers to pursue what Peters calls the 'wow market' when everything comes together and true excellence is achieved; chaotic and impressionistic, with no systematic approach.)

Peters, T.J. and Austin, N. (1985) *A Passion for Excellence: The Leadership Difference*, New York: Random House. (Largely a follow-up to *In Search of Excellence*.)

Peters, T.J. and Townsend, R. (1988) *Excellence in the Organization*, New York: Nightingale-Conant. (A further dissertation on the factors necessary for excellence.)

* Peters, T.J. and Waterman, R.H., Jr (1982) *In Search of Excellence: Lessons from America's Best-run Companies*, New York: Harper & Row. (The classic Peters, probably his best and certainly his best-known book.)

See also: BARNARD, C.I.; CHANDLER, A.D.; DRUCKER, P.F.; HANDY,C.; MAYO, G.E.;PORTER, M.E.; TAYLOR, F.W.

Related topics in the IEBM: BUSINESS SCHOOLS; CULTURE, CROSS-NATIONAL; EMPLOYEE DEVELOPMENT; ENTREPRENEURSHIP; GURU CONCEPT; LEADERSHIP; MANAGEMENT IN GERMANY; MANAGERIAL BEHAVIOUR; ORGANIZATION BEHAVIOUR; ORGANIZATION BEHAVIOUR, HISTORY OF; ORGANIZATION CULTURE; ORGANIZATION STRUCTURE; ORGANIZATIONAL PERFORMANCE; STRATEGIC COMPETENCE

Pettigrew, Andrew M. (1944–)

1 Introduction
2 The Centre for Corporate Strategy and Change
3 Contributions in recent years
4 Methodological contributions
5 Overall contribution

Personal background

- born Corby, Northamptonshire, United Kingdom, on 11th June 1944
- educated at Corby Grammar School, Liverpool University (BA social science) and Manchester Business School (PhD)
- married to Ethna Moores and has three sons
- worked as a research associate at Manchester Business School; visiting assistant professor at Yale University; lecturer in organizational behaviour at London Business School; professor of organizational behaviour at Warwick Business School
- created and directed the Centre for Corporate Strategy and Change at Warwick Business School, 1985–95
- held visiting posts at the European Institute for Advanced Studies in Management at Brussels, Harvard University and Stanford University
- co-founder and first chairman of the British Academy of Management, later becoming its second president

Major works

Politics of Organizational Decision Making (1973)

The Awakening Giant: Continuity and Change in ICI (1985)

Corporate Strategy Change and Human Resource Management (with C. Hendry and P.R. Sparrow) (1990)

Managing Change for Competitive Success (with R. Whipp) (1991)

Shaping Strategic Change: The Case of the NHS (with E. Ferlie and L. McKee) (1992)

The New Public Management in Action (with E. Ferlie, L. Ashburner and L. FitzGerald) (1996)

Summary

Professor Andrew M. Pettigrew has made, and continues to make, a significant contribution to our understanding of management and organizational processes in both substantive and theoretical terms as well as making a major contribution to the development of research methodologies for the study of the dynamic processes which occur in organizations.

To a greater extent than a majority of writers and researchers in the management area, Pettigrew has allowed us to come to terms with the sheer complexity of managerial and organizational processes. For this reason it is difficult to state in any simple terms the contribution that Pettigrew has made. It is certainly not possible to summarize it in terms such as 'he discovered X'. His methodological innovations have allowed him, and the readers of his very considerable published research output, to understand the multi-layered nature of the complex processes involved in organizational change with particular reference to corporate strategy and its implications for the operations of organizations.

1 Introduction

Pettigrew's early work which led to his doctorate and the later publication of his first book – *The Politics of Organizational Decision Making* (1973) was based on the use of a case study approach, using multiple methods, to examine in detail the political processes involved in specific organizational decisions. This book had a significant impact on the development of the subject and added greatly to our knowledge of the minutiae of organizational political processes and their implications.

In the period between 1975 and 1984 Pettigrew carried out a major empirical study of the management of change in a major British multinational company. This lead to his second book *The Awakening Giant: Continuity and Change in Imperial Chemical Industries* (Pettigrew 1985) which was an elaborate case history of the change processes affecting the main board of ICI and the changes occurring concurrently in the four major heavy chemicals divisions of the company. The book presented a detailed and elegant description of events and processes in ICI that went far beyond that in its thematic analysis of those events, and which allowed Pettigrew to draw conclusions of much greater generality than might be involved in the understanding of one company. This research also substantially illustrated developments in Pettigrew's research methodology which were to influence his own later work, as well as the work of many other researchers interested in organizational processes around the world. In particular, this research illustrated a methodology for analyzing time series data derived from multiple levels of analysis (the firm, the industrial sector, and the political and economic context). It was this ability to bring together processual data and contextual data relevant to lengthy periods of change and development from multiple levels which allowed Pettigrew to map the complexity of change in organizational systems. It also showed the way such changes depend on and interrelate with macro level change in the context in which the firm operates.

These two first major books and the many other significant publications that Pettigrew authored in the period up to 1985 were sufficient to establish Pettigrew not merely as one of the leading British academics in the area, but also as one of the significant researchers and writers on these topics world-wide.

2 The Centre for Corporate Strategy and Change

In 1985 Pettigrew founded the Centre for Corporate Strategy and Change in the Business School at Warwick University in the United Kingdom. He was its first director and continued in that role for ten years. The Centre has, through its research and many publications made a very significant contribution to our understanding of the complexity of change processes.

In his review of the contribution of the Centre during its first ten years up to 1995, Pettigrew described his view of the areas in which it had made significant theoretical contributions. He suggested that 'The Centre's theoretical contributions focused on process theories of changing; the development of quasi-markets; the role of power and ideology in change processes; the processual analysis of competitiveness; power and influence amongst elites; and the development of managerial idea systems'. It is a mark of the Centre's success that Pettigrew's claim that it contributed across such a wide range of areas, even allowing their inter-connectedness , would seem to be clearly justified. Indeed in most of these areas it can be legitimately stated that Pettigrew and his colleagues not only made contributions, but that these contributions were highly significant to the development of our understanding of such processes, and significantly influenced a range of researchers in North America, Europe and other parts of the world.

The creation of the Centre and its development marked a very significant change in Pettigrew's approach to research. Prior to 1985 he had largely been a lone researcher, with all the limitations in terms of rate of output that that placed upon him. From 1985 onwards, although he remained an active empirical researcher in his own right, he also became, significantly, a research manager with the ability to develop, manage and complete large processual studies at a much faster rate than he could have achieved on his own. The Centre's research is notable for its detailed description and analysis of processual phenomena. Its general approach has meant that most of its research topics have been of clear and critical importance to the practising managers in the organizations involved in the research, as well as more generally to practising managers in any organization. However, the feature which distinguishes Pettigrew's work from that of many others and has led to its major impact has been his continued ability, by means of developing his methodological approach, to derive, from such studies, thematic ideas and conceptually based theories of wide generalizability and applicability. The first major project conducted by the new Centre and funded by the ESRC led to a report, *Corporate Strategy Change and Human Resource Management* (Pettigrew, Hendry and Sparrow 1990), and to Pettigrew's third major book, *Managing Change for Competitive Success* (Pettigrew and Whipp 1991). This was part of the overall ESRC research initiative on competitiveness and was perhaps its most major single outcome. This book reported studies of the link between competitiveness, business strategy change and human resource change. This research showed clearly that firms operating in similar economic, political and institutional contexts vary considerably in their relative performance. Clearly the explanation of such differential performance had to involve factors internal to the individual firm and factors relating internal workings of the firm to the context in which it was operating. This research clearly established links between the change and learning capabilities of firms and their long-term performance.

The importance of this research was in some measure due to the way it linked to two of the major concerns of the late 1980s: namely, managing for competitiveness and new approaches to human resource management. Pettigrew's research clearly showed the importance of managing human resources for achieving competitiveness in the long term. The research also showed the importance for firm performance of processes that led to management understanding the environment in which the firm operated, and the way in which change was approached and managed within the strategic and other areas of operation of the firm. This book was rapidly followed by a further major contribution to our understanding of the management of change processes and the performance of individual organizations. When a year later Pettigrew, Ferlie and McKee (1992) published the results of their studies of the implementation of service changes in the British National Health Service in *Shaping Strategic Change: Making Change in Large Organizations, the Case of the NHS*. These two books further elaborated our understanding of the processes leading to the successful implementation of change and significantly extended our knowledge into an understanding of public sector as well as private sector organizations.

3 Contributions in recent years

In the early and middle years of the 1990s Pettigrew once again demonstrated his ability to combine his methodological and theoretical interests with the studies of issues of current significance amongst practising managers and policy makers with his research on the governance of UK firms and the examination of the implications of governance arrangements and the power and influence of board members in large companies. This research led importantly to the Pettigrew and McNulty (1995) article in *Human Relations* on 'Power and influence in and around the board-room'.

Paralleling this contribution Pettigrew continued his work in the British National Health Service and in 1996 published his consequential book on *The New Public Management in Action* (Ferlie, Ashburner, FitzGerald and Pettigrew 1996). This reported on studies of the implementation of the quasi-market in the British Health Service as a consequence of initiatives set in motion by the Conservative government of the early 1990s.

An additional extension of Pettigrew's work in recent years has involved the consideration of the internationalizing firm. In this area Pettigrew is not merely extending the theoretical compass of his research on strategy and change processes but is evolving extensions to his methodological approach. For the first time, in any significant way, he is combining his comparative case study approach with international comparative work using surveys and extant databases. Using this methodology and in partnership with colleagues in a variety of countries throughout the world he is examining the role and performance consequences of network organization and transformation of large enterprises in many parts of the world as they respond to 'global' markets.

4 Methodological contributions

Throughout his academic career up to the present time, Pettigrew has continuously developed his methodological approach in ways which not only influenced his own research and that of his colleagues in the Centre for Corporate Strategy and Change, but have had a profound influence on researchers interested in processual research in all parts of the world. His early case study research was based on his multi-method and detailed approach to studying organizational politics. In the next stage of development this approach was widened to bring in overtly his multi-layered consideration of change processes examining the interplay between organizational processes of change, the content of change processes and, importantly, the social political and economic context in which those change processes are worked out.

Pettigrew's development of his particular approach to longitudinal comparative case study analysis has been based on a combination of historical assessments of antecedent conditions and the real-time examination of on-going processes using a variety of methods. At the same time Pettigrew's ability to use theoretical ideas to guide his research has meant that he has been able to handle large amounts of detailed data in ways which have enhanced our understanding. In this respect he has avoided the trap of becoming buried in the detail of large quantities of data which has ensnared many other qualitative case study researchers such that their contribution has been little more than descriptive findings with insufficient methodological rigour reported for the reader to be able to assess the relative importance of different types of data for our understanding of the ongoing processes observed.

More recently, Pettigrew has further developed his methodological approach by seeking to combine his comparative longitudinal case study research method with survey methods and electronic databases. He is also increasingly becoming involved in large-scale multinational research consortia aimed at developing, in a theoretically rigourous way, international comparative research. However, it is probably too early to assess the contribution stemming from this on-going line of research and these latest extensions to his research methodology.

5 Overall contribution

It is very difficult to try and assess the overall contribution of a researcher who is still very clearly actively pursuing research of a fundamental and innovative kind. Not only is Pettigrew still actively working, but he continues to display a work rate which shames most of his contemporaries and their younger successors. The difficulty is substantially exacerbated, as noted above, by his ability to deal with the extreme complexity of social processes and their relationship to the historical and current context in which they take place.

Despite these difficulties, one can state with some confidence that Pettigrew has made a major contribution not only to the academic literature on organizational processes but to managerial understanding of such processes.

In a recent paper (Pettigrew and Webb 1996) he analysed how the very language of business strategy had to some extent become locked into a vocabulary appropriate to the description of static phenomena rather than for describing the active processes in which most managers are involved. Pettigrew and Webb went on to develop a typology of strategy expressed in the active language of consolidating, internationalizing, etc. His contribution, therefore, has not merely been to our substantive understanding of the various phenomena which he has studied but he has in part changed our way of talking and thinking about them by modifying the linguistic tools with which we approach the subject.

He has achieved this by developing both theory and method in ways which alternate between the study of particular historical processes and events and an appreciation of the general logic of process, as evidenced by the particular exemplars he has studied.

Although some of Pettigrew's early work was criticized on the grounds that his case study method provided inadequate grounds for generalization, it is a tribute to the later developments of his methodology and the rigour with which he has carried out his processual research that there are now few critics of either his methodological approach or of his conclusions. Pettigrew's determined development of conceptual ideas and his concentration on thematic theoretical developments coupled with the widening of his methodological approach has made it clear that his findings are capable of generalization beyond the particular. The developments in Pettigrew's work coupled with the changing shape of thinking on strategy and organizational behaviour has increasingly made the work mainstream and removes the basis for earlier misgivings.

Pettigrew's particular style of research and the quality and quantity of his published output mean that he has had a profound effect on the development of his subject as an academic endeavour and also a significant effect on the practice of management and the implementation of change amongst practitioners. The very nature of his research style has inevitably led to him and his colleagues in the Centre for Corporate Strategy and Change developing a wide variety of close and on-going contacts with senior management in a wide variety of both private and public sector organizations. This coupled with his energetic efforts to ensure the widespread dissemination of his research findings has meant that his input on managerial thinking is already significant and continuing to grow.

ROGER MANSFIELD
CARDIFF BUSINESS SCHOOL
UNIVERSITY OF WALES

Further reading

(References cited in the text marked *)

* Ferlie, E., Ashburner, L. FitzGerald, L. and Pettigrew, A.M. (1996) *The New Public Management in Action*, Oxford: Oxford University Press. (An examination of the changes to management in the public sector as a consequence of Conservative government policies in the early 1990s.)

* Pettigrew, A.M. (1973) *The Politics of Organisational Decision Making*, London: Tavistock. (A case study, based on multiple methods, of the politics surrounding a single decision in a particular organization.)

* Pettigrew, A.M.(1985) *The Awakening Giant: Continuity and Change in Imperial Chemical Industries*, Oxford: Basil Blackwell. (A major case study of the development of ICI in the particular social and economic context of the time.)

* Pettigrew, A.M. and McNulty, T. (1995) 'Power and influence in and around the boardroom', *Human Relations* 48, 8: 1–29. (A study of organizational elites examining the power and influence of boards of directors.)

* Pettigrew, A.M. and Webb, D. (1996) 'Espoused business strategy and structure changes in the UK and German insurance industries', Paper presented to the all Academy Symposium on the Evolution of New organisation Forms for the Information Age, Academy of Management, Cincinnati, August 12–14. (An article which suggests changes in terminology to make considerations of strategy more dynamic.)

* Pettigrew, A.M. and Whipp, R. (1991) *Managing Change for Competitive Success*, Oxford: Basil Blackwell. (A major study of processes of change and learning in organizations and how they contribute to competitive performance.)

* Pettigrew, A.M., Ferlie, E. and McKee, L. (1992) *Shaping Strategic Change: Making Change in Large Organisations, the Case of the NHS*, London: Sage. (An extension of Pettigrew's ideas and research methods to the public sector, specifically the National Health Service.)

* Pettigrew, A.M., Hendry, C. and Sparrow, P.R. (1990) *Corporate Strategy Change and Human Resource Management*, Sheffield: the Department of Employment, Training Agency. (A study of the importance of human resource management in the development of corporate strategy and its operationalization.)

535

See also: CHANDLER, A.D.; MINTZBERG, H.; SI-
MON, H.A.

Related topics in the IEBM: DECISION MAK-
ING; GLOBALIZATION; HEALTH MANAGE-
MENT; INDUSTRIAL ECONOMICS;
MANAGERIAL BEHAVIOUR; ORGANIZATION
BEHAVIOUR; ORGANIZATION BEHAVIOUR,
HISTORY OF; POWER; STRATEGY, CONCEPT
OF

Pfeffer, Jeffrey (1946–) and Gerald R. Salancik (1943–96)

Personal background

Jeffrey Pfeffer

- born in 1946
- received a BSc in administration and management science and an MSc in industrial administration from Carnegie-Mellon University, 1968
- graduated from Stanford University with a PhD in organizational behaviour, 1972
- assistant professor at the University of Illinois at Urbana-Champaign, 1971–3
- assistant and associate professor at the University of California, Berkeley, 1973–9
- Thomas Henry Carroll-Ford Foundation Visiting Professor of Business Administration at Harvard Business School, 1981–2
- Thomas D. Dee Professor of Organizational Behaviour at Stanford University, 1979–

Gerald R. Salancik

- born 29 January 1943 in Chicago
- received a BSc (1965) and a MSc (1966) in journalism from Northwestern University
- graduated from Yale University with a PhD in Social Psychology, 1970
- associate professor and professor at the University of Illinois at Urbana-Champaign)

- David M. and Barbara A. Kirr Professor of Organization at Carnegie Mellon University
- died 24 July 1996 in Pittsburgh, Pennsylvania, USA

Major works

Jeffrey Pfeffer

The External Control of Organizations (with Gerald R. Salancik) (1978)
Organizational Design (1978)
Power in Organizations (1981)
Organizations and Organization Theory (1982)
Managing with Power: Politics and Influence in Organizations (1992)
Competitive Advantage Through People (1994)
New Directions for Organization Theory (1997)
The Human Equation: Building Profits by Putting People First (1998)

Gerald R. Salancik

The Interview, Or The Only Wheel in Town (with Eugene J. Webb) (1966)
The Surprise Hunter, A Man-Computer Information System For Generating and Evaluating Future Marketing and Social Environments (with K.C. Ramond) (1969)
For The Days/For The Nights (1969)
On the Nature of Economic Losses Arising From Computer-Based Systems In The Next Fifteen Years (with T. J. Gordon and N. Adams) (1972)
New Directions in Organizational Behaviour (with Barry M. Staw) (1977)
The External Control of Organizations (with Jeffrey Pfeffer) (1978)

Summary

Jeffrey Pfeffer and Gerald Salancik are the founders of the resource dependency perspective on organizations. They were the first people to address the management of an organization's environment systematically and comprehensibly. Their work instigated a shift from viewing the environment as constraining to viewing the environment as facilitative, since it provides required resources. Both scholars have also contributed to other important issues in organization studies: Pfeffer notably to the practitioners' literature on how to manage with power; Salancik to the importance of social context in the analysis of organizational action.

1 Biographical data

Salancik was a first generation academic who began his career as a journalist before moving into the academic field of experimental social psychology. From this background it was a small step into the emergent field of organization studies with a focus on the social contexts of action. Pfeffer came from the more conventional organization theory background of an undergraduate and MBA degree at Carnegie-Mellon, before receiving a PhD from Stanford University. Salancik's PhD in social psychology was awarded by Yale University. When Pfeffer and Salancik joined the University of Illinois, a period of fruitful collaboration on management issues arising from the influences of an organization's environment on its actions began. In 1976 Salancik spent a summer visiting at the University of Bradford Management Centre, where he learned at first hand about the 'strategic contingency' approach that David Hickson and his colleagues were developing. *The External Control of Organizations* is the culmination of Pfeffer and Salancik's collaboration on managing organizations with an open eye to the external environment. Salancik's work maintained this focus on the social context of organizational action; for instance, one of his final articles investigated changes in the definition of 'death' in potential organ donors. This action was shaped by the resource needs

of transplant surgeons, patients, and other interested parties and subsequently shaped the external legal framework for further action by those parties. Weick (1996) very aptly named one of the legacies of Salancik: 'an appreciation of social context', in all its complexities. By contrast, Pfeffer's work developed in a manner that was more attuned to strategic issues, whether these were the management of power by practitioners or the management of knowledge by scholars.

2 Resource dependency perspective

The resource dependency perspective on organizations proposes that crucial external resource factors affect a large proportion of organizational actions. The environment is the source of resources for which the overall population of organizations competes. Where resources are scarce or controlled by a few organizations, those organizations who rely on obtaining resources become dependent on organizations who provide those resources: either they have to gain access to them in terms that the resource controllers determine, or they are denied access and have to find alternative suppliers. The notion of dependencies derives from 'exchange theory': when organization A cannot do without resources that organization B controls, and cannot obtain them elsewhere, then A will be dependent on B, and thus B will have power over A. Effective managers, therefore, will also manage such dependencies to the best of their organization. For instance, a company may appoint bankers or members from other financial institutions to its board of directors to deal with financial dependencies. The composition of a board of directors, consequently, often reflects the composition of the crucial resources that a company needs for long-term survival.

The basic theoretical claim starts from an open systems perspective: organizations require a continuing cycle of transactions with their environment for resources that they require. Organizations are viewed as active in determining their own fate (Scott 1987).

Managers scan the environment paying particular attention to potential threats and opportunities. They try to strike favourable bargains and to avoid costly entanglements. Organizations try to achieve rationality in their core production, maintain some degree of autonomy, overcome constraints introduced by dependencies, and solve problems of uncertainty by undertaking a variety of buffering and bridging strategies (Thompson 1967). Buffering strategies include coding, stockpiling, levelling, forecasting, and growth (larger organizations are more powerful and have more slack). Bridging strategies include bargaining, contracting, cooptation, joint ventures, mergers, associations, links with the state, and establishing/manipulating institutional linkages. Resource dependence theorists view organizations as 'capable of changing, as well as responding to, the environment. Administrators manage their environments as well as their organizations, and the former activity may be as important, or even more important, than the latter' (Aldrich and Pfeffer 1976: 93). It also acknowledges that organization environments are 'negotiated orders' produced through and by organizational exchanges.

The conceptualization is firmly rooted in and extends Thompson's (1967) model of organizations and organizational action. Thompson (1967: 29–30) argued that 'an organization is dependent upon some element of its task environment (1) in proportion to the organization's need for resources or performances which that element can provide, and (2) in inverse proportion to the ability of other elements to provide the same resource or performance'. Furthermore, there is a similarity with strategic contingency theory: effective control over strategic resources will predict power. Thus, one might characterize the resource dependence perspective as a union of strategic contingency and political models of organizations. It precedes the *population ecology* perspective (Hannan and Freeman 1989) chronologically, but has developed owing to it. Resource dependence and population ecology differ in their application to internal organizational decision making; a process mostly ignored by population ecologists. The

two perspectives also differ in their view of change processes. While population ecologists stress selective retention by organizations and organizational subunits that lead to long-term changes in the industry and the organization, respectively, resource dependence theorists stress the adaptation of organizations and subunits to their environments.

According to Scott (1987) resource dependency contributes to organization studies by describing strategies that help managers adapt to changing environments. Partly as a consequence of the resource dependency perspective organization theorists have revised their image of the environment. Rather than seeing it as an abstract configuration of laws, technological changes, and social norms, they are now more liable to regard it as a source of critical resources for organizations. A second important contribution concerns the effect of external dependencies on the internal distribution of power. According to resource dependency theory, subunits which manage crucial external dependencies are more powerful than others – a straight adoption of strategic contingency theory (Hickson *et al.* 1971). Environmental contingencies and constraints, however, change over time. As some subunits become more critical for managing change, the distribution of power within an organization shifts in their favour. Subunits that become more critical for organizational survival increase their power, while others lose it. This new distribution of power will be reflected in the selection of new chief executives from subunits which have acquired more power (see Fligstein 1985). The perspective and interests of these subunits will become represented in the organization structure as well as in decision making .

Empirical research on resource dependency has supported the general claims that: (a) dependence on external resources affects organizational action, and (b) subunits that manage crucial external dependencies gain power, but the evidence is not unequivocal. As Pfeffer (1982: 201) admitted, while 'the evidence on the ability of resource dependence considerations to predict patterns of inter-firm linkage and coordination tends to support the theory' there were also inconsistent findings. Support has mainly come from studies by Pfeffer, Salancik and their co-authors. For example, Pfeffer found a low correlation between the extent to which managers depend on the government and their willingness to pursue government policies. In a more specific test of the resource dependency perspective, Pfeffer and Salancik (1974) found that the more grants and contract funds departments brought into the university, the higher was their power. Moreover, the degree of 'paradigm' consensus within the knowledge-base of the department also affected the power of the department. Powerful departments were in a position to gain even more power by shaping structural changes in ways that enhanced their power.

3 The External Control of Organizations

The gist of this book is the argument that organizational action can be understood by looking at the context of the organization. The environment affects and constrains organizations. To ensure survival, organizations respond to and manage their environment successfully. The book consists of two main parts: a description of organizations, their social context, and interdependencies, followed by suggestions for managing those interdependencies.

According to Pfeffer and Salancik (1978: 2) the key to organizational survival is 'the ability to acquire and maintain resources'. This dependence on resources would not be problematic if resources were generated internally by the organization or obtainable from stable external sources. Most organizations, however, are not completely self-sufficient or self-contained, they rely on their environment for some or most of their resources. As the environment changes, new organizations enter and others go out of business: naturally occurring processes that affect the availability and ease of acquisition of resources. Thus, managers need not only concern themselves with internal processes such as motivation and leadership, but also with external

contingencies. Managing the external environment is as important as or even more important than managing the internal organization for long-term survival. It is for this reason that an important part of the manager's task is to be a symbolic manager: people who manage symbols effectively in order to signal the effective power and resourcefulness of the organization that they steer. In this way they strengthen their organizations through the ties that they are able to create with other organizations in their environments. Of course, these ties are inherently dynamic and potentially unstable, thus the politics of organizations knows no end.

When Pfeffer and Salancik refer to the environment they do not mean a 'real' thing, objectively there in its facticity, so much as something that is constituted or, in Weick's (1969) terms, 'enacted'. The meaning of the environment for the organization is created through interpretation. Different interpretations lead to different constitutions of the environment and shape the ways in which managers act upon their enactment of the environment. Such differences potentially generate power conflicts. Hence, Pfeffer and Salancik's view of organizations is inherently political because it assumes that it is the coalitions that form around different interpretations, rather than functional design, that will determine strategies followed. Organizations can avoid external influence attempts through the use of secrecy or restriction of information, balancing conflicting organizations against each other, attending to demands sequentially, claiming limited discretion, and developing norms or laws that limit discretion. Organization ends and the environment begins where the organization's control over activities diminishes and control of other organizations or individuals begins. Organizations can manage interdependence by extending their own control over vital areas (merging or acquiring), by increasing their own dominance (making others more dependent), or by decreasing their reliance on single critical exchanges.

The External Control of Organizations proposes a number of relationships between organizations and their environments which

Pfeffer and Salancik illustrate with data. For instance, they observe that formal trade associations were more likely to arise in industries with low levels of concentration. These associations were seen as device of communication and modest co-ordination under competition. Informal associations tended to arise in more concentrated markets to allow similar firms to act in concert and to protect their mutual interests. Additionally, they studied the occurrence of mergers, and argue that a merger is a mechanism used by organizations to restructure their environmental interdependence in order to stabilize critical exchanges. Therefore, organizations are more likely to merge with or acquire other organizations on which they depend for resources. Pfeffer and Salancik expected more mergers where exchanges were generally problematic and they interpreted findings from industry data to support this hypothesis.

4 Critique

One problem that comes up in almost any empirical study is the use of proxies for variables and the choice of the unit of analysis. For instance, in the merger study, aggregated data of the industry were used to predict organizational behaviour; also, the causality link was quite long and hardly convincing. In addition, the data were cross-sectional although the hypotheses were inherently dynamic. If correct, the cross-sectional data should also have explained divestiture among those organizations, where no resource dependency exists. Since mergers should only occur where competitive uncertainty is very high, divestiture should happen in situations of little or moderate uncertainty.

None of the resource dependency studies measures dependence or uncertainty directly. They are always inferred from some other sources or variables, where the inference is at best, dubious. The creation of new ties should be linked to changes in the resource dependency of organization A on organization B. Otherwise, the initiation of another new tie may not be caused by resource dependency. Such a study should be controlled for institutional effects, such as laws, or mimicking

other organizations, unless Pfeffer and Salancik intended to include legitimacy and good standing with the law as resources, which is doubtful.

The central concept of power in resource dependency is almost tautological and certainly overly narrow. Notions of cause and effect are difficult to untangle where the key terms are defined as the logical obverse of each other. Moreover, when Pfeffer and Salancik first published their resource dependency perspective, broader perspectives on power theory had already moved beyond such an exclusive emphasis on resource control (for example, Lukes 1974; Clegg 1989; Haugaard 1997). Pfeffer and Salancik avoided engagement with any of this debate. Rather than explore the role of non-decision making and non-issues, as well as the control of meaning, Pfeffer's managers are advised to manage with power principally in terms of controlling resources and setting agendas.

5 Recent work by Pfeffer and Salancik

Managing with Power: Politics and Influence in Organizations (1992) is Pfeffer's most recent foray into the politics of organizations. The book is designed to be useful to busy executives – teaching them how to manage with power – and is in many ways successful in terms of its avowed intentions. According to Pfeffer, executives obtain power from five primary sources: control over resources; ties to other powerful individuals; the formal authority attached to one's position; belonging to a strategic unit within the organization; and personal attributes. When executives use these sources wisely they will increase the probability of accomplishing their objectives. Wisdom resides in the attention shown to the framing and timing of their strategies, as well as the procedures that they employ to advance them. The shift towards a practitioner focus emerges even more clearly in *Competitive Advantage Through People* (1994).

Salancik's interest in the social context of action brought him closer to the neo-institutional perspective on organizations.

Together with Leblebici, Copay and King he studied institutional changes in the US broadcasting industry. He also investigated institutional processes in the increase of caesarean births, and in the changing definition of death for potential organ donors to name just a few. He died unexpectedly in the middle of several research projects.

6 Conclusion

The resource dependency perspective has played a significant role in opening up organization studies not only to issues of power but also of managing the environment. Pfeffer and Salancik have been instrumental in producing this body of enduring points of reference for the discipline. While one challenge of management concerns how 'to manage with power', one needs to recognize that this involves far more than merely juggling resource dependencies. Managers must be able to recognize, diagnose and deal with a diversity of interests. If managers were more aware of current streams of power theory they would be better able to manage (Hardy and Clegg 1996; Calás and Smircich 1996). However, within the limits that Pfeffer and Salancik placed round their conceptualization of power, it has been an influential body of work, albeit by now largely eclipsed. Intra-organizationally, its failure to engage with the debate about power in broader social and organizational theory, from Lukes (1974) onwards, marginalizes it as increasingly narrow in its focus; in terms of the inter-organizational world and the population level of organizations it has been effectively displaced by the concerns of organizational ecology.

STEWART R. CLEGG
AND THEKLA RURA-POLLEY
SCHOOL OF MANAGEMENT
UNIVERSITY OF TECHNOLOGY, SYDNEY

Further reading

(References cited in the text marked *)

* Aldrich, H.E. and Pfeffer, J. (1976) 'Environments of organizations', in A. Inkeles, J. Coleman and N. Smelser (eds) *Annual Review of Sociology* 2, Palo Alto, CA: Annual Reviews Inc, 79–105. (A discussion of organization environments that draws heavily on resource dependency theory.)

* Calás, M., and Smircich, L. (1996) 'From the women's point of view: feminist approaches to organization studies', in S.R. Clegg, C. Hardy and W.R. Nord (eds) *Handbook of Organization Studies*, London: Sage, 218–258. (Raises issues of power, and the analytic frameworks to address them, that resource dependence theory is unable to: shows the limits of the resource dependence perspective.)

* Clegg, S.R (1989) *Frameworks of Power*, London: Sage. (A wide-ranging discussion of social theory and organization theory approaches to the analysis of power.)

Clegg, S.R, Hardy C. and Nord, W.R. (eds) *Handbook of Organization Studies*, London: Sage. (The definitive 'state-of-the-art ' statement about the broad field of organization studies.)

Daft, R.L. (1998) *Organization Theory and Design*, Cincinnati, OH: South-Western College Publishing. (The classic and most-widely used textbook on organization theory, giving an excellent overview of the field and how to apply the knowledge as managers.)

* Fligstein, N. (1985) 'The spread of the multi-divisional form among large firms, 1919–1979', *American Sociological Review* 50: 377–391. (An empirically sophisticated test of resource dependency theory against some other organization theories, from which the perspective emerges as reasonably robust.)

* Hannan, M.T. and Freeman, J. (1989) *Organizational Ecology*, Cambridge, MA: Harvard University Press. (The classic statement of the population ecology perspective that has largely replaced resource dependency theory in addressing inter-organizational population level issues.)

* Hardy, C. and Clegg, S.R. (1996) 'Some dare call it power', in S.R. Clegg, C. Hardy and W.R. Nord (eds) *Handbook of Organization Studies*, London: Sage: 622–641. (An overview of the range of theoretical perspectives brought to bear to the analysis of power in organizations, including resource dependency theory.)

Hatch, M.J. (1997) *Organization Theory*, Oxford: Oxford University Press. (A current introduction to organization theory that stresses not only conventional but also cultural and postmodern perspectives.)

* Haugaard M. (1997) *The Constitution of Social Power*, Manchester: Manchester University

Press. (The most current overview available of social theory approaches to the analysis of power and dependency available in the literature.)

* Hickson D.J., Hinings, C.R., Lee, C.A., Schneck, R.L. and Pennings J.M. (1971) 'A strategic contingencies theory of intra-organizational power', *Administrative Science Quarterly* 16: 216–229. (The original statement of the strategic contingency perspective that was very influential in the shaping of Pfeffer and Salancik's own views.)

* Lukes, S. (1974) *Power: A Radical View*, London: Macmillan. (A concise, elegant introduction to all the currents of social theory that were available to Pfeffer and Salancik when they constructed 'resource dependency' theory but did not address.)

* Pfeffer, J. and Salancik G.R. (1974) 'Organizational decision-making as a political process: the case of a university budget', *Administrative Science Quarterly* 19, 2: 135–51. (A study of University departmental power from a resource dependency perspective.)

* Pfeffer, J. and Salancik, G.R. (1978) *The External Control of Organizations*, New York: Harper & Row. (An introduction into the resource dependency perspective.)

* Pfeffer, J. (1992) *Managing with Power: Politics and Influence in Organizations*, Cambridge, Mass: Harvard Business School Press. (A practitioner guideline to managing and managing with power.)

* Pfeffer, J. (1994) *Competitive Advantage through People*, Cambridge, Mass: Harvard Business School Press. (A practitioner guideline to effective people management.)

* Scott, W.R. (1987) *Organizations: Rational, Natural and Open Systems*, Englewood Cliffs, NJ: Prentice Hall. (An exhaustive integration of different schools of thought within organization theory written for both researchers and students.)

* Thompson, J.D. (1967) *Organizations in Action*, New York: McGraw-Hill. (An management classic on how managers achieve rationality and increase effectiveness by managing interdependencies.)

* Weick, K.E. (1969) *The Social Psychology of Organizing*, Reading, MA: Addison Wesley. (A classic discussion of organization theory from a social psychological perspective that addresses some issues of resource dependency cognitively.)

* Weick, K.E. (1996) 'An appreciation of social context: one legacy of Gerald Salancik', *Administrative Science Quarterly* 41: 563–573. (Gives an excellent overview and integration of Salancik's contribution to organization studies.)

See also: HANNAN, M. AND FREEMAN, J.; THOMPSON, J.D.; WEICK,K.

Related topics in the IEBM: CONTEXTS AND ENVIRONMENTS; DECISION MAKING; OCCUPATIONAL PSYCHOLOGY; ORGANIZATION BEHAVIOUR; ORGANIZATION BEHAVIOUR, HISTORY OF; ORGANIZATION STRUCTURE; ORGANIZATIONAL PERFORMANCE; ORGANIZING, PROCESS OF; POWER

Porter, Michael E. (1947–)

Personal background

- born Ann Arbor, Michigan, 23 May 1947
- served in US Army Reserve, 1969–77, reaching rank of captain
- BSE Princeton University, 1969; MBA Harvard University 1971, PhD 1973
- joined faculty of Harvard University in 1973, made full professor in 1981
- member, President's Commission on Industrial Competitiveness, 1983–5

Major works

Interbrand Choice, Strategy and Bilateral Market Power (1976)
Competitive Strategy: Techniques for Analyzing Industries and Competitors (1980)
Competitive Advantage: Creating and Sustaining Superior Performance (1985)
Competition in Global Industries (1986)
The Competitive Advantage of Nations (1990)

Summary

Michael Porter's primary goal has been to relate business strategy to applied microeconomics, two fields of study which had previously been considered independently, and build a set of models and tools for analysis. His second major book, *Competitive Strategy*, revolutionized approaches to business strategy; his third, *Competitive Advantage*, extended his thinking from analysing competition to creating sustainable creative advantage. More recently, Porter has concentrated on global applications of his strategic principles, including the nature of global competition and national determinants of competitive force.

1 Introduction

Arguably the single most influential writer on business strategy, Michael Porter has largely defined current mainstream thinking on strategy and competition, particularly in a global context. His books on competitive strategy and competitive advantage are read and discussed around the world, and there can be few MBA students in the West, at least, who have not studied his two best-known models, the 'five forces' and the value chain model. From these basic models, Porter has developed simple yet far-reaching analyses of the determinants of competition, the global forces affecting competition, and the ways and means of ensuring long-term competitive success.

2 Biographical data

Michael Porter was born in Michigan in 1947, the son of an army officer. His has been an academic career of great distinction. After taking an undergraduate degree at Princeton University, he took an MBA and then a PhD from Harvard University, winning honours and distinctions at every step. Soon after completing his PhD he was offered an academic post at Harvard; in 1981 at age thirty-four he was made a full professor. He has remained at Harvard ever since.

Porter's work throughout his career has been focused on competition, its elements and determinants. He has served as consultant and advisor to many blue chip companies and to the governments of Canada and New Zealand, among others; during the early 1980s he was a member of President Reagan's Commission on Industrial Competitiveness.

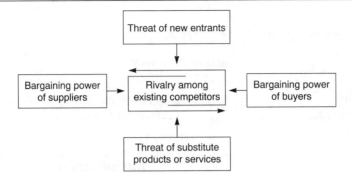

Figure 1 The five competitive forces that determine industry competition
Source: Porter (1980)

3 Main contribution

In *Competitive Strategy* (1980), Porter provided a revolutionary new approach to business strategy. Rejecting the either/or approaches which had hitherto characterized this field of study, Porter applied the principles of microeconomics to strategy. The first step was to see strategy as a principle which could be applied not just to individual companies but to entire industrial sectors. Analysing the strategic requirements of sectors led Porter to develop the first of his series of successful models, the *five forces* (see Figure 1).

The strength of each of the five forces can vary from industry to industry, but taken together they determine long-term industry profitability. They affect the prices firms charge, the costs they must accept and the level of investment required to compete in that particular industry. The threat of new entrants limits market share and therefore profit potential; powerful buyers or suppliers will erode margins; the presence of substitutes limits by price as increase could erode industry volume. The strength of each of the five forces is a function of 'industry structure', which is also defined as 'the underlying economic and technical characteristics of an industry' (Porter 1990: 35).

Porter's second model concerns *generic strategies*. Companies have, he believes, just four primary strategic options, as shown in Figure 2. In order to determine which generic strategy they will pursue, companies need to make just two choices: (1) they need to determine competitive scope, whether they will seek a broad market or target specific segments; (2) they need to determine competitive advantage, whether they will seek to compete through cost or differentiation.

Porter makes it clear that there is no one best strategy for any industry; indeed, in the industries he cites as examples, such as cars and shipbuilding, different firms pursue different strategies within the same industry framework. Although the five forces remain the same, responses to the pressures of those forces can vary along the lines noted above.

Finally, Porter introduced the concept of the *value chain* (see Figure 3). In essence, the value chain sums up the activities undertaken by the firm which add value to the product. The primary activities are those concerned with producing the product and delivering it to the consumer. The support activities are those that add value directly, such as technology development, or which allow the company to operate more efficiently: 'firms gain competitive advantage from conceiving of new ways to conduct activities, employing new procedures, new technologies, or

| | | COMPETITIVE ADVANTAGE | |
		Lower cost	Differentiation
COMPETITIVE SCOPE	Broad target	Cost leadership	Differentiation
	Narrow target	Cost focus	Focused differentiation

Figure 2 Generic strategies
Source: Porter (1980)

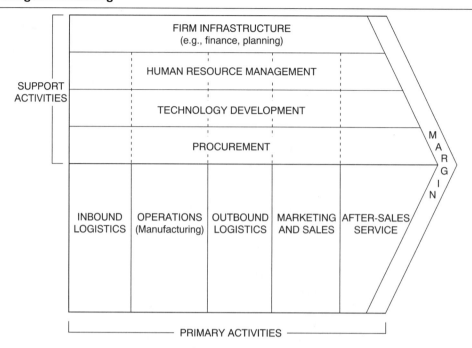

Figure 3 The value chain
Source: Porter (1985)

different inputs' (Porter 1990: 41). The value chain is crucial, Porter believes, because it demonstrates that a firm is more than just the sum of its activities; all activities are connected by linkages, through which trade-offs must be conducted. The firm must decide which of these activities are to be optimized in order to meet industry pressures and achieve competitive goals.

In *Competition in Global Industries* (1986), Porter and his colleagues set out to apply the principles of competitive strategy analysis to companies working in international markets. Again using industry analysis as his framework, Porter began by defining two types of international competition: there are *multi-domestic industries*, in which competition occurs on a country-by-country basis (such as consumer banking), and *global industries*. He defines a global industry as 'an industry in which a firm's competitive position in one country is significantly affected by its position in other countries, or vice versa' (Porter 1986: 18), citing the car and semiconductor industries as examples. The key

difference between these, he believes, is that international competition in multi-domestic industries is discretionary – companies can choose to compete internationally or not – while competition in global industries is compulsory.

What happens in international competition is that value chain activities are spread over a number of different countries. As well as choosing competitive scope and competitive advantage, therefore, companies can also choose strategic options based on configuration of value chain activities (where they take place; in other words, the degree of geographic concentration) and coordination of these activities (how closely they are linked with one another). Four options emerge:

1 high concentration, high coordination (a simple global strategy with value chain activities based in one region or country and centralized);

2 high concentration, low coordination (an export-based strategy with decentralized marketing);

3 low concentration, high coordination (a strong foreign investment strategy with dispersed operations but a high degree of coordination between them);

4 low concentration, low coordination (a country-centred strategy in which decentralized subsidiaries focus on their own market).

Again, there is no one best strategy; all these strategies have their applications, depending on circumstances such as the nature of competition in the industry, as determined by the five forces. There may be a case for dispersing some value chain activities and concentrating others; greater dispersal can on the other hand imply a need for greater coordination. It is important to remember that competitive advantage grows out of *how* each activity in the value chain is conducted, not necessarily where.

In *The Competitive Advantage of Nations* (1990), Porter has taken his analysis one step further to determine national as well as industry determinants of competition. Believing that 'ultimately nations succeed in particular industries because their home environment is the most dynamic and the most challenging, and stimulates and prods firms to upgrade and widen their advantage over time' (Porter 1990: 71), he sets out to find the fundamental determinants of competitive forces within nations. He lists four key determinants which can be applied to each industry in each nation:

1 factor conditions, or the availability within the nation of factors such as skilled labour or infrastructure which are necessary for production;

2 demand conditions, or the nature of market demand for a particular product or service;

3 the presence of related and supporting industries, such as suppliers and distributors, that are internationally competitive;

4 the nature of firm strategy, structure and rivalry, including the organizational and managerial climate and the level and nature of domestic competition.

These determinants serve as 'background' for competitive forces within industries: 'The determinants of national advantage reinforce each other and proliferate over time in fostering competitive advantage in an industry' (Porter 1990: 132). The nature of competitive advantage often leads to 'clustering', either in industries (machinery in Germany, electronics in Japan) or geographically within a country (such as the concentration of Italian industries in the north, or German industries in the Rhineland and Bavaria).

One point which Porter reinforces is that national competitive advantage is often obtained through adversity, as nations and industries respond to the challenges set for them. 'Selective factor disadvantages, powerful local buyers, early saturation, capable and international suppliers and intense local rivalry can all be essential to creating and maintaining advantage. Pressure and adversity are powerful motivators for change and innovation' (Porter 1990: 174). It is for this reason that nations rise and decline in terms of competitive advantage, as new industrial powers seek to challenge the domination of those already existing.

4 Evaluation

Valuable as they are, the fundamentals of competitive analysis which Porter first described are perhaps at their most useful and influential when it comes to analysing global competition and determining international competitive advantage. As Porter himself explains, his application of these fundamentals (the five forces, generic strategies, value chain) to international strategy has greatly broadened and enhanced perceptions of this subject:

International strategy has often been characterized as a choice between worldwide standardization and local tailoring, or as the tension between economic imperatives (large-scale efficient facilities) and the political imperative (local content, local production)...neither characterization captures the complexity of a firm's international strategy choices. A firm's choice of international strategy involves the search for competitive advantage from global configuration/coordination throughout the value chain .... The essence of international strategy is not to resolve tradeoffs between concentration and dispersion, but to eliminate or mitigate them.

(Porter 1986: 35)

By making redundant the argument that companies have to choose between full globalization and full localization and by providing a framework for developing the most advantageous strategy, Porter has offered international businesses a broader range of options and greater freedom of manoeuvre.

Criticisms can be raised about his work. His distinction between multi-domestic industries and global industries may be disappearing, as pressures for free trade and increasing exports bring international challenges to virtually every industry in its home market. His determinants of competition are regarded by some as being too simple and not allowing enough options; but the beauty of Porter's work lies in its simplicity, and he urges readers to use his models as a starting point and understand the trade-offs and linkages between different elements. Properly used, these are highly flexible tools of analysis which can clarify situations and help define strategic direction, especially in international strategy.

5 Conclusion

The work of Michael Porter has given firms a set of powerful tools for the analysis of competition and the determination of strategy, in both local and international markets. Standing at the intersection of economic forces and strategic pressures, he has defined how the two can be understood together. In doing so, he has greatly advanced our understanding of strategy and competition.

MORGEN WITZEL
LONDON BUSINESS SCHOOL
DURHAM UNIVERSITY BUSINESS SCHOOL

Further reading

(References cited in the text marked *)

Porter, M.E. (1976) *Interbrand Choice, Strategy and Bilateral Market Power*, Cambridge, MA: Harvard University Press. (Porter's first major work, which shows the beginnings of the thinking which would emerge more fully in his later work.)

* Porter, M.E. (1980) *Competitive Strategy: Techniques for Analyzing Industries and Competitors*, New York: The Free Press. (Perhaps Porter's most famous book, the source of the five forces and the value chain.)

Porter, M.E. (1982) *Cases in Competitive Strategy*, New York: The Free Press. (Comprehensive case book illustrating many of the concepts in Porter (1980).)

Porter, M.E. (1985) *Competitive Advantage: Creating and Sustaining Superior Performance*, New York: The Free Press. (Extends the principles of Porter (1980) from analysing the competitive environment to finding sources of sustainable competitive advantage.)

* Porter, M.E. (ed.) (1986) *Competition in Global Industries*, Boston, MA: Harvard Business School Press. (Expands the principles of competitive strategy to international competition.)

* Porter, M.E. (1990) *The Competitive Advantage of Nations*, London: Macmillan. (Goes beyond the competitive strategy of companies to look at the determinants competition in the world economy.)

Porter, M.E., Spence, A.M. and Caves, R.E. (1980) *Competition in the Open Economy*, Cambridge, MA: Harvard University Press. (Contains some of Porter's early thinking on competition, better developed in later works.)

See also: BARTLETT, C.A. AND GHOSHAL, S.; HAMEL, G. AND PRAHALAD, C.K.; OHMAE, K.; PETTIGREW, A.M.

Related topics in the IEBM: BUSINESS ECONOMICS; COMPETITIVE STRATEGIES, DEVELOPMENT OF; GLOBAL STRATEGIC PLANNING; GLOBALIZATION; INDUSTRIAL STRATEGY; INTERNATIONAL BUSINESS, FUTURE TRENDS; INTERNATIONAL TRADE AND FOREIGN DIRECT INVESTMENT; MARKET STRUCTURE AND CONDUCT; STRATEGY, CONCEPT OF ; TECHNOLOGY STRATEGY, INTERNATIONAL

Reich, Robert M. (1946–)

Personal background

- born Scranton, Pennsylvania, 24 June 1946
- studied economics: BA Dartmouth College (1968) and MA Oxford (1970, Rhodes Scholar)
- received doctorate in law from Yale (1973)
- Assistant Solicitor-General, US Justice Department (1974–6)
- Director of Policy Planning, Federal Trade Commission (1976–81)
- joined the faculty of the John F. Kennedy School of Government at Harvard University, 1981
- appointed Secretary of Labor in the Clinton administration, 1993
- professional appointment at Brandeis University 1996

Major works

Minding America's Business (with Ira C. Magaziner) (1982)
The Next American Frontier (1983)
New Deals: The Chrysler Revival and the American System (with John D. Donahue) (1985)
Tales of a New America (1987)
The Work of Nations (1991)

Summary

Reich regards strategy as the re-enactment of core beliefs and stories which exist in society. He uses this analysis to attempt to understand the fundamental nature of the US economy and, more importantly, the reasons for its steady decline since the 1960s. An economist and lawyer by training, he has attempted to synthesize a variety of disciplines including history and anthropology to arrive at a holistic view of attitudes in the USA to business, government, and the relations between them. During the 1980s his ideas gained broad acceptance among Democratic politicians in the USA, notably Michael Dukakis, the 1988 presidential candidate, and Bill Clinton (elected President in 1992). His analysis is broad-reaching and rich, but he has so far been less specific on solutions, concentrating on the need for a more cooperative, integrated business culture.

1 Introduction

Robert Reich makes a joke about his small physical stature: 'When I first began worrying about the American economy, I was over 6 feet tall'. Yet he has worried to considerable effect, and his intellectual stature is formidable. Educated in economics and the law, he has serious misgivings about the value of both disciplines and writes more in the style of a popular social anthropologist and political essayist. His writing shows a formidable grasp of the structure of polemic, ideology and myth, along with an extraordinary gift for the exposition of beliefs with which he profoundly disagrees, but which he describes with a marvellous coherence and inner consistency.

Like John Kenneth Galbraith, a colleague at Harvard, Reich is a critic of 'conventional wisdom' (see GALBRAITH, J.K.). His lectures on business and politics at the Kennedy School of Government are so popular that students enter lotteries to take his classes. Reich's chief contribution to our understanding of strategy lies in his grasp of the fact that the US experience is organized by the dominant culture stories people tell themselves and by the abiding myths by which they live.

2 Biographical data

After taking degrees in economics, Robert Reich studied law at Yale Law School under Professor Robert Bork, and later worked for Bork when the latter was Solicitor-General in the Nixon administration. However, increasingly finding that law was an abstraction removed from real life, he began searching for a synthesis between law and economics, and to this end accepted a job with the Federal Trade Commission.

His experience with the Commission taught him that economics, too, was something removed from the real life of businesses, which tended to be separated and divided into different mental and disciplinary departments. His conversations with more than a thousand business leaders convinced him that something had to be done to revitalize the economic future of the USA, and that some form of partnership between business and government was needed. With business consultant Ira Magaziner, Reich produced his first book, *Minding America's Business* (1982).

Minding America's Business was a grim catalogue of the USA's declining share of world trade and was the first book on the subject to recommend that the USA adopt a formal industrial policy. To Reich's surprise, the book provoked vigorous reaction from both opponents and supporters. There were similar reactions to his next book, *The Next American Frontier* (1983), in which Reich combined history and anthropology with economics to propose that the next challenge facing the USA was to build a strong economic future, securing jobs and prosperity for its citizens. Published as it was in 1983, when a Republican administration was in power and Reaganomics was the prevailing economic orthodoxy, the book became seen in strongly political terms; among the exponents of *The Next American Frontier* were leading Democrat politicians. Michael Dukakis, who was for a time a colleague of Reich at the Kennedy School of Government at Harvard, referred explicitly to 'the next American frontier' in his speech accepting the Democratic presidential nomination in 1988. In 1993, Reich was appointed US Secretary of Labor by the newly elected Democratic President, Bill Clinton.

Fearing that he was becoming too abstract, Reich descended into concrete case history for his next book, *New Deals* (1985), an account of how the US government rescued the Chrysler corporation. The book, based on extensive interviews with all involved, maintained that the so-called 'miracle' at Chrysler had been wrought not by the corporation's president, Lee Iaccoca, but by the government, which changed the competitive ground rules. Reich felt that the Chrysler case illustrated the way by which change was bound to come in the USA; not through national debate on industrial policy but through small, often local *ad hoc* adjustments.

Delving still deeper into how people in the USA perceive business and society, Reich set out to write a book which would explain how Americans think and the questions they ask (as well as those they do not ask). The result was *Tales of a New America* (1987b), which analyses the mythological structure of US socio-political thinking and the 'cycles of righteous fulmination' directed by turns at 'big business' and then at 'big government'. In this book, Reich was able to tap into the folklore and mythology which the USA and its people have built up around themselves to expose some of the fundamental concepts which affect thinking about and by businesses.

3 Main contribution

Reich sees strategy as the re-enactment of core beliefs and stories within each society. Americans, he believes, tell themselves stories and re-enact folklore about themselves; no matter how diverse and new their experiences, they continue to fit politics and business into received narrative moulds. Reich gives names to some of these stories or moulds: 'The Rot at the Top', 'The Mob at the Gates', 'The Benevolent Community', 'The Triumphant Individual', 'The Scientific Manager'. In his view, these basic themes intertwine to create some of the major blind spots and distortions from which the US economy has been suffering since the 1960s.

Reich starts from the premise that in the USA, as well as in Britain and Canada, there has been a fundamental split between business values and civic or political values. Instead of economic evolution and development constituting one process in which civic and liberal values play a major part and in which government has a vital role, the two sets of values are seen as being in opposition. The wealth created by business culture is taxed and redistributed by the political culture, an arrangement that reduces the influence of civic values on what is deemed affordable while narrowing business values to a mixture of scientism and philistinism. Americans, says Reich, have a long history of running away from government and civic issues, first by immigration and later simply by moving on to new frontiers. In the 'next frontier', they are going to have to confront decades of social issues left behind, but not as some unresolved residue; social, human and civic issues are the heart of the USA's economic malaise and are an inseparable part of creating wealth in knowledge-intense economy.

In order to succeed, therefore, the USA needs to adapt its organizations in order to help it confront new economic realities. Doing so will require not only the participation of government in business, but also a re-evaluation and reassessment of some of the prevailing myths.

One of the myths Reich attacks most strongly is that of the 'Scientific Manager' (see TAYLOR, F.W.). The scientific principles developed by Taylor in the early part of the twentieth century undoubtedly played a role in creating the wealth of the USA and developing its manufacturing base. Yet, as in a Greek tragedy, the very values that facilitated the hegemony of the USA from the 1920s to the 1960s are now contributing to the country's failure. In 1965 the USA's share of world trade was 26 per cent; by 1980 it had fallen to below 17 per cent.

Efficiency, specialization and the separation of planning from action were not enough to protect US industry from foreign competition, which could use these same virtues to produce goods at lower wages and sell them in the USA more cheaply than domestically produced goods. But scientific management did not die; on the contrary, according to Reich, it evolved into what he calls 'paper entrepreneurship', where the principles of scientific management are applied not to the making and selling of goods, but the making and selling of companies. The old scientific disciplines such as engineering were supplemented by new ones such as finance, accounting and law.

Individual fortunes continue to be made by the buying and selling of companies and the assembling of vast conglomerates such as Gulf and Western and ITT. Most of these companies have, however, failed to perform up to expectation. This is because, according to Reich, paper entrepreneurship does not create; it merely rearranges industrial assets. Managers preside over a symbolic economy where assets are rearranged on paper, and where the resources needed for research and development and for long-term product strategies are instead tied up in acquisitions and mergers. Paper entrepreneurism is a giant distraction from the genuine tasks of the company: creating, making and supplying.

The consequences of this syndrome are enormous. Employee turnover is increasing rapidly, particularly in firms which are taken over. This in turn has knock-on effects for innovation. Competitive advantage lies in accumulating and synthesizing experience, and there are few ways in which an organization can learn how to create and produce more effectively if more than 90 per cent of its employees depart within a three-year period. Another consequence is increasing tariff protection as companies, unable to compete with the flood of foreign imports, press government to discriminate against foreign competition.

In his article on US–Japanese joint ventures (Reich and Markin 1986), Reich contrasts the US approach to that of Japanese firms. In most of the joint ventures studied, the basic research behind new products was carried out in the US (usually at universities), but the commercial development and manufacture of the new products was carried out in Japan; US companies participate in the assembly and marketing stages. The latter make good short-term profits, but the long-term strategic consequences, Reich believes, are ominous; Japanese companies are ending up with a coherent body of integratable experience and learning which extends from development through to manufacture and includes the major portion of high value-added skills. When the joint venture comes to an end, the Japanese partners walk away with these skills; US corporations are left at the top and bottom of a sandwich without the meat. Corporations are left with an elaborate satire on scientific management in which a remote controller in the USA apparently 'calls the shots' in Japan but is in truth only the front man for a business whose essentials have moved across the Pacific. The distance between planning and action has reached its logical culmination.

Reich then asks, why is the USA so blind to these dynamics? The answer is, because it cannot see the wood for the trees or, more precisely, it cannot see the community for the individuals, the self-interests of whom are paramount in its mythology. It is here, Reich believes, that the heart of the problems lies. The myth of the 'Triumphant Individual' has been passed on in the USA from Benjamin Franklin to Horatio Alger to modern television. This spirit is still celebrated today, by authors such as George Gilder who lauds 'fighters, fanatics, men with a lust for contest, a gleam of creation and a drive to justify their break from the mother company' (Gilder 1992).

Reich attacks this point of view. For him, individualism ends not in triumph, but in traffic jams; this is what Thurow (1981) calls 'the zero-sum society'. Individualism, he says, begets rules, which begets lawyers to undo the rules, which begets more lawyers to tighten them, while everyone hates the government and regulations which are made necessary by these struggles to resist. The paradox is that, in a society which values free enterprise and choice, the USA is one of the most over-regulated economies in the world. It is this deadlock that Reich is convinced the USA must break if it is to halt its inevitable decline.

4 Evaluation

Reich is at his best attacking the prevailing myths in US business and society and identifying the sources of problems. Looking at the question of why the USA and the UK have consistently lost ground, particularly in the high value-added, knowledge-intense and complex-product sectors, Reich deduces five reasons:

1 because few business leaders have been trained or selected for the role of guiding product and process innovation;
2 because flexible system production requires for its success a radical reorganization of corporate hierarchies, and would require collaborative and power-sharing arrangements with workers and trade unions;
3 because the ability to upgrade human skills rapidly is well beyond the capacity of any one corporation (which would in any case hesitate to train employees who might move on to its competitors);
4 because scientific management sees quantities but misses qualities;
5 because US culture subscribes to the myth of 'entrepreneurs and drones', where brilliant 'Triumphant Individuals' create big ideas which are then implemented by drone workers, whose sole function is to operationalize genius as quickly and cheaply as possible.

Reich attacks this last view as fundamentally flawed. In the first place, genuine new ideas are quite few, and stem from the experience of complex development and manufacture; innovation is thus a group or collective skill, not an individual one. Attacking the 'drones', breaking their unions, putting pressure on their wages and endlessly exalting the individual above the common herd is a kind of national 'ghost dance' by which the USA will hasten its own decline.

He is perhaps less specific on solutions. Going back to the narrative stories in US folklore, Reich believes that the USA needs to choose the model of 'The Benevolent Community' to mould its future strategies. At the same time, however, he is highly critical of the liberal system of social benevolence of the 1960s and 1970s, arguing instead for a social system based on reciprocal obligation. Government should give incentives to business to train and develop human capital; market forces alone, he believes, will not achieve this aim.

It is this notion that market forces can be understood and aided, rather than opposed, that distinguished Reich from welfare liberalism and socialism. The market is not 'it', it is 'we'; it is for us to choose how we develop ourselves and adjust to the constantly shifting demands of the international market. Above all, he says, we have to grasp that the logic of economic development and complex creation is a cooperative one. In the world of information, it is the 'Triumphant Team', rather than the individual, which is best able to grasp the knowledge overload and create complexity. Collective entrepreneurialism is best suited to those seamless webs of information in which products are embedded. Integrated product systems are best created by integrated human systems, with the makers mimicking the structure of what is made. There are isomorphic patterns between the knowers and the known, who are joined by the same patterns.

Reich is oddly dismissive of all the embryonic idealism in US business, such as McGregor's views on managers' capacity to develop the growth of subordinates, and Mayo and Roethlisberger and the human relations movement. He appears only to regard such sentiments as genuine if they come from Japan. While it is true that these approaches have been largely coopted by the much stronger tide of Taylorism, they are not without significance or genuine insight. Nor is it the fault of the individuals concerned that their concepts were reduced to calculated techniques by the prevailing mind-set.

5 Conclusion

Society advances politically and socially by making creative syntheses between bodies of knowledge usually regarded as remote. Reich has reached out to the falsely dichotomized cultures of business and government, right and left, economics and humanity, West and East, hard and soft, competing and cooperative, and has created a skein of ideas of extraordinary promise and power. By analysing the myths of US culture, he has gone some way towards exposing the roots of that culture and has shown at least in outline one possible way in which the culture and the US economy can adapt and prosper.

CHARLES HAMPDEN-TURNER
JUDGE INSTITUTE OF MANAGEMENT STUDIES,
UNIVERSITY OF CAMBRIDGE

Further reading

(References cited in the text marked *)

* Gilder, G. (1992) *Recapturing the Spirit of Enterprise*, San Francisco, CA: ICS Press. (A study of the personal dynamics of enterprise.)
* Reich, R.B. (1983) *The Next American Frontier*, New York: Times Books. (Famous work in which Reich discusses the economic challenge facing the USA.)
  Reich, R.B. (1987a) 'Entrepreneurship reconsidered: the team as hero', *Harvard Business Review* May–June. (Argues for more team building at top level.)
* Reich, R.B. (1987b) *Tales of a New America*, New York: Times Books. (Describes how Americans see themselves and their organizations.)
  Reich, R.B. (ed.) (1988) *The Power of Public Ideas*, Cambridge, MA: Harvard University Press. (Argues for more debate in public on the future of the USA.)
  Reich, R.B. (1991) *The Work of Nations: Preparing Ourselves for Twenty-first Century Capitalism*, London: Simon & Schuster. (Lays out a blueprint for the USA in the future. This is the book which won Reich his post as US Secretary of Labor.)
* Reich, R.B. and Donahue, J.D. (1985) *New Deals: The Chrysler Revival and the American System*, New York: Times Books. (An incisive and challenging look at industry–government relations in the USA.)
* Reich, R.B. and Magaziner, I.C. (1982) *Minding America's Business*, New York: Harcourt Brace Jovanovich. (Reich's first book, arguing the need for an industrial policy in the USA.)
* Reich, R.B. and Markin, E.D. (1986) 'Joint ventures with Japan give away our future', *Harvard Business Review* March–April. (Contrasts US and Japanese approaches to joint ventures and innovation, reporting on twenty-two cases studies.)

* Thurow, L. (1981) *The Zero-Sum Society*, New York: Viking Press. (Sociological critique of Western society by a noted writer in the field.)

See also: GALBRAITH, J.K.; KOCHAN, T.; TAYLOR, F.W.

Related topics in the IEBM: BUSINESS ETHICS; BUSINESS AND SOCIETY; ENVIRONMENTAL MANAGEMENT; HUMAN RESOURCE MANAGEMENT; INDUSTRIAL AND LABOUR RELATIONS; INNOVATION AND CHANGE; MANAGEMENT IN JAPAN; MANAGEMENT IN NORTH AMERICA; STRATEGY, CONCEPT OF

Rivett, B.H.P. (1924–)

Personal background

- born 2 April 1924, Oswestry
- graduated from King's College, London in mathematics, 1944
- graduated from Birkbeck College, MSc in pure mathematics, 1947
- served in Ministry of Supply (Ordnance Board), 1943–51
- head of the Field Investigation Group, National Coal Board, 1951–60
- first secretary of the Operational Research Society, 1953–60
- operational research consultant at Arthur Andersen, 1960–3
- president of the Operational Research Society, 1960–1
- Silver Medallist, Operational Research Society
- first UK professor of operational research, Lancaster University, 1964–7
- professor of operational research, University of Sussex, 1967–87

Major works

A Manager's Guide to Operational Research (with R.L. Ackoff) (1963)
Concepts of Operational Research (1968)
Principles of Model Building: the Construction of Models for Decision Analysis (1972)
Model Building for Decision Analysis (1980)
The Craft of Decision Modelling (1994)

Summary

Patrick ('Pat') Rivett was a key member of the operational research community in the UK, from the 1950s to the 1980s, both as a practitioner and diffuser of the discipline. As head of the Field Investigation Group at the National Coal Board he was a notable advocate of methodological and technical advances in operational research (OR) drawing on his direct knowledge of North American practice. He was also a long-standing servant of the Operational Research Society from its inception and in that capacity was instrumental in forging links, both formal and informal, with overseas operational researchers, notably in the USA. From the early 1960s onwards, Rivett fulfilled a significant role in establishing OR as a university-level subject, being the first professor of operational research in a UK university. He will be remembered chiefly as an outstanding advocate and disseminator of OR as a guide to rational decision making in human organizations.

1 Biographical data

Pat Rivett was born in 1924 in Oswestry, the son of a former Baptist minister who became an NSPCC inspector. Educated at a grant maintained grammar school, he then proceeded to King's College, London in 1941, graduating in 1944 with a first class honours degree in mathematics. This was followed by part-time study at Birkbeck College resulting in the award (with distinction) of an MSc in pure mathematics. After completing his undergraduate studies Rivett joined the Ministry of Supply (Ordnance Board) as a statistician working on the tracking of aircraft, ground control of fighters, and anti-aircraft systems. In 1951 he was appointed head of the National Coal Board's Field Investigation Group (FIG), responsible to the Board's Director of Scientific Control (Donald Hicks) for the application of OR as an aid to effective managerial decision making. Under Rivett's leadership FIG's staff more than trebled in size from the original complement of eight operational researchers, fully reflecting the growing demand for the group's services in helping to expand the industry's productive capacity. Coincidentally, Rivett participated in the foundation of the Operational Research Society, serving as its first secretary from 1953 to 1960. This was followed by his election as president of the society in 1960. By that time Rivett had left FIG to join the American firm of management consultants, Arthur Andersen, in order to establish an OR facility in the London office. During his period of office as president of the Operational Research Society Rivett took a special interest in proclaiming the virtues of OR as a subject worthy of advanced study in the university sector. In 1964 he was offered, and accepted, the first dedicated UK Chair in OR at the newly-created University of Lancaster. This was followed by his appointment as the foundation professor of operational research at the University of Sussex in 1967, a post which he occupied until his retirement in 1987. From that time onwards, Rivett became interested in health and community care issues and in applying statistical analysis to the allocation of resources in the treatment of coronary heart disease.

2 Main contribution

Rivett's career has embraced two main themes. As a practitioner of OR he presided over the largest OR organization in UK industry with a remit to investigate and resolve a variety of production-oriented problems. Rivett was also one of the most effective advocates of OR as a quantitatively-based management tool: he was a founder member and officer of the Operational Research Society and was instrumental in securing greater awareness of North American OR techniques both before and after the first international conference of operational researchers held at Oxford in 1957. Rivett's commitment to OR was epitomized in his efforts to establish the discipline as a worthwhile university-level activity and it was entirely appropriate that he should have been appointed to the first chair at a UK university, responsible for innovative

teaching programmes in OR both at undergraduate and postgraduate levels.

In his role as an OR practitioner at the NCB almost all of Rivett's work was in the field of coal production with particular reference to coal winning and underground transport, and carried out on behalf of senior staff in the production department. Much of FIG's early work was of a straightforward costing or work study nature, although a major and continuing preoccupation was the collection of relevant and reliable data. Indeed, the only major investigation that employed a method of analysis that would now be recognized as 'operational research' was the study of underground communications. Arising from the Cresswell Colliery disaster of September 1950 in which 80 miners were killed, this was the first practical investigation to use manual and computer simulations (Tomlinson 1971). The former took nearly four months to examine the results of two weeks of observations and the researchers were thankful to gain access to computer facilities at the National Physical Laboratory for the final stages of the project. In 1957, however, the pattern of work began to change as FIG began to take on a remit beyond the production department. The major departure from previous work was an investigation into the wastage of men from the industry. The study set out to determine the leaving patterns for different categories of employee and then to establish how wastage varied in relation to the distance that men worked from their homes, whether housing was easily available to them, and other associated factors (Houlden 1964).

The year 1957 proved to be a watershed in FIG's work for another reason. In that year the first international conference of operational researchers, organized in large measure by Rivett and his colleagues in FIG, in collaboration with Sir Charles Goodeve, was held at Oxford and there can be no doubt that it had a traumatic effect on the whole British OR Community (Davies, Eddison and Page 1957). It is worth re-emphasizing that FIG's early work had not been based on any sophisticated mathematical techniques given that the group had been established at a time when there was no shame to be found in solving a problem by simple common sense if that would suffice. After the conference, however, the realization quickly dawned that there was a significant technical gap between British OR and its American counterpart. Within FIG, Rivett himself had visited the USA in 1954 in order to ascertain the scope and techniques of OR in the military and civilian sectors. Whilst there he 'discovered a thing called inventory control and linear programming and the transportation algorithm' and after returning to FIG 'bounded around like a retriever dog telling the lads all about this' (Rand 1995). Similar reactions were registered by Rivett's deputy, Steve Cook who, after visiting the USA in 1955, concluded that American operational researchers were armed with a battery of techniques unknown to or under-utilized by their British counterparts. The former were therefore capable of producing timely recommendations – a sensitive issue for FIG members in view of the typical 3–4 year length of their investigations. Nevertheless, it was the 1957 conference which provoked a searching appraisal of OR techniques and methodology within the wider UK OR community. In this respect, FIG was at the leading edge of debate, operating in a manner akin to speculative university researchers concerned to acquaint themselves with specific procedures as a prelude to wider seminar discussion of the possibilities of linear programming, queuing theory, inventory control and search theory. Rivett himself was by this time determined to publicize the value of OR to a wider audience. In the early 1960s he was the presenter of four BBC television programmes on OR in a prime-time slot and also acted as a consultant to Granada television with a view to assisting in the production of programmes on OR and computers in management. Informal talks with chambers of commerce were commonplace at the same time as Rivett addressed local groups of the Statistical Society on the virtues of OR. In 1960, when he was president of the Operational Research Society, he attempted to engage the interest of universities in OR. A particularly fruitful contact was Charles Carter, professor of economics at the University of Manchester. Following his appointment as

vice chancellor of the new University of Lancaster Carter invited Rivett to take up the first chair in OR at a British university. As an ardent admirer of the distinguished American operational researcher, Russell Ackoff (see ACKOFF, R.L.), and the OR activities that he presided over at the Case Institute, Rivett sought to model his new department on North American lines. In this task he was ably assisted by a small group of colleagues who joined him from FIG. Considerable media interest was expressed in Rivett's appointment and it served as a catalyst for the diffusion of OR into the wider university sector with Rivett himself proceeding to the University of Sussex in 1967 as the foundation professor of operational research.

3 Evaluation

In the 1950s and 1960s Rivett fulfilled critical roles as a practitioner and diffuser of OR using both formal and informal channels. His effectiveness may be gauged by the emergence of FIG as the largest OR group in the world and his catalytic role in promoting OR as a university-level activity. He also did much to disseminate US-derived OR techniques, most notably linear programming and mathematical modelling generally. In this respect, Rivett was an exponent of 'classical' OR whereby the application of the scientific method utilizing quantitative analysis could provide objective solutions to a wide range of managerial problems in human organizations. As a highly articulate proponent of tactical OR, therefore, Rivett was at the very centre of the diffusion of OR in the 1950s and 1960s. For Rivett, these were exciting years in which operational researchers had 'a rather easy life … because the national economies in which we worked were expanding, new job opportunities were being created and the *growth* of the organisations which we served … was more or less assured by the continuing *growth* of the economies in which we worked' (Rivett 1974). In this setting, classical OR had a legitimate role to play in enhancing the productive capacity of the economy, all the more so since the initial pay-off from quantitative evaluation could be considerable. After 1970, however, with the worldwide slowing down in economic growth and increasing awareness of the limitations of classical OR in resolving 'messy' problems where events are non-repeatable, Rivett joined with other leading operational researchers in expressing doubts about the relevance of OR in a world of increasing uncertainty, subject to multiplying constraints and incompatible sub-objectives. As early as 1974, he expressed the view that linear programming and other methodological developments had taken the OR community 'at high speed down a very attractive algebraic blind alley'. What was needed, therefore, was a new 'social dimension' to OR (Rivett 1974). Simplification of complex problems could be modelled but courses of action should be derived which do not depend upon mathematical manipulation. Rivett was thus one of the first UK operational researchers to question OR's 'hard science' ideal in advance of the movement towards 'soft' OR manifest in the 1980s.

Given that Rivett's career has spanned the worlds of industry and academia, it is apparent that he was more successful in the former than in the latter. Whilst at FIG he fulfilled his brief admirably, guiding the group's work effectively and sympathetically. For all of Rivett's expository gifts however, the transition to the university sector was marked by a degree of unease on his part in dealing with colleagues from more established academic disciplines. In view of the limited provenance of OR this was understandable, but it is to Rivett's credit that his robust defence of the discipline was a vital factor in establishing academic OR as a research-based discipline with an advancing frontier of new knowledge.

4 Conclusion

Pat Rivett has been one of the major figures in British OR since the early 1950s both as a practitioner and diffuser of the discipline. His status has rested, in large measure, on his presentational gifts – a high degree of articulacy reinforced by infectious enthusiasm. Whilst he himself was not responsible for any significant methodological innovations he fulfilled a critical role in disseminating advanced

practice. Although he eventually became disillusioned with the extreme mathematisation of the discipline he did not abandon it but sought to widen its scope to embrace a 'soft' science ideal.

MAURICE KIRBY
LANCASTER UNIVERSITY

Further reading

(References cited in the text marked *)

Ackoff, R. (1979) 'Resurrecting the future of operational research', *Journal of the Operational Research Society*, 30: 189–99. (A controversial article, attributing the author's disillusion with classical OR to the extreme mathematisation of the discipline at the hands of academic operational researchers.)

Dando, M.R. and Sharp, R.G. (1978) 'Operational research in the UK in 1977: the causes and consequences of a myth?', *Journal of the Operational Research Society* 29: 939–49. (A major article challenging OR's claim to be a 'hard' science.)

* Davies M., Eddison, R.T. and Page, T. (1957) *Proceedings of the First International Conference on Operational Research, Oxford 1957*, Baltimore: ORSA. (A compendium of papers from the first international conference of operational researchers, fully reflecting the methodological lead in the USA.)

Hicks, D. (1983) 'The origins of operational research in the coal industry: a tribute to Sir Charles Drummond Ellis, FRS 1895–1980', *Journal of the Operational Research Society* 34: 845–52. (An appreciation of the work of the NCB's first 'scientific member' in inaugurating OR in the coal industry.)

* Houlden, B. (1964) 'Operational Research in the National Coal Board', *Operational Research Quarterly* 15: 171–84. (A descriptive account of the work of FIG up to the early 1960s.)

Locke, R. (1989) *Management and Higher Education since 1940*, Cambridge: Cambridge University Press. (A magisterial study of the rise of management science generally which places the history of OR in its appropriate context.)

* Rand, G. (1994) Interview with Patrick Rivett. Operational Research Society Archive, Modern Records Centre, University of Warwick. (A wide-ranging interview covering all aspects of Rivett's career in OR.)

* Rivett, P. (1974) 'Perspective for operational research', *Omega* 2:. 225–33. (An appeal for a

wider remit for OR to embrace a 'social dimension'.)

* Tomlinson, R.C. (1971) *OR Comes of Age* (London: Tavistock). (A descriptive account of the work of the National Coal Board's Field Investigation Group.)

Tomlinson, R.C. (1974) 'O.R. is', *Operational Research Quarterly* 25: 346–60. (A vigorous defence of OR in the light of the doubts and uncertainties arising from economic recession.)

See also: ACKOFF, R.L.; BLACKETT, P.M.S.; BEER, S.; FORRESTER, J.W.; VICKERS, G.

Related topics in the IEBM: DECISION MAKING; LINEAR PROGRAMMING; MANAGEMENT SCIENCE; NON-LINEAR PROGRAMMING; OPERATIONS RESEARCH; OPTIMALITY AND OPTIMIZATION; SYSTEMS; WORK SYSTEMS

Samuelson, Paul Anthony (1915–)

1 Biographical data
2 Main contribution
3 Assessment

Personal background

- born 15 May 1915, in Gary, Indiana
- 1932–5 undergraduate student at University of Chicago
- 1935–40 graduate student and then junior fellow at Harvard University
- 1940–7 assistant and then associate professor of economics, Massachusetts Institute of Technology (MIT)
- from 1947, professor and then Institute Professor of Economics, Massachusetts Institute of Technology
- 1970 Nobel Prize for Economics

Major works

Foundations of Economic Analysis (1947)

Economics: An Introductory Analysis (1948; 14th edn, with W.D. Nordhaus, 1992)

Linear Programming and Economic Analysis (with R. Dorfman and R.M. Solow) (1958; 1987)

The Collected Scientific Papers of Paul A. Samuelson (5 volumes, 1966-1986)

Summary

Samuelson has arguably been the dominant figure in post-war economics, his publications extending to virtually all branches of economic theory: the theory of the consumer, production theory, general equilibrium, international trade, welfare economics, the business cycle, Keynesian economics, inflation, economic growth, the theory of capital and optimal capital accumulation and many others. Kenneth Arrow has described him as 'omnipresent in American and even world economics' (Arrow 1967: 730). However, whereas some economists are remembered primarily because of certain key ideas with which they are associated, Samuelson's contribution has been primarily to change the way in which economists have approached their subject. His early work, in particular his doctoral dissertation (1947), argued the case for a mathematical approach to problems that had traditionally been tackled using non-mathematical methods. While economists such as Hicks used mathematics, they kept it in the background. In contrast, Samuelson gave mathematics a much more prominent role. He emphasized, in a way no one had done before, the formal derivation of qualitative predictions concerning variables that could, at least in principle, be observed.

1 Biographical data

Samuelson studied economics at Chicago, notably under Jacob Viner. In 1935, the conditions attached to a graduate scholarship forced him to leave Chicago, and he moved to Harvard to undertake his doctoral work. He has argued that, as a result of this move, he had the luck to be in the right place at the right time. Harvard had Edward Chamberlin, responsible for the monopolistic competition revolution, and Alvin Hansen, soon to become the most prominent American convert to Keynes (see KEYNES, J.M.). In addition, Harvard boasted J.A. Schumpeter and Leontief. It was here that Samuelson, before the age of twenty-five, wrote many of his most influential articles, and the doctoral dissertation that became *Foundations of Economic Analysis*. Samuelson's youth perhaps explains the fervour with which he argued the case for using mathematical analysis in economic theory. In 1940, he moved to MIT, as he put it, 'because he got a better offer', though the reasons why Harvard let him go are not clear. Since 1940, Samuelson has spent his entire career at MIT, leaving only for very short periods. Many of his colleagues testify to his vital role in turning his department at MIT into what many would regard as the world's leading economics department. The 'MIT' style of economics is one that many departments, in the USA and in the rest of the world, seek to emulate.

Apart from 1944–5, when he worked in the MIT Radiation Laboratory, Samuelson has been an academic economist throughout his career. He has, however, been involved in public life. His textbook, *Economics*, is probably the most successful economics textbook ever. For many years he was a regular columnist in *Newsweek*, and he was an advisor to US President Kennedy. Although his main reputation lies in economic theory, he has made important contributions to debates over macroeconomic policy, such as his advocacy of using demand management to create full employment in the 1960s, and his analysis of inflation policy in terms of a short-run trade-off between inflation and unemployment.

2 Main contribution

Revealed preference

Since the so-called marginal revolution of the 1870s, economists had typically modelled consumer behaviour in terms of utility maximization, where utility (which depended on the quantities of various goods that were consumed) measured a consumer's level of welfare. One problem with this approach was that utility was unobservable. Using the language of logical positivism, it was a metaphysical concept. One response to this was the development by Hicks and Allen of indifference curve analysis, which enabled economists to dispense with the notion of measurable utility. Samuelson's approach was, at least at first sight, more radical. This was the theory of revealed preference.

The essential idea in revealed preference theory is very simple. The economist can observe prices, incomes and quantities purchased – nothing else. Suppose that a consumer has an income Y and is able to purchase two goods,

1 and 2, at prices P_1 and P_2. The budget constraint is that total expenditure is no greater than income: $P_1X_1 + P_2X_2 \leq Y$, where X_1 and X_2 are the quantities purchased. This can be represented by the budget line AB in Figure 1. Given this budget line, if the consumer chooses point C, we can conclude that the consumer prefers that combination of the two goods to all the other combinations that could have been chosen but were not: that C is revealed as preferred to all other points in the triangle OAB. Thus, if prices and/or income changes so that the budget line were to become A'B', we could conclude that the consumer would choose a point somewhere along the line CB' (assuming all income is spent). Points on A'C will not be chosen because the consumer could have chosen them when faced with AB, but did not do so.

The significance of this approach is that Samuelson was able to derive (with a few exceptions) the same results as Hicks and Allen, notably the negative substitution effect, without referring to anything that could not be directly observed.

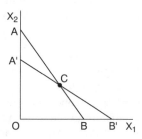

Figure 1 The consumer's choice of budget line

The business cycle

Samuelson's contribution here was to show how the business cycle might be analysed in terms of two simple relations: the multiplier and the accelerator. The multiplier is the relationship between investment and consumption (or income) that results from the process of income generation. Investment is spent, thereby generating income, which stimulates consumption. This gives rise to an equation of the form $C_t = cI_{t-1}$, where C_t is consumption in period t c is the multiplier and I_{t-1} is investment in the previous period. A lag is assumed on the grounds that when investment (and hence consumers' income) rises, consumption does not rise immediately, but only with some delay. The accelerator is the relationship between investment and the *change* in consumption that arises from capital being required to produce consumption goods. This can be written as $K_t = vC_t$, where K_t is the capital stock at time t and v is the capital-output ratio. Ignoring depreciation, investment is the change in the capital stock, from which it follows that:

$$I_t = \Delta K_t = (C_t - C_{t-1}).$$

Putting these two equations together, we obtain an equation that determines the time path of consumption:

$$C_t = cv(C_{t-1} - C_{t-2})$$

Given appropriate values of c and v this equation will generate a cycle.

The significance of Samuelson's contribution (1938) was to show the importance of formal, mathematical analysis. For the model to generate cycles, the multiplier and accelerator coefficients must have specific values. Furthermore, Samuelson was able to show that unless cv is *exactly* equal to one, the cycles will either become larger and larger, or smaller and smaller, depending on whether cv is greater or less than one. This shows that additional assumptions need to be introduced to explain the business cycle, for in the real world the business cycle neither dies away nor explodes. This is something that would be very difficult to show without formal mathematical analysis.

Although use of the multiplier–accelerator model has declined since rational expectations have become fashionable in macroeconomics, for over three decades it became the standard framework in which to analyse the business cycle. What distinguished business cycle research after Samuelson from the earlier literature was the central role of this simplified, formal model: the business cycle came to be conceived in terms of a second-order difference equation, something that would, with some justification, have been unpalatable to leading writers before Samuelson, such as W.C. Mitchell.

The theory of international trade

Until the development of theories based on imperfect competition and game theory in the 1980s, the theory of international trade was, from the 1940s, dominated by what has come to be known as the Heckscher–Ohlin–Samuelson model. This treats international trade as an application of general equilibrium theory. Though some of the results can be generalized to larger models, the basic tool of analysis is a model with two countries, two factors of production (labour and capital) and two goods. In a particularly influential paper, published in 1941, Samuelson and Wolfgang Stolper showed that protection would raise the price of the relatively scarce factor. Thus if labour was the relatively scarce factor, protection would, under certain circumstances, raise wages by more than the price of the imported good. The 'orthodox' view that protection, through raising prices, would reduce living standards was not necessarily correct. Shortly afterwards, Samuelson derived conditions under which free trade in goods would result in equalization of factor prices, even if factors cannot move from one country to another.

As with so much of Samuelson's work, the significance of this work was not so much the specific conclusions reached, but the method. He tackled these problems using a simplified, but formal, general equilibrium model. It was general equilibrium effects, whereby changes in one market affected other markets and hence the overall equilibrium, that enabled him to derive surprising results (that seemed obvious once they were understood). For many years the $2 \times 2 \times 2$ (countries, factors, goods) model, the results of which could be illustrated if not proved graphically, became the standard fare of international trade theory. Samuelson's contribution was to make formal, general equilibrium modelling central to the theory of international trade.

The Foundations of Economic Analysis

Perhaps the most significant feature of this book was its unashamed advocacy of mathematical methods. Laborious verbal analysis of essentially simple mathematical ideas, Samuelson claimed, was a particularly depraved form of unrewarding mental gymnastics. This attitude was in stark contrast to that of Alfred Marshall, author of what was still the dominant economics textbook (see MARSHALL, A.). This case was reinforced by Samuelson's argument that many economic problems were simply optimization problems. Consumers maximized utility subject to a budget constraint, and firms maximized profits subject to a production function. The theory of constrained optimization thus provided a unifying framework within which a range of diverse problems could be analysed. Equilibrium, in the sense of an optimum subject to constraints, was made central to economics.

The methodological principle underlying the *Foundations* was that economic theory should be concerned with the derivation of 'operationally meaningful' theorems. These were hypotheses about empirical data that might conceivably be refuted, if only under ideal conditions. This led Samuelson to emphasize the derivation of comparative-static predictions: predictions about how various changes would affect equilibrium values of economic variables. For example, instead of being content to list the factors on which the price of a commodity might depend, Samuelson required economic theory to predict whether changes in these factors would cause the price to rise or fall. Many such results could be derived from the conditions for an optimum. Samuelson went further, however, with his 'correspondence principle' where he argued that further comparative statics results could be derived from the assumption that equilibrium was stable – that starting from any arbitrary price, the market price will move towards the equilibrium price. It turned out, however, that for technical reasons, the correspondence principle was much less useful than Samuelson had hoped. The idea that theory should be aimed at deriving comparative statics results, however, became firmly established.

Economics: An Introductory Analysis

Samuelson's *Economics: An Introductory Analysis*, the fourteenth edition of which was published in 1992 (by which time W.D. Nordhaus had entered as a co-author), was the book that finally displaced Alfred Marshall's *Principles of Economics* (1890) as the leading introductory textbook on economics (see MARSHALL, A.). Enormous numbers have been sold, of both the English and foreign-language translations, of which there have been many. It is an introductory textbook, yet it is vast in scope, including some material that newcomers find difficult. Though it presents economic ideas in a simplified form, its remarkable success owes much to the principle Samuelson adopted, that it should contain nothing that students would subsequently have to unlearn. The book has been regularly revised, its contents list serving as a barometer of the topics in which economists have taken an interest over the intervening four decades.

This book played a major role in the spread of Keynesian macroeconomics (see KEYNES, J.M.). Two aspects of this are particularly important. The first is what is usually called either the 45° line model of the 'Keynesian cross' (the analogy being with the 'Marshallian cross', the supply and demand diagram), shown in Figure 2. This diagram plots expenditure against national income. Consumption,

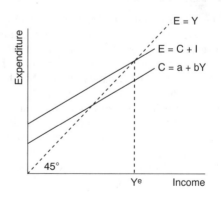

Figure 2 A rise in the equilibrium level of income

C, increases with income, Y ($C = a + bY$, where a is autonomous consumption and b is the marginal propensity to consume), and aggregate expenditure is consumption plus investment (assumed independent of income), I. Equilibrium income, Y^e, is where expenditure, E, equals income. It is easy to use the diagram to show, for example, that a rise in investment will cause the expenditure line, $E = C + I$ to shift upwards, leading to a rise in the equilibrium level of income.

The second important feature of Samuelson's *Economics*, dating from the 1950s, was what he termed the 'neo-classical synthesis'. At the level of economic theory this involved using neo-classical price theory (supply and demand, optimization – the economics of *Foundations*) for microeconomic and resource-allocation problems, and using Keynesian macroeconomics. At the level of policy it involved using monetary and fiscal policy to create full employment, varying the mix of the two types of policy to achieve the desired level of investment. Samuelson justified this approach, which is unacceptable to many economists because of its failure to provide a microeconomic underpinning for its macroeconomics, on the grounds that prices were, he believed, inflexible. He was thus prepared to take sticky prices as an assumption in doing macroeconomics. Samuelson is thus eclectic in his approach to economic theory in that he does not feel bound by a rigid set of assumptions.

3 Assessment

Samuelson's main contribution to economics has been to change the way in which economists have set about economic research. Perhaps more than any other economist, he represents the mathematical, model-building approach to economic theory. His early work, notably *Foundations of Economic Analysis*, but also his work on the consumer, welfare economics, the business cycle and international trade, was all aimed at establishing the vital role of mathematics in economics. His subsequent work, even in areas such as the history of economic thought that traditionally have been less affected by the phenomenon,

reinforces this, mathematics being used to analyse many new areas that would simply have been impossible to tackle without it. Outstanding examples are dynamics (how prices behave out of equilibrium, and the circumstances under which an economy will converge on an equilibrium) and optimal capital accumulation (given an initial and a desired terminal capital stock, what is the optimal time path for getting from one to the other?). Samuelson's emphasis on deriving comparative statics results concerning the effects of changes in policy or exogenous variables (assumed to be determined by non-economic factors) now pervades the whole of economics. Even where the economists are moving beyond the frameworks established by Samuelson (as in trade theory, where game theory is opening up new areas of research and new perspectives on old problems) the preference for formal methods and comparative static analysis has (for good or ill) remained.

ROGER E. BACKHOUSE
UNIVERSITY OF BIRMINGHAM

Further reading

(References cited in the text marked *)

* Arrow, K.J. (1967) 'Samuelson collected', *Journal of Political Economy* 75: 730–7. (The first two volumes of his collected papers surveyed, with a particularly interesting section on his views of the usefulness of neo-classical price theory.)

Brown, E.C. and Solow, R.M. (eds) (1983) *Paul Samuelson and Modern Economic Theory*, New York: McGraw-Hill. (Articles on Samuelson's contributions to various areas of economics, many written by colleagues or former students.)

Feiwei, G.R. (ed.) (1982) *Samuelson and NeoClassical Economics*, London: Kluwer. (Another collection of appraisals of Samuelson's contributions to economics.)

Fischer, S. (1987) 'Samuelson, Paul Anthony', in J. Eatwell, M. Milgate and P. Newman (eds), *The New Palgrave Dictionary of Economics*, London: Macmillan. (An excellent overview of Samuelson's contributions by a younger colleague at MIT.)

Lindbeck, A. (1970) 'Paul Anthony Samuelson's contributions to economics', *Swedish Journal of Economics* 72: 342–54. (The appraisal of Samuelson's work on the occasion of his being awarded the Nobel Prize in Economics.)

McCloskey, D.N. (1986) *The Rhetoric of Economics*, Brighton: Harvester Wheatsheaf. (Chapter 5 contains a brief analysis of Samuelson's rhetoric, considering the literary devices he uses to establish the authority of mathematical argumentation.)

* Samuelson, P.A. (1947) *Foundations of Economic Analysis*, Cambridge, MA: Harvard University Press. (Samuelson's doctoral dissertation which has had such a dramatic impact on modern economic theory.)

Samuelson, P.A. (1966-86) *The Collected Scientific Papers of Paul A. Samuelson*, 5 vols, London and Cambridge, MA: MIT Press. (Contains several hundred pieces covering all aspects of his work apart from popular writing. They give some idea of why Samuelson has made the impact on economics that he has.)

Samuelson, P.A. (1990) 'Paul A. Samuelson', in W. Breit and R.W. Spencer (eds), *Lives of the Laureates: Ten Nobel Economists*, 2nd edn, Cambridge, MA: MIT Press. (Samuelson's autobiographical reflections.)

Samuelson, P.A., Dorfman, R. and Solow, R.M. (1987) *Linear Programming and Economic Analysis*, New York: Dover Publications. (A look at modern methods of economic analysis.)

Samuelson, P.A. and Nordhaus, W.D. (1992) *Economics*, London: McGraw-Hill. (The 14th edition of the textbook through which many students have been introduced to economics.)

* Samuelson, P.A. and Stolper, W.F. (1941) 'Protection and real wages', *Review of Economic Studies* 9: 58–73. (Influential paper on international trade, in which the authors show that protection would raise the price of the relatively scarce factor.)

Wood, J.C. and Wood, R.N. (1989) (eds) *Paul Samuelson: Critical Assessments*, London: Routledge. (Four volumes of articles about Samuelson and his economics.)

See also: KEYNES, J.M.; MARSHALL, A.; SCHUMPETER, J.

Related topics in the IEBM: ARROW, K.J.; BUSINESS CYCLES; GAME THEORY AND GAMING; HICKS, J.R.; INTERNATIONAL TRADE AND FOREIGN DIRECT INVESTMENT; KEYNES, J.M.; MARKET STRUCTURE AND CONDUCT; MARSHALL, A.; MODELLING AND FORECASTING; NEO-CLASSICAL ECONOMICS; SUPPLY-SIDE ECONOMICS

Schein, Edgar (1928–)

1 Introduction
2 Main contributions
3 Evaluation and conclusions

Personal background

- Born 5 March 1928 in Zurich, Switzerland
- BA University of Chicaago (1947)
- MA Stanford University (1949)
- PhD in Social Psychology from Harvard University (1952)
- Served as a Captain in the US Army (1952–56)
- Professor at MIT since (1956)

Major works

Career Anchors: Discovering Your Real Values (1996)
'Culture: The Missing Concept in Organization Sciences', *Administrative Science Quarterly* (1996)
Organizational Psychology (1965)
Organizational Culture and Leadership (1992)
Process Consultation 3rd edition (1998)
The Clinical Perspective in Fieldwork (1987)

Summary

Besides an impressive academic background and achievements, Schein has consulted with many major corporations in the United States and Europe. These accomplishments were recognized in 1988 when he was named 'Consultant of the Year' by both the Consulting Division of the American Psychological Association and the American Society for Training and Development.

Schein has developed theory in four major areas, the first being culture and his book first published in 1992 *Organizational Culture and Leadership* is a classic in this area. In the area of organizational learning and change Schein has expanded on many of the traditional theories. Career dynamics, and in particular the concept of 'career anchors' was introduced in the late 1970s. Finally *Process Consultation* is the book which sets out, as a framework for consultants and researchers, one of the most used theories of Schein to this day.

1 Introduction

Edgar Schein received his undergraduate BA degree from the University of Chicago(1947), a masters (MA) degree from Stanford (1949), and his doctorate (PhD) degree from Harvard (1952) in social relations. He has written books on social and organizational psychology, however he is best known for his classic works *Process Consultation* (Addison-Wesley, 1969, rev. 1989), and *Process Consultation: Vol 2 Lessons for Managers and Consultants* (Addison-Wesley, 1987) as well as *Organization Culture and Leadership* (Jossey-Bass, 1985). In the area of Organization Development, he has proposed a new methodological approach to OD research called *The Clinical Perspective in Field Work* (Sage, 1987).

In addition to his impressive academic achievements, Professor Schein has consulted with many major organizations in the United States and Europe. He was recognized in 1988 as the 'Consultant of the Year' by both the Consulting Division of the American Psychological Association and the American Society for Training and Development.

Schein was born in Switzerland and spent some of his childhood in Czechoslovakia and Russia before his father settled at the University of Chicago as a physicist. Schein at one time entertained the idea of becoming a physicist, however his career eventually centred around social psychology. During his PhD at Harvard, he was exposed to a milieu that was very interdisciplinary. Social psychology, clinical psychology, sociology, and anthropology were on the daily menu. This exposure was to influence his subsequent thinking.

From Harvard Schein went into the army where he was involved with the repatriation of Korean prisoners of war. At the Walter Reed Army Institute of Research he did a study on 'brainwashing' and later wrote a paper and a book about Coercive Persuasion. After the Army, Douglas McGregor (Theory X and Y) invited him to consider a job at MIT in Boston. A scholarship to the National Training Labs workshop at Bethel, Maine followed, and it was here that Dr. Schein had some of his first exposures with individual and organizational development.

2 Main Contributions

Schein's work can be divided into the following categories: Organization Culture, Organizational Learning and Change, Career Dynamics and Process Consultation.

Organization culture

Culture is not an easy concept or process to define, however Schein often uses the definition 'culture is a pattern which shares basic assumptions'. He goes on to point out that it is learned by the members of a group in solving their external problems of survival in the environment and their internal problems of integration that work well enough to be taught to new group members. This behaviour is the correct way to perceive, think about and talk about all aspects of their daily lives. Once shared assumptions exist, the group functions to provide meaning to daily events that make life predictable, thus reducing anxiety.

Culture is a learned response(s) to external survival issues. As such culture is a shared definition of primary task, mission and strategy as well as shared goals. In this respect, the following shared aspects are obvious:

- sense of means to be used in goal accomplishment;
- definition of measurement systems to assess progress as well as error;

- sense of means to be used in error correction.

In addition to the survival issues mentioned above, culture is also learned responses to the problems of internal integration such as shared:

- language, concepts and processes;
- criteria for acquiring power and status;
- rules of face and intimacy;
- criteria for rewards and punishments;
- ideology and religion.

The group or organization often has a group of issues dealing with higher order abstractions where they may share assumptions about the nature of reality and truth; time and space; human nature, activity and relations. In addition to the nature and content of culture, one may look at the levels of culture. In this context, artefacts, shared values and shared basic assumptions are important. Artefacts include the visible, hearable, feelable manifestations of the underlying assumptions (e.g. behaviour patterns, rituals, dress codes, stories, myths, products, etc.). Shared values are the espoused reasons for why things should be as they are (e.g. charters, goal statements, norms, codes of ethics, and company value statements). Shared basic assumptions are the invisible but surfaceable reasons why group members perceive, think and feel the way they do about external survival and internal integration issues such as assumptions about mission, means, relationships, reality, time, space, human nature, etc.

To summarize this in an example, the culture of the USA would involve humans as optimistic, pro-active, perfectible and good. Relationships in the USA would involve rugged individualism, equality of opportunity, private property, task relationships and the rule of law (not men). Truth is pragmatism and diverse; time is scarce, monochromic and near future. Space is unlimited, open and shared.

Organizational learning and culture

Schein holds that organizational learning is 'in', but what do we mean by the term? Does learning involve individuals learning in organizational contexts? – or learning things relevant to their organizational roles? Do we mean that systems such as departments or entire organizations can learn? And how does one define learning? Is it an adaptation to environmental variation? or a way of coping with new and unexpected events? an increase in the capacity to be creative? – or all of the above.

Schein goes on to introduce 'coercive persuasion' as a conceptualization of organizational learning. The two extremes of this learning dimension are organization driven and individual driven. At the extreme of organizational driven learning, which is often thought of as socialization, acculturation, apprenticeships or training, learning is accomplished by teaching the organizationally defined skills, attitudes and values that are deemed by power centres in the organization to be relevant. Schein argues that this is 'coercive persuasion'. On the individual driven extreme learning is often thought of as creativity, sole innovation and creative individualism.

Schein's view of coercive persuasion stems from his work with the treatment of civilian prisoners in communist China after the Korean conflict in the 1950s. Some of the prisoners signed confessions under severe pressures but they were coerced and not persuaded. They never accepted their guilt. Schein defines the complex process these prisoners went through as cognitive redefinition, that is, some of them eventually came to understand the point of view of their captors.

On the other hand the essence of individually driven generative learning is the freedom to explore, to scan the environment for relevant information, to pick one's own identity models and integrate this with one's personality. The above has a huge implication for organizations, for if they succeed in creating a feeling of true choice and freedom, it will also create cultural deviants and undermine some of the organizations efforts to be more productive and innovative. Schein's article concludes with the paradox that the very concept of organization is to restrict some individual freedom in order to achieve a joint response.

Career dynamics

Schein often invited his former students back to MIT to have lunch with him and in that process the conversation often turned to career development. The concept of the 'career anchor' originated from the work Schein did in trying to get a better understanding of careers and the career process. A longitudinal study of 44 MIT alumni from the Master's program at the Sloan School of Management began in 1961. The initial surveys and interviews of values and attitudes were done in the period 1961–63 while all the respondents were second year students in the Masters program. A follow-up interview was conducted in 1973 and it was this material which produced the insights that led to the concept of the career anchor.

A career anchor is the self concept that emerges from the following questions:

- What are my talents, skills and areas of competence?
- What are my strengths and weaknesses?
- What are my main motives, needs, drives and goals in life?
- What do I want to do and how?
- What are the main criteria by which I judge what I am doing?
- Does the organization 'match' with my values?
- How do I feel about what I am doing?

The anchors Schein identified were:

- *Technical/Functional Competence* – where people build a sense of identity around the content of their work.
- *General Managerial Competence* – management is the main interest.
- *Autonomy/Independence* – people have an overriding need to do things in their own way.
- *Security/Stability* – some people organize their careers so they feel safe and secure.
- *Entrepreneurial Creativity* – often involves an overriding need to create new businesses of their own.

- *Sense of Service, Dedication to a Cause* – career decisions are based on a desire to improve the world in some fashion.
- *Pure Challenge* – a perception that one can conquer anything or anybody. Success is overcoming impossible obstacles, etc.
- *Lifestyle* – a matter of finding a way to integrate the needs of an individual, the family, and the career.

Schein concludes with three suggestions for organizations and managers:

- Create more flexible career paths, incentive systems, and reward systems.
- Stimulate more self-insight and self-management.
- Clarify what the organization needs from the individual.

Process consultation

Schein's works on Process Consultation are classics for consultants and researchers working in the qualitative methodologies. Schein begins by presenting three models of consultation:

1 The *Expertise Model* which is the most prevalent of the three. Here the client defines a need(s) and accepts the consultant's expert information or service. Often the organization (client) in question has concluded that they do not have the time and/or resources to fulfil the need(s).
2 The *Doctor–Patient Model* involves a consultant being brought into an organization to find out what is wrong, and like a physician recommend a solution. The consultant, like a typical doctor, has a great deal of power as he or she diagnoses and prescribes.
3 The *Process Consultation Model* can be summarized using the following assumptions:
    (a) The client often does not know what is wrong and asks for help.
    (b) The client is not sure of the kinds of help the consultant can give them.

(c) Clients often need help in identifying what to improve.
(d) Organization (clients) are usually more effective if they manage their own strengths and weaknesses.
(e) It is almost impossible, because of the time constraints, for a consultant to learn enough about the culture of an organization.
(f) Unless the client understands the problem, they may not assist in implementing a solution.
(g) Process Consultation then is a 'set of activities on the part of the consultant that help the client to perceive, understand, and act upon the process events that occur in the client's environment in order to improve the situation as defined by the client'. (p. 11)

3 Evaluation and conclusions

We would like to use Schein's article in the 40th Anniversary Special Issue of *Administrative Science Quarterly* 41 (1996): 229–240 as a summary of his present thinking on a variety of issues. The article begins with the view that organizational psychology is slowly moving from an individualistic point of view toward a more integrated view based on social psychology, sociology and anthropology. Schein goes on to point out that culture is a central dimension in this evolution and our failure to take culture seriously may stem from our methods of inquiry, which emphasize abstractions that can be measured. More ethnographic or clinical observations are needed.

Schein goes on to point out that Organizational Psychology was introduced in the early 1960s by Leavitt and Bass, as well as himself. At that time much of the emphasis was on the individual and lip service was paid to the organizational sociologists. Business schools adopted the field and called it Organizational Behaviour a term with which Schein has always been uncomfortable, calling OB an 'oxymoron'. The newly formed subject group at MIT was called Organization Studies at that time. Psychology has not paid enough attention to sociologists and anthropologists whose traditions have been to go out into the field and observe a phenomenon at length before trying to understand it. Schein goes on to stress that the field will only progress if we have a set of concepts that are 'anchored in and derive from concrete observations of real behaviour in real organizations'.

Another issue in this area of research is the connection between social needs and empirical research. This link became very apparent in Schein's study of the behaviour of prisoners of war in the Korean conflict. The concepts of psychology at that time were not capable of explaining the observed behaviour there. The phenomenon of 'coercive persuasion' subsequently developed can be used to explain why so many of the programmes of organization development and organizational learning that are launched with great enthusiasm do not seem to succeed.

Perhaps the biggest contribution in the *ASQ* article involves the three cultures of management. In a typical organization the *operators* are the line managers and the workers who make and deliver the products and services that fulfil the organization's basic needs. The *engineers* involve the core technology that underlines what the organization does. This group includes the technocrats and core designers in any functional group. Finally, there are the *executives* who share a common set of assumptions based on the daily realities of their status and role. The essence of this role is accountability to the owner-shareholders which usually involves share prices and financial results. Organization studies will not be mature until we begin to study, observe and absorb these three cultures.

PAT JOYNT
HENLEY MANAGEMENT COLLEGE
NORWEGIAN SCHOOL OF MANAGEMENT

Further reading

(References cited in the text marked *)

Schein, E.H. (1985) *Organizational Psychology*, USA: Prentice Hall. (Schein in many respects founded the Organizational Psychology School.)

* Schein, E.H. (1987) *The Clinical Perspective in Fieldwork*, Newbury Park, CA: Sage. (A must for all who are interested in field research.)

Schein, E.H. (1996) *Career Anchors: Discovering Your Real Values*, USA: Pfeiffer and Company. (A classic from the 1970s that is still applicable today.)

* Schein, E.H. (1996) 'Culture: The Missing Concept in Organization Sciences', *Administrative Science Quarterly* 41. (Perhaps the best available summary of the concept and process of culture.)

* Schein, E.H. (1997) *Organizational Culture and Leadership* San Francisco: Jossey-Bass. (An easy to understand summary of one of the most difficult concepts in our time.)

* Schein, E.H. (1998) *Process Consultation* (3rd edition) Addison Wesley. (Explains the three types of consultancy and then expands on the concept of process consultation which has been reviewed earlier in this piece.)

See also: ARGYRIS, C.; MCGREGOR, D; SCHON, D.

Related topics in the IEBM: CULTURE; HUMAN RELATIONS; HUMAN RESOURCE MANAGEMENT; MANAGERIAL BEHAVIOUR; OCCUPATIONAL PSYCHOLOGY; ORGANIZATION BEHAVIOUR; ORGANIZATION BEHAVIOUR, HISTORY OF; ORGANIZATION CULTURE; ORGANIZATION DEVELOPMENT; ORGANIZATIONAL LEARNING; ORGANIZING, PROCESS OF

Schmalenbach, Eugen (1873–1955)

Personal background

- born Halver, Germany, in 1873
- left secondary school prematurely in 1890 to work in his father's manufacturing business
- entered business school in Leipzig, 1898
- married Mariane Sachs, 1901
- appointed professor at Cologne Business School, 1906
- Schmalenbach Association formed, 1932, on the initiative of W. Minz
- retired from teaching in an attempt to escape Nazi harassment, 1933
- took refuge at the home of a former assistant following pressure from the Office for Racial Politics, 1944–45
- died 1955 at the age of 81

Major works

Finanzierungen (Financing) (1915)
'Selbstkostenrechnung' ('Cost calculation') (1919)
Goldmarkbilanz (Goldmark balances) (1922)
'Grundlagen dynamischer Bilanzlehre' ('Foundations of dynamic balance theory') (1919)
Der Kontenrahmen (Charts of Accounts) (1927)
Kapital, Kredit und Zins (Capital, Credit and Interest) (1933)
Über die Dienststellengliederung im Grossbetrieb (On the Division of Departments in Big Business) (1941)
Über die exakte Wirtschaftslenkung (On the Precise Management of the Economy) (1943)
Über pretiale Wirtschaftslenkung (On Decentralized Economic Management) (1947, 1948)

Summary

Eugen Schmalenbach was one of the most influential figures in the world of business economics and accountancy. Between the end of the nineteenth century and the middle of the twentieth he wrote more than twenty books and over two hundred articles. His memory is perpetuated in Germany by a powerful association named after him and a book of more than 400 pages devoted entirely to him, providing an irreplaceable source of information, co-authored in 1984 by Max Kruk, Eric Potthoff and Günter Sieben. The objective of this article is to trace a broad outline of his life and work.

Restricting itself to what appears to be the essential part of his scientific contribution, this entry will show that Schmalenbach promoted a theory of the evolution of capitalism, as well as writing a cost and price theory, advocating a particular method of general business organization, defending a balance sheet theory and designing a framework for a chart of accounts. All of this work is seen to amount to a coherent whole.

1 Biographical data

Eugen Schmalenbach was born in 1873 in Halver, Westphalia. His father owned a small hinge and lock manufacturing business. In 1890, because of the family's financial difficulties, the young Eugen was obliged to terminate his secondary school studies and work in his father's business.

In 1898, Schmalenbach gave up his job suddenly and enrolled in the first German business school, which had just opened in Leipzig. He attended the lectures of the management specialist Richard Lambert and the economist Karl Bücher. Around this time, he met Marianne Sachs, a young Jewish woman whom he was to marry in 1901, against his father's wishes.

Schmalenbach obtained his diploma and worked for a while as a journalist on the *Deutsche Metall Industrie Zeitung*, which gave him the opportunity in 1899 to publish his first essay on cost accounting. In 1901, he was taken on as an assistant to Bücher in Leipzig, and then, in 1903, appointed *Privat Dozent* at the Cologne Business School. His teaching abilities and extra-university activities were such that, in 1906, to ensure that his services were kept, it was decided to accord him the title of Professor. The fact that he did not even have a doctorate was counter to German university tradition and made this an extremely rare occurrence.

Besides his teaching job, Schmalenbach managed at the same time to work in a number of other areas. In 1906, for example, he founded the *Zeitschrift für handelswissenschaftliche Forschung* (ZfhF). This review became one of the three biggest publications on the new German discipline of business economics (first called *Privatwirtschaftslehre* and then *Betriebswirtschaftslehre*), which combines thinking on management and economics as an academic discipline at universities. (German business schools have not remained isolated from universities but, as in Cologne in 1919, have been integrated into the university system.) Schmalenbach also carried on research, publishing two fundamental articles on the theories of cost and transfer price calculation in 1909. He acted as business consultant to the Tietz company and the Reichsbahn, among others, was chair of the supervisory board of the audit company Treuhand A.G. (founded in 1909) and founded a small hardware company in 1913. Until 1926, he sat on the executive committee of the new Deutsche Demokratische Partei, where he mixed intimately with such figures as J. Hirsch, C.F. Siemens, W. Rathenau and M. Weber.

The opposition of Schmalenbach's ideas to those of the other great German representatives of business economics, like J.F. Schär, H. Nicklisch and F. Schmidt, gave rise to a whole series of publications which created a considerable stir in Germany as well as abroad. Among these were *Finanzierungen* (Financing) in 1915, 'Selbstkostenrechnung' ('Cost Calculation') in 1919, 'Grundlagen dynamischer Bilanzlehre' ('Foundations of dynamic balance theory') in 1919 and *Goldmarkbilanz* (Goldmark balances) in 1922, a book based on Schmalenbach's work at the *Reichswirtschaftsrat* (Economic Council of the Reich). His 1927 publication *Der Kontenrahmen* (Charts of Accounts) described work carried out within the framework of the *Reichskuratorium für Wirtschaftlichkeit* (RKW) (General Committee for Economic Efficiency).

Schmalenbach's university duties did not prevent him from playing a major role in the setting up of the Institute of German Auditors. In 1928, he was at the peak of his career. His works were known throughout continental Europe, with *Der Kontenrahmen* translated into Russian in 1928. He was to become still better known that year with his famous Vienna speech at the annual conference of the Association of German Business Economics Teachers, in which he explained the reasons for the appearance of a new economic order.

Schmalenbach's former assistants and students, who included directors and future directors of very big companies, such as H. Abs and F. Flick, decided in 1932, on the initiative of W. Minz, to form a Schmalenbach Vereinigung (Schmalenbach Association). This was not only to honour the 'old fellow' but also to apply his methods and ideas about work to economic thinking. The association merged in 1978 with the Deutsche Gesellschaft to become the Schmalenbach Gesellschaft.

When the Nazis came to power, Schmalenbach's problems began: in 1933, it was not well thought of to be married to a Jew. The Nazi authorities subjected him to official harassment. In an attempt to avoid this, he asked for and acquired the title of Professor Emeritus, which freed him from his teaching duties. Schmalenbach used his early retirement to work on his book *Kapital, Kredit und Zins* (Capital, Credit and Interest) (1933). He also produced various industrial inventions, such as the 'Tonisator' in 1936, and gave guest lectures in Scandinavia (1937).

In 1938, during *Kristallnacht*, there were attempts to break the windows of Schmalenbach's home. He asked for permission to take advantage of an invitation to go as visiting lecturer to Bern, but this was refused by the Ministry of Culture (1939). Thereafter, although Schmalenbach tried to create a 'normal' professional life – working on his books *Über die Dienststellengliederung im Grossbetrieb* (On the Division of Departments in Big Business) (1941) and *Über die exakte Wirtschaftslenkung* (On the Precise Management of the Economy) – he lived in anguish for the fate of his wife.

When the Rassenpolitische Amt (Office for Racial Politics) enjoined Schmalenbach to move house and share a flat with other *Mischehen* (mixed couples), he envisaged his death (letter to Minz 1943). In September 1944, after further threats from the Gestapo, he decided to flee, and accepted the invitation from L. Feist, a former assistant, to take refuge at his residence. During this period, until October 1945, Schmalenbach and his wife lived in secret, cut off from all news other than what the Feists and various friends, such as Eric Potthoff, brought them.

Schmalenbach continued to write and his book *Über pretiale Wirtschaftslenkung* (On Decentralized Economic Management) was written during his time of refuge, although its two parts were published only in 1947 and 1948. After the Nazis fell, Schmalenbach was bombarded with honours and was even asked to become minister of finance of Nordrhein Westphalia, an offer he refused. In 1950, he wrote his last article, a review of personnel management. He died in 1955 aged eighty-one, having written more than twenty books and over two hundred articles.

2 Main contributions

For Schmalenbach, the development of very large companies and their grouping together as cartels in order to regulate prices was a threat to what he called 'the free economy'. From 1909, he attacked those who viewed the cartels favourably, 'as organizations which

must grow … and allow a new economic period to begin that would apparently no longer be anarchic' (Schmalenbach 1909a: 166):

It is not correct to speak of anarchy as though our production of goods is not regulated. . . our economic organization based on dual competition, that of the producers and that of the consumers, is not without an ordered regulation of economic activity … it is certainly true that we do not have a human sovereign who rules over our companies, but we do have a sovereign principle regulating relations and that sovereign is prices.

(Schmalenbach 1909a: 166)

In 1919, he expressed his thinking a little more precisely, emphasizing, although indirectly, the role of businesses' fixed costs in the economic evolution of capitalism:

It is not surprising that in the sectors where the costs are highly degressive (as a result of the presence of fixed costs), the tendency to form cartels is particularly marked . . . . The impact of cost degression (the raising of unit fixed costs in case of below capacity activity and the resulting losses) can be so great and long-lasting that the companies suffering from it. . . are no longer able to cope with the system of free competition . . . and form cartels. . . in order to regulate production.

(Schmalenbach 1919a: 344)

It was in his famous 'Vienna speech', delivered on 31 May 1928 at the conference of German Business Economics Teachers, that Schmalenbach announced explicitly the appearance of a new economic system, giving his thesis that fixed costs acted as a nerve centre in this evolution. In his opinion, the free economy characteristic of the nineteenth century was being succeeded by a *gebundene Wirtschaft* (bound economy), as predicted by Karl Marx. The basic cause of this evolution was a transfer of production costs:

The proportion of variable costs in the production process is becoming progressively smaller while the proportion of fixed costs is growing ... such that the latter have become the determining factor in the organization of production .... As a large part of the proportional variable costs have become fixed, the economy is losing its capacity to adapt production to consumption. (Schmalenbach 1928: 2435)

According to Schmalenbach's theory, the formation of cartels during times of economic trouble, and the regulation of prices and production, contribute to economic rigidity (which means less competition) and excessive bureaucracy, and may also cause competent managers to be ousted (Schmalenbach 1928: 246). He had 'no sympathy with the features of the new bound economy', but recognized that 'a return to a free economy was not to be expected' (Schmalenbach 1928: 243). However, he considered it possible that business economics could help diagnose 'the ills of the new economy' (Schmalenbach 1928: 250).

Schmalenbach's economic writings would seem to have aimed essentially at suggesting ways of improving the management of the new bound economy. This led Schmalenbach to make contributions to cost and price theories, organization theory, balance sheet theory and the organization of accounting.

Contribution to cost theory

In the opinion of German specialists in cost theory, such as W. Kilger (1973) and G. Dorn (1961), Schmalenbach's essential merit in this field was that he worked very early on a typology of costs, set out the principle of differentiating between costs as a function of use, and contributed to thinking on the problem of the allocation of indirect costs.

Typology of costs
In 1899, Schmalenbach distinguished four overall types of costs: proportional (variable) costs, the overall level of which varies in proportion to the volume of production; fixed costs, which do not vary with production; degressive costs, which increase at a lower rate than the volume of production (because of fixed costs figuring within the overall costs); and progressive costs, which increase at a

higher rate than the volume of production does (Schmalenbach 1899 (15): 115–16).

In 1909, Schmalenbach stated that although fixed costs are independent of the quantity produced and appear as costs linked to the company's structure, this does not mean that they never vary. In 1919, he enlarged on all these points in his article 'Selbstkostenrechnung' ('Cost accounting'), a much broader study of the different cost categories (such as direct, indirect, fixed or variable).

Differentiating costs as a function of use
In 1899, Schmalenbach declared that 'the most important work when introducing cost calculation is having a clear idea of the reason for it' (Schmalenbach 1899 (22): 172). He points out that 'calculating merely the profit is just short of useless in that it does not give the necessary information for decision making, since the costs vary with the variation in production' (Schmalenbach 1899 (13): 99). In 1909, he again stressed: 'I think it cannot be said that the monthly production cost is right and the other costs are wrong. It is only as a function of the objective that it is possible to consider which is the best'. (Schmalenbach 1909b: 174). Schmalenbach's aim, therefore, was to work out which costs were relevant to each kind of decision. In an article published in 1909, he distinguishes 'three essential tasks' for calculating costs: fixing prices, management control and monitoring the result (Schmalenbach 1909a: 58).

On the subject of fixing prices, Schmalenbach put forth two main principles. First, a pricing policy independent of costing is necessary. 'It is the study of the market that is the determining factor. ... Fixing prices has only an indirect link with the calculation of costs' (Schmalenbach 1899 (17): 130-31). Second, it is appropriate to have two types of cost calculation to be able to develop an ideal pricing policy:

One type uses the average production cost as a possible calculation tool to come to a price. The other calculates only variable (proportional) costs. To the extent that the section of the company concerned has not reached its normal capacity (at which stage the costs cease to be fixed), the fixed costs will not be taken into account.

(Schmalenbach 1909a: 61)

Schmalenbach's idea is that during a period of below capacity production, a kind of cost calculation must be used that allows the lower price limit for accepting an order to be determined.

With regard to management control, Schmalenbach stressed in 1909 that 'the company manager must check on whether the costs are fixed or variable' (Schmalenbach 1909a: 46) and that cost control must concentrate on certain key elements for which a very detailed analysis is necessary. To avoid errors in calculation and to facilitate assessment, he suggested that the units produced be costed at variable cost and that fixed costs be treated as periodic costs. He also emphasized the need to compare the performance of companies with one another and to accept approximate data for quick decision making at work. It is chiefly when it comes to calculating the result that Schmalenbach admits that full costing is necessary, although this concerns only the company's overall result, which is subject to legal constraints.

The question of cost allocation

Schmalenbach was against the systematic allocation of all costs. When it proves necessary, he pointed out, the guiding principles of the allocation (which is 'decisive') must 'first of all be sought in a more precise study of how the indirect costs relate to the increase or fall in production' (Schmalenbach 1899 (14): 107). He explained the allocation of indirect costs as follows:

> The procedure whereby the (primary) direct costs are used as the basis for allocating all the (secondary) indirect costs ... is a simple way of calculating, but leads ... to an incorrect result ... there are (indirect) overheads which increase with weight, like materials, transport, others that increase with time, such as interest, machine maintenance, and yet others that do so with price, like reserves for bad debts. Lastly, some general production costs increase with the number of units (piece wages),

others with the length of time worked, such as time wages, and yet others with the period – day, week, year.

(Schmalenbach 1899 (19): 148)

Schmalenbach states as a principle that each of the indirect costs 'must be allocated with its own particular basis for allocation' (Schmalenbach 1899 (19): 148). Therefore, the 'bases may, as a function of the category of indirect costs, be very different' (Schmalenbach 1909a: 47).

Contribution to price theory

The guiding principles of Schmalenbach's ideas on how companies should fix prices were strongly influenced by the economic context of the time, which was marked by economic depression and the rising power of enormous groups and cartels. His central thesis was that at times of economic trouble, 'the regulation of prices linked to the formation of cartels is extremely unfavourable from a macroeconomic point of view' (Schmalenbach 1919a: 344). He argued that if all companies base their calculations on the average full cost formula, the effect of degressive and progressive costs will not be accounted for. Where this occurs, the economy loses its rudder, and the slump is therefore prolonged.

Schmalenbach thought that 'the completely free economy is based on the variable proportional cost rule' (Schmalenbach 1919a: 345), and suggested that companies systematically base their invoicing on the variable unit cost instead. Assessment based on variable costs was indicated as necessary, in 1899, and the principle concerning transfer prices was already partially formulated in 1909. However, it was not until 1919 that Schmalenbach outlined the principle clearly: 'It is not the average production cost but the variable proportional cost that must determine the calculation of prices' (Schmalenbach 1919a: 342). Schmalenbach was thus opposed to the full normal cost thesis advocated by some writers as the basis for calculating prices.

In short, for Schmalenbach, when a company is working at below its production capacity, it must take the variable cost of the last unit produced as the basis for calculating its minimum price, and when it is experiencing overcapacity problems, it must fix the price of the (additional) manufactured unit by 'adding to the purchase price the profit of the most profitable order sacrificed' (Schmalenbach 1919a: 279).

As Schmalenbach recognized, the variable cost per unit, which becomes a sacrificed utility when there is a bottleneck (overcapacity production), 'is similar to the marginal utility of the Austrian school' (including economists such as Böhm-Bawerk and Menger). This admission does not alter the fact that, very early on, Schmalenbach was able to show that an accounting system based on variable costs contained possibilities for solving problems encountered in optimizing production. For some German specialists, his reasoning approached that of modern mathematical models for decision-making theory, and he is considered to be the 'founder of direct costing' (Kilger 1973: 537).

Ideas about the general organization of companies

As his work with the Tietz company in 1907 shows, Schmalenbach was already interested in the organization of large-scale firms before the First World War. His basic idea was to avoid the potential bureaucratization of these companies by decentralizing their organizations and making the directors accountable. To this end, he suggested three measures:

1 split the company as much as possible into sub-companies;
2 introduce a system of transfer prices between the sub-companies so that the general interest of the firm may be ensured to the maximum;
3 consider managers as entrepreneurs and pay them according to two types of percentage, percentages based on overall profits and management percentages related to the result of the department concerned.

Regarding the second measure, Schmalenbach began, in an article published in 1909, to study systematically the advantages and disadvantages of four types of transfer price: the full cost of production, the normal cost of production (expected cost of production over an average period of time), the market price and the proportional variable cost. After rejecting the market price, 'which would not allow some of the advantages of the combination of companies to be realized', he showed that when a company is working below its production capacity, a variable cost system – as opposed to a real or standardized full cost system – should be used (Schmalenbach 1909b: 181).

In 1919, Schmalenbach specified that in the case of a bottleneck and constraint in supplies, a transfer price based on the concept of the sacrificed utility should be used. According to the German literature, and in particular W. Kilger: 'Schmalenbach's conception of cost assessment oriented towards decision making has been vividly borne out by operational research, in particular linear programming models' (Kilger 1973: 535).

Contribution to financial accounting theory

In 1908, Schmalenbach published an article in his review entitled 'Depreciation' in which he outlined diagrammatically his conception of accountancy. In 1919, also in his review, he devoted about a hundred pages to the bases of balance sheet theory from a dynamic point of view. This was published afterwards as a book, and was to make him famous.

Schmalenbach admitted that there may be several types of balance sheet and result as a function of different aims, but the only balance sheet that interested him, given his concern to develop a business mind, was the one that measures the result from an economic point of view. The profit given by the balance sheet 'must be a measure of the economic efficiency of the company' (Schmalenbach 1919b: 3). In so far as the objective of the balance sheet is to contribute to measuring (as accurately as possible) the flow of expenditure and revenue – that is, the movements that generate the result – Schmalenbach's 'dynamic' conception of the balance sheet was counter to those prevailing at the time.

In 1908, he showed that the dynamic balance sheet could not be a statement of property used to measure the company owner's wealth. As he made clear in 1919, he was opposed to V. Simon, who 'considered assets above all from the point of view of their utility value with respect to their future use' (Schmalenbach 1919b: 24). The 'dynamic balance sheet', he said, cannot be a legal or fiscal one, used to determine the distributable or taxable profit: 'What the law wants is not our concern' (Schmalenbach 1919b: 4).

'Dynamic balance sheets' of the kind prepared by practitioners of his era tended to under-assess by smoothing out the distributable result with the help of secret reserves. Schmalenbach condemned this practice, arguing that it distorted the movement of capital. As 'it is also a question of public interest that the result, the measure of efficiency, not be falsely evaluated' (Schmalenbach 1919b: 5), he thought that his dynamic balance sheet met the needs of the company's internal management as well as outside communication requirements.

In an attempt to define the dynamic balance sheet, Schmalenbach presented it as 'the bridge between expenditure and expenses on the one hand, and receipts and revenues on the other' (Schmalenbach 1919b: 16). To clarify what he meant, he drew up a table of the assets and liabilities components (see Table 1).

As many writers have pointed out, it is difficult to match the definition of the balance sheet given by Schmalenbach (the famous 'bridge') with all the items in the balance sheet presented above. In particular, Schmalenbach himself recognized that the cash entry under assets is a 'distinctive feature'. He experienced the same difficulties with the capital entry that he separated off in the liabilities side in the following editions of his book. In another work, however (Schmalenbach 1933), he contributed in an interesting way to the definition of capital in the macroeconomic sense. Schmalenbach thus failed to give a homogeneous definition of the concept of assets.

Nevertheless, Schmalenbach's merit is indisputable. By abandoning the principle of conservatism and reevaluating the assets on the basis of a general price index, he strengthened the school of thought that considered that the calculation of a result reflecting efficiency included putting items without patrimonial value in the assets column. Through this achievement, he kindled a fruitful debate in Germany and in German-speaking countries between the three different schools of thought on balance sheet theory: the dynamic theory, the static theory and the organic theory. The static theory, represented principally by H.V. Simon (1886), was against putting items without patrimonial value in the

Table 1 Components of the dynamic balance sheet

Assets		Liabilities	
1	Expenditure for the accounting period – future expenses	1	Expenses for the accounting period – future expenditure
2	Revenues for the accounting period – future receipts	2	Receipts for the accounting period – future revenues
3	Expenditure for the accounting period – future receipts	3	Receipts for the accounting period – future expenditure
4	Revenues for the accounting period – future expenses	4	Expenses for the accounting period – future revenues
5	Cash		

Source: Schmalenbach (1919b: 23)

balance sheet and the organic theory favoured replacement cost accounting, as represented by F. Schmidt (1921). The debate was extremely lively during Schmalenbach's time, judging from the famous confrontation between Schmalenbach and W. Rieger (1936), for example, and is still alive in the 1990s.

Schmalenbach's chart of accounts

In 1927, Schmalenbach published in his review a model for an accounting chart framework. It was to have a great influence on standards setting and the organization of accountancy in continental Europe. The model rested on two basic ideas, which were to 'sell' the notion of cost accounting and to create a databank as an aid to decision making.

Schmalenbach wanted to force industrial leaders to use cost accounting. Whereas there was an increasing tendency to dissociate financial and managerial accounting, he suggested a model for a chart of accounts based on two principles likely to encourage cost accounting:

(1) The principle of a systematic linking of managerial and financial accounting (single circuit accounting chart model). This principle is counter to that of dissociating the two kinds of accounting which characterizes some other German charts: Schmalenbach was an adherent of monism in accountancy.

(2) The principle of ordering the classes in the chart of accounts according to the circuit of goods in the company (schematically supplies, production, sale). This circuit principle is counter to the balance sheet principle (or condensed statement principle), according to which the structure of the classes in the chart of accounts follows as closely as possible the structure of the balance sheet and the profit and loss account (and gives priority to financial accounting).

Schmalenbach wanted to create a databank as an aid to decision making. Although it was only in 1948 that he formally set out the principle of keeping a 'neutral' information system (rich enough to give the different users the possibility of choosing the type of information they need), his 1927 chart of accounts appears to be a prototype of his future idea. It allowed for information on costs by degree of variability, by nature, function, section of the company and product, as well as differentiating between the costs for financial and managerial accounting.

3 Evaluation

Schmalenbach has always provoked lively interest. Nearly forty years after his death, his work is still the subject of keen debate. Kruk *et al.* (1984) are of the opinion that Schmalenbach belonged to the practical, normative school of business economics. Schneider (1987), on the other hand, considers that, from 1919, he adopted an ethical and normative stance, apparently evidenced in particular by this sentence drawn from the first edition of 'Selbstkostenrechnung' ('Cost calculation'): 'It is the effectiveness of a common, not a private, point of view that directs our work' (Schmalenbach 1919a: 258). Schneider deduces from this that the work carried out on this ethical basis could only end in a stalemate. The dynamic balance sheet apparently 'fell flat' and the theory that makes variable costs a basis for fixing prices would appear to be false (Schneider 1987).

The private/communal distinction does not mean that Schmalenbach defended the theses of a self-managing (*a fortiori* communist) economy by giving priority to the communal point of view. When he gave precepts, it was with the very concrete aim of helping capitalists in general not to make mistakes: he sought simply to find an information system that would enable every capitalist to make rational decisions. This would lead, in his opinion, to an overall optimum level of efficiency. For Schmalenbach, being on the communal side of the dichotomy meant rational management within the framework of capitalism.

Schmalenbach's precepts are therefore not the result of some metaphysical morality but of his thinking on the shortcomings of capitalism, and the 'bound economy' in particular. The fact that he was not interested in the legal or fiscal balance sheet cannot be interpreted, as it is by Schneider (1987), as a sign of a lack of realism. Schmalenbach may have had some very pragmatic reasons for advising capitalists to have a dynamic approach to accounting in order to avoid making wrong decisions. Moreover, such is the renown of Schmalenbach's works today that it could not be explained if it were not deeply anchored in the realities of the modern world.

In German-speaking countries, the dynamic balance sheet theory is still used as an introduction to works on balance sheet theory, and one could well consider that this viewpoint will grow as intangibles arise among the assets of the balance sheet. Schmalenbach's chart of accounts is an indispensable aid to understanding standardization in Europe, and it is likely that his 'monistic' theses have gained in strength with the development of data-processing and data banks. His strength is that he put forward a coherent approach in many fields (such as balance sheet and cost theory, and chart of accounts), and trained a generation who pay him tribute and perpetuate his work through a powerful organization which plays an essential role in the theory and practice of German business economics, the Schmalenbach Gesellschaft. Schmalenbach's work has also aroused interest in non-German-speaking countries, as can be seen in the fact that his *Foundations of Dynamic Balance Theory* has been translated into Japanese (1950), Spanish (1953), English (1959) and French (1961), and a book has been written about him in English (Forrester 1977).

JACQUES RICHARD
UNIVERSITÉ PARIS DAUPHINE

Further reading

(References cited in the text marked *)

Dorn, G. (1961) *Die Entwicklung der industriellen Kostenrechnung in Deutschland*, Berlin: Duncker und Humblot.
* Forrester, D.A.R. (1977) *Schmalenbach and After*, Glasgow: Strathclyde Convergencies.
* Kilger, W. (1973) 'Schmalenbachs Beitrag zur Kostenlehre', *Zeitschrift für handelswissenschaftliche Forschung*: 522–40.
* Kruk, M., Potthoff, E. and Sieben, G. (1984) *Eugen Schmalenbach: Der Mann–Sein Werk–Die*

Wirkung, Stuttgart: Fachverlag für Wirtschafts und steuerrecht Schäfer.
Moxter, A. (1984) *Bilanzlehre Band 1 Einführung in die Bilanztheorie*, Wiesbaden: Gabler.
Oberbrinkmann, F. (1990) *Statische und dynamische Interpretation der Handelsbilanz*, Düsseldorf: IDW-Verlag.
* Rieger, W. (1936) *Schmalenbachs Dynamische Bilanz*, Stuttgart and Cologne: W. Kohlhammer.
* Schmalenbach, E. (1899) 'Buchführung und Kalkulation im Fabrikgeschäft', *Deutsche Metall Industrie Zeitung* (nos 13–22).
* Schmalenbach, E. (1908) 'Die Abschreibung', *Zeitschrift für handelswissenschaftliche Forschung*: 81–8.
* Schmalenbach, E. (1909a) 'Theorie der Produktionkostenermittlung', *Zeitschrift für handelswissenschaftliche Forschung*: 41–65.
* Schmalenbach, E. (1909b) 'Über Verrechnungspreise', *Zeitschrift für handelswissenschaftliche Forschung*: 165–85.
* Schmalenbach, E. (1915) *Finanzierungen* (Financing), Leipzig: G.A. Gloeckner.
* Schmalenbach, E. (1919a) 'Selbstkostenrechnung' ('cost calculation'), *Zeitschrift für handelswissen schaftliche Forschung*: 257–99, 321–56.
* Schmalenbach, E. (1919b) 'Grundlagen dynamischer Bilanzlehre' ('Foundations of dynamic balance theory'), *Zeitschrift für handelswissenschaftliche Forschung*: 1–60, 65–101. (Published as a book entitled *Dynamische Bilanz*; 13th edn 1962, Köln und Opladen.)
* Schmalenbach, E. (1922) *Goldmarkbilanz* (Goldmark Balances), Leipzig: Julius Springer.
* Schmalenbach, E. (1927) *Der Kontenrahmen* (Charts of Accounts), Leipzig: G.A. Gloeckner. (Translated into Russian and Japanese, this book grew out of work performed within the framework of the *Reichskuratorium für Wirtschaftlichkeit* (RKW). It first appeared as a series of articles in *Zeitschrift für handelswissenschaftliche Forschung*.)
* Schmalenbach, E. (1928) 'Die Betriebswirtschaftslehre an der Schwelle der neuen Wirtschatsverfassung', *Zeitschrift für handelswissenschaftliche Forschung*: 241–51.
* Schmalenbach, E. (1933) *Kapital, Kredit und Zins* (Capital, Credit and Interest), Leipzig: Köln und Opladen.
* Schmalenbach, E. (1941) *Über die Dienststellengliederung im Grossbetrieb* (On the Division of Departments in Big Business), Leipzig: Köln und Opladen.
* Schmalenbach, E. (1943) *Über die exakte Wirtschaftslenkung* (On the Precise Manage-

ment of the Economy), unpublished manuscript.

* Schmalenbach, E. (1947, 1948) *Über pretiale Wirtschaftslenkung* (On Decentralized Economic Management), Bremen: Horn.

Schmalenbach, E. (1949) *Der freien Wirtschaft zum Gedächtnis*, Leipzig: Köln und Opladen.

* Schmalenbach, E. (1963) *Kosten und Preispolitik* (Costs and the Politics of Price), Leipzig: Köln und Opladen. (Prepared with the participation of R. Bauer, this book contains Schmalenbach's 1919 work 'Selbstkostenrechnung' (Cost Calculation), which first appeared in *Zeitschrift für handelswissenschlaftliche Forschung*.)

* Schmalenbach, E. (1966) *Die Beteiligungsfinanzierung*, Leipzig: G.A. Gloeckner. (Ninth edition of *Finanzierungen*, prepared by R. Bauer.)

* Schmidt, F. (1921) *Die organische Bilanz im Rahmen der Wirtschaft*, Leipzig: G.A. Gloeckner. (Re-edited by Th. Gabler Verlag in 1979.)

* Schneider, D. (1987) *Allgemeine Betriebswirtschaftslehre*, 3rd edn, Munich and Vienna: R. Oldenbourg.

* Simon, H.V. (1899) *Die Bilanzen der Aktiengesellschaften und der Kommanditgesellschaften auf Aktien*, 3rd edn, Berlin: Guttentag, Verlagsbuchhandlung.

See also: LIMPERG, T.; PACIOLI, L.; PATON, W.A.

Related topics in the IEBM: ACCOUNTING IN FRANCE; ACCOUNTING IN GERMANY; ASSET VALUATION, DEPRECIATION AND PROVISIONS; BUDGETARY CONTROL; COSTING; COST–VOLUME–PROFIT RELATIONSHIPS; TRANSFER PRICING

Schon, Donald (1930–97)

Personal background

- born 30 September 1930
- BA Yale University; graduate study at the Sorbonne; MA and PhD at Harvard University
- married sculptor Nancy Quint, 1952
- taught philosophy at University of Kansas, 1953–7
- joined Arthur D. Little in Boston, 1957
- director of Office of Technical Services, US Department of Commerce, 1973
- president, Organization for Social and Technical Innovation
- professor in the Department of Urban Studies and Planning, Massachusetts Institute of Technology
- died 13 September 1997

Major works

Beyond the Stable State (1971)
Theory in Practice: Increasing Professional Efficiency (with C. Argyris) (1974)
Organizational Learning: A Theory of Action Perspective (with C. Argyris) (1978)
The Reflective Practitioner (1983)
Educating the Reflective Practitioner (1987)

Summary

Often spoken of in the same breath as Chris Argyris, with whom he collaborated for over twenty years, Donald Schon was an original and important thinker in his own right. Philosopher to Argyris' psychologist, Schon's work reflected a deep thinking about the nature of organizations, individuals and creativity and contributed strongly to the theory and practice of action science. It also reflected a strong belief that existing scientific paradigms are inadequate for the explanation of what happens in business and organizations, and indeed in all of society.

1 Introduction

Much of Schon's work focused on organizational learning, particularly how learning is embedded in organizations. As an example, he described two kinds of error: undesigned error and designed error. Undesigned errors represent the common definition of the term 'error' and can be eliminated through training. Designed errors, on the other hand, have their origin in the defensive routines of organizations, which themselves often originate in the senses of threat or embarrassment felt by individuals. Organizations learn when their members jointly form a *polis* and share a task system and when their experience of that system is subject to evaluation; however, if the system contains designed errors, then organizations may be said to mislearn. Among the lessons that organizations therefore need to learn are the consequences of being organized in a particular way and of bypassing threats in order to ensure their own stability and comfort.

'Action science' is Schon's response to this problem. Action science, which includes concepts such as double-loop feedback, offers organizations the chance to learn by doing and to use feedback to correct mistakes as they are being made. Action science should be distinguished from normal scientific procedure which, in the view of Schon and Argyris (see ARGYRIS, C.), deals only with undesigned errors and offers no response to the problem of designed errors.

2 Biographical data

Donald Schon trained as a philosopher and lectured in the field for several years, at UCLA and then at the University of Kansas, before changing directions and moving into business. Joining the international consulting and information company Arthur D. Little in Boston, Schon founded the New Product Group in the firm's research and development division. From there, like many other leading management thinkers in the USA, he went to Washington. In 1973 he was appointed Director of the Office of Technical Services in the Department of Commerce. Finally he returned to academia, joining the Department of Urban Studies and Planning at the Massachusetts Institute of Technology (MIT).

He began distilling his experience and thinking into book form in the 1970s. *Beyond the Stable State*, published in 1971, won immediate attention around the world. His first joint work with Argyris, *Theory in Practice: Increasing Professional Efficiency*, was published in 1974; and their best-known work, *Organizational Learning: A Theory of Action Perspective*, appeared in 1978. Schon continued to work on his own as well, and *The Reflective Practitioner* (1983) has become a classic in its field.

3 Main contribution

Donald Schon was one of the creators of the theory known as action science, as distinguished from 'normal science'. The latter term, first coined by the philosopher of science T.S. Kuhn, refers to the rigorous types of laboratory or natural experimentation commonly used by organization behaviour researchers seeking to emulate the methodology of physics as the ideal of 'science'. Normal science takes the stance of a spectator and manipulator of the variables being studied; the investigator is concerned not to influence the subjects (managers) being studied and for that reason creates distance between the knowers and the known, along with an atmosphere of neutrality and detachment.

In contrast, the 'action scientist' sits beside managers and co-researches the problem with them. While normal science is concerned with discovery, action science aims to investigate the whole cycle of DIPE (discovery, invention, production and evaluation). While there is a gap between the discoveries of normal science and their adoption for practical use, action science follows the process through to its conclusion. Thus, action science might discover different performance standards among employees, invent a setting where this evaluation can be communicated and discussed, produce appraisals and then evaluate the effects of these on overall performance, all as part of a continuous process.

The problem with normal science is that based on what is known as 'Model I' behaviour. This model assumes that we must manipulate the physical and social world into compliance with our personal wishes. Human beings typically seek to control their relationships in order to attain those goals which they intended in the first place. We gain this control by wresting it from others and by winning conflicts. It is through Model I behaviour that many designed errors are introduced; individuals, fearing censure or embarrassment, create new routines which will excuse their behaviour, and these routines then become embedded in the company.

Schon, however, believed that most learning is – or should be – based on 'Model II' behaviour, in which relationships are managed through inquiry rather than through conflict. In *The Reflective Practitioner* (1983), Schon describes how learning involves reflection on prior action, while 'technical rationality' involves knowing before one acts what the consequences are likely to be. Learning and understanding thus become a virtuous circle. Model II behaviour also involves the introduction of double-loop learning: in Model I behaviour, employees would be criticized for failing to meet standards, while in Model II behaviour the manager would enquire as to why the employees had failed and what could be done to ensure improvement, perhaps by altering the standards by which performance is measured. Are the present standards used adequate indicators of employee potential? Do employees feel dedicated to reaching those standards, and if not, what standards would elicit such a commitment? The process becomes one not of saving face, and thus risking designed error, but of determining what is right.

Schon was quick to point out that learning Model II behaviour is not easy. Managers will, for example, subconsciously try to use employee participation as a means to making employees do what they the managers wished them to do in the first place. Action science has a role to play in helping managers and organizations learn new ways of interacting. Normal science confines itself to identifying and understanding the gap between goals and performance; action science intervenes in the problem and helps create a solution. By using double-loop feedback and understanding the process of learning and technical rationality, managers can understand not only their employees and themselves but the ways in which the organization functions.

4 Evaluation

Action science is a powerful theory, and Schon's work has many truths and profound insights. However, this philosophy does take a perhaps overly negative stance towards corporate defensive routines. Research of the kind described in action science theory itself creates defensive routines, as the many sneers about researchers being 'shrinks' testifies. Feedback loops do need to be designed to avoid causing offence, upset or embarrassment in employees or workers; failing to understand the need for this kind of sensitivity might itself fall into the category of designed error.

More recently, Schon (1988) commented on the tensions to be found within the design professions. These include tacit versus explicit forms of knowing, uniqueness versus generality, generativity versus cumulativeness and pluralism versus commonality. These dilemmas may well call for a Model II response, but routine problems are likely to call for technical rationality.

5 Conclusions

There is an urgent need for alternative visions of science, and Schon's work along with that of Argyris provides some of the best ideas and answers. Few have gone so far in reconciling the vigour of relevance and in building a bridge between the isolated academic fortresses of the sciences and the humanities.

CHARLES HAMPDEN-TURNER
JUDGE INSTITUTE OF MANAGEMENT STUDIES,
UNIVERSITY OF CAMBRIDGE

Further reading

(References cited in the text marked*)

Argyris, C. (1967) *Integrating the Individual and the Organization*, New York: Wiley. (Analysis of the way in which organizations and practices may be designed to benefit the growth of the individual.)

Argyris, C., Putnam, R. and Smith, D.M. (1986) *Action Science*, San Francisco, CA: Jossey Bass. (Expounds Argyris' theories of action science.)

* Argyris, C. and Schon, D. (1974) *Theory in Practice: Increasing Professional Efficiency*, San Francisco, CA: Jossey Bass. (First joint work with Argyris. Looks at the practical application of organization theory.)

* Argyris, C. and Schon, D. (1978) *Organizational Learning: A Theory of Action Perspective*, Reading, MA: Addison-Wesley. (Early text, offering examples of ways to diagnose and intervene at the organization and individual level.)

* Schon, D. (1971) *Beyond the Stable State*, New York: Random House. (First and best-known major work discussing the impact of change.)

Schon, D. (1979) 'Creative metaphor: a perspective on problem setting in social policy', in A. Ortny (ed.), *Metaphor and Thought*, Cambridge: Cambridge University Press. (A look at social policy research.)

* Schon, D. (1983) *The Reflective Practitioner*, New York: Basic Books. (Describes how learning hinges on understanding prior action.)

Schon, D. (1984) 'Making meaning: an exploration of artistry in psychoanalysis', *The Annual of Psychoanalysis* 14. (Discusses links between creativity and Freudian theory.)

Schon, D. (1987) *Educating the Reflective Practitioner*, San Francisco, CA: Jossey Bass. (Following on from Schon (1983), this book looks at applications for action learning.)

* Schon, D. (1988) 'Designing: rules, types and worlds', *Design Studies* 9 (3). (Article on design theory.)

Schon, D. and Rodwin, L. (eds) (1994) *Rethinking the Development Experience: Essays Provoked by the Work of Albert O. Hirschmann*, Washington, DC: The Brookings Institution. (Reflects Schon's more recent work on social policy and urban planning.)

See also: ARGYRIS, C.; SCHEIN, E.

Related topics in the IEBM: EMPLOYEE DEVELOPMENT; EMPLOYEE RELATIONS, MANAGEMENT OF; GURU CONCEPT; HUMAN RESOURCE MANAGEMENT; HUMAN RESOURCE MANAGEMENT, INTERNATIONAL; MANAGERIAL BEHAVIOUR; ORGANIZATION BEHAVIOUR; ORGANIZATION BEHAVIOUR, HISTORY OF; ORGANIZATION DEVELOPMENT; ORGANIZATIONAL LEARNING; ORGANIZATIONAL PERFORMANCE

Schuler, Randall S. (1945–)

Personal background

- born 29 April 1945 in Michigan, USA
- graduated with his Masters in Industrial Relations and his Ph.D. in Management from Michigan State University
- held faculty positions at Cleveland State University, Penn State University, the Ohio State University, the University of Michigan, the University of Maryland and New York University
- during this time he was also a Faculty Fellow at the US Office of Personnel Management in Washington, DC
- interests include strategic human resource management, global human resource management, organizational behaviour, and management consulting. His current interests focus on defining the human resource implications of critical business issues, and investigating the cultural imperative on human resource practices of multinational firms

Major works

'Linking competitive strategies with human resource management practices', (with Susan Jackson) *The Academy of Management Executive*, No. 2 (1987)

Human Resource Management: Positioning for the 21st Century, 6th edn. (1996)

'Technical and strategic human resource management effectiveness as determinants of firm performance', (with Mark Huselid and Susan Jackson) *Academy of Management Journal*, (1997)

'An integrative framework of strategic international human resource management', (with Peter Dowling and Helen Decieri)

Journal of Management 19 (2) 419–459 (1993)

1 Introduction

Randall Schuler is one of the most prominent American scholars in the area of human resource management. Since 1986 he has been Professor of Human Resource Management at the Stern School of Business, New York University. His main contributions have been in the areas of strategic human resource management; human resource management as a specialism, and international human resource management. He has authored or edited over thirty books including, most notably, *Human Resource Management: Positioning for the 21st Century*, and *Managing Human Resources*, and published over one hundred articles. He is Editor of the *Journal of World Business* and is on the Editorial Boards of some dozen other major journals including the *Academy of Management Review* and *Academy of Management Executive*.

2 Main contributions

Randall Schuler has made a significant contribution in three main areas of human resources: (1) strategic human resource management and its linkage with business strategy, (2) human resource management as a field and profession (3) international human resource management. His most sustained and significant contribution has been in the first of these and so this is where we will start and where also we will place the most emphasis. His work in the other two areas to a large extent flows out of his stance on the first.

Strategic human resource management and the link with business strategy

Schuler has explicated the linkages between HRM and organizational strategy choices in a number of different publications. His most well-known article on this theme was published (jointly with Susan Jackson) in the *Academy of Management Executive* in 1987 and was entitled 'Linking competitive strategies with human resource management practices'. This article is notable in that it makes a persuasive case for shaping HRM practices to fit the requirements of different business strategies. Randall Schuler thus firmly rejects the idea of universal best practice in HRM and opts instead for a best-fit approach. His analysis is built on Michael Porter's conceptual framework. For instance, the fundamental starting point is the idea that a firm's ability to grow or even survive is dependent upon gaining and maintaining some kind of 'competitive advantage'. Moreover, following Porter, it is suggested that there are three main forms of such advantage: innovation, low cost or superior quality.

Schuler's contribution is to show a theoretical linkage (what he terms a 'rationale') between competitive strategy and HRM practices. The basis of this rationale is the idea of focusing on what behaviours are required from employees under different competitive conditions. In other words, the attention is shifted from job specific technical skills and towards the idea of what he terms 'needed role behaviours' (that is, needed under specific circumstances). The rationale for these derives from Schuler's seminal research in the area of role conflict and role ambiguity (Jackson and Schuler 1985). These role behaviours relate to dimensions such as risk taking, creativity, concern for quality, tolerance of ambiguity and so on. Each one ranges across a continuum – for some situations one end of the continuum is more preferable whereas in other situations the opposite end is more appropriate (or some point elsewhere on the continuum).

For example, within a business strategy based on innovation, the role behaviours which are at a premium include a high degree of creativity, long- rather than short-term focus, relatively high levels of cooperative, interdependent behaviour and high tolerance of ambiguity. The implication for people management strategy are that recruitment and

selection may have to target highly skilled individuals, job design would have to be such that employees are given considerable autonomy and discretion, appraisal would be geared to long-term rather than short-term performance. 'Rather than managing people so that they work harder (cost reduction strategy) or smarter (quality strategy) on the same products or services, the innovation strategy requires people to work differently. This then is the necessary ingredient' (Schuler and Jackson 1987: 210).

A quality enhancement strategy requires a different set of needed role behaviours and by extension, a different set of HRM practices. The required behaviours include relatively repetitive and predictable performance, intermediate time focus, a modest concern for output, a high concern for process, low risk taking and a high commitment to the goals of the organization. The package of HRM policies associated with these requirements include the selection of employees comfortable with this profile, communication lines which allow employees to shape the process, wider job roles so that employees can use greater skills, and investment in training so that employees can learn the wider set of skills. Job redesign and compensation policies should underpin these practices.

A cost reduction strategy requires employee behaviour which is marked by focused application, tolerance of repetitive and predictable routines, short term focus, low risk taking and high concern for quantity of output. The HRM practices associated with this set of needs include stretching targets, tight controls, a focus on headcount reduction, low wage levels (possibly entailing relocation of plants to low-wage areas), increased use of contingent workers, and tight work rules.

There are a whole plethora of HRM tools or practices which can be deployed in pursuit of the required role behaviours. These 'practice choices' (Schuler 1987) are set out as a 'menu' as if one were choosing a starter and a main course and so on. In reality they are clusters of choices about pay, planning, staffing, evaluating and appraising, training and developing. As Schuler is at pains to point out, there is no one set of best practices here, rather these choices again should be viewed as constituting a continuum – for example, decisions about pay can be seen to comprise a whole set of choices including whether to offer few perks or many, a standard fixed package or a flexible one, short-term incentives or long-term, whether to focus on internal equity or external and so on. The central point is that different choices stimulate and reinforce different role behaviours.

Which is the best strategy will depend upon market conditions. Thus, if a product or service is relatively undifferentiated, such as overnight parcel delivery services, then a cost reduction strategy may be the way to gain competitive advantage: the HRM policies would then need to follow from that choice. However, if customers are demanding high quality then an emphasis on cost reduction may lead to a loss of market share and a quality enhancement strategy may be required.

This work is often criticized on the grounds that in practice firms often pursue more than one of these competitive strategies. They may pursue high quality and low costs. Schuler is not unaware of this. On the contrary, he explicitly points out examples of firms with these multiple strategies and contends that 'perhaps the top managers job is facilitated by separate business units or functional areas that have different competitive strategies'. And that managing the tensions 'may be the very essence of the top manager's job' (1987: 216).

Moreover, as competitive conditions change, so too there will be a need for an ever-changing employment relationship; employees may face different demands at different times. The key point is that managers need to make choices across the practice menu which reinforce the necessary employee behaviours. Thus, internal fit is just as vital as securing external fit.

Human resource management as a field and as a professional specialism

Schuler has made the case for the critical importance of HRM in corporate positioning for the twenty-first Century (Schuler and Jackson 1996). This case is based in part on

the idea that the new growth industries (such as biotechnology) are knowledge based industries but it is based also on the premise that sustained competitive advantage rests on resources not easily imitated – such as the skill to make better use of people. Using a multiple stakeholder framework, Schuler and Jackson garner evidence from a wide range of studies in order to demonstrate that good human resource management practice can pay in a whole range of ways (:financial bottom line, employee and customer satisfaction, union relations and suppliers. They emphasize that managing human resources effectively is important and is likely to become even more so in future years; that managing human resources effectively means responding to many stakeholders. Additionally, effective human resource management under contemporary conditions demands more than simple technical expertise in compensation management or selection. It requires a systematic and thoughtful approach which integrates sets of policies. Consistency and clarity are emphasized. Systematic management of human resources, Schuler maintains, means fitting HRM practices to the situation of particular companies. In this sense there is no one best way. 'In firms that manage their employees systematically, managers know why they manage their people the way they do: their entire set of HR practices has been explicitly developed to match the needs of their constituencies, their employees and their customers, and the strategies of the business. In this way they all fit each other and fit the qualities of the company' (Schuler and Jackson 1996). There is thus no one best way; some trial and error is inevitable and the practices must fit the changing circumstances. The contrast between this stance and the citation of Huselid's work which is used to emphasize the power of best practice is not however discussed – although it is just possible that a meaningful distinction could be drawn between general policies and specific practices, and that while Huselid addresses the former, Schuler has paid more attention to the latter.

The point is emphasized even more fully in Jackson and Schuler (1995). In that article they construct an integrated framework for understanding HRM in context. This seeks to take into account the external context such as laws and regulations, culture, politics, labour markets and the like as well as internal contextual features such as technology, organization structure, size, life cycle and business strategy. Above all however, the main message of Schuler's writing is that *human resource management matters*. Used wisely, he argues, HRM can transform a lacklustre company into a star performer; used unwisely it can create havoc.

This same upbeat message is echoed in a review of the place of world class HRM departments (Schuler 1994). In this piece Schuler locates the HRM department firmly in the top strategic team – world class organizations will need, he maintains, world class HRM departments. Schuler recognizes the role of line mangers in HRM but at the same time his analysis leads to the conclusion that HRM departments in effective organizations will become more important than ever in the future.

International HRM

Schuler has recently sought to extend his work into the international arena. The starting point is the increasing globalization of business and the need to operate across the world as one vast market while simultaneously being attentive to local conditions. An integrated framework of strategic international human resource management (SIHRM) is offered in Schuler *et al.* (1993). SIHRM is defined as 'human resource management issues, functions and policies and practices that result from the strategic activities of multinational enterprises and that impact the international concerns and goals of those enterprises' (1993:422). Schuler emphasizes the point that while many of the attributes of conventional human resource management are relevant to a study of multinational enterprises there are also some distinctive elements in the latter which call for special study.

The essential aspects of the integrated framework are the identification of the interplay between the key issues, the resulting functions and the required policies in HR

which pertain to SIHRM conditions. The main SIHRM *issues* are identified as inter-unit linkages (control and variety) and internal operations (remaining alert to local sensitivities and ensuring strategic fit). The main SHIRM *functions* revolve around the resources devoted to HRM and the location of these resources. The SIHRM *policies and practices* relate to questions of staffing, appraising, compensating and developing. A series of testable propositions are put forward which hypothesize the likely choices which different MNEs will make when balancing competing imperatives under different conditions.

This work is taken a stage further by Sparrow *et al.* (1994). Drawing upon an international survey by IBM and Towers Perrin they identify emerging trends across a number of country clusters. These include a predicted far greater emphasis on seeking competitive advantage through people and, most notably, in a drive for empowerment, equality, diversity management, flatter organizational structures, customer-based measures of performance and related remuneration, more training and development and greater communication of goals and objectives. In other words, a reaffirmation of the optimistic high commitment version of the HRM model. Thus, while cultural differences were certainly identified the most notable conclusion from this work is the idea that there are certain HRM policies and practices which are expected to travel well in future years. In the words of the authors: 'organisations seeking to have a truly global operation are likely to pursue the above stated key themes in the workplace with human resource practices that have some cross-cultural variation but that can all be fitted under a common policy umbrella' (1994: 296).

3 Evaluation

Schuler is evidently an articulate champion of the idea of the vital importance of HRM. He is most often cited for his work on making a connection between strategy and HRM. This work has been criticized on a number of fronts. The main criticism has been that the hypothesized connections between competitive strategies and HRM practices remain highly speculative and hypothetical. The connections have not been rigorously tested by Schuler though there was a fairly large-scale test of the link between innovation strategy and personnel practices and this did lend support to the hypotheses (Jackson *et al.* 1989). Much of his other work rests on the selective use of high profile cases which illustrate the argument rather than test it. More recent studies have moved towards the use of statistical tests of large data sets. While the links sound plausible it has proved to be very difficult to substantiate the propositions when they are subjected to statistical tests. Contemporary work has shifted to the exploration of the 'bundles' of HRM practices which are so mutually reinforcing that they provide true competitive advantage (Huselid 1995; MacDuffie 1995; Youndt *et al.* 1996). Some of these studies could be interpreted as supportive of Schuler's position, but the diversity of findings, the differences in the compositions of the bundles, the methodological problems associated with single respondent answers to tick-box questionnaires, and the tension between best practice versus best fit (to name just a few of the problems) suggest that the jury is still out.

Exploration of the link between HRM and business strategy was not of course confined to the work of Schuler. A number of other American scholars had sought to map the contours of the 'match' between them. Fombrun *et al.* (1984) published the best known version and this linked HRM with strategy and structure of businesses. Thus single product companies with functional structures were shown to require a different suite of selection, appraisal, rewards and development practices than, for example, companies in multiproduct divisionalized corporations. The added contribution of Schuler was the focus on the intermediate constructs of 'needed role behaviours' and an explicated 'menu' of human resource options: these provide a much needed *theoretical linkage* between HRM practices and business priorities under different strategic options.

There might also be some criticism that the analysis neglects the core–periphery characteristics of so much modern employment. The optimism reflected in the work on strategic HRM in large leading American corporations (and echoed in the international study which reflects on the data from IBM/Towers Perrin) tends to neglect the evidence which points towards the growing insecurity of employment, failure to invest more in training and declining scores on employee attitude surveys. The fact is that in large measure the expected diffusion of best practice in HRM has been notoriously slow to materialize. Some balanced attention to these practices is, hence, also required.

Although it is never made sufficiently explicit, there is a sense that strategy is a rational top-down process. It is implied that business strategy is reached in a rational, planned way and that with access to this strategy, the HR specialist can design a matching HRM strategy by selecting from the practice 'menu'. This view of strategy has been challenged by those who see strategy as an emergent process. It is also surprising perhaps that Schuler takes as a given that HR policies will necessarily be downstream of business strategy. Given the emphasis upon core competencies by the resource based view of the firm there could be scope for an alternative line of analysis which starts with comparative advantage based on competence and works backwards to the choice of markets and hence to the kind of business strategy. This dimension at least deserves some consideration.

Relatedly, it is not made entirely clear whether the analysis running through Schuler's work on strategy is descriptive or prescriptive. There is a sense that leading companies are already pursuing activities of this kind and that the author has educed the essence of these for others to emulate. But the evidence for this is rather thin. Detailed case-study work by Storey (1992) revealed that even in the leading blue-chip corporations where sophisticated HRM policies might have been most expected, there was evidence of the running being made by manufacturing directors and other non-HR players; of lack of integration between policies; of failure to sustain the implementation of new initiatives;

and of a rather insecure place for HRM in the wider corporate agenda – despite an ability of the senior team to recite the HRM rhetoric.

Despite such criticisms, the significance of Schuler's contribution in this area should not be underestimated. Schuler clarifies the linkages set out in more general terms in the model offered by Beer *et al.* (1982). While research has progressed in different directions there has been little evidence of major advances of a theoretical kind beyond that which has been achieved by Schuler. The need to build systematic theory and explanation concerning HRM and business strategy remains. His considerable reputation in this area is well deserved.

JOHN STOREY
THE OPEN UNIVERSITY

Further reading

(References cited in the text marked *)

* Beer, M., Spector, B., Lawrence,. P., Mills, D. and Walton, R. (1985) *Human Resource Management: A General Manager's Perspective.* New York: Free Press.
* Fombrun, C. J., Tichy, N.M., and Devanna, M.A. (1984) *Strategic Human Resource Management.* New York: Wiley.
* Huselid, M.A. (1995) 'The impact of human resource management practices on turnover, productivity and corporate financial performance', *Academy of Management Journal*, 38: 635–70.
* Jackson, S. and Schuler, R. S. (1985) 'A meta-analysis and conceptual critique of research on role ambiguity and role conflict in work settings', *Organizational Behavior and Human Decision Processes*, 36: 16–78.
* Jackson, S. and Schuler, R. S. (1995) 'Understanding human resource management in the context of organisations and their environments', *Annual Review of Psychology*, 46: 237–64.
* Jackson, S., Schuler, R.S., and Carlos Rivero, J. (1989) 'Organizational characteristics as predictors of personnel policies', *Personnel Psychology*, 42: 727–85.
* MacDuffie, J.P. (1995) 'Human resource bundles and manufacturing performance: organisational logic and flexible production systems in the world auto industry', *Industrial & Labor Relations Review*, 48 (2): 197–221
* Schuler, R.S. (1986) 'Fostering and facilitating entrepreneurship in organisations: implications for organisation structure and human resource management practices', *Human Resource Management*, 25: 607–29.
* Schuler, R.S. (1987) 'Human resource management choices and organisational strategy', *Human Resource Planning*, March: 1–19.
* Schuler, R.S. and Jackson, S.E. (1987) 'Linking competitive strategies with human resource management practices', *Academy of Management Executive*, 1 (3): 207–19
* Schuler, R.S.and Jackson, S. (1996) *Human Resource Management: Positioning for the 21st Century*, St Paul: West Publishing Co.
* Storey, J. (1992) *Management of Human Resources: An Analytical Review*, Oxford: Blackwell.

See also: DUNLOP, T.D.; HAMEL, G. AND PRAHALAD, C.K.; KOCHAN, T.; KOTTER, J.; PORTER, M.E.

Related topics in the IEBM: APPRAISAL METHODS; COMPETITIVE STRATEGY, DEVELOPMENT OF; GLOBALIZATION; HUMAN RESOURCE MANAGEMENT; HUMAN RESOURCE MANAGEMENT, INTERNATIONAL; JOB DESIGN; MOTIVATION AND SATISFACTION;ORGANIZATION BEHAVIOUR; PAYMENT SYSTEMS; SHORT-TERMISM; STRATEGY, CONCEPT OF; TRADE UNIONS; TRAINING

Schumacher, Ernst Friedrich (1911–77)

1 Introduction
2 Biographical data
3 Main contribution
4 Evaluation
5 Conclusions

Personal background

- born Bonn, Germany, on 16 August 1911
- moved to the UK in 1930 as a Rhodes Scholar at Oxford
- went to Columbia University, New York, in 1932
- returned to Germany in 1934 and worked in commerce
- married Anna Maria Petersen, 1936 (died 1960)
- returned to the UK, 1937
- married Verena Rosenberger, 1962
- advisor to the National Coal Board, 1950–70
- awarded CBE, 1974
- died on 4 September 1977

Major works

Small is Beautiful, A Study of Economics as if People Mattered (1973)
A Guide for the Perplexed (1977)

Summary

E.F. Schumacher was best known as a vigorous advocate of small-scale economic activities. But he was also a pioneer of modern thinking on environmental issues and the economics of developing countries, the latter coupled with an interest in land issues. Although an economist by training, his contributions to economic thinking did not fit easily into mainstream economics, and his major influence was on thinking outside conventional economics. While much of his writing was influenced by orthodox and unorthodox religious thinking and philosophy (from Eastern religions as well as Christianity), his most influential work challenged the economic and political ideas of his time on their own ground.

1 Introduction

In his most famous work, *Small is Beautiful, A Study of Economics as if People Mattered* (1973), Schumacher offered a sustained argument for small-scale human activities, emphasizing environmental and green issues. He also proposed the introduction of a system of 'intermediate technology' to help the economies of developing countries, and the phrase has since been adopted by many other theorists.

Schumacher's writing is marked by its accessibility, which enabled him to reach a much wider audience than most academics. Indeed, his influence on other academics was limited. Yet, his arguments, particularly in *Small is Beautiful*, were rigorously argued, and challenged the more conventional academic views of his time. However, his other major book, *A Guide for the Perplexed* (1977), is something of an *ad hoc* mixture of religion and philosophy that many academics could dismiss as having little to do with their concerns.

Schumacher's theories and arguments now appear less remarkable, since many have become part of mainstream thinking on green issues, sustainable economics and the virtues of small size. On the other hand, his thinking remains unconventional in one sense because it runs counter to the free-market philosophies that have come to dominate politics in advanced industrial countries such as the UK and the USA, and which have spread to the former command economies of eastern Europe and to some developing countries.

2 Biographical data

The son of a professor of economics, E.F. 'Fritz' Schumacher was born in Bonn, Germany, on 16 August 1911. In 1930, he moved to the UK to take up a Rhodes scholarship at Oxford University, and later went to the USA, where he was first a student and later a lecturer at Columbia University, New York.

Schumacher returned to Germany in 1934 but was unable to settle there. He moved back to the UK in 1937 and to Oxford in 1942. At the end of the Second World War, he became economic advisor to the British Control Commission in Germany. In 1950, he became economic advisor to the National Coal Board, the public corporation established to run the UK's coal industry. From 1963 to 1970, he was director of statistics for the Board. Schumacher had many other interests, including journalism, environmental issues and the economies of developing countries, particularly the rural aspects of such economies. In 1966, he founded the Intermediate Technology Group.

In 1973, Schumacher published *Small is Beautiful, A Study of Economics as if People Mattered*. Although the book (and especially its title) became very widely known, Schumacher never became a major media personality, unlike many other popular thinkers of the day. However, he inspired many who came into contact with him and his ideas have continued to be influential through a number of bodies with which he was associated or which were founded after his death. Among these are the Schumacher Society set up in 1977 in his memory, the Soil Association (of which he was president from 1970), the New Economics Foundation and the Schumacher College in Dartington, Devon, England. Schumacher died in 1977.

3 Main contribution

Virtually all of Schumacher's influential ideas are contained in *Small is Beautiful, A Study of Economics as if People Mattered*. These essays made an important contribution to thinking on organizational structures, environmental and green issues, forms of ownership, epistemology and the development of what were then termed 'Third World' countries.

The phrase 'small is beautiful' refers to Schumacher's strongly argued view that smallness in human affairs is to be preferred, whether in organizations or nation states. However, it was no simple matter to assert that small was always better. Schumacher argued that, given the complexity of human social, political and economic arrangements, there is no single answer to the size question and we may need very different kinds of structures for different purposes. For all human activities, there is an appropriate scale. In Schumacher's time, however, large structures and systems were assumed to be either inevitable or the most efficient means of organizing society. Schumacher questioned these assumptions and claimed that almost all large-sized structures destroy human dignity, democracy, self-realization and standards of living. Where economic arguments were offered, based, for example, on economies of scale, these could also be challenged and shown to be wanting.

On environmental and green issues, Schumacher was an early critic of nuclear energy. He saw it as a health danger and raised the issues of nuclear waste and the decommissioning of nuclear power stations once their productive life was over. Other energy sources, and especially coal, he stressed, should not be treated as simple market commodities to be produced only as long as it was profitable to do so. What was crucial was the long-term supply of energy and the fact that the supply of all fossil fuels is finite, while under existing economic arrangements the demand for energy was increasing rapidly. The solution he proposed was a shift to a locally focused economy based on self-sufficiency and renewable energy sources and materials.

Schumacher's notion of 'intermediate technology' also deserves attention since, again, it has become a much-used phrase. He proposed mixed technologies for any given project in order to achieve maximum local employment for modest inputs of capital. This might involve very sophisticated technology for some elements of production, but only where they were appropriate to the task. The object was not to be economically efficient simply in terms of capital output or labour productivity, but to involve as many local people as possible and to ensure self-sustaining local economic development. While modern knowledge can be applied in a great many ways, the capital-intensive technologies and economies of advanced industrial economies illustrate only a few possible applications.

Schumacher's epistemological arguments were unfashionable in his time but now receive more serious consideration. One example was his adoption of the distinction between *convergent* and *divergent* problems. Convergent problems are constructed problems, set by human beings and solved by logic and science. Once the solution has been written down it can be used by others. Divergent problems, on the other hand, cannot be solved by logic. They are common problems in politics, economics and social relations generally and involve attempts to overcome or reconcile opposites. For example, how can management reconcile the need for control over employees with increasing employee participation? In Schumacher's view, a divergent problem cannot be solved as if it was a convergent problem, although such solutions are attempted all the time.

Schumacher also attacked the epistemological assumptions underlying economic forecasting, particularly in the form of such measures as the five-year plan, which was popular in the economic management of command and developing economies of his time. In Schumacher's view, the fallacy of forecasting was that human freedom was being left out of the argument. Some prediction is possible because human beings often do behave in habitual ways, but some humans do not and their actions result in both unpredictable events and departures from previous patterns. The longer the period covered by the forecast, the greater the extent of such departures. National plans, in particular, presuppose the power to ensure they will be carried out. In a free society, concentration of power in this sense is rare and, even in other kinds of societies, it often fails because of human resistance or evasion. Schumacher's argument was a variant of what

is now called the anti-positivist position, a critique of attempts to explain human-centred activities and actions in terms of natural science models developed in the nineteenth century. Such models are considered inappropriate because they cannot incorporate the human attributes of freedom and purpose.

Schumacher also advocated 'feasibility studies', which differed fundamentally from forecasts or plans. Essentially, they consisted of explorations of the long-term effects of selected assumed tendencies. For instance, it could be assumed that some developing countries would attain living standards similar to those in advanced industrial societies by some year, *y*. A feasibility study might then be undertaken to work backwards from the assumed year in order to estimate the total energy, raw materials and capital required for such development. A study of this nature might well result in insights into what kind of developments were feasible, given assumptions about possible patterns of economic development. Feasibility studies were not forecasts or plans, therefore, but explorations of possible assumed trends.

Other themes in Schumacher's writing included organizations and ownership. He believed strongly in small organizations in which human beings do not feel alienated and in which they can realise their full potential. However, he accepted that large organizations were unavoidable in modern societies. The task, therefore, was to achieve smallness within the large organization. One principle he advocated was that of *subsidiarity*, that is, ensuring that decisions are made at the lowest level consistent with efficiency. Subsidiarity, he argued, enhanced human freedom and dignity and prevented the loss of self-worth that often results when people are involved in large-scale social structures.

Schumacher was a strong advocate of participation and cooperative ownership of enterprises. He was closely associated with the Scott Bader Cooperative, a plastic resin manufacturing company converted into a cooperative by its original owners. This became a much-cited example of a large-scale cooperative in the UK literature on cooperatives.

593

4 Evaluation

Schumacher's ideas – particularly on small-scale enterprise, environmental issues and epistemology – have now become part of wider arguments which have considerable influence. In some instances, the arguments have been amplified into major political and social messages, which have wide appeal in many countries, especially among young people.

Environmental groups have promoted the environmental message that Schumacher was among the first to articulate. In some countries, they have become the basis of new political parties often popularly called 'the Greens'. In other instances, existing political parties have adopted some of the ideas for their voter appeal. Some of Schumacher's other ideas have fared less well, however. For instance, dominant political parties in many advanced industrial societies still advocate the notion that economic growth is desirable as a solution to economic, social and political problems. The acceptance of green ideas of the kind advocated by Schumacher often sits uncomfortably alongside these older political ideas.

The promotion of the small-scale enterprise has become part of the ideologies of mainstream political parties in many countries. However, in this adaptation, the arguments have changed in ways that Schumacher would probably have found unacceptable. Governments in many advanced industrial societies actively support small businesses, but as the basis of a highly individualistic entrepreneurialism rather than as a vehicle for promoting human cooperation and dignity.

The anti-positivist epistemological stance of Schumacher has gained ground in many of the social sciences, although it is doubtful whether his writings have played a major role in bringing about such change. The change in interpretative and qualitative analyses in the social sciences has been particularly strong in sociology, for example. Even in Schumacher's own discipline, economics, there have been challenges to positivism and the associated emphasis on rational models of decision making and behaviour. In business and management studies, too, more attention is being given to qualitative issues, particularly in such areas as organizational behaviour.

Some of Schumacher's ideas have not made much headway. For example, his advocacy of new styles of ownership of economic organizations, particularly cooperatives, has clashed with the rise of economic individualism and the restoration of management power in the 1980s and 1990s.

Of the many books that have influenced business thinking in the twentieth century, a great number offer solutions to what Schumacher called divergent problems, that is, problems for which there are by definition no logical solutions because of their very nature. Schumacher's ideas, particularly in *Small is Beautiful*, are different, since he carefully avoids simple solutions and hence his ideas have greater lasting significance. In several key areas, he was able to pick out themes which later assumed great influence and which, in several instances, are still working themselves out. What Schumacher does share with many other popular management and business writers is a highly accessible writing style that enabled him to reach and influence a wide audience. On the other hand, his writing has not promoted any considerable critique among academics and often is referred to simply in footnotes.

5 Conclusions

Schumacher believed that achieving an appropriate scale in all human activities, and especially in economic affairs, is crucial to human self-realization and dignity. The most appropriate scale, he argued, is usually small. The simple maximization of economic growth cannot produce and, indeed, is inimitable to, human happiness since it cannot deliver what it promises – prosperity and self-realization for all.

On the issue of economic and growth strategies adopted by developing countries, Schumacher argued that most could not achieve their aims since they neglected the rural basis of most of the populations' way of life and employed inappropriate technologies. Likewise, analytical strategies used by many economists and political decision makers were based on false epistemological premises which excluded the key characteristics of human participants.

To counter such problems, Schumacher advocated a return to seeing human beings as ends in themselves and argued for the construction of organizations, political arrangements and communities that ensure human participation and self-worth. If we are to avoid destroying the planet, he said, we must structure the economy in a way that is consistent with concern for the environment and the use of renewable sources of energy.

JAMES CURRAN
KINGSTON UNIVERSITY

Further reading

(References cited in the text marked *)

* Schumacher, E.F. (1973) *Small is Beautiful, A Study of Economics as if People Mattered*, London: Blond and Briggs. (Schumacher's seminal work, in which he sets out his most influential ideas.)
* Schumacher, E.F. (1977) *A Guide for the Perplexed*, London: Jonathan Cape. (Dismissed by many academics, this book brings religious and philosophical ideas into the debates on social, political and economic issues.)
Wood, B. (1984) *Alias Papa: A Life of Fritz Schumacher*, London: Jonathan Cape. (A very readable biography of Schumacher.)

See also: BOUDLING, K.; ETZIONI, A.; FORRESTER, J.W.

Related topics in the IEBM: BUSINESS AND SOCIETY; BUSINESS ETHICS; ECONOMICS OF DEVELOPING COUNTRIES; ENVIRONMENTAL AND RESOURCE ECONOMICS; ENVIRONMENTAL MANAGEMENT; INDUSTRIAL DEMOCRACY; MODELLING AND FORECASTING; ORGANIZATION STRUCTURE; SMALL BUSINESS STRATEGY; TECHNOLOGY AND ORGANIZATIONS

Schumpeter, Joseph (1883–1950)

Personal background

- born in Moravia, in what is now the Czech Republic, on 8 February 1883
- studied law at the University of Vienna
- entered economics as a lecturer at Czernowitz
- married three times, to Gladys Ricarde Seaver (1907), Annie Reisinger (1926) and Elizabeth Broody (1937)
- briefly entered politics in 1919 as the finance minister for the new Austrian Republic
- the majority of his career was spent lecturing in economics at Czernowitz, Graz, Bonn and Harvard
- made numerous contributions to the development of economics, including his famous business cycles theory
- died in his sleep on 8 January 1950

Major works

Wesen und Hauptinhalt der Theoretischen Nationalökonomie (1908)

Theorie der Wirtschaftlichen Entwicklung (1912)

The Theory of Economic Development: An Inquiry into Profits, Capital, Interest, and the Business Cycle (1934)

Business Cycles (1939)

Capitalism, Socialism and Democracy (1942)

Summary

In comparison to his contemporaries, Joseph Schumpeter's work is most distinct. His works, particularly his early works, were characterized by a passionate and optimistic style and he had a vision that permeated every piece he wrote. Multilingual, he had a keen interest in history, politics and society. While a sceptic of aggregates, he recognized the importance of the mathematical component of economics. Moreover, he had the ability to incorporate all facets of his broad knowledge of history, politics and mathematics into his writing.

Schumpeter often proposed economic theories that were rejected by his colleagues, namely Walras and Böhm-Bawerk. This was particularly true for his views on interest rates. For example, he believed that interest rates were institutionally and dynamically determined, a view which was in direct conflict with the views of Böhm-Bawerk, who believed interest rates were independent of institutions. Schumpeter argued that because interest rates were institutionally determined they could be zero in a stationary or centrally planned economy.

Schumpeter also proposed that capitalism would falter and be replaced by socialism, another view that was rejected by his colleagues. While some of his contradictory views appeared unfounded, one was brilliant and is undoubtedly Schumpeter's greatest contribution to the development of economics – his business cycle theory. Schumpeter disagreed with the classical economists and demonstrated that the economy was not in a permanent state of equilibrium but rather experienced periods of disequilibrium. Although the classical economists accepted that significant events such as wars were responsible for pushing the economy out of equilibrium, Schumpeter believed more powerful forces worked in the economy to produce these fluctuations.

1 Biographical data

Joseph Schumpeter was born on 8 February 1883 in the province of Moravia, then part of the Austro-Hungarian Empire and now in the

Czech Republic. He was the only son of Alois Schumpeter, a cloth manufacturer who died when his son was young. His mother remarried a member of the Austro-Hungarian army at Kalksburg in Vienna in 1893. Schumpeter graduated with high honours in 1901 from the Theresianum, where he acquired a taste for foreign languages and learnt to speak Greek and Latin fluently. His time there, coupled with his exposure to French, English and Italian at home, allowed him to speak fluently a diverse range of languages.

In 1901 Schumpeter enrolled at the University of Vienna as a law student. By 1906 he was a doctor of both Roman and Canon Law. The law degree encompassed units in economics and politics. He practised law for a short time, but realized that his passion was economics. In 1907 he married his first wife, Gladys Ricarde Seaver. In 1909 he was made a professor at Czernowitz, the capital of Bukowina, and later in 1911 accepted a position at the University of Graz where he was head of the economics faculty and offered courses in economic democracy and the problems of the social classes which featured heavily in his work.

Schumpeter's first book was published in 1908 and titled *Wesen und Hauptinhalt der Theoretischen Nationalökonomie*. This was followed in 1912 by *Theorie der Wirtschaftlichen Entwicklung*. These initial books played a vital role in establishing Schumpeter as an economic theorist. His first book introduced his theory of interest the second book contained an expansion of this idea. In *Wesen und Hauptinhalt* he outlined that there was no direct relationship between the levels of income and savings. As the level of income rises it does not naturally follow that the levels of savings will also rise.

One of Schumpeter's greatest contributions to economics was his business cycle theory, the early indicators of which were outlined in his third book, *The Theory of Economic Development: An Inquiry into Profits, Capital, Interest, and the Business Cycle* (1934) an expanded version of *Theorie der Wirtschaftlichen Entwicklung*. Schumpeter's initial publications exhibit characteristics evident in all of his work. While rarely utilizing the mathematical component of economics, he embraced it; however, he never underestimated the importance of historical knowledge in economics.

After his appointment at Graz, he entered politics, albeit briefly, being appointed the finance minister in the socialist cabinet for the new Austrian Republic in 1919. His political career was a learning experience as he had great difficulty in counteracting the excess inflation that plagued post-war Europe. He and the socialists had conflicting views on the direction which the Austrian economy should take and he left politics due to the differences which arose between his conservative economic policies and the socialists' radical economic and financial policies.

Following his foray into politics Schumpeter returned to academia where he remained until his death in 1950. During this time he served at both the University of Bonn in Germany and later at Harvard University. In 1926 he produced a paper that critically analysed the work of Schmoller, and held the position of Chair of Public Finance. The year 1926 was however one of great sorrow for Schumpeter as both his new wife, Annie Reisinger, and his mother died. These blows changed him from a lively optimist to a pessimist.

In 1932 he accepted a full-time position at Harvard, initially living with F.W. Taussig, and in 1937 he married his third wife Elizabeth Broody, who was a fellow economist. Schumpeter was one of the founders of the Econometric Society and its president from 1937 to 1941. A great honour was bestowed upon him in 1948 when he became the first foreign-born president of the American Economic Association. During his time at Harvard he had a full teaching load and wrote *Business Cycles* (1939) and *Capitalism Socialism and Democracy* (1942) before dying on 8 January 1950. His monumental *A History of Economic Analysis* was published after his death.

2 Main contribution

When Schumpeter became interested in economics the classical theory of employment dominated economic thought. The classical economists argued that unemployment never existed and that the economy permanently achieved full employment. Their theory promoted pure capitalism and argued that the economy functioned in the absence of government intervention. The classical economists believed that the economy had built-in stabilizers that ensured the economy always returned to equilibrium, and they emphasized that underspending never occurred due to Say's law, which implied that supply created its own demand.

A neo-classical economist who greatly influenced Schumpeter's work was Böhm-Bawerk, who believed that the accumulation of capital was a simple process which involved few fluctuations. Böhm-Bawerk argued that a proportion of household income that had been saved would be invested. This investment would result in the expansion of the capital base, resulting in increased output, employment and national income. He recognized that fluctuations would occur due to inconsistencies in monetary policy, time lags or vagaries of the multiplier; however, appropriate policies would return the economy to equilibrium.

Schumpeter, however, believed that such fluctuations were not of little significance but rather of great importance to the economy. He argued that the economy was not permanently in a state of equilibrium but rather that it experienced significant fluctuations in economic activity. Schumpeter recognized that periods of low economic activity occurred that were characterized by high unemployment, low profit levels, decreases in the consumption of goods, decreases in business confidence and increases in the level of savings. While agreeing that the multiplier and acceleration principles contributed to these economic fluctuations, more powerful forces acted upon the economy including technological and organizational innovations, entrepreneurial activity and the credit mechanism. One can deduce that Schumpeter's understanding of the forces responsible for change in the economy was greater than that of his neo-classical colleagues.

In his work Schumpeter often outlined the importance of economics in shaping a society,

yet his analysis of society is often criticized. Like Karl Marx, he envisaged the destruction of the capitalist economic system. Schumpeter characterized capitalism by three features: the private ownership of the physical means of production; private profits and private responsibility for losses; and the creation of means of payments – bank notes and bank deposits – by private banks. He argued that the first two features suffice to define private enterprise. However, to Schumpeter no concept of capitalism could be satisfactory without including the set of typically capitalistic phenomena covered by the third.

Schumpeter believed that capitalism, despite its inability to achieve a greater equality in the distribution of income, was a very successful economic system and that it was responsible for greatly increasing the quality and quantity of goods and services consumed by society, leading to an increase in standards of living. However, he believed that capitalism would be destroyed because its success would result in a loss of its social structures. Despite being criticized for this belief, it illustrates the emphasis that Schumpeter placed upon the relationship between economics and society.

Schumpeter proposed a theory of interest rates that was in direct conflict with Böhm-Bawerk. He argued that a zero interest rate would exist in a static, semi-stationary or socialist economy. Moreover, to him, the rate of interest was institutionally and dynamically determined. This point conflicted with the view upheld by Böhm-Bawerk, who declared that the rate of interest was a basic economic category, independent of the concrete social and institutional arrangements. Schumpeter's interest theory is often criticized.

3 Conclusions

Joseph Schumpeter was a brilliant economist whose economic principles were revolutionary. While in academia he produced his great works, *The Theory of Economic Development*, *Capitalism, Socialism and Democracy* and *Business Cycles*. In these texts Schumpeter outlined his major contributions to economics, namely his theories on interest, capitalism and business cycles. His business cycle theory contradicted the accepted view that the economy was permanently in a state of equilibrium. Rather he argued that dynamic forces such as technological and organizational innovations, entrepreneurial activity and the credit mechanism are the primary causes of fluctuations in the economy.

JOHN CUNNINGHAM WOOD
UNIVERSITY OF NOTRE DAME AUSTRALIA

Further reading

(References cited in the text marked *)

* Schumpeter, J. (1908) *Wesen und Hauptinhalt der Theoretischen Nationalökonomie*, Munich and Leipzig: Duncker and Humblot. (Contains Schumpeter's theory of interest and argues that there was no direct relationship between the level of income and savings.)
* Schumpeter, J. (1912) *Theorie der Wirtschaftlichen Entwicklung*, Leipzig: Duncker and Humblot. (Expands on his theory of interest rates and argues that as the level of income rises it does not naturally follow that the level of savings will also rise.)
* Schumpeter, J. (1934) *The Theory of Economic Development: An Inquiry into Profits, Capital, Interest, and the Business Cycle* , Cambridge,

MA: Harvard University Press. (English language and revised edition of Schumpeter's 1912 book, containing his business cycle theory and his analysis of how economic growth occurs.)
* Schumpeter, J. (1939) *Business Cycles*, New York: McGraw-Hill. (Expands on his early ideas and highlights the critical role of entrepreneurs in the cyclical nature of economic development.)
* Schumpeter, J. (1942) *Capitalism, Socialism and Democracy*, New York: Harper and Brothers. (Integrates Schumpeter's political philosophy with his views on economics and provides an analysis of trends in capitalist and socialist political states.)
* Schumpeter, J. (1951) *A History of Economic Analysis*, New York: Oxford University Press. (Published after his death, this is an exhaustive survey of the development of economic ideas and analyses.)

See also: KEYNES, J.M.; MARSHALL, A.; MILL, J.S.; SAMUELSON, P.A.

Related topics in the IEBM: BUSINESS CYCLES; EMPLOYMENT AND UNEMPLOYMENT, ECONOMICS OF; ENTREPRENEURSHIP; INDUSTRIAL ECONOMICS; INNOVATION AND CHANGE; MARKETS; MARKET STRUCTURE; MARX, K.H.

Senge, Peter M. (1947–)

Personal background

- BSc in engineering, Stanford University
- Ph.D. in system dynamics from MIT (1978)
- wrote *The Fifth Discipline*, published in 1990
- co-founded the consulting firm Innovation Associates (1992)
- currently Director of the Systems Thinking and Organizational Learning Program at the Sloan School of Management, MIT

Major works

The Fifth Discipline: The Art and Practice of the Learning Organization (1990)

The Fifth Discipline Fieldbook: Strategies and Tools for Building a Learning Organization (with Charlotte Roberts, Richard Ross, Bryan Smith and Art Kleiner) (1994)

Summary

Peter Senge (1947–) became one of the most widely read and discussed management thinkers of the 1990s. His major work, *The Fifth Discipline*, articulated the concepts of systems thinking and the learning organization, terms which are now part of the standard management vocabulary. Systems thinking, 'the fifth discipline' of the title (the others are personal mastery, shared vision, team learning and mental models) can help organizations to view themselves as totalities and understand the interconnected natures of organizations themselves and their relationship with their environment. Senge's view of management is highly humanistic, and he contrasts his 'learning organization' which enables and grows people, with 'controlling organizations' which confine and limit them.

1 Introduction

Senge's background is in engineering, and he studied system dynamics at Massachusetts Institute of Technology where he was strongly influenced by the pioneer of that field, Jay Forrester. However, the experience of working with large companies on research programmes at MIT convinced him that the crucial systems in organizations were mental, not physical. Senge was also strongly influenced by studies carried out at Royal Dutch/Shell, which concluded that continuous learning was possibly a company's only sustainable form of competitive advantage (de Geus 1988). These two influences come together in *The Fifth Discipline*, Senge's major work which is now almost automatically identified with his name.

Senge has a strong philosophy of management which reaches out to encompass many disciplines besides organizations studies. Unlike other management gurus, he seeks not so much to revolutionize the organization as to revolutionize the thinking that goes into the organization. It is almost impossible to overemphasize the importance and value of thinking and learning in this philosophy. In *The Fifth Discipline*, Senge calls for a complete shift not only in thought but in approaches to thought. Principal to this change is the view that people and organizations must be proactive rather than reactive, and seek to create their own reality rather than waiting for events to happen. To do this, they need certain skills, the five disciplines, of which systems thinking is foremost.

Senge's approach is very humanist and human-centred. He sees the organization as having a responsibility to awaken and draw upon the human potential of its members. Only by harnessing the learning and thinking potential of everyone in the organization, from top to bottom, and combining all of this learning into an interconnected and systemic whole can the organization be sure of success.

2 Biographical data

After a bachelor's degree in engineering from Stanford University, Senge studied for a master's degree in social systems modelling followed by a doctorate from Massachusetts Institute of Technology. *The Fifth Discipline*, his major work, appeared in 1990 and was an instant success, having sold over 300,000 copies worldwide.

Following the success of *The Fifth Discipline*, Senge has become one of the most sought-after speakers and consultants in the USA. Much of the experience from his consultancy work went into *The Fifth Discipline Fieldbook* (1994) which seeks to expand the practical dimensions of the original work. He co-founded the consulting firm Innovation Associates, and is at present Director of the Centre for Organizational Learning at MIT. Married with two children, he lives in Massachusetts.

3 Main contribution

The concept of the learning organization emerged in the late 1980s, from work done at MIT and also at Royal Dutch/Shell, whose then Director of Planning, Arie de Geus wrote a seminal article on this subject for *Harvard Business Review* in 1988. Senge's definition of 'the learning organization' is deliberately fuzzy: learning organizations are 'organizations where people continually expand their capacity to create the results they truly desire, where new and expansive patterns of thinking are nurtured, where collective aspiration is set free, and where people are continually learning how to learn together' (Senge 1990: 3). Learning organizations happen when 'business strategy requires that you harness the collective intelligence and commitment of your workforce'; when 'top management can no longer supply the thinking for everyone in

the company', then organizational learning becomes essential (Innovation Associates Web Site 1997: 1). This aspirational model of the organization is contrasted with the 'controlling organization', which essentially functions by containing people, rather than growing them. Senge *et al.* (1994: 10) compare the learning organization concept with other managerial concepts such as TQM, empowerment, innovation and finding core competencies, and claims that they are all in fact part of 'the same fundamental purpose: to marry the individual development of every person in the organization with superior economic performance.'

The benefits of the learning organization are numerous, and not all have directly to do with business success. Reasons for developing a learning organization include to improve quality, to improve customer service, to gain competitive advantage, to increase employee commitment, to improve the management of change ('if there is one single thing a learning organization does well, it is helping people embrace change... Change and learning may not exactly be synonymous, but they are inextricably linked' (Senge *et al.* 1994: 11), to encourage truth in the organization, because the times demand it, and to help us better 'recognize our interdependence'. This last reason taps directly into the philosophical level of Senge's work. He sees organizations not just as money-making entities but as forms of human organization, through which individual human beings develop and reach for their own aspirations. As noted above, this is not a separate aspect of the organization; rather, by encouraging human development and harnessing that development to its own goals, the organization will prosper. By 'interdependence', Senge means not just the interdependence of employees and organization, but the fact that human beings are essentially social animals and that learning is a group rather than solitary activity.

At the heart of the organization lies the learning cycle (see Figure 1). Learning *new skills and capabilities* changes our way of seeing the world; new learning might cause us to view a customer in a different way, or question assumptions that underlie the firm's definition of its market. These *new aware-nesses and sensibilities* in time evolve into *new attitudes and beliefs*, new ways of seeing the world; in organizational terms, these can result in the development of new cultures. The confidence we acquire from our new and enhanced worldview leads us on towards new horizons and new learning.

In *The Fifth Discipline*, Senge begins by identifying five key 'component technologies' which, when brought together, will create the learning organization. These are personal mastery, mental models, building shared vision, team learning and systems thinking. It is systems thinking, the 'fifth discipline', to which he assigns primacy of place.

Personal mastery in Senge's view, respresents not dominance over others but mastery of oneself, as in mastering a skill or craft: 'personal mastery is the discipline of continually clarifying and deepening our personal vision, of focusing our energies, of developing patience, and of seeing reality objectively. As such, it is an essential cornerstone of the learning organization – the learning organization's spiritual foundation, (Senge 1990: 7). The building blocks of personal mastery are many and varied, ranging from a Western, quasi-Platonic commitment to truth to a Daoist-inspired acceptance of the 'power of power-lessness' (Senge 1990: 155). Critical to personal mastery are an understanding of the uses of the subconscious and the ability to see things in their interconnected states as parts of larger wholes.

Mental models represent the fundamental assumptions or generalizations that we make about our organizations, our work and ourselves. Everyone has these, Senge says; the important thing is to make sure that the mental models in place are helping, not hindering, the organization. Preconceptions or misconceptions about the organization are often responsible for holding it back. Part of the learning process must be an examination of these models, looking at ourselves in the mirror and scrutinizing our own views.

Building shared vision follows on from the above. It requires the deliberate creation and dissemination of a mental model that accurately represents the organization's goals and values. Creating and disseminating this vision is one of the tasks of leadership. Senge devotes a chapter of *The Fifth Discipline* to leadership for the learning organisation, where he characterizes the leader as designer, steward and teacher. He also believes that leaders who can fill these roles successfully cannot be made to order; developing these skills takes a lifetime of work to harmonize the five disciplines (Senge 1990: 359).

Team learning presents difficulties. Learning is a social activity, yet groups learn more slowly than individuals. This is the paradox which Senge confronts, not always successfully, throughout much of his writing. He argues that, contrary to much experience, teams can learn better than individuals, and cites as examples sports teams and teams in the performing arts and sciences 'where the intelligence of the team exceeds the intelligence of the individuals of the team'. The key to team learning, Senge says, is *dialogue*, 'the capacity of members of a team to suspend assumptions and enter into a genuine "thinking together"' (Senge 1990: 10). He cites the Greek origin of the word, *dia-logos*, meaning the free flow of thoughts through a group. Mastering the patterns of thoughts and interactions in groups is the key to successful team learning, which is in turn the key to successful organizational learning.

Systems thinking, the 'fifth discipline', is 'a discipline for seeing wholes', for seeing interrelationships rather than cause and effect, and for seeing cycles (what Senge calls 'circles of causality') rather than snapshots. To illustrate what he means, Senge devotes several pages (74–77) to describing and diagramming the workings of a water faucet. A man

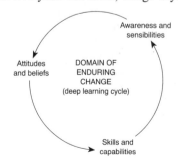

Figure 1

approaches a faucet with an empty glass. The man perceives a gap; the glass should be full. He initiates an action, turning on the faucet; the flow of water from the faucet fills the glass, closing the perception gap and completing the circle. In fact, few of us bother to deconstruct this action in such a way; we simply go to the faucet and fill the glass in an action that is largely subconscious. This is a relatively simple series of thoughts and actions, but Senge argues that we do many very complex actions in a similar way, such as driving a car or playing a piano.

In effect, then, systems thinking can help to overcome cognitive limitations. We programme our subconscious to perform certain actions not step-by-step but holistically and systemically. It is this type of thinking that Senge says we must transfer to organizational learning. To do so is not easy; we are used to thinking of organizations, particularly businesses, in a highly compartmentalized and functional way; because modern businesses are so large and complex, we tend to focus on the parts of it that affect us, at the time they affect us, and we fail to see the organization as whole. That is not to say that we should ignore the parts; true systems thinking encompasses both the detail and the big picture, what Senge calls 'the art of seeing the trees *and* the forest'.

Adopting systems thinking involves a complete mental shift to the new way of thinking. In a chapter entitled 'The Laws of the Fifth Discipline' (Senge 1990: 57–67), Senge sets out under a series of homilistic titles the principles of the new thinking that must be absorbed: 'today's problems come from yesterday's solutions', 'faster is slower', 'cause and effect are not closely related in time and space', 'dividing an elephant in half does not produce two small elephants' and so on, concepts which in fact violate much of recent perceived managerial wisdom.

These five disciplines, taken as an ensemble, help to create the learning organization. But there is one factor still missing: the drive or the will required to perform these disciplines. Senge acknowledges there are difficulties, some of which are ingrained in our culture. He suggests that modern people are perhaps generically less capable of meeting challenges than were their ancestors, for civilization has changed the nature of the challenges and made them less dramatic: 'there is no beast to slay, no villain to vanquish, no one to blame – just a need to think differently and understand the underlying patterns of dependency' (Senge 1990: 12). Innovation Associates, the firm Senge co-founded, comments: 'We have learned that organizational learning is an organic process, not a mechanical one. A learning organization is grown, not assembled. It grows from a fundamental assumption that the workforce genuinely wants the same things that management wants – real success, and the deep satisfaction that only real success can bring – and will eagerly work for these ends without manipulation or extrinsic motivation (Innovation Associates Web Site 1997: 2).

Since the publication of *The Fifth Discipline*, Senge has considered the question of motivation more closely. The motives to succeed, to work harder and to learn, he says, must come from internal rather than external incentives. As part of the 'disciplines' of learning, individuals and teams need to learn to do three basic things: '(1) recognize, articulate and align the goals which are most critical to them; (2) understand the genuine complexity of the modern business organization and the (often invisible) interconnectedness which, left unaddressed, can produce "unintended consequences" and otherwise sabotage operations and strategies; and (3) conduct conversations with each other around difficult and volatile issues in a way that creates deep understanding, empathy, innovation and cooperation rather than ducking and blaming' (Innovation Associates Web Site 1997: 2).

The architecture of the learning organization is represented by a distinctly unfashionable pyramid (Figure 2). At the top are what Senge calls 'guiding ideas'. It is the function of leadership, he says, to create and articulate these ideas. Vision, values and purpose must descend from the leadership to create a collective sense of purpose, what Nonaka (1991) calls 'organizational self-knowledge'. Senge suggests three key guiding ideas (24–28):

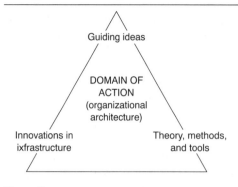

Figure 2

1 the primacy of the whole (in other words, interrelatedness);
2 the community nature of self, stressing the 'interrelatedness within us': through the recognition of our sense of self and our sense of place, we in turn recognize our fellows as human beings, not as tools for use;
3 the 'generative power of language'. Senge cites the philosophical principle of uncertainty (known to Confucian philosophers for millennia but only articulated in the West in the twentieth century), meaning that our descriptions of things in some way define those things. We can never completely grasp reality; language is the tool we use to define it. How we speak and write to describe things influences other people's perceptions of them.

At one corner of the pyramid's base are 'theory, methods and tools'. Senge sees these as interrelated as well, and deliberately blurs the boundaries between philosophy and practice. Of theory, he writes:

> It is a shame that we have lost this sense of the deeper meaning of theory today. For most of us, theory has to do with 'science'. It suggests something cold, analytic, and impersonal. Nothing could be further from the truth. The process whereby scientists generate new theories is full of passion, imagination, and the excitement of seeing something new in the world.
>
> (Senge *et al.* 1994: 29)

Theory is necessary to make tools work effectively, just as tools are required to make theory practical. Tools based on new theory 'have the power to change how we think' (Senge *et al.* 1994: 31).

4 Evaluation

The Fifth Discipline owes its popularity in part to its style. Written clearly and simply (at least, by comparison with other management textbooks) with much use of homely metaphor, the work is largely optimistic in tone. Compared with the works of Tom Peters (see PETERS, T.J.), for example, it is non-threatening; it suggests that organizations and people can and will succeed, and does not dwell overmuch on the consequences of failure.

It is also in many ways a profound work, which spills over the border from practice into philosophy. What Senge is trying to do is not so much reinvent the organization as reinvent the kind of thinking that goes into it. Indeed, in Senge's view the organization can almost be described as patterns of thought, rather than a mechanical or biological entity.

Senge himself is obviously passionate about thinking. His strength of feeling comes across, as for example when he defends the relevance of theory, and also in *The Fifth Discipline* when he talks about learning:

> Real learning gets to the heart of what it means to be human. Through learning we re-create ourselves. Through learning we become able to do something we were never able to do. Through learning we re-perceive the world and our relationship to it. . . . There is within each of us a deep hunger for this type of learning.
>
> (Senge 1990: 14)

Yet there is a gap here which is never quite closed. The assumption that everyone shares this view of and desire for learning is not proven. People can be taught to learn; but can they be taught to think? Ultimately, as Senge himself says, people will adopt this kind of thinking pattern, this mental shift, because they want to and because there are incentives for them to so. There might equally be many incentives – fear of change, perceived loss of status or material well-being in the event of change – for them not to do so. It is not clear what portion of the population are actively engaged in Senge's learning cycle; and for those who are not, it is equally unclear how the need to become engaged can be awakened within them. Certainly there are very few companies around the world that can truly claim to be learning organizations.

In *The Fifth Discipline*, Senge acknowledges that learning and gathering information are not the same thing. 'The problem with talking about 'learning organizations' is that the 'learning' has lost its central meaning in contemporary usage. Most people's eyes glaze over if you talk to them about 'learning' or 'learning organizations' (Senge 1990: 13). Yet he remains an optimist; and that surely is a good thing. As long as people like himself are prepared to continue to explain the learning organization and its benefits, there remains some chance that in time the concept will come to be truly adopted.

5 Conclusion

Summing up, we can see that Senge offers us a chance to re-think thinking, and to re-evaluate mental concepts of work and organizations. The learning organization offers a powerful conceptual framework for harnessing the knowledge and skills of employees, for developing those skills still further, and for creating networks of ideas and concepts that can lead to innovation and success. Systems thinking, along with the other four disciplines, offers a conceptual toolkit for building that organization. Though the indications are that Senge may have been ahead of his time, these two concepts are now part of the standard management vocabulary.

MORGEN WITZEL
LONDON BUSINESS SCHOOL
DURHAM UNIVERSITY BUSINESS SCHOOL

Further reading

(References cited in the text marked *)

Bryner, A., Markova, D. and Senge, P. (1996) *An Unusued Intelligence: Physical Thinking for 21st Century Leadership*, New York: Conari Press. (Later work by Senge on leadership.)

* Geus, Arie de (1988) 'Planning as learning', *Harvard Business Review*, March–April: 70–74. (Seminal article by the former director of planning at Royal Dutch/Shell, introducing the concept of continuous learning as competitive advantage.)

* Innovation Associates Web Site (1997) http://world.std.com/~ia/iabout.html. (Home page of the consultancy firm co-founded by Senge; contains a statement of purpose which summarizes the practical aspects of Senge's thought briefly and effectively.)

Kofman, F. and Senge, P. (1993) 'Communities of commitment: The heart of the learning organization', *Organizational Dynamics*, Fall. (Looks at what Senge calls 'guiding ideas' in the context of the learning organization.)

Kleiner, A. (1996) *The Age of Heretics: The Struggle for Truth in an Era of Change*, New York: Doubleday. (Work by one of Senge's colleagues.)

* Nonaka, I. (1991) 'The knowledge-creating company', *Harvard Business Review*, November–December. (Influential article on knowledge works by a prominent Japanese management thinker.)

* Senge, P.M. (1990) *The Fifth Discipline: The Art and Practice of the Learning Organization*, New York: Doubleday. (Senge's major work, describing the learning organization concept and the disciplines needed to create it.)

* Senge, P.M., Roberts, C., Ross, R.B., Smith, B.J. and Kleiner, A. (1994) *The Fifth Discipline Fieldbook: Strategies and Notes for Building a Learning Organization*, London: Nicholas Brealey. (Workbook with examples and case studies, expanding on the ideas of the original *The Fifth Discipline*.)

See also: ARGYRIS, C.; NONAKA,I.; PETERS, T.J.; SCHEIN, E.H.; SCHON, D.

Related topics in the IEBM: GROUPS AND TEAMS; MOTIVATION AND SATISFACTION; OCCUPATIONAL PSYCHOLOGY; ORGANIZATION BEHAVIOUR; ORGANIZATION BEHAVIOUR, HISTORY OF; ORGANIZATION STRUCTURE; ORGANIZATIONAL LEARNING; WORK AND LEISURE

Shingo, Shigeo (1909–1990)

Personal background

- born Saga City, Japan, 8 January 1909
- graduated with degree in Mechanical Engineering from Yamanashi Technical College (1930)
- joined Taipei Railway Company in Taiwan (1930)
- attended Industrial Engineering Training course presented by the Japanese Industrial Association (1937)
- transferred to Amano Manufacturing Company in Yokohama, Japan on orders of Ministry of Munitions (1943)
- joined the Japanese Management Association as a manufacturing consultant (1946)
- began assisting Taiichi Ohno at Toyota Motor Company in the development of the Toyota Production System (1955)
- left the Japanese Management Association to form his own consulting firm, the Institute for Management Improvement (1959)
- began consulting in Europe and America in the early 1970s
- awarded honorary Doctorate of Engineering degrees from Université de Toulouse in France and Utah State University in the USA (1988)
- annual 'Shingo Prizes for Manufacturing Excellence' established to recognize top North American manufacturing plants (1988)
- died in Tokyo 14 November 1990

Major works

A Revolution in Manufacturing: The SMED System (1985)

Zero Quality Control: Source Inspection and the Poka-yoke System (1986)

Study of the Toyota Production System from an Industrial Engineering Viewpoint (1989)

The Shingo Production Management System (1992)

Summary

Shigeo Shingo was a Japanese engineer and manufacturing consultant who made major contributions to the development of the Toyota production system (TPS) in post World War II Japan and to its subsequent global diffusion as just-in-time (JIT) manufacturing. He held a degree in mechanical engineering, but early in his career was attracted to industrial engineering by the writings of Frederick Taylor (see TAYLOR, F.W.). Shingo was impressed by Taylor's claim that low cost goods could be produced even if workers were paid high wages, if productivity were high enough; and he made the decision to 'devote my life to scientific management' (Shingo 1987: xvi).

In 1937 Shingo attended an Industrial Engineering training course sponsored by the Japanese Industrial Association, an experience which reinforced his commitment to devote his career to improving manufacturing. He was ideally suited to the task, possessing unbounded enthusiasm, a high level of inquisitiveness and excellent technical training. He used these skills to increase productivity in a Japanese weapons factory during World War II and after the war became a manufacturing consultant at the Japanese Management Association. It was in this role, as a consultant to the Toyota Motor Company, that he achieved his greatest success and established a worldwide reputation as a leading manufacturing management thinker.

1 Introduction

Shingo's choice of a consulting career exposed him to a wide variety of manufacturing processes and problems and gave him the oportunity to address these problems with an objectivity difficult for an operating manager to achieve. He capitalized on these opportunities by developing several innovative manufacturing concepts and techniques – some of them crucial 'building blocks' for the Toyota production system and modern manufacturing (see TOYODA FAMILY).

2 Biographical data

Shigeo Shingo was born in Saga, Japan on 8 January 1909. His technical education began at the Saga Technical High School where he was exposed to the 'scientific management' concepts of Frederick Taylor. He graduated from Yamanashi Technical College in 1930 with a degree in mechanical engineering and began his career at the Taipei Railway factory in Taiwan that same year.

The Taipei factory took an average of fifteen days to repair rail cars, compared to the five days common in Japanese plants. Shingo investigated and through self study of industrial engineering and the application of his analytical skills succeeded in gradually reducing the repair time to ten days. His process improvement skills were enhanced in 1937 when he attended an Industrial Engineering course sponsored by the Japanese Industrial Association. He describes the course as starting with 'emphasizing mastery of concepts', and moving on to the study of techniques of motion study and process analysis. The course developed both his technical capabilities and his operating philosophy. In his words: 'the experience forms the backbone of my philosophy; it is the foundation of my lifelong commitment to pursue improvement to its source' (Shingo 1987: xvi).

Shingo's application of his newly acquired skills dramatically improved the repair processes at Taipei Rail. His success led the Ministry of Munitions to assign him to the Amano Manufacturing plant in Yokohama at the start of World War II, where his improvements doubled production of torpedo depth guages. After the war Shingo joined the Japanese Management Association as a consultant, specializing in plant improvement projects. His work took him to the Toyota Motor Car Company in the mid 1950s where he teamed with Taiichi Ohno in the development of the Toyota production system – an innovative enhancement of Ford mass production (see OHNO, T.).

The Ohno–Shingo partnership benefited from their complimentary skills. Ohno was a visionary, relentlessly pursuing his goal of developing a more flexible, less 'wasteful' version of mass production. Shingo provided the technical expertise to help make Ohno's vision feasible. As Shingo's successes and reputation grew he began writing a series of books expounding his philosophy and describing his techniques. He also expanded the scope of his consulting activities by working with European and American firms, starting in the early 1970s.

In 1988 he was awarded honorary Doctor of Engineering degrees by both the Université de Toulouse in France and Utah State University in the USA, for his contributions to manufacturing. That same year the annual Shingo Prizes for Manufacturing Excellence were inaugurated, to recognize North American firms that achieve substantial improvements by applying Shingo's principles. The prizes are administered by the College of Business at Utah State University and the National Association of Manufacturers. Shingo continued to consult and write until his death in 1990 at the age of 81.

3 Main contributions

Shingo's major contributions are linked to his work with Taiichi Ohno in developing the Toyota production system. Ohno envisioned a continuous production flow of small quantities of parts; ideally a 'bucket brigade' flow. His aim was to eliminate all 'wasteful' production activities such as the storage and retrieval of work-in-progress inventory, material moves, machine setups and inspections – activities that add no value to the product. Shingo made key contributions to making Ohno's vision a reality by developing techniques to overcome some formidable obstacles to continuous, high value added work flow.

One such obstacle is the time needed to setup, or changeover a machine, such as a sheet metal forming press, in order to change the part being made. Different parts usually require different dies and it can take several hours to make a die change. For example, it may take two hours to change a forming die to shift from making Part A to Part B, and only 30 seconds to subsequently form each B. Large quantities of B must be made, to amortize the high changeover costs and provide a supply of Bs to cover the periods when the machine is producing large quantities of other parts. If, however, changeovers could be made in one or two minutes, it would be feasible to produce small quantities of parts as they are needed – 'just-in-time'.

During his consulting assignments Shingo developed two insights regarding machine changeovers. The first was the advantage of using standardized die holders. If all holders are the same height and operate with the same press stroke, time consuming machine adjustments are not needed after each changeover. If die holder locating pins are automatically located in recepticles on the machine and then quickly clamped into position, the setup time can be greatly reduced. The objective is to come as close as possible to an ideal design of self-locating, automatic clamping, interchangeable die holders – to achieve an ease of changeover comparable to that of a videocassette in a VCR machine.

Shingo's second insight was the identification of two types of setup activities: 'internal' tasks that can be done only when the machine is not running, and 'external' tasks that can be performed while the machine is running. A high percentage of changeover tasks are usually external. If they are performed while the machine is running the changeover time can be dramatically reduced. This can be illustrated with a videocassette changeover example:

Task		Time
1	Rewind cassette	120 seconds
2	Eject cassette, remove	3
3	Rebox cassette, carry to storage	10
4	Place cassette in storage location	5
5	Locate next cassette to be played	5
6	Carry cassette to player and unbox	10
7	Insert cassette into VCR	2
	Total	155 seconds

There is no need for the VCR to be idled for 155 seconds to make a changeover. Only tasks 2 and 7 are internal. All the others can be done while the VCR is running – by changing the task sequence and using an inexpensive cassette rewinder. This will cut the total changeover delay to 5 seconds – a reduction of 97%!

These concepts were employed by Shingo at Toyota to develop the SMED system – single minute exchange of die system, designed to achieve single digit changeover times of 9 minutes or less. The evolution of SMED illustrates the working relationship between Ohno and Shingo. In 1969 it took Toyota four hours to changeover a particular stamping press, compared to Volkswagen's two hours. Ohno wanted to better the VW performance and Shingo succeeded in reducing the changeover time to ninety minutes. Ohno then issued the further challenge of reducing it to three minutes! Shingo responded by refining his concepts and techniques to meet this new level of expectation. The three minute goal was met, initiating the SMED System. The dramatic reductions in changeover times achieved by SMED made continuous flow, small lot production feasible – reducing inventory, lowering production times, increasing the ability to respond to changes in customer demand, and improving quality. Shingo emphasizes the significance of the system when he states that 'Indeed, no transition to a Toyota production system can occur without drastic reductions in setup times' (Shingo 1989: 215) He also pays tribute to Ohno's role: 'Ohno's demand that [the] setup be further cut to three minutes sounded preposterous; but it was that demand that occasioned the birth of SMED' (Shingo 1987: 166).

Continuous production flow requires the elimination of stoppages caused by poor quality and waiting for quality checks to be made by inspectors. Shingo addressed these obstacles with his 'Zero Quality Control' system, aimed at achieving zero defects. The system integrates two elements: *poka-yoke*, or 'foolproof', product and process designs and inspections 'at the source', performed by the workers as part of their duties. *Poka-yoke* designs recognize the fallibility of humans in performing production tasks. Shingo describes the role of foolproof designs:

> Whenever I hear supervisors warning workers to pay attention or to be sure not to forget something, I cannot help thinking that the workers are being asked to carry out operations as if they possessed divine infallibility . . . we should recognize that people are human and will on rare occasions inadvertently forget things. It is more effective to incoporate a check – i.e., a *poka-yoke* into the operation so if a worker forgets something the device will signal that fact, preventing defects from occurring. This, I think, is the quickest road leading to zero defects.
>
> (Shingo 1986: 45)

Poka-yoke principles call for parts to be designed to permit assembly in only one way – the correct way. Any deviation is an unambiguous signal that something is wrong, enhancing the ability of workers to effectively perform 'source inspections' on their operations. This enlarges their jobs, eliminates the delays of waiting for available inspectors, and cuts overhead costs by reducing the number of inspectors. Parts that are easy to assemble properly help to maintain the consistency of production flow, reduce worker frustration, and improve product serviceability.

Shingo's SMED and Zero Quality Control systems were key factors in the implementation of the Toyota production system (TPS). He also contributed to the spread of the TPS through his writings, his consulting and his clarification of the role of the *kanban* system of parts replenishment used in the TPS. The *kanban* system employs the decision rule used in American supermarkets for refilling shelves – 'fill all empty spaces'. This rule takes advantage of the simplicity of visual signals and replaces stock based on actual rather than estimated demand. On the factory floor the *kanban* system often uses standard containers, sized to hold fixed quantities of a component. If, for example, a pump assembler uses the last pump housing from a container of ten, the empty container moves to the upstream work station where the housings are assembled. It is a visual signal to the work station to assemble ten more housings, fill the container and return it to the assembly area. Actual use, or demand, 'pulls' replenishment quantities to the using station to maintain production flow with low inventory levels and simple shop floor control.

Many authors mistakenly characterized the *kanban* system as being synonomous with the Toyota production system. Shingo, however, pointed out that 'the *kanban* system is merely a means of putting the Toyota production system into practice, and thorough rationalization of production cannot be achieved merely by applying it' (Shingo 1989: 222) The *kanban* system is a form of Reorder Point Inventory Control, and Shingo defined the fundamentals of the system through graphical and mathematical treatments in his writings. His clarification of the *kanban* system contributed to a better understanding of just-in-time production and its proper implementation.

Shingo's contributions go beyond those linked to Toyota. One of the most significant is his recognition of the relationship between production operations and production processes. While investigating rail car repair times at Taipei Railway Company he was surprised to learn that while the entire repair process at Taipei took three times as long as the Japanese factories, the labour time for the actual repair operations was only 20 percent higher. Clearly other factors were primarily responsible for the large gap in repair time. This led him to study the entire repair process from receipt of a car to its return to service. Traditional industrial engineering practice tended to focus on improving manufacturing operations – the tasks performed by humans or machines such as drilling, welding or assembly. Shingo came to realize that this narrow focus ignored the other activities involved in the process of transforming raw materials into finished products; activities such as materials storage, materials retrieval, inspections, moves and delays. These activities were viewed as a form of 'waste' by Ohno, since they do not add value to the product – only cost. Eliminating or reducing these sources of waste often yields much greater manufacturing improvements than is possible through improved operations. Shingo viewed the realization that production consists of a network of operations and processes as one of his most important contributions, stating that it 'frees us of our obsession with streamlining operations and focuses on making processes more rational' (Shingo 1992: 3). The potential of focusing on processes can be seen in the spread of process based work organization from the factory floor to the office, in the form of Business Process Reengineering.

4 Evaluation

During his long professional career Shigeo Shingo made lasting contributions to the practice of effective manufacturing management – particularly in the implementation of just-in-time production. His consulting activities improved manufacturing at many major firms including Toyota, Ford, Mitsubishi, Honda, Sharp, Peugeot, Citroën, Matsushita, Hewlett Packard, Nippon Steel, ATT and Mazda. His concepts and techniques have had a global impact, through his extensive lecturing and his many books. A review of his writings does reveal a shortcoming – a substantial amount of redundancy appears in his books, despite the differences in titles and emphasis. This is a relatively minor flaw, however, considering the quality of his ideas.

A more significant shortcoming in his writings is an absence of concern for the effects of JIT on worker job stress. In the late 1980s the negative effects of the production system developed by Ohno and Shingo led to unacceptably high levels of employee turnover and difficulties in recruiting workers at the Japanese Toyota plants. As a result, the Kyushu plant built in 1992 was based on a newly

adopted philosophy that 'the principle of just-in-time should not be applied to people' (Shimizu 1995: 383.) The plant incorporates features considered wasteful by Ohno and Shingo, such as small buffer inventories between work cells, in order to give the workers increased autonomy and reduce job stress. In his writings Shingo tended to focus on the macro economic benefits of JIT to workers, commenting in his final book that 'it is only on a foundation of increased productivity that we can build a wealthy nation and happy citizens' (Shingo 1992: 185).

5 Conclusion

Just-in-time (JIT) production, the generic version of the Toyota production system, has become the global competitive standard in the manufacture of products such as autos and appliances. It has the potential for simultaneously reducing costs and inventory, improving quality, and shortening delivery times. JIT represents a new paradigm for effective repetitive manufacturing and Shingo's key role in its development ensures his place among the leading contributors to the advancement of manufacturing theory and practice. His influence on modern manufacturing should continue through his many books and the annual competition for the Shingo Prizes.

ROBERT F CONTI
BRYANT COLLEGE, SMITHFIELD, RI

Further reading

(References cited in the text marked *)

Klein, J. (1989) 'The human costs of manufacturing reform', *Harvard Business Review*, March–April: 60–66. (Excellent discussion of the causes of JIT worker stress, with some practical prescriptions for minimizing the problem.)

Ohno, T. (1988) Toyota Production System, Beyond Large-Scale Production, Cambridge, MA: Productivity Press. (Discussion of the evolution and operation of the Toyota production system by the person who was the driving force behind its success.)

* Shimizu, K. (1995) Humanization of the production system and work at Toyota Motor Co and

Toyota Motor Kyushu, in A. Sandberg (ed.), *Enriching Production*, Avebury: Aldershot. (Detailed description of the Toyota plant built in 1992 at Kyushu, Japan, incorporating several design and operating features to reduce the stressful effects of the Toyota production system – creating a production system termed the 'New Toyotaism'.)

Shingo, S. (1985) *A Revolution in Manufacturing: The SMED System*, Cambridge, MA: Productivity Press. (In-depth coverage of the details of Shingo's ground breaking system for reducing setup times. Required reading for the implementation of JIT.)

* Shingo, S. (1986) *Zero Quality Control: Source Inspection and the Poka-yoke System*, Portland, OR: Productivity Press. (Detailed coverage of Shingo's approach to quality management – encompassing the major elements of poka-yoke, 'foolproof' designs and source inspections by the the workers.)

* Shingo, S. (1987) *The Sayings of Shigeo Shingo, Key Strategies for Plant Improvement*, Cambridge, MA: Productivity Press. (The first half of the book has an industrial engineering focus, outlining the details of Shingo's techniques, while the second half emphasizes applications of his techniques.)

Shingo, S. (1988) *Non-Stock Production, the Shingo System for Continuous Improvement*, Cambridge, MA: Productivity Press. (Descriptions of programs for continuously improving manufacturing, with a comparison of the 'non–stock' production system pioneered at Toyota and the traditional 'authorized stock' systems common in the West.)

* Shingo, S. (1989) *A Study of the Toyota Production System From an Industrial Engineering Viewpoint*, Cambridge, MA: Productivity Press. (Excellent technical coverage of the details of the Toyota system, including comprehensive treatment of the kanban system.)

* Shingo, S. (1992) *The Shingo Production Management System, Improving Process Functions*, Cambridge, MA: Productivity Press. (Shingo's last book. A summary of his life's work in process improvement, building on the ideas of past management thinkers such as Frank Gilbreth and Frederick Taylor.)

Shonberger, R. (1982) *Japanese Manufacturing Techniques,* New York: The Free Press. (Very readable introduction to the concepts and techniques of just-in-time production.)

Toyoda, E. and Toyoda, S. (1988) *Toyota – A History of the First 50 Years, Toyota City*: Toyota Motor Corporation. (Fascinating history of the growth of Toyota from 1933 to 1983. Describes the role of the Toyota Production System in the success of the company.)

See also: FORD, H.; ISHIKAWA, K.; OHNO, T.; TAYLOR, F.W.; TOYODA FAMILY

Related topics in the IEBM: INVENTORY AND JUST-IN-TIME MODELS; JUST-IN-TIME PHILOSOPHIES; MANAGEMENT IN JAPAN; MANUFACTURING SYSTEMS, DESIGN OF; PRODUCTIVITY; REENGINEERING; TOTAL QUALITY MANAGEMENT

Simon, Herbert Alexander (1916–)

Personal background

- born 15 June 1916 in Milwaukee, Wisconsin, the younger of two brothers
- father a German immigrant to USA, electrical engineer and inventor; mother an accomplished pianist
- BA in political science, University of Chicago, 1936
- married Dorothea Pye, 1937
- director of research group into municipal administration, University of California, Berkeley, 1939–42
- PhD in political science, University of Chicago, 1943, dissertation on decision making in organizations
- professor at Graduate School of Administration, Carnegie Institute of Technology, 1949
- Richard King Mellon Professor of Computer Science and Psychology, Carnegie Mellon University, 1966
- Nobel Prize in economics, 1978
- National Medal of Science, 1986

Major works

Administrative Behavior: A Study of Decision Making Processes in Administrative Organization (1947)

Organizations (with J.G. March) (1958)

The New Science of Management Decision (1960)

Human Problem Solving (with A. Newell) (1972)

Summary

In challenging classical economic theory, which ascribes business decision makers with near omniscience about options and with superhuman ability to compute the optimal choice, Herbert Simon has made a major impact upon our understanding of the processes of management. In place of a super-rational economic model of man assumed by classical economics, he advocates an administrative model, a person of much more modest ability who is incompletely informed about available options and their outcomes and who therefore 'satisfices'. Satisficing is accepting a satisfactory outcome rather than striving to maximize utilities through ever more comprehensive search and involved computations. It is a process whereby decision makers take short cuts, use rules of thumb and a whole range of intuitive methods.

The associated psychological condition is 'bounded rationality', a condition whereby it is accepted that perfect knowledge about options can never be achieved in complex decision making. However, minimum performance standards can be set and once this minimum standard is reached an appropriate choice is made and search for further options stopped.

In broader terms, Simon therefore challenged prevailing economic theories of management and led a reaction against the Harvard case method of teaching which had become dominant in US business schools. It was for his ability to apply so many different perspectives, emanating from psychology, computer science, economic theory and political science that he was awarded the Nobel Prize for economics in 1978.

1 Towards a science of administration

If there is one passion that could be said to infuse the work of Herbert Simon, it would be the drive to develop a science of decision making. After taking a typically satisficing approach in his choice of career, which he described as being settled 'as much by drift as by choice', his home, peopled by intellectually active parents and stocked with books, prepared him for academic life. Following graduation from the University of Chicago in political science, an early research assistantship in the field of public administration led to the directorship of a public administration research group at the University of California, Berkeley.

His doctoral dissertation at the University of Chicago was based upon his administrative studies at Berkeley and was published with modifications as *Administrative Behavior: A Study of Decision Making Processes in Administrative Organization*. This book founded his reputation in the field of business administration and is now a classic, as witnessed by its progression to three editions. It acknowledges its debt to Chester Barnard, who provides a foreword and who had previously advocated the need to move thinking about management beyond an overconcern with formal structures to a concern with decision making and cooperation (see BARNARD, C.I.). The book gives an outline of the problems with administrative theory as it then existed. For instance, in trying to determine which basis of specialization an organization would use, the choice was usually presented as a choice between organization by purpose, process, clientele or place. These are not mutually exclusive criteria, however, and in order to think more clearly about the problem it is preferable to see an organization in terms of the 'facts' and the 'values' that guide decision making. Facts and values nest together in a hierarchy whereby the values of one level set the facts for a lower level. Value (or ethical) statements set the parameters within which decisions are made and by which outcomes are judged. Decision making takes place within a framework of 'givens' which an organization provides; in deciding upon a new machine, the management of a shoe factory does not question the need to make shoes or to make a profit but take these as givens upon which more detailed search and extensive satisficing will ride. Rationality is therefore 'limited' or 'bounded'.

Administrative Behavior has the marks of a seminal work. It is not entirely coherent but is suggestive of the many avenues which Simon would later follow since engrained within this work are the three underlying concepts of bounded rationality, satisficing and search which are found throughout Simon's work.

This interest in the relationship between organizations and decision making was continued during his time at Carnegie Mellon through observation of decisions both in the field and laboratory. The second edition of *Administrative Behavior* further emphasized his belief that conventional economic assumptions about rationality were unrealistic and neglected the bounded rational nature of business decisions. These ideas were controversial and were attacked from a neo-classical viewpoint by economists such as Milton Friedman. For the neo-classicists the assumption of economic man gave a sufficiently accurate account of human behaviour to allow predictions to be made in the aggregate. Later, in his Nobel Lecture, Simon reaffirms his belief in the need to adopt a more realistic view of human decision making and to make empirical observations of actual business decisions.

The book, *Organizations*, which Simon co-authored with J.G. March (with the collaboration of H. Guetzkow) develops the idea of satisficing and its associated condition of bounded rationality through a series of propositions, which are in principle scientifically testable. Bounded rationality is a psychological condition whereby decision makers realize they cannot obtain all the necessary information to fully evaluate options and hence they satisfice. One aspect of bounded rationality is limited attention focus; decision makers have to cope with many problems simultaneously. Some decisions are programmed and can be made by routines while for unprogrammed decisions organizations use extensive search routines.

Organizations also concerns itself with the motivation of individuals to participate in organizations and with the ability of people to resolve conflict. A major source of conflict in organizations derives from attention to subgoals. In a study with Newell (1972), Simon showed how managers from different functions interpreted the main issues in business decisions in different ways. These different interpretations are largely perceptions learned during professional training and subsequent experience.

Bounded rationality is a residual, a failure of omniscience whereby all options are not known, there is uncertainty about exogenous events and an inability to calculate consequences. This notion forms also the basis for a behaviourial theory of the firm which was developed further by Cyert and March (1963) in a book of that name (see MARCH, J.G. AND CYERT, R.M.). In this sense the firm, or more generally the organization, is a node of bounded rationality, search and satisficing.

The importance of search behaviour in the theory of bounded rationality was taken up by Stigler (1961) through an attempt to equate the cost of extra search with the marginal return to that search through improved outcomes. But as Simon points out this requires decision makers to estimate marginal returns to extra search which, by the nature of the condition, cannot be done under bounded rationality. The theory of satisficing only requires that decision makers set a minimum aspiration as to the goodness required of those alternatives that come within their scope and choose the first that meets those aspirations.

2 Towards a science of problem solving

These ideas provided a base for a decade or so as a professor of administration at the newly founded Graduate School of Business Administration of the Carnegie Institute of Technology. After his concern with organizations, Simon's research in the mid-1950s turned increasingly to its psychological roots by examining the processes of human problem solving in greater depth and thereby contributing in a more general way to a behavioural theory of decision making.

An important aspect of Simon's thinking can be seen to have roots in Lewin's then fashionable field theory of psychology which points out that aspirations are not static but rise and fall with experience. With Newell, Simon came increasingly to explore these psychological roots by using computers as a central tool to simulate the way in which information is used in problem solving. Problem solving is seen to involve a highly selective search through a vast array of potentially available information. Selection of what is appropriate is based upon rules of thumb or heuristics in the manner of the previously developed idea of satisficing.

A central idea, whose origin can be seen in his earlier work on fact and value in decision making, is that problem solving is more effective if made within the structure of a hierarchy, what in one paper he described as the 'architecture of complexity'. Chess provided Simon with a major setting for testing propositions about these ideas. He has noted, through observation, that a chess grand master can solve chess problems more quickly than a novice because experience makes it possible to recognize patterns of standard moves that can be fitted together in a pattern. If pieces on a chess board are jumbled in a random way, thereby removing familiar learned patterns from the purview of the grand master, the difference between novice and grand master tends to disappear.

3 A stream of ideas

Through the breadth of his interests, teaching and writing and with fifteen books and over 500 articles to his name, Simon has been described as coming closest to the ideal Renaissance man. Although he has a reputation for being absent-minded ('part of the job description' as he said), it is impossible to ignore the influence that Simon has had when considering key sources of ideas about management and organization.

It is an influence that has also come about through a stream of ideas and an associated language finding a number of different niches also hewn by other scholars working on different problems across a range of disciplines. Sometimes the central ideas of the bounded rational model have been called the 'Carnegie School' of decision making due to Richard Cyert's as well as Simon's association with

Carnegie Mellon University. James March later developed (in conjunction with Cohen) decision making theory through a different, but not unrelated, set of ideas in the 'Garbage Can' model of decision making. Underlying these ideas is the contrast between economic and psychological views of decision making. Hence, Williamson (1975) places bounded rationality at the centre of an institutional economics in a theory attempting to understand the boundaries between market and hierarchical organizations in terms of a propensity to reduce transactions costs. A central problem of trying to conduct complex transactions in a market derives from bounded rationality in the sense that there can often be an asymmetry of knowledge between buyer and seller. Hierarchy is seen as a form of organization that allows greater flow of information than does a market and hence can ameliorate bounded rationality.

Although probably of greatest impact within North America, followed by other areas of the English-speaking world, the notions of bounded rationality, search and satisficing are likely to attract attention from scholars for years to come. Even if these ideas were to die today, Simon could be said to have been a major influence upon scholars of business and organization for over four decades.

RICHARD BUTLER
UNIVERSITY OF BRADFORD

Further reading

(References cited in the text marked *)

Barnard, C.I. (1938) *Functions of the Executive*, Cambridge, MA: Harvard University Press. (A foundation book for Simon, indicating the importance of decision making.)

* Cyert, R. and March, J.G. (1963) *The Behavioural Theory of the Firm*, Englewood Cliffs, NJ: Prentice Hall. (A pathbreaking book indicating the need to see the actions taken by firms in terms of bounded rationality.)

* March, J.G. and Simon, H.A. (1958) *Organizations*, New York: Wiley. (A classic book which builds a view of organizations from the microprocesses of decision making.)

* Newell, A. and Simon, H.A. (1972) *Human Problem Solving*, Englewood Cliffs, NJ: Prentice Hall. (A good statement of Simon's approach to problem solving.)

* Simon, H.A. (1947) *Administrative Behavior: A Study of Decision Making Processes in Administrative Organization*, New York: The Free Press. (The book that launched Simon; the third edition appeared in 1976.)

* Simon, H.A. (1960) *The New Science of Management Decision*, New York: Harper Row. (Still a refreshing airing of the move against an overrationalistic view of decision making.)

Simon, H.A. (1962) 'The architecture of complexity', *Proceedings of the American Philosophical Society* 106: 467–82. (An early statement of Simon's approach to problem solving.)

Simon, H.A. (1979) *Models of Thought*, New Haven, CT: Yale University Press. (A later statement of Simon's approach to problem solving.)

* Stigler, C.J. (1961) 'The economics of information', *Journal of Political Economy* 69: 213–25. (Application of economic theory to the cost of information).

* Williamson, O.E. (1975) *Markets and Hierarchies*, New York: The Free Press. (Builds upon the notion of bounded rationality to develop a theory of how transaction costs can lead to market or hierarchical institutions.)

See also: BARNARD, C.I.; COASE, R.H.; LEWIN, K.; MARCH, J.G. AND CYERT, R.M.

Related topics in the IEBM: DECISION MAKING, HABITUAL DOMAINS IN; DECISION MAKING, MULTIPLE-CRITERIA; DECISION SUPPORT SYSTEMS; MANAGERIAL BEHAVIOUR; MANAGERIAL THEORIES OF THE FIRM; PROBLEM SOLVING; PUBLIC SECTOR MANAGEMENT; ORGANIZATION BEHAVIOUR

Sloan, Alfred Pritchard, Jr (1875–1966)

Personal background

- born 23 May 1875 in New Haven, Connecticut
- eldest of four sons of a New Haven tea, coffee and cigar wholesaler and retailer
- grew up in Brooklyn, New York, from the age of ten
- graduated with degree in electrical engineering from Massachusetts Institute of Technology in 1895
- began career with Hyatt Roller Bearing Company, New Jersey, in 1895, becoming its president at the age of twenty-six
- after Hyatt was acquired by General Motors (GM) he became vice president and a member of its executive committee in 1918, then its operating vice president in 1920, then its president and chief executive officer in 1923
- reorganized GM from an untidy group of largely separate businesses into a widely emulated model of rational organization
- divided GM into five different divisions, each with its make of car in a different price range
- decentralized production while centralizing administration
- built up GM to surpass Ford's car sales in the USA in the late 1920s, and to become the largest company in the world
- funded several charities named after him, a centre for the advanced study of engineering and the prestigious Sloan School of Management at the Massachusetts Institute of Technology

Major works

Adventures of a White Collar Man (with B. Sparkes) (1941)
My Years with General Motors (1964)

Summary

Alfred P. Sloan, Jr (1875–1966) was an administrative genius who, with Henry Ford, brought the modern car industry into being. His successes followed Ford's with the Model T Ford, which was becoming increasingly obsolescent as General Motors (GM) began developing a wider range of cars. His very successful reorganization and development of GM along federal lines and evolving elaborate decentralization was and is imitated all over the world. Sloan used cost accounting, market analysis and internal competition as strong frameworks for a philosophy and style of management which was relatively fair, open, informal and democratic. Sloan joined GM in 1918 and retired in 1956, and was its chief executive officer from 1923 to 1946. Sloan's flexible and innovative approach to very large-scale organization and management was extremely successful, but elements of complacency and fear of change were apparent in GM by the 1960s. Habits of undue emphasis on economy and rather stereotyped approaches to marketing, as well as decreasing emphasis on technical innovation, combined with foreign competition to give the company problems from the 1970s onwards. Nevertheless most of the main elements of Sloan's philosophy are still widely praised for their administrative, economic, moral, political, psychological and social logic.

1 Introduction

Sloan is generally recognized as an organizational genius and, to a lesser extent, a marketing genius, who unified the efforts of a varied group of car manufacturing companies into the world's largest and most successful maker of cars. His achievements brought the car industry to its early maturity and were massively influential on other companies and in other sectors, and on the understanding and study of management.

The principles of decentralization and of the use of staff services in senior management developed under Sloan were not new but he and Pierre Du Pont (of Du Pont Chemicals), his helper and collaborator, applied and elaborated them extensively in large-scale private sector manufacturing for the first time. He was also responsible for influential developments in consumer marketing, for innovations in the use of specialist expertise in management, and for numerous developments in ways of obtaining, presenting and using data needed by decision makers.

The above achievements of Sloan have been built upon, but not genuinely superseded in spite of criticisms based on their somewhat inward-looking character. They were inward-looking in so far as they were strongly focused on GM's internal or immediate commercial concerns, and because GM faced little seriously effective competition during the 1920s, when its mould was made. They were sometimes described as being important building blocks for a democratic capitalist social order and then criticized for their narrowness, for the failure of GM executives to think beyond the corporation's relations with its suppliers, dealers and customers to its role in the wider society. However, Sloan's emphasis on fairness, on cooperation and competition used creatively in management, and on decision making based on rational discussion of facts, all within a very large, diverse, widespread and productive organization, continues to point the way forward for students and practitioners of management, industry and business, and of their roles in society.

2 Biographical data

Alfred P. Sloan, Jr was born into a middle-class business and professional family in New Haven, Connecticut on 23 May 1875. The family moved to Brooklyn in New York City when he was ten, and in 1895 he graduated from the Massachusetts Institute of Technology with a degree in electrical engineering. In the same year he began work for the Hyatt Roller Bearing Company of Harrison, New Jersey, which made tapered roller bearings, as a $10 per week draughtsman. After a short while Sloan left Hyatt to work for a firm which made one of the first electrical refrigerators, but after two years he returned to Hyatt, which was about to go out of business. However, the company was loaned $5,000 by Sloan's father and some friends while Sloan and a young bookkeeper, Peter Steenstrup, tried to change its fortunes. Steenstrup looked after Hyatt's finances and Sloan looked after design, engineering, production and sales, learning much about business management and something about mass production in the process. The latter occurred because when Sloan took Hyatt over the car industry was the main buyer of its products, and its demands were constantly growing and changing. Two particular lessons concerned the ever-growing precision of the parts used in cars, and the demand for price concessions from major buyers, which impressed on Sloan the need to look continually for lower costs and better methods, and thus the full value of systematic accounting, research and planning.

In 1916 the first major architect of General Motors, William C. Durant, then of the currently forming United Motors, suggested that Hyatt be sold to it. After some thought Sloan saw that because the future of Hyatt lay with large mass producers like Ford and GM, it was dependent on mass production and could only be profitable as long as it was selling to mass producers. Because Ford and GM were both capable of making their own roller bearings, the Durant proposal was accepted. Sloan became president of United Motors, which GM bought in 1918, when he also became a vice president of GM. At the same time the General Motors Company became the General Motors Corporation. This ended Chevrolet control of GM with Chevrolet remaining a major part of the new corporation. William C. Durant, the founder of GM, had foreseen, around 1900, the brilliant prospects for big vertically integrated companies making a variety of cars. GM was first founded in 1908 from Buick, Cadillac, Oakland (to become Pontiac) and Oldsmobile. Durant made two attempts to buy Ford at a time when Ford's great successes were imminent or starting, with Ford's responses making it hard to believe that he was doing any more than flirting with the idea of joining the corporation which was to overtake his company to become the USA's and the world's number one car producer from the mid-1920s onwards.

Durant had a whirlwind approach to business growth. He joined forces with Louis Chevrolet in 1911 to produce, around 1915, a popular car to challenge the rise of Ford's all-conquering Model T. Durant had lost control of GM and he began to try to recover it with the help of the Du Pont family which was making a great deal of money manufacturing chemicals during the First World War and which saw a potentially very good investment in the motor industry. The bankers' trust that controlled GM expired in 1916 and Durant returned to power, along with the Chevrolet company as the tail wagging the GM dog.

During the First World War and for most of the following decade until 1928, Ford's enormous success with the Model T swept almost all before it (see FORD, H.). Most cars apart from the Model T, however, were becoming more complicated and expensive to make, and newcomers to the industry found survival increasingly difficult. The First World War had given a big impetus to the mass production of motor vehicles. In 1919 Ford produced about 50 per cent and GM about 20 per cent of the cars made in the USA and the prospects for the industry seemed very bright. However the depression of 1920–1 began with most car manufacturers over-extended and led to major reorganizations in the industry which had long-term effects on its future structure. In 1919 the General Motors Acceptance Corporation was founded to help dealers with the finance of loans to customers and with handling used car sales. Dealers were thus supported through difficult periods by what was a very forward-looking measure for its time. However, while Durant was a very dynamic salesman and promoter with considerable energy, integrity and managerial ability, his management of so large and complex an organization

as GM tended to be too single-handed and impulsive.

Unlike Walter Chrysler, then head of Buick, Sloan did not quarrel with Durant about the effects of the latter's style of management. However Sloan reacted to it by producing a plan for the reorganization of GM which Durant approved but then did nothing to implement. The plan offered decentralization and delegation of authority to counteract the administrative chaos of Durant's approach to management. In 1920 Sloan saw how GM needed to cut its prices from wartime to peacetime levels. The ever-optimistic Durant could not see this and feared that price-cutting could put at risk his attempts to support GM on the stock market. Sloan saw this as an example of Durant's overemphasis on financing operations through the stock market and relative neglect of more mundane but important matters.

Sloan took a month's leave of absence in Europe to consider his future, as he could foresee ruin for GM. When he returned it was to find Durant gone. The Du Pont company had bought Durant's GM shares and paid off his obligations, and secured his resignation from the presidency of GM. Sloan and other executives got Pierre Du Pont to take over as president of GM to reassure the public about the company's basic soundness. Sloan became executive vice president and put his reorganization plan into effect.

By 1921 Ford was manufacturing about 60 per cent of all the motor vehicles made in the USA, whereas GM, which had just survived a near disaster, depended on two of its five models, Buick and Cadillac, for most of its sales. However, during the 1920s it replaced Ford as the industry's leading company. This was partly due to Henry Ford's idealization of the Model T and the assembly line. Ford mistook them for the culmination of car production, rather than as very important steps in its progress. The Model T of 1908 continued to sell on the basis of its low price for most of the 1920s, at a time when the rising affluence it was bringing into being was making price less and less important in the US public's buyer behaviour. Ford's failings combined with the success of Sloan's plan to engineer a sea change in the industry's structure.

Sloan's structural plan clearly distinguished GM's central planning and policy-making bodies from its operating divisions, which were autonomous, self-contained and competing within GM's general policy framework. This was a clear separation of staff and line functions. Following his experiences with Durant, but also by employing his own clear logic, Sloan recognized that no one person could ever manage a corporation of GM's size effectively. Careful analysis of relevant facts was needed as a basis for group judgement. While lines of authority were defined clearly, authority was nevertheless decentralized as much as possible. Managers at all levels were encouraged and empowered to make decisions. Each of GM's companies became an operating division under an executive with almost complete responsibility for its management. The services of the staff functions like financial and sales policy and research were available to all the constituent operating divisions but without direct authority over them.

All of GM's operations were covered by Sloan's changes. Thus Sloan spent a great deal of time visiting dealers in what was increasingly changing into a buyers' market. Mechanisms for managing the dealer relationship and giving financial support to dealers were developed way beyond those used by Ford. Sloan also built up an efficient and co-operative team at the top of GM. William S. Knudsen was in charge of the ailing Chevrolet Division and he made it Ford's main challenger. GM also introduced the annual model change, a sales technique designed to fight the ageing Model T and to encourage the growth of second-hand car sales. Knudsen became GM's production genius, the equivalent of Ford's Charlie Sorensen, and he eventually became Sloan's successor. GM developed an increasingly sophisticated range of cars at moderate prices. In 1927 the production of Ford's Model T ended and Chevrolet became the industry leader in terms of sales, a position which it generally retained for many years, even if Ford's Model A, first sold late in 1928, outsold Chevrolet in its first year.

In the 1930s the US car industry's three main firms, GM, Ford and Chrysler, all suffered but were never threatened with extinction. Chrysler survived by technical innovation and, especially, careful financial management. Ford was very badly managed but too big to go under. GM came through safely by efficient management and good financial planning, and expanded successfully into new areas, such as aircraft and diesel engines. Sloan resigned from the presidency of GM in 1937, remaining chairman of the board. When he stood down GM made over one-third of the world's output of motor vehicles, as well as aircraft engines, diesel locomotives and refrigerators. It had been the world's largest manufacturer of cars since 1925. Apart from the Chevrolet, the best-selling car in the USA, it also made the Cadillac and its La Salle version, the Oldsmobile, Pontiac and Buick, trucks and buses, and Opel cars in Germany and Vauxhall cars in the UK. It had grown into the biggest industrial concern of all time. The Du Pont Company owned nearly a quarter of its shares: otherwise GM's ownership was quite widely shared.

Sloan opposed trade unions in the USA in the 1920s and 1930s but accepted them as inevitable when Roosevelt was elected in 1936 along with the New Deal. Sloan was a businessman and engineer of his time and place in his suspicion and fear of trade unions and government intervention. On the other hand, he had strong and positive ideas on the contributions which business and industry made to society and his methodical and open-ended approach to management was far more than a matter of logically balancing centralization and decentralization.

Sloan was a very able selector of managers, a strong and effective advocate of research, and in some respects a marketing genius. Above all he was a great advocate and practitioner of teamwork, whose breadth of understanding and diplomacy had marked him out for the highest levels of management early in his career. He was a 'great empiricist, a complex personality and a tireless worker who made GM his all embracing interest. He let time, precision and an incisive appeal work for him' (Dale 1971: 86). He gave up being GM's chief executive officer in 1946, and finally resigned from the chairmanship in 1956, while remaining an honorary chairman and working as a strategic consultant. He had endowed the Sloan Foundation in the late 1930s and supported such philanthropic societies as the Memorial Sloan–Kettering Cancer Center, New York City, and the Sloan School of Management and a centre for advanced engineering at the Massachusetts Institute of Technology. In 1964, two years before his death, he outlined his management policy in great detail in *My Years with General Motors*. He had written the ebullient *Adventures of a White Collar Man* with Boyden Sparkes in 1941.

3 Main contribution

Sloan's greatest contribution to the practice and understanding of management is most closely summarized by one word, which he and others often called an oversimplification: decentralization. Schnapp (1979) described how decision making at GM under Sloan was informal and collaborative and how the company did not have a formal strategic planning function like that of the Ford Motor Company. Decisions were made partly through a complicated but logical grouping of senior committees and partly in an arguably very *ad hoc* way, rather democratically and 'more effectively than other companies because of some basic values deeply embedded in the GM organization' (Schnapp 1979: 145). Most people who knew GM would inevitably think of Sloan on reading this.

In the early 1920s Sloan saw that the overwhelming need at GM was for coordination of product and financial policies and of the activities of its five largely independent divisions. He and his team foresaw significant market growth because of the development of closed body (all weather) car designs, of the USA's systems of paved highways, of the used car market and of bank financing of car purchases. GM needed a more coordinated and rational product policy and strong central control, too, over finance. An integrated business policy which minimized overlap and waste was vital. This implied central control over all design, development, investment, location, production and promotional decisions. It meant genuine delegation of decision-

making power to genuinely competing product divisions. Divisional management could, therefore, only be overridden by decisions taken at the highest level of GM, so that central staff functions had to use persuasion, and not coercion, to influence divisional managers.

The power to finance projects was separated from their originators and advocates. This meant that GM's top decision-making group, the executive committee, had to pass on proposals that it had approved itself to the corporate finance committee for its separate approval, before they could be submitted to the board of directors. The executive and finance committees were thus deliberately set up partly in opposition to each other.

Writing soon after the end of the Second World War, Drucker explained how Sloan had developed decentralization in GM to 'satisfy the basic requirements of institutional life' (1946: 41). These requirements included survival as an efficient entity, which demanded a policy that harmonized the divergent claims of administration and of specific tasks, which facilitated change and rejected expediency, and which provided a suitable framework for local action. Thus responsibility and power had to be distributed appropriately, policy formulation and operational planning had to be both undertaken and balanced, and considerable attention had to be paid to the selection and development of all kinds of staff, at all levels and for almost every purpose. In the 1930s and 1940s GM consisted of three major product groups: cars and trucks; accessories and spare parts (also refrigerators); and non-automotive (diesel and aircraft) engines. These businesses were organized in around thirty divisions, some very large, such as Chevrolet cars, and some small single plant ones with fewer than a thousand employees.

Each division was organized and managed as an autonomous business unit and the three largest were represented at the most senior level of GM by their own top managers. The others were represented at that level of GM by individuals drawn from product-based groups. As part of GM's central management and side by side with the product management organization, functional service staffs with their own vice presidents (manufacturing, engineering, sales, research, personnel, finance, public relations, legal affairs and so on) advised both divisional (line managers) and central management, liaised between the divisions, and formulated corporate policies. The line or manufacturing organization of GM was headed by the president and two executive vice presidents, and the staff one was headed by the chairman of the board of directors, who was also the chief executive officer of GM, and by the vice chairman of the board.

These five formed a team that worked with and through two major committees, the administration and policy ones. These two committees were the 'government' of GM, the 'central organ[s] of co-ordination, decision and control' (Drucker 1946: 43). They were the final courts of appeal for disagreements about policy in GM. All the most senior people in GM and representatives of its major shareholders belonged to them and they combined all sorts of experiences and backgrounds into one policy. They were kept fully informed about all general and staff and line issues and decisions facing GM and their role was to discuss and decide about them.

Numerous, much smaller sub-committees formed from these members dealt with mainly functional matters on a regular basis, feeding information and recommendations upwards to the two main committees. GM had up to 500 senior executives and 250,000 employees (double the latter number in the second world war). Strong financial control had become one of the main ways of keeping divisional managements in line while encouraging them to have the prestige and to exercise the power of real bosses. Central management needed to know even minor details of divisional management but divisional managers needed to have real authority and standing, too. Drucker (1946: 47) called GM 'an essay in federalism', which successfully combined the highest levels of corporate unity with divisional autonomy and responsibility. Decentralization at GM under Sloan was far more than a division of labour. It was a philosophy of management and a system of local self-government which extended down to include

the level of first line supervision and externally to relations with business partners (especially car dealers).

The benefits of Sloan's system of decentralization appear to have included clear and reasonably quick decision making, a relative lack of internal conflict, an atmosphere of fairness, democracy and informality, a sense of management being a large-scale activity shared among many, a plentiful supply of experienced and able leaders, the early detection and timely resolution of problems and an absence of management by edict. Central policies were unified and coherent and set clear goals and gave clear guidance to divisions. Central management acted as the eyes and ears for the whole of GM, and it planned and governed the long-term future of the divisions. It obtained their capital and it handled many of their financial, legal and accounting tasks as well as most trade union negotiations and contracts. Central management's services staff also kept divisions up to date with developments in engineering, marketing, accounting and other specialist areas. Divisional managements were in complete charge of production and sales, almost all staffing, of engineering, investment planning, advertising, public relations, buying and relations with dealers and so on.

About 95 per cent of all division-level decisions were taken by divisional managers who were virtually in complete control of their own businesses. They operated a system of bonuses which gave them considerable independence within centrally determined limits designed to curb excesses of favouritism and spitefulness. There were many open and informal devices designed to maintain a two-way flow of information between the highest levels of central management and the lowest levels of the divisions' management. Twice a year, and at the GM headquarters in Detroit, between 200 and 300 senior managers from all over GM met, so as to ensure that all senior managers got to know something about the whole GM picture. Also, members of GM's central management regularly visited divisions for several days at a time.

GM's relations with car dealers were a further significant element in the decentralized approach. Dealers were often locally prominent businessmen who were nonetheless tied to GM and its fortunes. They had little control over their own costs, or over the price of cars or the manner of their sale. Also, while GM was mainly interested in dealers' new car sales, dealers got most of their profits from the sales of used ones. GM applied the philosophy of enlightened self-interest to support dealers through difficult times and to protect them against financial pressures from sales staff. GM established a Dealers Council in the mid-1930s, with nearly fifty members representing a geographical cross-section of GM's USA car dealers. It discussed such issues as the nature of GM's franchise, car design and advertising techniques. The less well-known Motor Holdings Division financially supported and encouraged about 300 good and improving dealers from the late 1930s onwards. GM–dealer relations typified GM's management policies through their emphasis on harmony, mutual self-interest and stability.

Managers at all levels were encouraged to criticize GM policies and practices. Criticisms were not penalized: they were taken seriously. Persuasion and rational arguments were used at virtually all times. However central management was the boss. There was a mixture of freedom and order; open management tended to ensure that issues, ideas, problems and decisions were discussed and decided upon thoroughly. Cost accounting and market analysis provided the necessary objective and impersonal background and framework for all this, with base pricing and competitive market standing respectively the main indices in use. Efficiency was thus measured, as well as debated thoroughly, with all measurements and discussions being related to production planning. The style of management mixed the informal and the impersonal and was based on the strong respect for facts which Sloan encouraged perhaps more than anything else.

When Sloan ceased to be GM's chief executive officer in 1946, he had used decentralization to manage and develop GM very effectively for a quarter of a century. Henry Ford II had just taken over his grandfather's ramshackle empire and was unashamedly copying GM's methods of organization. Sloan's methods were flexible and strongly entrenched enough to handle all but the most unusual and special problems which face very large companies. However, the experience of government control in the second world war had shown how decentralization within GM could be threatened, not just by the centralizing tendencies of government contracts and demands, but also by other external forces such as *one* very big and powerful trade union or the US motor industry becoming a cartel.

Sloan's main contribution to the practice and understanding of business and management was to demonstrate how to balance the conflicting interests of the central and the local in a very large and diverse company. He also made a major contribution to the development of the car industry through his recognition of the growing, if structured, diversity of its market. His organizational methods and some of his other innovations were copied widely, notably by the General Electric Company as well as by Ford in the USA, by Imperial Chemical Industries in the UK, and in the USSR, Japan and western Europe.

4 Evaluation

From the 1930s to the 1960s many GM managers saw GM as something of a model for a capitalist society's industrial and social order. A very diverse and large enterprise had practised diversity through decentralization, using many different kinds of training, team building, internal representation of interests, decentralization within its constituent divisions, various forms of autonomous group working, and so on. GM's management under Sloan was a good compromise between efficiency and personal freedom and development. Performance was measured objectively and improved by a reasonable mixture of discussion, persuasion and coercion. Decentralization under Sloan meant respect for small scale and to some extent, implementation of the belief that small is beautiful. Certainly a significantly higher proportion of GM's top executives than might be expected tended to come from its smaller divisions.

During the years from when Sloan, after the second world war, was largely part of GM's past, through that of his death in 1966 and until the 1970s and the rise of serious foreign competition, GM continued to prosper. From the 1960s until the 1980s at least, so-called liberal criticism of big US business grew louder and more strident. GM had been very effective at developing its expert management but since the 1920s it had also been more of a managed than a truly innovating company, and in almost every respect a domestic, US one rather than a true multinational, at least until long after 1945. By the 1970s it was no longer an unequivocal source of pride for most Americans, just as car ownership no longer symbolized their personal achievements. Decentralization had been a very positive thing, but GM and other large US organizations increasingly needed to work with the US and other governments, and with international agencies, and with each other, in an internationalizing and ever-more interdependent world.

There is a real if rather unfair sense, using hindsight, in which Sloan's policy of decentralization looks like one of insularity. In his book *My Years with General Motors* (1964) Sloan tells his story in a highly impersonal way, and focuses almost entirely on the internal management and organization of GM. By writing in such a way Sloan was clearly trying to set a strong example of his ideal of 'professionalism' in management. In one sense this was odd because Sloan was a very human and people-centred person. However, while he was very democratic in a typically demotic, ebullient and even slightly folksy American way, and while GM was a more or less unequivocal major success from the 1920s until the 1970s, it was increasingly under attack and out of touch with the views of many people from the 1960s onwards.

In many important respects GM was a prisoner of its own success. The affluence that it had played a big part in creating gave people the time and other resources to criticize the hands that were feeding them. Sloan appreciated business very well as a source of work, jobs, wealth, security and so on, but less well in terms of its wider roles as a source of power

and influence, within communities and within society in general. He understood its economic, technical, psychological, commercial and financial aspects both imaginatively and in great detail, but at least as far as GM and his own work was concerned, his historical, political and sociological imagination was rather limited from a later twentieth-century vantage point. However, they were far from limited from the appropriate one, that of the early to mid- twentieth century, a far less affluent period in which the scale of international economic cooperation and interdependence was much smaller than it is now.

Sloan has long been a hero figure in GM as much for the atmosphere that he encouraged as anything else (Kanter 1985: 347). Dale described him as 'the great empiricist. . . a complex personality and a tireless worker who made GM his all-embracing interest' (1971: 86). According to Kennedy (1941: 157, 158), Sloan was very much 'the type that does well with a big organization, provided that big organization is supplied for him'. He had been helped by being 'an accessory man, not an automobile man' in his big task of 'keeping peace among the various heads of the General Motors manufacturing divisions'. Until Sloan had the authority to do this, the very sound policy of each of the five car divisions being virtually independent was hampered by all attempts at control from head office. Sloan was very much a second-generation car industry leader, more of a team leader than an individualist, more pragmatic than romantic, more of a manager than an innovator.

Even so, Sloan's organization and management of GM was original in several respects through its very strong emphasis on facts, cooperation and 'system', in particular through the coordination and control of staff services. The line-staff distinction came from the military, and decentralization to partly autonomous sub-units had been practised by the Roman Catholic church for centuries when Sloan came to power in GM. But it was his dynamic combination of them in a commercial context (and that simultaneously taking place at du Pont Chemicals) which was new, along with the presentation and continued adaptation of his flexible 'framework of 'decentralized operations and co-ordinated control''' (Dale [1960] 1971: 106), mainly through oral tradition among Sloan and other GM founder members, over several decades. Sloan and his team were also innovative in marketing policy: their aim to offer 'a car for every purse and purpose' (Chandler 1964: 16), to reach every sector of the market, effectively superseded Ford's concentration on one model. Regular developments in the performance and styling of GM's cars and energetic advertising helped the company to expand market share. Sloan's policy of financing both its car dealers and customers was also highly innovative in its day, and also the opposite of Ford's policies.

Sloan and GM's other top managers of the 1920s and 1930s had to innovate because their company, their industry and the scale of their operations were all new. As a consequence, and while most of their ideas have stood the test of time, some elements have a dated quality. Their early success probably helped to curtail consideration of alternatives and to engender a certain conservatism. This tendency was discussed by Rothschild at some length in her discussion of 'Sloanism, or GM's variety marketing' (1973: 37–40). She noted how the company focused on sales techniques in the 1930s, at the expense of technical innovation. GM stimulated and developed the cyclical trading of used cars as down payments on new ones, so that 'USA auto marketing became a worldwide model for the selling of expensive consumer goods, showing businesses how to create and nourish demand' (1973: 40). However, while the US car industry 'led the expansion of consumer demand at the end of the Second World War' (1973: 41), the increasingly saturated car market became more and more jaded.

On the technical side, the industry was no longer a new one and GM's investment levels had fallen from around 25 per cent of total sales value from 1918 to 1920, to about 4 per cent in the early 1970s. Capital investment was increasingly seen as a 'regrettable necessity' (Rothschild 1973: 49), not as an exciting adventure, as it was viewed previously. Marketing techniques and cost-cutting had

increasingly been the main preoccupations of large USA car company head offices, at the expense of technical innovation. Also, ever-increasing 'Fordist regimentation' (1973: 33) of car production, aimed at cost-cutting, had long been alienating the workforce. Customers were often alienated, too, by the perpetual, generally marginal at best and expensively cosmetic at worst, upgrading of the product. For Rothschild (1973: 247), cars were the definitive US product, just as railways had been for the UK and as televisions and other electronic consumer goods were for Japan.

5 Conclusion

The main achievements of Sloan's work were: (1) the stabilization, restoration and very successful expansion of the fortunes of the major grouping of companies in a major industry; (2) the solution of many problems of very large-scale and diverse commercial management through elaborate and flexible systems of decentralization; (3) influential developments in techniques of consumer marketing; (4) the development of numerous techniques and structures for providing top managers with facts needed for making strategic policy and operational decisions; and (5) the dissemination of his experiences and achievements through example and informal education programmes, influencing management and organizational practices across the world.

Sloan's main achievement was to make the practice of management more sophisticated and to show how management could be a broadly responsible and socially benign activity. Affluence, the internationalization of production and markets, and foreign competition all eventually eroded Sloan's success at GM but others have continued to emulate and build on them for many years, both there and elsewhere.

IAN GLOVER
UNIVERSITY OF STIRLING

Further reading

(References cited in the text marked *)

Baughmar, J.P. (ed.) (1969) *The History of American Management: Selections from the Business History Review*, Englewood Cliffs, NJ: Prentice Hall. (Contains varied accounts of the development of US organizations and management which help to explain the influence of Sloan and GM in US industrial history.)

* Chandler, A.D., Jr (ed.) (1964) *Giant Enterprise: Ford, General Motors and the Automobile Industry: Sources and Readings*, New York: Harcourt, Brace and World. (Mainly consists of readings and discussions of their relevance, concerned with the development of GM and Ford from 1900 to the 1950s. Excellent on GM's innovations in management and marketing.)

* Dale, E. (1960) *The Great Organizers*, New York: McGraw-Hill, 1971. (On the development of systematic organization in US management: particularly stories on the contributions of Sloan and GM.)

* Drucker, P.F. (1946) *The Concept of the Corporation*, New York: John Day. (Considers the problems of large-scale capitalist organization and industry in the USA using GM under Sloan as its main source of evidence.)

* Kanter, R.M. (1985) *The Change Masters: Corporatist Entrepreneurs at Work*, Hemel Hempstead: Unwin. (Contains chapter on GM's problems of the 1970s and 1980s which includes a useful account of Sloan's legacy.)

* Kennedy, E.D. (1941) *The Coming of Age of Capitalism's Favourite Child*, New York: Reynal and Hitchcock. (Covers the period 1890 to 1940; rather descriptive but useful for understanding the roles of Sloan and GM in the US car industry in the years when it was established.)

Kuhn, A. (1986) *GM Passes Ford, 1918–1938: Designing the General Motors Performance-Control System*, University Park, Pennsylvania: State University Press. (Excellent on Sloan's design of GM's structure, the prototype of the modern managerial bureaucracy.)

Rae, J.B. (1959) *American Automobile Manufacturers: The First Forty Years*, Philadelphia: Chilton. (Excellent, balanced account of the history of the industry's companies until the mid-1930s; contains many useful comparisons between GM and its rivals.)

Rae, J.B. (1965) *The American Automobile: A Brief History*, Chicago: University of Chicago Press. (Covers the industry from the 1890s to the 1960s; includes a balanced account of the roles of Sloan and GM.)

* Rothschild, E. (1973) *Paradise Lost: The Decline of the Auto-Industrial Age*, New York: Random House. (On the problems of the US car industry in the early to mid-1970s, facing public scepticism, market saturation and foreign competition; excellent on the growing conservatism of GM.)

* Schnapp, J.B. (1979) *Corporate Strategies of the Automotive Manufacturers*, Lexington, MA: D.C. Heath & Co. (Covers the strategies of four American, one German and three major Japanese car companies in the mid-late 1970s; GM and its history are compared usefully with others.)

* Sloan, A.P., Jr (1964) *My Years with General Motors*, New York: Doubleday. (Impressively professional account of General Motors' story under Sloan, of the 'logic of management in relation to the events of the automobile industry' (p.xxiii).)

* Sloan, A.P., Jr and Sparkes, B. (1941) *Adventures of a White Collar Man*, New York: Books for Libraries. (Ebullient and endearing account of most of Sloan's life which offers much evidence of his integrity, enthusiasm, imagination and middle-class American folksiness.)

See also: CHANDLER, A.D.; DRUCKER, P.F.; FORD, H.; SCHUMACHER, E.F.; TAYLOR, F.W.; WILLIAMSON, O.E.

Related topics in the IEBM: ADVERTISING CAMPAIGNS; BIG BUSINESS AND CORPORATE CONTROL; CORPORATE STRATEGIC CHANGE; DECISION MAKING; ECONOMIC INTEGRATION, GROUPS AND TEAMS; INTERNATIONAL; GLOBALIZATION; INDUSTRIAL AND LABOUR RELATIONS; LEADERSHIP; LOGISTICS IN MANUFACTURING MANAGEMENT AND OPERATIONS; MANAGEMENT IN NORTH AMERICA; MANAGERIAL BEHAVIOUR; MARKETING; MARKETING, FOUNDATIONS OF; MARKETING STRATEGY; MULTINATIONAL CORPORATIONS, ORGANIZATION STRUCTURE IN; ORGANIZATION BEHAVIOUR, HISTORY OF; ORGANIZATION STRUCTURE; PUBLIC RELATIONS; STRATEGIC CHOICE; STRATEGY AND BUYER–SUPPLIER RELATIONSHIPS; STRATEGY, CONCEPT OF; TRADE UNIONS

Smith, Adam (1723–90)

Personal background

- born before 5 June 1723 in Kirkcaldy, Fife, Scotland, the son of a customs official
- educated at University of Glasgow, 1737–40
- Snell Exhibitioner, Balliol College, Oxford, 1740–6
- professor at University of Glasgow, 1751–64
- tutor to the Duke of Buccleuch, 1764–6
- Commissioner of Customs, 1778
- died in Edinburgh on 17 July 1790 of stomach cancer

Major works

The Theory of Moral Sentiments (1759)
Lectures on Jurisprudence (1762–3; first published 1978)
The Wealth of Nations (1776)

Summary

Adam Smith (1723–90), the leading figure in the classical school of economics and prominent in the Scottish Enlightenment, is one of the few economists to be credited with founding economics. In his compendious work, *The Wealth of Nations*, he integrated the information and ideas provided by historical and contemporary authors to explain how an economy operates and how it can grow. He set out a system of natural liberty for an economy, justified free trade and inspired subsequent value and distribution theories. Both socialist and libertarian economists look to him as a precursor.

1 Introduction

Adam Smith was born into a prosperous Scottish family and baptised on 5 June 1723. His father, the Clerk of the Court Martial and Comptroller of Customs at Kirkcaldy, died before his only son was born. Smith was educated at the local burgh school then entered the University of Glasgow in 1737 to study Latin, Greek, Logic, Moral Philosophy, Mathematics and Natural Philosophy for an MA degree. In 1740, without graduating, he left Glasgow when he was awarded a Snell Exhibition at Balliol College, Oxford. This minor scholarship was intended to enable young men to train for the ministry in the Church of England. Disgusted by the poor quality of the teaching at the University of Oxford, Smith embarked on an extensive course of self-education. Smith returned to Scotland in 1746, resigning the exhibition in 1749.

He had no intention of entering the church's ministry so he looked for a career in the law or elsewhere. Encouraged by the Lord Advocate, he gave private lectures in Edinburgh for three winters on rhetoric, *belles-lettres* and philosophy. Anticipating his later views, Smith told his audience: 'Little else is required to carry a state to the highest degree of opulence from the lowest barbarism, but peace, easy taxes, and a tolerable administration of justice; all the rest being brought about by the natural course of things' (Smith 1983).

In 1751 he was appointed Professor of Logic at Glasgow; in 1752 he was translated to the Chair of Moral Philosophy. He interpreted his academic remit widely to lecture on rhetoric, ethics, jurisprudence and economics. From reconstructions of students' lecture notes, it is possible to see the breadth of Smith's erudition. He was an enthusiastic teacher, lecturing eight hours weekly and involved in university administration, being Dean of the Faculty 1760–62. The University of Glasgow conferred the LLD degree on him in 1762. Residence in Glasgow enabled Smith to gain a detailed knowledge of the views and methods of merchants, putting that knowledge to use in his later economic writings.

The publication of *The Theory of Moral Sentiments* in 1759 brought him considerable fame. Charles Townshend, Secretary of State and stepfather of the eighteen-year-old Duke of Buccleuch, was sufficiently impressed by the book to invite Smith to leave the University of Glasgow to accompany the duke on a grand tour of Europe. Smith was given a life pension of £300 per annum, the same amount as his previous academic earnings. From January 1764 to November 1766 Smith travelled with the duke and his younger brother to Paris, Toulouse and Geneva, meeting François Quesnay (1694–1774) and other leading physiocrats, as well as Voltaire. The death of the duke's younger brother in Paris ended Smith's only journey beyond Britain.

Smith spent the winter of 1766–7 in London working on a revision of *The Theory of Moral Sentiments*, as well as advising Townshend, then Chancellor of the Exchequer, on the sinking fund. For six years to 1773, Smith stayed at his mother's home in Kirkcaldy gathering information for and preparing drafts of *The Wealth of Nations*. From 1773 to 1777 he resided in London, with a nine-month break in Scotland in 1776 to visit his dying friend David Hume and his ageing mother. In 1773 he was elected to the Royal Society. In London his opinions were eagerly sought. However, his view that the problem of the American colonies should be solved by a union of the colonies with Britain, with American representatives in the House of Commons, was rejected; later it was used as a model for the union with Ireland in 1800. *The Wealth of Nations* was published on 9 March 1776 to the immediate acclaim of contemporary thinkers. He received a flat fee of about £500 from his publishers.

He was appointed Commissioner of Customs at a salary of £600 in 1778, diligently attending board meetings at the Royal Exchange (now the City Chambers) of Edinburgh and residing at Panmure House, Canongate. It was strange for the apostle of free trade to administer a protectionist trade policy but it had no effect on his revisions to *The Wealth of Nations*. In his last years he revised his major works and took an active part in the social life of the city, becoming famous for his Sunday night supper parties. He died of a stomach cancer. His personal papers were burnt, on his orders, by his executors but his personal library substantially survives at Edinburgh University and in Tokyo. His grave in Canongate kirkyard, Edinburgh, has attracted respectful visitors from numerous countries.

2 Main contribution to economics

At the outset of his writing career, Smith wrote on moral philosophy. In *The Theory of Moral Sentiments* he set out to show that nature is a cosmic harmony and society is bound together by sympathy. Also, he introduced ideas which were to be central to *The Wealth of Nations*. He recognized that human behaviour is motivated by self-interest, but also by the contemplation of a grand and harmonious design for society. Nevertheless, there is an optimistic tone to the book. In his discussion of income distribution he states:

> The rich only select from the heap what is most precious and agreeable. They consume little more than the poor. . . . They are led by an invisible hand to make nearly the same distribution of the necessaries of life which would have been made, had the earth been divided into equal portions among all its inhabitants, and thus without intending it, without knowing it, advance the interest of the society and afford means to the multiplication.
>
> (Smith [1759] 1976: 184)

This passage is typical of the whole book. The underlying principles influencing society, including the idea of the 'invisible hand', are set out with economic mechanisms suggested but not discussed in detail.

As a professor of moral philosophy, he lectured on jurisprudence. Jurisprudence was regarded by Smith as including the study of trade, commerce, agriculture and manufactures as the police had the task of regulating markets. A copy of his lectures to the jurisprudence class for the winter of 1762–3 survives. It provides a clear insight into his early economic thinking. The influence of Francis Hutcheson (1694–1746), who had taught Smith in the 1730s at Glasgow, is strong but there is also a preview of Smith's later theories. Already there is a critique of the mercantilist policies of prohibiting the export of bullion and maintaining a favourable balance of trade. He uses a four-stage theory of economic development with human history divided into the four ages of hunters, shepherds, agriculture and commerce. He sets out the important principle of the division of labour and distinguishes natural price from market price. But in his theory of value he uses a straightforward notion of scarcity to explain paradoxes such as water being necessary but cheap and jewels with an immense price but little usefulness: 'cheapness is a necessary consequence of plenty' (Smith [1762–3] 1978: 333).

Smith's visit to France enabled him to have discussions on economics with the Physiocrats, the French school of economics which believed that agriculture was the only productive sector of an economy and that government regulation of economic life should be minimal. Subsequently Smith diligently collected information from numerous sources to write a detailed survey of economics. The full title of Smith's *magnum opus*, *An Inquiry into the Nature and Causes of the Wealth of Nations of 1776* indicates clearly that he wanted to analyse the nature of economic growth. At the outset he stated that the welfare of a state is measured by the ratio of produce to population, similar to the modern measure of economic welfare, per capita GDP. Smith attributes growth to the 'skill, dexterity and judgment with which its labour is generally applied' (Smith [1776] 1976: 10) and, less importantly, to the ratio of productive to unproductive labour.

The Wealth of Nations is divided into five books but has a continuous argument. He begins with determinants of productivity and income distribution then considers how capital is employed. He surveys the growth record of other nations, the diversity of economic systems and the activities of states in taxing and spending. The major themes are economic growth, value and distribution, the working of markets, international trade and the relationship between the State and the individual.

The human motive which starts an economy on a growth path is 'the desire of bettering our condition' (Smith [1776] 1976: 341) which prompts saving; the saving is invested to provide a capital fund which will make possible the employment of the labour force and the division of labour. Division of labour is a fundamental principle, the consequence of: 'a certain propensity in human nature. . .the propensity to truck, barter, and exchange one thing for another' (Smith [1776] 1976: 25). Using the example of pin-making he explains that by dividing the tasks of human labour into its component parts, the dexterity of the worker increases, the time lost in one piece of work to another is saved and machinery can be invented as a consequence of analysing work into its sub-operations. However, Smith did appreciate that economic growth has its costs. The effect of the division of labour is to make a person who spends his life on a few simple operations 'as stupid and ignorant as it is possible for a human creature to become' (Smith [1776] 1976: 782).

Again, in this work Smith makes use of his 'four stages' theory to explain how value is determined and the national product is distributed among the landlord, the capitalist and the labourer. The determination of value changes as the economy has progressed through its earliest stage. It is only in the most primitive of human societies, the age of the hunters, that goods (beavers and deer) are exchanged according to the quantities of labour required to obtain the goods. Only then do labourers obtain the whole produce of their labour. With population growth and the accumulation of capital, land becomes private property and the landlord receives a share of the national produce as rent and the capitalist profits. Like Aristotle before him, Smith distinguishes 'value in use' from 'value in exchange'. He also contrasts market prices and natural prices. The proportion between supply and demand determines the market price but the natural price is 'the central price to which the prices of all commodities are continually gravitating'

(Smith [1776] 1976: 75). This natural price is brought about by free competition and can be regarded as a long-run equilibrium price equal to the costs of production in the form of rent, profits and wages.

Smith's concept of the market mechanism is clear in his celebrated account of how in labour and capital markets there will be equilibrating flows in response to differentials: 'The whole of the advantages and disadvantages of the different employments of labour and stock must, in the same neighbourhood, be either perfectly equal or continually tending to equality' (Smith [1776] 1976: 116). But he was aware, too, of market imperfections. In product markets, businesses are constantly trying to engage in collusive oligopoly: 'People of the same trade seldom meet together, even for merriment and diversion, but the conversation ends in a conspiracy against the public, or in some contrivance to raise prices' (Smith [1776] 1976: 145).

In the labour market there is, according to Smith, unequal bargaining. Smith states that the workmen desire to get as much, the masters to give as little as possible. The masters, being fewer in number, can combine much more easily. Moreover, the law authorizes, or at least does not prohibit their combinations, while it prohibits those of the workmen (Smith [1776] 1976: 84–5)

After his discussion of the domestic economy, Smith turns his attention to different economic systems and to international trade. Having argued that the division of labour is the desirable course for the domestic economy, he justifies free trade in terms of the efficiency and productivity gains arising from a similar specialization internationally:

> The tailor does not attempt to make his own shoes . . . . All of them find it for their interest to employ their whole industry in a way in which they have some advantage over their neighbours and to purchase with a part of its produce. . . whatever else they have occasion for . . . . What is prudence in the conduct of every private family, can scarce be folly in that of a great kingdom . . . . Would it be a reasonable law to prohibit the importation of all foreign

wines, merely to encourage the making of claret and burgundy in Scotland?
>
> (Smith [1776] 1976: 456–8)

This trade theory based on 'absolute advantage' was part of Smith's attack on mercantilism. He also criticized the mercantilists for identifying wealth with gold and silver, not goods; also, for putting the interest of the producer above that of the consumer.

Smith disapproved of state intervention as subsidization of industry would divert economic activity away from its natural course. He saw the only justification for public institutions the benefits they conferred on society and the impossibility of the beneficiaries paying for them. Defence, law and order, the expenses of the sovereign and some public institutions were all that he recommended. As far as possible expenditure on the infrastructure was to be directly financed, for example, by tolls on roads and fees for education. Some taxation was necessary to finance this minimal state. The taxation should be according to ability to pay, certain, payable at the time of receipt of income and collected at minimum cost.

When faced with particular economic problems, Smith was willing to accept some departures from *laissez-faire*. Regulations on the issue of paper currency, support for the Navigation Acts which ruled that English trade be carried in English ships and a maximum interest rate of five per cent are all advocated. But the individual was more important than the government in economic life. At the heart of his analysis Smith maintained the beneficial effects of the pursuit of self-interest:

> By directing that industry in such a manner as its produce may be of the greatest value, he intends only his own gain, and he is in this, as in many other cases, led by an invisible hand to promote an end which was no part of his intention.
>
> (Smith [1776] 1976: 456)

3 Conclusions

Schumpeter, in a celebrated criticism of Smith, noted that Smith's admirers praised

The Wealth of Nations for the policies it advocated and for the fact that it contained 'no really novel ideas' but was a feat of coordination of previous economic writings. Also commended were Smith's accessible style and the fact that he 'was thoroughly in sympathy with the humours of his time' and 'advocated the things that were in the offing' (Schumpeter 1954: 185).

Gray, too, admitted that Smith was not a pioneer and could be confused, especially on value, but has the greatest name in the history of economics. He stated that 'before Adam Smith there had been much economic discussion; with him we reach the stage of discussing economics' (Gray 1980: 110). A more recent commentator on Smith, Hollander, sees in *The Wealth of Nations* 'not merely. . . the extraordinary range of topics treated, but also. . . Smith's demonstration of a high degree of interdependence between apparently unrelated variables culminating in his development of a more or less consistent 'model' of value and distribution' (Hollander 1973: 305).

Although Smith's method of economic exposition is literary, twentieth-century mathematical economists award him high marks. Samuelson (see SAMUELSON, P.A.) has written a strong defence of Smith and praises him for anticipating general equilibrium theory. The breadth of economic life discussed by Smith makes his work relevant to the discussion of modern business life: monetary economics, joint stock companies and entrepreneurship all commanded his attention (Laidler 1981; Anderson and Tollison 1982; Pesciarelli 1989). Smith's genius has been recognized throughout the world, with both ardent free marketers and socialists, even Lenin, acknowledging their debt to him (Mizuta and Sugiyama 1993).

DONALD RUTHERFORD
UNIVERSITY OF EDINBURGH

Further reading

(References cited in the text marked *)

* Anderson, G.M. and Tollison, R.D. (1982) 'Adam Smith's analysis of joint stock companies', *Journal of Political Economy* 90 (6): 1237–56. (An exposition of how corporations survive under competition through superior efficiency.)

Campbell, R.H. and Skinner, A.S. (1982) *Adam Smith*, London: Croom Helm. (A precise biographical summary of his life, principal lecture courses and books.)

* Gray, A. (1931, 1980 with A.E. Thompson) *The Development of Economic Doctrine*, London: Longman. (A stimulating general survey of economics placing Smith in the context of other leading economists.)

* Hollander, S. (1973) *The Economics of Adam Smith*, Toronto: University of Toronto Press. (Smith's analysis of the price mechanism and economic development in its historical context.)

* Laidler, D. (1981) 'Adam Smith as a monetary economist', *Canadian Journal of Economics* 14 (2): 185–200. (An explanation of how Smith integrated his banking theory into his theory of economic development.)

* Mizuta, H. and Sugiyama, C. (eds) (1993) *Adam Smith: International Perspectives*, London: Macmillan. (International symposium papers which trace Smith's past and present influence.)

* Pesciarelli, E. (1989) 'Smith, Bentham and the development of contrasting ideas of entrepreneurship', *History of Political Economy* 21 (3): 521–36. (Smith's view of the entrepreneur as a risk taker, planner and organizer of productive forces.)

Samuelson, P.A. (1977) 'A modern theorist's vindication of Adam Smith', *American Economic Review* 67: 42–9. (A mathematical proof that Smith's economic model survives the attacks of Ricardo and Marx.)

* Schumpeter, J.A. (1954) *History of Economic Analysis*, London: George Allen & Unwin. (A monumental study of how economic analysis developed from its earliest beginnings.)

Skinner, A. and Wilson, T. (1975) *Essays on Adam Smith*, Oxford: Clarendon Press. (A collection of articles which demonstrate the relevance of Smith to modern economic discussions.)

* Smith, A. (1759) *The Theory of Moral Sentiments*, ed. D.D. Raphael and A.L. MacFie, Oxford: Oxford University Press, 1976.

* Smith, A. (1762–3) *Lectures on Jurisprudence*, ed. R.L. Meek, D.D. Raphael and P.G. Stein, Oxford: Oxford University Press, 1978.

* Smith, A. (1776) *An Inquiry into the Nature and Causes of the Wealth of Nations*, ed. R.H. Campbell and A.S. Skinner, Oxford: Oxford University Press, 1976.

Smith, A. (1795) *Essays on Philosophical Subjects*, ed. I.S. Ross, Oxford: Oxford University Press, 1980.

Smith, A. (1977; 1987) *The Correspondence of Adam Smith*, ed. E.C. Mosner and I.S. Ross, Oxford: Oxford University Press.

* Smith, A. (1983) *Lectures on Rhetoric and Belles-Lettres*, ed. J.C. Bryce, Oxford: Oxford University Press.

See also: KEYNES, J.M.; MILL, J.S.; SAMUELSON, P.A.; SCHUMPETER, J.A.

Related topics in the IEBM: BUSINESS ECONOMICS; BUSINESS AND SOCIETY; CAPITAL MARKETS, REGULATION OF; DURKHEIM, .; INDUSTRIAL ECONOMICS; INTERNATIONAL MARKETING; INTERNATIONAL TRADE AND FOREIGN DIRECT INVESTMENT; LABOUR MARKETS; PRODUCTIVITY

Starbuck, William Haynes (1934–)

1 General appraisal
2 Early aspirations
3 Organizational growth and metamorphosis
4 Organizational design
6 Scientific methods
7 Conclusion

Personal background

- born 20 September 1934 at Portland, Indiana, USA
- graduated from Harvard University (AB Physics 1956), Carnegie Institute of Technology (MSc 1959; PhD 1964)
- held professorships in administrative sciences and economics (Purdue 1964–67), administration and sociology (Cornell 1967–71), and business administration (Wisconsin-Milwaukee 1974–84),
- held visiting professorships at Johns Hopkins University, (1966–67), London Business School (1970–71), International Institute of Management, Berlin (1971–74), Norwegian School of Economics and Business Administration, Bergen (1977–78), and Stockholm School of Economics (1977–78)
- Fellow, American Psychological Association (1975), Academy of Management (1986), American Psychological Society (1995)
- developed the concepts of self-designing organizations, organizational design, environmental niches, organizational equilibria composed of antithetical processes, relativity of aspirations through time
- contributed extensively to behavioural research methods and epistemology
- president, Academy of Management (1997–98)
- currently ITT Professor of Creative Management at New York University

Major works

'Organizational growth and development' in J. G. March (ed.), *Handbook of Organizations* (1965)

'Camping on seesaws: Prescriptions for a self-designing organization' 9with Bo L. T. Hedberg and Paul C. Nystrom) *Administrative Science Quarterly* (1976)

Handbook of Organizational Design (two volumes, edited with Paul C. Nystrom) (1981)

More than one hundred articles for leading scientific journals including *Administrative Science Quarterly, American Sociological Review, Behavioral Science, Journal of Management Studies*

Summary

William H. Starbuck has exerted a pervasive influence on three generations of behavioural scientists and management researchers. His works, which range over many topics, are distinguished by cautious inferences and constant reflexive interrogation. They investigate decision making, organizational design, learning, cognition, interaction between rationality and ideologies, forecasting, crises, and scientific methods. They emphasize the relativity of managers' perceptions, the interactions between rationality and ideologies, the use of experimental prescriptions, and crisis management through unlearning of behavioural and cognitive patterns. His writings assume a world filled with paradoxical, contradictory and antithetical processes. He has striven to foster prescriptive organizational design, and his four edited books include the classic *Handbook of Organizational Design* with Paul Nystrom (1981). During his term as the editor of *Administrative Science Quarterly (ASQ)*, he reoriented its focus on organization theory and enlisted an international editorial board.

1 General appraisal

'Self, career, family, organization and society tangle together. To abstract myself or my career from context would violate my scientific standards' (Starbuck 1993: 66).

William H. Starbuck's works stand among the most influential and most quoted in management sciences. Yet the range and depth of his contributions makes them difficult to describe, and the basic pattern of his research cannot be encapsulated in a single recurrent theme. His works range widely across applied mathematics and experimental psychology (1963, 1965a, 1965b, etc.), sociology and organizational theory (1974, 1983, etc.), information systems and man–machine interaction (1975, etc.), to scientific methods (1968, 1974, 1981: 9–13; 1988: 73–77, 1993, 1994)

Constant self-reflection and relentless interrogation of his own assumptions and values are key attributes of Starbuck's research. His autobiographical essay (1993) expresses extreme frankness. His research creates a paradoxical feeling because it is sometimes very prescriptive – such as works on managing crises (1978) – and sometimes very relativist, embodying astute wisdom and scepticism. This relativism is exemplified by the notion that organizations rely on antithetical processes that counterbalance and neutralize each other (1976).

Consistent with the behaviourist school – which is more attitude than doctrine, more philosophy and epistemology than specific assumptions – Starbuck's works are deeply rooted in a constant interrogation of concrete behaviours, extracting theoretical revolutions from singulars and exemplars. Human failures and weaknesses are particularly praised by Starbuck, who integrates his own life experiences (1993) into his theoretical constructions and his reflections on science.

Early aspirations

With a BA in Physics from Harvard University and three summers at IBM, the Starbuck was aiming for a doctorate in applied mathematics and a career as a computer designer. Then Richard Cyert, one of his professors at the Carnegie Institute of Technology, offered him financial aid for doctoral studies in Industrial Administration and advised him to focus on behavioural sciences. One result of this history is that Starbuck's writings reflect a tension between determinism and relativism. He sometimes does elegant acrobatics to avoid choosing between his intransigent and mathematical logic, on one hand, and the wisdom of a behaviourist who is willing to introduce fragility and relativity in the act of research, and consequently in theory construction.

From 1957 to 1960, Cyert and March mobilized students to conduct various studies in support of their forthcoming *A Behavioral Theory of the Firm* (1963). Starbuck ran an experiment in which three people had to cooperate to achieve joint results while also pursuing somewhat divergent individual goals (Cyert *et al.* 1961). The experiment drew two conclusions: (1) Individuals modify the information they transmit to pursue the rewards they expect from alternative group actions. (2) However, in the experimental situation, these manipulations do not affect the groups' performance.

Also, as part of the *Behavioral Theory of the Firm* project, Starbuck wrote a paper about aspiration levels that built upon Simon's notions. This student paper eventually turned into a published article in the highly prestigious *Psychological Review* (Starbuck 1963), debunked Festinger's theory that people set their aspirations so as to maximize subjective utility. The latter regarded a level of aspiration as a point of reference for feelings of success or failure; a performance exceeding the level of aspiration is a success, a performance that fails to reach this level is a failure. Starbuck pointed out that the utility-maximization model implies that, in this case, people should set their aspirations so low that every outcome would produce feelings of success. Starbuck argued, instead, that levels of aspiration change as goals are matched or missed. He also suggested that people construct their preferences ex-post so that behaviours and preferences interact continuously. This relative treatment of preferences was later echoed by March and Olsen's work.

This theme of antithetical processes that correct themselves in the course of events has been persistent throughout Starbuck's works, borrowing different clothes and disguises as the scope and focus shifts from very small to very large units of analysis. Organizing processes generate other processes that counterbalance them ('self-designing organizations' 1975–81). Decision making becomes a continuous collision between rationality and ideologies (1978). The ironies and bitter surprises of his life probably led him to study brutal and unilateral changes (such as social revolutions) and to develop a theoretical predilection for breakdowns and paradoxes, that revolve and self-dissolve.

3 Organizational growth and metamorphosis

The article that first made Starbuck well known was a chapter about Organizational Growth and Development in the *Handbook of Organizations* (1965b). This chapter began by reiterating the theme that behaviours and preferences interact continuously. Starbuck analysed motives for organizational growth – self-realization, risk, prestige, executives incomes, profit, cost, monopoly, stability and survival – and then he (1965b: 465) wondered: 'Do these goals produce growth, or does growth produce these goals?'.

He divided growth models into four categories : (a) cell-division models, which focus on growth as a change in percentage of size by adding cells and divisions; (b) metamorphosis models, which acknowledge that growth is not a regular process but incorporates abrupt changes; (c) will-o'-the-wisp models, which portray growth as the pursuit of opportunities that disappear as expansion is realized; and (d) decision–process models, which examine decision rules and decision-making procedures. Sometimes with an obvious lack of diplomacy, Starbuck unveiled brick by brick the flawed constructions of each model, picking up empirical weaknesses, shedding light on logical inconsistencies or methodological limits. He showed how cell-division models tend to concentrate on effects and to ignore

causes of growth; how metamorphosis models, although describing causes and effects of change fail to show their connections; how will-o'-the wisp models frame internal processes and external factors as 'chicken and egg'; and how decision–process models become harder to understand as they become more realistic.

'One problem with most models of organizational growth', Starbuck concluded, 'is that they imply a degree of autonomy and predestination which is difficult to reconcile with one's direct observation' (1965b: 494). Thus, Starbuck (1968, 1973) sought models that would embrace the totality of the phenomenon from its emergence to its extinction. Metamorphosis models seemed promising because they left room for unforeseen and fast adjustments, gave attention to details, and allowed for non-linearity and intrinsic regulation in the course of action. Starbuck's penchant for experimentation and his abilities in mathematics led him to the works of the Russian mathematician Pontryagin. The latter demonstrated that it is far more parsimonious to describe a revolution by three distinct groups of equations, instead of trying to integrate all phenomena into a single system of equations. These three systems describe (a) the slow transformation before the revolution, (b) the fast transformation during the revolution, and (c) a slow transformation after the revolution. This analysis also convinced Starbuck ('Tadpoles' 1973) that for any system capable of dramatic revolution, it is impossible to state precisely why the revolution occurs.

Starbuck's acute and cutting analyses, which leave little hope for the reviewed theories, have become as renowned as his generosity and commitment to young researchers. Starbuck's sharp scrutiny literally destroyed contingency theory ('A trip to view the elephants and rattlesnakes in the garden of Aston' 1981). In that case and many others, he has devoted enormous effort to producing evidence contradicting widely held theories, beliefs, or methods. For instance, he has repeatedly attacked tests of statistical significance (e. g 'On Behalf of Naïveté?' 1994).

4 Organizational design

George Box and Norman Draper were working on improving industrial processes in the late 1960s. The classical approach was, at that time, to establish the best possible design *a priori* given the state of current and exhaustive knowledge. Unfortunately, the constant improvement of industrial processes necessitated frequent interruptions and ad hoc fine tuning, so they proposed the use of evolutionary operation (EVOP). The philosophy of this method was to manage processes so that not only products were produced, but also the necessary information to improve the manufacturing processes. Box and Draper saw an analogy between EVOP and biological evolution, with natural selection operating to improve industrial processes.

This idea of a learning derived from incremental experiments eventually led Starbuck to the concept of 'self-designing organizations'. But first, it influenced a project for the German Federal Health Bureau. Starbuck and Wolfgang Müller (1972) were asked to design an information system that would help the Bureau to evaluate the efficacy of medicines (1993: 87). However, the rapid development of medical research would make any fixed system rapidly obsolete, as would the ever changing information about the efficacy and side-effects of medicines. So Starbuck and Müller proposed that the system be designed to support constant redesign. 'The central design challenge is to allow for solutions to an endlessly and rapidly evolving set of problems, taking into account changes in one's own comprehension of the problems as well as changes in the problems themselves' (1975: 219).

'Self-designing organizations' became the focus of a fruitful collaboration with Bo Hedberg and Paul Nystrom that extended over a decade and that continues to influence works on learning organizations and paradoxical change in organizations. An early statement of principles appeared as 'Camping on Seesaws: Prescriptions for a self-designing organization' (*ASQ* 1976). This article emphasized the roles of antithetical processes and contradictory prescriptions as sources of their inner balance for organizations. The deliberately prescriptive approach was itself a methodological prescription. By introducing changes in organization, they said, researchers can simultaneously generate better data, learn more about organizations' behaviour, and improve organizations.

Prevalent prescriptions for organizational design, said Starbuck *et al.*, were calling for 'organizational palaces' where specialization, clear objectives, and unequivocal structures would create differentiated yet harmonious ensembles, where rational procedures and delimited responsibilities would build rigid structures with 'refined and elegant' components. But such 'palaces' avoid experiments, praise certainties, ossify their behaviours, balk at reorientations, and intolerant despotic leaders. One method to sustain 'organizational palaces' is periodic redesign, but a procedure can itself become a routine of self-indulgent examinations and self-fulfilling prophecies. For Starbuck *et al.*, there was no reason an organization should behave more consistently than its environment. They proposed that 'organizational tents' should replace palaces. Indecisiveness can increase exploration, unlearning and relearning. More ambiguous roles can produce flexibility.

Not only should managers live in tents, they should pitch the tents on seesaws that balance antithetical organizational forces. Six seesaws interact: consensus and dissension, contentment and discontent, resource abundance and scarcity, faith in plans and doubt, consistency and experimentation, and rationality and imperfection. 'A self-designing organization can attain dynamic balances through overlapping, unplanned, and non-rational proliferation of its processes; and these proliferating processes, collide, contest and interact with one another to generate wisdom'(ASQ 1976: 63).

5 Crises: reframing and unlearning

Starbuck's organizational design theories are rooted in a distinctive analysis of the interactions between ideologies and rationality. The question that originally motivated this work was why organizations or people remain in stagnating environments. Starbuck (1982) attributed this inertia to the ideologies people invent to justify their actions. Ideologies are integrated aggregates of beliefs, values, rites and symbols. Environments are both products and sources of ideologies, as decision-making unfolds and intertwines people, ideologies and rationalization of upcoming events. The conformity of organizational ideologies to societal aspirations acts as a source of reassuring legitimacy for the organization.

Starbuck drew a distinction between problem solving, which aspires to rationality, and action generating, in which people observe the results of their actions and propose either new actions or new problems to fit the available solutions. He argued that the issue of whether problems are real or not is resolved by collective voting, in which clichés and quasi-theories play important roles. 'Organizations' characteristics create perceptual filters that strongly distort their attempts at rational analyses' (Starbuck 1982: 6). These ideas about cognition reflect the influence of Watzlawick, and colleagues who examined situations in which people invent solutions that make their problems worse. Before they can generate effective solutions, this view said that, the people must see the problems in entirely different frames. Likewise, argued Starbuck, organizations are often unable to respond appropriately to problems until they see the problems in new frames.

Starbuck's ideas on non-rational decision processes culminated in a paper of 'action generators,' which built on the writings of March and Simon (see also MARCH, J. AND CYERT, R. and SIMON, H.). 'Organizations' activities categorize in at least two modes: a problem-solving mode in which perceived problems motivate searches for solutions, and an action-generating mode in which action taking motivates the invention of problems to justify the actions. The problem-solving mode seems to describe a very small percentage of the activity sequences that occur, and the action-generating mode a large percentage' (Starbuck 1983: 91–92).

Hence, organizations build ideologies that turn into structures, language, actions or problems, and then become themselves sources for building new ideologies (Meyer and Starbuck 1993). Past successes are interpreted as criteria for the validity and consistency of current behaviours, as in the case of NCR, where eighty years of success in mechanical cash registers fused beliefs, strategies, structures, and action programmes into a self-reinforcing ensemble. Ideology then blinds the organization to signals of dramatic change, and crises materialize while organizations act in ways that make the crises worse (Starbuck et al. 1978).

Starbuck's longitudinal case studies – the Challenger disaster, Facit, Kalmar Verkstad, NCR – have made 'unlearning' a prescription for preventing and dealing with crises (Starbuck et al. 1976: 49–54; 1978;). As a prevention, unlearning counteracts the inertia of learning. Busy with applying old programmes, organizations fail to invent new behavioural patterns and they discount signs of trouble as being merely expected outcomes.

A finding of the Challenger study is that 'fine-tuning' can finally be the cause of failure because it creates sequences of experiments that test the limits of theoretical knowledge. Hence, if crises are occasions to learn, they are also occasions to discover that beliefs are failing to explain events (1983). Human and organizational flaws pervade Starbuck's theories as do behavioural programs that develop autonomously, showing his taste for relativity and indeterminateness.

6 Scientific methods

Managers are not the only people who take their objectivity for granted. Recognizing that researchers' perceptions, language and founding assumptions produce systematic interpretation biases, Starbuck turned his humble attitude towards knowledge into a life-long epistemological commitment, while he relentlessly combated theorizing that adopts a rational faade: 'Scientific rationality is a fantasy that appeals to us aesthetically, but it violates its own rules, distorts our observations, and extrapolates incomplete knowledge to ridiculous extremes' (1988b: 71).

Starbuck made such statements from experience. All of his theorizing has involved his questioning, without complacency or self-indulgence, his own epistemological assumptions. One result has been scepticism about clear-cut positions and theories presented as absolute truths. Even as he advocated the use of mathematics in social sciences, he pointed out that 'Symbolic representation can be as unspecific and as ambiguous as one chooses to make it' (1965a: 340). When James Price exhorted researchers to have more logical rigour, Starbuck protested, 'there are circumstances in which increases in logical rigor will decrease the value of a study' (1968: 135).

Instead of faking objectivity, a sincere researcher, Starbuck suggested, acknowledges the ambiguous border between prescription and prevision, between observation and interpretation. He or she does not reject paradigms, but understands their ideological nature (1974). He or she experiments and predicts in the course of experimentation, so as to surprise himself with errors (1981, Starbuck and Pant 1990). He or she acknowledges with humility that observations may say more about the researcher than about observed phenomena. He or she acknowledges that time series are autocorrelated and that one progresses faster by eliminating poor hypotheses than by defending plausible ones (1994).

7 Conclusion

Starbuck's contributions pervade management. Ideas and methods that he promoted are widely used everyday – action generator, computer simulation, environmental niche, evolution, knowledge-intensive firm, mathematical models, organizational design, prescription, fine-tuning, unlearning. Contingency theory is no longer popular, and he continues to wage campaigns against multiple regression, point null hypotheses, and significance tests. His most important contribution lies perhaps in the modesty that he assigned to the research act. He showed that scientists have personal values that impact

their research. Instead of adopting objective façades that look like grimaces, he invites us to constantly reconsider our descriptions with wisdom and our prescriptions with humility.

PHILIPPE BAUMARD
UNIVERSITY OF VERSAILLES

Further reading

(References cited in the text marked *)

* Cyert R.M., March J.G. and Starbuck W.H. (1961) 'Two experiments on bias and conflict in organizational estimation', *Management Science*, 7: 254–264. (Introduces the relativity of perception in decision situations. A breakthrough implicitly announcing March and Cyert's 'bounded rationality'.)

Hedberg, B.L. ; Nystrom P.C. and Starbuck, W.H. (1976) 'Camping on seesaws: Prescriptions for a self-designing organization', *Administrative Science Quarterly*, 21: 41–65. (A most influential and quoted paper, calling for wisdom in organizational studies. The core of the self-designing paradigm.)

Meyer A.D. and Starbuck W.H. (1993) 'Interactions between politics and ideologies in strategy formation', in K. Roberts (ed.), *New Challenges to Understanding Organizations;* Macmillan. (Based on NCR's case, this paper shows how ideologies can be collaterally stabilizers and destabilizers of organizations, impeding or fostering strategic reorientations.)

* Starbuck, W.H. (1963) 'Level of aspiration', *Psychological Review*, 70: 51–60. Based on Working Paper No. 7, Carnegie Institute of Technology 1958. (Suggests that levels of aspiration may be subject of changes over time, in contradiction of Festinger's maximization assumptions.)

* Starbuck, W.H. (1965a) 'Mathematics and organization theory', in J. G. March (ed.), *Handbook of Organizations*; Rand McNally. (Explores the limits of mathematical languages and theoretical apparatus when applied to social sciences.)

* Starbuck, W.H. (1965b) 'Organizational growth and development', in J. G. March (ed.), *Handbook of Organizations*; Rand McNally. (An extensive and critical review of classical growth models, that underlly their methodological pitfalls. Suggests broader and more detailed data could correct past theoretical failure.)

* Starbuck, W.H. (1968) 'Some comments, observations, and objections stimulated by Design of proof in organizational research', *Administra-*

tive Science Quarterly, 13: 135–161. (An offensive critique of Price's claim for logical rigour as a means of increasing the value of a study. A provocative invitation to consider small changes, idiosyncratic samples, and to resist to organization research methodological clichés.)

* Starbuck, W.H. (1973) 'Tadpoles into Armageddon and Chrysler into butterflies', *Social Science Research*, 2: 81–109. (Invites researchers to factor the study of large metamorphosis in time segments, and to concentrate on initial sparks rather than hazardous supposively complete understanding. A seminal paper on metamorphic changes.)

* Starbuck, W.H. (1974) 'The current state of organization theory', in J. W. McGuire (ed.), *Contemporary Management: Issues and Viewpoints*; Prentice-Hall. (A humourous invitation to broader the scope of organization theory.)

* Starbuck, W.H. (1975) 'Information systems for organizations of the future', in E. Grochla and N. Szyperski (eds.), *Information Systems and Organizational Structure*; de Gruyter. (Claims that restrained designs provide opportunities for adaptation. A true foresight on information systems two decades later.)

* Starbuck, W.H. (1982) 'Congealing oil: Inventing ideologies to justify acting ideologies out', *Journal of Management Studies*, 19 (1): 3–27. (A seminal paper on the interaction of ideologies and action in organizations).

* Starbuck, W.H. (1983) 'Organizations as action generators', *American Sociological Review*, 48: 91–102. (Action rationality prevails ideologies and decision-making in organizations.)

* Starbuck, W.H. (1988) 'Surmounting our human limitations', in R. Quinn and K. Cameron (eds.), *Paradox and Transformation: Toward a Theory of Change in Organization and Management*; Ballinger. (Points to the value, not the sin, of paradoxical settings in organizational research. An invitation to celebrate perceptual distortion, and to make it the ground for theoretical construction.)

* Starbuck, W.H. (1993) ' "Watch where you step!" or Indiana Starbuck amid the perils of Academe (Rated PG)', in A. Bedeian (ed.), *Management Laureates*, Volume 3; JAI Press. (Links his own experiences of brutal changes to the evolution of his research. A seminal paper on researchers' values and their influence on their practice and epistemological assumptions.)

* Starbuck, W.H. (1994) 'On behalf of naiveté', in J.A.C. Baum and J.V. Singh (eds.), *Evolutionary Dynamics of Organizations*; Oxford University Press. (A claim to take into account feeback into causal processes, and to carefully watch appearances of randomness in non-random process. A seminal contribution on researchers' values and influence on research process.)

Starbuck, W.H. and Milliken, F. (1988a) 'Challenger: Changing the odds until something breaks', *Journal of Management Studies*, 25: 319–340. (Suggests acclimatation and fine-tuning slowly degrade and impede sense-making.)

Starbuck, W.H. and Milliken, F. (1988b) 'Executives' perceptual filters: What they notice and how they make sense', in D. C. Hambrick (ed.) *The Executive Effect: Concepts and Methods for Studying Top Managers*; JAI Press. (A complete account on sense-making in organizations that set up a widely used framework in managerial cognition studies.)

* Starbuck, W.H. and Narayan Pant, P. (1990) 'Innocents in the forest: Forecasting and research methods', *Journal of Management*, 16(2): 433–460. (Least-square regression does not produce reliable findings. A call for simplicity in research and forecasting methods).

Starbuck, W.H. and Nystrom, P.C. (eds.) (1981) *Handbook of Organizational Design*, two volumes; Oxford: Oxford University Press. (Two volumes with major contributions to the management field. Installs organizational design as a new paradigm in management sciences.)

* Starbuck, W.H., Hedberg, Bo L. T. and Nystrom, Paul C. (1976) 'Camping on seesaws: Prescriptions for a self-designing organization', *Administrative Science Quarterly*, 21: 41–65.

Starbuck, W.H., Greve A. and Hedberg, B.L.T. (1978) 'Responding to crises', *Journal of Business Administration*, 9(2): 111–137. (Suggest unlearning and reframing can prevent organizations from crises, and foster reorientations).

See also: MARCH, J.G. AND CYERT, R.M.; NONAKA, I.; SIMON, H.A.

Related topics in the IEBM: BUSINESS ECONOMICS; DECISION MAKING; MANAGERIAL BEHAVIOUR; MANAGERIAL THEORIES OF THE FIRM; ORGANIZATIONA BEHAVIOUR; ORGANIZATION BEHAVIOUR, HISTORY OF; ORGANIZATIONAL INFORMATION AND KNOWLEDGE; ORGANIZATIONAL LEARNING

Strauss, George (1923–)

Personal background

- born 23 June 1923 at Manhattan, New York, USA
- served in US Army in Second World War
- graduated from Massachusetts Institute of Technology (1951)
- research associate, New York State School of Industrial and Labor Relations, Cornell (1951–54)
- assistant professor, latterly professor, School of Business, University of Buffalo (1954–61)
- professor of business administration, University of California-Berkeley (latterly Emeritus) (1962 onwards)
- Editor, *Industrial Relations*, for twelve years during the period 1964–1995
- President, Industrial Relations Research Association (1993)
- developed ideas on industrial relations, organizational behaviour, personnel management, and human resource management

Major works

The Local Union: Its Place in the Industrial Plant (with L.R. Sayles) (1953)

Personnel: The Human Problems of Management (with L.R. Sayles) (1960)

Human Behavior in Organizations (with L.R. Sayles) (1966)

Managing Human Resources (with L.R. Sayles) (1977)

The State of the Unions (with D. Gallagher and J. Fiorito) (1991)

Summary

George Strauss is a leading scholar in the fields of industrial relations and personnel management. In an academic career spanning more than 45 years, he has written numerous scholarly books and articles. Strauss has made an important contribution to thinking on trade union government, shaping understanding of local union organization, leadership and participation. He has also co-authored comprehensive textbooks integrating knowledge on personnel management, human resource management and organizational behaviour, including one of the first organizational behaviour textbooks published. Strauss has continued to influence thinking and research, particularly on industrial relations, through an extensive body of review articles on many topics including union government, comparative industrial relations, worker participation, human resource management in the United States (USA), collective bargaining and industrial relations theory.

1 Biographical data

George Strauss was born in 1923 and spent his childhood in Staten Island, new York. His mother was Belgian, the daughter of a long-shoreman who had been an active socialist. His father, a chemical engineer, was the son of a lawyer, later a judge in Pennsylvania (Strauss 1992). In 1940, Strauss embarked on a college education in economics and political science at Swarthmore. His studies were interrupted by 3 years service in the US Army, beginning in February 1943.

After graduating from Swarthmore in 1947, Strauss enrolled as a graduate student in the Department of Economics and Social Sciences at Massachusetts Institute of

Technology (MIT), Cambridge. Among Strauss's fellow students in the industrial relations stream was Leonard Sayles with whom Strauss subsequently collaborated on a series of projects, including four books and numerous articles on trade unionism. At MIT, Strauss was taught by scholars who were, or subsequently became, leading figures in economics, industrial relations and human resource management. These included John Dunlop, Bob Livernash, Douglas McGregor, Charles Myers, Paul Pigors and Paul Samuelson. It was at MIT that Strauss's ethnographic research skills were developed, as was his optimistic view that social science research can generate answers to most societal problems. The influence of MIT can also be seen in Strauss's interest in the development and dynamics of groups, formal and informal, which has characterized much of his scholarly work. In 1951, Strauss completed his dissertation, a study of the determinants of leadership and participation in a local union. This work was further developed in *The Local Union* Strauss's first book which he later wrote with Sayles.

His graduate studies finished, Strauss joined a research project on human relations in unions at the School of Industrial and Labor Relations, Cornell. William Foot Whyte, a leading human relations scholar, was the project's director and Sayles another researcher on the project. Whyte's work had had a major influence on Strauss's dissertation, with its stress on the way in which attitudes and behaviour at work are affected by the objective conditions of work. At Cornell, Strauss and Sayles wrote *The Local Union*, for which the Society for the Psychological Study of Social Issues awarded them the Marrow Prize in September 1952 for best contribution to 'scientific understanding of labour–management relations'. Strauss also wrote a number of scholarly articles on the internal life of trade unions in this period, as well as contributing to Whyte's study of economic incentives and human relations, *Money and Motivation* (1953).

In 1954, Strauss was appointed to the Business School at the University of Buffalo. There he taught labour relations, labour history and labour law, human relations, wage administration and personnel administration. In 1955, Strauss and Sayles began their collaboration on the textbook *Personnel: The Human Problem of Management*. Strauss married in Buffalo in 1957. Three years later, he completed *Personnel* with Sayles. In 1960, Strauss also accepted a visiting appointment for one year at the University of California-Berkeley. In 1962, he was appointed professor of business administration in the School of Business at Berkeley. He has remained there ever since, with the exception of one year as a Fullbright Scholar in Australia in 1979 and one year as visiting professor and Head of the Department of Industrial Relations at the University of Sydney, Australia, in 1986.

In the 1960s, Strauss researched and published on subjects as diverse as apprenticeship systems, professional associations, and industrial relations change in the USA, as well as completing *Human Behavior in Organizations* with Sayles. Organizational behaviour had emerged as a new field in the late 1950s and early 1960s, and this textbook was one of the first to comprehensively document the main elements of the field. At Berkeley, Strauss's teaching spanned the full range of organizational behaviour courses and he developed a popular Masters of Business Administration course on negotiation and conflict resolution. Strauss co-founded the Organizational Behavior Teaching Society in 1973. His administrative and other professional responsibilities also grew. These included appointments as editor of the Journal of Industrial Relations, for twelve years during the period 1964–95. Strauss was also Director of the Institute of Industrial Relations at the University of California-Berkeley in the years 1984–88, associate dean of the Business School, member and chairperson of the City of Berkeley Personnel Board for 5 years, and President of the Industrial Relations Research Association in 1993.

Since the 1970s, Strauss has collaborated with Sayles on their third textbook, *Managing Human Resources*, and the fourth edition of their first textbook, *Personnel* has been published. Human resource management had emerged in the US as a field of study and practice in the 1960s, following the application of organizational behaviour research to traditional personnel problems. In *Managing Human Resources*, Strauss and Sayles documented the main elements of human resource management, as they had done with personnel management seventeen years earlier. However, Strauss's work has increasingly focused on industrial relations rather than personnel or human resource management. He has written numerous review articles which summarize and critically evaluate knowledge on such matters as union government, comparative industrial relations, worker participation and industrial relations theory. While Strauss has continued to influence thinking and research in the fields of industrial relations, organizational behaviour and human resource management, this contribution will consider Strauss's early seminal contribution to these fields, *Personnel: The Human Problems of Management* and *The Local Union*, and his continuing work on union government.

2 Personnel: The Human Problems of Management

Personnel: The Human Problems of Management was the textbook which first made Strauss's reputation in personnel management and the field of organizational behaviour which had emerged in the late 1950s. This was the second book on which Strauss and Sayles had collaborated. They began writing *Personnel* in 1955 to assist their teaching in the fields of personnel management and organizational behaviour. At that time textbooks in these fields typically described practices and formal procedures, and treated personnel problems as clinical cases which managers could and should solve. The textbooks gave little attention to underlying organizational forces, behavioural science research or the politics of implementation. *Personnel* was the first textbook to comprehensively integrate these issues. The authors argued that managers needed analytical tools that went beyond the transitory practices of specific firms at

specific times, to provide an enduring understanding of personnel management.

Personnel consisted of 31 chapters, divided into seven parts. These included the nature of the personnel problem, supervisory functions, managerial skills, organizational structure, manpower and employee development, incentives for effective performance, and managerial responsibilities. Strauss and Sayles wove three threads through these chapters: an exploration of managerial techniques, consideration of the power relationships between management and union representatives, and an emphasis on relationships experienced by first-line supervisors, whose task it was to implement personnel techniques in the workplace.

This emphasis on the supervisor was unusual. Textbooks had previously concentrated on the role of specialist personnel departments. In contrast, Strauss and Sayles highlighted the staff administrative aspects of personnel management, the day-to-day responsibility of line managers for applying personnel policy and eliciting work group performance. Also unusual was the extent to which Strauss and Sayles made reference to empirical research in the behavioural and social sciences, including works by Hawthorne, Lewin, McGregor and Whyte, and such sociologists as Blau, Gouldner and Bendix. *Personnel* also included case problems at the end of many chapters, a device which subsequently became common to organizational behaviour and human resource management textbooks. An additional novel feature of *Personnel* was its emphasis on the politics of implementing personnel practices in complex organizations. This included study of the impact of such elements as hierarchical structures, trade unions and informal organization on the function of line management and methods for countering problems in order to effectively apply personnel practices. For Strauss and Sayles, an understanding of the problems associated with application and implementation was critical to effective personnel management. Strauss (1992) later said that when writing *Personnel*, he and Sayles had 'viewed implementation as a political process requiring endless accommodation'.

In subsequent years, Strauss and Sayles published two other textbooks which drew on and extended the themes of *Personnel*, while also charting the main elements of the younger and increasingly popular fields of organizational behaviour and human resource management. The first was *Human Behavior in Organizations* (1966). As one of the first textbooks to comprehensively canvass the concerns of organizational behaviour, a field which emerged in the late 1950s and early 1960s, this book placed Strauss and Sayles as leading commentators in the field. The other textbook was *Managing Human Resources* (1977) which integrated material on both human resource management and organizational behaviour. While US universities had continued to teach personnel management, human resource management had emerged as an increasingly popular field of study from the mid 1960s, built on the basis of the application of organizational behaviour research to traditional personnel practices. These two textbooks which Strauss co-authored with Sayles were unusual, like the earlier *Personnel*, because they applied and evaluated empirical research from a variety of disciplinary fields, emphasized the politics of implementation, and were exhaustively comprehensive.

Since writing *Managing Human Resources*, Strauss has continued to comment on human resource management in the USA. He has remained critical of most textbooks in the field. In 1989, Strauss wrote that most were too 'cookbooky', paid little attention to the problems of implementation and poorly integrated the various parts of the field. Strauss (1989) also lamented what he considered a continuing paucity of research on how to effectively implement human resource management techniques, the narrow psychological focus of the field and the concentration on staff specialists to the neglect of line managers.

3 *The Local Union* and Trade Union Government

With *The Local Union: Its Place in the Industrial Plant*, Strauss gained prominence as a leading scholar on trade union government, a subject on which he has continued to write throughout his career. Co-authored with Sayles, *The Local Union* was Strauss's first book. It was the first major study of the role of the local industrial union in the US labour movement. As such, it provided a richly detailed ethnographic study of life, leadership and participation in local unions. The book highlighted the importance of studying the 'local' for evaluating trade union democracy. In the process, it provided one of the earliest analyses of the factors which determine participation in local unions, the conditions for union democracy, and the involvement of women and minority groups in trade unions.

The Local Union was based on a study of 20 local unions primarily in the manufacturing sector. Over 16 chapters the book documented the role and function of the local union. Early chapters examined the role of union officers in the grievance process, the demands and pressures which they confront within the process and how they respond. The middle chapters of the book studied the personalities of union officers, their orientations to the role, and how they are selected. Strauss and Sayles classified shop stewards and local-wide officials, identifying three types of steward (social leaders, active unionists, self-seekers) and two types of local official (administrators and social leaders).

The last part of *The Local Union* was concerned with the problems of union democracy: the functions and problems of local meetings, patterns of participation, involvement of women and minority groups, employee attitudes towards unions and the conditions for democratic unionism. In explaining the differing participation patterns of work groups, Strauss and Sayles argued that groups participate because they obtain benefits from the unions, and continued participation is linked to union success. They identified four factors affecting the success of groups in union activity; the homogeneity of the group, its status or prestige in the plant, strategic position in the company, and the nature of the job. Strauss and Sayles found that work groups which are socially united, have high status within the plant community, a strategic position in the production line, and some free time usually obtain greater satisfaction from participation and are the more likely to participate in the 'local'. Another essential condition they identified is the existence of respected leaders within the group who are interested in taking on union activity.

In the final chapter, Strauss and Sayles discussed the meaning of the term 'union democracy', what makes locals democratic, and why some local unions are more democratic than others. In the process, they argued that many commonly used indicators of democracy are of limited value, including the union's constitutional structure, numbers of election candidates, turnover of officials, existence of organized parties and attendance at meetings. Strauss and Sayles suggested a more useful measure to be responsiveness of officers to demands of the membership. Their thesis was that local unions were typically more democratic than national bodies because participation and communication were easier at local level, leading to greater official responsiveness to members' concerns.

Finally, Strauss and Sayles identified three main reasons why some local unions are more democratic than others. These factors are the locus of control over collective bargaining, the history and organization of the union, and the collective bargaining relationship (or the degree of industrial peace). In a later edition of *The Local Union*, Strauss and Sayles extended this list to include geographical location and the character of work groups. They concluded that participation is greater in smaller local unions, in smaller urban centers, and when collective bargaining is relatively decentralized, there is a tradition of union democracy and the membership enjoys a sense of occupational community.

As the first comprehensive empirical study on local unionism, *The Local Union* had an immediate influence on academic research on union government, including Spinrad (1960) and Barbash (1967). It formed part of the body of early US literature on union government which focused on the informal life of unions, combining the concerns of human relations and industrial relations. The book also provided an early analysis of the influence of

occupational community and technology on union behaviour, and employee attitudes towards unionism, the latter subsequently becoming the subject of extensive union instrumentality studies. Some aspects of the book were overlooked in later scholarly work, including Strauss and Sayles's discussion of the impact of sex and ethnicity on participation rates.

Strauss has continued to comment on union government issues throughout his career. In 1977, he co-edited with Malcolm Warner 'Research on Union Government', a symposium edition of the journal *Industrial Relations*. The intention behind the symposium was to publish and spur interest in behavioural research on trade unions. Strauss contributed an article, 'Union Government in the US: Research Past and Present', which documented the history of empirical research on union government, reviewed literature on union behaviour published since 1960 and suggested a future research agenda. In the process, Strauss developed some of the ideas explored in *The Local Union*. In particular, he proposed a more systematic classification of the determinants of local union democracy, identifying three categories; legal, behavioural, and reponsiveness and control.

In 1991, Strauss co-edited *The State of the Unions* with Daniel Gallagher and Jack Fiorito. He also contributed chapters on participation and union democracy to the book. In his chapter on union democracy, Strauss extended the historical account of research on union government he had written in the 1977 symposium, and critically reviewed knowledge on the function and measurement of union democracy. Strauss began by asking why union democracy is important, a question to which most treatments of the topic give little attention. He followed by evaluating the findings of numerous studies conducted since the 1950s, in the process reaffirming many of the conclusions of *The Local Union*. In particular, he restated the central place of responsiveness as a criteria of democracy. Strauss also referred again to the factors which determine participation in local unions. He stressed the importance of occupational community in facilitating participation and the role of the activist core who undertake much of a union's work and can check the power of the leadership. Finally, Strauss discussed the factors which account for variations in participation, including occupational community, status, size of local, structure, degree of centralization, and history, tradition and ideology. In an important departure from his earlier writings, Strauss argued that while homogeneity may contribute to greater responsiveness in local unions, diversity may also foster democracy by engendering disagreement, electoral competition and officer turnover.

4 Conclusions

Strauss is one of the few early scholars of personnel management who has also had a continuing prominence in the field of industrial relations. He is also a leading commentator on organizational behaviour and human resource management. In his scholarly works, Strauss has provided an unusually sensitive blend of the concerns and insights of these fields. He has highlighted the importance of understanding unions and workplace politics in human resource management, for example, and of examining informal organization, leadership and attitudes in studies of union behaviour. Strauss's textbooks have played a significant role in defining the expanding fields of organizational behaviour and human resource management and his early and continuing work on union government has an enduring importance. Strauss has remained a leading commentator on industrial relations, his writings vigorously documenting the state of knowledge in the field and conveying his unceasing interest in the day-to-day realities of industrial life. Increasingly, Strauss has pointed to research needs and agendas, to encourage future scholars to expand the frontiers of knowledge in industrial relations and human resource management.

LOUISE THORNTHWAITE
GRIFFITH UNIVERSITY, AUSTRALIA

Further reading

(References cited in the text marked *)

* Barbash, J. (1967) *American Unions: Structure, Government and Politics*, New York: Random House. (A large US study of trade unions which examines union participation and government.)
* Gallagher, D., Fiorito, J., and Strauss, G. (eds.) (1991) *The State of the Unions, Madison*, Wisconsin: Industrial Relations Research Association. (A wide-ranging book which discusses union membership, growth and governance, and the tasks and challenges facing unions in the late twentieth century.)
* Sayles, L. and Strauss, G. (1953) *The Local Union: Its Place in the Industrial Plant*, New York: Harper & Brothers. (Strauss's classic work on leadership and participation in local unions.)
* Sayles, L. and Strauss, G. (1960) *Personnel: The Human Problems of Management*, New Jersey: Prentice-Hall. (Strauss's first comprehensive personnel management textbook, more than 700 pages.)
* Sayles, L. and Strauss, G. (1966) *Human Behavior in Organizations*, New Jersey: Prentice-Hall. (A textbook on organizational behaviour which integrates prescription, empirical research and critical analysis.)
* Sayles, L. and Strauss, G. (1977) *Managing Human Resources*, New Jersey: Prentice-Hall. (A textbook which draws on behavioural science research to explain the principles and processes of human resource management.)
* Spinrad, W. (1960) 'Correlates of trade union participation' *American Sociological Review*, 25 (2): 23–244. (An examination of union participation studies which identifies determinants of participation.)
* Strauss, G. (1977) 'Union Government in the US: Research Past and Future', *Industrial Relations*, 16 (1): 115–126. (Review article which evaluates knowledge in the field.)
* Strauss, G. (1989) 'Industrial relations as an academic field: What's wrong with it?', in J. Barbash and K. Barbash (eds.) *Theories and Concepts in Comparative Industrial Relations*, University of South Carolina Press: 241–260. (Analyses the roots and development of the industrial relations field, developments in the 1980s and future research directions).
* Strauss, G. (1992) 'Present at the beginning: Some personal notes on OB's early days and later', A. Bedeian (ed), *Laureates of Management Thought*, JAI Press: 145–190. (Strauss's reflections on his career and the development of or-

ganizational behaviour, including a list of Strauss's published works 1952–1992.)
* Whyte, W.F., with Dalton, M., Roy, D., Sayles, L., Collins, O., Miller, F., Strauss, G., Fuerstenberg, F., and Bavelas, A. (1955) *Money and Motivation: An Analysis of Incentives in Industry*, New York: Harper & Brothers. (A comprehensive study of the impact of monetary incentives in industry.)

See also: BARBASH, J.; DUNLOP, J.T.; KOCHAN, T.; MCGREGOR, D.; SCHULER, R.

Related topics in the IEBM: COLLECTIVE BARGAINING; EMPLOYEE RELATIONS; HUMAN RELATIONS; HUMAN RESOURCE MANAGEMENT; INDUSTRIAL DEMOCRACY; INDUSTRIAL AND LABOUR RELATIONS; OCCUPATIONAL PSYCHOLOGY; ORGANIZATION BEHAVIOUR; ORGANIZATION BEHAVIOUR, HISTORY OF; PAYMENT SYSTEMS; TRADE UNIONS

Sun Tzu

1 Introduction
2 The question of authorship
3 Sun Tzu's main principles
4 Evaluation
5 Conclusion

Overview

The emphasis in this entry is on the ancient Chinese book *Sun Tzu Ping Fa* – often called *Sun Tzu's Art of War* in English – rather than on the life of Sun Tzu himself. This choice of emphasis is due partly to the fact that the authorship of the book is an unsettled question. The aphorisms contained in the book have influenced generations of Chinese, Japanese and other east Asian peoples.

Predating Carl von Clausewitz's *On War* by some twenty-two centuries, *Sun Tzu Ping Fa* is the oldest extant systematic military treatise in the world, yet some of its fundamental ideas have been described as ageless by the great twentieth-century military strategist Captain B.H. Liddell Hart. Overall, the book demonstrates the Chinese emphasis on the concrete and specific, awareness of complex multiplicity and interrelationships, the eschewal of the abstract and absolute, and esteem for both hierarchy and nature (Nakamura 1964). However, many of the principles expounded in the text are considered to apply outside purely military spheres, in particular in diplomacy, interpersonal relations and business strategy.

1 Introduction

Many of the principles expounded in *Sun Tzu Ping Fa* have, over the centuries, become part of the intellectual make-up of generations of Chinese, Japanese and other east Asian peoples, both soldiers and civilians. The book was probably introduced to Japan by the middle of the eighth century (Griffith 1963). Its influence could be seen, for example, in slogans written on the battle banners of Takeda Shingen (a famous general of the sixteenth century): 'Swift as the wind, Calmly majestic as the forest, Plundering like fire, Immovable as the mountains'. These words are identical to part of a paragraph in the seventh chapter of *Sun Tzu Ping Fa*, entitled 'Manoeuvre'. When discussing business or personal strategy with friends, east Asians will often refer to Sun Tzu's aphorisms. Chinese-language books on the application of Sun Tzu to business and management are among the best-selling titles in Hong Kong, Singapore, Taiwan and China, while Miyamoto Musashi's *The Book of Five Rings* (written around 1645 and itself influenced by Sun Tzu) has become recommended reading for MBA students at leading US business schools.

2 The question of authorship

'Sun' is a family name and 'Tzu' is an ancient title of respect for a learned or virtuous man; thus, 'Sun Tzu' means simply 'venerable Mr Sun', leaving the question of Sun Tzu's identity open. The primary meaning of 'ping' is soldier or weapons, and 'fa' means method. A literal translation of *Sun Tzu Ping Fa* would therefore be 'The Military Method of Venerable Mr Sun'. The use of the expression 'art of war' probably owes much to Machiavelli, whose *The Art of War* was published in 1520, and to the Prussian general Carl von Clausewitz, who favoured the notion of the 'art of war' over the 'science of war'.

The authorship of *Sun Tzu Ping Fa* has been a controversial question since at least the Sung Dynasty (AD 960 to 1126), when the *Seven Military Classics* were codified, and it remains unsettled to this day. According to the traditional view – based on the *Shih Chi* (Historical Records), which were completed shortly after 100 BC by the grand historian Szuma Chien – Sun Tzu was Sun Wu, whose book gained him an audience with King Ho-lü of Wu. Sun Wu had the two leading concubines decapitated to demonstrate the principles of military discipline and went on to an illustrious career as a general. According to this account, the thirteen chapters of *Sun Tzu Ping Fa* would have been composed around 500 BC during the Spring-and-Autumn period. However, if the book was indeed written by a single person, a number of significant anachronisms identified by Griffith (1963) suggest that it must have been written later, during the Warring States period, possibly between 400 and 320 BC. These anachronisms include the emergence of the professional general, the use of the crossbow and the deployment of armoured troops.

It is also possible that the text was written by different people at different times. Szuma Chien's chapter dealing with Sun Wu is entitled 'The biographies of Sun Tzu and Wu Chi' and covers the life stories of three people: Sun Wu, Sun Pin (who was a descendant of Sun Wu and who lived more than a hundred years later) and Wu Chi. All three were brilliant generals who wrote military treatises. Furthermore, the text that has come down to this day is referred to as *Sun Tzu Ping Fa as Commentated by the Eleven Authorities*; the commentaries, consisting of explanations, further elaborations and examples drawn from later periods, follow each sentence or paragraph and exceed the original text in length. The principal commentator was Ts'ao Ts'ao (AD 155–220), a famous prime minister and general during the period of the Three Kingdoms; it appears that he not only commented on the text, but edited it to reduce the number of redundancies (Griffith 1963). It is this text which has been preserved together with the commentaries, and the influence of the book derives from both the text and the commentaries.

3 Sun Tzu's main principles

Sun Tzu urged moderation and caution in relation to war:

> A sovereign should not start a war out of anger, nor should a general give battle out of rage. For while anger can revert to happiness and rage to delight, a nation that has been destroyed cannot be restored, nor can the dead be brought back to life.
> (*Sun Tzu Ping Fa*, Chapter 12)

Indeed, the aim of war is not necessarily the destruction of the enemy's forces, as it is in Clausewitz's system:

> In war, it is better to take a nation whole rather than broken, an army whole rather than broken.... For to win one hundred victories in one hundred battles is not the acme of skill. To subdue the enemy's forces without fighting is the summit of skill. The best approach is to attack the other side's strategy; next best is to attack his alliances; next best is to attack his soldiers; the worst is to attack cities.
> (Chapter 3)

Although preparations for war may take a long time, once war breaks out speed is of the essence:

> What is precious in war is victory, not prolonged operations.... Thus, while one hears of blundering swiftness in war, one never sees skilfulness that is prolonged. For there never has been a case of prolonged war from which the nation profits.
> (Chapter 2)

Strategy, in the delimited sense of stratagems, ploys and deception, is an integral part of war. 'War is based on the method of deception. . . . Therefore when strong feign weakness, when using something appear not to use it, when near appear far away, when far away appear near'. The principle of deception is intimately linked to that of surprise: 'Attack where and when he is unprepared; sally out where and when attack is not expected' (Chapter 1).

Sun Tzu's views on strategy lead to another key principle, that of flexibility or adaptability:

> For the shape of an army is like that of water. The shape of water is to avoid heights and flow towards low places; the shape of the army is to avoid strength and to strike at weakness. Water flows in accordance with the ground; an army achieves victory in ac-

cordance with the enemy. Therefore the army has no constant shape just as water has no permanent form; it is an act of genius to achieve victory in accordance with changes in the enemy.

(Chapter 6)

These concepts of adaptability should not detract from the importance of the positional aspects of strategy:

> In the old days, the skilful generals first made themselves invincible and then waited for the enemy to become vulnerable. Invincibility depends on oneself – the possibility of victory depends on the enemy.... Therefore the skilful general stands on undefeatable ground and does not miss an opportunity to defeat his enemy.
>
> (Chapter 4)

Advantage on the battlefield does not depend on absolute numbers but on where, when and how one gives battle. To create a situation which assures victory is the ultimate responsibility of generalship:

> Generally, the army that occupies the field of battle first and awaits the enemy is at ease; the side that arrives later to the battlefield and rushes into the fight is exhausted. Therefore the skilful warrior drives the other side and is not driven by him.... If I can ascertain my enemy's shape while I have no shape (that is known to him), then I can concentrate my forces while he must divide his ... thus I can outnumber him by ten to one.
>
> (Chapter 6)

This puts a premium on 'intelligence'. Sun Tzu is remarkably forthright in his views on the use of spies, arguing that generals have a duty to use them:

> Armies confront each other for years to fight for victory on a single day. If, out of miserliness for ranks, emoluments and a hundred pieces of gold, one does not know the enemy's conditions, this is the ultimate in unkindness. Such a man is not fit to be a general, a support to his king, a master of victory.... Advance knowledge cannot be gained from ghosts and spirits ... but must be obtained from people who know the enemy situation.
>
> (Chapter 13)

According to Sun Tzu, one must also know the climate and, above all, the terrain. Much of chapters 8 ('The nine variations'), 9 ('Marches'), 10 ('Terrain') and 11 ('The nine types of ground') are devoted to discussions of ground and terrain.

4 Evaluation

To understand the tree, know the roots. The tap root of management strategy is war: its theory and practice. Indeed, the English word 'strategy' derives from the Greek words *stratos* (army) and *agein* (to lead), combined in the word *strategos* meaning generalship. Strategy has become an unconscious (and thus frozen) metaphor; a word which has become so familiar that it is treated as a literal term and our awareness of its metaphorical nature is lost. The meanings of unconscious metaphors tend to be discontinuously shifted rather than continuously developed. The reading of Sun Tzu and other classics can provide a way to breathe life into ossified metaphors; they can remind us of the essentially metaphorical (and hence open) nature of many of the concepts which guide business thinking.

In approaching Sun Tzu's work and its relevance for contemporary management, it is useful and illuminating to contrast his work with that of Clausewitz. The two generals' philosophies have quite different emphases. Clausewitz stressed the logical ideal, the abstract and the absolute. The metaphor underpinning his work might be that of the machine, planned, built and then put into inexorable, predetermined motion. His writings reflect the modernist enlightenment philosophies of mechanism, cause and effect, and the clear separation of thought and action. In contrast, the *Sun Tzu Ping Fa* stresses the pragmatic, the contextual and the emergent. A key metaphor underpinning Sun Tzu's writing is that of water, and in this sense his work resonates with the wider Chinese philosophy of Taoism.

The contrasting approaches of Sun Tzu and Clausewitz are reflected in contemporary strategic management. The 'design school' of strategy (Andrews 1971; Mintzberg 1990) stresses rational conscious planning, explicitness and clarity, and the clear separation of formulation and implementation. Internal strengths and weaknesses, external opportunities and threats are assessed; a strategy (with its sub-components of goals and action plans) is formulated and then implemented. This approach echoes Clausewitz's philosophy and, indeed, the wider modernist axioms. In contrast, the more recent 'process school' of strategy – which is part antithesis, part extension of the design school – stresses process, learning, adaptability and contextuality (for example, Quinn *et al.* 1988). In this respect, the process school is closer in spirit to Sun Tzu.

However, attempts to pigeonhole Sun Tzu or Clausewitz are in many ways misleading and the much-invoked dichotomy between West and East may be regarded as ephemeral. For example, early Greek strategists such as Pericles have much in common with Sun Tzu, stressing the paradoxical nature of strategy and the need for the great strategist to combine nominally antithetical attributes. Moreover, Clausewitz regarded prescriptive systems as inadequate, stressing that theory cannot tell a person how to act but may help in developing judgement. The writings of both authors prefigured the shift in emphasis from 'planning' to 'thinking' that is occurring in strategic management today.

Three dangers are inherent in contemporary readings of ancient texts such as *Sun Tzu Ping Fa*. First, there is the danger of projection. Ancient texts can take on the role of a Rorschach inkblot, in which people find meanings that correspond to strongly held views or ideas of their own. It is perhaps not surprising, therefore, that Sun Tzu has been interpreted from a number of different perspectives and used to support disparate schools of strategic thought (for example, Chen 1994; Tung 1994; Wee *et al.* 1991).

Second, there is the issue of literalization. It is interesting to note that in the East business is closely equated with war, a notion summarized in the saying 'the marketplace is a battlefield'. The war metaphor is taken quite literally by many business people. Metaphors are more than simple analogies: they become ways of seeing and acting. Thus, one must ask: is war an appropriate metaphor for strategic management in contemporary society? Any answer must be equivocal. Possibly, as intimated above, one fundamental problem lies in the fact that we are not consciously aware of the metaphorical nature of the language often used to talk about business and strategy.

Finally, there is the question of transferability. It is not difficult to collect cases and stories about business and management, to arrange them under headings borrowed from Sun Tzu and to call this 'the application of Sun Tzu to modern management'. However, there are two problems with such an approach. First, there is the question of the transferability (or otherwise) of concepts and principles to a different sphere (from war to management), to a different era and to different nations and cultures. Second, creative application requires the development of a new theoretical foundation on the basis of the old, just as Mao Tse-Tung articulated a theory of guerrilla warfare, which contains many concepts from Sun Tzu but which nevertheless offers new perspectives and insights appropriate to the conditions of time and place.

5 Conclusion

It is sometimes tempting to dismiss the writings of Sun Tzu as little more than 'common sense' aphorisms. However, the military strategist Captain B.H. Liddell Hart wrote: 'in that one short book was embodied almost as much about the fundamentals of strategy and tactics as I had covered in more than twenty books' (Griffith 1963). Yet, as suggested above, the paths to wisdom are not smooth. While reification (simplistic codification or literalization) of an ancient text may seem appealing, ultimately it is a sterile pursuit. It diminishes the past and impoverishes the present: the form of the original text is preserved but the essence lost. Essence cannot be reduced to mere theories or frameworks, but can only be approached with insight and inspiration. A careful study of texts such as *Sun Tzu Ping Fa* might pay dividends in providing the inspiration for a revisioning of contemporary strategic praxis.

YAO-SU HU
HONG KONG SHUE YAN COLLEGE

PIERRE BERTHON
CARDIFF BUSINESS SCHOOL

Note
All translations in this entry are by the contributors.

Further reading

(References cited in the text marked *)

* Andrews, K.R. (1971) *The Concept of Corporate Strategy*, Homewood, IL: Irwin. (Regarded by many as the quintessential text on the design school of strategic management.)
* Chen, M. (1994) 'Sun Tzu's strategic thinking and contemporary business', *Business Horizons* (March–April): 42–8. (An attempt to transfer some of Sun Tzu's principles directly to contemporary business.)
* Griffith, S.B. (1963) *The Art of War*, Oxford: Oxford University Press. (A good translation, by a US Army general, of *Sun Tzu Ping Fa* and selected commentaries; also includes chapters on the text and its background, and on Sun Tzu's influence on Mao Tse-Tung and Japanese military thinking.)
* Mintzberg, H. (1990) 'The design school: reconsidering the basic premises of strategic management', *Strategic Management Journal* 11: 171–95. (An insightful exposition of the assumptions of the design school which triggered an ongoing debate in the literature.)
* Nakamura, H. (1964) Ways of Thinking of Eastern Peoples, Honolulu, HI: University of Hawaii Press. (A magnum opus that compares the ways of thinking of China, India and Japan.)
* Quinn, J.B., Mintzberg, H. and James, B. (1988) *The Strategy Process*, Englewood Cliffs, NJ: Prentice Hall. (A definitive collection of articles stressing the process school of strategic thinking.)
* Tung, R.L. (1994) 'Strategic management in east Asia', *Organizational Dynamics* 22 (4): 55–65. (A description of four east Asian military classics: *Sun Tzu Ping Fa*, *The Book of Five Rings*, *The Three Kingdoms* and *The Thirty-six Stratagems*.)
* Wee, C.H., Lee, K.S. and Hidajat, B.W. (1991) *Sun Tzu: War and Management*, Singapore: Addison-Wesley. (A comprehensive discussion of Sun Tzu's ideas in terms of the traditional design-school model.)

See also: ANSOFF, I.; MINTZBERG, H.; OHMAE, K.; PETTIGREW, A.; TUNG, R.L.

Related topics in the IEBM: BUSINESS STRATEGIES, EAST ASIAN; COMPETITIVE STRATEGIES, DEVELOPMENT OF; CULTURE, CROSS-NATIONAL; MANAGEMENT IN CHINA; MANAGEMENT EDUCATION IN CHINA; MANAGEMENT IN PACIFIC ASIA; MILITARY MANAGEMENT; ORGANIZATION CULTURE; STRATEGY, CONCEPT OF; STRATEGY, IMPLEMENTATION OF

Tata, Jehangir Ratanji Dadabhoy (1904–93)

Personal background

- born 29 July 1904, Paris, of a French mother and an Indian (Parsi) father who belonged to a wealthy industrial family
- received his school education in Paris, Bombay, Yokohama and the UK but did not attend college
- became Bombay Flying Club's first pilot to obtain a flying licence in 1929
- participated in the Aga Khan Trophy in 1930, becoming the second Indian to fly UK–India or India–UK solo
- married Thelma Viccaji in 1930
- in 1932, his Karachi–Bombay flight for Tata Airlines inaugurated civil aviation in India
- in 1938, became chairman of Tata Sons, parent company of the Tata Group, the largest industrial group in India
- started the international airline Air India in 1948
- became the first national voice to call for the control of India's population in 1951 and started the Family Planning Foundation of India in 1970
- died 29 November 1993, in Geneva

Summary

Jehangir Ratanji Dadabhoy Tata (1904–93), better known as J.R.D., was the father of civil aviation in India and an industrialist. In 1938, he became chairman of the Tata Group of fourteen companies, comprising steel, electric power, textile, oils and soaps, and the famous Taj Mahal Hotel. When he stepped down in 1991 the Group had ninety-five companies – three of them among the ten largest in India.

From 1932 to 1978, J.R.D. remained active in the field of civil aviation. On the fiftieth anniversary of his inaugural flight launching India into civil aviation, at the age of 78, he repeated the performance in a vintage single-engine Leopard Moth.

1 Introduction

J.R.D. Tata's father, Ratanji Dadabhoy Tata, was an Indian industrialist related to Jamsetji N. Tata (1839–1904) who brought the industrial revolution to India through steel, hydroelectric power and the funding of its first university of science and technology. R.D. Tata was married to a French woman, Suzanne Brière. Their second child, Jehangir, was born in Paris. His school education was disrupted more than once as he spent a couple of years in Paris with his mother who then moved to India to be with her husband. In 1916, during the First World War, she suffered from tuberculosis and moved to Yokohama with her son, who was educated there.

After the war he returned to school in Paris. A place was reserved for him at Cambridge but prior to going there he was sent to a crammer to brush up on his English, his mother tongue being French. When he was ready to enter Cambridge the French authorities passed a conscription law and he joined a French cavalry regiment called 'Le Saphis' where, he complained, he was allowed to fire only five shots in one year! On completion of his conscription year his father summoned him to India. Eight months later his father died and J.R.D. had to step into his shoes as the director of Tata Sons (which prior to 1917 was called Tata & Sons). He was 22 years old.

2 Aviation

J.R.D. Tata's forty-six-year career in aviation began with the era of wood and fabric one-engined planes and ended with the jumbo jet.

His love for aviation was born on the coast near Boulogne in France where his father had a summer cottage. Their neighbour was Blériot, the first aviator to fly across the English Channel. When Blériot's plane landed J.R.D. would help to push it into a makeshift hangar. When he was 15 years old he was given his first joy ride in France and it was then that he decided he would one day become a pilot. Ten years later, in 1929, he joined the Bombay Flying Club and graduated as its first pilot; he also received the first licence awarded by the Fédération Aeronautique International (FAI). In 1930 he competed for the Aga Khan Trophy of £500 to be awarded to the first person to fly solo from India to England or from England to India. Tata was flying from Karachi to London, while one of his main competitors, the pilot Aspy Engineer, was flying from London to Karachi. At Alexandria, J.R.D. found his competitor stranded for want of a spark plug and lent him an extra one. The competitor went on to beat J.R.D. by a couple of hours.

Soon after the contest, an English pilot called Nevill Vintcent proposed that J.R.D. start an airline to connect with the Imperial Airlines flight from London to Karachi, which carried mail from Europe. On 15 October 1932, J.R.D. carried the first mailbag from Karachi to Bombay. He nursed Tata Airlines with care and established standards which he kept up when Air India International was launched in partnership with the government. His dream of such partnerships continuing in other industrial ventures did not come to fruition.

After the war, the government continued to license more airlines than could be sustained by the market, in spite of repeated warnings from J.R.D. Finally, the airline industry was in such a crisis that the government nationalized the industry. J.R.D. was invited to be the chairman of all the domestic airlines as well as of Air India. He chose to remain the chairman of Air India alone, and guided the enterprise with zeal and skill, often giving half his working day to aviation and the rest to his industrial empire. It was his desire that Air India should be one of the best airlines in service, if not the largest in size. He became President of IATA (International Air Transport Association) in

1958 and made a significant contribution to its deliberations for two decades as a member of the executive committee. Sir William Hildred, IATA's Secretary General, wrote how 'the Committee has benefited at every meeting from your questing mind, your knowledge and experience and commonsense…. I think without doubt there is no one geographically who could dream of replacing you' (Lala 1992a: 159). Air India won worldwide recognition under J.R.D.'s leadership but in 1978 he was relieved of the chairmanship:

Unpaid Air India Chief is Sacked by Desai

The air chief credited with making Air India one of the world's most successful airlines, basing its appeal on the beaming 'little Maharajah' emblem, has been fired by Mr Desai, the Prime Minister. His abrupt removal, apparently for political reasons, after 30 unpaid years at the helm of the national flag carrier, has left the business community in uproar and brought Mr Desai some of the worst publicity since he took office. Mr J.R.D. Tata, 73, is a legendary figure, known to legions of executives around the world and envied by most for his success…with a fleet of only 14 aircraft, Air India last year flew more than 1 million passengers and made a profit of £11 million pounds. But despite this, and without warning, Mr Tata was replaced.

(*Daily Telegraph* 27 February 1978)

Even if Prime Minister Desai did not recognize J.R.D.'s contribution, others did. A number of awards followed, including one in the name of Tony Jannus – the entrepreneur who started the world's first airline in Tampa, Florida, in 1914 – and among whose recipients were the founders of Pan-Am and Eastern Airlines, and the inventor of the jet engine, Sir Frank Whittle. In 1988, J.R.D. was awarded the Daniel Guggenheim Medal, the first recipient of which was Orville Wright.

In 1984, evaluating J.R.D.'s contribution, Anthony Sampson in his book *Empires of the Sky* wrote:

The smooth working of Air India seemed almost opposite to the Indian tradition on the ground – not least at its home base, Bombay Airport, with its chaotic huts, shouting porters and primitive equipment, which was one of the least alluring gateways to the East. Tata, a domineering but far-sighted tycoon, could effectively insulate Air India from the domestic obligations to make jobs and dispense favours; he could impose strict discipline and employ highly-trained engineers, of whom India has a surplus; and Air India could make more intensive use of its jets than most major airlines. Tata continued as chairman until 1977, the most long-lasting of all the pioneer aviators.

(Sampson 1984)

3 Industry

When he entered industry in his early twenties, unqualified in any technical field, J.R.D. felt that his major contribution would be in the context of people management, employing the finest people and encouraging their talent. He observed:

> Every man has his own way of doing things. To get the best out of them is to let them exploit their own instincts and only intervene when you think they are going wrong. Therefore all my management contributions were on the human aspect through inducing, convincing and encouraging the human being....As I had no technical training, I always liked to consult the experts....When I have to make a decision I feel I must first make sure that the superior knowledge of my advisors confirms the soundness of my decision; secondly, that they would execute my decision not reluctantly but being convinced about it; thirdly, I see myself in Tatas as the leader of a team, who has to weigh the impact of any decision on other Tata companies, on the unity of the group. I think this policy has paid off.

(Lala 1992b: 225)

On the question of consensus, he commented that when he became chairman of the group at the age of 34, all of the other directors were older than him, so he became a 'consensus man'. Consensus, he said, is weak in some respects but strong in the long run. Revealing the secret of his teamwork, he said:

> If I have any merit, it is getting on with individuals according to their ways and characteristics. At times it involves suppressing yourself. It is painful but necessary.... To be a leader you have got to lead human beings with affection.... Consensus never works 100 per cent but by and large I think I have succeeded.

(Lala 1992b: 225)

J.R.D. received his initial training in 1926 in Tata Steel which, prior to the Second World War was reputed to be the largest integrated steel plant in the British Empire. In 1943, he proposed in a note the need for a personnel management section, at a time when very few industries had such departments and it was left to the departmental heads to cope with their workers and staff. In 1938, when elected chairman of the Tata Group, he decided that he would get the best professionals from outside to run the organization. Among the people he picked was Dr John Matthai, later Finance Minister of India. Another of his directors, Sir Ghulam Mohammed, became Finance Minister and later Governor General of Pakistan.

J.R.D.'s unique contribution lay in trying to maintain ethical values in business and industry when all around him they were declining. Some critics argued that his value system inhibited the growth of the Tata Group at a time when latecomers were gaining ground. Even so, when he stepped down as chairman of Tata Sons, the parent company, there were ninety-five companies in the group, including India's largest automobile plant, TELCO, which J.R.D. himself had founded.

J.R.D. advocated liberal policies for business and a partnership between the government and private enterprise as he had earlier proposed for Air India. Instead, state control of the 'commanding heights of the economy' became the policy of the Indian Government. For thirty years, J.R.D. continued his struggle, hoping that his voice would have some influence on the socialist policies of successive governments. He lived to see the day, in 1991, when the Indian Government made a U-turn in its policies to encourage liberalization and privatization of the economy.

R. Venkataraman, who served as India's president from 1987–92, writes in his autobiography:

> J.R.D. Tata's contribution to the industrial development of India is unique. The Tata Group has expanded into every conceivable field of industrial activity and has set standards of enterprise, efficiency and integrity. J.R.D. Tata was the doyen among industrialists in India.
>
> I suggested to Prime Minister Narasimha Rao that we break the routine of honouring only politicians and confer *Bharat Ratna* (Jewel of India) on J.R.D. Tata. The Prime Minister readily agreed and for the first time an eminent industrialist was honoured with the highest award of *Bharat Ratna*.
>
> (Venkataraman 1994: 602)

J.R.D. was also a member of the Advisory Committee of the Chase Manhattan Bank which had one or two top industrialists from each country. He served there for twenty years and twice each year conferred with the top industrialists of the world. For all his accomplishments he was a humble man. To the end he regretted his lack of a university education, but it was this deprivation that gave him the drive to excel in all he attempted. Profit was never the driving force of his life. It was the joy of achievement.

At the age of 86, when he stepped down as chairman of Tata Sons in favour of his distant cousin Ratan N. Tata, *The Economic Times* wrote:

> Under Mr Tata's leadership, the group has earned a special place in India's corporate life in two important ways. First, it has professionalised management to a degree that few other indigenous business houses have done, and done it to a point where professionals have emerged as corporate stars in their own right. Second, it has consistently stayed in tune with national priorities, and ventured into the fields which urgently require private investment.... In J.R.D.'s own time, the group has diversified into auto-

mobiles, chemicals, exports and power. Throughout, the emphasis has been on building solid businesses, and not on seeking quick returns, capitalising on shortages, or manipulating government policy to personal advantage. This group culture should hold it in good stead in the future as well.... Mr J.R.D. Tata has ensured that a shared business vision and strong ethical traditions provide the bonds of partnership in a clutch of companies which see a mutual strength in staying together.

> (*The Economic Times*, Bombay and New Delhi, 26 March 1991)

4 Social contribution

J.R.D. Tata was known not only for his contribution to aviation and industry but for his social consciousness, which resulted in his raising the issue of family planning with Prime Minister Nehru. The Prime Minister's first reaction was to dismiss J.R.D.'s views with the words 'population is India's strength' – that was in 1951. Undeterred, J.R.D. continued to argue in favour of population control. In 1970, he started the Family Planning Foundation. He studied the problem for forty years and did all that he could to promote the implementation of the idea of population control.

As an industrialist, J.R.D. was concerned not only about the welfare of his employees, but in 1970 had the Articles of Association of some of his companies amended to enable them to serve people living in the areas where their industries were based. Around Jamshedpur, for example, where some of the biggest Tata factories for steel and automobiles are located, approximately 300 villages benefit from social and economic measures implemented by J.R.D.'s companies.

J.R.D. was associated with a number of major philanthropic institutions. He founded the Tata Institute of Fundamental Research, which was set up as a result of his support for a budding young scientist, Dr Homi Bhabha. This institution of higher physics and mathematics became the cradle of India's atomic energy programme. His support made possible the founding of the National Centre for the

Performing Arts at Bombay. In his later years, he established the National Institute of Advanced Studies in Bangalore.

A great advocate of exercise and good health, J.R.D. went skiing in the Alps each year until he was eighty-five years old. In 1991, he suffered from health problems and underwent four angioplasty procedures. He was fully active up until about three months before he died, aged 89, at a state hospital in Geneva on 29 November 1993.

R.M. LALA

SIR DORABJI TATA TRUST

Further reading

(References cited in the text marked *)

Harris, F.R. (1958) *J.N. Tata – A Chronicle of his Life*, Bombay: Blackie & Sons. (Interesting biography of J.N. Tata.)

Lala, R.M. (1984) *The Heartbeat of a Trust – Fifty Years of the Sir Dorabji Tata Trust*, New Delhi: Tata/McGraw-Hill. (The story the Sir Dorabji Tata Trust which founded many institutions of national importance.)

* Lala, R.M. (1992a) *Beyond the Last Blue Mountain – The Life of J.R.D. Tata (1904–1993)*, New Delhi: Penguin. (Detailed analysis of Tata's contribution to aviation and industry, and his philanthropy and social concerns.)

* Lala, R.M. (1992b) *The Creation of Wealth – The Tata Story*, Bombay: India Book House. (Covers the growth of the Tata organization and its effects on atomic energy, health, education, industrial relations and the performing arts.)

* Sampson, A. (1984) *Empires of the Sky*, London: Hodder & Stoughton. (Examines the politics, contests and cartels of world airlines.)

Tata, J.R.D. (1986) *Keynote*, edited by S.A. Sabavala and R.M. Lala, Bombay: Tata Press. (Excerpts from J.R.D.'s speeches and chairman's statements to shareholders.)

* Venkataraman, R. (1994) *My Presidential Years*, London: HarperCollins. (Autobiography of Venkataraman, India's President 1987–92.)

See also: BARNARD, C.I.; FAYOL, H.A.; KOTTER, J.; SLOAN, A.P.

Related topics in the IEBM: AIRLINE MANAGEMENT; BUSINESS ETHICS; GENERAL MANAGEMENT; HUMAN RESOURCE MANAGEMENT; LEADERSHIP; MANAGEMENT EDUCATION IN INDIA; MANAGEMENT IN INDIA; MANAGERIAL BEHAVIOUR; PRIVATIZATION AND REGULATION

Taylor, Frederick Winslow (1856–1915)

Personal background

- born 28 March 1856 in Philadelphia, Pennsylvania, into a middle-class Quaker family, but did not go to college
- trained as an apprentice and eventually studied at night school
- married Louise M. Spooner, 1884
- developed what he called the 'scientific' study of work
- formative influence on work-study and industrial engineering
- early death in Philadelphia on 21 March 1915 from pneumonia

Major works

Shop Management (1903)
The Principles of Scientific Management (1911)
Two Papers on Scientific Management (1919)

Summary

F.W. Taylor (1856–1915) was the initiator of scientific management and a major influence on the development of production management as a subject. He set out to systematize the study of workflow organization by breaking tasks into minute detail and devising ways to speed up their accomplishment. Taylor aimed at a 'mental revolution' in order to break down the barriers to good labour relations between workers and management. His ideas on efficiency were propagated by his disciples after his death through an international movement to promote such management techniques. While he was a controversial figure in his time, Taylor's contribution still continues to provoke lively debate in many management texts.

1 Introduction

Taylor is widely seen as the initiator of the scientific management movement, although his work has also been described as a synthesis of already existing notions. He has become one of, if not the, best known 'management guru' of all time. His contribution to the study of organizations has been described as original in that he set out to study jobs scientifically and to measure workflows in order to achieve higher productivity. He believed that management normally tried to push workers to achieve output, without an objective yardstick to measure a proper day's work. He therefore tried to devise a science of work to resolve this problem. Taylor thought that he was transforming what had previously been a crude art form into a firm body of knowledge.

Taylor set out to analyse tasks into their smallest details, diagnose the abilities of workers and then fit the two together to achieve greater efficiency. Job techniques would be redesigned to make maximum use of operatives' skills. In proposing these notions, he combined an engineer's outlook with an obsession for control. The main concept in Taylor's work was the 'task-idea', based on the principle that management should specify what must be done in the minutest detail and how it could be done. If these instructions were followed, industry would become more productive and trouble-free. While many writers have positively recognized Taylor's contribution (Merkle 1980; Kelly 1982), others have negatively referred to it as 'the degradation of work' (Braverman 1974).

2 Biographical data

Taylor was born into a Quaker, middle-class family on 20 March 1856, just outside the city of Philadelphia. Having completed his apprenticeship during the Depression in the 1870s, he went on to perform labouring work at the Midvale Steel Company in Philadelphia. In order to get out of this low-level employment, he decided to study engineering at the Stevens Institute's evening classes, eventually receiving his Master's Degree in Mechanical Engineering in 1883. Once qualified, he began a set of time studies at Midvale Steel in the early 1880s, out of which grew what was later called the Taylor System of Scientific Management. He started with the analysis of machine speeds in metal cutting in order to achieve greater efficiency.

In 1895, he gave a paper to the American Society of Mechanical Engineers entitled 'A piece-rate system: a step toward partial solution of the labor problem'. It was not the first paper on incentives, but it contained the basis of the distinctly Taylorist system and was founded on twelve years' experience at Midvale Steel, by which time he was chief engineer. It combined technical and organizational expertise, synthesizing several currents of efficiency management at hand. Taylor aimed to subdivide tasks, time them and find a way to speed them up. To prevent fatigue, carefully timed rest periods were to be built into the system. He continued his work in a new post at Bethlehem Steel, where he was made their management consultant in 1898, until 1901 when he lost his job on the sale of the company (Kanigel 1997).

After *Shop Management* was published in 1903, he became a well-known writer and lecturer and was elected President of the American Society of Mechanical Engineers. By this time, he had acquired several disciples, including C.G. Barth, H. Emerson and F.B. Gilbreth (see GILBRETH, F.B. AND GILBRETH, L.E.M.). An important implementation of his new methods of standardizing tools and tasks was later tried out between 1909 and 1912 at the Watertown Arsenal in Cambridge, Massachusetts (Aitken 1960). It led to the adoption of similar practices in arsenals all over the

USA. In 1911, he published his *Principles of Scientific Management* and became an increasingly public and controversial figure giving talks to top industrialists among others. He was invited as a visiting lecturer to the newly formed Harvard Business School and taught there once a year from 1909 until his death.

After organized labour tried to block rationalization techniques in industry influenced by Taylor's ideas in 1910–11, Taylor was confronted with Congressional investigation (Nelson 1980). A special House Committee summoned him as a leading witness in 1912. While the Committee conceded that Taylorism offered advantages to industry, it still believed Taylorism gave employers too much power. In the years following his death in 1915, Taylor's followers were to improve their relations with organized labour by recognizing the role of the unions in negotiating the introduction of new working methods, but still Taylor had gained a reputation as 'the enemy of the working man' (Morgan 1997: 22).

3 Main contribution

Taylor saw 'slacking' by workers as the main source of inefficiency in industry. The labourer, he reasoned, would not exert himself; the manager would use guesswork. Both had to be guided towards rational behaviour. To this end, he invented what he called a 'science of shovelling' while working in the steel industry in the early 1880s. To illustrate his notion of a fair day's work, he trained a labourer called Schmidt to increase by four times his workload of loading mouldings called 'pigs': the latter gained a bonus of 50 per cent as a result of the rationalization of his job. Piecework rates were devised to boost motivation, with what Taylor liked to call 'first-class men' setting the pace. He believed his system was more than a mere efficiency device: it involved a complete 'mental revolution' on the part of management as well as workers, and involved a coming together of capital and labour, a delusion according to his critics.

Taylor also tried to extend the division of labour to management, believing that there should be no fewer than eight kinds of functional foremen, dealing with work speed and repairs. He believed that 'a good organization with a poor plant will give better results than the best plant with poor organization' (Taylor 1903: 65). The planning department was to play a pivotal role in Taylor's schema, as it would work out the detailed work schedules for the employees to follow in order to increase output.

At the Congressional inquiry, Taylor argued that better production methods were not only in the interests of management but also of the workers. He believed that:

> The new way is to teach and help your men as you would a brother; to try to teach him the best way and show him the easiest way to do his work. This is the new mental attitude of the management toward the men, and that is the reason I have taken so much of your time in describing this cheap work of shovelling. It may seem to you of very little consequence, but I want you to see, if I can, that this new mental attitude is the very essence of scientific management; that the mechanism is nothing if you have not got the right sentiment, the right attitude in the minds of the men, both on the management's side and on the workman's side. Because this helps to explain the fact that until this summer, there has never been a strike under scientific management.
>
> (cited in Pugh 1991: 139)

Against the notion of the survival of the fittest which was prominent at the time, Taylor offered a strategy of collaboration. He argued that wasteful conflict was inefficient and therefore wrong. It was this moral element in his thought that inspired his disciples and generated a crusade for scientific management according to his defenders (Merkle 1980).

4 Evaluation

F.W. Taylor promoted not only systematic time-and-motion study, production control methods and incentive pay, but a wider philosophy and methodology of work organization. Scientific management would create an atmosphere of trust in industry based on a value-neutral approach, probably a dubious notion from the start. He always stressed the word scientific: he thought it would increase his credibility with managers and engineers and even ordinary workers who were sceptical about the impersonal forces of the market. Science, he thought, would create both high wages and high profits.

Taylorism has been criticized by many writers on organizational behaviour for its individualist assumptions that gave priority to distinctly individual motivation, rewards and controls in order to break the collective power of work groups. Furthermore, time-and-motion study techniques and financial incentives were seen as part of management's definition of what were appropriate workloads and work methods in order to increase managerial control. Other critics of Taylor's theories have argued that his work did not deserve the term scientific and that Taylorism took too narrow a view of work:

> Time-study; the confusion of human labour with the play of inanimate mechanisms; the ignorance of the physical and mental functioning of the organism and its own demands; the procedure adopted to stimulate and reward effort; the place of vocational guidance; the selection by output, and finally the empiricism of generalizations elevated to the status of 'laws' – everything proves that we have here a system created by a man who was doubtless a great technician but who could not see beyond the confines of his engineer's universe.
>
> (Friedmann 1955: 64–5)

None the less, Taylor carried out several important field experiments at both the Midvale Steel works and Bethlehem Steel, and later as an industrial consultant at Watertown Arsenal, for example, passing on his findings to meetings of bodies such as the American Society of Mechanical Engineers, although not without criticism and even Congressional scrutiny. The later phase of Taylor's work was, however, more linked with what were to become mainstream developments. For example, there was a considerable continuity between late Taylorism and early industrial psychology (Kelly 1982). During and after the First World War, industrial psychologists started to investigate the conditions for industrial cooperation. Union–management cooperation was encouraged as part of the war effort as were joint consultation mechanisms. In spite of proposing greater managerial control and increased specialization of tasks, Taylor emphasized many features of what later became subsumed under the human relations heading, including motivational factors, such as promotional prospects, friendly supervisors, positive work rhythms and clear working goals, which remain important concerns of managerial practice.

Taylorism evolved into an experimental approach which was to persist long after its founder's death in most capitalist economies. Japanese management was appreciably influenced by Taylorism in the inter-war years and in much of its post-1945 development (Warner 1994)(see UENO, Y.). Even in the Soviet Union, Taylorism was encouraged as part of an ambitious programme of social engineering as carried out by the Russian efficiency expert Gastev in the early 1920s. Taylor's name was openly used along with studies of work physiology, labour fatigue and selection methods. After initial opposition to such ideas, Lenin observed that 'Socialism plus Taylorism would equal Communism' because of businesslike methods and one-man management. Soviet and later Chinese industry continued to be influenced by scientific management as adapted to their respective systems (Kaple 1994).

5 Conclusions

Taylor's four Principles of Scientific Management (1911) are: (1) to establish a science of production; (2) to select and train workers to achieve this; (3) to apply such a science to operatives' tasks; and (4) to build cooperation between the workers and management to achieve common goals. Its impact on contemporary society and its so-called 'McDonaldization' (see Ritzer 1996) has been considerable. Taylorism was not a single innovation, but a series of notions and practices elaborated by the initiator and his collaborators. The movement promoted an international crusade for efficiency in the 1920s and 1930s with its effect being felt long after. Taylor's epitaph in Philadelphia reads: 'Father of Scientific Management' (Kakar 1970: 1). Without his innovations (and later those of Henry Ford), assembly-line mass production as we know it today would not have been possible (see FORD, H.). In anticipating the routinization of everyday life, 'History may judge that Taylor came before his time' (Morgan 1997: 26).

MALCOLM WARNER
JUDGE INSTITUTE OF MANAGEMENT STUDIES,
UNIVERSITY OF CAMBRIDGE

Further reading

(References cited in the text marked *)

* Aitken, G.H. (1960) *Taylorism at the Watertown Arsenal: Scientific Management in Action, 1908–1915*, Cambridge, MA: Harvard University Press. (A detailed monograph on a specific application of Taylor's work in arms manufacture, which is probably of interest mostly to specialists.)

* Braverman, H. (1974) *Labor and Monopoly Capital: The Degradation of Work in the Twentieth Century*, New York: Monthly Review Press. (A controversial work based on a critique of Taylorism from a Marxist perspective, which has played an important role in generating the de-skilling debate.)

Copley, F.B. (1923) *Frederick W. Taylor: Father of Scientific Management*, 2 vols, New York: Harper & Co. (A definitive, extended biography of Taylor, published not long after his death, which is dated but contains useful detail.)

* Friedmann, G. (1955) *Industrial Society: The Emergence of the Human Problems of Automation*, Glencoe, IL: The Free Press. (A well-known work on automation by a renowned French industrial sociologist who was a critic of Taylorism.)

* Kakar, S. (1970) *Frederick Taylor: A Study in Personality and Innovation*, Cambridge, MA: MIT Press. (A psychoanalytic biography of Taylor, which concisely examines the personal factors in his life that influenced his behaviour and the specific direction of his work.)

* Kanigel, R. (1997) *The One Best Way: Frederick Winslow Taylor and the Enigma of Efficiency*.

New York: Viking. (A new insightful, up-to-date biography of Taylor and his work which argues that his techniques owe more to 'guesswork' than to 'science'.)

* Kaple, D.A. (1994) *Dream of a Red Factory: The Legacy of High Stalinism in China*. Oxford: Oxford University Press. (An account of Taylorist influence on both Soviet and Chinese communist industrial practice.)

* Kelly, J. (1982) *Scientific Management, Job Design and Work Performance*, London: Academic Press. (This book constitutes an excellent critique of Taylor's work, which is distinctive in that it sees the later development of his thought as overlapping with the human relations school.)

* Merkle, J.A. (1980) *Management and Ideology: The Legacy of the International Scientific Management Movement*, Berkeley and Los Angeles, CA: University of California Press. (The author has written an interesting monograph on Taylorism as a social movement with reference to its influence on the UK, France, Germany and the Soviet Union.)

* Morgan, G. (1997) *Images of Organization*. Thousand Oaks, CA: Sage. (A provocative textbook which has attempted to re-write modern organizational theory.)

* Nelson, D. (1980) *Frederick Taylor and the Rise of Scientific Management*, Madison, WI: University of Wisconsin Press. (A more recent account of Taylor's life and work placing it in the context of US economic history.)

Pruijt, H.D. (1997) *Job Design and Technology: Taylorism-vs-Anti-Taylorism*. London: Routledge. (A timely account of anti-Taylorist innovations in European firms.)

* Pugh, D.S. (ed.) (1991) *Organization Theory: Selected Readings*, Harmondsworth: Penguin. (This is a set of useful readings covering more of the field and including detail on Taylor's evidence to the Congressional investigation.)

* Ritzer, G. (1996) *The McDonaldization of Society*. Newbury Park, CA: Sage. (An imaginative attempt to link Taylorism and later phenomena like McDonald's and Disney.)

Shingo, S. (1981) *The Toyota Production System*. Tokyo: Japanese Management Association. (Shingo describes the links between Taylorism and the Toyota system.)

* Taylor, F.W. (1903; 1919) *Shop Management*, New York: Harper Brothers. (Taylor's first major publication on work-study which made his reputation as a thinker and practitioner in the field.)

* Taylor, F.W. (1911) *The Principles of Scientific Management*, New York: W.W. Norton & Co. Inc. (Taylor's classic exposition of his views which has become internationally known as one of the classics of management theory.)

Taylor, F.W. (1919) *Two Papers on Scientific Management*, London: Routledge. (This book constitutes the late work of Taylor, which was published posthumously.)

* Warner, M. (1994) 'Japanese culture, Western management: Taylorism and Human Resources in Japan', *Organization Studies* 15: 509–533. (This paper explicitly points to the role of Taylorism in the development of the Japanese employment system.)

See also: BEDAUX, C.E.; FOLLETT, M.P.; FORD, H.; GILBRETTH, F.B. AND GILBRETH, L.E.; MAYO, G.E.; SMITH, A.; UENO, Y.

Related topics in the IEBM: COLLECTIVE BARGAINING; GROUPS AND TEAMS; GURU CONCEPT; HUMAN RELATIONS; HUMAN RESOURCE MANAGEMENT; INCENTIVES; INDUSTRIAL AND LABOUR RELATIONS; INDUSTRIAL CONFLICT; JOB DESIGN; JOB EVALUATION; LABOUR PROCESS; MANAGEMENT IN JAPAN; MOTIVATION AND SATISFACTION; OCCUPATIONAL PSYCHOLOGY; ORGANIZATION BEHAVIOUR; ORGANIZATION BEHAVIOUR, HISTORY OF; PAYMENT SYSTEMS; PRODUCTIVITY; RECRUITMENT AND SELECTION; SYSTEMS; TRADE UNIONS; WORK SYSTEMS

Thompson, James David (1920–73)

Personal background

- born 11 January 1920, Indianapolis, USA
- married Mary L. Mettenbrink, 1946
- earned doctorate at the University of North Carolina, 1953
- founded *Administrative Science Quarterly*, 1955
- specialized in the analysis of interdependence
- died September 1973 while at Vanderbilt University, Nashville, Tennessee

Major works

Comparative Studies in Administration (with P.B. Hammond, R.W. Hawkes, B.H. Junker and A. Tuden) (1959)
Organizations in Action (1967)
The Behavioral Sciences: An Interpretation (with D.R. Van Houten) (1970)

Summary

James David Thompson was a catalyst for the development of administrative science, specializing in the analysis of interdependence and its processes. He identified sources of interdependence and described their linkages with technology, power and authority, decision strategies and goal setting. Thompson presented typologies for interdependence and its dynamics which provide a strong conceptual base for further theory development and application.

1 Introduction

Thompson was instrumental in the development of the field of administrative science. He served as a catalyst for the field and contributed to theory through identifying and analysing sources and dynamics of interdependence and its essential nature in organized systems. Although many young scholars in the organizational sciences are unaware of his efforts, his commitment for a science of administration has taken root and borne fruit.

An early advocate of the study of administrative processes, Thompson championed this cause in publications and active work throughout his career. In 1955, he founded *Administrative Science Quarterly*, the first journal devoted specifically to the systematic study of administration, and served as editor for two years and on the editorial board until his death in 1973.

A key aspect of Thompson's work, particularly later in his career, was the application of his ideas on organizational processes to other fields, including education, social welfare, public administration and health care. Toward this end, he led the Pittsburgh area Committee on Common Elements in Administration (1959–60) and wrote essays and articles illustrating common elements in administration across academic fields (Thompson 1961, 1962a). However, Thompson's most recognized contribution to the study of organization theory lies in his analysis of interdependence and its premises and effects.

2 Main contribution

Contributions to theory

A dominant theme throughout Thompson's work is the importance of interdependence as both a source and a consequence of uncertainty, the management of which he saw as an essential function of administration.

'Uncertainty appears as the fundamental problem for complex organizations, and coping with uncertainty, as the essence of the administrative process' (Thompson 1967: 159).

Sources of interdependence

Thompson identified sources of interdependence arising both externally to the organization as well as internally. Sources of external interdependence he cited include general uncertainty, 'lack of cause/effect understanding in the culture at large' (Thompson 1967: 159) and contingency, in which organizational action outcomes are determined in part by the actions of environmental elements. He described internal interdependence as stemming from relationships between component parts within organizations and between parts and the whole organization. His differentiation of internal interdependence was based on the nature of the existing relationships and consisted of three types: pooled interdependence, sequential interdependence and reciprocal interdependence.

In the first internal interdependence type, pooled interdependence, 'each part renders a discrete contribution to the whole and is supported by the whole' (Thompson 1967: 54). Sequential interdependence is a serial form in which there is direct interdependence and the order of the interdependencies can be specified. Finally, reciprocal interdependence describes a situation in which outputs of each part become inputs for the others, that is, each unit or part poses contingencies on the others. Thompson felt that identifying the type of uncertainty was much more important than measuring the amount. The three types of internal interdependence he identified have implications for the coordination of technology and other processes within organizations.

Technology/interdependence linkages

Thompson defined technology as sets of man-machine activities or techniques that together produce a desired outcome. He identified three variations in technology and described their links to interdependence. First, mediating technology is a variation in which the primary purpose is to link clients or customers who seek to be interdependent, such as in a telephone company linking callers; thus, this technology is linked to pooled interdependence. Second, long-linked technology involves sequential interdependence in which each act or event rests on the completion of the preceding one, such as in a mass production assembly line. Finally, intensive technology draws on a variety of techniques to change an object, and the selection, combination and ordering of techniques are determined by feedback from the object itself, such as in a hospital emergency room in which the state of the patient suggests which techniques and actions are required. In intensive technology, actions by each part create contingencies for other parts; thus, this technology is linked to reciprocal interdependence.

The technology/interdependency linkages Thompson described are important in the modern context of rapid change. Much more emphasis is being placed on interdependence in companies that are increasingly pursuing lateral and team-based approaches as well as integration forward toward the consumer (Gailbraith and Lawler 1993).

Power and authority/interdependence linkages

Thompson also extended his analysis of interdependence and uncertainty to power and authority relationships (Thompson 1956b). Technology and the task environment continuously present sources of uncertainty. He described power as resulting from increased interdependence which arises from a desire and capacity to reduce this uncertainty. Individuals, units and organizations move in the direction of their dependency to pursue critical resources and create interdependencies to reduce uncertainty. The role of interdependence in defining power and authority and its relationship with the control of uncertainty have become increasingly prevalent in organization theory literature (Mackenzie 1986).

Task environment/interdependence linkages

Much of Thompson's discussion of interdependence focused on elements in the task environment, which he defined as 'parts of the environment which are relevant or potentially relevant to goal setting/attainment' (Thompson 1967: 27). He developed notions of buffering to absorb environmental fluctuations, smoothing or levelling to reduce fluctuations, and forecasting to adapt to anticipated fluctuations. His concepts of boundary and boundary-spanning roles which link organization members and non-members introduced key sources of organizational adaptation (Thompson 1962b). Many of his articles related task environment interdependencies to organization structure. He described disaster situations in which communities created temporary 'synthetic organizations' through allocation and integration processes in response to critical contingencies (Thompson and Hawkes 1962).

Thompson defined his domain broadly, applying his ideas on task-environment interdependencies to society as well (Thompson 1974a, 1974b). He believed that the number and variety of boundary-spanning groups related directly to the heterogeneity and dynamism of the task environment (Thompson 1968). The relevance of his boundary concepts is reflected in the increasing number of networked organizations and alliances worldwide, which serve as a testimonial to his accurate predictions.

Decision strategies/interdependence linkages – a typology

Thompson pioneered several typologies which led to the development of many contingency models, often pointing out previously unseen relationships between variables. Most notable is one that defines decision issues based on two dichotomized variables: preferences about possible outcomes and beliefs about cause and effect (Thompson 1974a). The two variables are analysed against the concepts of agreement or lack of agreement to yield a four-cell typology, as shown in Table 1. In the original presentation of the typology (Thompson *et al.* 1959), the latter concept was labelled as 'disagreement'; the later version reflects a move to a more general concept that includes, but is not limited to, cases of active disagreement. This revision demonstrates a concept refinement process that Thompson engaged in throughout his career.

The decision issues defined are linked to types of uncertainty and interdependence and appropriate strategies are suggested. Four strategies arise out of various combinations of agreement and lack of agreement on the two variables: computation, bargaining/compromise, judgement and inspiration. Thompson's focus on *how* decisions are made rather than *what* decisions are made is unique and differs from the usual approaches. In a later article, he further relates his typology to goal-setting strategies (Thompson 1964).

Goal-setting strategies/interdependence linkages

Thompson maintained a strong interest in goals in his work, and he saw goal setting as a necessary, recurring and dynamic aspect of organizational activity. He felt goals grew out of the interaction and interdependence within an organization and between an organization

Table 1 A typology of decision making

		Preferences about possible outcomes	
		Agreement	Lack of agreement
Beliefs about cause/effect	Agreement	Decision by computation	Decision by bargaining/ compromise
	Disagreement	Decision by majority judgement	Decision by inspiration

Source: Thompson et al. (1959)

and its environment. In 1958, he proposed his ideas in a well-known article with McEwen, which had been reprinted at least fifteen times by the mid-1990s. His proposed strategies for dealing with organizational environments include competition and cooperative strategies, with the latter further divided into bargaining, co-optation and coalition. His analysis placed goal setting in a more strategic form of reciprocal interdependence of the task environment and the organization.

Methodological contribution

Thompson's method of research often rested on creating innovative typologies and developing propositions stated in 'testable form' (Thompson 1960; Thompson 1967: 163). He felt administration was dynamic and that strategies for investigating organizations should focus on dynamics, not statics. Writing at a time when few researchers discussed process, Thompson referred often to patterned sequences of behaviour (Thompson 1967; Thompson *et al.* 1959), task environments (Thompson 1967, 1968) and the dynamics of organizations (Thompson *et al.* 1959).

A collaboratively written early article on the study of administration emphasized the importance of process – which the authors defined as 'how particular patterns bring about functional consequences' – and the need for process models (Thompson *et al.* 1959). The authors called for movement away from the reliance on 'spurious correlations' or associations and 'single-factor' analysis – statistical methods which dominated the field at the time. In fact, Thompson presented a process model for each of four transaction processes he analysed in an article on organizations and output transactions (Thompson 1962b). Given the dominant theme of his work – interdependence and its dynamics – his attraction to this approach is understandable. Leaders in the movement toward quality and organization redesign have pursued similar conceptual approaches (Deming 1982; Mackenzie 1986, 1991).

Although rarely an empiricist in practice, Thompson advocated the application of theory to experience and guided others in their pursuit of a science of administration that focused on simplified, testable models which considered unanticipated consequences and alternative means. He suggested that researchers seek out incidents which did not fit, as these were 'the only sure way of finding those points at which theory needs revision' (Thompson 1956a: 110).

Another aspect of Thompson's approach is his attempt to relate macro and micro structures and processes, seeing the field as a whole. He sought to define the field broadly, linking society, occupations, careers and families. This 'boundary-spanning' approach is currently being pursued under the label 'meso'.

3 Evaluation

Thompson was an early, effective and lifelong advocate of building a science of administration of complex organizations. He participated vigorously at the abstract, conceptual level but engaged less in the development of measurement, tools and the application of his concepts to the actual administration of organizations. He chose to lead by developing concepts for others to follow.

Citations of Thompson's work show 470 references in the period 1971 to 1975, 817 from 1981 to 1985 and 698 from 1989 to 1993. Clearly, others are beginning to follow him down the conceptual paths he pioneered. It is his ideas about the nature and types of technology, the impact of uncertainty on decision making and the nature of interdependence that continued to influence scholars two decades after his death. Thompson foretold the collapse of the large bureaucracy and the rise of networked organizations (Thompson 1967, 1973). These ideas are of central importance to organizations as they downsize, get re-engineered, implement increasingly sophisticated information management and movement systems, and adapt to regulation (Hammer and Champy 1993).

The globalizing effects of competition and the rapid transfer of technology are creating new interdependencies in the form of strategic alliances and networks. The rapid pace of change makes Thompson's discussion of goal setting, task environments and the nature of power and authority timeless. He continues to be well worth reading because his work has proven seminal.

Thompson was not enamoured with statistical thinking and static reasoning. He always emphasized the dynamics of administrative processes. Increasingly, managers and scholars are becoming more aware of the limitations of statistical reasoning and static comparison and are focusing more on processes and values (Keeney 1992). It could very well be that the most significant legacy of Thompson's work is the need to understand and use the processes of administration. After all, the action in organization lies in its processes.

4 Conclusions

In his writing, Thompson demonstrated how the concept of interdependence transcended academic disciplines and provided a reference point for a more holistic analysis of the behavioural sciences (Thompson and Van Houten 1970). Being an essential feature of all organized systems, interdependence is an important topic for research. Thompson's ideas, articulated in his classic propositions and typologies, provide a strong conceptual base for the further development of theory. Beyond that, they stimulate useful questions, the pursuit of which will lead to the refinement of administrative science and progression of the field that Thompson sought so fervently.

KENNETH D. MACKENZIE
ELAINE C. HOLLENSBE
UNIVERSITY OF KANSAS

Further reading

(References cited in the text marked *)

* Deming, W.E. (1982) *Quality, Productivity, and Competitive Position*, Cambridge, MA: MIT Press. (A useful account linking processes to quality; provides a bibliography for advanced study.)
* Gailbraith, J.R. and Lawler, E.E. (1993) *Organizing for the Future*, San Francisco, CA: Jossey Bass. (A useful book on lateral and team-based approaches for managing complex organizations.)
* Hammer, M. and Champy J. (1993) *Reengineering the Corporation: A Manifesto for the Business Revolution*, New York: HarperCollins. (An account of business process re-engineering through the radical redesign of process, organization and culture.)
* Keeney, R.L. (1992) *Value-Focused Thinking: A Path to Creative Decision Making*, Cambridge, MA: Harvard University Press. (An illuminating book on decision making and the need for integrating values and ethics in processes.)
* Mackenzie, K.D. (1986) *Organizational Design*, Norwood, NJ: Ablex. (An account of organizational audit and design technology, virtual positions, interdependence, boundaries and task processes.)
* Mackenzie, K.D. (1991) *The Organizational Hologram: The Effective Management of Organization Change*, Boston, MA: Kluwer. (A theory of the organizational hologram, a means of enhancing organization productivity, adaptability and efficient adaptability.)
Porter, M. (1990) *The Competitive Advantage of Nations*, New York: The Free Press. (A classic analysis of strategy and competition in an international environment.)
* Thompson, J.D. (1956a) 'On building an administrative science', *Administrative Science Quarterly* 1 (1): 102–11. (Thompson's arguments for developing a science of administration that focuses on simplified, testable models.)
* Thompson, J.D. (1956b) 'Authority and power in "identical" organizations', *American Journal of Sociology* 62: 290–301. (An analysis of relationships involving power and authority.)
* Thompson, J.D. (1960) 'Organizational management of conflict', *Administrative Science Quarterly* 4 (4): 389–409. (An analysis of conflict as a dynamic organizational phenomenon.)
* Thompson, J.D. (1961) 'Common elements in administration', in E.W. Reed (ed.), *Social Welfare Administration*, New York: Columbia University Press. (An essay that illustrates common elements in administration across academic fields.)
* Thompson, J.D. (1962a) 'Common and uncommon elements in administration', in *The Social Welfare Forum: Official Proceedings of the National Conference on Social Welfare*, New York: Columbia University Press. (An examination of the elements of administration.)
* Thompson, J.D. (1962b) 'Organizations and output transactions', *American Journal of Sociology*

68: 309–24. (A description of process models for four transaction processes.)

* Thompson, J.D. (1964) 'Decision-making, the firm, and the market', in W.W. Cooper, H.J. Leavitt and M.W. Shelly II (eds), *New Perspectives in Organization Research*, New York: Wiley. (An article that relates Thompson's typology of how decisions are made to goal-setting strategies.)

* Thompson, J.D. (1967) *Organizations in Action*, New York: McGraw-Hill. (A major work which identifies sources of interdependence and emphasizes the role of uncertainty.)

* Thompson, J.D. (1968) 'Models of organization and administrative systems', in *The Social Sciences: Problems and Orientations*, The Hague: Mouton/Unesco. (An outline of Thompson's views on boundary concepts.)

* Thompson, J.D. (1973) 'Society's frontiers for organizing activities', *Public Administration Review* 33: 327–35. (An article that predicts the collapse of the large bureaucracy and the rise of networked organizations.)

* Thompson, J.D. (1974a) 'Technology, polity, and societal development', *Administrative Science Quarterly* 19 (1): 6–21. (Discussion of a typology that defines decision issues based on two dichotomized variables.)

* Thompson, J.D. (1974b) 'Social interdependence, the polity and public administration', *Administration and Society* 6 (1): 3–21. (The application of Thompson's ideas on task-environment interdependencies to society.)

* Thompson, J.D., Hammond, P.B., Hawkes, R.W., Junker, B.H. and Tuden, A. (eds) (1959) *Comparative Studies in Administration*, Pittsburgh, PA: University of Pittsburgh Press. (A landmark work presenting comparative essays on the dynamics of administration.)

* Thompson, J.D. and Hawkes, R.W. (1962) 'Disaster, community organization, and administrative process', in G.W. Baker and D.W. Chapman (eds), *Man and Society in Disaster*, New York: Basic Books. (An analysis of organization processes at work in disaster situations.)

* Thompson, J.D. and McEwen, W.J. (1958) 'Organizational goals and environment: goal-setting as an interaction process', *American Sociological Review* 23: 23–31. (A well-known article that proposes strategies for dealing with organizational environments.)

* Thompson, J.D. and Van Houten, D.R. (1970) *The Behavioral Sciences: An Interpretation*, Reading, MA: Addison-Wesley. (An analysis comparing and relating behavioural sciences on a macro level.)

See also: ASTON GROUP; DEMING, W.E.; HAMMER, M.; HANNAN, M. AND FREEMAN, J.; SIMON, H.A.

Related topics in the IEBM: CONTEXTS AND ENVIRONMENTS; DECISION MAKING; GLOBALIZATION; OCCUPATIONAL PSYCHOLOGY; ORGANIZATION BEHAVIOUR; ORGANIZATION BEHAVIOUR, HISTORY OF; ORGANIZATION NETWORKS; ORGANIZATION STRUCTURE; POWER; STRATEGIC CHOICE; TECHNOLOGY AND ORGANIZATIONS

Toffler, Alvin (1928–)

Personal background

- born 4 October 1928 in New York City
- graduated from New York University (1949)
- associate editor of Fortune magazine (1959–61)
- member of faculty at the New School for Social Research (1965–67)
- since the publication of his *Future Shock* in 1970, a world renowned author and consultant
- developed the theme of The Third Wave, which offered a framework for understanding the global changes engulfing the world today

Major works

Future Shock (1970)
Third Wave (1980)
Power Shift (1990)

Summary

Since 1970, Alvin Toffler has co-authored with his wife Heidi Toffler some of the most influential books on the subject of change. His widely discussed trilogy of works – *Future Shock, Third Wave, Power Shift* – provide an unusually broad vision of the fundamental changes affecting societies throughout the world. Toffler has elaborated the concept of the Third Wave to illuminate what he considers to be three gigantic waves of change. *The First Wave* corresponds to the agricultural revolution which dominated human history for thousands of years. *The Second Wave* – industrial civilization – which began in the
seventeenth century and which soon dominated the globe is now facing exhaustion according to Toffler. *The Third Wave*, which began with the birth of the post-war service economy and the information technology of the 1950s now threatens the previous industrial civilization. The institutions, practices and values of industrialism face annihilation by the forces of the Third Wave. Toffler argues that it is the dynamic created by the clash between the second and third wave which helps explain most of the key developments that characterize contemporary societies.

1 Biographical Data

Alvin Toffler was born just before the outbreak of the Great Depression. The experience of economic stagnation and of inequalities had a radicalizing impact on him and led him towards leftist activism during his days as a university student. Indeed, after graduating from University in 1949, he and his wife Heidi worked on a factory production line. Apparently, this interest in union activism was motivated not only by his left-wing leanings but also by an early interest in technology and its effect on everyday life. This venture into the factory floor was followed by a career in journalism. He became a Washington correspondent for a number of newspapers in the late 1950s and during the years 1959 to 1961 he went on to serve as the associate editor of *Fortune* magazine. During this intense phase of journalistic work the Tofflers wrote for a wide variety of publications – from *Fortune* to *Playboy* through to the *Annals of the American Academy of Science*. This period of journalistic work was succeeded by a move into academia. Toffler went on to serve on the staff of a number of universities during the years 1965 to 1970.

The elaboration of the Tofflers' insights into the relationship between technology and social and economic change occurred in the 1960s, when IBM asked them to write a study of the long-term social and organizational consequences of the computer. This study initiated a phase of intense study into the wider socio-economic impact of technological change. Some of the key ideas that were to characterize the Tofflers' work in the decades ahead were the product of this period. Many of the themes were first presented in an article published in 1965, entitled 'The future as a way of life'. The thesis of the article was that change was likely to accelerate and that the outcome of this process would be to fundamentally disorient people who were unprepared for the future. The Tofflers coined the concept 'future shock' to underline the sense of dread that societies which were stuck in the past would experience. Alvin Toffler's *Future Shock* went on to become an international best seller and since that time he has never looked back. Toffler emerged as not only one of the most pre-eminent futurologists of our times; he also became one of the most successful popularizers of the notion of the information society. His contribution has been recognized internationally and he has won numerous awards for his writings in countries as varied as China, France, Italy and the United States.

2 Main Contribution

Toffler's main contribution has been to illuminate the outcome of the process of technological change to an unusually wide readership. Probably more than any one else he has also succeeded in sensitizing the business community to the profound implications of continuous change during the last three decades of the twentieth century. It was his educated intuition of the transformative impact of the knowledge industry, which allowed him to pinpoint at a relatively early stage what would become some of the most significant trends of our era. By the mid 1960s, he had grasped the central role which information technology would play in the economic life of the future. From this insight he concluded that technological change would be qualitatively more rapid than in the past.

Toffler's concept of *Future Shock* expressed a vision of society that was more and more torn apart by the premature arrival of the future. His thesis, that the pace of change was too fast for society to handle, reflected the mood of the sixties. This was a time when less and less could be taken for granted. The institutions and value systems associated with industrial civilization had become subject to the irresistible force of change, argued Toffler. He believed that change was fuelled by the growth of knowledge. This massive explosion of knowledge had created an environment, where the future would become virtually unrecognizable in the present. Transience had become a way of life – and this process was revolutionizing every aspect of life; from the economic to the realm of individual lifestyle. His advice to government and business was straightforward: be prepared for anything and certainly do not expect the future to be anything like the past. Today, this perspective has a strong influence on management theory, but back in the early seventies, Toffler's vision of unchanging change was often dismissed as somewhat bizarre and eccentric.

In his book *The Third Wave*, Toffler sought to elaborate a more comprehensive framework for making sense of the changes that were working towards the creation of what he considered to be a new post-industrial civilization. According to Toffler, The First Wave of change coincided with the agricultural revolution, which took off roughly ten millennium ago. But before this First Wave of change had exhausted itself, it was overtaken by the industrial revolution in Europe, which unleashed a Second Wave of planetary change. This Second Wave of change, swiftly engulfed most of the world, although the agricultural and industrial modes of culture continued to coexist and compete with each other in large parts of the world. The Second Wave of change rapidly transformed life and revolutionized the institutions of the economy and of society. The consequences of the Second Wave of changes are still experienced throughout the world.

But even as societies continue to be influenced by the institutions and practices of the

Second Wave, a new, even more significant process of change has begun to alter economic and social life. Toffler contends that industrialism, which peaked after the Second Wave has been succeeded by a Third Wave of change which has transformed virtually every aspect of the human experience. The Third Wave, symbolized by the computer, commercial jet travel, the birth control pill and high tech industry has fundamentally altered the way we live and produce. For Toffler, the dynamic of this process is most strikingly expressed in the shift from manufacturing to the knowledge industry.

Toffler's study of the dynamic of the interaction between the Second and Third Wave of change has been taken up by both academics, politicians and business mangers to make sense of their circumstances. Toffler's analysis is clearly focused on the fundamentals of wealth creation. He noted that the Second Wave of changes led to the emergence of a factory based system of wealth creation. Such a system depended on the principles of mass production, standardization, maximization and large bureaucratic business organizations. This industrial culture based on material factors of production has been severely undermined by changes brought about by the explosion of information technology. Toffler suggests that the Third Wave has fundamentally altered the very essence of wealth creation. Wealth today, according to Toffler's model, is based on instant communication and the dissemination of data, ideas and symbols.

Toffler has dismissed the idea of 'deindustrialization'. Instead, he argues that industry has been transformed by the knowledge revolution. In the Third Wave, the Tofflers coined the term 'de-massification' to describe trends that move economic life beyond mass production, mass distribution, mass media and mass homogeneity. The outcome of the process of *de-massification* is a shift from mass production towards increasing customization, from mass marketing towards niches and micro-marketing and from the monolithic hierarchical and control organization to a decentralized network.

Toffler's systematic study of the changing relations of power in his *Power Shift*, provides

intriguing insights into the role of knowledge in contemporary society. For Toffler, knowledge has become the essence of power. Both wealth and the means of physical violence depend on knowledge. His writings continually warn politicians and business managers about the danger of ignoring knowledge as a factor of production since economic success depends on a capacity to manipulate high-quality knowledge.

Toffler's theory of change has both a pessimistic and optimistic side. His work provides a detailed account of both the destructive and the constructive side of the Third Wave. He believes that most conflicts at both the global and the interpersonal level can be understood as a product of a clash between the forces steeped in the industrial civilization of the Second Wave and the forces which are the beneficiaries of the Third Wave. He argues that it is the shift in the foundation of power from violence and material wealth to knowledge which provides the impetus for these conflicts. Toffler projects a future where the scramble for the control of new knowledge resources becomes the foundation for the power struggles to come. There is also a democratic vision in this perspective. Since knowledge cannot be centralized or monopolized, a wide variety of interests have the potential to gaining access to this new source of power.

Knowledge as the source of power is Toffler's key idea for making sense of the tensions which afflict economic and political life throughout the world today. His work provides an important resource for making sense of the ways in which the knowledge industry has altered social and economic life.

3 Evaluation

Toffler's ability to integrate material and experience from a variety of subject areas is truly impressive. His key works have succeeded in synthesizing research from the fields of sociology, technology, science, cultural studies and psychology. The criticism made by academics that this feat is achieved at the expense of depth is undeniable. But despite all its shortcomings, Toffler has succeeded in putting forward the big picture and a framework for making sense of what other-wise appear as unconnected diverse processes.

Toffler's work also represents some of the finest examples of trend-spotting. He is at his best when he isolates developments before they have made an impact on the public imagi-nation and drawing our attention to their significance.

At the same time, Toffler's work suffers from the attempt to say too much too soon. His attempt to link together a variety of experi-ences – family breakdown, the rise of self-help groups, growth of new life styles, the rise of the paperless office, the home as the new place of work, the disintegration of the nation state – can only be sustained at the level of de-scription. But just because these experiences occur at roughly the same time, there is no rea-son to suppose that they are all products of the same processes. It appears that virtually any new or not yet comprehensible process be-comes integrated into the Third Wave pre-cisely because it is new.

In a sense, Toffler's strength also consti-tutes his weakness. His focus on change tends towards an exaggeration of its effects. It is dif-ficult to accept the view that everything from the family to the nation through to work has so fundamentally altered. Even in an age of in-formation, most people still work with their hands instead of their brains. And even in the service sector, many of the jobs involve the kind of unskilled, repetitive tasks that charac-terize the labour of the past. And certainly when we compare the experience of the sec-ond half of the twentieth century with the transformative experience of the industrial revolution, the intensity of our own pace of change may not appear all that unusual.

As a popularizer of other people's work, Toffler invariably overstates his case and sim-plifies the issues at stake. His work is littered with extravagant phrases and simplistic soundbites. But, unlike many academic works which deal with the issue of change, Toffler sticks his neck out and offers a stimulating argument.

4 Conclusion

In an important sense, Toffler personifies the temper of the late twentieth century. At a time when societies are prone to exaggerate the quality of change – terms like post-industrial, post historical, post-geographical, post mod-ern abound – Toffler provides a systematic statement of a future almost unconnected to the past. This disposition towards sensing change allows Toffler to help grasp some of the developments that will influence our future.

For the layperson, Toffler offers an exhila-rating and even democratic vision, where the dominance of knowledge gives an ever-widening section of society access to power. For the world of business, Toffler provides the important insight of 'do not live off the past'. And though he falls short of giving us answers, Toffler continually stimulates his reader to think the unthinkable.

FRANK FUREDI
UNIVERSITY OF KENT IN CANTERBURY

Further reading

(References cited in the text marked *)

Badham, R. (1984) 'The sociology of industrial and post-industrial societies', *Current Sociol-ogy*, 32: 1–36. (Reviews the contribution of Toffler and Daniel Bell to the establishment of the post-industrial perspective in sociology.)

Cohen, M.J. (1997) 'Risk society and ecological modernisation; alternative visions for post in-dustrial nations', *Futures*, 29: 105–119. *(Exam-ines how many of the trends outlined by Toffler are analysed by risk society theorists.)*

Frankel, B. (1987) *The Post-Industrial Utopians*, Oxford: Polity Press. (A useful critique of Toffler's work, which offers a balanced ac-count of the strength and weakness of Toffler.)

Gibson, R. (ed.) (1997) *Rethinking The Future*, London: Nicholas Brealey Publishing. (A col-lection of articles from leading business think-ers, which elaborate many of the insights found in Toffler's work.)

Kumar, K. (1995) *From Post-Industrial to Post-Modern Society*, Oxford: Blackwell. (This comprehensive survey of the post-industrial perspective helps situate Toffler within the wider sociological tradition.)

Marien, M. (1996) 'New Communications Technology – A Survey of Impacts and Issues', *Telecommunications Policy*, 20: 375–387. (An interesting biblioessay, which examines a wide range of literature on the impact of the new communications technologies on society.)

* Toffler, A. (1970) *Future Shock*, London: The Bodley Head Ltd. (Toffler's pioneering work which argues that the magnitude of change had become so great that its effects was a future of trauma.)

* Toffler, A. (1980) *The Third Wave*, London: William Collins Sons & Co. (This is Toffler's most important analysis of social transformation.)

* Toffler, A. (1990) *Power Shift*, New York: Bantam Press. (This work is devoted to the exploration of the relationship between knowledge and power, particularly economic power.)

Webster, F. (1995) *Theories of The Information Society*, London: Routledge. (Webster's study of theories of The Information Society helps situate Toffler in the wider discussion of the subject.)

See also: LEVITT, T.; MCLUHAN, H.M.; OHMAE, K.; PORTER, M.E.; WIENER, N.

Related topics in the IEBM: DECISION MAKING; FUTUROLOGY; GLOBALIZATION; GLOBALIZATION AND SOCIETY; INFORMATION REVOLUTION; INFORMATION TECHNOLOGY AND SOCIETY; ORGANIZATION BEHAVIOUR; ORGANIZATION BEHAVIOUR, HISTORY OF; POWER; SYSTEMS

Toyoda family

Summary

There is no one 'great person' who bears the name Toyota in the same way as Henry Ford. The Toyota Motor Company, which in 1982 became Toyota Motor Co. Ltd. (TMC), was founded by the Toyoda family. The company took on the name Toyota after staging a contest to select a new name in 1936. TMC has become the most powerful Japanese car manufacturer and one of the world's largest manufacturers of motor vehicles, third in size after General Motors (GM) and Ford. The success of TMC has been associated with its production system, which has given TMC the reputation of being highly efficient and of

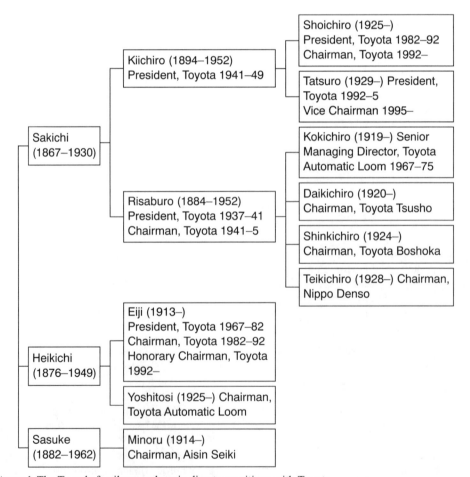

Figure 1 The Toyoda family: members in director positions with Toyota
Source: Adapted from Kamiya (1976: 100–1) and Cusumano (1985: 184) and personal

producing high quality cars and trucks. Much of TMC's success can be attributed to the achievements of the Toyoda family.

Personal background

See Figure 1 for details of the Toyoda family tree.

Major works

Toyota – Fifty Years in Motion: An Autobiography by the Chairman, Eiji Toyoda (1987)

Toyota, A History of the First Fifty Years (1988)

I Introduction

Toyota Motor Company was established in the summer of 1937, in 1952 it became the largest car producer , and it remains dominant. Since the mid-1980s, prompted by the rise in the value of the yen and of periodic tendencies towards protectionism in its export markets, the Toyota Motor Corporation (TMC) has made major investments in overseas manufacturing plants, including in the USA, Canada, the UK and Australia, but also in other countries.

In 1974 when most of the world's car companies were making losses, Toyota continued to make a modest profit. Competing manufacturers began making visits to Toyota to discover the key to that company's success. What they discovered was the Toyota production system which Toyota had continued to develop over forty years.

2 Biographical data

Sakichi Toyoda (1867–1930)

The founding father of the Toyota Group, Sakichi was born in Shizuoka Prefecture on 14 February 1867, the son of Ikichi Toyoda. As the first born, Sakichi was the *kacho*, or head of the household, and it was his duty to carry forward the obligations of his father and his trade as a carpenter. However, Sakichi was not interested in carpentry and in 1885 he decided instead to become an inventor. Over the next thirty-five years Sakichi worked on improving weaving looms. In 1907 he became a partner in Toyoda's Loom Works, from which he resigned in 1910. He later started his own business, Toyoda Spinning and Weaving Company. In 1924, with the aid of his son Kiichiro, he developed a fully automatic loom and in 1926 Sakichi formed another company, Toyoda Automatic Loom Works. In 1929 he granted the patent rights of the automatic loom to the British firm Platt Brothers & Co. Ltd, for £100,000. He was awarded the Imperial Order of Merit, Japan's highest civilian honour, by the Emperor in 1927, and died on October 30 1930.

When the people of the Nagoya region laid Sakichi to rest, they honoured him as a man who made his dreams reality, who had embraced the challenges and opportunities of the Meiji Restoration, and who had helped lead his country into the modern world.

(Togo and Wartman 1993: 39)

Kiichiro Toyoda (1894–1952)

The founder of Toyota Motor Company, Kiichiro, was born in Shizuoka Prefecture in 1894, the eldest son of Sakichi Toyoda. He graduated in 1920 from Tokyo Imperial University as a mechanical engineer and joined his father's company, Toyoda Spinning and Weaving Company, in that same year. In 1930, at the bequest of his father, Kiichiro began work to produce cars. He began by sectioning off an area of the Toyoda Automatic Loom Works in which to disassemble and study a small engine. In September 1933, the directors of Toyoda Automatic Loom agreed to fund an automotive department and in September 1934 Kiichiro and his staff completed their first prototype engine, type A. The A1-type passenger car was completed in May 1935 and the first truck prototype was completed in August 1935.

The cost of the automotive department was a great burden on the Loom company and Kiichiro reasoned that the only way to become established in the market was to expand. With the board's approval, the acquisition of credit and the sales of shares, Toyota Motor Company was formally established in the summer of 1937. Kiichiro was Executive Vice President and in 1941 he became President of the company. But by 1950 the company was in turmoil as the entire workforce went on strike, protesting against a proposed reduction in employees. In an attempt to smooth labour relations, Kiichiro resigned from the company. He was due to return as president in 1952 to oversee the production of cars, but unfortunately he died of a cerebral haemorrhage on 27 March 1952.

Eiji Toyoda (1913–)

Eiji was born in Nagoya in 1913, the eldest son of Heikichi Toyoda, Sakichi Toyoda's brother. He graduated from Tokyo Imperial University, where he had studied mechanical engineering, and joined the Toyoda Automatic Loom Works in 1936 at the newly established car research lab. Eiji lodged with Kiichiro and his family and became an integral part of their household. He transferred to Toyota Motor Company in 1937.

In 1950 Toyota and Ford were beginning talks of a joint venture; part of the deal was to accept Toyota trainees at Ford's facilities, and Eiji Toyoda was the first person sent by Toyota. In 1951, he redesigned Toyota's plants to incorporate more advanced methods and machines. Eiji became president in 1967 and, in 1982, Chairman of the new Toyota Motor Corporation (TMC). In this same year Eiji began talks with General Motors (GM) about an important joint venture, New United Motor Manufacturing Incorporated (NUMMI), which would produce a Corolla-type car (a Toyota model) at a recently closed GM plant in Fremont, California. The project was widely hailed as a success, and demonstrated that the Toyota production system could be adapted to a Western context.

Dr Shoichiro Toyoda (1925–)

Shoichiro, the eldest son of Kiichiro, was born in 1925. He graduated from Nagoya University in 1949 with a degree in engineering and joined Toyota Motor Company in 1952. In 1955 he earned a doctorate in engineering at Tokyo University, with a thesis on fuel injection systems. He assumed the presidency of TMC Sales Co., Ltd in 1981. After its merger with Toyota Motor Company the following year, he became the President of the new Toyota Motor Corporation and, in 1992, Chairman of the Board. He presided over Toyota's becoming a global corporation. In May 1994 he became chairman of Keidanren (Japan Federation of Ecomonic Organizations), the most powerful organization in Japan.

3 Main contributions

TMC's success reflects the foresight and determination of the Toyoda family. Each of the above members contributed to the development of the Toyota philosophy.

Sakichi Toyoda

Having no formal educational qualifications, Sakichi learnt by trial and error; he believed that he could learn all that he needed to know by working on machines with his hands. Sakichi also recognized that industry in Japan had to advance in small steps and to fill niche markets not met by Western companies. He came to recognize the importance of constantly improving machines regardless of what the competition was doing. Sakichi believed that no process ever reached a point where it could not be improved; this policy of *kaizen* (continuous improvement) became part of his basic philosophy.

Despite much opposition, Sakichi was sure that cars would be a worthwhile product of the future. When he sold the patent rights to Toyoda's automatic loom, he told his son, Kiichiro Toyoda, that he was giving him £100,000, but there was one condition: Kiichiro had to use the money for research on car production. Kiichiro agreed.

Kiichiro Toyoda

Kiichiro took on Sakichi's legacy and formally established Toyota Motor Company. However, his contribution to the Toyota story did not stop there. Kiichiro realized that in order to compete with such powerful Western companies as Ford and GM, Toyota needed to invest in research and development. Hence, in 1936, he established a research lab in Tokyo. Japan differed from the USA in its lack of space and other resources. The US manufacturers could afford to stockpile parts and could build big warehouses. Kiichiro wanted to develop a Japanese production system that reflected the country's lack of space and resources, as well as the flexibility and versatility of its people, so he bought general-purpose machines rather than specialized machines. His plan was to adapt them and make them multi-purpose.

In the past the process of building cars had been 'learning by doing'. This had generated waste, which the Japanese could not afford. Kiichiro envisaged a system in which no component would be produced unless it was needed, hence eliminating the need for stock piles and waste. Therefore, in his factory, he hung a sign that read JUST IN TIME. He told the workers that no component for a car should be produced before it was needed: in other words components should be made just-in-time (JIT) (Togo and Wartman 1993: 79). The practices of *kaizen* and JIT became an important part of the Toyoda philosophy. However the philosophy was not developed fully until Taiichi Ohno joined the team (see OHNO, T.).

Eiji Toyoda

In January 1951, Eiji Toyoda developed a five-year modernization plan. This plan involved the modernization of equipment and the transformation of production methods. Like Kiichiro and Sakichi before him, Eiji recognized that Toyota would have to do things differently from Western firms. Production would have to be streamlined; workers would have to search for continuous improvement and waste had to be minimized. Eiji employed Taiichi Ohno to implement these changes.

Ohno had begun his career with the Toyoda family in 1932 and was familiar with their philosophies. He introduced *kanban* cards (which keep track of stock), taught workers to understand *kaizen*, fully implemented the JIT system, rationalized the machinery and assembly lines, and introduced multi-skilling. Eiji was supportive of Ohno's work, and within two years Eiji had devised a radical new principle of factory operation. Whenever a problem developed in assembly, the production line was to be shut down, thus providing an incentive for a speedy and effective remedy.

By 1963 the JIT system had been instituted throughout the company and Toyota Motor Company began asking its suppliers to adopt the same system. It took Eiji Toyoda and Ohno more than twenty years to implement this set of ideas fully (including JIT) within the Toyota Motor Company supply chain.

Eiji also set another precedent. He decided that the future of the company depended on how well it built cars, even more than on how well it designed them. He proclaimed that production was the most important thing that happened at Toyota. The mission of designers and engineers was to enable the production staff to do their best. Accordingly, the status of assembly-line workers was elevated.

Shoichiro Toyoda

A novel production system had improved Toyota's efficiency and had enabled the company to put cars on the market at competitive prices. The quality, however, was still inadequate. Shoichiro Toyoda, then managing director of corporate planning, came to realize that the company was practising *kaizen* at too late a stage. Having to mend cars after they came on the market was damaging Toyota's reputation. In search of a means to improve quality, Shoichiro came across the work of Deming (see DEMING, W.E.). Toyota had instituted some aspects of Deming's approach in the early 1950s. Shoichiro realized that for Toyota Motor Company to improve, two aspects of their quality process needed to change: first, it had to become more systematic, and second it had to be extended to every department. Therefore, Shoichiro implemented a quality programme throughout the company and in 1965 Toyota Motor

Company won the coveted Deming Prize for quality.

Toyota Motor Company

Following the first 'oil crisis', by 1974 the international car industry was in a state of flux. Toyota was one of the few car manufacturers in the world that was consistently profitable. Competing manufacturers wanted to know how Toyota could be profitable in a bad market. Toyota was able to achieve extremely high levels of quality (few defects) and productivity in manufacturing (output per worker that was as much as two or three times higher than US or European plants in the late 1980s). Toyota was also able to achieve high levels of flexibility, producing relatively small batches of different models with little or no loss of productivity or quality. Accordingly, this Japanese style of manufacturing and product development has come to be studied and emulated around the world. By the mid-1990s the best US-owned car manufacturing plants appeared to have achieved relative parity with all but the most efficient Japanese plants.

Many believed that Toyota's most critical factor for success was its production system and underlying philosophies, sometimes known as 'Toyodaism'. The Toyota production system includes:

- JIT production
- minimal in-process inventories and efficient use of resources
- geographic concentration of assembly and parts production
- good communications
- elimination of waste
- manual demand-'pull' with *kanban* cards
- production levelling
- rapid set-up
- machinery and line rationalization
- work standardization
- foolproof automation devices
- multi-skilled workers
- high levels of sub-contracting
- selective use of automation

- continuous incremental process improvement (*kaizen*)
- teamwork

Since the publication of *The Machine that Changed the World* (Womack *et al.* 1990), Toyota's production system has also become known as 'lean production'. Lean production has been put forward as a model of 'best practice', which can be successfully implemented even in cultures very different from Japan, not merely in the car industry, but in other industries too.

4 Evaluation

The success of Toyota's production system has helped to transform Japan into one of the capitals of the automotive world and has also led to improved productivity and efficiency in Western manufacturing. For example, following a change to lean production at the GM–Toyota joint venture plant (NUMMI), performance in terms of quality, productivity and other indicators improved dramatically from one of the worst in the USA to one of the best. A typical body-stamping die-change time was reduced from twelve hours to less than ten minutes. Lean production involves significant differences from and advantages over Fordist and neo-Fordist mass-production factory regimes as illustrated in Table 1, and the key components of lean production can contribute to a major improvement in competitiveness (Shadur and Bamber 1994).

Nevertheless, as manufacturers around the world have tried to copy TMC's methods, there have inevitably been criticisms. Compared to Fordism, lean production systems place greater demands on managers and supervisory staff since they are responsible for managing a broader range of issues in their unit, such as human resource management, safety, absenteeism, and continuous improvement. There are also more demands on them to maintain extensive information systems for each work unit and optimize performance on each item they measure.

Critics argue that the pace of work in such Japanese production plants is frantic (for example, Kamata 1982; Williams *et al.* 1992).

Table 1 Critical differences between Fordism, neo-Fordism and lean production

	Fordism	Neo-Fordism	Lean production
Innovation	Wholly technocratic	Mostly technocratic	Technocratic/ continuous improvement
Quality control	Inspected in	Part inspected and built in	Built in
Operations management	Bulk supply	Bulk supply/JIT incipient	JIT
Throughput efficiency	Operational	Operational	Process
Approach to HR	Individual/plant	Individual/ some teams	Teams
Authority structure	Highly vertical	Vertical	Vertical/some decentralization
Information to workers	Minimal	Some provided	Extensive
Role of workers	Appendages of machines	Important part of production	Crucial part of production
Role of supervisory staff	Directive	Controlling/ organizing	Facilitating/ organizing/training
Company's role for union	Non-recognition	Adversarial	More cooperative

Source: Shadur and Bamber (1994)

The JIT system creates pressures for operators to maintain production at a pre-set rate, and the demands of smaller batches and shorter set-up times can lead to pressure on them to work harder. But advocates of Toyodaism hold that it requires people to work smarter, not necessarily harder. Others have argued that lean production uses labour as a buffer for a fragile production system, and that the workers have little real control over their job design. Such criticisms have led some authors to describe lean production as 'management by stress' (Parker and Slaughter 1988).

From the perspective typical of Toyota, however, such criticisms are merely seen to be a reminder that the lean notion itself should be subjected to continuous improvement. While US, European and other car makers continue to study and, at least in part, try to emulate Toyota's manufacturing and engineering practices, it has become apparent to many Japanese managers, policy-makers and industry observers that the notion of 'continuous improvement' – continually pushing for gains in manufacturing and engineering efficiency – can precipitate new problems and has some practical limits. *Kaizen* continues at TMC, as Toyota and other Japanese car makers are exploring ways to modify their approaches.

5 Conclusion

The Toyota Motor Corporation had its beginnings in 1930 when Sakichi Toyoda gave his son Kiichiro Toyoda a grant to produce cars. Since its establishment, TMC has grown to be the world's third-largest car manufacturer, with plants in many countries. Toyodaism has been emulated around the world and has been widely advocated as a paragon of best practice. TMC and its production system continue to attract much international acclaim. In spite of the rise in the value of the yen and economic recessions, Toyota has remained competitive, as it continues to improve its production system.

GREG J. BAMBER
GRIFFITH UNIVERSITY
KELLIE CAUGHT
QUEENSLAND UNIVERSITY OF TECHNOLOGY

Further reading

(References cited in the text marked *)

Berggren, C. (1992) *Alternatives to Lean Production: Work Organisation in the Swedish Auto Industry*, Ithaca, NY: Cornell University Press. (Also published in London by Macmillan under the title *The Volvo Experience: Alternatives to Lean Production in the Swedish Auto Industry*; challenges the superiority of Toyodaism, arguing for a more human-centred approach, contrasting and comparing the Swedish and Japanese styles.)

Clark, K.B. and Fujimoro, T. (1991) *Product Development Performance: Strategy, Organization and Performance in the World Auto Industry*, Boston, MA: Harvard Business School Press. (Shows that Toyota and other Japanese companies develop products more quickly and efficiently than Western manufacturers.)

* Cusumano, M.A. (1985) *The Japanese Automobile Industry: Technology and Management at Nissan and Toyota*, Cambridge, MA: Harvard University Press. (Provides an account of the developments of Nissan and Toyota, contrasts their different systems and highlights ways in which Japanese manufacturing diverged from US and European practices.)

* Kamata, S. (1982) *Japan in the Passing Lane*, New York: Pantheon. (A radical journalist's critique of working life in a Toyota plant in Japan, based on participant observation.)

* Kamiya, S. (1976) *My Life with Toyota*, Nagoya: Toyota Motor Sales. (A personal history of Shotoro Kamiya, his life with Toyota and the Japanese automobile industry.)

Kimoto, S. (1991) *Quest for the Dawn*, Milwaukee, WI: Dougherty. (An insight into the origins of Toyota Motor Company, based on translations of diaries, memos and other documents written by Sakichi and Kiichiro Toyoda and their contemporaries.)

Kochen, T., Lansbury, K.D. and MacDuffie, J.P. (1997) *After Lean Production: Changing Employment Practices in the World Auto Industry*. Ithaca: Cornell University Press. (Research based on car assembly plants in eleven countries includes the way work is organised, how workeers and managers interact, the way in which worker representatives respond to lean production strategies and the nature of the adaptation and innovation process.)

Krafcik, J.F. (1988) 'Triumph of the lean production system', *Sloan Management Review* 30 (1): 41–52. (An account of the superiority of the Toyota production system which manufactures a wide range of models but maintains high degrees of quality and productivity as revealed by research of the International Motor Vehicle Program (IMVP), Massachusetts Institute of Technology.)

MacDuffie, J.P. and Frits, K.P. (1995) 'The international assembly plant study: update on round two findings', IMVP Research Briefing Meeting, Toronto, 5 June (mimeo, Wharton School, University of Pennsylvania and International Motor Vehicle Program (IMVP), Massachusetts Institute of Technology.) (A comparison of the findings of IMVP's surveys conducted in 1989 and 1993 which show general improvements in plant performance, but Japanese plants in Japan appeared to be the most productive in both surveys.)

Monden, Y. (1983) *The Toyota Production System*, Atlanta, GA: Industrial Engineering and Management Press. (An explanation of Toyodaism dating from before it was popularized by the IMVP's publications.)

* Parker, M. and Slaughter, J. (1988) 'Management by stress', *Technology Review* 91 (7): 37–44. (A critique of Toyodaism by two radical critics based in Detroit with the Labor Education and Research Project.)

* Shadur, M.A. and Bamber, G.J. (1994) 'Toward lean management? International transferability of Japanese management strategies to Australia', *The International Executive* 36 (3): 343–64. (Reports a study of an attempt to transplant Toyodaism to Australia.)

* Togo, Y. and Wartman, W. (1993) *Against All Odds: The Story of the Toyota Motor Corporation and the Family That Created It*, New York: St Martin's Press. (An account of the Toyota family and the development of the Toyota Motor Corporation from 1867 to 1990.)

Toyoda, E. (1987) *Toyota – Fifty Years in Motion: An Autobiography by the Chairman, Eiji Toyoda*, New York: Kodansha International. (An account of the life of Eiji Toyoda, from birth to Chairman of Toyota.)

Toyota Motor Corporation (1988) *Toyota, A History of the First Fifty Years*, Japan: Toyota Motor Corporation. (An official synopsis of Toyota Motor Corporation's 50-year history, spanning 1937–87, with reference to Toyota's beginnings and the development of its management style.)

Toyota Motor Corporation (1995) *You ain't seen nuthin' yet!*, Japan: Toyota Motor Company. (Toyota Annual Report 1995: a review of operations, finances, Board of Directors and share information for the 1994–5 financial year.)

* Williams, K., Haslam, C., Williams, J. and Cutler, T., with Adcrost, A. and Sukhdev, J. (1992) 'Against lean production', *Economy and Society* 21 (3): 321–54. (A critique of the lean production system.)

* Womack, J.P., Jones, D.T. and Roos, D. (1990) *The Machine that Changed the World*, New York: Rawson/Macmillan. (Examines the differences between mass production and lean production in the automotive industry in Japan, North America and western Europe. Reports the results and implications of the International Motor Vehicle Program (IMVP) study.)

See also: DEMING, W.E.; FORD, H.; ISHIKAWA, K.; JURAN, J.M.; OHNO, T.; SHINGO, S.; SLOAN, A.P.; TAYLOR, F.W.

Related topics in the IEBM: BUSINESS STRATEGY, JAPANESE; INDUSTRIAL RELATIONS IN JAPAN; INVENTORY AND JUST-IN-TIME MODELS; JAPANIZATION; JUST-IN-TIME PHILOSOPHIES; MANAGEMENT IN JAPAN; PRODUCTIVITY; TEAMS IN MANUFACTURING; TOTAL QUALITY MANAGEMENT

Trist, Eric Lansdown (1909–93)

Personal background

- born 11 September 1909, Dover, England, into a maritime family
- educated at Dover County Boys' School and Pembroke College, Cambridge; took a First in English and in the Moral Sciences Tripos (1928–33)
- married Virginia Traylor (1900–60) in New York, 1935, while a Commonwealth Scholar at Yale University (1934–5); married Beulah Joyce Varney in London, 1959
- developed the sociotechnical approach to work design, the 'search conference', and the concepts of the turbulent environment and the social ecology of organizations
- died in Carmel, California, 4 June 1993

Major works

Exploration in Group Relations (with C. Sofer) (1959)

Organisational Choice: Capabilities of Groups at the Coal Face under Changing Technologies: The Loss, Rediscovery and Transformation of the Work Tradition (with G.W. Higgin, H. Murray and A.B. Pollock) (1963)

'The causal texture of organisational environments' (with F.E. Emery) (1965)

Towards a Social Ecology: Contextual Appreciations of the Future and the Present (with F.E. Emery) (1973)

Summary

Trist based his work as a management scholar on social science research. During the Second World War he designed War Office Selection Board procedures for officer selection and established Civil Resettlement Units for returning prisoners of war. He founded and later directed the Tavistock Institute of Human Relations, and studied work organization in British coal mines using a sociotechnical approach to work design, an alternative to traditional management. With his Australian colleague Fred E. Emery, Trist devised the 'search conference', a management tool for long-range planning; together they also presented a theory of organizational settings, among which was the 'turbulent' environment. In the USA and Canada, Trist developed his study of social ecology.

1 Introduction

Eric Trist's father was a master mariner and his mother was a Scot with a deep interest in education. Trist was educated in Dover at St Martin's School and the Dover County Boys' School. He won a scholarship to Cambridge, where I.A. Richards introduced him to humanistic psychology and Trist learned the social psychology of Kurt Lewin (see LEWIN, K.). A brilliant student, Trist graduated with a distinction star, and in 1934–5 he studied at Yale on a fellowship with the Commonwealth Fund. On returning to the UK, he and his wife researched the impact of structural unemployment in Dundee, Scotland, and for a year afterwards he headed the St Andrews University Department of Psychology.

In the Second World War, Trist worked at the Maudsley Psychiatric Hospital, studying the psychological effects of head injuries and the anxieties of those who suffered in the London blitz. He joined the army group of psychiatrists from the Tavistock Clinic and helped devise the experimental War Office Selection Boards, which selected officers for the army. Later, Trist contributed to the Civil Resettlement Unit scheme for prisoners of war. This involved the establishment of therapeutic communities with a radically different organization from the army. His experience in these army projects taught Trist that he could create social systems quite unlike those he had worked in before (Trist and Murray 1990).

With funds from the Rockefeller Foundation, Trist and his associates from the army established the Tavistock Institute of Human Relations in 1946. Trist went into psychoanalytic training so that he could work in groups and organizations with the detachment that clinicians normally have with patients. His aim was to use social psychological knowledge to resolve the problems in industry that faced the British government after the war. The Tavistock Institute secured government funds for one industrial project at the Glacier Metal Company, another to train young people in industrial fieldwork and a third to study groups of miners; this last would later bring Trist to the attention of organization theorists (Trist and Murray 1990). Trist also helped establish the journal *Human Relations*, because there was no British journal that would publish interdisciplinary social science. In 1951, Foundation funding ceased, so Institute members went directly to industry for support. Most of their work at this time centred on selection of executives (for which the experience with War Office Selection Boards was invaluable), studies in organizational change, and consumer research.

In 1960–1, while Trist was a Fellow at the Center for Advanced Studies in the Behavioral Sciences in Palo Alto, he co-wrote *Organisational Choice* (Trist *et al.* 1963). He was later invited to lead experiential groups at Bethal. In 1965, Trist, with Fred Emery, made a breakthrough in socio-organizational ecology in the famous paper 'The causal texture of organisational environments'. Trist joined the University of California at Los Angeles in 1966 as Professor of organizational behaviour and social ecology, and in 1969 he joined the faculty of the Wharton School at the University of Pennsylvania.

In Pennsylvania, Trist undertook a study of coal mines in the community of Rushton, and later did similar research in northwestern New York State, the Jamestown project (Trist and Murray 1993). Both were innovative programmes in industrial cooperation. In 1971, Emery joined Trist at Wharton, where the two drew their work together in *Towards a Social Ecology: Contextual Appreciations of the Future and the Present* (1973).

After supervising much postgraduate research, Trist retired from the Wharton School in 1978 and joined the Faculty of Environmental Studies at York University, Ontario, to teach organizational behaviour and social ecology. He consulted for Labour Canada, for projects concerned with the quality of working life and for community studies, and also introduced search conferences in Alberta as well as York. Trist's last efforts were directed to the publication of the three-volume *The Social Engagement of Social Science* (1990, 1993, 1997).

2 Main contribution

Trist's first contribution was as a psychologist on War Office Selection Boards. With the Directorate of Army Psychiatry, Trist studied morale among officer cadet training units, designed a psychological technique for selecting candidates and later advised on ensuing problems. His second contribution was to help establish Civil Resettlement Units for returning prisoners of war and others distressed by the return to civilian life. For this he developed the concepts of 'social reconnection' and 'de-socialization', and showed that therapeutic communities could be developed within the military authority structure. In both contributions, Trist used Wilfred Bion's ideas on group processes and followed Kurt Lewin's action research principles (Trist and Murray 1990).

Trist's next contributions were to British industry. These centred on the Glacier Metal project with Elliott Jaques, which showed how psychoanalytic ideas may be used to clarify conflicts at work, and on the coal projects with Ken Bamforth, which illustrated the productive value of semi-autonomous work groups (Trist *et al.* 1963).

Trist wrote on many subjects in management: the role of the absent leader, accidents as a means of withdrawal, diagnostic performance tests, communication issues, social structure and psychological stress, human relations training, systems theory, organizational democracy, quality of working life, action research methodology, and the weaknesses of scientific management. His most notable idea was the sociotechnical approach to organizations (Trist and Murray 1993).

The sociotechnical approach developed between 1946 and 1963 out of Trist's research and ideas from Emery. It was a practical alternative to the view of industrial organization that for generations had fused bureaucratic administration, technological imperatives, autocratic management and economic rationalism. The sociotechnical approach had the following features:

1. work was no longer to be considered as a list of discrete jobs, but as a system of activities that had a unity of its own;
2. the work group, not the job holder, was the central concern;
3. external regulation by supervisors was not appropriate – instead, internal regulation was more effective;
4. when work systems needed changes, the functions performed were to be regarded as redundant, not the people who performed the functions – consequently people would acquire many skills rather than just one;
5. work roles were no longer prescribed, but became alterable at the discretion of the job holder;
6. people complemented machines at work, rather than being mere extensions of them;
7. rather than standardizing operations, increasing their variety was the appropriate way to meet changing influences from outside the organization.

Redesigning work to these specifications was enormously productive, and was augmented by a closer, more rational commitment by employees to the organization's goals.

In 1960, Trist and Emery devised the search conference. Using concepts from applied social psychology and clinical skills acquired with small groups, Trist and Emery introduced a new use of group psychology

that has become accepted worldwide (Trist and Murray 1993).

In 1965, again with Emery, Trist published one of the most widely quoted papers in the social science of industrial management, 'The causal texture of organizational environments'. Until then it had been commonly thought that organizations functioned and were maintained largely by internal authorities. The impact of the environment – beyond mere market forces – was rarely considered, until their paper showed that organizations operate in four types of societal context. The most interesting of these was the 'turbulent environment', which now has a secure place in management theory (see ANSOFF, H.I.).

Trist's work thereafter centred on the quality of working life, the social ecology of organizations and the design of alternatives to the inward-looking and autocratic procedures of traditional management. His international experience as a researcher and consultant showed that modern industry operated in a turbulent environment. The steady-state and equilibrium theories were no longer useful for managing such turbulence because when organizations responded in accordance with these theories, they increased confrontational and defensive working relations; employees tended to feel infantilized and humiliated, and, like outsiders in their own workplaces, withdrew effort and commitment to workplace goals. Today's technocratic bureaucracies fail to work at high levels of complexity; because they curtail the participation of individuals and the use of innovative practices, and limit the quality of work experience, they fall perilously short of the productivity levels of self-regulating organizations. Failure to see this, Trist argued, would lead to a global industrial catastrophe from which recovery via conventional, entrenched, defensive, bureaucratic methods would be slow, impoverished and unproductive.

To overcome the problem, Trist recommended principles of co-designing organizations by working through the changes that turbulent environments bring about. The first step, he thought, was to understand the seriousness of the problem, to recognize the danger of a global industrial catastrophe. At the same time, it was important to realize that such a nightmarish scenario could not be managed by blaming others and treating them like hostile competitors, because that would perpetuate the conditions that promote irreversible disaster.

The solution was to consider the ordinary good life; it is this, with its ups and downs, that has to be valued, rather than the single-minded, popular and pathological pursuit of nothing but one goal (such as 'excellence'). Out of this, various productive imperatives emerge:

1 Variation in human capacity should be used to help tune into the turbulent environment, see new material as it appears and value ambiguous information. This leads to the idea that different procedures must be developed to match the changing effects of a turbulent environment.
2 The emotional upheaval and pain of seeing old securities and identities lose ground has to be accepted and tolerated. This is a great problem in entrenched industrial bureaucracies, and as yet there is no clear way to manage the pain except through findings from social science research.
3 People must recognize that a great cultural shift in organizational design will not happen by itself or be caused by outside forces such as the 'market'. People must accomplish it together, consciously and deliberately, with plans that have many evolving purposes, not just one.
4 These plans should be orientated towards ideas and purposes, and have a self-reviewing function attached to them.
5 Work has to be done openly, with organizations that have an overarching sense of community; the conventional form of control through autocratic bureaucracy must be rejected. Guidelines from social science research should be used to cope with the anxieties that will necessarily emerge with the move to open work systems.
6 A network of leaders and supporters is needed to turn negative identities and anxieties into positive images. This is another unknown for which social science offers appropriate methods and theory.

7 Finally, outsiders and consultants who are suited to tuning in to turbulent environments and redesigning organizations as internal resources should be brought in, along with co-contributors, co-learners, and action-research learners.

3 Evaluation

Trist's work was based on professional social research into changing organizations and not on the popular techniques and schemes that regularly dominate management fashions. As a result it is not possible yet to evaluate scientifically the impact of his efforts. Nevertheless, the academic recognition accorded to Trist in his later years indicates that his work has had a significant impact on professional management thought. On retirement, he was made Emeritus Professor of Organizational Behavior and Ecology at the Wharton School; Warren Bennis, one of the USA's most renowned organization theorists, described him as one of the few heroes of organizational psychology; in 1979, the International Academy of Management made Trist a Fellow for his outstanding contribution to the science and practice of management; in 1983, York University conferred the degree Doctor of Laws, *Honoris Causa*, on him; and in 1989, he was noted as the most outstanding organization development consultant of the year by the Organization Development Institute and the International Registry of Organizational Development Institutes.

While institutions honoured Trist generally, individual social scientists and co-workers valued him as a teacher, colleague, collaborator, guide and mentor: he could get people excited about their own ideas and make them feel clever in his presence; he motivated them to learn more; he encouraged them to think on their own, to be intellectually honest, and to see wisdom not in books or theories, but in honest reflection on their own lives, and on the connection between their own mental chaos and the turbulent world they were in. He was known by many for his relentless drive to create a better future.

Trist's work had four features that gave him his distinguished position in the field of organization and management. First, his ideas and concepts were thought-provoking, clear and unambiguous; among them he particularly advocated self-direction at work, socio-technical systems theory, open systems planning, ecology of work, and change processes. Second, he was always a collaborator; his power lay in cooperation with others and in demonstrating that social science had real human consequences. Third, Trist helped found a transnational network of colleagues, an alternative kind of global organization that openly spread ideas about human organization based on partnership and on new organization design principles that could replace autocratic bureaucracy. Finally, these elements were mediated by his personal qualities: quiet, impish humour, playfulness (especially with ideas), an acceptance of others, generosity of spirit and the courage to act quietly and simply in any situation.

4 Conclusion

Trist was one of the few prominent British social researchers in industry after the Second World War. He advanced the theory of socio-technical systems, practised what he learned from research and offered his work to overcome problems in modern management. He advocated the principle that social scientists had to earn the right to be consulted on management problems and strengthened the use of psychoanalysis and field theory in organization research. His intellectual and personal debts were to Ivor Richards for literary skills, Kurt Lewin for social psychology, Wilfred Bion for clinical insights into group dynamics and Fred Emery for systematic conceptualization of his work.

RICHARD TRAHAIR
LA TROBE UNIVERSITY

Further reading

(References cited in the text marked *)

Clark, A.W. (1976) *Experimenting with Organisational Life: The Action Research Approach*, New York: Plenum. (Reports several studies of action research in introducing and practising organizational change under the guidance of social scientists.)

Emery, F.E. and Thorsrud, E. (1976) *Democracy at Work*, Leiden: Martinus Nijhoff Publishers. (An account of field experiments in industrial democracy in Norway.)

Ketchum, L.D. and Trist, E.L. (1992) *All Teams Are Not Created Equal – How Employee Empowerment Really Works*, Newbury Park, CA: Sage Publications. (A study of work groups and how they function.)

Trist, E.L. (1993) 'Guilty of enthusiasm', in A.G. Bedeian (ed.), *Management Laureates: A Collection of Autobiographical Essays*, vol. 3, Greenwich, CT: JAI Press Inc. (This biographical entry includes the most comprehensive published list of Trist's publications.)

* Trist, E.L. and Emery, F.E. (1965) 'The causal texture of organisational environments', *Human Relations* 13 (1): 21–32. (A seminal theory of four types of environment – placid randomized, placid clustered, disturbed-reactive and turbulent – that affect an organization's change process.)

Trist, E.L. and Emery, F.E. (1973) *Towards a Social Ecology: Contextual Appreciations of the Future and the Present*, New York: Plenum. (Two substantial intellectual discussions of the concepts and methodology needed for an organization to reduce the complexity of and adapt to the vagaries of post-industrialism.)

* Trist, E.L., Higgin, G.W., Murray, H. and Pollock, A.B. (1963) *Organisational Choice: Capabilities of Groups at the Coal Face Under Changing Technologies: The Loss, Rediscovery and Transformation of the Work Tradition*, London: Tavistock Publications. (Reports on the first Tavistock coal-mining studies, which showed the value of cohesive primary groups committed to holistically organized tasks, and the power of responsible autonomy in work groups.)

* Trist, E.L. and Murray, H. (eds) (1990) *The Social Engagement of Social Science: A Tavistock Anthology*, vol. 1: *The Social-Psychological Perspective*, Philadelphia, PA: University of Pennsylvania Press. (Uses the object-relations approach of psychoanalysis for the study of groups and organizations.)

* Trist, E.L. and Murray, H. (eds) (1993) *The Social Engagement of Social Science: A Tavistock Anthology*, vol. 2: *The Socio-Technical Perspective*, Philadelphia, PA: University of Pennsylvania Press. (Offers an alternative to conventional management techniques and sug-

gests using action research to change organizations.)

Trist, B., Emery, F.E., and Murray, H. (eds) (1996) *The Social Engagement of Social Science: A Tavistock Anthology*, vol. 3: *The Sociao-Ecological Perspective*, Philadelphia, PA: University of Pennsylvania Press. (Gives an account of non-hierarchical forms of organizational relations in complex and ever-changing environments, and provides guidelines for future institution building.)

Trist, E.L. and Sofer, C. (1959) *Exploration in Group Relations*, Leicester: Leicester University Press. (Reports on the concepts and techniques discovered during the early development of group relations training at Leicester University by Tavistock workers.)

See also: ANSOFF, H.I.; EMERY, F.E.; LEWIN, K.

Related topics in the IEBM: GROUPS AND TEAMS; HUMAN RELATIONS; INDUSTRIAL DEMOCRACY; JOB DESIGN; OCCUPATIONAL PSYCHOLOGY; ORGANIZATION BEHAVIOUR; ORGANIZATION BEHAVIOUR, HISTORY OF; ORGANIZATION DEVELOPMENT; ORGANIZATION TYPES; ORGANIZATIONAL POPULATIONS; WORK SYSTEMS

Tung, Rosalie L. (1948–)

Personal background

- born in Shanghai, China, 2 December 1948
- raised and educated in Hong Kong, emigrated to Canada after finishing high school
- received BA in 1972 from York University, MBA in 1974 and Ph.D. in 1977 from the University of British Columbia
- served on the faculties of the University of Oregon (1977–80), Wharton School at the University of Pennsylvania (1981–86), and University of Wisconsin-Milwaukee (1986–90) before joining Simon Fraser University in 1991
- holder of Wisconsin Distinguished Professor (July 1988–December 1990) at University of Wisconsin-Milwaukee and The Ming & Stella Wong Professor of International Business (January 1991–present) at Simon Fraser University
- has served as a visiting professor at Harvard University, UCLA, University of Manchester (Institute of Science and Technology), Copenhagen Business School, Shanghai Jiaotong University (China), and the Chinese University of Hong Kong

Major works

Management Practices in China (1980)
U.S.–China Trade Negotiations (1982)
Key to Japan's Economic Strength (1984)
Business negotiations with the Japanese (1984)
Strategic Management in the United States and Japan (1986)
The New Expatriates (1988)

International Encyclopedia of Business and Management (subject editor for International Management) (1996)
IEBM Handbook of International Business (in progress)

Summary

Rosalie L. Tung is a pioneer and recognized authority in international management, a research area within the larger field of international business studies. Born in China, raised in Hong Kong, and educated at Canadian universities, Tung has made effective use of her cross-cultural background to integrate management thoughts and practices from the East and West. She is most widely recognized for her work in international human resource management and international comparative management studies. More recently, Tung has extended her research to investigate intra-national diversity and Chinese business networks both in and outside of China.

1 Introduction

Rosalie L. Tung was the first female scholar in business administration to be elected as a fellow of the Royal Society of Canada (established in 1882 under a charter of Queen Victoria of England), the first Asian-born management scholar to hold an endowed chair/professorship in a major university in both the U.S. and Canada, and the recipient of the Leonore Rowe Williams Award from the University of Pennsylvania. She was selected as one of the best 75 graduates from the University of British Columbia in that university's 75th anniversary celebration. According to the 1994 issue of *Journal of International Business Studies*, Tung was ranked among the world's top five most cited researchers in the field during 1989–93. In 1991, she was named by the same journal as the world's ninth most prolific author in the field. She is listed in many *Who's Who* and related honorific citations, including: *Who's Who in America*, *Who's Who in the World*, *Who's Who in Finance and Industry*, *Who's Who in Canadian Business*, *Who's Who of Canadian Women*, and *The Directory of Distinguished Americans*, among others. Most recently, Tung received the 1997 Outstanding Academic Contribution to Global Markets Research from the American Society for Competitiveness.

2 Main contribution

Tung's research has made original contributions to the theory and practice of cross-cultural understanding and communication within the context of economic collaborations between entities from different nations. There are two areas where her contributions are most widely recognized. First, in the area of international human resource management, her pioneering research on expatriate effectiveness has led to the development of a theoretical framework for the selection and training of personnel for international assignments. This framework was tested using data collected from samples of American, European, Japanese, and Australian multinational firms. Results support the theoretical framework and identify key factors that affect the success and failure of international assignments. These factors include: due consideration of the family situation, possession of good human relations skills in a cross-cultural setting, appropriate criteria for selection and training of personnel in different categories of international assignments, and use of effective repatriation programmes. Based on this research, Tung formulated a contingency paradigm for the selection and training of managers for international assignments. The recent explosion of research interests in international human resource management is largely a result of Tung's seminal work in this area. In 1997, with the assistance of Arthur Andersen Inc., she completed a major study of attitudes and experiences of American expatriates in 54 countries around the world. The study was based on a 14-page questionnaire survey of 409 expatriates in 49 multinationals. It investigated expatriates' motivations for undertaking international assignments, their mode of acculturation abroad, the mechanisms that they found most useful in coping with living and working in a foreign country, and their concerns about repatriation.

Second, in the area of international comparative management, Tung has conducted original and insightful research into the mindsets of East Asians as they affect management thoughts and practices. Until the early 1980s, much of the international comparative management literature was written by scholars who came from mono-cultural backgrounds. Mono-cultural researchers often lack the insight and perspective possessed by their bi-cultural colleagues in interpreting research findings and developing knowledge which can advance theory and research in new ways. Drawing upon her unique cultural background and upbringing, Tung has conducted path-breaking research on cross-cultural business negotiations between Americans and East Asians (Chinese, Japanese, and Koreans). This work has significantly advanced our theoretical and practical understanding of how people with different cultural mindsets can influence the way they communicate, process information, interact, compete, and collaborate. For example, following the Yin/Yang principle, East Asians are more adept at handling contradictions and appear to have a special ability to comprehend the interdependent relationships of situations, something not readily perceptible from a Western perspective. Given the increased involvement of firms in international strategic alliances and network organizations, these skills are becoming more important to meeting the managerial challenges of the twenty-first century.

3 Evaluation

As an Asian-born management scholar trained in the North American research traditions, Tung has distinguished herself as one who can effectively integrate management thoughts and practices from the East and West. This ability, coupled with her genuine concern for interpersonal effectiveness, have provided Tung with both the intellectual and motivational foundation for her pioneering research on cross-cultural understanding and communication. From the very beginning, she has been careful not to let the established theories and concepts from the West restrict her thinking and inquiry. In the best tradition of an empirical researcher, she collected systematic and reliable data from cross-national samples of managers and companies and let the data speak for themselves. The many contributions that Tung has made to the international management literature are the result of this investigative approach.

While Tung's work has been widely cited by colleagues in the international management field, it has also been criticized by some for lacking in methodological sophistication. These criticisms usually come from colleagues in the traditional organizational behaviour and human resource management areas who have a domestic research focus. Tung's supporters would argue that these traditional research areas are at a more advanced stage of paradigm development from that of international management. Thus, one should not use the same criteria to judge research work in a less developed area. Additionally, most of Tung's early work was done when international management was transitioning from case- to survey-based research, a stage where descriptive exploratory studies are most commonly conducted.

In recent years, Tung has extended her research in two major ways. First, she has applied her earlier research on cross-national interactions to theory development in the management of intra-national diversity, a challenge faced by the USA, Canada, and other countries. Intra-national diversity refers to the increasing multi-ethnic composition of the domestic workforce. Tung's research found that there are many similarities in the dynamics and processes associated with managing international and intra-national diversity, such as mode of acculturation and communication patterns.

Second, she has initiated new studies that investigate business networks in the Chinese society (both in and outside of China) and how these may affect foreign investors'

performance in the People's Republic of China. Given her outstanding prior research records, we can expect more and greater scholarly contributions from Tung in the coming years.

JOSEPH L. C. CHENG
UNIVERSITY OF ILLINOIS AT
URBANA-CHAMPAIGN

Further reading

(References cited in the text marked *)

Tung, R.L. (1994) 'Human resource issues and technology transfer', *International Journal of Human Resource Management*, 5 (4): 804–821. (Presents a theoretical framework highlighting the significant role that human resources play in the transfer of technology from one country to another.)

Tung, R.L. (1994) 'Strategic management thought in East Asia', *Organizational Dynamics*, 22 (1): 55–65. (Drawing upon the four ancient Chinese and Japanese works, this article presents the principles that guide strategic management thought in China, Japan, and Korea.)

Tung, R.L. (1993) 'Managing cross-national and intra-national diversity', *Human Resource Management Journal*, 23 (4): 461–477. (Examines the similarities and differences in the dynamics and processes associated with managing international and intra-national diversity. The article also offers suggestions on how to manage such diversity.)

Tung, R.L. (1987) 'Expatriate assignments: Enhancing success and minimizing failure', *Academy of Management Executive*, 1 (2): 117–125. (Compares and contrasts the expatriation process at US, West European, and Japanese multinationals. It also examines the reasons for the varying rates of expatriate failure among these firms.)

Tung, R.L. (1982) 'U.S.–China trade negotiations: Practices, procedures and outcomes', *Journal of International Business Studies*, Fall: 25–37. (Presents results from an empirical study of business negotiations between US and Chinese firms. It examines the major issues under negotiation and identifies success factors in collaborating with the Chinese.)

Tung, R.L. (1981) 'Selection and training of personnel for overseas assignments', *Columbia Journal of World Business*, Spring: 68–78. (Presents a contingency framework of selection and training of expatriates for international assignments. It also provides empirical data from US multinationals to support the framework.)

Yeung, I.Y.M. and Tung, R.L. (1996) 'Achieving business success in Confucian societies: the impact of guanxi connections', *Organizational Dynamics*, 24 (3): 54–65. (The study operationalizes the 'guanxi' construct and examines its relationship to firms' financial performance.)

See also: ADLER, N.; HOFSTEDE, G.; LUTHANS, F.; SUN TZU

Related topics in the IEBM: CULTURE, CROSS-NATIONAL; DIVERSITY; EQUAL EMPLOYMENT OPPORTUNITIES; GLOBALIZATION; HUMAN RESOURCE MANAGEMENT; HUMAN RESOURCE MANAGEMENT, INTERNATIONAL; MANAGEMENT IN CHINA; MANAGEMENT IN JAPAN; MANAGEMENT IN PACIFIC ASIA; MIGRANT MANAGERS; MULTINATIONAL; CORPORATIONS ORGANIZATION BEHAVIOUR; ORGANIZATION BEHAVIOUR, HISTORY OF; ORGANIZATION CULTURE

Ueno, Yôichi (1883–1957)

Personal background

- born Shiba, Tokyo, 28 October 1883, into a middle-class family; his father died when he was twelve years old
- gained a BA degree in psychology at the Tokyo Imperial University, 1908
- married Teruko Miimi, 1910; following her death in 1922, he married Shige Kochi
- promoted industrial efficiency movement, based on F.W. Taylor's notion of scientific management, in pre-war Japan
- established a school for industrial efficiency in 1942
- died at home of heart failure, 15 October 1957, aged 73

Major works

Shinrigaku tsûgi (Introduction to Psychology) (1914)

Hito oyobi jigyô nôritsu no shinri (Psychology of Efficiency of People and Business) (1919)

Jigyô tôseiron (Control of Enterprise) (1928)

Sangyô nôritsu-ron (Industrial Management) (1929)

Nôritsu gairon (An Introduction to Management) (1938)

Nôritsu handobukku (Management Handbook) (1939–41)

Nôritsu-gaku genron (Principles of Management) (1948)

Summary

Trained as a psychologist, Yôichi Ueno (1883–1957) was a pioneer in many fields in pre-war Japan. He is best remembered as the promoter in Japan of the notion of production efficiency based on the theory of scientific management devised by F.W. Taylor and developed by Taylor's followers. Ueno firmly believed in Taylor's idea that efficient work organization, informed by 'mental revolution', would reduce conflict and thereby lead to better relations between workers and management. Through consultancy, writing, lecturing and teaching, Ueno worked tirelessly to introduce the practice of industrial efficiency into the Japanese workplace. The philosophy of efficiency he developed was deeply influenced by the spiritual discipline of Zen Buddhist thought and could be extended to apply to life itself. Through pioneers like Ueno, Taylorism influenced Japanese management before the Second World War and provided the basis for further development in post-war Japan.

1 Introduction

Yôichi Ueno's professional life divides into four major phases. After his graduation in 1908 and until 1919, he worked to establish himself as a psychologist. Towards the end of this phase he became interested in industrial efficiency, introducing the works of F.W. Taylor and others to Japan (see TAYLOR, F.W.). From 1919 to 1925, he practised as an industrial efficiency consultant and visited the USA, where he contacted Taylor's followers. During the period 1925 to 1942, he established the Japanese chapter of the Taylor Society of America, participated in international activities and published Taylor's works. Later, when the official economic and industrial organizations became dominated by the military, Ueno concentrated on private consultancy work. During the final period of his life, he devoted himself to the development of his own school of industrial efficiency while continuing his writing and consultancy work.

2 Biographical data and main contributions

Ueno's family originated in Nagasaki, where his grandfather, Shunnojô Ueno (1791–1852), had been a scientist and industrialist. Shunnojô introduced the first camera into Japan and is today regarded as Japan's 'father of photography' (Misawa 1967). Ueno's father, a skilful photographic technician, left Nagasaki for Tokyo to establish himself as a professional photographer. However, this venture did not succeed and he changed jobs several times. He died in the year Ueno completed the eight years of his elementary education. The family returned to Nagasaki to live under the protection of Ueno's uncle, Hikoma, a successful photographer.

Ueno went to a missionary school where all the textbooks, except those used for Japanese and Chinese language studies, were in English. This early exposure to English was to serve him well. At the age of seventeen, he returned to Tokyo with a strong desire to study at Tokyo Imperial University, which was then the foremost educational establishment in Japan. Working as a live-in English language assistant to an eminent educationist, he also taught English in the evening to finance his admission to the university as an auditing student in 1903. Continuing to work throughout his years at university, he first acquired full student status and, finally, in 1908 gained a degree in psychology.

Psychology and industrial efficiency

The experience Ueno gained in his first job as an editor at Dôbunkan, a major publisher, was important for his subsequent activities. While he was with Dôbunkan, he began lecturing, writing, editing and publishing in psychology-based disciplines. Psychology was established as an academic subject in Japan by Ueno's teacher, Yûjirô Motora, a professor at the Tokyo Imperial University. Between 1909 and 1921, Motora and his graduates gave monthly public lectures to popularize psychology. The lectures, edited by Ueno and published by Dôbunkan, proved to be popular. The success of the venture led to the launch of a monthly psychological journal, *Shinri kenkyû* (The Study of Psychology) in 1912, with Ueno as its chief editor. In 1926, it amalgamated with another journal to become *Shinri-gaku kenkyû* (Journal of Psychological Studies), the journal of the Japan Psychological Society.

Ueno's comprehensive psychology textbook, published in 1914 for student teachers, became both the best seller among his early publications and a long-selling book. The first revision in 1926 incorporated new psychological developments, including Sigmund Freud's psychoanalytic theory, and by 1942 it had run to sixty-five editions. This success established Ueno's reputation as a psychologist and brought him financial independence (Saito 1983).

Turning his attention to the study of industrial efficiency, Ueno found the practical application of psychology to industry fascinating. At university he had read a journal from the USA in which Gilbreth, one of Taylor's followers, demonstrated the use of photography in the motion study (see GILBRETH, F.B. AND GILBRETH, L.E.M.). Ueno wrote to ask Gilbreth for further explanation and thus made contact with a leading exponent of scientific management. In 1912, he was asked to contribute to a special edition of the journal *Jitsugyôkai* (Business World), centred on scientific management. In writing this article, he studied the work of H. Münsterberg to establish a connection between psychology and scientific management and came to see Gilbreth's work in this light. To *Shinri-gaku kenkyû*, he contributed papers describing the accomplishments of Taylor, Gilbreth and Thompson and translated the work of Mûnsterberg. In 1919, using the material Gilbreth had sent, Ueno wrote and published his book *Hito oyobi jigyô nôritsu no shinri* (Psychology of Efficiency of People and Business). This achievement marked the end of the period when his study of industrial efficiency largely involved introducing the works of western scholars.

Industrial consultancy

From 1916, Ueno taught the psychology of advertising at Waseda University. In 1919, while working in this capacity, he came into contact with the director of marketing at the Kobayashi Company, the maker of Lion Brand tooth powder. The company wanted to improve its existing packing process, giving Ueno the opportunity to work on the practical application of theories of industrial efficiency to production. Using the time-and-motion technique, he introduced a change in the flow of work and a team-based work group and achieved a 20 per cent increase in output, a saving of 30 per cent in space, a reduction of waste and a decrease in the working hours. His success at Kobayashi established him as the first industrial consultant in Japan. The success of other assignments such as those at Nakayama Taiyôdô, a cosmetic firm, and Fukusuke Tabi Company, the maker of Japanese-style socks, helped to popularize the practical application of scientific management and brought Ueno a stream of speaking engagements and consultancy contracts.

In 1921, Ueno became the head of the *Sangyô Nôritsu Kenkyûsho* (Efficiency Research Institute), an arm of *Kyôchôkai*, a body established in 1919 to promote cooperation and adjustment between capital and labour through improvements in production efficiency. Ueno's achievements in industrial efficiency convinced the members of *Kyôchôkai* that there was a scientific basis to the notion of cooperation between capital and labour.

Before starting work at the institute, Ueno was sent to the USA and Europe on a ten-month fact-finding tour. The tour turned out to be immensely significant for the subsequent development of his career. Helped by Gilbreth, he visited many universities, businesses, governmental offices and private associations, mainly in the USA. He met many people, including F.W. Taylor's widow, the known followers of Taylor and many other exponents of scientific management. At the spring conference of the Taylor Society held in Philadelphia, Ueno gave an impressive speech to an audience of 500 people (Misawa 1967). The contacts he made with the members of the Taylor Society led to many lasting friendships. In Europe, he visited London, Paris, Munich and Berlin. He wrote *Nôritsu gakusha no tabinikki* (The Travel Diary of the Efficiency Management Scholar), describing his visits.

In the first part of the 1920s, Japan was ready to embrace the idea of industrial efficiency and Ueno was extremely busy running the institute, working as a consultant and writing. One of the institute's major achievements was its programme for training efficiency experts. Four courses held in 1923 qualified 450 people as efficiency supervisors, who became the backbone of the efficiency movement in subsequent decades (Misawa 1967). However, the institute was closed in March 1925, due mainly to lack of funds.

Keen to continue the institute's work, Ueno took it over as his personal consultancy business, with the same aims and staff, under the name of *Nihon Sangyô Nôritsu Kenkyûsho*, (Japan Institute of Industrial Efficiency). His activity extended to Manchuria, China, when it came under Japanese control. The institute's office moved, in 1933, to Ueno's home. In 1927, *Nihon Nôritsu Rengôkai*, (National Management Association of Japan), was formed as an amalgam of six existing regional efficiency institutes, with Ueno as one of its committee members and later as its director-general. He also edited the association's house journal, *Sangyô Nôritsu*. (In pre-war Japan, the term *nôritsu*, or 'efficiency', which was employed by Harrington Emerson, was more commonly used in Japanese industrial circles than the term *keikei*, or 'management'.)

Furthering the aims of scientific management

In 1925, Ueno established the Japan chapter of the Taylor Society, the first outside the USA. In the following five years, many leading US experts in scientific management came to Japan, and most of them were at the World Engineering Congress held in Tokyo in the autumn of 1929.

In the spring of 1929, Ueno attended the fourth *Comité International de l'Organisation Scientifique* (CIOS) congress in Paris, both as director-general of the National Management Association of Japan and as a representative of the Japan Branch of the Taylor Society. One item of interest at the congress was an historical map submitted by Ueno which showed the development of scientific management (*L'histoire graphique de l'organisation scientifique du travail, 1856–1929*). This map charted the four stages of the movement's development, the names of its major proponents, their publications and their contacts (Saito 1986).

A year later, the Taylor Society of America invited Ueno to lead a party of sixteen Japanese industrialists on a very successful tour of US factories. His next project was the publication of a three-volume comprehensive collection of works by Taylor and on Taylor. Only two volumes were published, however. The third volume, a projected biography of Taylor, was abandoned for financial reasons.

In 1934, Ueno extended his work to include the promotion of efficiency in the distribution/retail sector. Keen to introduce the idea of efficiency into people's lives, both at home and at school, he joined *Kanamoji-kai* (Phonetic Scripts Society), a society aimed at popularizing a simplified version of written Japanese which uses fewer Chinese script symbols. Aware of the implications for clerical and personal efficiency, Ueno also introduced the practice of writing Japanese from left to right.

In 1935, having received a grant from *Nihon Gakujutsu Shinkôkai* (the Japan Society for the Promotion of Learning), Ueno and the staff of the efficiency institute began the task of compiling a management handbook. Ueno wanted to produce a book on scientific management, framed within the Japanese concept, for the Japanese. The whole work was published in three volumes between 1939 and 1941.

Although Ueno enjoyed passing his knowledge and experience in management on to students, he remained largely outside mainstream management education at a higher education level in pre-war Japan, which was heavily influenced by the German tradition based on management economics. He taught at Waseda and Nihon Universities as a part-time lecturer, although from 1943 to 1945 he was professor in charge of the departments of Economics and Management at St Paul's University, Tokyo (now more commonly known as Rikkyô University). Of greater significance was his time at the Yokohama Polytechnical School (today's Kanagawa University), where he became the director of a newly inaugurated department of industrial management in 1939, after some years spent teaching the history of scientific management. The satisfaction Ueno got from contact with students there was an important factor in his decision to establish his own school of efficiency, *Nihon Nôritsu Gakkô*, in 1942.

Ueno's school of industrial efficiency

Ueno first discussed the idea of establishing a school of industrial efficiency in his book *Nôritsu gairon* (An Introduction to Management), published in 1938. In this text, he outlined the basic principles of efficiency as applied to the entire way people live and learn: 'The principle of efficiency is not just the method and technique but it is a philosophy and the way, and beyond learning one must act to disseminate the philosophy' (Saito 1983: 104).

In addition to being a writer and consultant, Ueno became directly involved in establishing his own teaching organization. The first stage of this development was the establishment of *Nôritsu dôjô* (the Efficiency Training Centre). This was underpinned by Ueno's emerging 'philosophy of efficiency', which rested on the five elements of: the right food, the right posture, learning without prejudice, the right belief and the right use of language. Followers of Ueno's efficiency activities in the Kyoto/Osaka region started several study circles called *Ochibo-kai* (the Society of Fallen Ears of Rice). The movement spread to Tokyo and Hakata in 1941. Based on this experience, Ueno opened a school in 1942, but it had to be closed the following year because of the Second World War.

In 1947, the Allied Occupation Force invited Ueno to serve on the *ad hoc* personnel committee for the creation of *Jinjiin* (the National Personnel Agency) and the civil service personnel structure. His post was equivalent to that of a cabinet minister, an unusual appointment for a person not connected with the government. During his four years in this post, he introduced the '*Jinjiin* Supervisory Training' (JST), a training programme for clerical supervisors. It was the 'first training programme made by the Japanese and for the Japanese' (Saito 1983: 124).

In 1948, Ueno published *Nôritsu-gaku genron* (Principles of Management), an original work on his philosophy which brings together the results of his life's work in management. In this book, the notion of three '*mu*', namely *muda* (waste), *muri* (inappropriateness) and *mura* (unevenness) – the avoidance of which is central to efficiency – is presented as an integral part of his philosophy.

While working for the occupation force, Ueno was elected chairman of the All-Japan Federation of Management Associations, which replaced the war-time association. He also played an important role in establishing the Japan Association of Management Consultants, which gave official recognition to management consultants' professional status in 1951.

Ueno's school, when it reopened in 1947, became a vocational school catering for the needs of adults through evening classes. In 1950, it obtained two-year junior college status, offering production and clerical efficiency programmes. In 1953, it introduced correspondence courses in four subjects, becoming Japan's only higher education institution providing working adults with part-time management education. After completing his tenure as a bureaucrat, Ueno devoted his remaining years to the development of the college *Sangyô Nôritsu Tanki Daigaku* (the Industrial Efficiency Junior College).

Ueno published over 100 books, particularly in the area of scientific management. Another area of publishing that was important to him as a communicator was his editorship of a succession of journals and the numerous articles he contributed to those publications.

Starting with *Shinri kenkyû* (The Study of Psychology), he went on to become involved in the publication of *Nôritsu Kenkyû* (Efficiency Review) by the Japan Efficiency Study Group from 1923 to 1927, followed by *Sangyô Nôritsu* (Industrial Efficiency), published by the National Management Association from 1927 onwards. These journals had a more public character than his previous work. In 1935, Ueno began publishing his own house journal, *Ochibo* (The Fallen Ears of Rice), which was renamed *Nôritsudô* (The Way of Efficiency) in 1942 and ran until his death. Through these journals, he communicated his experiences in consultancy work, introduced works of efficiency scholars from the USA and elsewhere and propounded his own philosophical views and educational ideas for the furtherance of scientific management.

Ueno's enthusiasm for the promotion of industrial efficiency never waned. He represented Japan at the tenth CIOS congress in Sâo Paulo, Brazil, in 1954. A year later, he travelled to India and Thailand as adviser on flood prevention and other matters for the Economic Commission for Asia and the Far East. Towards the end of his life, he worked on a book about creativity, which was published a month after his death. The evening before his death from heart failure, Ueno was teaching at his college.

3 Evaluation

Although he was not the first person to introduce Taylor's theories of scientific management to Japan (Greenwood and Ross 1982), within his own country, Ueno was probably the person who best understood what Taylorism truly stood for. Certainly, he worked steadfastly and passionately throughout his life to promote scientific management, which was encapsulated in the notion and practice of industrial efficiency. While mainstream Japanese management academics were concerned essentially with the textual interpretation of the German school of management economics represented by Nicklisch (Saito 1986), Ueno played a leading role in spreading the

American concept of 'efficiency' by applying at a practical level.

Perhaps, because it was in the pioneering stage, Ueno's work, although highly successful, began with small companies and did not involve large and heavy engineering concerns. Large companies tended to introduce 'Taylorist' practices through the mediation of their own trained industrial engineers, often in piecemeal fashion, with the result that their understanding of the principles of scientific management was often incomplete. Large companies were also suspicious of consultants such as Ueno, outsiders who offered their 'advisory' services for a pecuniary return, as it was customary for such 'non-concrete' expertise to be offered free of charge in Japan in the 1920s and 1930s (Saito 1983). Nevertheless, Ueno contributed enormously to raising the business community's concern for efficiency, by organizing the fragmented regional societies for the promotion of efficiency into a national-level organization.

A considerable part of Ueno's contribution to Japanese management was in the area of international exchange. Through the establishment of the Japan branch of the Taylor Society of the USA, he was able to organize an industrial mission to the USA and invite prominent disciples of Taylor (who were also Ueno's personal friends) to Japan to give talks to Japanese businessmen. Ueno was an active participant in international conferences on scientific management, raising the profile of Japanese management internationally.

Ueno's influence on efficiency activities at a national level waned from the early 1930s, when Japan was dominated increasingly by the military. This loss of influence was occasioned probably by his close association with the USA as well as by his lack of political adroitness (Saito 1983). However, the fertility of Ueno's mind was such that he continued to extend the notion of efficiency beyond the manufacturing sector, to advertizing, retailing, the service industry and clerical work, promoting it through his writing and consultancy. There is no doubt that his work prepared Japanese businesses for the promotion of productivity in the early 1950s.

Ueno's death in 1957 occurred just as enthusiasm for new management techniques gripped Japanese managers (Okazaki-Ward 1993). Industry was in the process of large-scale capital investment into new technology imported mainly from the USA (see TOYODA FAMILY). A flood of new American management ideas and techniques was to enter Japan, to be seized upon by managers and management academics (see DEMING, W.E.; JURAN, J.M.). Many American management experts were invited to Japan to give lectures, and hundreds of industrial missions were sent to the USA. It is hard to ignore the role played by the tradition of the Taylorist management practices, established in the pre-war Japan by people like Ueno, in providing a receptive climate for new American management ideas after the Second World War. However, because Ueno's work was concerned with the practical aspects of industrial management, his pioneering contribution to management in Japan is not properly appreciated by the academic community (Saito 1983).

Ueno never was a mere mouthpiece for Taylor's theory, nor was he a simple follower of the practitioners of scientific management in the USA. He stood equal to them in stature, and continued to evolve the practice of scientific management by incorporating the Japanese approach, not only to work but to the way of living, to create a unique synthesis. Once, he debated the possibility of such an approach to management being exported back to the USA (Saito 1983), presaging the worldwide interest which the so-called Japanese-style of management created in the 1980s.

4 Conclusion

As an early advocate and interpreter of American scientific management, Ueno worked tirelessly for its adoption into Japanese industrial culture. It was in recognition of this fact that he was given the title 'the Father of Industrial Efficiency' in Japan and also called 'Benefactor to the Efficiency Movement'. His work is carried on by his son, Ichirô Ueno, through the Sannô Institute of Business Administration, a unique educational organization that integrates undergraduate education in management, business education for adults and consultancy and research.

L.I. OKAZAKI-WARD
CRANFIELD SCHOOL OF MANAGEMENT

Further reading

(References cited in the text marked *)

Araki, T. (1955) *Nôritsu Ichidaiki – Keieikomon 30nen* (Record of a Life in the Efficiency Profession – Thirty Years as a Management Consultant), Tokyo: Nihon Keiei Nôritsu Kenkyûsho. (An account written by one of Ueno's junior colleagues.)

* Greenwood R.G. and Ross, R.H. (1982) 'Early American influence on Japanese management philosophy: the scientific management movement in Japan', in S.M Lee and G. Schwendiman (eds), *Management by Japanese Systems*, New York: Praeger. (Describes the early scientific management movement in Japan, in which Ueno figured prominently.)

* Misawa H. (ed.) (1967) *Ueno Yôichi-den* (Yôichi Ueno, a Biography), Tokyo: Sangyô Nôritsu Junior College Press. (A short biography/autobiography of Ueno, the first half of which is written by him.)

Nihon Nôritsu Kyôkai (ed.) (1982) *Nihon Nôritsu Kyôkai Konsarutingu 40 nen-shi* (The Forty-Year History of Consulting Activities at the Japan Management Association), Tokyo: JMA. (A collection of writings about the JMA's consultancy work, covering the period *c.*1940 to *c.*1980.)

* Okazaki-Ward, L.I. (1993) *Management Education and Training in Japan*, London: Graham and Trotman. (A comprehensive study of how managers are developed in Japan today, with some historical overview.)

Okuda, K. (1985) *Hito to keiei – Nihon keiei kanrishi kenkyû* (Men and Management – Research into the History of the Development of Scientific Management in Japan), Tokyo: Manejimento-sha. (A detailed history of the development of scientific management in Japan before the Second World War.)

* Saito, T. (1983) *Ueno Yôichi – Hito to gyôseki* (Yôichi Ueno – The Man and his Achievements), Tokyo: Sangyô Nôritsu University Press. (A work published to commemorate the centenary of Ueno's birth; includes full biographical details.)

* Saito T. (1986) *Ueno Yôichi to keieigaku no paionia* (Yôichi Ueno and the Pioneers of Management), Tokyo: Sangyô Nôritsu University Press. (A collection of documents and correspondence relating to Ueno and his colleagues in the scientific management movement, interspersed with the author's comments.)

* Taylor. F.W. (1911) *The Principles of Scientific Management*, New York: W.W. Norton & Co. Inc. (Taylor's exposition of his views which is widely regarded as a classic of management theory.)

Ueno, Y. (1914) *Shinrigaku tsûgi* (Introduction to Psychology), Tokyo: Dainihon Tokyo. (Comprehensive textbook written for students of teacher training. First to apply psychology to education.)

* Ueno, Y. (1919) *Hito oyobi jigyô nôritsu no shinri* (Psychology of Efficiency of People and Business), Tokyo: Dôbunkan. (The first half covers the effect of an individual's personal characteristics upon efficiency, while the second deals with topics such as scientific management.)

Ueno, Y. (1928) *Jigyô tôseiron* (Control of Enterprise), Tokyo: Dôbunkan. (Ueno advocates the practical application to Japanese business of the concept of planning and control which lies at the root of scientific management.)

Ueno, Y. (1929) *Sangyô nôritsu-ron* (Industrial Management), Tokyo: Chikura Shobô. (Comprehensive work on the theory and practice of management which incorporates practical wisdom distilled from Ueno's consultancy work.)

* Ueno, Y. (1938) *Nôritsu gairon* (An Introduction to Management), Tokyo: Dôbunkan. (Argues that the principle of efficiency must extend to all areas of human life, not simply factories and other organizations. Advocates the need to view efficiency as a philosophical principle which offers guiding precepts for behaviour.)

Ueno, Y. (1939–41) *Nôritsu handobukku* (Management Handbook), Tokyo: Dôbunkan. (Three-volume text designed to fulfil the need for a comprehensive handbook on scientific management written in Japanese, for the Japanese, based on the actual situation in Japan.)

* Ueno, Y. (1948) *Nôritsu-gaku genron* (Principles of Management), Tokyo: Nihon Nôritsu Gakkô. (Summarizing Ueno's life works on efficiency, this comes in two parts: the first dealing with the theory of management and the second with the history of industrial development and that of scientific management.)

Urwick L.F. (1984) 'Yoichi Ueno', in L.F. Urwick and W.B. Wolf (eds), *The Golden Book of Management*, New York: American Management

Association. (A collection of short biographies of 106 major international figures in management; Ueno is one of seven Japanese pioneers in management included in the collection.)

See also: DEMING, W.E.; FUKUZAWA, Y.; GIL-BRETH, F.B. AND GILBRETH, L.E.M.; JURAN, J.M.; TAYLOR, F.W.

Related topics in the IEBM: BUSINESS CULTURE, JAPANESE; BUSINESS HISTORY, JAPANESE; ECONOMY OF JAPAN; FREUD, S.; HUMAN RELATIONS; INDUSTRIAL RELATIONS IN JAPAN; JAPANIZATION; JUST-IN-TIME PHILOSOPHIES; MANAGEMENT EDUCATION IN JAPAN; MANAGEMENT IN JAPAN; MANAGEMENT IN PACIFIC ASIA; ORGANIZATION BEHAVIOUR; ORGANIZATION BEHAVIOUR, HISTORY OF; TOTAL QUALITY MANAGEMENT

Urwick, Lyndall Fownes (1891–1983)

Personal background

- born 3 March 1891 in Malvern, Worcestershire
- educated at Repton College, University of Oxford (New College) with History Exhibition; graduated BA (Oxon) in 1912, subsequently MA
- officer cadet service at Repton and Oxford
- 1912–14 worked in the family company; elected to partnership *in absentia* in 1916
- commissioned as Second Lieutenant in 1914 and served in British Army from August 1914 until December 1918; promoted to Captain; awarded Military Cross; selected for Divisional Staff appointment, 1916; promoted to Major, 1917, and appointed Officer of the Order of the British Empire (OBE)
- Fownes Brothers & Company, Worcester, 1919–21
- Rowntree & Company, York, 1922–6
- The Management Research Groups, 1926–8
- Director of the International Management Institute, Geneva, 1928–33
- founder, managing partner, and director of Urwick Orr & Partners, Consulting Specialists in Organisation and Management, 1934 onwards
- retired in 1965 and moved to Australia, where he died on 5 December 1983

Major works

Organising a Sales Office (assisted by E. Aston, F.H. Cordukes and C.H. Tucker) (1928)
The Meaning of Rationalisation (1929)
Management of Tomorrow (1933)
Committees in Organisation (1937)
Dynamic Administration (1941)
The Elements of Administration (1944)
The Making of Scientific Management (with E.F.L. Brech) (1946–8)
Patterns of Organisation (1946)
Morale (1947)
The Golden Book of Management (1956)
The Load on Top Management (1954)
Leadership in the Twentieth Century (1957a)
Is Management a Profession? (1958)
Sixteen Questions about the Selection and Training of Managers (1958)

Summary

Lyndall Urwick became interested in management during his early involvement with Army command and administration in the officer cadet service of the Territorial Army, and sought to apply positive lessons learned there into the industrial setting of the family manufacturing company. That approach was strengthened by experiences gained in his wartime Army service (1914–18), and he was manifestly successful in man-management during 1919–21. A wartime incident had brought to his attention the writings of F.W. Taylor, whose thinking he found closely concurrent with his own, and he set out to be a 'disciple' of the Taylor principles and doctrines. Through the ensuing four decades Urwick was unwavering in his promotion of sound managerial principles reflected into effective practice, with an accompanying urge towards management advancement. This was purveyed both in the sequence of employment roles and in an unstinting programme of voluntary service through the UK's institutional 'management movement' and the higher educational channels. He published a number of books as well as a plethora of papers, addresses and articles, the majority preserved in published reproductions.

1 Introduction

No other individual from the UK's industrial and commercial sectors, nor from the academic milieu, has made so extensive and varied a contribution as did Lyndall Urwick to the advancement of management in practice, as a subject or in specific education. While his three early books (Urwick *et al.*1928; Urwick 1929, 1933) made a significant presentation of his pioneering thinking and recommended practice (see below), by far the majority of his contributions were made through innumerable addresses and lectures given by invitation to the membership of managerial societies and educational conferences. His first such address came about in April 1921 when, in consequence of a recommendation from his own employees in the family-owned Fownes Brothers & Company, he was invited to address the Rowntree Lecture Conference in Oxford on the subject of 'Management as a science'. The content was an Urwick interpretation of the thinking and principles of F.W. Taylor, adapted to better understanding by a British audience (see TAYLOR, F.W.).

The impact of Urwick's lecture was such that Seebohm Rowntree invited him to join the Rowntree company in York to assist in determining and implementing a programme of managerial improvement in the sales and administrative offices. This Urwick accepted, effective from January 1922, taking on the role of 'organization and methods' investigator. He met with considerable success due to his capacity for gaining cooperation from the working people whose activities and methods were being changed by improvement. The Rowntree directors allowed the story of his efforts, *Organising a Sales Office* to be published in 1928. This book was an early contribution to ways and means of successfully carrying through the betterment of organization and methods, including the

innovation of setting timing norms for repetitive tasks, with full employee cooperation.

2 Management research groups

Urwick's involvement with Rowntree had an additional and more significant consequence when Seebohm Rowntree sought to use Urwick's talents to initiate experiments in the UK with a concept he had seen at work in the USA: manufacturers' research associations. These were informal groupings of non-competing companies for the purpose of strictly confidential interchange of experience and ideas at director and senior manager level, in matters of policy, marketing programmes, development, financial control and the like. Urwick's initial role was to visit top managers in a cross-section of larger manufacturing companies to ascertain and assess reactions to the concept and to the proposal to inaugurate an experimental development.

By mid-1926, Urwick had gained sufficient positive response to justify the Rowntree family's Social Research Trust putting up preliminary funding for a small London office, with Urwick himself working full-time to launch the experiment. Four groups were established early in 1927 with eight to ten participating companies in each, structured by size grades in order to sustain good comparability: the grades were large (over 2,000 personnel employed), medium (500–2,000) and small (under 500). Within the year the number of groups had doubled, with increasing numbers of participating companies, and the 'management research group' (MRG) nomenclature was adopted in preference over the US title.

Urwick's dedicated and enthusiastic promotional efforts brought a gradually expanding participation in all three grades, despite the traditional British conservative attitudes with regard to disclosure of information. The fundamental principle of strict confidentiality of proceedings was rigorously maintained, the only occasional public references being brief notes that the MRG had been formed and that interested company directors were invited to contact the secretariat at the London address. A governing council had been formed, with Seebohm Rowntree as Chairman, as a coordinating focus for policy and development, but each group had its own committee for the planning and conduct of programmes of activities including exchange visits. By the end of 1928 the network was firmly established and still expanding. The very nature of the objectives ensured that the more progressive companies and firms were those that joined, thus developing a strong background influence for managerial progress. This was to become significant during the 1930s and 1940s, especially in 'Group No. 1' whose membership included nearly thirty of the country's largest manufacturing concerns.

Whereas the idea for forming the MRGs came from Seebohm Rowntree, it was Urwick's two years of executive application that propelled the movement into permanent progress and success, with an in-built strength and momentum which meant that it continued onwards even after Urwick's own departure. In September 1928, he was appointed Director of the International Management Institute in Geneva. A successor secretary was appointed to the London office, and Urwick himself was co-opted onto the MRG Council. He was already undertaking a task ongoing from that setting, arising from the World Economic Conference in May 1927, where he had attended as a member of the British delegation. A major subject had been 'rationalization' in the sense of managerial and productivity improvement. For their reporting on the conference, the delegation decided that fuller explanation would be useful on the home scene and invited Urwick to undertake this. The outcome was *The Meaning of Rationalisation*, which was published until 1929. The content was a structured presentation of principles and practice for systematic managerial application.

Continuing involvement within the MRG, even though only part-time and from a distance, afforded Urwick further opportunities for contributing to managerial advancement in the UK. Three opportunities were particularly significant. First, arising from the Geneva Conference, the MRG Council had by 1929–30 reached the conclusion that the UK needed a public central institution in the managerial context, and invited Urwick to draft ideas and proposals, a task he gladly undertook. His memorandum submitted in mid-1930 was entitled 'The British Institute of Management' (Brech, forthcoming), and set down in full the rationale, a proposed constitution and suggested lines of action. This was circulated among the participating companies, but regrettably no further action ensued.

The second opportunity lay in bringing the UK overtly into the international scenario by securing an invitation to host a forthcoming session of the triennial International Management Congress. Urwick was hoping to secure the session for 1932, with the MRG Council as the focus, especially if the proposed institute had been initiated in the preceding year. By default of this, the only alternative host body had to be the Federation of British Industries, which needed more time for preparation. The invitation was accepted for the London venue for the Congress of 1935; this was successfully carried through, although British participation was both limited and unenthusiastic.

The third contribution again stemmed from the Geneva Conference, in that the success of the *The Meaning of Rationalisation* prompted its publishers to invite Urwick to compile a collected presentation of the many addresses and lectures that he had been delivering at home and abroad. In accepting this invitation, Urwick chose to adopt the form of a consolidated treatise rather than a collection of reproductions. The result was *Management of Tomorrow* (1933). While the content covered the broad spectrum of management principles and practice, the presentation was philosophical in mode rather than a textbook of action and technique. It had a remarkably perceptive and forward-looking content, portraying aspects of managerial thinking and development, and it set the foundations for the wide-ranging 'Urwick mentality' that was to become a predominating influence for the ensuing twenty years and more.

3 Professional consultant service

The closing of the International Management Institute in Geneva in December 1933 due to the prevailing financial crises brought Urwick back to the UK to start a new phase of his career. He was already a well-known name in the managerial context. His earlier successful re-organization service with the Rowntree Company suggested the initiation of a 'consultancy' practice, provided he could find a partner with comparable and even fuller experience in manufacturing managerial advancement. Fortuitous circumstances brought him this in the person of John L. Orr, who had a decade of industrial engineering background. Both had the goal of founding a well-rounded consultancy service covering, in due course, all aspects of managerial practice, and they shared both common and complementary characteristics.

The new jointly-owned company, Urwick Orr & Partners Limited, commenced business in September 1934, getting off to a good start with very commendable progress in the ensuing years, despite the relative novelty of a management consultancy service in the UK industrial and commercial scene. Within five years, thirty consultants were being employed by the company. All had substantial managerial experience and were given additional in-depth training by the two partners. The company described its service as 'consulting specialists in organization and management', indicative of the wide scope intended. Within those first five years specific teams had been developed for providing services in clerical methods and administration, in the effective process of delegation, in sales management and marketing, in the improvement of manufacturing productivity and in financial planning and control.

In all these services, a significant objective was the effective implementation of changes recommended for improvement of method and performance, involving preliminary and continuing consultation with the personnel concerned together with appropriate retraining for the changed and improved methods. One of the company's principles was the request for preliminary consultation with trades union representatives as and when pertinent. A second principle was to ensure that the supervisory personnel concerned in the assignments were competently trained in the improved organization and methods, as well as assisted to enhance their standards of man management in gaining cooperation.

4 Public institutional contributions

The company grew steadily in terms of service, size and reputation, becoming a nationally renowned institution. The personal standing which Urwick had attained, even by 1934–5, was a contributing factor. John Orr was a highly competent and successful industrial engineer and manufacturing management consultant, but he was a somewhat private person and not at ease in public display. He only rarely appeared in institutional programmes. Both partners were agreed that public contributions from the company, in the managerial institutional and educational context, formed an important obligation, as well as serving to foster promotion and reputation. This was to be primarily Urwick's sphere of activity in voluntary service towards the UK's emerging 'management movement', and he fulfilled the role comprehensively and generously. He had the personal advantage of language skills and fluency and an attractive personality, as well as the competence to advance progressive lines of thought and practice cogently and persuasively.

During the latter half of the 1930s Urwick was repeatedly invited by managerial societies and other institutions to address their meetings and conferences, and very frequently his contributions were subsequently reproduced in their journals or separately printed as booklets. Additionally, there were occasional articles (sometimes series) written for commercial magazines. The subject matter through all those contributions was customarily indicated or suggested by the institution concerned, but where the choice lay with himself, Urwick had the broad spectrum of *Management of Tomorrow* from which to select, knowing that his presentation would always be forward-looking. Among those many aspects and topics, two holding his particular personal interest were 'organization and delegation' and 'leadership in man management'. By any standards of assessment, Urwick's output during the 1930s in contribution to the advancement of managerial practice and of education for management can be described only as immense.

Fortuitous circumstances gave rise to two special contributions in the latter years of the decade. The first stemmed from the International Management Congress of 1938, held in Washington, DC. The aftermath of the 1935 London Congress had revealed a growing level of institutional activity in the UK, but this was only loosely coordinated. In January 1937 there was formed a new national framework for those institutions, the British Management Council. This included some thirty organizations, though still only in loose coordination.

An immediate task was to compose and brief the British delegation for the 1938 Congress, with a major item in that briefing being an overview of the background to the emerging 'management movement' and the current state of development attained. Urwick was invited to compile the background report and he used volunteer research assistance to pull together a comprehensive review. In 1937 he presented an interim report to an Oxford Management Conference, one of a series of conferences which provided a forum for the presentation of knowledge and know-how in management practice. The full document of July 1938, at over eighty pages *octavo*, was a remarkable historical *tour de force* under the title *The Development of Scientific Management in Great Britain*. Reproduced subsequently in *The British Management Review*, it represented an immensely valuable pioneering contribution to knowledge in the UK.

The second item of 1938 stemmed from that compilation, as it led Urwick to recommend the British Management Council to seek Leverhulme Research Trust funding for the inauguration of a specific project investigating the contemporary provision and development of facilities for the pursuit of management studies within the UK

educational system. The project was initiated late in 1938 with the service of a full-time research officer, E.F.L. Brech being the first such officer selected and appointed.

5 Education for management

During the Second World War, Urwick was on full-time service with government departments involved in developing and applying operational improvements in organization and methods, though he remained in office as chairman of Urwick Orr, in occasional attendance, while J.L. Orr took over the full general management role. Urwick did however continue with a restricted programme of voluntary institutional contributions, notably within the Institute of Industrial Administration (IIA) which was enjoying a marked revival of activities and membership growth.

One important non-institutional achievement early in the war period was to publish a collection of papers and addresses given over several years by Mary Parker Follett (see FOLLET, M.P.), an objective that Urwick had long had in his sights, despite the complexity arising from the necessity of having a US co-partner (H.C. Metcalfe). The volume was published in the UK in 1941 as *Dynamic Administration*. Within the IIA Urwick was an elected member of council, and in November 1944 he was appointed Chairman of the Institute's Education Committee, with a mandate to revise ('modernize') the professional diploma syllabus. Since 1928 this framework had been the UK's only structured system for promoting studies of 'the body of knowledge in management', a matter of long-standing special interest for Urwick himself. This committee setting afforded him opportunity for consultative contact with the higher educational authorities, enabling him to encourage national thinking towards a comprehensive approach in the advancement of management studies.

Urwick's standing and reputation among managerial societies and with the educational authorities ensured that his views were heard with respect. Within the new government (after the general election in July 1945) the Minister and Department of Education responded positively to his recommendation for a national review and acted promptly. In September 1945, the Minister invited all interested parties to an informal conference; representatives of eighteen institutions were in attendance, including the two senior educational authorities. Among those attending were some institutions that had already established programmes of management studies and some with schemes prepared and awaiting inauguration. The conference found consensus for the national review, recommending the Minister to appoint a committee and unanimously indicating preference for Urwick to serve as chairman. This recommendation was accepted and immediately implemented, with the committee formed and initiating deliberations in October 1945.

The leadership and outcome of the Departmental Committee on Education for Management could well be regarded as Urwick's biggest single contribution to the nation's advancement of management, especially because of the consensus that he achieved in the pattern of recommendations. The Committee's terms of reference were simple, as was the membership composition. There were six persons from the industrial and commercial milieu, selected to serve in personal capacity rather than as representatives, but with adequate familiarity with the existing situation in management studies. Two further members represented educational interests and there was a departmental secretary. The Committee worked expeditiously, enabling a report of review and recommendations to be completed by August 1946 and circulated as a draft for consultation among the eighteen institutions. In the following December the Minister reconvened the representatives to a conference whereat the draft report was unanimously approved and the Minister indicated intention for immediate implementation. The report was published by HMSO early in 1947 (Ministry of Education 1947).

The significance of the Urwick Committee's contribution lay in two features. First, there was now a national policy favouring, advocating, supporting and providing facilities for management studies and examinations covering all aspects and all regions of the country. Second, an integrated pattern of syllabuses had been promulgated, providing for cover of those subjects that were common among different functions and sections of the managerial process, together with appropriate attention to naturally arising differentiations. There was no doubt that Urwick's knowledge and leadership skill had secured unanimity in that pattern, attained through a simple formula of a two-tiered syllabus with an intermediate level and a final level. The former was common to all the managerial societies operating educational programmes, and it was structured into three 'parts' for which outline content was laid down in the report, respectively designated 'introductory subjects', 'background subjects' and 'the tools of management'. With regard to the Engineering Institutions and the Institute of Cost and Works Accountants, the committee recommended that their councils should align their incidental requirements in 'management' subjects to the structure and content of the common 'intermediate' syllabus; this was accepted.

The 'final' syllabus catered for specific managerial institutional requirements, to be determined and prescribed by the councils of the institutions concerned, but with one strong recommendation for serious inclusion of 'management principles' and a broad review of 'management practice' in all the specialist programmes. Within this pattern for a 'final' level, the Committee laid down a syllabus for 'general management' appropriate for the IIA and for the newly-founded British Institute of Management as and when that body was ready to embark on programmes of studies. The new pattern was initiated in the scholastic year 1948–9, requiring some three to four years for effective implementation. By then a new era had opened for the UK's industrial and commercial sectors, offering for the first time structured programmes of managerial studies and examinations. The credit for this belongs primarily to Urwick.

Contemporary circumstances, however, necessitated continuing active responsibility and involvement in that inauguration process during the ensuing few years. The new phenomenon in the UK's industrial and commercial sectors of widening interest in the reality of 'education for management' had encouraged a number of technical and commercial colleges in the major conurbations to initiate programmes of evening courses, even while the consultative procedures for the Committee's report were in progress (1946–7), when the Ministry of Education had no focus of coordination for policy and programme in implementing the recommendations. The natural focus should have been the newly-created (January 1947) British Institute of Management, but that body's slow progress in establishment during the first couple of years rendered it incapable of taking up a role of that kind. The Ministry's only alternative was to invite the Council of the IIA to undertake the advisory and coordination responsibility for an interim period: acceptance of the invitation put Urwick, as Chairman of their Education Committee, actively into the lead role until the end of the decade.

It was fortunate for the national development of managerial education that the Urwick Orr Company were willing to concede their Chairman the time, opportunity and support facilities for competent fulfilment of that public duty. Urwick allied it with his continuing institutional contributions to managerial advancement through addresses to the membership meetings of several societies, as well as to specific educational conferences where the further implications of the new national policy were being reviewed. For Urwick himself this became the satisfying achievement of a personal objective, in so far as he had been advocating and promoting the serious pursuit of structured managerial studies since his first public address in April 1921. It was a fitting climax that thirty years later he was invited to lead a selective team within the Anglo-American Productivity Council's programme to review and bring back ideas and pointers for further British development from a review of the widely established US policies, programmes and facilities for management education.

6 'Management movement' contributions

The ensuing fifteen years provided ample demonstration of Urwick's continuing contributions to the advancement of management thinking, practice and policies through addresses, lectures, articles and within the programmes of managerial societies, including the new national institute. He was recurrently invited to address their meetings and conferences, taking as subject matter the wide span of management principles and practice, oriented to the specific institutional slant involved. He had, of course, his own preferential or topics, two of which were 'organization and delegation' and 'leadership'. Both had roots in the presentation of his thinking in the 1933 book, and the former topic came forward again as an early postwar item in the Manchester Lecture and Monograph on *Patterns of Organisation* (1946), as well as in two or three London lectures in the following years.

Leadership of a US seminar in 1951–2 provided an opportunity for consolidating Urwick's thinking and presentation in the form of *Notes for Guidance on the Theory of Organisation*, reproduced as a booklet by the American Management Association. His second personal topic (leadership) was introduced in public contributions both incidental and specific, focusing on the high values that he had first placed on man management in the armed services, a feature that had underlain his thinking and attitudes since his first experience of it during his 1914–18 war service. An invited lecture series in London in November–December 1955 provided the opportune occasion for consolidation of his approach, and the presentation was preserved for permanent reference by reproduction in book form as *Leadership in the Twentieth Century* (1957a).

It was fortunate for the nation's progress in managerial advancement that the institutional councils as well as the commercial magazine companies readily sought and/or provided reproduction of his addresses; their extent and scope during the 1950–65 period was demonstrated by a printed bibliography of some twenty pages compiled by the Urwick Orr Company in that latter year. Among the items there were, at times, topics specifically written by Urwick for publication in the company's name, for example: *Is Management a Profession?* (1958a), *The Life and Work of Frederick Winslow Taylor* (1957b) and *Sixteen Questions About the Selection and Training of Managers* (1958b). An unusual commercial publication in 1956 arose from the invitation of the CIOS International Committee to Urwick personally to research and compile biographical and professional activity notes on seventy 'pioneers' (international in scope, but already deceased) contributing to the progressive evolution of managerial thinking and practice. This was published *The Golden Book of Management* (1956).

Increasingly from the mid-1950s, Urwick's institutional activities were becoming international in scale. He was regularly invited to address assemblies and conferences by national institutes and management education centres in a number of countries, and on many occasions these were published in translation in the local language. Some consequential curtailment of contributions at home was unavoidable, though there was no detriment to his established reputation or to the esteem with which he was held. His contributions abroad earned acknowledgements and awards, starting in 1951 when the CIOS International Gold Medal was awarded to him. He was the first Briton to be elected to Fellow of the International Academy of Management, founded in 1958, and in the following year was awarded the Gantt Memorial Gold Medal. He was by then enjoying a nationwide reputation and acclaim in the USA comparable with that already attained at home.

E.F.L. BRECH
THE OPEN UNIVERSITY BUSINESS SCHOOL

Further reading

(References cited in the text marked *)

* Brech, E.F.L. (1997) 'The concept and gestation of a central institute of management in Britain 1902–76'. (Includes appended reproduction of the Urwick memorandum of 1930 for the Council of the Management Research Groups proposing a 'British Institute of Management'.)

* Metcalf, H.C. and Urwick, L.F. (eds) (1941) *Dynamic Administration: The Collected Papers of Mary Parker Follett*, London: Management Publications Trust. (A collection of the addresses and papers given in the UK and the USA by Mary Parker Follett during 1921-32.)

* Ministry of Education (1947) *Education for Management:Report of the Departmental Committee*, London: HMSO. (The Committee was chaired by Urwick.)

* Urwick, L.F. (1929) *The Meaning of Rationalisation*, London: Nisbet & Co. (A review of the purposes and accomplishment of industrial and commercial company reorganization as discussed a the World Economic Conference in Geneva, May 1927.)

* Urwick, L.F. (1933) *Management of Tomorrow*, London: Nisbet & Co. (A consolidated exposition of the author's thinking on the principles and practice of management in the contemporary setting. Remarkably progressive.)

Urwick, L.F. (1937) 'Committees in organisation', *British Management Review* 2 (3). (A descriptive and critical review of the role that committees and formalized meetings can play in the conduct and coordination of managerial activity within a company.)

Urwick, L.F. (1938) 'Tthe development of scientific management in Great Britain'. *British Management Review* 3(4).

Urwick, L.F. (1944) *The Elements of Administration*, London: Pitman & Sons. (A structured analytical study of the principles and processes underlying and supporting the exercise of managerial and administrative responsibility.)

* Urwick, L.F. and Brech, E.F.L. (1946-8) *The Making of Scientific Management*, 3 vols: Management Publications Trust. (The first volume contains summary biographies and reviews of thirteen 'pioneers' in management thinking, principles and practice; the second records various aspects of pioneering development in management practice, literature and education within Britain's industrial and commercial sectors; the third is a summary presentation of the 'Hawthorne investigations' by the Western Electric Company 1925-33.)

* Urwick, L.F. (1946) *Patterns of Organization*. (Published as 'Monograph on Higher Management' by the University of Manchester. An exposition and review of the processes of delegation of managerial and supervisory responsibility within the organization structures of major industrial and commercial concerns.)

Urwick, L.F. (1947) 'Morale', published as 'Monograph on Higher Education', University of Manchester. (An exposition of the factors and features involved in maintaining good levels of morale and cooperation among managerial and supervisory colleagues within a company, as well as between those cadres and the employed personnel.)

* Urwick, L.F. (ed.) (1956) *The Golden Book of Management*, London: Newman Neame Limited. (Compiled for the International Committee on Scientific Management, comprising biographies and reviews of seventy contributors to the advancement of managerial principles and practice in several countries.)

* Urwick, L.F. (1957a) *Leadership in the Twentieth Century*, London: Pitman & Sons. (A compilation and review of contemporary observations on the nature and exercise of the leadership role, supplemented by the author's own thinking in that context.)

* Urwick, L.F. (1957b) *The Life and Work of Frederick Winslow Taylor*, address to the XIIth International Management Congress, London: Urwick Orr & Partners.

* Urwick, L.F. (1958a) *Is Management a Profession?*, London: Urwick Orr & Partners.

* Urwick, L.F. (1958b) *Sixteen Questions about the Selection and Training of Managers*, London: Urwick Orr & Partners. (Together with *The load on Top Management: Can it be Reduced?* (1954), these monographs discuss topics of contemporary interest in industrial and commercial circles.)

* Urwick, L.F., assisted by E. Aston, F.H. Cordukes, and C.H. Tucker (1928) *Organising a Sales Office*, London: Victor Gollancz. (Portraying the conduct and outcome of a major departmental reorganization within the Rowntree Company's Chocolate and Cocoa works.)

See also: FOLLET, M.P.; TAYLOR, F.W.

Related topics in the IEBM: EMPLOYEE DEVELOPMENT; EXECUTIVE TRAINING; MANAGEMENT DEVELOPMENT; MANAGEMENT RESEARCH, MANAGEMENT OF; MILITARY MANAGEMENT; TRAINING

Veblen, Thorstein Bunde (1857–1929)

Personal background

- born on 30 July 1857, the son of Norwegian immigrants, in Sheboygan County, Wisconsin
- educated at Carleton College, Johns Hopkins University, Yale University and Cornell University
- held various university posts at Chicago, Stanford, Missouri and New York
- developed a new 'institutionalist' approach to economics based on 'evolutionary' lines
- died in New Stanford, California on 3 August 1929

Major works

The Theory of the Leisure Class: An Economic Study of Institutions (1899)

The Instinct of Workmanship, and the State of the Industrial Arts (1914)

The Place of Science in Modern Civilisation and Other Essays (1919)

Summary

The work of the American institutional economist Thorstein Veblen (1857–1929) provides some of the most fundamental and radical criticisms of neo-classical economics. He is regarded as the founder of American institutionalism and was one of the first to apply evolutionary ideas from biology to economics.

1 Biographical data

Thorstein Veblen was born in 1857. He was the fourth son and sixth child of Norwegian immigrants who settled in eastern Minnesota in the USA when he was a young boy. Educated at Carleton College, Johns Hopkins University, Yale University and Cornell University, he held various university posts at Chicago, Stanford, Missouri and New York. As a student at Johns Hopkins University he came in contact with the brilliant philosopher and founder of pragmatism, Charles Sanders Peirce, while at Yale University he came under the influence of William Graham Sumner, the Social Darwinist. He read widely in biology, psychology and philosophy, as well as the social sciences. As well as Peirce and Sumner, the works of Charles Darwin, William James, Karl Marx, William McDougall and Herbert Spencer made an enduring mark.

Veblen's most important works date from the 1890s. In 1898 he published his classic article 'Why is economics not an evolutionary science?' in the *Quarterly Journal of Economics*. The following year saw the appearance of his first book *The Theory of the Leisure Class*. Although this is an original and sophisticated theoretical work, its satiric prose and mockery of the wasteful and idle practices of the rich turned it into a bestseller. Other academic articles followed in the *Quarterly Journal of Economics*, the *Journal of Political Economy* and elsewhere, the most important of which have been collected together in *The Place of Science in Modern Civilisation and Other Essays* (1919). Together these articles provide a devastating critique of neo-classical economics and the basis of a new approach to economics on 'evolutionary' lines. Neo-classical economics originated in the 1870s with the work of William Stanley Jevons, Alfred Marshall, Léon Walras and others, and is still the dominant school of thought in that subject. Veblen's critique was one of the first and most funda-mental of this emergent paradigm (see MAR-SHALL, A.).

In 1904 *The Theory of Business Enterprise* was published, followed by *The Instinct of Workmanship* in 1914, *Imperial Germany and the Industrial Revolution* in 1915, *An Inquiry Into the Nature of Peace and Terms of its Per-petuation* in 1917, *The Higher Learning in America* in 1918, *The Vested Interests and the State of the Industrial Arts* in 1919, *The Engi-neers and the Price System* in 1921 and *Ab-sentee Ownership and Business Enterprise in Recent Times* in 1923. Regrettably, the later works do not deliver the tacit promise of fur-ther theoretical development that is found in Veblen's writings from 1892 to 1915. He died in California in 1929.

Veblen was a radical and innovative thinker. He is remembered today as the founder of the school of 'institutional eco-nomics' which prospered in the USA between the First and Second World Wars. His writ-ings bristle with biting and satiric phrases, critical of the institutions and practices of modern capitalism. Nevertheless, Veblen and his followers did not construct an integrated system of economic theory to follow that of Karl Marx, Alfred Marshall or Léon Walras. After the 1930s the 'old' institutional eco-nomics lost ground to the rising generation of formal and mathematically inclined econo-mists, led by Kenneth Arrow, Paul Samuelson and others (see ARROW, K.J.; SAMUELSON, P.A.). By 1950 the institutional school was confined to a small minority of adherents. However, since the 1980s there are signs of a revival of the 'old' institutional economics in both Europe and America, and there is a re-newed interest in Veblen's works. A large number of themes arise in Veblen's writings and a comprehensive review is not possible. Instead, this entry concentrates on a few top-ics that are of particular relevance for business and management.

2 Veblen's critique of rational economic man

Veblen ([1919] 1990: 73) argues that neo-classical economics has a 'faulty conception of human nature' wrongly conceiving of the individual 'in hedonistic terms; that is to say, in terms of a passive and substantially inert and immutably given human nature'. Veblen's critique is directed at neo-classical economics and all theories in which the indi-vidual is taken as a given 'globule of desire', to use his satiric phrase. In *The Theory of the Leisure Class* and elsewhere, he argues that consumption is a 'conspicuous' and social rather than an individual process. Consump-tion is regarded as much more than the mechanical satisfaction of fixed individual needs, but as a cultural and communicative act by which humans signal status and social position, and thereby create further and future desires for others. Accordingly, tastes are malleable and the idea of 'consumer sover-eignty' is a myth. Indeed, Veblen's best-selling book is not only a major criticism of neo-classical economics but one of the found-ing texts in the modern science of marketing.

Veblen ([1919] 1990: 73) lambasts the neo-classical view of the economic agent as 'a lightning calculator of pleasures and pains'. He describes the economic man of the text-books as having 'neither antecedent nor con-sequent'. Neo-classical economics gives no account of how human wants were formed and developed and instead portrays human agents as utility-maximizing machines. Ve-blen proposes an alternative theory of human agency, in which 'instincts' such as 'workma-nship', 'emulation', 'predatoriness' and 'idle curiosity' play a major role. The emphasis on habitual and 'instinctive' behaviour replaces the utilitarian pleasure–pain principle.

Veblen's conception of the human agent is strongly influenced by the pragmatist phi-losophy of Peirce and James. Following them he rejects the Cartesian notion of the su-premely rational and calculating agent, in-stead seeing agents as propelled in the main by habits and routinized behaviours. Instead of the continuously calculating, marginally adjusting agent of neo-classical theory there is an emphasis on inertia and habit instead.

Veblen argues that habits give the point of view from which facts and events are apprehended and reduced to a body of knowledge. When they are shared and reinforced within a society or group, individual habits assume the form of socio-economic institutions. Institutions create and reinforce habits of action and thought:

> The situation of today shapes the institutions of tomorrow through a selective, coercive process, by acting upon men's habitual view of things, and so altering or fortifying a point of view or a mental attitude handed down from the past.
> (Veblen 1899: 190–1)

In neo-classical economics the self-contained, rational individual has autonomous preferences, seemingly formed apart from the social and natural world. He or she is seemingly capable of optimizing behaviour when faced with complex problems with enormous numbers of interdependent variables. In contrast, Veblen sees the individual's conduct as being influenced by culture and institutions and guided by habit. There is a radical break from the atomistic, individualistic and utilitarian assumptions associated with neo-classical economics.

3 Technology and institutions

One of Veblen's most important arguments against 'economic man' and other core assumptions of neo-classical theory is that they are inadequate for the theoretical purpose at hand. Veblen's intention is to analyse the 'evolutionary' processes of change and transformation in a modern economy. Neo-classical theory is defective in this respect because it indicated 'the conditions of survival to which any innovation is subject, supposing the innovation to have taken place, not the conditions of variational growth' (Veblen [1919] 1990: 176–7). But Veblen sees it as important to consider why such innovations take place and not to confine ourselves to a theory that dwells over equilibrium conditions with given technological possibilities. The question for Veblen was not how things stabilize themselves in a 'static state', but how they endlessly grow and change.

Accordingly, along with the assumption of fixed preference functions, Veblen also criticizes the widespread assumption of a fixed set of technological possibilities in economic theory. One of his concerns is to examine the conditions for human creativity. With ironic phrases such as 'idle curiosity' he rejects the view that business interests and the potential for technological advance are always positively correlated.

Veblen argues that technological change can often challenge established institutions and vested interests. In *The Theory of Business Enterprise* and elsewhere Veblen distinguishes between industry (making goods) and business (making money). This critical dichotomy parallels the earlier suggestion in *The Theory of the Leisure Class* that there is a distinction between serviceable consumption to satisfy human need and conspicuous consumption for status and display. Accordingly, Veblen is strongly critical of apologetic tendencies in social science which regard existing institutions as necessarily efficient or optimal. He rebuts the assumption that institutions must necessarily serve functional needs of society. Instead, he describes particularly regressive or disserviceable institutions as 'archaic', 'ceremonial' or even 'imbecile'.

4 Foundations of evolutionary economics

Veblen sees the evolutionary metaphor as crucial to the understanding of the processes of technological development in a capitalist economy. He is the first economist to apply the Darwinian evolutionary analogy from biology to economics. He argues that economics should become an 'evolutionary' and 'post-Darwinian' science. There is a current revival in 'evolutionary' approaches in economics but the Veblenian precedent is not always acknowledged.

In biology, evolution requires three essential components. First, there must be sustained variation among the members of a species or population. Variations may be blind, random or purposive in character, but without them, as Darwin insisted, natural selection cannot operate. Second, there must be some principle of heredity or continuity through which offspring have to resemble their parents more than they resemble other members of their species. In other words, there has to be some mechanism through which individual characteristics are passed on through the generations. Third, natural selection itself operates either because better-adapted organisms leave increased numbers of offspring, or because the variations or gene combinations that are preserved are those bestowing advantage in struggling to survive. This is the principle of the struggle for existence.

The same three principles can be found in Veblen's work. For instance, habits and institutions are regarded as relatively durable and the analogue of heritable traits:

> men's present habits of thought tend to persist indefinitely, except as circumstances enforce a change. These institutions which have so been handed down, these habits of thought, points of view, mental attitudes and aptitudes, or what not, are therefore themselves a conservative factor. This is the factor of social inertia, psychological inertia, conservatism.
>
> (Veblen 1899: 190–1)

Likewise, Veblen ([1914] 1990: 86–9) recognizes the role of creativity and novelty with his concept of 'idle curiosity'. Veblen's recognition of the open-endedness of the evolutionary process is evidenced in his conception of 'change, realized to be self-continuing or self-propagating and to have no final term' (Veblen [1919] 1990: 37). Finally, without drawing Panglossian or *laissez-faire* conclusions, Veblen subscribes to a notion of evolutionary selection in the socio-economic sphere:

> The life of man in society, just as the life of other species, is a struggle for existence, and therefore it is a process of selective adaptation. The evolution of social structure has been a process of natural selection of institutions.
>
> (Veblen 1899: 188)

In this respect Veblen is a more suited mentor for evolutionary economics than Joseph Schumpeter, who eschews all natural and physical metaphors and states in his *History of Economic Analysis* (1951: 789) that in economics 'no appeal to biology would be of the slightest use'. Schumpeter's frequent use of the word 'evolution' should not mislead us into believing that his work was a precedent for the employment of a biological analogy. He does not define the term in biological terms and we do not find in his work the use of the three principles of evolutionary change (heritable traits, generation of variety, and selection) as outlined above. Richard Nelson and Sidney Winter describe their seminal work *An Evolutionary Theory of Economic Change* (1982) as 'Schumpeterian', yet they make explicit use of a metaphor from evolutionary biology. In this respect there are strong resemblances with some of Veblen's ideas. Accordingly their work is better described as 'Veblenian', although they make no reference to the earlier economist.

5 Conclusions

During Veblen's lifetime, half-understood biological analogies were being widely applied to the social sciences in attempts to justify all sorts of ideological positions from socialism to capitalist competition. Veblen is a clear exception and his understanding of biology is much more sophisticated. Contrary to many of his contemporaries, Veblen saw that the idea of Darwinian evolution meant that the future was unknown, unpredictable and indeterminate. In this respect he treated Darwin not only as a critic of apologetic defenders of capitalism but also as a rebuttal of Marx's teleological suggestions that history was leading inevitably to a single and communist future.

Veblen's answer to both the Marxian suggestion of the inevitability of communism and his rebuff to the neo-classical concept of equilibrium is his theory of cumulative causation. He sees both the circumstances and temperament of individuals as part of the cumulative processes of change:

> The economic life history of the individual is a cumulative process of adaptation of means to ends that cumulatively change as the process goes on, both the agent and his environment being at any point the outcome of the last process.
>
> (Veblen [1919] 1990: 74–5)

Directly or indirectly influenced by Veblen, the notion of cumulative causation has been developed by a number of economists, notably Nicholas Kaldor and the Nobel Laureate Gunnar Myrdal. The idea relates to the modern notion that technologies and economic systems can get 'locked in' – and sometimes as a result of initial accidents – to relatively constrained paths of development. Hence there is 'path dependency' rather than convergence to a given equilibrium or track of development. History matters.

Veblen's concept of cumulative causation is an antidote to both neo-classical and Marxian economic theory. Contrary to the equilibrium analysis of neo-classical economics, Veblen sees the economic system not as a 'self-balancing mechanism' but as a 'cumulatively unfolding process'. As Myrdal and Kaldor argue at length, the processes of cumulative causation suggest that regional and national development is generally divergent rather than convergent. This contradicts the typical emphasis within neo-classical economic theory on processes of compensating feedback and mutual adjustment via the price mechanism leading to greater uniformity and convergence.

Contrary to much Marxist and neo-classical thinking, Veblen argues that multiple futures were possible. Equilibriating forces do not always pull the economy back onto a single track. This exposes a severe weakness in Marx's conception of history. Although Veblen has socialist leanings, he argues against the idea of finality or consummation in economic development. Variety and cumulative causation mean that history has 'no final term' (Veblen [1919]

1990: 37). In Marxism the final term is communism or the classless society, but Veblen rejects the teleological concept of a final goal. This means a rejection of the ideas of the 'inevitability' of socialism and of a 'natural' end-point in capitalist evolution. There is no natural path, or law, governing economic development. Accordingly, Veblen accepts the possibility of varieties of capitalism and different paths of capitalist development.

This standpoint is particularly relevant for the post-1989 debate about convergence versus divergence within capitalism itself. Veblen's emphasis on the importance of institutions and culture, along with his notion of divergent and cumulative causation, suggests that multiple futures and multiple varieties of capitalism are possible. Despite the lack of an integrated and systematic theory in his writings, his analytical outlook makes him one of the most relevant economists and social theorists today.

GEOFFREY M. HODGSON
JUDGE INSTITUTE OF MANAGEMENT STUDIES,
UNIVERSITY OF CAMBRIDGE

Further reading

(References cited in the text marked *)

Dorfman, J. (1934) *Thorstein Veblen and His America*, New York: Viking Press. (The classic intellectual bibliography of Veblen.)

Hodgson, G.M. (1988) *Economics and Institutions: A Manifesto for a Modern Institutional Economics*, Cambridge: Polity Press. (A critique of neo-classical economics from a perspective inspired by Veblen and other 'old' institutional economists; includes an extensive bibliography.)

Hodgson, G.M. (1993) *Economics and Evolution: Bringing Life Back Into Economics*, Cambridge: Polity Press. (An extensive discussion and analysis of various approaches to evolutionary economics where the work of Veblen is prominent.)

* Nelson, R.R. and Winter, S.G. (1982) *An Evolutionary Theory of Economic Change*, Cambridge, MA: Harvard University Press. (A now seminal application of the evolutionary analogy to the theory of the firm with aspects which are highly redolent of Veblenian institutionalism.)

Rutherford, M.C. (1994) *Institutions in Economics: The Old and the New Institutionalism*, Cambridge: Cambridge University Press. (An erudite and thoughtful account of institutional thought with extensive attention to Veblen.)

Samuels, W.J. (ed.) (1988) *Institutional Economics*, 3 vols, Aldershot: Edward Elgar. (A useful anthology of essays on Veblen and other 'old' institutionalists.)

Seckler, D. (1975) *Thorstein Veblen and the Institutionalists: A Study in the Social Philosophy of Economics*, London: Macmillan. (Contains a sympathetic critique of Veblen; sometimes misguided in its assessment, but with a number of useful points and extensive quotations.)

* Schumpeter, J. (1951) *A History of Economic Analysis*, New York: Oxford University Press. (Published after his death, this is an exhaustive survey of the development of economic ideas and analyses.)

Tilman, R. (1992) *Thorstein Veblen and His Critics, 1891–1963: Conservative, Liberal, and Radical*, Princeton, NJ: Princeton University Press. (A detailed perspective on Veblen through the eyes of his critics.)

* Veblen, T.B. (1899) *The Theory of the Leisure Class: An Economic Study of Institutions*, New York: Macmillan. (Veblen's classic and highly influential analysis of the consumer behaviour of the rich; with this work the 'old' institutional school was founded.)

* Veblen, T.B. (1904) *The Theory of Business Enterprise*, New York: Charles Scribners. (A major and influential work on modern capitalist enterprise. Reprinted 1975 by Augustus Kelley.)

* Veblen, T.B. ([1914] 1990) *The Instinct of Workmanship, and the State of the Industrial Arts*, New Brunswick, NJ: Transaction Books. (Regarded by Veblen as his most important book.)

* Veblen, T.B. (1915) *Imperial Germany and the Industrial Revolution*, New York: Macmillan. (A strikingly prescient and incisive work. Reprinted 1964 by Augustus Kelley.)

* Veblen, T.B. (1917) *An Inquiry into the Nature of Peace and the Terms of its Perpetuation*, New York: Huebsch. (An attempt to lay bare the causes of war.)

* Veblen, T.B. (1918) *The Higher Learning in America: A Memorandum on the Condust of Universities by Business Men*, New York: Huebsch. (A critique of business influence on universities.)

* Veblen, T.B. ([1919] 1990) *The Place of Science in Modern Civilisation and Other Essays*, New Brunswick, NJ: Transaction Books. (The most important collection of Veblen's essays, invaluable both for the economic and the social theorist.)

* Veblen, T.B. (1921) *The Engineers and the Price System*, New York: Harcourt Brace & World. (A work in which Veblen idiosyncratically sees the engineer as the agent of socialist revolution.)

* Veblen, T.B. (1923) *Absentee Ownership and Business Enterprise in Recent Times*, New York: Huebsch. (An early critique of the separation of ownership from both responsibility and control.)

See also: MARSHALL, A.; SAMUELSON, P.A.; SCHUMPETER, J.

Related topics in the IEBM: EVOLUTIONARY THEORIES OF THE FIRM; INSTITUTIONAL ECONOMICS; MARX, K.H.; NEO-CLASSICAL ECONOMICS; ORGANIZATIONAL EVOLUTION

Vickers, Sir Geoffrey (1894–1982)

1 **Biographical data**
2 **Main contribution**
3 **Conclusions**

Personal Background

- born 13 October 1894 in Nottingham, England
- served in First World War; awarded the Victoria Cross for exceptional gallantry
- graduated in Classics from Oxford University (1921)
- qualified as solicitor 1923; joined legal practice Slaughter & May (1926)
- in Second World War, became Deputy Director-General of the Ministry of Economic Warfare in charge of economic intelligence, for which work he was knighted in 1946
- returned to legal practice (1945)
- joined the National Coal Board as Legal Adviser (1947)
- became Director of manpower, training, education, health and welfare at the National Coal Board (1948)
- set up the Research Committee of the Mental Health Research Fund and was its chairman from 1951 to 1967
- was member of the London Passenger Transport Board (1941–46), the Council of the Law Society (1944–48) and the Medical Research Council (1952–60); also appointed to the Royal Commission on the Press (1947–49) and the Committee of Enquiry into the Cost of the National Health Service (1956)
- left the National Coal Board (1955)
- spent rest of his life mainly lecturing and writing on effective societal governance
- died 16 March, 1982 at Goring-on-Thames, England

Major works

The Art of Judgment (1965)
Towards a Sociology of Management (1967)
Value Systems and Social Process (1968)
Freedom in a Rocking Boat: Changing Values in an Unstable Society (1970)
Human Systems are Different (1983)

Summary

Sir Geoffrey Vickers was the doer/ thinker par excellence. His careers embraced the Army, the legal profession, public administration, public health, the world of business and the field of mental health research. To each, he brought formidable intellectual power, undivided attention and profound understanding of human behaviour. Then, when just over 60, he retired from the world of action to reflect on, and write about, what his experience had taught him and his views for effective organizational governance.

Vickers' contribution to systemic thinking, which flows into better management decision making, was his concept of the 'appreciative system', the element of *judgment*, unique to human systems, which enters into the decision-making process. His basic tenet was that every human decision has an appreciative content rooted in one's culture which influences that decision. The meaning we give an action, in fact, determines how we assess them. This meaning is affected by our history which informs our culture, both sources of moral and political standards. Systemic thinking is based on the *interdependence* of the parts making the whole. Interdependence liberates as well as constrains. The notion of the autonomous individual is unrealistic, 'man-in-society' being the indivisible reality; and dangerous, our Western culture of individual independence blinding us to our responsibilities to the others.

We should accept our factual interdependence and understand the contribution of history and culture to the decision-making process. In so doing, we evolve the more inclusive approach that leads to the more comprehensive and wiser decision and thus to more effective management and governance.

I Biographical data

Born on 13 October 1894, Geoffrey Vickers was brought up in a Victorian England at the height of its powers, in an environment of freedom and order, all of which gave him a strong sense of identity and stability. He had a very happy childhood. His father, a man of wide interests and large enthusiasms, instilled in him a love of nature, of learning and language. At 12, he was sent to Oundle, a typical English public school which conditioned him in many ways but could not change his inner sense of classlessness.

When Britain entered the war against Germany in August 1914, Vickers enlisted immediately. He showed exceptional gallantry in battle for which he was awarded the Victoria Cross and later the Croix de Guerre.

After the War, Vickers returned to Oxford and in 1921 took a degree in Classics. In 1923, he qualified as a solicitor. In 1926, by then an accomplished lawyer, he became a partner in the London legal practice of Slaughter & May. He specialized in international commercial law and was involved, in the 1930s, in the re-scheduling of the German debt. A highly successful lawyer, he enjoyed 'the comfortable, even pampered life of the self-employed professional who need not talk to anyone not willing to pay for the privilege', as he later described it (Vickers 1974: 185).

The events in Munich in 1938 made him politically conscious. He started 'The Association for Service and Reconstruction' through which he got to know many eminent academics, in the physical and social sciences, who influenced his burgeoning ideas on society and politics.

In the Second World War, Vickers re-enlisted, again immediately. Promoted colonel, he was seconded to the Ministry of Economic Warfare, as Deputy Director-General in charge of economic intelligence, for which work he was knighted in 1946.

At the end of the war, Vickers returned to his legal practice. In 1947, he was invited to join the National Coal Board (NCB) as Legal Adviser. He enthusiastically accepted the challenge, despite the loss of status and income involved. In 1948, he became directly involved in management, when appointed director for manpower, education, training, health and welfare, responsible for some 750,000 men – quite an undertaking, given the entrenched adversarial relations between the miners and their managers. His transition from being an international corporate lawyer to working in a nationalized industry was not easy. He reflected later that he felt more at home with the trade unionists than with his fellow directors, but he learnt a great deal at the NCB about motivation, industrial relations and the problems of operating a nationalized industry.

During his time there, his wife's ill health brought him into contact with psychiatrists which led him to study psychology, for him a new field of knowledge. He founded in 1951 the Research Committee of the Mental Health Research Fund, with scientists from various disciplines, which he chaired and kept going until 1967. It was the cognitive psychology he learnt here that enriched his systems thinking concepts and provided the foundation of the appreciative system he made his own in later years.

His other public appointments – to the London Transport Passenger Board, the Law Council, the Medical Research Council, the Royal Commission on the Press, the Committee of Enquiry into the Cost of the National Health Service – give an inkling of how much in demand he was and how much knowledge came his way as a result.

Important for Vickers, in the late 1940s, was discovering systems ideas, through the work of Norbert Wiener, Ludwig von Bertalanffy and Ross Ashby. Systemic thinking somehow liberated him, confirmed his own insights. It gave him a way of looking at a situation within the wider picture into which he could better fit its components and also see it in the context of its connections – of great help to him, as a manager, in his efforts to change the conflictual relationship dividing miners and managers into a cooperative one of joint effort and endeavour.

Systems ideas also gave him a new language with which to better understand and explain his diverse experiences – intellectually very exhilarating and inducing in him the urge to learn more about the discipline. In 1955, just over 60 years of age, Vickers decided to retire from the business arena, 'to contribute to what I believed to be a revolution in human thinking which had been reaching and exciting me for the previous ten years', as he reminisced to Bayard Catron in his letter of 19 January 1981.

The Director of the School of Social Work at the University of Toronto in Canada immediately snapped him up for three terms. This gave Vickers the academic time and space to work through, and formalize, his ideas. His address in 1956 to the School on 'Values and Decision-Making', showing how both individual and societal values shape the goals we set up, already presaged the comprehensiveness of his thought that joined aesthetic and ethical norms with calculable analyses – integration of tangible and intangible factors, the fundamental of all his later writings.

Systems thinking was the linchpin that fixed his ideas into a coherent framework, the tool of understanding that set him on a most exciting and productive intellectual voyage. Between 1955 and 1982, he wrote nine books and published 87 papers. His books – *inter alia The Art of Judgment* (1965), *Freedom in a Rocking Boat: Changing Values in an Unstable Society* (1970), *Human Systems are Different* (1983) – show the constancy of his interests and concerns. The diverse range of his papers can be gleaned from the publications in which they appeared – *Acta Psychologica*, the European Journal for Psychology, *The Lancet*, the British medical journal, *Futures*, the futurology publication, *Organizational_Dynamics*, *Human Relations* and *Policy Sciences* – to name but a few.

Vickers was much in demand in universities in the United States and made many friends there. In planning a Festschrift, their spokesman wrote him in January 1981 'we want to acknowledge more than the power of your intellect. The character of the man, his warm and gentle humanity, his indomitable curiosity, and zest for life – these have touched us. . . . Having known you as a person as well as author, we understand ourselves and our culture better.' No other words could have touched Vickers more.

In the UK, Vickers had been ignored, in the 1960s, by an academic community hidebound in its separate specialisms. But, in the 1970s, the growth of Systems Departments in the newer universities brought him admirers and followers. The Systems Groups of the University of Lancaster and of the Open University held him in high esteem. The latter invited Vickers as a regular speaker to its annual Summer School, commissioned a book which became *Human Systems are Different*, and edited, in 1984, in tribute, *The Vickers Papers*, a collection of his articles.

Vickers' wife had died in 1972. Unable to cope any longer on his own, he moved in 1977 to a residential home for the elderly. There, he spent his last years: serene and busy years during which he continued to write, receive visitors from home and overseas and, as always, carry on his extensive correspondence with friends, old and new.

2 Main contribution

Vickers was among the first, in the management field, to adopt and apply the concept of systems theory. He used systemic thinking to analyse situations, in their complex richness, in their internal and external relations, to better understand their workings, their reciprocal interactions and underlying commonalities.

The other systemic protagonists eschewed this inclusive approach. To acquire academic respectability, they followed the quantitative methods of the physical sciences, excluding all elements that were not measurable and treating all systems – natural, man-made and human – as identical.

Vickers fought long and hard against their reductionism. For him, human systems had the extra element of judgment. Each human system is a network of relations which reflects its historical past and culture. It develops its own ways of looking at the world, its own values and standards. This is its appreciative framework which substantially influences its decision-making. It is unique to the human system which cannot therefore be subsumed with the others.

In the *Art of Judgment*, (1965) Vickers showed that a judgment consists of three reciprocally interactive strands:

- a 'reality' judgment – (deciding what is) covering the whole range of factors from direct cause-and-effect facts to tacit beliefs;
- a 'value' assessment – (what might, or could or should be) taking into account self-interest, moral constraints, individual and collective set goals; and
- the instrumental means – (how do we get there?) of getting from 'what is' to 'what could or should be', within the available resources.

What facts we select out of all those in a situation, the meaning we give them, the means we use to reduce the mismatch between existing and desired situations – all this flows from our appreciative system. It is not to be disregarded because, partly tacit, it cannot be easily measured. We are culture-bound creatures. To ignore the effect of culture in the decision-making process is to disregard one of its essential components and thus arrive at the truncated and perforce inadequate solution. It is essential to understand how our belief systems affect our decisions, the better to make them for long-term effective performance.

In addition to culture, Vickers emphasized the fact of our interdependence. The basic unit of society is the interdependent 'man-in--society' not the independent, autonomous individual conceived by Western culture since the Enlightenment. Interdependence highlighted the double-sided coin of rights and responsibilities. To be a member of a healthy community involved fulfilling responsibilities as well as demanding rights.

Vickers always saw everything in terms of processes and reciprocal interactions. In *Value Systems and Social Process* (1968), Vickers was concerned about the effect of rapid technological advance on our social systems. In *Freedom in a Rocking Boat* (1970), it

was the threat to stable relations between human society and its ecological milieu that worried him. Underlying our multicultural diversity, we had to build a basic cultural consensus, to be able to agree on common action both in our social groupings and in relation to our environment – a difficult task but an urgent necessity.

3 Conclusions

Vickers' ideas were grounded in practical experience acquired through an unusually wide range of activities and backed by studies in both the physical and social sciences. Integrating theory and practice, his teaching has a breadth and depth of vision which startle by a foresight, which is in many instances, prophetic. In 1957, when the prevailing wisdom was that a health service was a self-limiting one, with little to do once the demands of health were fully met, Vickers was already warning of the effects of technology on expectations and of the conflict to arise between an ever increasing demand and the inability to meet it – a situation all the more intractable today, for having been ignored for so long.

Vickers' appreciative system concept was very much ahead of the times in the mid 1960s. Today, we recognize to some extent the incidence of culture in the decision-making process; here and there, 'soft' systems methodologies are complementing the 'hard' ones in place. But the full significance of the concept has yet to be realized. It is of primordial relevance to managers who, working in the multinational company or the global organization, must understand the value systems of those in their teams to better communicate with them. Failure to do so invariably leads to the weak, ineffective solution and therefore to unsatisfactory results.

Vickers' insistence on the need for some shared or compatible cultural values is similarly of basic importance to managers. Through reciprocal interchange, multiculturalism enriches its constituent cultures but these have to be underpinned by a basic commonality of norms to provide consensus and the will for joint action. It is of the essence of leadership, whilst respecting and indeed welcoming diversity, to bring to the fore those values which join us in our common humanity, to build the team spirit for effective and satisfying performance.

Yet another strand of Vickers' philosophy, that of interdependence, directly applies to managers. Steeped in the Western culture of individual independence, especially prevalent in the appreciative systems of those in authority, interdependence is felt as weakness. The command/obedience syndrome still lingers in the managerial consciousness. Managers need to absorb and act upon the irreducible fact of their interdependence with their followers. Leadership is not always with the manager; it is sometimes with the follower, the expert in that particular situation who knows what to do. The need between managers and their followers is reciprocal. It is that interdependence between <u>all</u> the members of the group which regulates their relationships, builds mutual knowledge and understanding and creates the initiative and enterprise that takes the group forward.

Vickers' teaching is not of course of value to managers only. It is of universal application and increasingly relevant in our fast-changing and pluralistic world. Understanding our diversity, developing a common culture to underlie it, recognizing our interdependence with each other as well as with our environment: these are the directions Vickers gives us to evolve the scientific art of human governance.

PAULINE GRAHAM
UNIVERSITY OF BRADFORD

Further reading

(References cited in the text marked *)

Blunden, M. (ed.) (1994) 'Rethinking public policy-making, questioning assumptions, challenging beliefs' *American Behavioral Scientist*, 38, September–October. *(Essays in honour of Sir Geoffrey Vickers on his centenary.)*

Open Systems Group (eds.), (1984) *The Vickers Papers*. London: Harper & Row. (A wide selec-

tion of his articles, in four parts, with an essay on 'Geoffrey Vickers – an intellectual journey' by Margaret Blunden and a bibliography of his books and articles.)

Vickers, J. (ed.) (1991) *Rethinking the Future: The Correspondence between Geoffrey Vickers and Adolph Lowe*, New Brunswick, NJ: Transaction. (The lifelong correspondence between Vickers and his friend, Adolph Lowe.)

* Vickers, G. (1965) *The Art of Judgment*, London: Chapman & Hall. (His seminal book, where he sets out his concept of the 'appreciative system'.)

* Vickers. G. (1967) *Towards a Sociology of Management*, New York: Basic Books. (On the basis that business is a social activity and management a form of social control.)

* Vickers, G. (1968) *Value Systems and Social Process*, New York: Basic Books. (His 1954–66 articles on the impact of technological change on social systems.)

* Vickers, G. (1970) *Freedom in a Rocking Boat: Changing Values in an Unstable Society*, New York: Basic Books. (Reflects his concern on the relations between human systems and their ecological milieu.)

Vickers, G. (1973) *Making Institutions Work*, New York: John Wiley. (To this end, we have to reduce our expectations from, and demands on, them.)

* Vickers, G. (1983) *Human Systems are Different*, London: Harper & Row. (A review why human systems are different from natural and manmade systems.)

Vickers, G. (1995) *The Art of Judgment*, Centenary Edition. Thousand Oaks, CA: Sage Publications, Inc. (With Foreword by G.B. Adams, B.L.Catron and Scott D.N. Cook; and 'The life of Sir Geoffrey Vickers' by Margaret Blunden.)

See also: ACKOFF, R.L.; BEER, S.; RIVETT, B.H.P.; SIMON, H.A; VON BERTALANFFY, L.; WIENER, N.

Related topics in the IEBM: CYBERNETICS; DECISION MAKING;INFORMATION REVOLUTION; MANAGEMENT SCIENCE; MANAGERIAL BEHAVIOUR; ORGANIZATION BEHAVIOUR; ORGANIZATION BEHAVIOUR, HISTORY OF; STRATEGY, CONCEPT OF; SYSTEMS

Von Bertalanffy, Ludwig (1901–1972)

Personal background

- born 1901 near Vienna, Austria
- Ph.D. from the University of Vienna (1926)
- Dozent and then Professor at the University of Vienna (1934–48)
- Professorships at the University of Ottawa, Canada; University of Southern California, USA; University of Alberta at Edmonton, Canada (1948–69)
- Professor at the State University of New York at Buffalo, USA (1969–72)
- first on the European continent to develop open systems theory in biology as a working hypothesis for research and a prime mover of general system theory, both considerably influencing the theory and practice of business and management

Major works in English

Modern Theories of Development (1933)
Problems of Life (1952)
General Systems (founding editor and co-editor) (1956–1972)
Robots, Men and Minds (1967)
Organismic Psychology and Systems Theory (1968)
General System Theory (1968)

Summary

Ludwig Von Bertalanffy was a biologist whose organismic conception of biology known as *open systems theory* came to pervade many disciplines, including business and management, the impact being vastly 'more than the sum of its parts'. He was the first person on the European continent to develop open systems theory in biology as a working hypothesis for research. It is central to his publications from the mid-1920s. Open systems theory profoundly influenced the way organizations are conceived and consequently managed. It helped shape management and organization theory in the 1950s and 1960s. It pervades management practice in the 1990s. Von Bertalanffy was also a prime mover of *general system theory* that emerged in his work in the late 1930s. In particular, his associated idea of the unity of science is still discussed in the 1990s. Von Bertalanffy from the 1950s until his death applied open systems theory and general system theory to a wide range of social sciences, the result becoming known as his *systems view of people*. Von Bertalanffy is one of those rare people who influenced widely the way Westerners conceive their relationship to each other (at work and elsewhere) and the world in which they find themselves.

1 Biographical data

Ludwig Von Bertalanffy was born near Vienna in Austria in 1901. He was awarded a Ph.D. from the University of Vienna in 1926, was appointed to Dozent there in 1934 and then Professor, remaining in post until 1948. Subsequently, Von Bertalanffy pursued his career in North America, initially as Professor and Director of Biological Research at the University of Ottawa in Canada, then Director of Biological Research at Mount Sinai Hospital and Visiting Professor at the University of Southern California in the USA, then Professor of Theoretical Biology (later University Professor) and member of the Centre for Advanced Study in Theoretical Psychology at the University of Alberta at Edmonton in Canada, finally (in 1969) moving as Faculty

Professor to the State University of New York at Buffalo in the USA.

Von Bertalanffy's career was distinguished. He was Fellow of the Rockefeller Foundation (1937–38), Fellow of the Centre for Advanced Study in Behavioural Sciences at Stanford in California (1954–55), Alfred P. Sloan Visiting Professor at the Menninger Foundation (1958–59), Honorary Fellow of the American Psychiatric Association, Member of the Deutsche Akademie der Naturforscher, Fellow of the International Academy of Cytology and Fellow of the American Association for the Advancement of Science.

Von Bertalanffy published extensively in English and German, with books being translated into many languages (see 'further reading'). A full list of major works is documented in (1972) *General Systems*, XVII: 221–228.

Von Bertalanffy's scholarly contribution to science can usefully be broken down into three interrelated categories: biology and open systems theory (from the mid-1920s), general system theory and the unity of science (from the late 1930s), and application of these theories to, for example, symbolism, psychology and education (from the mid-1950s). These categories reflect progression in his research. Concepts from each category influenced theory and practice in business and management to different degrees; the impact of open systems theory is profound, of general system theory is explosive; whilst work on symbolism, psychology and education, bear on those subject areas. Each category is presented below in an allocated space commensurate with its importance to business and management.

2 Open systems theory

A breakthrough in Western thought is credited in part to Von Bertalanffy's organismic biology. Until the late nineteenth century science was founded on concepts of physics. Physics advocated reductionism. Reductionism seeks of any system of interest analysis of fundamental parts. Analysis involves identification of fundamental parts and the behaviour of and forces acting upon each one. Coupled to reductionism is the Second Law of Thermodynamics which states that systems move from ordered to disordered states, known as entropy. Physics thus sees only closed, isolated systems moving ever closer to disorder. Phenomena defying explanation of this sort were dismissed as metaphysical, transcending the boundaries of science and not worthy of scientific study.

In the late nineteenth century researchers encountered limitations to reductionism. A counter position in biology took on a coherent form by mid-1920s. Several scientists began to think this way. Paul Weiss, Walter B. Cannon (credited with homeostasis) and in particular Ludwig Von Bertalanffy came to the fore. Von Bertalanffy demonstrated that concepts of physics were helpless in appreciating dynamics of organisms. Existence of an organism cannot be understood in terms of the behaviour of some fundamental parts. A whole organism is more than the sum of its parts, it exhibits synergy. Furthermore, much of an organism's existence is characterized by increasing or maintaining order, which is negentropic. Biology therefore required new concepts to explain phenomenon like synergy and negentropy.

In this regard, Von Bertalanffy developed a theory of open systems in biology, or organismic biology. Open systems theory employs functional and relational criteria rather than reductionist analysis of fundamental parts. Organisms exist in relation to an environment. Their functions and structure are maintained by a continuous flow of energy and information between organism and environment. An organism is a complex system comprising many interrelated parts resulting in a whole with integrity. Key concepts here include *self-organization* by way of progressive differentiation, *equifinality* as the independence of final state from initial conditions, and *teleology* as the dependence of behaviour of the organism on some future purpose 'known in advance'. Open systems theory and related ideas from biology swept across and challenged the basis of other disciplines like business and management as evidenced below.

Closed system thinking assumes the behaviour of organizations is based on fundamental principles and laws just like physics.

Closed organizations are like Newton's closed mechanical universe; their managers are governors and engineers. Operations are routine, repetitive and perform predetermined tasks. There is a strict hierarchy of control, exact obedience by standardized parts and much emphasis is placed on their efficiency.

Closed system, or machine, thinking resonates with and reinforces ideas of classical management theory. Classical management theory is a 'machine view' for organizations borrowed from physics. The machine view characterizes theories of bureaucracy (Weber), scientific management (Taylor) and administrative management theory (Fayol).

Open systems theory and other biological conceptions like homeostasis portray concepts of physics as helpless in appreciating dynamics of organizations as well as organisms. Rather, open systems theory observes organizations as complex systems made up of parts most usefully studied as a whole. An organization is open to its environment. Action is taken to hold an organization in the steady-state. The primary aim is to ensure survival, by transforming inputs and by adapting to changes when they occur. Since parts comprise people, management are concerned about the nature of people at work. Parts, or subsystems, have lists of needs that must be met. Individual motivation requires attention. For example, jobs can be enriched leading to greater satisfaction and productivity. The whole organizational structure may facilitate participation. Leadership can encourage democracy and autonomy.

Open systems theory and other biological conceptions echo and reinforce ideas of organizational systems theory and human relations theory (1950s–60s). These theories are to an extent the open systems view of organizations and their management borrowed from the biology of Von Bertalanffy. The open systems view helps characterize systems theories of Parsons, Selznick, Katz and Kahn, Barnard; and human relations theories of Roethlisberger and Dickson, Herzberg, and McGregor.

Open systems theory has attracted criticism. It suggests structure and function in bounded organizations and that they are physical entities just like organisms. This encourages people to seek and to identify systems in the world. Writers such as Churchman, Vickers and Checkland, in various ways, stated that human systems are different. Human systems, they argued, are better understood in terms of the systems of meaning (ideas, concepts, values, etc.) people ascribe to the world. To appreciate human systems therefore requires learning and understanding about systems of meaning and the conflict that arises between them. Organizational boundaries diminish in importance or at least are redefined in this way. Ideas such as open systems theory then are useful insofar as they stimulate learning and understanding as one possible model for analysis. This is precisely Gareth Morgan's approach, employing an open systems metaphor as one possible image of organizations.

Evidently, the impact of Von Bertalanffy's open systems theory on the theory of business and management is profound. It helped shape management and organization theory in the 1950s and 1960s. It pervades management practice in the 1990s. Planning and decision making is often couched in terms of differentiation, environment, functions, growth, interrelatedness and teleology (dependence of the behaviour of an organization on some future events planned in advance). Open systems theory also turned out to be the forerunner of general system theory.

3 General system theory

Von Bertalanffy generalized the open systems concept for other fields. This led him to the idea of general system theory and a new vision of the unity of science. General system theory aims to formulate and derive principles applicable to systems in general. General system theory was given its first oral presentation at the Seminar of Charles Morns in Chicago in 1937. Von Bertalanffy developed general system theory throughout the 1940s and into the 1950s.

In 1954 he and three other distinguished scholars with similar ideas spent time together as Fellows of the Centre for Advanced Study in the Behavioural Sciences in Palo

Alto, California. Von Bertalanffy along with Kenneth Boulding (economist), Ralph Gerard (physiologist) and Anatol Rapoport (mathematical biologist) became founding fathers of the systems movement. The systems movement, Kenneth Boulding recollects, began in conversations of four Fellows around a luncheon table.

Von Bertalanffy was a prime mover in organizing the systems movement. He was central in establishing the Society for the Advancement of General Systems Theory. It was initiated as a group of the American Association for the Advancement of Science at its Berkeley meeting in 1954. The society launched both a yearbook in 1956 and an annual conference (both still going today). The society was founded with the following aims:

- to investigate the isomorphy of concepts, laws and models from various fields, and to help in useful transfers from one field to another;
- to encourage the development of adequate theoretical models in fields which lack them;
- to minimize the duplication of theoretical effort in different fields;
- to promote the unity of science through improving communication among specialists.

Von Bertalanffy's main worry was increasing specialization leading to a breakdown in science as an integrated realm. He saw specialists encapsulated in their own private universe, finding it difficult to get messages from one cocoon to another. He wished to prevent closed, isolated research. He foresaw a system of laws and generalized theories to unify all sciences.

Robert Rosen (1979) described Von Bertalanffy's general system idea with forceful simplicity. If two systems S and S′ data are physically different but nevertheless behave similarly, then there is a sense in which we can learn about S through S′. Learning, Von Bertalanffy insisted, is through isomorphy or homology, not vague analogy.

For the record, Alexander Bogdanov (1873–1928; see further reading), a Russian

thinker, developed 'tektology' that is likened to general system theory. It was published in Russian 1912–28. 'Tektology' was suppressed by Soviet authorities. In the 1980s tektology became available in English.

4 Systems view of people

Consolidated in the book *A Systems View of Man* (edited by La Violette, 1981), Von Bertalanffy's reasoning on symbolism, psychology and education, illustrate applications of his systems theories. Besides certain biological differences, Von Bertalanffy states, what distinguishes human beings from other creatures is the creation of symbols. Symbols are freely created, representative of some content and transmitted by tradition. They are conscious representations such as thought and values. Von Bertalanffy's systems thinking sees systems of symbols, or symbolic universes. Through this conception he suggests language, science, art and other cultural forms, achieve existence transcending the personalities and lifetimes of their creators.

In the domain of psychology, Von Bertalanffy wrote of people as intrinsically active psychophysical organisms that possess autonomous behaviour. This challenged the reactive, mechanistic stimulus–response model. He emphasized many organismic principles from open systems theory.

In the domain of education, Von Bertalanffy saw a stifling of creativity in North American practices that taught within confines of disciplines. He recommended an interdisciplinary approach. Interdisciplinarity is a big topic in the 1990s, particularly in tertiary education.

5 Conclusion

In 1957 the Society for the Advancement of General Systems Theory changed its name to the Society for General Systems Research. Under this umbrella organization, systems thinking burgeoned into many offshoots including complexity theory, cybernetics, information theory, systems approaches to problem solving, systems engineering and systems philosophy. Offshoots then sprouted more offshoots; many national systems societies formed.

In 1980 the International Federation for Systems Research was incorporated, fittingly in Austria. The aim was to stimulate all activities associated with the scientific study of systems and to co-ordinate such activities at an international level. It launched the journal *Systems Research* (now incorporating *Behavioural Science*). The independent *International Journal of General Systems* was launched in 1974. In response to this growing plurality and competition, in 1988 the Society for General Systems Research changed its name to the International Society for the Systems Sciences. In 1988, the international journal *Systems Practice* (renamed *Systemic Practice and Action Research* in 1998) was launched in which many new possibilities for systems thinking have emerged. Systems thinking has become diverse yet remains vibrant.

Ludwig Von Bertalanffy was thus at the start of this remarkable movement. The systems movement began in 1954 at Palo Alto, California, in conversations of four Fellows around a luncheon table. Central to these conversations was Von Bertalanffy's open systems theory and general system theory. As seen, the outcome was vastly 'more than the sum of its parts'. As said, Von Bertalanffy is one of those rare people who influenced widely the way Western people conceive their relationship to each other (at work and elsewhere) and the world in which they find themselves.

ROBERT L. FLOOD
UNIVERSITY OF HULL

Further reading

(References cited in the text marked *)

Ashby, R. (1958) 'General system theory as a new discipline', *General Systems*, 3: 1–6. (Classic paper on general system theory.)

Bogdanov, A. (1996) *Bogdanov's Tektology*, Hull University: Centre for Systems Studies Press (translated by V.N. Sadovsky and V.V. Kelle, edited by P. Dudley). (The first full English Language translation of the Tektology.)

Boulding, K.E. (1956) 'General system theory: the skeleton of science', *Management Science*, 2: 197–208. (Classic paper on general system theory.)

Boulding, K.E. (1972) 'Economics and general systems'. In Laszlo, E. (ed.) *The Relevance of General System Theory*, New York: Braziller. (Reflections on the establishment of general system theory plus its relevance to economics.)

Gray, W. and Rizzo, N. (eds.) (1972) *Unity Through Diversity: A Festschrift in Honour of Ludwig Von Bertalanffy*, (2 volumes) London and New York: Gordon Breach. (A celebration of Von Bertalanffy's research.)

Klir, G. (1991) *Facets of Systems Science*, New York: Plenum. (Background and history of general system theory with contributions from many key researchers.)

* La Violette, P.A. (ed.) (1981) *A Systems View of Man*, Boulding, CA: Westview. (Collection of Von Bertalanffy's papers on symbolism, psychology and education.)

Laszlo, E. (1972) *Introduction to Systems Philosophy*, New York: Gordon and Breach. (Systems philosophy from a general system theory viewpoint, including a notable foreword from Von Bertalanffy.)

Rapoport, A. (1986) *General System Theory*, Tunbridge Wells: Abacus. (Recent general system theory from an old master.)

* Rosen, R. (1979). 'Old trends and new trends in General Systems Research', *International Journal of General Systems*, 5: 173–181. (Insightful reflections on general system theory with ideas for its development still relevant today.)

Von Bertalanffy, L. (1933) *Modern Theories of Development*, Oxford: Oxford University Press (translated from German by J.H. Woodger). (1962) Harper: New York. German original (1928) *Kritische Theorie der Formbildung*, Berlin: Gugrüder Borntraeger. Spanish translation (1934) *Teoria del Desarrollo Biologico*, Buenos Aires: Universidad de La Plata (in two volumes, translated by M. Biraben). (First conceptions of organismic biology and open system theory.)

Von Bertalanffy, L. (1950) 'The theory of open systems in physics and biology', *Science*, 11: 23–9. (Classic paper on organismic biology and open system theory.)

Von Bertalanffy, L. (1953) *Problems of Life: An Evaluation of Modern Biological Thought*, New York: Wiley, London: Watts. (1961) Harper: New York. German (1949) *Das Biologische Weltbild*, Bern: A Francke AG. Japanese translation (1954) Tokyo: Misuzu Shobo. French translation (1960) *Les Problèmes de la Vie*, Paris: Gallimard (translated by M. Deutsch). Spanish translation (1963) *Concepción Biológica del Cosmos*, Santiago: Ediciones de la Universidad de Chile (translated by F. Cordon). Dutch translation (1965) *Een Biologische Wereldbeeld. Het Verschijnsel Leven in Natuur en Wetenschap*, Utrecht: Holland, Bijleveld. (Includes a survey of his research on organismic biology and open system theory.)

Von Bertalanffy, L. (1956) 'General System Theory', *General Systems* 1: 1–10. (Classic paper on general system theory.)

Von Bertalanffy, L. (1967) *Robots, Men and Minds: Psychology in the Modern World*, New York: Braziller. German enlarged edition (1970) *aber vom Menschen wissen wir nichts* Düsseldorf: Econ Verlag. Japanese translation (1972) Tokyo: Misuzu Shobo (translated by K. Nagano). Italian translation (1971) *Teoria Generale dei Sistemi* Milano: Istituto Librario Internazionale (translated by L. Occhetto Baruffi). Spanish translation (1971) *Robots, Hombres y Mentes*, Madrid: Guadarrama (translated by F. Calleja). Czech translation (1972) *Clovek-robot a mysleni*, Prague: Svoboda (translated by J. Kamaryt). (Organismic biology and open system theory applied to psychology, plus detailed references to temporal sequence of development of organismic biology and open systems theory.)

Von Bertalanffy, L. (1968) *Organismic Psychology and Systems Theory*, Worcester, Mass: Clark University Press. (Organismic biology and open systems theory applied to psychology.)

Von Bertalanffy, L. (1968) *General System Theory: Foundations, Development, Applications*, New York: Braziller. Enlarged edition (1971) London: Penguin, (1972) New York: Braziller. Japanese translation (1971) Tokyo: Misuzu Shobo (translated by K. Nagano). Italian translation (1972) *Il Sistema Uomo: La Psicologia nel Mondo Moderno*, Milano: Istituto Librario Internazionale (translated by E. Bellone). Spanish translation (1972) Madrid: Guadarrama. French translation (1972) Paris: Dunod. Swedish translation (1972) Stockholm: Wahlstršm and Widstrand. German translation (1973) Braunschweig: Vieweg. (A consolidated account of general system theory.)

See also: ACKOFF, R.L.; BEER, S.; BOUDLING, K.; CHECKLAND, P.; CHURCHMAN, C.W.; FAYOL, H.; MORGAN, G.;TAYLOR, F.W.;VICKERS, G.;WEBER, M.; WIENER, N.

Related topics in the IEBM: BUSINESS ECONOMICS; CYBERNETICS; DECISION MAKING; MANAGEMENT SCIENCE; NEO-CLASSICAL ECONOMICS; ORGANIZATION BEHAVIOUR; ORGANIZATION BEHAVIOUR, HISTORY OF; OPERATIONS RESEARCH; SYSTEMS

Watson, Thomas (1874–1956)

Personal background

- born 17 February 1874 to a Methodist family of Scottish descent in rural New York State, USA
- early career as a travelling salesman paved the way for a meteoric rise through the ranks of National Cash Register (NCR), 1895–1913
- married 29-year-old Jeannette Kittredge in 1913
- hired as General Manager of the Computing Tabulating Recording company (CTR) in May 1914. CTR subsequently changed its name to International Business Machines (IBM) in 1924
- served 41 years as Chief Executive of CTR/IBM, releasing control to his eldest son, Thomas Junior, in 1956, six weeks before his death
- died 19 June 1956

Summary

Thomas J. Watson (1874–1956) was the progenitor of International Business Machines (IBM), formerly the world's most admired and profitable company. He was a persuasive salesman and, by all accounts, a charismatic leader, an autocratic man with a remarkable capacity for paternalistic benevolence. On the strength of IBM's success, Watson has been credited with operationalizing a code of management practice and a corporate culture which together represent a model for those grappling with the most crucial problems of business and administration in the late twentieth century. As IBM's fortunes have changed throughout the 1990s, such claims have become increasingly controversial, provoking intense debate among management theorists and consultants.

1 Introduction

Watson has left an indelible mark on the folklore and legend of the computer industry. He is frequently portrayed as a shrewd and skilful businessman who carries significant personal responsibility for its early development, its structure and indeed for some of its less appealing features via the corporate power and influence of International Business Machines (IBM). Historically, IBM has been the target of criticism for its pricing methods, for monopolizing key markets and restricting trade in its favour. Anti-trust officials with the US Justice Department have been particularly vigorous in pursuing the company with charges of pre-empting competitive processes, thereby stifling the innovative potential of smaller, entrepreneurial companies and limiting consumer choice in the market-place. Lengthy legal battles were fought over anti-trust suits filed in 1932, 1952 and 1969, the latter culminating in a dramatic withdrawal by the Reagan Administration in January 1982.

Watson himself joined the Computing, Tabulating and Recording company (CTR) with a conviction under US legislation, having been prosecuted with other National Cash Register (NCR) officials for earlier violations of the 1890 Sherman Anti-Trust Act. His penalty, a $5,000 fine and one-year jail sentence, was eventually quashed in March 1915 as the judgment was set aside on appeal. However, the experience undoubtedly left its mark, prompting the development of the clear and favourable corporate image that IBM projects to the outside world.

With lawsuits regularly fixing IBM in the public gaze, Watson and other officials have guarded information on how the company actually operates. Commentators have frequently expressed surprise that the internal workings of such a large and successful company should remain so remarkably opaque. This has lent a certain mystique to Watson's public persona, producing different evaluations of his status and his contribution to IBM's achievements and failures.

One popular interpretation employs the 'great man' theory of history, presenting Watson as a visionary who worked his way out of a farmyard to become 'an industrial giant', perhaps the most enlightened businessmen of his time (Sobel 1981). A related view concentrates on his managerial skills, his flair for motivating employees and success in crafting an organization with a clear sense of direction and a culture that has tended to be purposeful rather than reactive. Watson was apparently conscious of the need to monitor competitors' attempts at dictating market conditions and to minimize the dangers for IBM by responding pro-actively to ongoing events. For his critics, this amounted to a monopolists' charter, a philosophy of control that nurtured discriminatory practices, producing a company that ruthlessly crushed its rivals (DeLamarter 1988). For all the anti-trust interest in IBM, Watson had little truck with such a view. His self-image was not of a lawbreaker but rather of an individual who had lived the American dream. Hard work and dedication had delivered success, along with sound marketing and superior management of his production staff and sales force. Circumstances were also propitious, since IBM's growth coincided with epochs that were receptive to information processing and computing equipment. Another view of Watson's success suggests that he happened to be in the right place at the right time. More recent IBM executives have not been so fortunate, facing crises of morale, performance and profitability. Difficulties in the early 1990s notwithstanding, there is still a broad consensus that useful lessons can be gleaned from an understanding of Watsonian management at IBM. The debate centres on whether it constitutes an exemplar model, or a cautionary tale of unchecked corporate power.

2 Biographical data

Watson cut his business teeth as a teenager, selling pianos and sewing machines from the back of a wagon. After a few difficult years travelling the countryside, he took a job selling cash registers for NCR. Success came quickly, drawing the attention of Eugene Patterson, head of the company, who had installed Watson as his second-in-command by 1911. At NCR Watson established many of the convictions that later found expression in IBM's corporate culture. In fact he borrowed many of his concepts directly from Patterson, his own distinctive contribution relating to the missionary zeal with which they were refined and pursued. The armoury of sales techniques and paternalistic human resource strategies that later became synonymous with IBM have their roots in the quota systems, commission structures, company clubs and evangelistic pep talks that Patterson had pioneered as a way of motivating his sales force. Watson's antipathy for anti-trust legislation was also conditioned by his experience at NCR, his first brush with the authorities resulting from the aggressive sales tactics that Patterson favoured. Despite his admiration for Patterson, Watson was forced out of the company because his superior feared a challenge to his ultimate authority. With the anti-trust conviction of 1913 still hanging over him, his next step would be to CTR, the company that eventually became IBM.

Although Watson is often identified as the founder of IBM, its genealogy can actually be traced back to the inventor, Herman Hollerith. In 1896 Hollerith formally capitalized the Tabulating Machine Company, a business he had established by supplying US census agencies with 'statistical pianos' based on the Jacquard loom. With financial restrictions hindering its development, the company was subsequently absorbed into CTR, a conglomerate put together by Charles Flint, the so-called 'Trust King', who appointed Watson General Manager in 1914. While Hollerith had given the corporation innovative products, Watson's contribution centred on marketing, distribution and organizational arrangements. Due to the efforts of an increasingly professional sales force and highly motivated production staff, the company prospered through the early decades of the century, its change of name on 14 February 1924 signalling Watson's confidence about the prospects of trade outside the USA. By the end of the Second World War, IBM was an international icon, leading its industry with an annual revenue in excess of $140 million in 1948.

The post-war IBM was shaped under the leadership of three men, Thomas Watson, Sr and his two sons, Thomas, Jr and Arthur (known as Dick). In 1949, at the age of 75, Watson, Sr presided over its separation into a domestic US company and a subsidiary labelled IBM World Trade. The latter was controlled by Dick, while the parent company increasingly came under the direction of Thomas, Jr, who led the company fully into the computer age. Thomas, Jr was appointed Chief Executive Officer in May 1956, shortly before his father died of a heart attack (on 19 June 1956). Over the next fifteen years, IBM's gross income increased from $335 million to more than $7 billion, a rate of growth that prompted the August 1987 edition of *Fortune* magazine to proclaim Thomas Watson, Jr the greatest capitalist in history. Thomas, Jr retired in 1971 after a heart attack. In 1979 he was appointed US ambassador to Moscow by President Carter. He died in 1994.

3 Main contribution

IBM's success has been widely attributed to almost sixty years of continuous Watson management. Company brochures and business commentaries often project the image of an entrepreneurial family promoting a strong culture of managerial excellence through adherence to core values and behaviour patterns that were set out by Watson, Sr. The backbone of IBM's character is identified as the social creed that emerged from his sense of morality and his ethical fortitude. Three central principles are usually linked to this: respect for individual employees, a commitment to customer service and the pursuit of excellence in all spheres of operation. These found expression in personnel programmes promoting full employment and open communications, and also in pronouncements and slogans that set the tone for the company, at least through its first forty years. Legends such as 'Think' and 'The best supervision is self supervision', together with company anthems and personnel practices, ostensibly fostered a feeling of community, even family obligation, among employees. The consistent fairness of the culture was considered to be functional in creating corporate loyalty and identification. The message for other companies was reaffirmed by Thomas, Jr in 1963. In a book entitled *A Business and its Beliefs: The Ideas that Helped Build IBM*, he argued that there was simply no substitute for good human relations and for the high morale they bring.

More recently, through the 1970s and 1980s, prominent management theorists and consultants have taken the Watson lesson to heart, extolling the virtues of IBM's enlightened corporate culture. Peters and Waterman provide the most notable example, their 1982 book *In Search of Excellence* proclaiming IBM to be the epitome of excellence, the greatest corporation in the world. These authors attribute IBM's prosperity directly to its internal management systems and relationships, rather than to merger and monopoly activity, or even technical innovation. On this reading, autonomy and entrepreneurship within the company combined to create customer loyalty that made IBM invulnerable to competitors. Such a view has found enormous favour with company insiders. F. 'Buck' Rodgers, an ex-marketing executive who describes himself as 'a born-and-bred, dyed-in-the-wool IBMer' gives it a glowing commendation: 'Every now and then – about as often as Halley's Comet streaks across the sky – a book like *In Search of Excellence* comes along and gets right to the heart of things' (Rodgers and Shook 1986: 3). He maintains that 'To understand IBM's success and its unshakable optimism, one needs some insights into its marketing systems and philosophy, and its unique relationship with employees and customers' (1986: 4).

Others take a less complimentary stance, criticizing Peters and Waterman for accepting an IBM public relations spiel. For Richard DeLamarter, one of the US anti-trust officials on the 1969–82 investigation, Peters and Waterman operate at the level of superficial images:

> According to the authors, IBM has benefited from a strong central philosophy that was originally laid down by its charismatic leaders, the Watsons. They present a simple, appealing model for IBM's success – excellence in management. But this view is dead wrong. IBM's success comes from the power of monopoly.
>
> (DeLamarter 1988: xvii)

According to DeLamarter, few lessons can be learned from IBM on management, the work ethic or technological innovation. Under the Watsons, its growth was based on a strategy of holding a near monopoly market share in which customer interests were regularly and systematically sacrificed. This position is heavily endorsed by Rex Malik. In his 1975 publication, *And Tomorrow the World?: Inside IBM*, he wrote:

> This book is about control. It is about a sham: an American company which masquerades as a multinational and has dozens of foreign subsidiaries, each with a board packed full of local worthies and executive flunkies, but which in reality is a company, in all meaningful senses of the word, consolidated, and in which power is about as widely distributed as is power in the Kremlin.
>
> (Malik 1975)

Ex-IBM employees have also flagged the dangers of monopoly power at IBM, relating these to concerns about inferior products and weak management. Gene Amdahl, a leading technologist with the company in the 1960s, reported in 1975 that IBM was sidelining engineering talent, employing two-thirds of the Western world's computing engineers without producing leading edge technology. Similar pragmatic concerns about the limitations of IBM's logic of management have recently prompted business periodicals to caution against the emulation mentality encouraged by Peters and Waterman. *Business Age*

magazine is among the most prominent, noting in a March 1993 editorial that:

> *In Search of Excellence* provided many executives of companies that are now defunct with a false sense of security. It wasn't all wrong, but it just wasn't all right. There is a lot of responsibility on the shoulders of management gurus, especially those who write books and take peoples' money for it.
>
> (*Business Age* March 1993: 22–5)

4 Evaluation

So much has changed about IBM in the 1990s that efforts to attribute its record solely to superior management *or* monopoly power seem ill-informed and, ultimately, futile. Such absolutism deflects attention from contextual factors and contingencies, and downgrades the significance of reflective social action in formulating responses to environmental opportunities and constraints. In February 1993, when IBM announced a record corporate loss of $5.3 billion, it was clear that the information technology market had changed and that the company had failed to react. Regardless of whether the Watsons' management was essentially enlightened or monopolistic, the company was out of touch.

Ironically, given the mooted flexibility of IBM's culture, there was a broad consensus that bureaucratic priorities had taken hold. The dynamic organization had frozen. Perceptible rigidities enabled critics to hoist the company with its own petard. In their own analysis of the situation, senior IBM executives identified the core characteristics of the Watsons' management as a root cause of poor performance. Responding to early signs of a downturn in January 1988, then chairman John Akers announced a major reorganization, including changes to the open access policy that enabled employees to take their grievances progressively higher up the corporate ladder until they found an acceptable solution. By 1992, he was devolving decision making to the point where research and production centres could take responsibility for their own commercial well-being, changing employment and marketing policies if that was considered appropriate. Lou Gerstner, who assumed the mantle of chief executive in April 1993, was even more disdainful of the traditional culture, replacing Watson's three basic beliefs with eight objectives that would facilitate change. Respect for the individual came bottom of the list, confirming the new priorities to employees who had already lost the promise of lifetime employment when redundancies were instituted in early 1993.

Contrary to the views of Peters and Waterman, it would be easy to conclude from all of this that an over-indulgence in Watsonian management can be damaging to corporate health. There is another possibility, however. A more charitable theory is that Watson's principles were overridden by an expanding bureaucracy, stifled by complacency rather than causing cultural gridlock. From this angle, the axemanship involved in changing the traditional paternalism may create motivational difficulties which restrict the sense of entrepreneurship and process-ownership that Gerstner is trying to foster. Perhaps there is a danger of throwing something valuable out with the bureaucratic bathwater, in which case the management of Watson's legacy will be the subject of continuing debate.

5 Conclusion

Thomas J. Watson asserted that in order to respond to environmental contingencies, an organization must be willing to change everything about itself except its basic beliefs. Commentators on IBM's decline in the early 1990s have argued that its demise is inevitable given its inability or refusal to depart from Watsonian management. Bill Gates of Microsoft has predicted that it will be extinct by 2002. Paul Carroll, author of *Big Blues* (1994), argues that IBM will never again hold sway over the computer industry. The chorus of praise for the company may have been silenced, but its resilience and its attachment to Watson's logic should not be underestimated. IBM announced a modest profit in the summer of 1994.

MARTIN BEIRNE
UNIVERSITY OF GLASGOW

Further reading

(References in the text marked *)

* *Business Age* (1993) 'IBM: the death of the corporation', (March) 22–5. (Editorial which highlights the dangers of emulation mentality in corporate management.)

* Carroll, P. (1994) *Big Blues: The Unmaking of IBM*, London: Weidenfeld & Nicolson. (A timely review of IBM's predicament and responses.)

Cortada, J. (1993) *Before the Computer: IBM, NCR, Burroughs, and Remington Rand and the Industry They Created, 1865–1956*, Princeton, NJ: Princeton University Press. (Provides historical detail on the rise of IBM.)

* DeLamarter, R. (1988) *Big Blue: IBM's Use and Abuse of Power*, London: Pan Books. (A landmark text by an anti-trust investigator who articulates a penetrating critique of IBM's business practices.)

Evans, H.S. (1941) *Fellowship Songs of the International Business Machines Corporation*, New York: IBM. (Provides a taste of the corporate community spirit at IBM, which was fostered in part through company anthems, slogans and innovative personnel practices.)

Foy, N. (1974) *The IBM World*, London: Eyre Methuen. (Offers an informative, if now rather dated, insight into IBM's internal work systems.)

* Malik, R. (1975) *And Tomorrow the World?: Inside IBM*, London: Millington. (A useful counterweight to IBM in-house and officially endorsed publications.)

* Peters, T. and Waterman, R. (1982) *In Search of Excellence: Lessons from America's Best Run Companies*, New York: Harper & Row. (Initially influential with practitioners, this book illustrates the folly of de-contextualized, prescriptive advice in modern management consulting.)

* Rodgers, F. 'Buck' and Shook, R. (1986) *The IBM Way: Insights into the World's Most Successful Marketing Organization*, New York: Harper & Row. (A glowing endorsement of the 'IBM way' by a company insider.)

Rodgers, W. (1969) *Think: A Biography of the Watsons and IBM*, New York: Stein & Day. (An early account of the Watsons' influence at IBM.)

* Sobel, R. (1981) *IBM: Colossus in Transition*, New York: Times Books. (An interesting view of the pressures bearing on IBM as it entered the 1980s.)

* Watson, T., Jr (1963) *A Business and its Beliefs: The Ideas that Helped Build IBM*, New York: McGraw-Hill. (A straightforward commendation of Watsonian management through two generations.)

Watson, T., Jr (1990) *Father, Son and Co: My Life at IBM and Beyond*, New York: Bantam Books. (Thomas Watson, Jr offers some candid reflections on his family ties with IBM.)

See also: KOTTER, J.; PETERS, T.J.

Related topics in the IEBM: CULTURE; GURU CONCEPT; INFORMATION REVOLUTION; INFORMATION TECHNOLOGY AND SOCIETY; INTERNATIONAL MARKETING; MANUFACTURING MANAGEMENT; ORGANIZATION BEHAVIOUR; ORGANIZATION CULTURE

Weber, Max (1864–1920)

Personal background

- born into a middle-class family in Erfurt, Germany, 21 April 1864
- took his PhD and began his teaching career at the University of Berlin
- moved on to a position as Professor of Economics at the University of Heidelberg
- experienced a nervous breakdown in 1897 and was unable to do any serious work for several years
- began to re-emerge in 1904, coincident with a trip to the USA
- published his best-known work, *The Protestant Ethic and the Spirit of Capitalism*, in 1904–5
- most of his major works published in the next decade and a half, or posthumously
- died on 14 June 1920 while in the midst of his most important work, *Economy and Society*

Major works

The Protestant Ethic and the Spirit of Capitalism (1904–5)
Economy and Society (1921)
General Economic History (1927)

Summary

Max Weber (1864–1920) was a major social theorist whose ideas are of great relevance to business and management. Embedded in Weber's world historical studies is a general theory of the rationalization of society. Time has been kind to Weber's theory; society today is even more rationalized than it was in his day. His theoretical ideas are of particular relevance to the understanding of, among other things, modern formal organizations, the capitalist market, the professions and economies as a whole. Not only do Weber's ideas continue to be relevant today, but neo-Weberians are developing new ideas that have even greater applicability to modern society.

1 Introduction

After Karl Marx, Weber is the most important German social theorist. In fact, Weber had to grapple with, and distance himself from, Marxian theory. Weber, like Marx, had much to say about capitalism. However, to Weber capitalism was merely part of a much broader problem – modern rational society. Thus while Marx focused on alienation within the economic system, Weber saw alienation as a far larger problem occurring in many other social institutions. While Marx condemned the exploitation of the capitalist system, Weber was concerned with the increasing oppressiveness of the rationalized society. Marx was an optimist who felt that the problems of alienation and exploitation could be solved with the overthrow of the capitalist economy, but Weber was a pessimist who believed that the future held only increasing rationalization, especially if capitalism was overthrown. Weber was no revolutionary, but rather a careful and insightful analyst of modern society.

2 Biographical data

Max Weber was born into a middle-class family in which his parents had very different outlooks on life. His worldly father was a classic bureaucrat who ultimately rose to a position of some political importance in Germany; in contrast, Weber's mother was devoutly religious and even ascetic in her outlook. In a later biography, Weber's wife Marianne (Weber

1975) comments that Weber's parents confronted him with a difficult choice as a child, a choice that he agonized over for much of his life and one which had a profound effect on both his personal life and his scholarly work (Mitzman 1969).

Weber earned a doctorate from the University of Berlin in 1892 in his father's field (law) and began teaching at that university. However, his interests were already shifting towards his lifelong concerns – economics, history and sociology. His early work in these areas led to a position as Professor of Economics at the University of Heidelberg in 1896.

Not long after his appointment at Heidelberg, Weber had a violent argument with his father, who died shortly thereafter. Within a short period of time Weber suffered a nervous breakdown from which he was never to recover fully. However, by 1904–5 he had recuperated sufficiently to publish one of his best-known works, *The Protestant Ethic and the Spirit of Capitalism* (Weber 1904–5; Lehmann and Roth 1993). The subject-matter of this work, as reflected in the title, exhibited a concern for both his mother's religiosity (she was a Calvinist, the key Protestant sect in the rise of capitalism) and his father's worldly interests. It also demonstrated the ascendancy of his mother's orientation over his father's; an ascendancy that was to be manifest in a series of works focusing on the sociology of religion (Weber 1916, 1916–17, 1921), especially the impact of the major religions of the world on economic conduct.

In the last decade and a half of his life, Weber was able to publish his most important works. At the time of his death he was working on his most important book, *Economy and Society* (Weber 1921) which, although incomplete, was published posthumously, as was the also significant *General Economic History* (Weber 1927).

During his lifetime, Weber had a profound impact on scholars such as Georg Simmel, Robert Michels and Georg Lukacs. His influence remains strong to this day with the continuing, and perhaps even accelerating, production of a wide array of neo-Weberian scholarship (Collins 1985).

3 Main contribution

In the area of business and management, Weber has been best known for his work on bureaucracy. However, that work is but a small part of his broader theory of the rationalization of Western society and many elements of that theory beyond his paradigm of a bureaucracy are relevant to scholars working in the area of business and management.

At the broadest level, the question that informs Weber's work is, why did the Occident develop a unique form of rationalization and why did the rest of the world fail to develop such a rational system? The paradigm case of the West's distinctive rationality is the bureaucracy, but it is only one aspect, albeit a central one (along with capitalism), of a broad-based process of rationalization.

The rationalization concept in Weber's work is notoriously obscure, but the best definition of at least one key type – formal rationalization – is the process by which actors' choices of means to ends are increasingly constrained, if not determined, by universally applied rules, laws and regulations. The bureaucracy, a key domain of such rules, laws and regulations, is one of the defining products of this process of rationalization, but there are others such as the capitalistic market, systems of rational–legal authority, the factory and the assembly line. All have in common the fact that they are formally rational structures that constrain the individuals within them to act in a rational manner by pursuing ends through the choice of the most direct and efficient means. Furthermore, Weber saw more and more sectors of society coming under the domination of formal rationalization. Eventually, he envisioned a society in which people would be enslaved in an 'iron cage of rationality' made up of a near seamless web of these formally rational structures.

These structures, as well as the process of formal rationalization in general, can be seen as being defined by several dimensions (Eisen 1978). First, formally rational structures emphasize calculability, or those things that can be counted or quantified. The focus on quantity tends to lead to a de-emphasis on quality.

Second, there is a focus on efficiency, or finding the best means available to an end. Third, there is great emphasis on predictability, or being sure that things operate in the same way from one time or place to another. Fourth, there is an emphasis on the control over, and ultimately replacement of, humans by non-human technologies. Finally, and reflective of Weber's profound ambivalence about the rationalization process, is the tendency of formally rational systems to have irrational consequences, in other words, the irrationality of rationality.

Rationality has many irrationalities, but the foremost among them is dehumanization. Modern formally rational systems tend, in Weber's view, to be inhuman places in which to function and this goes for the bureaucrat, the factory worker, the assembly-line worker, as well as the participant in the capitalist market. For Weber, there is a basic conflict between these formally rational structures devoid of values and individuals imbued with his notion of 'personality,' that is, those defined and dominated by such values (Brubaker 1984: 63).

The modern analyst of business and management is left with several concerns derived from Weber's work. At the most general level is the continuing relevance of Weber's general theory of increasing formal rationalization to the modern business world. The business world in particular, as well as society as a whole, would seem to be even more rationalized today than it was in Weber's day. Thus, the process remains relevant and, in fact, we need to be attuned to its spreading influence throughout the business world and the larger society.

Beyond the broad theory are more specific aspects of Weber's work, the most important of which for our purposes is the process of bureaucratization and the resulting bureaucratic structure. As one aspect of the rationalization process, the process of bureaucratization persists and bureaucratic structures continue to survive and even spread throughout the West, as well as the rest of the world. At the same time, Weber's 'ideal type' of a bureaucracy continues to be useful as a heuristic device for analysing organizational structures. The goal is to see how well these structures measure up to the elements of the ideal-typical bureaucracy. The ideal-typical bureaucracy remains a useful methodological tool even in this era of radically new, debureaucratized organizational forms. The ideal type is of utility in determining how far these new bureaucratic forms have strayed from the form as it was first described by Weber.

While the bureaucracy continues to be important, one may question whether it still is the 'paradigm case' of the rationalization process. It could be argued, for example, that the fast-food restaurant is today a better paradigm for the rationalization process than the bureaucracy (Ritzer 1996).

The bureaucracy is the organizational form characteristic of one of Weber's three types of authority – rational-legal authority which rests on the legality of enacted rules. There is also traditional authority which is based on the sanctity of immemorial traditions. Finally, charismatic authority rests on the belief of followers that a leader has extraordinary qualities. These authority types remain relevant to thinking about those who lead businesses and other types of organizations. Since the three types of authority are ideal types, any given leader may have their authority legitimized on the basis of some combination of all three types.

With the rout of communism throughout most of the world, Weber's thoughts on the capitalistic marketplace take on renewed importance. The capitalist market was both a key site of the rationalization process and a formally rational structure defined by all of the key elements outlined above. Further, it was crucial to the dissemination of the principles of formal rationality to many other sectors of society.

Weber envisioned a mortal struggle taking place in the modern world between formal rationality and a second type of rationality, substantive rationality. While in formal rationality choices of means to ends are determined by rules, laws and regulations, in substantive rationality those choices are guided by larger human values. The Protestant ethic is an example of substantive rationality, while the capitalist system, which was an 'unanticipated consequence' of that ethic, is, as we have seen, an example of formal rationality. That they are in conflict is reflected in the fact that capitalism became a system that was inhospitable not only to Protestantism, but to all religion. To put it another way, capitalism, and more generally all formally rational systems, reflect the increasing 'disenchantment of the world'.

In the modern world, one of the places in which this conflict is being played out is in the struggle between formally rational systems like bureaucracies and the substantively rational professions like medicine and law. The classic professions are being threatened by both formally rational bureaucracies like those associated with the government or private enterprise as well as by increases in formal rationality within the professions. As a result, the professions as we have known them are embattled and in the process of losing much of their power, prestige and distinguishing characteristics. In other words, they are undergoing a process of deprofessionalization. This is nowhere clearer than in the most powerful profession of all, the American medical profession (Ritzer and Walczak 1988).

We have mentioned two of the types of rationality employed by Weber (formal and substantive), but it should be pointed out that there are two others: practical (the day-to-day rationality whereby people accept given realities and attempt to deal with them as best they can) and theoretical (the effort to master reality cognitively through increasingly abstract concepts) rationality. It could be argued that the USA achieved much of its economic success by creating and refining a wide range of formally rational systems, for example, assembly lines, time-and-motion systems, organizational principles such as General Motors' divisional system (see SLOAN, A.P.), and innumerable others. It also could be argued that its more recent failures are traceable to relying too long and too exclusively on such formally rational systems. In contrast, it could be argued that the Japanese have succeeded by using formally rational systems often developed in the USA (as well as developing their own such as the just-in-time system) and supplementing them with substantive rationality (importance of the success of the collectivity), theoretical ration-

ality (strong reliance on research and development, as well as engineering) and practical rationality (for example, quality circles). In other words, the Japanese have created a 'hyperrational' system and this gives them an enormous advantage over American industry that continues to rely heavily on only one form of rationality (Ritzer and LeMoyne 1991).

4 Conclusions

Weber's most lasting contribution has been his theory of rationalization. That theory posits four types of rationality (formal, substantive, theoretical and practical) and argues that formal rationality was a distinctive product of the Occident and one that has come to dominate it. This theory has proved useful in analysing such traditional issues as the bureaucracy, the professions and the capitalist market, as well as a series of recent developments such as the rise of the fast-food restaurant, deprofessionalization and the recent ascendancy of Japanese industry and the parallel decline of American industry. Thus, Weber's ideas continue to be relevant to an understanding of a variety of recent developments in the business world and in the world economy. Theorists continue to clarify and amplify his ideas and researchers continue to apply Weber's ideas to a wide range of social settings.

GEORGE RITZER
UNIVERSITY OF MARYLAND
AT COLLEGE PARK

Further reading

(References cited in the text marked *)

Bendix, R. (1960) *Max Weber: An Intellectual Portrait*, Garden City, NY: Anchor Books. (Now classic overview of the life and work of Max Weber.)

* Brubaker, R. (1984) *The Limits of Rationality: An Essay on the Social and Moral Thought of Max Weber*, London: Routledge. (The best single source on Weber's thoughts about rationality.)

* Collins, R. (1985) *Weberian Sociological Theory*, Cambridge: Cambridge University Press. (Excellent example of neo-Weberian theory.)

* Eisen, A. (1978) 'The meanings and confusions of Weberian "rationality"', *British Journal of Sociology* 29: 57–70. (Useful discussion of the various dimensions of formal rationality.)

Kalberg, S. (1980) 'Max Weber's types of rationality: cornerstones for the analysis of rationalization processes in history', *American Journal of Sociology* 85: 1145–79. (Excellent discussion of Weber's rationalization theory and the source for the four types of rationality employed in this biographical sketch.)

Lassman, P. (ed.) (1994) *Weber: Political Writings*, Cambridge: Cambridge University Press. (Essays dealing with another one of Weber's concerns – politics.)

* Lehmann, H. and Roth, G. (eds) (1993) *Weber's Protestant Ethic: Origins, Evidence and Contexts*, Cambridge: Cambridge University Press. (Collection of contemporary essays dealing with various aspects of Weber's classic work.)

* Mitzman, A. (1969) *The Iron Cage: An Historical Interpretation of Max Weber*, New York: Grosset & Dunlap. (A controversial psycho-biography of Weber which focuses on his often unsuccessful effort to work out the conflict between his mother and his father in his work and elsewhere.)

Parsons, T. (1937) *The Structure of Social Action*, New York: McGraw-Hill. (The work that introduced, many would say in a distorted manner, Weber's theory (and others) to an American audience and laid the basis for Parsonsian theory and structural functionalism.)

* Ritzer, G. (1996) *The McDonaldization of Society* (revised edition), Thousand Oaks, CA: Pine Forge Press. (The thesis of this book is that the fast-food restaurant is now a better paradigm of the rationalization process than the bureaucracy and that, if anything, that process is even more powerful today than it was in Weber's day.)

* Ritzer, G. and LeMoyne, T. (1991) 'Hyperrationality: an extension of Weberian and neo-Weberian theory', in G. Ritzer (ed.), *Metatheorizing in Sociology*, Lexington, MA: Lexington Books. (Creates the concept of hyperrationality to describe the co-existence of Weber's four types of rationality and uses that concept to explain Japan's economic successes and the recent failures of the USA.)

* Ritzer, G. and Walczak, D. (1988) 'Rationalization and the deprofessionalization of physicians', *Social Forces* 67: 1–22. (Argues that the medical profession is being swamped by formal rationalization and that this is leading to the deprofessionalization of medicine.)

Schluchter, W. (1981) *The Rise of Western Rationalism: Max Weber's Developmental History*, Berkeley, CA: University of California Press. (Important study of Weber's developmental history of rationalization.)

Sica, A. (1988) *Weber, Irrationality, and Social Order*, Berkeley, CA: University of California Press. (Unlike most other studies of Weber which focus on his work on rationality, this one deals with the issue of irrationality.)

* Weber, Marianne (1975) *Max Weber: A Biography*, trans. and ed. H. Zohn, New York: Wiley. (The definitive biography of Max Weber, by his wife.)

* Weber, M. ([1904–5] 1958) *The Protestant Ethic and the Spirit of Capitalism*, New York: Scribner's. (One of the classic works in sociology detailing the relationship between the ethos of Protestantism, especially Calvinism, and the rise of a spirit of capitalism in the West, a spirit that was ultimately connected to the development of capitalism and, more generally, formal rationality.)

* Weber, M. ([1916] 1964) *The Religion of China: Confucianism and Taoism*, New York: Macmillan. (Part of Weber's sociology of religion in which he discusses the barriers to the rise of capitalism and formal rationality within the major religions of China.)

* Weber, M. ([1916–17] 1958) *The Religion of India: The Sociology of Hinduism and Buddhism*, Glencoe, IL: Free Press. (Companion to *The Religion of China*. Here Weber shows how Hinduism and Buddhism served to impede the development of capitalism and formal rationality.)

* Weber, M. ([1921] 1963) *The Sociology of Religion*, Boston, MA: Beacon Press. (The most general statement of Weber's ideas on the sociology of religion.)

* Weber, M. ([1921] 1968) *Economy and Society*, Totowa, NJ: Bedminster Press. (Three volumes comprising the single best source for a sense of Weber's overall project and his general theoretical perspective.)

* Weber, M. ([1927] 1981) *General Economic History*, New Brunswick, NJ: Transaction Books. (Demonstrates that Weber saw the Protestant ethic as only one of many factors in the rise of Western capitalism and rationality.)

See also: CROZIER, M.; MICHELS, R.; SLOAN, A.P., JR

Related topics in the IEBM: JUST-IN-TIME PHILOSOPHIES; MANAGEMENT IN JAPAN; MANAGEMENT IN NORTH AMERICA; MARX, K.H.; OCCUPATIONAL PSYCHOLOGY; ORGANIZATION BEHAVIOUR; ORGANIZATION BEHAVIOUR, HISTORY OF; ORGANIZATION STRUCTURE; ORGANIZATION TYPES; POWER; TOTAL QUALITY MANAGEMENT

Weick, Karl E. (1936–)

1 *The Social Psychology of Organizing*
2 **Loosely coupled systems**
3 **Organizational cognition and learning**
4 **Enactment and crisis management**
5 *Sensemaking in Organizations*
6 **Modelling the discipline**

Personal background

- born 31 October 1936 at Warsaw, Indiana, USA
- graduated from the Ohio State University, Columbus, Ohio (1962, Ph.D. in Psychology),
- assistant professor of psychology at Purdue University, Lafayette, Indiana (1962–65)
- professor of psychology at the University of Minnesota, Minneapolis, Minnesota (1965–72)
- professor of psychology and organizational behavior, Cornell University, Ithaca, New York (1972–84)
- Harkins and Co. Centennial Chair in Business Administration, University of Texas (1984–88)
- Rensis Likert Collegiate Professor of Organizational Behavior and Professor of Psychology, the University of Michigan, 1988 onwards
- editor, *Administrative Science Quarterly* (1977–85)
- re-directed the focus of organization theory from structures to processes, from organizational behavior to sensemaking

Major works

Social Psychology of Organizing (1969, revised edition 1979)

'Educational organizations as loosely coupled systems', *Administrative Science Quarterly* (1976)
'Enacted sensemaking in crisis situations', *Journal of Management Studies*, (1988)
Sensemaking in Organizations (1995)

Overview

Karl E. Weick's work has had a central role in shaping the discipline of organization theory in the 1980s and 1990s. He launched a new style in organizational theorizing by combining a sophisticated use of systems theory with insights from the world of music and literature, which steadily acquired a growing circle of followers. Some of his concepts are widely used throughout organization theory, e.g. organizing, loosely coupled systems, enactment of environment and sensemaking. He is keenly interested in the concerns of organizational practice and combines an interest in concrete organizational events with an imaginative theorizing.

1 The Social Psychology of Organizing

The origins of organization theory can be placed as late as the early 1960s. Previous to this, there was business and public administration, industrial psychology and sociology, and other subdisciplines which dealt with somewhat similar issues within their disciplinary frames (Waldo 1961). An encounter with systems theory led to a need to establish an object with boundaries able to interact with its environment. Thus 'organization' became viewed not as a state of affairs but as an entity.

Among those works which attempted to make a massive loan from systems theory there was one which was especially prominent: Daniel Katz and Robert L. Kahn's *The Social Psychology of Organizations* (1966).

Weick's book – *The Social Psychology of Organizing* – published in 1969 but best known in its revised edition from 1979, clearly announced its intention to continue but also advance beyond their perspective. The reason for it was that the concept of open systems became the mainstay of organizational analysis, but remained underdeveloped (Weick and Sandelands 1990: 337). Weick undertook its development whilst simultaneously transcending it by the adoption of concepts related to autopoietic, i.e. self-regulating and self-reproducing systems (Maruyama 1974, Luhmann 1990). It is this later innovation that permitted him to extend biological metaphors to those coming from literature, poetry and the arts. Furthermore, it is Weick's understanding of how metaphors work which made him use biological concepts in organization theory so successfully.

He argued that the focus of organization theory must be set in the process of *organizing*, that is assembling 'ongoing interdependent actions into sensible sequences i.e. generate sensible outcomes' (Weick 1979: 3). The result of organizing is *interlocked* cycles which can be represented as *causal loops* rather than a linear chain of causes and effects.

Organizing runs through stages reminiscent of biological evolution and is triggered by a change in environment that is followed by an *enactment*: organizational actors bracket out a certain segment of their environment for active treatment. This stage corresponds to variation. The subsequent treatment consists of *selection*, i.e. attempts to reduce the ambiguity of the ongoing events by applying accessible cognitive schemes to them, which makes it possible to (temporarily) assemble them together; this is then followed by *retention*, i.e. storing of the successful results of such sensemaking that enlarges and renews the repertoire of cognitive schemes, but, paradoxically, also limits the possibility of noticing subsequent changes in the environment.

Organizing is thus an ongoing encounter with ambiguity, ambivalence and equivocality, being part of a larger attempt to make sense of life and the world. It is this assumption that sets Weick's theorizing organizations apart

from the rest of the field that evolved around the notion of 'uncertainty', which is a negative state which must be eradicated for organizing to take place. He cherishes ambiguity and gives it a central place in evolutionary processes. While organizing is an effort to deal with ambiguity, it never completely succeeds. Furthermore, the ordering it involves does not consist of imposing the rules of rationality on disorderly world, but is a far more complex and inherently ambiguous process of sensemaking.

Social Psychology of Organizing is exceptionally rich in metaphors, anecdotes, and pictures with everything from high to popular culture, jazz, business, politics and sports. The anecdote that is best remembered concerns three baseball umpires who represent the three most common variations of the theory of knowledge. Asked how they call balls and strikes, the objectivist says 'I calls them as they is'; the subjectivist says 'I calls them as I sees them', while the constructivist says 'They ain't nothin' till I calls them'. This last stance, together with the set of concepts introduced in this early work, was to characterize Weick's work in the years to come.

2 Loosely coupled systems

Like its outcomes, organizing itself does not develop along a linear sequence. Different stages are *loosely coupled* to one another in everyday organizational life. This loose coupling provides organizations with the flexibility and slack necessary for survival.

The idea of loosely coupled systems comes from Robert B. Glassman (1973) and was borrowed for organizational purposes by several organization scholars such as March and Olsen (1976) who used it in their notion of the garbage-can decision model. Weick originally applied the idea for understanding the erratic organizing typical of educational institutions (1976) and later for grasping the occurrence of disasters in high reliability organizations which tend toward tight coupling (Weick 1990). As the attention of organization researchers turned away from hierarchies and toward networks, the idea was then adopted by many researchers studying different organizational contexts. Its attraction lies in admitting the existence of both rationality and indeterminacy in the same system. There is a tendency, however, to mistake loosely coupled systems as the opposite of tightly coupled systems, rather than a combination of tightly coupled and decoupled systems: 'If there is responsiveness without distinctiveness, the system is tightly coupled. If there is distinctiveness without responsiveness, the system is decoupled. If there is both distinctiveness and responsiveness, the system is loosely coupled' (Orton and Weick 1990: 205). While the greatest promise of his notions is their ability to grasp complexity, the obvious danger awaiting Weick's followers is the one of simplifying these notions and thus forfeiting their power.

3 Organizational cognition and learning

When represented, causal loops resemble maps, thus the concept of *cause maps* that is present in his first major work and is later developed (Bougon *et al.* 1977, Daft and Weick 1984). Weick refused the concept of 'cognitive schemata' that was already in use in psychology in favour of 'cause maps' because it allowed him to tackle the paradoxical observation that 'a map is often a territory', which builds a bridge to the notion of enacted environments. But 'maps' were more in tune with the second umpire and his subjectivist stance 'I calls them as I sees them'. People may act according to their cause maps but if sensemaking is an ongoing process then how long is a given map valid? Does it survive the longish process of depicting it? Above all, does it capture complexity or does it trade it off for complication? Inscribing cause maps in research may well aid the reification and 'confusing the map with the territory' which he considers dangerous for managerial practice.

His later work on organizational learning (Weick 1991, Weick and Westley 1996) refutes the structuralist strain of cognitive psychology in favour of espousing the paradoxicality of organizational cognition

processes. Weick and Westley claim that 'organizational learning' is an oxymoron, as 'To learn is to disorganize and increase variety. To organize is to forget and reduce variety' (1996: 440). In order to grasp this paradox it is necessary to abandon the notion of organizational cognition as an aggregate of individual cognitive processes and focus the collective and embedded character of learning in organizations. Conceptualizing organizations as self-designing systems helps to reconcile the two opposing processes of learning and organizing in a picture of organizational change based on 'muddling through' (Lindblom 1959; in Weick's terms, 'small wins') rather than on stimulus–response or planned change models.

4 Enactment and crisis management

Another concept which turned out to be seminal in organization theory was that of enactment which is both the process of making ideas, structures, and visions real by acting upon them and the outcome of this process, 'an enacted environment' (Weick 1988). It reverses the idea of implementation – which is the putting of a plan into operation – by showing that people are able to act as if their ideas were already implemented. It exchanges the idea of environment as given for the one as constructed. This is not to be confused with wishful thinking as at best enactment is only partially successful, but the concept allows one a better understanding of the dynamics of collective undertakings.

The notion has been widely used as it blends well with the increasing constructivist strand in organization theory. Weick used it most spectacularly in studies on high reliability (or high risk) organizations. While crises are the everyday happening of all organizations, they become especially acute and visible in this kind of organization. The theory of crisis management, developed through the analysis of accidents, catastrophes and disasters (Turner 1978, Perrow 1984, Shrivastava 1987) conceptualized it in terms of reactions to the situation already existing. The perspective of enactment erases the division between crisis prevention and crisis management, revealing how enactment can produce a crisis-prone environment, but also how the understanding of it may help to avoid crises and to reduce danger (Weick 1988, 1990). One way of doing this in practice is by producing and exchanging stories, especially of the kind which he calls 'near-miss narratives', i.e. when an accident is prevented and there is therefore no one to blame but a lesson to be learnt. This is but one example of sensemaking – the core of all organizing.

5 Sensemaking in Organizations

Organizational sensemaking in this work is compared with interpretation, i.e. sensegiving and sense-taking. In the latter cases, a frame of meaning is already in place, and it is enough to connect a new cue to an existing frame. Where there is no frame or at least no obvious connection presents itself, one has to be created – and this is sensemaking. This distinction was not present in Weick's first book, where organizing equalled sensemaking, which seemed at the time to encompass all three processes.

Seven properties of organizational sensemaking were explored: 'identity, retrospect, enactment, social contact, ongoing events, cues, and plausibility' (Weick, 1995: 3). Most of these were known from his earlier writings, but here they are all brought together. After discussing plausibility – which in organizational practice is much more important than accuracy, the fetish of perception studies – Weick concludes:

If accuracy is nice but not necessary in sensemaking, than what is necessary? The answer is, something that preserves plausibility and coherence, something that is reasonable and memorable, something that embodies past experience and expectations, something which resonates with other people, something that can be constructed retrospectively but also can be used prospectively, something that captures both feeling and thought, something that allows for embellishment to fit current

oddities, something that is fun to contrast. In short, what is necessary in sensemaking is a good story.

(Weick 1995: 60–61)

This, in his opinion, is what is most needed 'in an equivocal, postmodern world, infused with the politics of interpretation and conflicting interests' (Weick 1995: 61). Such a postulate is consistent with another, also known from his earlier work: that of requisite variety, which suggests that complex objects must be met by complex models. Although stories simplify the world and are therefore useful as guides for action, they simplify it less than the kind of formal models which we learned to revere as true science.

Scientists may not always make sense, but practitioners constantly try to. Even though sensemaking is an ongoing activity, it is not always equally intensive. After all, there are routines, stereotypes, 'received ideas' and inherited truths. The activity of sensemaking increases with ruptures and discontinuities, shocks and interruptions.

What does sensemaking consist of? A frame, which is relatively large and lasting (Goffman 1974), a cue, and a connection. The frames can be usefully conceived as inherited vocabularies of society, organization, work, individual life projects and tradition.

Sensemaking can be driven by beliefs or by actions. Beliefs shape what people see, and give form to the actions they take. Disparity of beliefs in any social context leads to argument which is one form of sensemaking. Beliefs can also be projected onto the future thus forming expectations. In discussing this last point, Weick retrieves Merton's notion of the 'self-fulfilling prophecy' (Merton 1948) as a 'fundamental act of sensemaking' (Weick 1995: 148).

Action-driven sensemaking, in organizational practice irrevocably connected with the belief-driven kind, generally assumes two forms which are creating commitment and manipulating the world. Weick observes that organized anarchies are the ones which excel at creating commitment as in them there is a continuous need for sensemaking, unrelieved by routines, standard operating procedures or organizational memories.

The book as a whole fulfills two functions. It summarizes two decades of organization theory inspired by his work and it sets the platform for the works to come.

6 Modelling the discipline

Karl Weick has played a central role in shaping the discipline of organization theory in the 1980s and 1990s. This role is highly unusual in that he was never a part of the so called mainstream, and yet his influence was not exerted from the margins of the discipline. He is neither a school builder nor the critical deviant but more a constructive deviant, in the sense that his deviation from standard concerns and perspectives at any given time gives shape to the concerns and perspectives to come. For this reason, many other organization theoreticians tried to assess and understand his influence upon the field.

Weick himself was of the opinion that 'theorists often write trivial theories because their process of theory construction is hemmed in by methodological strictures that favour validation rather than usefulness' (Weick 1989: 516). Favouring usefulness, he suggests that theory making is an organizing process, a sensemaking process which consists of 'disciplined imagination'. A desired result brings out 'a plausible theory, and a theory is judged to be more plausible and of higher quality if it is interesting rather than obvious, irrelevant or absurd, obvious in novel ways, a source of unexpected connections, high in narrative rationality, aesthetically pleasing, or correspondent with presumed realities' (Weick 1989: 517).

His critics agree and use his work as the best example for just this kind of theory. John Van Maanen (1995) argues that, instead of following methodological strictures, Weick has developed a unique style, which fulfills both the requirement of a high narrative rationality and an aesthetical satisfaction. Van Maanen calls this style 'allegoric breaching'. Allegory consists of conveying an abstract message through the narration of a concrete set of events, while breaching concerns

conventional textual practices of the field. This style favours an essay form, ambiguity of reasoning, dialectic reconstruction, and a rhetorical strategy of presence (Van Maanen 1995). Much as these traits break against the recommended style of academic writing, the success of Weick's style speaks most eloquently for itself.

His influence on both form and context of theorizing organizations is profound. He turned the attention of organization students from structures to processes, from the relevance of academia to the relevance of the field, from mystification to imaginative interpretation. His exceptionally sophisticated use of biological metaphors permitted their combination with cultural metaphors in a seamless way. Although his importance for theory building is paramount, were managers to read only one book in organization theory in their lives, *Social Psychology of Organizing* is a serious candidate.

BARBARA CZARNIAWSKA
GOTHENBERG UNIVERSITY

Further reading

(References cited in text marked *)

* Bougon, Michel, Weick, Karl E. and Binkhorst, Din (1977) 'Cognition in organization: An analysis of the Utrecht Jazz Orchestra', *Administrative Science Quarterly* 22: 606–31. (Cybernetic analysis of cause maps held by the orchestra members.)
* Daft, Robert L. and Weick, Karl E. (1984) 'Toward a model of organizations as interpretation systems', *Academy of Management Review*, 9(2): 284–95. (A conceptual treatise on cognitive organization theory.)
* Glassman, Robert B. (1973) 'Persistence and loose coupling in living systems', *Behavioral Science*, 18: 83–98. (Adapts cybernetic terms and systems theory to behavioral and social sciences.)
* Goffman, Erving (1974) *Frame Analysis: An Essay on the Organization of Experience*, Boston: Northern University Press. (The most complete treatment of Goffman's theory of everyday's life.)
* Katz, Daniel and Kahn, Robert L. (1966) *The Social Psychology of Organizations*. New York:

Wiley. (A classic in the field; several editions exist.)

* Lindblom, Charles E. (1959) 'The "science" of muddling through', *Public Administration Review*, 19: 79–88 (An anti-reformist, incrementalist view of organizational change.)

* Luhmann, Niklas (1990) *Essays on Self-reference*, New York: Columbia University Press. (Explains the concept of self-perpetuating systems in the context of communication.)

* March, James G. and Olsen, Johan P. (1976) *Ambiguity and Choice in Organizations*, Bergen: Universitetsforlag. (A collection of studies using the garbage-can model of decision making.)

* Maruyama, Magorah (1974) 'Paradigms and communication', *Technological Forecasting and Social Change*, 6: 3–32. (Explains the notion of communication systems in cybernetics.)

* Merton, Robert K. (1948) 'The self-fulfilling prophecy', *Antioch Review*, 8: 193–210 (A classic article showing how collective beliefs can turn into reality.)

* Orton, J. Douglas and Weick, Karl E. (1990) 'Loosely coupled systems: A reconceptualization', *Academy of Management Review*, 15(2): 203–23. (A review of the works using the loosely coupled systems concepts after 14 years of its introduction.)

* Perrow, Charles (1984) *Normal Accidents*. New York: Basic. (Taking the Three Mile Island accident as a starting point, it suggests that accidents are normal rather than exceptional events in complex systems.)

* Shrivastava, Paul (1987) *Bhopal: Anatomy of a Crisis*, Cambridge, MA: Ballinger. (An attempt to formulate a theory of crisis origins and of crisis management.)

* Turner, Barry A. (1978) *Man-made Disasters*, (2nd edn. 1997), Oxford, UK: Butterworth/Heinemann. (The first book looking for systemic and organizational causes of disasters.)

* Van Maanen, John (1995) 'Style as theory', *Organization Science*, 6(1): 133–143. (A passionate defense of variety and creativity in organization theory against attempts to solidify and standardize it.)

* Waldo, Dwight (1961) 'Organization theory: An elephantine problem', *Public Administration Review*, 21: 210–225 (A review article signalizing the new era in organization theory.)

Weick, Karl E. (1976) 'Educational organizations as loosely coupled systems', *Administrative Science Quarterly*, 21: 1–19 (Introduces the concept of loosely coupled system to organization studies.)

* Weick, Karl E. (1979) *The Social Psychology of Organizing*, 2nd edn, New York: Addison-Wesley. (A classic, first published in 1969, for those interested in the concept of organizing.)

* Weick, Karl E. (1988) 'Enacted sensemaking in crisis situations,' *Journal of Management Studies*, 25(4): 305–17. (Argues that crisis management can be active instead of reactive.)

* Weick, Karl E. (1989) 'Theory construction as disciplined imagination', *Academy of Management Review*, 14(4): 516–31. (Presents a reflective view on the process of theory construction in organization studies.)

* Weick, Karl E. (1990) 'The vulnerable system: An analysis of the Tenerife air disaster', *Journal of Management*, 16(3): 571–93. (The collision of two plans in Tenerife in 1977 is analysed as a prototype of system vulnerability to crisis.)

Weick, Karl E. (1991) 'The nontraditional quality of organizational learning', *Organization Science*, 2(1): 116–124 (Criticizes the traditional definition of learning borrowed from psychology.)

* Weick, Karl E. (1995) *Sensemaking in Organizations*. Thousands Oaks, CA: Sage.

* Weick, Karl E. and Sandelands, Lloyd E. (1990) 'Social behavior in organizational studies', *Journal for the Theory of Social Behaviour*, 20(4): 323–346. (Summarizes main problems and achievements of organization research in the context of social science.)

* Weick, Karl E. and Westley, Frances (1996) 'Organizational learning: Affirming an oxymoron', In: *Handbook of organization studies*, Sage: London, 440–58. (Redefines the concept of organizational learning setting it in the context of culture and language.)

See also: LINDBLOM, C.E.; MARCH, J.G. AND CYERT, R.M.;MORGAN, G.

Related topics in the IEBM: DECISION MAKING; OCCUPATIONAL PSYCHOLOGY; ORGANIZATION BEHAVIOUR; ORGANIZATION BEHAVIOUR, HISTORY OF; ORGANIZATION PARADIGMS; ORGANIZATIONAL LEARNING; ORGANIZING, PROCESS OF

Wiener, Norbert (1894–1964)

Personal background

- born 26 November 1894, Columbia, Missouri, USA
- at the age of 10, wrote his first paper entitled 'The theory of ignorance'
- studied mathematics and philosophy at Harvard University
- at 19 he received a doctorate in philosophy from Harvard University
- married to Margaret Engelmann, 1926
- pioneer of the new science of cybernetics
- spent most of his academic life at the Massachusetts Institute of Technology (USA) as professor of mathematics
- was author of over 200 papers in mathematical and scientific journals and eleven books
- received five prizes and medals – including the National Medal of Science from the US president – and three honorary doctorates
- died of a heart attack in Stockholm on 18 March 1964

Major works

Cybernetics: or Control and Communication in the Animal and the Machine (1948)
The Human Use of Human Beings: Cybernetics and Society (1950)
Ex-prodigy (1952)
I am a Mathematician (1956)
God and Golem, Inc. (1964)
Invention: The Care and Feeding of Ideas (1993)

Summary

Norbert Wiener (1894–1964) was the father of cybernetics, an interdisciplinary new science that was born after the Second World War. Cybernetics created connections between wartime science and post-war social science by developing a non-causalistic and ecological view of systems, both physical and biological. In his books about cybernetics Wiener showed the existence of invariants in the communication and control mechanisms that are observed in both animals and machines. Cybernetic principles have provided, on the one hand, basic principles for the design of many sorts of machines such as radar, communication networks, computers and artificial limbs, and on the other hand, fundamental insights to the study of animal characteristics like learning, memory and intelligence. Cybernetic ideas have also been widely developed and used in the managerial sciences and in a much broader sociological context.

1 Introduction

Norbert Wiener was a mathematical prodigy who at the age of 19 obtained his doctorate in philosophy at Harvard University. He spent most of his academic life at the Massachusetts Institute of Technology (MIT) as professor of mathematics where he wrote over 200 papers in mathematical and scientific journals, and eleven books. Since his early scientific works in the development of a mathematical theory of Brownian motion and a mathematical interpretation of quantum mechanics, two of the more important research topics in theoretical physics at that time (1920s), Wiener appeared as an unusual mathematician because of the integration of the content of his mathematical work with his personal philosophy. For Wiener, mathematical theories were special instances in which general philosophical ideas are made concrete. His philosophical approach pointed to a unified view of the world, including human beings, where everything is connected to everything else, but in which the most general principles have an element of vagueness (Heims 1980: 140, 156). Such a holistic (or ecological) view of nature was well ahead of its time for an early twentieth-century scientist.

2 Main contribution

During the Second World War, the US Office of Scientific Research and Development gave priority to the solution of the long-range problem of atomic bomb construction and the more immediate problem of finding a way to attack German bomb-carrying aircraft. While the work on the atomic bomb was centred at Los Alamos, the problem of tracking and shooting down aircraft was concentrated at MIT where Wiener was in charge of developing the necessary mathematical foundations for solving it. Working with a young engineer, Julian Bigelow, Wiener developed a mathematical theory of great generality for predicting the future as best one can on the basis of incomplete information from the past. This theory helped revolutionize the whole field of communication engineering and formed the basis of modern statistical communication theory (Heims 1980: 184). At that time (1940s) the theory immediately led to great improvement in radar observations of aircraft and was successfully applied in the design of noise filters for radios, telephones and many other devices of common use (Wiener 1993). This work was carried out independently around the same time that Claude Shannon was developing his 'mathematical theory of communication' (Shannon and Weaver 1949).

One particularly interesting feature of the anti-aircraft problem was the cycle involving feedback: information from a radar screen was used to calculate the adjustments needed on gun controls to improve accuracy on the target, then the effectiveness of this adjustment was observed and communicated again via radar, and this new information used again to readjust the aim of the gun and so on. If the calculations are automated this is a self-steering device; if not, the whole system including the participating persons is a self-steering device. It was Wiener's crucial

insight that a similar feedback mechanism is involved in all voluntary activity, for example, in the act of picking up a pencil from a table. Here information perceived mainly through observation continually guides the movements of the muscles in our arm and hand until this particular task has been successfully achieved. Wiener discussed these ideas with the Mexican physiologist Arturo Rosenblueth, who suggested that some common disorders of the nervous system, generically known as ataxia, could possibly be explained in terms of failures of this feedback mechanism. If you offer a cigarette to a person suffering from ataxia, they will swing their hand past it in trying to pick it up. This will be followed by an equally futile swing in the opposite direction, and then by a third swing back, until the motion becomes nothing more than a vain and violent oscillation.

The idea that some parallels between engineering devices and living organisms could be found through mathematical formulations received extraordinary support from many scientists of quite diverse backgrounds. On 8 March 1946, in a hotel in New York, twenty-one scientists met to talk about these ideas. That was the first of a series of conferences sponsored by the Macy Foundation – a philanthropic medical foundation – out of which the principles of a new science were formulated: cybernetics. The group of scientists who met regularly during those years (from 1946 to 1953) is known as the 'cybernetics group' (Heims 1991), and included names such as the great mathematician John von Neumann, the neuropsychiatrist Warren McCulloch and the social scientist Gregory Bateson, along with Arturo Rosenblueth and Wiener himself.

In his classic book, *Cybernetics: or Control and Communication in the Animal and the Machine* (1948), Wiener named and presented the foundations of cybernetics, one of the youngest scientific disciplines of the twentieth century. Etymologically the name selected by Wiener came from the Greek or steersman. In choosing this term he wished to acknowledge that the first significant paper on feedback mechanisms was an article on governors written by Clerk Maxwell in 1868, and that 'governor' is derived from a Latin corruption of *gubernatur*. Plato had used this term to describe the science of the steering of ships, while in the nineteenth century the French scientist AmpÉre had also borrowed the term as a name for the science of government.

By showing the fact that some underlying unity did indeed exist between control mechanisms in different sciences, cybernetics made irrelevant the old philosophical controversy between vitalism and mechanicism, which had claimed that biological and physical systems were naturally distinct. In fact, cybernetics, in accordance with Wiener's philosophical standpoint, permitted a much broader classification of systems, reflecting its interdisciplinary nature (Wiener 1993: 84). A useful criterion for this classification is that of complexity. According to this category the main concern of cybernetics is the study of exceedingly complex (that is, so complex that they cannot be described in a precise and detailed fashion) and probabilistic (as opposed to deterministic) systems (Beer 1959: 18). Typical examples of these systems are the economy, the brain and the company.

To study the control and communication mechanisms of these sorts of systems Wiener and his colleagues developed a deep understanding of concepts like feedback, homeostasis and the 'black box'. Although the feedback mechanism has already been mentioned, it is interesting to look at its main characteristics in more detail. Each feedback loop involves some input information, such as the measurement of temperature, and some output, such as the heating of the room; moreover – and this is the crucial feature – the input information is affected by the output, for example, the output of the heater will determine the subsequent temperature reading, which in turn will determine whether the heater will be turned on or off. In this way it is continuously showing the difference between a desired situation and the existing one. If the control mechanism reduces this difference it is called a negative feedback (as in the case of the thermostat); if it increases the difference it is called a positive feedback (as in the case of power-assisted brakes which detect small manual movements

made and enlarge them until the force applied is capable of stopping the moving car).

In his *Cybernetics* book (1948), Wiener showed that feedback mechanisms are found in many systems of a totally different nature, from machines to economics and from sociology to biology. A special group of feedback loops which appears to be essential for the continuation of life is found in what is known as homeostasis. The classic biological example is the homeostasis of blood temperature in which the body temperature varies very little although the body passes from refrigerator to furnace-room. A homeostat is thus a control device for holding some variables between desired limits. The well-known Watt's governor of a steam engine, which serves to regulate its velocity under varying conditions of load, is a typical homeostat. What is important to understand here is that the movement of the controlled variable away from its desired value (the speed is too high or too slow in the steam engine) itself operates the regulatory feedback (the valves are closed or opened respectively in Watt's governor). In other words, for as long as the mechanism does not break, the feedback controller cannot fail. The corollary of this statement is extraordinary because it implies that the feedback controller not only is guaranteed to operate against a given kind of disturbance, but against all kind of disturbances (Beer 1959: 29). This special characteristic of control systems is commonly known as ultrastability (Ashby 1956).

By now it should be clear that 'control' in cybernetics does not refer to its naive interpretation as a crude process of coercion, but instead refers to self-regulation.

Another important concept in cybernetics that has permeated many other sciences is that of the black box. Cybernetics, as stated above, is mainly concerned with the study of control and communication mechanisms of exceedingly complex and probabilistic systems. To study control cyberneticians use the concepts of feedback and homeostasis; to deal with the probabilistic characteristics of systems they use the statistical theory of information; and to deal with extreme complexity they use black boxes. By representing a system as a black box cyberneticians are tacitly accepting their cognitive limitations in understanding the huge range of possible states which an exceedingly complex system can be in at any moment in time. However, they recognize some inputs that can be manipulated and some outputs that can be observed. If the outputs are continuously compared with some desirable values some responses could be determined to affect the inputs of the black box in order to maintain the system 'under control'.

By modelling a system as a black box four sets of variables are identified: a set 'S' of possible states in which the system can be, according to some purpose defining the nature of the study; a set 'P' of perturbations that effect the current state of the system; a set 'R' of responses to these perturbations; and a set 'T', or target set, determining the accepted states (according to some established criteria) of the system. The system is said to be 'under control' if at any time its states are elements of the target set T. An extremely important cybernetic principle is obtained from this modelling: indeed, for the system to be under control it is necessary that a response should exist for any perturbation taking the system out of its target set in such a way that after applying this response to the system its subsequent state is in the target set. This principle was established by the British cybernetician Ross Ashby and is known as the 'law of requisite variety', commonly phrased as 'only variety absorbs variety' (Ashby 1956).

Wiener's experiences with machines began very early in his scientific career (Wiener 1993). In the 1920s, long before computers existed, he devised a method for evaluating a general class of integrals by passing a beam of light through some screens and measuring the intensity of the resulting beam. This invention was in fact an analog computer that was known as the Wiener integraph. About twenty years later, in 1940, he wrote a memorandum for the government in which he proposed five points to be followed in the design of computer development: it should be digital, rather than analog; it should use binary numbers; it should be electronic; its logical structure should follow the principles of a Turing machine; and it should use magnetic tapes for data storage. Although this memorandum was ignored for many years the same ideas developed independently by other scientists gave rise to the modern high-speed digital computers.

3 Applications

Much of the early research associated with cybernetics involved the design and development of machines. The electronic tortoises built by the British neurologist Grey Walter were intended to demonstrate that by putting together a few simple mechanisms, with the correct system of feedback, extremely complex behaviour patterns could be produced of almost the same type as those seen in living systems. By the same time another British cybernetician, Gordon Pask, had developed a teaching machine initiating a process that years later gave rise to the development and publication of his *Conversation Theory* (1975). Pask's machine itself displayed the information that had to be learned, received the trainee's response and used this response as a feedback to proceed with the teaching process. In this way his machine was able to teach, by continuously adapting itself to the trainee's personal abilities to learn. Similarly, Wiener himself dedicated much of his time during the 1950s and early 1960s to the design of a device to replace an amputated limb, including its tactile sensibility. His work with a team of orthopedic surgeons, neurologists and engineers (although unsuccessful at that time) paved the way for the subsequent development of the effective prosthetic known as the Boston Arm.

This initial work on machines had the dual intention of demonstrating the practical applicability of cybernetic ideas and, at the same time, being used as a tool for studying complex systems like the human nervous system as well as understanding animal characteristics like learning, memory and intelligence. As an example of the latter Wiener – in a second edition of his book on cybernetics (Wiener [1948] 1961) – explained in some detail how to build a machine to play chess at an acceptable level. Now almost any personal computer can easily beat most non-professional chess players. Unfortunately, and perhaps because of the initial impact caused by these practical applications of cybernetic ideas, the whole scientific discipline has come to be associated with hardware, particularly with computers, despite its principles still being used in other disciplines.

In the area of management sciences perhaps the most important development of Wiener's original ideas has come from Stafford Beer who, by modelling a company as a set of interconnected homeostats and using Ashby's law of requisite variety, developed the viable system model (VSM) (Beer 1979, 1981, 1985). The VSM – an important achievement of the branch of cybernetics known as management cybernetics – has proved to be a useful tool for the diagnosis and even design of complex organizations, ranging from small companies to multinationals and from local government to the economy of a whole country (Espejo and Harnden 1989).

By the end of the 1970s some social scientists were trying to extend and enrich cybernetics by merging it with sociology in what they called 'socio-cybernetics'. However, some paradoxes were found which seemed very hard to solve (Geyer and Zouwen 1986). It was work in the field of the biology of cognition (see for example, Maturana and Varela 1987; Foerster 1984) that established the platform for the development of social cybernetics. This theory, known as 'second-order cybernetics' (Foerster 1979), is a non-objectivistic approach to scientific enquiry that emphasizes the role of the observer in social systems.

In this way, second-order cybernetics, by stressing the autonomy of individuals and studying the continuous processes by which they construct their shared reality, points to a new paradigm in social research which could lead to – recalling the title of one of Wiener's books – a more 'human use of human beings' (Wiener 1950).

RAUL ESPEJO
UNIVERSITY OF LINCOLNSHIRE AND
HUMBERSIDE

ALFONSO REYES
UNIVERSIDAD DE LOS ANDES

Further reading

(References cited in the text marked *)

* Ashby, R. (1956) *An Introduction to Cybernetics*, London: Chapman & Hall. (Explains the concepts of cybernetics, including the law of requisite variety, and contains exercises.)
* Beer, S. (1959) *Cybernetics and Management*, London: The English University Press. (The author explains cybernetics and shows how it can be used to study management problems.)
* Beer, S. (1979) *The Heart of Enterprise*, Chichester: Wiley. (Describes the development of a logical model for studying systems such as any enterprise.)
* Beer, S. (1981) *Brain of the Firm*, 2nd edn, Chichester: Wiley. (The original development of the viable system model (VSM), it starts from insights derived from the human nervous system.)
* Beer, S. (1985) *Diagnosing the System for Organizations*, Chichester: Wiley. (A manual of how to apply the VSM; full of explanatory graphics and methodological tips.)
* Espejo, R. and Harnden, R. (eds) (1989) *The Viable System Model: Interpretations and Applications of Stafford Beer's VSM*, Chichester: Wiley. (Contains a balanced, reflective and critical assessment of the VSM. Some practical applications are discussed.)
* Foerster, H. von (1979) 'Cybernetics of cybernetics', in K. Krippendorff (ed.), *Communication and Control in Society*, New York: Gordon and Breach. (Considers the importance of self-referential systems, such as social systems, and shows the necessity of a second-order cybernetics to study them.)
* Foerster, H. von (1984) *Observing Systems*, Seaside, CA: Intersystems Publications. (A collection of papers moving towards constructivism; that is, seeing reality as invented rather than discovered.)
* Geyer, F. and Zowen, J. van der (eds) (1986) *Socio-cybernetics Paradoxes: Observation, Control and Evolution of Self-Steering Systems*, London: Sage Publications. (A series of articles exploring the possibilities and limitations of socio-cybernetics in the study of social problems.)
* Heims, S. (1980) *John von Neumann and Norbert Wiener: From Mathematics to the Technologies of Life and Death*, Cambridge, MA: MIT Press. (A double biography of two brilliant and innovative scientists, critically analysing their

differences in personality and philosophy and their contributions to modern science.)

* Heims, S. (1991) *The Cybernetics Group*, Cambridge, MA: MIT Press. (The story of a remarkable group who met regularly between 1946 and 1953 to explore how to use cybernetics, information theory and computer theory as a basis for interdisciplinary alliances.)

* Maturana, H. and Varela, F. (1987) *The Tree of Knowledge: The Biological Roots of Human Understanding*, Boston, MA: Shambhala. (Presents an understanding of cognition not as reflecting an objective reality, but as a continuous bringing-forth of a world through our co-existence with others.)

* Pask, G. (1975) *Conversation, Cognition and Learning: A Cybernetic Theory and Methodology*, Amsterdam: Elsevier. (Describes a theory of person-to-person or person-to-machine conversations and cognitive processes.)

* Shannon, C. and Weaver, W. (1949) *The Mathematical Theory of Communication*, Urbana, IL: University of Illinois Press. (Contains a simple explanation of the theory of communication and develops a rigorous mathematical account of concepts like 'information', 'noise', 'coding' and 'communication'.)

* Wiener, N. (1948; 2nd edn 1961) *Cybernetics: or Control and Communication in the Animal and the Machine*, New York: Wiley. (A relatively short and easy book explaining cybernetics, contains examples and some mathematical sections. In the second edition Wiener adds chapters showing the relevance of cybernetics to learning, artificial intelligence, adaption and language.)

* Wiener, N. (1950) *The Human Use of Human Beings: Cybernetics and Society*, English edn, London: Eyre and Spottiswoode (1954). (Describes cybernetics for the layperson, showing Wiener's ethical considerations in relation to science and the application of cybernetics.)

Wiener, N. (1952) *Ex-prodigy*, paperback edn, Cambridge, MA: MIT Press, 1964. (The first volume of Wiener's autobiography, it concentrates on his years as a child prodigy and his relationship with his father.)

Wiener, N. (1956) *I am a Mathematician*, paperback edn, Cambridge, MA: MIT Press, 1964. (The second volume of Wiener's autobiography, it covers his mature personal and scientific career and intellectual development.)

Wiener, N. (1964) *God and Golem, Inc.*, Cambridge, MA: MIT Press. (The sequel to *The Human Use of Human Beings*, outlining how cybernetics impinges on society, ethics and religion.)

* Wiener, N. (1993) *Invention: The Care and Feeding of Ideas*, Cambridge, MA: MIT Press. (A historical account of discovery and invention showing the importance of the intellectual, technical, social and scientific climate for the development of original ideas.)

See also: ACKOFF, R.L.; BEER, S.; VICKERS, G.; VON BERTALANFFY, L.

Related topics in the IEBM: ARTIFICIAL INTELLIGENCE; CYBERNETICS; INFORMATION TECHNOLOGY; ORGANIZATIONAL BEHAVIOUR, HISTORY OF; SYSTEMS; SYSTEMS ANALYSIS AND DESIGN

Williamson, Oliver E. (1932–)

Personal background

- born on 27 September 1932
- professor of economics at University of Pennsylvania, 1965–83
- professor of economics at Yale University, 1983–88
- applied and developed the transaction cost analysis of Coase
- professor of business, economics and law at University of California at Berkeley

Major works

*Markets and Hierarchies: Analysis and Anti-Trust Implications: A Study in the Economics of Internal
Organization* (1975)
The Economic Institutions of Capitalism: Firms, Markets, Relational Contracting (1985)

Summary

The work of the US new institutional economist Oliver Williamson is one of the most important developments in the analysis of economic institutions. The main inspirations for Williamson have been the works of the two Nobel Laureates, Ronald Coase and Herbert Simon. Williamson developed the earlier transaction cost analysis of Coase to provide explanations of firm behaviour and structure. The behavioural economics of Simon are a key influence in Williamson's work. Williamson has made a theoretical attempt to compare the efficiency of different types of firm structure.

1 Biographical data

Oliver Williamson (born 1932) is former Professor of Economics at Yale University and is currently Professor of Business, Economics and Law at the University of California at Berkeley. Williamson came to prominence in an article published in the *American Economic Review* in 1963 that argued that managers will maximize their own utility rather than, for example, profits or sales. However, it was for his application and development of the transaction cost analysis of Nobel Laureate Ronald Coase (born 1910) that he is most well known (see COASE, R.). The first book in this genre was his *Markets and Hierarchies*, published in 1975. During the subsequent twenty years Williamson has developed and extended this approach in a large number of books and articles, most notably his *Economic Institutions of Capitalism*, published in 1985. His work is widely cited and has been inspirational for a large number of theoretical and applied researchers. His 1975 and 1985 books were two of the three most cited books in economics in the Social Science Citations Index in 1990. His influence has not been confined to economists and it has extended significantly to both legal and business studies.

2 Williamson and transaction costs

A key work in the general development of the mainstream economic thinking about institutions was Williamson's *Markets and Hierarchies*, published in 1975. Williamson was the first to coin the phrase 'new institutionalism' and used it to describe his approach. With this phrase he simultaneously underlined his focus on the inner structures and workings of the firm and his distance from the 'old' institutionalism of Veblen, Mitchell and Commons (see VEBLEN, T.B.). In the next few years this term achieved a wide currency and the study of institutions has become common-place for economists.

The main inspiration for Williamson was a much earlier and classic paper by Ronald Coase (1937). In this article Coase character-ized the firm as an organization that super-sedes the price mechanism and allocates resources by command rather than through price. As Coase himself put it:

> Outside the firm, price movements direct production, which is co-ordinated through a series of exchange transactions on the market. Within a firm, these market trans-actions are eliminated and in place of the complicated market structure with ex-change transactions is substituted the entrepreneur-co-ordinator, who directs production.
>
> (Coase 1937: 338)

Coase explained this phenomenon by arguing that the firm arises because of the relatively greater 'cost of using the price mechanism' (Coase 1937: 390).

Following on from Coase, Williamson de-veloped his central thesis that economic insti-tutions such as the firm 'have the main purpose and effect of economizing on transac-tion costs' (Williamson 1985: 1). The ap-proach of both Coase and Williamson can be characterized as contractarian because institu-tions are seen as emerging from contracts be-tween individuals. In particular, employment contracts emerge when the transaction costs of alternative market arrangements are too high.

However, the Coase–Williamson argu-ment contrasts with other contractarian ap-proaches that reduce all firm and market phenomena to identical types of contract. Wil-liamson recognizes a key polarity between 'markets' and 'hierarchies' and sees the latter as emerging because of specific asset and information-based efficiency considerations.

Much of Williamson's work is concerned with spelling out the implications of this ap-proach. For example, he argues that if two firms trade with each other and rely on assets that are highly specific to that relationship and cannot readily or cheaply be traded elsewhere – an example is a steel mill relying on a local supply of iron ore – then the transaction costs of an enduring relationship are likely to be high and the firms are likely to have an incen-tive to integrate vertically in order to reduce those costs. Much of the empirical work on transaction costs looks at this issue of 'asset specificity'.

As another important example, William-son compares two forms of hierarchical or-ganization, the unitary ('U-form') and multidivisional ('M-form') structures. He ar-gues that the M-form is often a more efficient way of administering particular types of transactions. It is argued that the M-form al-lows incentives to be aligned more closely to corporate goals and promotes the use of op-erational rather than functional criteria of managerial evaluation. On this basis it is claimed that the spread of the multidivisional form in modern capitalism is explained.

3 Williamson and behaviouralism

In its close attention to non-market forms of organization, Williamson departs from much of mainstream economics. Furthermore, Wil-liamson is influenced by Herbert Simon and the behaviouralist school; Simon is well known as a critic of mainstream assumptions of rationality (see SIMON, H.A.). However, on closer inspection it is evident that William-son's break from neo-classical theory is par-tial and incomplete, and much of the core apparatus of neo-classical economics is retained. In fact, Williamson's claimed depar-ture from orthodoxy sits uneasily alongside his repeated invocation that agents are marked by 'opportunism' (that is, 'self--interest seeking with guile'). As convention-ally presented, self-interested behaviour is a typical feature of 'economic man'.

Simon (1957) argued that complete or global rational calculation is ruled out, hence rationality is 'bounded'. Agents do not maxi-mize but attempt to attain acceptable minima instead. It is important to note that this 'sati-sficing' behaviour does not simply arise be-cause of inadequate information, but also because it would be too difficult to perform the calculations even if the relevant information was available. Contrary to a prevailing neo-classical interpretation of Simon's work, the recognition of bounded rationality refers primarily to the matter of computational capacity and not to additional 'costs'. Hence 'satisficing' does not amount to cost-minimizing behaviour. Clearly, the latter is just the dual of the standard assumption of maximization; if 'satisficing' was essentially a matter of minimizing costs then it would amount to maximizing behaviour of the neo-classical type.

Williamson (1990: 161) simply replicates this view when he accepts the term 'bounded rationality' rather than 'satisficing' because he regards the latter as 'a contentious and separate issue'. Clearly, Williamson adopts the neo-classical, cost-minimizing interpretation of Simon and not the one that clearly prevails in Simon's own work. In Williamson's work 'economizing on transaction costs' is part of global, cost-minimizing behaviour, and this is in fact inconsistent with Simon's idea of bounded rationality. The cost calculus remains supreme in his theory and there is no essential break with the neo-classical assumption of maximization.

4 Institutions and efficiency

According to Williamson, organizations with lower transaction costs are more likely to survive in a competitive world. In several passages Williamson (1975, 1985) asserts that because hierarchical firms exist, then they must be relatively efficient and more suited to survival. Thus, in his theoretical attempt to compare the efficiency of different types of firm structure, Williamson (1980: 35) concludes that 'it is no accident that hierarchy is ubiquitous within all organizations of any size. . . . In short, inveighing against hierarchy is rhetoric; both the logic and efficiency and the historical evidence disclose that nonhierarchical modes are mainly of ephemeral duration'.

However, this argument has been widely criticized, particularly for the neglect of path dependency. It also contrasts with the recent work of other 'new institutionalists' such as Douglass North, where path dependence is recognized. The explanation of emergence and survival in evolution is not the same thing as an explanation of efficiency, even if the latter may enhance the chances of survival in the future. Strictly, in order to explain the existence of a structure it is neither necessary nor sufficient to show that it is efficient. Inefficient structures do happen to exist and survive, and many possible efficient structures will never actually emerge or be selected.

Essentially, Williamson's transaction cost argument involves comparative statics. Typically, the incidence of transaction costs in equilibrium is compared in two or more governance structures, and the structure with the lowest costs is deemed to be more efficient. In fact Williamson (1985: 143–4) admits that a shift from considerations of static to those of dynamic efficiency is not encompassed by his theory: 'the study of economic organization in a regime of rapid innovation poses much more difficult issues than those addressed here. . . . Much more study of the relations between organization and innovation is needed.' It is questionable whether the comparative statics approach can do justice to important dynamic developments such as technological change. Particularly on this point, 'evolutionary' (Richard Nelson and Sidney Winter) and 'competence-based' (Edith Penrose) theorists of the firm claim they have overcome the limitations of comparative statics.

Transaction cost analyses reduce the interaction between individuals to the calculus of costs. Individuals act as utility-maximizing automata on the basis of given preferences. Social institutions bear upon individuals simply via the costs they impose. Consistent with the retention of the basic neo-classical model of optimizing behaviour, Williamson assumes that individual preferences are unchanged by the economic environment and the institutions in which individuals are located.

Importantly, the assumption of given individuals and preferences is antagonistic to the notion that institutions transform individual preferences, purposes, conceptions and beliefs. Clearly there is an important contrast here with the 'old' institutionalism of Veblen,

Commons, Mitchell, Galbraith and others (see GALBRAITH, J.K.; VEBLEN, T.B.). The contractarian emphasis in the new institutionalism means that non-contractual relations such as trust and loyalty are neglected. Just as seriously, the conception of the given individual cannot readily incorporate notions such as learning and personal development.

Williamson assumes that individual preferences are unchanged by the economic environment and the institutions in which individuals are located. However, it can be argued that an important difference between the market and the firm is that actors tend to behave in a different manner with differing goals. According to this alternative perspective, a key to understanding the nature of the firm is its ability to mould human preferences and actions so that a higher degree of loyalty and trust is engendered.

5 Conclusion

Whatever its limitations, Williamson's work is one of the most important developments in the analysis of economic institutions. It has been of enormous benefit in bringing questions of internal and intra-firm organization to the fore. Indeed, despite criticism, the Coase–Williamson argument for the existence of firms remains persuasive for many economists. Furthermore, recent work has gone a long way to bring empirical richness to the transaction cost story. Finally, transaction cost analyses have inspired key developments in corporate and competition policy.

GEOFFREY HODGSON
JUDGE INSTITUTE OF MANAGEMENT STUDIES,
UNIVERSITY OF CAMBRIDGE

Further reading

(References cited in the text marked *)

* Coase, R.H. (1937) 'The nature of the firm', *Economica* 4: 386–405. (The classic article that established the transaction cost approach to the theory of the firm – later developed by Williamson. Reprinted in L. Putterman (ed.) (1986) *The Economic Nature of the Firm: A Reader*, Cambridge: Cambridge University Press; and O.E. Williamson and S.G. Winter (eds) (1991) *The Nature of the Firm: Origins, Evolution and Development*, Oxford: Oxford University Press.)
Pitelis, C. (ed.) (1993) *Transaction Costs, Markets and Hierarchies*, Oxford: Blackwell. (A set of critical essays on the transaction costs approach.)
* Simon, H.A. (1957) *Models of Man: Social and Rational Mathematical Essays on Rational Human Behaviour in a Social Setting*, New York: Wiley. (An early statement of the behaviouralism that inspired Williamson.)
* Williamson, O.E. (1975) *Markets and Hierarchies: Analysis and Anti-Trust Implications: A Study in the Economics of Internal Organization*, New York: The Free Press. (Williamson's first major statement of the transaction costs approach.)
* Williamson, O.E. (1980) 'The organization of work: a comparative institutional assessment', *Journal of Economic Behavior and Organization* 1 (1): 5–38. (A notable attempt by Williamson to develop a theory of comparative organizational efficiency. Reprinted and revised in Williamson 1985, chs 9–10.)
* Williamson, O.E. (1985) *The Economic Institutions of Capitalism: Firms, Markets, Relational Contracting*, London: Macmillan. (A milestone development of Williamson's approach.)
* Williamson, O.E. (1990) 'Transaction cost economics', in R. Schmalensee and R.D. Willig (eds), *Handbook of Industrial Organization*, vol. 1, Amsterdam: North Holland. (A concise statement of Williamson's approach and analysis.)

See also: COASE, R.; GALBRAITH, J.K.; MARCH, J.G. AND CYERT, R.M.; MARSHALL, A.; SIMON, H.A.; VEBLEN, T.B.

Related topics in the IEBM: DECISION MAKING; GROWTH OF THE FIRM AND NETWORKING; INSTITUTIONAL ECONOMICS; MANAGERIAL THEORIES OF THE FIRM; NEO-CLASSICAL ECONOMICS; ORGANIZATION STRUCTURE; TRANSACTION COST ECONOMICS

Womack, James Potter, (1948–) and Jones, Daniel Theodore (1948–)

Personal background

Daniel Jones

- born in Sussex, England, 12 June 1948
- graduated in Economics from the University of Sussex, UK (1970)
- Voluntary service overseas on Lake Chad (1971–72)
- MSc in Economics, University of Manchester, UK (1973)
- Research Fellow, National Institute of Economic and Social Research, London (1973–77)
- Senior Research Fellow, University of Sussex (1977–89)
- Professor of Management, Cardiff Business School, UK (1989 onwards)
- developed and disseminated the idea of lean production

James Womack

- born in Little Rock, Arkansas, USA, 27 July 1948
- graduated in Political Science, University of Chicago (1970)
- time out travelling round the world, mainly in North West India (1971)
- read Transport Policy at the Kennedy School, Harvard (1973–75)
- Research fellow, MIT (1975–80)
- Principal Research Scientist, MIT (1980 onwards)
- received Ph.D. on comparative industrial policy in the auto industry in the US, Germany, France and Japan (MIT, 1983)
- developed and disseminated the idea of lean production

Major works

The Future of the Automobile (with Altshuler, A., Anderson, M. and Roos, D.) (1984)
The Machine that Changed the World (with Roos, D.) (1990)
Lean Thinking (1996)

Summary

James P. Womack and Daniel T. Jones are best known for their role in developing and disseminating the concept of 'lean production'. This concept evolved from two large scale studies on the international automotive industry in which Jones and Womack played leading roles. The best known of these was the 1985–90 International Motor Vehicle Programme (IMVP). This programme involved over 55 researchers world-wide, and demonstrated a substantial performance gap between Japanese and non-Japanese vehicle assemblers in terms of both productivity and quality. These performance differences were ascribed to a distinct set of organizing principles, found in their purest form in the Japanese automotive industry, termed 'lean production' principles. Womack and Jones argue that these principles apply not only to manufacturing operations, but to product development, distribution and retailing, and the organization of the supply chain.

Lean production quickly caught the imagination of academics and practitioners alike. The results of the IMVP sent shock waves around the automotive industry, prompting many companies to embark on programmes of manufacturing reform based on lean principles. These principles were eagerly adopted as the new best practice orthodoxy in operations management, though challenged by some, primarily from a critical social science perspective. During the 1990s the term lean production was gradually replaced by terms such as 'lean thinking' or the 'lean enterprise', as the principles were increasingly applied to contexts outside their original home in automotive manufacturing.

1 Biographical data

Pre 1980

Daniel Jones was born in Sussex, England in 1948. He graduated in Economics from the University of Sussex in 1970 and then embarked on voluntary service overseas for two years, running a Fisheries Extension project on Lake Chad. He undertook an M.Sc. in Economics at the University of Manchester, where he developed an interest in industrial performance. In 1973 Jones became a research fellow at the National Institute of Economic and Social Research in London, where he worked on two main projects. The first project investigated the innovation process in energy-related industries in the UK, Sweden and Germany. The second examined industrial performance and industrial structure in Germany, the UK and the USA, using both Industrial Census Data and detailed industrial case studies. Jones describes this work as a 'painstakingly rigorous piece of narrow, traditional industrial economics'. It was later written up in *Productivity and Industrial Structure* (Prais *et a.l* 1981).

In 1977 Jones returned to the University of Sussex, where he was to stay for 12 years, first at the Sussex European Research Centre, and later at the Science Policy Research Unit. Due in part to his previous experience with collaborative projects, and in part to his ability to speak German, Jones' activity in international research ventures continued. Between 1977 and 1981 he was a principal researcher on a project into European Industrial Policy and the evolution of large firms, involving

detailed studies of automotive, machine tool and chemicals industries in Europe.

In 1979 Dan Roos of MIT contacted Jones and invited him to participate in the International Automobile Programme, a project later written up in *The Future of the Automobile*. The project was initially funded by the German Marshall Fund in the USA as a study into environmental and social issues facing the automotive industry with many other governments and foundations later offering additional support. It was in the early stages of this project, in 1979, that Jones and Womack first met, and in Jones' words, 'hit it off from very early on'.

James Womack was born in 1948. He read political science at the University of Chicago, which exposed him to a wide variety of writers, including Marx and Weber. Having completed his degree he took some time out to travel around the world, spending some time in India in the process. On his return to the USA, Womack studied transport policy at the Kennedy School at Harvard, but perceived the field to be dominated by microeconomics, which led him to focus more on issues of network analysis and system optimization. In 1975 he took a research position in transport policy at MIT. At this time, urban transportation was a major issue, and the Nixon administration had a policy objective of promoting underground transportation systems in major cities in the USA. Womack analysed the policy alternatives to motor-vehicle dominant transport systems, largely from a political science perspective.

As the 1970s wore on, environmental and social concerns about motor vehicles grew. Womack's brother worked as a lawyer for the Federal Government's National Highway Traffic Safety Administration based in Washington. This meant that Womack was always close to someone involved in debates about improving vehicle safety and energy efficiency. In addition, by 1979 Womack had concluded that underground transportation systems would have little impact on transportation patterns in the USA. It therefore seemed appropriate to concentrate on the dominant technology, namely the automobile. This drew him to the International

Automobile Programme, co-ordinated out of MIT by Alan Altshuler and Daniel Roos. (Womack had worked with Altshuler in the late 1970s, contributing to Altshuler's *The Urban Transportation System*, published in 1979.) It was during the International Automobile Programme that the Womack/Jones partnership began.

1980 onwards

As with many large scale collaborative projects, the International Automobile Program was characterized by a variety of perspectives on the part of the collaborators, and inevitably conflict was a consequence of this. As project developed, the key issues to Womack and Jones (who had formed a good working relationship), was not the environmental impact of automobiles but the competitive gap opening up between the Japanese and Western car industries.

Both Womack and Jones describe how the early stages of this project were formative experiences for them. Womack describes how a visit to one of the Big Three's Auto Assembly plants in the USA was 'a defining moment' for him. At the end of the factory were two gates; one marked 'major repairs', the other marked 'minor repairs'. All cars went through one gate or the other, and there were as many people employed in rework and repair as were building the vehicles in the first place. Jones describes how he and Womack were amazed at the superiority of what they saw during visits to auto plants in Japan in 1982. This theme of the relative performance of the Japanese and Western car industries became a major element of the project.

At a conference called to launch *The Future of the Automobile* in 1984 a senior industry executive encouraged Jones and Womack to prove definitively the performance gap between Japan and the West. Jay Chai, the head of the Japanese trading company C Itoh (America) and his wife and leading auto industry analyst Maryann Keller helped mobilize Japanese and US auto industry support for the endeavour. First Japanese and then US firms joined in and the IMVP was born, with the first European players coming on board a

year later. Daniel Roos was the overall Director of the IMVP, Womack the Research Director and Jones the European Director.

The IMVP was completed in 1990, although there has been an IMVP II, in which Womack and Jones chose not to participate, feeling that they neither wanted to manage another huge project nor needed the MIT brand name. In 1989 Jones joined Cardiff Business School, initially as Professor of Motor Industry Management. Since then his interests have moved away from the motor industry to the application of lean principles in many different settings. In 1993 he founded the Lean Enterprise Research Centre (LERC) in Cardiff, which he has directed since then. By 1997 the LERC employed 18 full time researchers. Since 1991 Jones has been involved in variety of research programmes in different industries, including benchmarking in the autocomponents industry, supply chain development, automotive distribution and raw materials production and distribution.

Womack largely withdrew from academic life following the publication of *The Machine that Changed the World*, though he continues to have an affiliation with MIT. Having talked about lean principles and process improvement he felt it appropriate to try to put the words into action and so invested in a small, up-market bicycle manufacturing business, in which lean principles were successfully applied to cost reduction. Both Womack and Jones have been in great demand as speakers and consultants following the publication of *The Machine that Changed the World*, and spent much of their time advising companies on the implementation of lean principles. In addition to their consulting work, they spent much of time researching approximately 50 organizations for *Lean Thinking*, which was published in 1996. In 1997 Womack was tiring of consulting during the day, and trying to write during his spare time, and set up the Lean Enterprise Institute as a non-profit educational and research institution to encourage the dissemination of lean principles.

2 The Future of the Automobile

The Future of the Automobile (Altshuler, Anderson, Jones, Roos and Womack) was published in 1984, and summarized the findings of the 1980–84 International Automobile Programme. The initial focus of the project was on the future of the automobile in the light of increasing concerns about its environmental impact, but as the project developed the competitive imbalance between the world's major auto produced assumed increasing significance. The number of collaborators involved was huge (131 researchers under the overall direction of Altshuler and Roos), and the style and content of the book reflects the varied perspectives of those who contributed to it. The book sold over 40,000 copies in three languages.

The Future of the Automobile covers a wide range of issues: the development of the automotive industry, safety and energy issues, the relative performance of different car-making regions and international trade issues. Inevitably, the result is a rather chaotic piece. Womack comments: 'I don't look back on [the book] with any satisfaction'.

However, Womack and Jones' fascination with the production practices of the Japanese producers, in particular the manufacturing accuracy which these practices are able to deliver, clearly comes through in the book. The scene was set for a more thorough investigation of this issue, and it was this that culminated in the 1985–90 International Motor Vehicle Programme, and the subsequent publication of *The Machine that Changed the World* in 1990.

3 The Machine that Changed the World

This book sold over 400,000 copies in the seven years following its publication, has been translated into 11 languages, and has attracted extremes of praise and criticism. The book, voted business book of the year in 1990 by the *Financial Times*, is a synthesis of the findings of the 1985–90 International Motor Vehicle Programme.

Although IMVP covered all aspects of designing and producing automobiles, it was the study of the manufacturing performance of approximately 80 auto assembly plants across the world that captivated most readers and reviewers. This study revealed a substantial superiority – approaching 2:1 – between assembly plants in Japan and their non-Japanese counterparts on measures of productivity and quality. In addition to the assembly plant study, the IMVP covered new product development, relations with suppliers and retailing and distribution. The book has a strong story line, in which the traditional mass production methods of Henry Ford are portrayed as being swept away by the rise of 'lean production' methods – a new form of production organization, found in its purest form in Toyota in Japan. The book deals with processes of automotive design and development, manufacturing, supplier relationships and distribution, but it is manufacturing which takes centre stage.

Lean production principles include: integrated single piece production flow, with small batches made just-in-time; an emphasis on defect prevention rather than rectification; production which is pulled by consumption, not pushed to suit machine loading; team based work organization, with flexible, multiskilled operators; active involvement in problem-solving activities by all personnel, eliminating waste, interruptions and variability; and close integration of the whole supply chain from raw materials to retailing and distribution, back up by close buyer–supplier relationships based on trust and collaboration rather than competition.

The Machine that Changed the World proved to be a powerful cocktail for a number of reasons. Mass and lean production are set in a chronology, the latter addressing many of the acknowledged weaknesses of the former. The size of the performance gap between the Japanese producers and the rest of the world had a tremendous shock value, demonstrating to many that change was imperative. Lean production systems not only promised an answer to the performance problem, but also a more interesting and challenging work experience to those working within such systems, due to opportunities for problem-solving. Importantly, Womack, Jones and Roos argued that the successful implementation of lean production methods was not dependent on the Japanese cultural context, pointing to the Japanese auto transplant factories in North America, whose performance levels were not too far behind those of their Japanese parents.

> We believe that the fundamental ideas of lean production are universal – applicable anywhere by anyone – and that many non-Japanese companies have already learned this
>   (Womack, Jones and Roos, 1990: 9).

> We think it is in everyone's interest to introduce lean production everywhere, as soon as possible
>   (Womack, Jones and Roos, 1990: 256).

The sales of *The Machine that Changed the World* are a testament to the appeal of the book. However, there have been critical responses as well, the most ardent of which are represented by a group radical economists in the UK, who published a whole book as a rejoinder to lean production (Williams *et al*. 1994). They object to *The Machine that Changed the World* on both ideological and empirical grounds, accusing it of an 'unconscious managerialism' and claiming that the firm as the unit of analysis is overemphasized, to the neglect of economic and structural conditions. In addition, these critics allege that the IMVP method of plant productivity comparison is flawed, and that the 2:1 productivity superiority of the Japanese is not supported by secondary data. Furthermore, the exceptional performance of Toyota in Japan, rests on a unique interplay between its production system and the market conditions and therefore cannot be ascribed to a universally applicable set of principles. Commentators writing from a labour process perspective challenge the claim that lean production methods lead to a superior work experience, arguing that the lean production methods lead to more intense work, and by implication, a more exploitative employment relationship.

4 Lean Thinking

Lean Thinking represented a significant shift in style from the earlier work of Womack and Jones. It was the first book that they had produced that was not part of a large project involving many collaborators and it did not address major issues of *public* policy, such as environmental impact or relative competitiveness. Although *The Machine that Changed the World* had been written for practitioner audiences, the book blended the authority of large scale comparative empirical evidence with a strong story about the evolution of different approaches to the organization of production (and development, supply and distribution). In contrast, *Lean Thinking* was not concerned with international comparisons of productive performance, but was aimed at chief executives struggling with the implementation of lean principles. Perhaps it is this absence of a strong public story that explains the relatively muted response to the book by the media, though its appeal to practitioners may be seen from its sales over 100,000 in the year following publication – a faster rate of sales than *The Machine that Changed the World*. In 1997 the book was being translated into eight languages.

Lean Thinking identifies five key lean principles:

- The precise specification of value from the end customer's perspective, in terms of product capabilities, price and availability.
- The identification of the entire value stream for a product or product family, and the elimination of wasteful steps within this.
- The facilitation of flow between the value-creating steps which remain, eliminating waiting, downtime and scrap within and between steps.
- Control of flow by customer 'pull', not production 'push', providing only what the customer wants at the time it is wanted.
- The continuous pursuit of perfection – continuous effort to reduce effort, time, space and errors.

These principles are illustrated throughout the book with case studies of various organizations, including a bicycle manufacturer, Pratt and Whitney jet engines, and Porsche. The benefits which Womack and Jones claim typically accrue from the application of these principles are substantial – a doubling of labour productivity, a reduction in inventory and throughput times by 90 per cent and a halving of defect rates. These benefits may be expected during the first realignment towards lean principles; continuous improvement effort should result in a doubling of performance levels within two or three years (Womack and Jones 1996). In the light of this, it is not surprising that *Lean Thinking* sold so well in the months following its launch.

5 Conclusions

It is not easy to assess the long-term impact of work which has been relatively recently completed, or which is still ongoing. However, in their work so far, and particularly with *The Machine That Changed the World*, Womack and Jones and their collaborators have achieved something which is unusual amongst management writers. They have succeeded in leveraging the efforts of large international research teams, and (initially with the help of Dan Roos) have been very successful in raising substantial commercial sponsorship for these efforts. Their material has proved stimulating to both practitioners and to academics from many disciplines. Labour process academics have been intrigued by the implications of lean production principles for labour; operations management academics have eagerly, if uncritically, adopted lean principles as a best practice orthodoxy. Across the world managers have attempted to implement lean principles, sometimes supported, sometimes resisted, by labour unions. Lean production principles have excited evangelism on the part of their supporters, and challenges on the part of their critics, who argue that issues of market constraints and economic structures are given too little attention. Whatever view one favours, there is no doubt that Womack and Jones have stimulated extensive and fruitful debate about the

way humans organize for productive activity. In the course of their partnership, the emphasis has shifted from that of academic analysis to the active promotion of change, as the three books reviewed here demonstrate.

In 1997, both Womack and Jones were anticipating further joint work together. Womack, reflecting on the future, commented:

> The overt objective of the writing is to change the behaviour of the reader... we don't easily fit into the academic world . . . we're like two management priests or monks. We're catalysts, rather than analysts.

NICK OLIVER
JUDGE INSTITUTE OF MANAGEMENT STUDIES,
UNIVERSITY OF CAMBRIDGE

Further reading

(References cited in the text marked *)

* Altshuler, A. with Womack, J.P. and Pucher, J.R. (1979) *The Urban Transportation System: Politics and Policy Innovation*, Cambridge, MA: MIT Press. (Described by Jones as part of Womack's apprenticeship in writing books.)
* Altshuler, A, Anderson, M., Jones, D., Roos, D. and Womack, J. (1984) *The Future of the Automobile*, London: George Allen and Unwin, and Boston: MIT Press. (Initially concerned with the social and environmental challenges facing the automobile, but contains some early observations on the superiority of the Japanese automakers.)
Abo, T. (ed) (1994) *Hybrid Factory: The Japanese Production System in the United States*, Oxford: Oxford University Press. (Study of Japanese transplant factories. Concludes that Japanese firms adapt their practices when operating outside Japan.)
Clark, K.B. and Fujimoto, T. (1991) *Product Development Performance*, Boston: Harvard Business School Press. (Study of new product development patterns in the international automotive industry.)
Cusumano, M. (1985) *The Japanese Automobile Industry: Technology and Management at Nissan and Toyota*, Cambridge, MA: Harvard University Press. (Historical account of the development of Nissan and Toyota. Illustrates the differences between Japanese auto assemblers.)

Cusumano, M. (1994) 'The Limits of Lean', *Sloan Management Review*, Summer, 27–32. (Discussion of the factors that may limit the application of lean production principles.)

Fucini, J.J. and Fucini, S. (1990) *Working for the Japanese*, New York, Free Press. (Critical account of life inside Mazda's Flatrock assembly plant in the USA.)

Kenney, M. and Florida, R. (1993) *Beyond Mass Production: The Japanese System and its Transfer to the US*, Oxford: Oxford University Press. (Empirical account of the transfer of lean principles to the US, with an emphasis on Japanese transplant factories.)

Lillrank, P. (1995) 'The transfer of management innovations from Japan', *Organization Studies*, 16(6): 971–989. (Describes the process by which ideas from one context are transferred to other environments.)

Monden, Y. (1983) *Toyota Production System*, Atlanta, Georgia: Industrial Engineering and Management Press. (A dry but thorough description of the Toyota Production System.)

Ohno, T. (1988) *Just-in-Time for Today and Tomorrow*, Productivity Press: Cambridge, MA. (Description of the Toyota Production System by its chief architect.)

* Prais, S.J. *et al.* (1981) *Productivity and Industrial Structure*, Cambridge: Cambridge University Press. (Described by Jones as his apprenticeship in writing books.)

Wickens, P. (1993) 'Lean production and beyond: the system, its critics and the future', *Human Resource Management Journal*, 3(4): 75–90. (Observations on the lean production system by the ex Personnel Director of Nissan UK.)

Williams, K., Haslam, C., Williams, J., Cutler, T., Adcroft, A. and Johal, S. (1992) 'Against Lean Production', *Economy and Society*, 21(3): 321–354. (Rather polemical but stimulating critique of *The Machine that Changed the World*.)

* Williams, K., Haslam, C. Johal, S. and Williams, J. (1994) *Cars: Analysis, History, Cases*, Providence: Berghahn Books. (Argues the case for structural, rather than managerial explanations of company performance.)

* Womack, J.P., Jones D.T. and Roos, D. (1990) *The Machine that Changed the World: The Triumph of Lean Production*, New York: Rawson Macmillan. (The seminal work, containing dramatic performance comparisons tied together by a strong story line.)

Womack, J.P. and Jones, D.T. (1994) 'From Lean Production to the Lean Enterprise', *Harvard Business Review*, March/April. (Argues for the need to think about whole value chains rather than individual enterprises.)

* Womack, J.P. and Jones, D.T. (1996) 'Beyond Toyota: How to Root Out Waste and Pursue Perfection', *Harvard Business Review*, September/October. (Nice summary of the main points in *Lean Thinking*, with a case example.)

* Womack, J.P. and Jones, D.T. (1996) *Lean Thinking*, New York: Simon and Schuster. (The how-to-do-it version of lean production, with case examples.)

See aslo: HAMMER, M.; OHNO, T.; SHINGO, S.; TAYLOR, F.W.

Related topics in the IEBM: BUSINESS ECONOMICS ; BUSINESS HSITORY; GLOBALIZATION; INTERNATIONAL MARKETING; JAPANIZATION; JUST-IN-TIME PHILOSOPHIES; MANUFACTURING MANAGEMENT; ORGANIZATION BEHAVIOUR; ORGANIZATION BEHAVIOUR, HISTORY OF; RE-ENGINEERING; STRATEGY, CONCEPT OF; SUPPLY-CHAIN; WORK SYSTEMS

Woodward, Joan (1916–71)

Personal background

- born 19 June 1916
- 1936, BA (Hons), Class 1, philosophy, politics and economics, University of Oxford
- 1938, MA medieval philosophy, University of Durham
- 1939, diploma in social and public administration, University of Oxford
- 1939–46, Industrial War Service, Lancashire textiles, Buckinghamshire electronics, Royal Ordnance Factory, Bridgwater
- 1946–8, Administrative class of Civil Service, Ministry of Supply
- 1948–53, University of Liverpool, lecturer and senior research fellow
- 1951, married Leslie Thompson Blakeman, who became Director of Labour Relations for The Ford Motor Company and a member of the Commission on Industrial Relations
- 1953–7, Director, Department of Scientific and Industrial Research Human Relations Research Unit, South East Essex Technical College
- 1957–62, University of Oxford, lecturer and special tutor in industrial sociology
- 1962–71, Imperial College of Science and Technology: 1962–5 senior lecturer in industrial sociology; 1965–9 reader in industrial sociology; 1969 professor of industrial sociology
- 1960s, member of the Mallibar Committee on Government Industrial Establishments
- 1968–70, member of the Prices and Incomes Board
- died of cancer, 18 May 1971

Major works

Social Aspects of a Town Development Plan (with other members of the Department of Social Science, University of Liverpool) (1951)

Employment Relations in a Group of Hospitals (1951)

The Dockworker (with other members of the Department of Social Science, University of Liverpool) (1954)

Labour, Management and the Community (1956)

Management and Technology (1958)

The Saleswoman: A Study of Attitudes and Behaviour in Retail Distribution (1960)

Industrial Organisation: Theory and Practice (1965)

Experiment in Industrial Democracy: A Study of the John Lewis Partnership (with A. Flanders and R. Pomerantz) (1968)

Industrial Organisation: Behaviour and Control (1969)

Behaviour in Organizations (1970)

Summary

Joan Woodward was born on 19 June 1916. She gained a first-class degree in Philosophy, Politics and Economics at Oxford in 1936, in 1938 an MA in Medieval History from the University of Durham, and in 1939 a Diploma in Social and Public Administration from the University of Oxford. Her war service was spent in personnel and planning in industry, where she developed an abiding interest in seeking ways to improve the management process. This was confirmed in 1946 with a move to the Civil Service and a posting to the

Ministry of Supply. In 1948 she was appointed to a lectureship in Industrial Sociology at the University of Liverpool. Posts at South East Essex Technical College and Oxford University followed. In 1962 she was appointed to a senior lectureship in Imperial College, London, where, in an institution famous for its science and engineering, her ground-breaking work in bringing together technological and social analysis was recognized in 1969 by her appointment to the founding Chair in Industrial Sociology. Her commitment to finding practical solutions coupled with her keen analytical mind resulted in appointments as consultant to large companies, such as Tube Investments, Pilkington and the John Lewis Partnership, as well as to government departments and quasi-governmental organizations, such as the General Post Office, the Department of Employment and Productivity and the Prices and Incomes Board.

As a woman, Woodward was a rarity in her academic discipline and in Imperial College, where she was only the second woman to become a professor in its entire history. Her legacy to organizational analysis through surveys, case studies and practical experience is impressive for its breadth and depth. She led a generation of industrial sociologists in the pursuit of knowledge, in a field in which it was as important to be practically relevant as it was to be theoretically interesting and rigorous. Her name became synonymous in Britain with the recognition of a crucially important relationship between social and technical systems. Groundwork in this area had been undertaken at The Tavistock Institute of Human Relations, and contemporary scholars in the UK and USA were making similar observations, but it is her name which, in the UK, is most frequently associated with the discovery of relationships between production technology, organization structure and behaviour.

1 Early work

At the University of Liverpool, working with Professor Simey, Woodward tackled issues of social and organizational change with studies of employment relations in hospitals, social aspects of urban planning and industrial relations and management practices in the docks. Her monographs *The Dockworker* (1954) and *The Saleswoman* (1960) showed her to be a consummate field worker, able sensitively to establish different points of view, to locate them in a social and economic context and in particular to explore the human dimensions of technological and economic change.

As director of the Department of Scientific and Industrial Research's Human Relations Research Unit at South East Essex College of Technology, she began her work on management organization. Formal management education was in its infancy, and it was current practice to advocate 'one best way to manage'. There were, however, two competing views on what constituted the 'best way'. On the basis of the principles of scientific management, managers were urged to design formal structures with clear lines of authority, restricted spans of control and standardized working practices (see TAYLOR, F.W.). However, others espoused the human relations tradition associated with the work of Mayo and emphasized supportive supervision and group-based working (see MAYO, G.E.). Through her experience in textiles, retail, the docks and engineering, Woodward had witnessed a wide variety of management practices, which were not obviously related to degrees of commercial success. While formal hierarchies predominated, informal patterns of influence could also be found. Sometimes production line management was dominant, but other times technical or administrative specialists determined key points of strategy and operations. The contrast between the variety she observed and the emphasis on 'one best way' intrigued her. She embarked on a comprehensive study of all the firms employing more than a hundred people in her immediate locality of southeast Essex; 91 per cent agreed to cooperate, resulting in a study of 100 firms.

2 Discovering the relationship between technology and organization

The aim of the South East Essex study was to establish how and why industrial organizations varied in structure, and whether particular structures were associated with commercial success. General trends that emerged from the survey were to be explained in greater depth through case studies. Having looked in vain for an explanation of success in terms of any one particular set of organizational and managerial relationships, Woodward and her team discovered that systematic patterns could be discerned in the data when firms were grouped according to the complexity of their technology, which was also found to be related to the degree to which production processes were in themselves controllable and predictable, and the degree of uncertainty with which workers and their supervisors had to work. Taking a scale of technical complexity from unit prototype, craft or customized production, through the production of small, and then large, batches of products, on to the mass production of standardized goods and finally to continuous process production of liquids or gases, the research revealed two sets of relationships which, within each of the technologically based production groups, were strongly associated with commercial success. First, a set of linear relationships between technical complexity and a firm's organizational arrangements were established. For example, the number of direct workers to indirect workers decreased from unit to process, whereas the number of levels of management increased, and the ratio of managers to other staff decreased. However, not all relations were linear; curvilinear relationships were revealed between aspects of the social structure and technology. For example, the number of employees controlled by first-line supervisors was largest in mass production and lowest in both unit and process production. The classic 'one best way' principles of scientific management were found to be associated with success in the mass and large batch production of standardized goods, whereas the human relations emphasis on

supportive supervision and enhanced discretion, was better suited to unit and process production.

The survey findings were initially published in a Department of Scientific and Industrial Research pamphlet entitled *Management and Technology* (1958). They had a profound effect on practitioners, for whom they made immediate intuitive sense, and to whom they offered something more than generalized prescription. In the more detailed publication *Industrial Organisation: Theory and Practice* (1965), Woodward described the case studies as well as the survey and developed the idea that effective management depends on analysis of 'situational demands' and consideration about how they can best be met through creating appropriate organizational structures and developing appropriate managerial behaviour. For example, short lines of command within functions and strong interpersonal communication between functions were found to be most appropriate to unit production, but inappropriate to large batch and mass production, where, Woodward concluded, functions were best kept fairly distant and independent. She found that although there was considerable variation in structure within technological groups, where a firm's structure conformed to the median for that technological group, it was more likely to be successful than if it deviated from it.

3 Woodward's work as part of contingency theory

The findings supported work being undertaken coincidentally in the UK by Burns (1958), with his distinction between management systems which were organic and informal, and those which were mechanistic and formal. Meanwhile in the USA, Lawrence and Lorsch (1967), Perrow (1967), Thompson (1967), and Hage and Aiken (1969) were reaching compatible conclusions from their empirical work (see LAWRENCE, P.R. AND LORSCH, J.W.; THOMPSON, J.D.). Whereas Woodward had concentrated on the effects of technology, some of her contemporaries were equally concerned with the effects of the market, and the Aston School had demonstrated the importance of size (Pugh and Hickson 1976; Pugh and Hinings 1976) (see ASTON GROUP).

These scholars in the UK and the USA are credited with the development of contingency theory, with its basic tenet that a firm's industrial performance is influenced considerably by the extent to which structure and managerial behaviour 'fit' with the degrees of complexity and uncertainty which are displayed in contingent factors such as technology, market position, product diversity and size. The more uncertain and complex the context (as created by age, size, technologies, product, capital and labour markets), the more organic and flexible the structure needs to be and the more need there is for information to flow vertically between levels and horizontally between functions. In contrast, the more certain and less complex the context, the more structures can be mechanistic, with greater emphasis on hierarchy and standard rules and procedures. Woodward and her contemporaries were important in prompting further academic work (for example, the Harvard Organization and Environment Research Programme; see also Van de Ven and Joyce 1981; Mintzberg 1979). They also influenced generations of managers to see contingency theory as a useful guide for making decisions about the design of organization structures.

4 Limitations of the contingency approach

Notwithstanding its enormous impact, there are, however, a number of practical and theoretical limitations to contingency theory and they can be discerned in Woodward's work (Donaldson 1976; Wood 1979; Dawson 1992). Problems with the approach surround the hypothesized link between contingencies – including technology – and structures. First, different contingencies, such as technological complexity, product market characteristics and organizational size, may demand different and conflicting organizational responses. Which contingency is to dominate? Certainly not always technology. Second, the nature of

the contingencies evidenced in the technology or market will change over time, at different rates and in different directions. Third (and here Woodward readily acknowledged the limitation of any magic solution to organizational effectiveness), any 'fit' between contingencies and structures is the result of choices made by people within constraints which reflect decisions and actions taken at a previous time. Such choices reflect values and attitudes, not least about managerial effectiveness within the wider organizational context. Furthermore, at a general level, it is well established that many factors other than organization structure and managerial behaviour influence performance, for example, interest rates, commodity prices, international political change and so on. These points were first articulated by Child (1972).

Woodward's early death meant that she was unable to engage in debate about these issues. However, there is enough in her work to suggest that she did not favour an overly deterministic view of organizations. In her later work she was concerned to refine the concept of technology and so became interested in the exercise and limits of managerial choice, especially concerning the development of managerial control systems. She did not see organizations as static determined systems; she found scope for variability in organization design, particularly in the middle areas of batch production, and she attributed this to the exercise of choice.

5 Control systems in conjunction with technology

Working with colleagues at Imperial College, Woodward developed a typology of control systems based on two dimensions. First, the degree of personal direct control (for example, through the hierarchy) as opposed to impersonal control (for example, through technological or administrative systems). Second, the degree to which control systems were integrated, so that different standards and rules were presented in a common framework, or fragmented, with discrete sets of standards and rules applied by different departments to regulate and control performance. Reanalysis of the South East Essex data suggested that a consideration of control systems explained some of the curvilinear relationships. Unit and process production firms were found to operate to good effect with integrated control systems; in the former, the integration was through personal control, and in the latter through technologically integrated systems. In contrast, large batch and mass production firms operated with fragmented systems. This work is discussed in Woodward's edited collection *Industrial Organisation: Behaviour and Control* (1970).

Woodward suggested that types of technology and control systems determined and responded to the uncertainties and complexities in any organization. Both technologies and control systems were the creation of managers; relationships which existed were not somehow mechanistically created without human endeavour and were therefore influenced by different human interests. Furthermore, she readily acknowledged that control systems, although formally concerned with securing greater efficiency, also reflected and created differences of power and interest. However, she would only go so far in this analysis. She assumed that ultimately all parties engaged in one organization shared a common interest in working for the good of the organization. She wanted to help managers to identify things which they could, if possible, alter to increase effectiveness. She saw different interests arising from different locations in the product cycle of development, production and distribution, but she regarded the acceptance of overall goals and objectives as non-problematic. She was interested in challenging the ways in which management operated in order to increase their effectiveness but she was not interested in a critical reappraisal of the management function. Many, however, were far more prepared to take a more critical stance and subsequently several schools of radical or critical organization theory have become established (for example, Benson 1977; Reed and Hughes 1992) which stand in sharp contrast to Woodward's managerial approach.

6 Legacy

Woodward's immediate legacy was to stimulate work in the Industrial Sociology Unit which she had formed in Imperial College and which continued after her death under the leadership of Dorothy Wedderburn (Davies *et al.* 1973). Empirical studies were conducted of hospitals (Davies and Francis 1976), prison industrial workshops (Dawson 1975) and engineering companies, and a theoretical model of organizations as technically constrained bargaining and influence systems was developed (Abell 1975).

Woodward's work was ground-breaking and exciting. It showed managers that they should make informed choices on organizational design and gave them a framework for doing so. For scholars, she, together with Burns, established the basis for the empirical study of organizational effectiveness within the UK, and the importance of the relationship between technology, structure and performance. Her work stimulated intellectual debate and practical action. As such, she achieved her aim of wanting to bridge the gap between practising managers and academics; she fully expected further study and practice to lead to reappraisal of her work. Interestingly, in the years which have elapsed since her death no academic or manager considering organization theory or design has said that technology is unimportant. Some have emphasized the importance of other factors, some have stressed technology as a creature of human endeavour and therefore open to change, and others have challenged apolitical approaches to organizational development. Despite these caveats, most managers, when re-engineering their business or entering any period of major change, still have an eye on the human requirements generated by the technologies employed.

With increasing sophistication and penetration into all aspects of business and organization, technology as a constraint on action and as an opportunity for competitive advantage is of dual importance. When Woodward was conducting her research, technology was most obvious as a means of industrial production. It was based on mechanics and fairly simple electronics. With major developments in materials, electronics, telecommunications, genetics and the whole field of biomedical sciences, the relevance and use of technology in organizations has expanded beyond industrial production to lie at the heart of administration, distribution, decision making and communication. The speed and capacity underlying sophisticated analytical techniques have revolutionized managerial activity. As both the creature and creator of management systems, technology is now of ubiquitous importance and is a major factor when decisions are made about future structures and strategies for the vast majority of organizations. Woodward was the first person in the UK to draw attention to its practical and theoretical importance in management.

SANDRA DAWSON
JUDGE INSTITUTE OF MANAGEMENT STUDIES,
UNIVERSITY OF CAMBRIDGE

Further reading

(References cited in the text marked *)

* Abell, P. (1975) *Organizations as Bargaining and Influence Systems*, London: Heinemann. (A collection of papers showing work which continued at Imperial College after Woodward's death, with greater emphasis on power and control.)
* Benson, J.K. (ed.) (1977) *Organizational Analysis: Critique and Innovation*, Beverly Hills, CA: Sage Publications. (A radical approach, challenging the positivist view and stressing the importance of action, power and process.)
* Burns, T. (1958) *Management in the Electronics Industry – A Study of Eight English Companies*, Edinburgh: Social Science Research Centre, University of Edinburgh. (Subsequently elaborated and published as Burns, T. and Stalker, G. (1961) *The Management of Innovation*, London: Tavistock Publications.)
* Child, J. (1972) 'Organisational structure, environment and performance: the role of strategic choice', *Sociology* 6: 1–22. (The first article in the UK which challenged the static nature of contingency theory.)
* Davies, C., Dawson, S. and Francis, F.A.S. (1973) 'Technology and other variables', in M. Warner (ed.), *The Sociology of the Workplace*, London: Allen & Unwin. (A development of Woodward's work.)
* Davies, C., and Francis, F.A.S. (1976) 'Perceptions of structure in NHS hospitals', in M. Stacey (ed.), *The Sociology of the NHS*, Sociological Review Monograph 22, Keele: Keele University. (A development of Woodward's work.)
* Dawson, S. (1975) 'Power and influence in prison industries', in P. Abell (ed.), *Organizations as Bargaining and Influence Systems*, London: Heinemann. (A development of Woodward's work.)
* Dawson, S. (1992) *Analysing Organisations*, 2nd edn, London: Macmillan. (Chapters 3–5 give an overview of the development of contingency theory from Woodward and others, and a discussion of its limitations and contribution to practice and theory.)
* Donaldson, L. (1976) 'Woodward, technology, organisational structure and performance – a critique of the universal generalisation', *Journal of Management Studies* (October): 255–74. (Gives a critique of Woodward's work but concludes in broad support.)
  Hage, J. and Aiken, M. (1969) 'Routine technology, social structure and organizational goals', *Administrative Science Quarterly* 14: 366–76. (A study which resulted in conclusions similar to those of Woodward.)
* Lawrence, P.R. and Lorsch, J.W. (1967) *Organisation and Environment*, Boston, MA: Harvard Business School Press. (Placing greater emphasis on the environment, these authors developed a similar analysis to that of Woodward.)
* Mintzberg, H. (1979) *The Structuring of Organisations*, Englewood Cliffs, NJ: Prentice Hall. (A sophisticated development of contingency theory, developing five ideal structural models which are appropriate to five different technological and environmental scenarios.)
* Perrow, C. (1967) 'A framework for the comparative analysis of organisations', *American Sociological Review* 32: 194–208. (A similar emphasis on technology is found in this approach by a US author.)
* Pugh, D.S. and Hickson, D.J. (1976) *Organizational Structure in its Context*, The Aston Programme, vol. 1, Farnborough: Saxon House. (UK study which stressed size rather than technology as a determinant of structure.)
* Pugh, D.S. and Hinings, C.R. (1976) *Organizational Structure: Extensions and Replication*, The Aston Programme, vol. 2, Farnborough: Saxon House. (Companion volume to the above title.)
* Reed, M. and Hughes, M. (eds) (1992) *Rethinking Organization: New Directions in Organization*

Theory and Analysis, London: Sage Publications. (A series of papers challenging a positivist contingency paradigm.)

* Thompson, J.D. (1967) *Organizations in Action*, New York: McGraw-Hill. (A US scholar who was working at the same time as Woodward and producing compatible results.)

* Ven, A.H. Van de and Joyce, W.F. (eds) (1981) *Perspectives on Organisation Design and Behaviour*, New York: Wiley. (A development of contingency theory.)

* Wood, S. (1979) 'A reappraisal of the contingency approach to organisation', *Journal of Management Studies* 16 (3): 334–54. (Argues that if contingency theory is anything more than a statement that there is no one best way of organizing, it implies a technocratic systems approach and does not give adequate emphasis to the political realities of organizations and change.)

Woodward, J. (1951) *Employment Relations in a Group of Hospitals*, London: The Institute of Hospital Administrators.

Woodward, J. (1956) *Labour, Management and the Community*, London: Pitman.

* Woodward, J. (1958) *Management and Technology*, London: HMSO. (The initial findings of the South East Essex study.)

* Woodward, J. (1960) *The Saleswoman: A Study of Attitudes and Behaviour in Retail Distribution*, London: Pitman. (A fine example of field work.)

* Woodward, J. (1965; 2nd edn 1980; 3rd edn 1994) *Industrial Organisation: Theory and Practice*, Oxford: Oxford University Press. (Woodward's classic work containing the results of the South East Essex study.)

* Woodward, J. (1970; 2nd edn 1982) *Industrial Organisation: Behaviour and Control*, Oxford: Oxford University Press. (A book of papers with contributions from her colleagues at Imperial college, developing her work on technology and control.)

Woodward, J. (1970) *Behaviour in Organizations*, London: Imperial College of Science and Technology. (Woodward's inaugural lecture as Professor of Industrial Sociology.)

Woodward, J. *et al.* (1951) *Social Aspects of a Town Development Plan*, Liverpool: Liverpool University Press. (A study of the County Borough of Dudley, written in association with other members of Liverpool University's Department of Social Science.)

Woodward, J. *et al.* (1954) *The Dockworker*, Liverpool: Liverpool University Press. (An excellent piece of field work, written in association with other members of Liverpool University's Department of Social Science.)

Woodward, J., Flanders, A. and Pomerantz, R. (1968) *Experiment in Industrial Democracy: A Study of the John Lewis Partnership*, London: Faber & Faber.

See also: ASTON GROUP; LAWRENCE, P.R. AND LORSCH, J.W.; MAYO, G.E.; TAYLOR, F.W.; THOMPSON, J.D.

Related topics in the IEBM: CONTEXTS AND ENVIRONMENTS; HUMAN RELATIONS; MANAGERIAL BEHAVIOUR; OCCUPATIONAL PSYCHOLOGY; ORGANIZATION BEHAVIOUR; ORGANIZATION BEHAVIOUR, HISTORY OF; ORGANIZATION DEVELOPMENT; ORGANIZATION STRUCTURE; STRATEGY AND TECHNOLOGICAL DEVELOPMENT; TECHNOLOGY AND ORGANIZATIONS

Appendix

Entries by subject area

Accounting and finance
Benson, Harry
Hopwood, Anthony
Limperg, Theodore
Pacioli, Luca
Paton, William Andrew
Schmalenbach, Eugen

Business economics
Boulding, Kenneth
Coase, Ronald
Friedman, Milton
Galbraith, John Kenneth
Hayek, Friedrick
Keynes, John Maynard
March, James Gardiner and Cyert, Richard
    Michael
Marshall, Alfred
Means, Gardiner Coit
Mill, John Stuart
Samuelson, Paul Anthony
Schumacher, Ernst Friedrich
Schumpeter, Joseph
Simon, Herbert Alexander
Smith, Adam
Veblen, Thorstein Bunde
Williamson, Oliver E.

Comparative management
Hofstede, Geert
Luthans, Fred
Porter, Michael E.
Tung, Rosalie L.

General management
Barnard, Chester Irving
Drucker, Peter F
Fayol, Henri,
Fukuzawa, Yukichi,
Gulick, Luther Halsey
Handy, Charles
Kanter, Rosabeth Moss
Kotter, John
Nonaka, Ikujiro
Parkinson, Cyril Northcote

Peters, Thomas J.
Taylor, Frederick Winslow
Urwick, Lyndall Fownes

Industrial relations/HRM
Barbash, Jack
Braverman, Harry
Clegg, Hugh
Dunlop, John Thomas
Flanders, Allan David
Fox, Alan
Follett, Mary Parker
Gouldner, Alvin W.
Herzberg, Frederick
Ishikawa, Kaoru
Kochan, Thomas
Lawler, John,
Maslow, Abraham H.
Mayo, George Elton
Perlman, Selig,
Reich, Robert M.
Schuler, Randall S
Strauss, George
Taylor, Frederick Winslow
Ueno, Yôichi
Woodward, Joan

Manufacturing management
Bedaux, Charles E.
Deming, William Edwards
Ford, Henry
Gilbreth, Frank Bunker and Gilbreth, Lillian
    Evelyn Moller
Ishikawa, Kaoru
Iwasaki, Yataro
Juran, Joseph M.
Matsushita, Konosuke
Morita, Akio
Ohno, Taiichi
Shingo, Shigeo
Sloan, Alfred Pritchard, Jr
Taylor, Frederick Winslow
Toyoda Family
Watson, Thomas
Womack, James P. and Jones, Daniel
    Theodore

Marketing
Kotler, Philip
Levitt, Theodore
McLuhan, Herbert Marshall
Parasuraman, A., Zeithaml, Valerie, and Berry, Leonard L.
Sloan, Alfred Pritchard, Jr
Veblen, Thorstein Bunde

Organization behaviour
Argyris, Chris
Aston Group
Bennis, Warren
Boulding, Kenneth
Burns, Tom
Chandler, Alfred Dupont, Jr
Child, John
Crozier, Michael
DiMaggio, Paul and Powell, Walter W.
Downs, Anthony
Emery, Fred
Etzioni, Amitai Werner
Fiedler, Fred E.
Follett, Mary Parker
Foucault, Michel
Fox, Alan
Gouldner, Alvin W.
Hannan, Michael and Freeman, John
Herzberg, Frederick
Hofstede, Geert
Jaques, Elliott
Kotter, John
Lawler, John,
Lawrence, Paul Roger and Lorsch, Jay William
Lewin, Kurt
Lindblom, Charles Edward
McClelland, David C.
McGregor, Donald
March, James Gardiner and Cyert, Richard Michael
Maslow, Abraham H.
Mayo, George Elton,
Michels, Roberto
Miles, Raymond E. and Snow, Charles C.
Nonaka, Ikujiro
Pettigrew, Andrew M.
Pfeffer, Jeffrey and Salancik, Gerald R.
Schein, E. H.
Schon, Donald
Senge, Peter

Simon, Herbert Alexander
Starbuck, William
Taylor, Frederick Winslow
Thompson, James David
Toffler, Alvin
Trist, Eric Lansdown
Ueno, Yôichi
Weber, Max
Weick, Karl E.
Williamson, Oliver E.
Woodward, Joan

OR/Systems and MIS
Ackoff, Russell L
Beer, Stafford
Blackett, Patrick Maynard Stuart
Boulding, Kenneth
Checkland, Peter
Churchman, C. West
Forrester, Jay Wright
Rivett, B.H.P.
Vickers, Sir Geoffrey,
Von Bertalanffy, Ludwig
Wiener, Norbert

Strategy
Ansoff, , H. Igor
Bartlett, Christopher A., and Ghoshal, Sumantra
Chandler, Alfred Dupont, Jr,
Child, John
Deming, William Edwards
Hamel, Gary and Prahalad, C. K.
Hammer, Michael
Ibuka, Masaru
Ishikawa, Kaoru
Juran, Joseph M.
Mintzberg, Henry
Morita, Akio
Ohmae, Kenichi
Ohno, Taiichi
Pettigrew, Andrew M.
Porter, Michael E.
Shingo, Shigeo
Sun Tzu
Tata, Jehangir Ratanji Dadabhoy
Toffler, Alvin
Toyoda Family
Womack, James P. and Jones, Daniel Theodore

Index